D0034369

Italy

Damien Simonis, Duncan Garwood, Paula Hardy
Wendy Owen, Miles Roddis, Nicola Williams

Contents

Lonely Planet books provide independent advice. Lonely Planet does not accept advertising in guidebooks, nor do we accept payment in exchange for listing or endorsing any place or business. Lonely Planet writers do not accept discounts or payments in exchange for positive coverage of any sort.

Le pubblicazioni Lonely Planet provvedono consigli indipendenti. Lonely Planet non accetta nelle sue guide né inserzioni pubblicitarie né compensi per aver elencato o approvato qualsiasi luogo o impresa. Gli autori delle guide Lonely Planet non accettano sconti o pagamenti in cambio di recensioni favorevoli di qualsiasi tipo.

Destination: Italy

Italy is a movable feast of endless courses. No matter how much you gorge yourself on its splendours, you always feel you haven't made it past the antipasti. Few countries offer such variety and few visitors leave without a fervent desire to return.

The country's chequered history has engendered an astonishing regional variety. The great *città d'arte* (cities of art) are all intrinsically different. Rome bristles with reminders of its imperial past while Florence and Venice are compact but high-dosage shots of Renaissance art. Indeed, the entire country is strewn with artistic jewels, from the Arab-Norman and Byzantine wonders of Palermo in Sicily to the Baroque marvels of Lecce in Puglia.

Venture beyond the cities too. From the icy walls of the Alps to the turquoise coves of Sardinia, there is something for everyone. Ski with the chic in Cortina or get lost walking in Tuscany's Apuane Alps. Island-hop around the Aeolian and Egadi groups off Sicily, explore the coastal villages of the Cinque Terre or hang-glide above Umbria's Piano Grande plateau.

Your taste buds will demand equal attention. Hundreds of types of pasta are served up and down the country with a ceaseless variety of sauces. Regional specialities abound, such as basil-based pesto in the north, game-meat sauces and the truffles of Piedmont and Umbria in the centre, and Sicily's Arab-inspired spices in the south. All washed down with some of the world's greatest wines.

The Italians are not joking when they call their home *Il Belpaese*, the Beautiful Country. Come see for yourself!

JON DAVISON

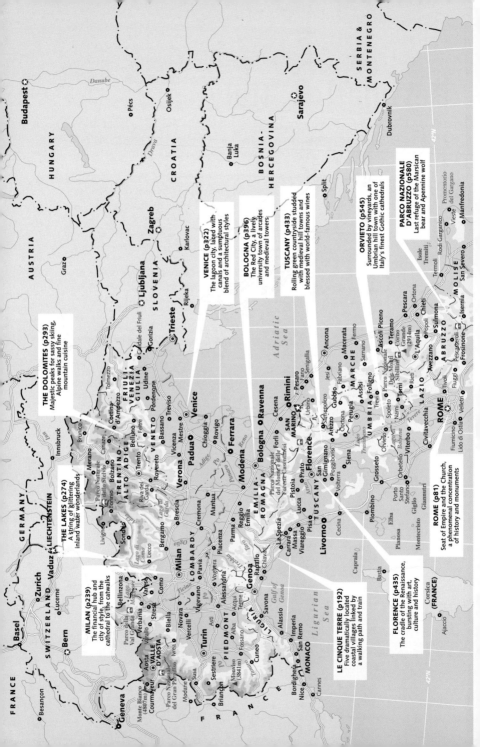

THE DOLOMITES (p293)
Majestic peaks for sassy skiing, Alpine walks and fine mountain cuisine

THE LAKES (p274)
A string of glittering inland water wonderlands

MILAN (p239)
The financial hub and city of style, from the cathedral to the catwalks

VENICE (p322)
The lagoon city, laced with canals and a sumptuous blend of architectural styles

BOLOGNA (p396)
The Red City, a lively university town of arcades and medieval towers

TUSCANY (p433)
Rolling green countryside studded with medieval hill towns and blessed with world-famous wines

ORVIETO (p545)
Surrounded by vineyards, an Umbrian hill town with one of Italy's finest Gothic cathedrals

PARCO NAZIONALE D'ABRUZZO (p580)
Last refuge of the Marsican bear and Apennine wolf

LE CINQUE TERRE (p192)
Five dramatically located coastal villages linked by a walking path and train

FLORENCE (p435)
The cradle of the Renaissance, bursting with art, culture and history

ROME (p81)
Seat of Empire and the Church, a phenomenal concentration of history and monuments

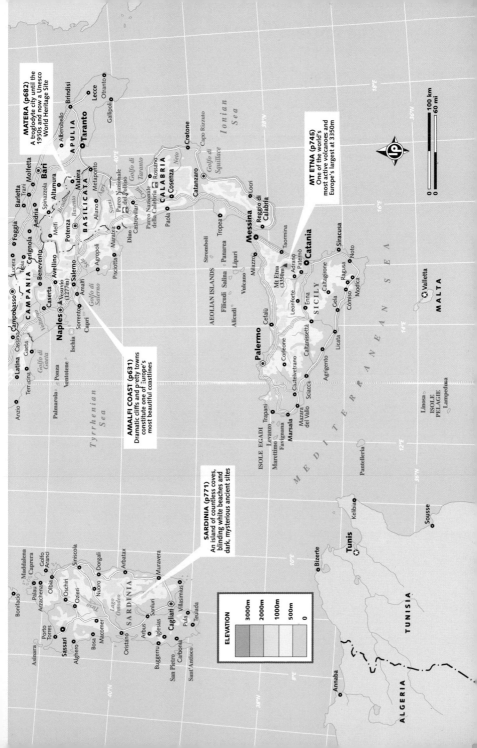

MATERA (p682)
A troglodyte city until the 1950s and now a Unesco World Heritage Site

MT ETNA (p745)
One of the world's most active volcanoes and Europe's largest at 3350m

AMALFI COAST (p631)
Dramatic cliffs and pretty towns constitute one of Europe's most beautiful coastlines

SARDINIA (p771)
An island of countless coves, blinding white beaches and dark, mysterious ancient sites

ELEVATION
3000m
2000m
1000m
500m
0

0   100 km
0   60 mi

Italy is a veritable treasure trove of ancient sites. There is always something to see around every corner.

Southern Italy is home to numerous ancient Greek sites, such as the temples of **Paestum** (p641) in Campania, and those of **Selinunte** (p760) in Sicily. The Greek temple and theatre of **Segesta** (p767) looks north from Sicily to Sardinia. Sardinia is home to the ancient towns of **Tharros** (p788) and **Nora** (p782), and is bespattered with 7000 Bronze Age fortresses like **Su Nuraxi** near **Barumini** (p789).

JOHN HAY

Head south of Naples to see the Roman town of **Pompeii** (p623) frozen in time by the eruption of Mt Vesuvius

Evidence of Rome's greatness can be found all over the country: Verona still uses its **Roman Arena** (p368) for entertainment today

GLENN BEANLAND

Start admiring the grandeur of Rome with the magnificent **Roman Forum** (p89)

JONATHAN SMITH

GREG ELMS

Rome's magnificent **Colosseum** (p93) is an ancient treasure in a modern setting

IZZET KERIBAR

Southern Italy is littered with ancient Greek sites, such as **Agrigento** (p757) in Sicily

Exquisite Roman mosaics can be seen at Sicily's **Villa Romana del Casale** (p256)

CHRISTOPHER WOOD

Italy's overwhelming man-made beauties are matched by its extraordinary variety of countryside. To the west the **Parco Nazionale del Gran Paradiso** (p233) is enticing. In the same northwest corner rises **Monte Rosa** (p225), one of the country's highest peaks. Lesser-known walking territory includes Tuscany's **Apuane Alps** (p478). Like your mountains more explosive? Feel the heat at **Mt Vesuvius** (p522) and the island of **Stromboli** (p732).

Breathtaking coastal stretches include the villages of the **Cinque Terre** (p192) and the **Amalfi Coast** (p631).

EMILY RIDDELL

Breathtaking coastal stretches include the incredible coves of Sardinia's **Golfo di Orosei** (p805)

Feel the heat at **Mt Etna** (p746)

FIONN DAVENPORT

The **Lakes** (p274) north of Milan provide some stunning scenery

THOMAS WINZ

DIANA MAYFIELD

Rolling hill country and vineyards of **Tuscany** (p433)

RICHARD NEBESKY

Mont Blanc (p225) straddles the Italo-French border

The north is closed off by grand Alpine ranges like the **Dolomites** (p293), which are equally a winter skiing draw and summer hikers' wonderland

DAVID TOMLINSON

Italy overflows with treasure. Where to begin? Gems abound. Seek out Leonardo da Vinci's **Cenacolo** (p245) in Milan, Mantegna's **Camera degli Sposi** (p270) in Mantua or Piero della Francesca's frescoes in Arezzo's **Chiesa di San Francesco** (p511).

For another side of the Renaissance coin you could head for the **Galleria dell'Accademia** (p453). The Byzantine-influenced art of mosaic decoration can be admired as far away as the cathedral of **Monreale** (p721) outside Palermo. Equally remarkable are those that grace Ravenna's churches, particularly the **Basilica di San Vitale** (p424).

Michelangelo's **Sistine Chapel** (p119)

RUSSELL MOUNTFORD

The Byzantine-influenced art of mosaic decoration can be admired in Venice's **St Mark's Basilica** (p331)

OLIVIER CIRENDINI

DOUG McKINLAY

Florence's **Uffizi Gallery** (p447) is crammed with Renaissance masterpieces

Right:
Michelangelo's exquisite statue of **David** (p452), in Florence
PHOTO BY GREG ELMS, GALLERIA DELL'ACCADEMIA

Italy is an epicurean's paradise and culinary traditions vary enormously. You'll find the best pesto sauce in **Genoa** (p185). For a big *bistecca alla fiorentina* (T-bone steak) meat eaters want to be in **Tuscany** (p461), or in **Sardinia** (p781) for *porcetto* (suckling pig). For dessert what about **Sicily's** (p716) cassata or sweet ricotta-filled *cannoli*?

ALAN BENSON

Naples (p602) is the home of the original pizza

ALAN BENSON

You'll find risotto in all its varieties in the **Veneto** (p350)

ALAN BENSON

Puglia (p647) is the home of abundant meals: try to squeeze in some magnificent *mozzarella di bufala*

Getting Started

You could keep visiting Italy for the rest of your life and still not exhaust all it has to offer. It's a treasure chest of art, a living tableau of human history from prehistoric to modern times, a culinary delight and a natural wonder with everything from craggy mountains to sparkling seas.

WHEN TO GO

The immediate response to this question is 'any time'! On a more serious note, the best time is April to June. The weather is sunny without being stiflingly hot, the countryside bursts with spring flowers, and the flood of summer tourism, largely dictated by school holidays, has yet to crash over the peninsula. Most Italians hit the road in July and August too, so those two months – in which prices soar and tempers flare and most of the country, bar the high mountains, broils – are best avoided.

See Climate Charts (pp813–14) for more information.

The cliched perception of Italy as the land of eternal Mediterranean sun is a trifle distorted. In the Alps, winters are long and severe. First snowfalls usually occur in November and freak falls in June are not unknown. Although the Alps shield northern Lombardy from the extremes of the northern European winter, cloud and rain are common. Milan comes close to being Italy's climatic version of London! Venice tends to be cool and wet in winter, and hot and humid in summer.

Florence's position, nestled in a valley surrounded by hills, creates oven-like conditions in summer. Rome experiences hot summers and mild winters. That tendency continues in the south; in Sicily and Sardinia you can expect very mild winters and long hot summers (a dip in the sea is possible from Easter to October), but in mountainous areas it can be surprisingly cold.

COSTS & MONEY

Italy isn't cheap, although compared with the UK and northern Europe the situation is not so bad. What you spend on accommodation (probably your single greatest expense) will depend on various factors, such as location (Milan is pricier than Taranto), season (August is crazy on the coast), the degree of comfort you want and old-fashioned luck. At the bottom end you will pay €13 to €18 per night in youth hostels, where meals cost around €8. The cheapest *pensione* (small hotel) is unlikely to cost much less than €25/40 for a basic single/double anywhere from Pisa to Palermo. You can stumble across comfortable rooms with en suite bathroom from around €45/70. Mid-range hotels in places like Rome, Florence and Venice can easily cost from €70/100 to €150/180 for singles/doubles.

Eating out is just as variable. In Venice or Milan you tend to pay a lot (and sometimes get little in return), while even such tourist magnets as

HOW MUCH?

Coffee at the bar
€0.90

Bowl of pasta & pesto
€6–9

Gelato
€1

Local newspaper
€0.90

Foreign newspaper
€1.50–2.80

Packet of 20 cigarettes
€3.30

City bus/tram ride
€1

10-minute taxi ride
€8

DON'T LEAVE HOME WITHOUT...

- Valid **travel insurance** (p820)
- Your ID card or passport and **visa** if required (pp827–5)
- Driving licence and car documents if driving, along with appropriate **car insurance** (p836)
- A set of smart casual clothes for evenings out: turning up to restaurants and bars in grimy T-shirts, shorts and dusty sandals doesn't cut the mustard in fashion-conscious Italy.

TOP TENS
OUR FAVOURITE FESTIVALS & EVENTS

Italians love to celebrate, and they do it in many different ways. From the baroque splendour of Venice's resuscitated Carnevale to Siena's exciting Il Palio, the gamut is enormous. The following list is our top 10, but for a comprehensive listing of festivals throughout the country, see pp818–19.

- Carnevale (Venice) February (p818)
- Festa dei Ceri (Candles Festival; Gubbio, Umbria) May (p818)
- Festa di San Gennaro (Naples, Campania) December (p818)
- I Candelieri (The Candlesticks; Sassari, Sardinia) August (p819)
- Il Palio (The Banner; Siena, Tuscany) July and August (p819)
- Palio delle Quattro Antiche Repubbliche Marinare (Regatta of the Four Ancient Maritime Republics; rotates each year between Venice, Pisa, Amalfi and Genoa) May/June (p819)
- Processione dei Serpari (Snake-Charmers Procession; Cocullo, Abruzzo) May (p818)
- Regata Storica (Historic Regatta; Venice) September (p819)
- Sa Sartiglia (Oristano, Sardinia) February (p818)
- Umbria Jazz (Perugia, Umbria) July (p818)

MUST-SEE ITALIAN MOVIES

Before you start your real trip, why not embark on a celluloid adventure through Italy? The following selection ranges from Italian cinema classics to classic Hollywood cheese. See pp48–9 for reviews.

- *Il Postino* (1994)
  Director: Michael Radford
- *La Dolce Vita* (1960)
  Director: Federico Fellini
- *La Vita è Bella* (1997).
  Director: Roberto Benigni
- *Ladri di Biciclette* (1948)
  Director: Vittorio de Sica
- *The Italian Job* (1968)
  Director: Peter Collinson
- *Death in Venice* (1971)
  Director: Luchino Visconti
- *Il Gattopardo* (1963)
  Director: Luchino Visconti
- *A Room with a View* (1986)
  Director: James Ivory
- *Nuovo Cinema Paradiso* (1988)
  Director: Giuseppe Tornatore
- *Three Coins in the Fountain* (1954)
  Director: Jean Negulesco

TOP READS

Before the advent of what the French call the 'seventh art' (cinema), writers conveyed the sights, feelings and sensibilities of Italians and their world. The following are just the tip of the literary iceberg. See p46 for reviews.

- *Cristo se è Fermato a Eboli* (Christ Stopped at Eboli; 1947) Carlo Levi
- *Il Gattopardo* (The Leopard; 1958) Giuseppe Tomasi di Lampedusa
- *I Promessi Sposi* (The Bethrothed; 1827) Alessandro Manzoni
- *Der Tod in Venedig* (Death in Venice; 1930) Thomas Mann
- *Il Giorno della Civetta* (The Day of the Owl; 1961) Leonardo Sciascia
- *La Romana* (The Woman of Rome; 1947) Alberto Moravia
- *The Aeneid* (19 BC) Virgil
- *La Storia* (History; 1974) Elsa Morante
- *Canne al Vento* (Reeds in the Wind; 1913) Grazia Deledda
- *Cronache di Poveri Amanti* by Vasco Pratolini

Florence and Rome still offer surprisingly affordable options. On average you should reckon on €20 to €30 for a full meal with house wine, although you can still find set lunch menus for as little as €10.

A backpacker sticking religiously to youth hostels, snacking at midday and travelling slowly could scrape by on about €40 per day. Your average mid-range daily budget, including a sandwich for lunch and a solid but not fancy dinner, as well as budgeting for a couple of sights and travel, might come to anything from €100 to €150 a day.

Public transport is reasonably priced, but car hire is expensive (as is petrol) and may be worth organising before you leave home (pp836–7). On trains it is cheaper to travel on the *regionale* (slow local train) and *diretto* (slow direct train) rather than the faster InterCity and Eurostar Italia trains.

TRAVEL LITERATURE

Reams have been written on Italy and it seems like everyone's been at it, from DH Lawrence to Hermann Hesse, from Charles Dickens to Henry James. Much has also been penned in more recent times giving lucid insight into all aspects of the country. For books on Italian history and society see Culture, pp46–7.

A Season with Verona (Tim Parks) Author of several books on Italy, Parks in his latest effort looks under the country's skin through the prism of Verona's second-rate football team.

A Small Place in Italy (Eric Newby) Long before it became habitual for Anglo-Saxon escapists to settle in Tuscany, one of the grand masters of travel scribbling was there resurrecting a tumble-down farmhouse in the 1960s.

Midnight in Sicily (Peter Robb) An intriguing and cleverly woven account of Sicily, part crime investigation, part culinary discourse and travelogue.

The Stones of Florence & **Venice Observed** (Mary McCarthy) With deceptive ease and flowing prose, McCarthy opens up all sorts of views on these two *città d'arte* (cities of art).

Heel to Toe: Encounter in the South of Italy (Charles Lister) Lister explores the glory and sadness of the south in his trip aboard a clapped-out moped from Brindisi to Reggio di Calabria.

Under the Tuscan Sun (Frances Mayes) A saccharine bestseller telling the story of starting life over in a Cortona house in disrepair. It was so successful that Mayes pumped out a couple more: *Bella Italia* and *In Tuscany*.

Venice (James Morris) Before he became Jan, Morris wrote this delicious personal ode to the lagoon city, treating with equal dexterity Venice's distant glorious past and troubled present.

INTERNET RESOURCES

Delicious Italy (www.deliciousitaly.com) Here's where to find that high-class cooking course in Venice, discover more about *mozzarella di bufala*, and generally immerse yourself in Italy's fabulous wine and food.

Ente Nazionale Italiano per il Turismo (www.enit.it) The Italian national tourist body's website has information on everything from local tourist office addresses to gallery and museum details and general introductions to food, art and history. Look for upcoming cultural events too.

Italian Art (www.angelfire.com/ok3/pearlsofwisdom/art.html) This site links to countless others delving into myriad aspects of Italian art and history, from ancient Roman life to Florence's Uffizi Gallery website.

Lonely Planet (www.lonelyplanet.com) Can get you started with summaries on Italy, links to Italy-related sites and travellers trading information on the Thorn Tree.

Trenitalia (www.trenitalia.it) Plan train journeys, check timetables and prices and book tickets on Italy's national railways website.

LONELY PLANET INDEX

Litre of gas/petrol
€1–1.10

Litre of bottled water
€0.65–1

Slice of pizza
€1.50–3

Beer – bottle of Peroni
€2.50–4

Souvenir T-shirt
€8–12

Itineraries

CLASSIC ROUTES

THE TIMELESS CLASSICS
1 week / Rome to Venice

A week is not a long time to spend in Italy but, with a bit of planning and a desire to make the most of every moment, it's possible to undertake a whistle-stop tour of the tried and tested.

Where to start but with a few days in the ancient capital of **Rome** (pp81–159), home to St Peter's dome, the Sistine Chapel and its famous ceiling, the world-renowned Colosseum, Trevi Fountain, Spanish Steps and much, much more. From Rome push onto **Florence** (pp435–68) for a mind-blowing collection of Italian art in the splendid Uffizi Gallery, squeezing in a day trip to **Siena** (pp491–8), a charming medieval town, or **Pisa** (pp479–85) with its renowned leaning tower and majestic cathedral. After two days in Tuscany it's time to head for the illustrious jewel of the Adriatic – **Venice** (pp322–57). Spend your last two precious days marvelling at the mosaics of St Mark's Basilica, exploring the picturesque waterways of the lagoon city and gazing in awe at the grand houses of the Grand Canal. If you don't have to travel back to Rome on the final day, stay in Venice to check out the attractive islands of the lagoon or move on to explore the beautiful streets of historic **Verona** (pp366–71) and possibly even cram in a quick visit to elegant **Bologna** (pp396–405) with its graceful monuments and bustling boulevards.

From Rome to Venice via Florence is a breathtaking 660km that you can do in a week but which easily merits as much time as you can give it.

SERIOUS ABOUT THE SOUTH

2 weeks / Naples to Palermo

With just a little more time available, exploring the Mezzogiorno makes for an incredible trip whether you want to live it up in a crazy, chaotic city, learn all about a rich heritage set in ancient ruins or discover a dazzling coastline at your leisure.

Sitting in the shadow of Mt Vesuvius, **Naples** (pp588–608) is a thriving metropolis where life is lived at a raucous and anarchic pace. Within striking distance of this fascinating city lie the ruins of two Roman towns, both of which offer a rewarding visit for the traveller. **Herculaneum** (pp620–2), which was once a Roman resort town, is still being excavated and **Pompeii** (pp623–7), Italy's premier tourist attraction offering an enthralling insight into the daily lives of the Romans, needs no introduction.

Don't even think about leaving the Gulf of Naples without making a sneaky visit to **Capri** (pp611–17), home to spectacular caves, lush vegetation and charming villages. The **Amalfi Coast** (pp631–44) is one of Europe's most dramatic coastlines incorporating beautiful towns such as **Positano** (pp632–4) and **Amalfi** (pp634–7) along its route, while **Paestum** (p641–3) boasts three Greek temples which are some of the world's best-preserved monuments of the Magna Graecia.

If you're being really serious about the south, extend your stay and continue onto **Reggio di Calabria** (pp696–9), where you can catch the boat to **Palermo** (pp708–20) on Sicily for a head-spinning combination of awe-inspiring artworks and architecture, fiery volcanoes, fabulous food, stunning beaches and enticing cities.

This route stretches 780km through Italy's sizzling south; two weeks is long enough to see everything but a month will allow you to really do the Mezzogiorno justice.

FROM TOP TO TAIL: THE GRAND TOUR   1 month / Milan to Palermo

Thankfully no longer the preserve of aristocratic young men, anyone with time on their side can make the most of a trip to Italy by starting in the north and working slowly south (or vice versa), taking in all the attractions of a traditional grand tour as you go.

A good starting point is the financial metropolis and shopping capital of Italy, **Milan** (pp239–58), from where you can head north to the beautiful **Italian lakes** (pp274–89) or south to lovely **Verona** (pp366–71) and the ever-stunning **Venice** (pp322–57).

Take time to gaze at the attractive architecture of 'red' **Bologna** (pp396–404), before progressing to **Florence** (pp435–68) for an art-infusion and then onto **Lucca** (pp474–8), a pretty town and excellent base from which to explore the delightful Tuscan countryside.

The enchanting town of **Siena** (pp491–8) is another worthwhile stop, as is the Umbrian hill town of **Perugia** (pp519–28) with its strong artistic and cultural tradition.

From Perugia let all roads lead you straight on to **Rome** (pp81–159) to discover the wonderful ancient city in all its glory before scampering on to **Naples** (pp588–608) and thereby glimpsing the other Italy, the Italy of the south. Don't miss the fascinating ruins of **Pompeii** (pp623–7) and make the most of the dazzling and alluring **Amalfi Coast** (pp631–44) before you head eastwards to **Lecce** (pp671–5) with its extravagant baroque palaces and graceful style or, if the mood takes you, further south to sizzling Sicily, with its wealth of history, culture and beautiful beaches, and **Palermo** (pp708–20) with its slowly emerging renovations.

This grand tour needs at least a month but can be extended for as long as you have available; enjoy an art-packed, history-infused 1720km from Milan to Palermo.

ROADS LESS TRAVELLED

MARCHE, ABRUZZO & MOLISE   2 weeks

The popularity of Italy as a tourist destination means you are hard pushed to find anywhere that doesn't swell with a steady influx of visitors. These three regions are by no means untouched by tourism but they do, for now, remain relatively off the beaten track. OK, so maybe they do have fewer artistic and cultural treasures than their more illustrious neighbours but instead there are breathtaking vistas, appealing hill towns and, perhaps most importantly, the feeling of being somewhere that most people are not.

Marche's undulating countryside is peppered with medieval towns and villages, the best known of which is **Urbino** (pp557–61), home to one of Italy's earliest and most complete Renaissance palaces (Palazzo Ducale). Avoid Pesaro during summer and head instead to **Macerata** (pp564–6), a beautiful hill town and an excellent base for exploring the scenic **Monti Sibillini** (pp570–1). Neighbouring Abruzzo has breathtaking mountainous terrain with the bald, craggy peaks of **Gran Sasso d'Italia** (p574), home to the Apennines highest mountain Corno Grande, as well as the interesting medieval city of **L'Aquila** (pp574–8) and charming **Sulmona** (pp578–9), Ovid's birthplace. In Molise you are well and truly on a road less travelled as you wander through one of Italy's least-visited Roman ruins at **Saepinum** (p583), hike the walking trails on the **Monti del Matese** (p583) and relax on the beach at **Termoli** (pp584–5), the jumping off-off point for the popular **Isole Tremiti** (pp656–7).

Taking anything from two weeks to a month, this route covers 635km through three unique regions known for their natural beauty.

SARDINIA

1 month

The attractions of Sardinia are no secret as the island's increasing popularity attests, but the majority of visitors to Italy have yet to include this spectacular island on their itinerary – making it the perfect place to come for fascinating historical sites, spectacular scenery and the all-essential beach R&R.

The capital, **Cagliari** (pp776–82), is an attractive city with a hilly medieval town centre and its own lovely beach. Moving up the west coast, you shouldn't miss the **Costa Verde** (pp785–6), a magnificent stretch of coastline which remains unspoilt and offers idyllic spots for swimming and sunning. The **Su Nuraxi** (p789) fortress, a vast nuraghic complex dating from 1500 to 400 BC, is just inland.

Alghero (pp790–3) is a pretty – albeit touristy – base to explore more of the island's superb coast and, further north, **Santa Teresa di Gallura** (p797) is the place to hang out if you fancy magnificent coves, rock pools and charming beaches.

The **Nuoro province** (pp801–7) has isolated inlets, spectacular gorges and wonderful walking trails, and will give you a unique taste of the island's traditional culture.

There are more coves and caves to discover by boat or on foot from **Cala Gonone** (pp806–7), an up and coming resort town, although if you don't feel that you've seen enough evidence of ancient man, you can always head back to the **Sinis Peninsula** (p788) and the ancient Roman city of **Tharros** (p788), which boasts ruins of significant archaeological interest.

Discover this spectacular island in a leisurely 820km round trip (as long or as short as you like) from Cagliari to Roman Tharros.

TAILORED TRIPS

TASTEBUDS ON TOUR

You don't need to go far in Italy to experience *cucina Italiana* at its best but if you're passionate about food and take your wine very seriously, a trip to the gastronomic heart of Italy – Emilia-Romagna, Tuscany and Umbria – is a must.

Stock up your cupboards at **Mercato delle Erbe** (fine food market; p403), in Bologna, and complete your store with a bottle of the finest balsamic vinegar from **Modena** (pp405–8). By now you'll be hungry so take your antipasto (starter) in possibly the most famous of foodie towns, **Parma** (pp411–16), home to Italy's best *proscuitto* (Parma ham) and *parmigiano reggiano* (Parmesan cheese).

For the *primo piatto* (first course) it's off to **Umbria** (pp517–49) for some *umbricelli* pasta served with shaved truffles, the elusive *tartufo nero* (black truffle) from around **Norcia** (pp544–5) if you're lucky.

For the *secondi piatto* (second course), what about sampling the famous *bistecca alla fiorentina* (steak) from **Florence** (pp435–68) or *porchetta* (an Umbrian speciality of suckling pig stuffed with its liver, wild fennel and rosemary) in **Perugia** (pp519–28)?

Wash it all down with a glass of red from the **Chianti region** (pp489–91) or a drop of white from **Orvieto's** (pp545–9) vineyards and finish off with **Siena's** (pp491–8) *panforte*, a flat, hard cake with candied fruits and nuts, or *cantucci e vin santo* (crisp *biscotti* dipped in the local sweet wine, *vin santo*), another Tuscan favourite.

WORLD HERITAGE SITES

With its vast historical legacy, it's no surprise that Italy is home to 35 World Heritage Sites. To see them all, put your historical hat on, allocate plenty of time and visit whc.unesco.org for a comprehensive list. If you prefer the past in smaller doses, you could try the following tour of a selection of Italy's World Heritage Sites.

Start at the Roman resort town of **Tivoli** (pp161–2) before pushing on for the world-famous historic towns of Tuscany – take your pick from **Florence** (pp435–68), **Siena** (pp491–8), **San Gimignano** (pp498–501), **Pisa** (pp479–85) and **Pienza** (pp505–6), as all their town centres are designated sites.

From Tuscany it's a short hop to **Modena's** (pp405–8) fine Romanesque cathedral, **Ravenna's** (pp422–7) stunning early Christian and Byzantine mosaics and the splendid Renaissance city of **Ferrara** (pp418–22).

Then turn your attention to **Urbino** (pp557–61), one of Italy's best-preserved and most beautiful hill towns, and finally finish in **Assisi** (pp531–6), the picturesque home of St Francis, which attracts millions of tourists and pilgrims each year.

SHAKESPEAREAN ITALY

The jury is out on whether Shakespeare actually made it to Italy but, with nearly a third of his plays set here, there's no doubt about the importance of the country to the Bard's works.

You don't need to be a literary genius to work out the connection with the *Merchant of Venice*, likewise *Two Gentleman of Verona*. But did you

know that *The Taming of the Shrew* was set in **Padua** (pp357–61), that *All's Well That Ends Well* has a couple of scenes in **Florence** (pp435–68) and that **Sicily** (pp703–70) features briefly in *The Winter's Tale*? **Rome** (pp81–159) has links to a veritable slew of big names: *Antony & Cleopatra, Coriolanus, Cymbeline, Julius Caesar* and *Titus Andronicus*, and let's not forget that *Othello* begins in the grand republic of **Venice** (pp322–57). But perhaps the most famous are the those star-crossed lovers from fair **Verona** (pp366–71) where you can actually visit Juliet's house and eagle eyes will spot a plaque declaring Romeo's abode, despite the fact that the famous duo never actually existed.

The Authors

DAMIEN SIMONIS

Damien still remembers listening to crackly shortwave Italian broadcasts years ago on many an Australian midsummer night. It all started in Rome, part of a typical backpacking tour, and carried on as a university obsession. Damien has explored Italy from Bolzano in the north to the island of Lampedusa, way south of Sicily. He has lived in Milan, Florence, Venice and Palermo and returns frequently for work and (especially) pleasure. Involved with this guide since its 2nd edition, he has also written for Lonely Planet on Venice, Florence, Tuscany and Sardinia.

Damien updated the Destination, Highlights, Getting Started, Snapshot, History, The Veneto and Sardinia chapters.

DAMIEN'S FAVOURITE TRIP

A two-week midwinter getaway draws me to northeast Italy, using **Venice** (pp322–57) as the gateway. January and February can be perfect for a few days' quiet canal-wandering. With luck the weather is cool but crisp and the lagoon city is never freer of tourists. From Venice, a quick ride west leads to **Verona** (pp366–71), a romantic two-night stopover (I like to splash out on dinner here and stroll along the Adige). Now it's time to get physical, turning north via **Bolzano** (pp306–8) for the **Val Gardena** (pp311–12), where the ski slopes are grand and the Italian-Tyrolean culinary mix intoxicating. A week's skiing has to include the **Sella Ronda circuit** (pp305–6). Then it's east to **Cortina d'Ampezzo** (pp315–17) for a chi-chi drink, and back to Venice.

DUNCAN GARWOOD

Duncan currently lives in the wine-rich hills overlooking Rome dividing his time between writing and teaching English to, among others, Miss World contestants. Prior to this, two years in Bari gave him a thorough introduction to the ways of southern Italian life. His first, and nearly last, taste of travelling came with a trip to India and Nepal where an inescapably intimate encounter with a pig almost put paid to any further travel. University and a spell in corporate journalism followed, but writing about sewage systems couldn't match the exotic lures of the Puglian capital which claimed him in 1997. Duncan updated the Culture, Abruzzo & Molise, Campania and Puglia, Basilicata & Calabria chapters.

PAULA HARDY

Having spent the last three years working on a cultural history of Libya, Paula retraced Arabian steps across the straits of Sicily. There she found the same contradictions between politics and politesse, poverty and pleasure amid a generous but guarded people, and as the war in Iraq raged on the international news Sicily proved an inspirational reminder of the fruits of oriental and occidental co-operation.

From the efficient bus service on the island, Paula moved on to chase less reliable airlines and transport links in a rapidly changing tourism market as well as reassessing useful facts for our Directory.

WENDY OWEN

Wendy studied English before joining Melbourne newspaper the *Age* as a journalist. She embarked on an odyssey of work and travel and fell hopelessly in love with Italy, staying for over seven years. After a glorious time as a freelance journalist, TV researcher and sometime English teacher, she decided (erroneously) that so much fun couldn't be good so she headed to London to work as a sub-editor for Reuters and for the *Independent*. When she returned home she joined Lonely Planet's editorial team. But old flames are hard to extinguish and she was delighted to return to Rome and find her love changed but *sempre bella*.

Wendy worked on the Art, Rome & Lazio and Umbria & Marche chapters.

MILES RODDIS

This is Miles' second Italian job for Lonely Planet. Having cut his teeth on a swath of Africa from Ghana in the west to Eritrea and Djibouti in the east, he writes these days mostly about Mediterranean lands. Living across the water in Valencia, Spain, he has written or contributed to over 20 Lonely Planet books including *Mediterranean Europe*, *France* and *Walking in France*, *Spain* and *Walking in Spain*.

Miles updated the Emilia-Romagna & San Marino and Tuscany chapters.

NICOLA WILLIAMS

A Latin leap for love from the Lithuanian capital of Vilnius to Lyon in France in 1997 proved a strategic move for travel writer and journalist Nicola Williams, who has nipped through the Mont Blanc tunnel numerous times since to feast on northern Italy's extraordinary cuisine, ski its slopes and shop Milanese-style. In 2001, Nicola spent several weeks in the region's cities researching the 1st edition of Lonely Planet's tri-city guide, *Milan, Turin & Genoa*. For this guide, she updated the Liguria, Piedmont & Valle d'Aosta, Lombardy & the Lakes, Trentino-Alto Adige and Friuli-Venezia Giulia chapters.

OTHER CONTRIBUTORS

Many thanks to current and former LPers Imogen Franks and Rachel Suddart, who stepped in to write the Itineraries and Environment chapters, respectively. The Food & Drink chapter was based on Lonely Planet's *World Food Italy* and the Health chapter was adapted from material written by Dr Caroline Evans.

Snapshot

'I didn't vote for him!' It is hard to find an Italian who openly admits having voted for media magnate Silvio Berlusconi's Casa della Libertà (House of Liberties) right-wing coalition back in 2001, but someone must have because they crushed their centre-left opponents!

Berlusconi, who owns most of the country's private TV stations and has artfully dodged rectifying this glaring conflict of interest, swept to power on a raft of promises to transform a country burdened with complex tax and labour laws, corruption and a stagnant public service. Pursued by the courts over a fraud case dating to the 1980s, Berlusconi has consistently claimed to be the victim of left-wing 'politicised' judges. In June 2003 he succeeded in pulling a rabbit out of the hat and passing a law guaranteeing the prime minister, and four other top political posts, immunity while in office. With the case against him thus stalled – and by the time he leaves office probably dropped altogether because of statutory limits – Berlusconi was able to crow: 'The law is equal for everyone but I am more equal than the rest!'

The opposition is in disarray and many Italians raise their eyes to the heavens in despair. Some hope Romano Prodi will return from his role as European Commission president. Others see the charismatic former trade union boss Sergio Cofferati, who since leaving his union post has hovered on the edge of Italian politics, as the only chance of unseating Berlusconi.

The trade unions themselves are furious with Berlusconi's attempts to reform state pensions and labour law (the latter reforms would allow more flexibility in hiring and firing), and regardless of the potential merits of these reforms – Italy's labour market is notoriously rigid – his disdain for consultation has led to massive country-wide demonstrations.

Berlusconi has also adopted a hard line on illegal immigration, tightening controls and accelerating expulsions of *clandestini* (illegal immigrants), who frequently turn up on Italy's coasts by the boatload from Albania, Kurdistan, Pakistan and Africa. For the separatist Lega Nord, led by the colourful Umberto Bossi, this is not enough: 'I want to hear cannons roar', he declaimed in the sweltering summer of 2003.

Italy has suffered as much as the rest of Europe from the economic downturn. Inbound tourism has been affected immensely and, with economic growth at its weakest since 1993, the atmosphere is one of increasing gloom. The death in 2002 of Gianni Agnelli, head of the once-mighty but now ailing FIAT car giant, seemed to epitomise the country's malaise.

An ongoing issue is the Mafia. In late 2002, a Perugia appeals court surprised everyone by sentencing former prime minister Giulio Andreotti to 24 years behind bars for collusion in the Mafia murder of a journalist in 1979. His advanced age means he faces, at most, house arrest.

A little light relief came with the return of the Italian royal family, Vittorio Emanuele & Co, exiled since the end of WWII. Parliament voted to let them return in 2002 and they have since made several somewhat uncomfortable appearances in Rome and elsewhere. The Jewish community, among others, is not overly pleased by their return.

Weary of politicians past and present, Italians nevertheless display boundless optimism. Endless talk of building an enormous suspension bridge across the Strait of Messina to link the mainland with Sicily may finally become reality. Planning is underway and the bridge may be opened in 2011. Some say that would be a miracle. Others say the idea is loopy. Only time will tell.

FAST FACTS

Population: 57.8 million

Area: 301,230 sq km

GDP: €1258.3 billion

GDP per head: €21,753

GDP growth: 1%

Inflation: 2.6%

Unemployment rate: 9%

Average life expectancy: 79

Highest point: Mont Blanc (Monte Bianco) de Courmayeur at 4748m

Annual pasta consumption: 28kg per person (the nearest rival is Switzerland with 10kg per person). In Sicily they eat 42kg per person every year!

HISTORY

Few countries have been on such a bumpy roller-coaster ride. The Italian peninsula lay at the core of one of the greatest world powers ever known, the Roman Empire; one of the world's great monotheistic religions, Catholicism, has its headquarters in Rome; and it was largely the dynamic city-states of Italy that set the modern era in motion with the insatiable curiosity for learning and artistic revolution that blossomed with the Renaissance. But Italy has known moments of chaos and suffering too. The collapse of the Roman Empire brought centuries of disruption. The rise of Europe's nation states from the 16th century left the divided Italian peninsula behind. Italian unity was won in blood, but many Italians have since lived in abject poverty, sparking great waves of internal migration. Only since the economic miracle of the 1960s has Italy truly begun to rise out of the mire. Today it is no superpower but a key, vibrant pillar in the construction of the EU.

'Today it is no superpower but a key, vibrant pillar'

PREHISTORIC ITALY

Stone Age nomadic hunter-gatherers were roaming across Italy at least 70,000 years ago and some researchers believe primitive humans may have lived in Sardinia as long as 400,000 years ago.

By around 4000 BC, the Neolithic humans entering Italy from the east were bringing with them the art of land cultivation. Agriculture meant staying in one spot and so fixed settlements emerged. It appears the Bronze Age reached Italy around 3000 BC (see the boxed text, p27).

By 1800 BC, Italy had been settled by numerous tribes united by the Indo-European origins of their Italic languages. North of the Apennines the main tribes were the Ligurians (in the northwest), the Raeti (later overrun by the Etruscans) and the Veneti. In Latium (Lazio today), the dominant tribes were the Latins, who later would come to dominate the entire peninsula. Most of central Italy was inhabited by a group of tribes collectively known as the Umbro-Sabellians; the south was dominated by the Oscans.

THE ETRUSCANS & THE GREEKS

Etruscan culture reached its height from the 7th to the 6th century BC. Etruria was based on city-states mostly concentrated between the Arno and Tiber rivers. Among them were Caere (Cerveteri), Tarquinii (Tarquinia), Veii (Veio), Perusia (Perugia), Volaterrae (Volterra) and Arretium (Arezzo). Most of what we know of these people has been deduced from artefacts and paintings unearthed at their burial sights, especially at Tarquinia near Rome.

While Etruscans dominated the centre of the peninsula, Greek traders settled in the south in the 8th century BC, setting up a series of independent city-states along the coast and in Sicily that together was known as Magna Graecia. They flourished until the 3rd century BC and the ruins of magnificent Doric temples in Italy's south (at Paestum) and on Sicily (Agrigento, Selinunte and Segesta) stand as testimony to the splendour of Greek civilisation in Italy.

TIMELINE	c70,000 BC	753 BC
	Palaeolithic hunter-gatherers roam across Italy.	Romulus, according to tradition, founds the city of Rome.

ÖTZI THE ICEMAN'S LAST MEAL

In 1991 tourists in the mountains near the Italo-Austrian border stumbled across the body of a prehistoric hunter, remarkably well preserved in ice, together with weapons, leather clothing and a basket. The hunter subsequently became known as Ötzi, the Iceman. DNA testing on Ötzi shows that, before he was killed by a rival's arrow (found lodged in his left shoulder), he had last dined on a healthy serving of venison, probably ibex or red deer.

The body, the oldest frozen mummy yet found, was taken to Innsbruck, in Austria, where scientists dated it to around 3000 BC. This forced a re-evaluation of when the Bronze Age arrived in Italy, which until this discovery had been put at around 1800 BC.

The Austrians were intent on keeping the body until surveyors confirmed that the site of its discovery is 11m inside the Italian border. After a six-year custody battle, in 1998 the Iceman was transported to Bolzano, where museum curators have created a refrigerated showcase to keep him in the same frozen state that preserved his body for 5000 years.

As the Etruscans spread south of the Tiber a clash was inevitable. The Greeks of Campania overcame them in a sea encounter off Cumae in 535 BC, setting the scene for Etruscan decline. The death knell, however, would come from an unexpected source – the grubby but growing Latin town of Rome.

ROMULUS & A LIKELY STORY

Aeneas, a refugee from Troy whose mother was the goddess Venus, is said to have landed in Italy in 1184 BC and established a kingdom based at Alba Longa. The last of this line produced the twins Romulus and Remus, allegedly sired by Mars himself and suckled by a she-wolf. Romulus then went on to found Rome in 753 BC.

All a shade far-fetched, but somewhere along the line myth gives way to fact. Seven kings are said to have followed Romulus and at least three were historical Etruscan rulers, indicating that Rome was under some degree of Etruscan control. The last of Rome's Etruscan chiefs, Tarquinius, was ejected in 509 BC by disgruntled Latin nobles and replaced by a republic.

The Republic got off to a rocky start, with infighting in Rome and a struggle to gain the ascendancy over neighbouring Latin towns. This accomplished, the Romans decided to deal with troublesome neighbouring Etruscans by conquering the town of Veii in 396 BC. During the ensuing century, Etruscan cities were either defeated or entered into peaceful alliance with the increasingly powerful Romans and their culture and language slowly disappeared.

THE REPUBLIC AT WORK

Under the Republic, *imperium*, or regal power, was placed into the hands of two consuls who acted as political and military leaders and were elected for nonrenewable one-year terms by an assembly of the people. The Senate, whose members were appointed for life, advised the consuls.

Although from the beginning monuments were emblazoned with the initials SPQR (*Senatus Populusque Romanus*; the Senate and People of Rome), the 'people' initially had precious little say in affairs. (The initials are still used and many Romans would argue that little has changed.) Known as

For a potted history of Italy see www.tricolore.net /history.htm

---

264–241 BC

Rome fights the First Punic War against rival Carthage.

202–218 BC

The second punic war on which Italy gained territory in Spain.

The Oxford History of the Roman World, edited by John Boardman, Jasper Griffin and Oswyn Murray, is a succinct and clearly set out introduction to the history of ancient Rome.

plebs ('the many'), the disenfranchised majority slowly wrested concessions from the patrician class in the more than two centuries that followed the founding of the Republic. Some plebs were even appointed as consuls.

Abroad, defeated city-states were not taken over directly but obliged to become allies. They retained their government and lands but had to provide troops on demand to serve in the Roman army. This increased the Republic's military strength and the protection offered by Roman hegemony induced many cities to become allies voluntarily.

The Romans were a rough and ready lot. Rome did not bother to mint coins until 269 BC, even though the neighbouring (and later conquered or allied) Etruscans and Greeks had long had their own currencies. The Etruscans and Greeks also brought writing to the attention of Romans, who found it useful for documents and technical affairs but hardly glowed in the literature department. Eventually the Greek pantheon of gods formed the bedrock of Roman worship.

WARS OF EXPANSION

In 264 BC Rome found itself at war with its Mediterranean rival, Carthage (in present day Tunisia). The bone of contention was Sicily and when the First Punic War was over in 241 BC, Rome had won control of Sicily. In the following decades Rome also embroiled itself in Greek affairs and marched north to evict the Gauls from the Po Valley. By 218 BC, all of Italy south of the Alps, except the northwest, was under Roman control.

The Carthaginians came back for more in the Second Punic War (218–202 BC). The young Carthaginian general, Hannibal, marched across North Africa, Spain and Gaul (modern France) to enter Italy over the Alps. He roamed the peninsula at will and inflicted several defeats on the Romans but had no access to reinforcements until his brother Hasdrubal arrived in 207 BC. The Romans struck back by landing in Spain; all of Iberia became Roman territory and Hannibal was recalled to Carthage.

It didn't stop there. By 146 BC, all of mainland Greece was under Roman control and in the same year an expeditionary force ended a three-year siege of Carthage and razed the city to the ground. Much of North Africa came under the Roman sphere of influence.

DEMISE OF THE REPUBLIC

As the 2nd century BC drew to a close, Rome slipped into a period of factional strife, exacerbated by problems abroad. Germanic tribes moving across northern Europe in search of land challenged Roman authority in client states and attacked Gaul. The result was the rise in political power of the generals and ultimately the proclamation in 82 BC of the dictatorship of Cornelius Sulla. The tendency to appoint dictators and so get around the limits placed on consuls eroded Rome's republican base. In the coming decades power was shared largely under the old pals act, with characters like Gnaeus Pompeius Magnus (Pompey the Great) dominating the scene. In 59 BC Pompey helped a rising military star, Gaius Julius Caesar, to the consulship, after which he left to conquer Gaul in 58–51 BC.

44 BC

Conspirators assassinate Julius Caesar after he is proclaimed dictator for life.

31 BC

Octavian defeats Antony and Cleopatra at Actium, Greece.

MARK ANTONY'S ILL-FATED EGYPTIAN AFFAIR

After their victory in Greece over Brutus and Cassius, who had assassinated Caesar in 44 BC to revive the Republic, Octavian returned to Rome and Mark Antony departed for the East, where he intended to lead a Roman army against Parthia. Before doing so he summoned the queen of Egypt, Cleopatra VII, for questioning on her alleged aid to Cassius.

Cleopatra turned up to the meeting dressed as Venus, goddess of love, and soon had Antony like a ball of putty in her erotic hand. Rather than set off for military exploits in Parthia, he wandered off to Alexandria for a roll in the hay. Meantime, his wife Fulvia was trying to maintain his influence in Rome, where Octavian's power was growing daily.

Antony finally returned to Italy in 40 BC and agreed with Octavian to divide power. Octavian would rule over Italy and Europe and Antony over Greece and the East. Fulvia had died so to seal the deal Antony married Octavian's half-sister, Octavia.

They moved to Athens and three years later Antony finally departed for Parthia. His campaign was a disaster and rather than go home to wife and children in Athens he headed straight for Alexandria, where he proceeded to hand over Roman territory to Cleopatra and declared his son by her the successor to Caesar. All this was too much for Octavian and the Senate, who declared war on Cleopatra and outlawed Antony. Antony led a fleet to Actium, off Greece, in 31 BC, but was soundly defeated – Cleopatra's 60 vessels turned tail almost from the outset. The following year Antony committed suicide. Several weeks later, having failed to seduce Octavian and unwilling to be paraded around the streets of Rome as a defeated enemy, Cleopatra too took her life.

Caesar's treatment of the Gauls was mild and the area became his power base. Pompey's jealousy of Caesar's success led to civil war and ultimately Caesar's proclamation as dictator for life – to all intents and purposes signalling the end of the Republic. He launched a series of reforms, overhauled the Senate and embarked on a building programme (of which the Curia and Basilica Giulia remain).

Grown too powerful for even his friends, Caesar was assassinated on the Ides of March (15 March) in 44 BC. One deed in blood seems to beget more and in the following years Caesar's lieutenant, Mark Antony (Marcus Antonius), and his nominated heir, great-nephew Octavian, plunged into civil war against Caesar's assassins. Things calmed down as Octavian took control of the western half of the empire and Antony headed east, but when Antony lost his head for Cleopatra VII in 31 BC, Octavian finally claimed victory over Antony and Cleopatra.

For more information on Julius Caesar see www.iol.ie/~coolmine /typ/romans/ romans6.html

A NEW ORDER

Octavian was left as sole ruler of the Roman world but, remembering Caesar's fate, trod carefully. In 27 BC he surrendered his powers to the Senate, which promptly gave them back. Four years later his position was regularised again, with the Senate voting him the unique title of Augustus (Your Eminence). By 19 BC, with all-important control of the army in his hands, Augustus had cemented his position as virtual emperor of Rome.

The new era of political stability that followed allowed the arts to flourish. Augustus was lucky in having as his contemporaries the poets Virgil, Horace and Ovid, as well as the historian Livy. He encouraged the visual arts, restored existing buildings and constructed many new ones.

AD 117–38	313
The Roman Empire reaches its greatest extent, from Britain to Parthia, under Hadrian	Emperor Constantine I ends persecution of the Christians and grants them freedom to worship.

I, Claudius and *Claudius the God*, by Robert Graves, delve into all sorts of aspects of imperial Rome at the time Claudius was in charge.

During his reign the Pantheon was raised and he boasted that he had 'found Rome in brick and left it in marble'.

Augustus reigned for 40 years and things remained stable under his successor Tiberius (AD 14–37). After that, things degenerated quickly. Gaius Caligula (37–45) was plain nutty, Claudius (46–53) unprepossessing but conscientious, and Nero (54–68) hell-bent on upsetting everyone with his obsession with all things Greek. With the provinces in uproar, the Senate impeached Nero, who committed suicide.

Stability was restored with Vespasian (69–79), who made a point of rebuilding the temple on the Capitoline Hill and constructing a huge amphitheatre in Nero's Domus Aurea.

PAX ROMANA

Despite the shenanigans of some wayward emperors, the Empire was never in any serious danger. Indeed, the long period of comparatively enlightened rule that started with Augustus brought about an unprecedented degree of prosperity and security to the Mediterranean. The Empire reached its maximum extent and was, in the main, wisely administered.

DID YOU KNOW?

Gaius Caligula, apart from engaging in incest with his sisters, is also said to have proposed making his horse a consul.

By AD 100, the city of Rome is said to have had more than 1.5 million inhabitants and all the trappings of the imperial capital – its wealth and prosperity were obvious in the rich mosaics, marble temples, public baths, theatres, circuses and libraries. An extensive network of aqueducts fed the baths and provided private houses with running water and flushing toilets.

The Empire extended from the Iberian peninsula, Gaul and Britain to a line that basically followed the Rhine and Danube rivers. All of the present-day Balkans and Greece, along with the areas known in those times as Dacia, Moesia and Thrace (considerable territories reaching to the Black Sea), were under Roman control. Most of modern-day Turkey, Syria, Lebanon, Palestine and Israel was occupied by Rome's legions and linked up with Egypt. From there a deep strip of Roman territory stretched along the length of North Africa to the Atlantic coast of what is today northern Morocco. The entire Mediterranean was a Roman lake.

Trajan (98–117) was an experienced general of Spanish birth who conquered the Parthians and devoted considerable energy to the upkeep and building of highways, aqueducts, bridges, canals and ports. He improved the postal system and instituted loans and grants to stimulate agriculture.

For a detailed run-down on Roman emperors, see www.roman-emperors.org

Hadrian (117–138) gave priority to the maintenance of a peaceful and prosperous Empire, well guarded by disciplined garrisons along its long frontiers. In Britain, for instance, he built Hadrian's Wall from the mouth of the River Tyne to the Solway Firth.

The reigns of Antonius Pius (138–161) and the philosopher-emperor Marcus Aurelius (161–180) were stable, but the latter spent 14 years fighting invaders along the Danube and from Parthia, stretching the Empire's resources to the limit. His inept successor, Commodus (180–192), managed to empty the imperial coffers and presided over a series of crises within the Empire as economic stagnation in Italy and Gaul pushed citizens to revolt. When the North African Septimius Severus (193–211) came to power, he was kept busy for four years by civil strife. He subsequently brought a steadying hand to imperial finances and defence.

476	568
German Odovacar proclaims himself king in Rome, sealing the end of the Roman Empire.	Lombards invade and occupy northern Italy.

DECLINE OF THE EMPIRE

By the time Diocletian (284–305) became sole emperor, the world had changed. Autocratic rule was the norm and the military wielded effective power. Attacks on the Empire from without and revolts within had become part and parcel of imperial existence. A disturbing new religious force was also rapidly gaining popularity. Christians had been a harmless minority, but in these trying times it became increasingly easy to target them as a cause of the Empire's problems. Although Empire-wide persecution occurred rarely, localised campaigns against Christians were not uncommon.

Constantine I (sole emperor 324–337) reversed Diocletian's policy of persecuting Christians, converted to the monotheistic religion and granted Christians full freedom of worship in 313.

Shortly thereafter Constantine founded Constantinople, on the Bosphorus in Byzantium, as a new strategic centre, but he still lavished attention on the ageing capital, Rome. His ambitious building programme included churches such as San Lorenzo Fuori le Mura and Santa Croce, Constantine's Basilica in the Roman Forum and his own triumphal arch, Constantine's Arch.

Constantine's successors were constantly engaged in defensive wars. Valentinian (364–375) and his brother Valens (364–378) split the imperial administration in two, with the elder and more capable Valentian taking the western half. Unity was preserved in name until the death of their successor, Theodosius, in 395. One of his sons, Honorius, ruled the Western Roman Empire, while his other son, Arcadius, ruled the Eastern Roman Empire.

The Western Empire collapsed under the weight of barbarian invasion and ceased to exist in 476 when the Germanic Odovacar proclaimed himself king. He was trounced by the Ostrogoth Theodoric in 493, who ruled in Italy until 526.

The Eastern Empire, with its capital in Constantinople, managed to survive. By the time Justinian I (527–565) came to the imperial throne, the Roman Empire (that is, what was left of its eastern half) stretched from parts of present-day Serbia and Montenegro across to Asia Minor, a coastal strip of what is now Syria, Lebanon, Jordan and Israel and down to Egypt and a strip of North Africa as far west as modern Libya.

Justinian, however, had a dream. He saw the glory of Rome restored and embarked on a series of wars of reconquest. At the height of his success he had retaken most of Italy and even extended imperial power as far as coastal Spain, but the gains proved short-lived.

In Rome, the western Church asserted itself as a spiritual and secular force. Pope Gregory I (590–604) set the pattern of Church administration that was to guide Catholic services and rituals throughout history.

Edward Gibbon's *History of the Decline and Fall of the Roman Empire* is the acknowledged classic work on the subject of the Empire's darker days. Try the abridged single-volume version.

LOMBARD ITALY & THE PAPAL STATES (600–800)

The Lombard invasion of Italy began shortly after Justinian's death. The Lombards were a Swabian people from the lower basin of the Elbe who settled around Milan, Pavia and Brescia and took over the south Italian duchies of Spoleto and Benevento. The Byzantines were left in nominal control over much of the rest.

In an effort to unseat the Lombards, Pope Stephen II invited the Franks to invade Italy, which they duly did in 754 and 756 under the

754–56	1130
Frankish Pepin the Short ousts Lombards and recognises power of popes over Papal States.	Norman Roger II crowned king of Sicily, creating a united southern Italian kingdom.

command of their king, Pepin the Short. The popes were, even at this early stage, an incredibly canny lot. The papacy invented the Donation of Constantine, a document in which Constantine I purportedly granted the Church control of the city of Rome and surrounding territories. At this point Rome was theoretically controlled by the Byzantine Duke of Rome. In return for the papal blessing and an ill-defined say in Italian affairs, Pepin marched into Italy, defeated the Lombards and at the same time declared the creation of the Papal States (ie, territories under the direct political control of the pope), to be made up of hitherto Byzantine-controlled lands.

Pepin's son and successor, Charlemagne, confirmed his father's backing for the Papal States. In return he was crowned emperor by Pope Leo III on Christmas Day 800 and the concept of the Holy Roman Empire came into being. The bond between the papacy and the Byzantine Empire was thus forever broken and political power in what had been the Western Roman Empire shifted north of the Alps, where it would remain for more than 1000 years.

Charlemagne's successors were unable to hold together his vast Carolingian Empire and Italy became a battleground of rival powers and states. The imperial crown was ruthlessly fought over; similarly Rome's aristocratic families engaged in battle for the papacy.

AN OASIS OF CALM

The rise of Islam in Arabia in the 7th century and its spread across North Africa led to a Muslim landing in Sicily, which was only fully occupied in 902. The Muslims (who in Italy were known as Saracens), a mix of Arabs and Berbers, established a splendid civilisation. The fundamentals of Greek culture were restored and elaborated on by Muslim scholars such as the physician and philosopher Avicenna, the astronomer and geographer Al-Battani and the mathematician Al-Khwarizmi. Cotton, sugar cane, oranges and lemons were introduced in the south, taxes were lower than elsewhere in Italy and the Sicilians lived relatively peacefully under their Arab lords for more than two centuries.

The Muslims were soon on the mainland, largely as mercenaries in the service of rival southern potentates, mostly Byzantine Greek in orientation if not always politically loyal or tied to Constantinople.

PAPACY VERSUS EMPIRE

Following the demise of the Carolingian Empire in 887, warfare broke out in earnest between north Italian rulers, who were divided in their support of Frankish and Germanic claimants (all of whom were absentee landlords) to the imperial title and throne. Finally, in 962 the Saxon Otto I was crowned Holy Roman Emperor in Rome, the first of a long line of Germanic rulers to hold the post until 1806.

Inevitably, the two protagonists in the creation of this illusory successor to the Roman Empire must end up in conflict. In the course of the 11th century, a heated contest over who had the right to invest bishops in Germany brought the popes and emperors to a stand-off. After Pope Gregory VII excommunicated Emperor Henry IV, the latter literally came to the pope on his knees to beg forgiveness. Gregory thus won

DID YOU KNOW?

The Arabs introduced spaghetti to Sicily, where 'strings of pasta' were documented by the Arab geographer Al-Idrissi in Palermo in 1150.

For more on the Holy Roman Empire, see www.heraldica.org /topics/national/hre.htm

1240–70	1309
Italian cities, among them Florence, Genoa, Milan, Pisa and Venice, rise as powerful city-states.	Pope Clement V shifts papacy to Avignon in France, where it remained for almost 70 years

enormous political power, since the pope would clearly only nominate bishops friendly to Rome.

In the following two centuries, imperial armies, on one pretext or another and frequently with the aim of underlining the Empire's theoretical authority over the cities of northern Italy, would descend on the peninsula with monotonous regularity. This conflict formed the focal point of Italian politics in the late Middle Ages and two camps emerged: Guelphs (Guelfi, in support of the pope) and Ghibellines (Ghibellini, in support of the emperor).

NORMAN CONQUEST OF THE SOUTH

As popes and emperors duelled in the north, Christian Norman zealots arrived in southern Italy in the early 11th century and in the following decades ably exploited local conflicts between Muslim, Byzantine and other independent rulers to gain control. Roger II was crowned king of Sicily in Palermo in 1130, thus creating a unified kingdom of the south.

The Normans assimilated and adapted local culture. The result could be seen in their architecture, in which elements of Romanesque simplicity, Muslim elegance and Byzantine decorative splendour all shone through. King Roger's magnificent Cappella Palatina (in Palermo) and the cathedral at Monreale (just outside Palermo) are excellent examples of the Norman genius for adaptation and fusion.

Norman rule gave way to Germanic as the son of Holy Roman Emperor Frederick I (Barbarossa), Henry, was married to Constance de Hauteville, heir to the Norman throne in Sicily. Barbarossa's grandson, Frederick II, became Holy Roman Emperor in 1220. An enlightened ruler, Frederick, who became known as Stupor Mundi (Wonder of the World), was a warrior and a scholar who also allowed freedom of worship to Muslims and Jews.

Charles of Anjou won the struggle for succession after Frederick II's death, but French dominion brought heavy taxes, particularly on rich landowners who did not accept such measures graciously. Despite his efforts to improve infrastructure, open silver mines and reform administration, the Sicilians loathed him and finally revolted in 1282. The rising came to be known as the Sicilian Vespers. Locals handed the crown to Peter III, the Catalano-Aragonese ruler of the Crown of Aragon (northeast Spain).

ITALY OF THE COMMUNES

While the south of Italy tended to centralised rule, the north was heading the opposite way. Port cities like Genoa, Pisa and especially Venice, along with internal centres such as Florence, Milan, Parma, Bologna, Padua, Verona and Modena, became increasingly insolent towards attempts by the Holy Roman Emperors to meddle in their affairs. Their growing prosperity and independence also brought them into conflict with Rome, which found itself increasingly incapable of exercising influence over them. Indeed, at times Rome's control over some of its own Papal States was challenged.

Between the 12th and 14th centuries, these city-states developed new forms of government. Venice adopted an oligarchic, 'parliamentary' system in an attempt at limited democracy. More commonly, the city-

History of the Italian People, by Giuliano Procacci, is one of the best general histories of the country in any language. It covers the period from the early Middle Ages until 1948.

DID YOU KNOW?

Dante Alighieri, considered the father of the Italian language, was exiled from his home town of Florence for being a Guelph.

For a range of topics on medieval Italy, see www.medioevoitaliano .org

1348	1469–92
The Black Death (bubonic plague) wreaks havoc across Italy, decimating the population.	Florence's Lorenzo de' Medici rules Italy's most flourishing Renaissance city.

The House of Medici: its Rise and Fall, by Christopher Hibbert, is a wonderfully told account of Florence's most-powerful dynasty, which was born in the splendour of the Renaissance but petered out rather ingloriously.

state created a *comune* (town council), a form of republican government dominated at first by aristocrats but then increasingly by the wealthy middle classes. These well-heeled families soon passed from business rivalry to internal political struggles in which each aimed to gain control of the *signoria* (government). In some of the cities, great dynasties, such as the Medici in Florence and the Visconti and Sforza in Milan, came to dominate their respective stages.

War between the city-states was also a constant and eventually a few emerged as small regional powers and absorbed their neighbours.

In Florence, prosperity was based on the wool trade, finance and general commerce. Abroad, its coinage, the *firenze* (florin), was king. By dint of war and purchase, Florence acquired control of almost all Tuscany by the 1450s – only Siena and Lucca remained beyond the city's grasp.

In Milan, the noble Visconti family destroyed its rivals and extended Milanese control over Pavia and Cremona, and later Genoa. Giangaleazzo Visconti (1351–1402) turned Milan from a city-state into a strong European power. The policies of the Visconti (up to 1450), followed by those of the Sforza family, allowed Milan to spread its power to the Ticino area of Switzerland and east to the Lago di Garda.

John Julius Norwich's A History of Venice is one of the all-time great works on the lagoon city in English and is highly readable. It covers the length and breadth of La Serenissima's colourful past.

The Milanese sphere of influence butted up against that of Venice. By 1450 the lagoon city had reached the height of its territorial greatness. In addition to its possessions in Greece, Dalmatia and beyond, Venice had expanded inland. The banner of the Lion of St Mark flew across northeastern Italy, from Gorizia to Bergamo.

HUMANISM

As the 15th century progressed, more universities and private schools were founded to educate a growing army of scholars, diplomats and public servants. A lively intelligentsia emerged, whose protagonists frequently moved from one court to another, enriching their knowledge and scholarly interchange.

As early as the 12th century, Averroës, a Muslim philosopher born in Córdoba (Spain), had resurrected Aristotle's doctrine that immortality was gained through individual efforts towards universal reason. This emphasis on the autonomy of human reason was a revolutionary philosophical position that by the 15th century became known as humanism.

The thirst for classical knowledge was accelerated by the arrival of Greek scholars from Byzantium, fleeing before the Turks (who took Constantinople in 1453). Through them, Western European scholars rediscovered the works of the ancients, especially key figures like Plato and Aristotle. A rigorous scientific approach to learning, frequently flying in the face of Church doctrine, characterised the *studia humanitatis* (study of the humanities).

The Church had grave misgivings about the new learning, which shifted the emphasis away from God to human reason (and hence potentially weakened the Church's authority) but could do little to stem it. The seats of Italian government increasingly sought the prestige of the presence of scholars in their midst. Venice, Florence, Milan and lesser cities frequently thumbed their noses at Rome and sheltered scholars considered heretics by the papacy.

1506	1562–63
Work starts on St Peter's Basilica, to a design by Donato Bramante, in Rome.	The Counter-Reformation is launched at the Council of Trent, confirming the split between Catholics and Protestants.

A WHOLLY UNHOLY POPE & HIS DANGEROUS CHILDREN

The popes of 15th-century Italy were a different breed. They fought wars to maintain their territories, indulged in political assassination, kept mistresses and had children by them. Most were motivated more by the desire for personal gain or dynastic interest than spiritual concerns.

The Spaniard Rodrigo Borgia, who became Pope Alexander VI in 1492 in probably the most corrupt election in papal history, took the biscuit. He established a notoriously licentious court and throughout his papacy maintained a mistress, Vannozza Catanei, who bore him several infamous offspring – all of whom the pope shamelessly manoeuvred into positions worthy of their descent!

Alexander's son Cesare, who killed his own brother, terrorised Italy in a campaign to consolidate and expand the Papal States. Ruthless, brilliant and an all-round nasty fellow (his victims were often found floating down the Tiber), Cesare went well until Pope Julius II – a bitter enemy of the Borgia family – came to the throne in 1503. Cesare, stripped of his territories and deported to Spain, died four years later.

His sister, Lucrezia, has gone down in history, perhaps unfairly, as the embodiment of Borgia cruelty, lust and avarice. It is said Pope Alexander was obsessed with his daughter to the point of incest. He ensured that she lived in incredible luxury and considered no man worthy of her. Nevertheless, Lucrezia married several times – one of her husbands was assassinated by Cesare and another was publicly declared impotent by Alexander. She finally ended up with Alfonso d'Este, the duke of Ferrara. In hindsight it appears she was, in the main, an instrument of her father's and brother's machinations rather than a willing participant.

Weakened by the Great Schism of the 14th century, during which the papacy found itself exiled in Avignon from 1309 to 1377 and then with rival popes in Avignon *and* Rome from 1378 to 1417, the Church was in no position to argue.

For details of the life of Michelangelo, Lorenzo de' Medici's most illustrious protégé, see www.michelangelo.com /buonarroti.html

THE RENAISSANCE

Indeed, the Church would embrace aspects of the new learning. Rome had suffered incredible neglect but after the schism the papacy initiated a programme of urban transformation. This coincided with the coming of the Renaissance, the inevitably explosive artistic offshoot of humanism.

The Vatican became one of the greatest Italian patrons of a new wave of artists, sculptors and architects. Donatello, Sandro Botticelli and Fra Angelico all lived and worked in Rome at this time. At the beginning of the 16th century, Pope Julius II asked Bramante to begin work on the second St Peter's Basilica. In 1508 Raphael started painting the rooms in the Vatican now known as Le Stanze di Raffaello, while between 1508 and 1512 Michelangelo worked on the Sistine Chapel.

Rome: the Biography of a City, by Christopher Hibbert, is a racy and anecdote-filled account of the long and often secretive past of the Eternal City.

Rome was a generous patron but the impulses for artistic creation and development in Renaissance Italy were multiple. Indeed the real stimulus came from the city-states. Wealth, humanistic thought and artistic revolution went hand in hand.

In Florence, the Medici family and especially Lorenzo Il Magnifico (the Magnificent), saw diplomatic value and prestige in patronising the fine arts. He enriched the city with the presence, and works, of the greatest artists of the time, particularly Michelangelo. Feudal lords such as Federico da Montefeltro in Urbino and Milan's Francesco Sforza competed with each other for the services of artists, writers, poets and musicians.

1582	1797
Pope Gregory XIII replaces the Julian with the modern Gregorian calendar.	Napoleon waltzes into Venice and so ends 1000 years of La Serenissima.

The Venice of the Doges, which had always tended to stand aloof from the rest of Italy, got on the Renaissance train and a distinctly northern, slightly melancholy, branch of the Renaissance took off.

THE COUNTER-REFORMATION & ITALIAN DECLINE

By the third decade of the 16th century, the broad-minded curiosity of the Renaissance had begun to give way to the intolerance of the Counter-Reformation. Art was one thing, but curious free-thinking quite another. No doubt many in Rome saw humanism as the cause of the Reformation, a term for the movement led by Germany's Martin Luther that aimed to reform the Church (and which led to the rise of Protestantism in its many forms).

The transition was epitomised by the reign of Pope Paul III (1534–49), who – in best Renaissance style – promoted the building of the Palazzo Farnese in Rome but also, in 1540, sanctioned the establishment of Ignatius Loyola's order of the Jesuits and, in 1542, of the Holy Office. The latter was the final (and ruthless) court of appeal in the trials of suspected heretics and part of the much-feared Inquisition.

For more on this great scientist, see http://galileo.imss.firenze.it/museo/b/egalilg.html

One Italian intellectual to suffer during the Counter-Reformation was Galileo Galilei (1564–1642). An advocate of Aristotelian science, Galileo was forced by the Church to renounce his approval of the Copernican astronomical system, which held that the earth moved around the sun rather than the reverse.

The latter years of the 16th century were not all counterproductive. Pope Gregory XIII (1572–85) replaced the Julian calendar with the Gregorian one in 1582, fixing the start of the year on 1 January and adjusting the system of leap years to align the 365-day year with the seasons.

By now Italy had ceased to be at the cutting edge of European culture. Italian ports and trade had declined with the discovery of the Americas and the growth of Atlantic trade. Much of Italy was dominated by foreign powers, especially Spain. Madrid's hold was wrenched loose in the wake of the War of the Spanish Succession (1701–14) and Austria moved in to Lombardy and much of the north (but not Venice and the Veneto). Tuscany was under the control of the Lorraine dynasty (and closely linked to Austria). The Bourbon dynasty installed in Naples meant the southern kingdom, or what was now known as the Kingdom of the Two Sicilies, had become independent.

THE LONG MARCH TO UNITY

The French Revolution at the end of the 18th century and the rise of Napoleon awakened hopes in Italy of an independent nation. The Napoleonic interlude (he created the Kingdom of Italy in 1804) helped foment the idea that a single Italian state could be created and many Italians hoped this would occur after Napoleon's demise. It was not to be. The reactionary Congress of Vienna restored all the foreign rulers to their places in Italy.

This backward step was bad news but did encourage the rapid growth of secret societies comprised, in the main, of disaffected middle-class intellectuals. In the south, the republican Carbonari society pushed hard

1861	1915–18
House of Savoy's Vittorio Emanuele II proclaimed king of a newly united Italy.	Italy joins Allies against Germany and Austria in WWI, beginning three years' heavy combat.

and often ruthlessly for a valid constitution, leading a revolutionary uprising in Naples in 1820. Several abortive uprisings were put down around the country during the 1830s and 1840s.

In 1848 revolts rocked almost every major city in Europe. In their newspaper, *Il Risorgimento*, nationalist writer Cesare Balbo and Count Camillo Benso di Cavour of Turin pressed for a constitution and published their parliamentary *Statuto* (Statute). Cavour, the prime minister of the Savoy monarchy that ruled Piedmont and Sardinia, became the diplomatic brains behind the Italian unity movement. He intrigued with the French and won over British support for the creation of an independent Italy. Meanwhile, revolutionary hero Giuseppe Garibaldi returned from South America and, in a daring stroke, he and his Red Shirts seized Sicily and Naples from the Bourbons in 1860 and handed them over to the Savoy King Vittorio Emanuele II.

The bloody Franco-Austrian war (also known as the war for Italian independence) unleashed in northern Italy (1859–61) led to the occupation of Lombardy and the retreat of the Austrians to their eastern possessions in the Veneto. With Lombardy and the south in the hands of the Italians, the new Italian kingdom was proclaimed. Tuscany joined in 1861 and Venice was seized in 1866. Rome was only wrested from French control during the Franco-Prussian war in 1870. Italian unity was complete and parliament moved from its temporary home in Florence to Rome.

The turbulent new state knew violent swings between socialists and the right. Giovanni Giolitti, one of Italy's longest-serving prime ministers (heading five governments between 1892 and 1921), managed to bridge the political extremes and institute male suffrage. Women were denied the right to vote until after WWII.

WWI

When war broke out in Europe in July 1914, Italy chose to remain neutral despite being a member of the Triple Alliance with Austria and Germany. Italy had territorial claims to make in Trent, the southern Tyrol, Trieste and even in Dalmatia, but the new country's weakness had compelled it to appease its powerful Austrian neighbour.

In April 1915, the government changed its mind and joined the Allies on the understanding that upon the successful conclusion of hostilities Italy would receive the territories it sought. From then until the end of the war, Italy and Austria engaged in a weary war of attrition. When the Austro-Hungarian forces collapsed in November 1918, the Italians marched into Trieste and Trent. But Rome was disappointed by the postwar settlement as not all its claims were met by the Treaty of Versailles.

The young country had been manifestly ill-prepared for this gruesome conflict. Not only did Italy lose 600,000 men but the war economy had produced a small concentration of powerful industrial barons and left the bulk of the civilian populace in penury. It was an explosive cocktail.

FASCISM & WWII

In 1919 Benito Mussolini, one-time socialist and journalist, founded the Fascist Party, with its hallmarks of the black shirt and Roman salute. These were to become symbols of violent oppression and aggressive nationalism

DID YOU KNOW?

Swiss Henri Dunant created the Red Cross after witnessing the horrors of the Battle of Solferino during the 1859–61 war.

Denis Mack Smith has produced one of the most penetrating works on Italy's dictator with *Mussolini*. Along with his career it assesses Mussolini's impact on the greater evil of the time: Hitler.

Novelist Rosetta Loy provides a fascinating personal view of life in Rome under the Fascists in *First Words: A Childhood in Fascist Italy*. Loy places special emphasis on the changes wrought by Mussolini's anti-Jewish race laws.

1922	1940
Mussolini and his Fascists march on Rome and take power.	Fascist Italy enters WWII on Nazi Germany's side and invades Greece.

For more on Fascist Italy, see www.thecorner.org /hists/total/f-italy.htm

for the next 23 years. After his march on Rome in 1922 and victory in the 1924 elections, Mussolini took full control of the country by 1925.

The great dictator also embarked on an aggressive if inept foreign policy and entered WWII on Hitler's side in 1940, a move Hitler must have regretted later. Germany found itself pulling Italy's chestnuts out of the fire in campaigns in the Balkans and North Africa and could not prevent Allied landings in Sicily in 1943. The Italians had had enough of Mussolini and his war and so the king, Vittorio Emanuele III, had the dictator arrested. In September, Italy surrendered and the Germans, who had rescued Mussolini, occupied the northern half of the country and re-installed the dictator.

The painfully slow Allied campaign up the peninsula and German repression led to the formation of the resistance. The Nazi response to partisan attacks was savage. In one of the most notorious reprisals, 1830 men, women and children were murdered by the SS at Marzabotto, south of Bologna, in October 1944.

Northern Italy was finally liberated in April 1945 and Mussolini strung up by resistance fighters in Milan's Piazzale Lotto.

THE REPUBLIC

In the aftermath of war, the leftwing Resistance was disarmed and Italy's political forces scrambled to regroup. The USA, through the economic largesse of the Marshall Plan, wielded considerable political influence and no doubt used this in attempts to keep the left in check.

Not long after WWII, Norman Lewis penned The Honoured Society, an intriguing study of Sicily, and in 2000 he returned to the subject and especially the Mafia with In Sicily.

Immediately after the war three coalition governments succeeded one another. The third, which came to power in December 1945, was dominated by the newly formed rightwing Democrazia Cristiana (DC; Christian Democrats), led by Alcide de Gasperi, who remained prime minister until 1953.

In 1946, following a referendum, the constitutional monarchy was abolished and a republic established. It was not until the elections of April 1948, when the Constituent Assembly had finished its work, that the first government was elected under the new constitution. De Gasperi's DC won a majority and excluded the left from power. Until then, the Partito Comunista Italiano (PCI; Communist Party), led by Palmiro Togliatti, and the Partito Socialista Italiano (PSI; Socialist Party), led by Pietro Nenni, had participated in ruling coalitions.

The Italians, by journalist Luigi Barzini, is a classic. Barzini pulls no punches in his assessment of his fellow Italians, their icons and their foibles past and present.

BOOM, TERRORISM & TANGENTOPOLI

By the early 1950s the country's economy had begun to recover and the Cassa per il Mezzogiorno (State Fund for the South) was formed to inject funds into development projects for the country's poorer regions (including Sicily and Sardinia).

In 1958 Italy became a founding member of the European Economic Community (EEC) and this signalled the beginning of the Economic Miracle, a spurt of growth that saw unemployment drop as industry expanded. A major feature of this period was the development of Italy's automobile industry and, more particularly, of Fiat in Turin, which sparked a massive migration of peasants from the south to the north.

Influenced by similar events in France, in 1967 and 1968 Italian university students rose up in protest, ostensibly against poor conditions in

1943	1946
Allies land in southern Italy, which later declares armistice and topples Mussolini from power.	Italians vote in national referendum to abolish the monarchy and create a republic.

the universities. However, the protests were really aimed at authority and the perceived impotence of the left. In 1969 the protests were followed a series of strikes that continued into 1971.

The 1970s, however, were dominated by the new spectre of terrorism. By 1970, a group of young left-wing militants had formed the Brigate Rosse (Red Brigades). Neo-Fascist terrorists had already struck with a bomb blast in Milan in 1969. They would outdo themselves with the Bologna train station blast in 1980, killing 84 people.

The Brigate Rosse, however, was the most prominent terrorist group operating in the country during the Anni di Piombo (Years of Lead) from 1973 to 1980, a period of considerable social unrest and regular protests, especially in the universities. In 1978 the Brigate Rosse claimed their most important victim – former DC prime minister Aldo Moro. His kidnap and murder shook the country.

However, the 1970s also produced much positive change. In 1970 regional governments with limited powers were formed in 15 of the country's 20 regions (the other five, Sicily, Sardinia, Valle d'Aosta, Trentino-Alto Adige and Friuli-Venezia Giulia already had strong autonomy statutes). In the same year divorce became legal and in 1978 abortion was legalised, following antisexist legislation that allowed women to keep their own names after marriage.

A spurt in the 1980s saw Italy become one of the world's leading economies but by the 1990s a new period of crisis had set in. High unemployment and inflation, combined with a huge national debt and an extremely unstable lira, led the government to introduce draconian measures to cut public spending. A series of left and centre-left governments maintained this tough course with the objective of joining European monetary union and, in 2001, entering the single currency. This it managed and the euro duly replaced the lira.

During the 1990s the PCI reached a watershed and split. The old guard now goes by the title Partito Rifondazione Comunista (PRC; Refounded Communist Party), under the leadership of Fausto Bertinotti. The bigger and moderate breakaway wing reformed itself as Democratici di Sinistra (DS; Left Democrats).

While the communists squabbled, the rest of the Italian political scene was rocked by the Tangentopoli ('kickback city') scandal, which broke in Milan in 1992 when a PSI functionary was arrested on bribery charges. The can of worms had been opened and no-one was terribly surprised by what they saw. Led by Milanese magistrate Antonio di Pietro, investigations known as Mani Pulite ('clean hands') implicated thousands of politicians, public officials and businesspeople. Charges ranged from bribery and receiving kickbacks to blatant theft.

Tangentopoli left two of the traditional parties, the DC and PSI, in tatters and demolished the centre of the Italian political spectrum. At the 1994 national elections, voters expressed their disgust by electing a new right-wing coalition comprised of media magnate Silvio Berlusconi's newly formed Forza Italia (Go Italy) party, the neo-Fascist Alleanza Nazionale (National Alliance) and Umberto Bossi's radical federalist Lega Nord. The turbulent Bossi scuppered the alliance nine months later and a series of left and centre-left governments took control.

Although much has happened since it was written, Paul Ginsborg's *A History of Contemporary Italy: Society and Politics 1943-1988* remains one of the single most readable and insightful books on postwar Italy.

1978	1993
Red Brigades kidnap and assassinate the former prime minister Aldo Moro.	Lonely Planet publishes the first edition of *Italy*.

THE RETURN OF IL CAVALIERE

Shortly after joining the euro, Rome's centre-left coalition collapsed and Berlusconi (dubbed Il Cavaliere, 'the Knight', in the press) got a second chance. The same coalition as in 1994 swept to power and this time Berlusconi's Forza Italia, which won a remarkable 30% of the vote, did not need to rely on its coalition partners. Two years into his mandate Berlusconi has disappointed many and continues to fight corruption charges arising from Tangentopoli investigations. For many politics-weary Italians, it all sounds like a very old record.

2001	2003
Silvio Berlusconi's rightwing Casa delle Libertà (Liberties House) coalition wins absolute majority in national polls.	Berlusconi appears in court in Milan in connection with corruption investigations.

The Culture

THE NATIONAL PSYCHE

Every one loves the Italians. How can you not? They do, after all, live in a land where the sun always shines and work is something done elsewhere. They ooze style, enjoy the best food in the world and drive with enviable abandon. But what's behind the polished veneer?

The Italian character is to a degree conditioned by campanilismo (literally, an attachment to the local bell tower). An Italian is first and foremost a Sicilian or Tuscan, a Roman or Neapolitan before being Italian. Confronted with a foreigner, however, Italians reveal a national pride difficult to detect in the cagey relationships they have with each other.

This deep-rooted caginess is the unsurprising result of a history of subordination to foreign masters and cultures which is most evident in the relationship (or nonrelationship) between citizen and state. For much of the population the state offers little and demands much. Tax evasion is consequently widespread and prompts the ingenuity of a nation for which *furbizia* (cunning) is a much-vaunted quality. To put one over on somebody marks you as a winner and this, to an Italian, is important. The maintaining of *la bella figura* (face) lies at the heart of much social behaviour.

Finding ways around rules is something at which Italians excel. Faced with ridiculous rules, as they are on an almost daily basis, Italians don't waste time complaining or trying to change the rule, they simply find the quickest way round it. This is a skill to which journalist Luigi Barzini pays lip-service when he describes his compatriots as a hard-working, resilient and resourceful people, optimistic with a good sense of humour. But, as he continues, it's only visitors to Italy who have clear ideas about the country and its people; the Italians themselves enjoy no such certainties.

LIFESTYLE

In a country where faith in officialdom is tepid at best, the family remains one institution on which Italians continue to depend.

It is still the rule rather than the exception for young Italians to stay at home until they marry. They say affordable housing is in short supply and unemployment a problem, but that doesn't totally convince. Cynics suggest it's a quid pro quo arrangement with parents booking a comfortable retirement courtesy of their children and the kids there to enjoy life before work, marriage and parenthood. Italy's highest appeals court seemed to sustain this in April 2002 when it ruled that a Neapolitan doctor continue to pay for his son (the son in question was a law graduate in his mid-thirties, had a trust fund of US$220,000 and had previously rejected more than one job offer).

However, the Italian family is shrinking. Nearly half of all families are ruled by a single child, childless couples are no longer the exception and with 39% of marriages finishing in divorce in 2000, single-parent families continue to grow. The church is not impressed.

The power of the church might not be what it once was, but it still counts, especially on social issues. Generously, the Vatican is never afraid to help when it feels Italians need a little moral guidance. It's not surprising therefore to hear the Pope reminding married couples that it's their duty to procreate; a sentiment much endorsed by politicians, who for their part worry that the world's lowest birth rate threatens the future tax returns necessary for paying the country's pensions.

For a light-hearted look at Italian life and culture, visit www.italiansrus.com More glitzy and serious www.italianculture.net has comprehensive information.

Italian women, it would seem, are increasingly choosing a career over children. Italy's maternity allowances are generous but still women, who today constitute 37.5% of the workforce, prefer to limit themselves to a single child at most. Italy's army of grandparents berate their children for this, grumbling that the younger generation simply won't make the sacrifices necessary to bring up kids. Certainly, the 'we can't afford children' argument seems difficult to sustain as incomes continue to rise. According to the Centre for Economic and Business Research the average disposable income of an Italian household in 2002 was €24,640 (compared to €35,270 in the UK and €32,757 in France).

But despite these changes, Italy remains a country of conservative mores. While, for example, cohabiting among unmarried couples is becoming more widespread and homosexuality is well tolerated in major cities, the idea of gay marriages has most politicians choking on their cappuccinos.

POPULATION

Italy's population is one of the oldest in the world and if it weren't for immigration would actually be shrinking. With nearly a fifth of the population over 65, Italians are dying quicker than they're arriving. An average of 2.1 children per woman is needed to keep the population stable, a feat which would require a procreative surge worthy of Casanova. Currently Italian women average 1.2 children a head.

DID YOU KNOW?

For every Italian grandchild there are six grandparents.

As of January 2001 foreign residents numbered 1,464,589, comprising some 2.5% of the population. The majority are based in the north, attracted by the healthy job market (see Multiculturalism, p44).

The cities of Rome, Milan and Naples continue to top the population charts, even if recent figures show a marked shift away from the cities. In 2001 cities of over 100,000 inhabitants registered a 7.8% decrease in population. Reasons for this ongoing trend include high city house prices, appalling bureaucracy and the notion that small towns offer a better quality of life.

SPORT
Football

With the right satellite dish it would now be possible to spend all and every weekend between October and May watching footy on the box. This, of course, is exactly what the TV execs who lord it over football would like you to do. No other sport in Italy enjoys anything like the

---

MUMMY'S BOYS

The rough charm of the unshaven Italian Lothario is an inescapable image. The truth is perhaps a little less alluring.

According to figures published in 2003 by Istat (Istituto Centrale di Statistica), the country's main statistics body, Italian men actually constitute an *esercito di mammoni* (army of mummy's boys). If you believe the figures, 67.9% of single Italian men remain at home with mum (and dad) up to the age of 34 at least. And even after the big move, one in three continue to see *la mamma* every day.

Not surprisingly this is not always appreciated by Italian wives. In fact nagging mother-in-laws are the direct cause of about 30% of all marriage breakdowns, and in March 2003 the Italian Supreme Court granted a woman from L'Aquila a divorce on the grounds of an invasive mother-in-law. Perhaps this shrewish relative would have benefited from the course for prospective mother-in-laws set up by an enterprising lawyer from Reggio Emilia. Lessons focused on the tricky art of how not to tell your daughter-in-law she shouldn't work, can't cook and doesn't know the first thing about bringing up your grandchild.

LOOK THE PART

In churches you are expected to dress modestly and if the guardians deem your dress indecent you don't get in. Pleading that you've travelled across the world just to see this very church simply doesn't cut it with the sartorial police. This means no shorts (for men or women) or short skirts, and shoulders should be covered. The major tourist attractions, such as St Peter's in Rome and San Francesco in Assisi, are particularly strict.

---

saturation coverage given *il calcio* (football). Formula One comes closest but even then only when Ferrari are winning.

After years of struggling to win a major European tournament it's suddenly all going right for Italian teams. In the 2003 Champions League final, AC Milan beat compatriots Juventus, while a third Italian side, Inter, reached the semifinals.

Italy's club teams have traditionally done well in European tournaments – 10 European Cups and nine UEFA Cups is the tally so far. The national team, the Azzuri (Blues), are also among the world's best, although a limp showing in the 2002 World Cup didn't impress many (see the boxed text, p44). Two years earlier they narrowly lost the final of the European championship to the French who'd also put them out of the 1998 World Cup. However, Italy has picked up the World Cup three times (1934, 1938 and 1982) and won the European Championship once (1968).

On the home front, the top division, Serie A, is dominated by an elite group of *squadre* (teams) from the north. In the last 12 seasons Juventus and AC Milan have taken the silverware every season bar two. In 2000 Rome-based Lazio grabbed the title only to lose it to city rivals AS Roma the following year.

Tickets for games start at around €15 for the lousiest positions and rise to well over €50. In most cities they are available from official agencies or directly from the stadiums. Italy's major stadiums are: **Stadio Meazza/San Siro** (☎ 02 48 70 71 23; Via Piccolomini 5, Milan) for AC Milan and Inter; **Stadio delle Alpi** (☎ 011 739 57 59; Viale Grande Torino, Turin) for Juventus and Torino; **Stadio Olimpico** (Map p99–100; ☎ 06 3 68 51; Viale del Foro Italico, Rome) for AS Roma and Lazio; and **Stadio San Paolo** (☎ 081 239 56 23; Piazzale Vincenzo Tecchio, Naples) for Napoli. For further details see the relevant city sections: Milan (p256), Turin (p205), Rome (p152) and Naples (p605).

Be warned, getting tickets for big games can be difficult, verging on the impossible.

Motor Racing

To an Italian there is Formula One and then there is Ferrari – the former furnishes the stage, the latter the spectacle. And with Ferrari, led by top driver Michael Schumacher, chasing their fifth consecutive title, interest in the sport is at a record high.

Italy hosts two races each year. The Italian Grand Prix is held at the Monza race track, just north of Milan, each September while the San Marino Grand Prix (to all intents and purposes, if not technically, an Italian race) is run at the 5km Imola circuit in April or May.

Tickets for the **Autodromo Nazionale Monza** (☎ 039 248 22 12; www.monzanet.it; Via Vedano 5, Parco di Monza) are sold at the **Automobile Club Italia** (Map pp248–9; ☎ 02 774 51, fax 02 78 18 44; Corso Venezia 43, Milan), at **ACP & Partners** (☎ 02 76 00 25 74; www.auto dromodimonza.com; Piazza Duse 1, Milan) and at the track. Tickets cost from €55 for a spot on the grass to €400 for the best grandstand seat.

Check out www.channel4.com /sport/football_italia/ for the latest from Serie A.

From the 'spend a year in Italy and write a book about it' school, the title of George Negus' book – *The World from Italy: Football, Food and Politics* – pretty much says it all. Light-hearted and entertaining.

GOOOOOOOOOAAAAAAAAAALLLLLLL!

The national love affair with *il calcio* encapsulates many aspects of Italian life. It's all about passion, fashion (check out the team strip or the centre forward's latest tattoo) and above all controversy. Apart from the lesser issue of national government, no other subject is so gloriously prone to conspiracy theories. When Italy lost in extra time to South Korea in the 2002 World Cup (ironically to a goal scored by a striker from the Italian club Perugia) the screams of indignation could be heard well beyond the national borders. Was it, shrieked the fans, a coincidence that Korea were playing on home soil and that they were co-organisers of the tournament? The bungling Ecuadorian referee who, it must be said, made some curious decisions suddenly became the human face of a sinister political conspiracy. The fact that South Korea then went on to beat Spain in a quarterfinal marred by yet more dodgy refereeing merely proved the point.

It was great fun and when, as always, interest waned, fans simply shrugged their shoulders and turned to the next outrage.

Tickets for the San Marino Grand Prix cost from €42 to €380 and are available via the **Consorzio San Marino** (☎ 0549 88 54 31). Full details are available online at www.formula1.sm.

Skiing
Given Italy's geography it's not surprising that skiing is popular, both as a sport and an excuse to dress up. For many, to miss *la settimana bianca* (literally 'white week') in January or February would be as unthinkable as working in August. Most of the chic resorts are in the north and in season fill quickly (see p295).

In 2006 Turin is set to host the Winter Olympics. Most of the mountain events are scheduled for resorts to the west of the city while construction is currently underway on city-centre venues for skating and ice-hockey. For further information consult the official website: www.torino2006.it.

Rugby Union
If the national football team is considered a dangerous predator, Italy's rugby braves are by comparison minnows. But interest in rugby is growing – thanks largely to Italy's plucky performance in the Six Nations Championship in 2003. In only their third year in the tournament they managed not to come last, finishing ahead of the Welsh.

The team play home international games at Rome's **Stadio Flaminio** (☎ 06 323 65 39; Viale Tiziano).

MULTICULTURALISM
Italy has traditionally been a country of emigrants, but in recent years the tables have turned and it's become a country of immigration. Long coastlines and fairly relaxed policing by Italian authorities have made it an easy point of entry into Europe. Of the estimated 1.4 million immigrants (about 2.5% of the total population), as many as half a million are reckoned to be clandestine. By some estimates more than 10% of the Italian population will be made up of immigrants by 2025.

This phenomenon has caught Italy ill-prepared. Apart from the obvious practical problems of processing such hitherto unseen numbers of immigrants, this influx of mostly young men has provided an easy target for the mindless 'immigration leads to crime' brigade. Add to this an increased suspicion of Muslims caused by the upsurge in international terrorism and you have an uneasy mix which has, at times, boiled over into acts of racism. Although it's highly unlikely that as a visitor to Italy you'll experience racism, like everywhere else the problem exists.

More than half of Italy's foreigners live in the north, some 22% in the northeast, the heartland of Umberto Bossi's secessionist Lega Nord party. It was at Bossi's instigation that parliament passed a new law on immigration where under its much debated terms, an immigrant can only enter the country with a valid work contract. Once the contract period is over the right to stay in Italy is automatically revoked. Critics note that the exception made of home-helps conveniently allows the rich to keep their army of formerly clandestine servants.

Italy is not, however, the final destination for many immigrants. The majority of them are trafficked into Italy by cut-throat rackets operating out of the Balkans, Turkey and north Africa on their way to other EU countries. The situation worries not only Italians, who have made repeated calls for an EU-wide police effort to curb the tide, but the rest of the EU as well.

Pilgrimages are big business

MEDIA

Silvio Berlusconi is the world's 45th-richest person, a media mogul supreme who just happens to be Italy's prime minister and a man who repeatedly claims not to see why his hold over much of the country's media should be a problem. Others are not so sure, pointing out that having a head of government control, either directly or indirectly, up to 90% of the nation's TV output is not ideal in a democracy.

There are seven main TV channels in Italy, of which the three state channels (RAI) and the three belonging to Mediaset, a Berlusconi company, enjoy almost total hegemony. Obviously, Mediaset is blatantly pro-Berlusconi but the question of RAI's neutrality depends on your political viewpoint: the right wing say it's objective, the left wing counter that it's pro-government.

Still, some facts speak for themselves. In 2002 Berlusconi accused two RAI journalists and a comedian of making 'criminal use' of the state broadcaster by speaking out against him in the run up to the 2001 election. 'I'm not interfering', he said, 'simply putting the record straight'. To date none of the three has worked on television again.

Berlusconi also owns the country's biggest publishing house, advertising agency and film production and distribution company. His wife and brother have a daily newspaper each.

RELIGION

Rome is synonymous with Catholicism. The Pope lives in the centre of town (OK, technically it's the Vatican) and every year millions come to Italy just to catch a glimpse of the octogenarian pontiff.

The role of religion in modern Italian life often appears to be more a matter of form than serious belief. But form counts in Italy and first communions, church weddings and religious feast days are an integral part of life. Church attendance stands at about 35%, compared with 70% after WWII, yet 84% of Italians consider themselves Catholic.

Pilgrimages are big business. Busloads of Italians still crisscross the country to venerate their favourite saint. Particularly popular is the recently beatified Padre Pio (see the boxed text, p653).

Of the non-Catholics in Italy, it's the Muslims who are making the farthest in-roads. Boosted by immigration – 36.5% of immigrants are Muslim – there are now anywhere between 580,000 and 700,000 Muslims in Italy, making Islam Italy's second religion. At number three are the

Jehovah's Witnesses with 400,000 adherents, followed by the 363,000 evangelical Protestants at number four.

ARTS

You don't need to be an expert to appreciate that Italy's artistic heritage has left an indelible mark, but what about the contemporary scene? Are Italy's modern architects, playwrights, film directors and composers worthy of their legendary predecessors? Here we offer a sweeping survey of Italy's arts, both past and present. For visual arts, such as painting and sculpture, see p58.

Literature

From his home in Verona, Tim Parks turns his breezy humour to the serious subject of Italian schooling in *Italian Education*. A good beach read, it'll make you laugh knowingly.

Italy's most recent publishing phenomenon hails from Sicily, where his stories of murder, long lunches and politicking bosses are all set. Andrea Camilleri (born 1925) has recently set booksellers' hearts racing with his novels, such as *Il Cane di Terracotta* (The Terracotta Dog), featuring the maverick detective Montalbano.

Another writer currently making waves is Roman Niccoló Ammaniti (born 1966). His latest novel, *Io Non ho Paura* (I'm not Scared), grippingly portrays the reaction of a nine-year-old to learning that his father is the perpetrator of a child kidnapping.

Children in Italy are taught that the first biggie of Italian literature was Dante Alighieri (1265–1321). His *Divina Commedia* (Divine Comedy) was the first major work written in Italian as opposed to classical Latin and tells of the author's search for God through hell, purgatory and paradise. With a supporting cast of Francesco Petrarca (Petrarch; 1304–74) and Giovanni Boccaccio (1313–75), the 14th century was something of a boom period.

Hold on, what about the Romans? interrupt the Classicists. You can't ignore Cicero (106–43 BC), Virgil (70–19 BC), Ovid (43 BC–AD 17), Horace (65–8 BC) and Livy (61 or 59 BC–AD 17). They're pre-Italian, reply the purists. Of their combined works arguably the most famous is Virgil's *Aeneid*. A rollicking epic, it tells of how Aeneas escapes from Troy only to finish up founding Rome.

Skip forward five hundred years to the Renaissance and you find that most of the artistic talent was either playing with paint or chipping away at blocks of marble. The 18th and 19th centuries, however, proved more fruitful. A landmark publication in the 1840s was *I Promessi Sposi* (The Betrothed) – written by Alessandro Manzoni (1785–1873), it's a heavy-going historical novel which uses a love story as cover for social critique.

Meanwhile south of Manzoni's Milan, in Marche, Giacomo Leopardi (1798–1837) is morosely penning verse heavy with longing and melancholy. In Florence, Carlo Collodi (1826–1890) provides a cheery interlude creating the world's most famous puppet, Pinocchio.

Suffering was a major theme of Primo Levi's work. A Jewish chemist from Turin, his internment in Auschwitz provided the horrific inspiration for his works, including *Se Questo é un Uomo* (If This is a Man*)*, the dignified story of his survival. Born in 1919, he committed suicide in 1987.

British journalist Charles Richards takes you through the murky backstage of modern Italian life in *The New Italians*. Packed with surprising revelations, not all of them bad, it's a fascinating eye-opener.

Fellow Turin writer Cesare Pavese (1908–1950) also took his own life, dying the year his greatest novel *La Luna e il Faló* (The Moon and the Bonfire) was published. Carlo Levi (1902–75), the third of this Turin triumvirate, is remembered for his haunting portrayal of southern Italy in *Cristo si é Fermato a Eboli* (Christ Stopped at Eboli).

A writer of a different ilk, Italo Calvino (1923–85) developed a unique fantastical style. *I nostri Antenati* (Our Ancestors) is a collection of three ingenious stories, featuring a viscount sliced in half, a baron who lives in the trees and a suit of armour worn by a nonexistent knight.

Rome is represented on the literary map by Alberto Moravia (1907–90) and long-time partner Elsa Morante (1912–85); her masterpiece is *La Storia* (History), the tough tale of an ill-fated family set against the poverty and desperation of wartime Rome.

Moving off-shore, Sardinia and Sicily have thrown up a number of major literary players. Nobel-prize winner Grazia Deledda's (1875–1936) novel *Canne al Vento* (Reeds in the Wind) portrays the difficulties of a Sardinian noblewoman in accepting the social changes surrounding her.

Similarly in *Il Gattopardo* (The Leopard), Giuseppe Tomasi di Lampedusa (1896–1957) describes the decline Italian unification forces on the feudal order in Sicily. A good read, it brilliantly encapsulates the island's wary mentality.

Taking the theme further, Leonardo Sciascia (1921–89) explores the Mafia's hold on Sicily in *Il Giorno della Civetta* (The Day of the Owl), his story of a murder investigation thwarted by the culture of silence.

Murder is also at the heart of bestseller *Il Nome della Rosa* (The Name of the Rose) which was written by Umberto Eco (born 1932) and filmed with Sean Connery; its prose often verges on the impenetrable.

> Very few books have captured the beguiling atmosphere of Venice as well as Salley Vickers' *Miss Garnet's Angel*, the critically acclaimed novel of a retired teacher's discovery of La Serenissima.

Cinema & Television

Images of Roberto Benigni jumping around like a loon at the 1999 Oscar ceremony, where he won Best Actor for *La Vita è Bella* (Life is Beautiful), did much for Italy's cinematic profile. However, modern Italian films still lack the verve of former pictures. Young directors like Gabriele Muccino (born 1967) and Paolo Virzí (born 1964) have enjoyed considerable success in Italy but their work tends not to travel well.

The real heyday of Italian film making was the immediate postwar period when cinematic tradition was shunned in the name of truth. The neorealists – namely, Luchino Visconti (1906–76), Roberto Rossellini (1906–77) and Vittorio de Sica (1901–74) – focused on the everyday struggles faced by Italy's war-battered citizens, rather than the muscular heroism so beloved of Hollywood.

> Everything you always wanted to know about Italian cinema is at www.cinecitta.it (Italian only).

The slippery art of *arrangiarsi* (getting by) features heavily in Italian films, particularly as a source of humour. The actor Totó (1898–1967) exploited it to great comic effect with his quick Neapolitan wit, while later exponents included three of Italy's most popular actors: Alberto

---

OUR THING

Five years after Giulio Andreotti had been acquitted for alleged Mafia links, the seven-time former prime minister was once again in the dock. This time, however, he faced a sentence of 24 years in prison for allegedly giving the order for the Mafia to kill an investigative journalist in 1979. (At the time of writing Andreotti was appealing the sentence.)

Whatever the truth, many people felt that the very fact of these trials was enough to darken the already murky waters surrounding the men of honour as well as Italy's top echelons. The power of the Mafia has long been the stuff of rumour although its reach is known to be long and usually deadly.

Italy's Mafia comprises five distinct groups: the original Sicilian Mafia, known as Cosa Nostra (Our Thing); the Calabrian 'ndrangheta; the Camorra of Naples; and the two Puglian contributions, the Sacra Corona Unita and La Rosa. Whether operating separately or together, they constitute a formidable economic power. In 2000 their combined annual turnover was estimated at US$133 billion, or about 15% of GNP, and they were said to control one business in five. Even if these figures are inflated, as critics maintain, they give a pretty good idea of the problem facing the Italian police.

DID YOU KNOW?

Rudolph Valentino's real name was Rodolfo Pietro Filiberto Guglielmi. He hailed from the small town of Castellaneta in Puglia.

Sordi (1920–2003), Massimo Troisi (1953–94) and Roberto Benigni (born 1952).

Although Italy's acting talent is, and has been, formidable with names like Rudolph Valentino (1895–1926), Marcello Mastroianni (1924–96) and Sofia Loren (born 1934) familiar to most, it's as a producer of films that Italy is better known.

Rome's vast studio complex Cinecittá was founded in 1937 and earned its place in cinematic history when epics such as *Ben Hur* and *Cleopatra* were filmed there. More recently Martin Scorcese used the same huge lots to recreate 19th-century New York for *Gangs of New York*.

The city of Rome has itself provided the background to many films. Federico Fellini (1920–94) in particular was inspired by the city. No such urban setting is evident in the spaghetti westerns of Sergio Leone (1929–89) – marked by their haunting soundtracks and eerie lack of dialogue these films made the name of both director and a certain Clint Eastwood.

At the same time, during the 1960s and '70s, Michelangelo Antonioni (born 1912) and Bernardo Bertolucci (born 1940) began to appear and an entire horror-movie industry was born. Output proved to be prolific and full of industrial-strength doses of exploitative sex and violence.

On television Italy doesn't score so well. Critics point to the quantity of imported quiz shows, the interminable variety shows and daily displays of female flesh as indicators of pretty awful standards. Apologists tartly respond that Italian TV is as good as anywhere else. (For more on television see Media, p45.)

Tobias Jones' *The Dark Heart of Italy* is a scathing study of the Berlusconi phenomenon; this fierce critique caused a scandal in Italy. 'What does he know?' critics said. Quite a lot, really.

For a sweeping panorama of postwar Italian cinema (and television) these films cover most angles.

- **Roma Cittá Aperta** (1945; Roberto Rossellini) Set in German-occupied Rome and starring Anna Magnani as a woman who loses her love to Fascism, it's a gritty testament to courage.
- **Ladri di Biciclette** (1948; Vittorio de Sica) A genuinely moving neorealist drama that traces the appalling fortune that follows the central character as he tries to support his family.
- **I Soliti Ignoti** (1958; Mario Monicelli) The cast of this classic crime caper runs like a Who's Who of Italian cinema – Totó, Vittorio Gassman, Marcello Mastroianni and Claudia Cardinale.
- **Il Gattopardo** (1963; Luchino Visconti) Burt Lancaster stars in this colourful adaptation of Tomasi di Lampedusa's melancholic drama of Sicilian nobility. The dance scene is the interminable highlight.
- **La Dolce Vita** (1960; Federico Fellini) Who hasn't seen Anita Ekberg cavorting in the Trevi Fountain? She plays Hollywood queen to Mastroianni's journalist in this slow-moving Roman classic.
- **The Good, the Bad and the Ugly** (1968; Sergio Leone) Leone's testosterone-laden spaghetti western introduces Clint Eastwood as the nameless gunslinger. It's the best of its type.
- **Profondo Rosso** (1975; Dario Argento) Not for the squeamish, this violent tale of bloody murder from Italy's king of horror paved the way for hundreds of lesser imitations.
- **Nuovo Cinema Paradiso** (1988; Giuseppe Tornatore) A small town in Sicily provides the atmospheric backdrop to a young child's relationship with a grizzly projectionist.
- **Caro Diario** (1994; Nanni Moretti) This self-indulgent autobiographical piece won Moretti the best director award at Cannes. Writer, actor and director Moretti's spiky personality makes for some entertaining viewing on screen.

All lingering shots and period costumes, *A Room with a View* (1986; James Ivory) – a romantic tale of love in pre-WW1 Florence – has done more for the city than a thousand tourist brochures.

- **Il Postino** (1994; Michael Radford) Filmed on the Aeolian islands and Procida, Massimo Troisi stars in this beautifully shot story of Chilean Pablo Neruda's exile to a southern Italian town.
- **La Vita è Bella** (1997; Roberto Benigni) Oscar-winner Benigni took something of a risk with this comedy set in a Nazi concentration camp. It paid off.
- **L'Ultimo Bacio** (2001; Gabriele Muccino) This Italian smash hit explores the lack of ideals and fears affecting Italy's 30-something generation.
- **San Remo Music Festival** (Rai 1) Italy's version of the Eurovision song contest has most Italians glued to their TV sets in February. It can have a curious kitsch appeal.
- **Blob** (Rai 3) Rai's most effective satire, this historic 15-minute programme consists of television clips cleverly edited and run without a soundtrack.

DID YOU KNOW?

Safe-sex campaigner Gabriele Paolini notched up 18,000 uninvited television appearances over a six-year period by sneaking up behind reporting journalists.

La Capa Gira (2000; Alessandro Piva) was a critical and cult success; this film of Bari's sordid underbelly was filmed entirely in dialect. This, along with a thumping soundtrack, makes it a joy to listen to.

Music

Italy and music surely means one thing – opera. What could be more Italian than Pavarotti singing Verdi?

Certainly Italy's 18th- and 19th-century opera composers rank with the best of them. Verdi (1813–1901) might be the most famous but Puccini (1858–1924), Bellini (1801–1835), Donizetti (1797–1848) and Rossini (1792–1868) are not exactly unknowns.

And then you have the great opera houses: La Scala (pp243–6) in Milan, San Carlo (p596) in Naples, La Fenice (p337; closed at the time of writing) in Venice, Teatro Massimo (p713) in Palermo and Rome's Teatro dell'Opera (p151) all count among the world's premier venues. For an outdoor performance you can do worse than Verona's Arena (p368).

Luciano Pavarotti (born 1935) is the top voice, although many see his career as a serious singer as all but over. Blind tenor Andrea Bocelli (born 1958) also sells well, having carved for himself a niche as a singer of popular classics. Italy also boasts two of the world's top conductors in Riccardo Muti (born 1941) and Claudio Abbado (born 1933).

But Italy's music heritage is not all opera-based. In fact, Antonio Vivaldi (1678–1741) created the concerto in its current form while also composing one of classical music's all time bestsellers, *Le Quattro Stagioni* (The Four Seasons).

Modern musicians are not, however, as famous as their illustrious predecessors. Part of the reason lies in the importance singers attach to their lyrics. Singer-songwriters like Francesco de Gregori, Fabrizio De Andrè and Pino Daniele simply don't translate well into English. Seventies idol Lucio Battisti tried to break into the American market but his soft, syrupy material just didn't cut it, while rockers Vasco Rossi, Ligabue and Irene Grandi fill home stadiums but offer international audiences nothing new.

Of the few who have enjoyed success outside of Italy, Zucchero (Adelmo Fornaciari) has had a few hits with his scratchy, bluesy voice and Eros Ramazzotti has made a small dent on the international pop scene.

But still homegrown talent thrives. Rappers Jovanotti and 99 Posse bang out songs with enviable energy, Carmen Consoli woos with her silky Sicilian voice and DJ's scratch and mix with the best of them. DJ Robert Miles (real name Roberto Concina) may have found success abroad but his musical schooling was pure Italian. His 1996 track *Children* was a hit throughout Europe.

Architecture

Italian architecture is more a matter of history than current affairs. True, Renzo Piano (born 1937) is one of the world's top architects, his auditorium in Rome considered an aesthetic and acoustic success; Paolo Portoghesi (born 1931) is highly regarded; and Pier Luigi Nervi (1891–1979) did original things with reinforced concrete, but still architecture in Italy isn't what it was.

Way back in the 8th century BC it was the Greek colonists of Magna Graecia who set the pace, creating an architectural heritage that's still visible in southern Italy. In Sicily, the Valley of the Temples (pp757–9) in Agrigento is a spectacular showcase while on the mainland Paestum (pp641–3) in Campania and the ruins of Metaponto (pp685–6) in Basilicata are well worth a visit.

Etruscan architecture, mostly aping Greek styles, didn't age so well. The Romans, however, were master builders, taking existing styles and blowing them up to massive proportions. Innovative construction techniques culminated in Rome's Colosseum (pp93–4) and the amphitheatres in Verona (p368) and Capua (p610).

'It's an architectural junkie's dream come true'

Fast forward to the 4th century AD and you find influences blowing in from the Holy Roman Empire's eastern provinces. The Byzantine style abounds in Ravenna and is most famously visible in Venice's St Mark's Basilica (pp331–4) – a hybrid mix of Byzantine, Romanesque and Renaissance styles, it's an architectural junkie's dream come true.

But with the collapse of the Empire, heightened insecurity and the rise of Christianity, the Romanesque period (c1050–1200) ushered in a style based on thick, plain walls, barrel-vaulted roofs and a profusion of semicircles. The Normans in Puglia were pretty good at this, leaving a series of cathedrals noted for their stark simplicity. In particular, the cathedral in Trani (p657) is considered a masterpiece.

In contrast there was nothing simple about the designs beloved of the Gothic architects. Going for size and decoration flowery even by a florist's standards, the style was considerably watered down in Italy – except for Milan's spiky cathedral (pp242–3) – with the clean lines of classical antiquity still an influence. Highlights include the Basilica di San Francesco (pp533–4) in Assisi, begun in the mid-13th century; Santa Maria Novella (pp449–50) and Santa Croce (pp452–3) in Florence; and the cathedrals of Siena (pp493–4) and Orvieto (pp546–7). Siena's, started in 1196, is arguably one of the greatest Gothic cathedrals ever built.

The dome spanning the cathedral (pp441–4) in Florence marked the arrival of the early Renaissance. Designed by Filippo Brunelleschi (1377–1446) it was original in both concept and construction and set off something of a fad. Of the domes that followed few could outdo the design Michelangelo Buonarroti (1475–1564) envisaged for St Peter's Basilica (pp115–17) in Rome. The Florentine genius was just one of a number of artists employed by the pope of the day to work on Rome's flagship church; notable names include Raphael (1483–1520), who also lent a hand with a spot of painting in the Vatican and, a century or so later, Gianlorenzo Bernini (1598–1680), the master of baroque. Bernini, when he wasn't transforming the face of Rome or chipping away at marble, designed the gigantic altar canopy above St Peter's grave.

Baroque also put the Puglian city of Lecce on the map. The most opulent of the city's churches is the Basilica della Santa Croce (p673).

No less elegant, although a little more restrained, were the works produced in the early 18th century. Rome's Spanish Steps (pp113–14; built 1726) and Trevi Fountain (p113) are two examples which pre-taste the neoclassicists. A reaction against the frivolous excesses of baroque, neoclassicism wasn't exactly low key. The Palazzo Reale di Capodimonte (pp597–8) in Naples, the royal palace designed by Luigi Vanvitelli (1700–73) in Caserta, La Scala (p243) in Milan and Teatro la Fenice (p337) in Venice don't stand out for their sobriety.

This period marks the last great era of Italian architecture. Art Nouveau, known in Italy as Stile Liberty, made a brief appearance in the early 20th century before Mussolini charged in with his grandiose vision of manly Fascist architecture. The Roman quarter of EUR (Esposizione Universale di Roma; p126) is a revealing example.

Theatre & Dance

The junior member of Italy's arts family, theatre and dance flourish without startling. Depending on your tastes you'll generally find the more experimental offerings in Bologna or Milan; Rome tends to the conservative while Naples enjoys a unique theatrical culture.

Italy's most famous playwright is Sicilian Luigi Pirandello (1867–1936). With such classics as *Sei Personaggi in Cerca d'Autore* (Six Characters in Search of an Author) he earned the 1934 Nobel Prize for Literature and influenced a whole generation of European writers.

Over the water in Naples, Eduardo De Filippo (1900–84) produced a body of often bittersweet work inspired by the everyday struggles of the average Neapolitan; *Sabato, Domenica e Lunedí* (Saturday, Sunday and Monday), a story of family jealousy around the Sunday lunch table, is a good example. Today De Filippo's son Luca continues the family tradition.

Of the contemporary scene, Nobel prize winner Dario Fo (born 1926) has been writing, directing and performing since the 1950s. His work is laced with political and social critique and has proved popular on London's West End. Hits have included *Morte Accidentale di un Anarchico* (Accidental Death of an Anarchist), *Non si Paga, Non si Paga* (Can't Pay, Won't Pay) and *Mistero Buffo*.

Dacia Maraini (born 1936) is one of Italy's most important feminist writers. She continues to work as a journalist while her all-women theatre company, Teatro della Maddalena, stages her 30-plus plays. Some of these, including the 1978 *Dialogo di una Prostituta con un suo Cliente* (Dialogue of a Prostitute with Client), have played abroad.

Dance is something that most Italians prefer to do rather than watch. Carla Fracci (born 1936) enjoyed a long dancing career with, among others, the Royal Ballet in England and the American Ballet Theatre, while Alessandra Ferri (born 1963) is today regarded as one of the world's premier ballerinas.

'Dance is something that most Italians prefer to do rather than watch'

Environment

THE LAND

DID YOU KNOW?

The biblical story of Noah and the great flood is thought to have originated from geological movements in the Mediterranean over 2 million years ago.

Italy's distinctive boot shape makes it one of the most easily recognisable countries in the world. It is made up of a long protruding mainland and two islands – Sicily (to the south) and Sardinia (to the west).

Bound on three sides by four seas (the Adriatic, Ionian, Ligurian and Tyrrhenian) this beautiful Mediterranean archipelago has over 8000km of coastline. Coastal scenery varies and you'll see lots of rocky cliffs interspersed with low-lying sandy beaches and bays.

Over 75% of Italy is mountainous with two chief ranges dominating the landscape. The most well known is the Alpine range, which stretches 966km from east to west across the northern boundary of the country. The highest mountains are in the western sector with peaks rising above 4500m. The stunning Valle d'Aosta includes Mont Blanc (Monte Bianco; 4807m), Monte Rosa (4633m), the Matterhorn (Monte Cervino; 4478m) and Gran Paradiso (4061m). The eastern sector is much lower but no less beautiful. It is here that you'll find the Dolomites – an area known worldwide for its spectacular scenery and natural beauty.

In the alpine foothills there are several large lakes; the largest of these include Lago di Garda, Maggiore and Como.

There are also over 1000 glaciers in the Alpine area, all of which are in a constant state of retreat. The most well known is the Marmolada glacier located on the border of Trentino and Veneto, popular with skiers and snowboard enthusiasts.

The second mountain chain is the Appenine range. It is often described as the 'backbone' of Italy due to its shape and extent. The range curves down in a southerly direction from Genoa to Calabria and runs for 1220km. The highest peak in the range is the Corne Grande (2912m) in the Gran Sasso d'Italia group (Abruzzo).

Only a quarter of Italy's land mass can be described as lowland. One of the largest areas is the Po valley plain. Located at the foot of the Alpine range, the plain is divided by the Po River, which at 628km is the longest river in Italy. The area is heavily populated and industrialised.

Italy has a complex geological history, characterised by marked environmental and climatic changes. Around 100 million years ago a tropical sea called the Tethys covered the area now occupied by the peninsula. Gradually the ocean began to recede and various types of materials were deposited, including limestones, dolomites and sandstones, as well as the extensive coral reefs to the northeast from which the Dolomite mountain range was later formed.

Although earlier volcanic activity had already resulted in the formation of the original core of the Alpine chain and other mountains further south, the crucial moment came around 40 million years ago when the African and European continental plates collided. The collision forced the respective borders of the plates and part of the bed of the Tethys to fold and rise up, beginning the formation of the Alpine and Apennine chains. The Alps rose up relatively quickly, at first forming an archipelago of tropical islands in the Tethys Sea. Both mountain chains underwent significant erosion, resulting in huge deposits of sand, gravel and clay at their feet and in part preparing the way for the development of lowland areas. By around two million years ago, after the landscape had been shaped and reshaped by the combined forces of continental

DID YOU KNOW?

A third of the world's population of Corsican seagulls can be found in the Parco Nazionale Arcipelago Toscano – which explains why it has become the park's mascot.

EARTHQUAKES & VOLCANOES

A fault line runs through the entire Italian peninsula – from eastern Sicily, following the Apennine range up into the Alps of Friuli-Venezia Giulia in the northeast of the country. It corresponds to the collision point of the European and African continental plates and still subjects a good part of the country to seismic activity. Central and southern Italy, including Sicily, are occasionally rocked by sometimes devastating earthquakes. The worst this century was in 1908 when Messina and Reggio di Calabria were destroyed by a seaquake (an earthquake originating under the sea floor) registering seven on the Richter scale. Almost 86,000 people were killed by the quake and subsequent tidal wave. In November 1980 an earthquake southeast of Naples destroyed several villages and killed 2570 people. An earthquake in the Apennine range in September 1997, which affected Umbria and Marche, killed 10 people and caused part of the vaulted ceiling of the Basilica di San Francesco d'Assisi, in Assisi, to collapse, destroying important frescoes. In late 2002 Molise hit the world headlines as a quake measuring 5.4 on the Richter scale destroyed a primary school in the hilltop town of San Giuliano di Puglia, killing 29 people.

Italy has six active volcanoes: Stromboli and Vulcano on the Aeolian Islands; Vesuvius, the Campi Flegrei and the island of Ischia near Naples; and Etna on Sicily. Stromboli and Etna are among the world's most active volcanoes, while Vesuvius has not erupted since 1944. However, this has become a source of concern for scientists who estimate that it should erupt every 30 years.

In 2001 officials were forced to close a tourist area and scientific monitoring station after lava flowed down Etna's southern slopes – further activity in 2002, including a quake measuring 5.6 on the Richter scale saw the temporary closure of Sicily's Catania airport. Stromboli was very active in spring 2003 when an eruption sent around 10 million cubic metres of volcanic rock plunging into the sea, setting off an 8m tidal wave that was felt more than 160km away.

Related volcanic activity produces thermal and mud springs, notably at Viterbo in Lazio and on the Aeolian Islands. The Campi Flegrei near Naples is an area of intense volcanic activity, which includes hot springs, gas emissions and steam jets.

plate movement and erosion, the Italian peninsula had almost arrived at its present-day form. The sea level continued to rise and fall with the alternation of ice ages and periods of warm climate, until the end of the last ice age around 10,000 to 12,000 years ago.

WILDLIFE

Italy is not renowned for its wildlife watching possibilities, but you'll be surprised by how many species naturally dwell in the country. As long as you don't confine yourself to urban areas you should certainly come across the more common mammals such as deer, chamois (mountain goats), ibex, wild boar, wildcats, hedgehogs, hares and rabbits. Touring the many national parks and nature reserves will increase your chances of seeing something a little more unusual.

Animals

Parco Nazionale dei Monti Sibillini is home to over 50 species of mammal including the wolf, porcupine, wildcat, snow vole and roe deer. As there are over 150 types of bird inhabiting the park you're sure to see a diversity of colourful plumage and hear a wide range of birdsong. Species include the golden eagle, peregrine falcon and rock partridge. There are also over 20 types of reptile and invertebrate living in the park, including the Orsini viper and *Chirocephalus marchesoni* (a small, extremely rare crustacean living exclusively in the Lago di Pilato).

In Parco Nazionale Dolomiti Bellunesi you should easily spot mouflon sheep and large numbers of chamois. Rather more elusive is the golden eagle and the rare alpine salamander.

DID YOU KNOW?

An Italian whale-loving group has created a sanctuary for *Balaenoptera physalus* (fin) whales in the area of the Mediterranean between Liguria, the French Cote d'Azur and Corsica.

Try Paul Sterry's *Complete Mediterranean Wildlife* for a general guide to the flora and fauna of the region.

Parco Nazionale Arcipelago Toscana occupies one of the main migratory corridors in the Mediterranean. The islands of Elba, Giglio, Capraia, Gorgona, Pianosa, Giannutri and Montecristo provide endless nesting possibilities for birds. Species include falcons, wall creepers, various types of swallow and the red partridge. Other unusual wildlife living in the park includes the tarantula gecko and the endemic viper of Montecristo.

Swordfish, tunafish and dolphins are also commonly found along the coastline.

The geographical positioning of Parco Nazionale del Circeo also coincides with the main migratory routes. The park is a good place to spot water birds such as the spoonbill and greater flamingo, as well as rare birds of prey such as the peregrine and osprey.

White sharks are known to exist in the Mediterranean (particularly in the southern waters) but attacks are extremely rare.

For more information on the National Parks, see p55.

Plants

The long human presence on the Italian peninsula has had a significant impact on the environment, resulting in the widespread destruction of original forests and vegetation and their replacement with crops and orchards. Aesthetically the result is not always displeasing – much of the beauty of Tuscany, for instance, lies in the combination of olive groves, vineyards, fallow fields and stands of cypress and pine.

Italy's plant life is predominantly Mediterranean. Three broad classifications of evergreen tree dominate – ilex (or evergreen oak), cork and pine. The occasional virgin ilex and oak forest still survives in the more inaccessible reaches of Tuscany, Umbria, Calabria, Puglia and Sardinia. These ancient woods are made up of trees that can reach up to 15m high and whose thick canopies block out light to the forest floor, preventing most undergrowth. Most common are ilex stands that have been created, or at least interfered with, by humans. They tend to be sparser, with smaller trees and abundant undergrowth.

ENDANGERED SPECIES

Changes to the environment, combined with the Italians' passion for *la caccia* (hunting), have led to many native animals and birds becoming extinct, rare or endangered. Hunters constitute a powerful lobby group in Italy and continue to win regular referendums on whether hunting should be banned.

In the 20th century 13 species became extinct in Italy, including the Alpine lynx. Under laws introduced progressively over the years, many animals and birds are now protected but the World Wide Fund for Nature (WWF) says 60% of Italy's vertebrates are at risk.

Among those slowly making a comeback after being reintroduced in the wild are the brown bear, which survives only in the Brenta area of Trentino; Marsican bear, which has been reintroduced in Abruzzo; and lynx, which is extremely rare and found mainly in the area around Tarvisio in Friuli-Venezia Giulia. Efforts are also underway to reintroduce the lynx in Abruzzo. Wolves are slightly more common, although you will still be hard-pressed to spot one in the wild. They can be seen in a large enclosure at Civitella Alfedena in the Parco Nazionale d'Abruzzo.

There are only about 100 otters left in Italy and most live protected in the Parco Nazionale del Cilento in Campania. Another extremely rare animal is the monk seal: only about 10 are thought to survive in sea caves on the eastern coast of Sardinia. The magnificent golden eagle was almost wiped out by hunters and now numbers about 300 pairs throughout the country. A colony of griffon vultures survives on the western coast of Sardinia, near Bosa. The bearded vulture, known in Italy as the *gipeto*, has been reintroduced in the Alps in the past decade.

Next to the ilex the most common tree is the cork. Corkwood has been prized since ancient times and there is not a cork tree standing today that is part of a virgin forest. Often they are mixed in with ilex and other oaks, although in Sicily and Sardinia it is possible to come across pure cork forests.

There are three types of pine: the Aleppo pine (the hardiest of the three); the domestic pine, especially common in Tuscany and also known as the umbrella pine for the long, flattened appearance of its branches; and the maritime pine, which, in spite of its name, is generally found further inland than the other two!

Ancient imports that are an inevitable part of much of the Italian countryside (especially from Tuscany south) are the olive and cyprus. The former comes in many shapes and sizes – the most striking of which are the robust trees of Puglia.

Much of the country is covered by *macchia* (maquis), which is a broad term that covers all sorts of vegetation ranging from 2m to as much as 6m in height. Typical *macchia* includes herbs such as lavender, rosemary and thyme as well as shrubs of the cistus family (gorse, juniper and heather), and if the soil is acidic there may also be broom. Orchids, gladioli and irises flower beneath these shrubs and are colourful in spring.

Where the action of humans and nature has been particularly harsh, or the soil is poor, the *macchia* becomes *gariga*, the very barest of scrub. This is dominated by aromatic herbs such as lavender, rosemary and thyme.

NATIONAL PARKS

Italy has 20 national parks, with four more on the way, and well over 400 smaller nature reserves, natural parks and wetlands. The national parks cover just over 1.5 million hectares (5%) of the country, but Italy's environmentalists are continually campaigning to increase the amount of land that is protected. The parks, reserves and wetlands all play a crucial part in the protection of the country's flora and fauna and there are regular conservation events and open days.

The national parks include:

- **Parco Nazionale dei Monti Sibillini**, Umbria/Marche (p544)
- **Parco Nazionale del Cilento e Vallo di Diano**, Campania (p643)
- **Parco Nazionale del Gargano**, Puglia (pp651–56)
- **Parco Nazionale del Gran Sasso e Monti della Laga**, Abruzzo (p578)
- **Parco Nazionale del Pollino**, Basilicata/Calabria
- **Parco Nazionale della Majella**, Abruzzo (p579)
- **Parco Nazionale della Val Grande**, Piedmont
- **Parco Nazionale dell'Arcipelago di la Maddalena**, Sardinia
- **Parco Nazionale Arcipelago Toscano**, Tuscany
- **Parco Nazionale dell'Asinara**, Sardinia
- **Parco Nazionale dell'Aspromonte**, Calabria
- **Parco Nazionale delle Cinque Terre**, Liguria (p192)
- **Parco Nazionale delle Dolomiti Bellunesi**, the Veneto (p373)
- **Parco Nazionale delle Foreste Casentinesi**, Emilia-Romagna
- **Parco Nazionale d'Abruzzo**, Abruzzo (pp580–1)
- **Parco Nazionale del Circeo**, Lazio
- **Parco Nazionale Gran Paradiso**, Piedmont/Valle d'Aosta (pp233–4)
- **Parco Nazionale della Calabria**, Calabria
- **Parco Nazionale dello Stelvio**, Lombardy(p289)/Trentino-Alto Adige (pp310–11)

Where to Watch Birds in Italy, published by the Italian Bird Protection League (LPIU), highlights over 100 recommendations for species spotting.

For the Italian Bird Protection League (LIPU), see www.lipu.it It has a UK branch at www.lipu-uk.org

Field Guide to Wildflowers of Southern Europe by Paul Davies and Bob Gibbons is a pocket-sized identification guide covering around 1200 species.

ENVIRONMENTAL ISSUES

The official Italian national parks website, offers comprehensive information on individual parks, useful publications, details of local wildlife, weather forecasts and educational initiatives. Check it out at www.parks.it

Italy is a dramatically beautiful country, but since Etruscan times humans have left their mark on the environment. The industrialised north of the country and major cities such as Rome, Milan and Naples currently suffer from high levels of air pollution. Sulphur dioxide levels have been actively reduced in recent years, primarily by substituting natural gas for coal, but this is not the whole cause of the problem. A large percentage of the smog and poor air quality can be attributed to the fact that Italy has one of the highest levels of car ownership per capita in the world. Visible evidence of the damage this causes can be seen on buildings where the stone has become blackened due to consistent exposure to exhaust fumes and emissions.

The Italian government's record on ecological and environment issues has not been good, although in the past few years things have begun to improve. The Ministry for the Environment, created in 1986, is now taking a tougher line concerning the environment, partly in response to EU directives. They are currently involved in and committed to many international agreements which include solving issues such as desertification, hazardous wastes, air pollution and marine dumping. They have also recently recognised the problems caused by the overuse of automobiles and have introduced programmes to minimise the damage. Initiatives include car-sharing programmes, car-free Sundays and the renovation of buildings that have been badly affected.

For details of Italy's cleanest beaches, see www.blueflag.org

Due to the inadequate treatment and disposal of industrial and domestic waste, the seas, and consequently many beaches, are polluted to some extent. Areas particularly affected include the Ligurian coast in the northern Adriatic (where there is an algae problem as a result of industrial pollution) and areas near major cities such as Rome and Naples. However, it is possible to find clean beaches, particularly on the islands of Sardinia and Sicily.

Aimed at amateur enthusiasts, Christopher Kilburn and Bill McGuire's *Italian Volcanoes* provides an in-depth account of Italy's key volcanic districts.

Litter-conscious visitors to the peninsula will be astounded by the widespread habit of Italians who dump rubbish when and where they like. In 2002 employees from Lever Faberge Italy teamed up with journalists and volunteers to clean up a glacier in the Italian Alps. The team dug into the ice and collected 20,000kg of plastic, cans and glass – some of which was 40 years old.

RESPONSIBLE TRAVEL

Visitors should travel responsibly at all times. Follow these common-sense rules:

- Always dispose of litter thoughtfully
- Do not discard items that could start a fire (cigarette butts, glass bottles etc) – forest fires are an annual torment
- Stick to footpaths wherever possible
- Close gates behind you
- Do not pick flowers or wilfully damage tree bark or roots – some of the species you see are protected
- Do not climb on walls or parts of buildings
- Respect landowners' property and do not trespass into private areas
- Take care when walking near cliffs – they can be dangerously slippery and quick to crumble
- Keep noise to a minimum and avoid disturbing wildlife
- Pay attention to signs and public warnings

In addition to the environmental problems caused by humans, the country is also affected by many natural hazards, including landslides, mudflows, earthquakes and volcanic eruptions. Environmental groups maintain that some of these natural disasters are exacerbated by human intervention. It seems that the increase in the number of devastating floods that have hit parts of northern Italy in recent years and landslides in Campania are due not only to increased rainfall, but also to deforestation and excessive building near rivers. Steps are being taken to reduce the damage but progress has been slow to date.

The World Wide Fund for Nature (WWF) has an Italian chapter at www.wwf.it

Italian Artistic Tradition

Almost all roads in the history of Italian art lead back to Rome – home of both the Caesars and the popes. Over the centuries, art in Italy has invariably been used as a propaganda tool, either in the service of the state or of the church.

Roman art covers a period of well over 1000 years, from Romulus to Constantine, and for most of this time art and politics were intimately connected. Monuments that recognised public service and buildings that met public needs formed the core of early Roman art. Civic leaders of the Roman Republic and later, of the Roman Empire, were well aware of the potential of art as a means of promoting their own ends.

Constantine's conversion to Christianity, which was adopted as the state religion in 313, began the trend of official art being used to glorify the Church rather than the emperor. This trend continued up to and beyond the 15th century and the Renaissance. Glorification of the church was almost the sole purpose of baroque artists during the Counter-Reformation. The artists of the Renaissance were drawn to the secular art of the early Roman Empire and their adaptation of these classical and Hellenistic forms had more effect on subsequent European art than early Christian art.

In 20th century Italy, under Benito Mussolini's dictatorship, art was once again pressed into the service of the state. Mussolini initiated an extensive programme of archaeology in Rome and North Africa, with the express purpose of showing his regime as an extension of imperial Rome. He used ancient Roman symbols for political purposes and had buildings designed in a style of classicism that conveyed imperial grandeur.

ART & THE INDIVIDUAL

In what art historians call the archaic period, Rome was on the fringe of the Etruscan realm, which had developed its own art forms. However, almost no Roman art has survived from this period. The Roman Republic began with the expulsion of the last Etruscan king in the 6th century BC, but it continued to look over its shoulder for artistic inspiration to the Etruscan heritage or to the Greeks. Roman society was essentially bourgeois and the wealthy were supplied with looted originals from the Greek world, which hindered progress in art. But eventually Roman art enlarged upon and almost utterly transformed the Greek tradition.

Unlike Hellenic art, Roman art was essentially secular and inextricably linked with its architectural development. There was much more emphasis on interior space and decoration than on the appearance of the exterior. The challenge was to create and adorn larger and more magnificent interiors to match imperial pride and the growing self-consciousness and importance of the individual.

Apart from their skills in architecture and engineering, the Romans are celebrated for three achievements in art: the development of portraiture; the narrative (most notably seen in historical relief sculpture); and landscape painting.

By the end of the 3rd century BC the Roman portrait was a firmly established tradition. Verism, a type of portraiture often referred to simply as the Republican portrait, is characterised by a stark realism in keeping with the Romans' interest in personality rather than type. It may initially have been inspired by Etruscan examples but is thought to owe much to the custom of storing death masks of family ancestors.

ART IN THE SERVICE OF THE STATE

Art during the Roman Empire was initially dominated by commemorative reliefs of successful generals and buildings financed by public figures. But soon the Romans found that they needed an art that served the state and not just the individual. Art and architecture were now instruments of propaganda for the state as guided by the imperial family.

Relief sculptures depicting historical events on the walls of public monuments became popular. Particular emperors or members of their families were shown in imposing positions. In contrast to the Greeks, who preferred to tell stories through myth, the Romans liked to depict historical events in a factual and secular way. The prowess of the supreme Roman, the emperor, who represented the grandeur of Rome but was also an individual, was of prime interest. Roman narrative sculpture was thus a particular extension of the trend in Roman portraiture.

'Augustus used art to remind the public of his success'

Many of the sculptural and architectural works made in the service of the first emperor, Augustus (27 BC–AD 14), had a propaganda message that was strengthened through associations with classical Greece and the golden age of Athens. In the 5th century BC Augustus used art to remind the public of his success in fulfilling the visions of Julius Caesar. His style and approach became a model for subsequent emperors because he was able to create a visual means of demonstrating the benefits he had brought to the Roman populace.

His most significant propaganda statement was the Ara Pacis Augustae (p120), the altar set up on the Campus Martius in Rome to commemorate the peace that Augustus had finally brought to the Empire. Flanked by tall screens, carved externally with life-size figures, the altar repeatedly reminds viewers, through myth and allegory as well as representations of contemporary events, of the greatness of the emperor.

Whereas the Ara Pacis depicts space in quite a sophisticated way through details of landscape, the sculptural reliefs on the Basilica Aemilia in the Roman Forum (pp89–91), illustrating the death of Tarpeia, a woman who turned traitor to her own city, are quite flat. These works exemplify two important strains in the art of the period, one idealised and elegant, the other, dramatic, intense and direct, and representative of the native Italic, or plebeian, style.

The Augustan Legacy

The emperors who followed Augustus always had his reputation and plans as a legacy. Each succeeding emperor set a new tone, which gave a special character to the artistic output of his time, although the framework of images and associations that Augustus had set up remained unaltered. The value of continuity for political purposes was put above personal taste.

A century after the reliefs on the Ara Pacis were carved, the whole perspective in portraiture was already undergoing significant and theatrical change. In the Arch of Titus (AD 81; p91) at the head of the Roman Forum, the Emperor is glorified even above Victory, who crowns him, and his chariot is twisted awkwardly to exhibit him in full face.

In the course of its search for new freedoms, Roman historical art seized upon and perfected a convention known as the 'continuous style' – where the same character is repeated from scene to scene in a single undivided composition – a sort of petrified strip-cartoon. The convention recurs in Roman reliefs, particularly in mythological stories on sarcophagi of the

2nd and 3rd centuries. The greatest manifestation of this type is Trajan's Column (p88), a sculptural document, erected in the Roman Forum in AD 113, which records in a breathtaking continuous spiral the campaigns and victories of Trajan over the Dacians, providing a constant reminder of the virtues of the emperor and by extension the success of the state.

The Last Roman Emperor

After 395 the Roman world was divided into an Eastern and a Western Empire. The rule of Constantine marked the end of an era. It was the last fanfare of the pagan empire and the prelude to the Christian state of Byzantium. Constantine turned to works of art, many of them colossal, to proclaim his own importance. But he also initiated the practice of removing sculptures from previous works and erecting them on his own monuments, hoping to acquire some of the honour and appeal of the predecessors whose sculptural panels he reused. The last great monument of Imperial Rome was the Arch of Constantine (p94).

In 330 Constantine renamed the ancient city of Byzantium Constantinople and made it his capital. Though the main imperial centre of gravity now lay in the east, the people of Constantinople still thought of themselves as Romans, and the guardians and true practitioners of Roman art, for several centuries. Pagan art traditions continued, though much of the imagery during the 4th century could be seen as imperial rather than pagan.

ART IN THE SERVICE OF THE CHURCH
Byzantine & Early Christian

The city of Constantinople now became the great cultural and artistic centre of Christianity; it was to remain so up to the time of the Renaissance, though its influence on the art of that period was never as fundamental as the art of ancient Rome. Byzantine art grew out of the same background as early Christian art and at times can hardly be separated from it. Christianity de-emphasised the naturalistic aspects of the classical tradition and exalted the spirit over the body. These new expectations joined the requirements of clarity and hierarchy, typical of this period, that were carried over into the art of Byzantium and the early medieval period. But though the Christian emphasis on the immaterial world gave art a new meaning, it did not give it a new style.

The Medieval World

The Italian Middle Ages have often been regarded as simply an age between the Roman Empire and the Renaissance. But such a view makes it very difficult to understand all subsequent Italian history, for Italy as we know it was born in the Middle Ages. The barbarian invasions of the 5th and 6th centuries began a process that turned a unified empire into a land of small independent city-states, the centres of political life and the focus of culture. Italian towns have always managed to incorporate the past into the present with a gradual process of adaptation and transformation. This process can be seen most clearly in the classical buildings adapted to new purposes from the 4th century onwards. Most of this adaptation and reuse of classical buildings, or bits of buildings, was motivated by convenience – it was easier and cheaper than having to quarry and rebuild – but not entirely. As the emperors had sought to glorify their rule, the bishops of Rome sought to glorify the new Church. However, the conversions played a vital role in preserving many buildings after their original function had disappeared. Ironically, the Renaissance architects were much more destructive, because they were seldom

'Christian emphasis on the immaterial world did not give art a new style'

content to adapt ancient buildings to new functions or to reuse marble without having it recarved.

Once more ideas of clarity and simplicity began to outweigh ideals of faithful imitation in art. One of the major influences on art of this time was Pope Gregory the Great (540–604). His declaration that: 'Painting can do for the illiterate what writing does for those who can read', was aimed at the iconoclasts of Byzantium. But it also had the effect of limiting artists. If the story had to be told as clearly and simply as possible, anything that might divert attention from this main and sacred aim had to be omitted. Thus, at first glance, many pictures of the period look rather stiff and rigid. There is nothing of the mastery of movement and expression that was the pride of Greek art, and which persisted until Roman times.

A Handbook of Roman Art by Martin Henig is a clear, readable introduction to the whole spectrum of Roman art.

THE ART OF ILLUSION – THE ITALIAN REVOLUTION IN PAINTING

The Byzantine painters in Italy knew how to make use of light and shade and had an understanding of the principles of foreshortening. It only required a genius to break the spell of their conservatism, to venture into a new world and translate the figures of Gothic sculpture into painting. This genius was the Florentine painter Giotto di Bondone (c1266–1337). Giotto's aims and outlook owed much to the great sculptors of the northern cathedrals, and his methods owed much to the Byzantine masters. But the Italians were convinced that he had initiated an entirely new epoch of art. Giotto's most famous works are frescoes (so called because they must be painted on the wall while the plaster is still wet). Around 1306 he covered the walls of the Cappella degli Scrovegni (p359) in Padua in northern Italy with stories of the life of the Virgin and Christ. Underneath he painted personifications of virtues and vices such as those sometimes used in northern cathedrals. Giotto's figure of Faith is a painting that gives the illusion of a statue in the round, with its foreshortening of the arm, modelling of face and neck, and deep shadows in the flowing folds of the drapery. Nothing like this had been done for a thousand years. Giotto had rediscovered the art of creating the illusion of depth on a flat surface.

THE WORSHIP OF NATURE

By the 14th century the aims of painting had shifted from telling a sacred story as clearly as possible to representing nature as faithfully as possible. In Italy, particularly in Florence, Giotto's art had changed the whole idea of painting. The old Byzantine manner suddenly seemed stiff and outmoded. The ideals of the Gothic painters of the north also began to have their effect on the southern masters, particularly in Siena. The greatest Sienese master of Giotto's generation, Duccio (c1255–1319), successfully breathed new life into the old Byzantine forms instead of discarding them altogether. *The Annunciation*, (now in the Uffizi, Florence; pp447–9) painted by Simone Martini and Lippo Memmi in 1333 for an altar in Siena's cathedral, successfully fitted figures into the complicated shape of the panel – an art learned from the medieval tradition. But when medieval artists arranged the symbols of the sacred stories to form a satisfying arrangement, they ignored the real shape and proportion of things, forgetting about space altogether. The Sienese artists worked differently, introducing light and shade.

Until this time artists had merely learned the ancient formulas for representing the main figures of the sacred stories and applied this knowledge in new combinations. Now they had to be able to make studies from nature. But soon even the newly acquired mastery of painting such details as flowers or animals did not satisfy them. They wanted to explore the laws of vision and to acquire sufficient knowledge of the human body to build it up in their statues and pictures, as the Greeks and Romans had done. Essentially, medieval art was at an end.

The Conquest of Reality – The Renaissance

The Penguin Book of the Renaissance by JH Plumb analyses the successes of this astounding movement.

In the 14th century the highest praise for an artist was to say his work was as good as that of the ancients. But many believed the northern 'barbarians' had almost destroyed the heritage of art, science and scholarship that had flourished in the classical period. It was time for a rebirth, a *renaissance*, of the glorious past. In Florence, in the first decades of the 15th century, a group of artists and architects deliberately set out to create a new art. Their leader was an architect, Filippo Brunelleschi (1377–1446), whose fame rests partly on an achievement of construction and design. The Florentines wished to have their cathedral crowned by a mighty dome and Brunelleschi devised a method to span the immense space between the pillars. He went on to develop a totally new way of building, using the forms of classical architecture to create harmony and beauty and his friends extended his interest in classical proportions and values to painting and sculpture.

Even the Greeks, who understood foreshortening, and the Hellenistic painters, skilled in creating the illusion of depth, did not know the mathematical laws by which objects appear to diminish as they recede from us. Brunelleschi gave artists the mathematical means of solving this problem and a whole new perspective.

THE NEW PERSPECTIVE

One of the first paintings made according to these mathematical rules was a wall painting in a Florentine church: *The Holy Trinity, the Virgin, St John & Donors*, in the Basilica di Santa Maria Novella (pp449–50), Florence, painted about 1428 by Masaccio (1401–28). He not only introduced the technical trick of perspective but used it to frame his figures so that startled viewers felt they were looking through a hole in the wall into a burial chapel with figures that looked like statues. After this the Florentine masters were no longer content to repeat the old formulae handed down by medieval artists. Like the Greeks and Romans they began to study the human body in their studios and workshops by asking models or fellow artists to pose for them.

The greatest sculptor of Brunelleschi's circle was the Florentine master Donatello (c1386–1466). His marble statue of St George, in the Chiesa di Orsanmichele (p445), Florence, shows how he wanted to replace the gentle refinement of his predecessors with a new vigorous observation of nature. In Siena, Donatello made a bronze relief called *Herod's Feast* (1427) for a font in San Giovanni. To people accustomed to the clear and graceful narrative of Gothic art this must have seemed shocking. Like Masaccio's figures, Donatello's are harsh and angular, their gestures violent.

Thus the Florentine masters had developed a method by which nature could be represented in a picture with almost scientific accuracy. They began with the framework of perspective lines and then they built up the human body through their knowledge of anatomy and the laws of foreshortening. The mastery of science and the knowledge of classical art remained for some time the exclusive possession of the Italian artists of the Renaissance. But the passionate will to create a new art more faithful to nature than anything ever seen before also inspired the artists of the same generation to the north of the country. The Flemish painter Jan van Eyck (c1390–1441) perfected the new technique of oil painting, substituting slow-drying oil for the egg which, until then, had been used as binder for coloured pigments. By the first decade of the 16th century, oil paint had become universally established as the prime painting medium in Italy.

The powers artists had gained now made it impossible to think of art only as a means to convey the meaning of sacred stories; they wanted to use these powers to add to the beauty and grace of life. Fascinated by the idea that art could be used to mirror a fragment of the real world, artists everywhere began to experiment and to search for new and startling effects.

For details on the movement and its artists, visit the site of the Italian Renaissance Art Project (IRAP), www.italian-art.org

NEW PROBLEMS

While artists elsewhere were applying the inventions of the Florentine masters, artists in Florence became aware of the new problems these innovations had created. Though medieval painters were unaware of the rules of draughtsmanship, this enabled them to distribute their figures over the picture in any way they liked in order to create the perfect pattern. Even 14th-century painters like Simone Martini (c1280–1344) were still able to arrange their figures to form a lucid design.

As soon as the new concept of making the picture a mirror of reality was adopted, however, this question of how to arrange the figures was no longer so easy to solve, particularly where large works like altar paintings were involved. These paintings had to be seen from afar and had to fit into the architectural framework of the whole church. Moreover, they had to present a sacred story to the worshippers in a clear and impressive outline. It was in finding a solution to this problem that Italian art reached its greatest heights a generation later.

Perfect Harmony – the High Renaissance

The beginning of the 16th century (what Italians call the Cinquecento), the time of Leonardo da Vinci (1452–1519) and Michelangelo Buonarotti (1475–1564), of Raphael (1483–1520), Titian (1485) and Correggio (1489–1534), is the most famous period of Italian art. By now cities competed with each other to secure the services of the great artists to beautify their buildings and to create works of lasting fame. The masters vied with each other for the commissions and sought social status to recognise the triumph of their skills.

The spirit of bold enterprise which made Donato Bramante's plan for St Peter's possible is characteristic of the period of the High Renaissance, which produced so many of the world's greatest artists. Nothing seemed impossible to them, and Leonardo da Vinci and Michelangelo Buonarotti set new standards in art of which nobody had ever dreamed.

THE CRISIS OF PERFECTION

Around 1520 all lovers of art in the Italian cities seemed to agree that painting had reached the peak of perfection. Michelangelo, Raphael, Titian and da Vinci had actually achieved everything that former generations had tried to do. No problem of draughtsmanship seemed too difficult, no subject matter too complicated. Now artists tried to beat the initiators of perfection at their own game, concentrating on the style and tending to neglect the meaning; this was derided by later critics as Mannerism. But artists such as Il Parmigiano (1504–1540) who deliberately sought to create something new and unexpected, even at the expense of the 'natural' beauty established by the great masters, were perhaps the first 'modern' artists.

In the late 16th century two artists of very different natures, who had grown tired of Mannerism, took very different approaches to painting in an attempt to break the deadlock caused by the achievements of their predecessors.

DID YOU KNOW?
Caravaggio often had to repaint commissions for churches because the saintly subjects were deemed too lifelike.

Annibale Caracci (1560–1609), from Bologna, had studied the art of Venice and Correggio and was entranced by the work of Raphael. He aimed to recapture something of their simplicity and beauty instead of deliberately contradicting them. He created magnificent frescoes of mythological subjects in the Palazzo Farnese (p112). The style followed by Guido Reni and the followers of Caracci, who formulated the programme of idealising nature according to the standards set by classical statue, has often been described as Neoclassical. Caracci's *Virgin Mourning Christ* altar painting (now in the Museo Nazionale in Naples) is as simple and harmonious as any early Renaissance painting. But the way he used light in a direct appeal to the emotions foreshadowed the new school of art that came to be known as baroque.

A website dedicated to the life and works of the artist can be seen at www.michelangelo .com/buonarroti.html

Michelangelo Merisi da Caravaggio (1573–1610), the *enfant terrible* of the late 16th century art world, had no liking for classical models or respect for 'ideal beauty'. Described by the writer Stendhal as a 'great painter…a wicked man' and centuries later by art critic Robert Hughes as 'saturnine, coarse and queer', his paintings were as controversial as his behaviour, and he was condemned by contemporaries for being a 'naturalist'. He used peasants and prostitutes as his models to give the Madonnas and saints of his paintings a realism that was not always welcome. But Caravaggio's way of handling light and shade to make his scenes glow with an uncompromising honesty has delighted and influenced artists for generations.

Baroque

The baroque style is perhaps the greatest example of art used to convey concepts – primarily faith in the Church and in its doctrines. Designed to combat the rapidly spreading Protestant Reformation and, at the same time, to emphasise the importance of the Catholic religion, the baroque was blatantly propagandistic: all the visual arts were used to make an appeal to the faithful that was both sensory and emotional.

The essential feature of baroque art was a fundamental ambiguity. baroque artists proclaimed themselves the heirs of the Renaissance and claimed to accept its norms, but they violated these systematically. Renaissance meant equilibrium, moderation, sobriety, reason, logic – baroque meant movement, desire for novelty, love of the infinite, of contrasts and the bold fusion of all forms of art. It was as dramatic, exuberant and theatrical as the preceding period had been serene and restrained. In fact the term baroque was used by critics of a later period to describe the tendencies of the 17th century that they found to be absurd or grotesque.

The baroque style in Italy is synonymous with Rome and the work of two rivals, Gianlorenzo Bernini (1598–1680) and Francesco Borromini (1599–1667), who helped to make the capital the series of stage sets it appears to be today. Architect Borromini was no longer content with decorating a wall using principles taken from classical architecture. His 'over-the-top' Chiesa di Sant'Agnese in Agone (p112) in Rome's Piazza Navona is a typical baroque church, curved as if it had been modelled in clay – ornate and highly theatrical.

In Giorgio Vasari's *Lives of the Artists*, the 16th-century painter reflects on the lives of his contemporaries in Florence.

Theatricality is also evident in the work of the great baroque sculptor Bernini, who dared to represent the vision of the Spanish Saint Theresa in a moment of ecstasy for a side chapel in Santa Maria della Vittoria, Rome. The artist deliberately used this work of religious art to arouse feelings of exultation and mystic transport. In this and many other works he achieved an intensity of facial expression which until then had never been attempted with art. Even his handling of draperies was, at the time, completely new. Instead of letting them fall in dignified folds in the approved classical manner, he made them writhe and whirl to add to the effect of excitement and movement. He was soon imitated all over Europe.

In the decoration of the ceiling of the Jesuit church in Rome, Chiesa del Gesù (p88), Giovanni Battista Gaulli (1639–1709), also known as Baciaccia, a painter of Bernini's following, gives us the illusion that the vault of the church has opened and that we are looking straight into the glories of heaven.

Rudolf Wittkower's Art & Architecture in Italy 1600–1750 is an excellent reference covering baroque art and architecture.

PAST & PRESENT: THE NEW ITALY

Travellers have been visiting Italy for centuries, primarily to admire the glories of her past greatness. Though the Roman past inspired great innovations in Italian art, the modern age could not rival these artistic achievements. By the 18th century, Italy was beginning to rebel against years of foreign rule – first the French under Napoleon and then the Austrians. But though new ideas of political unity were forming there was only one innovation in art – the painting and engraving of views, most notably in Venice, to meet the demand of travellers wanting souvenirs. Francesco Guardi's (1712–93) views of the Venetian lagoon show that the spirit of baroque, the taste for movement and bold effects, can express itself even in a simple cityscape.

Despite the slow movement towards Italian unity, at the beginning of the 19th century Italy's cities remained as they had been for centuries – highly individual centres of culture with sharply contrasting ways of life. Music was the supreme art of this period and the age of revolution in politics was an era of chaste refinement in the arts. Not surprisingly Neoclassicism, whose greatest exponent in Italy was the sculptor Antonio Canova (1757–1822), was most at home in the land that had produced classicism itself. Canova renounced movement in favour of stillness, emotion in favour of restraint, illusion in favour of simplicity, and he appealed to connoisseurs throughout Europe, notably Napoleon himself. Canova's most famous work is a daring sculpture of Pauline Bonaparte Borghese as a reclining *Venere Vincitrice* (Conquering Venus), in the Galleria Borghese (pp120–1) in Rome. But Canova was the last Italian artist to win overwhelming international fame. For some 400 years, Italian architecture, sculpture and painting had played a dominant role in the cultural life of Europe. With the death of Canova in 1822 this supremacy came to an end.

Modern Movements

The two main developments in Italian art at the outbreak of WWI could not have been more different. Futurism, led by Filippo Tommaso Marinetti and Umberto Boccioni, sought new ways to express the dynamism of the machine age; Metaphysical Painting, by contrast, looked inwards and produced mysterious images from the subconscious world.

Futurism demanded a new art for a new world and denounced every attachment to the arts of the past. Unlike many other movements, named by antagonistic critics, it chose its own name and was not born out of any dissatisfaction with a particular art form. It started with a general idea that was expressed in words, the first example of the modern artist's manifesto. It was some time before the movement, soon joined by Giacomo Balla (1871–1958) and Gino Severini (1883–1965), found a pictorial vehicle for its ideas. When the first major show of Futurist paintings opened in Milan in 1911, it was still the subject matter rather than the style of work that was new. Futurism has thus been described as an art movement that put ideas before style. In this it challenged not only traditional artistic values but also the aesthetic ambitions of most avant-garde art. Some art critics contend that without the Italian Futurists, Cubism

Check out
www.artcyclopedia.com
for a database describing
the artistic movements
and their major exponents.

could never have played so big a role in modern art. By showing bright colour joined to cubist broken forms the Italian Futurists encouraged the lesser Cubists of Paris to move away from a monochromatic idiom.

Futurism was the last wholly Italian movement. Though it did not last long, it was one of the most radical modern movements, noisily rejecting all traditions and institutions.

Metaphysical Painting also had a short life. Its most famous exponent, Giorgio De Chirico, lost interest in the style after the war, but his work held a powerful attraction for the Surrealist Movement, which developed in France in the 1920s. Stillness and a sense of foreboding are the haunting qualities of De Chirico's *Place d'Italie 1912*, showing disconnected images from the world of dreams in settings that usually embody memories of classical Italian architecture.

Though Giacomo Manzu (1908–91) later revived the Italian religious tradition in sculpture (his best-known work is a bronze door in St Peter's in Rome; pp115–17) the days when art in Italy was fully employed in the service of the church or the state seem finally to be over and art and the individual has taken on a new meaning in the modern age.

Food & Drink by Matthew Evans

To eat and drink in Italy is to be thrust into the heart of Italian life. Although this is a country that has exported its food culture around the world, Italian cuisine – *cucina italiana* – as such doesn't exist. Spend any time among the people of, say, Umbria and you'll hear an awful lot about Umbrian cuisine. But Italian cuisine? Well, that's not something they know about. The geography makes for many microclimates and the history for plenty of microcultures. The result is a range of food that is diverse, unexpected and intriguing.

The Art of Eating Well: Italy's Most Treasured Cooking is a translation of Pellegrino Artusi's great early text on Italian food, first published in 1891.

STAPLES
Despite the mind-boggling number of variations that exist, some common staples bind the regions of Italy.

Bread
Il pane (bread) is served at every meal apart from breakfast; you'll be given a basket of it in restaurants and freshly cut chunks in homes. Most of the time it will be white and fairly ordinary, although delicious speciality breads do exist. On restaurant tables you'll see *grissini*, thin sticks of crispy bread.

Pizza
Pizza is still a firm favourite at home and one of Italy's biggest exports, but don't expect it to be like the impostors you find around the globe. In Naples, where the modern pizza (round and baked to order) was born, the passion for eating it is only surpassed by its quality. All over Italy it has become the most popular fast food, baked in large rectangular trays and sold in slices as *pizza al taglio* (pizza by the slice).

Pasta
Although Liguria and Campania still dispute who made it first, pasta is now synonymous with Italian food the world over. It can be roughly divided into two groups: dried and fresh.

Pastasciutta (dried pasta) is usually made with *semolino* (durum wheat) and water. Most *pastasciutta* originated in the southern part of Italy (think spaghetti and penne) and suits predominantly vegetable-based sauces.

Pasta fresca (fresh pasta), also known as *pasta all'uovo* (pasta with eggs) or *fatto a mano* (hand-made), is made with eggs and flour. The egg pasta is usually served with richer, creamier sauces. The heartland of *pasta fresca* is Emilia-Romagna, but these days you will find tortellini, ravioli or thin-stripped tagliatelle all over Italy.

Grains & Pulses
One of the most popular of all grains is polenta, the cornmeal staple of the north and traditional belly-filler in poorer times. It's served hot and soft (referred to as 'wet polenta' in English) or left to set and then reheated in slices. Another popular grain is rice. In the north, rice usually means risotto, which is only made with the short-grained *arborio*, *carnaroli* and *vialone nano* rice varieties. Italians also love *lenticchie* (lentils), *ceci* (chickpeas) and dried beans such as borlotti and cannellini, which make a frequent appearance in soups.

Fruits & Vegetables

The variety of fresh produce available at any one time is reasonably limited. From north to south the ingredients you see are often the same: flattish *cipolle* (onions), ropes of *aglio* (garlic), mounds of *carciofi* (artichokes), deep-red *pomodori* (tomatoes) sold on the vine, and *melanzane* (aubergine or eggplant). It's what each region does with the ingredients that differs. Apart from cultivated produce, many Italians have a taste for the wild – *finocchio* (fennel) and *rucola* (rocket) – and a national obsession with *funghi* (mushrooms), of which there are over 50 edible species.

Olives & Olive Oil

The *olivo* (olive tree) has an almost philosophical importance to the people of Italy. Thousands of hectares are given over to growing olives, which are used both as eating and cooking (or 'table') olives, and – more importantly – for making oil. The quality depends on the region in which the olives are grown, their variety, the ripeness at which they're picked, how soon they're crushed and the crushing method. The best olive oil is *olio d'oliva extravergine* (extra-virgin olive oil).

A good search engine to find your perfect cooking course in Italy is www.italycooking schools.com For more recommendations see Courses, p814.

Meat & Poultry

Where for generations there was relative poverty in Italy, a new-found prosperity means that meat and poultry are now the focus of many meals. And, as natural feeding techniques are commonly used, they are often of a very high quality. Italians tend to serve most of their meats well done. Many cheaper cuts are *stracotto* (cooked for a long time, literally 'overcooked'), such as in a braise or ragu. And then there are Italy's famous cured meats. *Salumi* is a broad term that takes in all *prosciutto* (cured ham) and *salsiccia* (roughly translating as sausages), as well as other meat products such as salami.

Seafood

Frutti di mare (seafood), traditionally a mainstay of the Italian diet, has become a luxury item as pollution and overfishing have taken their toll. But spend any amount of time (and a bit of money) in Italy and you will invariably end up eating seafood. Italians favour *polpi* (octopus), *seppia* (cuttlefish) and tiny fish known in some areas as *neonati* or *bianchetti*, usually fried and eaten whole. Imported, preserved fish such as *stoccafisso* (air-dried cod) and *baccalà* (salted cod) are also popular.

Cheese

Italians love their *formaggio* (cheese) and produce nearly 450 different varieties, using it in every course throughout a meal. They make *formaggio* from the milk of cows (mainly in the north), goats (Piedmont and Valle d'Aosta), sheep (the centre and south) and even buffaloes (around Naples). While Parmesan and Gorgonzola have gained a name overseas, one of Italy's oldest and most versatile cheeses is *pecorino*, made from sheep's milk.

Gelati

No other nation today can boast such consistently good frozen desserts as the Italians. Gelati (singular: gelato) is the most lickably soft ice cream in existence. Look for *artigianale* (artisanal or home-made), *produzione propria* (proprietor's production) or *nostra produzione* (our production), and ask for a *cono* (cone) or a *coppa* (cup).

Desserts

Italian *dolci* (desserts) tend to fall into three categories: fruit, pastry or frozen. Cakes, while a must at any special occasion, are not often seen in day-to-day life. The end of a family meal will often include fruit or a home-made *crostata* (tart). Other preferences are for *biscotti* (biscuits) and treats from the *pasticceria* (pastry shop). The Italians are also champion *cioccolato* (chocolate) makers, with *gianduia* (a hazelnut and chocolate combination) now a speciality. Mass-produced Italian chocolate is well worth trying; the most famous brands are Perugina from Umbria and Ferrero from Piedmont.

Fred Plotkin's *Italy for the Gourmet Traveller* is an outstanding companion for your gastronomic tour of Italy.

REGIONAL SPECIALITIES

The food of Italy is a vast collection of regional dishes. This regional guide is meant as a map to help you find your way through the maze of disparate cuisines.

Campania

Naples is home to that most famous of Italian dishes, the pizza, and the general consensus is that Neapolitan pizza is the best. Take note of the basics – *mozzarella di bufala* (literally 'buffalo milk cheese') and the *conserva di pomodoro* (tomato sauce) are unequalled in flavour and appear in many other dishes besides pizza. A favourite sweet in Naples is *sfogliatella*, layers of flaky pastry with a ricotta filling.

Emilia-Romagna

The regional specialities of Emilia-Romagna, including *tagliatelle al ragù* (and its prosaic adaptation, spaghetti bolognese), lasagne and tortellini, are among the best-known Italian dishes abroad. Parma is the home of the best prosciutto and also of parmesan (see the boxed text, p412), while Modena is famed for balsamic vinegar (see the boxed text, p407).

Lazio

The food in this region sits heavily in the stomach but is no less mouthwatering for it. Traditional pasta dishes include *carbonara* (egg yolk, cheese and bacon) and *alla matriciana* (tomato, bacon and a touch of chilli).

Liguria

The cuisine of this coastal region makes good use of fresh herbs, olive oil and seafood. Culinary specialities include pesto – a delicious sauce of basil, garlic, oil, pine nuts and *pecorino* cheese – which is served with pasta or dolloped into the classic *minestrone alla genovese* (Genoese vegetable) soup.

Lombardy

Lombardy's dishes favour butter over olive oil. Risotto and polenta are staples, and are both often eaten instead of pasta. The cheeses are some of the most interesting in the country – Gorgonzola, *taleggio* and *stracchino*. Milan is the home of *panettone* (a yeast-risen sweet bread traditionally eaten at Christmas).

Piedmont

Often delicate and always flavoursome, the cuisine of Piedmont is influenced to some extent by nearby France. *Tartufo bianco* (white truffle) is used in a wide variety of dishes and the Piedmontese make good use

TRAVEL YOUR TASTEBUDS

As well as all the goodies you'll be expecting to find on the menu in Italy, there are a few more unusual items that you may not – turn the page now if you're feeling squeamish! In Rome, where their distinct cuisine was founded on the poverty of the general populace, you'll find the fifth quarter – offal – readily available. Order a dish with the word *coratella* in the name and you'll end up with lungs, kidneys and the heart. In Florence, *trippa* (tripe) is served up in buns to hungry hordes from mobile vans. Not to be outdone by the French, *carne equine* or *cavallo* (horse) is fairly common and you'll find *lumache* (snails) in Piedmont.

of game birds and animals, including chamois, pheasant, quail and even frogs. Chocolate is another regional speciality.

Puglia

The cuisine here is simple, often taking a single ingredient, capturing its special qualities and bringing it to the fore. Vegetable and seafood dishes are favourites. Try the *orecchiette* (pasta in the shape of 'little ears'), traditionally served with *cime di rapa* (turnip tops), or broccoli and anchovies. Another traditional dish is *fave a cicoria*, a puree of dried broad beans served with chicory and drizzled with extra-virgin olive oil.

Sardinia

Marcella Hazan's *The Essentials of Classic Italian Cooking* is a must-have on any cook's shelf: the recipes are inspiring.

One of the island's best-known dishes is *porcheddu* (baby pig roasted on a spit). Try the *carta musica* (a thin, crisp bread eaten warm and sprinkled with salt and oil) and the *bottarga* (dried pressed tuna roe which tops pasta instead of cheese). *Pecorino sardo* is a sharp, aged sheep's-milk cheese of which the Sardi are justifiably proud.

Sicily

The focus in Sicily is on seafood and fresh produce. Try the *pescespada* (swordfish), sliced into thick steaks and grilled, or the Palermo speciality *pasta con le sarde*, with sardines, wild fennel, pine nuts and raisins. Aubergines are popular, as are *capperi* (capers), both of which feature in *caponata*, a vegetable starter. Don't leave without trying *cassata*, a rich sponge cake filled with cream of ricotta, liqueur and candied fruits.

The Veneto

This region is renowned for its *bollito misto* (boiled meats) and the *radicchio trevisano* (a bitter red chicory). Don't miss *risotto nero* (risotto coloured and flavoured with squid ink) or the simpler dish of *risi e bisi* (rice and peas). And you must try the globally popular sweet tiramisu (sponge cakes soaked in coffee and Marsala and arranged in layers with mascarpone cheese).

Trentino-Alto Adige

The cuisine in this region has a considerable Austrian influence, so you will find *canederli* (noodle soup), bread dumplings, goulash and Wiener schnitzel. Local specialities include smoked meats and heavy, black-rye bread.

Tuscany

Regional specialities are noted for their simplicity and flavour. Try *bistecca alla fiorentina*, a huge T-bone steak. Among the staples of Tuscan cuisine are the popular small white cannellini beans, although all types of beans are widely used. There is also a range of soups, from the simple flavoured *acquacotta* (literally 'cooked water') to rich *minestrone alla fiorentina*, flavoured with pork and chicken giblets. Don't miss *panforte*, Siena's famous Christmas fruitcake.

Umbria

In Umbria both the *tartufo* and *porcini* mushrooms are abundant; they turn up in pasta, rice and much more. While many dishes are based upon vegetables, the locals also love their meat. A speciality is *porchetta*, a whole roast piglet stuffed with rosemary. Cakes and pastries stand out, as do chocolates such as the famous baci (chocolate-coated hazelnuts).

DRINKS
Wine & Spirits

Vino (wine) is an essential accompaniment to any meal and *digestivi* (liqueurs) are a popular way to end one. Italians are very proud of their wines and find it hard to believe that anyone else in the world could produce wines as good as theirs. Many Italians only drink alcohol with meals and the foreign custom of going out for a drink is still considered unusual.

There are now four main classifications of wine in Italy – DOC *(denominazione di origine controllata)*, DOCG *(denominazione d'origine controllata e garantita)*, IGT *(indicazione geografica tipica)* and *vino da tavola* (table wine) – which will be marked on the label.

A DOC wine is produced subject to certain specifications, although the label does not certify quality. DOCG is subject to the same requirements as normal DOC, but it is also tested by government inspectors for quality. IGT is a recent term introduced to cover wines from quality regions that are of a style or use grapes that fall outside the DOC and DOCG classifications.

For tasting notes and global events, see www.italianwine review.com

The style of wine varies throughout the country, so make a point of sampling the local produce during your travels. Try the many varieties of Tuscany's famous Chianti wines, the white Vernaccia of San Gimignano, the excellent Brunello of Montalcino, the Vino Nobile of Montepulciano, the Soave in Verona and Valpolicella around Venice. Piedmont and Trentino-Alto Adige both produce excellent wines, notably the Barolo in Piedmont. The wines of Orvieto in Umbria are also noteworthy. In Rome try the local Frascati and other wines of the Castelli Romani. Sicily is the home of sweet Marsala and the fragrant Moscato, but the region also produces feisty dry whites and reds full of sun-ripened fruit.

Before dinner Italians might drink a Campari and soda, or a fruit cocktail which is usually preprepared and is often without alcohol. After dinner, try a shot of grappa (a grape-based liqueur that is either an acquired taste or a relative of paintstripper, depending on your viewpoint) or an *amaro* (a dark liqueur prepared from herbs). If you prefer a sweeter liqueur, try the almond-flavoured *amaretto* or the sweet aniseed *sambuca*. On the Amalfi Coast and the islands of the Gulf of Naples, the fragrant local lemons are used to produce *limoncello*.

The Slow Food movement's annually updated *Guide to Italian Wines* is an excellent resource with region-by-region profiles of producers and their wines.

Beer

The most common Italian beers are crisp and light Pilsner-style lagers, and younger Italians are happy to guzzle them down with a pizza. The main local labels are Peroni, Dreher and Moretti, all very drinkable and cheaper than the imported varieties. If you want a local beer, ask for a *birra nazionale*, which will be either in a bottle or *alla spina* (on tap).

Coffee

Lonely Planet's *World Food Italy* takes an in-depth look at the country's food history and culture.

Coffee in Italy isn't like anywhere else in the world: it's better.

An espresso is a small shot of strong black coffee. It is also referred to simply as *un caffè*. You can ask for a *caffè doppio* (a double shot), *caffè lungo* (literally 'long coffee') or *caffè Americano*, although the last two will usually just be an espresso with extra water run through the grinds and they may taste bitter.

A *caffè corretto* is an espresso with a dash of grappa or some other spirit, and a *macchiato* ('stained' coffee) is an espresso with a dash of milk. You can ask for a *macchiato caldo* (with a drop of hot, foamed milk) or *freddo* (with cold milk). On the other hand, *latte macchiato* is warmed milk stained with a drop of coffee. *Caffè freddo* is a long glass of cold, black, sweetened coffee. If you want it without sugar, ask for *caffè freddo amaro*.

Then, of course, there is the *cappuccino* (coffee with hot, frothy milk). If you want it without froth, ask for a *cappuccino senza schiuma*. Italians tend to drink cappuccino only with breakfast and during the morning, never after meals. You will also find it difficult to convince bartenders to make your cappuccino hot rather than *tiepido* (lukewarm) – overheating the milk destroys its natural sweetness. If you must, ask for it *ben caldo*, *molto caldo* or *bollente* and wait for the same 'tut-tut' response that you'll attract if you order one after dinner.

Variations on the milky coffee menu include a *caffè latte*, a milkier version of the cappuccino with less froth. In summer the *cappuccino freddo*, a bit like an iced coffee, is popular. You will also find *caffè granita*, sweet and strong, which is traditionally served with a dollop of whipped cream.

Tea

Italians don't drink a lot of *tè* (tea) and generally do so only in the late afternoon, when they might take a cup with a few *pasticcini* (small cakes). You can order tea in bars, although it will usually arrive in the form of a cup of warm water with an accompanying tea bag. If this doesn't suit your taste, ask for the water *molto caldo* (very hot) or *bollente* (boiling).

Water

Despite the fact that tap water is reliable throughout most of the country, many Italians prefer to drink bottled *acqua minerale* (mineral water). This is available either *frizzante* (sparkling) or *naturale* (still) and you will be asked in restaurants and bars which you would prefer. If you just want a glass of tap water, you should ask for *acqua dal rubinetto*, although simply asking for *acqua naturale* will also suffice.

For recipes, extensive descriptions of regional specialities and booklets that can be downloaded, see www.italianmade.com

CELEBRATIONS

Italy celebrates an unprecedented number of festivals, many of them coming from each region's pagan past.

People on the peninsula have always celebrated something – whether it be a harvest, a god, a wedding or a birth – and when Christianity arrived they simply put their new god as the figurehead. Most of these festivals were wild affairs – such as the Saturnalia festival in Roman times, where a week of drunken revelry in honour of the god of disorder was marked by a pig sacrifice at the start and a human sacrifice at the end. Celebrations these days are more sedate affairs, but they can still be amazing. The biggest times for festivals these days centre around Natale (Christmas), Pasqua (Easter) and Carnevale (the period leading up to Ash Wednesday, the first day of Lent).

> **SMOKED OUT**
>
> Apparently there is a law in Italy that requires all restaurants to provide a nonsmoking area. We say 'apparently' because you will be very hard-pressed to find a nonsmoking section except in the most expensive of *ristoranti*. Smoking is a way of life – locals will puff energetically on cigarettes, and even cigars, just as your meal hits the table. As a visitor there's nothing you can do about it except request a nonsmoking area when you book. Don't be surprised, however, if you receive a total blank in response.

The classic way to celebrate any feast day is to precede it with a day of eating *magro* (lean) because the feast day is usually a day of overindulgence. While just about every festival has some kind of food involved, many of them are only about food. The general rule is that a *sagra* (feasting festival) will offer food, although you'll normally be expected to pay, and at a *festa* (festival or celebration) you may have to bring your own.

WHERE TO EAT & DRINK

A *tavola calda* (literally 'hot table') normally offers cheap, preprepared food which showcases local specialities and can include self-service pasta, roast meats, *pizza al taglio* and vegetable dishes.

A trattoria is basically a cheaper version of a *ristorante* (restaurant) with less-aloof service and simple dishes. A *ristorante* generally has a wider selection of dishes, printed menus, a higher standard of service and higher prices. The problem is that many establishments that are in fact *ristoranti* call themselves trattorie, and vice versa, usually to capture the spirit of the other establishment – sophisticated elegance or rustic charm respectively. It is best to check the menu, usually posted by the door, for prices. Don't judge the quality of a *ristorante* or trattoria by its appearance. You are likely to eat your most memorable meal at a place with plastic tablecloths in a tiny backstreet, a dingy piazza or on a back road in the country. And don't panic if you find yourself in a trattoria that has no printed menu: they are often the ones that offer the best and most authentic food.

A *pizzeria* will, of course, serve pizza but usually also has a trattoria-style menu. An *osteria* is likely to be either a wine bar offering a small selection of dishes with a verbal menu, or a small trattoria.

Bars are popular hang-outs, serving mostly coffee, soft drinks and alcohol. They often sell *brioche* (breakfast pastry), *cornetti* (croissants), *panini* (bread rolls with simple fillings) and *spuntini* (snacks) to have with your drink. You can round off a meal with a gelato from a *gelateria* – a crowd outside is always a good sign.

Most eating establishments have a cover charge (*coperto*; usually from around €1 to €2) and a *servizio* (service charge) of 10% to 15%. Restaurants usually open for lunch from noon to 3pm, but many are not keen to take orders after 2pm. In the evening, opening hours vary widely from north to south. In the north dinner starts at around 7.30pm, but in Sicily you will be hard-pressed to find a restaurant open before 8.30pm.

> More fun than instruction, *Around the Roman Table* by Patrick Faas details the exotic culinary habits of the ancient Romans. Anyone for roasted sows' nipples or stuffed dormice?

Quick Eats

There are numerous outlets where you can buy *pizza al taglio*. You could also try one of the *alimentari* (grocery stores) and ask them to make a *panino* with the filling of your choice.

Fast food is becoming increasingly popular in Italy and you'll find all the usual global chains, but seriously, why bother when Italian fast food – *arancini* (herby, deep-fried rice balls stuffed with meat or cheese) in

SLOW FAST FOOD

Fast food as a concept doesn't sit easily with Italians, and it was here in 1986 that the first organised, politically active group decided to tackle the issue head-on. Symbolised by a snail, the Slow Food movement now has groups in 48 countries and over 77,000 members. The movement promotes good food and wine to be consumed (slowly, of course) in good company, and champions traditional cuisine and sustainable agricultural practices. The volunteer-run groups organise social programmes of feasting and frivolity. For more information check out www.slowfood.com.

Sicily, *filetti di baccalà* (dried salted cod) in Rome and pizza all over the country – is so good?

VEGETARIANS & VEGANS

While menus around the country have an abundancy of vegetable-based dishes, vegetarians need to be aware of misleading names and the fact that many Italians don't think a little bit of prosciutto really counts as meat. Having said that, most eating establishments do serve a good selection of antipasti (starters) and *contorni* (vegetables prepared in a variety of ways), and the further south you go, the better the vegetable dishes get. Look for the word *magro* (thin or lean) on menus, which usually means that the dish is meatless. Vegans are in for a much tougher time. Cheese is used universally, so you have to say '*senza formaggio*' (without cheese) as a matter of course. Also remember that *pasta fresca*, which may also turn up in soups, is made with eggs. Vegetarian and vegan restaurants can be found in larger cities such as Rome and Milan.

Carlo Petrini, founder of the Slow Food movement, outlines the group's philosophy in *Slow Food: The Case for Taste*.

WHINING & DINING

You'll be hard-pressed to find a children's menu in most Italian restaurants. It's not that they're not welcome but because, more than anywhere, they are. Local children are treated very much as adults and are taken out to dinner from a very young age. You'll often see families order a *mezzo piatto* (half-plate) off the menu for their smaller members. Virtually all restaurants are perfectly comfortable tailoring a dish to meet your kid's tastes.

High chairs are available in many restaurants, but it would be a lot safer to bring one along if you can. While children are often taken out, and the owner's kids may be seen scrambling about the room, it's expected that kids be well behaved, and disciplined if they are not.

For more information on travelling with your little ones, see p812.

HABITS & CUSTOMS

Italians will rarely eat a sit-down *colazione* (breakfast). They tend to drink a cappuccino and eat a pastry while standing at a bar.

Pranzo (lunch) is traditionally the main meal of the day and many shops and businesses close for three to four hours every afternoon for the meal and the siesta that is traditionally supposed to follow. A full meal will consist of an antipasto, which can vary from bruschetta (a type of garlic bread with various toppings) to fried vegetables or *prosciutto e melone* (cured ham wrapped around melon). Next comes the *primo piatto* (first course), a pasta or risotto, followed by the *secondo piatto* (second course) of meat or fish. Italians often then eat an *insalata* (salad) or *contorno* (vegetable side dish) and round off the meal with fruit, or occasionally with *dolci* and coffee.

The delightful *Dear Francesca: An Italian Journey of Recipes Recounted with Love*, by Mary Contini, is a unique book full of recipes and tales of life.

Cena (evening meal) was traditionally a more simple affair, but in recent years habits have been changing because of the inconvenience of travelling home for lunch every day.

DOS & DON'TS

What constitutes 'good manners' alters – as it does everywhere – depending not only on whom you're with, but where you are eating, and the part of the country you're in. The good news is that Italians are so hospitable that they will forgive virtually anything you do unwittingly.

- *Buongiorno* or *buonasera* is the basic greeting in any bar or restaurant
- Italians tend to dress with impeccable style at most meals, so brush up when eating out
- When eating pasta, any bits hanging down should be bitten through rather than slurped up. You'll probably never be offered a spoon to eat your pasta with as this practice is considered to be quite rude
- If you are lucky enough to eat in an Italian home, remember that generosity at a meal is a sign of hospitality so refuse at your own peril! You should *fare la scarpetta* (make a shoe) with your bread and wipe plates clean of sauces – a sign you've really enjoyed the meal and one that won't go unnoticed

In general, Italians are not big snackers, although it is not uncommon for them to have a quick bite – usually a *tramezzino* (sandwich), *merendina* (cake or biscuit) or slice of pizza – halfway through the morning or afternoon.

EAT YOUR WORDS

Get behind the cuisine scene by getting to know the language. For pronunciation guidelines, see p844.

Useful Phrases

I'd like to reserve a table. — *Vorrei riservare un tavolo.*
vo-ray ree-ser-va-re oon ta-vo-lo

I'd like the menu, please. — *Vorrei il menù, per favore.*
vo-ray eel me-noo per fa-vo-re

Do you have a menu in English? — *Avete un menù (scritto) in inglese?*
a-ve-te oon me-noo (skree-to) een een-gle-ze

What would you recommend? — *Cosa mi consiglia?*
ko-za mee kon-see-lya

I'd like a local speciality. — *Vorrei una specialità di questa regione.*
vo-ray oo-na spe-cha-lee-ta dee kwe-sta re-jo-ne

Please bring the bill. — *Mi porta il conto, per favore?*
mee por-ta eel kon-to per fa-vo-re

Is service included in the bill? — *Il servizio è compreso nel conto?*
eel ser-vee-tsyo e kom-pre-zo nel kon-to

I'm a vegetarian. — *Sono vegetariano/a.*
so-no ve-je-ta-rya-no/a

I'm a vegan. — *Sono vegetaliano/a.*
so-no ve-je-ta-lya-no/a

Menu Decoder

SOUPS & ANTIPASTI

antipasti misto *(an-tee-pas-tee mees-to)* – mixed appetisers
carpaccio *(kar-pa-cho)* – very fine slices of raw meat
insalata caprese *(een-sa-la-ta ka-pre-ze)* – sliced tomatoes with mozzarella and basil
insalata di mare *(een-sa-la-ta dee ma-re)* – seafood, generally crustaceans
minestrone *(mee-nes-tro-ne)* – vegetable soup
olive ascolane *(o-lee-ve as-ko-la-ne)* – stuffed, deep-fried olives

prosciutto e melone *(pro-shoo-to e me-lo-ne)* – cured ham with melon
stracciatella *(stra-cha-te-la)* – egg in broth

PASTA SAUCES

There are literally hundreds of shapes of pasta and each region has its own variety. The straightforward long, thin strands of pasta (spaghetti), are omnipresent throughout the country and come with a variety of delicious sauces. Here are just a few – all equally delicious:

aglio e olio *(a-lyo e o-lyo)* – hot oil, garlic and sometimes chilli
amatriciana *(a-ma-tree-cha-na)* – salami, tomato, capsicum and cheese
arrabbiata *(a-ra-bee-ya-ta)* – tomato and chilli
bolognese *(bo-lo-nye-ze)* – a meat sauce (minced veal or pork), vegetables, lemon peel and nutmeg
cacio e pepe *(ka-cho e pe-pe)* – black pepper and sheeps cheese
carbonara *(kar-bo-na-ra)* – bacon, butter, cheese, beaten eggs and sheeps cheese
partenopea *(par-te-no-pe-a)* – mozzarella, tomato, bread crust, capers, olives, anchovies, basil, oil, chilli and salt
pescatora *(pes-ka-to-ra)* – fish, tomato and sweet herbs
pommarola *(po-ma-ro-la)* – simple tomato sauce
puttanesca *(poo-ta-nes-ka)* – garlic, anchovy, black olives, capers, tomato sauce, oil, chilli and butter
tartufo di Norcia *(tar-too-fo dee nor-cha)* – black truffle, garlic, oil and anchovies
vongole *(von-go-le)* – tomatos and clams

PIZZAS

All pizzas listed below have a tomato (and sometimes mozzarella) base:

capricciosa *(ka-pree-cho-za)* – olives, prosciutto, mushrooms and artichokes
frutti di mare *(froo-tee dee ma-re)* – seafood
funghi *(fun-gee)* – mushrooms
margherita *(mar-ge-ree-ta)* – oregano
napoletana *(na -pol-e-tan-a)* – anchovies
pugliese *(pu-lye-se)* – tomato, mozzarella and onions
quattro formaggi *(kwa-tro for-ma-jee)* – with four types of cheese
quattro stagioni *(kwa-tro sta-jo-nee)* – like a *capricciosa*, but sometimes with egg
verdura *(ver-doo-ra)* – mixed vegetables; usually courgette (zucchini) and aubergine, sometimes carrot and spinach

DID YOU KNOW?
The size and shape of each pasta is no accident: each one is designed for a specific type of sauce.

English-Italian Glossary

BASICS

bill/cheque	*conto*	*kon-to*
breakfast	*prima colazione*	*pree-*ma ko-la-*tsyo-*ne
dinner	*cena*	*che-*na
snacks	*cicheti*	ci-*che-*ti
fork	*forchetta*	for-*ke-*ta
knife	*coltello*	kol-*te-*lo
lunch	*ranzo*	*pran-*dzo
(non) smoking	*(non) fumatori*	(non) foo-ma-*to-*ree
spoon	*cucchiaio*	koo-*kya-*yo
waiter/waitress	*cameriere/a*	ka-mer-*ye-*re/a

METHODS OF PREPARATION

boiled	*bollito/a*	bo-*lee-*to/a
cooked	*cotto/a*	*ko-*to/a
fried	*fritto/a*	*free-*to/a
grilled	*alla griglia*	a-la *gree-*lya

raw	*crudo/a kroo*-do/a	
roasted	*arrosto/a*	a-*ro*-sto/a

STAPLES

bread	*pane*	*pa*-ne
butter	*burro*	*boo*-ro
cheese	*formaggio*	for-*ma*-jo
chilli	*peperoncino*	pe-pe-ron-*chee*-no
cream	*panna*	*pan*-na
egg/eggs	*uovo/uova*	*wo*-vo/*wo*-va
garlic	*aglio*	*a*-lyo
honey	*miele*	*mye*-le
jam	*marmellata*	mar-me-*la*-ta
lemon	*limone*	lee-*mo*-ne
milk	*latte*	*la*-te
oil	*olio*	*o*-lyo
olive	*olive*	o-*lee*-va
pepper	*pepe*	*pe*-pe
rice	*riso*	*ree*-zo
salt	*sale*	*sa*-le
sugar	*zucchero*	*tsoo*-ke-ro
vinegar	*aceto*	a-*che*-to

MEAT, FISH & SEAFOOD

anchovies	*acciughe*	a-*choo*-ge
beef	*manzo*	*man*-dzo
chicken	*pollo*	*pol*-lo
clams	*vongole*	*von*-go-le
cod	*merluzzo*	mer-*loo*-tso
crab	*granchio*	*gran*-kyo
cuttlefish	*seppia*	*se*-pya
kid (goat)	*capretto*	ka-*pre*-to
lamb	*agnello*	a-*nye*-lo
liver	*fegato*	*fe*-ga-to
lobster	*aragosta*	a-ra-*go*-sta
mackerel	*sgombro*	*sgom*-bro
mussels	*cozze*	*ko*-tse
octopus	*polpi*	*pol*-pee
oysters	*ostriche*	*os*-tree-ke
prawns	*gamberoni*	gam-be-*ro*-nee
rabbit	*coniglio*	ko-*nee*-lyo
sardines	*sarde*	*sar*-de
sausage	*salsiccia*	sal-*see*-cha
seafood	*frutti di mare*	*froo*-tee dee *ma*-re
snail	*lumache*	loo-*ma*-ke
squid	*calamari*	ka-la-*ma*-ree
steak	*bistecca*	bees-*te*-ka
swordfish	*pesce spada*	*pe*-she *spa*-da
tripe	*trippa*	*tree*-pa
tuna	*tonno*	*ton*-no
veal	*vitello*	vee-*te*-lo

For an excellent food and travel portal, visit www.deliciousitaly.com

FRUIT & VEGETABLES

apple	*mela*	*me*-la
artichokes	*carciofi*	kar-*cho*-fee

asparagus	asparagi	as-*pa*-ra-jee
aubergine	melanzane	me-lan-*dza*-ne
cabbage	cavolo	*ka*-vo-lo
carrot	carota	ka-*ro*-ta
cherry	ciliegia	chee-lee-*e*-ja
fennel	finocchio	fee-*no*-kyo
grapes	uva	*oo*-va
green beans	fagiolini	fa-jo-*lee*-nee
mushrooms	fungi	*foon*-gee
orange	arancia	a-*ran*-cha
peach	pesca	*pe*-ska
pears	pere	*pe*-ra
peas	piselli	pee-*ze*-lee
peppers	peperoni	pe-pe-*ro*-nee
potatoes	patate	pa-*ta*-te
rocket	rucola	*roo*-ko-la
spinach	spinaci	spee-*na*-chee
strawberries	fragole	*fra*-go-le
tomatoes	pomodori	po-mo-*do*-ree

DID YOU KNOW?

As well as being the world's largest producer of wine, Italy is also the largest consumer.

DRINKS

beer	birra	*bee*-ra
coffee	(un) caffè	ka-*fe*
tea	(un) tè	te
water	acqua	*a*-kwa
wine (red/white)	vino (rosso/bianco)	vee-no (*ros*-so/*byan*-ko)

Rome & Lazio

CONTENTS

Rome – the Eternal City, also known for centuries as Caput Mundi (capital of the world), attracts nearly 20 million visitors a year. Rome has always awed in its visitors, but its particular attraction is that it has managed to preserve impressive monuments and ruins from its varied past and incorporate them into the present. It is a living museum, an archaeological archive of Western culture, but also a constantly evolving, vibrant city still creating new architectural wonders.

The phenomenal concentration of history, legend and monuments coexists with an equally phenomenal concentration of people busily going about everyday life. Modern-day Rome is the noisiest city in Europe and even its citizens grumble about the traffic (and just occasionally about the huge numbers of tourists). But most will readily agree with the age-old phrase: *Roma, non basta una vita* (Rome, a lifetime is not enough).

In July and August the city is suffocatingly hot and humid – time to head out of town. The Lazio area, declared a region in 1934 has, since ancient Roman times, been an extension of Rome. Through the ages the rich built villas in the Lazio countryside and towns developed as fiefdoms of noble Roman families such as the Orsini, Barberini and Farnese families. Even today Romans build their holiday homes in the picturesque areas of the region. The ruins of Hadrian's Villa near Tivoli and the ancient Roman port at Ostia Antica are easy daytrips and a tour of the area that once formed the ancient land of the Etruscans is also recommended.

HIGHLIGHTS

■ **Dazzling Vista**

Climb up the dome of St Peter's (pp115–17) before seeing the splendours of the basilica, including Michelangelo's *Pietà*

■ **Holy Treasures**

Spend hours, if not days, in the magnificent Vatican Museums (pp117–18) and breathtaking Sistine Chapel (p119)

■ **Ancient Wonders**

Imagine the glory of ancient Rome as you wander the Roman Forum (pp89–91), Palatine (pp91–3) and Colosseum (pp93–4)

■ **Roman Road**

Stroll along Via Appia Antica (pp124–6) on Sunday, when it is closed to traffic, and visit the catacombs

★ Rome

■ **Green Haven**

Enjoy an afternoon in Villa Borghese park and marvel at the Galleria Borghese (pp120–1)

POPULATION:	■ ROME CITY 2.7 MILLION ■ ROME PROVINCE 3.8 MILLION ■ LAZIO 5.3 MILLION
AREA:	■ LAZIO 17,202 SQ KM

ROME (ROMA)

HISTORY

It is generally agreed that Rome has its origins in a group of Etruscan, Latin and Sabine settlements on the Palatine, Esquiline and Quirinale hills (three of the famous seven hills of Rome). The agreed date of the foundation of the city, when Romulus became its first king, is 21 April 753 BC, and archaeological discoveries have confirmed the existence of a settlement on the Palatine in that period. The city prospered and took shape under the Roman Republic; new temples, forums and buildings plus roads and aqueducts were constructed.

Under the first emperor, Augustus, Rome enjoyed a new era of political stability and artistic achievement. Augustus boasted that 'he found Rome in brick, and left it in marble'; monuments such as the Ara Pacis were built at this time. Much of the city was burnt to the ground in the Great Fire of AD 64. But by 100, the city of Rome had more than 1.5 million inhabitants, and trades and taxes from the Empire's vast domains brought wealth and prosperity. The Roman Forum was an active centre of municipal life and the Colosseum had been hosting gladiatorial contests for two decades. Rome was Caput Mundi (Capital of the World) until 330 when Constantine – the first Christian emperor – moved his power base to Byzantium.

Christianity had been spreading slowly through the Empire since the apostles Peter and Paul had joined a small group of Christians in Rome; they were persecuted but the religion flourished. The sites of many churches in Rome can be traced back to clandestine Christian meeting places. In the 5th century, the Goths and Vandals invaded the city but Gregory I's papacy (590–604) rescued Rome from its demise. Four of the city's great basilicas were built during his reign and missionaries were dispatched throughout Europe to encourage pilgrimages to Rome. In 774, Rome's place as centre of the Christian world was cemented when Pope Leo III crowned Charlemagne as Holy Roman Emperor.

Rome's fortunes oscillated as the papal states battled with city states throughout the Italian peninsula. Clement V moved the papal court to Avignon in 1309 and, while livestock grazed in the Roman Forum, the city became a battleground between the powerful Colonna and Orsini families. Pope Gregory XI returned to Rome in 1377 and chose to reside in the fortified Vatican area.

The popes of the 15th and early 16th centuries saw that the best way to ensure political power was to rebuild the city, which also brought incredible riches to their families – the Barberini, Farnese, Aldobrandini, Boncompagni and Pamphilj among others. The leading artists and architects of the Florentine Renaissance were summoned to Rome to work on the Sistine Chapel, St Peter's and other projects. Power struggles in Europe still affected the papacy and in 1527 Pope Clement VII was forced to take refuge in Castel Sant'Angelo in the Vatican when the troops of Charles V sacked Rome.

The broad-minded curiosity of the Renaissance gave way to the intolerance of the Counter Reformation. The Gesù was the prototype of Rome's great Counter-Reformation churches, built to attract and overawe huge congregations. In the 17th century, under the popes and grand families of Rome, the theatrical exuberance of the baroque found masterful interpreters in Bernini and Borromini. With their churches, fountains, *palazzi* and other architectural wonders, these two architects changed the face of the city.

Mass tourism in Rome, in the form of the Grand Tour, really took off in the 18th century when Italy started to rediscover its ancient past, and it hasn't stopped since. The building boom following the unification of Italy and the declaration of Rome as its capital also profoundly influenced the look of the city, and was only matched by the post-WWII spree to erect ugly apartment buildings in the growing suburbs.

Billions were spent preparing the city for the Jubilee Year in 2000, which attracted around 16 million Catholic pilgrims. Churches and *palazzi* were cleaned, roads and transport improved, car parks turned back into public spaces, museums completely reorganised and reopened. Rome, as its Tourist Board boasts, has changed its look. But the changes have also affected its infrastructure, and never has the city seen such organised information for its visitors. The ancient city lives on in the modern.

ROME & LAZIO

ORIENTATION

Rome is a vast city but the *centro storico* (historic centre) is relatively small, defined by the twisting River Tiber to the west, the sprawling Villa Borghese park to the north, the Roman Forum and Palatine to the south, and the central train station, Stazione Termini, to the east. The Vatican City and the characteristic area of Trastevere are on the west bank of the Tiber.

In ancient times, the city was enclosed by defensive walls but only traces of the Mura Serviane remain. From AD 271, Emperor Aurelian built a second defensive wall for the expanding city, most of which is still standing. Most major sights are located within the historic centre, making sightseeing relatively simple and walking the best way to get around town. Most of Rome's parks, some major churches and the catacombs lie outside the walls. Rome's best-known geographical features are its seven hills: the Palatine, Capitoline, Aventine, Caelian, Esquiline, Viminal and Quirinal. Two other hills, the Gianicolo (Janiculum), which rises above Trastevere, and the Pincio, above Piazza del Popolo, were never actually part of the ancient city.

Most new arrivals in Rome will end up at Stazione Termini (Map p106), which is the terminal for all international and national trains. The majority of cheap hotels and *pensioni* are concentrated around Stazione Termini. The main city bus station is on Piazza dei Cinquecento, directly in front of the station. Many intercity buses depart from and arrive at the front of Stazione Tiburtina in the east of the city, accessible from Stazione Termini on the Metropolitana Linea B. (This should not be confused with Piazzale Tiburtino, at the top of Via Tiburtina near Stazione Termini.) Buses serving towns in the region of Lazio depart from various points throughout the city, usually corresponding to stops on Metro lines (see p153 for details).

Maps

If you're planning to check out maps, try Lonely Planet's *Rome City Map*. Editrice Lozzi publishes a street map and bus guide entitled *Roma* (€3), available at just about any newsstand. It lists all major streets, with map references, as well as bus/tram routes. The slightly more expensive *Rome Today* (€5.50) version offers three maps in one – it also includes a map of the province of Rome and an enlarged plan of the city centre. Lozzi also publishes an excellent Roma Metro-Bus map (€5.50). You can find these maps in bookshops as well as at Stazione Termini and other news and magazine outlets.

If you're driving, the best road maps are published by the Touring Club Italia, available at all good bookshops.

For maps of Ancient Rome, Lozzi also publishes the very good *Archaeo Map*, a plan of the Roman Forum, Palatine and Colosseum and *Roma Antiqua* (€5). The smaller, *Ancient Rome* (€2), published by Electa is a good introduction and is available at most museum bookshops.

Rome's Tourism Board publishes a free handy pocket-sized map, available at tourism information centres.

INFORMATION
Airline Offices

All the airlines serving Rome have counters in the departure hall at Fiumicino. Many of the head offices are now based at or near the airport, although most have ticket offices in the area around Via Vittorio Veneto and Via Barberini, northwest of Stazione Termini (Map pp106–7).

Alitalia (☎ 06 650 11 437; www.alitalia.it; Via Marchetti Alessandro 111)

Air France (☎ 06 650 11 944; www.airfrance.com; Via Sardegna 40)

British Airways (☎ 06 650 01 513; www.british-air ways.com)

Air Canada (☎ 06 655 72 06; www.aircanada.ca; Via Veneziani 58)

Cathay Pacific (☎ 06 482 09 30; www.cathay pacific.com; Via Barberini 3)

Delta (☎ 06 420 10 336/339; www.delta.com; Via Sardegna 40)

Lufthansa (☎ 06 466 01; www.lufthansa.com; Via di San Basilio 41)

Qantas (☎ 06 524 82 725; www.qantas.com; Viale Citta d'Europa 681)

Singapore Airlines (☎ 06 48 79 44; www.singapore air.com; Via Bisosolati 24)

US Airways (☎ 06 420 14 322; www.usair.com; Via Bissolati 20)

Bookshops

Almost Corner Bookshop (Map pp108–9; ☎ 06 583 69 42; Via del Moro 45; ☼ 10am-1.30pm Mon-Sat,

11am-1.30pm & 3.30-8pm Sun) An excellent range of English-language fiction, non-fiction and travel guides.

Anglo-American Bookshop (Map pp102–4; ☎ 06 679 52 22; Via della Vite 102) Literature, travel guides and reference books; also sells the Thomas Cook European train timetable.

Bibli Bookshop (Map pp108–9; ☎ 06 588 40 97; info@ bibli.it; Via dei Fienaroli 28; ☑ 11am-midnight Tue-Sun) A few books in English; popular with English-speaking residents as it has a café, a cultural centre and Internet facilities (€4/6 per half/full hour).

Economy Book & Video Center (Map pp106–7; ☎ 06 474 68 77; Via Torino 136) Has a good selection of English-language books, including some second-hand paperbacks.

Feltrinelli International (Map pp102–4; ☎ 06 482 78 78; Via Orlando 84; ☑ 9am-8pm Mon-Sat, 10am-1.30pm & 4-7.30pm Sun) An extensive range in several languages plus lots of guidebooks.

Libreria del Viaggiatore (Map pp110–11; ☎ 06 688 01 048; Via del Pellegrino 78) A real find for travellers; it carries a huge range of maps.

Lion Bookshop (Map pp102–4; ☎ 06 326 54 007; fax 06 326 51 382; Via dei Greci 33-6) Good range of English-language books and magazines plus a little café.

Emergency

Main Police Station (Map pp106–7; ☎ 06 468 61; Via San Vitale 11)

Ufficio Stranieri (Foreigners' Bureau; Map pp106–7; ☎ 06 468 63 216; Via Genova 2; ☑ 24 hrs) Thefts can be reported here. This office can issue you with a *permesso di soggiorno* (see pp827–8).

Internet Access

Costs vary but are usually between €6 and €10 an hour, with hefty discounts or bonus hours if you take out a subscription.

Easy internet café (Map pp106–7; Piazza Barberini) More than 50 computers and it really is a café. Buy computer credit by putting money into a machine that displays the hourly rate; you can use as little as €1 worth of time.

Internet Cafè (Map pp106–7; ☎ 06 445 49 53; Via dei Marrucini 12; 1/10 hrs €4.15/31; ☑ 9-2am Mon-Fri, 5pm-2am Sat & Sun)

Netgate (€5.15/hr; ☑ 10.30am-9pm) Piazza Firenze (Map pp104–5; ☎ 06 689 34 45; Piazza Firenze 25); near St Peter's Basilica (Map pp102–4; ☎ 06 681 34 082; Borgo Santo Spirito 17-18); underground Forum shopping area (Map pp106–7; ☎ 06 874 06 008; Stazione Termini)

New Internet Point (Map pp108–9; ☎ 06 583 33 316; globalservice@mclink.it; Piazza Sonnino 27; €6/hr; ☑ 8am-midnight) Staff are helpful and speak English.

Sivet Internet point (Map pp104–5; ☎ 06 688 02 906; Via della Scrofa 73) Also offers photocopy services and laser printing.

Splashnet (Map pp106–7; ☎ 06 493 82 073; Via Varese 33; €3.10/hr) Kill two birds with one stone at this Internet café-cum-laundrette near Termini. If you're doing your washing you get 10 minutes free access.

TreviNet (Map pp106–7; ☎ 06 699 22 320; Via in Arcione 103; ☑ 10.30am-10pm Mon-Sat, 3-10.30pm Sun) Offers student discounts, photocopy facilities, scanning, free CD burning, digital and webcam picture downloads and direct connections for laptops.

Internet Resources

ATAC (www.atac.roma.it) Rome's transport service online.

Enjoy Rome (www.enjoyrome.com) Useful advice from independent tourist agency.

Trenitalia (www.fs-on-line.com) Check timetables and book tickets for trains.

Comune di Roma (www.capitolium.org) The official website of Rome's Imperial Forums – provided by the Comune di Roma (City Council).

Musei Online (www.museionline.it) Up-to-date information, in English, on exhibitions, events and news at all Italy's museums, sponsored by the Arts Ministry.

Roma Turismo (www.romaturismo.it) It provides a good overview of current and forthcoming major events, as well as listings and prices of all officially recognised accommodation options in Rome.

Vatican (www.vatican.va) Official site of the Vatican.

Wanted in Rome (www.wantedinrome.com) Listings and reviews of current exhibitions, cultural events and ads for apartments.

Laundry

In most cases, laundrettes are open 8am to 10pm daily; a 6kg to 8kg load costs around €3 to wash and €3 to dry. There are several self-service laundrettes in the streets northeast of Stazione Termini (Map 4). *Lavasecco* (dry-cleaning) costs range from around €3 for a shirt to €6 for a jacket.

Bolle Blu Via Palestro 59-61 (Map pp106–7); Via Malazzo 20b (Map pp106–7)

Oblo Service (Map pp106–7; Via Vicenza 50)

Splashnet (Map pp106–7; Via Varese 33) Gives you Internet access while you wash.

Onda Blu (Map p99; Via Vespasiano 50)

Wash & Dry Lavarapido Via della Chiesa Nuova 15-16 (Map pp104–5); cnr Via della Pellicia & Vicolo del Piede (Map pp108–9)

Left Luggage

Stazione Termini (Map pp106–7; 1st 5 hrs/per additional hr €3.10/0.52, 24hrs €13; ☑ 7am-midnight) Lower ground level under platform 24.

Fiumicino Airport (per item per day €2.15, luggage over 160cm long extra €2.15; ☑ 24 hrs) International arrivals area on the ground floor. Make sure you have your passport handy as a photocopy will be made when you leave your luggage.

Libraries

Biblioteca Nazionale Centrale Vittorio Emanuele II (Map pp106–7; ☎ 06 49 89; Viale Castro Pretorio 105; ☒ 8.30am-7pm Mon-Fri, 8.30am-1.30pm Sat) The national repository of books published in Italy; also has periodicals, newspapers, official acts, drawings, engravings and photographs. Readers need an identity document in order to get a day pass.

Santa Susanna Lending Library (Map pp106–7; ☎ 06 482 75 10; 1st fl, Via XX Settembre 15) For fiction in English; you have to pay a modest annual fee but you can then borrow all the books you want. Opening hours are irregular so phone to check first.

Media

Il Messaggero Rome-based daily newspaper with listings of theatre, cinema and special events.

Insiders Guide to Rome (www.nerone.cc) Online info; started as a weekly newspaper by an Italian for foreigners.

La Repubblica Rome-based daily newspaper with listings of theatre, cinema and special events.

Osservatore Romano Official daily newspaper of the Vatican.

Roma Cè (www.romace.it, Italian only) The most comprehensive entertainment guide with a small section in English; published every Thursday.

Wanted in Rome (☎ 06 0790190; www.wantedinrome .it) English-language magazine, available from newsstands, bookshops and on its website; published on alternate Wednesdays. Contains listings and reviews of the most important festivals, exhibitions and cinema as well as dance, classical music and opera performances.

Medical Services

A list of all-night pharmacies in the city centre is posted on www.romaturismo.it and in all pharmacy windows.

24-hour pharmacy (Map pp106–7; ☎ 06 488 00 19; Piazza dei Cinquecento 51) Opposite Stazione Termini.

Ospedale Santo Spirito (Map pp102–4; ☎ 06 683 51, first aid ☎ 06 650901; Lungotevere in Sassia 1) Hospital near the Vatican; several languages spoken.

Ospedale Bambino Gesù (Map pp102–4; ☎ 06 685 91, first aid for children ☎ 06 685 92 351; Piazza di Sant'Onofrio 4) Rome's paediatric hospital.

Ospedale di Odontoiatria G Eastman (☎ 84 48 31, first aid ☎ 06 844 83 232; Viale Regine Elena 287b) For emergency dental treatment.

Ospedale San Giacomo (Map pp100–1; ☎ 06 3 62 61, first aid ☎ 06 65 09 01; Via A Canova 29) Hospital near Piazza del Popolo.

Policlinico Umberto I (Map pp106–7; ☎ 06 499 71, first aid ☎ 06 499 72 01 00; Via del Policlinico 155) Hospital near Stazione Termini.

Money

There's a bank and several currency exchange booths at Stazione Termini (Map pp106–7). There is a Banca di Roma exchange booth and a couple of ATMs at Fiumicino airport (Map p99). There are numerous exchange booths throughout the city, including **American Express** (Map pp102–4) on Piazza di Spagna and **Thomas Cook** (Map pp102–4) on Piazza Barberini and Piazza della Repubblica.

Post

Main Post Office (Map pp102–4; Piazza di San Silvestro 20) Undergoing restoration at the time of writing. There are alternative **branches** (☒ 8.30am-6.30pm Mon-Fri, 8.30am-1pm Sat) at Piazza dei Capretti 69, Via Terme di Diocleziana 30, Via della Scrofa 61/63 and Via Arenula.

Vatican Post Office (Map pp102–4; Piazza San Pietro; ☒ 8.30am-7pm Mon-Fri, 8.30am-6pm Sat) Said to provide a faster and more reliable service than the normal Italian postal system. Letters can be posted in blue Vatican post boxes only if they carry Vatican stamps.

Telephone & Fax

There are Telecom offices at Stazione Termini (Map pp106–7), from where you can make international calls either direct or through an operator. There are public fax services at major post offices. Otherwise, there are numerous private services, usually in *tabacchi* and stationery stores.

Toilets

Most people use the toilets in bars and cafés – although you might need to buy a coffee first. However there are some public toilets at:

Piazza di Spagna (Map pp102–4; free; ☒ 10am-7.40pm)
Piazza San Silvestro (Map pp102–4; free; ☒ 10am-7.40pm)
Stazione Termini (Map pp106–7; €0.50) Lower ground level. The toilets on the Via Giolitti side also have showers (€7.80).

Tourist Information

Centro Servizi Pellegrini e Turisti (Map pp102–4; ☎ 06 698 84 466; Piazza San Pietro; ☒ 9am-5pm Mon-Sat) To the left of the basilica; general information about St Peter's and the Vatican, including times of daily Mass.

Comune di Roma Tourism Office (Map pp106–7; Stazione Termini; ☒ 8am-9pm) End of Platform 4. They also have a multilingual tourist **infoline** (☎ 06 360 04 399; ✆ 9am-7pm)

Enjoy Rome (Map pp106–7; ☎ 06 445 18 43; www.en joyrome.com; Via Marghera 8) This privately run tourist office is just a few minutes' walk northeast of the train station.

Rome Tourism Board (APT; Map pp106–7; ☎ 06 48 89 91; www.romaturismo.com; Via Parigi 5; ✆ 9am-7pm Mon-Sat) Publishes excellent information on accommodation, itineraries, activities and maps and guides to monuments within Rome and Lazio.

As well as an information point at Fiumicino (Map p99; Terminal B, Arrivals) there are 11 official **Tourist Information kiosks** (✆ 8am-9pm) dotted around the city:

Castel Sant'Angelo (Map pp102–4; Piazza Pia)

Trevi Fountain (Map pp102–4; Via Marco Minghetti)

Piazza dei Cinquecento (Map p106–7; outside Stazione Termini)

Piazza Navona (Map pp104–5; Piazza delle Cinque Lune)

Piazza San Giovanni in Laterano (Map pp110–11; opposite the basilica)

Piazza Santa Maria Maggiore (Map pp106–7 ; Via dell'Olmata)

Stazione Termini (Map pp106–7; Galleria Gommata)

Trastevere (Map pp108–9; Piazza Sonnino)

Via dei Fori Imperiali (Map pp106–7; near Largo C Ricci)

Via del Corso (Map pp102–4; Largo Goldoni)

Via Nazionale (Map pp106–7; next to the Palazzo delle Esposizioni)

Travel Agencies

CTS (www.cts.it, Italian only) Corso Vittorio Emanuele II 297 (Map pp102–4; ☎ 06 687 26 72); Via Genova 16 (Map pp106–7; ☎ 06 467 92 71); Via degli Ausoni 5 (Map pp106–7; ☎ 06 445 01 41; near La Sapienza university) Italy's official student travel service, offers discounted air, rail and bus tickets to students and travellers under 30 years old. CTS also issues ISICs (International Student Identity Cards). Note that to take advantage of CTS fares, if you are not a student, you must have a CTS card, which costs around €26 and is valid for a year.

Enjoy Rome (see above) This well-run private tourist office also operates as a travel agency selling discount tickets for air, bus and rail services and dealing with everything from car hire to Vatican tours.

Nouvelles Frontières (Map pp100–1; ☎ 06 322 24 63, ☎ 848 88 99 00; Via Angelo Brunetti 25) Off Via del Corso near Piazza del Popolo. Another popular travel agency catering for the youth and budget travel markets.

Passaggi (Map pp106–7; Stazione Termini; ✆ 7.15am-9pm) You can organise all your rail, ferry and car transport though Passaggi and it's the only authorised hotel booking service.

DANGERS & ANNOYANCES

Rome is a fairly safe city – you are most unlikely to be assaulted. However, thieves are very active around Stazione Termini, at major sights such as the Colosseum and in the city's more expensive shopping streets, such as those around Piazza di Spagna, especially in summer and during holiday and festival times. Pickpockets like to work on crowded buses (the No 64 from Stazione Termini to St Peter's is notorious). Beware of anyone, including children, who approach you with a printed sign – they usually try to use these to cover up their

---

CHEAP THRILLS

Roma, non basta una vita (Rome, a lifetime is not enough), goes the popular saying. When you calculate just what the city has to offer the sightseer, you can begin to see how this saying arose. Rome reputedly contains more than 900 churches – if you visited 17 per week for a year, you'd just cover them all – then there are the monuments and museums.

Where do you start? Well, they do say the best things in life are free and Rome itself is the world's biggest museum, where you can still see some of the most important and beautiful things in the world without paying. The Roman Forum, Capitoline Hill, Trevi Fountain, Spanish Steps, Pantheon, exterior of the Colosseum and Castel Sant' Angelo, the Mouth of Truth, Piazza Navona and St Peter's Basilica are all free. And inside many of those 900 or so churches, also all free, are some extraordinary masterpieces of art.

You'll find **Michelangelo** in San Pietro in Vincoli (p95), St Peter's Basilica (pp115–17), Chiesa di Santa Maria Sopra Minerva (p113) and Piazza del Campidoglio (p86); **Bernini** in Santa Maria della Vittoria (Map pp106–7; Largo S Sussana), Chiesa di San Francesco a Ripa (p98), St Peter's Basilica (pp115–17), outside Chiesa di Santa Maria Sopra Minerva (p113), on Ponte Sant' Angelo (Map pp102–4), at Sant'Andrea al Quirinale (Map pp106–7; Via Quattro Fontane) and Piazza Navona (p112); **Caravaggio** in Chiesa di Santa Maria del Popolo (p114), Sant'Agostino (Map pp104–5; Via della Scrofa) and Chiesa di San Luigi dei Francesi (Map pp104–5; Piazza San Luigi dei Francesi 5).

pilfering operations. Be careful in crowded shops and watch out for motorcycle-riding bag and camera snatchers. Avoid this by carrying bags away from the street side, across your body. Similarly, do not leave cameras or valuables unguarded on seats where they can be easily lifted as you sip your coffee. For more information on how to avoid being robbed, see pp815–16.

Although Rome's traffic is nowhere near as chaotic as that of Naples, some drivers, particularly motorcyclists, do not stop at red lights. Don't expect them to stop at pedestrian crossings either. The accepted mode of crossing a road is to step into the traffic and walk at a steady pace. Look the motorist straight in the eye. If in doubt, follow a Roman.

The heavy traffic also means heavy pollution, which can rise to such high levels in summer that elderly people, children and people with respiratory complaints are warned to stay indoors. Check with your hotel for daily information.

CAPITOLINE HILL   Map pp102–4

Capitoline Hill (Campidoglio), now the seat of the city's municipal government and home of the Capitoline Museums, was the centre of the government of ancient Rome and where Nelson hoisted the British flag in 1799 before he prevented Napoleon from entering the city.

The elegant Piazza del Campidoglio was designed by Michelangelo in 1538 and is bordered by three palaces: the **Palazzo Nuovo** on the north side, **Palazzo Senatorio** (admission free, bring identification; ⏰ 9am-4pm Sun) at the rear and **Palazzo dei Conservatori** on the south side. Together, Palazzo Nuovo and Palazzo dei Conservatori house the Capitoline Museums (see following).

For the greatest visual impact, approach the piazza from the west from Piazza d' Ara Coeli and ascend the Cordonata, a stepped ramp designed by Michelangelo. It is guarded at the bottom by two ancient Egyptian granite lions and at the top by two mammoth statues of Castor and Pollux, which were found in the nearby Ghetto area in the 16th century.

The bronze equestrian statue of Marcus Aurelius in the centre of the Piazza di Campidoglio is a copy. The original, which dates from the 2nd century AD, was badly damaged by pollution, weather and pigeon poo and was removed in 1981. It has been restored and is now housed behind glass in the Palazzo Nuovo.

In front of the Palazzo Senatorio's double staircase is a fountain displaying a marble and porphyry statue of a sitting **Minerva**, which dates from the time of Domitian. The statue sits uncomfortably on an elevated plinth and is about the only thing in the piazza that seems out of proportion. On either side of it are colossal statues representing the Tiber (on the right) and the Nile (on the left). Martino Longhi il Vecchio's bell tower replaced an old medieval tower in 1578.

To the left of the *palazzo* is Via di San Pietro in Carcere and (down the stairs) the ancient Roman **Carcere Mamertino** (Mammertine Prison), where prisoners were put through a hole in the floor to starve to death. St Peter was believed to have been imprisoned here and to have created a miraculous stream of water to baptise his jailers. It is now a church, San Pietro in Carcere.

At the bottom of Capitoline Hill, next to the staircase leading up to the Chiesa di Santa Maria in Aracoeli, are the ruins of a Roman apartment block or *insula*. Only the upper storeys are visible; three lower levels are buried below current street level. Buildings of this type were used to house the urban poor, who lived in cramped and squalid conditions.

Chiesa di Santa Maria in Aracoeli (☎ 06 679 81 55; Piazza Santa Maria in Aracoeli; admission free; ⏰ 7am-noon & 4-6.30pm) is between Piazza del Campidoglio and the Vittoriano monument (Il Vittoriano), at the highest point of the hill. Built on the site where, according to legend, the Tiburtine Sybil told Augustus of the coming birth of Christ, it features frescoes by Pinturicchio in the first chapel of the south aisle. The church is noted for a statue of the baby Jesus, said to have been carved from the wood of an olive tree from the garden of Gethsemane. The statue was stolen in 1994 and a replica is on display.

Capitoline Museums

This collection (Musei Capitolini; ☎ 06 399 67 800; Piazza del Campidoglio; admission €7.75; ⏰ 9am-8pm Tue-Sun) was started in 1471 with Pope Sixtus IV's donation of bronze sculptures to the city. The **Palazzo Nuovo** houses many important works, including statues of Roman emperors and other famous personages. Busts of philosophers, poets and politicians, among them Sophocles, Homer, Epicuros and Cicero, line the Sala dei Filosofi. The impressive *Galata Morente* (Dying Gaul) is a Roman copy of a 3rd-century-BC Greek original and the red-marble *Satiro Ridente* (a satyr holding a bunch of grapes) is the Marble Faun of Nathaniel Hawthorne's novel.

A tunnel links Palazzo Nuovo to **Palazzo dei Conservatori** opposite and gives access to the **Tabularium** beneath Palazzo Senatorio, where important inscriptions of the republic and Empire were kept.

The inner courtyard of the Palazzo dei Conservatori contains the head, a hand and foot of a colossal acrolith of Constantine originally in the Basilica di Massenzio in the Roman Forum. The highlight of the Palazzo dei Conservatori is the famous *Lupa Capitolina*, an Etruscan bronze statue of a she-wolf from the 6th century BC. The suckling figures of Romulus and Remus were added by Antonio Pollaiolo around 1509. Also of interest in this wing is the 1st-century-BC *Spinario*, a delicate bronze statue of a boy removing a thorn from his foot.

If the sculpture hasn't worn you out, head up to the **Pinacoteca**. Artists from the Venetian school, including Giovanni Bellini, Paolo Veronese, Titian and Tintoretto, are represented and there are also works by Guido Reni, Federico Zucchari, Salvator Rosa, van Dyck and Rubens. You can view paintings by Domenichino, Poussin, the Carracci, Pietro da Cortona and others. Highlights include Caravaggio's sensual *San Giovanni Battista* in his fully-fledged realist style, and Guercino's immense *Santa Petronilla*, a mosaic of which can be found in St Peter's Basilica. Both are in the Sala di Santa Petronilla.

PIAZZA VENEZIA   Map pp102–4

The **Vittoriano** (☎ 06 699 17 18; admission free; ☒ 9.30am-4.30pm) overshadows **Piazza Venezia**. This white, monolithic monument commemorates Vittorio Emanuele II and the united Italy, and is often dubbed the 'typewriter' or the 'wedding cake'. It's the biggest modern building in the centre of Rome, intentionally rivalling St Peter's in scale and visibility. It incorporates the Altare della Patria (Altar of the Fatherland), the tomb

of the unknown soldier and some lovely Art Nouveau murals and sculpture.

You can now go right up to the top for a magnificent view of the Roman Forum and all around Rome's golden buildings and distinctive cypresses. Photographic guides posted here will help you identify all the buildings you can see from the balcony. It's a popular place to be on a sun-filled Sunday and the rooftop cafés serve marvellous food under characteristic umbrellas. You can play the *dolce vita* here for little expense.

On the western side of the piazza is the Renaissance-era **Palazzo Venezia**, which was partially built with materials quarried from the Colosseum. Mussolini used it as his official residence and made some of his famous speeches from the balcony. Major art exhibitions are held here (the only way to get into the palace is by seeing one) and there is also a permanent museum, **Museo di Palazzo di Venezia** (☎ 06 699 43 18; entrance at Via del Plebiscito 118; adult/concession €4.15/2.05; ☒ 9.30am-5.30pm Tue-Sat winter, 9.30am-7pm summer). This often-overlooked museum has a superb collection of Byzantine and early Renaissance paintings, plus decorative arts from the medieval period to the 18th century: jewellery, tapestries, silver, ivories, ceramics, hundreds of 15th- to 17th-century bronze figurines spread over several rooms, 18th- and 19th-century pastels, carved wooden wedding chests as well as a collection of arms and armour.

Basilica di San Marco (Piazza di San Marco; admission free; ☒ 7am-noon & 4-6.30pm) was founded in the 4th century in honour of St Mark the Evangelist. After undergoing several major transformations over the centuries, the church has a Renaissance facade, a Romanesque bell tower and a largely baroque interior. The main attraction is the 9th-century mosaic in the apse, which depicts Christ with saints and Pope Gregory IV.

Galleria Doria Pamphilj

The **Palazzo Doria Pamphilj** (cnr Via del Corso & Via del Plebiscito) is just north of Piazza Venezia. Inside is the **Galleria Doria Pamphilj** (☎ 06 679 73 23; entrance at Piazza del Collegio Romano 2; adult/concession €7.30/5.70, private apartments extra €3.10; ☒ 10am-5pm). This collection was started by Pamphilj Pope Innocent X and is astounding even by Roman standards. Elaborate picture galleries – and the stunning private apartments – are crammed from floor to ceiling with paintings, although Velasquez's portrait of Innocent X dazzles in its own chamber. The excellent audio guide is by an English-educated member of the Pamphilj family (who recalls trying to skate on the centuries old floors, is included in the price).

Chiesa del Gesù

The first Jesuit church in Rome was **Chiesa del Gesù** (☎ 06 69 70 01, Piazza del Gesù; admission free; ☼ 6am-12.30pm & 4-7.15pm). Construction of the church began in 1551 and was completed in 1584. With an interior designed by Vignola and a facade by Giacomo della Porta, the Gesù represents the epitome of Counter-Reformation architecture. The Jesuits aimed to attract worshippers with splendour and breathtaking artworks. In Baciccia's astounding vault fresco, two and three dimensions merge, and the foreshortened figures appear to tumble onto the coffered ceiling. Baciccia also painted the cupola frescoes and designed the stucco decoration. St Ignatius' opulent marble and bronze tomb with lapis lazuli–encrusted columns is in the north transept.

The church was financed by Cardinal Alessandro Farnese, who was subsequently regarded as being the owner of the three most beautiful things in Rome – his family *palazzo*, his daughter and the church of the Gesù. This is one church definitely not to be missed.

To the east of the church are the **rooms** (admission free; ☼ 4-6pm Mon-Sat, 10am-noon Sun) where St Ignatius, founder of the Jesuits, lived from 1544 until his death in 1556. The rooms have been restored and display paintings and memorabilia, including a masterful trompe l'oeil perspective by Andrea del Pozzo.

IMPERIAL FORUMS

The **Fori Imperiali** – of Trajan, Augustus, Caesar, Nerva and Vespasian – were built between 42 BC and AD 112. In 1933 Mussolini built a grand thoroughfare as a symbolic link of the Fascist regime with the marvels of ancient Rome (and as a practical link between Piazza Venezia and the Colosseum). In the process, many 16th-century buildings were destroyed and the Imperial Forums were almost completely covered. Their hidden treasures are only now being fully

excavated and evaluated. You cannot enter any of these forums but you can view the excavations from Via dei Fori Imperiali.

The most extensively excavated of the Imperial Forums is **Foro di Traiano** (Trajan's Forum; Map pp102–4). Designed by Apollodorus of Damascus for Emperor Trajan and constructed at the beginning of the 2nd century AD, Trajan's Forum was a vast complex measuring 300m by 185m that extended from what is now Piazza Venezia. It comprised a basilica for the judiciary, two libraries (one Greek and one Latin), a temple, triumphal arch in honour of the emperor and the **Colonna di Traiano** (Trajan's Column; Map pp102–4). Restored in the late 1980s, the column was erected to mark Trajan's victories over the Dacians. It was used to house the ashes of the emperor, which were contained in a golden urn placed on a marble slab at the base of the column. The urn and ashes disappeared during one of the Saracen sacks of Rome.

The column is decorated with a series of reliefs depicting the battles that took place between the Roman and Dacian armies. These are regarded as among the finest examples of ancient Roman sculpture. A golden statue of Trajan once topped the column but it was lost during the Middle Ages and replaced with a statue of St Peter. Apart from the column, all that remains of the grand Imperial Forum are some of the pillars that once formed part of the Basilica Ulpia, the largest basilica built in the ancient city.

Mercati di Traiano (Trajan's Markets; Map pp106–7; ☎ 06 679 00 48, entrance IV Novembre 94; admission €6.20; ☼ 9am-7pm summer, 9am-4.30pm Tue-Sun winter) were also designed by Apollodorus. This complex, built in the early 2nd century, comprised six floors of shops and offices – the precursor to the modern shopping mall. Wine, oil, vegetables, flowers, imported silks and spices were all sold here. The tall red-brick tower above the market buildings, the Torre delle Milizie, was built in the 13th century.

Just to the southeast of Trajan's Forum and markets are the **Foro d'Augusto** (Map pp106–7) and the **Foro di Nerva** (Map pp106–7), although very little remains of either complex. The 30m-high wall behind the Foro d'Augusto was built to protect it against the fires that frequently swept through the area.

There is a delightful walkway beneath the loggia (colonnade) of the 12th-century Casa dei Cavalieri di Rodi (the ancient seat of the Knights of St John of Jerusalem), which is between the forums of Trajan and Augustus and accessible from either Via dei Fori Imperiali or Piazza del Grillo.

In summer the three forums are theatrically illuminated at night.

ROMAN FORUM & PALATINE
Roman Forum   Map Below
The ancient Roman commercial, political and religious centre, the **Roman Forum** (Foro Romano; ☎ 06 399 67 700; entrances at Largo Romolo e Remo, Piazza di Santa Maria Nova & Via di Monte Tarpeo; admission free; ☉ 9am-1 hr before sunset Mon-Sat) stands in a valley between the Capitoline and Palatine hills. The Forum was constructed over the course of 900 years, with later emperors erecting buildings next to those from the Republican era. Its importance declined along with the Roman Empire after the 4th century, and the temples, monuments and buildings constructed by successive emperors, consuls and senators

fell into ruin until eventually the site was used as pasture land. In the Middle Ages the area was known as the Campo Vaccino (literally 'cow field') – ironic, since the valley in which the Forum stood had been used as pasture land in the earliest days of the city's development.

During medieval times the area was extensively plundered for its stone and precious marbles. Many temples and buildings were converted to other uses, while other monuments lay half revealed. The physical destruction of Rome's ancient city can be blamed not on invaders or natural disasters but on the Romans themselves. Over the centuries, in the name of what they called progress, the Romans dismantled the city brick by brick and marble block by marble block in order to build their new palaces, churches and monuments.

During the Renaissance, with the renewed appreciation of all things classical, the Forum provided inspiration for artists and architects. The area was systematically excavated in the 18th and 19th centuries and the excavations continue.

As you enter the Forum from Via dei Fori Imperiali, to your left is the **Tempio di Antonino e Faustina**, erected in AD 141 by the Senate and dedicated to the Empress Faustina and later to the Emperor Antoninus Pius. It was transformed into the church of San Lorenzo in Miranda in the 8th century. To your right is **Basilica Aemilia**, built in 179 BC. The building was 100m long and its facade was a two-storey portico lined with shops. Destroyed and rebuilt several times, the basilica was almost completely demolished during the Renaissance, when it was plundered for its precious marbles.

The **Via Sacra**, which traverses the Forum from northwest to southeast, runs in front of the basilica. Continuing along Via Sacra in the direction of the Capitoline, you will reach the **Curia**, on the right just after the Basilica Aemilia. Once the meeting place of the Roman Senate, it was rebuilt successively by Julius Caesar, Augustus and Domitian and converted into a Christian church in the Middle Ages. The church was dismantled and the Curia restored in the 1930s. The bronze doors are copies – the Roman originals were moved by Borromini to Basilica di San Giovanni in Laterano (Map 6).

In front of the Curia is the famous **Lapis Niger**, a large piece of black marble that covered a sacred area which legend says was the tomb of Romulus. Down a short flight of stairs (rarely open to the public) under the Lapis Niger is the oldest known Latin inscription, dating from the 6th century BC.

The **Arco di Settimio Severo** (Arch of Septimus Severus) was erected in AD 203 in honour of the emperor and his sons, and is considered one of Italy's major triumphal arches. A circular base stone, the **umbilicus urbis**, beside the arch, marks the symbolic centre of ancient Rome. To the south is the **Rostrum**, used in ancient times by public speakers.

Just to the southwest of the arch is the **Tempio di Saturno** (Temple of Saturn), inaugurated in 497 BC and one of the most important ancient Roman temples. It was used as the state treasury and during Caesar's rule contained 13 tonnes of gold ingots, 114 tonnes of silver ingots and 30 million silver coins. Eight granite columns are all that remain. Behind the temple and backing onto the Capitoline are (from north to south) the ruins of the **Tempio della Concordia** (Temple of Concord), the three remaining

columns of **Tempio di Vespasiano** (Temple of Vespasian) and **Portico degli Dei Consenti**.

The remains of the **Basilica Giulia**, which was the seat of civil justice, are on Piazza del Foro. The piazza was the site of the original forum, which served as the main market and meeting place during the Republican era. The **Colonna di Foca** (Column of Phocus), which stands on the piazza and dates from AD 608, was the last monument erected in the Roman Forum. It honoured the Eastern Roman Emperor Phocas, who donated the Pantheon to the Church. At the southeastern end of the piazza is the **Tempio di Giulio Cesare** (Temple of Julius Caesar), which was erected by Augustus in 29 BC on the site where Caesar's body was burned and Mark Antony read his famous speech. Just to the southwest is the **Tempio di Castore e Polluce** (Temple of Castor and Pollux), built in 489 BC to mark the defeat of the Etruscan Tarquins and in honour of the Dioscuri – or Heavenly Twins – who miraculously appeared to the Roman troops during an important battle. Three elegant Corinthian columns from the temple, which at times served as a banking hall and also housed the city's weights and measures office, survive today.

South of the temple is the **Chiesa di Santa Maria Antiqua**, the oldest Christian church in the Forum. Inside the church are some early Christian frescoes. This area has been closed to the public since 1992. Back towards the Via Sacra is the **Casa delle Vestali** (House of the Vestal Virgins), home of the virgins who tended the sacred flame in the adjoining Tempio di Vesta. The six priestesses were selected from patrician families when aged between six and 10 years. They had to serve in the temple for 30 years and were bound by a vow of chastity during this time. If the flame in the temple went out it was seen as a bad omen and the priestess responsible would be flogged. If a priestess lost her virginity she was buried alive, since her blood could not be spilled. The offending man was flogged to death.

The next major monument is the vast **Basilica di Costantino**, which is also known as Basilica di Massenzio. Emperor Maxentius initiated work on the basilica and it was finished in AD 315 by Constantine. A colossal statue of Constantine was unearthed at the site in 1487. Pieces of this statue – a

---

LATIN IN V MINUTES

Can't tell an imperial measure from a republican ruin? If you're a millennium moron, here's a little Latin to help you figure things out:

I = 1; V = 5; X = 10; L = 50; C = 100; D = 500; M = 1000.

So when you read 'AB URB CON MMC CXXII', you know that building wasn't Roman at all, right? Well not ancient, anyway.

Still can't work it out? Here are the rules:

A smaller numeral placed in front of another is subtracted from the larger, eg IV = 4, XC = 90, CM = 900.

A smaller number placed after adds to the larger, eg VI = 6, CX = 110, MC = 1100.

When numbers are repeated, they double or triple, eg XX = 20, CC = 200.

If you still don't know when that building was erected, turn to p127, or ask a Roman.

---

head, hand and foot – are on display in the courtyard of the Palazzo dei Conservatori in the Capitoline Museums (see p86).

The **Arco di Tito** (Arch of Titus), at the end of the Roman Forum nearest the Colosseum, was built in AD 81 in honour of the victories of the emperors Titus and Vespasian against Jerusalem. Titus is represented with Victory on one of the reliefs on the inside of the arch. On the other side, the spoils of Jerusalem are paraded in a triumphal procession. In the past, Roman Jews would avoid passing under this arch, the historical symbol of the beginning of the Diaspora.

Basilica di SS Cosma e Damiano & Chiesa di Santa Francesca Romana

To the north of the Forum is the 6th-century **Basilica di SS Cosma e Damiano** (☎ 06 699 15 40; Largo Romolo e Remo; admission free; ☼ 9am-1pm & 4-7pm). The church once incorporated a large hall which formed part of Vespasian's Forum. In the apse are 6th-century mosaics which are among the most beautiful in Rome. In a room off the 17th-century cloisters is a vast Neapolitan *presepio*, dating from the 18th century.

Past the Basilica di Costantino there is a small stairway leading to the **Chiesa di Santa Francesca Romana** (☎ 06 679 55 28; Piazza di Santa Francesca Romana; admission free; ☼ 9.30am-12.30pm & 3.30-7pm). Built in the 9th century over an earlier oratory, the church incorporates part of the **Tempio di Venere e Roma** (Temple of Venus and Roma). In the apse is a 12th-century mosaic of the Madonna and child with saints. The skeleton of Francesca Romana,

patron saint of motorists, lies beneath the altar of this 9th-century church, holding a book and wearing black leather slippers. On 9 March each year, drivers park their vehicles as close as possible to be blessed. Note the lovely Romanesque bell tower and 12th-century mosaic.

Palatine   Map p92

The **Palatine** (Palatino; ☎ 06 399 67 700; entrances at Piazza di Santa Maria Nova & Via di San Gregorio 30; admission incl Colosseum €8; ☼ 9am-2 hrs before sunset) was the mythical founding place of Rome. Wealthy Romans built their homes here during the era of the Republic and it later became the realm of the emperors. Like those of the Roman Forum, the temples and palaces of the Palatine fell into ruin and in the Middle Ages a few churches and castles were built over the remains. During the Renaissance, members of wealthy families established their gardens on the hill, notably Cardinal Alessandro Farnese, who had elaborate gardens laid out over the ruins.

The largest part of the Palatine as it appears today is covered by ruins of a vast complex built for Emperor Domitian, which served as the main imperial palace for 300 years. This was an ambitious project to create an official imperial palace (the Domus Flavia), the emperor's private residence (the Domus Augustana) and a *stadio* (stadium). The complex was designed by the architect, Rabirius, who levelled a crest of land and demolished many Republican-era houses in the process. Some of these buried buildings have since been unearthed and excavations are continuing.

ROME & LAZIO

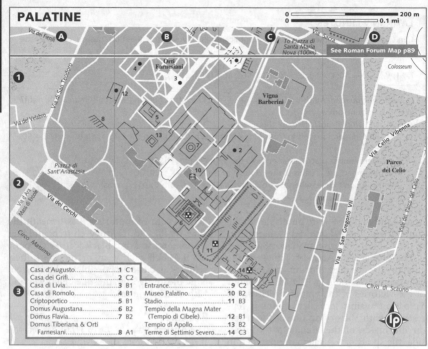

PALATINE

Casa d'Augusto	1 C1
Casa dei Grifi	2 C2
Casa di Livia	3 B1
Casa di Romolo	4 B1
Criptoportico	5 B1
Domus Augustana	6 B2
Domus Flavia	7 B2
Domus Tiberiana & Orti Farnesiani	8 A1
Entrance	9 C2
Museo Palatino	10 B2
Stadio	11 B3
Tempio della Magna Mater (Tempio di Cibele)	12 B1
Tempio di Apollo	13 B2
Terme di Settimio Severo	14 C3

The **Domus Augustana** was built on two levels with rooms leading off a peristyle or garden courtyard on each floor. You can't get down to the lower level but from above you can see the basin of a fountain and beyond it rooms that were paved with coloured marble. The *palazzo* had an elaborate colonnaded facade to the south overlooking Circo Massimo (Map 6), from where you get the clearest indication of the grand scale of the complex. Southeast of the Domus Augustana is the **stadio**, probably used by the emperors for private games and events.

Next to the stadium are the scant remains of baths built by Septimus Severus, the **Terme di Settimio Severo**.

The big white building (a former convent) between the Domus Augustana and the Domus Flavia houses the **Museo Palatino** (9am-3 hrs before sunset). It was established in the 1860s and contains artworks and artefacts found on the Palatine.

North of the Museo Palatino is the **Domus Flavia**, which was once connected to the Domus Augustana. The palace comprised three large halls to the north, the central one

of which was the emperor's throne room, and a large banqueting hall, or triclinium, to the south, which was paved in coloured marbles that can still be seen. The triclinium looked out onto an oval fountain, the remains of which are clearly visible. The Domus Flavia was constructed over earlier edifices, one of which is the **Casa dei Grifi** (House of the Griffins), so called because of a stucco relief of two griffins in one of the rooms. It is the oldest building on the Palatine and dates from the late 2nd or 1st century BC. It was excavated in the 18th century.

Among the best-preserved buildings on the Palatine is the so-called **Casa di Livia**, north of the Domus Flavia. It is well below current ground level and is reached by steps down to a mosaic-covered courtyard. Livia was the wife of Augustus; she owned this house and also a larger villa at Prima Porta to the north of Rome (see p123). The walls were decorated with frescoes – some of which can still be seen, although they have been detached from the walls in order to preserve them. In front of the Casa di Livia is the **Casa d'Augusto**, the actual residence of Augustus – the two constructions were most likely part of the same complex. Both these houses are being restored and can sometimes be visited, depending on what the archaeologists and restorers are up to.

Next to the Casa d'Augusto is the so-called **Casa di Romolo** (House of Romulus), where it is thought Romulus and Remus were brought up after their discovery by the shepherd Faustulus. Excavations carried out in the 1940s revealed evidence of supports for wattle and daub huts dating from the 9th century BC.

Northwest of the Casa di Livia is the **Criptoportico** (Cryptoporticus), a 128m tunnel built by Nero to connect his Domus Aurea (see p94) with the imperial palaces on the Palatine; unfortunately you can't walk into it. The tunnel had windows on one side, which provided light and ventilation. Elaborate stucco decorations once lined part of the Criptoportico.

The area west of this was once the **Domus Tiberiana**, Tiberius' palace, which Gaius Caligula extended further north towards the Forum; today it is the site of the **Orti Farnesiani**. Cardinal Alessandro Farnese, a grandson of Pope Paul III, bought the ruins of Tiberius' palace in the mid-16th century. He had the ruins filled in and asked the acclaimed and fashionable architect Vignola to design a garden for him. It was one of Europe's earliest botanical gardens. There are various paths, rose gardens and shady parasol pines – and it's a great place for a picnic. Twin pavilions stand at the northern point of the garden, from where the view over the Forum and the rest of the city is breathtaking.

COLOSSEUM
Map pp110–11

Construction of the **Colosseum** (Colosseo; ☎ 06 399 67 700; www.pierreci.it, Italian only; Piazza del Colosseo; admission incl Palatine €8; ☼ 9am-1 hr before sunset) was started by Vespasian in AD 72 in the grounds of Nero's private Domus Aurea. Originally known as the Flavian Amphitheatre, after the family name of Vespasian, it was inaugurated by his son Titus in AD 80. The massive structure could seat more than 50,000, and bloody gladiator combat and wild beast shows were held there (see the boxed text, p94). The splendid games held at the inauguration of the Colosseum lasted for

---

MUSEUM CARDS

Two combination tickets are available for sites administered by the Archaeological Superintendent. They can be purchased at any of the monuments or museums listed here:

Roma Archaeologica Card (€20, valid 7 days) for entrance to the Colosseum, the Palatine, Terme di Caracalla, Palazzo Altemps, Palazzo Massimo alle Terme, Terme di Diocleziano, Crypta Balbi, Tomba di Cecilia Metella and Villa dei Quintili.

Museum Card (€9, valid 7 days) for entrance to all venues of the Museo Nazionale Romano: Palazzo Altemps, Palazzo Massimo alle Terme, Terme di Diocleziano and Crypta Balbi.

---

100 days and nights, during which some 5000 animals were slaughtered. Trajan once held games that lasted for 117 days, during which 9000 gladiators fought to the death.

The outer walls of the Colosseum have three levels of arches, which are articulated by columns topped by capitals of the Ionic (at the bottom), Doric and Corinthian (at the top) orders. The external walls were covered in travertine, and marble statues once filled the niches on the second and third storeys. The upper level, punctuated by windows and slender Corinthian pilasters, had supports for 240 masts that held up a canvas awning over the arena, shielding the spectators from sun and rain. The 80 entrance arches allowed the spectators to enter and be seated in a matter of minutes.

The interior of the Colosseum was divided into three parts: the arena, cavea and podium. The **arena** originally had a wooden floor, which was covered in sand to prevent the combatants from slipping and to soak up the blood spilled. It could also be flooded for mock sea battles. Trapdoors led down to the underground chambers and passageways beneath the arena floor, which can be clearly seen today. Animals in cages and sets for the various battles were hoisted onto the arena by a very complicated system of pulleys. The **cavea**, for spectator seating, was divided into three tiers. Knights sat in the

ROME & LAZIO

lowest tier, wealthy citizens in the middle and the populace in the highest tier. The **podium**, a broad terrace in front of the tiers of seats, was reserved for emperors, senators and other VIPs.

With the fall of the Empire, the Colosseum was abandoned and gradually became overgrown. Exotic plants grew there for centuries; seeds had inadvertently been transported from Africa and Asia with the wild beasts (including crocodiles, bears, lions, tigers, elephants, rhinos, hippos, camels and giraffes) that appeared in the arena. In the Middle Ages the Colosseum became a fortress, occupied by two of the city's warrior families: the Frangipani and the Annibaldi. Its reputation as a symbol of Rome, the Eternal City, also dates to the Middle Ages, with Bede writing that 'while the Colosseum stands, Rome shall stand, but when the Colosseum falls, Rome shall fall – and when Rome falls, the world will end'.

Damaged several times by earthquakes, it was later used as a quarry for travertine and marble for other buildings. Pollution and the vibrations caused by traffic and the underground railway have also taken their toll.

Arco di Costantino

On the western side of the Colosseum is the triumphal arch built to honour Constantine following his victory over Maxentius at the battle of the Milvian Bridge (near the Zona Olimpica, northwest of the Villa Borghese) in AD 312.

DOMUS AUREA

Nero didn't do things by halves. His massive **Domus Aurea** (Golden House; Map pp106–7; ☎ 06 399 67 700; www.pierreci.it, Italian only; Viale della Domus Aurea; admission €6; ⏰ 9am-8pm Tue-Sun), built after the fire of AD 64, extended over the Palatine, Oppian and Caelian hills. The gold paint that covered the facade gave the Domus Aurea its name. Its banqueting halls, nymphaeums, baths and terraces were decorated with frescoes and mosaics, a few of which remain. The extensive grounds had vineyards, game and an artificial lake.

After Nero's death in 68, his successors were quick to remove all trace of his excesses, razing much of the Domus Aurea to

---

GLADIATORS

Gladiatorial combat originated as part of Etruscan funerary rites, as a form of human sacrifice. By the 1st century BC, gladiatorial games had far outstripped this ritual context; Caesar exhibited 320 pairs of gladiators in 65 BC, while Augustus and Trajan each showed 5000 pairs of gladiators on different occasions.

Gladiators were prisoners of war, slaves sold to gladiatorial schools or volunteers. Some were equipped with heavy swords and shields, while others were almost naked, armed only with a net and a trident. Pairings were made to match a heavily armed gladiator against a lightly armed one.

Bouts were not necessarily to the death. A defeated gladiator could appeal to the crowd and the presiding magistrate, who could signal that he had fought well and deserved to be spared. Thumbs down, however, meant death, which the defeated man was expected to face with quiet courage.

Although gambling was technically illegal in Rome, vast sums were wagered on gladiatorial combats. Successful gladiators were popular heroes and lived to enjoy a comfortable retirement, with some running their own training schools.

As with the other blood sports held in Rome, gladiatorial games were more than just particularly gruesome entertainment. This state-run public spectacle was a demonstration of Empire through the display of exotic beasts and prisoners of war. It also allowed the people to share in the Roman State's judgement of the defeated by sticking their thumbs up or down according to whether the prisoners should live or die.

Inspired as much by award-winner Russell Crowe in the box office hit *Gladiator* as by the history of ancient Rome, the Gruppo Storico Romano, an association of history enthusiasts, has established Rome's first gladiator school on Via Appia. Romans are enrolling in courses lasting several months to transform themselves into gladiators under the direction of a *magister*. Short intensive courses have also been introduced to cater for tourists keen to get a grip on gladiatorial combat in three days. For more information see www.gsr-roma.com.

the ground. Vespasian drained the lake and built the Colosseum in its place, Domitian built his palace on the Palatine, and Trajan constructed a baths complex on top of the Colle Oppio ruins (this is this area that has been excavated).

Many of the original loggias and halls were walled when Trajan's baths were built and, significantly, the light which filtered through the Domus Aurea's pavilions was completely lost. It is quite confusing trying to identify the parts of the original complex and the later baths.

The baths and the underlying ruins were abandoned by the 6th century. During the Renaissance, artists (including Ghirlandaio, Perugino and Raphael) lowered themselves into the ruins in order to study the frescoes. Some left their own graffiti – not quite 'Pinturicchio woz 'ere', but not far off – and all copied motifs from the Domus Aurea frescoes in their work in the Vatican and other parts of Rome.

ESQUILINE   Map pp106–7

The largest and highest of Rome's seven hills is **Esquiline** (Esquilino). It stretches from the Colosseum to Stazione Termini, encompassing Via Cavour (a major traffic artery between Stazione Termini and Via dei Fori Imperiali), the charming residential area of Monti, Basilica di Santa Maria Maggiore, the market square of Piazza Vittorio Emanuele II and the Colle Oppio (Oppian Hill). The Esquiline originally had four summits. In ancient times the lower slope of the western summit, the Suburra, was occupied by crowded slums, while the area between Via Cavour and the Colle Oppio was a fashionable residential district for wealthier citizens. Much of the hill was covered with vineyards and gardens, many of which remained until the late 19th century, when they were dug up to make way for grandiose apartment blocks.

From the Colle Oppio, follow Via delle Terme di Tito and turn left into Via Monte Oppio to reach the **Basilica di San Pietro in Vincoli** (☎ 06 488 28 65; Piazza di San Pietro in Vincoli 4a; admission free; ☯ 7am-12.30pm & 3.30-7pm), built in the 5th century by the Empress Eudoxia, wife of Valentinian III, to house the chains of St Peter. Legend has it that when a second part of the chains was returned to Rome from Constantinople, the two pieces miraculously joined

together. The church also offers another great treasure – Michelangelo's unfinished tomb of Pope Julius II, with his powerful Moses and unfinished statues of Leah and Rachel on either side. Michelangelo was frustrated for many years by his inability to find time to complete work on the tomb; in the end, Pope Julius was buried in St Peter's Basilica without the great tomb he had envisioned. A flight of steps through a low arch leads down from the church to Via Cavour.

Basilica di Santa Maria Maggiore

One of Rome's four patriarchal basilicas, **Santa Maria Maggiore** (☎ 06 48 31 95; Piazza Santa Maria Maggiore; admission free; ☯ 7am-6.30pm) was built on Esquiline Hill in the 5th century, during the time of Pope Sixtus III. Its main facade was added in the 18th century, although the mosaics of an earlier 13th-century facade were preserved. The interior is baroque and the bell tower Romanesque. The basilican form of the vast interior, a nave and two aisles, remains intact and the most notable feature is the cycle of mosaics dating from the 5th century that decorate the triumphal arch and nave. They depict biblical scenes; in particular, events in the lives of Abraham, Jacob and Isaac (to the left), and Moses and Joshua (to the right). Note also the Cosmatesque pavement, dating from the 12th century. The sumptuously decorated Cappella Sistina, last on the right, was built in the 16th century and contains the tombs of popes Sixtus V and Pius V. Opposite is the Cappella Borghese (or Cappella Paolina), also full of elaborate decoration, erected in the 17th century by Pope Paul V. The Madonna and Child above the altar is believed to date from the 12th to the 13th century.

Basilica di San Clemente

At the base of Esquiline Hill, near the Colosseum and Caelian Hill, is the **Basilica di San Clemente** (Map pp110–11; ☎ 06 704 51 018; Via di San Giovanni in Laterano; admission church/lower levels free/€2.10; ☯ 9am-12.30pm & 3-6pm Mon-Sat, 10am-12.30pm & 3-6pm Sun). Dedicated to one of the earliest popes, the church exemplifies how history in Rome exists on many levels. The 12th-century church at street level was built over a 4th-century church which was, in turn, built over a 1st-century Roman house, to which was added a late 2nd-century temple to the pagan god Mithras (imported to Rome by soldiers returning from the east). Furthermore, it is believed that foundations from the era of the Roman Republic lie beneath the house.

It is possible to visit the first three levels. In the medieval church, note the marble choir screen, originally in the older church below, and the early Renaissance frescoes – which depict the life of Santa Caterina of Alexandria – by Masolino in the Cappella di Santa Caterina. The stunning mosaics in the apse date from the 12th century. On the triumphal arch are Christ and the symbols of the four Evangelists. There is also a depiction of the Triumph of the Cross, with 12 doves symbolising the apostles. Figures around the cross include the Madonna and St John, as well as St John the Baptist and other saints, encircled by a vine growing from the foot of the cross.

The church below was mostly destroyed by Norman invaders in 1084 but some Romanesque frescoes remain. Descend further and you reach the Roman house and temple of Mithras.

BASILICA DI SAN GIOVANNI IN LATERANO

Founded by Constantine in the 4th century, the **Basilica di San Giovanni in Laterano** (Map pp110–11; ☎ 06 698 86 452; Piazza San Giovanni in Laterano 4; admission church free; 🕑 church 7am-7pm summer, 7am-6pm winter) was the first Christian basilica constructed in Rome. It is Rome's cathedral and the pope's seat as Bishop of Rome. It has been destroyed by fire twice and rebuilt several times. In 1425 Martin V had the floor inlaid with stone and mosaic looted from other derelict Roman churches.

Borromini transformed the interior in the mid-17th century. The **bronze doors** of the eastern facade were moved here from the Curia in the Roman Forum. Alessandro Galilei's **portico** (porch; built 1736) is surmounted by colossal statues representing Christ with Sts John the Baptist as well as John the Evangelist and the 12 apostles. The Gothic **baldacchino** over the papal altar contains relics that include the heads of Sts Peter and Paul. The apse was rebuilt in the 19th century; its mosaics are copies of the originals.

Fortunately the beautiful 13th-century **cloister** (admission €2.10; 🕑 9am-6pm summer, 9am-5pm winter) escaped the fires. Built by the Vassalletto family in Cosmati style, the cloister has columns and an architrave that were once completely covered with inlaid marble mosaics. The outer walls are lined with sarcophagi and sculpture, including an inscription of a Papal Bull of Sixtus IV.

The domed **baptistry** (admission free; 🕑 9am-1pm & 4-6pm Mon-Thu, 9am-1pm Fri & Sat), near Domenico Fontana's northern facade, was also built by Constantine, but has been remodelled several times. Sixtus III gave it its present octagonal shape, which became the model for many baptistries throughout the Christian world. The **Cappella di Santa Rufina** is decorated with a stunning 5th-century mosaic of vines and foliage against a deep-blue background, while the vault of **Cappella di San Giovanni Evangelista** has a mosaic of the Lamb of God surrounded by birds and flowers. **Cappella di San Venanzio** was added by Pope John IV in the 7th century. It has extremely well-preserved mosaics; in the apse are Christ with angels and the Madonna and saints, and on the triumphal arch are Christian martyrs. Right at the top are views of Jerusalem and Bethlehem.

The **Palazzo Laterano**, which adjoins the basilica, was the papal residence until the popes moved to Avignon early in the 14th century. It was largely destroyed by fire in 1308 and most of what remained was demolished in the 16th century. The present building houses offices of the diocese of Rome.

The building on the eastern side of Piazza San Giovanni in Laterano contains the **Scala**

THE SAINTLY SEVEN

While the Roman Emperors recognised seven hills, Pontifical Rome recognises seven pilgrim churches associated with important saints or their relics. Pilgrims who managed to visit all seven churches during the medieval and Renaissance periods were granted a special plenary indulgence. To win this, they visited the four patriarchal basilicas – St Peter's (San Pietro; pp115–17), San Giovanni in Laterano (pp96–7), Santa Maria Maggiore (p95) and San Paolo Fuori-le-Mura (p124) – then San Lorenzo Fuori-le-Mura (p124), Chiesa di Santa Croce in Gerusalemme (p97) and San Sebastiano (p126) on the Appian Way.

Santa (Holy Staircase; admission free; ☺ 6.15am-noon & 3.30-6.45pm Apr-Sep, 6.15am-noon & 3-6.15pm Oct-Mar) and the **Sancta Sanctorum** (admission €2.60; ☺ 10.30-11.30am & 3-4pm Tue, Thu & Sat). The Scala Santa is said to come from Pontius Pilate's palace in Jerusalem and people are allowed to climb it only on their knees. The Sancta Sanctorum was the popes' private chapel and contains 13th-century frescoes and mosaics.

East of Piazza di San Giovanni is the **Chiesa di Santa Croce in Gerusalemme** (☎ 06 701 47 69; Piazza Santa Croce in Gerusalemme 12; admission free; ☺ 6.30am-12.30pm & 3.30-7.30pm). This pilgrimage church was founded in AD 320 by St Helena, Constantine's mother, who brought Christian relics, including a piece of the cross on which Christ was crucified, to Rome from Jerusalem. The bell tower was added in 1144, the facade and oval vestibule in 1744.

CELIO   Map pp110–11

Celio (Caelian Hill) is accessible either from Via di San Gregorio VII to the west or from Via della Navicella to the east. The **Villa Celimontana** (Via della Navicella; admission free; ☺ sunrise-sunset) is a large public park on top of the hill, perfect for a quiet picnic; there is also a children's playground. The 4th-century **Chiesa di SS Giovanni e Paolo** (Piazza SS Giovanni e Paolo) is dedicated to Sts John and Paul, two Romans who had served in the court of Emperor Constantine II and were beheaded by his anti-Christian successor, Emperor Julian, for refusing to serve as officers in his court. The church was built over their **houses** (☎ 06 704 54 544; www.caseromane.it; adult/concession €6/4; ☺ 10am-1pm & 3-6pm Thu-Mon winter, 10am-1pm & 4-7pm summer), which have recently been reopened to the public and reveal fascinating aspects of daily Roman life. There are more than 20 rooms, many of them richly decorated. Entrance to the archaeological site is through the door on the Clivo di Scauro.

The 8th-century **Chiesa di San Gregorio Magno** (Via di San Gregorio) was built in honour of Pope Gregory the Great on the site where he dispatched St Augustine to convert the people of Britain to Christianity. The church was remodelled in the baroque style in the 17th century.

The fascinating circular **Chiesa di Santo Stefano Rotondo** (☎ 06 704 93 717; Via di S Stefano Rotondo 7; admission free; ☺ 1.50-4.20pm Mon, 9am-1pm & 1.50-4.20pm Tue-Sat, 9am-noon 2nd Sun of each month in summer), built between 468 and 483, is one of Rome's earliest churches. Inside are two rings of antique granite and marble columns. The wall is lined with frescoes depicting the various ways in which saints were martyred. The vivid scenes are quite grotesque and you might not make it through all 34 of them.

Around Celio

The refurbished **Chiesa di Santa Maria in Cosmedin** (Map pp108–9; ☎ 06 678 14 19; Piazza Bocca della Verità 18; admission free; ☺ 9am-1pm & 2.30-6pm) is regarded as one of the finest medieval churches in Rome. It has a 12th-century, seven-storey bell tower and its interior, including the beautiful floor, was heavily decorated with inlaid marble. There are 12th-century frescoes in the aisles. Under the portico is the famous Bocca della Verità (Mouth of Truth), a large, round, marble mask that probably served as the cover of an ancient drain. Legend says that if you put your right hand into the mouth while telling a lie, it will snap shut. Opposite the church are two tiny Roman temples: the round Tempio di Ercole Vincitore and the Tempio di Portunus.

Just off the piazza are the **Arco di Giano** (Arch of Janus), a four-sided Roman arch that once covered a crossroads, and the medieval church of **San Giorgio in Velabro**.

Teatro di Marcello (Map pp110–11; Via del Teatro di Marcello) was built around 13 BC to plans by Julius Caesar and dedicated by Emperor Augustus. It was converted into a fortress and residence during the Middle Ages, and a palace built on the site in the 16th century preserved the original form of the theatre.

Isola Tiberina

Across the **Ponte Fabricio**, which was built in 62 BC and Rome's oldest standing bridge, is **Isola Tiberina** (Map pp102–4). The island has been associated with healing since the 3rd century BC, when the Romans adopted Aesculapius, the Greek god of healing, as their own and erected a temple to him on the island. Today it is the site of one hospital, the **Ospedale Fatebenefratelli**. **Chiesa di San Bartolomeo** (Map pp102–4) was built on the island in the 10th century on the ruins of the Roman temple. It has a Romanesque bell tower and a marble well-head, believed to have been built over the same spring that provided healing waters for the temple. The Ponte Cestio, built in 46 BC, connects the island to Trastevere to the south. It was rebuilt in the late 19th century. Also to the south of the island are the remains of part of the **Ponte Rotto** (Broken Bridge), ancient Rome's first stone bridge.

TERME DI CARACALLA

These **baths** (Map pp110–11; ☎ 06 399 67 70; www .pierreci.it; Via delle Terme di Caracalla 52; admission €5; ☼ 9am-1 hr before sunset Tue-Sat, 9am-2pm Mon) are south of the Celio, accessible by bus Nos 160 and 628 from Piazza Venezia. Covering 10 hectares, Caracalla's Baths could hold 1600 people and had shops, gardens, libraries and entertainment. Begun by Antonius Caracalla and inaugurated in AD 217, the baths were used until the 6th century AD. Excavations of the baths in the 16th and 17th centuries unearthed important sculptures, which found their way into the Farnese family collection.

AVENTINE HILL

South of the Circo Massimo is **Aventine Hill** (Aventino; Map pp108–9), best reached from Via del Circo Massimo by Via di Valle Murcia or from Clivo de Publici by Via di Santa Sabina. It is also easily accessible by bus No 27 from Stazione Termini and the Colosseum, or on the Metro Linea B, disembarking at Circo Massimo (Map pp110-11). Nearby is the **Roseto Comunale**, a beautiful public rose garden best seen in spring and summer, and the pretty, walled **Parco Savello**, planted with orange trees. There is a stunning view of Rome from the park.

Next to the park is the 5th-century **Basilica di Santa Sabina** (Via di Santa Sabina; ☼ 6.30am-12.30pm & 4-6pm). Of particular note is the carved wooden door to the far left as you stand under the 15th-century portico facing the church. Dating from the 5th century, the door features panels depicting biblical scenes; the crucifixion scene is one of the oldest in existence.

TRASTEVERE

Separated from the historic centre by the river, **Trastevere** (Map pp108–9) is one of the most picturesque parts of Rome. The many bars and restaurants tucked into its labyrinthine lanes make it the most popular area

of the city for eating and hanging out. Its traditionally proletarian nature is changing as crumbling old *palazzi* become gentrified and wealthy foreigners move in.

A lovely way to arrive in Trastevere (which means across the Tiber) is to cross over the historic **Ponte Fabricio** onto the Isola Tiberina and then over the Ponte Cestio into Piazza in Piscinula (named after the ancient baths that once stood here). This leads into Via della Lungaretta and across busy Viale di Trastevere to Santa Maria in Trastevere. But on the way it's worth visiting two other churches.

In **Basilica di Santa Cecilia in Trastevere** (Map pp108–9; ☎ 06 589 92 89; Piazza di Santa Cecilia; admission church/Cavallini fresco free/€1.10; ☼ church 10am-noon & 4-5.30pm, fresco 10-11.30am Tue & Thu, 11.15-11.45am & after Mass Sun) there's a magnificent 13th-century fresco of the *Last Judgement* by Pietro Cavallini in the nuns' choir, entered through the convent.

Towards the end of Via delle Luce is the **Chiesa di San Francesco a Ripa** (Map pp108–9; Piazza di San Francesco d'Assisi) and tucked away inside is one of the Bernini ecstasy sculptures, *Blessed Ludovica Albertoni*.

Follow the Via di San Francesco a Ripa across Viale Trastevere, through Piazza San Calisto and into the heart of Trastevere and the lovely **Piazza Santa Maria in Trastevere**. It's a true Roman square – by day it's full of mothers with prams, chatting locals and guidebook-toting tourists, by night there are artisans selling their craftwork, young Romans looking for a good time and the odd homeless person looking for a bed.

The **Basilica di Santa Maria in Trastevere** (Map pp108–9; ☎ 06 581 94 43; Piazza Santa Maria in Trastevere; admission free; ☼ 7.30am-12.30pm & 3.30-7.30pm) is believed to be the oldest place of worship dedicated to the Virgin Mary in Rome. Although the first basilica was built on this site in AD 337, the present structure was built in the 12th century and contains a Romanesque bell tower and facade, with a mosaic of the Virgin from the 12th century. The impressive interior features 21 ancient Roman columns. Of particular interest are the 17th-century wooden ceiling, and the vibrant mosaics in the apse (dating from 1140) and on the triumphal arch. Note the richly patterned dress of the Madonna in the apse. A badly deteriorated painting of

(Continued on page 112)

0 — 1 km
0 — 0.5 mi

INFORMATION

Australian Embassy	**1** D2
Canadian Embassy	**2** D2
New Zealand Consulate	**3** D2
Onda Blu	**4** A2
St John's University	**5** A3
Swiss Embassy & Consulate	**6** C1
UK Embassy	**7** C2

SIGHTS & ACTIVITIES pp86–126

Basilica & Catacombs of San Sebastiano	**8** D6
Catacombs of San Callisto	**9** D5
Catacombs of San Domitilla	**10** D5
Catacombs of Santa Priscilla	**11** C1
Centro Linguistico Italiano Dante Alighieri	**12** D2
Chiesa del Domine Quo Vadis?	**13** C5
Mausoleo delle Fosse Ardeatine	**14** D6
San Lorenzo Fuori-le-Mura	**15** D3
San Paolo Fuori-le-Mura	**16** B5
Tomba di Cecilia Metella	**17** D6
Tomba di Romolo	**18** D5

SLEEPING pp131–9

Hotel Lady	**19** B2
Ostello Foro Italico	**20** A1
Pensione Nautilus	(see 19)
Pensione Paradise	**21** B2

EATING pp139–47

Archeologia	**22** D6
Emporium Naturae	**23** A2
Croce Osteria Con Cucina Angelo	**24** A2
Pommidoro	**25** D3
Tram Tram	**26** D3

ENTERTAINMENT pp149–52

Alexanderplatz	**27** A2
Alpheus	**28** B5
Auditorium Parco della Musica	**29** B1
Goa	**30** B5
Stadio Olimpico	**31** A1
Accademia Filarmonica Romana	**32** B1

INFORMATION
Austrian Consulate......................... 1 F3
Dutch Embassy & Consulate........... 2 E2
Nouvelles Frontières...................... 3 B6
Ospedale San Giacomo.................. 4 B6

SIGHTS & ACTIVITIES pp86–126
Bioparco....................................... 5 E3
Chiesa di Santa Maria dei Miracoli.. 6 B5
Chiesa di Santa Maria del Popolo.... 7 B5
Chiesa di Santa Maria in
   Montesanto............................... 8 B5
Explora... 9 B4
Galleria Borghese......................... 10 G4
Galleria Nazionale d'Arte Moderna..11 D3
Museo Nazionale Etrusco di Villa
   Giulia....................................... 12 C3

SLEEPING pp131–9
Hotel de Russie............................ 13 C5
Hotel Ercoli................................. 14 H6

Hotel Locarno.............................. 15 B6
Hotel Margutta............................ 16 C6
Hotel Tizi................................(see 14)
Parco dei Principi......................... 17 F3

EATING pp139–47
Edy.. 18 C6
GS.. 19 D6
Margutta Vegetariano.................. 20 C6

DRINKING pp147–9
Caffè delle Arte......................(see 11)
Canova.. 21 C5
Rosati.. 22 B5

ENTERTAINMENT pp149–52
Alien... 23 H5

TRANSPORT pp153–9
Avis... 24 F6
I Bike.. 25 E6

E   F   G   H

1

Villa Grazioli

Via C Antonelli

Viale dei Parioli

Via Romania

Via A Stoppani

Piazza
Cuba

Piazza
Ungheria

Via F Siacci

Viale   Bruno   Buozzi

Via Liegi

Via Cavalieri

Via G D'Arezzo

Via Aterno

2

Via Michele
Mercati

Via U. Aldrovandi

Viale G Rossini

Piazza
G Verdi

Via Metauro

V. G. Carissimi

Via S Mercadante   Via N Porpora

Via G Paisiello

Via Po

3

Via Frescobaldi

17

Via Pergolesi

Largo N
Spinelli

Via Basento

Viale del Giardino

Piazza
Giardino
Zoologico

Zoologica

1

Piazzale
dei Daini

Villa
Borghese

Viale dell' Uccelliera

Viale dei Due Mascheroni

Via G Vasanzio

Villa Torlonia
(Già Albani)

4

Largo
Acqua Felix

Piazza
di Siena

Viale Pietro Canonica

Piazzale dei
Cavalieri Marini

Piazzale
Scipione
Borghese

10

Via di Villa Albani

Cavalli Marini

Via Salaria

Via Po

Via Savola

Via Wolfango Goethe

Piazzale
Sienkiewicz

Via Pinciana

Via G Puccini

Via
Isonzo

Via Teresa

Via Tevere

Via Veletri

23

Via Anieni

Via Salaria

5

Viale San Paolo del Brasile

Villa
Borghese

Viale del Museo Borghese

Via Pinciana

Corso d'Italia

Via Campania

Piazza
Fiume

Galoppatoio

Porta
Pinciana

Piazzale
Brasile

25

Largo   Via Campania
Federico Fellini

24

Via Sardegna

Via Piemonte

Via Abruzzi

Via Toscana

Via Romagna

Via Puglie

Via Lucania

Via Calabria

Via Valenziani

Via
Via Plave

Porta
Pia

6

Via Lazio

Via
Vittorio Veneto

Via Marche

Via Sicilia

Via Boncompagni

Sallustiano

Via Boncompagni

Piazza
Sallustio

14

Via Belisario

Via Cadorna

Via Lombardia

0 — 200 m
0 — 0.1 mi

See Around Villa Borghese
Map pp100-1

See Centro Storico Map pp104-5

See Roman Forum and Esquiline
Map pp106-7

E **F** **G** **H**

1
2
3
4
5
6

Via Ennio Quirini Visconti
Tiber
Via Pietro Cossa
Via Marianna Dionigi
Via Vittorio Colonna
Lungotevere Mercati — Prati
Ponte Cavour
Lungotevere Marzio
Piazza dei Tribunali
Ponte Umberto I

Via A Canova
Via della Frezza
Via di Ripetta
Via del Corso
Piazza Augusto Imperatore
Largo degli Schiavoni
Largo San Rocco
Via Tomacelli
Via dell'Arancio
Largo della Piazza Fontanella di Borghese
Piazza Monte d'Oro
Piazza Nicosia
Via di Monte Brianzo
Via della Scrofa

Via di San Giacomo
Via del Greci
Via di Ripetta
Via Vittoria
Via della Croce
Via delle Carrozze
Via Bocca di Leone
Via Condotti
Via Borgognona
Via Frattina
Via della Vite
Via del Gambero
Via Belsiana
Via Mario de' Fiori
Via Santa Andrea delle Fratte
Piazza di San Lorenzo in Lucina
Largo Goldoni
Via delle Mercede
Piazza di San Silvestro
Piazza di San Claudio
Via del Tritone

Campo Marzio
Spagna
Piazza della Trinità dei Monti
Piazza di Spagna
Piazza Mignanelli
Via Sistina
Via Gregoriana
Via Due Macelli
Via Capo le Case
Via del Nazareno
Via Accademia di San Luca
Via della Panetteria
Piazza dei Crociferi
Via del Lavatore
Largo di Santa Maria in Via
Largo Chigi
Piazza Colonna

Colonna

Piazza Sant'Apollinare
Piazza di Sant'Agostino
Via delle Coppelle
Piazza delle Coppelle
Via della Stelletta
Via degli Uffici del Vicario
Piazza del Parlamento
Piazza del Monte Citorio
Piazza di Monte Citorio
Via in Lucina
Via della Guglia
Via Canova
Via Aquiro
Piazza Capranica
Via dei Pastini
Piazza di Pietra
Piazza Sant'Ignazio
Via del Seminario
Via del Corso
Via delle Muratte
Via Marco Minghetti
Piazza dell'Oratorio
Via dell'Umiltà
Piazza di San Marcello
Via del Corso
Piazza dei Santissimi Apostoli
Via IV Novembre
Via della Vergine

Via dei Coronari
Piazza Lacellotti
Via G Zanardelli
Piazza Ponte Umberto I
Via dell'Orso
Piazza di Tor Sanguigna
Piazza delle 5 Lune
Corso del Rinascimento
Piazza Navona
Via di Santa Maria dell'Anima
Via del Governo Vecchio
Piazza del Fico
Piazza di Pasquino
Corso Vittorio Emanuele II

Pariome
Via del Pellegrino
Via dei Cappellari
Piazza Aula Cancelleria
Piazza della Chiesa Nuova
Largo Febo
Piazza Monte Vecchio
Piazza del Fico
Via del Teatro Valle
Via di Torre Argentina
Via Monterone
Largo del Teatro Valle

Sant'Eustachio
Piazza Sant'Eustachio
Via G Toniolo
Piazza Rondanini
Piazza della Rotonda
Piazza della Minerva
Via di Pie di Marmo
Piazza della Pigna
Via della Pigna
Piazza del Collegio Romeno
Piazza di Grazioli
Piazza del Gesù
Via di San Marco

Pigna
Via dei Barbieri
Largo di Torre Argentina
Via del Sudario
Corso Vittorio Emanuele II
Piazza Vidoni
Piazza Pollarola
Piazza Paradiso
Piazza Campo de' Fiori
Piazza Farnese
Piazza della Quercia
Via dei Baullari
Via Monserrato
Via dei Giubbonari
Piazza del Largo del Biscione
Piazza del Pallaro
Via de' Chiavari
Via di Sant'Anna
Via Arenula
Via Florida
Piazza Paganica
Piazza del Monte di Pietà
Via del Falegnami
Piazza B Cairoli
Via di Santa Maria del Pianto
Via dei Funari
Piazza Mattei
Via de' Delfini
Piazza Capizzucchi
Piazza Margana
Piazza d'Ara Coeli
Via delle Botteghe Oscure
Via di San Marco
Piazza San Marco
Piazza Venezia
Piazza della Madonna di Loreto
Via Cesare Battisti
Piazza di San Marco
Via dei Fori Imperiali
Via di San Pietro in Carcere
Cordonata di Michelangelo
Piazza del Campidoglio

Ponte Sisto
Piazza SV Pallotti
Lungotevere dei Vallati
Piazza Trinità Pellegrini
Via delle Zoccolette
Piazza Cenci
Via San Bartolomeo dei Vaccinari
Via Arenula
Via San Bartolomeo de' Cenci
Lungotevere de' Cenci
Piazza di Monte Savello
Piazza delle Cinque Scole
Via del Portico d'Ottavia
Via Catalana
Piazza Campitelli
Piazza di Monte Savello
Via del Foro Piscario
Via del Teatro di Marcello
Via della Villa Caffarelli

Capitoline Hill
Via di Monte Caprino
Piazza della Consolazione
Piazza Monte Savello

Ponte Garibaldi
Ponte Fabricio
Ponte Cestio

Piazza Trilussa
Lgt Sanzio Raffaello
Via dei Pettinari

E F G H

CENTRO STORICO (p105)

0 **100 m**
0 **0.1 mi**

A **B** **C** **D**

1
2
3
4
5
6

Ponte Umberto I

Piazza Cardelli

V di Prefetti

29

Piazza Firenze

2 @

Via di Monte Brianzo

Via della Scrofa

Via d'Ascanio

11
Piazza Ponte Umberto I

Via dell'Orso

40

23

Via dei Portoghesi

43

Via della Stelletta

Lungotevere Tor di Nona

Via di Tor di Nona

Via G. Zanardelli

Via di Acquasparta

12

Via dei Tre Archi

Piazza Lacellotti

Piazza Sant'Apollinare

37

Piazza delle Coppelle

Via degli Uffici di Vicario

35

Piazza di Salvatore in Lauro

Via dei Coronari

Piazza Tor Sanguigna

8

Piazza di Sant'Agostino Agostino

46

Via delle Coppelle

34

Piazza di San Simeone

Piazzella di San Simeone

Piazza delle Cinque Lune

4

3

@

66

Piazza della Maddalena

36

Via delle Colonnelle

67

Vicolo delle Volpe

L'Arco della Pace

Via di Monte vecchio

45

9

Largo Febo

Via dei Lorenesi

Via San Giovanni d'Arco

Largo G Tonioli

Via del Pozzo

Piazza Rondanini

42

64

41

17

Via delle Vacche

53

52

61

Piazza del Fico

57

Via della Pace

Via di Santa Maria dell'Anima

Piazza Navona

Corso del Rinascimento

Piazza di San Luigi

6

Via del Salvatore de'Francesi

31

Via Giustiniani

Piazza della Rotonda

3

Via di Tor Millina

Via del Teatro Pace

69

10

7

Via de Cupis

Salita de'Crescenzi

Via della Dogana Vecchia

16

Via del Grana

Piazza Sant' Eustachio

55

56

Via di Santa Chiara

39

Piazza Santa Chiara

Piazza della Minerva

24

49

5

Piazza della Chiesa Nuova

Via del Governo Vecchio

Via degli Staderari

Via dei Sediari

Via del Teatro Valle

63

Corso Vittorio Emanuele II

Piazza di Pasquino

65

Via della Vecchia Posta

Via dei Canestrari

Via de'Nari

Via Arco della Ciambella

Largo di Stimmate

Parione

Pasquino

Via di Parione

Piazza dei Massimi

Largo del Teatro Valle

Sant'Eustachio

13

25

Piazza di San Pantaleo

Piazza di Sant'Andrea della Valle

Corso Vittorio Emanuele II

Largo di Torre Argentina

Via del Pellegrino

Via dei Cappellari

32

47

Via dei Baullari

Piazza Pollarola

38

Piazza Vidoni

Via del Sudario

62

Corso Vittorio Emanuele II

Via di Montoro

33

Piazza Campo de'Fiori

44

21

Piazza del Paradiso

19

Via del Chiavari

50

54

60

48

18

20

Largo del Pallaro

70

Via Giulia

Via del Monserrato

Piazza Farnese

59

Piazza del Biscione

Piazza dei Satiri

22

Via di Sant'Anna

Largo Arenula

Via Florida

14

28

58

30

Piazza della Quercia

Via del Giglio

Via delle Grotte

Via di Giubbonari

Via del Monte della Farina

Via dei Barbieri

Via Paganica

Via Arenula

Via dei Falegnami

15

Piazza del Monte di Pietà

27

Piazza B Cairoli

68

Piazza Trinità Pelegrini

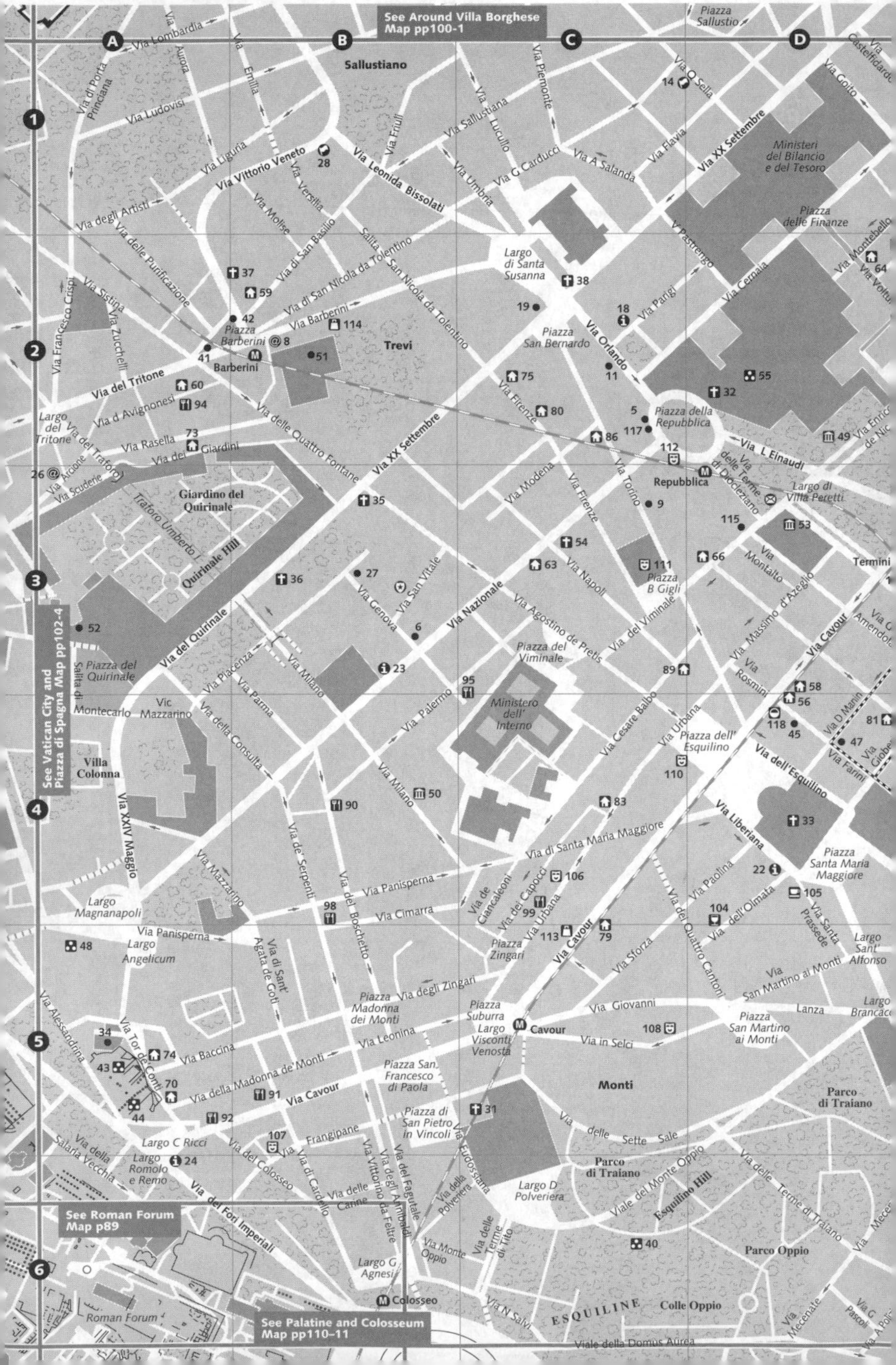

See Around Villa Borghese Map pp100-1
See Vatican City and Piazza di Spagna Map pp102-4
See Roman Forum Map p89
See Palatine and Colosseum Map pp110-11
A
B
C
D
1
2
3
4
5
6
Piazza Sallustio
Sallustiano
Via Lombardia
Via Aurora
Via Emilia
Via di Porta Pinciana
Via Ludovisi
Via Liguria
Via Vittorio Veneto
Via Friuli
Via Sallustiana
Via Lucullo
Via Piemonte
Via Q Sella
Via Goito
Via Castelfidardo
Via Leonida Bissolati
Via Veneto
Via Versilia
Via Molise
Via Umbria
Via G Carducci
Via A Salanda
Via Flavia
Via XX Settembre
Ministeri del Bilancio e del Tesoro
Piazza delle Finanze
Via degli Artisti
Via delle Purificazione
Via di San Basilio
Salita di San Nicola da Tolentino
Via di San Nicola da Tolentino
Largo di Santa Susanna
V Pastrengo
Via Cernaia
Via Montebello
Via Volturno
Via Francesco Crispi
Via Sistina
Via Zucchelli
Piazza Barberini
Barberini
Via Barberini
Trevi
Via Pargi
Piazza San Bernardo
Via Orlando
Via del Tritone
Via d Avignonesi
Via Firenze
Piazza della Repubblica
Largo del Tritone
Via del Traforo
Via Rasella
Via dei Giardini
Via delle Quattro Fontane
Via L Einaudi
Via delle Terme di Diocleziano
Via Enrico de Nicola
Via Arcione
Via Scuderie
Giardino del Quirinale
Traforo Umberto I
Quirinale Hill
Via Modena
Via Torino
Repubblica
Largo di Villa Peretti
Via Montalto
Termini
Via Napoli
Piazza B Gigli
Via San Vitale
Via Genova
Via Nazionale
Via del Quirinale
Via Agostino de Pretis
Via del Viminale
Via Massimo d'Azeglio
Via Cavour
Via Amendola
Salita di Montecarlo
Piazza del Quirinale
Via Piacenza
Via Milano
Piazza del Viminale
Via Rosmini
Vic Mazzarino
Via Parma
Via della Consulta
Via Palermo
Ministero dell' Interno
Via Cesare Balbo
Via Urbana
Piazza dell' Esquilino
Via D Manin
Via Farini
Via Gioberti
Villa Colonna
Via XXIV Maggio
Via dell'Esquilino
Via Liberiana
Via de' Serpenti
Via di Santa Maria Maggiore
Piazza Santa Maria Maggiore
Via Mazzarino
Via Panisperna
Via del Boschetto
Via de Ciancaleoni
Via dei Capocci
Via Paolina
Via dell'Olmata
Via Santa Prassede
Largo Magnanapoli
Via Cimarra
Via Urbana
Via dei Quattro Cantoni
Largo Angelicum
Via di Sant' Agata de Goti
Piazza Zingari
Via Sforza
Largo Sant' Alfonso
Via Alessandrina
Piazza Madonna dei Monti
Via degli Zingari
Piazza Suburra
Largo Visconti Venosta
Via Giovanni Lanza
Via San Martino ai Monti
Largo Brancaccio
Via Tor de' Conti
Via Baccina
Via Leonina
Cavour
Via in Selci
Piazza San Martino ai Monti
Via della Madonna de' Monti
Piazza San Francesco di Paola
Monti
Parco di Traiano
Piazza di San Pietro in Vincoli
Via delle Sette Sale
Largo C Ricci
Via Frangipane
Via della Salaria Vecchia
Largo Romolo e Remo
Via del Colosseo
Via di Cardello
Via delle Carine
Via Vittorino da Feltre
Via degli Annibaldi
Via del Fagutale
Via Eudossiana
Via della Polveriera
Largo D Polveriera
Viale del Monte Oppio
Esquilino Hill
Via delle Terme di Traiano
Via del Fori Imperiali
Via Monte Oppio
Via delle Terme di Tito
Parco Oppio
Largo G Agnesi
Colosseo
Roman Forum
Via N Salvi
ESQUILINE
Colle Oppio
Via Mecenate
Via G Pascoli
Viale della Domus Aurea

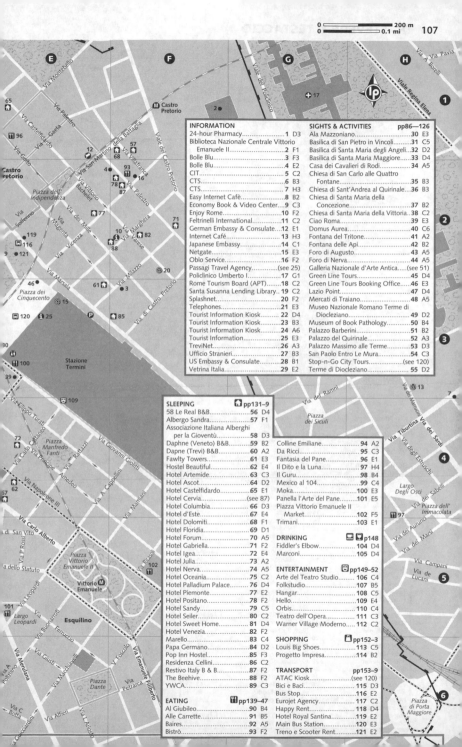

INFORMATION

24-hour Pharmacy	**1** D3
Biblioteca Nazionale Centrale Vittorio Emanuele II	**2** F1
Bolle Blu	**3** F3
Bolle Blu	**4** E2
CIT	**5** C2
CTS	**6** B3
CTS	**7** H3
Easy Internet Café	**8** C2
Economy Book & Video Center	**9** C3
Enjoy Rome	**10** D2
Feltrinelli International	**11** C2
German Embassy & Consulate	**12** C1
Internet Café	**13** H3
Japanese Embassy	**14** C1
Netgate	**15** E3
Oblo Service	**16** F2
Passagi Travel Agency	(see 25)
Policlinico Umberto I	**17** G1
Rome Tourism Board (APT)	**18** C2
Santa Susanna Lending Library	**19** C2
Splashnet	**20** F2
Telephones	**21** E3
Tourist Information Kiosk	**22** D4
Tourist Information Kiosk	**23** B3
Tourist Information Kiosk	**24** A6
Tourist Information	**25** E3
TreviNet	**26** A3
Ufficio Stranieri	**27** B3
US Embassy & Consulate	**28** B1
Vetrina Italia	**29** E2

SIGHTS & ACTIVITIES   pp86—126

Ala Mazzoniano	**30** E3
Basilica di San Pietro in Vincoli	**31** C5
Basilica di Santa Maria degli Angeli	**32** D2
Basilica di Santa Maria Maggiore	**33** D4
Casa dei Cavalieri di Rodi	**34** A5
Chiesa di San Carlo alle Quattro Fontane	**35** B3
Chiesa di Sant'Andrea al Quirinale	**36** B3
Chiesa di Santa Maria della Concezione	**37** B2
Chiesa di Santa Maria della Vittoria	**38** C2
Ciao Roma	**39** E3
Domus Aurea	**40** C6
Fontana del Tritone	**41** A2
Fontana delle Api	**42** B2
Foro di Augusto	**43** A5
Foro di Nerva	**44** A5
Galleria Nazionale d'Arte Antica	(see 51)
Green Line Tours	**45** D4
Green Line Tours Booking Office	**46** E3
Lazio Point	**47** D4
Mercati di Traiano	**48** A5
Museo Nazionale Romano Terme di Diocleziano	**49** D2
Museum of Book Pathology	**50** B4
Palazzo Barberini	**51** B2
Palazzo del Quirinale	**52** A3
Palazzo Massimo alle Terme	**53** D3
San Paolo Entro Le Mura	**54** C3
Stop-n-Go City Tours	(see 120)
Terme di Diocleziano	**55** D2

SLEEPING   pp131–9

58 Le Real B&B	**56** D4
Albergo Sandra	**57** F1
Associazione Italiana Alberghi per la Gioventù	**58** D3
Daphne (Veneto) B&B	**59** B2
Dapne (Trevi) B&B	**60** A2
Fawlty Towers	**61** E4
Hostel Beautiful	**62** E4
Hotel Artemide	**63** C3
Hotel Ascot	**64** D2
Hotel Castelfidardo	**65** E1
Hotel Cervia	(see 87)
Hotel Columbia	**66** D3
Hotel d'Este	**67** C4
Hotel Dolomiti	**68** F1
Hotel Floridia	**69** D1
Hotel Forum	**70** A5
Hotel Gabriella	**71** F2
Hotel Igea	**72** E4
Hotel Julia	**73** A2
Hotel Nerva	**74** A5
Hotel Oceania	**75** C2
Hotel Palladium Palace	**76** D4
Hotel Piemonte	**77** E2
Hotel Positano	**78** F2
Hotel Sandy	**79** C5
Hotel Seiler	**80** C2
Hotel Sweet Home	**81** D4
Hotel Venezia	**82** F2
Marello	**83** C4
Papa Germano	**84** D2
Pop Inn Hostel	**85** F3
Residenza Cellini	**86** C2
Restivo Italy B & B	**87** F2
The Beehive	**88** F2
YWCA	**89** C3

EATING   pp139–47

Al Giubileo	**90** B4
Alle Carrette	**91** B5
Baires	**92** A5
Bistrò	**93** F2
Colline Emiliane	**94** A2
Da Ricci	**95** C3
Fantasia del Pane	**96** E1
Il Dito e la Luna	**97** H4
Il Guru	**98** B4
Mexico al 104	**99** C3
Moka	**100** E3
Panella l'Arte del Pane	**101** E5
Piazza Vittorio Emanuele II Market	**102** F5
Trimani	**103** E1

DRINKING   p148

Fiddler's Elbow	**104** D4
Marconi	**105** D4

ENTERTAINMENT   pp149–52

Arte del Teatro Studio	**106** C4
Folkstudio	**107** B5
Hangar	**108** C5
Hello	**109** E4
Orbis	**110** C4
Teatro dell'Opera	**111** C3
Warner Village Moderno	**112** C2

SHOPPING   pp152–3

Louis Big Shoes	**113** C5
Progetto Impresa	**114** B2

TRANSPORT   pp153–9

ATAC Kiosk	(see 120)
Bici e Baci	**115** D3
Bus Stop	**116** E2
Eurojet Agency	**117** C2
Happy Rent	**118** D4
Hotel Royal Santina	**119** E2
Main Bus Station	**120** E3
Treno e Scooter Rent	**121** E2

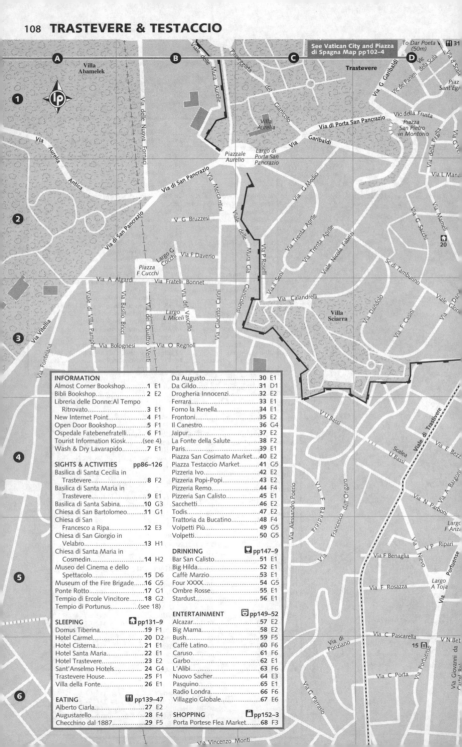

See Vatican City and Piazza
di Spagna Map pp102-4

To Dar Poeta
(50m)

Trastevere

INFORMATION
Almost Corner Bookshop	**1** E1
Bibli Bookshop	**2** E2
Libreria delle Donne:Al Tempo Ritrovato	**3** E1
New Internet Point	**4** F1
Open Door Bookshop	**5** F1
Ospedale Fatebenefratelli	**6** F1
Tourist Information Kiosk	(see 4)
Wash & Dry Lavarapido	**7** E1

SIGHTS & ACTIVITIES pp86–126
Basilica di Santa Cecilia in Trastevere	**8** F2
Basilica di Santa Maria in Trastevere	**9** E1
Basilica di Santa Sabina	**10** G3
Chiesa di San Bartolomeo	**11** G1
Chiesa di San Francesco a Ripa	**12** E3
Chiesa di San Giorgio in Velabro	**13** H1
Chiesa di Santa Maria in Cosmedin	**14** H2
Museo del Cinema e dello Spettacolo	**15** D6
Museum of the Fire Brigade	**16** G5
Ponte Rotto	**17** G1
Tempio di Ercole Vincitore	**18** G2
Tempio di Portunus	(see 18)

SLEEPING pp131–9
Domus Tiberina	**19** F1
Hotel Carmel	**20** D2
Hotel Cisterna	**21** E1
Hotel Santa Maria	**22** E1
Hotel Trastevere	**23** E2
Sant'Anselmo Hotels	**24** G4
Trastevere House	**25** F1
Villa della Fonte	**26** E1

EATING pp139–47
Alberto Ciarla	**27** E2
Augustarello	**28** F4
Checchino dal 1887	**29** F5
Da Augusto	**30** E1
Da Gildo	**31** D1
Drogheria Innocenzi	**32** E2
Ferrara	**33** E1
Forno la Renella	**34** E1
Frontoni	**35** E2
Il Canestro	**36** G4
Jaipur	**37** E2
La Fonte della Salute	**38** F2
Paris	**39** E1
Piazza San Cosimato Market	**40** E2
Piazza Testaccio Market	**41** G5
Pizzeria Ivo	**42** E2
Pizzeria Popi-Popi	**43** E2
Pizzeria Remo	**44** F4
Pizzeria San Calisto	**45** E1
Sacchetti	**46** E2
Todis	**47** E2
Trattoria da Bucatino	**48** F4
Volpetti Più	**49** G5
Volpetti	**50** G5

DRINKING pp147–9
Bar San Calisto	**51** E1
Big Hilda	**52** E1
Caffè Marzio	**53** E1
Four XXXX	**54** G5
Ombre Rosse	**55** E1
Stardust	**56** E1

ENTERTAINMENT pp149–52
Alcazar	**57** E2
Big Mama	**58** E2
Bush	**59** F5
Caffè Latino	**60** F6
Caruso	**61** F6
Garbo	**62** E1
L'Alibi	**63** F6
Nuovo Sacher	**64** E3
Pasquino	**65** E1
Radio Londra	**66** F6
Villaggio Globale	**67** E6

SHOPPING pp152–3
Porta Portese Flea Market	**68** F3

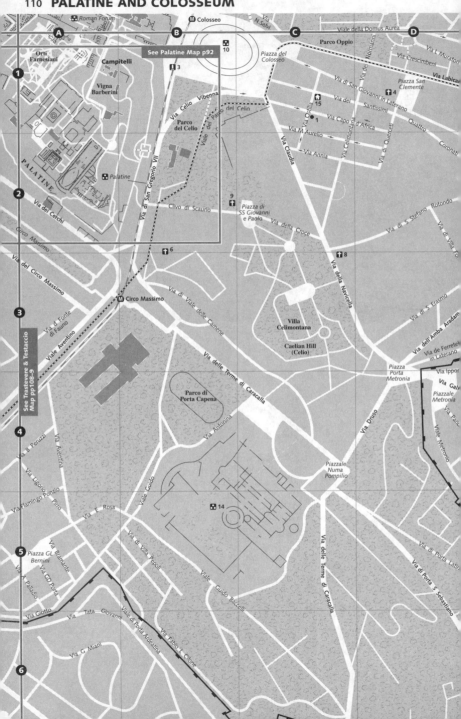

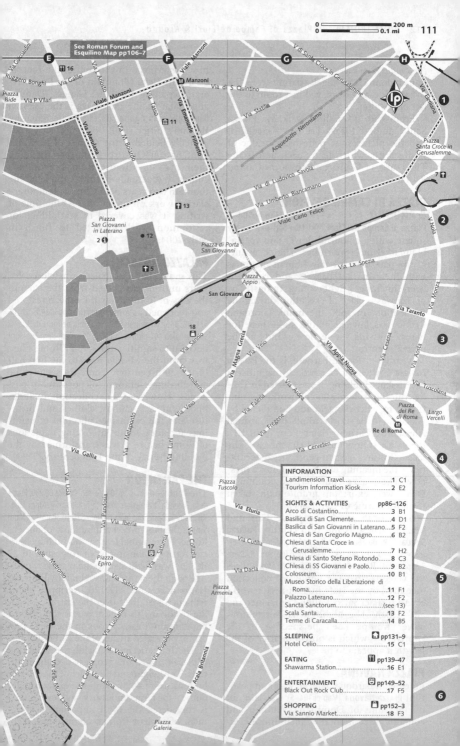

0 ——— 200 m
0 ——— 0.1 mi

INFORMATION

Landimension Travel	**1** C1
Tourism Information Kiosk	**2** E2

SIGHTS & ACTIVITIES pp86–126

Arco di Costantino	**3** B1
Basilica di San Clemente	**4** D1
Basilica di San Giovanni in Laterano	**5** F2
Chiesa di San Gregorio Magno	**6** B2
Chiesa di Santa Croce in Gerusalemme	**7** H2
Chiesa di Santo Stefano Rotondo	**8** C3
Chiesa di SS Giovanni e Paolo	**9** B2
Colosseum	**10** B1
Museo Storico della Liberazione di Roma	**11** F1
Palazzo Laterano	**12** F2
Sancta Sanctorum	(see 13)
Scala Santa	**13** F2
Terme di Caracalla	**14** B5

SLEEPING pp131–9

Hotel Celio	**15** C1

EATING pp139–47

Shawarma Station	**16** E1

ENTERTAINMENT pp149–52

Black Out Rock Club	**17** F5

SHOPPING pp152–3

Via Sannio Market	**18** F3

(Continued from page 98)
the Madonna and angels, dating from the Byzantine era, is displayed in a room to the left of the altar.

From here it's a short walk, via Piazza Sant'Egidio, to Piazza Trilussa (Map pp102–4) and the picturesque pedestrian bridge of Ponte Sisto, which leads back across the Tiber to Via Giulia and towards Campo de' Fiori.

PIAZZA DI CAMPO DE' FIORI & AROUND   Map pp104–5

Piazza di Campo de' Fiori (😊 Mon-Sat) is a lively square with a colourful flower and vegetable market most mornings. The occupants of the piazza are by day Roman mammas with their market baskets and by night beer-clutching bright young things. The piazza was a place of execution during the Inquisition. In 1600 the monk Giordano Bruno was burned at the stake here for heresy and his statue now stands at the piazza's centre.

Nearby, in Piazza Farnese, is the **Palazzo Farnese** (😊 closed to the public). A magnificent Renaissance building, it was started in 1514 by Antonio da Sangallo and work was continued by Michelangelo and completed by Giacomo della Porta. Built for Cardinal Alessandro Farnese (later Pope Paul III), the palace is now the French embassy. The facade features elegant geometrical decorations, the meaning of which remains a mystery. The piazza contains two fountains, which were enormous granite baths taken from the Terme di Caracalla.

South of Piazza di Campo de' Fiori and Piazza Farnese is the 16th-century **Palazzo Spada** (😊 06 686 11 58; Piazza Capodiferro 13; adult/concession €5.20/2.60; 😊 9am-7pm Tue-Sun, 8.30am-7.30pm Sun). Rome's prettiest *palazzo* houses the Galleria Spada, a family art collection (acquired by the state in 1926) with works by Andrea del Sarto, Guido Reni, Guercino and Titian. The highlight is Borromini's clever trompe l'oeil perspective in the courtyard – which is only a quarter of the length it appears to be.

PIAZZA NAVONA

Lined with baroque *palazzi*, vast and beautiful **Piazza Navona** (Map pp104–5) was laid out on the ruins of Domitian's stadium and contains three fountains, including Berni-

ni's masterpiece in the centre, the **Fontana dei Quattro Fiumi** (Fountain of the Four Rivers), depicting the Nile, Ganges, Danube and Plata. Facing the piazza is the **Chiesa di Sant'Agnese in Agone**, its facade designed by Bernini's bitter rival, Borromini. It's traditionally held that the statues of Bernini's Fontana dei Quattro Fiumi are shielding their eyes in disgust from Borromini's church, but actually Bernini completed the fountain two years before his contemporary started work on the facade. At the time of writing it was covered in scaffolding for restoration work expected to finish in early 2004.

PALAZZO BRASCHI

This grand baroque palace was closed for years until it was passed from the state to the City of Rome. Now it has been restored and reopened as a **museum** (Map pp104–5; 😊 06 671 08 346; www.museodiroma.comune.roma.it; Via di San Pantaleo 10; admission €6.20; 😊 9am-7pm Tue-Sun) devoted to significant issues in Rome's history from the Middle Ages to the first half of the 20th century. There do seem to be an inordinate amount of portraits of past popes. However, the collection includes photographs, etchings, clothes and furniture and the extensive collection of paintings includes some interesting depictions of Rome before it was transformed by the building frenzy of the 17th century.

THE PANTHEON

The **Pantheon** (Map pp104–5; 😊 06 683 00 230; Piazza della Rotonda; admission free; 😊 8.30am-7.30pm Mon-Sat, 9am-5.30pm Sun, mass 6.30pm Sat, 10.30am & 6.30pm Sun) is the best-preserved building of ancient Rome. The original temple was built by Marcus Agrippa, son-in-law of Augustus, in 27 BC and was dedicated to the planetary gods. Although the temple was rebuilt by Emperor Hadrian around AD 120, Agrippa's name remained inscribed over the entrance, leading historians to believe it was the original building until excavations in the early 19th century revealed traces of the earlier temple.

The dramatic, imposing interior is the kind of place that inspires people to become architects. The height and diameter of the interior both measure 43.3m, and the extraordinary dome – the largest masonry vault ever built – is considered the most important achievement of ancient Roman architecture. Light is provided by the oculus – a 9m opening in the dome – and small holes in the marble floor beneath it allow any rain that enters to drain away. The weight of the dome is supported by brick arches embedded in the structure of the walls – evident from the exterior. Rivets and holes in the brickwork indicate where the original marble veneer panels have been removed. The 16 massive Corinthian columns of the portico are each a single block of stone.

After being abandoned under the first Christian emperors, the temple was given to the Church by the Eastern Emperor, Phocus, in AD 608 and dedicated to the Madonna and all martyrs. Over the centuries the temple was consistently plundered and damaged. The gilded bronze roof tiles were removed by an Emperor of the Eastern empire and in the 17th century Pope Urban VIII had the bronze ceiling of the portico melted down to make the *baldaccino* (canopy) over the main altar in St Peter's and 80 cannons for Castel Sant'Angelo. The Italian kings Vittorio Emanuele II and Umberto I and the artist Raphael are buried here.

CHIESA DI SANTA MARIA SOPRA MINERVA

Just east of the Pantheon, this 13th-century Dominican **church** (Map pp102–4; ☎ 06 679 39 26; Piazza della Minerva; admission free; ☽ 7am-7pm) was built on the site of an ancient temple of Minerva. It was heavily restored in Gothic style in the 19th century and contains a number of important art treasures, including superb frescoes by Filippino Lippi in the Cappella Carafa (c.1489), which depict events in the life of St Thomas Aquinas and (left of the high altar) Michelangelo's statue of Christ Bearing the Cross (c.1520). The body of Santa Caterina di Siena, minus her head (which is in Siena) lies under the high altar. In the piazza in front of the church is a delightful Bernini statue of an elephant supporting an Egyptian obelisk.

TREVI FOUNTAIN

This high-baroque **fountain** (Fontana di Trevi; Map pp102–4) is one of Rome's most famous monuments. Completely dominating a tiny piazza, it was designed by Nicola Salvi in 1732. Its water is supplied by one of the city's earliest aqueducts. It is where Marcello Mastroianni and Anita Ekberg frolicked in Fellini's film

La Dolce Vita. Neptune's chariot is led by Tritons with sea horses – one wild, one docile – representing the moods of the sea. The word Trevi refers to the three roads (*tre vie*) which converged at the fountain.

The famous custom is to throw a coin into the water (over your shoulder while facing away) to ensure you return to Rome. Toss a second coin and you'll fall in love with an Italian. Chuck a third and be happy you've donated to charity.

PIAZZA DI SPAGNA & THE SPANISH STEPS   Map pp102–4

The piazza, church and famous **Spanish Steps** (Scalinata della Trinità dei Monti) have long provided a gathering place for tourists. The piazza was named after the Spanish Embassy to the Holy See, although the staircase, built with a legacy from the French in 1725, leads to the French church, Trinità dei Monti.

IL TRIDENTE – THE OPEN AIR MUSEUM

The best of Renaissance and baroque art in Rome is enclosed in an area known as Il Tridente (the Trident), around three roads which radiate out from Piazza del Popolo (p114), the northern entrance to the city: Via del Corso, the continuation of Via Flamina, which leads to Piazza Venezia; Via Ripetta which becomes Via della Scrofa and leads past the Pantheon (pp112–13), Santa Maria Sopra Minerva (left) to the Chiesa del Gesù (p88); and Via del Babuino, leading to Piazza di Spagna (see above), on to the Fontana di Trevi (left) and the Chiesa di SS Apostoli.

This free museum contains sculpture, architecture, paintings and objects belonging to different historical and artistic eras. They include numerous fountains and obelisks brought to Rome during the imperial era from ancient Egyptian civilisations. You can just wander and gasp, or you can follow one of the 'theme' itineraries – baroque art (Bernini, Borromini and Pietro da Cortona), Renaissance artists (Sansovino, Raffaello and Michelangelo), neoclassical (Canova) – outlined by the Superintendency of Historic and Fine Art, and available from the tourist information centre in Palazzo Doria Pamphilj (pp87-8).

ROME & LAZIO

To the right as you face the steps is the house where Keats died in 1821, now the **Keats-Shelley House** (☎ 06 678 42 35; Piazza di Spagna 26; admission €2.60; ☺ 9am-1pm & 3-6pm Mon-Fri, 11am-2pm & 3-6pm Sat). In the piazza is a fountain of a sinking boat, the **Barcaccia**, believed to be by Pietro Bernini, father of the famous Gian Lorenzo.

PIAZZA DEL POPOLO   Map pp100-1

Vast **Piazza del Popolo** was laid out in the early 16th century at the point of convergence of the three roads – Via di Ripetta, Via del Corso and Via del Babuino – which form a trident at what was the main entrance to the city from the north. The two baroque churches between the three roads are **Santa Maria dei Miracoli** and **Santa Maria in Montesanto**. The piazza was redesigned in the neoclassical style by Giuseppe Valadier in the early 19th century. In its centre is an obelisk brought by Augustus from Heliopolis, in ancient Greece, and moved here from the Circo Massimo in the mid-16th century. To the east is a ramp leading up to **Pincio Hill**, which affords a stunning view of the city.

The **Chiesa di Santa Maria del Popolo** (☎ 06 361 08 36; Piazza del Popolo; admission free; ☺ 7am-noon & 4-7pm Mon-Sat, 8am-2pm & 4.30-7.30pm Sun) next to the Porta del Popolo at the northern side of the piazza, is a smorgasbord of art treasures dating from 1099. Bramante designed the apse and the vault frescoes (c.1509) are by Pinturicchio, who also painted the lunettes and the *Adoration* in the Della Rovere chapel. Raphael designed the Cappella Chigi, which features a macabre mosaic of a kneeling skeleton, but it was completed by Bernini 100 years after Raphael's death. Don't miss Caravaggio's *Conversion of St Paul* and *Crucifixion of St Peter* in the Cerasi chapel.

THE VATICAN

The **Vatican City** (Map pp102-4; Città del Vaticano) is the smallest independent state in existence, though its influence is considerable. After Italian unification in 1861, the Papal States of central Italy became part of the new Kingdom of Italy. The church thus lost much of its former temporal power and a considerable rift developed between the church and the state. In 1929 Mussolini signed the Lateran Treaty (or Concordat) with Pius XI, giving the pope full sovereignty over what is now the Vatican City. The Lateran Treaty

also granted extra-territoriality to the basilicas of San Giovanni in Laterano (as well as the Palazzo Laterano), Santa Maria Maggiore and San Paolo Fuori-le-Mura.

The Vatican has its own postal service, currency, newspaper, radio station and train station (now used only for freight). It also has its own army of Swiss Guards, responsible for the pope's personal security. The corps was established in 1506 by Julius II to defend the Papal States against invading armies. The guards still wear the traditional eye-catching red, yellow and blue uniform (not, as legend would have it, designed by Michelangelo) and brandish unwieldy 15th-century pikes, but they are in fact highly trained soldiers. The guards are at the pope's side whenever he appears in public and accompany him on all overseas trips.

Dress regulations are stringently enforced at St Peter's Basilica and throughout the Vatican. It is forbidden to enter the church wearing shorts (men included) or short skirts, or with bare shoulders.

Building the Vatican

Nero built a circus in the Ager Vaticanus in the 1st century AD and it was probably in this stadium that St Peter and other Christians were martyred between AD 6 and 67. The body of St Peter was buried in an anonymous grave next to the wall of the circus. In AD 160 the stadium was abandoned and later a small monument was erected on the grave of St Peter. Then, in 315, Emperor Constantine – the first Christian ruler of Rome – ordered the construction of a basilica on the site and in 326 the first St Peter's was consecrated.

The first pope to establish a fixed papal residence in the Vatican was Pope Symmachus (498-514). In 846, Pope Leo built the protective walls, now know as the Leonine Walls, to protect the palace from Saracen invaders. In the 12th century, Eugenius III constructed a new palace, which Innocent III enlarged and fortified, surrounding it with a wall and towers. More land was acquired and in 1277 a walled passageway was built to link the palace with Castel'Sant Angelo, allowing an escape route to the fortress for the popes, when under attack.

However, the Vatican Palace was considered a secondary residence, linked to the liturgical functions of St Peter's Basilica.

The official residence of the Pope was the Palace of San Giovanni in Laterano. It was only after 1377, when Pope Gregory XI returned from Avignon, where the Papacy had been based during the Great Schism, that the Vatican Palace became the official residence of the Popes.

Subsequent popes then began to expand and enlarge on the palace, most notably Nicholas V (1447–55) who extended the palace around the Cortile dei Pappagalli, and Sixtus IV (1471–84) who employed some of Renaissance Italy's most famous heroes, most notably the Florentine artist Michelangelo Buonarotti, who decorated the ceiling of the chapel now known after its benefactor as the Capella Sistina, or Sistine Chapel.

The Belvedere pavilion was added under Innocent VIII in the late 15th century and when Julius II decided to use it to house his impressive collection of classical sculpture, he had Donato Bramante design a new entrance to the palace. It included a spiral staircase up which horses could be ridden. Then Bramante created the Cortile del Belvedere, connecting the pavilion to the Vatican Palace and the Sistine Chapel with long corridors. This courtyard was later divided into three smaller sections after Pope Sixtus V built the Biblioteca Apostolica (Vatican Library) and Pope Pius VII added the Braccio Nuovo. The northern courtyard came to be called the Cortile delle Pigne after the 1st or 2nd century bronze pine cone that was placed there in 1608 by Paul V.

In the late 18th century the Belvedere was converted into a museum with a new entrance, the Attio dei Quattro Cancelli, and a monumental staircase by Michelangelo Simonetti.

The 20th century saw more additions. Pius XI unveiled a new pinacoteca (art gallery) and a new entrance to the museums in 1932. New galleries of modern religious art in the Borgia apartments were opened in 1973, and in the same year the Museo Missionario-Ethnologico (Ethnological Missionary Museum) was inaugurated. Under John Paul II, a new entrance to the museums was opened in 2000. The magnificent Simonetti staircase is now the exit.

Piazza San Pietro

Bernini's piazza is considered a masterpiece. Laid out in the 17th century as a

AN AUDIENCE WITH THE POPE

At 11am Wednesday, the pope meets his flock at the Vatican (in July and August he does so in Castel Gandolfo). For permission to attend an audience, go to the **Prefettura della Casa Pontificia** (☎ 06 69 88 46 31; ✆ 9am-1pm), through the bronze doors under the colonnade to the right of St Peter's as you face the church. You can apply on the Tuesday before the audience (or, at a push, on the morning of the audience). You can also apply in writing to the Prefettura della Casa Pontificia, 00120 Città del Vaticano or fax 06 6698 85 863. Specify the date you'd like to attend and the number of tickets (free) required. If you have a hotel in Rome, the office will forward the tickets there.

place for the Christians of the world to gather, the immense square is bounded by two semicircular colonnades, each of which is made up of four rows of Doric columns. In the centre of the piazza is an obelisk brought to Rome by Caligula from Heliopolis in ancient Egypt.

St Peter's Basilica
(Basilica di San Pietro)   Map p116

By the mid-15th century, after more than a thousand years, the church that had been erected on the site of St Peter's tomb in the 4th century by the Emperor Constantine was in a poor state of repair. Pope Nicholas V put architects, including Leon Battista Alberti, to work on its reconstruction, but it was not until 1506, when Pope Julius II employed Donato Bramante, that serious work began. Bramante designed a new basilica on a Greek cross plan, with a central dome and four smaller domes. He oversaw the demolition of much of the old basilica and attracted great criticism for the unnecessary destruction of many of its precious works of art.

It took more than 150 years to complete the new basilica, still the biggest in the world. Bramante, Raphael, Antonio da Sangallo, Michelangelo, Giacomo della Porta and Carlo Maderno all contributed, but it is generally held that St Peter's owes most to Michelangelo, who took over the project in 1547 at the age of 72 and was responsible for the design of the dome.

ST PETER'S BASILICA (BASILICA DI SAN PIETRO)

400 m
0.2 mi

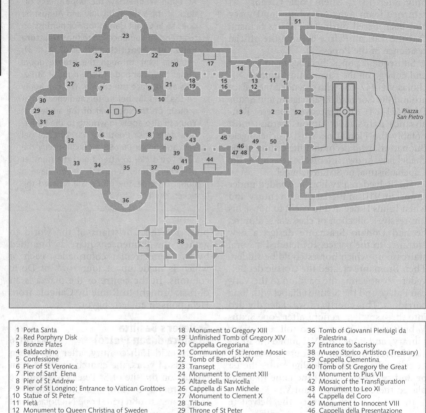

1 Porta Santa
2 Red Porphyry Disk
3 Bronze Plates
4 Baldacchino
5 Confessione
6 Pier of St Veronica
7 Pier of Sant' Elena
8 Pier of St Andrew
9 Pier of St Longino; Entrance to Vatican Grottoes
10 Statue of St Peter
11 Pietà
12 Monument to Queen Christina of Sweden
13 Statue of Leo XII; Entrance to Cappella del Crocifisso
14 Cappella di San Sebastiano
15 Monument to Innocent XII
16 Monument to Countess Matilda of Tuscany
17 Cappella del Santissimo Sacramento
18 Monument to Gregory XIII
19 Unfinished Tomb of Gregory XIV
20 Cappella Gregoriana
21 Communion of St Jerome Mosaic
22 Tomb of Benedict XIV
23 Transept
24 Monument to Clement XIII
25 Altare della Navicella
26 Cappella di San Michele
27 Monument to Clement X
28 Tribune
29 Throne of St Peter
30 Monument to Urban VIII
31 Monument to Paul III
32 Monument to Alexander VIII
33 Cappella della Colonna
34 Monument to Alexander VII
35 Transept
36 Tomb of Giovanni Pierluigi da Palestrina
37 Entrance to Sacristy
38 Museo Storico Artistico (Treasury)
39 Cappella Clementina
40 Tomb of St Gregory the Great
41 Monument to Pius VII
42 Mosaic of the Transfiguration
43 Monument to Leo XI
44 Cappella del Coro
45 Monument to Innocent VIII
46 Cappella della Presentazione
47 Monument to John XXIII
48 Monument to Benedict XV
49 Stuart Monuments
50 Baptistry
51 Entrance to Dome
52 Portico

The facade and portico were designed by Maderno, who took over the project after Michelangelo's death. He was also instructed to lengthen the nave towards the piazza, effectively altering Bramante's original Greek cross plan to a Latin cross. Restoration work on the facade was carried out between 1997 and 1999 – this mainly consisted of cleaning the travertine marble and repairing damage caused by age and pollution.

The cavernous interior, decorated by Bernini and Giacomo della Porta, can hold up to 60,000 people. It contains art treasures, including Michelangelo's superb **Pietà**, sculpted when he was only 25 years old and the only work to carry his signature (on the sash across the breast of the Madonna), at the beginning of the right aisle. It is now protected by bulletproof glass after a hammer-wielding vandal attacked it in 1972. The **red porphyry disk** just inside the main door marks the spot where Charlemagne and later Holy Roman Emperors were crowned by the pope.

Bernini's baroque **baldacchino** (canopy) stands 29m high in the centre of the church and is an extraordinary work of art. The bronze used to make it was taken from the Pantheon. The high altar, which only the pope can use, stands over the site of St Peter's grave.

To the right as you face the high altar is a famous bronze **statue of St Peter**, believed to be a 13th-century work by Arnolfo di Cambio. The statue's right foot has been worn down by the kisses and touches of many pilgrims.

Michelangelo's dome, a majestic architectural masterpiece, soars 119m above the high altar. Its balconies are decorated with reliefs depicting the Reliquie Maggiori (Major Relics) – the lance of San Longino, which he used to pierce Christ's side; the cloth of Santa Veronica, which bears a miraculous image of Christ; and a piece of the True Cross, collected by Sant'Elena, the mother of Emperor Constantine. Entry to the dome is to the right as you climb the stairs to the atrium of the basilica. Access to the roof of the church is by elevator or stairs; from there, you ascend the stairs to the base of the dome for a view down into the basilica. A narrow staircase leads eventually to the top of the dome and St Peter's lantern, from where you have an unequalled view of Rome. It is well worth the effort, but bear in mind that it's a long and tiring climb.

The **Vatican Grottoes** (Sacre Grotte Vaticane) below the church are the resting place of numerous popes. The tombs of many early popes were moved here from the old St Peter's, and more recent popes, including John XXIII, Paul VI and John Paul I, are also buried here. The entrance is next to the pier of San Longinuson (one of four piers supporting the arches at the base of Michelangelo's cupola), to the right as you approach the papal altar.

Vatican Museums

The incredible collection of art and treasures accumulated by the popes can be seen at the **Vatican Museums** (Musei Vaticani; Map pp102–4; ☎ 06 698 84 947; www.vatican.va/museums; adult/concession €10/7, last Sun of the month free; ◷ 8.45am-4.45pm (last admission 3.30pm) Mon-Fri, 8.45am-1.45pm (last admission 12.45pm) Sat mid-Mar–late Oct, 8.45am-1.45pm (last admission 12.20pm) Mon-Sat rest of the year, 9am-1pm last Sun of month). You will need several hours to see the most important areas and museums.

ST PETER'S TOMB

The excavations beneath St Peter's, which began in 1940, have uncovered part of the original church, an early Christian cemetery and Roman tombs. Archaeologists believe they have also found the tomb of St Peter; the site of the empty tomb is marked by a shrine and a wall plastered with red. Nearby is another wall, scrawled with the graffiti of pilgrims; in 1942 the bones of an elderly, strongly build man were found in a box placed in a niche behind this wall. In 1976, after many years of forensic examination, Paul VI declared the bones to be those of St Peter. John Paul II had some of the relics transferred to his hospital room when he was recovering from the 1981 assassination attempt. The bones were then returned to the tomb and are kept in hermetically sealed Perspex cases designed by NASA.

The excavations can be visited only by appointment, which can be made in writing or in person at the **Ufficio Scavi** (☎ 06 698 85 318; fax 06 698 85 518; Piazza Braschi; ◷ 9am-5pm Mon-Fri). Address your letter to Ufficio Scavi, 00120 Città del Vaticano, and stipulate the date you'd like to visit. The office will then contact you to confirm the time and date. You need to book at least one week ahead; tickets cost €5.20. Small groups are taken most days between 9am and noon and 2pm to 5pm.

Make sure you pick up a floor-plan leaflet. There are four 'one-way' itineraries, which have been mapped out with the aim of simplifying visits and containing the huge number of visitors. It is basically compulsory to follow the itineraries (which vary in duration from 1½ to five hours), but you can make some deviations if you want. The new entrance (with every facility you could want) leads up to the area known as the Quattro Cancelli, where each of the separate itineraries starts.

Another point to note is that the Sistine Chapel comes towards the end of each itinerary. If you want to spend most of your time in the chapel or you want to get there early to avoid the crowds, it is possible to walk straight there. However, if you want to visit the Stanze di Raffaello, you'll need to do so first, because you can't backtrack once you're in the Chapel. Most tour groups (and there are many!) head straight to the chapel and it is almost always very crowded. You can also hire CD audio guides.

The museums are well equipped for disabled visitors; there are four suggested itineraries, several lifts and specially fitted toilets. Ask for a folder at the ticket window or information desk or call in advance on ☎ 06 698 84 341. Wheelchairs can be reserved. Parents with young children can take pushchairs into the museums.

The buildings that house the Vatican Museums, known collectively as the Palazzo Apostolico Vaticano, cover an area of 5½ hectares. Their construction has been a work in progress since the 5th century. The buildings to the west of the Quattro Cancelli are the most recent and house the Museo Gregoriano Profano (Gregorian Museum of Pagan Antiquities), Museo Pio-Cristiano (Pio Christian Museum), Pinacoteca, Museo Missionario-Etnologico (Missionary and Ethnological Museum) and a carriage museum. These galleries come last on the longer itineraries and are probably the ones to miss if you run out of time.

The **Museo Gregoriano Egizio** (Egyptian Museum) contains pieces taken from Egypt in Roman times. The collection is small but there are fascinating exhibits including the Throne of Rameses II, part of a statue of the seated king.

The Vatican's enormous collection of ancient sculpture is contained in a series of galleries. The long corridor that forms the **Museo Chiaramonti** contains hundreds of marble busts, while the **Braccio Nuovo** (New Wing) contains some important works. These include a famous statue of Augustus, and a carving depicting the Nile as a reclining god with 16 babies (which are thought to represent the number of cubits the Nile rose when in flood) playing on him.

The **Museo Pio-Clementino** is in the Belvedere Pavilion. In the Cortile Ottagono (Octagonal Courtyard) is part of the Vatican sculpture collection: the Apollo Belvedere, a 2nd-century Roman copy in marble of a 4th-century-BC Greek bronze, considered one of the great masterpieces of classical sculpture; and, notably, the *Lacoön*, depicting a Trojan priest of Apollo and his two sons in mortal struggle with two sea serpents. This statue was excavated from the Domus Aurea area.

In the **Sala delle Muse** (Room of the Muses) is the Belvedere Torso, a Greek sculpture from the 1st century BC, which was found in the Piazza Campo de' Fiori during the time of Pope Julius II and was much admired by Michelangelo and other Renaissance artists. In the **Sala a Croce Greca** (Greek Cross Room) are the porphyry sarcophagi of Constantine's daughter, Constantia, and his mother, Sant'Elena.

Up one flight of the Simonetti staircase is the **Museo Gregoriano Etrusco** (Etruscan Museum), which contains artefacts from Etruscan tombs in southern Etruria. Of particular interest are those from the Regolini-Galassi tomb, discovered in 1836 south of Cerveteri. Those buried in the tomb included a princess, and among the finds on display are gold jewellery and a funeral carriage with a bronze bed and funeral couch. A collection of Greek vases and Roman antiquities is also displayed in the museum.

Through the superb **Galleria delle Carte Geografiche** (Map Gallery) and the **Galleria degli Arazzi** (Tapestry Gallery) are the magnificent **Stanze di Raffaello**, the private apartments of Pope Julius II. Raphael painted the Stanza della Segnatura and the Stanza d'Eliodoro, while the Stanza dell'Incendio was painted by his students to his designs and the ceiling was painted by his master, Perugino. In the Stanza della Segnatura is one of Raphael's masterpieces, *La Scuola d'Atene* (The School of Athens), featuring philosophers and scholars gathered around Plato and Aristotle. Opposite is *La Disputa del Sacramento* (Disputation on the Sacrament), also by Raphael. In the Stanza d'Eliodoro is another Raphael masterpiece, *Expulsion of Heliodorus* from the Temple, on the main wall (to the right as you enter from the Sala dei Chiaroscuri), which symbolises Julius' military victory over foreign powers. To the left is *Mass of Bolsena*, showing Julius II paying homage to a relic from a 13th-century miracle in that town. Next is *Leone X ferma l'invasione di Attila* (Leo X Repulsing Attila), by Raphael and his school, and on the fourth wall is *Liberazione di San Pietro* (Liberation of St Peter), which depicts the saint being freed from prison but is actually an allusion to Pope Leo's imprisonment after the battle of Ravenna (also the real subject of the Attila fresco).

MICHELANGELO AND THE POPES

Michelangelo Buonarotti came to work in Rome for Pope Julius II, who wanted him to create a grand marble tomb for his own burial. Although the tomb, intended by the Pope to surpass any funerary monument in existence, preoccupied Michelangelo for most of his life, it was never completed.

Michelangelo's passion was sculpture and he was reluctant to take on the job for which he is now most famous – the painting of the ceiling frescoes of what is now known as the Sistine Chapel, after Pope Sixtus, who commissioned the work. But when the Florentine artist did take it on, he did so with passionate obsession, dismissing all assistance and working lying down on scaffolding lodged high under the windows for four years, pushing himself to artistic and physical limits and bickering constantly with the Pope and his court who wanted the job finished.

Despite this unhappiness as a Vatican-employed painter, Michelangelo returned to Rome again almost 20 years later, at the age of 59, to work on another painting commission in the Sistine Chapel. This time it was at the request of Pope Clement VI, who wanted the Florentine artist to paint *The Last Judgement* on the altar wall.

When Clement VIII died, his successor, Paul III, was determined to have Michelangelo work exclusively for him. He wanted the Sistine Chapel finished. In 1535 he appointed Michelangelo as chief architect, sculptor and painter to the Vatican.

When *The Last Judgement* was finally completed and unveiled in 1541, its depiction of a swirling mass of predominantly naked bodies caused quite a scandal. But though Pope Pius IV had Daniele da Volterra, one of Michelangelo's students, add fig leaves and loin cloths, Michelangelo's work was claimed by many to be one of his best, surpassing all the other paintings in the chapel, including his own ceiling frescoes.

The artist spent his last years working – unhappily (he felt that it was a penance from God) – on St Peter's Basilica. He disapproved of the plans that had been drawn up by Antonio da Sangallo the Younger before his death, claiming they deprived the basilica of light, and argued with Sangallo's assistants, who wanted to retain their master's designs. Instead Michelangelo created the magnificent light-filled dome based on Brunelleschi's design for the cathedral in Florence, and a stately facade.

He continued to direct the work until his death on 18 February 1564, and the dome and facade of St Peter's were completed to his designs by Vignola, Giacomo della Porta and Carlo Fontana.

Sistine Chapel

The **Sistine Chapel** (Capella Sistina) was completed in 1484 for Pope Sixtus IV and is used for the conclave that elects the popes. It is best known for two of the most awe-inspiring acts of individual creativity in the history of the visual arts: Michelangelo's **frescoes** on the barrel-vaulted ceiling (painted 1508–12), and **The Last Judgement** on the end wall (completed in 1541). Restorations carried out over the past two decades have brought back to life Michelangelo's rich, vibrant colours.

The frescoes down the middle represent nine scenes from the book of Genesis, including the Division of Day from Night, the Creation of Adam, the Expulsion of Adam and Eve from the Garden of Eden and the Flood. These main images are framed by the **Ignudi**, athletic male nudes; next to them, on the lower curved part of the vault,

are large figures of Hebrew **Prophets** and androgynous pagan **Sibyls**. In the lunettes over the windows are the ancestors of Christ.

The walls of the chapel were painted by important Renaissance artists, including Botticelli, Domenico Ghirlandaio, Pinturicchio and Luca Signorelli. Try to drag your attention away from Michelangelo's frescoes to appreciate these other late-15th-century works, depicting events in the lives of Moses and Christ; thanks to careful restoration they are as stunning as the ceiling. Botticelli's *Temptation of Christ* and the *Cleansing of the Leper* (the second fresco on the right) is particularly beautiful, with its typical Botticelli maiden in a diaphanous dress. The first frescoes in each cycle, *Finding of Moses* and *Birth of Christ* by Perugino, were destroyed to make way for *The Last Judgement* – a great controversy at the time.

CASTEL SANT'ANGELO

Originally the mausoleum of Emperor Hadrian, this building was converted into a fortress for the popes in the 6th century AD. It was named **Castel Sant'Angelo** (Map pp102–4; ☎ 06 681 91 11; Lungotevere Castello; admission €6.50; ☺ 9am-8pm Tue-Sun) by Pope Gregory the Great in AD 590, after he saw a vision of an angel above the structure heralding the end of a plague in Rome. The fortress was linked to the Vatican palaces in 1277 by a wall and passageway, often used by popes to escape in times of threat. During the 16th century sacking of Rome by Emperor Charles V, hundreds of people lived in the fortress for months.

Hadrian built the **Ponte Sant'Angelo** across the River Tiber in AD 136 to provide an approach to his mausoleum. It collapsed in 1450 and was subsequently rebuilt, incorporating parts of the ancient bridge. In the 17th century, Bernini and his pupils sculpted the figures of angels which now line the pedestrian-only bridge.

ARA PACIS

The **Ara Pacis Augustae** (Altar of Peace; Map pp102–4; ☎ 06 688 06 848; closed to the public) was inaugurated in 13 BC to commemorate the peace that Augustus had established both at home and abroad. The actual altar is enclosed by a marble wall decorated with reliefs – historical scenes on the north and south friezes and mythological scenes at the east and west. It is one of the most important works in the history of ancient Roman sculpture and represents the point at which Roman art emerged as a distinct entity. Panels excavated from the 16th century onwards ended up in the Medici collection, the Vatican and the Louvre; in 1937, under Mussolini, the remaining parts were reassembled in the present location. A new, state-of-the-art museum complex designed by Richard Meier is still under construction.

East of the monument is **Mausoleo d'Augusto** (Mausoleum of Augustus; Map pp102–4; ☺ closed to the public), built by the emperor for himself and his family. It was originally faced with marble and was converted into a fortress during the Middle Ages. It served various purposes until restored to its original state in 1936.

VILLA BORGHESE & AROUND

This beautiful **park** (Map pp100–1), just northeast of the Piazza del Popolo, was once the estate of Cardinal Scipione Borghese. The main entrance is from Piazzale Flaminio but it is also accessible through the park at the top of Pincio Hill. It's a good place to have a picnic or to take children for a break from sightseeing. You can hire rollerblades (including helmets and kneepads). There are also various forms of bicycles for hire – for one or more people.

Also in the park is the **Bioparco** (☎ 06 36 08 211; www.bioparco.it; Viale del Giardino Zoologico 1; admission €3.10; ☺ 9.30am-5pm 29 Oct–24 Mar, 9.30am-6pm 25 Mar–28 Oct, 9.30am-7pm holidays & weekends May-Oct), the flashy new name for the former Zoological Gardens, at the northern end of the park. There are better ways to spend your money but kids might enjoy it.

Galleria Borghese

This place is so popular that entrance to the **Galleria Borghese** (Map pp100–1; ☎ 06 3 28 10; www.ticketeria.it; Piazzale Scipione Borghese; admission €8.50; ☺ 9am-7pm Tue-Sun) is restricted to those who have pre-booked, and visitors are only admitted at two-hourly intervals. Once you've called the booking phone number, dial 2 for an English-speaking assistant. The collection was formed by Cardinal Scipione Borghese, the most passionate and knowledgeable connoisseur of his day. The collection and the mansion were acquired by the Italian state in 1902; a lengthy restoration took place in the 1990s.

The ground floor contains some important classical statuary, intricate Roman floor mosaics and Antonio Canova's daring sculpture of Paolina Bonaparte Borghese as a reclining *Venere Vincitrice* (Victorious Venus), her diaphanous drapery leaving little to the imagination. But Bernini's spectacular carvings – flamboyant depictions of pagan myths – are the stars. His precocious talent is evident in works such as *Ratto di Proserpina* (Rape of Persephone), where Pluto's hand presses into Persephone's solid marble thigh, and in the swirling *Apollo e Dafne*, which depicts the exact moment when the nymph is transformed into a laurel tree, her fingers becoming leaves, her toes turning into tree roots, while Apollo watches helplessly.

There are six Caravaggio paintings including several early works, as well as masterpieces by Giovanni Bellini, Giorgione, Veronese, Botticelli, Guercino, Domenichino and Rubens, among others. Highlights are Raphael's *Deposizione di Cristo* (Christ Being Taken Down from the Cross) of 1507 and Titian's early masterpiece *Amor Sacro e Amor Profano* (Sacred and Profane Love).

Galleria Nazionale d'Arte Moderna

The belle époque *palazzo* housing the **Galleria Nazionale d'Arte Moderna e Contemporanea** (Map pp100–1; ☎ 06 32 34 000; www.gnam.arti.beniculturali .it; Viale delle Belle Arti 131; admission €6.50; ☼ 8.30am-7.30pm Tue-Sun) was built for the 1911 Rome international exhibition. It now showcases 19th- and 20th-century painting and sculpture, including work by De Chirico, Carrà, Fontana and Guttuso; the futurists Boccioni and Balla; artists of the so-called Transavanguardia Clemente, Paladino and Cucchi; as well as Degas, Cézanne, Kandinsky and Mondrian. There's also a modern international collection which includes works by Henry Moore and Cy Twombly.

The latest works (from 1987) are now being displayed in the **Ala Mazzoniana** (Map pp106–7; ☎ 06 478 26 414; www.romatermini.it; admission €2; ☼ 10am-8pm Tue-Sun) at Stazione Termini.

Museo Nazionale Etrusco di Villa Giulia

Situated in the 16th-century villa of Pope Julius III, at the northern end of the Villa Borghese, this **museum** (Map pp100–1; bookings ☎ 06 32 810; www.ticketeria.it; Piazzale di Villa Giulia 9; admission €4.15; ☼ 8.30am-7.30pm Tue-Sun) houses the national collection of Etruscan treasures, many of which were found in tombs at sites throughout Lazio. If you plan to visit Etruscan sites near Rome, a visit to the museum before setting out will give you a good understanding of Etruscan culture. There are thousands of exhibits, including domestic objects, cooking utensils, terracotta vases and amphorae, distinctive black *bucchero* tableware, bronze mirrors engraved with mythological scenes, and the remains of a horse-drawn chariot. An Etruscan tomb has been reconstructed, complete with burial objects, and armchairs sculpted into the rock.

Of particular note is the polychrome terracotta statue of Apollo and other pieces found at Veio, dating from the late 6th century or early 5th century BC. Another highlight is the *Sarcofago degli Sposi* (sarcophagi of the husband and wife) made for a husband and wife, from a tomb at Cerveteri.

AROUND VIA VITTORIO VENETO

The **Chiesa di Santa Maria della Concezione** (Map pp106–7; ☎ 06 487 11 85; Via Vittorio Veneto 27; admission by compulsory donation; ☼ 9am-noon & 3-6pm Fri-Wed) is an austere 17th-century church, but the Capuchin cemetery beneath (access is to the right of the church steps) features a bizarre display of the bones of some 4000 monks, used to decorate the walls of a series of chapels between 1528 and 1870.

In the centre of Piazza Barberini, at the southern end of Via Vittorio Veneto, is the spectacular **Fontana del Tritone** (Fountain of the Triton), created by Bernini in 1643 for Pope Urban VIII, patriarch of the Barberini family. It features a Triton blowing a stream of water from a conch shell. In the northeastern corner of the piazza is another fountain, the **Fontana delle Api** (Fountain of the Bees), created by the same artist for the Barberini family, whose crest, which features three bees, can be seen on many buildings throughout Rome.

The 17th-century **Palazzo Barberini** (Via delle Quattro Fontane) is well worth a visit. Carlo Maderno was commissioned to build the *palazzo* by Urban VIII, and both Bernini and Borromini worked on its construction for the Barberini family. The building houses part of the **Galleria Nazionale d'Arte Antica** (Map pp106–7; ☎ 06 481 45 91; www.galleriaborghese.it/barberini/en; entrance at Via Barberini 18; admission €6.20; ☼ 9am-7pm Tue-Sat, 9am-8pm Sun), which includes paintings by Raphael, Caravaggio, Guido Reni, Guercino, Bronzino, Bernini, Filippo Lippi and Holbein. A highlight is the ceiling of the main salon, entitled the *Triumph of Divine Providence* and painted by Pietro da Cortona.

QUIRINALE   Map pp106–7

The **Palazzo del Quirinale** (☎ 06 46 991; www.quirinale.it; Piazza del Quirinale; admission €5.20; ☼ 8.30am-12.30pm Sun Sep-Jul, closed holidays) is the official residence of the president of the Republic. Built and added to from 1574 to the early 18th century, it was the summer residence of the popes until 1870, when it became the royal palace of the kings of Italy.

The obelisk in the centre of the piazza was moved here from the Mausoleo di Augusto in 1786. It is flanked by the large statues of the Dioscuri, Castor and Pollux, which are Imperial-era copies of 5th-century-BC Greek originals.

BUT WAIT, THERE'S MORE

Apart from the more obvious and famous museums covered elsewhere, here are some of the lesser known options:

For those who like the macabre, the Crypt of the Capuchin Friars in the **Chiesa di Santa Maria della Concezione** (Map pp106–7; ☎ 06 487 11 85; Via Vittorio Veneto 27; entrance by donation; ⏰ 10am-noon & 3-6pm) comprises five chapels whose walls are decorated with skeletons, the mortal remains of 4000 Capucin friars who died between 1528 and 1870. Then there's the **Museum of Souls in Purgatory** (Piccolo Museo delle Anime del Purgatorio; Map pp102–4; ☎ 06 688 06 517; Chiesa del Sacro Cuore del Gesu, Lungotevere Prati 12; admission free; ⏰ 7-11am & 4.30-7pm Mon-Sat) which displays pieces of cloth, wood tables and breviaries that have allegedly been marked with traces of fire from those poor souls languishing in purgatory. And if these nasties haven't sated your appetite, you can visit **Dario Argento's Horror Museum** (Map pp100–1; Museo degli Orrori di Dario Argento; ☎ 06 32 11 395; www.profondorossoshop.com; Via dei Gracchi 260; admission €3; ⏰ 10.30am-1pm & 4-7.30pm Mon-Sat), a collection of sets and special effects from horror and fantasy films.

The **International Museum of Film & Entertainment** (Museo Internazionale del Cinema e dello Spettacolo; ☎ /fax 06 370 02 66; www.mics.pagehere.com; Via Portuense 101; ⏰ guided visits in English by appointment only) puts things a bit more in perspective. It's full of souvenirs from when Rome was capital of the cinema world: cameras, projectors, posters for international film productions as well as an important collection of Italian and European silent films.

For those interested in how things are put together, or taken apart, there's a **Museum of the Central Institute for Book Pathology** (Museo dell'Istituto Centrale di Patologia del Libro; ☎ 06 48 29 11; Via Milano 76; admission free; ⏰ 9am-6pm Mon-Fri), which demonstrates book manufacturing and restoration techniques, and one containing ancient surgical instruments – **National Historic Museum of the Medical Arts** (Museo Storico Nazionale dell'Arte Sanitaria; ☎ 06 689 30 51; http://utenti.quipo.it/asas; Lungotevere in Sassia 3; admission €3; ⏰ 10am-noon Mon, Wed & Fri) – and other related curiosities.

Along the Via del Quirinale are two excellent examples of baroque architecture: the churches of **Sant'Andrea al Quirinale** (☎ 06 489 03 187; Via del Quirinale 29; admission free; ⏰ 9am-noon & 4-7pm Mon-Fri, 9am-noon Sat), designed by Bernini, and **San Carlo alle Quattro Fontane** (☎ 06 488 32 61; Via del Quirinale 23; admission free; ⏰ 9.30am-12.30pm), designed by Borromini. Sant'Andrea is considered one of Bernini's masterpieces. He designed it with an elliptical floor plan and with a series of chapels opening onto the central area. The interior is decorated with polychrome marble, stucco and gilding. Note the cherubs that adorn the lantern of the dome. San Carlo was the first church designed by Borromini in Rome and it was completed in 1641; the small cloister was also designed by Borromini. The church stands at the intersection known as Quattro Fontane, after the late-16th-century fountains at its four corners.

San Paolo Entro Le Mura

If you've been tramping around the Via Nazionale area, you might be longing for a bit of peace and quiet. The little sculpture garden in this Anglican Episcopal **church** (Map pp106–7; ☎ 06 420 31 21; cnr Via Nazionale & Via Napoli) is a haven. Sit for a few minutes and contemplate the marvellous examples of modern sculpture which are collected here.

MUSEO NAZIONALE ROMANO

The archaeological collection of the **Museo Nazionale Romano** is among the most important in the world. For years most of these treasures were locked up in storerooms and underground cellars. But with the revolution in the care and administration of Rome's museums that has taken place in the last few years, the collection has been moved into several magnificent spaces where it is well displayed and can be truly admired.

Museo Nazionale Romano

TERME DI DIOCLEZIANO   Map pp106–7

The complex of baths, libraries, concert halls and gardens that made up the **Terme di Diocleziano** (Diocletian's Baths; entrance on Piazza della Repubblica) was completed in the early 4th century. It was the largest of its kind in ancient Rome, covering about 13 hectares and with a capacity for 3000 people. The

There's a **Napoleonic Museum** (Museo Napoleonico; Map pp104–5; ☎ 06 688 06 286; www.comune.roma it/museonapoleonico, Italian or French only; Piazza Ponte Umberto I 1; closed for restoration) that traces the rise of the Bonaparte family back to the second Roman Empire and, to prove that not everyone fiddled while Rome burned, a **Museum of the Fire Brigade** (Museo dei Vigili del Fuoco; Map pp108–9; ☎ 06 574 68 08; Via Galvani 2; admission free; ⏲ 9.30am-12.30pm & 4.30-7.30pm, closed mornings Mon), which documents the history of Rome's fire-fighting efforts, from the age of Augustus, with photos, sound effects and videos. Was Nero really a pyromaniac?

The **National Postal Museum** (Museo Storico delle Poste e Telecomunicazioni; ☎ 065 422 1673; Viale Europa 190; admission €1; ⏲ 9am-1pm Mon-Fri) is not a place where they store all those letters you sent from Rome that never arrived, but a collection of stamp printing matrixes, telephone and telegraphic equipment.

You are also able to visit a **museum** (Museo del Risorgimento; Map pp102–4; ☎ 06 678 06 64; Via San Pietro in Carcere; admission free; ⏲ 10am-6pm Tues-Sun) devoted to the period of the Risorgimento right up until WWI, a **museum** (Museo Storico della Liberazione di Roma; Map pp110–11; ☎ 06 700 38 66; Via Tasso 145; admission free; 9.30am-12.30pm Tues-Sun, 4-7pm Tue, Thu & Fri) dedicated to the Liberation of Rome, which is housed in what was once the headquarters of the notorious SS Kommandatur, where members of the Roman Resistance were interrogated, tortured and imprisoned and a **Museum of Jewish Art** (Synagogue, Lungotevere Cenci; Map pp102–4; ☎ 06 684 00 661; fax 06 68 40 06 84; admission €6; ⏲ daily except Sat and Jewish holidays: Mon-Thu 9am-4.30pm Mon-Thu winter, to 7.30pm summer, 9am-1.30pm Fri, 9am-noon Sun, closed Jewish holidays), which documents the relations of Rome's Jews with the state of Italy and the Nazis.

And then there's the **National Pasta Museum** (Museo Nazionale delle Paste Alimentari; Map pp102–4; ☎ 06 699 11 19; www.pastainmuseum.com; Piazza Scanderberg 117; admission €9; ⏲ 9.30am-5.30pm) – the only museum in the world to document the history of the Italian staple diet from the Etruscans to the present.

complex fell into disrepair after the aqueduct that fed the baths was destroyed by invaders in about AD 536.

Michelangelo incorporated the main hall and tepidarium of Diocletian's Baths into the design of the **Basilica di Santa Maria degli Angeli** (☎ 06 488 08 12; Piazza della Repubblica; admission free; ⏲ 7.30am-12.30pm & 4-6.30pm), although only the great vaulted ceiling remains from his original plans. The meridian in the transept traces both the polar star and the time of the sun's zenith (visible at noon).

The **Museo Nazionale Romano Terme di Diocleziano** (☎ 06 39 96 77 00; Viale Enrico di Nicola 78; admission €5; ⏲ 9am-7.45pm Tue-Sun) is housed in the ancient charterhouse built on the ruins of the original baths. Ancient epigraphs and artefacts from Italian protohistory are the focus of this section of the Museo Nazionale Romano, although its elegant Renaissance cloister is lined with classical sarcophagi, capitals and (mostly headless) statues.

The **Aula Ottagona** (Octagonal Hall; ☎ 06 399 67 700; Via G Romita; ⏲ 9am-2pm Tue-Sat, 9am-1pm Sun) contains important sculptures from the Roman baths complex.

PALAZZO MASSIMO ALLE TERME
Part of the Museo Nazionale Romano collection, **Palazzo Massimo alle Terme** (Map pp106–7 ☎ 06 39 96 77 00; Largo di Villa Peretti 1; adult/concession €6.20/3.10; ⏲ 9am-7.45pm Tue-Sun) boasts some of the best examples of Roman art in the city. The commissioned sculptural portraits of emperors, statesmen and their families (in the ground-floor galleries) are idealised representations of the ruling classes. Realism had little to do with these busts and statues; self-glorification was the order of the day.

The highlights of the museum are the sensational Roman paintings and mosaics, including frescoes (dating from at least 20–10 BC) from the excavated Villa Livia, which belonged to the wife of Augustus. These stunning frescoes depict an illusionary garden with cypresses, pines, oleander, myrtle and laurel, and fruit trees abundant with ripe pomegranates and quinces.

CRYPTA BALBI
The underground ruins of the theatre built by Balbus in 13 BC have now been converted into a **museum of ancient and medieval**

art (Map pp102–4; ☎ 06 399 67 700; Via delle Botteghe Oscure 31; admission €4; ☒ 9am-7.45pm Tue-Sun) forming the latest addition to the Museo Nazionale di Roma's complex. After the 4th century and throughout the Middle Ages, the ruins of the ancient theatre were used as tombs, artisans' workshops and for religious purposes.

PALAZZO ALTEMPS

The prestigious Ludovisi collection forms the main body of the exhibits in the Renaissance and baroque former cardinal's palace, **Palazzo Altemps** (Map pp104–5; ☎ 06 683 35 66; Piazza Sant'Apollinare 46; adult/concession €5.20/2.60; ☒ 9am-7.45pm Tue-Sun). The *palazzo* was designed by Antonio da Sangallo the Elder, Baldassarre Peruzzi and Martino Longhi for generations of the noble Altemps family.

Cardinal Ludovico Ludovisi, a nephew of Pope Gregory XV, was a ravenous collector of ancient sculpture, which was regularly unearthed in the building boom of Counter-Reformation Rome. He employed leading sculptors – including Bernini and Alessandro Algardi – to repair and 'enhance' the works, replacing missing limbs or sticking a new head on a headless torso.

Baroque frescoes provide a decorative backdrop for the sculpture. Landscapes and hunting scenes are seen through trompe l'oeil windows in the Sala delle Prospettive Dipinte, and a fresco by Melozzo da Forlì (in the Sala della Piattaia, once the main reception room of the *palazzo*) displays a cupboard full of wedding gifts.

The Trono Ludovisi, discovered in the late 19th century, is one of the prize exhibits. Most scholars believe the carved marble throne came from a Greek colony in Italy and dates from the 5th or 6th century BC.

In the Sala del Camino, intricate carvings graphically depict a Roman battle scene on a giant marble sarcophagus. The expression and movement extracted from a lump of stone is astonishing. Equally impressive is the Galata Suicida. Blood spurts out of his flesh as the Gaul knifes himself to death.

SAN PAOLO FUORI-LE-MURA

The basilica of **San Paolo Fuori-le-Mura** (St Paul's Outside the Walls; Map p99; ☎ 06 541 03 41; Via Ostiense 186; admission free; ☒ 7am-6.30pm) was built by Constantine on the site of St Paul's burial and was destroyed by fire in 1823. The

5th-century mosaics on the triumphal arch, a Romanesque paschal candlestick and the marble tabernacle (c1285) by Arnolfo di Cambio survived. The reconstruction recreates some sense of the huge scale of the original; until the construction of the present-day St Peter's, this was the largest church in the world. The **cloisters** survived the fire and are a masterpiece of Cosmati work, with elaborate mosaic-encrusted columns. To get there take the Metro Linea B to San Paolo.

SAN LORENZO FUORI-LE-MURA

Constantine's 4th-century church, built over the martyred St Laurence's burial place, was joined with another early Christian church nearby; medieval additions and later WWII bombing raids gave us the basilica of **San Lorenzo Fuori-le-Mura** (St Lawrence Outside the Walls; Map p99; ☎ 06 49 15 11; Piazzale del Verano 3; admission free; ☒ 3.30-7pm) we see today, highlights of which are the Cosmati floor, 13th-century frescoed portico, and the catacombs of Santa Ciriaca where St Laurence was buried.

VIA APPIA ANTICA & THE CATACOMBS   Map p99

Known to ancient Romans as the *regina viarum* (queen of roads), the **Via Appia Antica** (Appian Way) runs from the Via di Porta San Sebastiano, near the Terme di Caracalla, to Brindisi on the coast of Puglia. It was started around 312 BC by the censor Appius Claudius Caecus, but did not connect with Brindisi until around 190 BC. The first section of the road, which extended 90km to Terracina, was considered revolutionary in its day because it was almost perfectly straight.

Every Sunday a long section of the Via Appia Antica becomes a car-free zone. You can walk or ride a bike for the several kilometres from Via Porta di Sebastiano. To get to Via Appia Antica and the area of the catacombs, catch bus No 218 from Piazza San Giovanni in Laterano or Metro Linea A from Stazione Termini to Colli Albani and then bus No 660 to the Via Appia Antica. ATAC's Archeo Bus (€7.75) departs Piazza Venezuia every hour daily (see p129).

Monuments along the road include catacombs (see pp125–6) and Roman tombs. The **Chiesa del Domine Quo Vadis?** (Via Appia Antica) is built at the point where St Peter, while fleeing Rome, is said to have met Jesus. The saint consequently returned to Rome, where he was martyred.

Circo di Massenzio

Archaeologists believe this **arena** (☎ 06 780 13 24; Via Appia Antica 153; admission €2.60; ☺ 9am-5pm Tue-Sun winter, 9am-7pm Tue-Sun summer), built by Maxentius around AD 309, was never actually completed. It is well preserved and starting stalls for the chariots can still be made out. In front is the **Tomba di Romolo**, a tomb built for Maxentius' son Romulus, and next to it are ruins of an imperial residence.

Tomba di Cecilia Metella

Farther along Via Appia is this famous **tomb** (☎ 06 780 24 65, Via Appia Antica; admission €2.10; ☺ 9am-1 hr before sunset Tue-Sun) of a Roman noblewoman. Money talked in Roman times and Cecilia Metella's fabulously

wealthy in-laws made sure she was buried in style. This grand tomb was used as a fortress by the Caetani family in the early 14th century. Not far past it is a section of the original Via Appia.

Mausoleo delle Fosse Ardeatine

When a brigade of Roman partisans blew up 32 German military police in WWII, the Germans retaliated by taking 335 random prisoners to the Ardeatine Caves, where they were shot. The Germans then used mines to explode sections of the caves and thus bury the bodies. This moving **mausoleum** (☎ 06 513 67 42; Via Ardeatina 174; admission free; ☺ 8.15am-5.15pm Mon-Sat, 8.45am-5.45pm Sun) honours the dead.

The Catacombs

There are several catacombs along Via Appia Antica – kilometres of tunnels carved out of the soft tufa rock (see the boxed text, below).

ROMAN UNDERWORLD

The catacombs are underground corridors and passageways that were built as communal burial grounds. The best known are the Christian catacombs along the Via Appia Antica, although there are Jewish and pagan ones as well. Scholars are divided as to whether the catacombs were also clandestine meeting places of early Christians in Rome, as well as useful places for secreting important relics from Christian persecutors.

Catacombs were often established in areas where there were existing quarries or underground passages; the soft volcanic earth of the Roman countryside enabled the Christians to dig to a depth of 20m or so.

During the periods of persecution, martyrs were often buried in catacombs beside the fathers of the Church and the first popes. Many Christians wanted to be buried in the same place as the martyrs and consequently a trade in tomb real estate developed, becoming increasingly unethical until Pope Gregory I issued a decree in 597 abolishing the sale of graves. However, Christians had already started to abandon the catacombs as early as in 313, when Constantine issued the Milan decree of religious tolerance.

Increasingly, Christians opted to bury their dead in catacombs near the churches and basilicas that were being built (often above pagan temples). This became common practice under Theodosius, who made Christianity the state religion in 394. The catacombs became sanctuaries for remembering the martyrs buried there.

In about 800, after frequent incursions by invaders, the saintly bodies of the martyrs and the first popes were transferred to the basilicas inside the city walls. The catacombs were abandoned and eventually many were forgotten and filled up with earth. In the Middle Ages only three catacombs were known. Those of San Sebastiano were the most frequented as a place of pilgrimage, since they had earlier been the burial place of Sts Peter and Paul.

The catacombs of Santa Priscilla on Via Salaria were discovered by chance at the end of the 16th century, following the collapse of a tufa quarry. From that time on, groups of curious aristocrats began to lower themselves into the dark underground passages on a regular basis, often risking losing themselves permanently in the underground labyrinths. From the mid-19th century onwards, passionate scholars of Christian archaeology began a programme of scientific research and more than 30 catacombs in the Rome area have been uncovered.

Corpses were wrapped in simple white sheets and usually placed in rectangular niches carved into the tunnel walls, which were then closed with marble or terracotta slabs. For further information, contact the **Vatican authorities** (☎ 06 4465619, ☎ 06 44 56 10; www.vatican.va/roman_curia).

CATACOMBS OF SAN CALLISTO

These **catacombs** (☎ 06 513 01 580; Via Appia Antica 110; admission by guided tour €5; ☺ 8.30am-noon & 2.30-5.30pm Thu-Tue, to 5pm winter, closed Feb) are the largest and most famous, and contain the tomb of the martyred Santa Cecilia (although her body is now in the Basilica di Santa Cecilia in Trastevere). There is also a crypt containing the tombs of seven popes martyred in the 3rd century. In the 20km of tunnels explored to date, archaeologists have found the sepulchres of some 500,000 people.

BASILICA & CATACOMBS OF SAN SEBASTIANO

These **catacombs** (☎ 06 788 70 35; Via Appia Antica 136; admission €5; ☺ 8.30am-noon & 2.30-5.30pm Mon, to 5pm winter, closed mid-Nov–mid-Dec) were a safe haven for the remains of Sts Peter and Paul during the reign of Vespasian. The first level is now almost completely destroyed but frescoes, stucco work, epigraphs and three perfectly preserved mausoleums can be seen on the 2nd level. The basilica above them dates from the 4th century and preserves one of the arrows used to kill St Sebastian.

CATACOMBS OF SAN DOMITILLA

Among the largest and oldest in Rome, these **catacombs** (☎ 06 511 03 42; Via delle Sette Chiese 283; admission €4.20; ☺ 8.30am-noon & 2.30-5.30pm Wed-Mon, closed late Dec–Jan) were established on the private burial ground of Flavia Domitilla, niece of the Emperor Domitian and a member of the wealthy Flavian family. They contain Christian wall paintings and the underground church of SS Nereus e Achilleus.

GIANICOLO & VILLA DORIA PAMPHILJ

If you're after a panoramic view of Rome, go to the top of **Gianicolo Hill** (Map pp102–4) between the St Peter's Basilica and Trastevere. At the top of the hill, just off Piazzale Giuseppe Garibaldi, there are pony rides and a permanent merry-go-round, as well as a small bar. Puppet shows are often held here on Sunday. Take bus No 870 from Via Paola at the end of Corso Vittorio Emanuele II where it meets the Lungotevere or alternatively walk up the steps from Via Mameli in Trastevere.

The bus will also take you within easy walking distance of the nearby **Villa Doria Pamphilj** (Map p99; Via Aurelia; ☺ sunrise-sunset). It is the largest park in Rome and a lovely quiet spot for a walk and a picnic. Built in the 17th century for the Pamphilj family, it is now used for official government functions.

EUR
Map p99

This acronym, which stands for Esposizione Universale di Roma, has become the name of a peripheral suburb south of Rome, interesting for its many examples of Fascist architecture. These include the **Palazzo della Civiltà del Lavoro** (Palace of the Workers), a square building with arched windows known as the Square Colosseum.

Mussolini ordered the construction of the satellite city for an international exhibition, which was to have been held in 1942. Work was suspended with the outbreak of war and the exhibition never took place; however, many buildings were completed during the 1950s.

The **Museo della Civiltà Romana** (☎ 06 59260 41; www.pigorini.arti.beniculturali.it, Italian only; Piazza G Agnelli; admission €4.20; ☺ 9am-6.45pm Tue-Sat, 9am-1.30pm Sun) reconstructs Roman history using a magnificent scale model of the ancient city. This amazing museum, which also contains scale models of its monuments and military operations, will appeal to the kids. It was set up by Mussolini's mob to glorify Imperial Rome, and it certainly does that.

Also of interest is the **Museo Nazionale Preistorico Etnografico Luigi Pigorini** (☎ 06 54 95 21; Piazzale G Marconi 14; admission €4.20; ☺ 9am-8pm). The prehistoric section covers the development of civilisation in the region, while the ethnographic collection includes exhibits from around the world.

WALKING TOUR

This is a short route through the heart of Rome, an area dense with important monuments, where Renaissance buildings and the impressive ruins of classical antiquity coexist. It explores the courtyards of patrician *palazzi* and the narrow streets of one of the city's more characteristic areas.

Start on the southeast corner of the large and noisy Largo di Torre Argentina, from

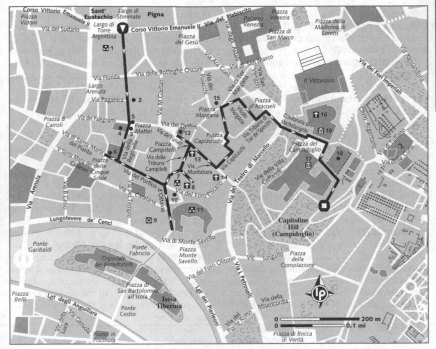

where you can admire the **Largo Argentino (1)** archaeological zone and its numerous cats, and walk south. Cross Via delle Botteghe Oscure to Via Paganica, skirting the elegant **Palazzo Mattei di Paganica (2)**, built in 1541. This is one of five *palazzi* in the area built by the patrician Mattei family, causing it to be renamed L'isola dei Mattei (Mattei Island) in the mid-16th century.

Continue south to the charming Piazza Mattei with its elegant **Fontana delle Tartarughe (3)**, or Fountain of the Tortoises. In the piazza at No 10 is the 16th-century **Palazzo Costaguti (4)**, and at Nos 17–19 is **Palazzo di Giacomo Mattei (5)**. The building on the right has a beautiful 15th-century courtyard with a staircase and an open gallery.

The area just south of here, around Via del Portico d'Ottavia, is known as the Jewish **Ghetto**. In the 16th century, Pope Paul IV ordered the confinement of Jewish people to this area, marking the beginning of a time of intolerance that continued well into the 19th century.

From Piazza Mattei, take narrow Via della Reginella, which is lined with artisan workshops, framers and bookshop – a reminder of what the area would have once looked like. A few paces to the right along Via del Portico d'Ottavia bring you to the curious **Casa di Lorenzo Manilio (6)** at Via del Portico d'Ottavia 1. The building was constructed in 1468 or, according to the Latin inscription on its facade, 'AB URB CON MMC CXXII', 2222 years after the traditional founding of Rome in 753 BC. Another Latin inscription on the doors on the ground floor tells us the owner's name: LAUR MANLIUS. There is also an inscription in Greek and fragments of Roman sculpture set into the wall, including a relief depicting a lion killing a fallow-deer, a Greek stela with two dogs and a funereal relief with four busts.

Walk southeast down Via del Portico d'Ottavia (en route noting the medieval and Renaissance houses) until you reach the ruins of the **Portico d'Ottavia (7)**. In AD 755 this portico was remodelled to incorporate the **Chiesa di Sant'Angelo in Pescheria (8)**. A medieval fish market established in the portico was operational until the end of the

19th century. At the end of Via del Portico d'Ottavia, you'll also find, on the Lungotevere dei Cenci, the 19th century **synagogue** and **Jewish museum (9)**.

Beyond the portico is the 14th-century **Casa dei Valati (10)**, housing the X Circoscrizione of the Comune di Roma, which oversees the city's cultural patrimony. Unusually for this area, the building stands in isolation, since the surrounding buildings were demolished in 1927 during the restoration of the Teatro di Marcello at the rear.

A narrow passage to the left of the portico opens onto the deserted Via Sant'Angelo in Pescheria. Go around the back of the church and then bear right at a water fountain until you come to a dead end. From this isolated spot you get a view of the arches of the **Teatro di Marcello (11)**. Only 12 of the original 41 arches, which are made of large travertine blocks, remain. You can also see the three marble columns with Corinthian capitals and beams of the Tempio di Apollo Sosiano, dedicated in 431 BC and rebuilt in 34 BC.

Retrace your steps out of the dead end street, and take Via della Tribuna Campitelli to the right. On the corner, at No 23, there is a house incorporating a medieval portico with granite columns and Ionian capitals. After a short walk you'll come to Piazza Campitelli.

If you detour back down Via de' Funari you'll find the **Palazzo Mattei di Giove (12)** at No 3. Built by Carlo Maderno in 1598, today it houses the Centro Italiano di Studi Americani (Italian Centre for American Studies); sections are open to the public. The *palazzo*, which is adorned with numerous pieces of ancient Roman sculpture, bas-reliefs and stuccos, is a good example of the taste of the Renaissance noble classes for all things classical. The private courtyards contain ancient Roman bas-reliefs set into the walls, and busts and statues from what remains of the Mattei collection, once one of the most valuable collections of Roman antiquities. The monumental staircase decorated with classical stucco and ancient sculpture leads to a library; the balustrade is decorated with 16th-century busts of numerous emperors.

Back in Piazza Campitelli, on the west and northeastern sides stand a row of fine *palazzi* belonging to five noble families.

About half-way along the piazza is the **Chiesa di Santa Maria in Campitelli (13)**, built by Carlo Rainaldi and a masterpiece of late-baroque style, with an elegant travertine facade. The church was built in 1662 in honour of the Virgin Mary, who was believed to have halted the plague of 1656. Inside, on the main altar, there is an image of the miraculous Madonna in silver leaf and enamel. In front of the church, on the piazza, there is a pretty fountain designed in 1589 by Giacomo della Porta.

Slightly further on is the **Chiesa di Santa Rita da Cascia (14)**, now deconsecrated. It was built by Carlo Fontana in 1665 at the foot of the nearby Scalinata dell'Aracoeli and rebuilt on this spot in 1940 to allow for an urban revamp. Take Via Capizucchi to the left off the Piazza Campitelli. This takes you through deserted narrow streets into Piazza Capizucchi, and then to the left into Piazza Margana with the **Torre dei Margani (15)**. Together with the surrounding buildings, the tower looks like a fortified medieval residence. Set in the wall is an ancient column with an Ionic capital. In the door next to it are large pieces of cornice from buildings of the late Empire.

Turn right into Via di Tor Margana and then right again into the darkness of Vicolo Margana. Go under an arch to emerge in Via Tribuna di Tor de' Specchi. Here, at No 3, there is another medieval tower. Turn left to reach the chaotic Piazza d'Aracoeli, from where you have a splendid 180° view extending from Palazzo Venezia to Capitoline Hill. Turn right and go past the 16th-century facade of Palazzo Pecci-Blunt, at No 3, and the 17th-century Palazzo Massimo di Rignano.

Cross the busy Piazza d'Aracoeli using the pedestrian crossing but beware, cars don't always stop! This brings you to the **Cordonata di Michelangelo**, the monumental flight of steps designed by Michelangelo, which lead up to the Piazza del Campidoglio. The Cordonata is guarded at the bottom by two Egyptian basalt lions (turned into fountains in 1588), and almost touches the older staircase on the left, which leads up to the **Chiesa di Santa Maria in Aracoeli (16)**, also accessible from Piazza del Campidoglio. Climb the Cordonata, noting the shift in perspective as you approach the colossal Dioscuri, Castor and Pollux, at the top. These statues date from the late Empire and were found in a temple complex dedicated to them near Monte dei Cenci.

On the same balustrade in a symmetrical arrangement are the **Trofei di Mario** (Trophies of Mario), representing barbarian weapons that date back to the reign of Domitian, and statues of Constantine and his son Constans, found at the Terme di Costantino. There are also two milestones taken from the Via Appia Antica, which bear inscriptions of Nerva and Vespasian.

Once at the top of the stairs, the piazza, designed by Michelangelo, will take your breath away. It is bordered by the **Palazzo dei Conservatori (17)** on the south side, the **Palazzo Senatorio (18)** at the rear, and the **Palazzo Nuovo (19)** on the north side, and in its centre stands a very good copy of an original bronze equestrian statue of Marcus Aurelius (see pp86–7 for details).

Take the road going downhill to the right of the Palazzo Senatorio. This brings you to a (usually) crowded terrace overlooking the ancient Roman Forum and the Colosseum against the backdrop of the city and the Colli Albani – definitely one of the best views in Rome. If you want to visit the **Roman Forum** (see pp89–91), there is an entrance to the right of the terrace.

COURSES

Arco di Druso (Map pp102–4; ☎ 06 397 50 984; www .arcodidruso.com; Via Tunisi 4) Courses in Italian language and culture.

Centro Linguistico Italiano Dante Alighieri (Map p99; ☎ 06 442 31 400; www.clidante.it; Piazza Bologna 1) Four-week Italian language courses (four hours per day) run throughout the year and cost from €540.

Italiaidea (Map pp102–4; ☎ 06 699 41314; www.italia idea.com; 1st fl, Via dei Due Marcelli 47) Four-week intensive Italian language courses (three hours a day) costing about €415.

ROME FOR CHILDREN

Sightseeing in Rome will wear out adults, so imagine how the kids feel! If it's not too hot, they'll probably enjoy a wander through the Roman Forum. The enterprising Rome Tourism Board has several brochures with itineraries and activities especially for children, available at the Tourist Information booths. There's even a museum, **Explora** (Map pp102–4; ☎ 06 361 377; www.mdbr.it; Via Flaminia 82; adult/child €5/6; ☺ 9.30-11.30am & 3-5pm Tue-Fri, 10am-noon & 3-5pm Sat & Sun & 1 Jul–30 Sep), especially for children up to 12. It's close to Piazza del Popolo.

But if museums and ancient ruins bore them, you can count on the amazing **Time Elevator** (Map pp102–4; Via dei Santissimi Apostoli 20; ☎ 06 69 90 053; www.time-elevator.it; adult/child €11/9.20; ☺ sessions every 15 mins 9.30am-midnight), a 45-minute, four-dimensional multimedia experience to delight even the most worldweary child (or adult). The flight simulator covers 3000 years of Roman history, putting the audience right in the middle of the action. You'll find this ingenious crowd pleaser three minute's walk from Piazza Venezia, just off Via del Corso.

The **Villa Borghese** (see pp120–1) gardens is a great place for a picnic. **Bioparco** (see p120) is there and near the Porta Pinciana there are bicycles for hire, as well as pony rides, train rides and a merry-go-round. In the **Villa Celimontana** (p97), on the western slopes of the Celio (entrance from Piazza della Navicella), is a lovely public park and a children's playground. See also the **Gianicolo** (p126) and **Villa Doria Pamphilj** (p126). There is a Luna Park at EUR.

TOURS
Bus
ATAC (Map pp106–7; ☎ 06 469 52 252, lines open 9.30am-6pm; www.atac.roma.it; Piazza dei Cinquecento; Non-Stop €7.80, Stop & Go €12.91) has the Roma 110 City which is a good hop-on, hop-off bus tour of the city's major monuments. You can spend as much (or as little) time as you'd like at each sight. The non-stop loop takes 1½ hours, and tours leave every 30 minutes, daily 9am to 8pm (April to end Sept); 10am to 6pm (October to end March). Buy tickets at Piazza dei Cinquecento, in front of Termini Station, at ATAC kiosks or on the bus (cash only). If you're keen to visit Rome's four major basilicas as well as the other monuments, take the 2½ hour Major Basilicas Tour. It leaves Piazza dei Cinquecento at 10.30am and 2.30pm (summer 10.30am and 3pm).

Archeobus (☎ 06 46952343; tickets €7.75; ☺ hourly 10am-5pm Apr-Sep, 10am-4pm Oct-Mar) is another Stop & Go bus, sponsored by Rome's municipal government and operated by Trambus, which takes groups of up to 16 down the Appian Way, stopping at other places of archaeological interest such as Circo Massimo and Terme di Caracalla. Bus tickets are valid for the entire day, and may be purchased on board; buses depart from Piazza Venezia. They do not cover entrance fees to archaeological and historic sights, however.

Stop-n-Go City Tours (Map pp106–7; ☎ 06 478 26 379; Piazza dei Cinquecento 44/48; www.romecitytours.com; 1-/2-/3-day ticket €12/18/24) is a private company which offers tours to the major basilicas, monuments, the catacombs, Appian Way and Ostia Antica.

Ciao Roma (Map pp106–7; ☎ 06 489 76 161, Via Giovanni Giolitti 34; tickets €18) operates buses (some of which are painted to look like old trolley cars) that zip you around Rome. Hop on/off at one of the many stops including Vatican, Colosseum, Piazza Venezia, Piazza Navona, Stazione Termini and Villa Borghese.

Green Line Tours (☎ 06 482 74 80; www.greenline tours.com; Via Farini 5a, Piazza dei Cinquecento) offers a 90-minute Shuttle Tour (€18) as well as half-day tours of Classical, Imperial, Christian and Illuminated Rome (from €30) among others.

Cycling

Enjoy Rome (Map pp106–7; ☎ 06 445 18 43; www.enjoy rome.com; Via Marghera 8; under/over 26 years €20/25) runs three-hour bike tours which are a huge hit, but you have to be aged 18–35 to participate. The route includes Villa Borghese, the Bocca della Verità and the Colosseum.

Landimension Travel (☎ 06 700 36 22; www.landim ensiontravel.it; Via Ostilia 10; groups of 2/3/4-6 people per person €50/45/39) offers 'Rome by Electric Bicycle'. These people take the slog out of sightseeing. The three-hour tours have experienced guides and all equipment is provided.

Walking

Through Eternity Rome (☎ 06 700 93 36, ☎ 0347 336 52 98; www.througheternity.com) employs enthusiastic 'storytellers', who are passionate about their subject (and native English speakers to boot) to make Rome come alive on their walking tours. Twilight tours of Renaissance and baroque Rome show the city in arguably its best light, and 'Feast of Bacchus' wine-sampling tours combine aesthetic pleasures with gastronomic ones.

Enjoy Rome (Map pp106–7; ☎ 06 445 18 43; www.enjoyrome.com; Via Marghera 8) tours are designed for the budget traveller. Their three-hour walking tours (under/over 26yrs €14/20) cover ancient Rome (by day or night), the Vatican, Trastevere and the Ghetto. Tours to the Catacombs and Appian

Way (€30/35) and the Vatican cost extra to cover entrance costs. All guides are native English speakers or hold degrees in archaeology or related areas.

Scala Reale (☎ 06 474 5673; www.scalareale.org) organises archaeological walks in small groups with knowledgeable guides, often American graduate students specialising in art history and archaeology. Tours are tailor-made and by prior arrangement only.

Archimede Association (☎ 06 84 18 271; www .archimede.info; Via Clitunno 28; tours free) offers guided tours in Italian and English with entrance tickets to the chosen sites the only cost.

FESTIVALS & EVENTS

There's always something happening in the streets and piazzas of Rome. Sometimes the public protests – *manifestazioni* – are every bit as theatrical as the more orthodox festivals on Rome's official calendar. But in spring, things really take off.

There are so many festivals celebrating Holy Week that you have to check with the tourist office, which publishes itineraries. There are marvellous free concerts in some of the Eternal City's most-famous and atmospheric churches, with musicians and singers of international renown.

January

New Years (1 Jan) A candlelit procession takes place in the Catacombs.

March

Festa di San Giuseppe (Feast of St Joseph; 19 Mar) Celebrated in the Trionfale neighbourhood, between the Vatican and Monte Mario. Little stalls are set up to serve *fritelle* (fried pastries) and there's usually a special market set up near the church of San Giuseppe.

April

Procession of the Cross (Easter) A candlelit procession to the Colosseum on Good Friday evening led by the Pope. At noon on Easter Sunday he gives his traditional blessing from the balcony in St Peter's Square, which is packed with pilgrims.

April

Rome's Birthday (21 Apr) To celebrate her birthday, the City of Rome provides processions, fireworks and free entry to lots of museums.
La Festa di Primavera (Spring Festival; late Apr/May) The Spanish Steps are decorated with masses of pink azaleas.

GAY & LESBIAN ROME

Rome's main cultural and political gay organisation is the **Circolo Mario Mieli di Cultura Omosessuale** (☎ 06 541 39 85; www.mariomieli.it, Italian only; Via Efeso 2a), off Via Ostiense near the Basilica di San Paolo, which organises debates, cultural events and social functions. It also runs a free AIDS/HIV testing and care centre. Its website has information and listings of forthcoming events, both social and political, including Rome Pride, which takes place every year in June. Mario Mieli also publishes a free monthly magazine *AUT* (predominantly in Italian), available from gay bookshops and organisations.

The national organisation for lesbians is **Co-ordinamento Lesbiche Italiano** (CLI; Mapp102–4; ☎ 06 686 42 01; cli_network@ iol.it; cnr Via San Francesco di Sales & Via della Lungara, Trastevere), also known as the Buon Pastore Centre.

Libreria Babele (Map pp102–4; ☎ 06 687 66 28; Via dei Banchi Vecchi 116) is an exclusively gay and lesbian bookshop and a good first stop for information about Rome's gay scene. Forthcoming gay and lesbian events are listed on the shop's notice board. The **Libreria delle Donne: Al Tempo Ritrovato** (Map pp108–9; ☎ 06 581 77 24; Via dei Fienaroli 31d), in Trastevere, is a women's bookshop with a well-stocked lesbian section, including material in English, and a notice board full of information and events.

Rome has several gay bars and discos and there is even a gay beach. These can be tracked down through local gay organisations and publications such as *Pride* (€3.10), a national monthly magazine, and *AUT* (free), both available at gay and lesbian organisations and in bookshops. The magazine *Time Out Roma* (€1.05), which is published weekly (in Italian) and is available from bookshops, has good coverage of gay and lesbian venues and events. The international gay guide, *Spartacus*, also has listings of gay venues in Rome.

The lesbian scene is less active than the gay scene and there is not yet any permanent lesbian nightclub, although there are various associations that organise events.

May

International Horse Show A marvellous show jumping display by some of the international greats at the lovely Piazza di Siena in the Villa Borghese gardens.

June

Feast of San Pietro e Paolo (St Peter and St Paul; 29 Jun) This feast, for the patron saints of the city, includes major celebrations at St Peter's.

Birth of John the Baptist (23-24 Jun) Many celebrate the birth of St John the Baptist, particularly around the Basilica di San Giovanni in Laterano, where there are special market stalls set up and lots of lovely *porchetta* (pork) to eat.

Estate Romana (until Sep)The big event in summer, this is a series of outdoor cultural events and activities for the few people who have remained in the capital. Two of the most popular summer events take place on Caelian Hill: Villa Celimontana Jazz and Massenzio (see p149).

July

Festa de'Noantri (3rd week in Jul) A traditional working-class festival, originally with food, wine and dancing, though it's become a little less authentic of late.

October

Ottobrata Romana Musical events take place throughout the month in Trastevere.

Sagra dell'Uva (1st Sun of the month) Outside the city in Marion in the Castelli Romani, you can sample free white wine at this festival. For a full list of country fairs and festivals in the province of Rome, get hold of the *Roma C'è* guide *Sagre & Fiere* (in both English and Italian). It costs €3.50, available from newsstands or the Tourist Office.

December

Toy Fair (1st week in Dec; Piazza Navona) Christmas time in Rome sees a toy fair, with lots of handmade *presepi* (Christmas Nativity Scene) characters and rustic touches like bagpipe players, bright lights and fun.

Feast of San Silvestro (31 Dec) The Pope visits the Chiesa del Gesù and sings the Te Deum, while the Mayor presents a chalice to the presiding priest. Romans eat, drink and merrily throw a few plates out the window to welcome the New Year.

SLEEPING

Rome has a vast number of hotels and other accommodation options on offer. While spring, particularly around Easter and autumn, are the peak periods, tourists and pilgrims flock to Rome year-round, so it's always best to book your room ahead. Rome's municipal government has a full list of accommodation options (in English), including prices, on its excellent website www.romaturismo.it.

There is a free hotel **reservation service** (☎ 06 699 10 00; Stazione Termini, opposite platform 21; ☺ 7am-10pm). A good alternative is the private tourist office Enjoy Rome (see p85).

Avoid the people hanging around at the train station who claim to be tourism officials and offer to find you a room. They usually lead you to pretty seedy accommodation for which you end up paying more than the official rate.

Most of the budget *pensioni* and larger hotels that cater for tour groups are located near Stazione Termini. The area southwest (to the left as you leave the platforms) can be noisy and unpleasant. The city authorities have gone to some lengths to clean it up in recent years but pickpockets are active in this area and women alone may feel uncomfortable at night. To the northeast of Stazione Termini, you can find accommodation in a quieter and more pleasant residential area and there are several decent hotels in the streets around Via Nazionale, a busy traffic thoroughfare and shopping area. However, the historic centre of Rome is far more appealing and the area around the Vatican is much less chaotic; both of these areas are only a short bus or Metro ride away from Stazione Termini.

You will often find three or four budget hotels in the same building. Most hotels will accept bookings in advance, although some demand a deposit or credit card details.

Although Rome does not have a low season as such, the majority of hotels offer significant discounts in July and August and from November to March (excluding the Christmas and New Year period). A lot of mid-range and top end hotels also offer special deals for families, and discounts for extended stays. If you're thinking of staying a week or more in Rome, you'll probably find it cheaper, and more convenient, to stay in a short-let apartment, sometimes called a Residence (see following).

Rental Accommodation

Apartments near the centre of Rome are not cheap, but it can often turn out to be less expensive to rent than to stay in a hotel for more than a week and there are lots of short-term lets available. Some are mini-apartments in hotel blocks, often

called a residence. The Rome Tourism Board has a list of these, with prices, available at www.romaturismo.com. There are also an increasing number of attractive apartments available through specialised agencies, known as *agenzie immobiliari*. They charge a hefty commission but most speak good English. You'll need to book well ahead and many advertise their properties on the Internet. There are also quite a few private apartments available for short-term lets. You'll find a good selection of private and agency properties advertised in Rome's English-language magazine *Wanted in Rome* and on its website (www.wantedinrome.com).

Hostels

Associazione Italiana Alberghi per la Gioventù (☎ 06 487 11 52; www.ostellionline.org; Via Cavour 44) The Italian youth hostels association has information about all the youth hostels available in Italy and will assist with bookings to stay at universities during summer. You can also join Hostelling International (HI) here.

Ostello Foro Italico (Map p99; ☎ 06 323 62 79; aigsedenazionale@uni.net; Viale delle Olimpiadi 61; dm €16) This place is nothing flash. It has a bar, self-service restaurant and a garden but no kitchen. Bookings must be made one month in advance, otherwise you have to turn up at 10am. However, you cannot enter the dorm until 2pm and there is a midnight curfew. It's also a long way from the action.

Marello (Map pp106–7; ☎ 06 482 53 61; fax 06 481 9743; Via Urbana 50; B&B €22-27) Conveniently located in the Esquilino district, but at a cost.

YWCA (Map pp106–7; ☎ 06 488 04 60; fax 06 487 10 28; Via Cesare Balbo 4; s/d €37/62, with bathroom €47/74, tr/q per person €26) Centrally located, accepts men, women and couples, but book well in advance. This is the place for early risers but best avoided by night-owls as there's a midnight curfew. Breakfast is included, but credit cards are not accepted.

Hostel Beautiful (Map pp106–7; ☎ 06 446 58 90; fax 06 493 84 134; www.hostelbeautiful.com; Via Napoleone III, 35; dm €20; ▣) A recent and obviously very welcome addition to Rome's budget accommodation; we've had numerous rave reports about this cheap, clean and friendly place, just around the corner from the main train station.

Bed & Breakfast

The influx of pilgrims during the Jubilee year 2000 and the demand for really good budget accommodation has brought the concept of B&B accommodation to Italy. Italian houses are invariably spotlessly clean, but staying in someone's home means you may be expected to operate within the family's timetable and keys may not always be provided. However, many of the new B&B establishments are really what was once known as *pensioni*, often run by young Italians who have travelled and speak English. The tourist office publishes a full list of B&Bs, with prices.

Lists of authorised private B&B operators in and around Rome can be obtained from the tourist information offices and are also available on www.romaturismo.it. Private B&B operators are listed in the magazine *Wanted in Rome*, although not all of these are registered (and therefore insured) by the city authorities.

Bed & Breakfast Italia (Map pp102–4; ☎ 06 68 80 15 13; www.bbitalia.it; Corso Vittorio Emanuele II 282) This is the longest established B&B network. It has accommodation throughout Rome in three categories: 2 Crowns single/double/triple per person without bathroom €37/30.50/28.40; 3 Crowns single/double/triple with bathroom €50.60/43.40/40.80; 4 Crowns luxurious single/double/triple with bathroom €66.60/57.80/51.10. You can view apartments and book online via the website.

Bed & Breakfast Association of Rome (☎ 06 553 02 248; www.b-b.rm.it; Via A Pacinotti 73) offers a similar service, and can also arrange high-quality, fully furnished apartment rentals for brief periods, usually a minimum of three nights.

A useful online accommodation agency which has a large number of very good B&Bs or *affittacamere* (virtually the same thing but without the breakfast) on its books is **Cross Pollinate** (www.cross-pollinate.com). This website allows you to view pictures and maps of the accommodation (most of which are in the centre of the city) and tells you if the place is already booked. A credit card deposit reserves the room and you'll have a confirmation in 24 hours. The young American couple who run the site also manage the excellent Beehive hostel (see opposite).

Camping

All Rome's camp sites are a hike from the centre.

Seven Hills (Map p99; ☎ 06 303 10 826; fax 06 303 10 039; Via Cassia 1216; sites per person/tent €7.30/5; P ⚊) From Stazione Termini: catch the Metro Linea A to Ottaviano, then take bus No 907 (ask the driver where to get off). From Via Cassia it is a 1km walk to the camping ground.

Flaminio Village (Map p99; ☎ 06 333 26 04; info@villageflaminio.com; Via Flaminia Nuova 821; sites per adult/child/tent €11/7.90/12.50, bungalows from €54; P ⚊) This place has its own bar, restaurant and washing machines. Take Metro Linea A to Flaminio, change to the Roma-Nord train line and get off at Due Ponti station, or take bus No 910 to Piazza Mancini then No 200 to the camp site.

Hotels Northeast of Stazione Termini   Map pp106–7
BUDGET

Fawlty Towers (☎ 06 445 03 74; www.fawltytowers.org; Via Magenta 39; dm with/without shower €24/19, s/d €39/66, with bathroom €47/82) As far as budget accommodation goes, this is one of Rome's best options. Added bonuses are the sunny terrace, satellite TV with a set in every room, communal fridge and microwave. Advance bookings are accepted only for the private (non-dorm) rooms. To reserve a dorm bed, you have to call (either in person or by phone) at 9pm the night before you wish to stay there and they'll hold the bed until around 10am the following morning. It's also a good place to go if you've arrived in Rome late at night and the accommodation agencies are all closed as the staff can usually recommend a *pensione* with vacancies.

The Beehive (☎ 06 447 04 553; www.the-beehive.com; Via Marghera 8; dm €18, d with/without bathroom per person €40/30) The Beehive is the place for the discerning budget traveller. It has clean, attractive rooms and kitchen use is included. You must book ahead as walk-ins are not accepted and party animals positively discouraged.

Pop Inn Hostel (☎ 06 495 98 87; www.popinn hostel.com; Via Marsala 80; dm €16-22, s €35-90, d €18-46) Clean and comfortable with friendly and helpful management, this is several steps above the usual hostel conditions for a place as cheap as this. Additional features include no lock out, free breakfast, hot showers, free luggage storage, multilingual staff and access to the Internet and a laundry.

Restivo Italy B & B (☎ 06 445 26 29; www.italy bnb.it; Via Palestro 49; d €45-62, tr €59-85; ✗) This spotlessly clean, though rather ramshackle *pensione* was established by a former *carabinieri* (police) officer and his wife. Thank-you letters from past guests are proudly displayed. Some rooms (over a restaurant) can be noisy and there is a midnight curfew.

Hotel Cervia (☎ 06 49 10 57; fax 06 49 10 56; Via Palestro 55; dm €19-21; s €20-70, d €30-80, d with bathroom €35-120, breakfast €5) The rooms in this 19th-century building have high vaulted ceilings and seem enormous. There are four- and five-bed dorms on the 3rd floor.

Albergo Sandra (☎ 06 445 26 12; albergosandra@ libero.it; Via Villafranca 10; s/d €43/75) This medium-sized *pensione* with clean and pleasant rooms is run by a house-proud Italian mamma and her English-speaking son.

MID-RANGE
Hotel Gabriella (☎ 06 445 01 20; www.gabriellahotel .com; 1st fl, Via Palestro 88; s €80-115, d €135; ✗) This two-star hotel is an unassuming place, family-run and friendly. Rooms have recently been renovated and there's a TV, safe and telephone in every room. There is also a restaurant and buffet service.

Hotel Floridia (☎ 06 481 40 89; www.sebraeli.it; Via Montebello 45; s with bathroom €47-166, d with bathroom €62-207) There's an elegant entrance area on the ground floor but many of the 44 rooms are quite small and decorated in mock-elegant style.

Hotel Positano (☎ 06 49 03 60; www.hotelpositano .it; Via Palestro 49; s €20-50, d €35-75, s with shower €35-75, d with shower €40-100) This family-run hotel with English-speaking staff is particularly good for families, as they don't charge for children under six. All credit cards are accepted.

Hotel Dolomiti (☎ 06 49 10 58; www.hotel-dolo miti.it; Via San Martino della Battaglia 11; s €62-77, d €80-119; ✗) Two hotels have been turned into one and though the outside looks a bit shabby, the hotel is spotless with elegant and airy rooms (all with private bathroom, minibar, TV, telephone, double glazing, safe and hairdryer). There's a small bar and English, French and Spanish are spoken. Air-conditioning is €13.

Hotel Venezia (☎ 06 445 71 01; www.hotelvenezia .com; Via Varese 18; s €110-189, d €149-208) At the

upper end of the mid-range scale, the Venezia is beautifully furnished with antiques and attractive fabrics. The multilingual staff are charming and it is the nicest place to stay in this area. Prices drop by about 10% in the low season.

Hotel Piemonte (☎ 06 445 22 40; piemonte@italy hotel.com; Via Vicenza 34; s €70-140, d €80-200, tr €100-220, q 120-230; ✗) The pleasant Hotel Piemonte is convenient if you have to take an early morning train, but, unlike most places close to the station, is quiet and stylish. There's double glazing throughout and the bathrooms are particularly nice as is the management. One room has disabled access.

Hotels Northwest of Stazione Termini
BUDGET
Papa Germano (Map pp106-7; ☎ 06 478 69 19; info@hotelpapagermano.it; Via Calatafimi 14a; dm/s/d €19/47/68; 🖳) A good budget choice, Papa Germano has a friendly family atmosphere which is very popular with travellers. There are telephones and TVs in each room, but try to avoid the windowless single room on the top floor. The staff speak English and French.

Hotel Castelfidardo (Map pp106-7; ☎ 06 446 46 38; castelfidardo@italmarket.it; Via Castelfidardo 31; s/d €44/64, with bathroom €55/74) Off Piazza dell' Indipendenza, this is one of Rome's better one-star hotels. The English-speaking staff are friendly and helpful.

Hotel Ercoli (Map pp106-7; ☎ 06 474 54 54; www.hotelercoli.com; Via Collina 48; s with bathroom €52-75, d with bathroom €75-105) This comfortable hotel is about a 10-minute walk from Stazione Termini. Its quality rooms are at the upper end of the budget scale and have TV, telephone and hairdryer.

Hotel Tizi (Map pp100-1; ☎ 06 482 01 28; fax 06 474 32 66; Via Collina 48; s €23, d €37-62, d with bathroom €42-62) This hotel offers light and spacious rooms, which have all been renovated recently. Check for discounts in low season and for stays of more than five days. This hotel accepts cash only.

Hotel Ascot (Map pp106-7; ☎ 06 474 16 75; fax 06 474 01 65; Via Montebello 22; s with bathroom €30-55, d €50-80) The hotel itself is fine – as long as you're not concerned about the porn cinemas and sex shops in the surrounding area. Ask for room No 24, which still has its original parquet floor.

Hotels Southwest of Stazione Termini   Map pp106–7

BUDGET

Hotel Sandy (☎ 06 488 45 85; www.sandyhostel.com; Via Cavour 136; dm €18) Hotel Sandy is probably the closest thing in Rome to a backpackers crash pad. It's on the 5th floor (no lift), there are metal lockers but no keys and the hotel lacks adequate bathroom facilities – so be prepared to queue. Payment is by cash only. You can book via email if you guarantee to arrive before 2.30pm, by phone if you arrive before 11.45am.

58 Le Real B&B (☎ 06 48 23 566; www.58viacavour.it; Via Cavour 58; s €50-100, d €70-180; ⌘) Clean and spacious rooms, near the Colosseum, in a lovely apartment with panoramic views and a sun-terrace. Guests have appreciated friendly management and free access to fridge with juices, yoghurt and water.

MID RANGE

Hotel Sweet Home (☎ 06 488 09 54; www.hotelsweet home.it, Italian only; Via Principe Amedeo 47; s €42-52, with bathroom €77-92, d €72-73, with bathroom €82-104; ⌘) The rooms here vary in size and comfort; ask for one facing away from the street as these are larger and quieter. Air-conditioning is an extra €10.30.

Hotel Igea (☎ 06 44 66 913; igea@venere.it; Via Principe Amedeo 97; s €45-90, d €70-140; ⌘) The fancy entrance suggests a great interior, but the rooms are simple, with basic furniture. They all have satellite TV, double-glazed windows and air-conditioning.

TOP END

Hotel Palladium Palace (☎ 06 446 69 18; www.hotel palladiumpalace.it; Via Gioberti 36; s €71-186, d €82-284; ⌘) This hotel's stylishly refurbished rooms are all individually decorated with parquet floors and gilded ceilings. There are four rooms for disabled travellers and a roof garden with sauna.

Hotel d'Este (☎ 06 446 56 07; d.este@italyhotel.com; Via Carlo Alberto 4b; s €37-129, d €41-165; ⌘) A stone's throw from Piazza Santa Maria Maggiore, this is one of the better hotels in the area, with beautifully furnished rooms and a pleasant roof garden.

Hotels on the Aventino

TOP END

Sant'Anselmo Hotels (Map pp108–9; ☎ 06 574 3547; www.aventinohotels.com; Piazza Sant'Anselmo 2; s €42-109,

d €78-166; ⌘ P) Five separate turn-of-the-century villas make up this group of hotels, situated in a predominantly residential area but still only a stone's throw from the historic centre (to the north) and the restaurants of Testaccio (to the south). These hotels offer both two-star and three-star accommodation and are the perfect place if you prefer quieter surroundings or if you have a car, as street parking is fairly easy to find. There are some facilities for disabled people.

Hotels Near Via Nazionale   Map pp106–7

BUDGET

Daphne B&B (☎ 06 478 23 529; www.daphne-rome .com; Via degli Avignonesi 20; d €68-110, tr €81-135) This clean, convenient and well-equipped place has been described as a 'home sweet home' by a number of travellers, who have enthused over the warm and helpful owners.

Residenza Cellini (☎ 06 4782 5204; www.residenza cellini.it; Via Modena 5; d €145-240, ste €165-260) Readers have raved about this small, 'charming, upscale and friendly' luxury hotel. With its six beautifully appointed rooms overlooking a courtyard is quiet, despite the central location. Flowers, Jacuzzi, and warm and friendly management are extra fringe benefits.

MID-RANGE

Hotel Seiler (☎ 06 488 02 04; www.hotelseiler.com; Via Firenze 48; s €45-90, d €60-145, extra bed €20) A friendly, helpful management and clean, comfortable rooms are the selling points of this hotel. Ask for room 405, known as *la camera degli angeletti* (room of the angels) for its ceiling fresco of angels dating from 1885.

Hotel Oceania (☎ 06 482 46 96; www.hoteloceania.it; Via Firenze 38; s €51-103, d €62-134) This small hotel stands out for the unbeatable hospitality offered by the delightful owners, and nice touches such as English newspapers for guest use.

Hotel Columbia (☎ 06 48 83 509; www.hotel columbia.com; Via del Viminale 15; s/d/tr €189/208/260; ⌘) Rooms in this charming hotel, run by the same people as the Venezia, are large, bright and elegantly furnished with telephone, minibar, satellite television and room safe. There's also a very nice roof terrace.

TOP END

Hotel Artemide (Map 4; ☎ 06 48 99 11; www.venere.it /roma/artemide; Via Nazionale 22; s €216-235, d €300-325; ⌘) This elegant, four-star hotel has

ROME & LAZIO

attractive extras, including free mineral water, soft drinks and daily newspapers. There is one twin room with facilities for disabled people. Ask about low-season discounts.

Hotels in the City Centre
BUDGET   Map pp104–5
Really economical hotels away from the noisy central station area don't exist. But in the areas around Piazza di Spagna, Piazza Navona, the Pantheon and Campo de' Fiori you do have the convenience and pleasure of staying right in the centre of historic Rome.

Albergo Abruzzi (☎ 06 679 20 21; Piazza della Rotonda 69; s €55-75, with bathroom €125-150, d €90-115, with bathroom €175-195) The position, directly opposite the Pantheon, is fantastic. There's nothing fancy about the rooms and they can be very noisy until late at night when the piazza is finally deserted. The chatty management make it a perennial favourite, however. No credit cards.

Albergo della Lunetta (☎ 06 686 10 80; fax 06 689 20 28; Piazza del Paradiso 68; s/d/tr €57/85/115, d/tr with bathroom €110/130) Just east of Campo de' Fiori, this is a Roman *pensione* of the old school, run by three rather cantankerous but somewhat charming *signori* (gentlemen). The labyrinthine corridors and staircases lead to small but spotless rooms. It is popular with young foreign students who stay for months at a time. Breakfast is not available here.

MID-RANGE
Albergo del Sole (Map pp104–5; ☎ 06 687 94 46; www.soldalbiscione.it; Via del Biscione 76; s/d €65/95, with bathroom €83/125; ℗) Just off Campo de' Fiori, this place dates from 1462 and is claimed by some to be the oldest hotel in Rome. It has comfortable rooms, some with antique furniture. There is lots of communal space, including a TV room, an internal patio and a roof terrace, which is open to guests until 11pm. Credit cards are not accepted and parking is €18.

Hotel Campo de' Fiori (Map pp104–5; ☎ 06 688 06 865; www.hotelcampodefiori.com; Via del Biscione 6; s with bathroom €113, d with bathroom €100-150, 3-/4-/5-person apartments €200/230/260) The decor at this quirky establishment – garish blue carpet and clashing floral wallpaper – is not recommended if you have a hangover. In some

cases the 'bathroom' is merely a shower stall plonked unceremoniously in the room, but you pay a bit less. The six-storey, no lift setup might worry some, but it gets 10 points for position and you can take the sun on the top-floor *terrazzo*.

Pensione Primavera (Map pp104–5; ☎ 06 688 03 109; fax 06 686 92 65; Piazza San Pantaleo 3; d €81-95, d with bathroom €100-115, d/tr with bathroom €109/135; ✜) Just south of Piazza Navona, this centrally located hotel has clean and comfortable rooms, all with double glazing to keep out the (considerable) traffic noise. Bathrooms, added to the rooms as an afterthought, are a bit cramped. No credit cards.

Hotel Pomezia (Map pp104–5; ☎ /fax 06 686 13 71; hotelpomezia@openaccess.it; Via dei Chiavari 12; s/d/tr €78/114/130) A good lower mid-range choice, especially after its recent renovation, with one room equipped for disabled travellers.

Hotel Margutta (Map pp100–1; ☎ 06 322 36 74; fax 06 320 03 95; Via Laurina 34; s/d €88/99, d with shared/ private terrace €124/135) Near Piazza del Popolo, off Via del Corso, Hotel Margutta has small and dark rooms but they're spotlessly clean. Book well in advance for a terrace room.

Hotel Forte (Map pp102–4; ☎ 06 320 76 25; forte@venere.it; Via Margutta 61; s €113-160, d €142-232; ✜) Near Piazza di Spagna, the pleasant Hotel Forte is perfect if you like antiques, as Via Margutta is lined with antique shops and artists' studios.

Hotel Julia (Map pp106–7; ☎ 06 488 16 37; www.hoteljulia.it; Via Rasella 29; s €55-145, d €80-170; ✜) Close to busy Piazza Barberini, Hotel Julia offers simple comfort in a tranquil environment. There's a small bar and all rooms have satellite TV.

TOP END
Casa Howard (Map pp102–4; ☎ 06 699 24 555; www.casahoward.com; Via Capo le Case 18; s €120-160, d €160-190; ▣) More guesthouse than hotel, Casa Howard has only five rooms, each individually decorated with gorgeous fabrics and paintings (you can see them on their website). There are 10 more rooms at Via Sistina 149 at a slightly higher rate. Computer connection is available. Both establishments offer the possibility of a Turkish bath.

Hotel Scalinata di Spagna (Map pp102–4; ☎ 06 679 30 06; www.hotelsscalinata.com; Piazza della Trinità dei Monti 17; s €150-300, d €200-350, tr €250-380; ✜) Magnificently located at the top of the

Spanish Steps, with views over the Roman rooftops. Room No 18 has a private terrace and connects with an adjoining room to make a family suite.

Hassler Villa Medici (Map pp102–4; ☎ 06 69 93 40; www.hotelhasslerroma.com; Piazza della Trinità' dei Monti 6; s €435, d €589-781; ste from €1,772; P ☒) Rome's class act for over a century can claim among its past guests the royal families of Sweden, Greece and Britain, John F Kennedy, Elizabeth Taylor and Francis Ford Coppola. If you can't afford to join them for a night then at least go for Sunday brunch costing just €45.

Hotel Locarno (Map pp100–1; ☎ 06 361 08 41; www .hotellocarno.com; Via della Penna 22; s €90-120, d €130-310) Near Piazza del Popolo, the Locarno is a friendly alternative to some of the more impersonal top-end hotels. Popular with both tourists and business travellers, it also has an attractive Art Deco lounge-bar.

Hotel de Russie (Map pp100–1; ☎ 06 32 88 81; www.roccofortehotels.com; Via del Babuino 9; s €418-510, d €572-1050; ☒ P) Rome's newest luxury hotel is opulent, minimal and tasteful. The enormous bathrooms are complete with mosaic tiles and fine linens. But it is the terraced gardens behind the hotel and the various rooftop spaces that take your breath away.

Grand Hotel de la Minerve (Map pp102–4; ☎ 06 69 52 01; minerva@pronet.it; Piazza della Minerva 69; s €326-410, d €410-570; ☒) Opposite Bernini's Elefantino statue near the Pantheon, this deluxe hotel, part of the Crowne Plaza chain, is located in a 17th-century palace redesigned in the 1980s by the Italian architect Paolo Portoghesi. One of his additions was a magnificent Art Deco–style coloured-glass ceiling in the lobby.

Hotel Santa Chiara (Map pp104–5; ☎ 06 687 29 79; www.albergosantachiara.com; Via Santa Chiara 21; s/d €143/212) Attractively positioned behind the Pantheon, Santa Chiara is a very pleasant, comfortable hotel. Some rooms have small balconies overlooking the street, although the rooms around the internal courtyard are quieter.

Hotel Portoghesi (Map pp104–5; ☎ 06 686 42 31; www.hotelportoghesiroma.com; Via dei Portoghesi 1; s €129-1145, d €170-185; ☒) The delightful Portoghesi is superbly positioned in a quiet street lined with craft shops and jewellers. Prices include breakfast on the lovely roof terrace.

Albergo Teatro di Pompeo (Map pp104–5; ☎ 06 687 28 12; hotel.teatrodipompeo@tiscalinet.it; Largo del Pallaro 8; r €95-190; ☒) Parts of this hotel, just off Campo de' Fiori, go back as far as the Roman Republic; guests have breakfast in the remains of Pompey's Theatre (dating from 55 BC).

Hotel Ponte Sisto (Map pp102–4; ☎ 06 68 63 13 68; www.hotelpontesisto.it; Via dei Pettinari 64; s/d/tr €150/310/362; ste €340-420; ☒ ☐ P) An extensive renovation has turned this hotel, close to Campo de' Fiori and the lovely Via Giulia, into a city-centre delight; several of the elegant rooms have their own terraces with unrivalled Roman rooftop views.

Hotel Forum (Map pp106–7; ☎ 06 679 24 46; www.hotelforum.com; Via Tor de' Conti 25; s €145-225, d €220-320, tr €290-365; ☒ P) This former convent very near the Roman Forum has a reception area filled with antiques. The hotel's best asset, however, is its delightful roof-garden restaurant with views to take your breath away.

Hotel Nerva (Map pp106–7; ☎ 06 678 18 35; Via Tor de' Conti; s €50-160, d €60-220; ☒) Rooms in this cosy establishment, named after the Roman emperor and just off Via dei Fori Imperiali, aren't huge, but what they lack in size is made up for by the friendly management. Two rooms have facilities for disabled travellers.

Hotel Celio (Map pp108–9; ☎ 06 704 95 333; www .hotelcelio.com; Via dei Santi Quattro 35c; s €120-230, d €170-290) Just southeast of the Colosseum, this is a little slice of heaven in an area with few accommodation options. A small fortune has been spent on meticulous renovations: stunning mosaic floors decorate corridors and guest rooms, and large-screen TVs feature in most rooms.

Hotels Around Villa Borghese
TOP END

Parco dei Principi (Map pp100–1; ☎ 06 845 421; www.parcodeiprincipi.com; Via G Frescobaldi 5; s €400, d €540-620; P ☒ ☒) This is a gorgeous place anytime, but in summer it's particularly good as it has poolside waiters to serve you iced drinks. The rooms have all been redecorated and have marvellous views across the park. From the top floor you can see as far as Saint Peter's.

Hotels Near the Vatican
BUDGET

Although there aren't many bargains in this area, it's comparatively quiet and close to the main sights. Bookings are an absolute necessity because rooms are often filled with people attending Vatican conferences.

Colors Hotel (Map pp102–4; ☎ 06 687 40 30; www.colorshotel.com; Via Boezio 31; dm €20, d/tr €73/83, with shower €83/89; 💻) Run by the people at Enjoy Rome (see p85). Colors offers good quality accommodation, helpful English-speaking staff, a fully equipped kitchen, and mini-gym. There is no curfew and no lock-out period.

Pensione Nautilus (Map p99; ☎ 06 324 21 18; 2nd fl, Via Germanico 198; s €26-52, with shower €41-78, d €37-77, with shower €52-93) This place has clean, simple rooms and a small lounge-TV area.

Hotel Lady (Map p99; ☎ 06 324 21 12; fax 06 324 34 46; 4th fl, Via Germanico 198; d with/without shower €124/88) A quiet, old-fashioned *pensione* with pleasant rooms and spotless bathrooms. Ask for room No 4 or 6, both of which still have the original beamed ceiling. The eccentric owner and his wife do not speak English, but their eager conversation will give you lots of practice in Italian.

Pensione Paradise (Map p99; ☎ 06 360 04 331; www.hotelpandaparadise.com; Viale Giulio Cesare 47; s/d with shower €52/88) Located near the Lepanto metro stop, this place has simple but bright rooms.

MID-RANGE   **Map pp102–4**
Hotel Adriatic (☎ 06 688 08 080; www.adriatichotel.com; Via G Vitelleschi 25; s €40-60, with bathroom €50-80, d €50-80, with bathroom €60-105; 🔛 🅿) Hotel Adriatic is on the continuation of Via Stefano Porcari, off Piazza del Risorgimento, and has simple but comfortable rooms. The large terrace is a bonus for guests and makes up for the somewhat unfriendly management. Parking is €11.

Hotel Joli (☎ 06 324 18 54; www.hoteljoliroma.it; 6th fl, Via Cola di Rienzo 243; s €45-67, d €60-100) This is a family-friendly hotel with pleasant rooms, although the bathrooms are small and the hand-held showers are liable to soak everything in the room. Readers have reported that the walls are not well soundproofed.

Hotel Florida (☎ 06 324 18 72; www.hotelfloridaroma.it; 2nd fl, Via Cola di Rienzo 243; s €50-90, d €85-113, tr €144) Popular with families, the Florida is small and quiet with pleasantly furnished rooms. There are some cheaper rooms with shared bathroom. Discounts are given in low season.

Hotel Amalia (☎ 06 397 23 356; www.hotelamalia.com; Via Germanico 66; s €95-130, d€150-210; 🔛)

A stone's throw from the Vatican, this is one of the best-value, mid-range hotels in the area. There's nothing special about the rooms but they are bright, spacious and spotlessly clean. Staff is friendly and helpful. Air-conditioning is an extra €20.

TOP END   **Map pp102–4**
Hotel Bramante (☎ 06 688 06 426; www.hotelbramante.com; Via delle Palline 24; s €93-145, d €130-197; 🔛) This is one of the most charming hotels in Rome. Located in a restored 16th-century building, it has superbly decorated bedrooms and antique furniture and carpets throughout. The original building was designed by the Swiss architect, Domenico Fontana, who lived in it until he was expelled from Rome by Pope Sixtus V.

Hotel dei Mellini (☎ 06 32 47 71; www.hotelmellini.com; Via Muzio Clementi 81; s €280, d €320-350; 🔛 🅿) Near the River Tiber, between the Lepanto and Flaminio metro stops, this hotel has large, comfortable rooms (some equipped for disabled access). There's a roof terrace overlooking the Palazzo della Giustizia and a snack bar serving light meals.

Hotel Columbus (☎ 06 686 54 35; hotel.columbus@alfanet.it; Via della Conciliazione 33; s €100-200, d €150-330; 🔛 🅿) The deluxe Hotel Columbus is in a magnificent 15th-century palace in front of St Peter's. It is a Renaissance curiosity with splendid halls and frescoes by Pinturicchio.

Hotels in Trastevere
BUDGET
La Foresteria Orsa Maggiore (Map pp102–4; ☎ 06 684 01 724; www.casainternazionaledelledonne.org, Italian only; Via San Francesco di Sales 1a; s with/without bathroom €57/47, d/tr per person €31/29, 8-bed r €21) For women only, this lovely guesthouse in a beautifully restored 16th-century convent, offers 35 beds in single or multiple rooms which mostly face an internal garden. It provides a peaceful stay in the most elegant surroundings right in the heart of busy Rome. It's run by the *Casa Internazionale delle Donne* (International Women's House), which has its headquarters here. There is a communal room with TV, newspapers and a library. Breakfast (included in the price) and other meals are served in the beautiful garden restaurant which offers regional, ethnic and international cuisine and is usually packed full of lively women, both local and not-so.

There are special rates for group bookings of a minimum of eight women for stays exceeding one week.

MID-RANGE   Map pp108–9
Hotel Trastevere (☎ 06 581 47 13; hoteltrastevere@ tiscalinet.it; Via L Manara 24a-25; s €77-83, d €103-119, tr/q €129/154) One of the best deals in the area (if not the city), with three-star quality at excellent prices. Most of the spotlessly clean rooms look out over the market square of Piazza San Cosimato.

Hotel Carmel (☎ 06 580 99 21; reservations@hot elcarmel.it; Via Mameli 11; s/d/tr €85/100/140) This is a quirky place with a shady roof terrace that can be used by guests. Offers kosher conditions and proximity to Rome's main synagogue.

Hotel Cisterna (☎ 06 581 72 12; fax 06 581 0091; Via della Cisterna 7-9; s/d/tr €105/130/155) Located in a pretty street around the corner from the busy Piazza Santa Maria in Trastevere, Hotel Cisterna has obliging management. Some of the rooms are larger and airier than others.

Villa della Fonte (☎ 06 580 37 97; fax 06 580 37 96; Via della Fonte d'olio 8; s/d €95/145; 🅿) Just a jump from popular Piazza Santa Maria in Trastevere, this fully renovated old building offers five charming and pristine little rooms, with all modern conveniences, including Internet access for personal computers. There's a lovely sunny garden terrace for breakfast and just dozing.

Domus Tiberina (☎ /fax 06 58 03 033; www.hotel seiler.com; Via in Piscinula 37; s/d/tr €95/130/150) This little place has a marvellous position at the non-noisy end of Trastevere and very close to the lovely Ponte Cestio that will lead across the river to Teatro Marcello. Rooms are cosy, if a little twee.

Trastevere House (☎ /fax 06 588 37 74; www .hotelseiler.com; Vicolo del Buco 7; s €40-60, with bathroom €65-120, d €60-90, with bathroom €75-130) Pretty rooms in a quaint little building in the heart of the old Roman quarter, within walking distance of all the sights and close to traditional restaurants. Quiet, safe and comfortable.

EATING
Rome offers a pretty good range of places to eat. There are some excellent establishments offering typical Roman fare to suit a range of budgets, as well as some good,

---

THE AUTHOR'S CHOICE
Hotel Santa Maria (Map pp108–9; ☎ 06 589 46 26; www.htlsantamaria.com; Vicolo del Piede 2; s €124-155, d €145-207, tr €166-233; 🅿 🅾) This gorgeous place is a recently renovated former 17th-century cloister and its 19 rooms, all with spanking new en suite bathrooms, telephone, and TV as well as heating and air-con, are built around a delightful courtyard garden, just around the corner from what was once, in Trastevere's truly working-class days, a den of thieves. It's a beautiful, quiet haven enclosed behind a protective fence in the heart of a popular area , within walking distance of most of the important sights and numerous restaurants and nightspots. Management is young, polite, efficient and English-speaking.

---

but usually fairly expensive, restaurants specialising in international cuisines such as Indian, Vietnamese and Japanese. Generally the restaurants near Stazione Termini are to be avoided if you want to pay reasonable prices for good-quality food. The side streets of the historic centre around Piazza Navona and Campo de' Fiori harbour many good-quality, low-priced trattorie and *pizzerie*, and the areas of San Lorenzo (to the east of Stazione Termini, near the university) and Testaccio are popular eating districts with the locals. Trastevere is full of restaurants, trattorie and *pizzerie*. Very few of them offer great dining and, as the once working-class Roman area has become more and more popular with foreigners, increasingly the so-called authentic restaurants have begun to offer indifferent food in five languages for increasingly higher prices, often accompanied by 'authentic' orchestras playing Neapolitan sob songs.

During summer, however, these areas are lively and atmospheric and there is certainly plenty of choice. Most establishments have outside tables. Be warned, however, that many restaurants close for several weeks during the traditional summer holiday month of August, although new Rome city council laws mean that they must consult with local colleagues to ensure that a similar business is open no more than 300m away.

ROME & LAZIO

Budget Restaurants
AROUND STAZIONE TERMINI & SAN LORENZO

If you have no option but to eat near Stazione Termini, try to avoid the places offering overpriced tourist menus – the food is rarely good. There are many *tavole calde* (self-service eateries with ready-cooked food) in the area, particularly to the west of the train station, which offer *panini* (filled bread rolls) and pre-prepared dishes for reasonable prices.

Moka (Map pp106–7; ☎ 06 474 22 11; Via Giovanni Giolitti 34; ☒ 24 hrs) Brilliant for train travellers (and others), Moka, next to platform 24 at Stazione Termini, offers really tasty ready-made food – pastas, salads and snacks.

Trimani (Map pp106–7; ☎ 06 446 96 630; Via Cernaia 37) This is Rome's biggest *enoteca* (wine bar) and has a vast selection of Italian regional wines with excellent soups, pasta and *torta rustica* (quiche) on offer for lunch and dinner.

Il Dito e la Luna (Map pp106–7; ☎ 06 494 07 26; Via dei Sabelli 49-51; meals around €35; ☒ dinner Mon-Sun) The excellent Sicilian-inspired menu serves interesting dishes such as anchovies marinated in orange juice, a savoury tart made with onions and melted parmesan and *caponata* (a sort of Sicilian ratatouille).

Fantasia del Pane (Map pp106–7; ☎ 06 495 83 37; Via Goito 9; ☒ 7am-2.30pm & 4.30-7.30pm, closed afternoon Sat) This is really a sophisticated bread shop, but it serves delicious *pizza a taglio* (by the slice), if you're eating on the run.

Pommidoro (Map p99; ☎ 06 445 26 92; Piazza dei Sanniti 44; full meals €30; ☒ Mon-Sat) This place is one of the area's more famous trattorie, popular with artists and intellectuals. Specialities are grilled meats and, in winter, game.

Tram-Tram (Map p99; ☎ 064 470 25 85; Via dei Reti 44; meals €16-25) In the heart of San Lorenzo, this warm and friendly little trattoria specialises in seafood dishes from Southern Italy. Swordfish dishes are great, so are the wines.

CITY CENTRE –
NEAR PIAZZA NAVONA   Map pp104–5

Da Gino (☎ 06 687 34 34; Vicolo Rosini 4; full meals €24; ☒ Mon-Sat) A trattoria of the old school, with old-fashioned prices. Off Via di Campo Marzio, it's always full and is popular with politicians and journalists, especially at lunchtime. Try the home-made fettuccine pasta cooked with peas and *guanciale* (bacon made from the pig's cheek) or the *coniglio al vino bianco* (rabbit cooked in white wine).

Pizzeria da Baffetto (☎ 06 686 16 17; Via del Governo Vecchio 114; pizzas €8; ☒ dinner) A Roman institution, its large pizzas would feed an army and deserve their reputation for being among the best (and best value) in Rome. Expect to join a queue if you arrive after 9pm and don't be surprised if you end up sharing a table full of gesticulating locals.

Da Sergio alla Grotta (☎ 06 686 42 93; Vic delle Grotte 27; meals €25; ☒ Mon-Sat) You don't need to see a menu here; decide what takes your fancy by looking at the pictures on the walls, then enjoy enormous helpings of traditional Roman pasta and sauces – *cacio e pepe* (pecorino cheese and ground black pepper), *carbonara*, *amatriciana* (with pancetta, tomato and chilli) – as well as good meat and fish dishes. The pizza oven and grill cater to all tastes. It's got a great atmosphere and has tables outside in summer.

CITY CENTRE – CAMPO MARZIO

Insalata Ricca (Map pp104–5; ☎ 06 68 803 656; Largo dei Chiavari 85; full meals €12.90) King-sized salad meals, and hearty pasta dishes. Fast food with speedier waiters.

MONTI & CELIO

This is a good area for cheap eateries. Stroll around Via del Boschetto, Via dei Serpenti, Via Panisperna, Via Urbana or Via Madonna de' Monti and you're bound to find something to whet your appetite. Many of the best ethnic eateries are located here.

Alle Carrette (Map pp106–7; ☎ 06 679 27 70; Vicolo delle Carrette 14; full meals €10.30) A decent *pizzeria* off Via Cavour near the Roman Forum, well placed to rest weary legs after a hard day's sightseeing.

Al Giubileo (Map pp106–7; ☎ 06 481 88 79; Via del Boschetto 44; full meals €12.90; ☒ Tue-Sun) This is Neapolitan pizza comes to Rome. Waiters dash around this high-energy *pizzeria* punching orders into computer handsets, pizza is piled onto wooden slabs and hungry punters dig in. There's plenty of other stuff on the menu, including melt-in-your-mouth *gnocchi alla sorrentina* (Sorrento-style).

Da Ricci (Map pp106–7; ☎ 06 488 11 07; Via Genova 32; pizzas from €7; ☒ Tue-Sun) Reputed to be the oldest *pizzeria* in Rome, Da Ricci started up as a wine shop in 1905 and has been run by the same family ever since. The pizzas turned out here have a slightly thicker crust than the normal Roman variety but some say it's the best pizza in town. There are also good salads and home-made desserts.

Shawarma Station (Map pp110–11; ☎ 06 48 81 216; Via Merulana 271) Basta la pasta? This is a kind of Middle Eastern *tavola calda* serving kebabs, felafel and other oriental fast foods.

Mexico al 104 (Map pp106–7; ☎ 06 474 27 72; Via Urbana 104; set menu €15) It's hardly Acapulco but it's the closest you'll get in the centre of Rome. Tuck into tacos, burritos, tamales or enchiladas.

GHETTO

Sora Margherita (Map pp102–4; ☎ 06 687 4216; Piazza delle Cinque Scole 30; full meals €20; ☺ lunch Tue-Sun) In the heart of the old Ghetto, Sora's is so well known and popular with the locals that there isn't even a sign over the door. Don't let the formica table tops put you off, you're here for the traditional Roman and Jewish fare – and the bargain prices. Get here early to avoid a queue (especially on Thursday if you want the fresh gnocchi).

TRASTEVERE

Jaipur (Map pp108–9; ☎ 06 580 39 92; Via San Francesco a Ripa 56; full meals €24; ☺ Tue-Sun & dinner Mon) An excellent Indian restaurant.

Bibli (Map pp108–9; ☎ 06 58 14 534; www.bibli.it; Via dei Fienaroli 28; meals €8-16; ☺ 11am-midnight, closed lunch Mon) It's a bookshop, it's a cultural centre, it does lunch and great weekend brunches (from 12.30pm) and there's a buffet at night. Favours vegetarian, but not exclusively.

Da Augusto (Map pp108–9; ☎ 06 580 37 98; Piazza de'Renzi 15; full meals €20; ☺ lunch & dinner Mon-Fri, lunch Sat Sep-Jul) One of Trastevere's favourite trattorie, complete with paper tablecloths and stereotypical down-to-earth funny, snarling Roman staff. Honest fare at prices you only read about. Enjoy your home-made fettuccine pasta or *stracciatella* (clear broth with egg and parmesan) at one of the rickety tables that spill out onto the piazza in summer.

Da Gino (Map pp104–5; ☎ 06 580 3403; Via del la Lungaretta 85; meals €20; ☺ Thu-Tue) No frills *pizzeria*/trattoria.

Pizzeria San Calisto (Map pp108–9; ☎ 06 581 82 56; Piazza San Calisto 9a; pizzas €5.15-7.25; ☺ Tue-Sun)

SOMETHING SPECIAL

Albistrò (Map pp102–4; ☎ 06 686 52 74; Via dei Banchi Vecchi 140a; full meals around €30; ☺ dinner Thu-Tue) This cosy little restaurant serves great food, beautifully presented by the hospitable Swiss host, who is passionate about the food and wine he serves. Each dish is original, and beautifully presented, and you can ask about its origins and seek advice on the wines in Italian, French or English. Excellent value for money.

The enormous pizzas here just about fall off your plate. Dine at one of the outdoor tables in summer and watch the passing parade.

Dar Poeta (Map pp102–4; ☎ 06 58 80 516; www.darpoeta.it; Vicolo del Bologna 46; meals €16-25; ☺ dinner) Quality pizzas, great bruschette and a *calzone* to die for – with ricotta and nutella. Expect a crowd and an elbow in your face.

Pizzeria Popi-Popi (Map pp108–9; ☎ 06 589 51 67; Via delle Fratte di Trastevere 45; pizzas €4.15-6.20; ☺ Fri-Wed) A popular haunt among the youth of Rome, which is hardly surprising since its pizzas are good, big and cheap.

Pizzeria Ivo (Map pp108–9; ☎ 06 581 70 82; Via di San Francesco a Ripa 158; pizzas from €4.65) This *pizzeria* has outdoor tables but the pizza could be bigger for the price. The bruschetta is an excellent start to the meal.

TESTACCIO   Map pp108–9

Pizzeria Remo (☎ 06 574 62 70; Piazza Santa Maria Liberatrice 44; meals around €8.25) You won't find a noisier, more popular *pizzeria* anywhere in Rome. The pizzas here are huge but tend to have a very thin crust. You make your order by ticking your choices on a sheet of paper.

Augustarello (☎ 06 574 65 85; Via Giovanni Branca 98; pasta €5.70, mains €6.70-7.75; ☺ Mon-Sat) If sweetbreads and oxtail aren't your thing, then don't come here. Virtually every dish (other than the pasta) in this old-fashioned trattoria has some correlation to the innards of an animal.

Trattoria da Bucatino (☎ 06 574 68 86; Via Luca della Robbia 84; pasta €5.15-6.20, pizzas €5.15-6.20, full meals around €15.50; ☺ Tue-Sun) This restaurant is a popular Testaccio eating place, with pizza, pasta and Roman fare.

ROME & LAZIO

Mid-Range Restaurants
AROUND STAZIONE TERMINI
Bistrò (Map pp106–7; ☎ 06 44 702 868; Via Palestro 40; meals €50; ☾ dinner Mon-Sat) Attractive and welcoming in an unprepossessing area, this restaurant offers a huge range of dishes, though some of the pastas are a bit disappointing. Seconds and desserts offer better value. Service is cordial, if a bit slow.

CITY CENTRE
L'Eau Vive (Map pp104–5; ☎ 06 688 01 095, Via Monterone 85; full meals from €35; ☾ Mon-Sat) L'Eau Vive is quite unique. It is run by the Domus Dei order of nuns – who drop everything to sing a tuneful Ave Maria in the middle of the dinner service. The food is French/international, but it's not great.

Thien Kim (Map pp102–4; ☎ 06 683 07 832; Via Giulia 201; full meals from €24; ☾ dinner Mon-Sat) This place offers an Italian take on Vietnamese cooking, with tasty dishes that are lighter and more strongly flavoured than other Vietnamese restaurants in Rome.

CITY CENTRE – TRIDENTE
'Gusto (Map pp102–4; ☎ 06 322 62 73; Piazza Augusto Imperatore 9; meals around €40) When you're tired of trudging around the shopping streets nearby, stop here for a 21st-century meal that's a little different from your usual run-of-the-mill Roman offerings. Great cooking. Excellent wines.

Otello alla Concordia (Map pp102–4; ☎ 06 679 11 78; Via della Croce 81; pasta/mains €5.15/15.50; ☾ Mon-Sat) The faithful following of local artisans and shopkeepers keeps Otello away from the tourist trap tag. Cannelloni and *pollo alla romana* (chicken with capsicums) are among the many dishes they do well. A glassed-in courtyard is used as an attractive winter garden in the colder months.

Mario (Map pp102–4; ☎ 06 678 38 18; Via della Vite 55; full meals €31; ☾ Mon-Sat, closed Aug) The very popular Mario's offers Tuscan food – fabulous bean soups, grilled meat and game. We've had some reports saying the service was fantastic, others that it was dreadful.

Sogo Asahi (Map pp102–4; ☎ 06 679 87 82; Via di Propaganda 16; full meals from €36.15; ☾ Mon-Sat) A separate sushi bar, teppanyaki room and *sakura* (with tatami mats) preserve the atmosphere and ritual of Japanese dining. Tasting menus are excellent value and sushi lovers should try the Saturday sushi buffet.

Al 34 (Map pp102–4; ☎ 06 679 50 91; Via Mario de' Fiori 34; full meals around €31; ☾ Tue-Sun) The menu here combines Roman cooking with regional dishes from throughout Italy. Try the rigatoni with *pajata* (chopped veal intestines) if you can stomach it, or the spaghetti with courgettes if you can't. For those with a really large appetite, a *menu degustazione* (gourmand's menu) is also available.

Osteria Margutta (Map pp100–1; ☎ 06 323 10 25; Via Margutta 82; full meals €40; ☾ Mon-Sat) In pretty Via Margutta, Osteria Margutta has a good selection of vegetable antipasto dishes, and pasta with tasty sauces such as broccoli and sausage.

Edy (Map pp102–4; ☎ 06 360 01 738; Vicolo del Babuino 4; full meals €30; ☾ Mon-Sat) Residents and shopkeepers of upmarket Via del Babuino make up Edy's regular clientele – they know it's a good bet in an area not known for great value. Try the house speciality, *spaghetti al cartoccio*, a silver-foil parcel of pasta and seafood. Fettucine with artichokes is also worth writing home about.

Colline Emiliane (Map pp106–7; ☎ 06 481 75 38; Via degli' Avignonesi 22; full meals around €31; ☾ Sat-Thu) A small trattoria near Piazza Barberini serving superb Emilia-Romagnan food. Try the home-made pasta stuffed with pumpkin and the *vitello* (veal) with mashed potatoes – both are delicious.

Osteria dell'Ingegno (Map pp102–4; ☎ 06 678 06 62; Piazza della Pietra 45; pasta from €8.25, full meals around €30; ☾ Mon-Sat) Popular with local politicians, this modern-looking place contrasts strongly with the ancient Hadrian's Temple opposite. The cuisine is central Italian with an international twist. Antipasti include porcini mushroom salad and warm goat's ricotta with grilled vegetables. There's a good selection of salads and an excellent wine list.

Il Bacaro (Map pp104–5; ☎ 06 686 41 10; Via degli Spagnoli 27; meals around €31; ☾ Mon-Sat) Just north of the Pantheon, Il Bacaro is a tiny restaurant where miracles are performed in a minute kitchen. The pasta and risotto dishes are imaginative and delicious, and they do great things with beef and veal. Booking is essential.

Ristorante Monserrato (Map pp104–5; ☎ 06 687 33 86; Via del Monserrato 96; full meals €39; ☾ Tue-Sun) An unassuming neighbourhood eatery that does marvellous things with fish and seafood. The *spaghetti alle vongole* (with clams) and *risotto con scampi* (with prawns) are among the best in Rome. Shady outdoor tables and a great wine list (with excellent whites from northeast Italy) encourage long, relaxed summer lunches.

L'Orso 80 (Map pp104–5; ☎ 06 686 4904; Via dell Orso 33; around €35; ☺ Tue-Sat) In the Camp Marzio area, this place specialises in delicious antipasti. Sit down and let the waiters do it all for you. There's so much variety you can't help but like something and there'll be no room for seconds. This place is popular, so get there early, or book.

Ditirambo (Map pp104–5; ☎ 06 687 16 26; Piazza della Cancelleria 74; full meals €32; ☺ Tue-Sun & dinner Mon) Ditirambo has a rustic feel with its wood-beamed ceilings and wooden floors. The food is traditional Italian with a dash of innovation (such as tortelli with mint) and a good selection of vegetable-only dishes. The home-made bread and pasta add to its charms.

Da Giggetto (Map pp102–4; ☎ 06 686 11 05; Via del Portico di Ottavia 21-2; full meals €35-40; ☺ Tue-Sun) Good food and the Ghetto go hand in hand, and Giggetto is a local institution which combines the two well. It has been serving Roman Jewish cooking for years (the deep-fried artichokes are especially good). In the heart of the Ghetto, right next to the ancient Portico d'Ottavia, its location can't be beaten.

VEGETARIAN

Vegetarians will have no problems eating in Rome. Most traditional Roman pasta dishes are suitable for vegetarians. Other dishes to look out for are: *pasta e fagioli*, a thick soup made with borlotti beans and pasta; *pasta al pesto*, with basil, parmesan, pine nuts and olive oil; and *orecchiette ai broccoletti*, ear-shaped pasta with a broccoli sauce, often quite spicy. Risotto is usually a good choice, although sometimes it is made with a meat or chicken stock. For a dedicated vegetarian restaurant, try one of the following.

Naturist Club – L'Isola (Map pp102–4; ☎ 06 679 25 09; 4th fl, Via delle Vite 14; full meals from €20; ☺ Mon-Sat) Also known as the Centro Macrobiotico Italiano, this place has a double life: at lunch it's a semi self-service vegetarian eatery serving veggie pies and wholegrain risottos; by night it's a la carte dining with fish as the speciality.

Margutta Vegetariano (Map pp100–1; ☎ 06 32 65 05 77; Via Margutta 118; full meals from €20.65)

Unfortunately the vegetarian specialities here are bland and disappointing; stick with veggie versions of Italian staples – pizza and pasta – and you'll eat well. The bizarre decor features black '70s-style love couches. There's another branch of the same operation near the Pantheon, **Le Cornacchie** (Map pp104–5; ☎ 06 681 34 544; Piazza Rondanini 53).

NEAR THE VATICAN

Croce Osteria Con Cucina Angelo (Map p99; ☎ 06 372 94 70; Via G Bettolo 24; meals €20-30; ☺ lunch Tue-Fri, dinner Mon-Sat) This restaurant is in an area little frequented by tourists, and serves authentic traditional Roman fare like *salsicce al cinghiale, rigatoni all pajata, coda all vaccinara* (the latter two based on offal). It's so popular you'll need to book in advance.

TRASTEVERE

Da Gildo (Map pp108–9; ☎ 06 580 07 33; Via della Scala 31a; meals around €25; ☺ Fri-Wed) A cosy, busy little *pizzeria*/trattoria, always full of locals.

Checco Er Carrettiere (Map pp102–4; ☎ 06 581 70 18; Via Benedetta 10; meals €30-40; ☺ lunch Mon-Sun) A charming trattoria with all those romantic touches – bunches of garlic, photos of past famous visitors. It specialises in fish and typical but delicious dishes like *carciofi fritti* (fried artichoke). The home-made bread is particularly good too.

Ferrara (Map pp108–9; ☎ 06 583 33 920; Via del Moro 1a; full meals €52; ☺ Mon-Sat) Ferrara is a compulsory stop on any foodie itinerary for dishes such as *orecchiette* ('little ears') pasta with courgettes and ginger-scented prawns or warm rabbit salad with spicy couscous. Expert advice is on tap for choosing wine from the encyclopaedic lists – this is one of Rome's best *enoteche* (wine bars) after all – and the vaulted, whitewashed dining room is decorated with old barriques. Book a courtyard table.

Paris (Map pp108–9; ☎ 06 581 53 78; Piazza San Calisto 7a; full meals €45; ☺ Tue-Sat & lunch Sun) Paris is the best place outside the Ghetto proper to sample true Roman-Jewish cuisine. The delicate *fritto misto con baccalà* (deep-fried vegetables with salt cod) is memorable, as are simpler dishes such as *pasta e ceci* (a thick chickpea soup in which the pasta is cooked) and fresh grilled fish.

Ristorante L'Una è L'Altra (Map pp102–4; ☎ 06 684 01 727; Casa Internazionale delle Donne, Via S Francesco di Sales, meals around €20; ☺ 1-2.30pm & 8.30pm-midnight

Mon-Sat) In the grounds of a restored convent that is the headquarters of the International Women's House, women can dine in the lovely garden or in the warm and friendly interior. Great food, good wines.

Sora Lella (Map pp102–4; ☎ 06 686 16 01; Via Ponte Quattro Capi 16; meals €30-50; ☺ Mon-Sat) On the Isola Tiberina, in the middle of the Tiber, this elegant little place serves authentic Roman dishes and is extremely popular with the locals, so it's best to book.

NEAR COLOSSEUM & AROUND
VIA NAZIONALE
Baires (Map pp106–7; ☎ 06 692 02 164; Via Cavour 315; meals around €29) One of a chain of fun, funky Argentinian restaurants, which serves up steaks as big as Sardinia, meat any which way and flavoursome soups based on legumes and pulses. Knock it all back with the excellent organic house wine. It's a good place for a rowdy, hungry group. There's another near the Pantheon at Corso Rinascimento.

Il Guru (Map pp106–7; ☎ 06 489 04 656; Via Cimarra 4-6; full meals from €25) Gurus in the know and those who just want a good Indian meal eat here. The menu offers tandooris, curries (of every strength) and great vegetarian choices. The exotic decor will transport you eastwards and the friendly proprietor will steer you clear of curries that are too hot to handle.

Oliphant (Map pp104–5; ☎ 06 686 14 16; Via della Coppelle 31; full meals from €41.95) Rome's first 'Tex-Mex' restaurant is still one of the best and is a good place for a meat fix if that's what you want. Go Tex with hot dogs or buffalo wings or Mex with tortillas and enchiladas. A good range of beers makes it a popular hangout.

TRASTEVERE
Surya Mahal (Map pp102–4; ☎ 06 589 45 54; Piazza Trilussa 50; full meals around €25.85) This Indian restaurant has a delightful garden terrace right next to the fountain on Piazza Trilussa. Set menus – vegetarian, meat or fish – provide an opportunity to try almost everything.

ATM Sushi Bar (Map pp102–4; ☎ 06 683 07 053; Via della Penitenza 7; full meals from €23.25) This sushi bar is tucked away in the quiet backstreets of Trastevere. Chill out amid the minimalist decor, soft lighting and relaxed music, and chow down on excellent sushi, sashimi, nori rolls, tempura and other Japanese classics.

APPIA ANTICA & CATACOMBS
Archeologia (Map p99; ☎ 06 788 04 94; Via Appia Antica 139; meals €36-51; ☺ Wed-Mon) This is by far the best restaurant in this tourist-frequented area. Set in an ancient country house in a lovely garden it offers reasonable food at reasonable prices.

Top End Restaurants
CITY CENTRE
Camponeschi (Map pp104–5; ☎ 06 687 49 27; Piazza Farnese 50; full meals €87; ☺ dinner Mon-Sat) You cannot find a more perfect setting for a restaurant than that of Camponeschi on the beautiful (and, delightfully, car free) Piazza Farnese. It is a favourite with politicians, diplomats and the glitterati.

La Rosetta (Map pp104–5; ☎ 06 686 10 02; Via della Rosetta 8-9; full meals around €115; ☺ Mon-Sat, closed lunch Sat) Near the Pantheon, La Rosetta is without doubt the best seafood restaurant in Rome. The menu features innovative combinations – how about shrimp, grapefruit and raspberry salad or fried *moscardini* (baby octopus) with mint? Owner-chef Massimo Riccioli is regarded as one of the best in Italy. Expensive but memorable. Booking is essential.

Piperno (Map pp102–4; ☎ 06 688 06 629; Via Monte de' Cenci 9; full meals from €41.30; ☺ Tue-Sat & lunch Sun) In the heart of the Ghetto, Piperno has turned deep frying into an art form; the house special is a mixed platter of deep-fried fillets of *baccalà*, stuffed courgette flowers, vegetables and mozzarella cheese. Offal eaters will be well satisfied.

Vecchia Roma (Map pp102–4; ☎ 06 686 46 04; Piazza Campitelli 18; full meals €45; ☺ Thu-Tue) The terrace of Vecchia Roma is one of the prettiest in Rome, and it's an extremely pleasant spot to pass a few hours. The pan-Italian menu is extensive and changes seasonally. In summer there are imaginative salads, in winter lots of dishes based on polenta, plus good pasta and risotto year-round.

Montevecchio (Map pp104–5; ☎ 06 686 1319; Piazza di Montevecchio 22a; full meals around €52; ☺ dinner Tue-Sun) Intimate and welcoming atmosphere, good wine list and excellent food. Try *sfogliatine di foie gras* (small pastries) with black truffle sauce.

TRASTEVERE
Alberto Ciarla (Map pp108–9; ☎ 06 581 86 68; Piazza San Cosimato 40; mains €50-60; ☺ Mon-Sat) Alberto is

well-known for his (at times tempestuous) passion for getting the food just right. It must have paid off, as Italy's food critics hold him in high esteem. Fish is his speciality, but the menu offers lots to choose from.

TESTACCIO

Checchino dal 1887 (Map pp108–9; ☎ 06 574 38 16; Via di Monte Testaccio 30; full meals around €55; ☺ Tue-Sat) This family-run eatery provides constant fodder for travel magazines seeking the best places for traditional Roman dining. Its location near the former abattoir is appropriate, given that offal – from calves' heads to pigs' trotters and sweetbreads – is its trademark. The great wine cellar is a bonus.

Quick Eats

Fast food Roman style usually consists of a hearty *panino* (filled bread roll), a slice of piping hot *pizza bianca* (plain focaccia-like bread; around €0.75 per slice) or a tasty slice of *pizza a taglio* (also known as pizza rustica).

There are hundreds of bars around the city that are good options for cheap, quick meals. *Gastronomie* are often found in conjunction with a bar, meaning *tramezzini* (premade refrigerated sandwiches, usually white bread with no crusts and lots of mayonnaise) which cost around €1.90 to €4 (maybe more if you sit down). You can also buy a delicious freshly made sandwich from an *alimentari* with meat and cheese for about €1.50 to €2. At a takeaway *pizzeria*, a slice of freshly cooked pizza, sold by weight, can cost as little as €1.50. There are numerous bakeries in the Campo de' Fiori area which are good for a cheap snack.

M & M Volpetti (Map pp104–5; Via della Scrofa 31) Near Piazza Navona, this upmarket sandwich bar-cum-deli-cum-*rosticceria* (specialising in grilled meats) sells gourmet lunch snacks (and takeaway dinners) for above-average prices.

Antico Forno (Map pp102–4; ☎ 06 679 28 66; Via delle Muratte 8) Your wishes won't necessarily come true by throwing a coin into the Trevi Fountain, but a few coins spent in this famous bakery opposite will assure you of a delicious slice of pizza or a hearty filled *panino*.

Forno di Campo de' Fiori (Map pp104–5; ☎ 06 688 06 662; Campo de' Fiori 22) People come from all over the city for this bakery's *pizza bianca*. Drizzled with extra virgin olive oil

and sprinkled with crunchy grains of sea salt, it proves the maxim that less is more. Buy it by the metre.

Forno la Renella (Map pp108–9; ☎ 06 581 72 65; Via del Moro 15-16) Trastevere's famous bakery has been producing Rome's best bread for decades. As the embers die down in the wood-fired ovens, the bakers turn their hand to slabs of thick, doughy pizza with toppings such as tomato, olives and oregano, or potato and rosemary. This *pizza a taglio* is worth crossing rivers for.

Frontoni (Map pp108–9; Viale di Trastevere) Among the city's more famous sandwich outlets, Frontoni makes its *panini* with both *pizza bianca* and bread, and offers an enormous range of fillings. Sandwiches are sold by weight and it has good *pizza a taglio*. There is now a restaurant upstairs as well.

Volpetti Più (Map pp108–9; Via A Volta 8) It's worth making a special trip to Testaccio just to eat lunch at Volpetti Più. It's a *tavola calda* so you don't pay extra to sit down. The *pizza a taglio* is extraordinarily good and there are plenty of pasta, vegetable and meat dishes.

Zi' Fenizia (Map pp102–4; Via di Santa Maria del Pianto 64; ☺ Fri-Wed, closed afternoon Fri, Sat & Jewish holidays) Better known as the kosher pizzeria, Zi' Fenizia makes, arguably, the city's best *pizza a taglio*. There's no cheese on this kosher variety but you don't miss it, and the toppings are not the usual suspects either – this is *pizza a taglio* par excellence.

There are numerous *pizza a taglio* outlets all over the city. Some good places are around Campo de' Fiori: **Pizza Rustica** (Map pp104–5; Campo de' Fiori) and **Pizza a Taglio** (Map pp104–5; Via Baullari), between Campo de' Fiori and Corso Vittorio Emanuele II. Just off Piazza di Trevi is **Pizza a Taglio** (Map pp102–4; Via delle Muratte).

GELATERIE

Gelateria Giolitti (Map pp104–5; Via degli Uffici del Vicario 40; ☺ 7am-midnight) Gelateria Giolitti has long been a Roman institution – on summer evenings it's packed. There are more than 70 exotic flavours to choose from, Pope John Paul II's favourite flavour, marrons glacé (glacé chestnuts), used to be specially delivered. There's a great selection of cakes and pastries as well.

Gelateria della Palma (Map pp104–5; Via della Maddalena 20) You could be forgiven for thinking you'd stumbled into Willy Wonka's factory here, and choosing from the 100 flavours is surprisingly difficult. The house specialities are the extra creamy (and rich) mousse gelati, and the *meringata* varieties with bits of meringue dotted through them.

La Fonte della Salute (Map pp108–9; Via Cardinal Marmaggi 2-6) Whether this Trastevere *gelateria* really is a fountain of health (as its name translates) is debatable, although the soy- and yoghurt-based gelati support the theory. The fruit flavours are superb and the marron glacé so delicious that it has to be good for you. Scoops are more generous than at *gelaterie* in the historic centre.

CAKES & PASTRIES

Bernasconi (Map pp104–5; Piazza B Cairoli 16) There's always a tempting selection of cakes and pastries at Bernasconi; the *cornetti alla crema* (custard-filled pastries) are to die for.

Bella Napoli (Map pp104–5; Corso Vittorio Emanuele II 246a) You won't get better Neapolitan-style pastries outside Naples. Try stopping at just one *sfogliatelle* (ricotta-filled sweet pastry).

La Dolceroma (Map pp102–4; Via del Portico d'Ottavia 20d) Right next to the Portico d' Ottavia, La Dolceroma specialises in Austrian cakes and pastries, and American treats such as cheesecake, brownies and chocolate-chip cookies.

Il Forno del Ghetto (Map pp102–4; Via del Portico d'Ottavia 2) You'll lose all self-control when you see what the all-female team in this tiny kosher bakery can produce. People come from all parts of Rome for the ricotta-and-damson tart. Buy a slice and you'll know why.

Sacchetti (Map pp108–9; Piazza San Cosimato 61) Sacchetti is a Trastevere favourite with shoppers and stallholders at Piazza San Cosimato market. Ignore the grumpy proprietors; these cakes – especially the chestnut and cream confection called *monte bianco* – are something special.

Panella l'Arte del Pane (Map pp106–7; Largo Leopardi 2-10) On Via Merulana, near Stazione Termini, this place has a big variety of pastries and breads.

Self-Catering

For groceries and supplies of cheese, prosciutto, salami and wine, shop at *alimentari*, generally open 7am to 1.30pm and 5pm to 8pm every day except Thursday afternoon and Sunday (during the summer they are often closed Saturday afternoon instead of Thursday).

For fresh fruit and vegetables, there are numerous outdoor markets, notably the lively daily markets in Campo de' Fiori (Map pp104–5), Piazza Testaccio (Map pp104–5), Piazza San Cosimato (Map pp108–9), Piazza Vittorio Emanuele (Map pp108–9) and Via Andrea Doria (north of the Vatican). Supermarkets are few and far between, though a few more have sprung up recently, such as: **Di Meglio** (Map pp102–4; Via Giustiniani 18b-21) which is near the Pantheon and **GS** (Map pp102–4; Via del Galoppatoio 33), near Villa Borghese.

Todis (Map pp108–9; Via Natale del Grande 24), in Trastevere, is a discount supermarket which costs less than a normal supermarket, but doesn't usually have fresh fruit and vegetables.

The following are some of Rome's better-known gastronomic establishments.

Castroni (Map pp102–4; ☎ 06 687 43 83; Via Cola di Rienzo 196) Castroni, in Prati near the Vatican, has a wide selection of gourmet foods, packaged and fresh, including international foods (desperate Aussies will find Vegemite here). There are other outlets around the city, at Via Flaminia 28 and Via Ottaviano 55.

Gino Placidi (Map pp104–5; Via della Maddalena 48) This place, near the Pantheon, is one of central Rome's best *alimentari*.

Volpetti (Map pp108–9; ☎ 06 574 23 52; Via Marmorata 47) Volpetti, in Testaccio, is famous for its gastronomic specialities, including a large selection of unusual cheeses from throughout Italy.

Volpetti alla Scrofa (Map pp104–5; ☎ 06 688 06 335; Via della Scrofa 3) A great selection of cheese, sausage, salmon and truffles as well as a *tavola calda* where you can try them out.

Billo Bottarga (Map pp102–4; Via Sant'Ambrogio 20) This store, near Piazza Mattei, specialises in kosher food and is famous for its *bottarga* (roe of tuna or mullet).

Drogheria Innocenzi (Map pp108–9; ☎ 06 581 27 25; Piazza San Cosimato 66; 6.30am-1.30pm & 4.30-8pm Mon-Wed, Fri & Sat) This is a thrilling place where you'll find everything from sacks of beans, rice and Corn Flakes, to gourmet chocolates. Every conceivable food product from Italy and the world can be found here.

HEALTH FOODS

Buying muesli, soya milk and the like can be expensive in Italy. The following outlets have a good range of products, including organic fruit and vegetables, at relatively reasonable prices.

L'Albero del Pane (Map pp102–4; ☎ 06 686 50 16; Via di Santa Maria del Pianto 19) In the Jewish quarter, this store has a wide range of health foods, both packaged and fresh.

Emporium Naturae (Map p99; ☎ 06 375 11 415; Viale delle Milizie 7a) This is a well-stocked health-food supermarket.

Il Canestro Testaccio (Map pp108–9; Via Luca della Robbia 47) Trastevere (Map pp108–9; Via San Francesco a Ripa 105) This shop has a large selection of health foods, as well as fresh fruit and vegetables and takeaway food.

DRINKING
Cafés & Bars
Coffee aficionados have a wealth of choice. There are several excellent bars near the Pantheon that are known for their excellent caffeine beverages, including **La Tazza d'Oro** (Map pp104–5; ☎ 06 679 27 68; Via degli Orfani 84-6; ☼ Mon-Sat), **Camilloni a Sant'Eustachio** (Map pp104–5; ☎ 06 686 49 95; Piazza Sant'Eustachio 54-5) and **Caffè Sant' Eustachio** (Map pp104–5; ☎ 06 686 13 09; Piazza Sant'Eustachio 82). The latter makes gran caffè, a wonderful, almost bubbly, coffee made by beating the first drops of espresso and several teaspoons of sugar into a frothy paste, then adding the coffee on top.

Bar della Pace (Map pp104–5; ☎ 06 686 12 16; Via della Pace 5) A lovely, old fashioned, Art Nouveau place on the inside, great for coffee and *cornetto* in the winter or lazing outside with a cool cocktail in the summer.

Café dei Musei (Map pp102–4; ☎ 06 32 65 12 36; Musei Capitolini, Piazza del Campidoglio 19; ☼ 9am-6pm Tue-Sat) A nice terrace for a drink, snack and stunning views of the ruins of ancient Rome.

Caffé delle Arte (Map pp100–1; ☎ 06 32 65 12 36; Via Gramsci 72/75; ☼ 7.30am-6pm Mon, 7.30am-midnight Tue-Sun) One of the nicest cafés in the city, popular with families, this place is part of the Galleria Nazionale d'Arte Moderna in the middle of Villa Borghese. There are tables outside on a lovely terrace and it's a great place for Sunday brunch.

Rosati (Map pp100–1; Piazza del Popolo 5) A well-known meeting place and an elegant place for coffee, tea, snack or gelato. The cocktails are great and you can look out over the lovely piazza for the rest of the day. Not the cheapest bar in town, but the cakes are magnificent. It's equally well-known rival

opposite, **Canova** (Map pp100–1; Piazza del Popolo 16), is not quite so sophisticated.

Caffè Greco (Map pp102–4; ☎ 06 679 17 00; Via dei Condotti 86; ☼ 8am-9pm Mon-Sat) This elegant place opened in 1760 and was the meeting place for artists and writers. Keats ate here, as did Casanova. The food's not great and the prices are high, but it's worth visiting for the atmosphere. Bear in mind if you sit down for even just a coffee and cake you'll pay about as much as you would for a meal.

Caffè Farnese (Map pp104–5; ☎ 06 688 02 125; Via dei Baullari 106) On one corner of the lovely Piazza Farnese, this is a great spot for people watching, especially on Saturday morning when the Campo de' Fiori market is at its busiest.

Caffè Marzio (Map pp108–9; Piazza Santa Maria in Trastevere) You will pay around €3 for a cappuccino if you sit down outside (compared with €0.90 at the counter inside), but it's worth it as this café looks onto one of Rome's most beautiful and atmospheric piazzas.

Caffè Doria Tea Room (Map pp102–4; ☎ 06 679 38 05; Palazzo Doria Pamphilj, Via della Gatta 1a) This lovely, old fashioned café, with its cooling fountain and antique furniture is a good place to relax after you've wandered around the gallery upstairs.

Bar San Calisto (Map pp108–9; ☎ 06 583 58 69; Piazza San Calisto) Seedy and cheap, the perennially popular but decidedly unglamorous Bar San Calisto attracts Trastevere locals, the arty set, people apparently doing drug deals and a few well-known winos. It's famous for its to-die-for hot chocolate in winter and chocolate gelato (arguably the best in town) in summer.

Pubs
The pub scene isn't huge as Italians don't drink a lot of alcohol, especially without meals, and pubs are not traditionally part of Roman culture. But since the early 1990s they have proliferated to cater to the growing numbers of young travellers and students. Most are styled after traditional English or Irish pubs, although there are also places with Australian or American themes.

Trinity College (Map pp102–4; ☎ 06 678 64 72; Via del Collegio Romano 6) There's a good selection of imported beers, great food and an easy-going ambience in this stalwart of the pub scene. It gets packed to overflowing on Fridays and at weekends.

Four XXXX (Map pp108–9; ☎ 06 575 72 96; Via Galvani 29) This eclectic Testaccio Tex-Mex haunt has undergone a bit of 'Latinisation' and has something for everyone: Castlemaine XXXX beer on tap for homesick Aussies, Tequila cocktails if you want something stronger, tasty South American food and good live jazz or a DJ most nights.

Big Hilda (Map pp108–9; ☎ 06 580 33 03; Vic del Cinque 33-4) Murphy's stout and bitter on tap and a few good wines are the attractions here in this smoky, buzzing, music-filled Trastevere pub.

Marconi (Map pp106–7; ☎ 06 486 636; Via Santa Prassede 9) Regulars come here as much for the food as the booze. It's a bit of an international smorgasbord, with Irish breakfasts and stodgy English fish'n'chips alongside Hungarian goulash. Oh, and then there's the beer…

Fiddler's Elbow (Map pp106–7; ☎ 06 487 21 10; Via dell'Olmata 43) The Guinness, darts and chips formula has been working well here for over 20 years, and there is often spontaneous live music. This was one of the first Irish pubs to hit Rome, and it's still popular with foreigners and locals.

Bars

If you prefer bars to pubs, try one of the following.

Sloppy Sam's (Map pp104–5; ☎ 06 688 02 637; Campo de' Fiori 9-10) A cross between an Italian bar and an English pub, Sloppy Sam's is friendly and relaxed. Settle into a repro antique chair, choose your beer from the selection on tap, grab a plate of nachos and take it from there.

Bar del Fico (Map pp104–5; ☎ 06 687 55 68; Piazza del Fico 24) Popular with local actors and artists, this bar buzzes until the early hours, and crowds spill out the door and block the neighbouring streets.

Jonathan's Angels (Map pp104–5; ☎ 06 689 34 26; Via della Fossa 18) Rome at its quirky best is on display here. Run by an artist, the whole bar – even the loo – is covered with pictures and decorations. It's a relaxed place for a late-night drink.

Stardust (Map pp108–9; ☎ 06 583 20 875; Vicolo dei Renzi 4) A cross between a pub and a jazz venue, Stardust often has live jazz and jam sessions. It's a real neighbourhood place

that tends to close when the last customers fall out the door.

Friends Art Café (Map pp102–4; ☎ 06 581 61 11; Piazza Trilussa 34) A fashionable and lively drinking spot that has Internet access and staff with attitude.

Bartaruga (Map pp102–4; ☎ 06 689 22 99; Piazza Mattei 9) Named – in a fashion – after the Fontana delle Tartarughe opposite, this combined cocktail bar, tearoom and pub is original, decked out in bright colours, including oriental furniture, velvet cushions and a Turkish harem feel.

Ombre Rosse (Map pp108–9; ☎ 06 588 4155; Piazza San Egidio 12-13; ☯ 7-2am Mon-Sat, 5pm-2am Sun) Right next to the revamped Pasquino English-language cinema complex, this bar attracts an international crowd.

Wine Bars

Enoteche (wine bars) are a feature of most Roman neighbourhoods. They sell wine, spirits and olive oil, and are often frequented by groups of elderly locals enjoying a glass of wine and a chat in much the same manner as they might have a coffee at a bar. In recent years a more sophisticated breed of *enoteche* has been attracting a different crowd from the regular pub-goers. Many of these offer snacks or light meals in addition to an extensive range of wines that you can taste by the glass (ask for it *alla mescita* or *al bicchiere*) or buy by the bottle.

Vineria (Map pp104–5; ☎ 06 688 03 268; Campo de' Fiori; ☯ 9.30am-2pm & 6pm-1am Mon-Sat, to 2am Sun) Also known as Da Giorgio, this *enoteca* was once the gathering place of the Roman literati. Today the crowd that spills out into the piazza is decidedly less bookish, but it's still a fun place to drink with a wide selection of wine and beers.

L'Angolo Divino (Map pp104–5; ☎ 06 686 44 13; Via dei Balestrari) This charming *enoteca*, with wooden beams and terracotta floors, has been run by the same family for three generations. It's a lovely place for a quiet glass of excellent wine, a nibble of cheese or a light meal.

Il Goccetto (Map pp102–4; ☎ 06 686 42 68; Via dei Banchi Vecchi 14) Most customers of this club-like wine bar, considered one of the best, are regulars who drop in for a drink after work. Wines from all over the world share shelf space with the top Italian drops and there's a choice of around 20 wines by the glass.

Trimani (Map pp106–7; ☎ 06 446 96 61; Via Cernaia 37) Rome's biggest *enoteca* with a vast selection of Italian regional wines.

ENTERTAINMENT

You don't have to look far to be entertained in Rome. Whether it's opera or football, dance or drinking, the Eternal City has something for everyone. Most of the activity is in the historic centre. Campo de' Fiori is especially popular with younger crowds, while the alleyways near Piazza Navona hide some interesting late-night hang-outs. The Trastevere, Monti and Esquilino districts are also full of bars, pubs and gay venues.

The clubbing scene is less active in Rome than in other European capitals. Still, there is something for all tastes, with some clubs retaining a certain sophisticated glamour and others priding themselves on being the latest in hip and groovy.

Estate Romana (☎ 06 807 26 25; www.massenzio.it, Italian only) Rome comes alive in summer with its many dance, music, opera, theatre and cinema festivals. Many of these performances take place under the stars, in parks, gardens and church courtyards, with classical ruins and Renaissance villas as the backdrop. Catch one of these productions and it will undoubtedly be the highlight of your trip. Autumn is also full of cultural activity with specialised festivals dedicated to dance, drama and jazz.

Roma C'è (www.romace.it) would have to be the city's most comprehensive entertainment guide, published every Thursday, and has a small section in English. *Wanted in Rome* (www.wantedinrome.it), published on alternate Wednesdays, contains listings and reviews of the most important festivals, exhibitions, dance, classical music, opera and cinema. Both magazines are available from newsstands. The daily newspapers *Il Messaggero* and *La Repubblica* have listings of theatre, cinema and special events.

For theatre, opera and sporting events you often have to book well ahead. These agencies can do it for you:

Hello (Map pp106–7; ☎ 800 90 70 80, ☎ 06 808 83 52; www.amitonline.it, Italian only; Stazione Termini; ⏰ 10am-6pm Mon-Sat) Tickets for music, sport and theatre; opposite the travel agency near Via Giolitti.

Orbis (Map pp106–7; ☎ 06 474 47 76; Piazza dell' Esquilino 37)

> ### LEND ME YOUR EARS
>
> Rome's auditorium has been slow moving and costly. The project of three concert halls and an outdoor amphitheatre, designed by Renzo Piano, as a multifunctional space to host jazz and classical concerts as well as art exhibitions, has been, like most building projects in Rome, constantly halted as ancient ruins appear during the course of construction. In fact, the remains of a 5th-century-BC Roman villa have now been incorporated into the architecture.

Cinemas

Films are shown regularly in English at the following cinemas. Expect to pay around €6 to €7, with some discounts on Wednesdays.

Pasquino (Map pp108–9; ☎ 06 580 36 22; Piazza Sant' Egidio) The super revamped complex shows films in English daily.

Quirinetta (Map pp102–4; ☎ 06 679 00 12; Via Marco Minghetti 4) Films in English daily.

Alcazar (Map pp108–9; ☎ 06 588 00 99; Via Merry del Val) Films in English on Monday.

Nuovo Sacher (Map pp108–9; ☎ 06 581 81 16; Largo Ascianghi 1) Owned by director/actor Nanni Moretti, it shows films in their original language Monday and Tuesday.

Warner Village Moderno (Map pp106–7; ☎ 06 477 79 202; Piazza della Repubblica 45) Five cinemas showing Hollywood blockbusters (both in English as well as dubbed into Italian) and major release Italian films.

A popular form of entertainment in the hot Roman summer is outdoor cinema.

Isola del Cinema (Map pp108–9; ☎ 06 583 33 113; www.isoladelcinema.com) This international film festival takes place on the Isola Tiberina during July and August and features independent films.

Massenzio (Map pp110–11; ☎ 06 428 14 962; www.massenzio.it, Italian only) Massenzio is one of Rome's most popular summer festivals. Several films, both current release and old favourites, are shown each night on a huge screen under the stars on Caelian Hill, opposite the Colosseum. Check the listings magazines or the daily press for details of these events.

Classical Music

Accademia di Santa Cecilia (Map pp102–4; ☎ 06 361 10 64; Via della Conciliazione 4) World-class international performers join the highly regarded Santa Cecilia Orchestra. Short festivals dedicated to a single composer are a feature of the autumn calendar. In June the orchestra and its guest stars move to the beautiful gardens of the Renaissance Villa Giulia (Map pp100–1) for its summer concert series.

Accademia Filarmonica Romana (Map p99; ☎ 06 323 48 90; Teatro Olimpico, Piazza Gentile da Fabriano 17) The Filarmonica programme features mainly chamber music, with some contemporary concerts and multimedia events. The academy was founded in 1821 and its members have included Rossini, Donizetti and Verdi.

Free concerts are often held in many of Rome's churches, especially at Easter and around Christmas and New Year. Seats are available on a first come, first served basis and the programmes are generally excellent. Check newspapers and listings press for programmes.

San Paolo entro Le Mura (Map pp106–7; ☎ 06 488 33 39; www.stpaulsrome.it; Via Nazionale) Often hosts musical events.

Auditorium Parco della Musica (Map p99; ☎ 06 806 93 444; Viale Pietro di Coubertin) The first of three concert halls in Rome's long-awaited Auditorium complex, designed by architect Renzo Piano, opened in April 2002. It's off Via Flaminia, north of the historic centre and you can get there on Tram 2 or by the new bus line, M, that travels to/from Stazione Termini (every 15 minutes daily) from 5pm to the last performance.

Clubs & Live Music Venues

In terms of dance clubs – discos to the locals – Rome falls way behind Berlin or London. Still, there's plenty of choice, from grungy clubs with live music or cool DJs to upmarket discos frequented by jet-set types. The latter can be expensive; expect to pay up to €20 to get in, which may or may not include one drink.

Alien (Map p100–1; ☎ 06 841 22 12; Via Velletri 13) The distinctive decor of Alien is like something out of a science fiction film. Dancers on raised platforms groove to the rhythm of house, techno and hip-hop. For the retros among us, one of the two dance areas features '70s and '80s revivals.

Gilda (Map pp102–4; ☎ 06 678 48 38; Via Mario de'Fiori 97; ☽ from 11pm Tue-Sun, closed summer) Appealing to a slightly older, wealthier and, some might say, 'less-than-cool' clientele, Gilda has plush decor, state-of-the-art lighting and a huge dance floor. Despite all this, it has a sterile, formal atmosphere – not helped, perhaps, by the dress code, which requires jackets.

Goa (Map p99; ☎ 06 574 82 77; Via Libetta 13; ☽ Oct-May) The far-from-central location near San Paolo Fuori-le-Mura hasn't affected the popularity of Goa. It's decked out in ethnic style, with comfy couches to sink into when your feet need a break from the dance floor. The bouncers rule – you might not get in if they don't like the look of you.

Black Out Rock Club (Map p99; ☎ 06 704 96 791; Via Saturnia 18) Known as the club for punk, rock and indie music, Black Out occasionally has gigs by British (and American) punk and rock bands.

Locale (Map pp104–5; ☎ 06 687 90 75; Vicolo del Fico 3) Off Via del Governo Vecchio, near Piazza Navona, this live music/dance venue is very popular among young foreigners and Italians. Expect to queue on Friday and Saturday night.

Bush (Map pp108–9; ☎ 06 572 88 691; Via Galvani 46) This Testaccio club has a reputation for excellent DJs, especially on Thursday which is hip-hop, R&B and soul night.

Radio Londra (Map pp108–9; ☎ 06 575 00 44; Via di Monte Testaccio 65b) Decked out like an air-raid shelter, Radio Londra has live music four nights a week.

Caruso (Map pp108–9; ☎ 06 574 50 19; Via di Monte Testaccio 36) There's live music twice a week at Caruso, and good DJs playing Latin, rock and hip-hop the rest of the time.

Caffè Latino (Map pp108–9; ☎ 06 572 88 556; Via di Monte Testaccio 96) As you might expect, this venue has live Latin American music most nights, followed by a disco of Latin, acid jazz and funk. There are also cabaret and film screenings.

Villaggio Globale (Map pp108–9; ☎ 06 575 72 33; Lungotevere Testaccio) Located in a former slaughterhouse, Villaggio Globale is one of Rome's *centri sociali* (community centres), once a squat, frequented by ageing hippies, new-age types and people into punk and 'grunge'. Many big acts perform here.

Dance

There's an active dance scene in Rome and many of the world's best companies tour Italy, although quality home-grown companies are few and far between. See the listings magazines and daily press for details. The Teatro dell'Opera (see right) includes a few classical ballets in its season. These productions are generally worth seeing only if there are important guest stars.

Gay & Lesbian Venues

Details of Rome's gay and lesbian bars and clubs are provided in gay publications and through local gay organisations (see pp819–20).

Hangar (Map pp106–7; ☎ 06 488 13 97; Via in Selci 69) Rome's oldest gay bar, run by an American, is still one of its most popular. The varied clientele – international and Italian, all age groups – includes a significant portion of gym bunnies. Monday is gay video night.

L'Alibi (Map pp108–9; ☎ 06 574 34 48; Via di Monte Testaccio 44) L'Alibi is regarded by many as Rome's premier gay venue.

Edoardo II (Map pp102–4; ☎ 06 699 42 419; Vicolo Margana 14) There's amusing decor (it's done up like a medieval torture chamber) and a mixed clientele (mostly dressed in black) at this gay club just off Piazza Venezia. There's no dancing – it's just a bar – but it's a good cruising spot.

Garbo (Map pp108–9; ☎ 06 583 20 782; Vicolo di Santa Margherita 1a) Rome's first (and not only) gay café/bar catering to couples rather than cruisers. The clientele is a mix of Italians and foreigners.

Goa (Map p99; ☎ 06 574 82 77; Via Libetta 13; ☼ Oct-May) Tuesday is 'Gorgeous Goa Gay' night. Women get their day with 'Venus Rising' on the last Sunday of the month.

Alpheus (Map p99; ☎ 06 574 7826; Via del Commercio 271b) It's a fair way from the centre, but this is where it happens for gays and lesbians on Friday night. Often has good jazz.

Casa Internazionale delle Donne (Map pp102–4; ☎ 06 684 01 720; www.casainternazionaledelledonne .org; Palazzo del Buon Pastore, Via della Lungara 19) This place, with its entrance at Via San Francesco di Sales 1a, is one of the few spaces available to lesbians in Rome. There's a café and a women-only restaurant, **Le Sorellastre**. Drop in for Sunday brunch at noon.

Jazz & Blues

Alexanderplatz (Map p99; ☎ 06 397 42 171; Via Ostia 9) Top international (particularly American) musicians and well-known Italian artists feature on the programme nightly. In July and

August the club moves to the grounds of the Renaissance Villa Celimontana (Map pp110–1) on Caelian Hill for **Villa Celimontana Jazz** (☎ 06 589 78 07) one of Rome's popular summer festivals.

Folkstudio (Map pp106–7; ☎ 06 487 10 630; Via Frangipane 42; ☼ 7pm-1am Tue-Sun) This place, near Via Cavour, is an institution in the Roman music scene and provides a stage for folk, jazz and world music as well as young artists just starting out.

Big Mama (Map pp108–9; ☎ 06 581 24 51; Via San Francesco a Ripa 18; ☼ 9pm-1am Wed-Sun) The 'home of the blues', although it also plays host to rock and jazz artists, both Italian and international.

Opera

Teatro dell'Opera (Map pp106–7; ☎ 06 481 60 28 706; www.opera.roma.it; Piazza Beniamino Gigli; ☼ box office inquiries 9am-2pm Mon-Fri) Rome's opera season starts in December and continues until June. Tickets are expensive: the cheapest upper balcony seats (not recommended for vertigo sufferers) start at around €22 and prices go up to €120. First-night performances cost more.

In summer, opera is performed outdoors, often at the Terme di Caracalla (p98).

Theatre

Italian theatre is often more melodramatic than dramatic. There are over 80 theatres in the city, many of them worth visiting as much for the architecture and decoration as for the production itself. Some performances are in English.

Teatro Argentina (Map pp104–5; ☎ 06 688 04 601; Largo di Torre Argentina 52) This state-funded theatre, the official home of the Teatro di Roma, stages major theatre and dance productions.

Teatro dell'Orologio (Map pp102–4; ☎ 06 683 08 735; Via dei Filippini 17a) Fringe theatre and works by contemporary Italian playwrights are staged here.

Teatro Valle (Map pp104–5; ☎ 06 688 03 794; Via del Teatro Valle 23a) This theatre shows English-language works translated into Italian plus some excellent international productions.

Off-Night Repertory Theater (Map pp106–7; ☎ 06 444 13 75; Arte del Teatro Studio, Via Urbana 107) An international theatre company that performs a mix of contemporary one-act plays and full-length dramas in English every Friday.

The Miracle Players (☎ 06 446 98 67; www.miracle players.org) This group performs classic English drama such as *Everyman* and *Julius Caesar*, usually in abridged form, near the Roman Forum and other atmospheric open-air locations.

SPECTATOR SPORTS
Football
If you want passion, you should not leave Rome without a trip to the *stadio* to watch one of the city's two soccer teams: AS Roma and Lazio. The Romanisti fans – *giallorossi* (yellow and red) – and the Laziali – *biancazzuri* (white and blue) – tackle, hug and kiss each other on alternate weekends between September and late May at the end of the aptly named Avenue of the Gladiators, in the **Stadio Olimpico** (Map p99; Foro Italico, Viale dei Gladiatori 2) to the north of the city centre. Games are usually held at 3pm on Sunday. Tickets range in price from €16 to €95 and can be bought at the Lottomatica (lottery centres), at the stadium box office, ticket agencies or at one of the many Roma or Lazio stores around the city: try **AS Roma Store** (Map pp102–4; ☎ 06 692 00 642; Piazza Colonna 360) or **Lazio Point** (Map pp106–7; ☎ 06 648 26 688; Via Farini 34).

Horse Riding
The Concorso Ippico – the International Horse Show, takes place every year at Piazza di Siena in the Villa Borghese gardens. See some of the world's top show jumpers in action.

SHOPPING
Shopping in Rome is fun, if exhausting. You don't even have to buy anything, just wander. It's a popular local pastime, particularly on Saturday, when traffic is banned to accommodate thousands of window shoppers who saunter down the three ancient Roman roads radiating from Piazza del Popolo (Map pp100–1) that constitute not only Rome's best outdoor museum but also its main shopping district. If it's designer clothes you're lusting after, then the area around Piazza di Spagna (Map pp102–4) will help to feed your fantasies. The top names in shoes and leather goods are there too, but for more affordable versions, Via del Corso (Map pp102–4) is the place to go. Via Nazionale (Map pp106–7) and surrounds are also good for affordable, fairly run of the mill clothing

– every second shop seems to have 'discount' leather jackets. Via del Governo Vecchio (Map pp104–5) has more off-beat clothes, and a few interesting second-hand clothes shops. If it's antiques that attract, wander down Via dei Coronari (Map pp104–5; near Piazza Navona), Via Giulia (Map pp104–5) and Via del Babuino (Map pp102–4). For jewellery there's a whole street that runs from the Ponte Sisto (Map pp102–4) to the area around Camp de'Fiori (Map pp104–5). If you can time your visit to coincide with the *saldi* (sales), you'll pick up some marvellous bargains. The winter sales run from early January to around mid-February and the summer sales from July to August.

Antique Photos & Prints
Alinari (Map pp102–4; ☎ 06 679 29 23; Via Alibert 16a) Photographic prints (mostly views of Rome) are reproduced from the archives of more than a million glass-plate negatives of 19th-century photographs by the famous Alinari brothers.

Nardecchia (Map pp104–5; ☎ 06 686 93 18; Piazza Navona 25) This Roman landmark is only marginally less famous than Bernini's Fontana dei Quattro Fiumi opposite. It sells antique prints, including 18th-century etchings of Rome by Giovanni Battista Piranesi, and less expensive 19th-century views of the city.

Clothing, Shoes & Leather Goods
The big designer names need no introduction; all are located around Via dei Condotti and the Spanish Steps. Good diffusion ranges include:

Artigianato del Cuoio (Map pp102–4; ☎ 06 67 84 435; 2nd fl, Via Belsiana 90) Bags, belts luggage – anything handmade and hand stitched to your own design in 24 hours.

Bruno Magli (Map pp102–4; ☎ 06 692 02 264; Via dei Condotti 6) Shoes and leather accessories.

Emporio Armani (Map pp102–4; ☎ 06 699 14 60; Via dei Condotti 77)

Fendi (Map pp102–4; ☎ 06 69 96 61; Via Borgognona 36-40)

Gucci (Map pp102–4; ☎ 06 67 90 405; Via Condotti 8) Shoes and leather accessories.

Il Calzalaio (Map pp104–5; Vicolo delle Volpe 14) Shoes and leather accessories.

L'antica Sartoria (Map pp104–5; ☎ 06 683 39 23; Piazza Mattei 13) For a made-to-measure outfit you'll need a month and €315 to €390 to spare for a fine suit (male or female).

Louis Big Shoes (Map pp102–4; ☎ 06 679 16 77; www.louisbigshoes.com; Via Cavour 309) Shoes and leather accessories for those podiatrically challenged.

MaxMara (Map pp102–4; ☎ 06 679 36 38; Via Frattina 28) Also at Via dei Condotti 17 & Via Nazionale 28.
Versace for women (Map pp102–4; ☎ 06 67 80 521; Via del Bocca di Leone 26/27); for men (Map pp102–4; ☎ 06 67 95 037; Via Borgognona 24)

Design & Homewares

Art'è (Map pp102–4; ☎ 06 683 39 07; Piazza Rondanini 32) Lamps, furnishings, pens, watches, kitchen utensils and appliances by Alessi.
C.U.C.I.N.A. (Map pp102–4; ☎ 06 679 12 75; Via Mario de' Fiori 65) The stainless-steel look has become ubiquitous, but good quality kitchenware can still be snapped up here.
House & Kitchen (Map pp102–4; ☎ 06 699 25 592; Corso Vittorio Emanuele II 20) Affordable style.
Leone Limentani (Map pp102–4; ☎ 06 683 07 000; Via Portico d'Ottavia 47) This warehouse-style shop has an unbelievable choice of kitchenware and tableware. High-priced fine porcelain and crystal sits alongside bargain basement items. It also stocks plenty of Alessi.
Spazio Sette (Map p104–5; ☎ 06 686 97 08; Via dei Barbieri 7) All the top names in modern design beautifully displayed in a former 17th-century cardinal's palace.

For Children

Bertè (Map pp104–5; ☎ 06 687 50 11; Piazza Navona) The patriarch of the family that runs this fabulous toy shop bears a striking resemblance to Pinocchio's Geppetto. So it's rather appropriate that the toys here include beautifully made wooden dolls and puppets, finely crafted scooters in wood and metal, and high-quality educational games.
Città del Sole (Map pp104–5; ☎ 06 687 54 04; Via della Scrofa 65) When only the best-quality educational and creative toys will do, this is the place for kids and adults alike.
Mel Giannino Stoppani (Map pp102–4; ☎ 06 699 41 045; Piazza dei Santissimi Apostoli 59-65) The best children's bookshop in Rome stocks mainly Italian books but one corner is devoted to French, Spanish, German and English titles.

Haberdashery & Fabric

Merceria Alfis (Map pp102–4; ☎ 06 688 01 970; Largo Ginnasi 6) High-quality wedding fabrics, needlepoint and embroidery threads, buttons etc.

Markets

Everyone flocks to the **flea market** (Map pp108–9; Piazza di Porta Portese) on Sunday morning. A mishmash of new and old, the market has all manner of incredible deals but you have to be prepared to drive a hard bargain. The market extends along the side streets parallel to Viale Trastevere. Be extremely aware of pickpockets.

The excellent **market** (Map pp110–11; Via Sannio; ⏱ to 1pm Mon-Sat), near Porta San Giovanni, sells new and second-hand clothes.

For prints, antiques and books, head for the **market** (Map pp102–4; Largo della Piazza Fontanella di Borghese; ⏱ mornings Mon-Sat).

Stationery, Office Goods, Art & Craft

Campo Marzio Penne (Map pp102–4; ☎ /fax 06 688 07 877; Via Campo Marzio 41) This charming little shop specialises in pens and ink as well as other related objects, perfect for unusual gifts
Ditta G Pozzi (www.poggi1825.it, Italian only) Via del Gesù 74-5 (Map pp102–4; ☎ 06 678 44 77); Via Pie di Marmo 38/41 (Map pp102–4) This fine-art supply shop, has been in business since 1825
Progetto Impresa (Map pp106–7; ☎ 06 488 01 39; Via Barberini 40) Stocks a range of attractive leather filofax holders, credit card wallets and leather briefcases as well the more usual stationery items.
Vertecchi (Map pp102–4; ☎ 06 6790155; www.ver tecchi.com; Via della Croce 70a & 38) Beautiful notebooks, pens, boxes, upmarket stationery goods and fine art and papers and materials.
Vertecchi (Map pp102–4; Via della Croce 38) Another branch of this stationery shop.

GETTING THERE & AWAY
Air

Rome's main airport is **Leonardo da Vinci** (FCO; ☎ 06 65 95 4471/6074, ☎ 06 54 6591; www .aeroportidiroma.com), more usually referred to as Fiumicino after the town nearby. The city's other airport is **Ciampino** (CIA; ☎ 06 79 49 4225), where many national and some international (including charter) flights arrive. See pp155–6 for details on getting to and from the airports.

Bus

The main **bus station** (Map p99) for buses to and from cities outside the Lazio region is on Piazzale Tiburtina, in front of Stazione Tiburtina. Take Metro Linea B from Stazione Termini to Tiburtina, or bus Nos 649 or 492 from the piazza in front of the station. Various bus lines run services to cities throughout Italy; all depart from the same area and the relevant ticket offices or agents are next to the bus terminus.

Cotral buses (☎ 800 15 00 08; www.cotralspa.it, Italian only) service the Lazio region and depart from numerous points throughout the city, depending on their destination. The company is linked with Rome's public transport system, which means that you can buy one Metrebus ticket that covers city buses, trams, metro and train lines, and regional buses and trains (see pp837–8). Ask for the *Brief Ticket Guide*, published by ATAC in English and Italian, available at the tourist information offices or the ATAC stand at Piazza dei Cinquecento.

Most buses to places outside the Lazio region leave from or around Piazza Tiburtina (Map p99). For information and to make bookings it's best to contact a travel agent (see p85).

Train

Almost all trains arrive at and depart from Stazione Termini (Map pp106–7). There are regular connections to all the major cities in Italy and Europe.

The **train information office** (7am-9.45pm) at Stazione Termini, where English is spoken is very helpful, though it's often crowded and you have to take a ticket and wait till your number is called. They will print out various train options for you, with fare prices. However, they cannot make reservations. These must be made outside at Sportello 8. If you speak Italian, you can **book by phone** (848 88 80 88; 7am-9pm), then pick up the ticket from the automatic machines in most stations.

If this is not going to be convenient, most travel agents with a TrenItalia sign in the window can do this for you. But better still, see the Trenitalia website (www.trenitalia.it), which has an English-language option and allows you to give details of where you want to go and when to find out all available train services and costs. You can also do this at the automatic ticket machines, where you can pay with cash, credit or ATM card.

An *orario* (timetable) of all trains can be bought at most newsstands in and around Stazione Termini for €4 and is particularly useful if you are making multiple train journeys. Remember to validate your train ticket in the yellow machines on the station platforms. If you don't, you may be forced to pay a fine on the train.

There are eight other train stations scattered throughout Rome. Some trains depart from or stop at the Stazione Ostiense (Map p99) and the Stazione Tiburtina (Map p99).

Car & Motorcycle

More than two thousand years of urban development and restrictions on traffic in the *centro storico* (historical centre) have made it very difficult for modern vehicles to reach the central tourist areas of Rome. If, however, you are determined to make the journey to Rome by car, you should expect some pretty hectic and chaotic driving experiences. You'll find plenty of one-way streets that are never going the way you want to go and you may, at times, think you will have to spend the rest of your trip circling around the city trying to find a place where you can legally park your vehicle.

Still game? Then to reach the centre, if you travelling are on the A1 highway coming from the north, take the exit marked Roma Nord. If you are coming from the south, take the Roma Est exit. After a few kilometres, both of these exits take you to the Grande Raccordo Anulare (GRA), the ring road around the city that links the highways and the *strade statali* (SS; state roads). The most important roads for the traveller are:

Via Cristofero Colombo To Ostia.

Via Pontina To Ostia.

Via Aurelia (S1) Starts at the Vatican and leaves the city to the northeast, following the Tyrrhenian coast to Pisa, Genoa and France.

Via Cassia (S2) Starts at the Ponte Milvio and heads northwest to Viterbo, Siena and Florence.

Via Flaminia (S3) Starts at the Ponte Milvio; goes northwest to Terni, Foligno and over the Apennines into Le Marche, ending on the Adriatic coast at Fano.

Via Salaria (S4) Heads north from near Porta Pia in central Rome to Rieti and into Marche, ending at Porto d'Ascoli on the Adriatic coast.

Via Tiburtina (S5) Links Rome with Tivoli and Pescara, on the coast of Abruzzo.

Via Casilina (S6) Heads southeast to Anagni and into Campania, terminating at Capua near Naples.

Via Appia Nuova (S7) The most famous of the consular roads, it heads south along the coast of Lazio, via Ciampino airport and the Castelli Romani and into Campania, then inland across the Apennines into Basilicata, through Potenza and Matera to Taranto in Puglia and finally on to Brindisi.

From the GRA you will also find the exit for the Autostrada Fiumicino for Leonardo da Vinci (Fiumicino) airport and the A24 highway to the Parco Nazionale d'Abruzzo and Pescara.

GETTING AROUND
To/From the Airport

Getting to and from the main airport, **Leonardo da Vinci** (commonly known as Fiumicino), about 30km southwest of the city centre, is quite straightforward (see following)

Getting to/from **Ciampino** airport, 15km southeast of the city centre, is not simple and is time consuming and uncomfortable by public transport (Cotral bus and metro) as buses run infrequently, finish early and do not connect well with the metro trains.

Several charter firms, such as Ryan Air and Easy Jet now charter their own buses to Ciampino, which leave from Via Magenta outside Satzione Termini two hours before each scheduled flight and from Ciampino soon after the arrival of each flight. You can buy tickets, which cost around €8, from the **Hotel Royal Santina** (Via Marsala 22), which is located opposite the bus stop, or at Ciampino airport.

Otherwise, to get to Rome take the Cotral bus (€1.30, buy a ticket from a *tabacchi* inside the airport) to the Metro A stop Anagnina (about 30 minutes), then take the metro (€0.77) to Stazione Termini. If you miss the bus and it's after 11pm, you'll have to take a taxi around €39 plus surcharges for luggage.

TRAIN

The *Leonardo Express*, the direct Fiumicino–Stazione Termini train (follow the signs to the train station from the airport arrivals hall), costs €8.80, which you buy from selected *tabacchi* – there's one (open 6am to 7.30pm Monday to Saturday) at the Via Giolitti entrance of the station. The train arrives at and leaves from platform Nos 25–29 at the Termini (a fair walk from the main concourse) and takes about 30 minutes. The first direct train leaves the airport for Termini at 6.37am, then trains run half-hourly until the last one at 11.37pm. From Termini to the airport, trains start at 5.51am and run half-hourly until the last train at 10.51pm.

Another train from Leonardo da Vinci (look for the train destination Orte or Fara Sabina) stops at Trastevere, Ostiense and Tiburtina stations, but NOT at Termini (€4.65). From the airport, trains run about every 20 minutes from 5.57am to 11.27pm, and from Tiburtina from 5.06am until

10.36pm. You should allow more time on Sundays and public holidays.

BUS

From midnight to 5am, an hourly bus runs from Stazione Tiburtina (accessible by bus No 42N from Piazza dei Cinquecento, in front of Termini) to Fiumicino airport (€4.65).

If you arrive at Ciampino airport, infrequent Cotral buses (operating from 5.45am to 10.30pm) will take you to the Anagnina Metro station, from where you can get to Stazione Termini.

CAR

If you have decided to brave the Roman traffic and hire a car (see p157). you'll need to follow the signs for Rome out of the Leonardo da Vinci airport complex and onto the autostrada that connects the airport to the city. Exit the autostrada at EUR, then follow the *centro* signs, or else ask directions, to reach Via Cristoforo Colombo, which will take you directly into the centre of Rome.

Ciampino airport is connected to Rome by Via Appia Nuova.

TAXI

You'll find plenty of people who want to offer you a ride. Official taxis leave from outside the arrivals hall at Fiumicino. They are white or yellow and you can be sure they have the blessing of the Rome City Council when you see the letters SPQR on their door. Make sure the meter is on and try to act cool and experienced at Roman taxi riding. Even when legitimate they are expensive: a taxi to the centre of Rome will cost from €36.15 (including an airport surcharge of €7.75, plus surcharges for luggage, at night and on public holidays).

Several private companies run limousine services which work out about the same price as a taxi but are usually a lot more comfortable. **Airport Connection Services** (☎ 06 338 32 21; www.airportconnection.it) has two deals – a shuttle service in a minivan to either airport for €25 per person (minimum two passengers) or a chauffeur driven Mercedes for €39.

Airport Shuttle (☎ 06 420 14 507; www.airportshuttle.it) offers transfers to/from Fiumicino in a minivan for €28.50 for one or two passengers, €34 for three, and €45.50 for four.

ROME & LAZIO

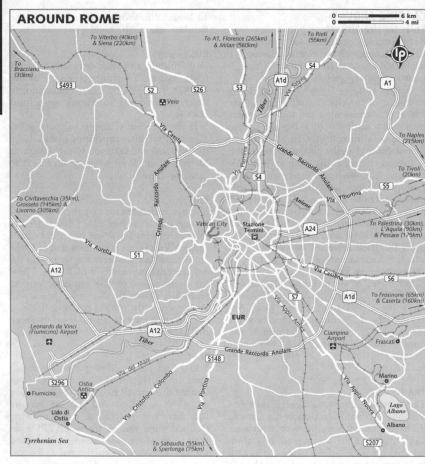

AROUND ROME

Each additional passenger costs €5.50. To/from Ciampino costs €39.50 for one to two people with €5.50 for each additional person. A 30% surcharge is added between 10pm and 7am.

Car & Motorcycle

Negotiating Roman traffic by car is difficult enough, but you may be taking your life in your hands if you ride a motorcycle or moped in the city. The rule in Rome is to look straight ahead to watch the vehicles in front and hope that the vehicles behind are watching you!

Most of the historic centre of Rome is closed to normal traffic. Police control some of the entrances to the centre, while other entrances have electronic gates. You are not allowed to drive to the centre of Rome from 6.30am to 6pm Monday to Friday and 2pm to 6pm Saturday, unless you are a resident or have special permission.

All 22 streets accessing the so-called 'Limited Traffic Zone' have been equipped with electronic-access detection devices. To avoid a fine, tourists wishing to drive to hotels in these areas should first contact the hotel management who will fax authorities with your number plate. For further information visit www.sta.roma.it (Italian only) or call ☎ 06 57 118 333 8am to 6pm Monday to Friday and 2pm to 6pm Saturday.

A parking system operates around the periphery of Rome's city centre whereby spaces are denoted by a blue line in most areas including the Lungotevere (the roads beside the Tiber; Map pp108–9) and near Stazione Termini (Map pp106–7). You'll need small change to get tickets from machines, otherwise scratch tickets are available from *tabacchi*.

Traffic police are getting very tough on illegally parked cars. At best you'll get a heavy fine (around €105), at worst a wheel clamp or your car towed away. In the event that your car goes missing after it was parked illegally, always check first with the **traffic police** (☎ 06 67 69 11). You will have to pay about €95 to get it back, plus a hefty fine.

The major parking area closest to the centre is at the Villa Borghese; entry is from Piazzale Brasile at the top of Via Vittorio Veneto (Map pp100–1). There is also a supervised car park at Stazione Termini (Map pp106–7). Other car parks are at Piazzale dei Partigiani, just outside Stazione Ostiense (Map p99) and at Stazione Tiburtina (Map p99), from where you can also catch the metro into the centre.

CAR RENTAL

The major rental companies have representatives in Rome.

Avis (24-hr booking ☎ 800 86 30 63; www.avis.com) Ciampino Airport (Map p99; ☎ 06 793 40 195); Leonardo da Vinci Airport (Map p99; ☎ 06 650 11 531); Via Sardegna 38a (☎ 06 420 10282)

Europcar (central booking ☎ 800 014410; www .europcar.com) Leonardo da Vinci Airport (Map p99; ☎ 06 650 10 287); Ciampino Airport (Map p99; ☎ 06 793 40 387); Stazione Termini (Map pp106–7; ☎ 06 488 28 54)

Maggiore National (central booking ☎ 848 86 70 67; www.maggiore.it, Italian only) Leonardo da Vinci Airport (Map p99; ☎ 06 650 10 678); Ciampino Airport (Map p99; ☎ 06 79 340 368); Stazione Termini (Map pp106–7; ☎ 06 488 00 49)

Hertz (www.hertz.com) Leonardo da Vinci Airport (Map p99; ☎ 06 592 27 42); Ciampino Airport (Map p99; ☎ 06 650 10256); Stazione Termini (Map pp106–7; ☎ 06 4740389)

Sixt (central booking ☎ 800 90 06 66, ☎ 06 650 04 751; www.e-sixt.com)

Allow plenty of time if you're dropping off hire cars at Leonardo da Vinci airport or at a station. There are usually dedicated *autonoleggio* (parking areas for hire cars) but these aren't always easy to find.

MOTORCYCLE & BICYCLE RENTAL

If you want to do as the Romans do, of course you'll want to scoot around on a motor scooter. But you'll really have to do as the Romans do if you want to stay alive. If you think you can handle your vehicle among all the Scooterone traffic, then there are plenty of places around town where you can rent one. If you'd prefer to cycle around the city, be careful, Romans are not used to seeing bicycles on the roads; you may be wise to venture forth on a Sunday, when much of central Rome is closed to traffic. However, the Rome City Council has published a useful brochure, *Exploring By Bike*, available from the Tourist Information kiosks, that offers some suggestions for cycling around Rome. On Sundays you can hire bikes at Via Appia Antica, when the ancient road is closed to traffic and cycle around the catacombs and ancient Roman ruins.

Here are some places where you can hire two-wheeled vehicles:

Appia Antica (Map p99; ☎ 06 512 63 14; ✦ 9.30am-5pm)

Bici e Baci (Map pp106–7; ☎ 06 482 84 43; Via del Viminale 5; scooters per day from €18.50, bicycles/500cc motorbikes per day €7.50/93) Located near Piazza della Repubblica.

Happy Rent (Map pp106–7; ☎ 06 481 81 85; Via Farini 3; bicycles per hr/week €2.60/62, 600cc motorcycles per day around €103, 50cc-125cc scooters & mopeds €31-68) Also rents cars and minivans. Baby seats are available for both cars and bicycles.

I Bike (Map pp100–1; ☎ 06 322 52 40; Villa Borghese underground carpark, 3rd sector, Via Vittorio Veneto 156; ✦ 9am-7pm Mon-Sun; scooters per day from €60, bicycles €10-18)

Scoot Along (Map pp106–7; ☎ 06 678 02 06; Via Cavour 302; scooters per day €30-40)

Treno e Scooter Rent (Map pp106–7; ☎ 06 489 05 823; Stazione Termini; scooters per day from €30, bicycles €5.50-9.50)

Public Transport

Travel on Rome's buses, trams, metro and suburban railways is part of the same system, and the same **Metrebus** (www.metrebus.it) ticket – also known as *biglietto integrato a tempo* (BIT) – is valid for all modes of transport. You can buy tickets at *tabacchi*, newsstands and from vending machines at main bus stops. Single tickets cost €0.75 for 75 minutes. Daily tickets cost €3.10, weekly

ROME & LAZIO

tickets €12.40; children up to 1m tall travel free. Tickets must be purchased before you get on the bus or train and then validated in the machine once on the bus or tram (at the entrance gates for the Metro). You risk a €52 fine if you're caught without a valid ticket – being an 'ignorant' tourist won't get you off the hook. For information on public transport in Rome and Lazio (ATAC-Cotral and Trenitalia) call ☎ 800 431 784 (8am to 6pm Monday to Friday)

BUS & TRAM

ATAC (☎ 800 43 17 84; www.atac.roma.it) is the city's public transport company. Many of the main bus routes terminate in Piazza dei Cinquecento at Stazione Termini (Map pp106–7) where there's an information booth (on the stand in the centre of the piazza). Largo di Torre Argentina, Piazza Venezia and Piazza San Silvestro are other hubs. Buses generally run from about 6am until midnight, with limited services throughout the night on some routes. Pick up a free transport map from the ATAC information booth at Termini or from any tourist information booth. Useful routes are listed below.

No 40 Stazione Termini, Via Nazionale, Piazza Nazionale, Piazza Venezia, Largo Argentina, Chiesa Nuova, Piazza Pia (for Castel St Angelo) and St Peter's (Express route with fewer stops than No 64).

No 64 Stazione Termini to St Peter's. It takes the same route as above but is more crowded and has more stops.

H Stazione Termini, Via Nazionale, Piazza Venezia, Largo Argentina, Ponte Garibaldi, Viale Trastevere and into the western suburbs.

No 8 (tram) Largo Argentina, Trastevere, Stazione Trastevere and Monteverde Nuovo.

No 492 Stazione Tiburtina, San Lorenzo, Stazione Termini, Piazza Barberini, Piazza Venezia, Corso Rinascimento, Piazza Cavour, Piazza Risorgimento and Cipro-Vatican Museums (Metro Linea A).

No 175 Stazione Termini, Piazza Barberini, Via del Corso, Teatro di Marcello, Aventino and Stazione Ostiense.

No 23 Piazzale Clodio, Piazza Risorgimento, Ponte Vittorio Emanuele II, Lungotevere, Ponte Garibaldi, Lungotevere, Via Marmorata (Testaccio), Piazzale Ostiense and Basilica di San Paolo.

No 170 Stazione Termini, Via Nazionale, Piazza Venezia, Via del Teatro Marcello and Bocca della Verità (then south to Testaccio and EUR, ending at Piazzale dell'Agricoltura).

No 714 Stazione Termini, Piazza Santa Maria Maggiore, Piazza San Giovanni in Laterano and Viale delle Terme di Caracalla (then south to EUR, ending at Piazzale P L Nervi).

No 660 Largo Colli Albani, Via Appia Nuova and Via Appia Antica (near Tomba di Cecilia Metella).

No 910 Stazione Termini, Piazza della Repubblica, Via Piemonte, Via Pincians (Villa Borghese), Piazza Euclide, Palazzetto dello Sport and Piazza Mancini.

No 590 Follows the route of Metro Linea A and has special facilities for disabled passengers.

ELECTRIC BUSES

In an effort to minimise pollution in the small backstreets of the historic centre, the city has established several electric bus lines to navigate alleyways barely wide enough for a Vespa.

116 Via Vittorio Veneto, Piazza Barberini, Piazza di Spagna, Corso Rinascimento, Campo de' Fiori, Via Farnese, Via Monserrato, Via Giulia, Terminal Gianicolo, Campo de' Fiori, Corso Rinascimento, Piazza della Rotonda, Piazza Colonna, Piazza Barberini and Via Vittorio Veneto.

117 Piazza San Giovanni in Laterano, Piazza del Colosseo, Via dei Serpenti, Largo Tritonem, Piazza di Spagna, Piazza del Popolo, Via del Corso, Piazza Venezia, Piazza del Colosseo, Via Labicana and Piazza San Giovanni in Laterano. Weekdays only.

119 Piazza del Popolo, Via del Corso, Largo Goldoni, Piazza Venezia, Via del Tritone, Piazza Barberini, Via Veneto, Piazza Barberini, Piazza di Spagna, Via del Babuino and Piazza del Popolo (on Saturday and Sunday it ends at Via Vittorio Veneto).

METRO & TRAIN

Rome's metro system is very useful and quite safe as long as you are alert. The Metropolitana (Metro) has two lines: Linea A and Linea B. Both pass through Stazione Termini and operate 5.30am to 11.30pm (one hour later on Saturday).

All the metro stations on line B have facilities for the disabled except Circo Massimo, Colosseo and Cavour (direction Laurentina). There are trains from 5.30am until 10.30pm every day (12.30am Saturday), which run approximately every five to 10 minutes.

In addition to the Metro, Rome has an overground rail network. It is useful only if you are heading out of town to the Castelli Romani, the beaches at Lido di Ostia or the ruins at Ostia Antica (see p161).

NIGHT BUSES

There are 23 night bus lines. The main terminal stations are Termini (Piazza dei Cinquecento) and Piazza Venezia. From these two piazzas buses leave every 30 minutes. You can recognise bus stop for the night buses by signs with a owl on the top and N is written after number.

Here is a list of the most useful routes and their major stops:

78N Piazzale Clodio, Piazzale Flaminio, Piazza Cavour, Corso Rinascimento, Via delle Botteghe Oscure (Largo di Torre Argentina), Piazza Venezia, Via Nazionale and Stazione Termini.

40N Same route as metro Linea B which runs every 30 minutes. Good connection to Testaccio (use the stop at Piramide, in Piazzale Ostiense) and Termini; there's also a night train at Tiburtina Station.

55N Same route as Metro Linea A. It runs every 30 minutes.

29N Piramide (Piazzale Ostiense), Ponte Vittorio Emanuele II, Piazza Risorgimento, Viale Belle Arti, Piazza Ungheria, Viale Regina Margherita, Piazza Porta Maggiore, Piazza Porta San Giovanni, Piazza Colosseo and Piramide

80N Same route as train Rome – to Ostia Lido.

Taxi

Taxi drivers all over the world have a reputation for trying to fleece foreigners and the Romans always like to play in the top league. Make sure you understand the rules of the game before you throw your bags, and yourself, into the fray.

Make sure your taxi is licensed and metered, and always go with the metered fare, never an arranged price. Daytime trips within the centre of Rome can cost anywhere from €5 to €15. Any more and you can be pretty certain you're being taken for a ride.

If you have a dispute over a fare, you can take down the driver's name and licence number (written on a metal plaque on the inside of the rear door of the cab) and call his taxi company, the number of which will be on the outside of the driver's door.

Away from the airport, it's not always easy to find a cab. You cannot hail them in the street: they have to operate out of special taxi stands throughout the city. In the *centro storico* you can find these at: Largo Argentina, the Pantheon, Corso del Rinascimento and Piazza Navona, Piazza di Spagna, Lorgo Goldoni, Piazza del Popolo, Piazza Venezia, the Colosseum, at Piazza GG Belli in Trastevere and near the Vatican at Piazza del Pio XII and Piazza Risorgimento. You can also call one of the many **Radio Taxi companies** (☎ 06 35 70, ☎ 06 66 45, ☎ 06 88 22, ☎ 06 41 57, ☎ 06 49 94, ☎ 06 55 51). If you can hear and understand each other

over the roar of traffic, an operator will contact the nearest taxi to you and then tell you the name and number and how long it will take to reach you. The driver will turn on the meter immediately and you will pay the cost of travel to reach you.

LAZIO

A tour of Etruria, the ancient land of the Etruscans (which extended into northern Lazio), is highly recommended. Visits to the tombs and museums at Cerveteri and Tarquinia provide a fascinating insight into Etruscan civilisation. The ruins of Villa Adriana (Hadrian's Villa), near Tivoli, and of the ancient Roman port at Ostia Antica, are both easily accessible from Rome, as is the medieval town of Viterbo, north of the capital. In summer, tired and overheated tourists can head for the lakes north of Rome, which are somewhat preferable to the polluted beaches near the city, or head south to the relatively clean and sandy beaches of Sabaudia or Sperlonga.

There are some hill-top towns to the southeast of Rome that are worth visiting, such as Anagni (which has remarkable frescoes in its Romanesque cathedral), Alatri and those included in the Castelli Romani (see p169) in the hills just past Rome's outskirts. Those interested in Italy's involvement in WWII might want to visit Monte Cassino, the scene of a major battle during the last stages of the war.

If you have your own transport, try to avoid day trips out of Rome on Sunday during the summer. On your return in the evening, you are likely to find yourself in traffic jams extending for many kilometres, including on the autostrada.

The Provincia di Roma publishes a useful guide to ecological tours, *From Green*

CHEAP BUS & TRAIN TICKETS

If you are travelling around Lazio by Cotral bus and trains, check out the daily BIRG tickets, which allow unlimited use of city and regional transport, including the metro in Rome. The cost depends on the distance travelled but ranges from around €4.50 to €10. Tickets are available from *tabbachi*.

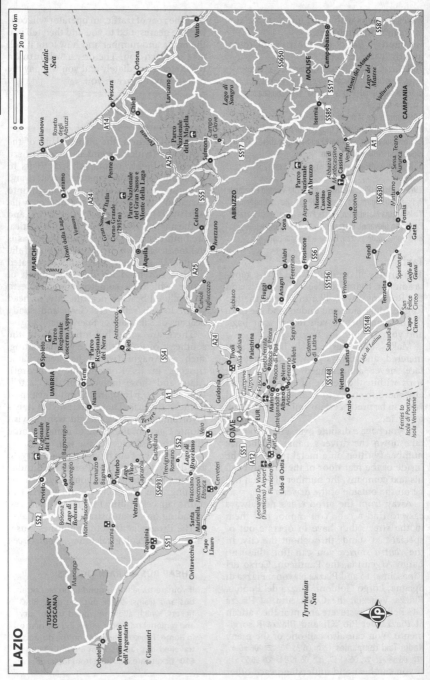

LAZIO

0   40 km
0   20 ml

to Green, which covers most of the areas mentioned in this section.

OSTIA ANTICA

The Romans founded this port city at the mouth of the River Tiber in the 4th century BC and it became a strategically important centre for defence and trade. It was populated by merchants, sailors and slaves, and the ruins of the city provide a fascinating contrast to the ruins at Pompeii, which was a resort town for the wealthy classes. Barbarian invasions and the outbreak of malaria led to the city's eventual abandonment, and it slowly became buried – up to 2nd-floor level – under river silt, which explains its excellent state of preservation. Pope Gregory IV re-established the town in the 9th century AD.

Information about the town and ruins is available from the Rome Tourism Board office in Rome (see p85).

There is a good **café/restaurant** within the complex, but it's also an atmospheric spot for a picnic.

Sights

The **ruins** (☎ 06 563 58 099; Viale dei Romagnoli 717; admission €4.20; ⏰ 9am-7pm Tue-Sun Feb-Oct, 9am-5pm Tue-Sun Nov-Mar) are quite spread out and you will need a few hours to see them all.

The clearly discernible ruins of restaurants, laundries, shops, houses and public meeting places give a good impression of everyday life in a working Roman town. The main thoroughfare, the **Decumanus Maximus**, runs over 1km from the city's entrance (the Porta Romana) to the Porta Marina, which originally led to the sea. Behind the restored **theatre**, built by Agrippa and later enlarged to hold 3000 people, is the **Piazzale delle Corporazioni**, the offices of Ostia's merchant guilds, which display well-preserved mosaics depicting the different interests of each business.

The 2nd-century **Casa di Diana** is a pristine example of ancient Rome's high-density housing, built when space was at a premium. Nearby the **Thermopolium** bears a striking resemblance to a modern bar.

Ostia once had several baths complexes, including the **Terme di Foro**, which were also equipped with a roomful of stone toilets (the *forica*) which still remain pretty much intact.

Continue along the Via dei Dipinti to reach the **museum**, which houses statuary and sarcophagi excavated on site.

Getting There & Away

From Rome, take the Metro Linea B to Piramide or Magliana, then the Ostia Lido train from Stazione Porta San Paolo (next to the Metro station). Trains leave about every 30 minutes and the trip takes approximately 30 minutes. It is covered by the standard BIT tickets (see pp158–9).

The ruins are also easy to reach by car from Rome. Take the Via del Mare, a fast superstrada (superhighway), which runs parallel to the Via Ostiense.

TIVOLI

Set on a hill by the Aniene river, Tivoli was a resort town of the Romans and became popular as a summer playground for the rich during the Renaissance. While the majority of tourists are attracted by the terraced gardens and fountains of the Villa d'Este, the ruins of the spectacular Villa Adriana, built by the Roman Emperor Hadrian, are far more interesting.

The **tourist office** (☎ 0774 31 12 49; Largo Garibaldi; ⏰ 8.30am-2.30pm Tue-Sat, 3-6pm Tue-Thu) is near the Cotral bus stop.

Sights
VILLA ADRIANA

Emperor Hadrian's summer residence, **Villa Adriana** (☎ 0774 53 02 03; admission €6.50; ⏰ 9am-1hr before sunset) was built between AD 118 and 134 and was one of the largest and most sumptuous villas in the Roman Empire. A model near the entrance gives you some idea of the scale of the massive complex, which you'll need several hours to explore.

Hadrian travelled widely and was a keen architect, and parts of the villa were inspired by buildings he had seen around the world. The massive **Pecile**, through which you enter, was a reproduction of a building in Athens, and the **Canopo** is a copy of the sanctuary of Serapis near Alexandria, with a long canal of water, originally surrounded by Egyptian statues, representing the Nile.

Highlights of the excavations include the fish pond encircled by an underground gallery where Hadrian took his summer walks, and the emperor's private retreat, the **Teatro Marittimo**, on an island which could be reached only by a retractable bridge, in an artificial pool. There are also nymphaeums, temples and barracks, and a museum displaying the latest discoveries from ongoing excavations. Archaeologists have found features such as a heated bench with steam pipes under the sand and a network of subterranean service passages for horses and carts.

VILLA D'ESTE
There's a sense of faded splendour about **Villa d'Este** (☎ 0774 31 20 70; Piazza Trento; admission €6.50; ☼ 8.30am-6.45pm Tue-Sun Apr-Sep, 8.30am-4pm Tue-Sun Oct-Mar). This former Benedictine convent was transformed in 1550 by Lucrezia Borgia's son, Ippolito d'Este, into a sumptuous pleasure palace with a breathtaking formal garden full of elaborate fountains and pools. From 1865 to 1886 the villa was home to Franz Liszt and inspired his composition Fountains of the Villa d'Este.

The Mannerist frescoes in the villa are worth a fleeting glance but it's the garden you come for – terraces with water-spouting grotesque heads, shady pathways and spectacular fountains powered solely by gravitational force. One fountain once played the organ, another imitated the call of birds. Don't miss the Rometta fountain, which has reproductions of the landmarks of Rome.

Getting There & Away
Tivoli is 30km east of Rome and is accessible by Cotral bus from outside the Ponte Mammolo station on Metro Linea B. Buses depart at least every 20 minutes, stopping at Villa Adriana, about 1km from Tivoli, along the way; the trip takes about one hour. Local bus No 4 goes to Villa Adriana from Tivoli's Piazza Garibaldi.

The fastest route by car is on the Rome–L'Aquila autostrada (A24).

ETRUSCAN SITES
Lazio has several important Etruscan archaeological sites, most within easy reach of Rome by car or public transport. These include Tarquinia, Cerveteri, Veio and Tuscania (four of the major city-states in the Etruscan League).

If you have the time, a few days spent touring at least Tarquinia and Cerveteri, combined with visits to their museums (and the Museo Nazionale Etrusco di Villa Giulia in Rome – see p121), should constitute one of your most fascinating experiences in Italy. A useful guidebook to the area, The Etruscans, is published by the Istituto Geografico de Agostini and has a map. If you really want to lose yourself in a poetic journey, read DH Lawrence's 'Etruscan Places' in DH Lawrence and Italy (Penguin).

Cerveteri
Cerveteri, ancient Caere, was one of the most important commercial centres in the Mediterranean from the 7th to the 5th century BC. In 358 BC, the city was annexed to Rome and the inhabitants granted Roman citizenship. This colonisation of the city (as of the other cities in the Etruscan league in the same period) resulted in the absorption of the Etruscan culture into Roman culture and its eventual disappearance. After the fall of the Roman Empire, the spread of malaria and repeated Saracen invasions caused further decline. In the 13th century there was a mass exodus from the city to the nearby town of Ceri, further inland and Caere became Caere Vetus ('Old Caere'), from which its current name derives. The first half of the 19th century saw the first tentative archaeological explorations in the area and in 1911 systematic excavations began in earnest.

The main attraction here is the atmospheric **Necropoli di Banditaccia** (Banditaccia Necropolis; ☎ 06 994 00 01; Via del Necropoli; admission €4.20; ☼ 9am-7pm Tue-Sun summer, 9am-4pm Tue-Sun winter) and its remarkable *tumoli* (mounds of earth with carved stone bases) in which the Etruscans entombed their dead. The *tumoli* are laid out in the form of a town, with streets, squares and terraces of 'houses'. The best example is the 4th-century-BC **Tomba dei Rilievi**, decorated with painted reliefs of cooking implements and other household items.

Treasures taken from the tombs can be seen in the Vatican Museums (pp117–18) and Villa Giulia (p121) in Rome, and also at the **Museo Nazionale di Cerveteri** (☎ 06 994 13 54; Piazza Santa Maria; admission free; ☼ 9am-7pm Tue-Sun) in Cerveteri town centre, which has an interesting display of pottery and sarcophagi.

To get to the main necropolis area, take the (infrequent) local bus from the main square. Otherwise it is a pleasant 2km walk west from the town. There is a **tourist office** (☎ 06 995 51 971; Piazza Risorgimento 19).

Many Romans make the trip to Cerveteri just to eat at the **Antica Locanda Le Ginestre** (☎ 06 994 06 72; Piazza Santa Maria 5), near the museum. The *panzerotti in salsa* d'ortiche (stuffed pasta parcels in a creamy, herby sauce) are especially good, and there's a nice outdoor terrace.

Cerveteri is easily accessible from Rome by Cotral bus (75 minutes, every half hour) from outside the Lepanto stop on Metro Linea A. Buy a regional ticket (BIRG) for €4.50 covering the return bus journey, public transport in Cerveteri and the metro and buses in Rome. By car take either Via Aurelia (S1) or the Civitavecchia autostrada (A12) and exit at the Cerceteri-Ladispoli exit. The journey takes approximately 40 minutes.

Tarquinia

Believed to have been founded in the 12th century BC, and home of the Tarquin kings who ruled Rome before the creation of the Roman Republic, Tarquinia was an important economic and political centre of the Etruscan League. The town has a small medieval centre with a good Etruscan museum but the major attractions here are the painted tombs of the burial grounds.

ORIENTATION & INFORMATION

By car or bus you arrive at the Barriera San Giusto, just outside the main entrance to the town (see Getting There & Away, right). The **tourist information office** (☎ 0766 85 63 84; info@tarquinia@apt.it; Piazza Cavour 1; ☺ 8am-2pm Mon-Sat) is on your left as you walk through the medieval ramparts.

It's a long day-trip from Rome to Tarquinia; if you prefer to stay overnight in the medieval town, it is advisable to book accommodation (see right).

SIGHTS

The 15th-century Palazzo Vitelleschi houses the **Museo Nazionale Tarquiniese** (☎ 0766 85 60 36; Piazza Cavour; admission incl necropolis €6.20; ☺ 9am-7pm Tue-Sun), a significant collection of Etruscan treasures, including frescoes removed from the tombs. There is a beautiful terracotta frieze of winged horses, taken from the Ara della Regina temple. Numerous sarcophagi found in the tombs are also on display.

The famous painted tombs are at the **necropolis** (☎ 0766 85 63 08; admission incl Museo Nazionale Tarquiniese €6.20; ☺ 9am-1hr before sunset Tue-Sun), a 15- to 20-minute walk away (get directions from the museum). Almost 6000 tombs have been excavated, of which 60 are painted, but only a handful are open to the public. Excavation of the tombs started in the 15th century and continues today. Unfortunately, exposure to air and human interference has led to serious deterioration in many tombs and they are now enclosed and maintained at constant temperatures. The painted tombs can be seen only through glass partitions.

If you have time, wander through the pleasant medieval town of Tarquinia, where there are several **churches** worth a look.

If you have a car, you can get to the remains of the Etruscan acropolis of **Tarxuna**, on the crest of Civita Hill nearby. There is little evidence of the ancient city, apart from a few limestone blocks that once formed part of the city walls, since the Etruscans generally used wood to build their temples and houses.

However, a large temple, the **Ara della Regina**, has been excavated.

SLEEPING & EATING

There are no budget options in the old town and it can be difficult to find a room if you don't book in advance.

Tuscia Tirrenica (☎ 0766 86 42 94; tuscia@tin.it; Viale delle Neriedi; ☺ May-Sep; 🐾) This camp site, 5km from the medieval town, is by the sea at Tarquinia Lido. It has a restaurant and is well equipped for various activities.

Hotel San Marco (☎ 0766 84 22 34; Piazza Cavour 10; s/d €52/67) This hotel has pleasant rooms and is in the medieval section of town, near the museum.

Hotel all'Olivo (☎ 0766 85 73 18; info@hotel -allolivo.it; Via Togliatti 13/15; s/d with breakfast to €52/78) In the newer part of town, Hotel all'Olivo is a 10-minute walk downhill from the medieval centre.

There are few places to eat in Tarquinia, but for a good, cheap meal go to **Trattoria Arcadia** (Via Mazzini 6) or **Cucina Casareccia** (Via Mazzini 5).

GETTING THERE & AWAY

Cotral buses leave approximately every hour for Tarquinia from outside the Lepanto stop on Metro Linea A, arriving at Tarquinia at the Barriera San Giusto, a short distance from the tourist office.

By car, take the autostrada for Civitavecchia and then the Via Aurelia (SS1). Tarquinia is about 90km northwest of Rome.

CIVITAVECCHIA

There is little to recommend this busy port and industrial centre to tourists, other than the fact that it is the main point of departure for the daily ferries to Sardinia.

Established by Emperor Trajan in AD 106 as the port town of Centumcellae, it was later conquered by the Saracens, but regained importance as a papal stronghold in the 16th century. The medieval town was almost completely destroyed by bombing during WWII. In 1995, the town hit the headlines when a 43cm-high statue of the Madonna, located in the private garden of a local family (but now in Sant'Agostino church), started crying tears of blood. Tests revealed the tears were in fact human blood and the statue continues to attract crowds of pilgrims, although the Vatican is yet to rule on the authenticity of the miracle.

Orientation & Information

The port is a short walk from the train station. As you leave the station, turn right into Viale Garibaldi and follow it along the seafront.

Getting There & Away

Cotral buses from Rome to Civitavecchia leave from outside the Lepanto station on Metro Linea A about every 40 minutes.

Civitavecchia is on the main train line between Rome (1½ hours) and Genoa (2½ hours).

By car, it is easily reached from Rome on the A12. If arriving from Sardinia with your car, simply follow the A12 signs from Civitavecchia port to reach the autostrada for Rome.

FERRIES TO/FROM SARDINIA

Tirrenia operates ferries to Olbia (eight hours), Arbatax (10 hours) and Cagliari (14 to 17 hours). Departure times and prices change annually and it is best to check with a travel agency or with **Tirrenia** (☎ 199 12 31 99; www.tirrenia.it) for up-to-date information

The company operates fast boats (in summer only) from Civitavecchia to Olbia and from Fiumicino to Golfo Aranci (about 20km north of Olbia and accessible by bus or train) in Sardinia. They take only 3½ to four hours but are considerably more expensive than the slower ferries. Tickets can be purchased at travel agencies, including CIT, and at the Stazione Marittima in Civitavecchia. In high season it is advisable to book well in advance.

Trenitalia (previously Ferrovie dello Stato or FS) also runs two daily ferries to Sardinia, docking at Golfo Aranci; the fare is only €13 if you are prepared to stand. The downside is that you cannot book in advance and availability cannot be guaranteed. Go to the port at Civitavecchia and try your luck.

VITERBO
pop 60,000

Founded by the Etruscans and eventually taken over by Rome, Viterbo developed into an important medieval centre, and in the 13th century became the residence of the popes.

Papal elections were held in the town's Gothic Palazzo Papale and stories abound about the antics of impatient townspeople anxious for a decision. In 1271, when the college of cardinals had failed to elect a new pope after three years of deliberation, the Viterbesi locked them in a turreted hall of the *palazzo*, removed its roof and put the cardinals on a starvation diet. Only then did they manage to elect Gregory X.

Although badly damaged by bombing during WWII, Viterbo remains Lazio's best-preserved medieval town and is a pleasant base for exploring northern Lazio. For travellers with less time, Viterbo is an easy day trip from Rome.

Apart from its historical appeal, Viterbo is famous for its therapeutic hot springs. The best known is the sulphurous Bulicame pool, mentioned by Dante in his Divine Comedy.

Orientation

As is the case with most historic centres in Italy, the town of Viterbo is neatly divided between newer and older sections. Hotels are in the newer part of town; you must walk south and cross the Piazza del

Plebiscito, with its *palazzi*, before reaching medieval Viterbo and the real reason for your visit. There are train stations north (Stazione Porta Fiorentina) and southeast (Stazione Porta Romana) of the town centre; both are just outside the town walls. The intercity bus station is somewhat inconveniently located at Riello, a few kilometres out of town.

Information

Tourist Information (☎ 0761 30 47 95; infoviterbo@ apt.viterbo.it; Piazza San Carluccio; ⊗ 9am-1pm Mon-Sat) In the medieval quarter of Viterbo.

Post Office (Via F Ascenzi) Off Piazza del Plebiscito.

Province of Viterbo Tourist Information (☎ 0761 29 10 03; www.apt.viterbo.it; Piazza dell'Oratorio 2)

Telecom Office (Via Cavour 28)

Sights

PIAZZA DEL PLEBISCITO

The piazza is enclosed by 15th- and 16th-century palaces, the most imposing of which is the **Palazzo dei Priori** (Piazza del Plebiscito; admission free; ⊗ 9am-1pm & 2-7pm), with an elegant 17th-century fountain in its courtyard. Many rooms are decorated with frescoes, notably the Sala Reggia, which is decorated with a late-Renaissance fresco depicting the myths and history of Viterbo.

CATHEDRAL & THE PALAZZO PAPALE

The 12th-century **cathedral** (Cattedrale di San Lorenzo; ☎ 0761 32 54 62; Piazza San Lorenzo; admission incl Sala del Conclave in Palazzo Papale €2.60; ⊗ 9am-12.30pm & 3.30-6pm) was rebuilt in the 14th century to a Gothic design, although the interior has just been restored to its original Romanesque simplicity.

Also on the piazza is the **Palazzo Papale** (⊗ 9am-12.30pm & 3.30-6pm), built in the 13th century with the aim of enticing the popes away from Rome. Its beautiful, graceful *loggia* (colonnade) is in the early Gothic style. The part facing the valley collapsed in the 14th century but the bases of some of the columns remain. The hall, the **Sala del Conclave**, in which papal conclaves were held, is at the top of the steps. Admission is included with your ticket to the cathedral museum.

CHIESA DI SANTA MARIA NUOVA

This Romanesque **church** (Piazza Santa Maria Nuova) was restored to its original form after bomb damage in WWII. The cloisters, which are believed to date from an earlier period, are worth a visit.

MEDIEVAL QUARTER

Via San Pellegrino takes you through the medieval quarter into **Piazza San Pellegrino**. The extremely well-preserved buildings that enclose this tiny piazza comprise the finest group of medieval buildings in Italy.

OTHER SIGHTS

Built in the early 13th century, the **Fontana Grande** (Piazza Fontana Grande) is the oldest and largest of Viterbo's Gothic fountains.

At the old northern entrance to the town is the **Chiesa di San Francesco** (Piazza San Francesco; admission free; ⊗ 8am-noon & 3.30-7pm), a Gothic building that was restored after suffering serious bomb damage during WWII. The church contains the tombs of two popes: Clement IV (died 1268) and Adrian V (died 1276) – both are lavishly decorated, notably that of Adrian, which features Cosmati work.

There's no shortage of museums in town. The **Museo della Macchina di Santa Rosa** (☎ 0761 34 51 57; Via San Pellegrino; admission €1.05; ⊗ 10am-1pm & 4-8pm Wed-Sun) documents the history of the festival that takes place on 3 September each year, when the Viterbesi parade a 30m-high tower around the town.

The **Museo Civico** (☎ 0761 34 82 75; Piazza Crispi; admission €3.10; ⊗ 9am-7pm Tue-Sun) is housed in the restored convent of the church of Santa Maria della Verità, just outside the Porta della Verità, on the eastern side of town. Among the works in the museum are Iron age Etruscan artefacts, a lovely *Pietà* by Sebastiano del Piombo and a Roman sarcophagus which is said to be the tomb of Galiana, a beautiful and virtuous woman murdered by a Roman baron after she refused his advances.

Sleeping & Eating

Hotel Roma (☎ 0761 22 72 74; fax 0761 30 55 07; Via della Cava 26; s/d €40/57, with bathroom €41/60; **P**) Just off Piazza della Rocca, Hotel Roma offers one-step-up from budget accommodation in pleasant rooms. Prices include breakfast; there's a restaurant and free parking.

Hotel Tuscia (☎ 0761 34 44 00; fax 0761 34 59 76; Via Cairoli 41; s/d up to €55/86) For more comfortable

ROME & LAZIO

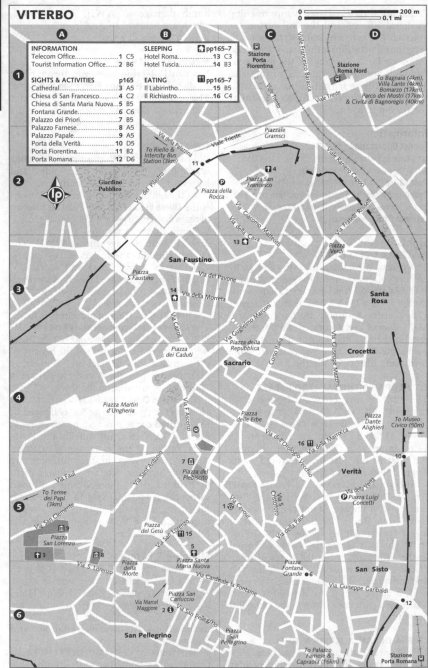

VITERBO

0 — 200 m
0 — 0.1 mi

A	**B**	**C**	**D**

INFORMATION
Telecom Office.....................1 C5
Tourist Information Office......2 B6

SLEEPING 🏠 pp165–7
Hotel Roma....................13 C3
Hotel Tuscia...................14 B3

SIGHTS & ACTIVITIES p165
Cathedral.........................3 A5
Chiesa di San Francesco.........4 C2
Chiesa di Santa Maria Nuova...5 B5
Fontana Grande...................6 C6
Palazzo dei Priori................7 B5
Palazzo Farnese..................8 A5
Palazzo Papale...................9 A5
Porta della Verità...............10 D5
Porta Fiorentina.................11 B2
Porta Romana....................12 D6

EATING 🍴 pp165–7
Il Labirintho...................15 B5
Il Richiastro...................16 C4

accommodation, including breakfast, Hotel Tuscia is a good choice.

Il Labirinto (☎ 0761 30 70 26; Via San Lorenzo 46; pizzas/pasta €6.20/6.20, mains €4.65-8.25) Typical Roman pasta dishes such as carbonara and all'amatriciana are good here, but the pizzas and excellent desserts also draw the crowds.

Il Richiastro (☎ 0761 22 80 09; Via della Marrocca 18; meals €25.30) This restaurant serves hearty food based on ancient Roman recipes and has outside tables in summer.

Getting There & Away

Direct, if slow, Trenitalia trains depart hourly from Rome's Ostiense, Trastevere and San Pietro stations, stopping at both the Porta Romana and Porta Fiorentina train stations. Porta Romana is closer to the sights. Trains take at least 1½ hours.

The other way to get to Viterbo from Rome is by Cotral bus. There are several daily, leaving Rome from the Saxa Rubra (1½ hours, every 30 minutes) station on the Ferrovia Roma-Nord train line. Catch the train to Saxa Ruba from Piazzale Flaminio (just north of Piazza del Popolo).

The intercity bus station is at Riello, a few kilometres northwest of Viterbo. However, buses also stop at the Porta Romana and Porta Fiorentina entrances to the city, so get off at one of them. If you find yourself at Riello, catch city bus No 11 into Viterbo.

By car, the easiest way to get to Viterbo from Rome is on the Via Cassia (S2, about 1½ hours). Enter the old town through the Porta Romana onto Via Giuseppe Garibaldi, which becomes Via Cavour. There are numerous public car parks scattered throughout the town; the best is probably Piazza della Rocca in the modern town.

AROUND VITERBO

Viterbo's **thermal springs** are about 3km west of town. They were used by both the Etruscans and Romans, and the latter built large bath complexes, of which virtually nothing remains. Travellers wanting to take a cure or relax in the hot sulphur baths will find the **Terme dei Papi** (☎ 0761 35 01; www.termedeipapi.it, Italian only; Strada Bagni 12; admission pool €12.90; ☾ year-round, pool Wed-Mon) the easiest to reach. Take city bus No 2 from the bus station in Piazza Martiri d'Ungheria, near-ish the tourist office. Specialist and therapeutic mud and water treatments cost much more than the entrance fee and must be booked in advance.

At Bagnaia, 4km northeast of Viterbo, is the beautiful 16th-century **Villa Lante**, noted for its fine gardens. The two superficially identical *palazzi* are closed to the public, but you can wander in the large **public park** (☎ 0761 28 80 08; admission €2.05; ☾ 9am-1hr before sunset Tue-Sun). Guided tours of the gardens leave every half hour; unfortunately, picnics aren't allowed in the park. From Viterbo, take city bus No 6 from Piazza dei Caduti.

At Caprarola, southeast of Viterbo, is the splendid **Palazzo Farnese** (☎ 0761 64 60 52; admission €2.05; ☾ 9am-6.30pm Tue-Sun summer, 9am-4pm Tue-Sun winter). Designed by Vignola, it is one of the most important examples of Mannerist architecture in Italy. You will need to wait for an attendant to take you through rooms which were richly frescoed in the 16th century by artists such as Taddeo and Federico Zuccari. Seven buses daily leave from the Riello bus station just outside Viterbo for Caprarola; the last bus returns from Caprarola at 6.35pm.

The **Parco dei Mostri** (☎ 0761 92 40 29; admission €7.75; ☾ 8am-sunset) at Bomarzo, 17km northeast of Viterbo, is especially entertaining – for children and adults alike. The park of the 16th-century Palazzo Orsini, created for the Orsini family, is scattered with gigantic and grotesque sculptures, including an ogre, giant and even a dragon. Also of interest here are the octagonal *tempietto* (little temple) and the crooked house, built without using right angles. From Viterbo, catch the Cotral bus from the stop near Viale Trento to Bomarzo, then follow the signs to Palazzo Orsini.

Another interesting detour from Viterbo is the tiny, medieval hilltop town of **Civita di Bagnoregio**, near its newer Renaissance sister, Bagnoregio (north of Viterbo). Civita, in a picturesque area of tufa ravines, is known as the 'dying town' because continuous erosion of its hill has caused the collapse of many buildings. Abandoned by its original residents, who moved to Bagnoregio, most of the buildings in the town were purchased by foreigners and artisans, and Civita has been restored and developed as a minor tourist attraction. Regular Cotral buses serve Bagnoregio from Viterbo. From the bus stop, ask for directions to Civita; a pedestrian bridge links Civita with Bagnoregio's outskirts.

THE LAKES

There are several large lakes just to the north of Rome, all of which are popular recreational spots in summer. The lake shores never seem to get as crowded as Lazio's beaches and their hilly, leafy environment makes them more attractive swimming destinations.

Lago di Bracciano

Lago di Bracciano, 40km north of Rome, is easily accessible by public transport. Visit the **Castello Orsini-Odelscalchi** (☎ 06 998 04 348; Piazza Castello; admission free; ✆ 10am-noon & 3-5pm Tue-Sun) in the medieval town of Bracciano or head straight for the lake for a swim. On the northern edge of the lake is the picturesque town of Trevignano Romano, with its pretty waterfront and modest beach.

There are a couple of good places to eat in the area.

Trattoria del Castello (☎ 06 998 04 339; Piazza Castello) This place, near the castle, has excellent food; if *funghi porcini* (porcini mushrooms) are on the menu, have them.

La Tavernetta (☎ 06 999 90 26; Via Garibaldi 62, Trevignano Romano; full meals from €15.50) On the shores of the lake, this rustic, family-run restaurant serves simple but tasty fare.

Vino e Camino (☎ 06 99803433; Piazza Mazzini 11; meals €20-30) This is an *enoteca* so you can have a good wine with their good food.

Cotral buses, which depart roughly every hour from outside the Lepanto Metro station in Rome, serve Bracciano directly, arriving in Piazza Roma in the middle of town. By car, take Via Braccianense (S493) for Bracciano, or take Via Cassia (S2) and then follow the signs to Trevignano Romano.

Lago di Bolsena

This elliptical lake, 100km from Rome, is too far to reach in a day but is close to Viterbo (see pp164–7). The town of Bolsena was the scene of a miracle in 1263 – a doubting priest was convinced of transubstantiation when blood dripped from the host he was holding during a mass. To commemorate the event, Pope Urban IV founded the festival of **Corpus Domini**: each June the townspeople hold a 3km procession and decorate the town with flowers.

Castello Monaldeschi (☎ 0761798630; ✆ 9.30am-1.30pm & 4-8pm Tue-Fri, 10am-1pm & 3-6pm Sat & Sun summer, 9.30am-1.30pm Tue-Fri, 10am-1pm & 3-6pm Sat & Sun winter) in the medieval quarter has an interesting history. The original structure dates from between the 13th and 16th centuries. However, it was pulled down by the locals in 1815 to prevent it from being taken by an invading Luciano Bonaparte. It now houses a **museum** and a **tourist office** (☎ 0761 79 99 23).

Also of interest in the medieval quarter are the 11th-century **Chiesa di Santa Cristina** and the **catacombs** beneath it. Just before the entrance to the catacombs is the **altare del miracolo**, where the miracle of Bolsena occurred. The catacombs are noteworthy because they contain tombs that are still sealed.

There are many hotels and camp sites by the lake.

Villaggio Camping Lido (☎ 0761 79 92 58; sites per adult/child/tent €7.75/4.15/5.15) This large camp site 1½km from Bolsena has a bar, restaurant and bungalow facilities.

Hotel Eden (☎ 0761 79 90 15; fax 0761 79 60 56; Via Cassia; s/d €46.50/62) This hotel is by the lake.

If you're touring the area by car, it is worth heading on to **Montefiascone**, which is noted for its white wine, Est, Est, Est. Local history has it that on his travels a monk wrote 'est' (it is) to indicate the places where the wine was good. On arriving at Montefiascone he was so overcome by the quality of the wine that he exclaimed 'Est! Est! Est!'. Visit the cathedral and the nearby Romanesque church of Sant' Andrea. On the Orvieto road, just outside Montefiascone, in Umbria, is the Romanesque church of **San Flaviano**.

In summer, Cotral runs a direct bus service travelling to Bolsena from the Saxa Rubra stop on Ferrovia Roma-Nord (catch the train from the station in Piazzale Flaminio); otherwise you need to change at Viterbo. There are regular Cotral buses, Monday to Saturday, to Bolsena from Viterbo leaving from the bus station at Riello. On Sunday there is only one bus that leaves around 9am (returning at around 6pm). By car, take the Via Cassia (S2) to Viterbo and follow the signs from the Riello bus station.

SOUTH OF ROME
The Castelli Romani

Just past the periphery of Rome are the Colli Albani (Alban Hills) and the 13 towns which make up the Castelli Romani. A summer resort area for wealthy Romans since the days of the Roman Empire, its towns were mainly founded by popes and patrician families. Castel Gandolfo and Frascati are perhaps the best known; the former is the summer residence of the pope and the latter is famous for its crisp white wine. The other towns in this group are Monte Porzio Catone, Montecompatri, Rocca Priora, Colonna, Rocca di Papa, Grottaferrata, Marino, Albano Laziale, Ariccia, Genzano and Nemi.

The **tourist information office** (☎ 06 942 03 31; Piazzale Marconi 1; ☻ 8am-2pm Mon-Sat, plus 3.30-6.30pm Tue-Fri) is at Frascati. For information on B&B accommodation contact www.promonetonline.it/b&b/ or ☎ 00 76 81 70.

The area has numerous villas, including the 16th-century **Villa Aldobrandini** (Frascati), designed by Giacomo della Porta and built by Carlo Maderno, which has a beautiful garden. Admission is granted by a permit which is available from the tourist office. Just outside Frascati is the site of the ancient city of **Tusculum**. Imposing and impregnable, Tusculum remained independent until 380 BC, when it came under Roman domination. Today, scant evidence of the city remains. There is a small amphitheatre, the remains of a villa as well as a stretch of ancient Roman road leading up to the city.

At Grottaferrata there's a 15th-century **abbey** (abbazia; ☎ 06 945 93 09; Viale San Nilo; admission free; ☻ 8.30am-noon & 4.30-6pm Tue-Sat, 8.30-10am & 4.30-6pm Sun), founded in the 11th century and which is home to a congregation of Greek monks. There is also a museum situated here.

Nemi is worth a visit just to see the pretty **Lago di Nemi** located in a volcanic crater. In ancient times there was an important sanctuary here beside the lake, where the goddess Diana was worshipped. Today, very little remains of this massive temple complex but it is possible to see the niche walls of what was once an arcade portico. New excavations at the site have just started. The incongruous-looking building at the edge of the lake, near the ruins of the temple, has an interesting story attached to it. It was built by Mussolini to house two ancient Roman boats (one 73m long, the other 71m), which were recovered from the bottom of the lake when it was partly drained between 1927 and 1932. The official story is that retreating German troops burned the ships on 1 June 1944. Locals tell a different story, but you'll have to go there to find out!

In Nemi, the delightful **Trattoria la Sirena del Lago** (☎ 06 936 80 20; Via del Plebiscito 26) serves simple but excellent meals. It is situated right on the edge of a cliff and overlooks the lake. Signs direct you from the centre of town.

It is really best to tour this area by car: you could see most of the more-interesting sights on an easy day trip from Rome. However, most of the towns of the Castelli Romani, including Nemi, are accessible from Rome by Cotral bus from the Anagnina station on Metro Linea A. Access between them, though, is well-nigh impossible. Trains also leave from Stazione Termini for Frascati, Castelgandolfo and Albano Laziale, from where you can catch a bus to Nemi.

Palestrina

The town of Palestrina is dominated by the massive **Santuario della Fortuna Primigenia**. Built by the ancient Romans on a series of terraces on the slope of Monte Ginestro, the sanctuary was topped by a circular temple with a statue of the goddess Palestrina on the top. On a clear day, the view from the sanctuary is sensational. The 17th-century **Palazzo Colonna Barberini** was built on the site and houses the **Museo Nazionale Archeologico Prenestino** (☎ 06 953 81 00; Piazzadella Cortina; admission €4.15; ☻ 9am-8pm, shorter hrs winter). The museum houses an important collection of Roman artefacts and is one of Lazio's best. Of particular interest is the spectacular Nile mosaic, a masterpiece of Hellenistic art, which came from the most sacred part of the temple (where the cathedral with its Romanesque belfry now stands). It depicts the Nile in flood from Ethiopia to Alexandria.

Apart from its historical and archaeological importance, Palestrina is also renowned for being the birthplace of the 16th-century choral composer, Giovanni Pierluigi da Palestrina. His former home, the **Casa di Palestrina** (admission €4.15; ☽ 9.30am-12.30pm Tue-Sun), is now a museum and important music library. Craft lovers can purchase locally produced beaten copper work in the shape of shells and 'Palestrina point' embroidery.

The **tourist office** (☎ 06 957 31 76; Piazza Santa Maria degli Angeli 2; ☽ 9.30am-1pm & 3.30-5.30pm) is close to the Museo Nazionale Archeologico Prenestino in the town centre.

Palestrina is accessible from Rome by Cotral bus (€2, 30 minutes, every half hour) from the Anagnina stop on Metro Linea A. At Palestrina, you can either walk uphill to the Santuario or save your legs and take the small local bus. By car it is a straightforward 39km along the Via Prenestina (S155). If you're driving, you might like to do as many Italians do, and detour to Labico for lunch at **Antonello Colonna** (☎ 06 951 0032; Via Roma 89; meals €75), one of Lazio's best restaurants. It's definitely not cheap, but it's run (and named after) one of the top chefs in the country.

Anagni & Alatri

These medieval towns are in an area known as the Ciociaria, and are 40 minutes' drive southeast of Rome. **Anagni**, birthplace of several medieval popes, is of particular interest for its 11th-century Lombard-Romanesque cathedral. Its pavement was laid in the Middle Ages by renowned Cosmati marble workers. The crypt has an extraordinary series of vibrant frescoes, painted by Benedictine monks in the 13th century. Depicting a wide range of subjects, the frescoes are considered to be a major example of medieval painting at the crucial stage of its transition from the Byzantine tradition to the developments culminating in the achievements of Giotto. The frescoes have been restored and certainly deserve a look. The crypt's pavement was also laid by the Cosmati.

Alatri has a couple of interesting churches, including the 13th-century Santa Maria Maggiore in its main piazza. Its ancient acropolis is ringed by huge 6th-century-BC walls, built by the town's original inhabitants, the Ernici.

To get to Anagni by bus you will have to change at Colle Ferro. Cotral buses for Colle Ferro leave from the Anagnina stop on the Metro Linea A approximately every half hour. From here take the bus to Anagni. Otherwise take the Frosinone train from Stazione Termini (leaving approximately every hour) and get off at Anagni-Fiuggi. To get to Alatri, catch the train to Anagni and then take the Cotral bus to Alatri.

Along the Coast

Beaches close to Rome include Fregene, the Lido di Ostia and the long stretch of dune-lined beach which is between Ostia and Anzio. However, they really are not terribly inviting and the water tends to be heavily polluted. You'll need to head further south to beaches such as Sabaudia and Sperlonga to find cleaner and more-attractive spots for a swim. Sabaudia has the added attraction of sand dunes and the **Parco Nazionale del Circeo**, a wetlands nature reserve along the coast. It is accessible by Cotral bus from outside the EUR-Fermi station on Metro Linea B.

SPERLONGA

The small coastal town of Sperlonga is a good destination to take a weekend break, with two long, sandy beaches on either side of a rocky promontory jutting out into the sea. The town is divided into two separate parts. Medieval Sperlonga Alta is situated on top of the promontory and, with its whitewashed buildings, seems more Greek than Italian, Modern Sperlonga Bassa is at sea level.

Other than the beach, the main attraction is the **Grotta di Tiberio** (admission €2.60; ☽ 9am-7pm summer, 9am-4pm winter), a cave with a circular pool used by the emperor Tiberius. The remains of his villa are in front of the cave. Statues found in the cave are housed in the nearby museum and include a large group in the style of the *Lacoön* (now in the Vatican Museums, pp117-18).

For a place to stay and somewhere to eat, try one of the places listed below.

Albergo Major (☎ 0771 54 92 44; Via Romita I 4; s/d low season €56.80/67.15, half-board high season per person €77.50) All the above prices include access to sun loungers and umbrellas on the private beach area.

Lido da Rocco (☎ 0771 5 44 93; Via Spiaggia Angelo 22) For a snack on the beach, try this seafront spot, which does very tasty rolls filled with mozzarella, tomato and basil.

Agli Archi (☎ 0771 5 43 00; Via Ottaviano 17; full meals €45) In the heart of the medieval town, this restaurant specialises in fish and there are a lot of dishes to choose from.

To get to Sperlonga from Rome, take a *diretto* regional train (not the Intercity) from Stazione Termini towards Naples and get off at Fondi. From here take the connecting Cotral bus (or a taxi) to Sperlonga. The return bus leaves from the main piazza at the top of the hill in the centre of Sperlonga Alta.

Sperlonga is 120km from Rome by car. Take the Via Pontina (S148) from EUR going south and follow signs to Terracina. From Terracina it is a short drive on the S213.

Isole Pontine

International tourists are only just beginning to discover this group of small islands between Rome and Naples. Only two of the islands – Ponza and Ventotene – are inhabited and both are popular summer holiday spots for Italians; they are especially crowded on summer weekends. Prices are not cheap and budget travellers are best to go out of season when the islands are more affordable – although beware that many services shut down.

The history of the islands goes back a long way. Homer refers to Ponza in the *Odyssey*, attesting to the presence of the ancient Greeks, confirmed by the remains of the tombs on the bluff overlooking Chiaia di Luna. In 313 BC, the archipelago came under Roman rule, and later came the building of sumptuous villas for the emperor and his circle. The collapse of the Empire brought about a period of decline on the islands, during which time they sustained violent attacks by the Saracens and by groups from mainland Italy and the nearby Aeolian islands. Unfaithful wives, promiscuous daughters and persecuted Christians counted among the large number of people exiled to the islands at this time.

The recent history of the islands begins in 1734, when surrender to the Bourbon ruler Charles III gave rise to a wave of migration to Ponza that was to last for the rest of the century. Commerce on the island flourished at the expense of the natural habitat, which was largely destroyed in the locals' rush to build and to cultivate. The island of Ponza is ecologically in pretty poor shape. Almost every inch of the hilly island was terraced and used for farming, and now there's a lot of erosion. Bird hunting is virtually an obsession for the locals; migrating birds pass over on their journeys between Europe and Africa. However, all the islands are now under National Park protection.

There is a **tourist information office** (☎ 0771 8 00 31; Via Molo Musco; ☺ 9am-1pm & 4-7.30pm summer, 10am-noon spring & autumn, 10am-noon Sat & Sun winter) near the port, on Ponza in the main town. On Ventotene, go to the private travel agency **Bemtilem** (☎ 0771 8 53 65; Piazza Castello 16) for information.

SLEEPING & EATING

Many of the locals rent out individual rooms to tourists for much less than the Hotel Mari (listed below) and you'll find them touting at the port; otherwise go to the tourist information office for an authorised list.

Hotel Mari (☎ 0771 8 01 01, fax 0771 8 02 39, Corso Pisacane 19; s/d high season €56.80/103.50, low season €41.30/72.30) You'll need to book ahead for this hotel, and make sure you ring to check that the hotel is open in low season. Prices include breakfast.

The Pontine Islands are renowned for their fish-based cuisine. Lentil soup is also a local speciality.

Ristorante da Ciro (☎ 0771 80 83 88; Via Calacaparra; ☺ lunch & dinner) One kilometre or so past the town of Le Forna on Ponza, this is the place to go for a good seafood meal. There is a west-facing terrace with a view of Palmarola.

GETTING THERE & AROUND

Ponza and Ventotene are accessible by car ferry or hydrofoil from Anzio, Terracina or Formia. Timetable information is available from most travel agents. During the summer the timetables are also published in the Cronaca di Roma section of the national daily newspapers *Il Messaggero* and *Il Tempo*. There is a hydrofoil that runs between Ponza and Ventotene. In both cases get information from the port or the Pro Loco office.

Cars and large motorbikes are forbidden on Ponza during the high season, but there is a good local bus service that covers all the main points of interest in town. Otherwise, you can rent a scooter at the port, either at one of the numerous outlets around or from one of the touts who will meet you at the ferry.

ERIC L WHEATER

Climb the narrow steps to the top of **St Peter's Basilica** (p115) in Rome, still the largest dome in existence today

A dizzyingly ornate staircase at the **Vatican Museums** (p117)

GREG ELMS

GREG ELMS

Admire the ornate frescoes of the **Galleria delle Carte Geografice** (p118) in the Vatican Museums

MARTIN MOOS

Take a breath of fresh air in the tranquil surrounds of **Villa Borghese** (p120)

ROME METRO MAP

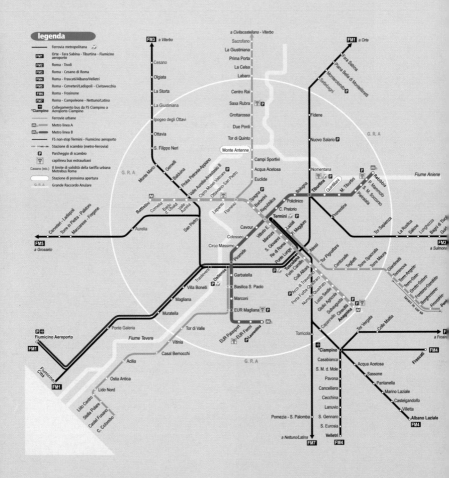

Liguria, Piedmont & Valle d'Aosta

CONTENTS

Italy's northwestern corner has long been the country's political, economic and intellectual engine room. It was here that the movement for Italian unity took wing. Piedmont (Piemonte) was the cradle of Italy's industrial success and the birthplace of its labour movements. For much of the 20th century, the Piedmontese capital, Turin, was a hotbed of intellectual activity. Further south Genoa was once a major city port, open to the rest of the world for centuries. Today it is regaining importance.

Turin (which touts itself as Europe's capital of baroque, chocolate and cars) and Genoa (birthplace of Christopher Columbus and European City of Culture 2004) resonate with past glories. But these two wildly contrasting cities – one oh-so-elegant, the other downright chaotic – are but one side of the coin. At the feet of Europe's two greatest mountains, Mont Blanc and the Matterhorn, is the Valle d'Aosta, a quiet valley of hilltop castles and quaint mountain villages where French (and German in parts) is spoken alongside Italian. There's mountains of on- and off-piste adventures to be had in the ski resorts both here and in northern Piedmont, while mountain bikers and walkers seeking one more trail better than the last won't be disappointed.

From the treasured white truffles and red wines of the southern Piedmont kitchen table, to the Ligurian coast with its sweet dessert wines and magical five lands known as the Cinque Terre, this extraordinary corner of the country is a microcosm of Italy's best.

HIGHLIGHTS

- **Wining**
  The Asti vineyards (white; pp221–2) & the Langhe hill villages around Alba (red; pp220–1)

- **Dining**
  Genoa's backstreet trattorie (pp185–6) & Piedmont's *agriturismo* restaurants (pp203–37)

- **Must-Sees**
  The Holy Shroud in Turin (p209)

- **Sugary Sweet**
  Turin's chocolate shops & coffee houses (p205); Cinque Terre's Lovers' Lane (p194)

- **Wild Encounters**
  White truffle hunting near Alba (p221); whale watching in the Ligurian Sea (p185)

- **Adrenaline Rush**
  Skiing the Milky Way or legendary off-piste Vallée Blanche (p232); mountain biking around Courmayeur (p232); scaling new heights atop Monte Rosa (p221), Mont Blanc (p204) or in the Parco Nazionale del Gran Paradiso (p227)

- **Festive Frolic**
  Orange-dodging at Ivrea's Carnival (p223)

★ Courmayeur

Ivrea ★

Turin ★

Asti ★
Alba ★

★ Genoa

Ligurian Sea

★ The Cinque Terre

POPULATION:	■ LIGURIA 1.6 MILLION	■ PIEDMONT 4.2 MILLION	■ VALLE D'AOSTA 120,589
AREA:	■ LIGURIA 5,413 SQ KM	■ PIEDMONT 25,399 SQ KM	■ VALLE D'AOSTA 3,262

LIGURIA

The Ligurian coast was inhabited by Neanderthals about one million years ago and many remains have been unearthed. Locals say these early inhabitants were lured by the beaches, which still exert a hold over thousands of tourists who flock to this narrow coastal region.

There is more to Liguria, however, than just beaches. Stretching from the French border in the west to La Spezia in the east, the coast is dotted with medieval towns; the mountainous hinterland hides hilltop villages, and holds plenty of scope for walkers. Genoa, regional capital and one-time sea power, is an important port and much-overlooked attraction in its own right.

A railway line follows the coast from the French border to La Spezia and beyond, connecting all points along the way. By road you have the choice of motorways or the Via Aurelia, an often congested but more picturesque state speedway.

GENOA (GENOVA)

pop 632,350

Travellers who write off Genoa as a dirty, lusty, noisy and chaotic port town (which it is) do the city an injustice. Once a mighty maritime republic and the birthplace of Christopher Columbus, the city known as *La superba* (literally 'the proud' or 'haughty') might have lost some of its gloss over the centuries – but none of its fascination.

Genoa might have had a greater story to tell had its town founders lent an ear to Columbus' exploration ideas; instead he turned to Spain for patronage, which became a Renaissance superpower on the back of wealth taken from the New World. Nonetheless this did not stop Genoa from marking the 500th anniversary of the discovery of America with an Expo in 1992, which transformed the ancient Genoese harbour from black sheep of the city to queen bee. Genoa's best-known contemporary product, world-renowned architect Renzo Piano (see the boxed text, p184), was the man behind the brilliant face-lift that left Genoa with a clutch of lasting portside attractions and the confidence to stand proud once more. In 2004 the city stepped back into the limelight as a European City of Culture.

Genoa exudes a gregariousness typical of southern Europe. It straddles Italy's most alluring strip of Mediterranean coastline and is filled with gangs of easy riders who fly through the streets helmetless on Vespa scooters. At the heart of its old town, its infamous labyrinth of *caruggi* (dark narrow alleys), punctuated with medieval churches and Renaissance palaces, bear witness to the back-stabbing dramas and intrigues of Genoa's golden age and the bickering dynasties which made the city the spellbinding place it is today.

History

Genoa was founded in the 4th century BC and possibly derives its name from the Latin *ianua* (door). A Roman port, it later became a mercantile power. Genoa was occupied by the Franks in 774, the Saracens in the 10th century and the Milanese in 1353. A famous victory over Venice in 1298 led to a period of rapid growth, but quarrels between the Grimaldis, Dorias, Spinolas and other noble families of the city caused much internal disruption.

Genoa peaked in the 16th century under the rule of imperial admiral Andrea Doria, and benefited from Spain's American fortunes by financing Spanish exploration. This golden age lasted into the 17th century and produced innumerable magnificent palaces and great works of art. The feverish activity attracted masters such as Rubens, Caravaggio and Van Dyck. Galeazzo Alessi (1512–72), who designed many of the city's splendid buildings, is regarded as highly as Andrea Palladio, perhaps the greatest architect of 16th-century northern Italy. The Age of Exploration came as a terrible blow, though, and as the Mediterranean's importance declined so did Genoa's.

A leading participant in the Risorgimento (the process of Italian unification and independence in the 19th century), Genoa was the first northern city to rise against the Germans and the Italian Fascists towards the close of WWII, liberating itself before the arrival of Allied troops.

After the war the city expanded rapidly along the coast. After the boom years of the 1960s it began to decline as big industries folded, port activity dropped and the waterfront and city centre fell into decay. Since then, the city has turned a sharp corner,

LIGURIA

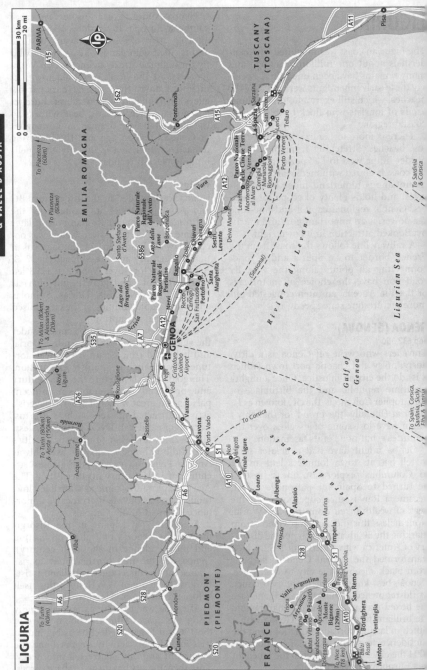

kick-started by the 1992 Expo, which saw vast amounts of money poured into returning the historic port area to its former glory – and backed up by its 2004 cultural city status. Genoa's hosting of the 2001 G8 summit turned sour when three days' violent protests by 100,000 antiglobalisation protestors left one dead and dozens injured.

Orientation

Genoa stretches along the coast for 30km and is served by 15 train stations. The centre is tucked between the two main train stations, Stazione Principe and Stazione Brignole. The main shopping boulevard, Via XX Settembre, starts a short walk southwest of Stazione Brignole and spills into the city's focal point, Piazza de Ferrari. West towards the port and stretching around the waterfront towards Stazione Principe you'll find the oldest Genoese quarters.

Information

BOOKSHOPS

La Feltrinelli (Map pp180–2; ☎ 010 54 08 30; Via XX Septembre 231-233r) English-language novels on the 1st floor.

Touring Club Italiano Genoa (TCI; Map pp180–2; ☎ 010 56 21 35; info@in-centro.it; Via XX Septembre 19r) Maps and guides, including Lonely Planet titles.

EMERGENCY

Police Station (Map pp180–2; ☎ 010 5 36 61; Via Armando Diaz 2)

GAY & LESBIAN

ArciGay (Map pp180–2; ☎ 010 545 02 24; www.arcigay.it/genova, Italian only; Salita Salvator Viale 15r)

INTERNET ACCESS

First-time users need a passport to register at these places; online access costs around €5 an hour.

Nonedove Internet Point (Map pp180–2; ☎ 010 570 48 78; cnr Corso Buenos Aires & Piazza Borgo Pila; 9.30am-8.30pm)

Superba Internet Caffè (Map pp180–2; ☎ 010 25 50 29; Salita San Giovanni di Prè 25r) Opposite Stazione Principe.

Touring Club Italiano Genoa (Map pp180–2; ☎ 010 56 21 35; Via XX Septembre 19r; 10am-7.30pm Mon-Fri, 10am-1.30pm & 3-7.30pm Sat)

Virgin Megastore (Map pp180–2; Magazzini del Cotone, Via Magazzini Generali 1; €2/hr; 11-1am)

LAUNDRY

Washing a 7kg load costs around €4.50.

La Maddalena (Map pp180–2; Via della Maddalena 2; 8am-8pm)

Le Bolde di Sapone (Map pp180–2; Molo Ponte Morosini 26; 6am-11pm)

LEFT LUGGAGE

Expect to pay around €3 per 24 hours.

Stazione Brignole (Map pp180–2; Piazza Giuseppe Verdi; 7am-9pm)

Stazione Principe (Map pp180–2; Piazza Acquaverde; 6am-midnight)

MEDICAL SERVICES

Ghersi (Map pp180–2; ☎ 010 54 16 61; Corso Buenos Aires 18) Night pharmacy.

Guardia Medica (☎ 010 35 40 22) Emergency doctor.

Ospedale San Martino (Map p178; ☎ 010 55 51; www.hsanmartino.liguria.it, Italian only; Largo Rosanna Benci 10) Hospital.

MONEY

Banks riddle Via Fieschi, off Via XX Settembre. ATMs likewise abound throughout the city.

POST

Main Post Office (Map pp180–2; Piazza Piccapietra 67-9; 8am-6.30pm Mon-Sat)

Branch Post Office (Map pp180–2; Via di Brera 10; 8am-6.30pm Mon-Fri, 8am-12.30pm Sat)

Branch Post Office (Map pp180–2; Stazione Principe; 8am-6.30pm Mon-Fri, 8am-12.30pm Sat)

TOURIST INFORMATION

Port Antico (Map pp180–2; Piazza delle Fieste; 9am-8pm) Run by the port authorities.

Port Antico (Map pp180–2; in front of Magazzini del Cotone; 9am-8pm) Run by the port authorities.

City Centre (Map pp180–2; ☎ 010 24 87 11; www.apt.genova.it; Piazza Giacomo Matteotti; 9am-1pm & 3-6pm)

Stazione Principe (Map pp180–2; ☎ 010 246 26 33; 9.30am-1pm & 2.30-6pm Mon-Sat)

Ferry Terminal (Map p178; ☎ 010 246 36 86; 9.30am-12.30pm & 1.30-5.30pm)

Airport (Map p178; ☎ 010 601 52 47; iat.aeroporto@apt.genova.it; 9.30am-12.30pm & 1.30-5.30pm)

TRAVEL AGENCIES

Geotravels (Map pp180–2; ☎ 010 59 28 37; geotravels@statcasale.com; Piazza della Vittoria 30r)

Pesci Viaggi e Turismo (Map pp180–2; ☎ 010 56 49 36; pesciros@tin.it; Piazza della Vittoria 94r)

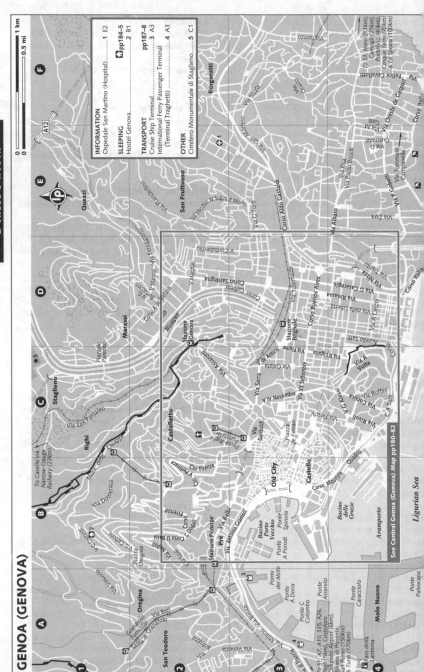

GENOA (GENOVA)

See Central Genoa (Genova) Map pp180–82

Ligurian Sea

0   0.5 mi
0   1 km

LIGURIA, PIEDMONT
& VALLE D'AOSTA

Touring Club Italiano (TCI; Map pp180–2; ☎ 010 695 52 91; negozio.genova@touringclub.it; Palazzo Ducale, Piazza Giacomo Matteotti 62r)

Sights

PIAZZA DE FERRARI

With its elegant cast of the Art Nouveau **Palazzo della Borsa** (the former stock exchange), **Palazzo Ducale**, the neoclassical facade of the WWII-bombed **Teatro Carlo Felice** and **Museo dell'Accademia Ligustica di Belle Arti** (Map pp180–2; ☎ 010 58 19 57; Largo Pertini 4; adult/child €3/1.50; ☽ 3-7pm Tue-Sun), with its 14th- to 20th-century art works, this square is the place to start.

The main entrance to the **Palazzo Ducale** (Map pp180–2; ☎ 010 557 40 00; www.palazzoducale.genova.it, Italian only; Piazza Giacomo Matteotti 9; variable admission; ☽ exhibitions 9am-9pm Tue-Sun) is on adjoining Piazza Giacomo Matteotti. Once the seat of the city's rulers, today the palace hosts temporary art exhibitions, a bookshop, café (see p186) and restaurant. You can wander around its neoclassical atrium, flanked by two porticoed courtyards. Its medieval **Torre Grimaldina** which was a prison for intellectuals, nobles and aristocrats under the Republic.

CATTEDRALE DI SAN LORENZO

Genoa's **cathedral** (Piazza San Lorenzo) – with its black-and-white-striped Gothic marble facade, fronted by twisting columns and almost gaudy decoration – is a shock every time you see it. It was consecrated in 1118, but its two bell towers and cupola didn't go up until the 16th century.

Inside, the **Cappella del San Giovanni Battista** (Piazza Matteotti), built 1450-65, once housed relics of St John the Baptist. In the sacristy, the **Museo del Tesoro** (Map pp180–2; ☎ 010 247 18 31; adult/child €5/3; ☽ guided tours 9am-11am & 3-5.30pm Mon-Sat) safeguards the Sacro Catino, a cup allegedly given to Solomon by the Queen of Sheba and used by Jesus at the Last Supper (how did a humble prophet/deity manage to get hold of such a cup for his evening nosh-up?). Other relics include the polished quartz platter upon which Salome is said to have received John the Baptist's head.

PORTA SOPRANA & CASA DI COLOMBO

A short stroll southeast from the Cattedrale di San Lorenzo through Piazza Matteotti brings you to the only remaining section of the city's 12th-century defensive walls. **Porta Soprana** was built in 1155, but what you see

today is a restored version – as is **Casa della Famiglia Colombo** (Map pp180–2; ☎ 010 246 53 46; Piazza Dante; admission free; ☽ 9am-noon & 2-6pm Sat & Sun), the supposed birthplace of Christopher Columbus (1451-1506).

VIA GARIBALDI

Skirting the northern edge of what was once the city limits, Via Garibaldi (designed by Galeazzo Alessi) marks a break between the Middle Ages and Renaissance, and between the poor and rich. Lined with magnificent palaces it's the place to admire the pick of Genoa's museums.

Palazzo Rosso (Red Palace; Map pp180–2; ☎ 010 271 02 36; Via Garibaldi 18; adult/child €3.10/free, Sun free; ☽ 9am-7pm Tue-Fri, 10am-7pm Sat & Sun) boasts works from the Venetian and Genoese schools and several paintings by van Dyck. Opposite, **Palazzo Bianco** (White Palace; Map pp180–2; ☎ 010 247 63 77; Via Garibaldi 11), which is temporarily closed but should be open by the end of 2004 once extensive renovation works are complete, features works by Flemish, Spanish and Dutch masters, and home-grown material by Caravaggio and Antonio Pisanello.

Inside **Palazzo Grimaldi Doria Tursi** (Via Garibaldi 9), built between 1565 and 1579 for aristocrat banker Niccolò Grimaldi, is one of Niccolò Paganini's violins (made in 1742). The prized instrument is played at concerts; otherwise call ☎ 010 55 71 11 to book a **viewing** (admission free). The palace has housed Genoa's town hall since 1848. **Palazzo Spinola** (Via Garibaldi 5), home to Deutsche Bank, has magnificent frescoes in its courtyard.

A short walk east of Via Garibaldi, a path from Piazza Corvetto twists through tiered gardens to the **Museo d'Arte Orientale** (Map pp180–2; ☎ 010 54 22 85; Piazzale Mazzini 1; adult/child €3.10/free; ☽ 9am-1pm Tue & Thu-Sun), home to one of Europe's largest collections of Oriental art. Heading southwest, elegant **Via Roma**, with its Art Nouveau boutiques and adjacent glass-covered **Galleria Mazzini**, is Genoa's finest shopping street. It links Piazza Corvetto with Piazza de Ferrari.

OLD CITY

Medieval Genoa is famous for its historic maze of *caruggi* – twisting lanes and dank blind alleys that spill in a bewildering spaghetti formation across the oldest part of Genoa. Its core is bounded by Porta dei Vacca, the waterfront streets Via Cairoli,

Via Garibaldi and Via XXV Aprile, and the Porta Soprana around the inland periphery. Most of the old city's lowlife (prostitution, drugs, and so on) is concentrated in the zone west of **Via San Luca**, with Piazza Bianchi at its southern end. East of the piazza is **Via Orefici**, where you'll find market stalls.

The **Palazzo Reale** (Map pp180–2; ☎ 010 271 02 72; Via Balbi 10; adult/child €4/free; ☺ 9am-7pm Thu-Sun, 9am-1.30pm Tue & Wed) features Renaissance works and terraced gardens. A combined ticket also covering admission to **Galleria Nazionale** (Map pp180–2; ☎ 010 270 53 00; Piazza Superiore di Pellicceria 1; adult/child €5/free; ☺ 9am-8pm Tue-Sat, 2-8pm Sun), costs €6.50. The latter –

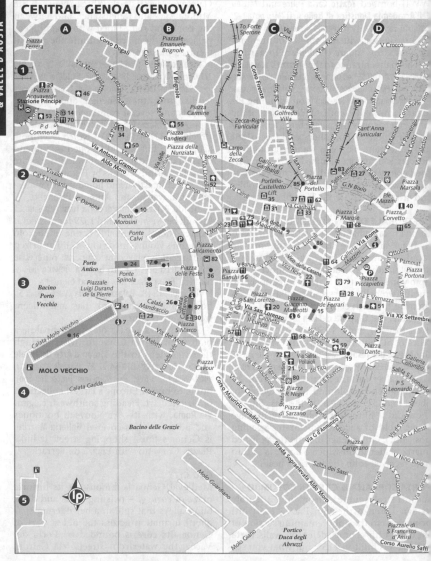

CENTRAL GENOA (GENOVA)

a 16th-century mansion – was owned by the Spinolas, one of the Republic's most formidable and feared dynasties. Their ancestral home displays Italian and Flemish Renaissance art.

Dozens of medieval churches and palaces were built by the ruling families, who staked out pockets of the old city for themselves and their *alberghi* (clan), defying rival families (with death, pillage and so on) to set foot on their patch. The Sarzanos controlled 11th-century **Chiesa di San Donato** (Map pp180–2; Strada Sant'Agostino), built in pure Romanesque style, while the church of the Doria family, **Chiesa di San Matteo** (Map pp180–2; Piazza San Matteo) was founded in 1125. Andrea

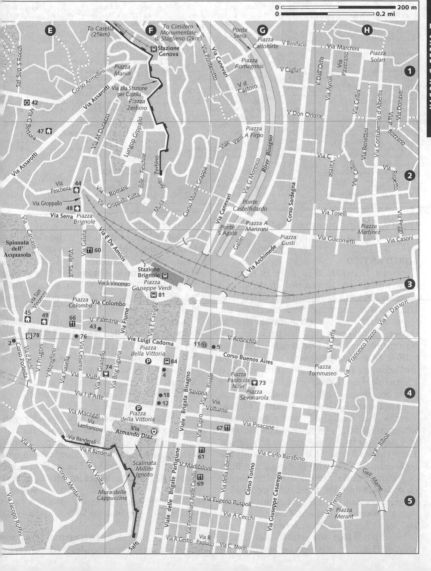

INFORMATION		
Alimar	1	B3
ArciGay	2	E4
Club Alpino Italiano	3	D3
Cooperativa Battellieri del Porto di Genova	(see 1)	
Geotravels	4	F4
Ghersi Pharmacy	5	G4
Information Booth	6	C3
Information Booth	7	B3
La Feltrinelli	8	D3
La Maddalena Laundrette	9	C3
Le Bolde di Sapone Laundrette	10	B2
Nonedove Internet Point	11	F4
Pesci Viaggi e Turismo	12	F4
Port Information Booth	13	B3
Superba Internet Caffè	14	A1
Touring Club Italiano	15	C3
Virgin Megastore	16	A3

SIGHTS & ACTIVITIES	pp179–84	
Acquario	17	B3
AMT Bus Office	18	F4
Casa della Famiglia Colombo	19	D4
Cattedrale di San Lorenzo	20	C3
Chiesa di San Donato	21	C4
Chiesa di San Matteo	22	C3
Città dei Bambini	(see 16)	
Galleria Nazionale	23	C2
Grande Blu Nave	24	B3
Ice-Skating Rink	25	B3
Il Bigo	26	B3
Magazzini del Cotone	(see 16)	
Museo d'Arte Orientale	27	D2
Museo del Tesoro	(see 20)	
Museo dell'Accademia Ligustica di Belle Arti	28	D3
Museo Luzzati	29	B3
Museo Nazionale dell'Antartide	30	B3

Padiglione del Mare e della Navigazione	(see 16)	
Palazzo Bianco	31	C2
Palazzo della Borsa	32	D3
Palazzo Ducale	(see 15)	
Palazzo Grimaldi Doria Tursi	33	C2
Palazzo Reale	34	B2
Palazzo Rosso	35	C2
Palazzo San Giorgio	36	B3
Palazzo Spinola	37	C2
Porta Siberia	(see 29)	
Porta Soprana	(see 19)	
Renzo Piano's Sphere	38	B3
Statue of Christopher Columbus	39	A1
Statue of Vittorio Emanuele II	40	D2
Swimming Pool	41	B3
Synagogue	42	E1
Torre Grimaldina	(see 15)	
Touring Club Italiano Genoa	43	E3

SLEEPING	pp184–5	
Albergo Carola	44	E2
Albergo Soana	45	E3
Hotel Acquaverde	46	A1
Hotel Assarotti	47	E2
Hotel Astoria	48	E2
Hotel Bel Soggiorno	49	E3
Hotel Bologna	50	B2
Hotel Bristol Palace	51	D3
Hotel Cairoli	52	B2
Hotel Chopin	53	A1
Hotel Cristoforo Colombo	54	D4
Hotel Crocicchio	55	B2

EATING	pp185–6	
A Ved Romanengo	56	C3
Antica Sà Pesta	57	C3
Café degli Specchi	58	C3

Café di Barbarossa	59	D4
Cuxinn-E	60	E3
Enoteca Sola	61	F5
La Ligura in Cucina	62	C2
La Taverna di Colombo	63	C2
Le Dolcezze Salate di Angelo	64	C3
Mangini	65	D2
Mentelocale Café	(see 15)	
Mercato Orientale	66	E3
Taverna Da Michele	67	G4
Trattoria da Maria	68	D2
Trattoria Lombarda	69	F5
Trendy	70	A1

DRINKING	pp186–7	
La Maddeleine Café Teatro	71	C2
Le Corbusier	72	C4
Liquid Art Café	73	G4
Maddox Rock Café	74	F4
Quattro Canti	75	C2

ENTERTAINMENT	p187	
FNAC (Event Tickets)	76	E3
Politeama Genovese	77	D2
Ricordi Mediastore (Event Tickets)	78	E3
Teatro Carlo Felice	79	D3
Teatro della Tosse	80	C4

TRANSPORT	pp187–7	
AMT Buses to Airport	81	F3
Bus Terminal	82	B3
Funicolare St Anna	83	D2
Main AMT Bus Terminal	84	F4

OTHER		
Ascensore Portello-Castelletto	85	C2
Nuovo Centro Sportivo	86	C3
Sul Fronte del Porto	87	B3

Doria's sword is preserved under the altar and his tomb is in the crypt.

PORTO ANTICO

Genova's ancient Greek port is Genoa's drawcard. It was revamped in 1992 and again in 2004 as a European City of Culture. Unfortunately, nothing can detract from the Sopraelevata, the flyover that slashes straight through the old port area. Just back from the waterfront, frescoed **Palazzo San Giorgio** (Map pp180–2; Piazza Caricamento) was built in 1260 and became a prison in 1298; inmate Marco Polo worked on *Il Milione* within its walls. It hosts occasional exhibitions today.

A must-see is Genoa's **Acquario** (Aquarium; Map pp180–2; ☎ 010 234 56 78; www.acquario.ge.it; Ponte Spinola; adult/child €12/7; ☓ 9.30am-7.30pm Mon-Wed & Fri, 9.30am-10pm Thu, 9.30am-8.30pm Sat & Sun Sep-Jun, 9.30am-11pm Jul & Aug). Sharks are among the 5000 animals that swim in six million litres of water, in tanks protected by 25cm-thick glass. **Grande Nave Blu**, the adjoining floating barge, takes visitors on a voyage through the Age of Discovery (Darwin, Columbus et al) and into a Madagascan rain forest.

Nearby is **Il Bigo** (Map pp180–2; Calata Cattaneo; adult/child €3.30/2; ☓ 10am-6pm Tue-Sun), built for

the sole purpose of hoisting a cylindrical container 200m into the air, thereby giving its occupants a bird's-eye view of the Porto Antico. It was designed by Renzo Piano. Behind it is an **ice-skating rink** (Map pp180–2; ☎ 010 246 13 19; Piazza delle Feste; adult/child €6.79/ 5.50; ☓ 12.30pm-midnight Mon, 8am-midnight Tue-Fri, 10-2am Sat, 10am-midnight Sun Dec-Mar).

A chilly addition to the waterfront is **Museo Nazionale dell'Antartide** (Map pp180–2; ☎ 010 254 36 90; Palazzino Millo, Calata Cattaneo; adult/child €5.16/4.13; ☓ 10.30am-6.30pm Tue-Sun Jun-Sep, 9.45am-5.30pm Tue-Fri, 10am-6pm Sat & Sun Oct-May). Multimedia devices encourage visitors to explore the 98% ice-covered continent of Antarctica.

Walking west along Calata Mandraccio you pass **Porta Siberia** (1550), a city gate named after *cibaria*, a derivation of the Italian word for food (alluding to the port's grain warehouses). Inside, exhibitions on Genoese artist and scenographer Emanuele Luzzati (born 1921) fill the **Museo Luzzati** (Map pp180–2; ☎ 010 253 03 28; Calata Mandraccio; adult/child €3.50/2.50; ☓ 9.30am-12.30pm & 2.30-6.30pm Tue-Fri, 10am-1pm & 2-6pm Sat & Sun Sep-Jun, 3-11pm Tue-Sat Jul & Aug).

Further west still are **Magazzini del Cotone** one-time cotton warehouses since converted

THE GENIUS OF GENOA

Niccolò Paganini (1782–1840) played a mean violin. Extracting chords, arpeggios and rhythms hitherto undreamed of, the Genoese musician revolutionised violin technique with his use of harmonics and left-handed pizzicato. He was also a virtuoso on the guitar and a prolific composer, writing six concertos, 24 quartets for violin, viola, guitar and other strings, 12 sonatas for violin and guitar, and a long list of further sonatas in a career that took him to every corner of Italy and all of Europe's great stages.

Raised by a tyrannical father, Paganini knew just about all there was to know about the violin by the age of 13. In 1798 he fled his father's cruelty, running away to Lucca where he scraped together a living giving concerts. Loose women and gambling became part of the 16-year-old's life for a short while, leading on more than one occasion to the violinist pawning his violin to pay off a debt.

Between 1805 and 1813 Paganini worked for the princess of Lucca as court violinist and engaged in some of his greatest experiments with violin technique at this time. In 1828 he performed for the first time in Vienna – a coup that coincided with a public defence of himself in the *Revue Musicale*. This was intended to squash rumours claiming that the genius of Genoa was, in fact, demonically inspired.

Diabolical rumours did not diminish Paganini's popularity, although the adjectives capricious, greedy, mean and egotistical were all piled on the somewhat eccentric genius. At the height of his fame in the late 1820s, everything from hats and shawls to foodstuffs were named after him. Hundreds of adoring fans mobbed him when he left concert halls, while Chopin and Liszt (who is supposed to have said of the virtuoso 'what torture in those four strings!') applied much of what they learned from Paganini's genius to the piano.

Paganini spent the last days of his eccentric life further along the coast from his native Genoa in Nice, France, where he died penniless in 1840. Four years previously he had blown the entire fortune he'd amassed in the opening of a casino (which failed) in Paris.

into an entertainment area with nine-screen cinema and shopping centre. On the 1st floor the **Città dei Bambini** (Map pp180–2; ☎ 010 27 57 02; Magazzini del Cotone; child aged 3-5/6-16 yrs €4.65/5.16; ♥ 10am-6pm Tue-Sun) is an interactive space aimed at showing kids the wonders of play, science and technology. On the 2nd floor, Genoa's maritime history is celebrated in **Padiglione del Mare e della Navigazione** (Map pp180–2; ☎ 010 246 36 78; Magazzini del Cotone; adult/child €5.40/2.80; ♥ 10.30am-7pm Mon-Fri, 10.30am-7.30pm Sat & Sun).

A sweeping view of Porto Antico and its **lighthouse** (1543) can be enjoyed from Molo Vecchio, the westernmost tip of the peninsula behind Magazzini del Cotone. The lighthouse can be visited by guided boat tour; the tourist office has details.

CITY WALLS, WALKS & CEMETERIES
The high country leaning protectively over the city bears a 13km-long scar of city walls, built between 1626 and 1632 to shield the port's landward side. These **Mura Nuove** (New Walls) covered a much larger area than their 12th-century predecessors which stretched west to the lighthouse, east to Piazza della Vittoria and north to **Forte Sperone** (490m), the largest of the remaining defensive forts. The fortress hosts to plays and concerts in summer and can be visited by pre-arranged guided tour; **Aster** (☎ 010 98 101; www.astergenova.it; Via XX Settembre 15) has details.

The easiest way to reach the walls is by **cable car** from Largo della Zecca to Righi (300m). From Largo Giorgio Caproni (the square in front of Righi funicular station), walking trails lead to Forte Sperone. Contact **Club Alpino Italiano** (CAI; ☎ 010 59 21 22; www.cailigure.it, Italian only; Galleria Mazzini 7/3, Via Roma).

A **narrow-gauge railway** snakes from **Stazione Genova** (Map pp180–2; ☎ 010 83 73 21; www.ferroviagenovacasella.it, Italian only; Via alla Stazione per Casella 15), 25km north to **Casella** (405m; one hour, single/return €1.80/2.50, nine to 11 daily), a village in the Scrivia Valley. The railway has been in operation since 1929 and offers passengers great views of Genoa's forts and its **Cimitero Monumentale di Staglieno** (Map p179; ☎ 010 87 01 84; Lungo Bisagno; ♥ 7.30am-5pm), a monumental cemetery dating to 1840. Revolutionary Giuseppe Mazzini (1805–72) and Constance Lloyd (1858–98), whom Oscar Wilde wed in 1884 and later abandoned, are buried here. To visit the cemetery take bus No 34 from Stazione Principe.

RENZO PIANO

A daring use of glass is the distinctive trademark of world-renowned Genoese architect, Renzo Piano (born 1937). Son of a builder and graduate of the architecture school of the Polytechnic Institute of Milan, he raised eyebrows for the first time with Paris' Centre George Pompidou (1971–7) – a 'shocking' state-of-the-art construction at odds with the historic city quarter in which it boldly stood. Since then eyebrows have stayed raised.

The maverick of world architecture has trotted around the globe: the Menil Museum in Houston, Texas (1992–7); Beyeler Foundation Museum in Switzerland (1992–7); Lyons' Cité Internationale and contemporary art museum, France (1996–ongoing); and Japan's Kansai airport (1988–94), built on a 15km sq man-made island in Osaka Bay. Piano's been overseeing the transformation of Berlin's Potsdamer Platz since 1992.

Closer to home Piano converted Turin's FIAT (Fabbrica Italiana di Automobili Torino) factory at Lingotto into a conference centre (1983–ongoing) topped, no less, with a bright blue bubble of glass; and revamped Genoa's Porto Antico area (1985–92), transforming cotton warehouses into a shopping and congress centre, building an aquarium and other waterside attractions. In 2001 world leaders attending the G8 Summit in Genoa saw Piano's latest creation unveiled – a glass bubble floating on water by the side of the aquarium at the Porto Antico (currently closed for renovation).

Piano masterminds his architectural wonders from the Renzo Piano Building Workshop, his glass office on rocks overlooking the sea, mid-way between Voltri and Vesima, west of Genoa. He has a second office (and home) in Paris. In 1998 he won the Pritzker Architecture Prize – the highest accolade an architect can achieve – and in 2003 won the gold medal for Italian architecture at the Milan Triennale.

Tours

Information and tickets for boat trips are available from the **ticket booths** (Map pp180–2; ☎ 010 25 67 75; Ponte Spinola; ☺ 9.30am-6.30pm Sep-Jun, 9am-8pm Jul & Aug), beside the aquarium at Porto Antico.

Port tours (45 minutes) by **Cooperativo Battellieri del Porto di Genova** (Map pp180–2; ☎ 010 26 57 12; www.battellierigenova.it; Calata degli Zingari; adult/child €6/4) depart at 10am from Ponte Spinola. June to September it runs excursions to San Fruttuoso, Portofino, the Cinque Terre and Porto Venere. **Alimar** (Map pp180–2; ☎ 010 25 67 75, ☎ 010 25 59 75; www.alimar.ge.it, Italian only; Calata degli Zingari) runs boat trips to the Cinque Terre (€23), Portofino/San Fruttuoso (€15) and Portovenevre (€25).

Festivals & Events

Genoa is one of four historical maritime cities that race each other in the **Palio delle Quattro Antiche Repubbliche Marinare** (Regatta of the Four Ancient Maritime Republics) in June. The city will host the race in 2004 and 2008.

Sleeping

BUDGET

Although the old city, Stazione Principe and the port areas have a fair smattering of budget hotels, you'll get better value and a greater sense of security near Stazione Brignole.

Hostel Genova (Map p178; ☎ 010 242 24 57; hostelge@iol.it; Via Costanzi 120; dm €13, dm in 4-bed room with private bathroom €18; ☺ reception 9am-3.30pm & midnight-7am Feb–mid-Dec; **P**) Dorms have eight beds and some quadruple rooms have disabled facilities at Genoa's only hostel, 2km north of the old centre in Righi. Rates include breakfast and sheets. Catch bus No 40 from Stazione Brignole to the end of the line or No 35 from Stazione Principe to Stazione Brignole, and then connect with No 40.

Hotel Crocicchio (Map pp180–2; ☎ /fax 010 251 23 76; Piazza Bandiera 3; d with shared bathroom €36) This little-known hotel with lime-green wooden shutters and a peach facade slumbers behind a hulk of a church. Despite its simplicity the place is friendly, fun and a steal.

Albergo Carola (Map pp180–2; ☎ 010 839 13 40; albergocarola@libero.it; Via Groppallo 4; s/d from €21/33, with bathroom from €31/41) Albergo Carola's clean, well-kept rooms can be found on the 3rd floor of a lovely old building near Stazione Brignole.

Dirt-cheap dives in dodgy Prè include: **Hotel Acquaverde** (Map pp180–2; ☎ 010 26 54 27; www.hotelacquaverde.it; Via Balbi 29/4; s/d/tr/q from €35/72/93/98; **P**))

WHALE WATCH LIGURIA

There's no guarantee that you'll see one. In fact, those aboard whale-spotting excursions organised by the Cooperativa Battellieri del Porto di Genova (see p184) are advised to bring binoculars.

Trips, run in consultation with the Worldwide Fund for Nature (WWF) who plant a biologist on board, sail from Genoa into a 96,000 km sq protected zone wedged between the Côte d'Azur (France) and Tunisia. Some 12 cetacean species are known to exist here, the long-finned pilot whale and sperm whale among them. In summer its striped dolphin population peaks at 25,000. Its whale population is estimated at 2000.

Whale-spotting **expeditions** (☎ 010 26 57 12; www.whalewatchliguria.it, Italian only; adult/child from Genoa €33/18, from Savona €30/15) depart at 9am from Genoa's Porto Antico, 9.15am from Genoa's Calata degli Zingari (the waterfront near Stazione Principe) and at 10.30am from Savona's Pontile Marinetta three to 10 times a month, on a seemingly random selection of days (listed on its website) during June and September. Advance reservations by telephone are obligatory.

Hotel Bologna (Map pp180–2; ☎ 010 246 54 47; Piazza Superiore del Roso 3; s/d €30/40, with bathroom €40/50)
Hotel Chopin (Map pp180–2; ☎ 010 25 52 87; Via A Doria 4/2; s/d €21/31, with bathroom €31/37)

MID-RANGE & TOP END
Hotel Cairoli (Map pp180–2; ☎ 010 246 14 54; www.hotelcairoligenova.com; Via Cairoli 14/4; s/d/tr from €47/68/78; 🕸 🅿) The 12 rooms in this 3rd-floor hotel are worth more than the two stars bestowed on them. Guests seeking a suntan can lounge amid rooftops on its plant-filled terrace.

Hotel Assarotti (Map pp180–2; ☎ 010 88 58 22; www.hotelassarotti.it; Via Assarotti 40c; s/d €45/70; 🕸 🅿) This simple, twin-starred hotel is a family-run place offering a bit of a getaway from the hubbub of central Genoa. Bus No 36 links the hotel with Piazza Ferrari and Via XX Settembre.

Hotel Cristoforo Colombo (Map pp180–2; ☎ 010 251 36 43; www.hotelcolombo.it; Via di Porta Soprana 27; s/d/tr from €47/75/98) Christopher Columbus is a charming choice in what is probably the nicest part of the old city. Advance reservations are essential.

Hotel Bel Soggiorno (Map pp180–2; ☎ 010 58 14 18; www.belsoggiorno.com; Via XX Settembre 19; s without bathroom €44, s/d with bathroom €73/93; 🕸) This reliable option puts you to bed in a turn-of-the-19th century townhouse, smack-bang in the middle of Genoa's busy shopping street. The family which runs it speaks French, English and German.

Albergo Soana (Map pp180–2; ☎ 010 56 28 14; www.hotelsoana.it; Via XX Settembre 23/8; s/d/tr €70/85/113; 🕸) A weary stone-faced pair of atlantes (columns in the form of male figures) prop up the entrance to this two-star hotel. Cheaper promotional rates kick in at vari-

ous times of the year – so bargain! Breakfast costs €5.

Hotel Astoria (Map pp180–2; ☎ 010 87 33 16; www.hotelastoria-ge.com; Piazza Brignole 4; s/d €93/140; 🅿 🕸) This restful hotel, with a warm ochre facade on a quiet square, is a popular place with briefcase-carriers. Rates drop at weekends when the suits go home.

Hotel Bristol Palace (Map pp180–2; ☎ 010 59 25 41; www.hotelbristolpalace.com; Via XX Settembre 35; d low/high season Mon-Fri €142/160, d weekends year-round €125; 🅿 🕸 💻) A former 19th-century mansion, this hotel has a breathtakingly beautiful staircase topped by a fab stained-glass ceiling – both dramatically visible from reception. Most rooms have a Jacuzzi.

Eating
Don't leave town without eating pasta doused in *pesto genovese* (a sauce of basil, garlic, parmesan cheese and pine nuts), *torta pasqualina* (a spinach, ricotta cheese and egg tart), *pansotti* (spinach ravioli with a thick, creamy hazelnut sauce), *trenette al pesto* (a spaghetti with pesto and potato) and, of course, focaccia and *farinata*.

CAFÉS
Café degli Specchi (Map pp180–2; ☎ 010 246 81 93; Salita Pollaiuoli 43r; 1st/2nd courses €8/10; ❤ Mon-Sat) Genoa's Café of Mirrors is an Art Deco joint where the literati hung out in the 1920s. Its original vaulted interior was used as a backdrop for some scenes of Dino Risi's film *Scent of a Woman* (1974). Upstairs is a great restaurant.

Café di Barbarossa (Map pp180–2; ☎ 010 246 50 97; Piano di Sant'Andrea 21-3r) This simple but stylish café-cum-bar basks in the shade of towering 12th-century Porta Soprana. It is tucked in the basement of a palace dating to 1250 and has a red-brick cellar.

Mentelocale Café (Map pp180–2; ☎ 010 595 96 48; Palazzo Ducale, Piazza Giacomo Matteotti 9; brunch/lunch menu €11.50/12) Newspapers to read, designer chairs to pose in and computer terminals to check the latest happenings in town are all part-and-parcel of this ultra-modern café run by the cyber team responsible for Genoa's most up-to-date online city guide (www.mentelocale.it, Italian only).

Opposite Stazione Principe, **Trendy** (Map pp180–2; Salita San Giovanni di Prè; 🕑 lunch Mon-Sat) is a self-service spot to eat on the cheap. In the old city, pull in at **Le Dolcezze Salate di Angelo** (Map pp180–2; Via XXV Aprile 22-4; 🕑 Mon-Sat), a sandwich shop stocked with well-stuffed *panini* (bread rolls), quiches and salads to take away.

Most cake shops sell *kranz* (honey-glazed raisin bread baked in a twist and topped with sugar crystals) and *pandolce genovese* (traditional Genoese fruit bread). Genoa's finest, **Mangini** (Map pp180–2; ☎ 010 56 40 13; Piazza Corvetto 3r), dating to 1876, and **A Ved Romanengo** (Map pp180–2; ☎ 010 247 29 15; Via Orefici 31-33), open since 1805, both have small sit-down areas to coffee 'n' cake-it.

RESTAURANTS

A clutch of popular lunch-time spots are within an easy walk of Stazione Brignole.

Taverna Da Michele (Map pp180–2; ☎ 010 59 36 71; Via della Libertà 41r; pizzas €4-7.50, 1st/2nd courses €8/12) Enjoy a wholemeal pizza beneath creeping vines at this little-known spot with a peaceful green terrace – a rarity in this traffic-crazy city.

Enoteca Sola (Map pp180–2; ☎ 010 59 45 13; Via Carlo Barabino 120; 1st courses €7-12, 2nd courses €9-13; 🕑 Mon-Sat) Dine in style at this fabulous wine shop. The wine list is extensive, the staff knowledgeable and typical Genoese dishes star on its handwritten menu.

Trattoria Lombarda (Map pp180–2; ☎ 010 59 46 29; Via Finocchiaro Aprile Camillo 26; 1st/2nd courses €7/10; 🕑 Mon-Sat) Feast on the cheap at this charming bistro. *Stoccafisso alla genovese* (stockfish) is among the traditional local delights.

Cuxinn-E (Map pp180–2; ☎ 010 595 98 39; Via Galata 35r; 1st courses €5.50-8, 2nd courses €6.50-11; 🕑 Mon-Sat) Traditional Genoese fodder might well be cooked up at Cuxinn-E, but its minimalist modern decor – all aglow in warm amber

and ochre – makes a refreshing change from the rustic, bottle-lined norm.

Cheap deals are not to be had at the Porto Antico, although atmosphere ranks high in the sushi bar and American-style diner on the 3rd floor of **Sul Fronte del Porto** (Calata Cattaneo), the building behind Il Bigo.

Old-city gems include:

La Ligura in Cucina (Map pp180–2; ☎ 010 277 00 54; Via del Portello 16r; full meals from €20; 🕑 Mon-Sat) Mario Rivaro's Ligurian kitchen, one of Genoa's oldest restaurants, oozes atmosphere. Bring your sweetheart to this bottle-filled trattoria where the 1919 interior alone speaks more than words can say.

La Taverna di Colombo (Map pp180–2; ☎ 010 246 24 47; Vico della Scienza 6; 1st/2nd courses €2.85/3.60; menus from €7) This charming bistro dishes up simple but delicious cuisine to a young and hungry clientele that packs out its cosy red cellar.

Trattoria da Maria (Map pp180–2; ☎ 010 58 10 80; Vico Testa d'Oro 14; lunch menu €8) Off Via XXV Aprile, Maria's trattoria exudes a simple charm with its checked tablecloths (often hanging outside to dry), handwritten menu and hearty dishes served by granny in pinny. The fixed lunch menu includes bread and 25cl of wine.

Antica Sà Pesta (Map pp180–2; Via del Giustiniani 16r; full meals from €10; 🕑 9am-9pm Mon-Sat) *Sale pestato* (ground salt) used to be sold here, hence the name of this shop-turned-trattoria where giant platters of *torte* (tarts) and *farinata* are baked in an open wood-stoked oven. The walls still bear the original ceramic tiles.

Drinking

Quattro Canti (Map pp180–2; ☎ 010 25 29 97; Via Ai Quattro Canti di San Francesco 28) This old-city bar dishes up *panini*, bruschette (toasted bread spread with a variety of toppings) and good music to a mellow crowd. Bring a beer mat from home to woo the bar staff.

Le Corbusier (Map pp180–2; ☎ 010 246 86 52; Piazza San Donato 36-38) Despite its name this cocktail bar and café seemingly has nothing to do with the architect of the same name. Its style is hip-modern.

Liquid Art Café (Map pp180–2; ☎ 347 488 68 25; Piazza Savonarola 28) A steely interior decorates this industrial music bar where punters breakfast from 6.30am and move to DJ tunes from 10pm; Saturday is generally house.

MARKET DAY

Nowhere is there a better place to sniff up Genoa's scents and pongs than at its central market, a sprawling maze of stalls and sellers inside **Mercato Orientale** (Map pp180–2; entrances on Via XX Settembre & Via Galata). Flower stalls in front of the covered market on Via XX Settembre sell blooms for your sweetheart. In the old town, fruit and veg stalls are set up on Piazza Banchi and Via degli Orefici, immediately east.

Works by local artists and second-hand books can be picked up from the open-air stalls beneath the arcades on Piazza Colombo, a pretty square at the southern foot of Via Galata. On the first Saturday and Sunday of the month October to July, an antique market fills the interior courtyards of Palazzo Ducale.

Maddox Rock Café (Map pp180–2; ☎ 010 56 58 96; Via Malta 15) American-style Maddox shakes a mean aperitif, matched by an endless supply of complimentary pizza slices, fries, tortilla chips and olives. Sport is screened on a big screen.

La Madeleine Café Teatro (Map pp180–2; ☎ 010 246 53 12; Via della Maddalena 103) A red-brick interior greets drinkers at this fabulous café theatre-cum-music bar where live bands blast their stuff from 10pm most nights.

Entertainment

Tickets for cultural and sporting events are sold at box offices inside the **Ricordi Mediastore** (Map pp180–2; Via alla Porta degli Archi 88-94) and **FNAC** (Map pp180–2; Via XX Settembre 58). English-language films are shown at **Multi-Sala Ariston** (Map pp180–2; ☎ 010 247 35 49; www.cinema-online.net, Italian only; Vico San Matteo 14-16).

In summer, open-air events are held at Forte Sperone; the tourist office has details. Otherwise, take in a play or opera at **Teatro Carlo Felice** (Map pp180–2; ☎ 010 538 12 24/7; www.carlofelice.it, Italian only; Passo E Montale 4), Genoa's four-stage opera house. Casanova walked the boards at **Teatro della Tosse** (Map pp180–2; ☎ 010 247 07 93; www.teatrodellatosse.it, Italian only; Piazza Renato Negri 4), the city's oldest theatre dating to 1702.

Getting There & Away
AIR
Regular domestic and international flights use **Christopher Columbus airport** (GOA; Aeroporto Internazionale di Cristoforo Colombo; ☎ 010 601 54 10; www.airport.genova.it), 6km west in Sestri Ponente.

BOAT
Ferries sail to/from Spain, Sicily, Sardinia, Corsica and Tunisia from Genoa's **passenger terminal** (terminal traghetti; Map p178; 24-hr information ☎ 166 152 39 393; www.porto.genova.it; Via Milano 51). Only cruise ships use the 1930s terminal on Ponte dei Mille.

Fares listed are for one-way, low/high season deck-class tickets. Ferry operators based at the passenger terminal include: **EnerRnaR** (☎ 899 20 00 01, ☎ 199 76 00 03) Ferries to/from Sardinia (Palau €35/59) April to September. **Grandi Navi Veloci** (toll-free ☎ 800 46 65 10, ☎ 010 254 65; www.gnv.it) Ferries to/from Sardinia (Porto Torres year-round €31/74; Olbia June to September €38/77) and year-round to/from Sicily (Palermo €69/109) and Spain (Barcelona €55/91). **Moby Lines** (☎ 010 254 15 13, ☎ 056 593 61; www.mobylines.it) Ferries year-round to/from Corsica (Bastia €15/30) and Sardinia (Olbia €30/65). **SNCM Ferryterranée** (☎ 058 621 05 07; www.sncm.fr) Weekly boats, June to late September, to/from Tunisia (Tunis €108/214). **Tirrenia** (toll-free ☎ 800 82 40 79, ☎ 99 12 31 99; www.tirrenia.it) Ferries and high-speed boats year round to/from Sardinia (Porto Torres €25/50, Olbia €27/37, Arbatax €30/40, Cagliari July to September €45), with connections to Sicily.

June to September, **Cooperativa Battellieri del Golfo Paradiso** (Map pp180–2; ☎ 0185 77 20 91; www.golfoparadiso.it, Italian only; Via Scalo 3) operates boats from the Porto Antico to Camogli (€8/10.50 single/return), Recco (€8/10.50), Portofino (€8/10.50), the Cinque Terre (€15.50/23.50) and Porto Venere (€19/25) on the Riviera di Levante (see p188).

BUS
Buses to international cities use Piazza della Vittoria, as do buses to/from Milan's Malpensa airport (€15.50, two hours, twice daily) and other inter-regional services. Tickets are sold at Geotravels and/or Pesci Viaggi e Turismo (see p177).

TRAIN
Genoa is linked by train (Intercity fares quoted) to Turin (€15.86, 1¾ hours, seven to 10 daily), Milan (€12.86, 1½ hours, up to eight daily), Pisa (€15.86, two hours, up to

eight daily) and Rome (€34.51, 5¼ hours, six daily) and it makes little difference which of the two train stations (Principe or Brignole) you choose, except for trips along the two Rivieras. Going west to San Remo (€7.65, 2¼ to three hours, five daily) and Ventimiglia (€8.80, 2½ hours, six daily) however, there are more departures from Stazione Principe.

Getting Around
TO/FROM THE AIRPORT
AMT's **line No 100** (☎ 010 558 24 14) departs from Piazza Giuseppe Verdi, outside Stazione Brignole (€3 one way, 25 minutes, every 30 minutes 5.30am to 11pm). It stops at Stazione Principe en route to the airport.

BICYCLE
Nuovo Centro Sportivo (Map pp180–2; ☎ 010 254 12 43; Piazza dei Garibaldi 16-22; ☻ 3.30-7.30pm Mon, 9am-12.30pm & 3.30-7.30pm Tue-Sat) rents bicycles for €6 a day.

BUS
AMT (toll-free ☎ 800 085 352, ☎ 010 599 74 14; www.amt.genova.it, Italian only) operates buses throughout the city and has an **information office** (Piazza della Vittoria; ☻ 7.15am-6pm Mon-Fri, 7am-7pm Sat & Sun). Bus line No 383 links Stazione Brignole with Piazza de Ferrari and Stazione Brignole. A ticket valid for 90 minutes costs €1 (10-ticket carnet €9.50) and an all-day ticket costs €3. Tickets can be used on mainline trains within the city limits (as far as Voltri and Nervi).

RIVIERA DI LEVANTE
The coast east of Genoa's unfortunate portside sprawl unfolds in a sprinkling of seaside villages, which, despite their evident popularity, ensure pretty walking, dramatic scenery and charm. The green lands around Portofino, Italy's wealthiest promontory 38km east of Genoa, are protected by the Parco Naturale Regionale di Portofino.

Camogli
pop 5740
Wandering Camogli's alleys and cobbled streets, 25km east of Genoa, it is hard not to be taken aback by the painstaking trompe l'oeil decoration. The main esplanade, Via Garibaldi, is a colourful place, especially on the second Sunday in May when fishermen

celebrate the **Sagra del Pesce** (Fish Festival) with a big fry-up – hundreds of fish are cooked up in 3m-wide pans along the busy waterfront. Camogli, meaning 'house of wives', takes its name from the days when the women ran the town while their husbands were at sea.

From here, boats nip across to **Punta Chiappi**, a rocky crop on the Portofino promontory where you can swim and sunbathe. The **tourist office** (☎ 0185 77 10 66; iat.camogli@apt.genova .it; Via XX Settembre 33; ☻ 9am-12.30pm & 3.30-6pm Mon-Sat, 9am-1pm Sun) has a list of diving schools and boat-rental places. Overpriced restaurants and cafés line the waterfront and Piazza Colombo; delve down the lanes away from the water to escape the lunchtime crowd and get a better deal.

GETTING THERE & AWAY
Tigullio (☎ 0185 23 11 08) runs buses to/from Rapallo and Santa Margherita (both €1, every 20 minutes) from the stop just past the tourist office on Via XX Settembre.

Camogli (€2, 30 minutes from Stazione Principe, hourly) is on the Genoa–La Spezia train line.

Year-round, **Cooperativa Battellieri del Golfo Paradiso** (☎ 0185 77 20 91; www.golfoparadiso.it, Italian only) runs boats to/from Punta Chiappi (€4/5.50 single/return), San Fruttuoso (€5.50/8), Portofino (€8/12, June to September), Porto Venere (€13/20, June to September) and the Cinque Terre (€12/19, June to September).

San Fruttuoso
Fascinating San Fruttuoso, 5km southeast, is dominated by the **Abbazia di San Fruttuoso di Capodimonte** (☎ 0185 77 27 03; adult/child €4/2.50; ☻ 10am-6pm Jun-Sep, 10am-4pm Tue-Sun Mar-May & Oct, 10am-4pm Sat & Sun Dec-Feb). The Benedictine abbey was built as a final resting place for Bishop St Fructuosus of Tarragona, martyred in Spain in 259, and rebuilt in the mid-13th century with the assistance of the Doria family, who used it as a family crypt. It fell into decay with the decline of the religious community, and in the 19th century was divided into small living quarters by local fishermen.

In 1954 a bronze statue of Christ was lowered 15m to the sea bed by locals as a tribute to divers lost at sea and to bless the waters. Dive to see it or view it from a boat if the waters are calm (the Cooperativa Battellieri del Golfo Paradiso can provide details, p187). A replica, in a fish tank, is displayed in the church adjoining the abbey. A religious ceremony is held over the statue each August.

San Fruttuoso is only accessible on foot from Camogli or Portofino – a stiff but exhilarating 5km-long cliffside walk that takes up to 2½ hours one way from either town – or by boat – year-round from Camogli; summer only from Santa Margherita (pp190–1), Portofino (following) and Rapallo (p191).

Portofino
pop 556
Exclusive Portofino, 38km east of Genoa, is Liguria's most chichi spot where Europe's movers and shakers come to wheel, deal, play and pose – poet Petrarch, writers Guy de Maupassant and Truman Capote, and English photographer Cecil Beaton all sojourned here. A haughty disdain by residents lends the place a healthy air of restraint, and the huddle of pastel-coloured houses around the portside square is a delight. In summer the waterfront cafés and designer boutiques glitter with glitterati, while motorists sit it out in the searing heat, waiting to enter the village. A digital clock, 2km north in the seafront hamlet of Paraggi, flashes how much longer they can expect to sweat.

The **tourist office** (☎/fax 0185 26 90 24; Via Roma 35; ☼ 10.30am-1.30pm & 2.30-5.30pm Tue-Sun) has plenty of information on Portofino and its protected green surrounds.

SIGHTS & ACTIVITIES
At the port a flight of stairs signposted 'Salita San Giorgio' leads past the **Chiesa di San Giorgio** to 16th-century **Castello Brown** (☎ 0185 26 71 01; Via alla Penisola; adult/child €3.50/free; ☼ 10am-7pm). Built by the Genoese over an existing fort, the castle occasionally saw action, particularly when occupied by Napoleon and taken by the English in 1814. A visit takes in a couple of furnished rooms, a temporary exhibition and great views. For a better outlook continue along the same track through olive groves to the **lighthouse**; it's an hour's walk there and back.

Sailing and motorboats can be hired from **Giorgio Mussini & Co** (☎ 0185 26 93 27; www.giorgiomussini.com, Italian only; Calata Marconi 38). **Garage Portofino Motonoleggio** (☎ 0185 26 90 39; Piazza della Libertà 27) rents mountain bikes (around €15 per day) and the tourist office distributes free maps of **walking** and **biking**

trails around Monte di Portofino (610m) in the Parco Naturale Regionale di Portofino.

Heading north along the coastal road is the **Abbazia della Cervara** (Abbazia di San Girolamo; ☎ 0185 29 31 39; www.cervara.it; Lungomare Rossetti, Via Cervara 10; ☼ guided tours 1st & 3rd Sun of month 10am, 11am & noon Mar-Oct), built in 1361, which is surrounded by monumental gardens. Benedictine monks lived here from the 14th to 18th centuries and French Trappist monks in the 19th century; it has been a private residence since 1937. Guided tours (by reservation only) take in the gardens, 15th-century chapterhouse, 16th-century cloister and the Saracen Tower built to safeguard the abbey against Saracen attacks in the 1500s.

SLEEPING & EATING
Eden (☎ 0185 26 90 91; www.hoteledenportofino.com; Vico Dritto 18; s/d from €100/200; P ✗) Run by the same family for the last 40-odd years, this 12-room hotel with palm trees in its garden and polished wooden floors is Portofino's cheapest place to stay.

Piccolo Hotel (☎ 0185 26 90 15; www.dominapiccolo.it; Via Duca degli Abuzzi 31; s/d from €180/230; P ✗) The Little Hotel comes in the guise of a three-storey villa with signature palm trees and a tiny beach. It's a short walk from the port.

Hotel Splendido (☎ 0185 26 78 01; www.splendido.orient-express.com; Salita Baratta 16; d low/high season from €798/916; P ✗ ☞) Taylor, Burton, Sting and Madonna have all stayed at Portofino's plushest pad – a splendid villa in the hills above the port. It also runs the portside **Splendido Mare** (☎ 0185 26 78 06; Via Roma 2; d low/high season from €536/594; P ✗ ☞).

Ö Magazin (☎ 0185 26 91 78; Calata Marconi 34; 1st/2nd courses €18/20) Decked out like the cabin of a boat, this waterfront eatery is a tad more authentic than the rest. Look for the handful of tables romantically perched away from it all at the far end of the port.

GETTING THERE & AROUND
Portofino is an easy bus ride from Santa Margherita (see pp190–1 for details).

April to October, **Servizio Marittimo del Tigullio** (see pp190–1) runs daily ferries from Portofino to San Fruttuoso (€5.50/8 single/return) and Santa Margherita (€3.50/6).

Motorists must park at the village entrance and pay €4.50/12 per one/three hours (cash only) for the privilege.

Santa Margherita

pop 10,600

Once home to a coral-fishing fleet that roamed as far afield as Africa, Santa Margherita, 32km southeast of Genoa, is known for its orange blossoms and lace. In a sheltered bay on the eastern side of the Portofino promontory on the Golfo di Tigullio, its waterfront is a jumble of one-time fishing cottages, elegant hotels with Liberty facades and moored million-dollar yachts.

Lemon trees and other flora typical to Santa Margherita's hot climate grow in the parklands around **Villa Durazzo** (☎ 0185 29 31 35; villa.durazzo@comunesml.org; entrances Piazzale San Giacomo 3, Via San Francesco d'Assisi 3 & Via Principe Centurione; admission free; ⏱ 9am-7pm Jun-Sep, 9am-5pm Oct-Apr), a 17th-century villa.

Sailing, **water-skiing**, **scuba diving** and **walking** opportunities abound, especially in the **Parco Naturale Regionale di Portofino** which has its **headquarters** (☎ 0185 28 94 79; it.parcodiportofino@libero.it; Viale Rainusso 1) in Santa Margherita.

ORIENTATION

From the **train station** (Via Roma), head downhill to the palm-tree-clad port, then along Corso Doria to Piazza Vittorio Veneto, from where most buses depart. Boat trips use the jetty off the adjoining square, Piazza Martiri della Libertà.

INFORMATION

Internet Point (☎ 0185 29 30 92; liguriacom@tigullio.it; Via Giuncheto 39; €4/hr)

Post Office (Via Giunchetto 45; ⏱ 8am-6pm Mon-Fri, 8am-1.15pm Sat)

Tourist Office (☎ 0185 28 74 85; www.apttigullio.liguria.it; Via XXV Aprile 2B; ⏱ 9.30am-12.30pm & 2.30-5.30pm Mon-Sat).

SLEEPING

Annabella (☎ 0185 28 65 31; Via Costasecca 10; s/d/tr €44/68/90) This is a clean place, signposted from Piazza Mazzini. Look for a deep-red terracotta building. Rooms have a washbasin and bidet, but share one of several corridor showers.

Fasce (☎ 0185 28 64 35; www.hotelfasce.it; Via Luigi Bozzo 3; s/d/tr with breakfast €82/92/118; ℗ 🐾) Tucked off Corso Matteotti, this stylish two-star Anglo/Italian-run hotel has 16 ultra-clean modern rooms, a roof terrace for sunbathing, bicycles to borrow and a peaceful bar out back.

EATING & DRINKING

Simple but appealing food is the order of the day in these eateries.

Caffè del Porto (☎ 0185 28 70 44; Via Bottaro 32; 1st/2nd courses €6.20/15.50) Oodles of charm can be found here, making it *the* place to sniff and swill local wines. Lunch on a simple *panino* (filled roll; €3.50), a lip-smacking plate of finger-licking fried fish (€10.50) or crayfish flambéed in oil, paprika and whisky (€17). *Spaghetti al cartuccio* (spaghetti in a cardboard box; €9.50) is the dish for the culinary curious.

Trattoria dei Pescatori (☎ 0185 28 67 47; Via Bottaro 43-44; 1st courses €10, 2nd courses €20-25; ⏱ Wed-Mon) This simple but soulful seafood restaurant dates to 1911 and serves rustic dishes with a fishy flavour. *Moscardini affogati* (stewed baby octopus) is a speciality. A note on the menu adds 'our prices are high because portions are abundant'.

Bar Colombo (☎ 0185 28 70 58; Via Pescino 13) Do what Burton, Taylor and other Hollywood greats did and pass a few hours at this historic Art Nouveau place on the waterfront. An espresso costs €2.20.

La Vaca Loca (☎ 0185 29 03 16; Vico Masaniello 5; ⏱ Wed-Mon) Never been to a beerhouse resembling a mad cow (*la vaca loca* in Spanish)? Then this wild 'n wacky *paninoteca* (sandwich bar) and bar is the place for you. The crowd is young, fun and friendly.

Zinco of London (Piazza Vittorio Veneto; 1st/2nd courses €15/15, pizzas €9) This self-marketed 'American bar' and art café with large windows overlooking the central square reflects the modern – and happening – face of Santa Margherita.

Shop for the day's catch at the **fresh fish market** (Corso Marconi; ⏱ 4pm-7pm Mon-Fri).

GETTING THERE & AROUND

Tigullio Trasporti (toll-free ☎ 800 01 48 08; www.tigulliotrasporti.it, Italian only) runs buses to/from Portofino (€1, every 20 minutes) and Camogli (€1.10, every 30 minutes). Buy tickets at its information kiosk (☎ 0185 28 88 34; Piazza Vittorio Veneto), at the bus terminal.

By train, there are hourly services to/from Genoa (€2, 45 minutes) and La Spezia (€3.80, 1½ hours).

Servizio Marittimo del Tigullio (☎ 0185 28 46 70; www.traghettiportofino.it; Via Palestro 8/1b) runs seasonal ferries to/from Porto Venere (€17/26 single/return), San Fruttuoso (€7/11.50,

Portofino (pp189–90) and the Cinque Terre (p192).

Get around by **taxi** (☎ 0185 28 79 98), bicycle or moped – hire the latter two from **Noleggio Cicli e Motocicli** (☎ 330 87 86 12; Via XXV Aprile 11; per 4hrs/day €7/10; ☻ Mon-Sat).

Rapallo
pop 29,360
Rapallo, overlooking the Gulf of Tigullio, has an air of bustle independent of tourists that towns further down the promontory lack – all the more so on Thursday when market stalls fill central Piazza Cile. Bright blue changing cabins line its sandy beach and lend the palm-tree-studded waterfront an old-fashioned air. The little castle by the sea, built in 1550, hosts art exhibitions.

With its Roman origins Rapallo boasts a bridge supposedly used by Hannibal during the Carthaginian invasion of Italy in 218 BC. In the 19th century the town became known for its lace and a century later for its treaties: in 1920, the Italo-Yugoslav Treaty that defined the borders of the two countries was signed here, and in 1922 Russia and Germany sealed a peace deal that would last 19 years.

Since 1934 a **cable car** (☎ 0185 27 34 44; funivi a.rapallo@libero.it; Piazzale Solari 2; single/return €5.20/7.75; ☻ 9am-12.30pm Mon-Fri, 8.30am-12.30pm Sat & Sun Mar-Oct) has trundled up to **Santuario Basilica di Montallegro** (612m), a sanctuary built on the spot where, on 2 July 1557, the Virgin Mary was reportedly sighted. Walkers and mountain bikers can follow an old mule track (5km, 1½ hours) to the hilltop site. The **tourist office** (☎ 0185 23 03 46; Lungo Vittorio Veneto 7; ☻ 9.30am-12.30pm & 2.30-5.30pm Mon-Sat) has details of other **walks** in the area and stocks walking maps.

SLEEPING & EATING
Il Pellegrino (☎ 0185 23 90 03; Santuario di Montallegro; B&B from around €35, full meals around €15; ☻ May-Aug, Easter & Christmas) Stunning views of Rapallo and the coastline star at this highly atmospheric hotel and restaurant, perched behind Montallegro and popular with walkers. A footpath leads from the hotel to the sanctuary.

Albergo La Vela (☎ /fax 0185 5 05 51; Via Milite gnoto 21/7; d with/without bathroom from €55/45) Friendly, simple and soulful are attributes of La Vela, one of Rapallo's cheapest hotels. Situated above a bar, look for the 'we speak English' sign.

Hotel Ambra (☎ /fax 0185 23 41 35; Via Monsignore Boccoleri 2-4; s/d low season €45/57, high season €52/67) Down an alley off Rapallo's main boulevard, this terracotta-coloured hotel with green shutters and lots of pot plants promises a peaceful stay.

The waterfront is lined with places to eat, drink and snack. Foodies should browse **Parla Come Mangi** (☎ 0185 23 49 93; Corso Italia 60), a fabulous wine, cheese and sausage shop.

GETTING THERE & AWAY
Tigullio Trasporti (toll-free ☎ 800 01 48 08, 0185 23 11 08; www.tigulliotrasporti.it; Italian only; Piazza delle Nazioni) runs regular buses to/from Santa Margherita (€1, every 20 minutes) and Camogli.

Servizio Marittimo del Tigullio runs year-round boats to/from Santa Margherita (€2/3 single/return), Portofino (€5/8) and San Fruttuoso (€7.50/12.50), and seasonal boats to Genoa (€10.50/15.50), the Cinque Terre (€17/26) and Porto Venere (€17/26).

Chiavari to Levanto
The stretch of coast between the Portofino promontory and the Cinque Terre can be a letdown, wedged as it is between two such beauty spots. It does have some of the Riviera di Levante's best beaches, although the rash of resorts – **Chiavari, Lavagna, Sestri Levante, Deiva Marina** and **Levanto** – get packed out in summer.

Inland you can OD on fresh mountain air in the **Parco Naturale Regionale dell'Aveto**, a nature reserve at the northern end of the **Val d'Aveto**. The tranquil valley, frequented mainly by walkers on the prowl for peace and quiet, starts 12km north of the coast in **Borzonasca**. Heading north, **Santo Stefano d'Aveto** (population 1281) is a small cross-country skiing centre and the main village in the valley. Between the two is **Lago delle Lame**, a glacial lake whose shallow waters have preserved fir-tree stumps from 2500 years ago. Information on walks is covered by the **park office** (☎ 0185 34 03 11; Via Marre 75a) in Borzonasca and Santo Stefano d'Aveto **tourist office** (☎ 0185 8 80 46; Piazza del Popolo 1). From Borzonasca point your compass east to get to the short **Valle Sturla.**

Chiavari (population 28,280), with an arcaded old town, 12km east of Santa Margherita, is the main access point inland; by car, follow the signs in town for Carasco.

LIGURIA, PIEDMONT & VALLE D'AOSTA

Chiavari **tourist office** (☎ 0185 532 51 98; Corso Assarotti 1) is opposite the train station.

The Cinque Terre

If you miss the five villages that make up the Cinque Terre (literally 'five lands'), you will have bypassed some of Italy's most extraordinary countryside (it is a Unesco World Heritage site and on the World Monument Fund list). But blink as the train zips between tunnels and you will miss them.

The mountains, covered by terraced vineyards and 7000km of dry-stone walls, drop precipitously into the Mediterranean. Wine growers use monorail mechanisms to ferry themselves up and the grapes down, while olive groves – tinted orange with nets in November when the black fruits fall – embrace the lower slopes. Tourism long ago overtook fishing and viniculture as the mainstay industry (100 hectares are farmed today, compared to 1400 in its heyday), prompting fears for these unique lands: if the terraced hillsides are not worked, they will quite literally slide into the sea.

Although the **Parco Nazionale delle Cinque Terre** was created in 1999, it was not until 2002 that any real protective measures were taken. Information centres have now been set up and walkers pay to use trails which the park authorities close when numbers get too great.

Hotels are scarce but numerous villagers have rooms to rent: look for signs reading *camere* (rooms) or *affittacamere* (rooms for rent).

INFORMATION

National park offices sell the Cinque Terre Card (€3), valid for 24 hours and allowing unlimited use of footpaths. Cards covering rail travel (see following) also cover trails. Park offices sell maps and have information on walking and cycling.

The main **Parco Nazionale delle Cinque Terre office** (☎ 0187 92 06 33, ☎ 0187 76 00 91; parconazionale5terre@libero.it; Piazza Rio Finale 26; ☼ 6.30am-8pm Oct-Apr, 6.30am-10pm Jun-Sep) is outside Riomaggiore train station, with smaller offices at train stations in **Monterosso** (☎ 0187 81 70 59), **Vernazza** (☎ 0187 81 25 38), **Corniglia** (☎ 0187 81 25 23) and **Manarola** (☎ 0187 76 05 11), all open 7am to 8pm.

A useful Internet resource is www.cinqueterre.it.

The only self-service **launderette** (Via Colombo 111; ☼ 9am-7pm) is in Riomaggiore.

GETTING THERE & AROUND

The Cinque Terre's saving grace is its lack of motorised traffic. Cars are not allowed beyond village entrances, meaning a hefty hourly parking fee (about €1) and a strenuous hike of 1km or more. In some villages park authorities run minibus shuttles (€1.50/2.50 single/return) between the car park and village entrance.

The easiest way to get there and around is the Genoa–La Spezia train service which trundles along the coast every 15 to 30 minutes between 6.30am and 10pm. Journey time between one village and another is no more than a few minutes and a single fare typically costs €1.10. Alternatively, unlimited 2nd-class rail travel between Levanto and La Spezia is covered by the Cinque Terre Card, a one-/three-/seven-day pass sold by national park offices for €5.20/12.40/19.60 (child €2.60/6.20/9.80).

In summer **Cooperativa Battellieri del Golfo Paradiso** runs boats to the Cinque Terre from Genoa; see p187. Seasonal boat services to/from Santa Margherita (€14/21 single/return) are handled by **Servizio Marittimo del Tigullio** (see pp190–1).

Late March to October, La Spezia-based **Navigazione Golfo dei Poeti** (see p196) runs daily shuttle boats between all the villages (except Corniglia). A one-day 'village-hopping' ticket costs €10.50/6.50 per adult/child and a single/return fare to one village is €2.70/4.50. The same company operates boat excursions to the Cinque Terre from Porto Venere (p197) and La Spezia (p196).

You can hire bicycles to pedal around from the national park office in Riomaggiore (see pp193–4).

MONTEROSSO AL MARE
pop 1604

Huge statues embedded into the rocks overlook one of the few Cinque Terre beaches, a grey, pebbly affair.

In the historic centre **Enoteca Internazionale** (☎ 0187 81 72 87; Via Roma 62) and **Cantina du Sciacchetrà** (☎ 0187 81 78 28; Via Roma 7) are two of several wine bars where the Cinque Terre's renowned white wines can be tasted and bought. Be sure to sniff and swill the sweet dessert wines Morasca, Chiaretto del

Faro and the sweeter-than-sweet Sciacchetrà while you're here. Die-hards can down shots of *limoncino*, a potent lemon liqueur made from Monterosso lemons and guaranteed to make your heart race.

Anchovies are the other Monterosso tradition. Eat them fresh from the sea, fried, raw with lemon juice, pickled in brine, salted in glass or in a *tian* (oven-baked with potatoes and tomatoes).

VERNAZZA
pop 1110

Possibly the most fetching village Vernazza makes the most of the sea with a piazza on the water and the remains of an 11th-century castle. Heading inland, the road is choked with vineyards and lemon groves.

Vernazza's main cobbled street, Via Roma, links seaside Piazza Guglielmo Marconi with the train station. On the main street, there's a tasty *focacceria* at No 3 and Internet access inside the **Blue Marlin Café** (☎ 0187 82 11 49; bmarlin@tin.it; Via Roma 43; Internet access €0.15/min ☺ 7am-11pm Fri-Wed), a café-cum-bar.

Vernazza has a couple of hotels and numerous rooms to let. If you dine at **Trattoria da Sandro** (☎ 0187 81 22 23; Via Roma 69; full meals around €25) don't miss its mixed fried-fish platters or *insalata di polpo* (octopus salad).

CORNIGLIA

Balanced precariously along a ridge high above the sea, Corniglia is a postcard of four-storey houses, narrow lanes and stairways woven into a hill by **La Torre**, a medieval lookout. From the central square, Via Fieschi cuts through the village heart to **Belvedere Santa Maria**, another lookout with a coastal panorama. In summer minibuses shuttle tourists between the station and village – otherwise, it's a strenuous, 363-step zig-zag uphill.

La Posada (☎ 0187 82 11 74; la_posada@libero.it; Via alla Stazione 11; d from €65) Standing tall at the top of the steps linking the station and village, La Posada has one of Cinque Terre's loveliest terraces – white table-clothed tables perched on a lawn beneath olive trees, with breathtaking ocean views. Rooms are equally seductive.

A Cantina de Mananan (☎ 0187 82 11 66, accommodation ☎ 0187 81 23 20; Via Fieschi 117; 1st/2nd courses €7/12.50, r €60) This charming pocket-sized *osteria* (wine bar), in an 18th-century

wine cellar, is the place to taste Cinque Terre wines and munch homemade pasta. It has a handful of rooms above.

MANAROLA

More grapes are grown around Manarola than any other Cinque Terre village. A 13th-century church, a bell tower used as a defensive lookout in the 14th century, and an oratory that once served as a leper hospital line the central square at the northern end of steep Via Discovolo. Those game for a climb can follow a path off nearby Via Rollandi that leads through vineyards to the top of the mountain.

Ostello 5 Terre (☎ 0187 92 02 15; www.cinqueterre.net /ostello; Via Riccobaldi 21; dm low/high season €18/20, 4-bed f low/high season €84/80, breakfast/dinner €3.50/12; ☺ hostel 7am-1pm & 5pm-1am mid-Apr–Sep, 7am-1pm & 4pm-midnight Oct–mid-Apr) The Cinque Terre's only hostel rents out mountain bikes, kayaks and snorkelling gear. Reservations at least one week in advance are advised and guests don't need an HI card. Each single-sex, six-bed dorm has its own bathroom. Note the guest lockout times.

Marina Piccola (☎ 0187 92 01 03; Via Lo Scalo 16; s/d from €60/80, full meals around €25) The Little Marina overlooks Manarola's little marina no less. *Zuppa di datteri* (date soup) and a shoal of fishy dishes are the house specialities. Some rooms have sea views.

RIOMAGGIORE
pop 1823

A mess of houses slithering down a ravine to form the main street, Riomaggiore is the main village in the Cinque Terre. Tiny fishing boats bob by the shore or sit stacked on the small waterside square when seas are rough. Outside the train station – a short walk through a tunnel or ride in a lift from town – wall murals by Argentinian artist Silvio Benedetto (born 1938) depict the hard graft of Cinque Terre farmers who, over the centuries, built the Cinque Terre with their bare hands.

Marine life can be viewed through a mask with the **Cooperative Sub 5 Terre** (☎ 0187 92 05 96; Via San Giacomo), a diving centre which rents snorkels and canoes/kayaks. Walkers with a keen eye for nature should make a beeline for **Torre Guardiola** (☎ 0187 76 00 52; ☺ 9am-1pm Aug, 9am-1pm & 4-7pm Sep, Feb-Oct), a nature observation and birdwatching centre on **Fossola**

LOVERS' LANE

For those with time or a romance on their hands, there's the **Via dell'Amore** (Lovers' Lane; national park's department ☎ 0187 92 10 26, ☎ 0187 76 05 11; viadellamore@libero.it; ☼ 9am-9pm), a well-paved coastal path linking Manarola with Riomaggiore (1km). Picnic areas stud it and stone benches, embedded in the cliffside, abound for those keen to feast their eyes on sweeping ocean views. At either end steps lead up from the train station to the path – checkpoints along the way ensure no one sneaks by without a €3 trail pass (see p192).

The Via dell'Amore is part of the 12km-long *sentiero azzurro* (blue trail; trail No 2) that runs the length of the coast between Monterosso and Riomaggiore. Unlike Lovers' Lane (which is flat, well-paved and suited to walkers of all abilities, including children and pushchairs), the rest of the footpath is only for the sure-footed and well equipped. The first stretch between Monterosso and Vernazza (4km) is particularly difficult – lots of ups and downs – and is the least scenic. Further east dramatic coastal views and pretty little coves with crystal-clear water (bring your swimming gear) compensate for any sweat and tears – count on 1¾ hours to cover the 4km-long Vernazza–Corniglia section, and one hour to walk from Corniglia to Manarola (3km).

Of the dozens of national-park trails suitable for experienced walkers, trail No 1 is the most memorable. The 12km-long footpath links Riomaggiore to Port Venere and takes walkers up into the mountains before plummeting back down to the coast.

Beach, immediately southeast of Riomaggiore marina. From the centre a botanical trail leads along the coast.

A clutch of B&Bs, room- and apartment-rental agencies litter Via Colombo, including **La Dolce Vita** (☎ 0187 76 00 44; agonatal@tin.it; Via Colombo 120), **Edi** (☎ 0187 92 03 25; edi-vesigna@iol.it; Via Colombo 111), **Roberto Fazioli** (☎ 0187 92 09 04; robertofazioli@libero.it; Via Colombo 94) and extra-friendly **Mar Mar** (☎ 0187 92 09 32; www.marmar.5terre.com; Via Colombo 234; d low/high season from €40/60, d with breakfast, TV & terrace from €50/90; ☼ 8.30am-8pm). Mar Mar has dorm beds (read: share an apartment with backpackers) for a €15/20 in low/high season as well as rooms and apartments for rent. Dorm beds can't be reserved in advance. Mar Mar also has a couple of terminals to access the Internet (€0.10/minute) and, between April and September, rents one-/two-person kayaks for €4/8 an hour or €20/30 a day.

La Spezia
pop 99,090

La Spezia, 100km southeast of Genoa, sits at the head of the gulf of the same name – also known as the Gulf of Poets in deference to Byron, Dante, DH Lawrence, Shelley, George Sand and others drawn here by its beauty.

The construction from 1860 to 1865 of Italy's largest naval base propelled La Spezia from minor port to provincial capital, its street grid and venerable public buildings largely a product of that time. It's still a navy town, with the ubiquitous blue sailor's uniform a constant reminder. The city centre is sandwiched between the naval base (west) and the commercial port (east).

INFORMATION

Phone Centre (Via Paleocapa 1a; Internet access €5/hr)
Police Station (☎ 0187 56 71; Viale Italia 497)
Post Office (Piazza di Giuseppe Verdi; ☼ 8am-6.30pm Mon-Sat)
Tourist Office (☎ 0187 25 43 11; www.aptcinqueterr e.sp.it; Viale G Mazzini 47; ☼ 9am-1pm & 2.30-5.30pm Mon-Sat, 9am-1pm Sun)

SIGHTS

La Spezia's star attraction is the **Museo Amedeo Lia** (☎ 0187 73 11 00; Via Prione 234; adult/child €6/3; ☼ 10am-6pm Tue-Sun, admission free guided tours 3.30pm every 2nd Sun), a fine art museum in a restored 17th-century convent. The private collection covers the 13th to 18th centuries and contains 2000 works by masters such as Tintoretto, Tiepolo, Titian, Bellini and Sansovino.

Next door, the Palazzina delle Arti dates to the 19th century. Inside, the **Museo del Sigillo** (Seal Museum; ☎ 0187 77 85 44; Via Prione 236; adult/child €3.10/2; ☼ 4-7pm Tue, 10am-noon & 4-7pm Wed-Sun) displays dozens of seals (for letters rather than of the breathing variety).

A mixture of booty is stashed inside **Castello di San Giorgio** (☎ 0187 75 11 42; sangiorgio@castagna.it; Via XXVII Marzo; adult/child €6/3; ☼ 9.30am-12.30pm & 2-5pm Tue-Sun winter, 9.30am-12.30pm & 5-8pm Tue-Sun

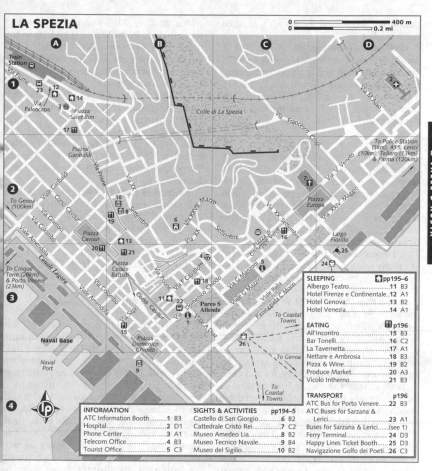

LA SPEZIA

0 _____ 400 m
0 _____ 0.2 mi

SLEEPING	pp195–6
Albergo Teatro.................11	B3
Hotel Firenze e Continentale.12	A1
Hotel Genova...................13	B2
Hotel Venezia..................14	A1

EATING	p196
All'Incontro....................15	B3
Bar Tonelli.....................16	C2
La Tavernetta..................17	A1
Nettare e Ambrosia 18	B3
Pizza & Wine...................19	B2
Produce Market.................20	A3
Vicolo Intherno................21	B3

TRANSPORT	p196
ATC Bus for Porto Venere......22	B3
ATC Buses for Sarzana &	
Lerici.......................23	A1
Buses for Sarzana & Lerici....(see 1)	
Ferry Terminal.................24	D3
Happy Lines Ticket Booth.......25	D3
Navigazione Golfo dei Poeti...26	C3

INFORMATION			SIGHTS & ACTIVITIES	pp194–5
ATC Information Booth..........1	B3		Castello di San Giorgio........6	B2
Hospital......................2	D1		Cattedrale Cristo Rei..........7	C2
Phone Center..................3	A1		Museo Amedeo Lia...............8	B2
Telecom Office.................4	B3		Museo Tecnico Navale...........9	B4
Tourist Office.................5	C3		Museo del Sigilio.............10	B2

LIGURIA, PIEDMONT & VALLE D'AOSTA

---

summer). A hotchpotch of Bronze Age and Iron Age relics and ancient Ligurian statue-stelae are among its archaeological treasures.

A ticket covering admission to the above three museums costs €8/4 and is valid for 48 hours. You can purchase a ticket from any of the participating museums.

Next to La Spezia's naval base is the **Museo Tecnico Navale** (Naval Museum; ☎ 0187 78 30 16, Viale Amendola 1; admission €1.55; ⏲ 8.30am-6pm Mon-Sat, 10.15am-3.45pm Sun), founded in 1870. It hosts a phalanx of *polene* (colourful busts or statuettes that graced the prows of vessels) and lots of model ships. The naval base itself only opens to the public for one day of the year – 19 March, the festival of the town's patron saint, Joseph.

SLEEPING

Albergo Teatro (☎ 0187 73 13 74; www.albergo teatro.it; Via Carpenino 31; s/d without bathroom low season €20/35, high season €28/46, d with bathroom low/high season €45/61) Cheap and down-to-earth sums up La Spezia's Theatre Hotel where spartan rooms ensure a sound sleep nonetheless.

Hotel Venezia (☎ 0187 73 34 65; Via Paleocapa 10; s/d/tr low season €42/62/78, high season €51/87/103) Orange trees front this modern three-star hotel where a mustard facade shields a hotchpotch of furnishings inside.

Hotel Genova (☎ 0187 73 29 72; hgenova@col.it; Via F Rosselli 84; s/d €70/105; ☒) A charming reno-vated exterior dresses a modern interior at this courteous three-star pad, on a quiet pedestrian street near La Spezia's covered food market.

Hotel Firenze e Continentale (☎ 0187 71 32 10; www.hotelfirenzecontinentale.it; Via Paleocapa 7; s/d €76/ 114; 🏖) The Florence is La Spezia's grand train-station option. New it might be, but a grand job has been made of making the marble floors, wood panelling and brass fittings match the 1900 facade.

EATING

Bar Tonelli (Via XX Settembre 27; 1st/2nd courses €5.70/10) Red, white, green and blue walls stand bold in this modern Art Deco–styled café. It offers an inspired range of cheese and salami to munch, and the tobacconist next door is the only place in town to sell English-language newspapers and magazines.

La Tavernetta (☎ 0187 70 41 47; Via Fiume 57; 1st/2nd courses €5.70/10, pizzas €2.60-6.50) A tavern is exactly what this cavernous, wooden-clad bar is. Pub grub includes too many pizzas to choose from and a €10 tourist menu.

Pizza & Wine (☎ 0187 217 12; Via Prione 237; meals around €15; 🕐 12.30pm-3.30pm & 7pm-3am Tue-Fri, 7pm-3am Sat & Sun) Pizza and wine are the mainstays of this self-marketed 'music meeting bar', above a street-fashion clothes shop on La Spezia's main window-shopping avenue. Its modern interior is bright, cheerful and chic.

Vicolo Intherno (☎ 0187 239 98; Via della Canonica 22; meals around €15.50; 🕐 Tue-Sat) Sit around solid wooden tables beneath a hefty beamed ceiling and wash down *torte di verdure* (Ligurian vegetable pie) or stockfish with a tongue-tickling choice of local vintages.

Nettare e Ambrosia (☎ 0187 73 72 52; Via Fazio 85 & 86; meals €15; 🕐 Mon-Sat) It might well appear a tad shabby and simple from the outside, but Nectar & Ambrosia is *the* place to sample great wines in an authentic La Spezian atmosphere. Its cuisine is equally inspiring.

All'Incontro (☎ 0187 2 46 89; Via Sapri 10; 1st course €5.20-6.70, 2nd course €7.75-13; 🕐 Mon-Sat) Tuck into a plate of *spaghetti alla chitarra ai 'batti batti' di Monterosso* (chunky spaghetti in a sauce topped with flavoursome local sea critters), followed by a juicy slab of kangaroo or bison. Exotic animals aside, fish is said to be the speciality.

A daily food market fills Piazza Cavour.

GETTING THERE & AWAY

Towns close to La Spezia can only be reached by buses run by **Azienda Trasporti Consortile** (ATC;

toll-free ☎ 800 32 23 22; www.atclaspezia.it, Italian only); these include Porto Venere (€1.32, up to five daily from Via Domenico Chiodo), Lerici (€1.32, two or three daily from the train station) and Sarzana (€1.43, two or three daily from the train station).

La Spezia is on the Genoa–Rome railway line and is also connected to Milan (€20.97, three hours, four daily), Turin (€18.90, three hours, several daily) and Pisa (€6.25, 50 minutes, almost hourly); Intercity fares are quoted. The Cinque Terre and other coastal towns are easily accessible by train.

Navigazione Golfo dei Poeti (☎ 0187 96 76 76; www.navigazionegolfodeipoeti.it; Via Don Minzoni 13) runs boat services to Genoa and other coastal towns. See those sections for details.

April to October, **Happy Lines** (☎ 0187 56 44 28; Via Maralunga 45), with a ticket booth at the port, runs daily ferries to Bastia in Corsica.

Porto Venere
pop 4250

It's worth the trip to Porto Venere, a 12km wiggle south of La Spezia, simply to sample its razor-clam soup. The Romans built Portus Veneris on the western shore of the Golfo della Spezia as a base en route from Gaul to Spain. From the waterfront, narrow steps and cobbled paths lead uphill to the **Chiesa di San Lorenzo** (1116). In the church's shadow lies **Castello Doria** (adult/ child €2.60/1.50; 🕐 10.30am-1.30pm & 2.30-5.30pm Fri-Sun), built in the 16th century as part of the Genoese Republic's defence system and offering magnificent views from its terraced gardens.

At the end of the quay a Cinque Terre panorama unfolds from the rocky terraces of **Grotta Arpaia**, a former haunt of Byron who once swam across the gulf from Porto Venere to Lerici. George Sand also stayed here. Traces of a pagan temple believed to date from before 6 BC have been uncovered inside **Chiesa di San Pietro** (1277), built in the typical Genoese Gothic fashion with black-and-white bands of marble, on the quay. Just off the promontory lie the tiny islands of **Palmaria**, **Tino** and **Tinetto**.

The **tourist office** (☎ 0187 79 06 91; www.portovenere.it; Piazza Bastreri 7; 🕐 10am-noon & 3-6pm Thu-Tue) sells a couple of useful maps and walking guides in English.

SLEEPING & EATING

Albergo Genio (☎ /fax 0187 79 06 11; Piazza Bastreri 8; s/d low season €65/83, high season €76/88; ☺ mid-Feb–mid-Jan) This small, seven-room hotel run by an elderly couple is simple but atmospheric. From Piazza Bastreri, scale the spiral stairs in the round tower to get here. Breakfast (alfresco beneath vines in summer) costs an extra €5 to €6.50, depending on the season.

Grand Hotel Portovenere (☎ 0187 79 26 10; ghp@rphotels.com; Via Garibaldi 5; d low/high season from €85/125, with sea view from €125/165; P ☒ ☐) This fabulous four-star oasis of charm and luxury, inside what was a 12th-century monastery, is Porto Venere's grand choice.

A half-dozen or so restaurants line Calata Doria, by the sea. A block inland Porto Venere's main old-town street, Via Cappellini, proffers several tasty choices, including **La Piazzetta** at No 56 where you can dunk plates of *cantuccini* (hard almond biscuits) into your cuppa.

Antica Osteria del Caruggio (☎ 0187 79 06 17; Via Cappellini 94; meals around €20) Sample razor-clam soup and other traditional dishes at this old-world place crammed with antique knick-knacks.

Shop for *pesto alla Genovese*, *trofie* (pasta shaped in a tiny squiggle) and succulent slabs of focaccia at **Bajeicò La Bottega del Pesto** (☎ 0187 79 10 54; Via Cappellini 70).

GETTING THERE & AWAY

Porto Venere is served by bus from La Spezia (see p196).

Late March to October, La Spezia–based Navigazione Golfo dei Poeti sails from Porto Venere to/from Lerici (€8 return, six daily), La Spezia (€6 return), the Cinque Terre (€14 to €20 return) and Portofino (€24 return, mid-June to mid-September). It also runs boat excursions to Palmaria, Tino and Tinetto (€8).

Lerici & Around

pop 11,750

At the southeastern end of the Riviera di Levante, 10km from La Spezia, Lerici is an exclusive summer refuge for wealthy Italians. Magnolia, yew and cedar trees grow in its 1930s public gardens and pool-clad villas cling to the cliffs along the beach. For outstanding views make your way on foot or by public lift to 12th-century Castello di Lerici, home to the ferociously fascinating **Museo**

Geopaleontologico (☎ 0187 96 90 42; Piazza San Giorgio 1; adult/child €4.60/3.10; ☺ 10.30am-1pm & 2.30-6pm Tue-Sun Mar-Jun & Sep–mid-Oct, 10.30am-12.30pm Tue-Fri, 10.30am-12.30pm & 2.30-5.30pm Sat, Sun & holidays mid-Oct–Feb, 10.30am-12.30pm & 6.30pm-midnight Jul & Aug). Earthquakes, robots and dinosaurs feature in the museum's futuristic exhibits.

Lerici **tourist office** (☎ 0187 96 73 46; info@aptcinqueterre.sp.it; Via Biaggini 6; ☺ 9am-1pm & 2.30-5.30pm Mon-Sat, 9am-1pm Sun) can advise on walking and cycling in the area. From Lerici a scenic 3km coastal stroll leads north to **San Terenzo**, a seaside village with a sandy beach and Genoese castle. The Shelleys hung out here in the 1820s – the couple stayed at the waterfront Villa Magni (privately owned and closed to visitors) and Percy Bysshe's boat sank off the coast here in 1822 on a return trip from Livorno (Leghorn), costing him his life.

Another coastal stroll, 4km south, takes you past magnificent little bays to **Tellaro**, a fishing hamlet with pink-and-orange houses cluttered about narrow lanes and tiny squares. Weave your way to Chiesa San Giorgio, sit on the rocks and imagine an octopus ringing the church bells – which, according to legend, it did to warn the villagers of a Saracen attack. Novelist DH Lawrence stayed in Tellaro the year before WWI broke out.

Val di Magra

Southeast of La Spezia the Magra Valley forms the easternmost tongue of Ligurian territory. **Sarzana** (population 20,120), a short bus or train ride from La Spezia, was an important outpost of the Genoese republic. In its cathedral you can see the world's oldest crucifix, painted on wood. The phial in the chapel is said to have contained the blood of Christ. Nearby, the fortress of Sarzanello (built by Castruccio Castracani) offers magnificent views. Take a pretty detour to hillside **Castelnuovo Magra** (population 7978) which has a medieval castle.

Die-hard fans of all things Roman may be interested in **Luni** (☎ 0187 6 68 11; adult/child €2.05/free; ☺ 9am-7pm Tue-Sun), 6km southeast of Sarzana. Established as a Roman colony in 177 BC on the site of an Etruscan village, it thrived until the 13th century. Excavations have revealed an amphitheatre, forum, temple and other remnants of a classic Roman town.

Nature walks abound in this pretty region, much of which is protected by the **Parco di**

Montemarcello-Magra which has an **information centre** (☎ 0187 69 10 71; www.parcomagra.it, Italian only; Via Paci 2) in Sarzana.

RIVIERA DI PONENTE

Stretching southwest from Genoa to France, this part of the Ligurian coast is more heavily developed than the eastern side. However, some of the resorts are not bad; several of Genoa's historical maritime rivals retain the architectural trappings of a more glorious past, and the mountains, hiding a warren of hilltop villages, promise cool air and pretty walking and driving circuits.

Savona
pop 61,910

When you approach Savona from the southwest or northeast, it is the sprawl of the port's facilities that strikes you first – a sprawl that scarcely matches the chaos of its long-time rival, Genoa. The two cities were steady opponents from the time of the Punic Wars and the Genoese destroyed the town in 1528, proving their dominance.

Its medieval centre, dominated by the baroque **Cattedrale di Nostra Signora Assunta**, still survives, as does Savona's lumbering **Fortezza del Priamàr** (Piazza Priamàr), built in 1528 to protect the town. Within the fortress's impressive walls is an art gallery displaying 16th- to 20th-century works, a couple of sculpture museums and the **Civico Museo Storico Archeologico** (☎ 019 82 27 08; Piazza Priamàr; adult/child €2.10/1.05; ☾ 10am-noon & 4-6pm Tue-Sat, 4-6pm Sun), displaying archaeological treasures.

The **tourist office** (☎ 019 840 23 21; iatsavona@infocomm.it; Via Guidobono 23; 9am-12.30pm & 3-6pm Mon-Sat, 9am-12.30pm Sun) is near Savona's sandy beach. Restaurants, trattorie and cafés dot Via Paleocapa. **Vino e Farinata** (Via Pia 15r) is a good spot to sample *farinata*. Stacks of wood waiting to fire the open oven fill its entrance.

GETTING THERE & AROUND
SAR (☎ 0182 215 44) and **ACTS** (☎ 019 220 11) buses, departing from Piazza del Popolo and the train station, are the best options for reaching points inland. Bus No 2 links the train station and the fortress. On foot, Via Collodi and Via Don Minzoni lead from the station, across the River Letimbro, towards Piazza del Popolo, from where Via Paleocapa runs to the marina.

Trains run along the coast to Genoa (€2.95, 45 minutes, almost hourly) and San Remo (€5.35, 1¾ hours, eight daily).

Corsica Ferries (☎ 019 21 55 11) runs up to three boats daily between Savona's Porto Vado and Corsica. A high-season single deck fare to Bastia/Calvi/Île Rousse costs €44/33/33.

Noli
pop 2900

Noli has little of the Riviera di Ponente's made-to-measure resort atmosphere. It was an independent republic for 600 years, a history hinted at by the ruined medieval walls which run up a hill behind the old town and peak in a fort designed to watch for invaders from North Africa. The town sells itself as the original home of a Ligurian culinary singularity, *trofie*. Fishing remains one of Noli's mainstays and the waterfront is often converted into an impromptu seafood market.

The waterfront **tourist office** (☎ 019 740 90 03; iatnoli@italianriviera.com; Corso Italia 8) stocks information on accommodation, although don't expect any bargains in high season. One of the cheapest is **Albergo Rino** (☎ 019 74 80 59; Via Cavalieri di Malta 3; s/d from €45/55).

Buses run from Finale Ligure and Savona.

Finale Ligure
pop 12,300

With a good beach and affordable accommodation, Finale Ligure is a handy base for exploring the Riviera di Ponente. Its historic centre known as Finalborgo – a clutter of twisting alleys behind medieval walls – is away from the coast on the River Pora. Finale Marina, on the waterfront, is where most hotels and restaurants languish, while Finale Pia – towards Genoa – runs along the River Sciusa and is suburban.

From the **train station** (Piazza Vittorio Veneto), at Finale Marina's western end, walk down Via Saccone to reach the sea and the **tourist office** (☎ 019 68 10 19; iatfinale@italianriviera.com; Via San Pietro 14; ☾ 9am-12.30pm & 3-6.30pm Mon-Sat, 9am-noon Sun). The promenade lining Via San Pietro and Via Concezione, as well as pedestrian Via Roma a block inland, are crammed with places to eat. Come aperitif time head for the cocktail and ice-cream bars overlooking the beach between Via San Pietro 19 and 29.

SAR (☎ 0182 215 44) buses yo-yo every 30 minutes along the coast to/from Savona (€2, 50 minutes), stopping en route in

Finalborgo (€1, five minutes) and Noli (€1.25, 20 minutes). Buses use the stop in front of the train station.

Albenga
pop 22,760

Albenga's medieval centre sets it apart from the resorts further west. Settled as far back as the 5th century BC, Albenga grew from its Roman roots to become an independent maritime republic in the Middle Ages. In the 13th century it threw in its lot with Genoa.

Albenga's **Museo Diocesano di Arte Sacra** (Via Episcopio 5; adult/child €3/1; ⏰ 10am-noon & 3-6pm Tue-Sun), featuring a painting by Caravaggio, is near a 5th-century **baptistry** and Romanesque **cathedral**. The baptistry is somewhat unusual, if only because the 10-sided exterior breaks with the octagonal shape that characterises its counterparts throughout northern Italy.

A collection of 1st-century amphoras (wine urns), recovered in 1950 from the wreck of a Roman cargo vessel found 4km offshore (one of the world's oldest discovered shipwrecks), is showcased in the **Museo Navale Romano** (Roman Naval Museum; ☎ 0182 5 12 15; Piazza San Michele 12; adult/child €3/1; ⏰ 10am-12.30pm & 2.30-6pm Tue-Sun).

From the **train station** (Piazza Matteotti), turn left and then left again beneath the railway bridge, then bear east along tree-lined Viale Italia to get to the sea. To get to the historic centre from Piazza Matteotti, walk straight ahead (west) along Viale Martiri della Libertà. The **tourist office** (☎ 0182 55 84 44; iatalbenga@italianriviera.com; Viale Martiri della Libertà 1; ⏰ 9am-12.30pm & 3-6.30pm Tue-Sat) can guide you if you get lost.

SLEEPING & EATING

There are around 20 camp sites in the area.

Albergo Torino (☎ 0182 5 08 44; Viale Italia 25; s/d €24/36, with bathroom €30/48) Rates rise by around €5 a night in high season but Hotel Turin still offers a solid price-quality ratio. Its flower-filled terrace, a stone's throw from the sea, is welcoming indeed.

Hosteria Sutta Ca' (☎ 0182 5 31 98; Via Rolandi Ricci 10; full meals about €20; ⏰ Dec-Sep) Dare to try *ventre* (stomach of tuna fish baked in a pine kernel sauce) at one of medieval Albenga's most traditional eating houses.

Don't leave Albenga without sampling a slice of *panciucco al limoncello*, the sweetest, moistest, most succulent lemon cake you're ever likely to taste – **Pasticceria Fili** (Via Venezia 8), off Viale Italia, is the place to buy it. Tasty tip: turn your cake upside down and leave for 30 minutes before devouring.

GETTING THERE

Albenga is served by trains and SAR buses (main stop on Piazza del Popolo) along the coast.

Alassio
pop 11,365

In addition to 3km of white beaches pretty Alassio boasts its own variety of *baci* (literally 'kisses'), sugary concoctions comprising two biscuit whirls sandwiched together with chocolate cream. Delightfully narrow alleys cut from Via XX Settembre, the *budello* (main pedestrian street in the old centre), to the beach. A couple of streets inland, between the sea and the Art Nouveau train station, is the **Muretto di Alassio**, a wall of fame engraved with visiting celebrities' autographs – Roosevelt, Louis Armstrong and playwright Dario Fo. Hemingway's is stuck on the facade of the building opposite at Corso Dante 312 (a legendary café in the 1930s).

Alassio is one of the prettier beach resorts on this mountainous stretch of the Ligurian coast. Should you decide to stay, the **tourist office** (☎ 0182 64 70 27; iatalassio@italianriviera.com; Piazza della Libertà 5) can assist.

Cervo

Past Capo Cervo, southwest on the way to Imperia, this small fishing village, surrounded by a ring of walls and towers around the medieval centre, makes a pretty stop.

Imperia
pop 40,250

Dominated by lines of hothouses on the surrounding hillside, Imperia is the main city of Liguria's westernmost province, commonly known as the Riviera dei Fiori because of the area's flower-growing industry which is among Italy's most extensive. Imperia was founded in 1923 by Mussolini when he bridged the River Impero and unified the towns of Porto Maurizio (west) and Oneglia (east) – they still retain the air of separate towns. The resort's outlying apartment blocks and smoke stacks can hardly be described as appealing, but Porto Maurizio – the older of the two – dominated by a large neoclassical cathedral, merits an afternoon stroll.

From Porto Maurizio train station, head uphill to Viale G Matteotti or through an underpass to the waterfront, which eventually leads to Corso Garibaldi. The **tourist office** (☎ 0183 66 01 40; Viale G Matteotti 37) can advise on accommodation, including the resort's numerous camp sites.

San Remo

pop 55,970

San Remo gained prominence as a resort for Europe's social elite, especially Brits and Russians, in the mid-to-late 19th century, when the likes of Tsarina Maria Alexandrovna (mother of Nicholas II, the last tsar) held court there. Today, although a few hotels thrive as luxury resorts, many from that period are long past their prime and are cut off from the beach by the railway line.

The poetically named maze of an old centre, La Pigna (literally 'pine cone'), is just north of Corso Matteotti, San Remo's main strip, where the wealthy shop for Armani designs by day and take their evening stroll at dusk. Corso Matteotti meets San Remo's other famous strip, Corso Imperatrice, at Piazzale Battisti near the train station.

September sees speed-fiends hit town for the **Rallye San Remo** (www.rally.sanremo.it, Italian only), a 1407km-long rally first held in 1926.

INFORMATION

Hospital (☎ 0184 53 61; Via Giovanni Borea 56)
Internet Resource (www.sanremoguide.com)
Police Station (☎ 0184 5 90 81; Via del Castillo 5)
Post Office (Via Roma 156; ⏰ 8am-6pm Mon-Sat)
Tourist Office (☎ 0184 5 90 50; aptsanremo@sistel.it; Largo Nuvoloni 1; ⏰ 8am-7pm Mon-Sat, 9am-1pm Sun)

SIGHTS & ACTIVITIES

The **Chiesa Russa Ortodossia** (Piazza Nuvoloni; admission €0.50; ⏰ 9.30am-noon & 3-6.30pm) was built for the Russian community that followed Tsarina Maria Alexandrovna to San Remo. The Russian Orthodox church – with its onion-shaped domes and simple, candle-scented interior – was designed in 1906 by Alexei Shchusev who, 20 years later, planned Lenin's mausoleum in Moscow.

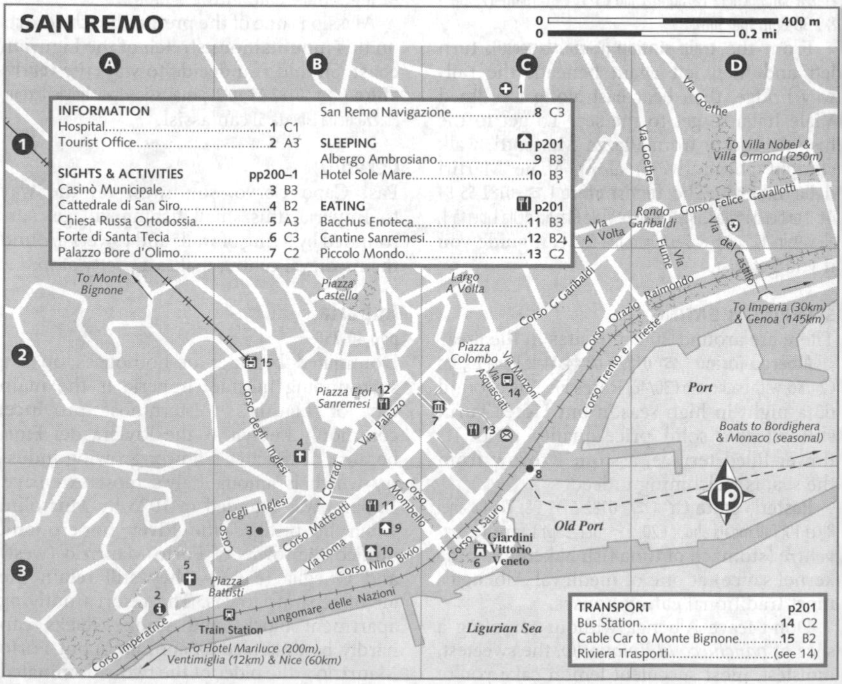

A stroll along shop-lined Corso Matteotti brings you to the sumptuous **Palazzo Borea d'Olimo** (☎ 0184 55 19 42; Corso Matteotti 143; ☺ 9am-12.30pm & 3-6pm Tue-Sat), built in Genoese style in the 15th century. Inside there are small archaeological, art and local history museums. From here you can cut west through the narrow streets to get to **La Pigna**.

Northeast along Corso Matteotti you reach Italy's principal **flower market** (Corso Garibaldi; ☺ 6-8am Jun-Oct) – go to watch the frenetic bidding. Further east still, Corso Felice Cavallotti leads to a rash of elegant villas and gardens, perfect for romantic picnics. The Moorish **Villa Nobel** (Corso Felice Cavallotti 112) is the former home of Alfred Nobel, the Swedish inventor of dynamite after whom the Nobel prize is named. Occasional art exhibitions are held in **Villa Ormond** (☎ 0184 50 57 62; Corso Felice Cavallotti 51; admission free; ☺ gardens 8am-7pm), better known for its Japanese gardens.

A short drive northwest from the centre, **Monte Bignone** (1299m) offers views over San Remo and as far west as Cannes in France. March to September, **San Remo Navigazione** (☎ 0184 50 50 55; www.rivieraline.it, Corso Nazario Sauro), at the old port, runs twice-daily 1½ hour boat trips to Bordighera (adult/child €11/6).

SLEEPING

San Remo is stuffed with hotels, although summer can be difficult and many places shut in September. Palatial four- and five-star pads are clustered at the more exclusive, western end of the resort.

Albergo Ambrosiano (☎ 0184 57 71 89; www.hotel ambrosiano.it; Via Roma 36; d low/high season €42/78) This two-star, 4th-floor place is one of the best deals in town. Its eight rooms are clean and spacious, and some tout a fridge-bar.

Hotel Sole Mare (☎ 0184 57 71 05; fax 0184 53 27 78; Via Carli 23; s/d/tr/q low season €57/77/100/120, high season €54/89/122/145; ℗ ⌘) Sole Mare is a bright and airy option on the 4th floor of a blue-painted building.

Hotel Mariluce (☎ 0184 66 78 05; Corso Matuzia 3; d without bathroom from €50, s/d with bathroom from €40/60; ℗) A short walk from the centre at the 'seaside' end of San Remo, this excellent-value hotel is an attractive option with a small garden.

EATING

Cheap trattorie fill the old-town alleys around Piazza Eroi Sanremesi and open-air snack bars stud the length of Corso Nazario Sauro, the promenade overlooking the old port.

Cantine Sanremesi (☎ 0184 57 20 63; Via Palazzo 7; 1st/2nd courses from €5/7; ☺ Mon-Sat Aug–mid-Jul) Try the local cuisine at this old tavern, about the only place in San Remo with a time-worn character. The *stoccafisso alla sanremasa* (stockfish with tomato and potatoes) is delicious.

Piccolo Mondo (☎ 0184 50 90 12; Via Piave 7; 1st/2nd courses from €5/10; ☺ Mon-Tue, Thu & Fri) Feast on *trippe alla ligure* (Ligurian tripe), *polpo con patate* (octopus with potatoes), osso buco (veal shanks) or *fonduta* (fontina cheese melted with butter and egg yolks, then fried on toast) at San Remo's most traditional dining spot. What's cooking depends on what's at the market.

Bacchus Enoteca (☎ 0184 53 09 90; Via Roma 65; 1st/2nd courses from €7/10) For modestly priced food and a few glasses of tastebud-tickling wine, try this atmospheric wine bar and *grapperia* (grappa bar).

GETTING THERE & AROUND

Riviera Trasporti (☎ 0184 59 27 06; Piazza Colombo 42) buses leave from the train station and the bus station (Piazza Colombo 42) for the French border, Imperia (€1.70, 45 minutes, at least hourly) and inland destinations such as Taggia (25 minutes, at least hourly) and Triora (€2.25, 1¼ hours, four daily).

From San Remo **train station** (Piazza Battisti 1), there are trains to/from Genoa (€7.65, three hours, hourly), Ventimiglia (€1.20, 15 minutes, hourly) and the stations in between.

Valle Argentina

The Silver Valley stretches from **Taggia** (population 13,622), a charming place a few kilometres inland from the San Remo–Imperia road, into thickly wooded mountains that seem light years from the coastal resorts. Quaint villages abound in this neck of the woods, each seeming even more impossibly perched on a hill crest than the one before.

Buses from San Remo go as far as **Triora** (population 425, elevation 776m), 33km north of San Remo. This haunting medieval village, the scene of celebrated witch trials and executions in the 16th century, dominates the surrounding valleys and the trip is worth the effort. Gruesome tales of witches being burned alive are portrayed in its **Museo Etnografico e della Stregoneria** (Museum of Ethnography & Witchcraft; Corso Italia 1; adult/child €2/1; ☺ 2.30-6pm Mon-Fri, 10.30am-noon & 2.30-6pm Sat & Sun Oct-Apr, 3-7pm Mon-Fri, 10.30am-noon & 3-7pm Sat & Sun Jun, Jul & Sep, 10.30am-noon & 3-7pm Aug).

Triora's **tourist office** (☎ 0184 9 44 77; Corso Italia 7) has information on the valley.

Valle Nervia

From Triora, a stunning 25km-long series of hairpin bends brings you to **Pigna** (population 989, elevation 280m) in the upper Valle Nervia. Riddled with alleys and narrow streets criss-crossing in all directions, the medieval village is a delight to get lost in. Its fortified neighbour and traditional rival, **Castel Vittorio** (population 395, elevation 420m), 5km to the southeast, is equally medieval in outlook.

Isolabona (population 690, elevation 106m), a former stronghold of the Doria family 10km south, is dominated by a half-ruined 15th-century castle where concerts are held in summer. From here you can pick up the scenic drive from Ventimiglia to San Remo on the coast (see the boxed text, below).

Monet was a frequent visitor to **Dolceacqua** (population 1910, elevation 51m) and painted the medieval village's plentiful *palazzi* several times. The Doria's family castle tops off the old upper part of the village on the left bank of the River Nervia. Theatre performances are held here in July and August. Cross the late-medieval, single-span bridge – 33m wide – to get to Il Borgo, Dolceacqua's newer quarters. The **tourist office** (☎ 0184 22 95 07; Via Patrioti Martiri 22) has a list of places where you can taste and buy the village's well-known Rossese, ruby-red wine. Black olives are grown in abundance here.

Buses (four to six daily) link Ventimiglia with Pigna, Castel Vittorio, Apricale, Isolabona and Dolceacqua; Ventimiglia tourist office has updated schedules.

Bordighera
pop 10,735

A few kilometres west of San Remo is built-up Bordighera. Apart from being a one-time favourite haunt of rich British seaside lovers – the collection of charming and costly hotels attests to this – Bordighera's fame rests on a centuries-old monopoly of the Holy Week palm business. The Vatican selects its branches exclusively from the palms along the promenade, Lungomare Argentina. The **tourist office** (☎ 0184 26 23 22; Via Vittorio Emanuele 172) has accommodation details.

SCENIC DRIVE FROM VENTIMIGLIA TO SAN REMO

A scenic drive from Ventimiglia takes motorists 10km north along the Valle Nervia to **Isolabona**, then 4km east to **Apricale** (population 575, elevation 275m). In this hilltop village known literally as the 'village of the sun', a maze of medieval streets wends it way to the 11th-century feudal **Castello della Lucertola** (Castle of the Lizard; admission free; ☺ 4-7pm & 8-10pm Tue-Sun Jun-Sep, 2-8pm Tue-Sat, 10.30am-noon & 2-7pm Sun Oct-Apr). Artisan workshops abound in the village and olive groves carpet its surrounding slopes. Lunch on *pansarole* (fried aniseed pastries) and other regional specialities at **La Favorita** (☎ 0184 20 81 86; Strada San Pitero 1), a trattoria in the village with a handful of rooms above.

Continuing 10km east along the same road, you reach the hilltop village of **Baiardo** (population 310, elevation 896m) where, on Whit Sunday, villagers dance in circles around a giant tree in their central square. This is to honour the Count of Baiardo who, so legend says, was sentenced to death with his loved one on Whit Sunday. Immediately east, the **Passo Ghimbegna** mountain pass loops through chestnut trees and pine groves to **Ceriana** (population 1340, elevation 900m), a pretty medieval village a few kilometres south of the pass, known for its olive oil.

Make **Bussana Vecchia**, 5km or so further south, your final stop before hitting the coast just east of San Remo. On 23 February 1887, Bussana Vecchia was wiped out by an earthquake and abandoned for 60 years. In 1963 eccentric British socialite Elizabeth Wilmot, along with a host of artists and other bohemians, moved into the ruined village and gradually rebuilt it to make Bussana the appealing 'medieval artists village' it is today. In 2000 the Italian Cultural Ministry declared Bussana a historical monument, hence state property, and tried to evict them, prompting the artists to take their case to the Supreme Court. The case continues.

Ventimiglia

pop 26,725

If you are coming in from the splendidly rich end of the French Riviera, you may find Ventimiglia a letdown. The town is jaded, the beach grey and pebbly and the limpid blue water of Nice seems far away. Typically in this frontier area, French seems to have almost equal status with Italian.

Ventimiglia's Roman ruins (which can't be visited) include an **amphitheatre** dating from the 2nd and 3rd centuries when the town was known as Albintimulium. Its medieval town, crowned with a 12th-century **cathedral** (Via del Capo), squats on a hill on the western bank of the River Roia.

Corso Genova is the main eastern exit from the city, while its continuation to the west, Via Cavour, runs past the **tourist office** (☎ /fax 0184 35 11 83; Via Cavour 61; ⏰ 9am-12.30pm & 3-7pm Mon-Sat) and into France. From the **train station** (Via della Stazione), Corso della Repubblica leads to the beach. Trains connect the city with Genoa (€8.80, two to 3½ hours, hourly), Nice (50 minutes, hourly) and beyond into France.

Villa Hanbury

Overlooking the coast by the village of **Mortola** are the **Giardini Botanici Hanbury** (☎ 0184 22 95 07; adult/child €6/3.50; ⏰ 9.30am-6pm Jun-Sep, 9.30am-5pm Thu-Tue Oct-Apr). Established in the 19th century by Sir Thomas Hanbury, an English noble, the tumbledown gardens surround his Moorish-style mausoleum on the 18-hectare estate. Take bus No 1a from Via Cavour in Ventimiglia; the bus goes on to the Ponte San Lodovico frontier post, from where you can walk down to the Balzi Rossi.

PIEDMONT (PIEMONTE)

The region's position against the French and Swiss Alps has helped forge an identity for Piedmont that is quite separate from that of the rest of Italy. Its neat and tidy northernmost reaches could easily be Swiss, while Turin's grand squares, arcades and sophisticated café life owe more to French influence than to anything typically Italian.

The House of Savoy (originally a feudal family from southeast France), which ruled Piedmont in the early 11th century, created one of Europe's grand cities in Turin. Vittorio Emanuele II and the Piedmontese statesman Count Camillo Cavour were instrumental in achieving Italian unification and succeeded in making Turin the capital of Italy, albeit briefly, for three years from 1861.

Much of Italy's industrial boom last century had its roots in the region, particularly in and around Turin where Fabbrica Italiana di Automobili Torino (FIAT) started making cars. Today, Piedmont is second only to Lombardy in industrial production and is one of the country's wealthiest regions.

Piedmontese cuisine is heavily influenced by French cooking and uses marinated meats and vegetables. *Bagna caoda* (meat dipped in oil, anchovies and garlic) is popular during winter, and the white truffles of Alba are considered Italy's best. The region accounts for two-thirds of Italy's rice production, so it comes as no surprise that risotto is popular in Piedmont. The crisp climate is no hindrance to wine making and you can find some good reds, notably those from the vineyards of Barolo and Barbera, and sparkling wines from Asti.

Central Turin is an ideal base for exploring the region. The area's main attraction is the Grande Traversata delle Alpi, a walk of more than 200km through the Alps from the Ligurian border to Lago Maggiore in the northeast of the region.

Activities

For walkers the big hike is the two-week Grande Traversata delle Alpi (GTA), starting near Viozene in southern Piedmont, and following a network of Alpine rifugi (mountain huts) north through the province of Cuneo, the Valle di Susa and the Parco Nazionale del Gran Paradiso. It continues across the north of the region before ending on the banks of Lago Maggiore at Cannobio. Tourist offices and branches of Club Alpino Italiano in the region have maps, itineraries and lists of rifugi (generally open July to September).

Horse riding is a popular summertime activity. Many places organise treks and less-exacting rides through some of the region's valleys and national parks. A popular approach is to book a place in an *agriturismo* where horse riding is an option. Contact **Agriturismo Piemonte** (☎ 011 53 49 18; www.agriturismopiemonte.it, Italian only; Via Lagrange 2) in Turin for a list of 75-odd farms which offer a

LIGURIA, PIEDMONT
& VALLE D'AOSTA

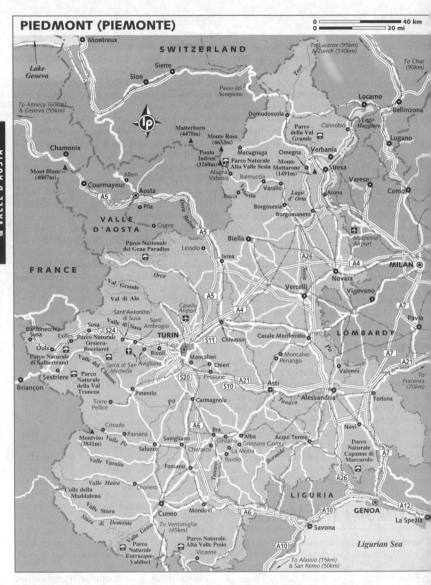

PIEDMONT (PIEMONTE)

range of activities as well as accommodation and dining opportunities.

White-water rafting, **bungee jumping** and **mountain-bike treks** are organised by various groups throughout Piedmont, mainly in summer; the main tourist office in Turin has a list of organisations. Alternatively, contact the Guide Alpino (Alpine guide associations) in any of Piedmont's numerous ski resorts. Some of Europe's most glamorous Alpine **skiing** pistes and greatest peaks – Mont Blanc and the Matterhorn – are spitting distance west of Turin, while the generous sprinkling of Piedmontese resorts and villages in between will host the 2006 Winter Olympics.

DALLAS STRIBLEY

Admire some of the 135 spires of Milan's **cathedral** (p242)

NEIL SETCHFIELD

Shop 'til you drop in Italy's most-fashionable capital, **Milan** (p256)

DENNIS JONES

Ski in one of the resorts dotting the **Bergamo Alps** (p261) in Lombardy

Feed a hungry flock of pigeons on Milan's **Piazza del Duomo** (p242)

JON DAVISON

JEFF CANTARUTTI

Immerse yourself in ancient Ladin culture in **Val Badia** (p313)

ANDREW

The stunning backdrop of the **Dolomites** (p293) provides some unique climbing and walking opportunities

Alto Adige (p306) is a heady paradise for keen walkers

ALAI

TURIN (TORINO)

pop 900,985 / elevation 240m

A gracious city of wide boulevards, elegant arcades and grand public buildings, Turin rests in regal calm beside a pretty stretch of the River Po. Touting itself as Europe's capital of baroque, the city has the air of a capital manqué rather than some provincial outpost. Although much of the industrial and suburban sprawl west and south of the centre is predictably awful, there's actually an enormous green belt in the hills east of the river, proffering splendid views to the snow-covered Alps west and north.

Turin, the Savoy capital from 1574, was the seat of Italy's parliament for a brief period after unification. It was also the birthplace of Italian industry – giants like FIAT lured hundreds of thousands of impoverished southern Italians to Turin and housed them in vast company-built and owned suburbs like Mirafiori to the south. FIAT's owner, the Agnelli family (which also happens to own the champion Juventus football club, Turin's local newspaper and a large chunk of the national daily *Corriere della Sera*), is one of Italy's most powerful establishment forces. But Turin itself is a left-wing bastion. Industrial unrest on FIAT's factory floors spawned the Italian Communist Party under the leadership of Antonio Gramsci and, in the 1970s, the left-wing terrorist group called the Brigate Rosse (BR; Red Brigades).

There's much more to Turin than FIAT cars, however – which is where the city's element of surprise kicks in. Often written off as 'industrial', its oddball collection of world-famous products includes the Holy Shroud, Ferrero Rocher chocolates, Tic Tacs, Nutella and Lavazza coffee.

History

It is unclear whether the ancient city of Taurisia began as a Celtic or Ligurian settlement. Like the rest of northern Italy it eventually came under the sway of the Roman Empire, which was succeeded by the Goths, Lombards and Franks.

When Turin became capital of the House of Savoy, it pretty much shared the dynasty's fortunes thereafter. The Savoys annexed Sardinia in 1720, but Napoleon virtually put an end to their power and occupied Turin in 1798. Turin suffered Austrian and Russian occupation before Vittorio Emanuele I restored the House of Savoy and re-entered Turin in 1814. Nevertheless, Austria remained the true power throughout northern Italy until unification when Turin became the capital, an honour it passed on to Florence three years later.

Turin adapted quickly to its loss of political significance, becoming first a centre for industrial production during the WWI years and later a hive of trade-union activity. Today, it is Italy's second-largest industrial city after Milan.

Orientation

Stazione Porta Nuova is the main point of arrival. Busy Corso Vittorio Emanuele II

LIGURIA, PIEDMONT & VALLE D'AOSTA

CHOCOLATE

Feasting your way around Turin's fiesta of old-fashioned sweet shops and chocolate makers is the sweetest way to tour the city.

Peyrano (☎ 011 53 87 65; www.cioccolato-peyrano.it; Corso Vittorio Emanuele II 76), creator of *Dolci Momenti a Torino* (Sweet Moments in Turin) and *grappini* (chocolates filled with grappa), is Turin's most-famous chocolate house. Others include **Gerla** (Corso Vittorio Emanuele II 88) and **Giordano** (Piazza Carlo Felice 69).

Turin's best-known confectioner, **Leone** (www.pastiglie-leone.com), has made sweets since 1857. Favourites include fruity bonbons inscribed with the word *allegria* (meaning 'happiness') on the outer wrapper; old-fashioned 'matchboxes' filled with tiny *pastiglie* (lozenges) in mint, mandarin and a myriad of other flavours; and its gold-wrapped *gianduiotti*, chocolates filled with hazelnut cream first concocted in 1875. Historic shops selling Leone bonbons, chocolates and jellied fruits include **Stratta** (☎ 011 54 79 20; Piazza San Carlo 191), founded in 1836; **Abrate** (Via Po 12a), with its lovely 1920s shop; and **Avvignano** (Piazza Carlo Felice 50), founded in 1883 and known for its *sorrisi di Torino* (literally, 'smiles from Turin').

The city celebrates **Cioccolatò**, a three-week chocolate festival with chocolate workshops, sculptures, films and the like each year in March.

TURIN (TORINO)

LIGURIA, PIEDMONT & VALLE D'AOSTA

To Docks Home,
Castello di Rivoli
(12km) & Valle
di Susa (52km)

Corso Francia

Piazza
Statuto

Stazione
Porta Susa

Piazza
XVII Dicembre

Giardino
Cittadella

To Bus Station (700m)
& Hospital (6km)

Corso Giacomo Matteotti

Corso Vittorio Emanuele II

To Ospedale Mauriziano Umberto I (1.5km),
Palazzina di Caccia di Stupinigi (10km),
Asti (60km), Alba (65km) & Genoa (170km)

INFORMATION	
1PC4YOU	1 G3
Circolo Culturale Maurice	2 F2
City Tourist Office	3 F2
Club Alpino Italiano	4 F3
CTS Viaggi	5 G3
Farmacia Boniscontro	6 D4
Fnac	7 F3
Informacittà	8 E2
Internet Train	9 F4
Lava e Asciuga	10 H3
Lava e Asciuga	11 E5
Libreria Druetto	12 F3
Libreria Luxemburg	13 F3
Telecom Booth	14 F3
Touring Club Italiano Bookshop	15 E2
Vetrina per Torina	16 F3

SIGHTS & ACTIVITIES	pp208–11
Abrate	17 G3
Armeria Reale	18 F2
Avvignano	19 E4
Castello del Valentino	20 F6
Chiesa di Gran Madre di Dio	21 H4
Chiesa di San Carlo	22 E3
Chiesa di San Lorenzo	23 F2
Chiesa di Santa Cristina	24 E3
Galleria Civica d'Arte Moderna e Contemporanea	25 C4
Galleria Sabauda	26 F3
Gerla Chocolate House	27 C4
Giordano Chocolate House	28 E4
Mole Antonelliana	29 G3
Museo d'Antichità	30 F1
Museo della Sindone	31 D1
Museo Egizio	(see 26)
Museo Nazionale del Cinema	(see 29)
Museo Nazionale del Risorgimento Italiano	32 F3
Museo Regionale di Scienze Naturale	33 G4
Palazzo Bricherasio	34 E4
Palazzo Carignano	(see 32)
Palazzo Cavour	35 F3
Palazzo dell' Accademia delle Scienze	(see 26)
Palazzo Madama	36 F2
Palazzo Reale	37 F2
Peyrano Chocolate House	38 D4
Porta Palatina	39 F2
Prefecture	40 F2
Roman Amphitheatre	41 F2
State Archives	42 F3
State Archives	(see 40)
Statue of Emanuele Filiberto	43 F3
Statue of Vittorio Emanuele II	44 C4
Stratta Confectioner	45 F3
Synagogue	46 E5

SLEEPING	pp212–13
Albergo Sila	47 F4
Grand Hotel Sitea	48 F4
Hotel Bologna	49 E4
Hotel Canelli	50 E2
Hotel des Artistes	51 G3
Hotel Dogana Vecchia	52 E2
Hotel Genio	53 E5
Hotel Montevecchio	54 D5
Hotel Piemontese	55 E5
Hotel Roma e Rocca Cavour	(see 47)
Hotel Solferino & Artuá	56 D3
Hotel Versilia	57 E5
Ostello Torino	58 H6
Turin Palace Hotel	59 F4
Victoria Hotel	60 F4

EATING	pp213–15
Baratti & Milano	61 F3
Barrumba	62 G3
Bokaos Dining Club	63 H4
Brek	64 F3
Caffè Fiorio & Gelateria Fiorio	65 F3
Caffè Milassano	66 F3
Caffè Miretti	67 E4
Caffè San Carlo	68 E3
Caffè Torino	69 E3
Fratelli La Cozza	70 H1
Free Vélo	71 E1
Gatsby's	72 E3
Hafa Café	73 E1
I Tre Galli	74 E1
Il Bagatto	75 E1
Il Granaio	76 E3
Kirkuk Kafè	77 F3
La Focacceria Tipica Ligure	78 F4
Mamma Mia	79 D4
Mamma Mia	80 H3
Mare Nostrum	81 H4
Montagne Viva	82 E1
Mood	83 F3
Olsen	84 E2
Pastis	(see 71)
Platti	85 D4
Porto di Savona	86 G4
Société Lutéce	87 F4

DRINKING	pp214–15
Al Bicerin	88 E1
Caffè Elena	89 H4
Cantine Barbaroux	90 E2
Frog	91 E3
La Drogheria	92 H4
La Focacceria	93 E2
Lobelix	94 E2
Roar Roads	95 F3
Taberna Libraria	96 F3
Vinicola Al Sorij	97 H4

ENTERTAINMENT	pp215–16
Alcatraz	98 G5
Beach	99 H5
Cinema Massimo	100 G3
Jammin'	101 H5
Pier 7-9-11	102 H5

Teatro Regio Torino & Teatro Piccolo Regio	103 F3
Theatró	104 E3

SHOPPING	p216
La Rinascente Department Store	105 F4
Ricordi Media Store	106 E4

TRANSPORT	pp216–17
Bus Stop for Airport	107 E4
Caffè Cervino (Sadem tickets for Airport bus)	108 E4
Imbarco Murazzi	109 G5

OTHER	
University (Humanity Faculty)	110 H3

LIGURIA, PIEDMONT & VALLE D'AOSTA

is the main tram and bus route, running southeast–northwest, while Via Roma links the station (southwest) with Piazza Castello (northeast). Piazza Carlo Felice, the square in front of the station, and Via Nizza, which continues southwest past it, are the main axes of Turin's seedier side of life.

The Mole Antonelliana dominates the horizon to the east, near Via Po (the university area), Piazza Vittorio Veneto and the mighty River Po. Nightlife is centred round the riverside Murazzi del Po and the Quadrilatero Romano, the old-town patch of Turin west of Piazza Castello.

Information

BOOKSHOPS
Libreria Druetto (☎ 561 91 66; drulib@tin.it; Via Roma 227) Art, architecture and design books.
Libreria Luxemburg (☎ 011 561 38 96; Via Battisti 7) Anglo-American bookshop.
Touring Club Italiano (☎ 011 562 72 07; Via San Francesco d'Assisi 3) Excellent range of maps and guides.

EMERGENCY
Police Station (☎ 011 5 58 81; Corso Vinzaglio 10)

INTERNET ACCESS
1PC4YOU (☎ 011 83 59 08; Via Giuseppe Verdi 20g; €6/hr; ☯ 9am-10pm Mon-Sat, noon-10pm Sun)
Fnac (Via Roma; €2/3 per 30/60 mins; ☯ 9.30am-8pm Mon-Sat, 10am-8pm Sun)
Internet Train (☎ 011 54 30 00; Via Carlo Alberto 18; ☯ 9.30am-10pm Mon-Fri, 9.30am-8pm Sat) Free surfing 1pm to 1.30pm and 7pm to 7.30pm.

INTERNET RESOURCES
Extra Torino (www.extratorino.it) Comprehensive, up-to-date listings guide in English.

GAY & LESBIAN
Circolo Culturale Maurice (☎ 011 521 11 16; www .mauriceglbt.org, Italian only; Via della Basilica 3/5) Gay and lesbian information and happenings.

LAUNDRY
Lava e Asciuga (Via Vanchiglia 10; €3.20/6.40 per 7/16kg load; ☯ 8am-10pm)
Lava e Asciuga (Via Sant'Anselmo 9; €3.20/6.40 per 7/16kg load; ☯ 8am-10pm)

LEFT LUGGAGE
Stazione Porta Nuova (opposite platform No 16; €3/2 for 1st 12/subsequent 12 hrs; ☯ 6am-midnight)

MEDICAL SERVICES
Farmacia Boniscontro (☎ 011 53 82 71; Corso Vittorio Emanuele II 66; ☯ 3pm-12.30pm) Night pharmacy
Ospedale Mauriziano Umberto I (☎ 011 5 08 01; Largo Turati 62) Hospital.
Pharmacy (☎ 011 659 01 00; Stazione Porta Nuova; ☯ 7am-7.30pm)

MONEY
Stazione Porta Nuova shelters a bank, ATM and exchange booth. Other banks dot Via Roma and Piazza San Carlo. There's a 24 hour automatic banknote change machine outside **Banca CRT** (Piazza CLN) and another in front of **Banca San Paolo** (Via Santa Teresa 1g).

POST
Post Office (Via Alfieri 10; ☯ 8.30am-7pm Mon-Fri, 8.30am-1pm Sat)

TOURIST INFORMATION
Airport Tourist Office (☎ 011 567 81 24; ☯ 8.30am-10.30pm)
City Tourist Office (☎ 011 53 59 01, ☎ 011 53 51 81 www.turismotorino.org; Piazza Castello 161; ☯ 9.30am-7pm Mon-Sat, 9.30am-3pm Sun)
Informacittà (☎ 011 442 28 88; Via Palazzo di Città 9a; ☯ 8.30am-6pm Mon-Fri, 9am-1pm Sat) City information service on the metro, new hotels and other ongoing project
Vetrina per Torina (toll-free ☎ 800 01 54 75; www .torinocultura.it, Italian only; Piazza San Carlo 159; ☯ 11am-7pm Mon-Sat) Cultural information and ticketin service.

TRAVEL AGENCIES
CTS Viaggi (☎ 011 812 45 34; Via Montebello 2h) Student and youth travel.

Sights
PIAZZA CASTELLO
At the heart of the historic centre, Turin grandest square houses a wealth of museums, theatres and cafés in its porticoed promenades. Essentially baroque, the piazza was laid out from the 14th century to serve as the seat of dynastic power for the House of Savoy. It is dominated by **Palazzo Madama** a part-medieval, part-baroque castle built in the 13th century on the site of the old Roman gate. Madama Reale Maria Cristina, the widow of Vittorio Amedeo I, used it as her residence in the 17th century, hence it name. The rich baroque facade was added in the following century. Today, part of the palace houses the **Museo Civico d'Arte Antica**

THE HOLY SHROUD

The *sindone* (Holy Shroud) is Christianity's greatest icon of faith and object of devotion, luring millions of pilgrims to Turin when it is publicly displayed every few years or so. Only the pope and the bishop of Turin can decide when the sacred cloth will next be hauled out – its last public appearances were 1978, 1998 and 2000.

For centuries experts and fanatics have argued over the authenticity of the Shroud of Turin, said to be the burial cloth in which Jesus' body was wrapped. Tests in 1981 uncovered traces of human blood (type AB) and pollen from plants known to exist only around Jerusalem. Many guessed the shroud as being from AD 1260 to 1390; carbon dating carried out in 1988 seemed to confirm this, tying it to the 13th century and making it far from sacred. Most agree that the white cloth – 4.37m long and 1.10m wide – was woven in the Middle East.

How the image of a human body – with fractured nose, bruised right cheek, lance wound on chest, scourge marks on back, thorn wounds on forehead and nail wounds on both wrists and feet – was formed on the cloth remains the biggest mystery. Antishroudies claim it's neither the blood of Christ nor a medieval fake but, rather, the first ever attempt at photography (using a camera obscura) by Leonardo da Vinci.

Crusaders first brought the shroud to Europe. It belonged to Louis of Savoy from 1453 who folded the cloth into squares and stashed it in a silver treasure trove in Chambéry in France. The tie dye–style brown patterns visible on it today were caused by a fire in 1532 that saw a drop of hot silver fall into the casket and through the folded layers. Safe-guarded in Turin since 1578, the shroud is laid out flat today in a vacuum-sealed box, which in turn is stored in a controlled atmosphere.

LIGURIA, PIEDMONT & VALLE D'AOSTA

011 442 99 12; Piazza Castello; adult/child €6.20/3.10; 10am-8pm Tue-Fri & Sun, 10am-11pm Sat). Restoration of the entire palace continues.

In the northwestern corner of the square the baroque **Chiesa di San Lorenzo**, designed y Guarino Guarini. The richly complex interior compensates for the spare facade.

Statues of the Roman deities Castor and ollux guard the entrance to the **Palazzo eale** (011 436 14 55; Piazza Castello; adult/child .50/free; 9am-7pm Tue-Sun). An austere, apcot-coloured building erected for Carlo manuele II around 1646, its lavishly ecorated rooms house an assortment of rnishings, porcelain and other bits and eces, including a collection of Chinese ses. The surrounding **Giardino Reale** (Royal rden; admission free; 9am-1 hr before sunset), st of the palace, was designed in 1697 André le Nôtre, who also created the rdens at Versailles.

The entrance to the Savoy **Armeria Reale** yal Armoury; 011 518 43 58; Piazza Castello; adult/child free; 8.30am-2pm Mon, Wed & Fri, 1.30-7.30pm Thu, & Sun) is under the porticoes just right of the lace gates. It contains what some claim to Europe's best collection of arms.

Under the porticoes in Piazza Castello's ortheastern corner, you'll find the **state hives** (1730–34), **prefecture** (1733–57), and e **Teatro Regio & Piccolo Regio** (see p216).

DUOMO DI SAN GIOVANNI

Turin's **cathedral** (Piazza San Giovanni), built from 1491 to 1498 on the site of three 14th-century basilicas, houses the **Shroud of Turin** (see the boxed text, above). The **Cappella della Santa Sindone** (1668–94), the rightful home since 1694 of the cloth in which Christ's body was supposedly wrapped after his crucifixion, has been closed for restoration since 1997 when it was severely damaged by fire. A decent copy of the cloth is on permanent display in front of the cathedral altar.

The Romanesque **bell tower**, standing alone to the left of the cathedral, was designed by Juvarra and built from 1720 to 1723. Just to the north lie the remains of a 1st-century **Roman amphitheatre** and, a little further to the northwest, **Porta Palatina**, the red brick remains of a Roman-era gate. Across the road is the **Museo d'Antichità** (Museum of Antiquity; 011 521 22 51; Via XX Settembre 88c; adult/child €4.50/free; 9am-7pm Tue-Sun), a trip down 7000 years of memory lane to the earliest Po valley settlements.

MUSEUMS

Baroque Palazzo Carignano was the birthplace of Carlo Alberto and Vittorio Emanuele II, and the seat of Italy's first parliament from 1861 to 1864. You can see the parliament as part of the **Museo Nazionale** del Risorgimento Italiano (☎ 011 562 11 47; Via Accademia delle Scienze 5; adult/child €5/3.50; ⏱ 9am-7pm Tue-Sun), which has an extensive display of arms, paintings and documents tracing the turbulent century from the revolts of 1848 to WWII. It's one of the best of this genre in northern Italy (and there are many) but is of limited interest to those who don't read Italian.

On the topic of the Risorgimento, one of its prime architects, Camillo Benso di Cavour, was born and died at **Palazzo Cavour** (☎ 011 53 06 90; Via Camillo Cavour 8; adult/child €6.50/free; ⏱ 10am-7.30pm Tue-Sun). The baroque palace dates to 1729 and can be visited during temporary exhibitions held in its grandiose interior.

On the same street as Palazzo Carignano is **Palazzo dell'Accademia delle Scienze** (Via Accademia delle Scienze 6), home to the **Museo Egizio** (☎ 011 561 77 76; adult/child €6.50/free; ⏱ 8.30am-7.30pm Tue-Sun). Established in the late 18th century it's considered to have one of the best collections of ancient Egyptian art, second only to those in London and Cairo. In the same building is **Galleria Sabauda** (☎ 011 561 83 91; adult/child €4/free; ⏱ 8.30am-7.30pm Tue-Sat mid-Sep–May, 8.30am-7.30pm Tue-Fri, 8.30am-11pm Sat Jun–mid-Sep), housing the Savoy collection of art, which includes works by Italian, French and Flemish masters. A combination ticket covering admission to both museums costs €8 for adults (children free).

Shroud fiends should search no farther than **Museo della Sindone** (☎ 011 436 58 32; www .sindone.it, Italian only; Via San Domenico 28; adult/child €5.50/2.50; ⏱ 9am-noon & 3-7pm). Despite its informative displays and unexpected 'shroud' paraphernalia – such as the first camera used to photograph the cloth (1898), and test tubes used to store traces of human blood removed from the shroud in 1978 – the museum does little to unravel the mystery of the Holy Shroud. Guided tours are in Italian only; ask for an English-language audioguide (free).

An Alaskan brown bear greets those who dare enter the animal-stuffed **Museo Regionale di Scienze Naturale** (Natural Science Museum; ☎ 011 432 30 80; Via Giovanni Giolitti 36; adult/child €5/2.40; ⏱ 10am-7pm Wed-Mon), inside a monumental 17th-century hospital with four inner courtyards and a chapel.

Further afield the **Galleria Civica d'Arte Moderna e Contemporanea** (GAM; ☎ 011 562 99 11; www.gamtorino.it; Via Magenta 31; adult/child €5.50/free;

⏱ 9am-7pm Tue-Sun) is dedicated to 19th- an 20th-century artists, including Reno Courbet, Klee and Chagall. More moder art exhibitions are held in **Palazzo Bricheras** (☎ 011 517 16 60; www.palazzobricherasio.it; Via Lagran 20; adult/child €6.50/free, audioguide 1/2 people €3.50 ⏱ 2-8pm Mon, 9am-8pm Tue & Wed, 9am-11pm Thu-Su The art gallery in a 17th-century palace h hosted surrealist Dali and been 'wrapped' l Christo and Jeanne-Claude in its time.

For modern art of a metallic sheen, hea for the **Museo dell'Automobile** (☎ 011 67 76 € www.museoauto.org, Italian only; Corso Unità d'Italia ₄ adult/child €5.50/4; ⏱ 10am-6.30pm Tue-Sat, 10a 8.30pm Sun). Among its 400 masterpiec are one of the first FIATs, and the Isot Franchini driven by Gloria Swanson in th film *Sunset Boulevard*. Take bus No 34 fro beside Stazione Porta Nuova.

PIAZZAS

It is the great squares and elegant boulevar that lend Turin its air of reserved majest Via Roma, Turin's main shopping tho oughfare since 1615, stretches south fro **Piazza Castello** to the grandiose Stazione Por Nuova, built by Mazzucchetti in 1865.

Walking south from Piazza Castell you emerge on **Piazza San Carlo**. Known Turin's drawing room, and home to seven renowned cafés, the square is surround by characteristic porticoes (central Tur has some 18km of them) and is capped its southern end by two baroque church **Chiesa di San Carlo** and **Chiesa di Santa Cristi** Further down Via Roma you reach **Piaz Carlo Felice**, at once square and garden. Li Via Nizza, which continues south past t train station, it has seen better days.

Now the main axis of Turin's seedier si of life, Via Nizza and the surrounding ar is worth exploring but is dodgy territo at night. If you do happen to be wande ing around here, head east a few blocks admire the Oriental strangeness of the 19 century **synagogue** (Piazzetta Primo Levi).

VIA PO & AROUND

The hip young· scene, revolving arou Turin's university, can be freely enjoyed the cafés along and around Via Po, whi connects Piazza Castello with the river way of Piazza Vittorio Veneto.

Turin's single most remarkable sig is the **Mole Antonelliana** (Via Montebello 20),

TORINO CARD

Serious sightseers can invest €15/17 in a Torino Card, valid for 48/72 hours and covering admission to most monuments and museums in town, a ride up the Mole Antonelliana panoramic lift, a return trip on the Sassi-Superga cable car, and all public transport costs including ATM boats on the River Po and the Turismo Bus Torino (see p212). Tourist offices sell the Torino Card.

ouple of blocks north of Via Po. Intended s a synagogue when it was started in 1863 his extraordinary structure – 167m tall – is we inspiring when you first see it from the urrounding narrow streets. Capped by an luminium spire it is engineering as art orm (in a similar vein to the Eiffel Tower) nd quite a spectral sight when lit at night. nside you'll find the riveting **Museo Nazion-e del Cinema** (☎ 011 812 56 58; adult/child €5.20/ ee; ☺ 9am-8pm Tue-Fri & Sun, 9am-11pm Sat). The National Cinema Museum takes visitors n an interactive tour of Italian cinematic istory. Its glass **Panoramic Lift** (adult/child €3.62/ 58, lift & museum ticket €8/2.58) silently whisks isitors 85m up to the Mole's stunning oof terrace in 59 seconds.

Walking southwest along the River Po, ou come to **Castello del Valentino** (closed to e public), a mock French-style chateau built the 17th century. The carefully designed rench-style **Parco Valentino** around it opened 1856 and is one of the most celebrated arks in Italy – particularly by rollerbladers, clists and smooching young romancers. A ttle further southwest is a minor Disney-yle medieval **Rocca** (Castle; Viale Virgilio 107; adult/ ild €2.60/1.55; ☺ 9am-7pm Oct-Mar, 9am-8pm Apr-Sep) nd **village** (admission free), collectively known **Borgo Medievale**. They were built for the alian General Exhibition in 1884.

Southeast of Piazza Vittorio Veneto, across e Po, is **Chiesa di Gran Madre di Dio** (closed to the blic), built between 1818 and 1831 to com-emorate the return of Vittorio Emanuele from exile. Set into the hills, the church's ome is an unmistakable landmark.

ASILICA DI SUPERGA
 1706 Vittorio Amedeo II promised to uild a basilica to honour the Virgin Mary Turin was saved from besieging French

and Spanish armies. The city was indeed saved, and architect Filippo Juvarra built the church on a hill across the River Po to the northeast of central Turin. It became the final resting place of the Savoys, whose lavish tombs make for interesting viewing. In 1949 a plane carrying the entire Turin football team crashed into the basilica in thick fog. Their tomb lies at the rear of the church.

To get there take tram No 15 from Piazza Vittorio Veneto to the Sassi-Superga stop on Corso Casale, then walk 20m to **Stazione Sassi** (toll-free ☎ 800 01 91 52; Strada Communale di Superga 4; ☺ 9am-noon & 2-8pm Mon & Wed-Fri, 7am-midnight Tue, 9am-8pm Sat), the cable car station from where an original tram dating to 1934 rattles the 3.1km up the hillside (18 minutes, hourly).

LA PALAZZINA DI CACCIA DI STUPINIGI
A visit to the Savoys' sprawling hunting lodge, in manicured grounds beyond Mirafiori, is a must. The Juvarra creation, a rococo de-light, was designed for Vittorio Amedeo II in 1729. Many parts of the building are in original condition and the rest is slowly being restored with FIAT money. Pieces of art and furniture from Savoy palaces are displayed in the **Museo di Arte e Ammobiliamento Storia** (☎ 011 358 12 20; pstorico@mauriziano.it; adult/child €6.20/5.20; ☺ 10am-6pm Tue-Sun Apr-Oct, 9am-5pm Tue-Sun Nov-Mar).

Take bus No 4 from along Via San Sec-ondo (near Stazione Porta Nuova) or along its southbound route from Piazza della Re-pubblica to Piazza Caio Mario, then bus No 41 to the palace.

CASTELLO DI RIVOLI
The preferred residence of the Savoy family from the 14th century onwards lies outside central Turin in Rivoli. The 17th-century **castle** (☎ 011 956 52 22; www.castellodirivoli.org; Piazza Mafalda di Savoia; adult/child €6.20/free; ☺ 10am-5pm Tue-Fri, 10am-7pm Sat & Sun, 10am-10pm every 1st & 3rd Sat of the month) now houses a contemporary art gallery filled with daring installations.

Take ATM bus No 36 from Piazza Statuto to Rivoli bus station, then bus No 36n or any No 36 marked 'Castello' up the hill. Journey time is about one hour (€1.25).

Tours
The tourist office runs guided city tours (€6, 1½ hours), departing on Saturday at 10am from the Piazza Castello office.

Turismo Bus Torino (1-day ticket adult/child €5/3; ☻ 10am-6pm) A hop-on hop-off bus service, run by public transport company ATM, has an on-board hostess and serves 14 different points around central Turin. Buy tickets on board; a pass valid for 48 hours is also available.

ATM also operates **Navigazione sul Po** (adult return Mon-Fri/Sat & Sun €1.55/2.07) boat trips on the River Po. Boats to the Borgo Medievale in Parco Valentino depart from **Imbarco Murazzi** (Murazzi del Po 65) six times a day Tuesday to Sunday (six times per day weekends only May to mid-June; three times per day Sunday and holidays only October to April).

Sleeping

BUDGET

Villa Rey (☎ /fax 011 819 01 17; Strada Val San Martino Superiore 27; person/tent/car €5/4/1.10; ☻ Mar-Oct) Take bus No 61 from Piazza Stazione Porta Nuova to the end of the line, then bus No 54 from the corner of Corso Casale and Corso Gabetti to get to this camp site in the hills east of the River Po.

Ostello Torino (☎ 011 660 29 39; hostelto@tin.it; Via Alby 1; dm B&B €12, dm in family room B&B €13-16; ☻ mid-Jan–mid-Dec) Turin's 76-bed hostel, 1.8km from the train station, can be reached by bus No 52 (No 64 on Sunday) from Stazione Porta Nuova. Family rooms have their own bathroom and dormitories sleep three to eight. A nightly heating charge of €1 is charged between October and April. Non HI-card holders can buy a one-night stamp or annual card on arrival.

Hotel Versilia (☎ /fax 011 65 76 78; Via Sant'Anselmo 4; d with/without bathroom €55/43) Near Stazione Porta Nuova, opposite a synagogue, Hotel Versilia is basic but not bad value.

Hotel Canelli (☎ 011 54 60 78; Via San Dalmazzo 5b; s/d/tr €24/32/39) Little motorised traffic passes by this ageing place, on the fringe of cobbled Turin. Rooms with bathroom are bare and old but serviceable. Staff only speak Italian.

Hotel Bologna (☎ 011 562 02 90; www.hotelbologna srl.it, Italian only; Corso Vittorio Emanuele II 60; s/d/tr €57/88/100) Just across from Stazione Porta Nuova, this busy two-star pad is a friendly and smiling place to stay – if you can bag a room, that is.

Albergo Sila (☎ 011 54 40 86; Piazza Carlo Felice 80; s/d with shower €43/55, s/d with shower & toilet €55/68) Decent, maniacally clean rooms are found on the 3rd floor of this porticoed building handy for Stazione Porta Nuova.

MID-RANGE & TOP END

The city boasts three-star hotels galore but those seeking five-star comfort will be dis appointed. Many mid-range and top-end hotels tout special rates at weekends, in August and during other holidays when business travellers steer clear of the city.

Hotel Montevecchio (☎ 011 562 00 2 montevecchio@email.it; Via Montevecchio 13; d low/hig season €58/63; ✗) Hovering between budge and mid-range, this family-run place in quiet residential area is hard to beat for sound night's sleep.

Hotel Roma e Rocca Cavour (☎ 011 561 27 7 hotel.roma@tin.it; Piazza Carlo Felice 60; s/d without showe €48/66, economy s/d/tr €69.50/87.50/98.50, comfort s/d/ €84/102/113, s/d/tr Fri, Sat & Aug €57/75/86) Piedmon novelist Cesare Pavese is said to have spen some of his last days at this historic hote (before committing suicide in 1950), on th square in front of the train station. 'Econ omy' rooms simply sport older furnishing than the modern 'comfort' rooms. Breakfa costs €7.

Hotel Piemontese (☎ 011 669 81 01; www.hot piemontese.it; Via Berthollet 21; s/d Mon-Thu €89/113, Fr Sun €59/89; P ☒ ✗) Brandishing three sta and a Best Western label, you really can go wrong at this lovely Liberty-style hote which languishes inside a late-19th-centur townhouse. Pricier rooms with Jacuzzi an hydromassage are available.

Hotel Dogana Vecchia (☎ 011 436 67 52; fax 0 436 71 94; Via Corte d'Appello 4; s/d from 78/100; P ☒ Mozart and Verdi were among the mo distinguished guests to stay at this elegan three-star pad – a 17th-century inn.

Hotel Solferino & Artuá (☎ 011 517 53 01; ww .hotelartuasolferino.it; Via Brofferio 1 & 3; s/d from €75/9 P ☐ ✗) Artuá is one of two hotels run b the same team, just off the grand and lea Corso Re Umberto I. Ride the fantastic ol wooden lift with glass doors to the 4th floo A laptop is available at reception for gues to surf in their room.

Victoria Hotel (☎ 011 561 19 09; fax 011 561 18 0 Via Nino Costo 4; s/d €102/147) Marble-clad wall racing green carpets, floral sofas and lo of wood panelling add to the charm of th English country–styled hotel, beautiful placed on a pedestrian lane around th corner from the congress centre.

Hotel des Artistes (☎ 011 812 44 16; www.desartistes otel.it; Via Principe Amedeo 21; s/d €125/160; P ⊠ ⊠) A reassuring choice with no surprises up its sleeve, Hotel des Artistes offers good-value accommodation. Rates fluctuate (watch for special offers' on its website) and drop by 20% on nonholiday weekends.

Hotel Genio (☎ 011 650 57 71; www.hotelgenio.it; Corso Vittorio Emanuele II 47; d €134; P ⊠ ⊠) This Best Western hotel is tucked beneath the arcades, not far from Stazione Porta Nuova. A minor detail – bedspreads and curtains are very floral.

Grand Hotel Sitea (☎ 011 517 01 71; sitea@thi.it; Via Carlo Alberto 35; s/d Sun-Thu €184/246, Fri & Sat €171/145; P ⊠ ⊠) This top-notch oasis of calm and sophistication is apparently where the champion Juventus football team is put up when in town.

Turin Palace Hotel (☎ 011 562 55 11; palace@thi.it; Via Sacchi 8; s/d €205/251; P ⊠ 🖵 ⊠) A hotel since 1872, this is Turin's last word in late-19th-century luxury.

Eating

Turin's cuisine is heavily influenced by the French, and the massive migration of southern Italians to the city brought traditions of cooking unmatched anywhere else in the north. Try *risotto alla Piemontese* (with butter and cheese) or *zuppa canavesana* (turnip soup), and finish with a Savoy favourite, *panna cotta* (a kind of crème caramel).

CAFÉS

Partly due to Turin's legacy of French and Austrian involvement, the city has a flourishing café life. Come early evening all these places lay out a succulent banquet of snacks to accompany aperitifs.

Caffè San Carlo (☎ 011 53 25 86; Piazza San Carlo 156; 1st/2nd courses from €5.50/7) Host to a gaggle of Risorgimento nationalists and intellectuals in the 1840s, this sumptuous café, dating to 1822, is where suited folk network today. It offers cocktails, toasted snacks and 28 types of coffee.

Caffè Milassano (☎ 011 54 79 90; Piazza Castello 15) Milassano (built 1907–09) is an Art Nouveau gem, lined with a marble floor, mirrored walls, a coffered ceiling and – yes – four tables. As in days gone by, the theatre mob from nearby Teatro Regio adore this relic.

Baratti & Milano (☎ 011 561 30 60; Piazza Castello 27) Elegant Baratti & Milano, with a stunning interior dating to 1858, serves coffee, cakes and light lunches. Crowds flock here on Sunday to buy cakes, sweets and biscuits – boxed and ribbon-wrapped – from its old-fashioned shop counter.

Platti (☎ 011 506 90 56; platti1875@tin.it; Corso Vittorio Emanuele II 72; lunch menu €15.50) The original Art Nouveau interior (1870) remains firmly intact at this sweet-laden coffee, cake and liquor shop. Skip the noisy terrace and lunch beneath gold-leaf inside.

Caffè Torino (☎ 011 54 51 18; Piazza San Carlo 204; 1st/2nd courses from €10.50/12.50) Torino has served coffee beneath its chandelier-lit, frescoed ceiling since 1903. Stand with the gaggle of Turinese at the bar or pay a fortune for silver service – a glass of wine costs €6.80. When leaving, rub your shoe across the brass bull embedded in the pavement for good luck.

Al Bicerin (☎ 011 436 93 25; Piazza della Consolata 5) Cavour, Dumas et al came here to drink *bicerin* (€4), a hot mix of coffee, chocolate, milk and cream. Other chocolate goodies cooked up at this café dating to 1763 include chocolate on toast, and hot chocolate with ice cream. Its terrace at the foot of a 14th-century church bell tower is one of Turin's most peaceful.

Caffè Elena (☎ 011 812 33 41; Piazza Vittorio Veneto 5; ⊗ Thu-Tue) Easily the trendiest of Turin's historic bunch, Elena lures a chic set with its wood-panelled interior and Starck-designed chairs on a terrace overlooking one of the city's hippest (and most traffic-packed) squares.

Contemporary cafés include:

Olsen (☎ 011 436 15 73; Via Sant' Agostino 4b; lunch menus €5 & €6.50) Tummy-tickling strudels, muffins, banoffee pie and cherry clafoutis (French baked-custard pastries) are baked at this down-to-earth, jam-packed lunchtime spot. Look for the cherry-topped fairy cake outside.

Pastis (☎ 011 521 10 85; Piazza Emanuele Filiberto 9; ⊗ 9am-3.30pm & 6pm-2am) Food design is what this boldly painted café-cum-bar prides itself on. Pop here any time of day for any type of drink, to be downed between geometric patterns inside or beneath trees outside. French-inspired Free Vélo next door lures a similar clientele.

Mood (☎ 011 566 08 09; Via Battisti 3e; ⊗ 8am-9pm Mon-Sat) Flick through design and art books while sipping a cappuccino or munching brunch at this modern reading café.

RESTAURANTS

There are several excellent places to dine around Piazza Carlo Emanuele II and Stazione Porta Nuova.

Il Granaio (☎ 011 562 10 03; Via San Francesco d'Assisi 87; meals around €8; ☒ noon-2.30pm Mon-Sat) Walk through the *pastificio* (pasta shop) to uncover this cheap self-service restaurant, packed full with Torinese. Predictably, the pasta dishes are superb, as is its Tuscan *castagnaccio* (chestnut-flour cake topped with pine kernels and rosemary).

Brek (☎ 011 53 45 56; Piazza Carlo Felice 22; meals around €8; ☒ 11.30am-3pm & 6.30-10.30pm) Italy's very luxurious version of fast food is a quick stumble from the train station and heaves at lunch-time. Its interior courtyard beats many of the better restaurants' outside dining areas in the charm stakes.

Société Lutéce (☎ 011 88 76 44; Piazza Carlo Emanuele II 21; dish/menu of the day €5/10) A definite *ciao* rather than *arrivederci* place, this trendy bistro sports retro furnishings, weekend brunch and a fab pavement terrace.

Kirkuk Kafè (Via Carlo Alberto 16bis; meals around €15; ☒ 6.30pm-midnight Mon, Tue, Sat & Sun, noon-3pm & 6.30pm-midnight Wed-Fri) For a real change, munch on Kurdish, Turkish, Iraqi and Iranian cuisine. Call to book as it's popular, cheap and tiny.

In the fashionable Quadrilatero Romano quarter west of Piazza Castello are some fine spots to eat and drink well.

I Tre Galli (☎ 011 521 60 27; Via Sant' Agostino 25; meals around €15) This one is spacious, rustic and full of light. It serves food until 12.30am, although wine and its fantastic array of aperitif snacks served on a buzzing pavement terrace are the main reason why most come here.

Il Bagatto (☎ 011 436 88 87; Via Sant' Agostino 30a; 1st/2nd courses from €4/6; ☒ 5pm-2am or 3am Tue-Sun) Another late opener, this wine bar serves a spoilt-for-choice range of vintages. Ochre-washed walls add a warm touch.

Hafa Café (☎ 011 436 70 91; Via Sant'Agostino 23c; meals around €15; ☒ 11-2am Tue-Sat, 11am-8pm Sun) For a taste of Morocco eat spicy couscous and grilled meats, slumber on floor cushions or sip mint tea at this atmospheric restaurant adjoining a shop. Spend a Saturday afternoon here learning how to paint your hand with henna.

Montagne Viva (☎ 011 521 78 82; Piazza Emanuele Filiberto 3a; meals around €15; ☒ Mon-Sat) Piedmontese fare (honey, meats, wine) can be sampled in a variety of dishes cooked with strictly loca farm at this innovative *agriturismo* restau rant, run by the regional consortium fo typical agricultural products.

One of Turin's trendiest spots is in th equally fashionable Piazza Vittorio Venet area.

Bokaos Dining Club (☎ 011 812 89 31; Piazza Vitto rio Veneto 23; 1st/2nd courses from €9/11; ☒ 8pm-3.30a Tue-Sun) No wonder the adjectives 'chic' an 'beautiful' bounce off guests' lips here s often – the young and wealthy crowd tha spill into this contemporary London-styl restaurant bar is, indeed, chic and beautifu The riverside entrance on Murrazzi del P is its final word in hipness.

Mare Nostrum (☎ 011 839 45 43; Via Matteo Pesc tore 16; 1st/2nd courses from €8/10; ☒ evenings) There nothing fishy about this place. An upmarke lip-licking choice, Mare Nostrum is Turin' most-respected and prized fish restaurant.

Porto di Savona (☎ 011 817 35 00; Piazza Vittor Veneto 2; 1st/2nd courses from €5.50/10; ☒ Tue-Su Some of Turin's most classic Piedmontes dishes are cooked up at this old and au thentic little trattoria. A different specialit is served each day of the week.

PIZZERIAS

Fratelli La Cozza (☎ 011 85 00 99; ciro@lacozza.con Corso Regio Parco 39; pizzas from around €5) This leg endary pizzeria is famed as much for it owner – Turinese comic TV presenter Pier Chiamretti – as its delicious Napoli-inspire pizzas and wacky chandelier-lit interior dec orated with a giant-size hot pepper, amon other things.

Mamma Mia (☎ 011 88 83 09; Corso San Mauriz 32; pizzas €4-8, pasta €4.50-8.50) Ask a Turines where to eat pizza and the answer wi often be Mamma Mia! Some 45 varietie are dished up on large wooden boards a both pizzerie – one around the corner fror the university and a **branch** (Via Parini 7) a sho stroll from Stazione Porta Nuova.

La Focacceria Tipica Ligure (☎ 011 53 01 85; V Sant'Agostina 6 & Via Giovanni Gioliiti 4) Bite into a slic of *farinata* (€1.05), a traditional Liguria focaccia with one of 13 different topping (€0.75 per slice) or a pizza (from €12.90) this quick-eat, munch-on-the-move optior

Drinking

Bar-wise, there are two pockets where hi Turinese flock – the riverside area aroun

---

ICE-CREAM LEGENDS

The Turinese have bestowed legend status on just three of its many *gelaterie* (ice-cream parlours).

Caffè Fiorio (☎ 011 817 32 25; Via Po 8) A nationalist haunt favoured by Count Camillo Benso di Cavour and other pro-unification patriots, who ate ice cream here. Fiorio first opened its doors in 1780. Since then it has never looked back as the place in Turin to wrap your tongue around a ball of creamy pistachio or pesky peach.

Caffè Miretti (☎ 011 53 36 87; Corso Giacomo Matteotti 5; cone/cup from €1.50/1.70, €17 per kg; ☯ 7.30-1.30am Tue-Sun) Flavours here include yoghurt, peach, nougat, chestnut, zabaglione with amaretti, and minty After Eight – licked on the move or on its sunny pavement terrace.

Gatsby's (☎ 011 562 25 45; Via Soleri 2; ☯ 8am-midnight Mon-Sat) Turin's swish modern spot to go suck ice. Come dark, feast on a vanilla and strawberry ice cream doused in champagne.

Piazza Vittoria Veneto and the so-called Quadrilatero Romano district east of Piazza Savoia.

Lobelix (☎ 011 436 72 06; Via Corte d'Appello 15f; ☯ Mon-Sat) The leafy terrace beneath trees on Piazza Savoia is a favourite with the in' crowd for *aperitivi* (aperitifs; €6) – its banquet of snacks laid out from 6pm is one of Turin's most extravagant.

Cantine Barbaroux (Via Barbaroux 13f; ☯ 6pm-2am) This rustic *cantina con cucina* (wine cellar with kitchen), with its entrance on pedestrian Via Mercanti, is the place to sip wine in the traditional style. Its red-brick, checkered-tiled cellar is original.

The Frog (☎ 011 440 77 36; Via Mercanti 19; ☯ Tue-Sun) The Frog is a large music bar and restaurant with a typical pub-style interior – dark wooden panelling, table lamps, curtains et al.

Vittorio Veneto drinking spots include:

La Drogheria (☎ 011 812 24 14; Piazza Vittorio Veneto 18; ☯ 8-2am) So hip it hurts – the dips, salads and other 'snacks' served with early evening drinks are a meal in themselves.

Taberna Libraria (☎ 011 83 65 05; Via Bogino 5; ☯ 10am-9pm) The mainstay of this new-style *nolibreria* (wine bookshop) is its excellent

array of wines available to taste and buy – a definite highlight for wineophiles at that favourite Turinese time of day – aperitif hour!

Vinicola Al Sorij (☎ 011 83 56 67; Via Matteo Pescatore 10c; ☯ 6pm-2am Mon-Sat) Another wine bar hot on the trail of Turin's more moneyed crowd, this tiny spot just behind Piazza Vittorio Veneto has a cellar of more than 500 different wines to taste.

Near Stazione Porta Nuova there are a clutch of English- and Irish-inspired pubs, also serving pub grub, along the eastern end of Corso Vittorio Emanuele II. Elsewhere, quench that thirst at:

Roar Roads (☎ 011 812 01 71; Via Carlo Alberto 3; dishes around €5) Roar Roads is a good spot for a very un-Italian selection of beers, served on an odd wooden contraption, and pub grub.

Entertainment

Entertainment listings are included in *Torino Sette*, the Friday insert of newspaper *La Stampa* (www.lastampa.it, Italian only). Cinema, theatre and exhibition listings are also included in its daily *Spettacoli Cronaca* section. Also worth picking up at the tourist office and in many bars is the free 80-page *News Spettacolo* (www.newspettacolo.com, Italian only), a weekly booklet listing several hundred entertainment venues, ranging from straight and gay to innocent and downright naughty.

Tickets for rock concerts are sold at the **Ricordi Media Store** (☎ 011 562 11 56; Piazza CLN 251). For other events, go to Vetrina per Torina (see Tourist Offices, p208).

DISCOS, CLUBS & LIVE MUSIC

Most Turinese clubs shower punters with a mix of tunes spun by resident DJs and late-night live music gigs. Things get particularly heated on Murazzi del Po (also called Lungo Po Murazzi), the arcaded riverside area stretching between Ponte Vittorio Emanuele I and Ponte Umberto I. Names to look for here include:

Pier 7-9-11 (☎ 011 83 53 56; Murazzi del Po 7-11)
The Beach (Murazzi del Po 18-22)
Jammin' (☎ 011 88 28 69; Murazzi del Po 17-19)
Alcatraz (☎ 011 83 69 00; Murazzi del Po 37)

Venues elsewhere include:
Theatró (☎ 011 518 71 07; Via Santa Teresa 10) Artsy venue in an old cinema.

Zoo Bar (☎ 011 819 43 47; Corso Casale 127; ☾ Tue-Sat) Industrial bar across the water.
Barrumba (☎ 011 819 43 47; Via San Massimo 1; ☾ Tue-Sat) Hip indie-guitar rock club.

Away from the centre there's a twin set of thumping venues:

Docks Home (☎ 011 28 02 51; Via Valprato 68) The real star of Turin's music scene is set in a converted 1912 warehouse complex.

Hiroshima Mon Amour (☎ 011 317 66 36; Via Bossoli 83; admission free-€15) The other big name in the dance and music circuit, HMA plays everything from folk and punk to tango and techno.

CINEMAS
Near the Mole Antonelliana, **Cinema Massimo** (☎ 011 812 56 06; Via Giuseppe Verdi 18; admission €5.20 or €6.20) offers an eclectic mix of films, mainly in English or with subtitles. One of its three screens only screens classic films.

THEATRE
Teatro Regio Torino (☎ 011 881 52 41; www.teatro regio.torino.it, Italian only; Piazza Castello 215; h ticket office 10.30am-6pm Tue-Fri, 10.30am-4pm Sat & one hour before performances) Sold-out performances can sometimes be watched for free live on TV in the adjoining **Teatro Piccolo Regio** (☎ 011 881 52 41) where Puccini premiered La Bohème in 1896.

Shopping
Every morning until noon, Piazza della Repubblica is filled with a food and clothes market. On Saturday the area north of the square becomes an antique collector's heaven known as Il Balôn. On the second Sunday of every month it becomes Il Gran Balôn, with antique dealers from far and wide.

Porticoed Via Roma is the place to shop for designer fashion. Chic boutiques also stud parallel Via Lagrange, home to the city's department store **La Rinascente** (Via Lagrange 15; ☾ 1-8.30pm Mon, 9.30am-8.30pm Tue-Fri, 9.30am-9pm Sat, 10am-8pm Sun).

Getting There & Away
AIR
Turin airport (TRN; ☎ 011 567 63 61; www.turin-airport .com), 16km northwest of the city centre in Caselle, is served by connections to European and national destinations. Several budget no-frills airlines fly here – see pp829–30.

BUS
Most international, national and regional buses terminate at the **bus station** (☎ 01 433 25 25; Corso Castelfidardo). You can also get t Milan's Malpensa airport from here.

TRAIN
The main train station is **Stazione Porta Nuov** (Piazza Carlo Felice). Regular daily trains con nect Turin with Milan (€14.57, 1¾ hours) Aosta (€6.82, two hours), Venice (€25.09 five hours), Genoa (€15.86, 1¾ hours) an Rome (€40.44, seven hours). Most stop a **Stazione Porta Susa** (Corso Inghilterra) too.

Getting Around
TO/FROM THE AIRPORT
Sadem (☎ 011 300 01 66; www.sadem.it, Italian only runs buses to the airport from Stazion Porta Nuova (40 minutes), stopping als at Stazione Porta Susa (30 minutes). Buse depart every 30 minutes between 5.15an and 10.30pm (6.30am and 11.30pm fron the airport). Single tickets costing €5 ar sold at Porta Nuova at **Caffè Cervino** (Cors Vittorio Emanuele II 57). Buses use the stop o the corner of Corso Vittorio Emanuele I and Via Sacchi.

BICYCLE
The only wheels to be rented are thos available from informal stalls which are se up at various spots in Parco Valentino ir summer. Count on paying around €3/6 half/full day.

PUBLIC TRANSPORT
The city boasts a dense network of buses trams and a cable car which is run b **Azienda Torinese Mobilità** (ATM; toll-free ☎ 80 01 91 52; www.atm.to.it, Italian only), which has als an **information office** (☾ 7am -9pm) at Stazion Porta Nuova. Buses and trams run fron 6am to midnight and tickets cost €0.90 (€12.50 for a 15-ticket carnet, €3 for a one day pass). By 2006, Turin will be graced with a metro line; one line will link Port Nuova with Lingotto.

CAR & MOTORCYCLE
Motoring information, road maps and guides are provided by the **Automobile Clu Torino** (ACT; ☎ 011 5 77 91; Via San Francesco da Paol 20a). Major car-rental agencies have office at Stazione Porta Nuova and the airport.

TAXI
Call (☎ 011 57 37, ☎ 011 57 30, ☎ 011 33 99)

VALLE DI SUSA & VALLE DI CHESONE

Ripping down snow-packed slopes in the legendary Via Lattea (Milky Way) is why most visit these two parallel valleys immediately west of Turin. The more northern Valle di Susa meanders past a magnificent abbey, the old Celtic town of Susa and a clutch of pretty mountain villages. Its southern counterpart, the Valle di Chesone, is pure ski resort – of which slick Sestriere reigns.

During the ski season and in summer, Turinese flock here in droves for fresh mountain air. The main Italy–France highway (the A32) and railway line roar furiously along the Valle di Susa, making this traffic-busy valley easily accessible by public transport and car.

Sacra di San Michele

Perched on a hill above the road from Turin is the **Sacra di San Michele** (☎ 011 93 91 30; adult/child €2.50/1.50; 🕑 9.30-12.30am & 3-5pm Tue-Fri, 9.30am-noon & 2.40-5pm Sat & Sun mid-Oct–mid-Mar, 9.30-12.30am & 3-6pm Tue-Fri, 9.30am-noon & 2.30-6pm Sat & Sun mid-Mar–mid-Oct), a mean and moody, brooding Gothic-Romanesque abbey which has kept sentry atop Monte Pirchiriano (962m) since the 10th century. Inside, don't miss the so-called 'Zodiac Door', a 12th-century doorway sculpted with cheeky cherubs pulling each other's hair (and tongues in one instance). Sunday mass is celebrated at noon and 6pm.

The only way to get to the abbey from **Avigliana** (population 11,110), the abbey's closest town 12km west (and a 26km train ride from Turin), is by car or on foot. Avigliana **tourist office** (☎ 011 932 86 50; avigliana@montagnedoc.it; Piazza del Popolo 2; 🕑 9am-noon & 3-6pm Mon-Fri, 9am-noon Sat) has route maps and information on walking and mountain biking in the area, including around the two lakes and marshlands in the **Parco Naturale dei Laghi di Avigliana**. This protected area is on the town's western fringe.

A 30km-long circular bike trail hoops from Avigliana to the abbey and back. By foot the shortest walk is actually from Sant'Ambrogio, a village further west, from where an old mule track leads from the foot of the hill to the abbey – a strenuous 90-minute climb. Another route passes by

Il Sentiero dei Franchi (☎ 011 96 31 747; ilsentierodeifranchi@tiscali.it; Borgata Cresto 16; 1st/2nd courses €6.70/6.70; 🕑 9am-3pm & 7pm-midnight Wed-Mon), a hiker-friendly bar and restaurant in Borgata Cresto (2km north of Sant'Antonino di Susa) where you can grab a plate of home-dried *salami* or tasty spinach gnocchi in gorgonzola sauce between kilometres. Its antipasti – an exquisite, tastebud-titillating sequence of six different dishes – will thrill. Advance reservations are essential.

Susa & Oulx

On the busiest route between Turin and France, **Susa** (population 6550, elevation 205m) started life as a Celtic town (a Druid well remains as testimony) before falling under the Roman Empire's sway. The modest Roman ruins make it a pleasant stop on the way to the western ski resorts. In addition to the remains of a Roman **aqueduct**, a still-used **amphitheatre** and the triumphal **Arco d'Augusto**, the town's early-11th-century **cathedral** is among Piedmont's rare medieval survivors.

Worth a brief pitstop is the forbidding **Forte di Exilles** (☎ 0122 5 82 70; adult/child €5/1.50; 🕑 10.30am-6.30pm Tue-Sun May-Sep), overlooking the quiet village of Exilles 15km west of Susa. Its military role only ended in 1943. Opening hours do vary so check with Susa **tourist office** (☎ /fax 0122 62 24 70; Corso Inghilterra 39).

Nothing much in itself, **Oulx** (population 2725), 21km further west, is the main stepping stone to the ski resorts of the Milky Way. Its **tourist office** (☎ 0122 83 15 96; oulx@montagnedoc.it; Piazza Garambois 2) is one of the valley's largest and can help with accommodation, walking and cycling itineraries and other sporting activities.

Sapav buses (toll-free ☎ 800 80 19 01, in Susa 0122 62 20 15; www.sapav.com, Italian only) connect Susa with Oulx (20 minutes), Avigliana (35 minutes), Turin (1¼ hours) and the Milky Way resorts (see following).

Sestriere & the Milky Way
pop 885 / elevation 2035m

Conceived by Mussolini and built by the Agnelli clan of FIAT fame in the 1930s, Sestriere ranks among Europe's sexiest ski resorts – in part no less due to its enviable location in the eastern realms of the vast Via Lattea (Milky Way) ski domain. Embracing 400km of pistes and five interlinked ski resorts – Sestriere,

LIGURIA, PIEDMONT & VALLE D'AOSTA

Sauze d'Oulx (1509m), Sansicario (1700m), Cesano Torinese (1350m) and Claviere (1760m) in Italy, and Montgenèvre (1850m) in neighbouring France – this prestigious area entices skiers and boarders of all abilities with its enormous range of slopes and exceptionally reliable snow conditions. In February 2006 it will stage the Winter Olympics.

Sestriere **tourist office** (☎ 0122 75 54 44; www .sestriere.it; Via Louset; 🕙 9am-12.30pm & 2.30-7pm) has mountains of information on every conceivable summer and winter sport, including **heli-skiing**, **bobsledding** and **mushing**, **golfing** on Europe's highest golf course, **walking**, **free-climbing** and **mountain biking**. It also makes hotel reservations, although only a couple of three-star hotels open out of season. There is a small tourist office in **Sauze d'Oulx** (☎ 0122 858 009; Piazza Assietta 18) and **Claviere** (☎ 0122 87 88 56; claviere@montagnedoc.it; Via Nazionale 30).

A six-day ski pass covering the entire Milky Way domain costs €117/133/149 in low/mid/high season and skiing lessons start at €31 per hour for private tuition and €26.50/130 for one/six two-hour group lessons. Ski or snowboard/boot/pole hire costs upwards of €10/6/3 a day. Oodles more Milky Way information is online at www.vialattea.it.

Sestriere's central square, Piazza Fraiteve, is loaded with sports shops and places to eat and drink, including popular pizzeria **The Pinky** (☎ 0122 76 441; Piazza Fraiteve 5n) and traditional **Osteria Barabba** (☎ 0122 76 402; Piazza Fraiteve 2i).

Caffè La Torteria (☎ 0122 77 141; Pizzale Fraiteve 3d; 🕙 8am-7.30pm; ✗) This bar-cum-café is nothing special beyond the fact (a) it's packed year-round; (b) has great aperitif nibbles and; (c) serves the thickest hot chocolate (killer-calorie whipped cream optional) this side of Mont Blanc.

Sapav buses (toll-free ☎ 800 80 19 01, ☎ 0122 75 54 44 Sestriere; www.sapav.com, Italian only) connect Sestriere up to five times daily with Cesana (€2.10, 25 minutes), Oulx (€3, 45 minutes) and Turin (€5.10, two to three hours).

SOUTHERN PIEDMONT

If foodies thought they were in heaven in Turin, they'll quickly realise they weren't the minute they hit Piedmont's tasty south. Noble red wines, hazelnuts, precious white truffles and mushrooms are among the gastronomic pleasures this region dishes up.

MARTINI & ROSSI

Martini (an alcohol salesman) and Rossi (a distillery supplier) were two men from Turin who teamed up in the 1850s to create a wine and liqueur distillery of their own in 1879. What happened after that can be discovered at the **Museo Martini di Storia dell'Enologia** (☎ 011 941 92 17; Piazzale Luigi Rossi 1; admission free; 🕙 2am-5pm Tue-Fri, 9am-noon & 2-5pm Sat & Sun Sep-Jul), about 20km southeast of Turin in Pessione. The museum is housed in the cellars of an 18th-century villa. One of Martini's largest production plants is also here but guided tours and tasting sessions have to be arranged in advance.

Better still it remains relatively unexplored. Numerous valleys slice paths westwards to France and the mountains provide excellent walking, cycling and skiing.

Cuneo & Around
pop 54,600 / elevation 543m

Cuneo is a mildly interesting provincial capital with a small but pleasant old town in the northern wedge of the city. Its **tourist office** (☎ 0171 69 32 58; www.cuneotourism.com; Corso Nizza 17) has extensive information on the entire Cuneo province.

From here a clutch of valleys radiate west towards the southern French Alps. The longest, the **Valle Stura**, leads 70km to the Colle della Maddalena (1996m), a mountain pass linking Italy with France. When snowfalls are good skiing is possible, both here and on the bare rock mountain slopes characteristic of the more southern **Valle Gesso**. Northwest of Cuneo, the dead-end **Valle Maira** climbs past **Dronero** (population 7035, elevation 622m), a pretty medieval village with houses topped by precarious-looking grey slate roofs.

Cuneo's big plus is transport, with regular trains from its central **train station** (Piazzale Libertà) to Saluzzo (€2.45, 35 minutes, up to six daily), Turin (€4.70, 1¼ hours, up to eight daily), San Remo (€5.73, 2¼ hours, three daily), Ventimiglia (€4.65, two hours, around four daily) and Nice (2¾ hours, at least six daily) in France. There is a second train station for the Cuneo–Gesso line serving small towns in that valley to the southwest.

Saluzzo

pop 15,740 / elevation 395m

Once a feisty medieval stronghold, Saluzzo, 32km north of Cuneo and 60km south of Turin, maintained its independence until the Savoys won it in a 1601 treaty with France. One of its better-known sons was General Carlo dalla Chiesa, whose implacable pursuit of the Mafia led to his assassination in the early 1980s.

The burnt-red tiled rooftops of Saluzzo's charming old town make a pretty picture from the top of the **Torre Civica** (☎ 0175 4 14 55; Via San Giovanni; admission €1.50; ☉ 9am-noon & 2pm- or 3-5.30pm or 6.30pm Wed-Sat, 9am-noon & 2pm- or 3-5.45pm or 6.45pm Sun), a 15th-century tower where the town administration once sat. The Marchesi, Saluzzo's medieval rulers, meted out justice from **La Castiglia** (Piazza Castello), the sombre castle nearby; while the **Museo Civico di Casa Cavassa** (☎ 0175 4 14 55; Via San Giovanni 5; adult/child €2.50/1.50; ☉ 9am-12.15pm & 2pm- or 3-5.15pm or 6.15pm Wed-Sat, 9am-12.15pm & 2pm- or 3-5.45pm or 6.45pm Sun) is a fine example of a 16th-century noble's residence.

The **tourist office** (☎ 0175 4 67 10; iat@comune .saluzzo.it; Piazza dei Mondagli 5; ☉ 9am-12.30pm & 3-6.30pm Mon-Sat, 9am-noon & 3-7pm Sun Apr-Sep, 9am-12.30pm & 2-5.30pm Mon-Sat, 9am-noon & 2-6pm Sun Oct-Mar) is in the house where 19th-century writer Silvio Pellico was born in 1789.

SLEEPING & EATING

Hotel Astor (☎ 0175 4 55 06; fax 0175 4 74 50; Piazza Garibaldi 39; s/d €60/93; ☒ **P**) Ring the bell to enter this three-star hotel, overlooking one of main squares in the new part of town but just a few minutes' walk from Saluzzo's medieval treasures.

Trattoria Përpôin (☎ 0175 4 23 83; Via Spielberg 19-27; s/d from €40/70, menus €12-25; **P**) Enjoy hearty homecooking at shared tables in this cheerful eating and sleeping option. There is no hotel reception; call ahead if you intend arriving outside restaurant opening hours.

Taverna dell'Artista (☎ 0175 4 20 31; Via Gualtieri 8; 1st/2nd courses €5/10, pizzas €4-6) Sink your teeth into a plate of *gnocchi al castelmango* (gnocchi baked in a nutty blue cheese unique to Piedmont) at this simple but satisfying eating spot.

A divine selection of cheese, sausages, dried meats, wines and oils are displayed at **I Formaggi** (☎ 0175 24 82 62; Piazza XX Settembre 6; ☉ 8am-12.30pm & 4-7.30pm Tue-Sat).

GETTING THERE & AWAY

There are **buses** (information ☎ 0175 4 37 44) from Saluzzo to/from Turin (1½ hours, hourly). Otherwise, take a train to Cuneo (€2.45, 30 minutes, up to six daily), from where there are connections for Turin.

Around Saluzzo

Castello di Manta (☎ 0175 8 78 22; adult/child €5/2.50; ☉ 10am-1pm & 2-6pm Tue-Sun Dec-Sep, 10am-1pm & 2-5pm Tue-Sun Oct-Jan, free guided tours 3pm Sun) is 5km south of Saluzzo in Mantua.

West of town, the River Po doglegs along the Valle Po to its source on the Pian del Re, below the **Montviso** (3841m) peak. **Paesàna** (population 3060, elevation 614m) and **Crissolo** (population 212, elevation 1338m) are the main mountain resorts in this enticing valley, laden with walking (and less so) skiing opportunities. There are a couple of Alpine ski resorts in the more southern **Valle Varaita**, while the **Valle Maira**, south again, provides a weekend escape for Saluzzo's cross-country skiers.

Alba

pop 30,000 / elevation 172m

Solid red-brick towers rise above the heart of Alba, a wine town with a medieval past. The town was settled during Neolithic times and during WWII citizens proclaimed an independent republic for 23 days after partisans liberated it from the Germans.

Alba's modern claims to fame are its white truffle crop, celebrated each October/November with a **truffle fair**, and a **donkey race** in the same month. The latter was inaugurated in 1932 as a snub, much to the horror of nearby Asti, its rival in all things, including wine production (see pp221–2). Hazelnuts harvested here end up in Gianduiotti chocolates and in the more contemporary product, that nutty chocolate spread Nutella. The latter is produced in Alba by Ferrero no less. (From the train station, sniff out the factory – quite literally – by bearing left along Corso F Bandiera, then left along Via Vivaro.)

With picturesque vineyards to see and wine cellars to visit, **cycling** and **walking** in the surrounding Langhe hills is a true pleasure. Alba **tourist office** (☎ 0173 3 58 33; Piazza Medford 3; ☉ 9am-12.30pm & 2.30-6.30pm Mon-Fri, 9am-12.30pm Sat) sells walking maps and a booklet with six cycling itineraries (€1.50).

SLEEPING & EATING

Via Vittorio Emanuele II, Alba's main street and pedestrian zone, is lined with cafés and delicatessens selling fresh truffles – black and white – in season. Out of season, opt for a €30/kg wedge of *crutina al tartufo* (a hard cheese with specks of black truffle).

Albergo Leon d'Oro (☎ 0173 44 19 01; fax 0173 44 05 36; Piazza Marconi 2; s/d €26/40, with bathroom €40/58) Overlooking the fresh food market, the Golden Lion surprises. White wooden shutters hide a flower-filled interior terrace and spotlessly clean, if old fashioned, rooms. The cheap self-service restaurant on the ground floor has nothing to do with the hotel. High-season rates work out €7 more per person.

Vincafé (☎ 0173 36 46 03; Via Vittorio Emanuele II 12; cheese & meat platters €8-16) A clever mix of old and new, this contemporary wine bar cooks up a splendid feast of mixed cheese and meat platters in a vaulted stone cellar. The wine list stretches beyond the 350 mark. Risotto and other typical Piedmontese dishes appease a hungry lunch-time clientele.

GETTING THERE & AROUND

From the **bus station** (☎ 800 21 72 16; Corso G Matteotti 10) there are frequent buses to/from Turin (€3.70, 2¼ hours, up to 10 daily) and sporadic buses to/from Barolo (€1.60, 25 minutes, two daily) and other surrounding villages.

From Alba **train station** (Piazza Trento e Trieste) there are hourly trains to/from Turin (€3.90/5.10 via Bra/Asti, 50 minutes, hourly). From the station walk left along Corso F Bandiera and its continuation, Corso G Matteotti, to reach the tourist office.

Around Alba

Some of Italy's best reds come from the gently rolling Langhe hills around Alba. Barbaresco, Barolo and La Morra – named after the surrounding pinprick villages that produce them – are big names to look for. Some of the most sought-after wines are stashed in the prestigious Cavour Regional Piedmontese wine cellar in **Castello Grinzane Cavour** (☎ 0173 26 21 59; Piazza Castello 5; admission €3.50; ☺ guided castle tours 7 times per day 10am-5.30pm Wed-Mon), one of many hilltop castles in this area, 5km south of Alba. Italian statesman Camillo Cavour lived here in the 1850s.

CINZANO

Cinzano is concocted and bottled 10km west of Alba in Cinzano, below the hilltop Santa Vittoria d'Alba area on the busy S231. The monstrous distilling plant of United Distillers & Vintners (UDV) cannot be visited but individuals can try to hook up with a group to tour the **Villa Cinzano** and its vast **cellars** (☎ 0172 47 71 11; ☺ pre-arranged group tours only). Artefacts chronicling the history of a company that started as a small distilling operation in Turin's hills in 1757 are displayed in the villa, a former hunting lodge of Carlo Alberto.

CHERASCO

pop 7140 / elevation 288m

Lumache (snails) are an integral part of Langhe cuisine. And nowhere more so than in Cherasco, Italy's self-proclaimed snail capital 23km west of Alba where the molluscs are not actually grown (it's too cold) but simply marketed and sold.

Snails in this neck of the woods are never served as a starter or curled up in their shells. Rather, they are dished up *nudo* (nude). They can be pan-fried, roasted on a spit, dressed in an artichoke sauce or minced inside ravioli. Dishes typical to Piedmont include *lumache al barbera* (snails simmered in Barbera red wine and ground nuts), *lumache alla Piemontese* (stewed with onions, nuts, anchovies and parsley in a tomato sauce) and *lumache di bobbio* (fried with leeks then bubbled in wine and herbs).

Two tasty trattorie to try these dishes are **La Lumaca** (☎ 0172 48 94 21; cnr Via San Pietro & Via Cavour; 1st/2nd courses €5/8-10; ☺ noon or 12.30-2pm & 8-9.30pm Wed-Sun) and **Osteria della Rosa Rossa** (☎ 0172 48 81 33; Via San Pietro 31; 1st/2nd courses €5/8; ☺ 12.30-2pm & 8-9pm Fri-Tue). Advance reservations are essential at both.

Cherasco's **Istituto Internazionale di Elicicoltura** (☎ 0172 48 92 18; www.lumache-elici.com; Via Vittorio Emanuele 55) has more heliciculture facts.

BAROLO

pop 680

Robust, velvety, truffle-scented with orange reflections and the 'wine of kings and king of wine' are among the compliments piled onto this extraordinary red wine, produced around Barolo, 20km southwest of Alba. The village celebrates wine fairs in mid-September and October, and you can taste and buy wine in the **Enoteca Regionale del Barolo**

LIGURIA, PIEDMONT & VALLE D'AOSTA

TRUFFLE HUNTING WITH A PIEDMONT CHAMP

When autumn comes to Piedmont, it's time to *andare a funghi* – mushroom-pick. Mushrooms, especially the popular *porcini* (boletus) and the harder to find *tartufo* (truffle), also known as *Tuber magnatum*, are considered something of a delicacy. Black truffles are precious, but it is the white truffle of Alba *(Tuber magnatum pico)* – which can range from white with pink veins to brownish-grey in colour – that is the most prized of all.

The white truffle is celebrated in the town of Alba each year with the **Fiera del Tartufo Bianco d'Alba** (Alba White Truffle Fair), held every Saturday and Sunday for four weeks from early October to early November. This is a delightful occasion for the palate, when Alba's best wines and rival vintages from Asti and the Langhe are brought out to accompany mouthwatering mushroom and truffle recipes dating from the 17th century. The open-air truffle feast – open to everyone – fills Piazza Medford, while truffle and mushroom traders haggle over whopping 2kg slabs of porcini and fist-sized truffles at the market in Coro della Maddalena (Maddelena Courtyard). The fair closes with a world white truffle auction at Castello di Grinzane Cavour (see p220). In 2003 white truffles sold for around €200 per 100g (compared to around €40 for 100g of black).

Porcini and other mushroom specimens sprout in the dark oak and chestnut forest floors on sunny days immediately following a good burst of rain. White truffles, on the other hand, incubate for several months beneath birch, lime, poplar and willow trees. *Trifolao* (truffle hunters) only hunt for truffles, with the help of a specially trained truffle-sniffing dog, at night. Piedmont's champion dog, Bricciola, is one of three dogs that sniff out black and white truffles with Signore Ezio on the land around **Tra Arte e Querce** (☎ 0173 79 21 56; www.traarteequerce.com; Via Monchiero Alto 11, Monchiero; d with truffle breakfast low/high season €80/120, meals €20-30; ☿ on reservation Mar-Dec), a 17th-century stone house with a truffle restaurant and several stylish rooms above. Guests can feast on Signora Clelia's truffle-inspired homemade cooking, and join Signore Ezio on a truffle-hunting expedition. He hunts white truffles between September and December, and black truffles in spring, winter and autumn.

(☎ 0173 5 62 77; www.baroloworld.it; ☿ 10am-12.30pm & 3-6.30pm Fri-Wed), inside Castello di Barollo.

No, you aren't that drunk. **Capella Sol Le-Witt-David Tremlett** (☎ 0173 28 25 82), a chapel on top of a vine-covered hill between Barolo and **La Morra**, really is painted all the colours of a rainbow. Built by a farmer in 1914, the ruined church (never consecrated) was restored and painted with symmetrical patterns in red, blue, green, yellow and orange by English and American artists in 1999. The chapel is 1.6km southeast of La Morra along a dust track, signposted off Via Roma at the southern end of the village. It can be accessed from Barolo too. You need your own wheels to get there.

EASTERN & NORTHERN PIEDMONT

East of Turin sits Asti, a name most link with sparkling white wine. From here wide plains fan out north to Ivrea and northeast towards Milan. The gentle green hills and vineyards of Monferrato aside, this is a largely barren landscape typical to eastern and northern Piedmont. Approaching **Vercelli** (population 480,015), a large town on the west bank of the River Sesia, the land becomes so flat (and

soggy) in fact that rice – no less than 100 different types – is grown. Following the river north past **Varallo** to **Monte Rosa** and the Swiss frontier, flat plains fizzle out and Alpine slopes kick in. **Skiing**, **walking**, **biking** and **white-water rafting** are among the many ways to explore this mountainous terrain.

The last main stop before Switzerland in northern Piedmont is **Domodossola** (population 18,650, elevation 277m), a once-attractive pre-Alpine town swallowed up by suburban sprawl. From here you can jump aboard a charming train to the Swiss town of Locarno (see p274).

Asti

pop 73,175 / elevation 123m

Asti has a rocky history. Its original settlers became part of a Roman colony in 89 BC. Then, after existing as an independent city-state in the 13th and 14th centuries, it was passed around between Spain, Austria, Napoleon's France and finally the Savoys, prior to unification. During the late 13th century the region became one of Italy's wealthiest with 150-odd towers springing up in Asti alone to show off different families' wealth.

Only 12 remain today as reminders of its glorious past. One of them – 38m-tall **Torre Troyana o Dell'Orologio** (☎ 0141 39 94 60; Piazza Medici; ✆ 10am-1pm & 4-7pm Apr-Sep, Oct 10am-1pm & 3-6pm Sat & Sun) – can be scaled.

Since the 1850s the grapes grown on the largely flat plains around Asti have produced Italy's top sparkling wine – Asti (better known, incorrectly since 1993, as Asti Spumante). The sweet white wine is best drunk young and at a chilled 6° to 8°C, like its less-fizzy cousin Moscato d'Asti. There are numerous places to sample it, either in town or out of town in Asti's 9120 hectares of vineyards tended by 6800 wine growers. The **tourist office** (☎ 0141 53 03 57; atl@axt.it; Piazza Alfieri 29; ✆ 9am-1pm & 2.30-6.30pm Mon-Sat, 9am-1pm Sun) has a complete list.

September's flurry of wine festivals offers ample tasting opportunities: the 10-day **Douja d'Or** (a *douja* being a terracotta wine jug unique to Asti) is followed by the one-day **Delle Sagre** food festival on the 2nd Sunday of the month (a mind-blowing 500,000 people sat down to eat on Piazza Campo del Palio in 2002). The **Palio** held the 3rd weekend in September sees 21 jockeys race their horses around Piazza Alfieri.

At Asti's chaotic Wednesday- and Saturday-morning market on Piazza Alfieri and Piazza Campo del Palio everything from food and clothes to tractors, vines and lawn-mowers is sold.

SLEEPING & EATING
Hotel Reale (☎ 0141 53 0240; fax 0141 3 43 57; Piazza Alfieri 6; s €60, d €110-130) The Royal Hotel is by no means budget but it does languish in a majestic 18th-century mansion and is one of Asti's few hotels to languish slap bang in the centre of the wine-tasting town. Rates for doubles reflect the extent of renovation the room has earned in recent years.

Tacaband (☎ 0141 53 09 99; osteria.tacaband@tin.it; Via al Teatro Alfieri 5; 1st/2nd courses €8/10; ✆ noon-2pm & 8-9.30pm Thu-Tue) Pick and choose from 500 different wines at this select wine bar, next to the theatre off pedestrian Corso Alfieri. To aid the tasting process it offers a good-value range of fixed lunch-time menus Monday to Friday (€12 to €18), a *menu degustazione* (€30) and a superb stand-alone antipasti (€20).

3 Bicchieri (☎ 0141 32 41 37; Piazza Statuto 37; mixed platters €6, salads €3.60-5.20; ✆ 7.30am-last customer

Tue-Sun) This one might well be nestled inside a 16th-century red-brick family tower (restored in 1898) but its interior is strictly contemporary. Clean-cut minimalist furnishings (read lots of Philippe Starck's transparent *La Marie* chairs) set off its platters of mouth-melting *bresaola* (dried seasoned meat), mixed salami and cheese to perfection. Wine by the glass costs €2.60 to €6.20.

GETTING THERE & AWAY
Asti is on the Turin–Alessandria–Genoa railway line and is served by regular trains (hourly) in both directions. Journey time to/from Turin is 30 to 55 minutes (€3.50) and 1¾ hours to/from Genoa (€5.73).

Monferrato
Bright, young and intensely red is how critics sum up the Barbera del Monferrato wines produced in Monferrato, a cluster of wine-producing villages spread-eagled between Asti and **Casale Monferrato** (population 37,000, elevation 116m), 20km north-east. Little visited and beautiful, this green pocket amid an otherwise barren scape is ideal wine-tasting territory.

At the **Cooperativa Sette Colli** (☎ 0141 91 72 06; www.vinisettecollimoncalvo.it, Italian only; ✆ 9am-noon & 3-6pm Mon-Sat, 9am-noon Sun) in Moncalvo 15km north of Asti along the S457, you can taste wine (free) and buy. Otherwise many of the dozens of *agriturismi* in this rural region run informal cellar tours; the **Consorzio Operatori Turistici Asti e Monferrato** (☎ 0141 53 03 57; www.terredasti.it, Italian only; Piazza Alfieri 29) in Asti has a list.

Tenuta del Barone (☎ 0141 91 01 61; Via Barone 18, Penango; www.tenutadelbarone.com; s/d with break-fast low season €44/62, high season €55/77.50, dinner with wine €25; Ⓟ) Very much a family affair, this old and rambling farm dating to 1550 has been converted over the past decade into a cheery and down-to-earth B&B. Sleep in the old stables and feast on enormous amounts of homemade food cooked up by Mother.

Penango, 2km from Moncalvo, is signposted from Moncalvo's southern end.

Locanda del Sant'Uffizio (☎ 0141 91 62 92; santuffizio@thi.it; Strada Sant'Uffizio 1, Cioccaro di Penango; Ⓟ ✖ ▢ ▣) This haven of peace comes in the form of a restored 17th-century convent with 4 hectares of working vineyards. Stylish rooms – some with original frescoes –

THE BATTLE OF ORANGES

The story goes that, back in the 12th century, a miller chose Violetta, another miller's pretty young daughter for his wife. But Ranieri, the nasty Count of Biandrate who ruled at the time, like many feudal overlords, reserved for himself the right to the first round with any local woman who was about to be married. A feisty individual, the miller's daughter was so upset by this that she sparked a revolt against the tyrant by the impoverished townspeople. On foot and armed only with stones, they launched themselves against the tyrant's troops, pelting them as they rode around the town in horse-drawn carts. This desperate uprising went down in the town's folk history and centuries later provided an excuse for rival gangs from different parts of town to stage an annual riot around carnival.

When Napoleon occupied this part of Italy at the beginning of the 19th century, his administrators ordered everyone to wear red revolutionary bonnets. They also put a stop to the fatal nature of the brawling, ordering that from then on the re-enactment of the famous uprising was to be carried out with oranges.

And so today, for three consecutive days, nine teams of 'revolutionaries' (3500 in all) wait on foot at four different squares for 30 roaming carts, each laden with 10 helmeted 'soldiers' – and they pound each other with 400,000kg of oranges imported from Sicily for the occasion. *Anyone* slipping and sliding on the slimy carpet of squashed orange (well-mixed with horse manure) without some kind of red headgear is considered fair game for a massive orange assault by the 'rebel' squads – and will be pelted.

The Battle of Oranges is part of the **Ivrea Carnival** which traditionally starts on the Thursday before Lent with a masked ball on Piazza Ottinetti. On Saturday evening the *mugnaia* (miller's daughter) is presented to the town, along with the other costumed medieval characters and Napoleonic troops who parade through town amid fireworks and torchlight. The next morning the so-called 'distribution of beans' on Piazza Maretta is followed by the solemn 'Preda in Dora' ceremony, whereby the town leader throws a stone into the Dora River to symbolise the town's uprising against tyrannical feudal rule. Sunday afternoon sees the main costumed procession with drums, flag bearers and a band – and the start of the orange battles! The final battle of Shrove Tuesday is followed on Ash Wednesday by a great open-air feast of polenta and salted cod in the Borghetto quarter of town. This marks the start of Lent.

reflect the colour of the flowers after which they are named.

To reach Monferrato, you need your own wheels or a sturdy set of boots.

Ivrea

pop 24,250

The mildly charming plains town of Ivrea, 55km northeast of Turin, explodes in early February to celebrate its absolutely wild **Battaglia delle Arance** (Battle of Oranges). Bags of fun!

The River Dora Baltea runs through the centre of town, neatly dividing the historic old town (north bank), with its arcaded squares and medieval red-brick **castle** (closed), from the new town (south bank) where Olivetti typewriters were manufactured in the 1950s and 1960s. In its heyday Olivetti – founded by Ivrea entrepreneur Camillo Olivetti (1868–1943) in Ivrea in 1896 – enjoyed a 27% and 33% share of the world typewriter and calculator market respectively. Today its Bauhaus-inspired factory and offices with their giant glass facades form part of **MAAM** (Museo a Cielo Aperto dell'Architettura Moderna; ☎ information centre 0125 64 18 15; mam@comune.ivrea.to.it; Via Jervis 26; admission free; ☺ museum 24 hrs, info centre 9am-1pm Tue-Sat), an open-air museum of modern architecture. Seven numbered information panels in English lead visitors on a tour of the Olivetti building facades (all still in use); the canteen was designed in 1953 'not just as a place to eat but a place for a moment in the day'.

Ivrea tourist office (☎ 0125 61 81 31; www .canavese-vallilanzo.it; Corso Vercelli 1; ☺ 9.30am-noon & 3-5.30pm Mon-Fri, 10am-noon & 3-5.30pm Sat) has more information.

SLEEPING & EATING

Trattoria Residence Monferrato (☎ 0125 64 10 12; monferrato@iol.it; Via Gariglietti 1; s/d €45/55, 1st/2nd courses €6.20/6.20; ☺ Mon-Sat, lunchtime Sun) Typical Piedmontese cuisine characterises this excellent value trattoria with a handful

---

KOSHER CUISINE

La Miniera (☎ 0125 5 86 18; www.laminiera.it, Italian only; Via delle Miniera 9, Calea di Lessolo; meals including wine €23-28, breakfast €6, s/d with shared bathroom €23/46, d with bathroom €52, 3-person self-catering cottage per night/week €66/440; ⊙ B&B Mar–mid-Aug & mid-Sep–Dec, kitchen Fri-Sun) The tasty Piemontese kitchen of Signora Roberta Anau is the place for extraordinary kosher cuisine and traditional Piedmont dishes, fresh from the farm. Accommodation is inside the main house or in a separate little cottage with a wood-burning stove, a trickling stream outside and fabulous green views. Only lunch is served on Sunday. Advance reservations are essential. From Lessolo, 10km west of Ivrea, follow the signs for Calea, from where La Miniera is 1.5km up a dirt track.

---

of kitchenette-equipped rooms above. Its eight-dish antipasti (nine if you opt for snails too) costing €15.50 is a meal itself and ensures you'll never forget the place. (Where else have you eaten deep-fried apple fritters, veggie balls, frog legs and chocolate marzipan all on one plate?) Otherwise, try a plate of *plin* (the local version of tortellini).

Enoteca Vino e Dintori (☎ 0125 64 12 23; Via Arduino 126; ⊙ Tue-Sat) Simple wooden tables between bottle-lined shelves stage serious wine-tasting in Ivrea. The traditional wine bar hosts thematic tasting evenings on Friday and Saturday, focusing on regional specialities (risotto evenings are quite frequent) as well as wine.

Bodegà Lounge Restaurant (☎ 0125 4 55 52; bodega.ivrea@virgilio.it; Via Arduino 121; 1st/2nd courses €4/6; ⊙ noon-2.30pm & 9pm-2am Tue-Sun) For the absolute antithesis to Ivrea's best wine bar, look no further than this contemporary lounge bar directly opposite. Designer plastic chairs seat a buoyant and trendy crowd.

GETTING THERE & AWAY
From Ivrea **train station** (cnr Corso Jervis & Corso Nigra), in the new town, there are direct trains to/from Aosta (€3.50, one hour, hourly), Chivasso (€2.45, 30 minutes, at least hourly) and Turin (€3.90, one hour, eight daily). Both the historic centre and MAAM are an easy walk from here.

Varallo
pop 7500 / elevation 451m

Varallo marks the start of the Valsesia, one of the less-crowded Piedmontese valleys which – together with the Valle d'Aosta's Val d'Ayas and Val di Gressoney – forms part of the Monte Rosa ski area (see p225). White-water rafters, canoeists and kayakers take to the Sesia's wild rapids May to September.

The Passion and death of Jesus dramatically unfolds in a cinematic fashion at Varallo's **Sacro Monte di Varallo** (☎ 0163 5 39 38; riservasacromonte@laproxima.it; admission free), a series of 45 chapels dating to the 16th century. Inside each numbered chapel, life-size statues capture – often in bloody detail – a biblical episode, be it the original sin, Herod's massacre of Bethlehem's innocents or Christ's crucifixion. Work started on the first chapel in 1491 and the entire project took 250 years to complete. The wooded complex, above the town, is protected by the Riserva Naturale Speciale del Sacro Monte di Varallo and a half-day stroll here is a must. In summer a cable car links the Sacro Monte with Piazza G Ferrari in town.

The **tourist office** (☎ 0163 5 12 80; fax 0163 5 30 91; Corso Roma 38; ⊙ 9am-1pm & 2.30-6.30pm Mon-Fri 9.30am-1pm & 2.30-7pm Sat) has lots more on Varallo and its surrounds and has details on white-water sport associations along the valley, including Varallo's **Accadueo Scuola di Sport Fluviali** (☎ 347 58 36 888; www.accadueo-sesia.it Italian only; Crevola Varallo).

GETTING THERE & AWAY
Autoservizi Novarese (☎ 011 90 31 003) operates buses from Varallo to Turin (2¼ hours, two daily). For information on buses to/from Alagna Sesia (one hour, up to five daily) contact **ATAP** (☎ 015 84 88 411).

By car a narrow winding road links the valley directly with the pretty **Lago d'Orta** (see p227).

VALLE D'AOSTA

Covering just 3262 sq km and with a population of only 120,589, the Valle d'Aosta is the smallest – and wealthiest – Italian region. It enjoys self-governing status meaning that 90% of local taxes are spent in the province. Its inhabitants, known as Valdostans, speak a Franco-Provençal patois, with French sharing equal rights with Italian. (Italian was only introduced into the region after it was incorporated into the newly united Italian state in 1861.) To the east the Walser villagers cling to their German dialect, Tich.

Human settlement in the Valle d'Aosta dates to 3000 BC. Neolithic and early Bronze Age remains have been discovered and early Roman sites dot the valley. For a century the Valle d'Aosta was part of the French kingdom of Bourgogne, and was later made a part of Republican France, and then of Napoleon's Imperial France. Under Mussolini's regime massive immigration from other parts of Italy was encouraged in an attempt to bury the region's separate identity.

Always an important passageway through the Alps, the valley is lined with castles. The opening of the Traforo Monte Bianco (Mont Blanc Tunnel) in 1965 connected Courmayeur at the western end of the valley with the French resort of Chamonix – and transformed a quiet valley into a major road-freight thoroughfare and premier skiing area.

Valle d'Aosta cuisine makes liberal use of the local cheese *fontina* (see the boxed text, p230). Traditional dishes include *seupa valpellinentze*, a thick soup of cabbage, bread, beef broth and *fontina*, and *carbonada con polenta*, another thick soup traditionally made with the meat of the chamois although beef is now generally used. *Mocetta* (dried beef) is popular. The valley also boasts small, government-subsidised cooperative vineyards, mostly producing dry and fruity reds and rosés. Chambave, named after the village at the valley's eastern end which produces it, is a sweet dessert or aperitif wine.

The region shares Europe's highest mountain, Mont Blanc (Monte Bianco; 4807m), with France and the Matterhorn (Monte Cervino; 4478m) with Switzerland. It also takes in Monte Rosa (4633m) and the Gran Paradiso (4061m), which it shares with Piedmont.

Activities

The mountains here ensure formidable **downhill skiing**, with thundering off-piste opportunities for experienced skiers: Courmayeur (from where you can cable-car it to the French resort of Chamonix) and Breuil-Cervinia (from where you can ski to Zermatt, Switzerland) are by far the best known resorts, but smaller spots like Pila (immediately south of Aosta), the Valtournenche and Valle di Gressoney resorts all offer scenic off-the-beaten-track skiing for intermediates and beginners. Skiers seeking a spot to stay without motorised vehicles should plump for Chamois, a traditional mountain hamlet that can make a refreshing change from the après-ski merry-go-round of bigger resorts. The Valle di Cogne in the Gran Paradiso national park and the Valle di Gressoney at the southern foot of Monte Rosa are leading **cross-country skiing** centres.

Information on ski schools, mountain guides and individual-resort ski-lift passes are detailed under Activities in the respective resort sections. A three-/six-day lift pass covering the entire Valle d'Aosta, Alagna Valsesia (Piedmont) and Zermatt (Switzerland) costs €90/169; a 4+2 Around Mont Blanc pass is valid in the Four Valleys skiing area (Switzerland) and Chamonix (France) as well as the Valle d'Aosta and covers four days of skiing in the resort area where the pass was bought and two days of skiing in the other two; while a Mont Blanc Snow Safari pass costs €210 and covers six days of skiing in all three ski areas. For more information, see www.skivallee.it.

A pair of boots, poles and nothing-special/top-notch skis will set you back around €10/25 a day or €40/100 for six days. Boarders will pay around €15/25 for a standard/superior snowboard and boots.

THE BATTLE OF THE QUEENS

Every October thousands of Valdestans gather in Aosta to watch cow fights. Known traditionally as the Bataille de Reines (Battle of the Queens), the event is organised along the lines of a beauty contest. Knockouts start around the valley in March, when locals from across the region prime their best bovines for battle, and end with the Aosta-based finals on the third Sunday in October, when the queen of the cows is crowned. This might seem a bit strange, but it is a tradition from the days when cows returning from mountain fields would tussle with each other. The losing cow is not injured and the match ends when one pulls away. The queen sells for wads of cash.

VALLE D'AOSTA

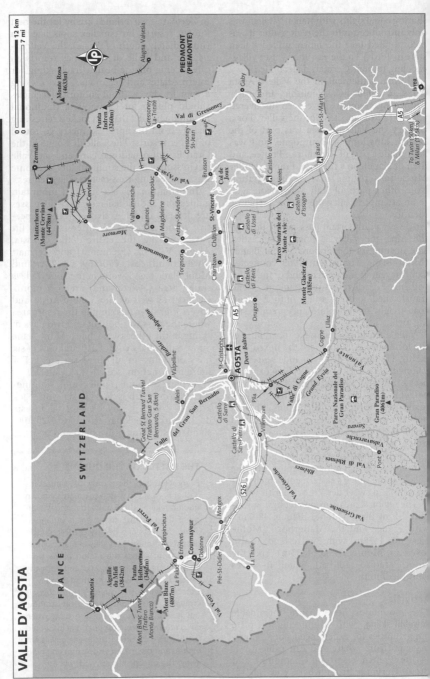

While expert mountaineers set off across the ice to tackle Mont Blanc from Courmayeur, walkers should settle for one of the dozens of half- and full-day **walks** and rambles at lower altitudes offered by the region. Many trails in the valley are suitable for **mountain biking** and there are some particularly interesting **nature trails** in the **Parco Nazionale del Gran Paradiso**. Details on walks, huts and mountain guides are listed under Activities in the respective resort sections; tourist offices have mountains more information.

AOSTA

pop 34,644 / elevation 565m

Aosta is the so-called 'Rome of the Alps'. Sitting in all its faded splendour at the centre of the valley, this is the Valle d'Aosta's capital and only major city. The River Dora Baltea licks its southern boundary and the River Buthier, its eastern side. Attractions are thin on the ground but good transport links make it a natural jumping-off point to the region's 11 valleys and their green wonders.

Information

BOOKSHOPS

Brivio (Piazza Chanoux 34)
Libreria Minerva (Via de Tillier 34)

EMERGENCY

Police Station (☎ 0165 26 21 69; Corso Battaglione Aosta 169)

INTERNET ACCESS

Voyelles Librairie de la Francophone (☎ 0165 4 36 49; info@librairiedelafrancophone.it: Via di Tillier 28; €1.50/hr) French book shop with Internet access.

MEDICAL SERVICES

Farmacia Centrale (☎ 0165 26 22 05; Piazza Chanoux 35)
Hospital (☎ 0165 54 31; Viale Ginevra)

MONEY

Banks abound on and around Piazza Chanoux.
Change Exact (Via E Aubert 77; ⏱ 10am-1pm & 2.30-6.30pm Mon-Sat) Currency exchange and Western Union money transfer.

POST

Post Office (Piazza Narbonne; ⏱ 8.15am-6pm Mon-Fri, 8.15am-1pm Sat)

TOURIST INFORMATION

Aosta tourist office (☎ 0165 23 66 27; www.regione .vda.it/turismo, Italian only; Piazza Chanoux 2; ⏱ 9am-1pm & 3-8pm Jun-Sep, 9am-1pm & 3-8pm Mon-Sat, 9am-1pm Sun Oct-May) Information on the entire region, including comprehensive lists of *rifugi*, B&Bs, farmhouses, hotels and camp sites.

Sights

ROMAN RUINS

Deemed the city's symbol, the lumbering **Arco di Augusto** (Piazza Arco d'Augosto) has been strung with a crucifix in its centre since medieval times. From Piazza Arco di Augusto, nip east across the River Buthier bridge to view the cobbled **Roman bridge** – continually in use since the 1st century – then backtrack west 300m along Via Sant'Anselmo to **Porta Praetoria**. This is the main gate to the Roman city.

North along Via di Bailliage takes you to Aosta's **Roman theatre** (Via Porta Praetoria; admission free; ⏱ 9am-6.30pm Oct-Feb, 9am-8pm Mar-Sep). Part of its 22m-high facade is still intact. In summer, performances are held in the better-preserved lower section. All that remains of the **Roman forum**, another couple of blocks west, beneath Piazza Giovanni XXIII, is a colonnaded walkway known as the **Criptoportico**. The foreboding **Torre dei Balivi**, a former prison, marks one corner of the Roman wall and peers down on the smaller **Torre dei Fromage** (☎ 0165 44 23 38; admission free; ⏱ 9.30am-noon & 2.30-6.30pm Tue-Sun) – named after a family rather than a cheese – which today hosts temporary art exhibitions.

CATTEDRALE SANTA MARIA ASSUNTA

Aosta's **cathedral** (☎ 0165 40 251; Piazza Giovanni XXIII; ⏱ 6.30am-noon & 3-7pm) has a neoclassical facade that belies the impressive Gothic interior. Inside, the carved 15th-century walnut-wood choir stalls are particularly beautiful. Two mosaics on the floor, dating from the 12th to the 14th centuries, are also worth studying, as are the religious art treasures displayed in the **Museo del Tesoro** (☎ 0165 40 413; adult/child €2.10/0.75; ⏱ 9-11.30am & 3-5.30pm Mon-Sat, 8.30-10am & 10.45-11.30pm Sun Apr-Sep, 8.30-10am, 10.45-11.30am & 3-5.30pm Sun Oct-Feb), in the cathedral's deambulatory.

CHIESA DI SANT'ORSO

This **church** (Via Sant'Orso; ⏱ 10am-12.30pm & 1.30-5pm Mon-Fri, 10am-12.30pm & 1.30-6pm Sun

AOSTA

0 — 300 m
0 — 0.2 mi

INFORMATION
Aosta Tourist Office.............1 B3
Brivio Bookshop..................2 B3
Change Exact.....................3 A3
Farmacia Centrale...............4 B3
Hospital............................5 A2
Libreria Minerva.................6 B3
Telecom Office....................7 B2
Voyelles Librairie de la
  Francophone.....................8 B3

SIGHTS & ACTIVITIES pp227–9
Arco di Augusto....................9 D3
Basilica di San Lorenzo..........10 C3
Cattedrale Santa Maria Assunta...11 B3
Chiesa di Sant'Orso...............12 C3
Meinardi Sport....................13 A3
Porta Praetoria...................14 C3
Roman Bridge......................15 D3
Roman Forum (Criptoportico)......16 B3
Roman Theatre.....................17 C3
Torre dei Balivi..................18 C3
Torre dei Fromage.................19 C3

SLEEPING p229
Hotel Europe......................20 B3
La Belle Époque...................21 A3

EATING p229
Brasserie du Commerce.............22 B3
Superfresco Standa................23 A3
Taverna da Nando..................24 B3
Trattoria degli Artisti..........25 A3

DRINKING p229
Ad Forum..........................26 B3
Le Grand Paradis..................27 B3

SHOPPING pp229–30
IVAT Craft Shop...................28 B3
La Madison de la Fontana.........29 B3

TRANSPORT p230
Aosta-Pila Cable Car..............30 B4
Bus Station.......................31 C4
Europcar..........................32 B4

To Great St Bernard
Pass & Tunnel (25km)

To Police Station,
Club Alpino Italiano,
Interguide, Courmayeur
(35km) & Mont Blanc
Tunnel (40km)

Via Parigi

To Milleluci
Camping (1km)
& St-Christophe
(3km)

Via Federico Chabod

To Ivrea
(45km), Turin
(110km) &
Milan (185km)

Piazza
Giovanni
XXIII
Via Mons. de Sales

Via Xavier de Maistre

Via de Baillage

Via des Morrales

Via Sant'Orso

Piazza
Arco
d'Augusto

To Questura
(Police Station)
& Club Alpino Italiano

Via d'Avise

Via E. Aubert

Piazza
della
Repubblica

Via Croce di Ville

Piazza
Chanoux

V Porta Praetoria

Piazza
Narbonne

Via Sant'Anselmo

Via Torino

Via de Tillier

Via Bonifacio Festaz

Via Ribitel

Via Olietti

Piazza
Manzetti

Train Station

Strada Paravera

Via Giorgio Carrel

Via Caduti del Lavoro

To Pila (18km)

Strada
Pont
Suaz

Oct-Feb, 9am-7pm Mar-Jun & Sep, 9am-8pm Jul & Aug)
dates to the 10th century but was altered
on several occasions, notably in the 15th
century when Giorgio di Challant of the
ruling family ordered the original frescoes
covered and a new roof installed. Remnants
of these frescoes can be viewed by clambering up into the cavity between the original
and 15th-century ceilings. Ask the church
attendant for a tour. The interior and
the magnificently carved choir stalls are
Gothic, but excavations have unearthed
the remains of an earlier church, possibly
dating from the 8th century. The Romanesque cloister, with its ornately carved
capitals representing biblical scenes, is to
the right of the church.

Activities

SKIING

The small resort of **Pila** (1800m), accessible
by **Aosta–Pila cable car** (☎ 0165 363 615; www.pila.it
half-/full-day pass €19/27.50; ☻ mid-Dec–mid-Apr) from
Aosta or an 18km drive south, is quick and
easy to reach from the town. Its 70km of
runs, served by 13 lifts, form one of the
valley's largest ski areas. Its highest slope, in
the shadow of Gran Paradiso, reaches 2700m
and sports a snow park with half pipe, fun
box, jump and slide for boarders. The ski
station is a village of sorts, but services such
as the tourist office, police and medical services are handled from Aosta. For details on
ski-passes covering other resorts in the Valle
d'Aosta, see pp225–7.

WALKING & MOUNTAIN BIKING

The lower slopes leading down from Pila into the Dora Baltea valley provide picturesque and easy walks and rides. Mountain bikes can be transported for free on the **Aosta–Pila cable car** (adult single/return €2.60/4.20; ☼ 8am-12.15pm & 2-5pm or 6pm Jun-Aug) and mountain bikers can buy a one-day pass (€13), allowing unlimited use of the cable car and chair lifts. The tourist office gives advice on mountain biking itineraries and walking trails and has lists of Alpine guides and mountain accommodation.

Recommended walking clubs which, among other things, organise treks and provide mountain guides include:

Club Alpino Italiano (CAI; ☎ 0165 4 01 94; www .caivda.it, Italian only; Corso Battaglione Aosta 81; ☼ 6.30-8pm Tue, 8-10pm Fri)

Interguide (☎ 0165 4 09 39; www.interguide.it, Italian only; Via Monte Emilius 13; Corso Battaglione Aosta 81; ☼ 6.30pm-8pm Tue, 8pm-10pm Fri)

Meinardi Sport (☎ 0165 4 06 78; Via E Aubert; ☼ 3-7.30pm Mon, 9am-12.30pm & 3-7.30pm Tue-Sat) A well-stocked sports shop with walking supplies and maps.

Festivals & Events

The **Fiera di Sant'Orso**, the annual wood fair held around Porta Praetoria on 30 and 31 January, honours the town's patron saint. Craftspeople from all over the valley gather to display their carvings and present an item to the saint at the Chiesa di Sant'Orso.

Sleeping

Accommodation in Aosta can be expensive and hard to find. Cheaper (and often more charming) lodgings lie in the hinterland. Aosta can easily be visited from Cogne and Valnontey, 24km and 27km respectively south of Aosta on the northern fringe of the Gran Paradiso national park; see pp233–4 for accommodation details.

Camping Milleluci (☎ 0165 4 42 74, ☎ 0165 23 52 78; www.campingmilleluci.com, Italian only; Porossan-Roppoz 15; person/tent & car €5.50/10.50) Milleluci is about 1km east of Aosta and can be reached by bus No 11. It adjoins a hotel of the same name.

La Belle Époque (☎ 0165 26 22 76; fax 0165 26 11 96; Via d'Avise 18; s/d €23/46, with bathroom €25/50) Fifteen basic rooms above a simple pizzeria clock in as Aosta's cheapest; they all share a toilet on the corridor.

Hotel Europe (☎ 0165 23 63 63; hoteleurope@tis calinet.it; Piazza Narbonne 8; s/d low season €64/92, high season €98/160) Elegant style and service sees that Europe lives up to its four-star reputation.

Eating & Drinking

Plenty of open-air café terraces spring up on sun-baked Piazza Chanoux in summer.

Taverna da Nando (☎ 0165 4 44 55; Via de Tillier 41; 1st/2nd courses €7/10, menus €12-28; ☼ Tue-Sun) Nando's *menu turistica* (tourist menu) might be a tad overpriced, but its hearty plates of polenta (€8 to €13), spaghetti (€7) jumbo salads (€5 to €9) and traditional pizzas (€4 to €7) are guaranteed to fill the noisiest of tummies. With 15 different types of polenta or pizza alone, there's something for everyone here.

Brasserie du Commerce (☎ 0165 3 56 13; Via de Tillier 10; 1st/2nd courses €8/13) Dip into a steaming fondue, mouth-melting *raclette* (hot, melted cheese scraped from a block in front of a grill) or hefty *choucroute* (sauerkraut) – all around €10 a tummy-filling plateful – at this busy brasserie. The *piatto Valdostano* (a meal of regional bites; €12) is a must for traditionalists.

Ad Forum (☎ 0165 4 00 11; Via Mons de Sales; 1st courses €6.50, 2nd courses €7.50-18; ☼ 11am-midnight Tue-Sun) Tickle those tastebuds with a bottle of valley vintage at this fabulous café-cum-wine bar, complete with a Roman cellar full of wine. Cheese platters cost €9, there's a sinful selection of gooey cakes and it throws tasting evenings with live music. Bask in the garden for lunch in the sun.

Trattoria degli Artisti (☎ 0165 4 09 60; Via Maillet 5-7; 1st courses €5-8.10, 2nd courses €6.70-8.50; ☼ Tue-Sat) Antipasti fiends flock here in droves to tuck into this rustic kitchen's imaginative appetisers. Tucked down an alleyway off Via de Tillier, it serves plenty of traditional regional fodder too.

Self-caterers and picnic partiers can shop for mainstream products at **Superfresco Standa** (Corsa Battaglione Aosta 5; ☼ 9am-1pm & 3.30-7.30pm Mon-Sat); dried mushrooms at any of the tourist shops lining Via Sant'Anselmo; and grappa and wine at wine bar **Le Grand Paradis** (☎ 0165 4 40 47; Via Sant'Anselmo 121).

Shopping

Tradition has it that Sant'Orso gave carved wooden shoes known as *sabi* to the city's poor. Valdestans continue to carve shoes, tiny houses and ceremonial pots, all widely used. Tacky shops throughout the city, particularly along Via Porte Praetoria, sell

---

VALDOSTAN CHEESE

A curious cross between Gouda and Brie best sums up *fontina*, Valdostans' favourite cheese honoured with its own DOP (designation of protected origin) since 1996. It must be made from the full-cream unpasteurised milk of Valdostan cows that have grazed on pastures up to 2700m high. One hundred litres of milk makes 10kg of cheese. During the three months it matures in underground rock tunnels, it is turned daily and brushed and salted alternate days. This and other age-old traditions dating to the early 13th century can be discovered first-hand at the **Valpelline Vistors Centre** (☎ 0165 7 33 09; Frissonière; admission free; ☺ 8.30am-12.30pm & 2.30-6.30pm Mon-Fri, 9am-noon & 3-6pm Sat & Sun mid-Jun–mid-Sep, 9am-noon & 2.30-5.30pm Mon-Fri mid-Sep–mid-Jun). To get to the centre from Aosta, follow the S28 for 7km north to Valpelline, turn left (west) towards Ollomont and after 1.5km, turn left again along a mountain road to Frissonière.

In Aosta, **La Madison de la Fontana** (☎ 0165 23 56 51; Via Mons de Sales 14), a cheese shop established in 1937, stocks an outstanding selection of regional cheese. Once bought, *fontina* (€14.95 per kg) is best kept outside the fridge. The curiosity of the culinary inquisitive will be aroused by Stravecchio di Montagna (€14.25 per kg), an extremely strong, salty and potent hard cheese – eat it *before* asking how it is made.

---

these goods, as does **IVAT** (☎ 0165 4 14 62; ivat.vda@tin.it; Via Xavier de Maistre 1) overlooking the central square.

Getting There & Away

Buses to Milan (€12, 1½ to 3½ hours, two daily), Turin (€7, two hours, up to 10 daily) and Courmayeur (€3, one hour, up to eight daily) leave from Aosta **bus station** (☎ 0165 26 20 27; Via Giorgio Carrel), virtually opposite the train station. To get to Breuil-Cervinia, take a Turin-bound bus to Châtillon (30 minutes, eight daily), then a connecting bus (one hour, seven daily) to the resort.

Aosta **train station** (Piazza Manzetti) is served by trains from most parts of Italy via Turin (€6.30, two to 2½ hours, more than 10 daily).

Aosta is on the A5, which connects Turin with the Mont Blanc Tunnel and France. Another exit road north of the city leads to the Great St Bernard tunnel and Switzerland.

Getting Around

Aosta's sites are easily reached on foot. Shuttle buses run through town from the train station. Book a **taxi** (☎ 0165 3 18 31) or hire your own wheels from **Europcar** (☎ 0165 4 14 32) at the train station.

AOSTA VALLEY CASTLES

If you need a break from the slopes, the Aosta valley is peppered with castles, many of them Romanesque and Gothic, just waiting to be explored. Each castle is within view of the next, and messages used to be transferred along the valley by flag signals. From Aosta follow the scenic S26 that runs parallel to the busy A5.

East from Aosta is the magnificently restored **Castello di Fénis** (☎ 0165 76 42 63; adult/child €5/free; ☺ 9am-6.30pm Mar-Jun & Sep, 9am-7.30pm Jul & Aug, 10-11.30am & 2-4.30pm Wed-Sat & Mon, 10-11.30am & 2-5.30pm Sun Oct-Feb). Formerly owned by the Challant family it features rich frescoes as well as period graffiti. It was never really used as a defensive post but served as a plush residence.

Past St Vincent is the sober **Castello di Verrès** (☎ 0125 92 90 67; adult/child €3/free; ☺ 9am-6.30pm Mar-Jun & Sep, 9am-7.30pm Jul & Aug, 10am-noon & 1.30-4.30pm Fri-Wed, 10am-noon & 1.30-5.30pm Sun Oct-Feb). More the real thing, this castle does sentinel duty high on its rocky perch.

About 1km southwest of the River Dora Baltea, below the town of Verrès, is the 15th-century **Castello d'Issogne** (☎ 0125 92 93 73; adult/child €5/free; ☺ 9am-6.30pm Mar-Jun & Sep, 9am-7.30pm Jul & Aug, 10am-noon & 1.30-4.30pm Thu-Tue, 10am-noon & 1.30-5.30pm Sun Oct-Feb). This building was a castle though you'd hardly know it – it looks like a stately home.

Further down the valley still, towards Pont-St-Martin, the fortress of **Bard** (closed) was a no-nonsense military outpost given short shrift by Napoleon on his first campaign into Italy. Once you are at Pont St-Martin, you could strike north to **Castel Savoia** in Gressoney-St-Jean; see pp235–6.

Heading west towards Mont Blanc from Aosta, you quickly hit **Castello di Sarre** (☎ 0165 25 75 39; adult/child €5/free; ☺ 9am-6.30pm Mar-Jun & Sep

---

A FARMHOUSE FEAST

Lo Ratelë di Conchatre Paola (☎ 0165 7 82 65; Allein; d with breakfast €39, dinner per person €29; ☺ only with advance reservation) Sheep, cows and chickens are raised at this remote farmstead where farm-made 1st courses are dished up, so hearty, wholesome and numerous that there's really no knowing when the 1st course ends and the 2nd begins.

The feasts starts with an aperitif of Chambave, followed by three types of salami and wafer-thin *lardo* (herb-scented pork fat); a plate of prosciutto and apple fritters; a prune wrapped in bacon; farm-made ricotta cheese with herbs and balsamic vinegar; a pear, celery and *fontina* cheese salad; hot chestnuts in butter; boiled potatoes with *contechino* (a big, fat farm-made sausage built from pig skin, fat, garlic and a smidgen of pork meat); cabbage-laden *seupa valpellinentze* and another type of thick soup made from bread, milk and courgette; a choice of wine-braised deer or veal with polenta… and an espresso with grappa. Dessert is generally skipped on account of exploding stomachs.

Each dish is trolleyed to the table by a hot-from-the-kitchen, pinny-clad Signora Paola. Traditionally at great social events, Valdostans round off a meal with a *caffè valdostana* – coffee, grappa and sugar mixed and served in a communal drinking pot with several spouts. A couple of such pots sit on the side in the dining room, as do racks of *copa*, loaves of rye bread baked, as tradition demands, a week before Christmas and dried for months until rock-hard. Credit cards are not accepted.

9am-7.30pm Jul & Aug, 10am-noon & 1.30-4.30pm Tue-Sat, 10am-noon & 1.30-5.30pm Sun Oct-Feb). Built in 1710 on the remains of a 13th-century fort, King Vittorio Emanuele II bought it in 1869 to use as a hunting residence. The Savoys sold the castle in 1972 and it now serves as a museum of the royal presence in the region.

Castello di San Pierre (☎ 0165 90 34 85; adult/child €3/1.50; ☺ 9am-7pm Apr-Sep), home to a natural history museum, is the last main sight of interest on Aosta's castle route.

COURMAYEUR

pop 2956 / elevation 1224m

Set against the backdrop of Mont Blanc and with much of the original village intact, Courmayeur is one of the Valle d'Aosta's more picturesque skiing resorts. It is also one of the priciest. Out of season, wealthy Milanese and Turinese women leave their fur coats in a local furrier's vault – minks and ermines are too valuable to be worn in the streets of their home cities.

The resort has more than 140km of downhill and cross-country ski runs and a feast of summer activities, including **skiing**, **horse riding**, **hang-gliding**, **canoeing** and 280km of footpaths in the mountains. Year-round a cable car links La Palud, near Courmayeur, with Punta Helbronner (3462m) on Mont Blanc – an extraordinary 20-minute ride. From here another cable car (April to September only) takes you on a breathtaking 5km transglacial ride across the Italian border to the Aiguille du Midi (3842m) in France (from where the

world's highest cable car transports you into the French ski resort of Chamonix).

Information

Ambulance (☎ 0165 84 46 84)

Ospedale Regionale d'Aosta (hospital; ☎ 0165 30 42 56, 0165 54 32 90).

Tourist Office (☎ 0165 84 20 60; www.courmayeur.net, Italian only; Piazzale Monte Bianco 13; ☺ 9am-12.30pm & 3-6.30pm)

Activities

The **Società delle Guide Alpine di Courmayeur** (☎ 0165 84 20 64; www.guidecourmayeur.com; Piazzale Monte Bianco 14), founded in 1859, is Italy's oldest guiding association. In winter its guides lead adventure seekers off-piste, up frozen waterfalls and on **heli-skiing** expeditions. In summer **via ferrata**, **rock climbing**, **canyoning**, **canoeing**, **kayaking** and **hiking** are among its many activities. The association's dramatic history is unravelled in the **Museo Alpino Duca degli Abruzzi** (☎ 0165 84 20 64; Piazza Henry 2; admission free).

SKIING

Courmayeur is served by four cable cars, two gondolas and numerous drag lifts, all run by **Funivie Courmayeur Mont Blanc** (☎ 0165 84 66 58; www.courmayeur-montblanc.com; Strada Regionale 47). Count on paying at least €32.50/169 for a one-/six-day ski pass; for passes for Courmayeur and other resorts, see pp225–7. Skiing lessons with the **Scuola di Sci Monte Bianco** (☎ 0165 84 24 77; www.montebianco.maestridisci.com, Italian only;

Strada Regionale 51), founded in 1922, start at €30 for a one to three hour, private or group lesson. For advanced skiers the legendary Vallée Blanche off-piste descent from Punta Helbronner into Chamonix (France) is a must. Ability aside an experienced guide is essential for the challenging 24km-long run.

SWIMMING
For an exhilarating summertime experience take a heady dive into Courmayeur's open-air alpine **swimming pool** (☎ 0165 84 66 58; adult/child under 5 €10/free, pool & return cable-car ticket €16/free; 🕑 9.30am-5.30pm mid-Jun–early Sep), tucked in the heart of the mountains at the top of the Courmayeur cable car on Plan Checrouit (1709m). Admission to the pool includes use of the sauna.

WALKING & MOUNTAIN BIKING
In July and August the resort's Courmayeur and Val Veny **cable cars** (☎ 0165 84 66 58; single/return €6/10) and the Maison Vieille **chairlift** (☎ 0165 84 66 58; adult single/return €4/5) whisk walkers and mountain bikers into the mountains; transporting a bike is free. All three run from around 9.15am to 1pm and 2.15pm to 5.15pm June to August.

The **La Palud-Punta Helbronner cable car** (☎ 0165 8 99 25; www.montebianco.com; return €30.50; 🕑 8.30am-12.40pm & 2-4.30pm) departs every 20 minutes in each direction. From mid-station **Pavillon du Mt Fréty** (elevation 2173m; return €11.50), nature lovers can take a flowery stroll around the **Giardino Alpino Saussurea** (☎ 0165 8 99 25; adult/child €2.10/1.50; 🕑 9.30am-6pm Jul-Sep). From this Alpine garden – at 2175m, Europe's highest – the stunning views of the Mont Blanc range alone make a visit worthwhile. Walking trails around here are numerous and many fall within the **Pavillon du Mt Fréty Nature Oasis**, a protected zone of 1200 hectares tucked between glaciers and populated by ibexes, marmots and deer.

Even if it's sweltering in the valley be prepared for it to be as bone-chillingly cold (not to mention downright windy) as -10°C at **Punta Helbronner** (3462m). Take heavy winter clothes, sunglasses and head up early in the morning to avoid the heavy weather that often descends onto the summit area in the early afternoon. Bring your passport (and check if you need a visa) if you intend making the glacial crossing (€17.50/39 return to Aiguille du Midi/Chamonix) into France.

Mountain bikes can be hired at **Noleggio Ulisse** (☎ 0165 84 22 55), in front of the Courmayeur chair lift; **Lo Caraco** (☎ 0165 84 41 52; Via Roma 150) in town; or **Club des Sports** (☎ 0165 8 95 70) in Planpincieux, 5km north of Courmayeur. Hire costs around €10 a day.

Those seeking a guide should contact the Società delle Guide Alpine di Courmayeur (see p231) or the **Associazione Accompagnatori della Natura Courmayeur-Mt Blanc** (☎ 0165 86 21 40; Strada La Palud 1).

Sleeping & Eating
Peak-season accommodation in Courmayeur can cost up to 50% more than in low season, but hotel rates in towns along the valleys – La Palud, Dolonne, Entrèves, La Saxe, Plan Ponquet, Val Ferret, Pré-St Didier and Morgex – soar less dramatically. For mountain-hut accommodation ask the tourist office for a list of rifugi. In the old part of Courmayeur quality food shops and restaurants line Via Roma.

Camping Monte Bianco La Sorgente (☎ 0165 86 90 98; www.campinglasorgente.net; Peuterey-Val Veny; person/tent/car €4.30/3.20/3.20, bed in shared hut €11, 2-person bungalow with/without kitchen €47/32; 🕑 mid-Jun–mid-Sep; [P]) This well-equipped camp site, in the middle of a forest 5km from Courmayeur, has a great range of budget accommodation and rallies campers together with a host of activities, organised walks etc.

Rifugio Pavillon (☎ 0165 84 40 90; Pavillon du Mt Fréty; 🕑 10am-5pm Dec-Oct) At a heady height of 2173m and promising a dramatic mountain panorama from any deck chair you flop on, this mountain bar-café-restaurant makes an exhilarating lunch stop for those travelling up to Punta Helbronner or walking around Mt Fréty. It has 24 dorm beds should your legs refuse to shift another inch.

Hotel Edelweiss (☎ 0165 84 15 90; Via Marconi 42; s/d low season €40/70, high season €60/100; 🕑 Dec-Apr & May-Sep) Quietly placed in a green part of town, this two-star hotel with garden and sun loungers is not a bad deal. An almost stereotypical alpine chalet-style exterior shelters 30 comfy rooms.

Getting There & Away
Three trains daily from Aosta terminate at Pré-St Didier, with bus connections (20 to 30 minutes, eight to 10 daily) to **Courmayeur bus station** (☎ 0166 84 13 97; Piazzale Monte Bianco), outside the tourist office. There are up to eight

direct Aosta–Courmayeur buses daily (€3, one hour) and long-haul buses serve Milan (€16, 4½ hours, three to five daily) and Turin (€9, 3½ to 4½ hours, two to four daily).

Immediately north of Courmayeur, the 11.5km-long Mont Blanc Tunnel leads to Chamonix (France).

PARCO NAZIONALE DEL GRAN PARADISO

Gran Paradiso was Italy's first national park, established in 1922 after Vittorio Emanuele II gave his hunting reserve to the state. By 1945 the ibex (wild goat) had been almost hunted to extinction in the park and there were only 419 left. Today, as the result of a conservation policy, almost 4000 live here.

The national park incorporates the valleys around the Gran Paradiso (4061m), three of which are in the Valle d'Aosta: the Valsavarenche, Val di Rhêmes and beautiful Valle di Cogne. On the Piedmont side of the mountain, the park includes the valleys of Soana and Orco.

The main stepping stone into the park is the lovely village-resort of **Cogne** (population 1469, elevation 1534m), a former iron-ore mining village on the park's northern fringe which, since the late 1970s, has devoted itself to greener activities. It is also known for its lace-making. The **tourist office** (☎ 0165 7 40 40; www.cogne.org, Italian only; Piazza Chanoux 36; ☼ 9am-12.30pm & 2.30-5.30pm Mon-Sat) has stacks of information on the entire park and a list of emergency contact numbers.

In summer, the national park runs a visitors centre in the Alpine Botanical Garden 3km south of Cogne in Valnontey (see Activities, following). Otherwise its Turin-based **headquarters** (☎ 011 86 06 211; Via Della Rocca 47) provides information.

Activities

Excellent **cross-country skiing** trails line the Valle di Cogne, one of the Valle d'Aosta's most picturesque, unspoiled valleys. There are 80km of well-marked cross-country trails in Cogne, also the starting point for 9km of downhill slopes. A one-/two-day ski pass covering use of Cogne's one cable car, chairlift and drag lift costs €18/30. Individual/group skiing lessons with the **Scuola Italian Sci Gran Paradiso ski** (☎ 0165 7 43 00; Piazza Chanoux 38) typically cost €31/9.50 an hour.

Come summer more than 1000 species of Alpine flora and butterflies typical to the mountains here can be discovered at the fascinating **Giardino Alpino Paradisia** (☎ 0165 7 41 47; Valnontey; adult/child €2.10/1.10; ☼ 9.30am-12.30pm & 2.30-6.30pm Jun–mid-Sep), a botanical Alpine garden in Valnontey (1700m). Otherwise, hook up with a naturalist through the **Associazione Guide della Nature** (☎ 0165 7 42 82; Piazza Chanoux 36; ☼ 9am-noon Mon, Wed & Sat). Between July and September it runs a rash of half- and full-day guided walks.

From Cogne an easy walking trail (3km, one hour) leads southeast through forest to Lillaz and its waterfall. Another path (2.8km, 45 minutes) meanders through grassland south to Valnontey. From the top of the **Cogne–Montzeuc cable car** (☎ 0165 7 40 08; adult single/return €4/6; ☼ 9am-noon & 2-5.30pm Jul–mid-Sep), there's a nature trail (4km, three hours) with information panels and 15 observation posts. The main point of departure for the Gran Paradiso peak is Pont in the Valsavarenche. Climbers and walkers wanting someone to lead the way can contact the **Società Guide Alpine di Cogne** (☎ 0165 7 42 82; geoabel@libero.it; Piazza Chanoux 40).

Sleeping & Eating

Wild camping is forbidden in the park, but there are 11 alpine *rifugi*; the tourist office has a list. Hotels are most plentiful in Cogne, but those seeking true peace and tranquillity should plump for Valnontey, 3km south.

Camping Lo Stambecco (☎ 0165 7 41 52; camping stambecco@tiscali.it; Valnontey; person/tent/car €4.50/3.50/ 2.50; ☼ May-Sep; P) Bang in the heart of the national park, this well-run and friendly site should keep most campers smiling. Rent wheels or blades from its sister hotel La Barme (see following).

Petit Dahu (☎ 0165 7 41 46; Valnontey 27; s/d low season from €25/50, high season from €40/80) Small but sweet sums up this unusual place to stay and eat, housed inside two interlinked alpine huts dating to 1729. Interior furnishings are rustic, the cuisine is strictly homemade, and the exterior is as quaint as quaint can be.

La Barme (☎ 0165 74 91 77; www.hotellabarme.com; Valnontey; d half-board low/mid/high season €84/92/98, menus €11-23; P ✗) What was a traditional stone-and-wood dairy in the 1830s has been transformed into a delightful 15-room hotel with wooden furnishings and a roaring winter fire. None of the barn's

LIGURIA, PIEDMONT & VALLE D'AOSTA

original old-world charm has been lost in the makeover, making it a dream to stay in. The hotel rents cross-country skis in winter, mountain bikes in summer and rejuvenates weary bones with a sauna and massages.

Hotel Bellevue (☎ 0165 7 48 25; www.hotelbellevue .it; Via Grand Paradis 22, Cogne; d low/mid/high season €115/ 145/260, 2-person chalet €131/147/178; ☺ mid-Dec–mid-Oct; **P** ☒) Cogne's top four-star choice – a fabulous, green-shuttered mountain hideaway from the 1920s – is the stuff honeymoons are made of. Its old-world charm, complete with weighty cow bells strung from hefty old beams, bathtubs with legs, a 1920s limousine and cheese cellars, will take your breath away. The views will too.

Getting There & Around
There are up to seven buses daily to/from Cogne and Aosta (50 minutes), from where many more services can be picked up. Cogne can also be reached by cable car from Pila.

Valley buses (up to 10 daily) link Cogne with Lillaz (€0.80, five minutes) and Valnontey (€0.80, five minutes).

VALTOURNENCHE
Stretching from the Valle d'Aosta to the Matterhorn (4478m), the 25km-long Valtournenche is synonymous with **Breuil-Cervinia** (2050m), a ski resort which – despite its bristling modern, purpose-built facade – offers some of Europe's finest skiing. Skiing across into Zermatt (Switzerland) or simply in view of what English poet Byron described as 'Europe's noble rock' is unforgettable. Smaller skiing areas include **Antey-St-André** (1080m), **La Magdeleine** (1644m) and **Valtournenche** (1524m), 9km short of Breuil-Cervinia. Nature lovers seeking a flashback in time should make a beeline for **Chamois** (1800m), a mountain hamlet accessible only by cable car or on foot.

Information
There are tourist offices in **Breuil-Cervinia** (☎ 0166 94 91 36; www.cervinia.it; Via Carrel 29; ☺ 9am-noon & 3-6.30pm); **Valtournenche** (☎ 0166 9 20 29; valtournenche@montecervino.it; Via Roma 45; ☺ 9am-noon & 3-6.30pm) and **Antey-St-André** (☎ 0166 54 82 66; antey@montecervino.it; Piazza A Rolando 1; ☺ 9am-noon & 3-6.30pm).

For Internet access go to **Lino's Bar** (☎ 0166 94 82 80; linosbar@yahoo.com; €5/hr ☺ 9am-1am

mid-Nov–May & Jul–mid-Sep), next to the ice-skating rink.

Activities
Plateau Rosa (3480m) and the Little Matterhorn (3883m) in the Breuil-Cervinia ski area offer some of Europe's highest skiing while the Campetto area has introduced the Valle d'Aosta to night skiing. A couple of dozen cable cars serve the 200km of downhill pistes that can be skied here in all, four of which originate in Breuil-Cervinia. Three types of ski pass are available: a one-/six-day ski pass covering just Breuil-Cervinia for €30/155; equivalent passes covering the entire Breuil-Cervinia Valtournenche and the Matterhorn zone of Zermatt for €36/180; and passes covering the latter plus all of Zermatt is €40/198.

Contact Breuil-Cervinia's **Scuola di Sci de Breuil Cervinia** (☎ 0166 94 09 60; www.scuolasc breuil.com) or **Scuola Sci del Cervino** (☎ 0166 94 8 44; www.scuolacervino.com) for skiing and snowboarding lessons, and its mountain guide association **Società Guide del Cervino** (☎ 0166 9 81 69; www.guidedelcervino.com; Via J Antoine Carrel 20) to make the most of Matterhorn's wild off-piste opportunities.

Between July and September several cableways and lifts to Plateau Rosa continue to operate, allowing the truly dedicated to ski all year round. A one-day ski pass for glacier summer skiing costs €23 (€33 if you want to ski on the Swiss side too). In October cableways only run at the weekend. A one-day lift pass for mountain bikers costing €18 is also available.

Basic walking maps are available at the APT offices, but if you want to tackle the Matterhorn you need to be properly dressed and equipped. Get a 1:25,000 walking map such as the Instituto Geographico Centrale (IGC) map No 108 (available from book shops in Aosta, see p227), and consider a guide – contact the **Società Guide del Cervino** (☎ 0166 94 81 69; guidedelcervino@hotmail.com; Via Antoine Carrel 20) in Breuil-Cervinia.

Sleeping & Eating
Rifugio Guide del Cervino (☎ 0166 9 21 01; giorgio.ca rel@galactica.it; Plateau Rosa) Breathtakingly nestled up high at 3480m on Plateau Rosa, thi mountain hut gets rammed with skiers i winter and walkers in summer. Ride the Plateau Rosa cable car to get here. At full moon

t throws dinners, followed by a torch-lit ski
descent down into Breuil-Cervinia.

Hotel Pub Grivola (☎ 0166 94 82 87; Breuil-
ervinia; s/d from €50/70, 1st/2nd courses €10/14) Well-
placed at the top of Breuil-Cervinia's main
pedestrian street, this three-star hotel-
restaurant-bar caters to all tastes. Its 21
rooms warrant zero complaints, the €10
Grivoli pizza (mozzarella, tomato, rocket
and truffle oil) or venison stew served in
its Vieux Grenier (Old Attic) restaurant
will tickle the trickiest of tastebuds, while
its pint-driven Irish pub rocks.

Hotel The Dragon (☎ 0166 94 94 80 85; hoteldragon@
ostanet.com; Via JB Bich 3, Breuil-Cervinia; s/d low season
31/62, high season €52/124, half-board per person low/high
season €45/65; ☾ Nov-Mar, Jul & Aug) Balconies with
Matterhorn views and a one-step stumble
away from the slopes are star assets of this
young fun hotel, conveniently placed directly
opposite the bustling slopes and above a busy
Scottish and Welsh pub. Guests are definitely
closer to 20 than 50.

Hotel Punta Maquignaz (☎ 0166 94 91 45; www
.puntamaquignaz.com; Breuil-Cervinia; half-board per person
w/mid/high season €70/95/105) Half-board is a
must at this handsome four-star hulk of a
hotel, complete with stacked logs in the hall-
way alongside cow bells and bear skins. The
decor is strictly rustic – think verrrry large
mountain chalet. A buoyant après-ski crowd
fills the hotel's American-styled Ymeletrob
bar and grill.

etting There & Away

avda (☎ 0165 36 12 44) operates buses from
Breuil-Cervinia to Châtillon (one hour,
seven daily), from where there are connecting buses to/from Aosta and trains to other
destinations in Italy. Longer-haul seasonal
bus services from Breuil-Cervinia include
to/from Turin, Milan and Genoa.

ALLE D'AYAS, VAL DI GRESSONEY & ALSESIA

ast of Valtournenche, the Val di Gres-
oney, Val d'Ayas and Valsesia (in Piedmont) snake splendidly north to the feet
f majestic Monte Rosa (4633m), a mas-
ve hulk of a mountain shared by Italy
nd Switzerland. It was to these southern
Monte Rosa valleys that the Walsers – an
hnic group of Germanic descent – mi-
rated from Switzerland's Valais region in
e 13th century.

Today, the Val di Gressoney and Valsesia
particularly remain Walser strongholds: German is the mother tongue of many in these
rural climes today where village names are
written trilingually and quaint Walser *Stadel* (wood-slatted houses built from larch
on short stilts) dot the hillsides. Walsers
don traditional dress each year on Midsummer's Day (24 June) to celebrate mass.
Other Walser traditions can be discovered
in the small **Museo Walser** (☎ 0163 92 29 88; admission free; ☾ 2-6pm Sat & Sun Sep-Jun, 2-6pm Mon, Jul,
10am-noon & 2-6pm Aug), in Piedmont, on Alagna
Valsesia's northern edge.

In the Valle d'Ayas, **Champoluc** at the head
of the valley is the main resort, although
Brusson makes a handy base for those seeking easy half-day ambles. Pretty lakeside
Gressoney-St-Jean (population 816, elevation
1385m) and **Gressoney-La-Trinité** (population
306, elevation 1637m), a few kilometres
north, are the main mountain villages in
the Val di Gressoney. The more sprawling
Valsesia helter-skelters big-dipper style all
the way from the relatively low-lying ski resort of **Alagna Valsesia** (1191m) in the north
to urban Vercelli, 50km west of Milan.

Online see www.monterosa-ski.com.

Information

There are tourist offices in:
Brusson (☎ 0125 30 02 40; infobrusson@libero.it;
Piazza Municipio 2; ☾ 9am-12.30pm & 3-6pm)
Champoluc (☎ 0125 30 71 13; monterosa.info@libero.it;
Via Varasc 16; ☾ 9am-12.30pm & 3-6pm) In the Valle
d'Ayas.
Gressoney-St Jean (☎ 0125 35 51 85; www
.aiatmonterosawalser.it; Villa Deslex; ☾ 9am-12.30pm &
2.30-6.30pm Mon-Sat, 9am-12.30pm & 2.30-6pm Sun)
Gressoney-La Trinité (☎ 0125 36 61 43; info@
aiatmonterosawalser.it; Piazza Tache; ☾ 9am-12.30pm &
2.30-6.30pm Mon-Sat, 9am-12.30pm & 2.30-6pm Sun) In
the Valle di Gressoney.
Alagna Vaisesia tourist office (☎ 0163 92 29 88;
www.alagna.it; Piazza Grober 1) The main information
source for mountain activities in the Valsesia.

Sights

Before heading to the hills brush up on
your alpine fauna at Gressoney-St-Jean's
Museo Regionale della Fauna Alpina (☎ 0125 35
54 06; adult/child €3/free; ☾ 9am-12.30pm & 3-6.30pm
Thu-Tue), at the southern end of the village.

In 1894 Queen Margherita picked Gressoney-St-Jean as the location for **Castel Savoia**

(☎ 0125 35 53 96; adult/child €3/free; ☺ 9am-6.30pm Mar-Jun & Sep, 9am-7.30pm Jul & Aug, 10am-noon & 1.30-4.30pm Fri-Wed, 10am-noon & 1.30-5.30pm Sun Oct-Feb), a fairy-tale mansion enjoyed by the Italian royals well into the 1900s.

Activities

The Ayas, Gressoney and Sesia valleys form **Monterosa Ski**, a ski area sporting 180km of downhill runs (predominantly red and best suited to intermediate skiers) and 38 ski lifts. From Alagna Valsesia a cable car climbs to Punta Indren (3260m). A one-/six-day Monterosa ski pass costs €30/135.

Of the three valleys the Val di Gressoney is the place to cross-country ski: the 25km-long Gressoney-St-Jean piste takes skiers past Castel Savoia (see pp235–6) and dozens of traditional wooden Walser houses. Lower down the valley the 15km-long trail linking the villages of Gaby and Issimeis an easy one to do, and picturesque at that.

Walks abound in this neck of the woods. In summer you can ride a cable car from Gressoney-La-Trinité to Lago Gabiet, an Alpine lake at 2357m from where numerous trails can be picked up. The tourist offices have more details as well as lists of local mountain guides.

Sleeping & Eating

Rifugio Gabiet (☎ 0125 36 62 58; fax 0125 80 61 52; Lago Gabiet; d half-board low/high season €72/80; ☺ mid-Dec–mid-Apr & mid-Jun–mid-Sep) This attractive mountain hotel, named after the family who opened it several decades ago, stands tall and alone at 2880m. It peers down on Lago Gabiet and can be reached by cable car from Gressoney-La-Trinité. Its 25 cosy double rooms are generally filled

by walkers, heli-skiers and other mountain enthusiasts. You can dine here too.

Hotel Favre (☎ 0125 30 71 31; albergo.favre@flas net.it; Via Quaille 1, Champoluc; half-board per person low high season €40/65) Top a fun, down-to-earth staff with a busy sun-drenched bar terrace designed strictly with sun-basking and drinking in mind, and you have one great sleeping 'n eating spot.

Hotel Stadel (☎ 0125 35 52 64; edmond@libero.i Bieltschöcke, Gressoney-St-Jean; d low/high season pe week €170/225) If you're still not sure what a typical Walser house looks like, then sta here…because Hotel Stadel is a *stadel* no less! Its 12 rooms are cosy, snug and toast and more than live up to the two star someone gave them.

Albergo Breithorn (☎ 0125 30 87 34; www.breithor hotel.com; Route Ramey 27, Champoluc; d low/high seaso €75/110, half-board per person €72/125, 1st/2nd courses €1 15; ☺ Dec-Sep; ℗) A carved wooden exterio shields an oasis of rustic mountain charm a this four-star chalet hotel. But just what di happen to the wearers of those fantastic co bells in reception? Breithorn's restaurar and less-expensive brasserie are enticin – its sauna and Turkish bath even more s Those seeking a romantic getaway shoul stay at Breithorn's **Hotellerie de Mascognaz**, luxurious seven-room chalet in the moun tains, with transfers to/from Champoluc b snowmobile or off-road vehicle.

Getting There & Away

Trains running through Aosta stop in S Vincent and Verrès, from where you ca catch a bus to either valley. **Valdostan Impresa Trasporti Automobilistici** (VITA; ☎ 012 96 65 46) operates buses from Verrès trai station to Champoluc (€2.10, one hour, u to nine daily).

Lombardy & the Lakes

From the Alps to the lush plains of the River Po, Lombardy's (Lombardia) often fractious political history is reflected in its geographical diversity. Beyond the chic financial metropolis of Milan, the region is peppered with affluent towns that preserve pretty old centres and a distinct character inherited from the days of city-states: Mantua, Cremona, Bergamo, Brescia and Pavia are wealthy and stylish. Green escape routes for the city folk from Italy's richest, most industrial and developed region include a stretch of enchanting lakes from Lago d'Orta to Lago di Garda.

Lombardy formed part of Gallia Cisalpina (Cisalpine Gaul) before it fell to Saracen tribes and later to Germanic Lombards. Interference by the Franks under Barbarossa (Frederick I) in the 12th century ended when the cities united under the Lega Lombarda (Lombard League). After the League collapsed Lombardy was divided between the Visconti, Sforza, Gonzaga and Scaliger families and was later invaded by the Venetians, Austrian Habsburgs and Napoleon.

Lombard cuisine relies heavily on rice and polenta and features butter, cream and cheese from its Alpine pastures. Gorgonzola originated just outside Milan, while it was in the great city that Italy's best-known cake, *panettone*, was first baked. Meats are predominantly pork and veal – *cotoletta alla milanese* (fillet of veal fried in breadcrumbs) is famous. Lombardy's sparkling wines are among Italy's best; the Franciacorta red is mellow, while the white is fruity and dry.

HIGHLIGHTS

- **Hot Date**
  An opera at Milan's La Scala (p243)

- **Old Town Stroll**
  Bergamo (pp261–5) or Cremona (pp268–9)

- **Down-to-earth Milanese Cooking**
  Trattoria da Pino (p252), Antica Osteria Milanese (p252) & Antica Trattoria della Pesa (p253)

- **Trend Setters**
  Milan's Corso Como bars and clubs (p254)

- **Altitude Encounter**
  Cable car up Monte Baldo (p284)

- **Kidding Around**
  Feeding pigeons on Milan's Piazza del Duomo (pp242–3), Lago di Garda's Disney-style amusement parks (p285), boats on the lakes (pp274–9)

- **Treasure Trove**
  Leonardo's Cenacolo Vinciano (p246); Mantegna's Camera degli Sposi (p270), Certosa di Pavia (pp259–60), Cremona's violins (pp268–9), Rovereto's MART art collection (p287)

- **World Events:**
  Milan's fashion weeks (p257), World Windsurf Championships on Lago di Garda (p287)

■ POPULATION: 9.1 MILLION	■ AREA: 23,835 SQ KM

MILAN (MILANO)

pop 1.3 million \ elevation 122m

Milan is synonymous with style. Smart and slick at work and play, the Milanese run their busy metropolis with efficiency and aplomb. It is Italy's economic engine room, the powerhouse of world design and Paris' arch-rival on the catwalk. The city wrenched Europe's international fashion shows away from Florence in the 1980s and has long mocked Rome for losing out on the country's stock market – to who else but Milan. Most of the country's major corporations and the nation's largest concentration of industry are likewise here.

Milan is strictly for city lovers. Shopping is of religious significance. The world's most-famous designers have their flagship stores here, the city is top of most international music tour programmes, its clubbing scene is hot and hip and theatre and cinema flourish in this oasis of sophistication.

Food is another Milan joy. Historical cafés where Verdi and other eminent composers sank espresso shots are plentiful, while sweet *panettone*, Italy's quintessential Christmas cake, is modelled on the lofty domes of a Lombardy cathedral. Milan's cathedral, incidentally, is the world's fourth largest.

Milan's smog is almost as legendary as London's. Should you get to see the sun, note that a sultry pair of dark shades is an essential fashion item. Despite many Milanese talking endlessly of escaping Milan and moving to the country, most are staunchly proud of their city and few leave – except in August when city dwellers depart en masse to escape the stifling heat. And you'd do well to stay away then too.

HISTORY

Milan is said to have been founded by Celtic tribes who settled along the River Po in the 7th century BC. In 222 BC Roman legions marched into the territory, defeated the Gallic Insubres tribe and occupied the town, which they knew as Mediolanum ('middle of the plain'). Mediolanum's key position on the trade routes between Rome and northwestern Europe ensured its continued prosperity and it was here in AD 313 that Constantine I made his momentous edict granting Christians freedom of worship.

In the 11th century a *comune* (town council) was formed. The city-state, ruled by a council including members of all classes, entered a period of rapid growth but soon started bickering with neighbouring towns. Holy Roman emperor, Barbarossa (Frederick I), exploited these local conflicts and besieged Milan in 1162. Milan and its allies formed the Lega Lombarda and exacted revenge in 1176.

From the mid-13th century the city was governed by a succession of families – the Torrianis, Viscontis and finally Sforzas. It fell under Spanish rule in 1535 and passed to Austria with the Treaty of Utrecht of 1713. Legacies of the reign of Maria Theresa of Austria are still evident, particularly in the dull-yellow (her favourite colour) facades of the Palazzo Reale.

Napoleon made Milan the capital of his Cisalpine Republic in 1797 and, five years later, of his Italian Republic, crowning himself king of Italy in 1805. Austria returned in 1814 but troops under Vittorio Emanuele II and Napoleon III quickly crushed the Austrian forces in 1859 and Milan became part of the nascent Kingdom of Italy.

After WWI Mussolini, then in Milan as editor of socialist newspaper *Avanti!*, turned the city into a hotbed of fascism, founding the Fascist Party in 1919. Party meetings were held in Milan's Palazzo Castini. Allied bombings during WWII destroyed much of central Milan.

Swift post-war economic recovery saw Milan become an industrial mean machine. The 1960s gave rise to neofascist terrorist groups and in December 1969 a bomb exploded in a Milan bank, killing 16 people. In the late 1980s, protest by Milan's business and political leaders against inefficient and corrupt government in Rome and subsidies directed to the south spawned the separatist party, the Lega Nord (Northern League). In 1992 the Tangentopoli scandal broke, implicating thousands of Milanese politicians, officials and businesspeople, fashion designers Gianni Versace and Giorgio Armani among them. A year later a Sicilian mafia terrorist bomb exploded outside Milan's contemporary art museum and in 1995 fashion tycoon Maurizio Gucci was shot outside his office on the same street.

Nine murders in nine consecutive days in 1999 prompted Milan's centre-right mayor

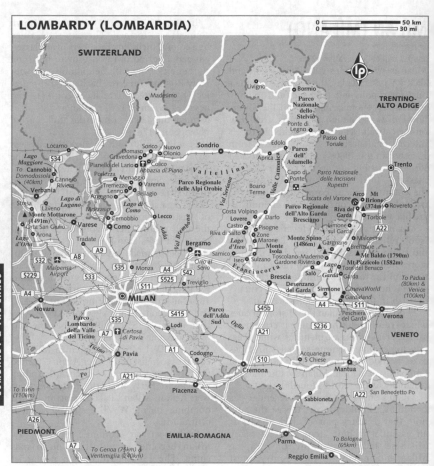

LOMBARDY (LOMBARDIA)

Gabriele Albertini to seek advice from New York hardliner Rudolph Giuliani. Milan's self-made big shot (and Italy's richest man), Silvio Berlusconi, was elected Italian prime minister in 2001. Terrorism fears returned with a vengeance in 2002 when a small plane crashed into the 25th floor of the city's 30-storey Pirelli skyscraper building, killing two lawyers inside.

ORIENTATION

Most of Milan's attractions are concentrated between the cathedral and Castello Sforzesco, either accessible from the train stations by underground railway, the Metropolitana Milanese (MM). Other parts of town likely to be frequented are Brera –

immediately north of the cathedral – which encompasses many galleries and fashionable shopping streets; Navigli to the south; and the Porta Garibaldi area north of town where the city's fashionable Corso Como bars and clubs lie.

INFORMATION
Bookshops

American Bookstore (Map pp248–9; ☎ 02 87 89 20; Via M Camperio 10) Only English books.

English Bookshop (Map pp244–5; ☎ 02 469 44 68; www.englishbookshop.it; Via Mascheroni 12) English titles.

La Scala Bookstore (Map pp248–9; ☎ 02 869 22 60; Piazza della Scala 5) Opera bookshop inside the Trussardi shop.

Rizzoli (Map pp248–9; ☎ 02 864 61 071; Galleria Vittorio Emanuele II) Unbeatable range of translated works by Italian writers and Italy-inspired travel literature in its basement.

Touring Club Italiano (Map pp248–9; ☎ 02 535 99 71; Corso Italia 10) Guidebooks and walking maps.

Cultural Centres

British Council (Map pp248–9; ☎ 02 77 22 21; www.british council.it; Via Alessandro Manzoni 38)

Emergency

Foreigners' Police Office (Map pp248–9; ☎ 02 6 22 61; Via Montebello 26)

Police Station (Map pp248–9; ☎ 02 6 22 61; Via Fatebenefratelli 11)

Gay & Lesbian

Centro d'Iniziativa Gay – ArciGay Milano (Map pp244–5; ☎ 02 541 22 225; www.arcigaymilano.org, Italian only; Via Bezzeca 3) The main point of contact for gays and lesbians; organises Milan's annual Gay Pride march.

Internet Access

Internet Enjoy (Map pp244–5; ☎ 02 835 72 25; Alzaia Naviglio Pavese 2; €3.10/hr; ☽ 9am-1am Mon-Sat, 8pm-1am Sun) Sit in a blue booth and surf.

Extremelot (Map pp244–5; ☎ 02 454 91 469; Ripa Porta Ticinese 9; €6/hr) Seemingly never full and definitely the most comfortable.

Le Point Contact (Map pp248–9; ☎ 02 671 01 061; Via Pergolesi 21; €4/hr; ☽ 9am-10pm) Cheap telephone calling centre with Internet access.

Virgin Megastore (Map pp248–9; ☎ 02 880 01 200; Duomo Centre, Piazza del Duomo 8; ☽ 10am-midnight) Buy a one/two hour coded slip of paper for €2/4 from the sales desk and wait until a computer frees up; type in the code (valid one month) to access the Net.

Laundry

Washing 7/16kg costs around €3.50/6.

Onda Blu (Map pp244–5; Via Savona 1; ☽ 9am-10pm)
Lavanderia Self Service (Map pp244–5; Via Tadino 4; ☽ 8am-9pm)

Left Luggage

Stazione Centrale (Map pp244–5; ☽ 6am-1.30am; €3/1st 12 hrs)

Stazione Nord (Map pp248–9; ☎ 800 55 77 30; ☽ 5.15am-11.30pm) Safety-deposit lockers next to the Malpensa Express ticket office.

Stazione Porta Garibaldi (Map pp244–5; €4/24 hrs; ☽ 7am-8.30pm)

Media

The comprehensive listings guide, *Milano* - *Milano*, sold at the tourist office for €3, is worth buying. The online edition of *Hello Milan* (www.hellomilano.it) is meatier than its monthly print edition (free). *Easy Milano* (www.easymilano.it) is another dual print-electronic publication for Anglophones. The free Italian newspapers distributed on the underground are handy for what's on listings. Book-wise, *Milanopass* (€12) is a hip annual Italian-only listings guide, essential for clubbers and night owls.

Medical Services

24-hour Pharmacy (Map pp244–5; ☎ 02 669 09 35; Stazione Centrale)

Farmacia Carlo Erba (Map pp248–9; ☎ 02 87 86 68; Piazza del Duomo 21; ☽ 9pm-8.30am) All-night pharmacy.

Milan Clinic (Map pp248–9; ☎ 02 760 16 047; www.milan clinic.com; Via Cerva 25) One of several private clinics with English-speaking doctors.

Ospedale Maggiore Policlinico (Map pp248–9; ☎ 02 5 50 31, foreigners ☎ 02 550 33 171; Via Francesco Sforza 35)

Money

There are bureaux de change at both airports and a couple on the western side of Piazza del Duomo.

American Express (Map pp248–9; ☎ 02 721 04 010; Via Larga 4; ☽ 9am-5.30pm Mon-Fri)

Banca Cesare Ponte (Map pp248–9; Piazza del Duomo 19) 24-hour automatic banknote exchange machine here and at Stazione Centrale.

Banca Commerciale Italiana (Map pp248–9; Piazza della Scala) 24-hour booth with currency exchange machine and ATMs.

Post

Central Post Office (Map pp248–9; Piazza Cordusio; ☽ 8am-7pm Mon-Fri, 8.30am-noon Sat)

Stazione Centrale (Map pp244–5; Piazza Duca d'Aosta; ☽ 8am-7pm Mon-Fri, 8.30am-12.30pm Sat)

Tourist Information

Central tourist office (Map pp248–9; ☎ 02 725 24 301; www.milanoinfotourist.com; Via Marconi 1; ☽ 8.45am-1pm & 2-6pm Mon-Sat, 9am-1pm & 2-5pm Sun)

INFORMATION DIAL-UP

Call these local information numbers (Italian only) for location, opening times and anything else you want know about:
Pharmacies ☎ 1100
Cinemas & Museums ☎ 1101
Hotels & ATMs ☎ 1102

LOMBARDY & THE LAKES

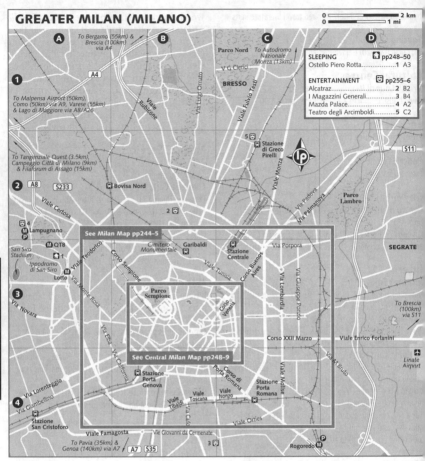

GREATER MILAN (MILANO)

Linate Airport (Map p242; ☎ 02 702 00 443; ⏱ 9am-5pm Mon-Fri)

Malpensa Airport (Map p242; ☎ 02 748 67 213; ⏱ 9am-5pm Mon-Fri)

Stazione Centrale (Map pp244–5; ☎ 02 725 24 360; ⏱ 8am-7pm Mon-Sat, 9am-noon & 1.30-6pm Sun)

Travel Agencies

CIT (Map pp248–9; ☎ 02 863 70 227; milano.gve@ cititalia.net; Galleria Vittorio Emanuele II; ⏱ 9am-7pm Mon-Fri, 9am-1pm & 2-6pm Sat) Plane, train and boat reservations – but none by telephone! Currency exchange service.

CTS (Map pp244–5; ☎ 02 837 26 74; Corso di Porta Ticinese 100) Student and budget travel.

Voyages Wasteels (Map pp244–5; ☎ 02 669 00 20; Galleria di Testa, Stazione Centrale)

DANGERS & ANNOYANCES

Pickpockets and thieves haunt Milan's main shopping areas, train stations and busiest public-transport routes – pay particular attention on metro Line 3 between the Stazione Centrale and Duomo stops.

Beware bird-seed sellers on Piazza del Duomo who flog seeds to unsuspecting tourists by sneakily popping seed in their pockets, prompting pigeons to dive-bomb the victim – the victim is forced to buy seed to escape further bombardment.

SIGHTS
Cathedral

Milan's impressive navel, **Piazza del Duomo** (Map pp248–9), home to Milan's most visible monument, the cathedral, has been Milan's social, geographical and pigeon centre since medieval times. Feeding the thousands of pigeons that fill this square is a definite highlight for any kid visiting Milan.

Commissioned in 1386 by Gian Galeazzo Visconti, the **cathedral** holds a congregation of 40,000. The first glimpse of this late-Gothic wonder is memorable, with its marble facade (under renovation) shaped into pinnacles, statues and pillars, the whole held together by a web of flying buttresses. Some 135 spires and 3200 statues – built between 1397 and 1812 – are crammed onto the roof and into the facade. The central spire, 108m tall, is capped by a gilded copper statue of the **Madonnina** (literally 'our little Madonna'), the city's traditional protector. The surrounding forest of spires, statuary and pinnacles distracts from an interesting omission – the cathedral has no bell tower.

The brass doors at the front bear the marks of bombs that fell near the cathedral during WWII. Inside the cathedral showcases 15th-century stained-glass windows on the right and later copies on the left. High above the altar is a nail, said to have come from Christ's cross, which is displayed once a year in September. Originally lowered using a device made by Leonardo da Vinci called the *nigola*, the nail is now retrieved by more modern means. The *nigola* is stored near the roof on the right-hand side as you enter the cathedral by the main entrance off Piazza del Duomo. Next to the main entrance a stairwell leads to an early Christian **Battistero di San Giovanni** (admission €1.50; 9.45am-12.45pm & 2.45-5.45pm Tue-Sun), the baptistry that predates the Gothic church.

The 165-step (some say 158) climb to the **roof of the cathedral** (admission €3.50; 9am-5.30pm) is worth the effort, if only to view one of Milan's more memorable skyscrapers, the 20-storey **Torre Velasca**, which is topped by a six-storey protruding block and was designed in the late 1950s by Studio BBPR. The **lift** (admission €5; 9am-5.30pm) is kinder on the thigh muscles. Entrances to both are outside the cathedral on the northern flank.

Shorts, uncovered shoulders and bare chests are forbidden inside the cathedral.

Around the Cathedral
Map pp248–9

The southern side of Piazza del Duomo is dominated by the **Palazzo Arcivescovile** and

Palazzo Reale, the traditional seats of Milan's ecclesiastical and civil rulers from the 11th and 12th centuries. At the **Museo del Duomo** (02 86 03 58; Piazza del Duomo 14; adult/child €6/3; 10am-1.15pm & 3-6pm), in the palace's left wing, you can study the six centuries of cathedral history in more detail.

Virtually destroyed in bombing raids during WWII, the cruciform **Galleria Vittorio Emanuele II** – known as *il salotto di Milano* (Milan's drawing room) thanks to its elegant cafés (see the boxed text, p251) – leads north off Piazza del Duomo. The covered arcade, designed by Giuseppe Mengoni, was one of the first buildings in Europe to employ mainly iron and glass as structural elements. The four mosaics around the central octagon represent Europe, Africa, Asia and North America. Rub the sole of your shoe across the bull's worn-away testicles for good luck.

Southwest of Piazza del Duomo, the **Pinacoteca Ambrosiana** (Ambrose Art Gallery; 02 806 92 225; www.ambrosiana.it, Italian only; Piazza Pio XI 2; adult/child €7.50/4; 10am-5.30pm Tue-Sun) is one of the city's finest galleries. It contains Italy's first real still life, Caravaggio's *Canestra di Frutta* (Fruit Basket), as well as works by Tiepolo, Titian and Raphael. Da Vinci's *Musico* (Musician) is also on show.

La Scala & Around
Map pp248–9

Walk north through the Galleria Vittorio Emanuele II from Piazza del Duomo to Piazza della Scala, dominated by a **monument** dedicated to Leonardo da Vinci, and Milan's legendary opera house, **La Scala** (Teatro alla Scala) – closed until 2005 for renovation. The fabulous playhouse opened on 3 August 1778, was practically destroyed during WWII but reopened in 1946 under the baton of Arturo Toscanini, who returned from New York after a 15-year absence. Learn more at the Museo Teatrale alla Scala (p246). See p255 for ticket details.

Palazzo Marino, between Piazza della Scala and Piazza San Fedele, was begun in 1558 by Galeazzo Alessi and is a masterpiece of 16th-century residential architecture. Milan's municipal council has sat here since 1859. There are more than 60 other grand palaces scattered about the city centre – a far cry from the several hundred that stood at the end of the 19th century.

Northeast, the **Museo Poldi-Pezzoli** (02 79 48 89; Via Alessandro Manzoni 12; adult/child €6/4;

MILAN (MILANO)

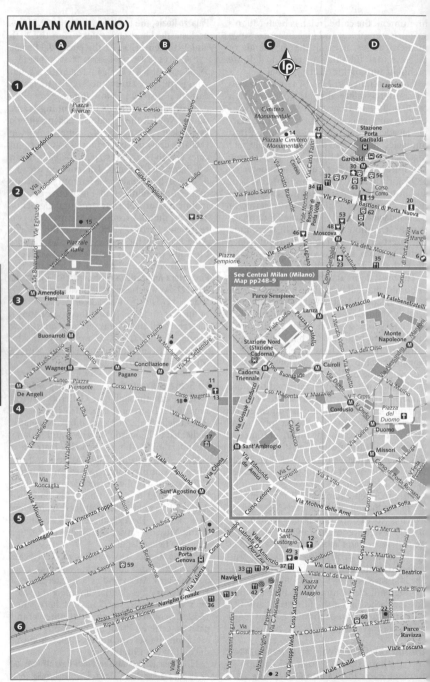

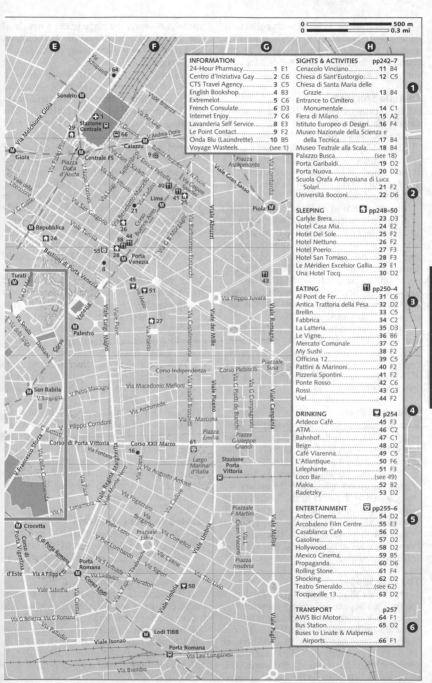

LOMBARDY & THE LAKES

10am-6pm Tue-Sun) is filled with collections of jewellery, porcelain, sundials, tapestries, ancient armaments, period furniture and paintings – including Botticelli's *Madonna and Child* among others.

Castello Sforzesco

At the northern end of Via Dante looms **Castello Sforzesco** (Map pp248–9; ☎ 02 884 63 700; www.milanocastello.it; Piazza Castello; admission free; 9.30am-5.30pm Tue-Sun), home to some excellent museums. Originally a Visconti fortress, it was remodelled by Francesco Sforza in the 15th century and Leonardo da Vinci helped design the defences.

A vast collection of Lombard sculptures is displayed in the **Museo d'Arte Antica**. In the **Pinacoteca e Raccolte d'Arte** is an applied arts display and a picture gallery, featuring works by Bellini, Tiepolo, Mantegna, Correggio, Titian and van Dyck. Another museum is devoted to prehistoric and ancient Egyptian artefacts, while the **Museo degli Strumenti Musicali** enchants visitors with its musical instruments.

Behind the red-brick castle is **Parco Sempione**, a 47-hectare park featuring a neoclassical arch, a neglected arena inaugurated by Napoleon in 1806 and the Torre Branca (1933), a 103m-tall steel tower near the rather ugly Palazzo dell'Arte.

Palazzo di Brera

East of Castello Sforzesco, sprawling 17th-century Palazzo di Brera houses the **Pinacoteca di Brera** (Map pp248–9; ☎ 02 894 21 146; info@amicidibrera.milano.it; Via Brera 28; adult/child €5/2.50; 8.30am-7.15pm Tue-Sun). Its extensive treasury of paintings has grown since the gallery was inaugurated at the start of the 19th century, with Andrea Mantegna's masterpiece *The Dead Christ* being one of the better-known works on display. Raphael, Bellini, Rembrandt, Goya, Caravaggio and van Dyck are others represented.

The Last Supper

Leonardo da Vinci's masterful mural depicting the Last Supper decorates one wall of the Cenacolo Vinciano, the refectory adjoining **Chiesa di Santa Maria delle Grazie** (Map pp244–5; Corso Magenta; 8am-7.30pm Tue-Sun). Painted between 1495 and 1498, Leonardo's work captures the moment when Jesus uttered the words 'One of you will betray me'. The word *cenacolo*

means refectory, the place where Christ and the 12 Apostles celebrated the Last Supper, and is also used to refer to any mural depicting this scene.

Restoration of the Last Supper began in 1977 and was completed in 1999. Centuries of damage from floods, bombing and decay had left the mural in a lamentable state. The method employed by restorers in the 19th century caused the most damage – their alcohol and cotton wool removed a layer from the painting. Even so, Leonardo must take some of the blame, as his experimental mix of oil and tempera was not durable. The Dominicans did not help matters in 1652 by raising the refectory floor, callously chopping off a lower section of da Vinci's scene – including Jesus' feet.

To see the Last Supper, you have to book ahead by phone (☎ 02 894 21 146; adult/child €6.50/free, €1 booking fee); call at least three or four days in advance if you want to guarantee a ticket. Once through to an operator, you'll be allotted a visiting time and a reservation number which you present 30 minutes before your visit at the refectory ticket desk. Turn up late and your ticket will be resold.

The ticket desk at the refectory rents English-language audioguides (one/two people €2.50/4.50). Guided tours (15 minutes) in English cost €3.25 and depart at 9.30am and 3.30pm Tuesday to Sunday. Again, places must be booked in advance.

Occasionally you can turn up at and snag a cancellation or unfilled place for a tour that day. If this happens, you will be allocated a time, made to pay on the spot and told to return 10 minutes before the scheduled visit starts.

Museo Teatrale alla Scala

This enchanting **museum** (Map pp248–9; ☎ 02 469 12 49; Corso Magenta 71; adult/child €5/4; 9am-6pm) inside Palazzo Busca, takes theatre lovers on a whirlwind tour of La Scala's fabulous past. Precious collections of antique musical instruments, curtain designs and theatrical costumes worn by Maria Callas and other greats are among the memorabilia to be seen. Among the 60-odd gramophones and phonographs from the 19th and early 20th centuries is the phonolamp (1925) – a gramophone cunningly disguised as a table lamp.

LOMBARDY & THE LAKES

THE HONEY-TONGUED DOCTOR

When the future St Ambrose (Sant'Ambrogio) was appointed bishop of Milan in 374 his credentials were hardly in order – he hadn't even been baptised. Small matter. This former governor of Liguria had impressed everyone with his skills in umpiring between Catholics and the Christian Arians that denied Christ's oneness with God (so slick was he with his words that he was dubbed 'the honey-tongued doctor'), so he received all the sacraments and the mitre in an unusually accelerated procedure.

At that time Milan was the effective capital of the western half of the crumbling Roman Empire and Ambrose became a leading figure in imperial politics. He and the emperor of the Western Roman Empire, Gratian, embarked on a crusade to eradicate paganism and the Arian heresy.

His influence grew to such an extent that he was later able to challenge the authority of Theodosius – the eastern emperor and guarantor of the Western Empire after Gratian's assassination – with impunity. In one incident the emperor ordered Christians to rebuild a synagogue they'd burned. Ambrose demanded the order be revoked and, threatening to thump the pulpit and stir popular feeling, convinced the emperor to see things his way.

Ambrose, the public functionary who was never a priest, was a powerful and charismatic bishop. He was the incarnation of the triumph of spiritual over secular power. He presaged the Church's future political role in European affairs and inspired the composition of the *Te Deum*. He died in 397.

South of Castello Sforzesco

Housed in the Monastero Maggiore, a 9th-century Benedictine convent rebuilt in the 1500s, the **Civico Museo Archeologico** (Map pp248–9; ☎ 02 864 50 011; Corso Magenta 15; admission free; ☽ 9am-5.30pm Tue-Sun) has substantial Roman, Greek, Etruscan, Gandhara (ancient northwest Indian) and medieval sections. Adjoining it is **Chiesa di San Maurizio** (Map pp248–9) with 16th-century frescoes by Bernardino Luini.

A short stroll south is Romanesque **Basilica di Sant'Ambrogio** (Map pp248–9; Piazza Sant'Ambrogio 15), dedicated to Milan's patron saint, St Ambrose (see the boxed text above). Founded in the 4th century by Ambrose, Bishop of Milan, the church on Piazza Sant'Ambrogio has been repaired, rebuilt and restored several times since and is a hotchpotch of styles. The shorter of the two bell towers dates to the 9th century, as does the remarkable ciborium (freestanding canopy over the altar) under the dome inside. The saint himself is buried in the crypt.

For proof that Leonardo da Vinci did more than paint, check the fascinating displays at the **Museo Nazionale della Scienza e della Tecnica** (Map pp244–5; ☎ 02 48 55 51; www.museoscienza.org; Via San Vittore 21; adult/child €6.20/4.20; ☽ 9.30am-4.50pm Tue-Fri, 9.30am-6.20pm Sat & Sun).

Around Piazza Cavour   Map pp248–9

The **Civica Galleria d'Arte Moderna** (GAM; ☎ 02 760 02 819; Via Palestro 16; admission free; ☽ 9.30am-5.30pm Tue-Sun), in the 18th-century Villa Reale which Napoleon temporarily called home, has a wide collection of 19th-century works, including many from the Milanese neoclassical period. More recent works can be enjoyed in the neighbouring **Padiglione d'Arte Contemporanea** (PAC; ☎ 02 760 09 085; www.pac-milano.org; Via Palestro 14; adult/child €5.20/2.60; ☽ 9.30am-7pm Fri-Sun, Tue & Wed, 9.30am-10pm Thu).

TOURS

The tourist office sells tickets for three-hour city bus tours (€40, including admission to the Last Supper) and for less-formal city tours by tourist tram (€15.50). Bus tours depart at 9.30am from in front of the main tourist office, and trams depart up to three times daily from Piazza Castello. With the latter you can hop on and off as you please; tickets are valid all day.

FESTIVALS & EVENTS

The **Festa di Sant'Ambrogio** on 7 December is Milan's biggest feast day. Celebrations take place at the **Fiera di Milano** (Map pp244–5; ☎ 800 82 00 29, ☎ 02 480 08 061; www.fieramilano.com; Largo Domodossola 1), the trade, conference and exhibition centre northwest of the city centre. La Scala marks the solemn occasion by opening its opera season on this day.

The first 10 days of June are devoted to the **Festa del Naviglio**, a smorgasbord of parades, music and other performances. The **Milan Jazz Festival** rocks through the city in November. Make the tourist office your first port of call for finding out more about these and other festivals and events. See the boxed text above,

LOMBARDY & THE LAKES

CENTRAL MILAN (MILANO)

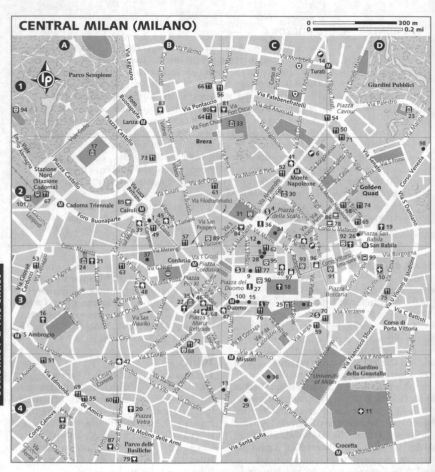

for information on the international fashion and furniture shows.

SLEEPING

Milan's hotels are among Italy's most expensive and finding any room (let alone a cheap one) can be impossible – especially during the fashion weeks and furniture fair when hotels hike up their prices and get booked up months in advance. The tourist office distributes *Milano Hotels*, a annual 70-page listings guide (free) to Milan's 350-odd hotels, and can put you in touch with accommodation agencies that make hotel reservations.

There are a couple of budget options towards the outer edge of town.

Ostello Piero Rotta (Map p242; ☎ 02 392 67 095; fax 02 330 00 191; Viale Angelo Salmoiraghi 1; B&B €16; ❧ reception 7-9am & 3.30-11.30pm) The city's only HI hostel is a two-minute walk south along Viale Angelo Salmoiraghi from the QT8 underground stop. HI cards (€15.50) are compulsory.

Campeggio Città di Milano (☎ 02 482 00 999; www.parcoaquatica.com, Italian only; Via G Airaghi 61; per person/tent/car €7/6/6, 2-/3-/4-person bungalow €37/47/62, with bathroom €78/88/98; ❧ 8am-8pm Feb-Nov) This camp ground, a good few kilometres west of the centre, keeps campers happy with its wide range of facilities and a water amusement park. Take the underground to the De Angeli station, then bus No 72 from Piazza de Angeli to the Di Vittorio stop, from

INFORMATION		
American Bookstore	1	B2
American Express	2	C3
Banca Cesare Ponte	3	C3
Banca Commerciale Italiana	4	C2
British Consulate	5	C3
British Council	6	C2
Central Tourist Office	7	C3
CIT Travel Agency	8	C3
Farmacia Carlo Erba	9	C3
La Scala Bookstore	(see B4)	
Milan Clinic	10	D3
Ospedale Maggiore Policlinico	11	D4
Rizzoli	12	C2
Touring Club Italiano	13	C4
US Embassy	14	C1
Virgin Megastore	15	C3

SIGHTS & ACTIVITIES	pp242–7	
Basilica di Sant'Ambrogio	16	A3
Castello Sforzesco	17	A2
Cathedral	18	C3
Chiesa di San Babila	19	D2
Chiesa di San Lorenzo Maggiore	20	B4
Chiesa di San Maurizio	21	A3
Chiesa di San Sepolcro	22	B3
Civica Galleria d'Arte Moderna	23	D1
Civico Museo Archeologico	24	A3
Civico Museo d'Arte Contemporanea	25	C3
Conservatorio Giuseppe Verdi	26	D2
Equestrian Statue of Vittorio Emanuele II	27	C3
Galleria Vittorio Emanuele II	28	C3
International House	29	C4
Museo degli Strumenti Musicali	(see 17)	
Museo del Duomo	(see 25)	
Museo d'Arte Antica	(see 17)	
Museo Poldi-Pezzoli	30	C2
Museo Teatrale alla Scala	31	C2
Padiglione d'Arte Contemporanea	(see 23)	
Palazzo Arcivescovile	32	C3
Palazzo di Brera	33	C1
Palazzo Marino	34	C2
Palazzo Reale	(see 25)	

Pinacoteca Ambrosiana	35	B3
Pinacoteca di Brera	(see 33)	
Pinacoteca e Raccolte d'Arte	(see 17)	
Statue of Leonardo da Vinci	36	C2
Stock Exchange	37	B3
Teatro alla Scala	(see 31)	
Torre Velasca	38	C4

SLEEPING	pp248–50	
Genius Downtown	39	B2
Grand Hotel Duomo	40	C3
Grand Hotel et de Milan	41	C2
Hotel Ariston	42	B4
Hotel de la Ville	43	C2
Hotel Gritti	44	B3
Hotel London	45	B2
Hotel Spadari	46	B3
Hotel Speronari	47	C3
Hotel Vecchio Milano	48	B3

EATING	pp250–4	
Antica Osteria Milanese	49	B2
Armandola	50	D1
Baci & Abbracci	51	A4
Bar Biffino	52	C2
Boccondivino	53	A3
Brek	54	D1
Caffè della Pusteria	55	A4
Centro Botanico	56	B1
Ciao	(see 15)	
Coco's	57	B2
Cova	58	D2
Duomo Centre	(see 15)	
Flash	59	C3
Gelateria Ecologica Artigiana	60	A4
Il Coriandolo	61	B2
Il Salotto	62	C3
Marchesi	63	B3
Orient Express	64	B2
Paper Moon	65	D2
Pattini & Marinoni	66	C3
Pattini & Marinoni	67	A2
Peck	68	B3
Pizzeria Naturale	69	A4

Poker	70	C3
Princi: Il Bread & Breakfast	(see 47)	
Rêve	71	D2
Spizzico	(see 15)	
Superfresco Standa	72	B3
Tintero	73	B2
Trattoria Bagutta	74	D2
Trattoria da Pino	75	D3
Viel	76	C3
Zucca in Galleria	77	C3

DRINKING	pp254	
Bar Centro	78	D2
Coquetel	79	B4
Ice & Dreams	80	B1
Jamaica	81	C1
Le Biciclette	82	A4
Le Trottoir	83	B1
Marino alla Scala	84	C2
Pubblicittà	85	B2
Sunflower Bar	86	D2
Tabloid	87	A4

ENTERTAINMENT	pp255–6	
FNAC	88	B3
La Banque	89	B2
La Scala Box Office	90	C3
Messaggerie Musicali	91	D3
Milan Point	92	D2
Odeon	93	C3
Old Fashion Café	94	A1
Ricordi Mediastore	95	C3

SHOPPING	pp256–7	
Galleria Mode	96	C3
Godiva	(see 41)	
La Rinascente Department Store	97	C3

TRANSPORT	p257	
Automobile Club Italia	98	D2
Bus Stop for ATM Buses to Linate Airport	99	D3
Info Point	100	C3
Malpensa Express Bus	101	A2

where it is a 400m walk to the camp ground. By car, leave the Tangenziale Ovest at San Siro-Via Novara.

Around Stazione Centrale   Map pp244–5
BUDGET
Although handily placed, some budget hotels in the Stazione Centrale area double quietly (or not so quietly) as brothels. Places not appearing to sport a dual trade are listed.

Hotel Nettuno (☎ 02 294 04 481; nettunomilano@ libero.it; Via Tadino 27; s/d €38/55, with shower €50/75) A tad on the grim side but dirt cheap, these rock-bottom rooms are a 10-minute walk southeast of Stazione Centrale. Room rates rise by €3 to €5 a night in high season.

Hotel Casa Mia (☎ 02 657 52 49; hotelcasamia@ libero.it; Viale Vittorio Veneto 30; s/d from €46/56) Down near Piazza della Repubblica, renovated Hotel Casa Mia has something of a family atmosphere. Rates don't appear to be fixed, so try to bargain.

Hotel San Tomaso (☎ 02 295 14 747; hotelsan tomaso@tin.it; Viale Tunisia 6; s with/without bathroom €45/30, d with shower/bathroom €65/75) Hotel San

Tomaso touts a friendly English-speaking staff and basic but sleepable-in rooms. Should it be full, there's another hotel in the same building.

Hotel Poerio (☎ 02 295 22 872; Via Poerio 32; s/d from €47/75) Tucked down a quiet residential street, Hotel Poerio is Milan's most peaceful budget option.

MID-RANGE & TOP END
Hotel Del Sole (☎ 02 295 12 971; delsolehotel@tiscali.it; Via Gaspare Spontini 6; d/tr €70/90, with shower €85/90) Wend your way up the spiral mirrored staircase to the 1st-floor reception where a friendly smile greets travellers. Prices quoted are maximum rates – they do vary, depending on how full or empty the hotel is.

Le Méridien Excelsior Gallia (☎ 02 6 78 51; www .excelsiorgallia.it; Piazza Duca d'Aosta 9; s/d €387/465; P ⓧ ⬛) Ernest Hemingway and Maria Callas stayed at this elegant Art Nouveau hotel, a stroll back in early 20th-century splendour opposite Stazione Centrale. The hotel opened its doors in 1932.

Around the Cathedral   Map pp248–9

MID-RANGE

Hotel Speronari (☎ 02 864 61 125; fax 02 720 03 178; Via Speronari 4; s/d from €44/73, with bathroom from €68/98) Rooms with bathroom are substantially more comfortable than those without. Nonetheless, rooms are good value, given their central location a stone's throw from the cathedral.

Hotel Gritti (☎ 02 80 10 56; www.hotelgritti.com; Piazza Santa Maria Beltrade 4; s/d/tr €99/142/199; P X) Half-way down Via Torino from the cathedral, this three-star place overlooks a quiet(ish) square and often has rooms available when others don't. Unusually, it touts a single set of prices year-round. Garage parking costs €25 a night.

Hotel Vecchia Milano (☎ 02 87 50 42; hotelvecchiamilano@tiscalinet.it; Via Borromei 4; s/d €100/145) Old-world charm exudes from Old Milan, appropriately placed in a atmospheric cobbled street off Via Torino.

Hotel Ariston (☎ 02 720 00 556; ariston@brerahotels.com; Largo Carrobbio 2; s/d/tr €129/185/210; P X 🖵 X) Ariston is Milan's first ecological hotel – purified air in hotel rooms, purified water in the herbal teas at breakfast, recyclable paper and biodegradable cleaning products throughout, oh…and a free bicycle at the door for guests to breathe in some of those delicious carbon dioxide–polluted traffic fumes outside.

Hotel Spadari (☎ 02 720 02 371; www.spadarihotel.com; Via Spadari 11; s/d €190/208; P X 🖵) A wall fresco by Milan-born Valentino Vago and other worth-stealing originals by Italian artists and designers are modestly displayed in this design hotel.

Hotel London (☎ 02 720 20 166; hotel.london@traveleurope.it; Via Rovello 3; s/d €80/120, with bathroom €95/140) Off Via Dante, Hotel London looks swanky but charges reasonable rates. Payment in hard cash yields a 10% discount.

Genius Downtown (☎ 02 720 94 644; downtown@geniusresort.it; Via Porlezza 4; s/d from €100/140; X) In a quiet alley off Via Camperio, Milan's ingeniously named Genius hotel is a stone's throw from Castello Sforzesco. The newspaper (take your pick when you check-in) delivered to your room each morning is a nice touch.

TOP END

Hotel de la Ville (☎ 02 879 13 11; Via Hoepli 6; www.delavillemilano.com; s/d €273/318; P X 🖵) Unattractive from the outside but stunning inside, Hotel de la Ville has long lured the long-legged catwalk set. The decor is strictly 'old dwelling England' (to quote its own brochure); there's a tasty oyster bar for aphrodisiac seekers and the pool is on the roof.

Grand Hotel et de Milan (☎ 02 72 31 41; www.grandhoteletdemilan.it, Via Alessandro Manzoni 29; s/d from €300/372; P X 🖵) Milan's most prestigious hotel – an eclectic affair dating to 1863 – was home to Verdi for the last few years of his life. When the much-loved composer lay on his deathbed here in 1901, straw was laid on the street outside to stop the rattle of carriages disturbing him. Much of the original furniture remains in suites No 105 and No 106 where Verdi lived.

Grand Hotel Duomo (☎ 02 88 33; www.grandhotelduomo.com; Via San Raffaele 1; s/d from €227/320; P X 🖵) Sipping tea amid orange trees on the roof terrace or admiring paintings by Brunelleschi are but some of the pleasures awaiting guests inside this beautiful marbled palace dating to 1860.

Around Porta Garibaldi   Map pp244–5

Una Hotel Tocq (☎ 02 620 71; una.tocq@unahotels.it; Via A De Tocqueville 7d; s/d €216/253; P X 🖵 🖳) It might be part of a luxurious four-star Italian hotel chain but Una Hotel Tocq is Milan's temple to contemporary design. Its hip location between the city's most happening bars and clubs lures famous faces. Week-day high-season prices jump around €100.

Carlyle Brera (☎ 02 290 03 888; brerahotels@cityligtnews.com; Corso Garibaldi 84; s/d €235/270; P X 🖵) Brera's four-star hotel has all the mod cons, including an à la carte pillow menu. Pick your pillow (eight different shapes and stuffings) upon arrival – the 'sleep in a meadow' pillow filled with flowers and herbs sounds particularly dreamy.

EATING

Italians say Lombard cuisine is designed for people in a hurry. The result? Opting for the Full (four-course) Monty in restaurants is neither expected nor obligatory, while sandwich bars and quick-eat places litter the streets around the cathedral and Stazione Centrale. At the top end of the scale, you can blow a small fortune on dining in the hippest of designer joints.

The city has a strong provincial cuisine. Polenta is served with almost everything

HISTORICAL CAFÉS

These institutions are classic places for breakfast, lunch or an aperitif in the company of a lavish array of never-ending hors d'oeuvres.

Cova (Map pp248–9; ☎ 02 760 05 578; Via Monte Napoleone 8) Founded in 1817 by a soldier in Napoleon's army, this elegant tearoom has languished in Monte Napoleone since 1950 (the original was destroyed during WWII). Sip champagne amid Japanese tourists.

Marchesi (Map pp248–9; ☎ 02 87 67 30; Via S M alla Porta 11a) The legendary marchioness has been in the cake-and-coffee business since 1824. Her heavily wood-panelled interior shelters luscious displays of chess and draughtboards made from chocolate.

Il Salotto (Map pp248–9; Galleria Vittorio Emanuele II; 1st/2nd courses €11/15, pizzas €10) Milan's 'drawing room' is generally filled with tourists and harassed waiters. An outrageous €3.60 for a cappuccino (sitting down) is the price you pay for its historical location and easy-to-read five-language menu.

Zucca in Galleria (Map pp248–9; ☎ 02 864 64 435; Galleria Vittorio Emanuele II 21; 1st/2nd courses €10/15) Milan's most historic café overlooks Piazza del Duomo and touts an Art-Deco mosaic interior dating to 1867.

and risotto – traditionally scented with saffron (hence its bold yellow colour) and bone marrow to become *risotto alla milanese* – dominates the first course of many menus. Meaty dishes worth sinking your teeth into include *fritto misto alla milanese* (fried slices of bone marrow, liver and lung), *busecca* (sliced tripe boiled with beans) and *cotoletta alla milanese* (a breaded and fried veal cutlet offering fewer surprises).

The cover charge imposed by restaurants is around €2, though it can creep up to €5. Few places tout a fixed-priced multicourse menu.

Bar snacks are a Milanese institution, with most bars laying out their fare from around 5pm daily.

Cafés

Milan's café scene is a mix of old (see the boxed text above) and new.

Bar Biffino (Map pp248–9; ☎ 02 80 43 23; Via Andegari 15) Grab a sandwich and ultra-frothy cappuccino (€6.70) between sights at this friendly tobacconist (entrance on Via Alessandro Manzoni) – if you're looking for pretensions of any sort, you won't find them here.

Rêve (Map pp248–9; ☎ 02 76 00 15 05; Via della Spiga 42; 1st/2nd courses €10/20) Fabulous sums up chic Dream (*rêve* meaning 'dream' in French) where some of Milan's most creative café food is complemented by the charm and gaiety of owners Ivar and Mesa. The spruce branches and apples in the hand basin are 7.inspired. And where else is couscous served in a grapefruit?

Caffè della Pusteria (Map pp248–9; ☎ 02 894 02 146; Via Edmondo de Amicis 22; salads €4-7, panini €4.50) An old-fashioned, jazz-inspired interior and a terrace beneath vines manages to lure a young and trendy crowd to this busy lunchtime café.

Pubblicittà (Map pp248–9; Piazza Cadorna; ⏰ 7am-2am) This huge contemporary space makes for a modern, clean-cut pit-stop between sights. Should conversation lack or be slack, buy a €5 Internet card (which is cashed in for a drink) and surf on a flat screen embedded in the wall.

Other central venues to slam espresso shots or linger over an aperitif and bar snacks include:

Sunflower Bar (Map pp248–9; ☎ 02 760 22 754; Via Pietro Verri 8) Terrace bar beneath arches.

Bar Centro (Map pp248–9; ☎ 02 760 01 415; Corso G Matteotti 3) Eclectic decor and cocktail-quaffing crowd.

Marino alla Scala (Map pp248–9; ☎ 02 806 88 295; Piazza della Scala 5) Watch the fire rage!

Quick Eats

Pattini & Marinoni (⏰ 7am-8pm Mon-Sat) Stazione Central (Map pp244–5; Corso Buenos Aires 53); Stazione Nord (Map pp248–9; Piazza Cadorna 10); Brera (Map pp248–9; Via Solferino 5) This bread shop sells great breads, cakes and pizza slices (€1.55). The Brera branch gets packed with suits standing up eating cardboard plates of pasta.

My Sushi (Map pp244–5; ☎ 02 204 07 41; Via Felice Casati 1; sushi trays €2.50-22.80; ⏰ 11.30am-11.30pm Mon-Sat) For something different in the central station area – take away some sushi.

Brek (Map pp248–9; ☎ 02 65 36 19; Piazza Cavour) Refuel on quality fodder for less than €8 at this canteen-style chain – a superior alternative to a hamburger joint.

LOMBARDY & THE LAKES

Poker (Map pp248–9; ☎ 02 58 30 75 30; ittem@libero.it; Piazza Santo Stefano 5; 1st/2nd courses €2.40/3.70; ☺ 7am-5pm Mon-Sat) Rub elbows with a Milanese workforce at this cheap and cheerful self-service restaurant, a stone's throw from the cathedral.

Armandola (Map pp248–9; ☎ 02 760 21 657; Via della Spiga 50) Shoppers can indulge in a bowl of pasta standing up at this delicatessen shop. Pick the right day and white Alba truffles might just end up (at a price) on your plate. Balsamic vinegar is the other house speciality – invest €480 in a 100-year-old bottle (100ml) of the real McCoy from Modena.

Coco's (Map pp248–9; ☎ 02 45 48 3253; Via San Prospero 4; pasta €4.30) Italy's first vegetarian chain fries up veggie burgers (€3.20 or €3.70 with cheese) and other soul food in a soulful wooden interior. The down-sized kiddies' area makes it a great one for kidding around.

The **Duomo Centre** (Map pp248–9; Piazza del Duomo 8) eating mall on Piazza del Duomo houses **Spizzico** (☺ 10.30am-midnight) and **Ciao** (☎ 02 86 42 67; ☺ 11am-11pm), two late-night fast-food restaurants where you can fill up on 1st/2nd courses sitting down for around €3.50/5.

PIZZERIAS
Pizzeria Spontini (Map pp244–5; ☎ 02 204 74 44; Via Gaspare Spontini; normal/big pizza slice €3.50/4, pasta €4) This busy little pizza joint has cooked up the best pizza in the Stazione Centrale area – and much of Milan – since 1953. Munch standing up or on the move.

Flash (Map pp248–9; ☎ 02 583 04 489; Via Bergamini 1; pizzas €10; ☺ 24 hrs) This pizzeria on the corner of Via Larga draws a young crowd. Unusually for a place that never closes, its pizzas are worth the trip any time of day or night.

Pizzeria Naturale (Map pp248–9; ☎ 02 839 57 10; Via Edmondo de Amicis 24; pizzas €5.20-9.30) Tea infusions and wholemeal pizzas are among the non-naughty options cooked up here for the health-conscious.

Fabbrica (Map pp248–9; ☎ 02 655 27 71; Via Pasubio 2; pizzas €10; ✗) With its low-hanging steel table lamps and brown paper table mats, trendy Factory exudes a definite industrial feel. The pizzeria is nicely located near the Corso Como bars and nightclubs.

Restaurants
AROUND THE DUOMO   Map pp248–9
Trattoria da Pino (☎ 02 760 00 532; Via Cerva 14; lunch €13, 1st/2nd courses €4.50/5.50; ☺ 8am-8pm

Mon-Fri, 8am-4pm Sat) Nowhere can you beat the cost-quality ratio dished up at this authentic trattoria where strangers dine at shared tables. Its three-course lunch menu is built solely from hearty homemade cooking and includes a 25cl jug of wine or 50cl jug of mineral water.

Trattoria Bagutta (☎ 02 760 02 767; Via Bagutta 14-16; 1st/2nd courses €12/18; ☺ Mon-Sat) In the 1950s the infamous Gucci clan frequently dined at this fashionable 1920s trattoria, a scissor-snip away from their then-Via Monte Napoleone boutique.

Paper Moon (☎ 02 796 083, ☎ 02 760 22 297; Via Bagutta 1; 1st/2nd courses €10/15; ☺ Mon-Sat) Minimalist Paper Moon lures a well-dressed crowd. Its fresh asparagus (in season) topped with two fried eggs is a must-taste, as is its grilled cheese served piping hot and gooey on a bed of rocket.

Baci & Abbracci (☎ 02 890 13 605; Via Edmondo De Amicis 44; ☺ noon-2am) Contemporary design fronts this stunning eating and drinking space, worth a wait in line purely to let yourself be bowled over by the sheer minimalism of it all. Traditional Italian dishes as well as 700 different types of pizzas star on the far-from-minimalist menu.

Boccondivino (☎ 02 86 60 40; Via Giosuè Carducci 17; 1st/2nd courses €14/18; ☺ 8pm-midnight Mon-Sat) Dine here for a gastronomic voyage through Italy – pick from 40 different cheeses, dozens of smoked and dried meats and over 900 wines. Sign up for a wine-tasting course if the whole experience leaves you feeling somewhat inadequate.

Antica Osteria Milanese (☎ 02 86 13 67; Via M Camperio 12; 1st courses €6.50-14, 2nd courses €11-13) Some places just don't change as this traditional, frill-free trattoria testifies. Suits (predominantly male) fill it up every lunchtime. The *meneghina alla griglia al Grand Marnier* (Milanese sponge cake soaked in liqueur and baked) is a sweet must.

BRERA
Hip Via Fiori Chiari is known for its summer pavement terraces.

La Latteria (Map pp244–5; ☎ 02 659 76 53; Via San Marco 24; 1st/2nd courses €8.30/12.50; ☺ 12.15-2.30pm & 7.30-9.30pm Mon-Fri) Otherwise known as the 'Milk Bar', this pocket-sized trattoria might have been around for what seems like centuries but nothing has changed – thankfully. Original white-and-blue bar tiles, flowery wallpaper and no more than a dozen tables add up to one very charming, very tasty lunch spot. Arrive dot-on to snag a seat.

Centro Botanico (Map pp248–9; ☎ 02 290 13 254; Piazza San Marco 1; ☒ 1-8pm Mon, 10am-2.30pm & 3.30-8pm Tue-Fri, 10am-8pm Sat) This green temple to bio products draws a down-to-earth crowd with its unpretentious lunch dishes, served at small tables between clothes racks and bookshelves.

Il Coriandolo (Map pp248–9; ☎ 02 869 32 73; Via dell'Orso 1; 1st/2nd courses €9-12/16) Dine on delicious *risotto alla vecchia maniera Milanese* (old Milanese risotto) beneath an ornate moulded ceiling at this upmarket restaurant, on the edge of Brera.

Tintero (Map pp248–9; ☎ 02 86 14 18; Via Q Sella; 1st/2nd courses €10/15) A bold interior paying homage to contemporary design contrasts starkly with the traditional exterior of this popular restaurant near Castello Sforzesco. In summer, sit on the flowery pavement terrace and watch the cars whizz by.

NAVIGLI & PORTA TICINESE   Map pp244–5
Options abound in this area, renowned for its late opening hours and innovative cuisine cooked up by a mixed bag of chefs. Canalside Ripa di Porta Ticinese makes for a particularly tasty evening stroll.

Le Vigne (☎ 02 837 56 17; Ripa di Porta Ticinese 61; 1st courses €3.50-4, 2nd courses €6) Those seeking nothing more than a feast of local cheese and wine are heartily welcomed at Le Vigne, French for The Vine.

Al Pont de Fer (☎ 02 894 06 277; Ripa di Porta Ticinese 55; 1st/2nd courses €5.20/7.75; ☒ 12.30-2.15pm & 8pm-1am) Sip wine and discover ecstasy with a sublime slice of caramel-and-honey tart.

Brellin (☎ 02 581 01 351; Alzaia Naviglio Grande 14; 1st/2nd courses €7.20/14; ☒ 12.30-2.30pm & 7pm-2am Mon-Sat, noon-3pm Sun) The main draw of Brellin is its canalside flower-filled garden – unique among Milanese restaurants. Dark wooden panels furnish the less-appealing interior.

Officina 12 (☎ 02 894 22 261; Alzaia Naviglio Grande 12; 1st/2nd courses €8.50/12; ☒ 7pm-2am Tue-Sat, 12.30-3pm & 7pm-midnight Sun) The new kid on this attractive waterfront block is a modern minimalist affair. Its cobbled patio overlooking the canal is particularly appealing – as is its hangover-sympathetic Sunday brunch.

Ponte Rosso (☎ 02 837 31 32; Ripa di Porta Ticinese 23; 1st/2nd courses €10/15; ☒ Thu-Sat & Mon-Wed) The

Red Bridge is run by a wine and balsamic vinegar connoisseur who also collects corkscrews, cocktail shakers and miniature toys. Attempt to order anything less than the four-course dining experience and you'll be severely frowned upon.

CORSO COMO
Antica Trattoria della Pesa (Map pp244–5; ☎ 02 655 57 41; Viale Pasubio 10; 1st courses €10, 2nd courses €15-20; ☒ Mon-Sat) This traditional trattoria with the signature, bottle-filled windows, lures a chic crowd thanks to its hip location a meal away from the Corso Como nightlife scene. The place has been feeding hungry Milanese since 1880.

Self-Catering
Via Speronari, just off Piazza del Duomo, is the best street around the cathedral for bread, cakes, salami, cheese, fruit and wine.

Peck (Map pp248–9; Via Spadari 7-9; ☒ 3-7.30pm Mon, 8.45am-7.30pm Tue-Sun) Established in 1883, this is one of Europe's elite food outlets, famous since 1920 for its homemade ravioli, 3200 variations of *parmigiano reggiano* (parmesan) and wine cellar.

Princi: Il Bread & Breakfast (Map pp248–9; ☎ 02 87 47 97; Via Speronari 6) This busy bakery sells filling slabs of warm pizza and foccacia (around €2.50 a slice) to eat in or on the move. There's also a superb choice of cakes, tarts, bread and fresh pasta.

COOL IT, BOY!

Need to wrap your tongue around an ice? A trio of *gelaterie* stand out:

Gelateria Ecologica Artigiana (Map pp248–9; ☎ 02 581 01 872; Corso di Porta Ticinese 40; ☒ Thu-Tue) Ecologically friendly artisan ice creams are made in a rainbow of unusual – and natural, of course – flavours.

Rossi (Map pp244–5; ☎ 02 73 04 92; Viale Romagna 23; ☒ Wed-Mon) Rossi is reckoned to be Milan's ice-cream queen – if the crowds are anything to go by, it could be true.

Viel (2-/3-scoop cone €1.50/2.10; ☒ 8am-2am Wed-Mon) Duomo (Map pp248–9; Via Manzoni 3e); Stazione Centrale (Map pp244–5; ☎ 02 295 16 123; Corso Buenos Aires 15) Ice creams and *frullati di frutta* (fruit shakes; €1.80/2.60/3.60 small/medium/large) are packed with fruit, as the lush fruity displays waiting to be mushed up testify.

Stock up on supermarket produce at **Superfresco Standa** (Map pp248–9; Via della Palla 2a) and fresh fruit, vegetables and fish at the covered market, **Mercato Comunale** (Map pp244–5; Piazza XXIV Maggio; 8.30am-1pm Mon-Thu, 4-7.30pm Fri, 8.30am-1pm & 3.30-7.30pm Sat).

DRINKING

There is a trio of spots in particular to search for a drink, music and a madding Milanese crowd in a chic and trendy setting. Most bars open until 2am or 3am and a beer can cost anything from €5 to €10. Many places serve food too.

Heading towards Stazione Centrale, **Lelephante** (Map pp244–5; 02 295 18 768; Via Melzo 22; Tue-Sun) and **Artdeco Café** (Map pp244–5; 02 295 24 720; Via Lambro 7) are a twin set of hip bars.

BRERA   Map pp248–9

Le Trottoir (02 80 10 02; Corso Garibaldi 1; pasta €4, burgers €5) Aspiring artists hang wild art on the walls of this wacky bar. Its small stage hosts alternative bands (often jazz) and food is dished up upstairs.

Jamaica (02 87 67 23; Via Brera 32) Lap up Brera street life on the pavement terrace of this ageing bar where artists and intellectuals have lamented the world's woes since 1921.

Ice & Dreams (02 80 53 612; Via Brera 23) This art café and ice-cream bar, with its orange plastic chairs and spiky-haired waiters, beams brazenly across at Jamaica from the other side of the busy pedestrian street.

NAVIGLI & PORTA TICINESE

Several bars in this canalside area float alongside Via Ascanio Sforza, but there's plenty of others to choose from.

Coquetel (Map pp248–9; 02 836 06 88; Via Vetere 14; 8am-2am) Closed but a few hours a day, this relaxed and laid-back bar lies on the southern fringe of Milan's central ring. Its pavement terrace, at the end of a dead-end street on the grassy edge of Parco delle Basiliche, makes it an ideal summertime spot.

Tabloid (Map pp248–9; 02 894 00 709; Corso di Porta Ticinese 60; 6pm-4am) A panther and leopard guard the entrance to this cocksure disco bar where misted windows hide what happens inside. One thing is sure – dress up or look good to get in here. Don your dancing shoes, Friday to Sunday.

Loco Bar (Map pp244–5; 02 832 28 02; Corso di Porta Ticinese 106; 7am-2am) This cross

between a traditional milk bar and a train no less (hence its name) is a steaming success. Squash any hunger pangs between shots with a well-filled *panino* (€3.60).

Café Viarenna (Map pp244–5; 02 839 22 11; Piazza XXIV Maggio; 7am-3pm Mon, 7am-2am Tue-Sun) Happy punters make this music bar, next door to the Loco, throb. You can also lunch here (1st/2nd courses €4/5).

Le Biciclette (Map pp248–9; 02 581 04 325; Via Torti 1; 6pm-2am Mon-Sat, 12.30-4.30pm & 6pm-2am Sun) In a converted bicycle workshop with a well-worn mosaic floor, Le Biciclette is an ode to two wheels – 'cuisine, art & design' is the house motto, brunch is served every Sunday and art exhibitions change monthly.

East of the Navigli district is **L'Atlantique** (Map pp244–5; 02 551 93 925; Viale Umbria 42), where the interior design is hi-tech. Sunday brunch is served at this hip bar, oh so *alla moda*.

CORSO COMO   Map pp244–5

This fashionable patch is conveniently close to Stazione Porta Garibaldi and is laden with many of Milan's best nightclubs (see p255). **10 Corso Como** (see the boxed text, p257) is worth an aperitif for the fashion-conscious.

Radetzky (02 657 26 45; Corso Garibaldi 105; 7-2am) This long-favoured haunt is a must for one drink at least, purely to absorb its marbled and minimal Art Deco interior.

Beige (02 659 94 87; Largo di Foppa 5; noon-4pm & 6pm-2am Mon-Sat) Flick through the latest issue of *The Face* or *Wallpaper* while enjoying a weekday lunch (€10), dusk aperitif or early morning nightcap at this stylish wine bar. Look for the beige door with 12 round windows.

Makia (02 336 04 012; Corso Sempione 28) Furnishings at this drinks and food bar reflect the latest in contemporary design. The headquarters of RAI TV are a flick-of-the-hair away, making it a drawcard for Milan's hobnobbing set.

ATM (02 655 23 65; Bastioni di Porta Volta 15) The ungainly bunker sandwiched between speeding cars on a traffic island was an ATM terminal until Milanese glamour queens transformed it into the chic place it is today.

Bahnhof (02 290 01 511; Via Giuseppe Ferrari) In the pits overlooking the tracks into Stazione Porta Garibaldi, trendy Bahnhof's stainless-steel interior and moderately priced food are worth the hike.

WHERE TO SCORE TICKETS

Tickets for concerts, sporting events and the theatre can be booked through **Ticket One** (☎ 02 39 22 61, ☎ 840 05 27 20; www.ticketone.it, Italian only) or **Ticket Web** (☎ 02 760 09 131; www.ticketweb.it). **Milano Concerti** (☎ 02 487 02 726, www.milanoconcerti.it, Italian only) only handles ticketing for international rock concerts. **Box Tickets** (☎ 02 847 09 750; www.boxtickets.it, Italian only) sells tickets for musicals at Teatro Smeraldo, sporting events at the San Siro stadium and pop concerts at Milan's live music venues (see below).

In Milan itself, try the *biglietteria* (ticket office) inside **FNAC** (Map pp248–9; ☎ 02 72 08 21; fnac@ticketweb.it; Via della Palla 2), on Via Torino; **Virgin Megastore** (Map pp248–9; ☎ 02 880 01 200; Duomo Centre, Piazza del Duomo 8); **Messaggerie Musicali** (Map pp248–9; ☎ 02 79 55 02; Galleria del Corso 20) with an entrance on Corso Vittorio Emanuele II; and **Ricordi Mediastore** (Map pp248–9; ☎ 02 864 60 272; www.ricordimediastores.it, Italian only; Galleria Vittorio Emanuele II).

ENTERTAINMENT

Milan has some of Italy's top clubs, several cinemas screening English-language films and a fabulous year-round cultural calendar, topped off by La Scala's opera season. The main theatre and concert season opens in October.

Other than those mentioned in this guide, there are at least another 50 active theatres in Milan; check the newspapers and ask at the tourist office. The latter also stocks the free monthly entertainment guide (in English), *Milano Mese* – an essential reference for culture buffs.

For club listings, *Corriere della Sera* (www.corriere.it, Italian only) runs a reasonable supplement, *ViviMilano* (www.corriere.it/vivimilano, Italian only), on Wednesday. *La Repubblica* (www.repubblica.it, Italian only) counters on Thursday with *Tutto Milano*. Both papers run cinema listings.

Cinemas

English-language films are shown at **Anteo** (Map pp244–5; ☎ 02 659 77 32; www.anteospaziocinema.com, Italian only; Via Milazzo 9), **Arcobaleno Film Centre** (Map pp244–5; ☎ 02 294 06 054; Viale Tunisia 11) and **Mexico** (Map pp244–5; ☎ 02 489 51 802; www.cinemamexico.it, Italian only; Via Savona 57). Tickets at all three cost €6/4 for evening/afternoon screenings.

Live Music

Propaganda (Map pp244–5; ☎ 02 583 10 682; Via Gian Carlo Castelbarco 11; ☽ Thu-Mon) and **Rolling Stone** (Map pp244–5; ☎ 02 73 31 72; Corso XXII Marzo 32; ☽ Tue-Sat) are live rock-band venues to watch out for.

The biggest names play at **Alcatraz** (see following), **Mazda Palace** (Map p242; ☎ 02 334 00 551; Viale Sant'Elia 33), near the San Siro stadium, and **Filaforum** (☎ 02 48 85 71; www.filofarum.it, Italian

only), further out of town. To get to the latter take the MM2 line to Romolo and pick up a special shuttle bus laid on for concerts.

Box Tickets (see boxed text above) sells tickets for concerts at all these venues.

Nightclubs

Milan boasts dozens of places to dance, although the scene for Milanese social butterflies revolves around 10 or so clubs, generally open until 3am or 4am Tuesday to Sunday. The Corso Como area is particularly well endowed with fashionable venues.

La Banque (Map pp248–9; ☎ 02 869 96 565; Via Porrone 6; ☽ Tue-Sun) Among the most central of clubs, this was a bank before the clerks moved out and the clubbers in.

Old Fashion Café (Map pp248–9; ☎ 02 805 62 31; www.oldfashion.it, Italian only; Viale Emillio Alemagna 6) Look for the discreet red canopy at the rear of the Palazzo dell'Arte to uncover this club where the fashion-conscious mingle. DJs mix most nights and you can eat here.

Alcatraz (Map p242; ☎ 02 690 16 352; Via Valtellina 21) An excellent live-concert venue north of the centre near the Cimitero Monumentale, Alactraz is transformed into one of the city's biggest clubs on Friday and Saturday nights.

I Magazzini Generali (Map p242; ☎ 02 552 11 313; Via Pietrasanta 14; ☽ 9pm-3am Wed-Sun) This thumping space, happily housed in a 1930s converted warehouse, is a fair hike south of the city centre.

Casablanca Café (Map pp244–5; ☎ 02 626 90 186; Corso Como 14; ☽ 6pm-2am Wed-Sun) In the same spirit as its Old Fashion counterpart, Casablanca – dubiously located in what very much resembles a portacabin – is one of a clutch of places to drink and club in this happening patch of town.

Other fashionable Corso Como clubs where face control counts include:

Gasoline (Map pp244–5; ☎ 02 290 13 245; www.disco gasoline.it, Italian only; Via Bonnet 11a; admission €13-16; 😊 Thu-Sun) Gay tea dances and other events, straight and gay.

Hollywood (Map pp244–5; ☎ 02 655 55 75; Corso Como 15; 😊 Tue-Sun)

Shocking (Map pp244–5; ☎ 01 265 51 240; Bastioni di Porta Nuova 12) Tucked beside Teatro Smeraldo.

Tocqueville 13 (Map pp244–5; ☎ 02 290 02 973; Via Alessio da Tocqueville 13; 😊 Tue-Sun) On the ground floor of an unattractive high rise – inside, blue.

Opera & Theatre

La Scala's opera season runs from 7 December through to July but – with the exception of the last two weeks in July and all of August – you can see theatre, ballet and concerts here year-round. Until 2005 however, while the original 18th-century opera house on Piazza della Scala is being renovated, all performances will be staged at the modern purpose-built **Teatro degli Arcimboldi** (Map p242; ☎ 02 647 08 76; Viale dell'Innovazione) in Milan's Bicocca district. To get here, take a train from either Stazione Centrale or Stazione Porta Garibaldi to Stazione di Greco Pirelli (five to six minutes) or hop aboard a shuttle bus, departing every five minutes between 6.45pm and 7pm from Piazza del Duomo. A regular ATM underground ticket covers either journey.

Scoring opera tickets (€10 to €155) requires luck and perseverance. About two months before the first performance, tickets can be bought by **telephone** (☎ 02 86 07 75; 😊 24 hrs) and online at www.teatroallascala .org; these tickets carry a 20% surcharge. One month before the first performance, any remaining tickets are sold (for a 10% surcharge) at the main **La Scala box office** (Map pp248–9; ☎ 02 72 00 37 44; Galleria del Sagrato, Piazza del Duomo; 😊 noon-6pm Sep–mid-Jul) in the metro underpass beneath Piazza del Duomo – walk down the underground entrance opposite the Galleria Vittorio Emanuele II. On the actual day of the performance, tickets for any unsold seats – a rare occurrence – are sold (at half-price) at the Teatro degli Arcimboldi box office at the theatre. To find out what tickets are available when, call **Infotel Scala** (☎ 02 72 00 37 44), consult the computer terminal in the La Scala box office or look online.

Musicals are staged at **Teatro Smeraldo** (Map pp244–5; ☎ 02 290 06 767; www.smeraldo.it, Italian only; Piazza XX Aprile 10).

Sport

The Italian Grand Prix tears around the **Autodromo Nazionale Monza** (☎ 039 2 48 21; www .monzanet.it; Parco di Monza, Via Vedano 5) in September. The track, 20km north of central Milan, can be reached along Viale Monza from Piazzale Loreto.

Milan's two football clubs, AC Milan and FC Internazionale Milano (known simply as Inter) play on alternate Sundays in season at the **San Siro Stadium** (Stadio Giuseppe Meazza; ☎ 02 487 00 457; sansirotour@tin.it; Via Piccolomini 5; museum & guided tour adult/child €12.50/10; 😊 10am-5pm on non-match days), built in 1926. Take tram No 24, bus No 95, 49 or 72, or the underground to the Lotto station (MM1), from where a free shuttle bus can run you to the stadium. Tickets are available at the stadium or, for AC Milan matches, from **Milan Point** (Map pp248–9; ☎ 02 894 22 711; Corso San Gottardo 2) and branches of the Cariplo bank. For Inter matches try Banca Popolare di Milano branches or Ticket One (see the boxed text, p255).

SHOPPING

Anything that money can buy can be snapped up in Milan's Golden Quad (see the boxed text, p257). Streets for more affordable fashion lie behind the cathedral around Corso Vittorio Emanuele II, and between Piazza della Scala and Piazza San Babila. In the 1960s Giorgio Armani dressed the windows of Milan's main department store **La Rinascente** (Map pp248–9; Piazza del Duomo; 😊 9am-10pm Tue-Sat, 10am-8pm Sun). Seeking an unusual gift to take home? Spell out his (or her) name in chocolate letters or invest in a chocolate watch from the decadent **Godiva** (Map pp248–9; ☎ 02 864 61 857; Via Manzoni 29).

Markets fill the canal-side Viale Papiniano in the southwest of the city on Tuesday and Saturday mornings. There is a flea market in Viale Gabriele d'Annunzio on Saturday and an antique market in Brera on Via Fiori Chiari every third Saturday of the month. A huge market where you can buy anything is held on the last Sunday of each month on the Alzaia Naviglio Grande and Ripa di Porta Ticinese.

FASHION & DESIGN

Milan's meteoric rise to European fashion and design capital rode on a wave of creative activity that the city witnessed from the 1960s. With the departure of many haute-couture fashion houses from Florence in the mid 1950s, coupled with the emergence of a new mass market in high fashion, Italy's largest fashion show – a twice-yearly Florentine event since 1951 – made a leggy leap to the industrial north.

The first international fashion show waltzed down Milan's cat walk in 1971. In 1982 Milan-born designer Giorgio Armani revolutionised the industry with his more wearable and affordable *prêt à porter* ('ready to wear') collection. The Giorgio Armani empire set another precedent in 2000 with the opening of its flagship store, Milan's **Emporio Armani** (☎ 02 723 18 630; Via Manzoni 31) – 6000 sq m of space pioneering designer shopping for fashion, flowers and wine 'under one roof'. Former Italian *Vogue* contributor Carla Sozzani had already experimented with the idea in 1991 with the launch of the seriously trendy **10 Corso Como** (☎ 02 290 02 674; Corso Como 10), a cutting-edge art gallery, fashion shop and restaurant rolled in to one.

Gucci (☎ 02 77 12 71; Via Monte Napoleone 5 & 27), the industry's other big name, moved to Milan in 1951, launching the birth of Milan's legendary **Golden Quad** (Map pp248-9; Quadrilatero d'Oro) – a quadrangle of pedestrian streets, sketched out by Via della Spiga, Via Sant'Andrea, Via Monte Napoleone and Via Alessandro Manzoni, and crammed with boutiques of the world's best-known designers: Prada, Versace, Roberto Cavalli, Dolce & Gabbana, Gian Franco Ferré, Chanel, Moschino, Kenzo and Brit Paul Smith are all here, to name but a few. Girls seeking diamonds as a best friend can visit **Tiffany & Co** (Via della Spiga 19a), **Cartier** (cnr Via Montanapoleone & Via Gesu) or **Damiani** (Via Monte Napoleone 16), Italy's leading diamond house founded here in 1924. Pick up a pair of pretty-in-pink, slip-on Jimmy Choo shoes (€222 instead of €449.83) and other last-season designs for a mere snip of the original price at **Dmagazine** (☎ 02 760 06 027; Via Monte Napoleone 26), a designer seconds outlet.

The Milan fashion shows are seasonal. The world's top designers unveil their ready-to-wear women's collections in February/March and September/October, while the men's fashion show takes place in January and June/July. Shows last 10 to 12 days and are held at the Fiera di Milano.

Milan is also the world's design capital but you wouldn't know it unless you search it out. Showrooms and galleries are spread throughout the city and most products are made for export. The latest designs are unveiled each year at the five-day Salone Internazionale del Mobile (furniture fair), hosted by Milan at the Fiera dei Milano since 1961. Magazines with listings to look out for in newspaper stands include *Domus* and *La Casa Bella*, both founded by Gio Ponti (1891–1979) – the considered architect of Italian design – in 1928; and *Interni*, a monthly design magazine published since 1954.

The original beanbag created by Milan's Zanotta in 1968, Panton chairs, the Milan-designed Carlton stack of shelves (1972) produced by the Milanese furniture house Memphis, and the lush-lipped Bocca sofa form part of the awe-inspiring collection at **Galleria Mode** (Via San Paolo 1). **Nilufar** (Via della Spiga 32) is another place dealing exclusively in rare and original furniture designed between 1950 and 2000. **Area Design** (☎ 02 869 84 584; Via Borromei 11) deals in designer furniture made in the 1960s, 1970s and 1980s. Notable designs to come out of the world's design capital in the 1990s included Ron Arad's Bookworm book shelf, produced in 1994 by Milanese pioneer of plastic **Kartell** (☎ 02 659 79 16; Via Carlo Porta 1) and one of the many pieces sold in its large white flagship store.

GETTING THERE & AWAY
Air
Most European and other international flights use **Malpensa airport** (www.malpensa.com), 50km northwest of the city. Most (but not all) domestic and a handful of European flights use **Linate airport** (www.sea-aeroportimilano.it), 7km east of the city centre.

For all flight information call ☎ 02 748 52 200 (both airports). For a computerised information service with details about flight departures only, call ☎ 02 585 83 497 (for both airports).

Bus
Bus stations are scattered across the city so unless you know exactly where you're going, you're better off travelling by train.

Buses (which are operated by numerous different companies) to many national and

LOMBARDY & THE LAKES

international points leave from the **bus station** (Map pp244–5; ☎ 02 63 79 01; Piazza Sigmund Freud) opposite the main entrance to Stazione Porta Garibaldi. **Eurolines** (☎ 02 637 90 299; Piazza Sigmund Freud) has a ticketing desk here.

Train
You can catch a train from **Stazione Centrale** (Map pp244–5; Piazza Duca d'Aosta) to all major cities in Italy. Check schedules at its **information office** (☎ 147 88 80 88; ☺ 7am-9pm). Daily trains (Intercity train fares quoted) run to/from Venice (€19.15, 3½ hours), Florence (€21.70, 3½ hours), Genoa (€12.85, 1½ hours), Turin (€16.65, 1½ hours), Rome (€38.15, 5¾ hours) and Naples (€48.50, 8 hours). This is also a good point to pick up international connections to/from Switzerland (with the Cisalpino train) and France (with the TGV).

Ferrovie Nord Milano (FNM) trains from **Stazione Nord** (Map pp248–9; Stazione Cadorna, Piazza Luigi Cadorna) connect Milan with Como (€2.85, one hour, hourly) and Desanzano (€5.70, 1¼ hours, hourly). Regional services to many towns northwest of Milan are more frequent from **Stazione Porta Garibaldi** (Map pp244–5; Piazza Sigmund Freud).

GETTING AROUND
To/From Malpensa Airport
The **Malpensa Express** (☎ 02 20 222, ☎ 02 277 63; www.malpensaexpress.it; ☺ ticket office 6am-8.20pm) train links Stazione Nord with Malpensa airport (adult/child one-way €9/4.50, if purchased on train €11.50/7.50, adult/child day return €12/6, 40 minutes, every 30 minutes). Some early morning and evening services are provided by bus (single €6.70, 50 minutes) instead; the stop is on Via Paleocapa.

The airport is also served by **Malpensa Shuttle** (Map pp244–5; ☎ 02 585 83 185; www.malpensa-shuttle.com; ☺ ticket office 7am-9pm) coaches, departing from Piazza Luigi di Savoia, outside Stazione Centrale (every 20 minutes 5am to 10.30pm). A one-way ticket per adult/child costs €4.50/2.25 for the one-hour journey. **STAB** (☎ 02 339 10 794) runs hourly buses between 4.45pm and 8pm to Orio al Serio airport (€6.70, one hour, nine daily) near Bergamo.

A taxi from Malpensa airport to Milan city centre will cost at least €75.

To/From Linate Airport
From Milan's Piazza Luigi di Savoia, in front of Stazione Centrale, **STAM** (☎ 02 748 52 757)

buses run to Linate airport (one way €2, 25 minutes, every 30 minutes between 5.40am and 9.35pm). Tickets are sold on board by the driver. You can also get local ATM bus No 73 (€1 one-way, 20 minutes, about every 15 minutes between 5.30am and 8pm) from Piazza San Babila (on the corner of Corso Europa).

A taxi from Linate airport to Milan city centre should cost no more than €15.

Bicycle
Hire a bicycle for around €5 a day from **AWS Bici Motor** (Map pp244–5; ☎ 02 670 72 145; Via Ponte Seveso 33), on the corner of Via Schiaparelli.

Car & Motorcycle
Entering central Milan by car is a major hassle – plus there's talk of a fee being imposed on every car driving into the centre. Street parking costs €1.30 per hour (flat rate of €2.60 8pm to midnight) and is limited to two hours. To pay, buy a SostaMilano card from a tobacconist, scratch off the date and hour, and display it on your dashboard.

Motoring information is provided by the **Automobile Club Italia** (ACI; Map pp248–9; ☎ 02 774 51; Corso Venezia 43). Hertz, Avis, Maggiore and Europcar have offices at Stazione Centrale and both airports.

Public Transport
Milan's public transport system, run by **ATM** (☎ 800 01 68 57; www.atm-mi.it) is efficient. The underground consists of four underground lines (red MM1, green MM2, yellow MM3 and blue Passante Ferroviario) which run 6am to midnight.

A ticket costs €1 and is valid for one underground ride or up to 75 minutes travel on ATM buses and trams. You can buy a book of 10 tickets (five double-journey tickets) for €9.20 or unlimited one-/two-day tickets for bus, tram and MM costing €3/5.50. Tickets are sold at underground stations, tobacconists and newspaper stands.

Free public transport maps are available from ATM's **Info Point** (Map pp248–9; ☺ 7.45am-8.15pm Mon-Sat), in the Duomo underground station.

Taxi
Don't bother trying to hail taxis – they don't stop. Head for a taxi rank or call ☎ 02 40 40, ☎ 02 69 69 or ☎ 02 85 85.

SOUTH OF MILAN

PAVIA

pop 73,893 \ elevation 77m

Pavia is an industrial and agricultural centre on the banks of the River Ticino, known for its university. Originally the Roman Ticinum, Pavia rivalled Milan as the capital of the Lombard kings until the 11th century. Like many northern cities, Pavia became a pawn of power politics as the Renaissance dawned. Spain occupied it in the early 16th century, followed immediately by the Austrians from the early 18th century. Interrupted by a few years of Napoleonic French control from 1796, Austrian rule lasted until 1859.

The province produces about one-third of Italy's rice, making risotto the thing to eat – don't miss *risotto con le rane* (risotto peppered with small frogs). Top it off with a slice of *torta paradiso* (moist sponge cake topped with icing sugar).

Information

Banca Nazionale del Lavoro (BNL; Via Mentana)
Farmacia Fapa (Corso Strada Nuova 100) Historic pharmacy (1828) with night service.
Ospedale San Matteo (☎ 0382 50 11; Piazza Golgi 2) Hospital.
Police Station (☎ 0382 51 21; Viale Rismondo 68)
Post Office (Piazza della Posta 2; ☺ 8.30am-7pm Mon-Sat)
Tourist Office (☎ 0382 2 21 56; www.apt.pavia.it, Italian only; Via Fabio Filzi 22; ☺ 8.30am-12.30pm & 2-6pm Mon-Sat)
Travel Agency CTS (☎ 0382 3 51 95; Via Bossolaro 27) Student and youth travel.

Sights

OLD TOWN

Pavia once boasted some 100 medieval **watchtowers**; the trio on Piazza di Leonardo da Vinci is all that remain today. The forbidding **Castello Visconteo** watches over the northern end of medieval Pavia. Only ever used as a residence, it was built in 1360 for Galeazzo II Visconti and now houses the **Museo Civico** (☎ 0382 30 48 16; museocivici@comune .pv.it; Viale XI Febbraio; adult/child €6/4; ☺ 9am-1.30pm Tue-Fri, 10am-7pm Sat & Sun Mar-Jun & Sep-Nov, 9am-1.30pm Tue-Sat, 9am-1pm Sun Dec-Feb, Jul & Aug). The museum's archaeological, ethnographic and art collections cover pretty much everything about Pavia's past.

The medieval centre is dominated by the **University of Pavia** (☎ 0382 50 41; www.unipv.it, Italian only; Corso Strada Nuova 65), built as a school in the 9th century. It became a university in 1361, with Christopher Columbus being among its rash of notable graduates. Self-taught physicist Alessandro Volta, who invented the electric battery, lectured here. Discover other facts in the **Museo per la Storia dell'Università di Pavia** (☎ 0382 2 97 24; Corso Strada Nuova 65; admission free; ☺ 3.30-5pm Mon, 9.30am-noon Fri), the small museum in the academic complex.

The other old-town landmark is the **cathedral**, a short walk south of the university along pedestrian Corso Strada Nuovo. Work started on the hulk of a church – topped by Italy's third-largest dome – in 1488 but it wasn't completed until the 19th century. Both Leonardo da Vinci and Donato Bramante contributed to the church's design. In 1989 its bell tower fell over, killing four people.

Continuing south along Corso Strada Nuova, and then east along Corso Garibaldi brings you to the **Basilica di San Michele** (Piazzetta Azzani 1), built in the Romanesque style in 1090 and, for a long time, a preferred location for European coronations. Barbarossa was crowned Holy Roman Emperor here in 1155. Although deteriorated, the soft sandstone facade remains a Romanesque masterwork.

CERTOSA DI PAVIA

One of the most notable buildings produced during the Italian Renaissance was Pavia's splendid **Certosa** (Charterhouse; ☎ 0382 92 56 13; Viale Monumento; admission by donation; ☺ 9-11.30am & 2.30-4.30pm Tue-Sun Nov-Feb, 9-11.30am & 2.30-5pm Tue-Sun Mar & Oct, 9-11.30am & 2.30-5.30pm Tue-Sun Apr & May-Sep), a Carthusian monastery 10km north of Pavia. Founded by Gian Galeazzo Visconti of Milan in 1396 as a private chapel for the Visconti family and a home for 12 monks, the Certosa soon became one of northern Italy's most lavish buildings.

The interior is Gothic, although some Renaissance decoration is evident. In the former sacristy is a giant sculpture, dating from 1409 and made from hippopotamus teeth, including 66 small bas-reliefs and 94 statuettes. Behind the 122 arches of the larger cloisters are 24 cells, each a

LOMBARDY & THE LAKES

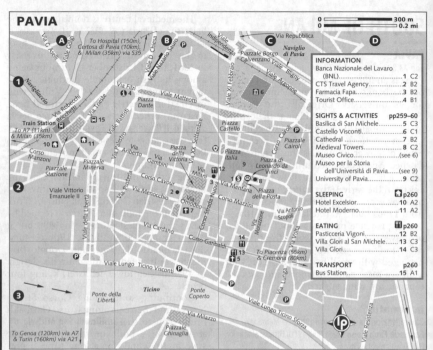

PAVIA

INFORMATION	
Banca Nazionale del Lavaro	
(BNL)..1 C2	
CTS Travel Agency...................2 B2	
Farmacia Fapa.........................3 B2	
Tourist Office..........................4 B1	

SIGHTS & ACTIVITIES	pp259–60
Basilica di San Michele............5 C3	
Castello Visconti.....................6 C1	
Cathedral...............................7 B2	
Medieval Towers.....................8 C2	
Museo Civico.......................(see 6)	
Museo per la Storia	
dell'Università di Pavia......(see 9)	
University of Pavia..................9 C2	

SLEEPING	p260
Hotel Excelsior.....................10 A2	
Hotel Moderno.....................11 A2	

EATING	p260
Pasticceria Vigoni.................12 B2	
Villa Glori al San Michele.......13 C3	
Villa Glori............................14 C3	

TRANSPORT	p260
Bus Station..........................15 A1	

Sleeping & Eating

Hotel Excelsior (☎ 0382 28 596; www.excelsiorpavia.com; Piazzale Stazione 25; s/d €50/73) Three-star interior comforts make the Excelsior, across from the train station, decidedly more inviting from the inside than out.

Hotel Moderno (☎ 0382 30 34 01; www.hotelmoderno.it; Viale Vittorio Emanuele 41; s/d/tr €100/135/149; P 🕸) Hotel Moderno is Pavia's upmarket choice, nestled in an old family palace from the 19th century. Traditional fodder is served in its Liberty restaurant.

Cafés abound beneath the arches on Piazza della Vittoria. Sample a slice of *torta paradiso* (€1) at **Pasticceria Vigoni** (☎ 0382 2 21 03; Corso Strada Nuova 110), a cake shop and tearoom dating to 1878 in front of the university.

Villa Glori (☎ 0382 2 07 16; Via Villa Glori 10; meals €25; 🕑 Wed-Mon) Feast on Pavian culinary pleasures on a cobbled terrace. Taste local

self-contained living area for one monk. Several are open to the public.

SGEA buses to Milan stop at the Certosa. See opposite for details.

vintages around the corner at **Villa Glori al San Michele** (next to the Basilica San Michele), which is a wine bar run by the same team.

Getting There & Around

SGEA buses (☎ 0382 37 54 05; www.sgea.it) linking Pavia **bus station** (Via Trieste) and Viale Bligny in Milan (€2.75, 35 minutes, seven daily) stop en route at Certosa di Pavia (€1.20, 10 minutes, seven daily). To reach the charterhouse (a 10-minute walk) from the bus stop, turn right at the traffic lights then continue straight ahead. Pavia–Milan buses continue to Malpensa airport (€10, 1½ hours). Updated schedules are on the SGEA website.

Direct trains run from Pavia train station to Milan (€2.40, 30 minutes, up to eight daily), Genoa and beyond.

Pavia is small and easy enough to get around. Bicycles are popular and most summers the city council plants several bicycle stands – including at Hotel Moderno and the university – around town, from where cyclists can borrow a bike for free.

LOMBARDY & THE LAKES

EAST OF MILAN

BERGAMO

pop 117,415 \ elevation 249m

Virtually two cities, Bergamo's walled hilltop *città alta* (upper town) is surrounded by the *città bassa* (lower town), a sprawling modern addition to this magnificent former outpost of the Venetian empire. Although Milan's skyscrapers to the southwest are visible on a clear day, historically Bergamo was more closely associated with Venice, which was in control of the city for 350 years until Napoleon arrived at the gates. Although long dominated by outsiders, Bergamo has retained a strong sense of local identity, perhaps demonstrated most colourfully by the local dialect, which is all but incomprehensible to visitors.

Bergamo, with its wealth of medieval, Renaissance and baroque architecture, was one of Europe's little-known secrets until the third millennium when no-frills airlines started flying from London in and out of Orio al Serio airport, just 4km southeast of the city. Several small ski resorts speckle the Bergamo Alps around the town.

Information

BOOKSHOPS

Galleria Internazionale del Libro (☎ 035 23 01 30; Via XX Settembre 83) Travel guides (in English and Italian) and English-language novels.

Libreria di Dimetra (☎ 035 21 00 86; Viale Papa Giovanni XXIII 28) Walking and cycling guidebooks (in Italian) and city maps.

EMERGENCIES

Police Station (☎ 035 27 61 11; Via Alessandro Noli)

LAUNDRY

Pay €3/5 to wash 6/14kg of socks 'n smocks.

Lavanderia Self-Service (Via Angelo Maj 39b; ☼ 7.30am-8pm)

Wash & Dry (Via San Bernardino 11d; ☼ 7.30am-8pm)

MEDICAL SERVICES

Ospedale Riuniti (☎ 035 26 91 11; Largo Barozzi 1)

MONEY

You'll find several banks in the lower town and a couple on Via B Colleoni, near the upper town tourist office.

POST

Lower Town Post Office (Via Masone 2a; ☼ 8.30am-7pm Mon-Sat)

Upper Town Post Office (Via S Lorenzo; ☼ 8.30am-2pm Mon-Fri, 8.30am-12.30pm Sat)

TOURIST INFORMATION

Lower Town (☎ 035 21 02 04; www.apt.bergamo.it; Viale Vittorio Emanuele II 20; ☼ 9am-12.30pm & 2-5.30pm Mon-Fri)

Upper Town (☎ 035 24 22 26; iat.bergamo@apt.bergamo.it; Vicolo Aquila Nera 2; ☼ 9am-12.30pm & 2-5.30pm)

TRAVEL AGENCIES

CTS (☎ 035 24 41 67; bergamo@cts.it; Via Pignolo 16a; ☼ 9.30am-12.30pm & 3-7pm Mon-Fri, 9.30am-12.30pm Sat)

Sights

PIAZZA VECCHIA

Medieval Bergamo's heart is hard to miss. Whichever way you enter the walled hilltop town, you'll soon find yourself in this gracious square. The white porticoed building on Via B Colleoni, which forms the northern side of the piazza, is the 17th-century **Palazzo Nuovo**, now a library and the square's least interesting feature. Turn south and you face the imposing arches and columns of the **Palazzo della Ragione**, first built in the 12th century. The lion of St Mark is a reminder of Venice's long reign. Note the sun clock in the pavement beneath the arches. Next to the palace, the **Torre del Campanone** (Piazza Vecchia; adult/child €1/0.50; ☼ 10.30am-4pm Sat & Sun Nov-Feb, 10am-12.30pm & 2-6pm Tue-Fri, 10am-6pm Sat & Sun Mar, Apr & Oct, 10am-8pm Sat & Sun May-Sep) tolls the old 10pm curfew. Scale the tower for wonderful views.

Tucked in behind these secular buildings is the core of Bergamo's spiritual life, the Piazza del Duomo. Oddly enough, the modest baroque **cathedral** (☎ 035 21 02 23; Piazza del Duomo; ☼ 7.30-11.45am & 3-6.30pm) plays second fiddle to neighbouring **Basilica di Santa Maria Maggiore** (☎ 035 22 33 27; Piazza del Duomo; ☼ 9am-12.30pm & 2.30-5pm Mon-Fri, 9-11am & 2.30-5pm Sat, 9-11am & 2.30-6pm Sun), a Romanesque church begun in 1137. Gaetano Donizetti, a 19th-century composer and son of Bergamo, is buried here. The gaudy Renaissance **Cappella Colleoni** (Funeral Chapel; ☎ 035 21 00 61; Piazza del Duomo; ☼ 9am-12.30pm & 2-4.30pm Tue-Sun Nov-Mar, 9am-12.30pm & 2-6.30pm Tue-Sun Apr-Oct) is an extravagant addition to the church.

LOMBARDY & THE LAKES

LOMBARDY & THE LAKES

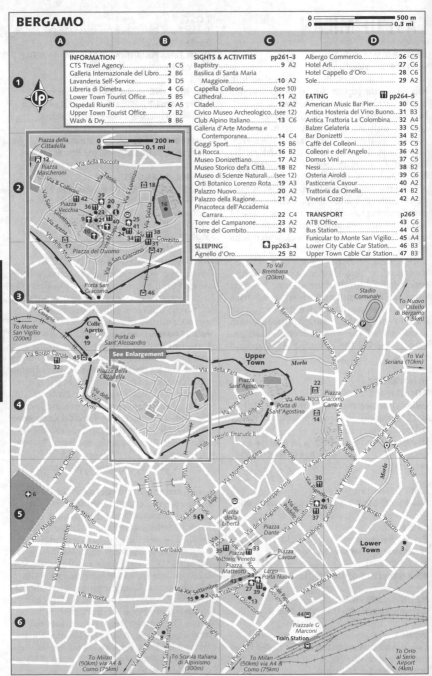

BERGAMO

0 ──────── 500 m
0 ──────── 0.3 mi

INFORMATION
CTS Travel Agency.....................1 C5
Galleria Internazionale del Libro....2 B6
Lavanderia Self-Service.............3 D5
Libreria di Dimetra....................4 C6
Lower Town Tourist Office.........5 B5
Ospedali Riuniti.......................6 A5
Upper Town Tourist Office........7 B2
Wash & Dry..............................8 B6

SIGHTS & ACTIVITIES   pp261–3
Baptistry.................................9 A2
Basilica di Santa Maria
    Maggiore.............................10 A2
Cappella Colleoni...............(see 10)
Cathedral...............................11 A2
Citadel...................................12 A2
Civico Museo Archeologico....(see 12)
Club Alpino Italiano................13 C6
Galleria d'Arte Moderna e
    Contemporanea.................14 C4
Goggi Sport............................15 B6
La Rocca...............................16 B2
Museo Donizettiano...............17 A2
Museo Storico della Città.......18 B2
Museo di Scienze Naturali....(see 12)
Orti Botanico Lorenzo Rota...19 A3
Palazzo Nuovo......................20 A2
Palazzo della Ragione...........21 A2
Pinacoteca dell'Accademia
    Carrara.............................22 C4
Torre del Campanone............23 A2
Torre del Gombito.................24 B2

SLEEPING   pp263–4
Agnello d'Oro.......................25 B2

Albergo Commercio................26 C5
Hotel Arli..............................27 C6
Hotel Cappello d'Oro.............28 C6
Sole.....................................29 A2

EATING   pp264–5
American Music Bar Pier..........30 C5
Antica Hosteria del Vino Buono...31 B3
Antica Trattoria La Colombina...32 A4
Balzer Gelateria.....................33 C5
Bar Donizetti.........................34 B2
Caffè del Colleoni..................35 C5
Colleoni e dell'Angelo.............36 A2
Domus Vini...........................37 C5
Nessi....................................38 A2
Osteria Airoldi......................39 C6
Pasticceria Cavour.................40 A2
Trattoria da Ornella................41 B2
Vineria Cozzi........................42 A2

TRANSPORT   p265
ATB Office.............................43 C6
Bus Station...........................44 C6
Funicular to Monte San Vigilio...45 A4
Lower City Cable Car Station.....46 B3
Upper Town Cable Car Station...47 B3

Piazza della
Cittadella
0 ──────── 200 m
0 ──────── 0.1 mi

Piazza
Mascheroni

Via della Boccola

Via B. Colleoni
Via Tassis
Via S. Lorenzo

Piazza
Vecchia

Via Salvatore

Via Arena

Via delle Mura

Piazza del Duomo

Via di San Giacomo

Porta San
Giacomo

To
Brembana
(20km)

Stadio
Comunale

To Nuovo
Ostello
di Bergamo
(1.5km)

Via Giulio Crescenzi

Via Baioni

Via Mazzano Sauro

See Enlargement

Colle
Aperto

Porta di
Sant'Alessandro

To Monte
San Vigilio
(200m)

Via Borgo Canale

Piazza della
Cittadella

Via delle
Mura

Tre Armi

Upper
Town

Via della Fara

Piazza
Sant'Agostino

Via Porta Dipinta

Porta di
Sant'Agostino

Morla

Piazza
Giacomo
Carrara

Via della Noca

To Val
Seriana (10km)

Viale Giulio Cesare

Via Borgo S. Caterina

Viale Vittorio Emanuele II

Via C. Battisti

Via San Giovanni

Viale
Muraine

Via Pignolo

Viale Gianforte Suardi

Alessandro Noli

Via D. Chiesa

To
Monte
San Vigilio

Via F. Cavagnis

Via dello Statuto

Via XXIV Maggio

Via Quattro Novembre

Via Mazzini

Via San Alessandro

Viale Vittorio Emanuele II

Via Brigata
Lupi

Piazza
della
Libertà

Via Giuseppe Verdi

Via di Borgo
Palazzo

Morla

Via Pignolo

Via Masone

Via Torquato Tasso

Via Gabriele Camozzi

Lower
Town

Via Garibaldi

Via Tasca

Viale Roma

Piazza
Vittorio Veneto

Piazza
Dante

Piazza
Cavour

Largo
Porta Nuova

Via Angelo Mai

Via Broseta

Piazza
Matteotti

Via XX settembre

Via Tiraboschi

Via Ghislanzoni

Viale Papa
Giovanni XXIII

Piazzale G
Marconi

Train Station

Via Gian Battista Moroni

Via San Bernardino

To Scuola Italiana
di Alpinismo
(300m)

Via Pietro Paleocapa

Via Quarenghi

To Milan
(50km) via A4 &
Como (75km)

To Milan
(50km) via A4 &
Como (75km)

To Orio
al Serio
Airport
(4km)

The octagonal **baptistry** was built inside the Basilica di Santa Maria Maggiore in 1340 but moved outside in the late 19th century.

CITADEL

The upper city's western tip is filled by the defensive hulk of Bergamo's **citadel**, occupied today by two small museums, the **Museo di Scienze Naturali Enrico Caffi** (☎ 035 28 60 11; msnbg@tiscalinet.it; Piazza Citadella 10; admission free; 🕑 9am-12.30pm & 2.30-6pm Tue-Fri, 9am-7pm Sat & Sun Apr-Sep, 9am-12.30pm & 2.30-5.30pm Tue-Sun Oct-Mar) and the **Civico Museo Archeologico** (☎ 035 24 28 39; Piazza Citadella 12; admission free; 🕑 9am-12.30pm & 2.30-6pm Tue-Fri, 9am-7pm Sat & Sun Apr-Sep, 9am-12.30pm & 2.30-6pm Tue-Sun Oct-Mar). However, a wander through the citadel's impressive courtyard is just as interesting.

MUSEO STORICO DELLA CITTÀ

In the former Convento di San Francesco (founded in the 13th century), this **museum** (☎ 035 24 71 16; www.museostoricobg.org; Piazza Mercato del Fieno 6a; admission free; 🕑 9.30am-4pm Tue-Sun) traces the city's history, with emphasis on the period 1797 to Italian unification in the 1860s.

MUSEO DONIZETTIANO

A collection of furnishings and objects belonging to the city's favourite musical son, Gaetano Donizetti (1797–1848), can be seen at the **Museo Donizettiano** (☎ 035 39 92 69; Via Arena 9; admission free; 🕑 10am-1pm Mon-Fri, 10am-1pm & 2.30-5pm Sat & Sun).

LOOKOUTS

A stroll downhill along Via B Colleoni and Via Gombito takes you past **Torre del Gombito**, a 12th-century tower. Carry on along medieval Bergamo's main street towards the cable-car station and then turn left to **La Rocca** (adult/child €1/0.50; 🕑 10.30am-4pm Sat & Sun Nov-Feb, 10am-6pm Sat & Sun Mar, Apr & Oct, 10am-8pm Sat & Sun May-Sep), a fortress set in a park. The views from the **park** (admission free; 🕑 9am-8pm Apr-Sep, 10am-6pm Oct & Mar, 10am-4pm Nov-Feb) are worth the effort, as is a stroll around the fortress.

For more spectacular views, trudge uphill along Colle Aperto and bear left (following the yellow signs) up a steep flight of stone steps to Bergamo's **Orti Botanico Lorenzo Rota** (☎ 035 39 94 66; botanico@cyberg.it; Scaletta di Colle Aperto; admission free; 🕑 9am-noon & 2-5pm Mar & Oct, 9am-noon & 2-6pm Mon-Fri, 9am-7pm Sat & Sun Apr-Sep).

More than 900 species grow in the hillside botanical garden.

PINACOTECA DELL'ACCADEMIA CARRARA

Make time to visit the art gallery of **Accademia Carrara** (☎ 035 39 96 43; www.accademiacarrara.bergamo.it, Italian only; Piazza Giacomo Carrara 82a; adult/child Mon-Sat €2.58/1.55, Sun free; 🕑 9.30am-1pm & 3-6.45pm Tue-Sun Apr-Sep, 9.30am-1pm & 2.30-5.45pm Tue-Sun Oct-Mar), reached pleasantly on foot from the upper town through **Porta di Sant' Agostino** and down Via della Noca. Founded in 1780, it contains an impressive range of Italian masters. An early St Sebastian by Raphael is worth looking out for, as are works by Botticelli, Canaletto, Lorenzo Lotto, Andrea Mantegna, Giovanni Tiepolo and Titian.

On the opposite side of the square is the academy's **Galleria d'Arte Moderna e Contemporanea** (GAMeC; ☎ 035 39 95 28; www.gamec.it; Piazza Giacomo Carrara). Admission prices and opening hours vary, depending on the exhibition.

Activities

Club Alpino Italiano (CAI; ☎ 035 24 42 73; www.caibergamo.it, Italian only; Via Ghislanzoni 15) has details about winter sports, walking and gentle strolls in the nearby Bergamo Alps. It also runs a small library specialising in walking, outdoor activity and other mountain-related titles. Buy forgotten gear at **Goggi Sport** (Via XX Settembre 73-77).

Guided climbing expeditions up frozen waterfalls, sheer rock faces or mere mountains are run by the **Scuola Italiana di Alpinismo** (☎ 035 32 30 511; www.guidealpinebergamo.it, Italian only; Via San Berdardino 145).

Sleeping

Bergamo is an easy day trip from Milan. If you want to stay, arrive early or reserve as hotels fill up distressingly quickly.

LOWER TOWN

Nuovo Ostello di Bergamo (☎ 035 36 17 24; hostelbg@spm.it; Via Galileo Ferraris 1; dm/s/d with breakfast €14/19/33; 🕑 reception 7am-midnight) Bergamo's hostel is about 4km north of the train station. Take bus No 14 from Largo Porta Nuova or follow Viale Giulio Cesare north past the stadium and take the fourth turning on the right after crossing the large Circonvallazione Fabriciano intersection.

Albergo Commercio (☎ 035 22 40 96; hotelcommercio@jumpy.it; Via Torquato Tasso 88; s or d €50, s/d/tr with bathroom €70/80/100; ☒) This well-worn hotel lures a youngish budget crowd with its basic rooms and happy family atmosphere.

Hotel Arli (☎ 035 22 20 14; www.arli.net; Largo Porta Nuova 12; s/d €90/123; ☒) The Arli is a comfortable, three-star hotel with nothing staggering to remember or forget. Top that with a friendly staff and highly successful web marketing, and you have one very busy hotel.

Hotel Cappello d'Oro (☎ 035 23 25 03; www.hotel cappellodoro.it, Italian only; Viale Papa Giovanni XXIII 12; s/d €176/190; ℗ ☒) With four stars and a Best Western label, the comfort levels are hard to beat at Bergamo's most upmarket choice. Service is formal and flattering.

UPPER TOWN

Bergamo's most charming options – each with a superb restaurant – are on the hill.

Sole (☎ 035 21 82 38; fax 035 24 00 11; Via B Colleoni 1; s/d €51/67) Soulful Sole is just off Piazza Vecchia. Simple lino floors, coupled with big windows and brightly coloured bedspreads, lend rooms a country feel. Out back there's a garden restaurant.

Agnello d'Oro (☎ 035 24 98 83; Via Gombito 22; s/d €52/92; ☒) With the incredible clutter of objects adorning every wall, this 17th-century spot could easily pass for a (very full) antique shop. Rooms are attractive and you can dine al fresco in summer.

Eating

The Bergamaschi are passionate about polenta and eat it as a side dish or dessert – *polenta e osei* are little cakes filled with jam and topped with yellow icing and chocolate birds. Bergamo contributed *câsonséi*, a ravioli stuffed with meat, to the Italian table and the area is noted for its fine red wines, including Valcalepio. Taste the latter with some fine slices of *carne salata di cavallo* (salted horse meat).

LOWER TOWN

Caffè del Colleoni (☎ 035 22 55 62; Portici del Senti-erone 33-34; cappuccino €1.15) Sink your teeth into a well-filled pastry or sip tea at this elegant café-cum-*salon de thé*.

Osteria Airoldi (☎ 035 24 44 23; Viale Papa Giovanni XXIII 18) This bright, breezy and spacious *enoteca*/coffee house is a modern break from the traditional norm. Perch on a bar stool or splay out on a low bench.

American Music Bar Pier (☎ 035 24 73 73; Via Pignolo 23; ☾ Mon-Sat) Mingle with locals at this hybrid tobacconist/American-styled bar where local bands play.

Domus Vini (☎ 035 21 08 67; Passagio Canonici Lateranensi, Via Torquato Tasso 70; ☾ 10am-2.30pm & 5.30pm-midnight Tue-Sat, 9.30am-2.30pm Sun) This stylish wine bar, tucked beneath of arches of the cloistered Chiostro di Santo Spirito, prides itself on its foie gras (duck liver pâté), fresh meats, rare cheeses and chocolates.

Balzer Gelateria (☎ 035 23 40 83; Piazza Cavour 42) Lip-smacking jams, chocolates and chestnut creams have been concocted since 1850 at this temple for the sweet-toothed. On Sunday morning, what feels like half of Bergamo crams in here for coffee, cake and ice cream.

UPPER TOWN

Dining is tasty but not cheap in medieval Bergamo.

Nessi (☎ 035 24 70 73; Via Gombito 34) Killer-calorie apple strudel and *torta trentina al cioccolato* (a heavy chocolate sponge encased in pastry) are among the sweet goodies displayed in Nessi's window. Equally sweet are its pizza and focaccia slices to eat on the move.

Pasticceria Cavour (☎ 035 24 34 18; Via Gombito 7a; 1st/2nd courses from €9/11; ☾ Thu-Tue) Plump little cherubs frescoed on the walls add to the charm of this late 19th-century tea room where the sweet-toothed have splurged since 1850. Come Sunday, plump for brunch (€16) or a choice of fish and meat dishes from its all-day buffet.

Bar Donizetti (☎ 035 24 26 61; Via Gombito 17a; ☾ Wed-Mon) Wine, cheese and cold cuts are the prime temptations of this shop-cum-bar and lunchtime spot where you can dine al fresco – in a stunning loggia overlooking the upper town's main street, no less. A mixed platter of cold meats/cheese for one/two people costs €8.30/13.

Trattoria da Ornella (☎ 035 23 27 36; Via Gombito 15; 1st/2nd courses from €6/10) *Polenta taragna* (polenta cooked with butter, cheese and a choice of rabbit, chicken or veal; €14) is the house speciality at this traditional no-frills eating house. Kickstart your dining experience with a starter-sized plate of *lardo Bergamasco* (slices of Bergamo pork fat) with polenta (€6).

Antica Hosteria del Vino Buono (☎ 035 24 79 93; Piazza Mercato delle Scarpe; 1st/2nd courses €6.50/9;

Tue-Sun) Feast on cheese-sprinkled *cason-celli* (homemade pasta cushions filled with a spicy sausage meat and laced with a buttery sage sauce) followed by a guaranteed-to-fill €8 plate of *polenta del Bergami* (polenta and mushrooms) – two dishes typical to Bergamo – at this *trattoria tipica* (typical inn).

Colleoni e dell'Angelo (☎ 035 23 25 96; colleonid ellangelo@uninetcom.it; Piazza Vecchia 7; 1st/2nd courses from €10/15; Tue-Sun) A wallet-cruncher it might be but this tasteful place dishes up a rainbow of gastronomic surprises: balsamic vinegar-scented pigeon breast with apple salad; braised leek and foie gras lasagne; venison fillet with red wine-scented pears and chestnut cream; or veal with quail eggs and black truffle sauce.

Antica Trattoria La Colombina (☎ 035 26 14 02; Via Borgo Canale 12; 1st/2nd courses €5.50/8.50; Wed-Sun;) A humble exterior (so humble you'd miss it if you weren't wielding this guide) ensures Bergamo's best-kept secret stays well under wraps. Step inside and boom – the buoyant chatter of a polenta- and wine-fuelled crowd at shared tables almost bowls you over.

Getting There & Away
AIR
The local airport, **Orio al Serio** (☎ 035 32 63 23), is 4km southeast of the train station. A handful of international flights land here, including daily flights to/from several European cities with no-frills airlines.

BUS
From Bergamo's bus station on Piazzale G Marconi, **SAB** (☎ 035 24 02 40; www.sab-autoservizi.it, Italian only) operates services to the lakes and mountains as well as to/from Milan's Piazza Castello (€4, every half-hour).

TRAIN
From the Piazzale G Marconi train station, there are almost hourly trains to/from Milan's Stazione Centrale (€3.75, 45 minutes) and less-frequent trains to Brescia (€3.25, 50 minutes, four daily) and Cremona (€5, two hours, two daily).

Getting Around
TO/FROM THE AIRPORT
Autoservizi Zani (☎ 035 67 86 78; www.zaniviaggi.it, Italian only) operates buses to/from Orio al Serio airport, departing every 20 minutes

from platform No 12 at Bergamo bus station. A one-way ticket costs €1.05 (€1.50 from the driver) and journey time is 10 minutes. The airport is also served by direct buses to Milan – see p257 for details.

PUBLIC TRANSPORT
ATB buses (☎ 035 36 42 11; atb@ita.flashnet.it; Via Tiraboschi) serve the city. Bus No 1 connects the train station with the cable car to the upper city and Colle Aperto. From the latter, either bus No 21 or a second cable car continues uphill to San Vigilio. Bus No 3 runs from Porta di Sant'Alessandro in the upper city to Via Pietro Paleocapa in the lower city. Buy tickets, valid for an hour's travel on buses and cable cars for €0.90 from machines at the train and cable-car stations; a 10-ticket carnet costs €6.80 and an all-day ticket allowing unlimited travel is available for €2.80.

Car-rental agencies at Orio al Serio airport include:
Hertz (☎ 035 31 12 58)
Avis (☎ 035 31 01 92)
Europcar (☎ 035 31 86 22)
Sixt (☎ 035 31 88 62)

VALTELLINA
Covering the band of Alps across Lombardy's north, the Valtellina is one of Italy's least-attractive Alpine regions, although it does have some acceptable skiing and is well set up for walking.

The **Valtellina tourist board** (www.valtellinaonline .com, Italian only) has information points in the following towns:
Sondrio (☎ 0342 51 25 00; aptvaltellina@provincia.so.it; Via Trieste 12)
Aprica (☎ 0342 74 61 13; aptaprica@provinica.so.it; Corso Roma 150)
Madesimo (☎ 0343 5 30 15; aptmadesimo@provinicia .so.it; Via alle Scuole)
Livigno (☎ 0342 99 63 79; www.aptlivigno.it; Via de la Gesa 65)

See Lonely Planet's *Walking in Italy* for more guidance. For information on the Alpine ski resort of Bormio, in Valtellina's far eastern realms, see the Parco Nazionale dello Stelvio (pp310–11).

Trains leave Milan for Sondrio (€7.05, two hours, hourly), a regional transport hub from where buses connect with the resorts and towns.

LOMBARDY & THE LAKES

BRESCIA

pop 194,700 \ elevation 149m

Brescia is a scruffy provincial capital, arms production centre and transport hub. Although rough around the edges, its student life gives the place a bit of buzz and there are a few sights worth seeing.

When the Romans took control of the Gallic town in 225 BC, Brescia (the name derives from a word meaning hill) already had hundreds of years of now obscure history behind it. Charlemagne and his successors were in the driver's seat in the 9th century, followed for 1000 years by a parade of outside rulers. As revolutionary fervour swept Europe in 1848–49, Brescia was dubbed 'The Lioness' for its 10-day uprising against Austria – an unsuccessful prelude to its participation in the movement towards Italian unification a decade later.

Risotto, beef dishes and *lumache alla bresciana* (snails cooked up with parmesan cheese and fresh spinach) are common in Brescia and the region offers many good wines, including those from Botticino, Lugana and Riviera del Garda.

Information

Brixia Web (☎ 030 375 93 31; www.brixiaweb.it, Italian only; Via Antiche Mura 6a; €4/hr; 🕙 11am-8pm Mon-Fri, 11am-7.30pm Sat, 2-7pm Sun) Users need a passport to gain access.

Ospedale Civile (☎ 030 3 99 51; Piazzale Ospedale)

Police Station (☎ 030 3 74 41; Via Botticelli)

Post Office (Piazza della Vittoria; 🕙 8.30am-7pm Mon-Sat)

Tourist Office (☎ 030 4 34 18; www.bresciaholiday.com; Corso Zanardelli 34; 🕙 9am-12.30pm & 3-6pm Mon-Fri, 9am-12.30pm Sat)

Branch Tourist Office (☎ 030 240 03 57; Piazza della Loggia 6; 🕙 9.30am-6.30pm Mon-Sat)

Castle

Brescia's historic centre is dominated by a hill, **Colle Cidneo**, topped by a rambling **castle** which has been the core of the city defences for centuries. **Torre Mirabella**, the main round tower, was built by the Viscontis in the 13th century. The castle hosts two museums, the **Museo delle Armi Antiche** (☎ 030 29 32 92; Al Castello; adult/child €3/2; 🕙 9.30am-1pm & 2.30-5pm Tue-Sun Oct-May, 10am-5pm Tue-Sun Jun-Sep) and the **Civico Museo del Risorgimento** (☎ 030 4 41 76; Al Castello; adult/child €3/2; 🕙 9.30am-1pm & 2.30-5pm Tue-Sun Oct-May, 10am-5pm Tue-Sun Jun-Sep). The former

contains one of Italy's most extensive collections of weapons while the latter deals with Italian unification history.

Cathedrals & Piazzas

The most compelling of Brescia's religious monuments is the **Duomo Vecchio** (Old Cathedral; Piazza Paolo V I; 🕙 9am-noon & 3-7pm Wed-Tue Apr-Oct, 9am-noon & 3-6pm Sat & Sun Nov-Mar), an 11th-century Romanesque basilica built over a 6th-century circular structure. Next door, the Renaissance **Duomo Nuova** (New Cathedral; Piazza Paolo VI) dwarfs its elderly neighbour but is of less interest. Also on the square is **Il Broletto**, the medieval town hall with an 11th-century tower.

Northwest of Piazza Paolo VI is **Piazza della Loggia**, dominated by the squat 16th-century loggia in which Palladio had a hand. The **Torre dell'Orologio**, with its exquisite astrological timepiece, is modelled on the one in Venice's St Mark's Square.

Finally, the Fascist-era **Piazza della Vittoria** is worth a look. Laid out in 1932 by Piacentini, the square and its buildings (like the post office) are a perfect example of the period's monumentalism.

Roman Ruins & Museums

Evidence of the Roman presence in Brescia remains. Along Via dei Musei are the now partly restored and impressive remains of the **Tempio Capitolino**, a Roman temple built in AD 73. The **Palazzo Martinengo** (☎ 030 280 79 34; Via dei Musei 30; adult/child €6.50/5; 🕙 9.30am-7.30pm Tue-Sun), opposite the small 18th-century **Chiesa di San Zeno di Foro** (Piazza del Foro), is the majestic host to temporary art exhibitions.

About 50m east of the Tempio Capitolino along Via de Musei, cobbled Vicol del Fontanon leads to the ruins of a **Roman theatre**. Continuing east you reach Brescia's most intriguing sight – the jumbled **Monastero di Santa Giulia and Basilica di San Salvatore**. Inside the rambling complex is the **Museo della Città** (☎ 030 297 78 34; Via dei Musei 81b; adult/child €8/4; 🕙 9.30am-5.30pm Tue-Sun Oct-May, 10am-6pm Tue-Sun Jun-Sep) where Roman mosaics have also been unearthed. The star piece of the collection is the 8th-century Croce di Desiderio, a Lombard cross encrusted with hundreds of jewels.

Pinacoteca Civica Tosio-Martinengo (☎ 030 377 49 99; Via Martinengo da Barco; adult/child €3/2; 🕙 9.30am-1pm & 2.30-5pm Tue-Sun Oct-May, 10am-5pm

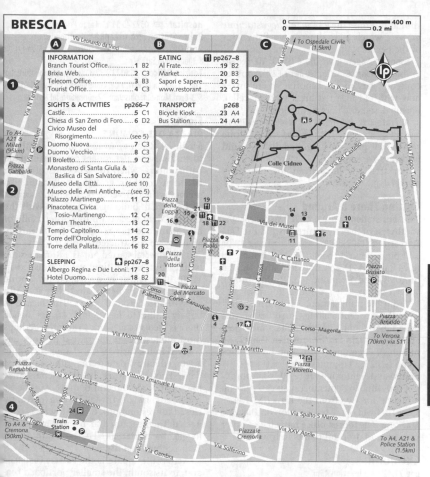

BRESCIA

INFORMATION	
Branch Tourist Office	1 B2
Brixia Web	2 C3
Telecom Office	3 B3
Tourist Office	4 C3

SIGHTS & ACTIVITIES	pp266–7
Castle	5 C1
Chiesa di San Zeno di Foro	6 D2
Civico Museo del Risorgimento	(see 5)
Duomo Nuova	7 C3
Duomo Vecchio	8 C3
Il Broletto	9 C2
Monastero di Santa Giulia & Basilica di San Salvatore	10 D2
Museo della Città	(see 10)
Museo delle Armi Antiche	(see 5)
Palazzo Martinengo	11 C2
Pinacoteca Civica Tosio-Martinengo	12 C4
Roman Theatre	13 C2
Tempio Capitolino	14 C2
Torre dell'Orologio	15 B2
Torre della Pallata	16 B2

SLEEPING	pp267–8
Albergo Regina e Due Leoni	17 C3
Hotel Duomo	18 B2

EATING	pp267–8
Al Frate	19 B2
Market	20 B3
Sapori e Sapere	21 B2
www.restorant	22 C2

TRANSPORT	p268
Bicycle Kiosk	23 A4
Bus Station	24 A4

LOMBARDY & THE LAKES

Tue-Sun Jun-Sep) features works by artists of the Brescian school as well as works by Raphael.

Festivals & Events

The **International Piano Festival**, held from early April until June, is staged in conjunction with nearby Bergamo, while the **Estate Aperta** festival of music occupies the summer months.

Sleeping & Eating

Hotel Duomo (☎ 030 375 86 69; duomosas@virgilio.it; Via Cesare Beccaria 17; s/d €45/70) Cheerfully decorated and well-kept rooms come as a surprise at this 15-room two-star choice, slap-bang between medieval palaces in Brescia's old town. In summer guests can breakfast al fresco in the interior courtyard.

Albergo Regina e Due Leoni (☎ 030 375 78 81; Corso Magenta 14; d with/without bathroom from €50/35) Ageing fails to aptly describe this spartan but friendly pad, firmly trapped in some strange time warp. The entrance is on Vicola Ambrosioni – look for the credit card stickers on the unmarked door.

Brescia's culinary patch is around Piazza della Loggia; Via Beccaria, which runs off the east side of the piazza, is well-endowed with places to eat.

www.restorant (☎ 030 375 22 54; Vicolo Sant' Agostino 3b; 1st/2nd courses €8/13; ☼ noon-1.30pm & 8pm-2am Mon-Sat) Looks count at this stylish and modern fish restaurant. Seafood lovers should not miss the €33 *menù degustazione di pesce* which takes diners on a fishy tour of the ocean.

Sapori e Sapere (☎ 030 4 00 73; Via Beccaria 11; 1st/2nd courses €8.50/15, set menu €28) Another contemporary choice, Sapori e Sapere mixes new with old in a red brick vaulted cellar. Plastic designer chairs sit outside.

Al Frate (☎ 030 375 14 69; Via dei Musei 25; 1st courses €8, 2nd courses €12-15; ☽ Tue-Sun) Al Frate serves well-presented regional dishes – and is always packed.

For fresh produce head for the daily **market** (Piazza del Mercato).

Getting There & Around

The **bus station** (☎ 030 44 915; Via Solferino) is southwest of the city centre. From here **SAIA Trasporti** (☎ 030 230 88 11; www.saiatrasporti.it, Italian only) buses serve Verona (€7, two hours, 10 to 14 daily) via Desenzano del Garda (€3, 50 minutes), and Sirmione (€3.60, one hour), and Cremona (€4, 1¼ hours, hourly).

From the train station, a 10-minute walk from the city centre along Corso dei Martiri della Libertà and Viale della Stazione, there are regular trains to/from Milan (€6.92, 50 minutes), Cremona (€3.75, one hour), Bergamo (€3.25, 30 minutes), Venice (€8.99, 2¼ hours) and Ventimiglia (€17.40, six hours).

From June to September, you can pick up a bicycle for free from the **kiosk** (☽ 7.30am-8.30pm) in front of the train station on Piazzale Stazione. The tourist office has a list of other pick-up and drop-off points in town.

CREMONA

pop 71,420 \ elevation 45m

Home of the Stradivari violin, Cremona jealously maintains its centuries-old status as premier exponent of the delicate art of making the perfect string instrument. All of the great violin-making dynasties started here – Amati, Guarneri and Stradivari – and there are plenty of opportunities to get acquainted with the art of violin making. For centuries an independent city-state, Cremona boasts a compact but impressive city centre, meriting a stopover, if not necessarily an overnight stay. Cremona is an easy day trip from Milan, Mantua and Brescia.

Information

Banca Popolare di Cremona (Piazza del Comune) 24-hour banknote exchange machine and ATM.

Hospital (☎ 0372 40 51 11; Largo Priori)
Police Station (☎ 0372 48 81; Via Tribunali 6)
Post Office (Via Verdi 1; ☽ 8.30am-5.30pm Mon-Fri, 8.30am-noon Sat)
Tourist Office (☎ 0372 2 32 33; www.cremonaturismo .com, Italian only; Piazza del Comune 5; ☽ 9am-12.30pm & 3-6pm Mon-Sat, plus 9am-12.30pm Sun Jul & Aug)

Sights

PIAZZA DEL COMUNE

Medieval Cremona, like most Lombard towns, was an independent *comune* until the 14th century, when the Viscontis of Milan added it to their growing collection. To maintain the difference between the secular and spiritual, buildings connected with the Church were erected on the eastern side of the square, and those concerned with earthly affairs were constructed across the way.

The **cathedral** started out as a Romanesque basilica but, by the time it was finished in 1190, it was heavily overtaken by Gothic modishness (best demonstrated by its Latin cross-shaped ground plan). The facade is largely faithful to the original concept. Inside there is plenty of artwork to admire. Perhaps most interesting are the partial frescoes uncovered in the early 1990s – some, including a winged harpy, date to the cathedral's first days. Look for work by the Renaissance masters Boccaccino and Bembo.

The adjoining 111m-tall **Torrazzo** (currently closed for restoration), or bell tower, is connected to the cathedral by a Renaissance loggia, the **Bertazzola**. To the south is the 12th-century **baptistry**.

Across the square is the **Palazzo Comunale** and, to its south, the smaller porticoed **Loggia dei Militi**; both date to the 13th century. The former was, and remains, the town hall; the latter housed the town's militia.

MUSEUMS & VIOLINS

The **Museo Stradivariano** (☎ 0372 46 18 86; Via Palestro 17; adult/child €8/4; ☽ 8.30am-6pm Tue-Sat, 10am-6pm Sun) features items from the Stradivari workshop. Around the corner the **Museo Civico** (☎ 0372 40 77 64; Via Ugolani Dati 4; admission incl in Museo Stradivariano ticket ☽ 8.30am-6pm Tue-Sat, 10am-6pm Sun) houses a small violin collection – the stars of which are two Amatis dating to 1566 and 1658, two Guarneris and a 1715 Stradivari. A local maestro occasionally plays the instruments to keep them in working order.

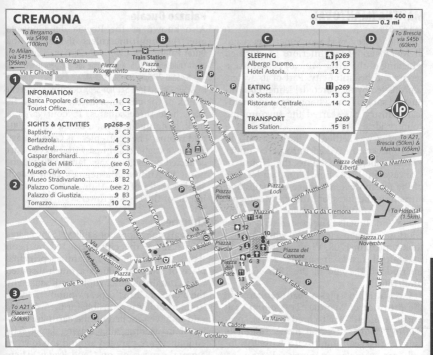

CREMONA

0 — 400 m
0 — 0.2 mi

Gaspar Borchiardi (☎ 0372 3 19 69; Piazza San Antonio) is one of several violin- and bow-making workshops sprinkled in the streets around Piazza del Comune. Cremona has some 90-odd in all; the tourist office has a list.

Festivals & Events
The **Triennale Internazionale degli Strumenti ad Arco** (International String Instrument Expo) is held every third October; the next will be in 2006.

Sleeping & Eating
Albergo Duomo (☎ 0372 3 52 55; fax 0372 45 83 92; Via Gonfalonieri 13; s/d €40/60) Set in the heart of old Cremona and ablaze with wrought-iron flower boxes in spring, Albergo Duomo is among Cremona's most pleasing places to stay. It runs its own pizzeria.

Hotel Astoria (☎ 0372 46 16 16; fax 0372 46 18 10; Via Bordigallo 19; s/d/tr €45/70/95) Down a small lane near Piazza Cavour, rooms brandish three-star mod cons.

Cremona's gifts to Italian cuisine include *bollito* (boiled meats) and *cotechino* (boiled

pork sausage) with polenta. *Mostarda*, often served with *bollito*, is fruit in a sweet mustardy goo.

La Sosta (☎ 0372 45 66 56; Via Sicardo 9; full meals around €25; ❧ Tue-Sun Sep-Jun) Surrounded by violin-makers' workshops, this is a beautiful place to feast on regional delicacies. Its *lumache gratinate* (oven-baked snails) should not be missed.

Ristorante Centrale (☎ 0372 2 87 01; Viccolo Pertusio 4; full meals €25; ❧ Fri-Wed) Centrale is a popular spot, oozing history and charm, where you can try *cotechino*, admire human-size jars of *mostarda* and drool over huge drums of fresh local cheese. It does not accept credit cards.

Open-air market stalls on the Piazza del Pace sell fresh fruit and veg every morning.

Getting There & Away
The city can be reached by train from Milan (€5, one hour, several daily), Mantua (€4.15, one hour, hourly) and Brescia (€3.75, one hour, hourly) or from the south by changing at Piacenza.

LOMBARDY & THE LAKES

MANTUA (MANTOVA)

pop 47, 970

On the shores of Lago Superiore, Lago di Mezzo and Lago Inferiore (a glorified widening of the River Mincio) is Mantua, a serene and beautiful city. Part of its waters is protected by the Parco del Mincio but industrial sprawl from a booming petrochemical industry has scarred the surrounding countryside.

Mantua was settled by the Etruscans in the 10th century BC and prospered under Roman rule. It passed to the House of Gonzaga in 1328, flourishing under one of the foremost Renaissance dynasties and attracting the likes of Andrea Mantegna, Petrarch, Antonio Pisanello, Giulio Romano and Rubens. The golden days of 'La Gloriosa' came to a mean end when Austria took control in 1708. Vienna's troops were in control (aside from the Napoleonic interlude at the end of the 18th century) until 1866.

Over a million pigs a year are reared in the province of Mantua. Try *salumi* (salt pork), pancetta (salt-cured bacon), *prosciutto crudo* (salt-cured ham), *salamella* (small sausages) and risotto with the locally grown *vialone nano* rice. Pasta-wise, *tortelli di zucca* (pumpkin-stuffed square cushions of pasta) is *the* dish, while the sweet-toothed will enjoy *torta sbrisolona* (a buttery cake with almonds). Wines such as red Rubino dei Morenici Mantovani from the hills around Lago di Garda are highly palatable.

Markets stalls selling everything from fruit, flowers, pots, pans and clothes to useless clutter fill Piazze Sordello, Broletto and Erbe and their surrounding streets on Thursday morning.

Information

Banks are scattered throughout the city centre and there's a currency exchange and ATM inside the post office.

Hospital (☎ 0376 20 14 34; Via Albertoni)

Mailboxes etc (☎ 0376 32 53 00; mbe280@libero.it; Via Cavour 5/7; €7.80/hr) Internet access.

Post Office (Piazza Martiri di Belfiore; ⏱ 8.30am-7pm Mon-Sat)

Police Station (☎ 0376 20 51; Piazza Sordello 46)

Tourist Office (☎ 0376 32 82 53; www.aptmantova.it; Italian only; Piazza Mantegna 6; ⏱ 8.30am-12.30pm & 3-6pm Mon-Sat, 9.30am-12.30pm Sun)

Palazzo Ducale

Also known as the Reggia dei Gonzaga after the long-time rulers of Mantua, the **Ducal Palace** (☎ 0376 38 21 50; Piazza Sordello 40; adult/child €6.50/3.25, audioguide for 1/2 people €4/5.50; ⏱ 8.45am-7.15pm Tue-Sun Oct-May, 8.45am-7.15pm Tue-Fri & Sun, 8pm-11pm Sat Jun-Sep) occupies a great chunk of the city's northeastern corner. Its walls hide three squares, 15 courtyards, a park, hanging gardens, a basilica and 500-odd rooms. The centrepiece is **Castello di San Giorgio**, a castle crammed with pieces of art collected by the Gonzaga family. The highpoint is Andrea Mantegna's **Camera degli Sposi**, a series of fine 15th-century frescoes in one of the castle's towers.

Churches

The baroque cupola of **Basilica di Sant' Andrea** looms above the city. Designed by Leon Battista Alberti in 1472, Mantua's principal place of worship houses a much-disputed relic: containers said to hold earth soaked by the blood of Christ's spear wound. The very Roman soldier responsible for the wound is said to have scooped up the earth and buried it in Mantua after leaving Israel. The containers are paraded around the town in a grand procession on Good Friday. There is no dispute, though, about the tomb of the painter Andrea Mantegna, also to be found inside the basilica.

South of the basilica, across 15th-century colonnaded Piazza delle Erbe, is the 11th-century Romanesque **Rotonda di San Lorenzo** (Piazza delle Erbe; admission free; ⏱ 10am-1pm & 2-6pm Mon-Fri, 10am-6pm Sat & Sun), sunk below the level of the square and believed to stand on the site of a Roman temple dedicated to Venus. In the **Palazzo della Ragione**, which runs the length of the square from the Rotonda and was once the seat of secular power in the city, you can see exhibitions of varying interest (usually free).

The **cathedral** (Piazza Sordello 16) pales before the magnificence of the basilica. The facade was erected in the mid-18th century, while the decoration inside was completed by Giulio Romano after a fire in 1545.

On Lago Superiore, 8km from Mantua in Grazie di Curtatone, is the Lombard Gothic-style **Santuario di Santa Maria delle Grazie** (☎ 0376 3 10 02; Grazie di Curtatone), built in 1406 in thanks for the end of the Black Death. Inside are 53 life-size papier-mâché statues.

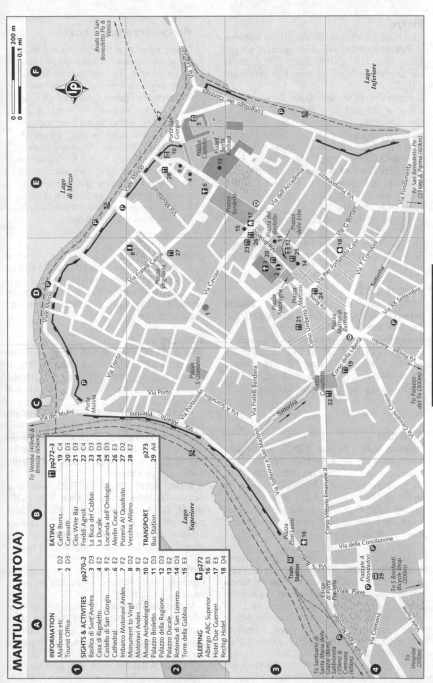

MANTUA (MANTOVA)

LOMBARDY & THE LAKES

Piazze

Past the 13th-century Palazzo della Ragione is **Palazzo Broletto**, which dominates neighbouring Piazza del Broletto. In a niche on the facade is a figure said to represent Virgil.

Enter Piazza Sordello from the south and on your left you have the grand house of the Gonzagas' predecessors, the Bonacolsi clan. Hapless prisoners used to be dangled in a cage from the tower, aptly called the **Torre della Gabbia** (Cage Tower). Behind the cathedral lies **Casa di Rigoletto** (☎ 0376 44 94 62; Piazza Sordello; admission free; 10am-12.30pm & 3-6pm), which Verdi used as a model set for most of his operas.

Opposite, inside what was once a covered market, is a **Museo Archeologico** (☎ 0376 32 92 23; Piazza Castello 5; admission free; 8.30am-6.30pm Tue-Sat). It unearths Mantua's archaeological past.

Palazzo del Te

Mantua's other Gonzaga palace, **Palazzo del Te** (☎ 0376 32 32 66; Viale Te; adult/child €8/5.50; 1-6pm Mon, 9am-6pm Tue-Sun), at the southern edge of the centre, is a grand 16th-century villa built by Giulio Romano. It has many splendid rooms, including the **Camera dei Giganti**, one of the most fantastic and frightening creations of the Renaissance. It also houses a modern art collection and an Egyptian museum.

Activities

Motonavi Andes (☎ 0376 32 28 75; www.motonaviandes.it; Italian only; Via San Giorgio 2) organises 1¼-hour boat tours of the lakes (adult/child €10/8), five-hour excursions to San Benedetto Po (adult/child €18/15) and day trips to Venice (adult/child €68/57). Boats arrive/depart from the Imbarco Motonavi Andes, behind Castello di San Giorgio on Lago di Mezzo's shore.

The tourist office stocks an excellent booklet in English detailing cycling itineraries along the Po River, in the **Parco del Mincio** (☎ 0376 36 26 57; Via Marangoni 36) and around the lakes. One route takes cyclists around Lago Superiore to the Santuario di Santa Maria delle Grazie (see p270). In town, **S Bonfanti** (☎ 0376 22 09 09; Viale Piave 22b; 8.30am-12.30pm & 2.30-7.30pm Mon-Sat) rents bicycles.

For an informative stroll visit the **Parco dell Scienza** (☎ 0376 33 83 37; Viale Mincio), a riverside

THE CHASTE & ROYAL POET

Dryden called Virgil 'the chastest and royalest of poets'. Born 70 years before Christ on his parents' farm just outside Mantua, Virgil, the city's favourite son, was one of ancient Rome's greatest poets. Of the three works he left behind, *The Aeneid* is the most exalted. An epic in the great tradition of the ancient Sumerian myth *Gilgamesh*, and Homer's *Iliad* and *Odyssey*, the tale is a fantastic account of the foundation of Rome, loaded with symbolism and told with unsurpassed virtuosity. The inspiration of countless poets since, Virgil comes to life as Dante's 'sweet master' in the *Divine Comedy*, 14 centuries after Virgil's death.

promenade stretching along the shore of Lago di Mezzo, from Porta San Giorgio to Porta Molina. Information panels and various gadgets along the way illustrate various physical and scientific phenomena in a kid-friendly fashion.

Sleeping

Albergo ABC Superior (☎ 0376 32 33 47; Piazza Don Leoni 25; s/d €66/99) This hotel has a variety of rooms, ranging from pokey to reasonable, and is one of a trio lined up opposite the train station.

Hotel Due Guerrieri (☎ 0376 32 15 33; Piazza Sordello 52; s/d €61.95/98.15;) The gleam might well have rubbed off this ageing hotel's three stars a while back but its impressive location at the feet of Torre del Gabbia makes it a worthy mid-range option.

Rechigi Hotel (☎ 0376 32 07 81; www.rechigi.com; Via Pier Fortunato Calvi 30; s/d/tr €114/176/190;) A stark marble interior provides a stunning backdrop for the Le Corbusier designer chairs and contemporary art displayed at this fabulous four-star, art hotel.

Eating

Open-air cafés abound on Piazze Sordello, Broletto and Erbe.

Locanda dell'Orologio (☎ 0376 36 97 57; Piazza delle Erbe 15; 1st/2nd courses from €6/12) One of a bunch of tasty places to eat outside on this square, Locanda is known for its designer decor and refreshing use of vegetables.

Pizzeria Al Quadrato (☎ 0376 36 88 96; Piazza Virgiliana 49; pizzas €5.50-18, 1st/2nd courses €5.80/8.50;

Tue-Sun) Fill up on fishy delights at this flower-filled terrace pizzeria, overlooking the city park. Fish dishes aside, there's 30-odd pizzas to pick from.

Vecchia Milano (☎ 0376 32 97 20; Piazzo Sordello 26; 1st/2nd courses €6/9.50; Thu-Tue) Dine on Mantua's favourites at this old-world *osteria* (snack bar) – *tortelli di zucca* (pumpkin-stuffed pasta cushions), followed by *stracotto d'asino* (donkey stew) with polenta. Big eaters can invest a few hours in Old Milan's *menu tipico mantuvano* (€25) built solely of Mantuan specialities.

Clos Wine Bar (☎ 0376 36 99 72; www.closwinebar.it; Corte del Sogliari 3; 1st/2nd courses €9/9, cheese/meat platters €9/10; 10am-10pm Tue-Sun) This innovative wine bar-cum-eating space is Mantua's most contemporary choice. Heave open the giant glass door to discover a minimalist interior with a high ceiling and more glass.

La Buca del Cabbai (☎ 0376 36 69 01; Via Cavour 98) and neighbouring **Merlin Cocai** (Via Cavour 98) are two vaulted wine cellars which ooze atmosphere and locals swilling, sniffing and swallowing local vintages. Sensibly, both serve food too – the *risotto alla Mantovana* (rice with pumpkin, mushrooms and shrimps) at La Buca is particularly tasty.

For a contemporary choice away from the tourist zone, try **Caffè Borsa** (☎ 0376 32 60 16; Corsa della Libertà 6; 7am-midnight Mon-Thu, 7-2am Fri-Sun) with its contrasting Kartell and Liberty-style chairs, funky bar and resident DJ who spins tunes at the weekend.

Buy a *torta sbrisolona* and other sweet Mantuan specialities from **Caravatti** (Piazza delle Erbe 18) or **La Ducale** (Via Pier Fortunato Calvi 25), both dating to 1865, and fresh *tortelli di zucca* (€19 per kg) from **Freddi Agnoli** (Piazza Cavallotti 7).

Getting There & Around

From the **bus station** (Piazzale A Mondadori), **APAM** (☎ 0376 32 72 37) operates buses to/from Sabbioneta (see below) and San Benedetto Po (see opposite).

From the **train station** (Piazza Don Leoni), there are direct trains to/from Cremona, Milan and Verona. ARV buses serve Peschiera del Garda on Lago di Garda (see p284).

AROUND MANTUA

Sabbioneta

Some 30km southwest of Mantua, the surreal town of Sabbioneta was created in the 16th

century by Vespasiano Gonzaga Colonna in a failed attempt to build Utopia. A city *'misura d'uomo'* ('made to man's measure') was the idea.

Within the heavily restored star-shaped walls are four 16th-century monuments to visit. Of these, the **Teatro all'Antica** (Antique Theatre; adult/child €2.60/1.20; 10am-1pm & 2.30-5.30pm), constructed 1588–90, with statues of Olympic gods topping a loggia held up by Corinthian pillars, and the 90m-long **Galeria degli Antichi** (Gallery of the Ancients; adult/child €2.60/1.20; 10am-1pm & 2.30-5.30pm), constructed 1583–84, with its frescoed walls and painted wood ceiling, are the most interesting. The duke of Sabbioneta resided in **Palazzo Giardino** (Garden Palace; adult/child €2.60/1.20; 10am-1pm & 2.30-5.30pm), built 1578–88 and ruled the dukedom from the 1554 **Palazzo Ducale** (Ducal Palace; adult/child €2.60/1.20; 10am-1pm & 2.30-5.30pm).

Sabbioneta's **ticket office** (☎ 0375 22 10 44; comune.sabbioneta@unh.net; Piazza d'Armi 1; 10am-1pm & 2-5.30pm), inside Palazzo Giardino, sells tickets covering admission to all four monuments (adult/child €7.20/3.10) and doles out maps and general information on the town.

The **tourist office** (☎ 0375 5 20 39; www.sabbioneta.org, Italian only; Via Vespasiano Gonzaga 27; 10am-12.30pm & 2.30-5.30pm) has information on other Sabbioneta sights to see, including a 19th-century **synagogue** (Via Bernardino Campi 1; adult/child €2/1.50; 10am-noon & 2.30-5.30pm Sat & Sun); and the **Museo A Passo d'Uomo** (☎ 0375 22 02 99; adult/child €3/1.50; 9.30am-12.30pm & 2.30-5pm Tue-Fri, 9.30am-12.30pm & 2.30-6pm Sat & Sun), which includes a treasury (with a Golden Fleece found in the tomb of Vespasiano Gonzaga).

Sabbioneta's red-brick city walls shelter three restaurants and two hotels, including the **Albergo Ristorante Al Duca** (☎ 0375 5 24 74; al.duca@tin.it; Via della Stamperia 18; s/d/tr rooms €38/60/75), where a knight in shining armour (motionless) greets the guests. Rooms are clad in three-star comforts while the dishes cooked up in the restaurant are typically Mantuan in taste – think rice, pike and pumpkin.

APAM (☎ 0376 23 03 46) buses link Sabbioneta with Mantua (€5.10, 50 minutes, up to five daily).

San Benedetto Po

This Benedictine **abbey** (☎ 0376 62 30 36; Piazza Matteotti; admission free; 2.30-6pm Mon-Fri) in this small Po valley town, 21km southeast of Mantua, was founded in 1007. Little remains

LOMBARDY & THE LAKES

of the original buildings, although Chiesa di Santa Maria still sports a 12th-century mosaic. The star attraction is the Correggio fresco discovered in the refectory in 1984.

There are buses to the town from Mantua (€2.10, 35 minutes, around 10 daily).

THE LAKES

Where the Lombard plains rise into the Alps, northern Italy is pocked by a series of lakes – long-time playground for the Milanese rich and tourists from all over northern Europe.

LAGO MAGGIORE

A captivating lake, Maggiore (also known as Lago Verbano) is stunning in parts, although its shores are flatter and less spectacular than its pre-Alpine counterparts. Fed principally by the Rivers Ticino and Tresa, this lovely lake is about 65km long and lures stifling crowds in July and August. Stresa is the main lakeside town.

Getting There & Around

Buses leave from the waterfront at Stresa for destinations around the lake and elsewhere, including Milan, Novara and Lago d'Orta. The daily Verbania Intra-Milan bus service operated by **SAF** (☎ 0323 40 15 26; www .safduemila.com) links Stresa with Arona (€1.75, 20 minutes), Verbania Pallanza (€1.75, 20 minutes), Verbania Intra (€1.75, 25 minutes) and Milan (€4.85, 1½ hours).

Stresa – the main town on the lake – sits on the Domodossola–Milan train line and is well-served by hourly trains from both Milan (€4.23, one hour) and Domodossola (€2.65, 30 minutes).

Ferries and hydrofoils around the lake are operated by **Navigazione Lago Maggiore** (☎ 0323 3 03 93, ☎ 800 55 18 01; www.navigazionelaghi.it, Italian only), which has its main ticket office and landing stage next to the Stresa **tourist office** (Piazza Marconi 14-16). Boats connect Stresa with Arona (adult/child return €8/4), Angera (€8/ 4), Baveno (€4.80/4) and Pallanza (€6.80/ 3.40). Visiting a single island costs €4.80/4 adult/child return. Various one-day pass are also available – a ticket covering Isola dei Pescatori, Isola Bella and Baveno costs €6/3 per adult/child, a ticket covering the three Borromean islands, Pallanza and Baveno is €9/5 per adult/child, and a ticket covering

the latter plus the Villa Taranto is €10/5 per adult/child. More expensive one-day passes include admission to the various villas too. Services are reduced in autumn and winter.

The only car ferry connecting the western and eastern shores for motorists sails between Verbania Intra (the Swiss end of Verbania) and Laveno. Ferries run every 20 minutes; and one-way transport costs €4 for a small car and driver or €2.90 for a bicycle and cyclist.

A good trip is the circular excursion from Stresa to Domodossola by train, from where you get a charming little train to Locarno (Switzerland – take your passports) and a ferry back from Locarno to Stresa. The 'Lago Maggiore Express' package deal costs €27/13.50 per adult/child; Navigazione Lago Maggiore sells tickets.

Stresa

pop 4885 \ elevation 205m

Extremely popular with Germans and Brits, Stresa, 80km northwest of Milan on the lake's western shore, is like one great English tearoom – prim and not unattractive but staid and insipid. It's commonly touted as a base for visiting the Borromean Islands (see p275), although they can easily be reached from other resorts around the lake too.

Hemingway was among the rash of writers to seek inspiration on Maggiore's shores. He first set foot in Stresa in 1918 to convalesce from a war wound, and part of one of his novels, *A Farewell to Arms*, is set here.

INFORMATION

Banks and ATMs abound on Corso Italia the road running along Stresa's waterfront. **Post Office** (Via Anna Bolongaro 44; ☺ 8.30am-7pm Mon-Fri, 8.30am-1pm Sat)
Tourist Office (☎ 0323 13 08; proloco.stresa@libero .it; Piazza Marconi 16; ☺ 10am-12.30pm & 3-6.30pm Mar-Oct, 10am-12.30pm & 3-6.30pm Mon-Fri, 10am-12.30pm Sat Nov-Feb)

SIGHTS & ACTIVITIES

Apart from visiting the Borromean Islands (see p275), you can ride the **Funivia Stresa Mottarone** (☎ 0323 3 02 95; Piazzale della Funivia; adult return Alpino/Mottarone €6.50/11.50; ☺ departure every 40 minutes 9.20am-5pm) to the top of Monte Mottarone (elevation 1491m). The cable car takes 40 minutes to reach the top. At the Alpino mid-station (803m), 700 Alpine species flourish in the **Giardino Botanico Alpinia** (☎ 0323 3 02 95; adult/child €1.50/1.20; ☼ 9.30am-6pm Tue-Sun Apr–mid-Oct), a botanical garden dating to 1934.

The mountain itself offers good **biking** trails and **walking** opportunities. **Mountain bikes** (☎ 0323 3 03 99, ☎ 338 839 56 92; www.bicico.it) can be rented from the lower Stresa cable-car station. Rates include a helmet and road book detailing a 25km panoramic descent (two to three hours) from the top of Mottarone back to Stresa. A one-way trip with bike on the cable car to Alpino/Mottarone costs €5.50/9.

Walkers should ask at the cable-car station for a copy of *Trekking on the Slopes of Mont Mottarone*, a free brochure compiled by the Club Alpino Italiano (CAI), which outlines a two-hour walk from Stresa to the Alpine garden and a four-hour walk to the top of Mottarone. Walks further afield are mapped out in the free multilingual *Nature Hikes* brochure, available at tourist offices.

Most winters, skiers and boarders can cruise down the gentle slopes of Mottarone from late December to early March. **Skiing** is limited to five green and two blue slopes. Gear can be hired from the station at the top of Mottarone. A one-day ski pass costs €7.

Parco Zoologico di Villa Pallavicino (☎ 0323 3 24 07; adult/child €6/4.50; ☼ 9am-6pm Mar-Nov), at Stresa's southern end, is a kid-friendly park where animals roam relatively freely.

SLEEPING & EATING
There are 40 camp grounds up and down the lake's western shore; the tourist office has a list.

Hotel Luina (☎ 0323 3 02 85; luinastresa@yahoo.it; Via Garibaldi 21; s/d €35/55) In the heart of Stresa's cobbled streets, Luina is a simple but friendly place with quiet rooms and a restaurant. Some have a lake view.

Hotel Elena (☎ 0323 3 10 43; www.hotelelena.com; Piazza Cadorna; d €80) Adjoining a café, old-fashioned Hotel Elena is slap-bang on Stresa's pedestrian central square. Rooms are small but well kept and each has a balcony overlooking the square.

Grand Hotel des Iles Borromees (☎ 0323 93 89 38; www.borromees.it; Corso Umberto I; d from €295; Ⓟ ☼ 🖳 🏊) Rockefeller, Bernard Shaw, Hemingway, Clark Gable and Mussolini are among the illustrious guests to have stayed at Stresa's most fabulous hotel, built

in 1861 and furnished precisely as it would have been in the belle époque.

Osteria degli Amici (☎ 0323 3 04 53; Via Anna Maria Bolongaro 33; 1st/2nd courses from €5.20/9.50, pizzas €3.70-7.80) Dine under vines on one of Stresa's most delightful terraces. Expect to queue as it's always packed.

Borromean Islands (Isole Borromee)
The Borromean Islands can be reached from various points around the lake but Stresa and Baveno are the best departure points. The four islands – Bella, Madre, Pescatori (or Superiore) and San Giovanni – form the lake's most beautiful corner. San Giovanni is off-limits to tourists.

Bella was named after Charles III's wife, the *bella* (beautiful) Isabella, in the 17th century and has courted a number of famous holiday-makers – Wagner, Stendhal, Byron and Goethe among them. **Palazzo Borromeo** (☎ 0323 3 05 56; www.borromeoturismo.it, Italian only; adult/child €8.50/4; ☼ 9am-5.30pm mid-Mar-Sep, 9am-5pm Oct) is its main draw card. Built in the 17th century for the Borromeo family, the sumptuous palace contains works by Giovanni Tiepolo and Anthony Van Dyck as well as Flemish tapestries and sculptures by Canova. Mussolini tried to stave off WWII here at the Conference of Stresa in April 1935. The fossilised boat displayed behind glass in one of the palace grottoes is 3000 years old. The actual grottoes – studded with pebbles from the lake bed – took 25 years to complete and were used by the Borromeo family as their cool (literally) hang-out. What's left of the island (little) swarms with stalls selling ice cream, pizza slices and tacky island souvenirs.

Madre provides fertile ground for Italy's tallest palm trees. The entire island is taken up by the fabulous, 16th- to 18th-century **Palazzo Madre** (☎ 0323 3 12 61; adult/child €8/4; ☼ 9am-5.30pm Apr-Sep, 9am-5pm Oct) and its lavish peacock-filled gardens which are even more lavish than those of Palazzo Borromeo. Period furnishings cram the palace interior; highlights include Countess Borromeo's doll collection, a neoclassical theatre designed by a scenographer from Milan's La Scala and smaller theatre starring hell on centre stage. A combined ticket covering admission to the Borromeo and Madre palaces costs €12/7 per adult/child.

LOMBARDY & THE LAKES

Beyond an 11th-century apse and a 16th-century fresco in the **Chiesa di San Vittore**, there are no real sights to see on **Isola dei Pescatori**, making it most visitors' port of call for lunch. Despite the many places to eat, there are no snack stalls and the tiny island retains some of its original fishing-village atmosphere. Count on eating (and paying) much the same in whichever waterfront restaurant you plump for – grilled fish 'fresh from the lake' for around €14. If you want to stay on the island the romantic **Albergo Verbano** (☎ 0323 3 04 08; www.hotelverbano.it; s/d/tr €100/140/160; Mar-Dec) will impress your sweetheart.

Western Shore

It was the once-fortified Rocca di Arona in **Arona** (population 15,900), 20km south of Stresa that French novelist Stendhal vividly depicted in prose after witnessing its demolition in 1800. Ruins of the 9th-century fortress, an early Romanesque chapel and a couple of storehouses are all that remain in the vast parkland today (off-limits to visitors). Below the castle, an attractive waterfront unfolds with an appealing line-up of hip and trendy cafés (see opposite) to eat and drink at – and enjoy an eagle-eyed view of the magnificent Rocca di Angera across the water. The **tourist office** (☎ 0322 24 36 01; Piazzale Duca d'Aosta; 9am-12.30pm & 3-6pm Mon-Fri, 9am-12.30pm Sat) is opposite the train and bus stations. Rocca di Angera is a medieval castle whose magnificent walls today shelter the 12-room **Museo della Bambola** (Dolls Museum; ☎ 0331 93 13 00; adult/child €6.50/4; 9.30am-12.30pm & 2-6pm Apr-Sep, 9.30am-12.30pm & 2pm-5pm Oct) today.

Heading towards Switzerland, **Verbania** (population 30,300), the biggest town on the lake, offers plenty of accommodation in most classes. Split into three districts, it is Verbania Intra – the Swiss end with an attractive old town and car ferry port to cross the lake – and Verbania Pallanza – the middle chunk – that are of the most interest. In Pallanza the green-fingered can stroll the grounds of the late-19th-century **Villa Taranto** (☎ 0323 40 45 55; www.villataranto.it; adult/child €7/5; 8.30am-7.30pm mid-Mar-Oct). In 1931 royal archer and Scottish captain Neil McEacharn bought the villa from the Savoy family and planted some 20,000 species over 30 years, creating what are today considered to be among Europe's finest botanical gardens.

Boats stop at Pallanza and at the landing stage in front of the villa. There is a **tourist office** (9am-12.30pm & 2-5.30pm Fri-Sun) at the car ferry terminal and on the waterfront in **Verbania Pallanza** (☎ 0323 50 32 49; Corso Zanitello 6-8; 9am-12.30pm & 3-6pm Mon-Sat, 9am-12.30pm Sun).

Cannero Riviera (population 1200) is a tranquil lakeside village. Just off the coast lie some tiny islets that, before being taken over by the Borromeo family in the 15th century, served as a den for thieves who operated in the area during the 12th century. See the boxed text, p277, for a memorable dining venue.

More interesting is **Cannobio** (pop 5100), 5km short of the Swiss border. The tiny toy town's spotless cobblestone streets retain something of a village flavour. It has an active sailing and surfing school, **Tomaso Surf & Sail** (☎ 0323 7 22 14; www.tomaso.com) next to a patch of gritty beach at the village's northern end, and mountain bikes can be hired per hour/day €3/11 from **Cicli Prezan** (Viale Vittorio Veneto 9), opposite the **tourist office** (☎ /fax 0323 7 12 12; Viale Vittorio Veneto 4; 9am-noon & 4.30-7pm Mon-Fri, 9am-noon Sat & Sun).

SLEEPING & EATING

Ostello Verbania (☎ 0323 50 16 48; Via alle Rose 7, Verbania; dm/d B&B €13/32; reception 7am-11am & 3.30-11.30pm Mar-Oct & Christmas) Backpackers should make a beeline for Verbania's only hostel. Rates include sheet hire.

Hotel Pironi (☎ 0323 7 21 84; hotel.pironi@cannobio .net; Via Marconi 35, Cannobio; s/d from €70/100) Languishing in a 15th-century *palazzo* amid Cannobio's cobbled maze, this is one of several charming hotels in Cannobio.

Ostello del Castello (☎ 0323 51 65 79; Piazza Castello 9, Verbania Intra; 1st courses €6.50, 2nd courses €12-18; Mon-Sat) With its flower-topped pergola terrace overlooking a quaint old-town square, Ostello del Castello's location – 20m from the ferry port – is hard to beat. Wine is plentiful and dishes are rustic and regional – the mixed plate of meat melts in your mouth, as does the salmon trout fillet dressed in asparagus cream.

La Latteria (☎ 0348 371 24 06; Piazza San Rocco 20, Verbania Intra; 1st courses €6.50, 2nd courses €12-18; Tue-Sat) Around the corner next to the Chiesa San Vittore is Verbania Intra's other tasty find – a cow-inspired trattoria overlooking a quite traffic-free square.

Arona has a trio of trendy waterfront places: mellow **Café de la Sera** (☎ 0322 24 15 67;

THE AUTHOR'S CHOICE

Cà Bianca (☎ 0323 78 80 38; Via Casali Cà Bianca 1, Cannero; 1st/2nd courses €8/12, menus from €25; ⊗ Thu-Tue) Take an old stone house perched on a rock close to the water, a rambling garden with sweeping lake views, and a couple of ruined 15th-century castles built on a twin set of islets in the middle of a lake and what do you have – a fantastically atmospheric and peaceful place to eat. Pasta is strictly *in casa* (homemade) and the *gnocchi al radicchio e gorgonzola* (gnocchi with chicory and gorgonzola cheese) is a real mouth-melter. Fish dishes bulk out the choice of 2nd courses, while afternoon tea – with homemade cakes – is served on the lakeside terrace between 2.30pm and 6pm. Look for the house on the water, 1km north of Cannero Riviera at foot of Monte Carza.

Lungo Lago Marconi 85; 1st/2nd courses €6.50/7) which offers a simple choice of four dishes for each course; **Ul Boc** (☎ 0322 4 46 58; Lungo Lago Marconi 71; ⊗ 8am-3am Thu-Tue) with a dazzling Art Deco–inspired decor; and **Gym Café** (☎ 0322 24 36 84; Lungo Lago Marconi 47) for those who prefer a 1950s US diner feel.

LAGO D'ORTA

Only 15km long and about 2.5km wide, Lago d'Orta is actually in the Piedmont region and is separated from its more celebrated eastern neighbour, Lago Maggiore, by Monte Mottarone. Orta is surrounded by lush woodlands and, unlike the larger lakes, the area does not swarm with visitors 365 days a year.

The main town on the lake is **Orta San Giulio** (population 1133; elevation 293m), an idyllic spot with no real sights but lots of cobbled lanes to stroll and medieval squares to sip coffee on. From the main waterfront square, regular launches make the short trip to the **Isola San Giulio**, named after a Greek evangelist who earned his saintly status by ridding the island of an assortment of snakes and monsters late in the 4th century. The island, dubbed the 'island of silence', is dominated by the 12th-century **Basilica di San Giulio**, from where a single footpath – La Via del Silenzio (The Way of Silence) – encircles the island. There is one museum to see, the **Museo del Regio Esercito Italiano** (☎ 0322 90 52 24; museo_regio_esercito@libero.it; adult/child €5/2.60;

⊗ 9.30am-6pm), dedicated to military history from 1861 to 1945, and one pocket-size pebble beach to speak of.

Sacro Monte, behind Orta San Giulio, is dotted with a series of 20 small chapels erected to St Francis of Assisi over a 200-year period from 1591. It makes for a pleasant stroll above the town. Other lakeside spots, accessible by boat from Orta San Giulio, include **Omegna**, popular for its Thursday market; and **Pella**, a village with a factory that churns out taps and valves on the lake's western shore. The small village of **Armeno**, at the foot of Monte Mottarone, is worth visiting, not least for its umbrella museum. From here, the narrow road that perilously wiggles to the mountain peak (and down to Stresa on Lago Maggiore) makes for a splendid drive.

SLEEPING & EATING

Piccolo Hotel Olina (☎ 0322 90 56 56; Via Olina 40; d with bath/spa €67.15/72.30, 2-/4-person attic €72.30/108.45) Rooms here are cosy but charming. There are self-catering apartments to rent too, plus a tasty restaurant.

Hotel San Rocco (☎ 0322 91 19 77; www.hotel sanrocco.it; Via Gippini 11; s/d from €102.50/159; P ⊗ ☐ ☒) Giuseppine nuns lived a life of seclusion at this 17th-century convent until 1960, when it was transformed into a luxurious place to stay. Moor your motorboat outside and cruise into this pool-filled oasis of luxury.

Villa Crespi (☎ 0322 91 19 02; www.slh.com/crespi; s/d from €115/165; P ⊗ ☐ ☒) Secular decadence was lived out to the full by 19th-century Lombard industrialist Benigno Crespi who made a fortune trading cotton – and had this oriental extravaganza built in 1879. Its lavish gardens and opulent Moorish interior are breathtaking.

GETTING THERE & AWAY

Orta Miasino train station, a short walk from the centre of Orta San Giulio, is just off the Novara–Domodossola train line.

Navigazione Lago d'Orta (☎ 0322 84 48 62) runs boats to numerous other lakeside spots from its landing stage on Piazza Motta to Isola San Giulio (single/return €1.50/2), Omegna (€3.50/5) and Pella (€2/3.50). Island boats simply leave when there are sufficient passengers to warrant the five-minute crossing.

LAGO DI COMO

Marie Henri Beyle first set foot on the shores of Lake Como (also known as Lago Lario) as a 17-year-old conscript under Napoleon. Years later, as Stendhal, he wrote in *La Chartreuse de Parme* that the blue-green waters of the lake and grandeur of the Alps made it the most beautiful place in the world. Pliny the Elder and Pliny the Younger were born here but are not known to have gushed about the area to the same degree as Stendhal. Another of Como's famous sons, Alessandro Volta, born in 1745, came up with the battery.

This immense body of water, which sprawls in an upside down 'Y' shape at the foot of the Rhaetian Alps, is enchantingly beautiful. **Isola Comacina**, the lake's sole island, is where Lombard kings took refuge from invaders. Bathers wanting to wash the city dust right out of their hair should note that Lago di Como's waters are murky and swimming is not advised.

Getting There & Around

Como-based **Società Pubblica Trasporti** (SPT; ☎ 031 24 72 47; www.sptcomo.it, Italian only) operates regular buses around the lake. Key routes include Como–Colico (1½ hours, three to five daily), via all the villages on the western shore mentioned in this section (some with a change of bus in Menaggio); Menaggio–Lugano (one hour, hourly), via Lago di Piano; Como–Bellagio (one hour, hourly); and Como–Erba–Lecco (one hour, almost hourly). Further afield there are buses to/from Como and Bergamo (€5, 2¼ hours, around six daily); Como and Malpensa airport (€11, one hour, two to six daily); and Menaggio and Malpensa airport (€13, two hours, one or two daily). Updated schedules are online.

Como's main train station (listed as Como San Giovanni on train timetables) is the lake's main point of arrival/departure. Trains from Milan's Stazione Centrale (€2.85, one hour, at least hourly) stop here and continue to many Western European cities. Trains from Milan's Stazione Nord (€2.85, one hour, hourly) use Como's lakeside Stazione FNM (listed on timetables as Como Nord Lago). From Lecco local trains run the length of the less-popular eastern shore.

Ferries operated by Como-based **Navigazione Lago di Como** (☎ 031 57 92 11, ☎ 800 55 18 01; www.navigazionelaghi.it; Piazza Cavour) criss-cross the lake year-round. Hydrofoils only sail April to September. Single fares range from €1.30/2 (Como–Cernobbio by ferry/hydrofoil) to €7.70 (Como–Lecco by ferry). A whole host of other tickets are available, including those for day cruises with lunch and those which include admission to various lakeside villas.

Motorists can cross the lake with a car ferry on the western shore at Cadenabbia and on the eastern shore at Varenna. There are also limited car ferries from Bellagio to Cadenabbia, Menaggio and Varenna. Transporting a small car/bicycle one way on any one crossing costs €5.10/3.20.

Como

pop 82,890 \ elevation 202m

Como, 50km north of Milan, is the main access town to the lake and sits at the foot of the 146 sq km body of water. On the last Saturday of the month its streets are filled with a huge antique market. Otherwise, the town has few attractions in its own right but makes a good base for exploring the fairy-tale lakeside villages.

INFORMATION

Banca d'Italia (Via Boldoni 15) Currency exchange and ATM.
Coreweb (Via Malta 23; €6/hr; ⏰ 9am-noon & 2-7pm Mon-Fri)
CTS Travel Agency (☎ 031 26 68 60; Via Vitani 35)
Ospedale Sant'Anna (☎ 031 58 51 11; Via Napoleona 60) Hospital.
Police Station (☎ 031 31 71; Viale Roosevelt 7)
Post Office (Via T Gallio 6; ⏰ 8.30am-7pm Mon-Sat) Also has currency exchange.
Branch Post Office (Via Vittorio Emanuele II 99; ⏰ 8.30am-12.30pm Mon-Sat)
Tourist Office (☎ 031 330 01 11; www.lakecomo.org; Piazza Cavour 17; ⏰ 9am-1pm & 2.30-6pm Mon-Sat)
Tourist Kiosk (☎ 031 26 42 15; Piazza del Duomo; ⏰ 10am-12.30pm & 2.30-6pm Mon-Fri, 10am-6pm Sat & Sun)

SIGHTS & ACTIVITIES

From Piazza Cavour, the main square overlooking the water, walk south along arcaded Via Caio Plinio to Como's marble-faced **cathedral** (Piazza del Duomo), built from the 14th to the 18th centuries. Elements of baroque, Gothic, Romanesque and Renaissance styles are crowned with a high octagonal dome. Next to it the polychromatic **town hall** was altered in 1435 to make way for its sacred neighbour. Continue south to get to the

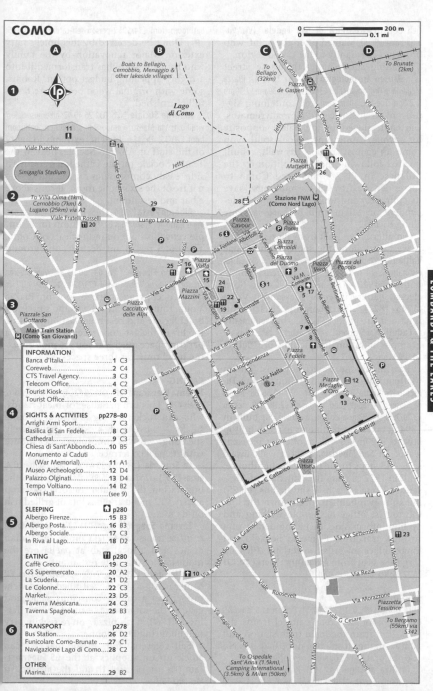

COMO

| 0 | 200 m |
| 0 | 0.1 mi |

Boats to Bellagio,
Cernobbio, Menaggio &
other lakeside villages

To
Bellagio
(32km)

To Brunate
(2km)

Lago
di Como

Viale Puecher

Sinigaglia Stadium

To Villa Olma (1km),
Cernobbio (7km) &
Lugano (25km) via A2

Viale Fratelli Rosselli

Lungo Lario Trento

Piazzale San
Gottardo

Main Train Station
(Como San Giovanni)

Piazza
de Gasperi

Piazza
Matteotti

Lungo Lario Trieste
Stazione FNM
(Como Nord Lago)

Piazza
Cavour

Piazza
Roma

Piazza
Grimoldi

Piazza
del Duomo

Piazza
Verdi

Piazza del
Popolo

Piazza
Volta

Piazza
Mazzini

Piazza
Cacciatori
delle Alpi

Piazza
S Fedele

Piazza
Medaglie
d'Oro

Piazza
Vittoria

Piazzetta
Tessitrice

To Bergamo
(55km) via
S342

To Ospedale
Sant'Anna (1.5km),
Camping International
(3.5km) & Milan (50km)

LOMBARDY & THE LAKES

6th-century **Basilica di San Fedele** (Via Vittoria Emanuele II), named after the saint who brought Christianity to the Como region.

Heading south along the same street is a **Museo Archeologico** (☎ 031 27 13 43; Piazza Medaglie d'Oro; adult/child €3/free; ⏰ 9.30am-12.30pm & 2-5pm Tue-Sat, 10am-1pm Sun), containing significant prehistoric and Roman remains. Garibaldi stayed in the palace opposite for a while. Continuing a block south, you come up against Como's **city walls**, rebuilt in 1162 following their demolition by the Milanese in 1127 who forced Como to surrender, destroy all its buildings (save its churches) and walls, and become a dependent on Milan until Barbarossa came along in 1152.

An alternative walk from Piazza Cavour is westward along the shore to the **Tempo Voltiano** (☎ 031 57 47 05; Viale Marconi; closed for restoration), a lakeside neoclassical temple built in 1927. The relics of Como-born electric battery inventor Alessandro Volta (1745–1827), after whom the electric unit is named, are inside. The nearby **Monumento ai Caduti** (War Memorial; Viale Puecher 9) is a classic example of rationalist architecture dating to 1931.

East along the waterfront, past Piazza Matteotti and the train station, is the **Funicoloare Como-Brunate** (☎ 031 30 36 08; Piazza de Gasperi 4; adult/child one way €2.10/1.40, return €3.70/2.30; ⏰ 6am-midnight), a cable car built in 1894. It takes seven minutes to reach hilltop **Brunate** (720m), a village offering pleasant walks. In **San Maurizio**, a short walk away, scale 143 steps to the top of the lighthouse, built in 1927 to mark the centenary of Alessandro Volta's death. A shuttle bus (€0.75) links the two hamlets. Back down the hill, the tourist office has ample walking and cycling information, including details of a two-day trail from Como to Bellagio and longer hikes towards Switzerland. Pick up forgotten gear from **Arrighi Armi Sport** (☎ 031 26 22 95; Via Indipendenza 20).

SLEEPING

Villa Olmo (☎ 031 57 38 00; Via Bellinzona 6; dm B&B €12.50; ⏰ Mar-Nov) Como's hostel fronts the lake, 1km from the main train station and 20m from the closest bus stop. Take bus No 1, 6, 11 or 14. HI cards are obligatory.

In Riva al Lago (☎ 031 30 23 33; www.inrivaallago.com; Piazza Matteotti; s/d from €24/34, with bathroom from €34/50, 2-person self-catering flats €65; Ⓟ) Don't be deceived by this hotel's tatty exterior. Major renovation by the family who runs the hotel has transformed it into a highly appealing budget option. Rooms, some with original wood beams, are tastefully furnished.

Albergo Sociale (☎ 031 26 40 42; albergosociale@virgilio.it; Via Maestri Comacini 8; s/d without bathroom from €20/35; ⏰ Sep-Jul) The extreme joviality of the staff at Albergo Sociale, next to the Teatro Sociale on the cathedral's southern side, easily compensates for the unexciting nature of the six simple rooms it runs above a bar and restaurant.

Albergo Posta (☎ 031 26 60 12; www.hotelposta.net; Via G Garibaldi 2; s/d from €42/52) Plump for a simple yet stylish option in the heart of Como. The hotel restaurant occupies the ground floor.

Albergo Firenze (☎ 031 30 03 33; www.albergofirenze.it; Piazza Volta 16; s/d €73/120; ✂ Ⓟ) This hotel, occupying a prime spot on Piazza Volta, touts what must be Como's prettiest hotel facade and best breakfast buffet. Ride the lift to the 1st-floor reception and bag a parking space quickly if you are motoring – the hotel only has three spaces!

EATING

Taverna Messicana (☎ 031 26 62 04; Piazza Mazzini 6; meals €20) This is a paradise for meat fiends, who can tuck into big and juicy T-bone steaks – alive and kicking (figuratively speaking) – in this atmospheric steakhouse with its packed terrace.

La Scuderia (☎ 031 30 43 22; Piazza Matteotti 4; pizzas €5-9, 1st/2nd courses €5/9) Tucked behind the bus station, this popular trattoria cooks up a tasty €12 menu and has lots of grilled fish on its menu.

Taverna Spagnola (☎ 031 27 24 60; Via Grassi 8; 1st/2nd courses from €6/12) Competent Italian dishes and a local stab at paella are the mainstays of this little restaurant.

Caffè Greco (☎ 031 27 10 74; Piazza Mazzini 13) You can bite into a well-filled sandwich, munch on a calorie-conscious salad and gaze at the impressive beamed ceiling dating to 1760. If it's pizza you're seeking, try neighbouring Le Colonne.

Self-caterers and picnic-makers can stock up on supplies at the **GS Supermercato** (Via Fratelini Rosselli 11) and the **market** (Via Mentana 15).

LOMBARDY & THE LAKES

Western Shore

Lago di Como's western shore stretches a handsome 80km from Como (south) to Sorico (north), from where you can continue north into Switzerland or east into Trentino-Alto Adige (see p290). The wiggly S340 snakes along Como's shore for most of the way, making driving or cycling along this route an invigorating experience.

In **Cernobbio** art exhibitions can be viewed in the **Villa Bernasconi** (☎ 031 334 72 09; Via Regina 7) and the Mannerist 19th-century **Villa Erba** (☎ 031 34 91; www.villaerba.it, Italian only; Largo Luchino Visconti). Down by the water, thrill seekers can rent a waterscooter/motorboat (10/30/60 minutes €18/50/99), a *pedalo*/rowing boat (€11 an hour) or a bicycle (hour/day €3.50/ 15) from **Non Solo Barche di Riccardo** (☎ 329 219 68 37; 9am-1pm & 3-7pm).

From Cernobbio a lower lakeside road (Via Regina Vecchia) skirts the lake shore, past a fabulous row of 19th-century villas around **Moltrasio** and a couple of charming lunch-time spots on Laglio's north fringe. A few kilometres further north in **Argegno**, venture into the mountains with the **Funivia Argegno-Pigra** (single/return €1.88/2.95, single with bicycle €2.90; 8am-noon & 2-6pm Apr, Jun & Sep, 8am-noon & 2-7pm Jul & Aug, 8am-noon & 2-5pm Oct-Mar). The cable car makes the five-minute climb to the village of Pigra (elevation 860m) every 30 minutes.

Scenes from *Stars Wars Episode II* were filmed at **Villa del Balbianello** (☎ 0344 5 61 10; adult/child €5/2.50; gardens 10am-12.30pm & 3.30-6.30pm Tue, Thu & Fri, 10am-6pm Sat & Sun Apr-Oct), a villa built by Cardinal Angelo Durini in **Lenno** in 1787. Bizarrely, visitors are only allowed to walk the 1km from the Lenno landing stage to the estate on Tuesday and at weekends; other days, you have to take a **taxi boat** (☎ 333 410 38 54; www.taxiboat.net) from Lenno.

In **Tremezzo** (population 1300), pergolas knitted from orange trees and some of Europe's finest rhododendrons, azaleas and camellias (April to May) bloom in the botanical gardens of 17th-century **Villa Carlotta** (☎ 0344 4 04 05; Riva Garibaldi; adult/child €6.50/free; 9am-6pm Apr-Sep, 9-11.30am & 2-4.30pm Mar & Nov). The villa, strung with paintings and tapestries, takes its name from the Prussian princess who was given the place as a wedding present by her mother in 1847. The Tremezzo **tourist office** (☎ 0344 4 04 93; infotremezzo@tiscalinet.it; Via Statale Regina; 9am-noon & 3.30-6.30pm Wed-Mon Apr-Oct) adjoins the boat jetty.

Motorists can cross the lake by car ferry in Cadenabbia, 3km south of **Menaggio** (population 3200). A popular centre for walking, the **tourist office** (☎ 0344 3 29 24; www.menaggio.com; Piazza Garibaldi; 9am-noon & 3-6pm Mon-Sat) sells several excellent brochures on walking and biking. The hostel (see following) rents bikes and arranges treks around Lago di Piano in the Val Menaggio, a remote valley connecting Lake Como with Lake Lugano in Switzerland. The small lake is protected by the **Riserva Naturale Lago di Piano.** Three marked nature trails, 4km to 5.3km long, encircle the lake and the **visitors centre** (☎ 0344 7 49 61; riservalagopiano@yacc.it; Via Statale 117, Piano di Porlezza; 9am-noon Mon, Tue & Sat, 2-4pm Wed May-Oct), on the lake's northern shore, rents mountain bikes (€5/hour) and rowing boats (€10/hour) and arranges guided visits on foot (€2.50) and on horseback (€30).

A glimpse of Como's silky past – mulberry trees were grown in the area (to feed silk worms) from 1554 – can be enjoyed at the **Museo della Barca Lariana** (2.30-5.30pm Sat, 10.30am-12.30pm & 2.30-5.30pm Sun Easter-Jun & mid–Sep-Nov, 2.30-5.30pm Fri-Wed Jul–mid-Sep), a boat museum inside a 19th-century silk-weaving mill in **Pianello del Lario**, 15km north of Menaggio.

North of here plush villas and manicured gardens turn into rugged terrain and real working mountain communities.

SLEEPING

The lake offers literally hundreds of accommodation possibilities. Stand-outs (from south to north) are listed.

Albergo Centrale (☎ 031 51 14 11; www.albergo-centrale.com; Via Regina 39, Cernobbio; s/d/tr €50/85/110;) A typical wooden-shuttered place, this pretty little choice away from the water on Cernobbio's main street has a flowery terrace, a red-brick cellar, tavern serving pizzas baked in a wood-fired oven and 20 mid-range rooms warranting zero complaints. High-season prices jump around €30.

Villa d'Este (☎ 031 34 81; www.villadeste.it; Via Regina 40, Cernobbio; s/d from €275/450;) This splendid 120-year-old villa, Lago di Como's most famous hotel, is ideal for honeymooners with a bottomless bank account and a taste for queenly pleasures. Rooms are dressed in Como silk and its outdoor pool floats on the lake. High-season prices increase over €100.

Hotel Villa Marie (☎ 0344 4 04 27; Via Regina 30, Tremezzo; d with garden/lake view €80/95; P 🅿 🕸 🕭) Take a short stroll south from Tremezzo's boat jetty, past the gloriously apricot Chiesa di San Lorenzo, to find this stunning 19th-century villa hotel which – better still – is geared to a mid-range pocket.

Grand Hotel Tremezzo (☎ 0344 4 24 91; www.grand hoteltremezzo.com; Via Regina 8, Tremezzo; d with/without lake view from €247/200; P 🅿 🕸 🖳 🕭) A glass lift whisks guests from the lake shore up to one of Lago di Como's most romantic hotels. The dreamy Liberty style hotel opened its doors in 1910 and remains family run. Its vast gardens are magnificent.

Ostello La Primula (☎ 0344 3 23 56; Via IV Novembre 106, Menaggio; B&B dm €12.50, 4- to 6-bed f with bathroom €13; 🕑 reception 8-10am & 5-11.30pm mid–Mar-early Nov) A gem of a hostel, run by a gem of a guy, this garden-clad hillside villa will welcome you with open arms. Dine here for €10, including drinks, wash your dirties (€3.50), rent a bicycle/kayak (€10.50 per day) and get 30 minutes of Internet access free with this guide! To get to the hostel from the boat jetty, walk up to main road, cross it, then bear left up the pedestrian ramp. Non HI cardholders must buy a €2.58 one-night stamp.

Hotel Garni Corona (☎ 0344 3 20 06; Largo Cavour 3, Menaggio; s/d from €37/55; 🕑 Mar-Nov) This small two-star hotel is tucked in an alley off Menaggio's central square, Piazza Garibaldi, and offers exceptionally good-value accommodation for this neck of the woods.

Camping OK La Rivetta (☎ 0344 7 07 15; www .campingoklarivetta.com; Via Calbiga 30, Porlezza; person/ tent/car from €4/8/4, 2-/4-person bungalow from €30/50; 🕑 Apr-Oct; P 🕭) Peace perfect peace – with mountains of nature thrown in – is what this clean and green camp ground, 3km east of Porlezza in the Lago di Piano nature reserve, offers. Some bungalows are equipped for disabled guests. Minimum stay is one week in July and August.

EATING

Many eateries are dotted around the lake; a few interesting choices are listed.

Tom & Jerry (☎ 031 34 23 17; Via Regina 33b, Cernobbio; 1st/2nd courses €7/12) This wine bar, decked out 1950s style, even touts an old-fashioned petrol pump between bottles. Fantastic wines aside, Tom & Jerry has a lovely garden overlooking a quiet park.

Red & White (☎ 0344 4 00 95; Via Portici Sampietro 18, Tremezzo) Red & White is an authentic wine bar where you can sample local wines over lunch. Its hot chocolate is thick enough to spoon. Popular demand has seen it extend its repertoire to bruschette (toasted bread with variety of savoury toppings), omelettes and pasta dishes (€9).

Alberghetto e Lal Cucina della Marianna (☎ 0344 4 30 95; www.la-marianna.com; Via Regina 57, Cadenabbia di Griante; meals €20; 🕑 Wed-Mon) Freshly baked bread and a lakeside terrace are highlights of this tempting trattoria where Paolo cooks up traditional lake cuisine. Eat until you can eat no more, then flop into a sweet world of dreams in one of eight stylishly furnished rooms above.

At the pocket-size **Osteria Vecchio Mol** (☎ 031 40 07 30; Via Regina 93, Laglio; meals €20; 🕑 Thu-Tue), strung with fishing nets, fresh fish from the lake is the most likely thing to end up on your plate. Drink wine and beer next door at **Lal Ocand del Cantiere** (Via Regina 91, Laglio; 🕑 10.30am-2.30pm & 6pm-3am Wed-Mon).

Eastern Shore

Como's eastern shore is the least scenic – the lakeside S36 is an old military road and a motorway blasts its way along the entire 40km length from just north of Colico (north) to Lecco (south), en route to the Lombardian capital. The **Abbazia di Piona** (🕑 9am-noon & 2.15-4.45pm), a Cistercian abbey, is a pocket of peace 10km south of Colico. From the lakeside S36, follow the mountain road for 2.5km; the last stretch is cobbled.

Pretty **Varenna** (population 850), 13km south, is crowned by a castle and studded with extravagant villas. The gardens of **Villa Monastero** (☎ 0341 83 12 81; Piazza Venin 1; adult/child €2/1.30; 🕑 9am-6pm Mar-Oct), a former monastery, and **Villa Cipressi** (☎ 0341 83 01 13; Via IV Novembre 18; adult/child €2/1.30; 🕑 9am-7pm Mar-Oct) can both be visited. Magnolias, camellias and yucca trees are among their blooming wonders. A combined ticket to both costs €3.50/2.50. To get to both villas from Piazzale Martiri Libertà, the square next to the boat jetty, follow the **lakeside promenade** around the shore then bear left (inland) up the steps to Piazza San Giorgio, the village square. Both villas are signposted from here.

The **tourist office** (☎ 0341 83 03 67; Piazza San Giorgio; 🕑 10am-12.30pm & 3-6pm Tue-Sat, 10am-12.30pm Sun) has information on the plentiful sleeping and eating options on the lake's eastern shore. Try **Vecchia Varenna** (☎ 0341 83 07 93; www.vecchiavarenna.it; Contrada Scoscesa 10, Varenna; 1st/2nd courses €11/15; ☺ Tue-Sun Feb-Dec) where you can sit on a delightful little terrace bobbing on the water and dine on pickled lake trout with citrus fruit and fennel, perch fish risotto or fish stew – to mention a few of the delicious dishes cooked up at this old-world, lakeside restaurant.

Few sights tempt visitors further south towards **Lecco**, a largely industrial centre where Milanese writer Alessandro Manzoni (1785–1803) famously set his epic novel *I Promessi Sposi* (The Betrothed).

Southern Shore

The so-called 'southern shore' (the V stretch of Lago di Como's Y) embraces the pearl of the lake, **Bellagio** (population 3000) – a pretty little town indeed, sitting square on the point where the lake's western and eastern arms split and head south. The 32km drive to Como (west) is itself rewarding, the 22km trip down the eastern side towards Lecco is less so.

The lavish gardens of **Villa Serbelloni** (☎ 031 95 15 55; Via Garibaldi 8; visits by guided tour only, adult/child €6.50/3; ☺ 11am-4pm Tue-Sun Apr- Oct) cover much of the promontory on which Bellagio sits. Tours are limited to 16 people and tickets are sold 10 minutes in advance from the small **tourist office** (Piazza Chiesa 14) near the church. Garden lovers can also stroll the grounds of neoclassical **Villa Melzi D'Eril** (☎ 339 644 68 30; Via Melzi D'Eril; adult/child €5/3; ☺ 9am-6.30pm Mar-Oct), built in 1808 for one of Napoleon's assistants and known in horticultural circles for its springtime azaleas and rhododendrons.

Bellagio **tourist office** (☎ 031 95 02 04; Piazza Mazzini; www.bellagiolakecomo.com; ☺ 9am-noon & 3- 6pm Apr-Oct, Mon & Wed-Sat Nov-Mar), next to the boat landing stage, has mountains of information on water sports, mountain biking and other lake activities. Dry-land surfers can log-on at **Il Sorbetto** (ilsorbetto@tiscalinet.it; Salita Serbelloni 34) for €6 per hour.

SLEEPING & EATING

Bellagio boasts a couple of outstanding spots to sleep.

Residence La Limonera (☎ 031 95 21 24; www .residencelalimonera.com; Via Bellosio 2; 2-/3-/4-person apartments €60/78/85; ☐) This elegant villa with garden, in the heart of cobbled Bellagio, has been cut into several spacious and thoughtfully furnished self-catering apartments. Rentals are generally by the week but turn up in low season and you could well snag an apartment for a night or three. High-season prices rise by about €40.

La Pergola (☎ 031 95 02 63; www.lapergolabellagio .it; Piazza del Porto 4; s/d from €60/110, 1st/2nd courses €7/9; ☺ restaurant Wed-Mon; P) Scenically set in the fishing hamlet of Pescallo, on the eastern shore of the Bellagio promontory, La Pergola peers out towards Lecco from its 16th-century waterfront perch. Its terrace restaurant adds to its natural old-world charm.

Grand Hotel Villa Serbelloni (☎ 031 95 02 16; www.villaserbelloni.com; Via Roma 1; s/d from €160/240; P ☒ ☐ ☒) This rich man's villa was built in 1852 and has been a very very grand hotel since 1872. Private landing stage, beach, tennis courts, fitness centre, sauna, poolside restaurant and beauty farm are but some of luxurious facilities available to amuse guests. Its restaurant is renowned. High-season prices are around €50 higher.

Far/out (☎ 031 95 17 43; farout.bellagio@virgilio.it; Salita Mella 4; meals around €20) The modernity of this self-marketed 'fancy restaurant' comes as a breath of fresh air in a village where tradition far outweighs innovation. Clean cut and minimalist is the name of the game here.

LAGO DI GARDA

Lago di Garda is the largest, most over-developed, least scenic – and ironically most popular – of the Italian lakes. Lying between the Alps and the Po valley, the 370-sq-km pool of murky water enjoys a temperate climate and is revered by windsurfers across Europe for its extraordinary Ora (southerly) and Peler (northerly) winds. At its northern reaches the lake is hemmed in by craggy mountains and resembles a fjord. As it broadens towards the south, the lake takes on the appearance of an inland sea.

Villages liberally stud the shoreline. The lake's trio of towns – picturesque but Disneyland–like **Sirmione** on the particularly crowded and noisy southern shore, **Gardone Riviera** on its western edge and **Riva del Garda**, a popular base for walking in the nearby Alps at the quieter northern end – form a neat triangle around the lake. Surfers hang out around Torbole and Malcesine, two nice and windy windsurfing spots south of Riva del Garda on the eastern shore. From the latter, walkers and mountain bikers can ride a state-of-the-art glass bubble of a cable car up to Monte Baldo (2200m), from where trails abound. In winter you can ski on its slopes.

Getting There & Around

From Desenzano del Garda train station, **Azienda Provinciale Trasporti Verona** (ARV; ☎ 045 805 79 11) runs buses to Riva del Garda (€4.90, two hours, up to six daily) via Salò (30 minutes), Gardone Riviera (35 minutes) and Limone sul Garda (1½ hours). Peschiera del Garda train station is on the Riva del Garda–Malcesine–Garda–Verona ARV bus route, with hourly buses to both Riva (€4.50, 1½ hours) and Verona (€2, 20 minutes). Buses also run to/from Mantua (1¼ hours, up to eight daily) from Peschiera del Garda train station. The Riva del Garda–Milan (€10.10, 3¾ hours, three daily) bus route operated by **Società Italiana Autoservizi** (SIA; ☎ 02 864 62 350; www.sia-autoservizi.it, Italian only) also serves Limone, Gardone Riviera, Salò and Brescia; schedules and fares are online. **Atesina** (☎ 046455 23 85; www.atesina.it, Italian only) runs hourly buses from Riva del Garda to/from Arco (€0.80, 20 minutes), Rovereto (€2.50, 45 minutes) and Trento (€3.40, 1¾ hours).

The lake is served by train stations in Desenzano del Garda and Peschiera del Gard, both on the Milan–Venice train line with almost hourly trains in each direction. A single fare to Desenzano from Milan/Venice (1½ hours/two hours) costs €6.25/7.90.

Navigazione sul Lago di Garda (☎ 800 55 18 01; www.navigazionelaghi.it; Piazza Matteotti 2, Desenzano del Garda) operates passenger ferries year-round between all towns mentioned in this section and others. Motorists can cross the lake using the car ferry that yo-yos between Toscolano-Maderno (9km north of Salò on the western shore) and Torri del Benaco (8km north of Garda on the eastern shore), or seasonally between Limone (11km south of Riva del Garda on the western shore) and Malcesine (15km south of Riva on the eastern side). Lakeside ticketing booths and tourist offices have timetables. Transporting a small car/bicycle on either ferry route costs €5.80/4.20 one way. Passenger one-way fares on a ferry/hydrofoil range from €1.30/2.50 (Riva–Torbole) to €9.10/12.30 (Riva–Peschiera). A one-day ticket allowing unlimited travel costs €21.60/10.80 per adult/child and a day ticket covering the

lower/upper half of the lake only is €14.20/12.20 (child €7.10/6.10).

Sirmione
pop 6500 \ elevation 68m

The Roman poet Catullus celebrated Sirmione – a narrow peninsula jutting out from the southern shore of the lake – in his writings and his name is still invoked in connection with the place. It is a popular bathing spot and jammed tight with tourists but does retain a comparatively relaxed atmosphere. The area of interest (watch for the castle) is an islet attached by a bridge to the rest of the peninsula.

The **tourist office** (☎ 030 91 61 14; Viale Marconi 8; ☼ 9am-9pm) adjoins a bank and the bus station. Motorised vehicles are banned from the historic centre.

SIGHTS & ACTIVITIES

The Roman villa and baths, the **Grotte di Catullo** (☎ 030 91 61 57; adult/child €5/free; ☼ 8.30am-7pm Tue-Sun Mar–mid-Oct, 8.30am-4.30pm Tue-Sun mid–Oct-Feb) probably had nothing to do with the Roman poet, although Catullus and his family did have a villa somewhere round here. The ruins occupy a prime position on the northern, quieter end of the Sirmione island. En route you pass a path leading to **Lido delle Bionde**, a beach with deck chairs and pedal boats to rent.

Castello Scaligero (☎ 030 91 64 68; adult/child €5/free; ☼ 8.30am-4.30pm Tue-Sun) was built by Verona's ruling family, the Scaligeri, as a stronghold on the lake in 1250. There's not a lot inside but the views from the tower are good.

From the jetty near the castle, all sorts of vessels will make any manner of trip around the lake – at a price – and an array of water activities can be arranged. Massages, saunas and other sensuous delights can be enjoyed at the **Terme di Sirmione** (☎ 030 9 99 04 23, ☎ 800 80 21 25; www.termedisirmione.com; Piazza Virgilio 1). A 25-/45-minute massage typically costs €44/68.

Two wheelers can rent mountain bikes/50cc scooters for around €10/32 per day from **Adventure Sprint** (☎ 030 91 90 00; Via Brescia 15; ☼ 9am-6.30pm).

SLEEPING & EATING

It is hard to believe 90-odd hotels are crammed in here, many of which close from the end of October to March. Four camp grounds lie near the town and the tourist office can advise on others around the lake.

Albergo Degli Oleandri (☎ 030 990 57 80; hoteloleandri@libero.it; Via Dante 31; s/d €38.75/51.65) Stay near the castle in a shady, pleasant location. Spotlessly clean rooms with TVs promise to be even better after a massive face-lift.

Hotel Speranza (☎ 030 91 61 16; fax 030 91 64 03; Via Casello 6; d €70; 🐾) Tucked in the maze of tourist shops, Hotel Speranza is a reliable and friendly two-star bet. Better still, it stays open year-round.

Palace Hotel Villa Cortine (☎ 030 990 58 90; www.hotelvillacortine.com; Via Grotte 6, s/d €260/300; P 🐾 💻 🐾) The five-star neoclassical villa, built in the 1880s, languishes in a fabulous park with statues of Neptune, Narcissus et al. Half-board and a minimum stay of three nights is compulsory in high season, when you'll pay an extra €65 to €130.

There are loads of takeaway food outlets to be found, especially around Piazza Carducci, where the bulk of cafés, ice-cream parlours and restaurants are located.

Wara Warda (☎ 030 91 62 87; Piazza Carducci 9/10; pizzas €8, 1st/2nd courses €8/12) Sit here in relative tranquillity and watch the mayhem of Sirmione's main square and boat dock. Pizzas are particularly tasty, authentic and laden with cheese.

Antica Trattoria La Speranzana (Via Dante 16; 1st/2nd courses €8/15) A gem of a find, this lovely little trattoria near the church is tucked well away from the waterfront circus – eat in peace on a quiet terrace, between olive trees by the lake.

Around Sirmione

Sirmione is 5km east of **Desenzano del Garda** (population 24,385), a transport hub but not really worth a visit. Further north from Desenzano is **Salò** (population 9980) which gave its name to Mussolini's puppet republic in 1943, after the dictator was rescued from the south by the Nazis.

Larger-than-life dinosaurs, Burmese forests, buddhas, pirate ships, roller coasters and a dolphinarium are part of the excitement at kid-orientated **Gardaland** (☎ 045 644 97 77; www.gardaland.it; day ticket adult/child €22/18.50; 🕙 10am-6pm Apr–mid-Jun & last 2 weeks of Sep, 9am-midnight mid-Jun–mid-Sep, 9am-6pm Sat & Sun Oct). Multiday tickets are also available.

Next door, **CanevaWorld** (☎ 0457 59 06 22; www.canevaworld.it; Via Fossalta 1) features an **aqua park** (adult/child €17/13; 🕙 10am-7pm mid-May–mid-Sep) **medieval shows** (adult/child €20/13; 🕙 once or twice daily Apr-Sep) and a **Rock Star Cafe** (admission free; 🕙 6pm-2am), crammed with rock memorabilia. CanevaWorld's **Movie Studios** (adult/child €15/12; 🕙 10am-7pm May-Sep) can be found next door. Stunt-packed Rambo-action shows that thrill audiences are part of the attractions here.

Free buses shuttle visitors the 2km to both parks to/from Peschiera del Garda train station.

Gardone Riviera
pop 2520 \ elevation 85m

On the western edge of the lake at the head of a small inlet is Gardone Riviera, once one of the lake's most elegant holiday spots. No longer quite so fashionable, it lures the crowds today with **Il Vittoriale** (☎ 0365 29 65 11; www.vittoriale.it; Piazza Vittoriale; adult/child d'Annunzio's house €6/4, house & grounds or war museum €11/8, house, grounds & war museum €16/11; 🕙 grounds 8.30am-8pm Apr-Sep, 9am-5pm Oct-Mar, house & museum 9.30am-7pm Tue-Sun Apr-Sep, 9am-1pm & 2-5pm Tue-Sun Oct-Mar). This fabulous estate belonged to Italy's controversial 20th-century poet and screeching nationalist, Gabriele d'Annunzio (1863–1938), who moved here in 1922 because, he claimed, he wanted to escape the world, which made him ill. He slept in a coffin-shaped bed.

Visits to d'Annunzio's house are by guided tour only (25 minutes, departures every 10 minutes). **Museo della Guerra** (War Museum) records d'Annunzio's WWI antics – one of his most triumphant and more bizarre feats was to capture, with a band of his soldiers, a battleship from the fledgling Yugoslavia shortly after WWI when Italy's territorial claims had been partly frustrated in postwar peace talks. In July and August classical concerts, ballets, plays and operas are staged in the **open-air theatre** (☎ 0365 29 65 19; teatro.vittoriale@tiscalinet.it) in the villa grounds.

Sigmund Freud, David Bowie and Peter Gabriel, among others, have strolled through Gardone's **Giardino Botanico Fondazione André Heller** (☎ 336 41 08 77; Via Roma; adult/child €6/3; 🕙 9am-6pm Mar–mid-Oct). The gardens were laid out in 1900 and redesigned in the late 1990s by multimedia artist André Heller. They include sculptures by

Keith Haring, Roy Lichtenstein and other contemporary greats, and some 8000 plant species grow here.

The **tourist office** (☎ 0365 2 03 47; www.brescia holiday.com; Corso Repubblica 8; ☼ 9am-12.30pm & 3.30-6.30pm Jul-Sep, 9am-12.30pm & 3.30-6.30pm Fri-Sat & Mon-Wed, 9am-12.30pm Thu Oct-Jun) stocks a wealth of information on lake accommodation and activities around the lake.

SLEEPING & EATING

Villa Fiordaliso (☎ 0365 2 01 58; www.villafiordaliso.it; Via Zanardelli 150; d from €200; P ⊠ ⬚ ⬚) Historically furnished rooms are named after flowers at this 1903 waterside palace. D'Annunzio lived here from 1921 to 1923, as did Mussolini's mistress, Clara Petacci, from 1943 to 1945. The villa also has an acclaimed restaurant.

The waterfront is lined with plenty more places to eat, drink and be merry. Otherwise, **Trattoria Agli Angeli** (☎ 0365 2 08 32; Piazza Garibaldi 2; meals €20), en route to Il Vittoriale, is a pretty little trattoria overlooking a quintessentially Italian piazza. It has a handful of simple rooms above.

Around Gardone Riviera

About 12km north of Gardone, past the car ferry port at Toscolano-Maderno, is **Gargnano** (population 3004) where Mussolini was based during the short life of his Repubblica Sociale Italiana (or Repubblica di Salò). He was guarded by German SS units and the republic was, in fact, fictitious, as northern Italy was occupied territory after Italy signed an armistice with the Allies in September 1943. The republic lasted until 25 April 1945 when the last German troops were finally cleared from Italy. Mussolini was killed three days later near Lago di Como.

The finest place to stay without a doubt on the entire lake is the **Grand Hotel a Villa Feltrinelli** (☎ 0365 79 80 00; www.villafeltrinelli.com; d from €200; P ⊠ ⬚ ⬚), a fairy-tale villa built as a lakeside residence for the Feltrinelli family in 1892 and host to Mussolini before his fall from glory. Guests are waited on hand and foot by their own personal butler. Get a load of the look-alike American 1920s riverboat, moored on the lake shore and the Magnolia room, which overlooks a magnificent magnolia tree, no less.

Riva del Garda

pop 14,725 \ elevation 70m

Riva del Garda, on the lake's northern edge, has a pleasant old centre of cobbled lanes and squares. Links with the Germanic world are evident, not only in the bus and car loads of Germans and Austrians but also in the town's history. Riva was part of Habsburg Austria until it was incorporated into Italy after WWI and was annexed briefly by Nazi Germany in the closing years of WWII. Central European luminaries such as Nietzsche, Kafka and Thomas Mann put their feet up in Riva.

Riva, along with Torbole (see p287), is a popular windsurfing spot and has several schools that runs courses, hire equipment and so on. The main **tourist office** (☎ 0464 55 44 44; Giardini di Porta Orientale 8; ☼ 9am-noon & 3-6.15pm Mon-Sat Apr–mid-Jun, 9am-noon & 3-6.15pm Mon-Sat, 10am-noon & 3-6.30pm Sun mid-Jun–Sep, 9am-noon & 2.30-5.15pm Mon-Fri Oct-Mar) and its **kiosk** (☎ 0464 55 07 76; Lungolago d'Annunzio 4c; ☼ 9am-noon & 3-6.15pm Apr-Oct), overlooking Piazza Catena where boats dock, both have a list. They can also advise you everything from climbing and paragliding to wine tasting and touring flea markets.

Riva is a popular starting point for walks around **Monte Rocchetta** (972m), which dominates the northern end of Lago di Garda. Immediately south of the village, the shore is laced by a long shingle beach, overlooked by a wide green park.

At hip and trendy **Caffè Italia** (☎ 0464 55 25 00; www.caffeitalia.it, Italian only; Piazza Cavour 8; ☼ 7am-1am) you can surf for €6 an hour.

SIGHTS

Guarding the waterfront is the **Museo Civico** (☎ 0464 57 38 69; Piazza Cesare Battisti 3; adult/child €3/1.50; ☼ 9.30am-12.30pm & 2.30-6.30pm Tue-Sun), a typical city museum inside the Rocca di Riva built in 1124. The castle touts photographic exhibitions, an art gallery and various archaeological finds from Arco and ancient Magna Graecia.

The 34m-tall **Torre Apponale** is Riva's other century post. Scale its steep 165 steps for a stunning panorama. The sturdy square 13th-century tower is topped by an angel-shaped weather vane and is named after *ponale* – the southwest direction of the port that it faces. Tickets for the Museo Civico cover admission to the tower.

Three kilometres north of town and a pleasant 45-minute stroll is **Cascata del Varone** (☎ 0464 52 14 21; adult/child €4/free; ☽ 10am-12.30pm & 2-5pm Mar, Oct & school holidays Nov-Feb, 9am-6pm Apr & Sep, 9am-7pm May-Aug). The impressive 100m waterfall is fed by Lago di Tenno, a tiny lake northwest of Lago di Garda.

SLEEPING & EATING

Riva's hotel reservation centre **Consorzio Garda Trentino Hotel** (☎ 0464 55 36 67; www.gardat rentinohotels.com; Via Bastoni 7) makes reservations (free) for hotels with three or more stars.

Campeggio Bavaria (☎ 0464 55 25 24; camping bavaria@yahoo.it; Viale Rovereto 100; person/tent/car from €8/6/5; **P**) One of four camp grounds to dot Riva's lakeside, this one is part of the Marco Segnana Surf Center (see below) and is generally packed with surfers and mountain bikers.

Albergo Ancora (☎ 0464 52 21 31; fax 0464 55 00 50; hotelancora@riavdelgarde.com; Via Montanara 2; s/d with breakfast €57/88) This is a satisfying mid-range option, tucked well away from the boat-clambering crowds. Unlike most other lake hotels, it sports no half-board deals but does give guests 15% discount in its tasty restaurant.

Hotel Sole (☎ 0464 55 26 86; fax 0464 55 28 11; www.hotelsole.net; Piazza 3 Novembre 35; r with breakfast low/mid/high season from €59/64/75) Despite its four contemporary stars, this once-elegant waterfront hotel – where Nietzsche stayed – has clearly seen better days. Rooms with a lake view cost more.

Riva has dozens of takeaway places and delicatessens for picnic supplies, and a mind-boggling choice of lakeside cafés, pastry shops and *gelaterie*. For an exceptional pizza that flops off either side off your plate, head straight for **Bella Napoli** (☎ 0464 55 21 39; Via Armandi Diaz 29; pizzas €5-10, 1st/2nd courses €6/8), away from the water.

Around Riva del Garda

There's plenty to see and do around Riva del Garda. Northbound, the 20-minute stroll through olive groves from the medieval village of **Arco** (population 14,438) to **Castello di Arco** (☎ 0464 51 01 56; adult/child €2.50/1.50; ☽ 10am-7pm Apr-Sep, 10am-4pm Oct-Mar) limbers up the muscles for the more strenuous terrain awaiting walkers a few kilometres north in neighbouring Trentino-Alto Adige.

ROVERETO
pop 34,200

For contemporary art lovers, the 22km-long trip east from Riva to Rovereto is a must. Its **Museo d'Arte Modern e Contemporanea** (MART; ☎ 0464 43 88 87; www.mart.trento.it, Italian only; Corso Berttini 43; adult/child €8/5; ☽ 10am-7pm Tue-Thu, 10am-9pm Fri-Sun) displays dozens of priceless and fun pieces from the early 20th century to present day, including Andy Warhols' *Four Marilyns* (1962), Tom Wesselman's *Seascape* (1966), several Picassos and various wrapped or glass-boxed creations by Christo and New Realist Arman. Temporary exhibitions fill the 2nd floor of the building – a work of art in itself with its monumental glass dome designed by Swiss-born architect Mario Botta.

The **Museo Storico Italiano Della Guerra** (Italian War Historical Museum; ☎ 0464 43 81 00; Via Castelbarco 7; adult/child €5.20/1.60; ☽ 8.30am-12.30pm & 2-6pm Tue-Sun) is worth a peek, as is the **Campana della Pace** (Bell of Peace; adult/child €1/0.30; ☽ 9am-noon & 2-6pm Nov-Feb, 9am-noon & 2-7pm Mon-Fri, 9am-7pm Sat & Sun Apr-Jul & Sep, 9am-7pm Aug), a bell of peace cast in 1924 from bronze canons from the 19 countries who fought in WWI. The 3.36m-tall bell – the world's largest ringing bell – tolls every evening around 9pm from its perch atop Miravelle Hill on Rovereto's eastern fringe. To get here, follow the signs in town from Via Santa Maria.

Free guided tours (in English) of the small old town, visited by Dante in 1303, Mozart in 1769 and Goethe in 1786, depart from outside MART on Saturday at 10am. Reserve at least a day before at the **tourist office** (☎ 0464 43 03 63; www.apt.rovereto.tn.it; Corso Rosmini 6a; ☽ 8.30am-12.15pm & 2.30-6pm Mon-Fri).

Scala della Torre (☎ 0464 43 71 00; Via Scala della Torre 7; meals €20) In the medieval heart of old Rovereto, this cosy decades-old trattoria and *birraria* (beer house) is the place to swill with the locals and feast on typical mountain fodder.

TORBOLE
pop 5000 \ elevation 67m

Host to the **World Windsurf Championships** in June or July, and a huge **Surf Festival** at the end of May, this is *the* place to ride the wind. Garda-fan Goethe described Torbole as 'a wonder of nature, an enchanting sight', and indeed the village still retains much of its original fishing-village charm. Picturesque strolls aside, most people come here to surf.

The **Marco Segnana Surf Center** (☎ 0464 50 59 63; www.surfsegnana.it; Foci del Sarca), with bases at lakeside Lido di Torbole in Torbole and on Porfina beach in Riva del Garda, is a large surfing centre (board rental per hour/day from €15/38, three-hour lessons from €45) which rents catamarans (hour/half day €33/83) and mountain bikes (hour/day €5/15) too. Water fiends can canyon (half/full day from €36/65), enjoy a night-time canyoning adventure (€62) and rock climb (half/full day €40/65) with **Canyon Adventures** (☎ 0464 50 54 06; www.canyonadv.com; Via Matteotti 22). Sports gear can be picked up at **Flipper** (☎ 0464 50 50 72; Via Matteotti 57b), a well-equipped sports shop.

The **tourist office** (☎ 0464 50 51 77; Via Lungolago Verona 19; ☺ 9am-noon & 3-6.30pm Jun-Sep, 9am-noon & 3-6.30pm Mon-Sat Oct-May) has a complete list of surfing schools, distributes free mountain-bike and walking maps and has information on accommodation.

MALCESINE

Garda's other surfing centre, 15km south, is a village of cobbled streets crowned by the **Castello e Museo Scaligero** (☎ 045 740 08 37; Via Castello; adult/child €4/1; ☺ 9.30am-7pm Apr-Nov, 9am-6pm Sat & Sun Dec-Mar), immortalised by German novelist Goethe on canvas. Inside the castle walls there are stunning lake views and a couple of natural history museums to be seen as well as a collection of Goethe's books. Olives harvested around here are turned into extra-virgin olive oil by the **Consorzio Olivicoltori di Malcesine** (☎ 045 740 12 86; Via Navene); buy a litre of oil from their shop for €16.

Malcesine's other must is the **Funivia Malcesine-Monte Baldo** (☎ 045 740 02 06; adult/child under 1.4m return €14/11, with bike/paraglider €15/11; ☺ 8am-7pm), a cable car which offers an eagle-eye mountain view from its rotating glass cabins during its panoramic 10-minute journey up to 1790m. Pick up trail information and maps from Malcesine **tourist office** (☎ 045 740 00 44; wwww.malcesinepiu.it; Via Capitanato; ☺ 9am-noon & 3-6pm Mon-Sat) and rent a mountain bike from **Furioli Bike** (☎ 045 740 00 89; Piazza Matteotti). In winter you can ski on Monte Baldo.

Shuttered **Albergo Aurora** (☎ 045 740 01 14; Piazza Matteotti 10; d low/high season €49/59) is an exceptionally good-value, one-star choice in the cobbled village heart of the town. Nearby is **Osteria Santo Cielo** (Piazza Quirico Turazza; ☺ 8am-2am),

an atmospheric wine bar with no more than half a dozen tables inside and a few more outside on the tiny cobbled square.

LAGO D'ISEO

Lago d'Iseo is the least known and least attractive of the lakes. Shut in by mountains, it is scarred by industry and a string of tunnels at its northeastern end around **Castro** and **Lovere**, although driving through the blasted rock face at the water's edge can be enjoyable. Heading south, the Franciacorta – a patch of rolling countryside that produces good wine – spills around the lake shore, while the mountainous hinterland offers interesting walking possibilities. **Riva di Solto** (population 825) and **Sarnico** (population 5875), with its lovely Liberty villas towards the southern end of the lake, are a couple of fairly unspoiled villages on the western shore with a sprinkling of hotels and restaurants.

The River Oglio winds to the lake through the **Valle Camonica** between two national parks. Walking is the main attraction both here and around **Marone** on the eastern shore, from where a road winds into the mountains to **Zone**. Small and quiet **Sulzano** (population 1475), 12km south of Marone, is linked by ferry to the lake island of Monte Isola.

Getting There & Around

SAB (☎ 035 28 90 00; www.sab-autoservizi.it, Italian only) buses trundle between Sarnico and Bergamo (50 minutes, up to six daily), and trains link Iseo train station with Brescia (€2.40, 30 minutes, hourly).

Navigazione sul Lago d'Iseo (☎ 035 97 14 83; www.navigazionelaghi.it) operates up to eight ferries daily between (south to north) Sarnico, Iseo, Monte Isola, Lovere and Pisogne. Single fares range from €1.70 (Sulzano–Peschiera Maraglioli on Monte Isola) to €5.20 (Iseo–Lovere). In winter there are substantially fewer sailings.

Iseo
pop 8383 \ elevation 198m

A pleasant, if somewhat dull, spot fronting the southern end of the lake, Iseo boasts the first monument erected to Garibaldi. South of the small town lies a 2-sq-km protected wetland, formed from 18th-century peat beds. In late spring the pools are smothered in water lilies. Grilled sardines and smoked salami are the things to eat here.

From Iseo you can catch a boat to **Monte Isola**, Europe's largest lake island at 5 sq km. Few vehicles are allowed on the streets – cycling is the preferred means of getting around, making the fishing village a peaceful place to stay. Ask at Iseo **tourist office** (☎ 030 98 02 09; Lungolago Marconi 2) for details of the 15km-long trail – suitable for cyclists and walkers – that encircles the island.

Motorists have to dump their cars on the other side of the water before heading to the island camp ground **Campeggio Monte Isola** (☎ 030 982 52 21; Via Croce 144; person/tent €43.30/5.15; ☯ year-round).

Ambra Hotel (☎ 030 98 01 30; Via Porta Rosa 2; s/d €47/75, lake view supplement €5) is beautifully situated overlooking Iseo's lovely little harbour square. This solid mid-range choice is guaranteed to please. Some rooms are balcony-clad.

Valle Camonica

The Valle Camonica weaves its way from the north of Lago d'Iseo to the vast **Parco dell'Adamello** and, further north, to the **Parco Nazionale dello Stelvio**. The area borders on Trentino-Alto Adige and takes in the better parts of the Lombard Alps. The two national parks offer many walks and are dotted with Alpine huts to rest weary bones – see p290 for details.

About halfway between Darfo and Edolo, lovers of rock art will have a field day. The **Parco Nazionale delle Incisioni Rupestri** (☎ 0364 4 21 40; adult/child €4.50/2.50; ☯ 9am-6.30pm Tue-Sun summer, 8.30am-4.30pm Mon-Fri & 9am-4.30pm Sat & Sun winter), at Capo di Ponte, is a 30-hectare open-air museum containing a representative array of rock engravings going as far back as the Bronze Age. The valley is littered with such carvings.

The area north of Edolo offers some reasonable winter **skiing**, particularly near Ponte di Legno, at the northern end of the valley, and the nearby Passo del Tonale. Brescia's tourist office (see p266) stocks plenty of walking, camping and mountain hut information. In the valley there are tourist offices at **Darfo Boario Terme** (☎ 0364 53 16 09; Piazza Einaudi 2) and **Ponte di Legno** (☎ 0364 9 11 22; Corso Milano 41).

Trentino-Alto Adige

CONTENTS

TRENTINO-ALTO ADIGE

This autonomous Alpine region, incorporating much of the spectacular Dolomite range, embraces Trentino and Alto Adige – two vastly separate provinces.

Alto Adige, or South Tirolo (Südtirol), in the north was part of the Tirolo province of Austria until ceded to Italy in 1918. The people, mostly of Germanic descent, favour German (68%) over Italian (28%), although Ladin (4%), an ancient Latin-based language, is spoken in some valleys, mainly the Val Badia (Gadertal) and Val Gardena (Grödnertal). Trentino, to the south, was a reluctant part of the Austrian and Austro-Hungarian empires for about a century until it was returned to Italy after WWI. The population here has a stronger Italian identity, although German is widely spoken too.

The marriage of Trentino to Alto Adige, Italian to Tirolean, has at times created friction. In Alto Adige, the Südtiroler Volkspartei (SVP) is easily the most popular party. One of its primary aims is the development of German and Ladin ethnic groups, but extreme elements want to secede from Italy. Bombings in the 1950s, 60s and 80s were attributed to radical secessionists. Politics aside, tourism is highly organised and travellers can enjoy inexpensive accommodation and extensive information on activities from walking to scaling frozen waterfalls. Many hotels close from mid-April to late June and mid-October to mid-December, transforming many mountain resorts into ghost towns.

HIGHLIGHTS

■ **Wildlife Watch**

Bear-watching in Spormaggiore, Parco Naturale Adamello-Brenta (p301)

■ **Traditional Pastime**

Tracking down the Ladins (p314)

■ **Guaranteed Stunner**

Bolzano's ice man Ötzi (p307)

■ **Grass Roots**

Hay bathing (p313)

■ **High Life**

Après-ski in Cortina d'Ampezzo (pp315–16); high-altitude music concerts around a *malghe* (p295)

■ **Spills & Thrills**

Skiing in the Brenta group, Val di Fassa or the Dolomites (p295); biking in Alpe di Siusi (p312–13)

■ **Tummy Tickler**

The region's farm restaurants: Oberraut (Brunico, p318), Maso-Marocc (Molveno, p300), Malga Venegiota (San Martino di Castrozza, p304)

■ POPULATION: 943,123 | ■ AREA: 13,613 SQ KM

TRENTINO-ALTO ADIGE

TRENTINO-ALTO ADIGE

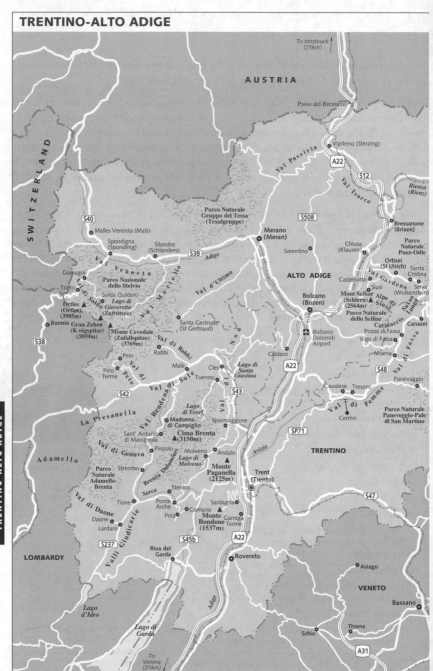

To Innsbruck
(25km)

AUSTRIA

Passo del Brennero

Vipiteno (Sterzing)

Val Passiria

A22

S12

Rienza
(Rienz)

S508

Val Isarco

Parco Naturale
Gruppo del Tessa
(Texalgruppe)

Bressanone
(Brixen)

S40

Merano
(Meran)

Parco
Naturale
Puez-Odle

Malles Venosta (Mals)

Spondigna
(Spondinig)

Silandro
(Schlanders)

Chiusa
(Klausen)

Sarentino

Ortisei
(St Ulrich)

Santa
Cristina

S38

Adige

ALTO ADIGE

Castelrotto

Val Gardena

Selva
(Wolkenstein)

Val Venosta

Val d'Ultimo

Siusi

Sasso
Lungo

Gomagoi

Parco Nazionale
dello Stelvio

Val Martello

Mont Sciliar
(Schlern)
(2564m)

Alpe di
Siusi

Trafoi

Solda (Sulden)

Bolzano
(Bozen)

Parco Naturale
dello Sciliar

Catinaccio

Canazei

Lago di
Gioveretto
(Zufrittsee)

Santa Gertrude
(St Gertraud)

Pozza di Fassa

Ortles
(Ortler)
(3905m)

Bormio

Gran Zebrù
(K nigspitze)
(3859m)

Monte Cevedale
(Zufallspitze)
(3769m)

Non

Vigo di Fassa

Bolzano
Dolomiti
Airport

Moena

S38

Peio

Caldaro

Val di Fassa

Rabbi

Val di Rabbi

S48

Cles

Lago di
Santa
Giustina

A22

Panevaggio

Peio
Terme

Val di Peio

Malè

Tuenno

Val di Sole

Cavalese

Tresero

S42

S43

Val di Femme

Parco Naturale
Paneveggio-Pale
di San Martino

La Presanella

Lago
di Tovel

Spormaggiore

Cermis

Madonna
di Campiglio

TRENTINO

Adamello

Sant' Antonio
di Mavignola

Cima Brenta
(3150m)

SP71

Val di Genova

Pinzolo

Molveno

Andalo

Avisio

Lago di
Molveno

S47

Parco
Naturale
Adamello-
Brenta

Strembo

Monte
Paganella
(2125m)

Trent
(Trento)

Brenta Dolomiti

Stenico

Sarca

Tione

Ponte
Arche

Comano

Sardagna

Val di Daone

Poia

Monte
Bondone
(1537m)

Garniga
Terme

Daone

Valli Giudicarie

S45b

A22

Lardaro

LOMBARDY

S237

Riva del
Garda

Rovereto

Asiago

VENETO

Lago
d'Idro

Bassano

Lago di
Garda

Adige

Thiene

Schio

To
Verona
(25km)

A31

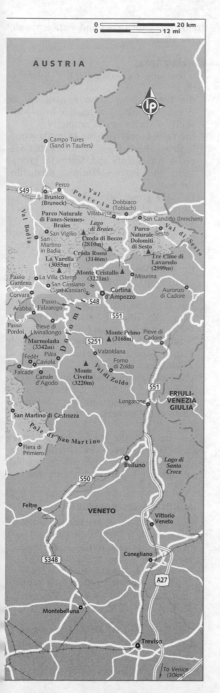

INFORMATION

The provincial tourist offices in Trent (p296) and Bolzano (p306) stock loads of practical information, including updated lists of *rifugi* (mountain huts) and farmhouses offering B&B. The regional **Trentino tourist board** (toll-free ☎ 800 01 05 45, ☎ 0461 49 73 53; www.trentino.to; Via Romagnosi 11) in Trent also has an office in **Milan** (☎ 02 864 61 251; apt.milano@trentino.to; Piazza Diaz 5).

GETTING THERE & AROUND

Bolzano airport (p308) in the region is only served by a couple of European flights. Otherwise the nearest airports are Verona and Innsbruck (Austria) or Munich (Germany), from where you can train it south to Bolzano.

Public transport is managed by two main companies: **Atesina** (☎ 0461 98 36 27; www.atesina.it, Italian only) in Trentino and **Servizi Autobus Dolomiti** (SAD; toll-free ☎ 800 84 60 47; www.sii.bz.it) in Alto Adige. The main towns and many ski resorts can be reached directly from major Italian cities – including Rome, Florence, Bologna, Milan and Genoa. Information about these services is available from tourist offices and bus stations throughout Trentino-Alto Adige, or from bus stations in the respective cities.

WALKING IN THE DOLOMITES

The Dolomites, stretching across Trentino-Alto Adige into the Veneto, provide the most spectacular and varied opportunities for walkers in the Italian Alps – from half-day rambles to more demanding routes that require mountaineering skills.

Trails are generally well marked with numbers on red-and-white painted bands (on trees and rocks along the trails) or inside different coloured triangles for the Alte Vie (High Routes). Numerous *rifugi* offer overnight lodging and something to eat. Tourist offices usually have maps with roughly marked trails, but walkers planning anything more than the most basic itinerary should buy detailed walking maps from bookshops and tobacconists (listed under Information in the relevant town sections).

Those wanting to undertake guided walks or tackle more difficult trails that combine mountaineering skills with walking (with or without a guide) can seek information

TRENTINO-ALTO ADIGE

AN ALPINE CORAL REEF

The Dolomites are, in fact, ancient coral reefs reincarnated as Alpine peaks. Accounting for a vast portion of the eastern Alps, the spiky peaks take their name from French geologist De Dolomieu, the first to identify their composition of sedimentary limestone formed from calcium carbonate and magnesium. Around 100 million years ago, the entire area was covered with tropical forest and a shallow, warm sea. After millions of years, the sea receded at the same time as the Alps were being formed, raising what had once been the seabed to heights of between 2000 and 3000m. During the Ice Age, the coral reefs and rocks were eroded by glaciers that, together with normal atmospheric erosion, shaped the fantastic and spectacular formations seen today in the Dolomites. It is not unusual to find marine fossils among the pinnacles, towers and dramatic sheer drops of these mountains.

at Guide Alpine (mountain guide) offices in the region (also listed under Information in the relevant town sections).

For more information on walking the Dolomites, see Lonely Planet's *Walking in Italy* guide.

Preparations

The walking season runs from the end of June to the end of September (sometimes into October, depending on the weather). Most mountain huts close from mid-September.

Among the many maps available are the *carte topografiche per escursionisti* maps published by Tabacco at a scale of 1:25,000. These topographic maps provide extensive details of trails, altitudes and gradients, as well as marking all mountain huts, and are widely available in bookshops throughout this mountainous region. Those in the equally reputable Kompass series are also widely available.

Always check the weather predictions before setting out (see the boxed text, this page), ensure you're prepared, have the correct gear and the correct equipment for high-altitude conditions and set out early; the weather can change suddenly in the Alps, even in hot August when it can dramatically turn cold and wet, especially in the afternoon.

Walking Areas

The best areas for walking in the Dolomites include:

- the **Brenta** group (also known as the Brenta Dolomites), accessible from Molveno or Madonna di Campiglio
- the **Val di Genova** and the **Adamello** group, both accessible from Madonna di Campiglio (the Brenta and Adamello groups form the Parco Naturale Adamello-Brenta)
- the **Sella** group, accessible from the Val Gardena, Val Badia, Pieve di Livinallongo and the Val di Fassa
- the **Alpe di Siusi, Sciliar** and **Catinaccio** group, all are accessible from Siusi and Castelrotto
- the **Pale di San Martino**, accessible from San Martino di Castrozza and Fiera di Primiero
- the area around **Cortina** that straddles Alto Adige and the Veneto and features the magnificent Parco Naturale di Fanes-Sennes-Braies and, to the south, Monte Pelmo, Monte Civetta and the Val di Zoldo area
- the **Sesto** group (also called the Sesto Dolomites) north of Cortina towards Austria, accessible from San Candido or Sesto in Val Pusteria

There are four Alte Vie in the Dolomites, each taking up to two weeks. Routes link existing trails and incorporate new trails which make difficult sections easier to traverse.

MOUNTAIN EMERGENCIES

Many towns and resorts have local telephone numbers (listed under Information) to call for mountains rescue; wherever you are however, calling ☎ 118 will get you out of trouble. Before setting out always check the **weather forecast, snow conditions and avalanche warnings** (☎ 0461 23 89 39; fax 0461 23 70 89; www.meteotrentino.it). Reports are updated at 4pm daily. The **14th Delegation-SAT Alpine Rescue team** (☎ 0461 23 31 66; Via Manci 57), the largest of 35 Alpine rescue stations manned by 350 volunteers in the region, is based in Trent.

Each route links a chain of *rifugi*, and you can opt to only walk certain sections:

- **Alta Via No 1** crosses the Dolomites from north to south, from Lago di Braies to Belluno
- **Alta Via No 2** extends from Bressanone to Feltre and is known as the 'High Route of Legends' because it passes through Odle, the mythical kingdom of ancient Ladin fairy tales
- **Alta Via No 3** links Villabassa and Longarone
- **Alta Via No 4** goes from San Candido to Pieve di Cadore

The Alte Vie are marked by numbers inside triangles – blue for No 1, red for No 2 and orange/brown for No 3; No 4 is marked by normal numbers on red-and-white bands. Booklets with the routes in detail are available at most tourist offices in the region.

SKIING IN THE DOLOMITES

The Dolomites boast innumerable excellent ski resorts, including fashionable Cortina d'Ampezzo for drop-dead gorgeous people and their weighty wallets, Madonna di Campiglio, San Martino di Castrozza and Canazei, as well as the extremely popular resorts of the Val Gardena.

Accommodation and ski facilities are abundant and you have plenty of scope to choose between downhill and cross-country skiing, as well as *sci alpinismo*, combining skiing and mountaineering skills on longer excursions. Snowboarding and other white-stuff activities are equally well catered for.

High season runs from mid-December to early January and February to mid-March.

Ski passes range from those covering use of lifts in one resort and its immediate neighbours – ideal if you only have one or two days or don't intend venturing far – to the **Dolomiti Superski ski pass** (www.dolomitisuperski.com) which allows access to 464 lifts and some 1220km of ski runs across 12 regions. It costs around €88/154 for a three-/six-day pass (high season €100/175). Prices for passes covering individual resorts and areas are listed in the respective sections in this chapter.

Several ski schools operate at every resort; they all offer boarding lessons as well as classic downhill skiing. A six-day course (three hour's group tuition per day) costs

TAKING MUSIC TO NEW HEIGHTS

Every summer Trentino's regional tourist board organises a string of free high-altitude concerts, embracing everything from classical and blues to jazz, ethnic and funk sounds. Most performances start at 2pm, allowing audiences ample time to ramble uphill to the respective venue – always a *rifugio* or mountain pass. Some venues are better reached with the aid of the local Alpine guide; most run free guided treks to the concert.

The culturally inclined who prefer a tad more wrist-action can limber up with a spot of wine-tasting in a traditional Trentino wine cellar, followed by an evening concert. Local wine can likewise be sampled during the musical events held in a *malghe* – an Alpine hut on a hill where butter and cheese are traditionally made.

For more information call ☎ 0461 83 90 00, look online at www.trentino.to or contact the tourist office in Trent.

about €120, and private lessons average €35 per hour. The average cost of ski and boot hire ranges from €12 to €25 per day for downhill skis and up to €12 for cross-country skis and boots. In more expensive resorts such as Cortina, prices can jump to as high as €270 for a six-day group ski tuition and €40 per day to hire downhill skis and boots. When hiring skis it always pays to ask exactly what is available – generally, you do end up paying for what you get, ie a pair of the latest VIP carving blades naturally cost more than a run-of-the-mill pair from three seasons ago.

Tourist offices abound across the region, but the best for getting general information, including more on ski-pass prices and accommodation packages, are those in Trent (p296) and Bolzano (p306).

OTHER ACTIVITIES

Summer pastimes include mountain biking, hang-gliding and rock climbing. Tourist offices can help find trails, bike-rental outlets and hang-gliding schools. Mountain guide associations (under Information in relevant sections) arrange guided excursions, ranging from family rambles to challenging walks of several days at high altitudes.

TRENTINO

TRENT (TRENTO)
pop 105,942 / elevation 194m

This calm capital is a fine starting point for forays into the province and the neighbouring Parco Naturale Adamello-Brenta. Its tourist offices have extensive information on the town and Trentino, and its public transport network is efficient and extensive. **Castel Toblino**, a remote lakeside castle with a restaurant and café, some 17km west of town along the S45b, makes for a romantic lunchtime spot for those with wheels at hand. Heading south, vineyards are strung the length of the pretty road linking Trent with Rovereto (see p284).

Known by the ancient Romans as Tridentum, Trent later passed from the Goths to the Lombards and was eventually annexed by the Holy Roman Empire when it became known as Trento or Trient. From 1027 until the early 19th century, it was an episcopal principality during a period marked by political and territorial conflict with the rulers of Tirolo. The Council of Trento (1545–63) considered the restructuring of the Catholic Church and dreamed up the ideals of the Counter-Reformation here.

Information

BOOKSHOPS
Ancora Libreria (Via Santa Croce 35) Kompass walking maps.
Libreria Viaggeria (☎ 0461 23 33 37; Via S Vifilio 20) Excellent travel bookshop.
Rizzoli (Corso III Novembre) English-language novels in its basement.
Touring Club Italiano (☎ 0461 22 11 61; Via Garibaldi 27) Maps and guides galore.

EMERGENCY
Police Station (☎ 0461 89 95 11; Piazza della Mostra)

INTERNET ACCESS
Wireless Internet Café Olimpia (☎ 0461 98 24 45; Via Belenzani 33; ☼ 7am-9pm Mon & Tue, 7am-midnight Wed-Sat)

MEDICAL SERVICES
Guardia Medica (☎ 0461 91 58 09) Emergency doctor.
Hospital (☎ 0461 90 31 11; Largo Medaglie d'Oro 9) Hospital southeast of the centre.

POST
Post Office (Via Calepina; ☼ 8.30am-6.30pm Mon-Fri, 8am-12.30pm Sat)

TOURIST INFORMATION
Tourist Office (☎ 0461 98 38 80; www.apt.trento.it; Via Manci 2; ☼ 9am-7pm Mon-Sat)
Trentino Agritur (☎ 0461 23 53 23; Via Aconcio 13; ☼ 9am-5pm Mon-Fri) Info point for *agroturismi*, places to eat and activities in the Trentino countryside.

Sights

Flanked by the Romanesque **cathedral** and 13th-century **Palazzo Pretorio** and its tower, Piazza del Duomo is the natural place to start a tour of Trent. Host to the Council of Trent, the cathedral displays fragments of medieval frescoes inside its transepts. Two colonnaded staircases flank its nave, and the foundations of an early Christian church form part of an archaeological area.

Illuminated manuscripts, icons depicting the Council of Trent, liturgical vestments and other 15th- to 19th-century treasures form part of the awe-inspiring collection in the **Museo Diocesano** (☎ 0461 23 44 19; Piazza del Duomo; adult/child €2.50/free; ☼ 9.30am-12.30pm & 2.30-6pm Mon-Sat), inside the former bishop's residence of Palazzo Pretorio. Admission includes entry to the cathedral's archaeological zone and treasury.

On the other side of the piazza are two Renaissance houses, known as the **Casa Cazuffi-Rella**, with fresco-decorated facades. The 18th-century **Fontana di Nettuno** gushes in the piazza's centre. Southeast of here is the **Museo Tridentino di Scienze Naturali** (Natural Science Museum; ☎ 0461 27 03 11; www.mtsn.tn.it, Italian only; Via Calepina 14; adult/child €2.50/1.50; ☼ 9am-12.30pm & 2.30-6pm Tue-Sun).

A short walk north of the Piazza del Duomo, subterranean Trent can be unearthed at the fascinating **Tridentum La Città Sotterranea** (☎ 0461 23 01 71; Piazza Cesare Battisti; adult/child €2/1; ☼ 10am-noon & 2-6pm Tue-Sun Sep-May, 10am-noon & 2.30-7pm Jun-Aug). Archaeological remains of Roman Trent can be viewed at the underground site.

An easy stroll northeast through pedestrian streets takes you to **Castello del Buonconsiglio** (☎ 0461 23 37 70; Via Bernardo Clesio 5; adult/child €3/1.50; ☼ 9am-noon & 2-5pm Tue-Sun Oct-Mar, 10am-5.30pm Tue-Sun Apr-Sep), home of the bishop-princes who once ruled Trent. The fortified complex incorporates the old

TRENTINO-ALTO ADIGE

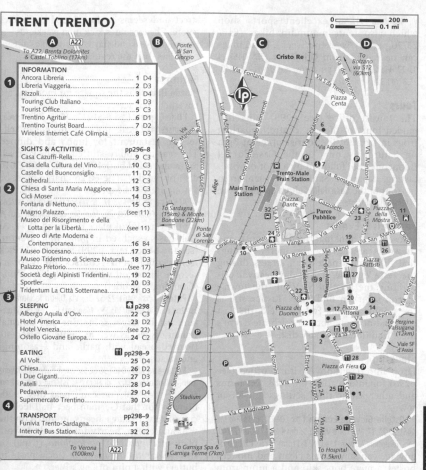

TRENT (TRENTO)

INFORMATION
Ancora Libreria	1 D4
Libreria Viaggeria	2 D3
Rizzoli	3 D4
Touring Club Italiano	4 D3
Tourist Office	5 C3
Trentino Agritur	6 D1
Trentino Tourist Board	7 D2
Wireless Internet Café Olimpia	8 D3

SIGHTS & ACTIVITIES   pp296–8
Casa Cazuffi-Rella	9 C3
Casa della Cultura del Vino	10 C3
Castello del Buonconsiglio	11 D2
Cathedral	12 C3
Chiesa di Santa Maria Maggiore	13 C3
Cicli Moser	14 D3
Fontana di Nettuno	15 C3
Magno Palazzo	(see 11)
Museo del Risorgimento e della Lotta per la Libertà	(see 11)
Museo di Arte Moderna e Contemporanea	16 B4
Museo Diocesano	17 D3
Museo Tridentino di Scienze Naturali	18 D3
Palazzo Pretorio	(see 17)
Società degli Alpinisti Tridentini	19 D2
Sportler	20 D3
Tridentum La Città Sotterranea	21 D3

SLEEPING   🏠 p298
Albergo Aquila d'Oro	22 C3
Hotel America	23 D2
Hotel Venezia	(see 22)
Ostello Giovane Europa	24 C2

EATING   🍴 pp298–9
Al Volt	25 D4
Chiesa	26 D2
I Due Giganti	27 D3
Patelli	28 D4
Pedavena	29 D4
Supermercato Trentino	30 D4

TRANSPORT   pp298–9
Funivia Trento-Sardagna	31 B3
Intercity Bus Station	32 C2

13th-century castle, the Renaissance bishops' residence **Magno Palazzo** and a **Museo del Risorgimento e della Lotta per la Libertà**.

Impressively showcased in the regal Palazzo delle Albere is Trent's enjoyable **Museo di Arte Moderna e Contemporanea** (☎ 0461 23 48 60; Via Roberto da Sanseverino 45; adult/child €4/3; ☯ 10am-6pm Tue-Sun), part of the MART in Rovereto (see p287). Works displayed inside range from 19th-century impressionist pieces to futurist photography, cityscapes and contemporary state-of-the art installations.

Activities

From Trent you can ride the **Funivia Trento-Sardagna** (☎ 0461 23 21 54; Via Montegrappa 1) to Sardagna, a pleasant year-round strolling territory. From here 15km of wiggly road brings you to the small ski station of **Vaneze di Monte** (1350m), connected by cable car to its higher counterpart **Vasòn** – where most ski schools and ski hire shops are – and the gentle slopes of **Monte Bondone** (1537m). The latter is criss-crossed by 37km of cross-country ski trails and nine downhill runs. Its slopes are more famed in the region however for their extraordinary grass (see the boxed text, p313). For walking information, including itineraries and *rifugi* in Trentino, contact local Alpinist society, **Società degli Alpinisti Tridentini** (SAT; ☎ 0461 98 18 71; Via Manci 57; ☯ 8am-noon & 3-7pm Mon-Fri).

Some 2500 sq m of sports gear can be ogled and bought at **Sportler** (☎ 0461 98 12 90;

TRENTINO-ALTO ADIGE

Via Mantova 12), an excellent sports shop which also rents mountain bikes (€15/25/70 per day/weekend/week). Road bikes can be rented from **Cicli Moser** (☎ 0461 23 03 27; Via Calepina 37; per day/weekend/week €15.49/25.82/41.32).

Tours

The tourist office (see p299) runs free guided tours of the city centre, departing from in front of the tourist office at 3pm on Saturday. Tours of the Castello del Buonconsiglio, followed by a spot of wine-tasting, depart on Saturday at 10am from in front of the **Casa della Cultura del Vino** (House of Wine; Via Suffragio).

Festivals & Events

Goose races, dunkings, medieval jousts and fireworks are among the merry-makings that fill Trent's pedestrian streets during the **Feste Vigiliane**, a five-day festival celebrating the feast of St Vigil (the town's patron saint) in mid-June. Tastier still is the annual **Polenta Festival**, held the last weekend of September to celebrate Trent's most traditional culinary dish.

Sleeping

Drop into Trentino Agritur's office (see p296) for information on B&Bs on farms and other idyllic rural settings outside of town.

Ostello Giovane Europa (☎ 0461 26 34 84; fax 0461 22 25 17; Via Torre Vanga 9; dm €13-17, s/d €25/40; ☻ reception 7.30am-11am & 3-11pm) Travellers of any age can stay at this clean and modern hostel, a mere hop, skip and a jump from the bus and train stations. Mountain views, cheap canteen food and excellent bathrooms facilities are other assets. HI cards are obligatory.

Hotel Venezia (☎ /fax 0461 23 41 14; Piazza del Duomo 45; s/d from €40/50) This 1950s-style hotel is split across two buildings; rival Albergo Aquila d'Oro forms the filling in the sandwich.

Albergo Aquila d'Oro (☎ 0461 98 62 82; www.aquiladoro.it, Italian only; Via Belenzani 76; s/d from €50/60) This quiet, family-run hotel with 20 rooms is spitting distance from the hubbub of the central square.

Hotel America (☎ 0461 98 30 10; www.hotelamerica.it; Via Torre Verde 50; s/d/tr €60/90/110; P ☻) This 1920s pad is situated on a busy non-pedestrian street and seems to lure kid-clad families galore. Cheaper rates kick in at weekends – a two-night weekend stay lands doubles at €7 a night less than the regular rate.

Eating

Piazza Battisti is the square for modern café pavement terraces.

I Due Giganti (☎ 0461 23 75 15; Via del Simonino 14; courses €4) Locals flock to this cheap self-service restaurant for lunch and dinner. The eat-till-you're-stuffed, help-yourself pizza and salad buffet is a steal, as its €3.10 dish of the day. The €0.26 charge must be among Italy's cheapest!

Al Volt (☎ 0461 98 37 76; Via Santa Croce 16; 1st/2nd courses from €6.20/7.70; ☻ Mon-Sat, closed lunch Thu) A simple yet soulful place dating to 1894, Al Volt has specialised in *piatti tipici trentini* (see the boxed text, p299) since 1894. Pick from a couple of first courses and five or six second. Finish off with *strudel della nonna* (Grandma's strudel).

Patelli (☎ 0461 23 52 36; Via Dietro le Mura 1/5 1st/2nd courses €7.40/11; ☻ Mon-Sat) Off Via Mazzini, Patelli serves some fine and unusual Italian dishes, as well as lighter bruschette (toasted bread with garlic and seasoning) and salads.

Pedavena (☎ 0461 98 62 55; www.birreriapedavena .com, Italian only; Piazza di Fiera 13; 1st/2nd courses from €5/6; ☻ Wed-Mon) You can't beat this 1920s brewery for that German beer-hall feeling, complete with stags' heads mounted on the wall and cheap, hearty food. Swill down a plate of *trippa alla parmigiana* (tripe) or *strangolapreti alla Trentina* (local pasta in butter) with a pint of Lag's Bier.

Chiesa (☎ 0461 23 87 66; Via Marchetti 9; 1st/2nd courses from €8/10) With a bird-twittering terrace in Parco San Marco, the Church dishes up finely presented and imaginative dishes. Look out for the artistic happenings it hosts and don't miss the metres-deep well in the ladies' loo.

Pick up picnic supplies at **Supermercato Trentino** (Corso III Novembre 4-6).

Getting There & Away

Regular trains connect Trent **train station** (Piazza Dante) with Verona (one hour, hourly), Venice (2½ hours, up to six daily), Bologna (3¼ hours, four daily) and Bolzano (30 minutes, at least hourly). The Trent-Malè train line (station next to the main station)

GASTRONOMIC ORGASMS

Tuck into the following for a titillating taste of Trentino-Alto Adige. Remains of the plate can be mopped up with a hunk of bread – often dense, scented with caraway or rye and almost always brown. Dry palates can be whetted with a mug of Forst, the local beer brewed in Merano.

canederli – Germanic Alto Adige's answer to pasta: large bread dumplings, known as *knödel* by good Germans who, like those in Alto Adige, are reared on platefuls of the hefty tummy-filling balls

cotto e cren – cooked ham with horseradish; *salsa al cren* is a sausage variation – both are antipasti

formaggio grigio – a most bizarre cheese from the Val Pusteria, concocted from unpasteurised milk and guaranteed to thrill the most fanatic of foodies. The Gasthof-Albergo Oberraut near Brunico is one of the few farms where one can still sample it; season with apple vinegar, olive oil and salt 'n' pepper

gulasch – a thinner version of spicy Hungarian goulash, either served as a soup or with *canederli* as a blood-stirring main course

polenta e coniglio – game is all the rage in Trentino-Alto Adige as this dear little rabbit, cooked up with polenta, would attest

polenta e crauti – cornflour meal and sauerkraut, two staple ingredients set to stuff the stoutest of stomachs

risotto ai funghi – risotto laced with *brisa* mushrooms, locally picked and known for their extraordinarily strong and distinctive flavour

trippa alla parmigiana – tripe with parmesan cheese

spàtzle – little flour and egg dumplings, topped with melted gorgonzola to make a tasty antipasto or dished up alongside meat as a main course

strangolapreti – spinach-flavoured gnocchi

strudel – sliced and cooked apples rolled in a thicker, less-refined pastry than one finds in Vienna.

connects the city with Cles in the Val di Non.

From the **bus station** (Via Andrea Pozzo), local bus company **Atesina** (☎ 0461 98 36 27; www .atesina.it, Italian only) runs buses to/from various destinations, including Madonna di Campiglio (€4), San Martino di Castrozza (€4.60), Molveno (€3.20), Canazei (€4.60) and Rovereto (€2.20).

BRENTA DOLOMITES (DOLOMITI DI BRENTA)

Northwest of Trent and part of the **Parco Naturale Adamello-Brenta**, this majestic group of peaks is isolated from the main body of the Dolomites and provides dramatic walking opportunities – best suited to those keen to test their mountaineering skills. Harnesses and ropes are essential for most high-altitude trails, including one of the group's most famous trails, Via Bocchetta di Tuckett – opened up by 19th-century climber Francis Fox Tuckett from Molveno to Cima Brenta, and including gruelling sections of *vie ferrate* trails with permanent steel cords).

Lakeside Molveno and Madonna di Campiglio make suitable bases from which to delve into the Brenta Dolomites. The wiggly S421, S237 and S239 linking Molveno to Madonna make for a scenic, if perilous, drive.

Molveno

pop 1080 / elevation 864m

This pretty village, 38km northwest of Trent by road, languishes in a picturesque position by Lago di Molveno, overshadowed by the towering Brenta Dolomites. It became famous in the 19th century as a base for English and German mountaineers who came to open up trails into the group. In winter, skiers and snowboarders fly down the slopes of **Monte Paganella** (2125m), linked by cable car to **Andalo** (population 1026), 4km northeast of Molveno, and **Fai della Paganella** (population 900), 10km north.

INFORMATION

Andalo Tourist Office (☎ 0461 58 58 36; www .aptandalo.com; Piazza Dolomiti 1; ⏰ 9am-12.30pm & 3.30-7pm Mon-Sat, 9.30am-12.30pm Sun)

Fai della Paganella Tourist Office (☎ 0461 58 31 30; Via Villa; ☺ 9am-12.30pm & 3.30-7pm Mon-Sat, 9.30am-12.30pm Sun)

Guardia Medica (☎ 0461 58 56 37; ☺ 8pm-8am) Night medical aid.

Molveno Iniziative Turistiche (☎ 0461 58 60 86; Piazza Marconi 1; ☺ 9am-12.30pm & 3-6.30pm Mon-Fri) Hotel reservations, information on the Molveno Card and mountain-bike itineraries.

Molveno Tourist Office (☎ 0461 58 69 24; www.apt molveno.com; Piazza Marconi 5; ☺ 9am-12.30pm & 3-6.30pm Mon, Wed, Fri & Sat, 9am-12.30pm Tue & Thu, 9.30am-12.30pm Sun)

Tourist Medical Service (☎ 0461 58 60 45) Daytime medical aid.

ACTIVITIES

Cyclists, mountain bikers and walkers needing a guiding hand should touch base at Molveno's **Guide Alpine Brenta Est** (☎ 0461 58 69 24, ☎ 320 022 43 60; guidealpine@aptdolomitipag nella.com; Piazza Marconi 1; ☺ 8.30-10pm Jul & Aug). It can organise rock-climbing and guided walks in summer and ski-mountaineering, frozen waterfall climbing and snow-shoeing excursions – which are suitable for all abilities – in the Parco Naturale Adamello-Brenta in winter.

The Paganella ski area – Molveno's winter playground – is accessible from Andola (by cable car) and Fai della Paganella (by chair lift). It sports two cross-country **skiing** trails and 50km of downhill ski slopes, ranging from beginner-friendly greens to heart-thumping blacks. Plenty of sports shops in Andola and Fai della Paganella rent gear. A Skipass Paganella allowing unlimited use of the resort's one cable car, chairs and drag lifts costs €13/16/18 for two/three/four hours (high season €16/19/21) or €21.50/42 for one/two days (high season €28/49). The Skirama and Superskirama Adamello-Brenta passes (see p301) are both valid here, as is the Dolomiti Superski pass.

From the top of Molveno village, a two-seater **cable car** (☎ 0461 58 69 81; single/ return €4.70/5.30) transports you in two stages up to Pradel (1400m), from where trail No 340, which is a pleasant and easy one-hour walk, leads to the **Rifugio Croz dell'Altissimo** (1430m; ☎ 0461 58 61 95). Several other trails – many tough – kick off from here. Tourist offices have complete lists of mountain huts.

SLEEPING & EATING

There are numerous farmhouses to sleep in and eat at around Molveno, best suited for travellers with wheels wanting to get away from it all.

Camping Spiaggia (☎ 0461 58 69 78; camping@ molveno.it; Via Lungolago 25; person/tent & car from €5/8; ☺ reception 9am-noon & 2-7pm) Rates on Molveno's lakeside camp site, open all year, include free admission to the neighbouring outdoor swimming pool, tennis court and table-tennis tables as well as to the numerous forms of on-site entertainment.

Azienda Agrituristica Maso-Marocc (☎/fax 0465 70 20 98; d B&B per person from €30, 1st/2nd courses from €5/7; ☺ Tue-Sun mid-Nov–Sep) Fabulously perched at the top of a dirt track, this rustic farmhouse offers guests charming rooms with a view, an inspirational summer terrace overlooking the mountains, and hearty home cooking. It's 20km south of Molveno along S421 to Ponte Arche, then 2km along SP213 to Poia, at end of village left towards Comano then immediately right onto dirt track.

Almost a dozen hotels in Molveno subscribe to the Molveno Card scheme – guests staying at these hotels are entitled to free mountain-bike hire, among other things. Most only open between Christmas and New Year, for Mardi Gras in February and from Easter to mid-October. Full board is generally obligatory in December, July and August.

Hotel Belvedere (☎ 0461 58 69 33; www.belvedere online.com; d half-board per person low/high season from €41/74; P ✖) Note that full board costs just €6 more per person a night, making it by far the best-value option at this large hotel – one of a handful to keep its doors open all year. Mountain-bike rental is free to guests and a bus shuttles skiing guests from the hotel to Andola in season.

Grand Hotel Molveno (☎ 0461 58 69 34; fax 046 58 61 76; Via Bettega 18; s/d from €65/75; ☺ Jul-Sep) Slightly out of town this grandiose, ochre coloured mansion sits astride the lake shores, south of Molveno on the S421.

GETTING THERE & AWAY

From Molveno, **FTM** (☎ 0461 23 83 50) run buses to/from Trent (€3.20, 3½ hours, up to nine daily). **Atesina** (☎ 0461 98 36 27) operate services from Molveno to/from Madonna di Campiglio (€8.10) and Riva del Gard (€5.10) on Lago di Garda.

Madonna di Campiglio & Pinzolo

elevation 1522m

One of the top ski resorts in the Alps, Madonna di Campiglio (known locally simply as Madonna) sprawls along the Val Rendena on the northwestern side of the Brenta Dolomites. Less expensive, family-orientated Pinzolo is 16km south of the resort. Austrian emperor Franz Joseph and his wife were frequent visitors to Madonna at the end of the 19th century – an era relived in late February when fireworks blaze and costumed pageants waltz through town during the annual Habsburg Carnival.

As with most resorts in the region, Madonna and Pinzolo are dead out of season.

INFORMATION

Guardia Medica (☎ 0465 44 08 81, ☎ 0465 80 16 00) Emergency doctor.

Madonna Tourist Office (☎ 0465 44 20 00; www .campiglio.to; Piazza Brenta Alta; 🕑 9am-noon & 3-6.30pm Mon-Sat, 9am-noon Sun)

Pinzolo Tourist Office (☎ 0465 50 10 07; www .pinzolo.to; Piazzale Ciciamimo; 🕑 9am-noon & 3-6.30pm Mon-Sat, 9am-noon Sun)

Tourist Medical Service (☎ 0465 44 30 73) Only functions in season.

ACTIVITIES

A network of chair lifts and several **cable cars** (☎ 0465 44 77 44) takes skiers and boarders from Madonna to its numerous **ski runs** and a **snowboarding park** (with half pipe, slide park and boarder cross) in winter, and to **walking** and **mountain-biking trails** in summer. In Pinzolo there is just one **cable car** (☎ 0465 50 12 56; www.funiviepinzolo.it, Italian only; Via M Bolognini 84; 🕑 8.30am-12.30pm & 2-6pm mid-Dec–Apr & Jun–mid-Sep) which climbs the mountain to Doss del Sabion (2100m; single/return €5/8, 20 minutes), stopping at mid-station Pra Rodoni (1530m; €5/6; 10 minutes) en route. Mountain bikes can be hired at this cable-car station in summer.

In winter, a one-/three-/six-day ski pass for Madonna di Campiglio costs €29/83/144 (high season €32/89/153) and the equivalent for Pinzola is €23/49/87 (high season €26/ 60/110). Six-day Skirama Adamello-Brenta passes covering either resort, plus one day in the other are also available; while the less-restrictive one-/three-/six-day Superskirama Adamelo-Brenta pass covering both resorts and others in the valley costs €31/87/153 (high season €34/96/172). Dolomiti Super-ski passes are also valid.

PARCO NATURALE ADAMELLO-BRENTA

The Italian Alps' last remaining brown bears mingle with ibex (wild goats), red deer, marmots (rodents belonging to the squirrel family) and chamois (mountain-dwelling goats) in Trentino's largest protected area, the 618-sq-km Parco Naturale Adamello-Brenta. Brown bears can be viewed at close quarters at the **Centro Visitatori Spormaggiore** (☎ 0461 65 36 22; Via Alt Spaur 6; admission free; 🕑 10am-noon & 3-7pm Sat, 3-7pm Sun) in **Spormaggiore** (population 1176), 15km northeast of Molveno. Three of the park's 12 brown bears (10 of which have been introduced into the park from Slovenia since 1999) live in a large enclosure at the bear-watching visitors centre – park authorities closely monitor the others with the aid of a radio collar.

Some 82 bird species nest in the Parco Naturale Adamello-Brenta. Spot some around the banks of **Lago di Tovel**, set deep in a forest some 30km north of Spormaggiore in the park's heart. An easy walking trail encircles the lake (one hour). The lakeside **visitors centre** (☎ 0463 45 10 33; 🕑 9am-1pm & 2-6pm Jul & Aug, 9am-1pm & 2-6pm Sat & Sun Sep) has extensive information on other walks in the park. Those with a particular penchant for fauna should make time to visit the **Centro Visitatori Fauna** (☎ 0465 62 20 75; adult/child €2.50/1.50; 🕑 10am-noon & 2-6pm Tue-Sat, 9am-noon & 2-7pm Sun Jul-Sep), in the park's southern realms in **Daone** (population 591), 45km south of Madonna di Campiglio and 50km west of Riva del Garda in Lombardy. The fauna centre organises numerous nature walks and activities in summer.

More information on the park, including lists of mountain huts, Alpine guides, and walking and mountain biking maps and itineraries can be obtained from the helpful **visitors centre** (🕑 9am-noon & 4-8pm Apr-Sep) in **Sant'Antonio di Mavignol**, 15km south of Madonna di Campiglio, or from the **park headquarters** (☎ 0465 80 46 37; www.parcoadamellobrenta.tn.it, Italian only; Via Nazionale 12; 🕑 8.30am-noon & 2-7pm Jul & Aug, 8.30am-noon & 4-6pm Mon-Fri Sep-Jun), a few kilometres south in **Strembo** (population 442).

TRENTINO-ALTO ADIGE

Walking opportunities are endless. Particularly enchanting are the guided walks (€10) to a traditional Alpine pasture hut in the national park, run once on Wednesday mid-July to September, by the tourist office and Parco Naturello Adamello-Brenta. The culinary minded can combine a walk in the mountains with the discovery of a traditional gastronomic dish – chefs prepare, for example, a local dish with honey, salami, milk, mushrooms or forest fruits. Reserve a place at Madonna tourist office.

In Campo Carlo Magno, 2km north of Madonna, the **Cabinovia Grosté** (single/return €8/13; ☻ 8.30am-12.30pm & 2-5pm mid-Dec–Apr & Jun–mid-Sep) cable car takes walkers up, in two stages, to the Passo Grostè (2440m), from where you can set off into the Brenta Dolomites. The Via delle Bocchette (trail No 305) – the **via ferrata** for which the Brenta group is famous – also leaves from the cable-car station; only experienced mountaineers with the correct equipment should attempt it. Otherwise take trail No 316 to **Rifugio del Tuckett** (☎ 0464 44 12 26; ☻ mid-Jun–mid-Sep) and Q Sella (2271m). From there take trail No 328 and then No 318 (*sentiero* Bogani) to the **Rifugio Brentei** (☎ 0465 44 12 44) at 2182m. All trails heading higher into the group from here cross glaciers and need special equipment.

Pinzolo's 16th-century **Chiesa di San Vigilio** merits a visit for its external painting entitled *La Danza Macabra* (The Dance of Death), 20m in length. North of Pinzolo is the entrance to the **Val di Genova**, often described as one of the Alps' most beautiful valleys. A series of spectacular waterfalls along the way enhances its reputation as great walking and picnic country. Four mountain huts strung out along the valley floor make overnight stays an option – Pinzolo tourist office has details.

Descending into the **Val Rendena** a few kilometres southwest of Madonna brings you to the **Valli Giudicarie** area near Lardaro. The area is not served by public transport and you need your own car to explore the spectacular side valleys here. The 25km-long **Val di Daone** road, southwest of Lardaro, brings you to a reservoir, from where a two-hour stroll along the reservoir edge ends at the peaceful **Rifugio Val di Fumo** (☎ 0465 67 45 25; ☻ mid-Jun–mid-Sep) at 1918m, at the foot of the imposing Carè Alto in the Adamello

group. This old-style 1960s mountain hut recalls the mountain-lovers' paradise before tourists discovered the Dolomites. This, and most other huts in the region, are managed by the Trent-based Società degli Alpinisti Tridentini – see p297.

SLEEPING & EATING
Few places to stay in Madonna suit budget travellers' pockets. Most demand half or full board and in the high season are reluctant to accept bookings for less than seven days. Most hotels open mid-December to Easter, and mid-June to mid-September.

Camping Parco Adamello (☎ 0465 50 17 93; ivbeltra@tin.it; Carisolo; person/tent & car low season €7/8, high season €8/11, d with TV & bathroom low/high €18/24; P) Open all year, this camp site, 1km north of Pinzolo, reclines amid mountains in the national park, making it a natural starting point for walking and cycling forays in nature.

Hotel Bellavista (☎ 0465 50 11 64; www.bella vistanet.com, Italian only; Pinzolo; d half-board per week per person low/mid/high season €268/280/308; full board per night €40/57/66; P) Pinzolo's 57-room 'Beautiful View' hotel – one of the few hotels to open all year – can prove a life-saver for mountain travellers passing through Pinzolo out of season.

Caola (☎ 0465 50 10 29; Via Mons Perli 11, Pinzolo) This succulent delicatessen and grocery dating to 1921 stocks a specialist and enticing range of olive oil, balsamic vinegar, preserved chestnuts and fruits, honey, jams, cheese, meat, wine and so on.

GETTING THERE & AWAY
Madonna di Campiglio and Pinzolo are accessible by bus from Trent and Milan (3¾ hours, one daily in each direction mid-December to March). Mid-December to mid-April **shuttle buses** (☎ 0465 50 10 07) run from Milan's Malpensa and Linate airports and Verona's Villafranca airport to/from Madonna and Pinzolo.

VAL DI NON, VAL DI SOLE & VALLE DI PÉIO
The **Val di Non** is a picturesque valley of apple orchards and castles accessible from Trent by Trent–Male train or bus. The main town is **Cles**, dominated by Castel Cles. The **tourist office** (☎ 0463 42 13 76; Corso Dante) is just off the main road through town, and there

is another in the nearby village of **Fondo** (☎ 0463 83 01 33). You may want to stay here on your way north, although accommodation choices are limited.

West from Cles, the scenic S42 thrusts motorists into the **Val di Sole**, a pretty valley which traces the course of the River Noce. The tourist office in **Malè** (☎ 0463 90 12 80; www.valdisole.net; Piazza Regina Elena 19; ⏱ 9am-noon & 3.30-6.30pm Mon-Sat, 10am-noon Sun) has extensive accommodation, transport and sporting activity information for the entire valley, and can advise on walking trails and ski facilities. The **Liberty Hotel Malè** (☎ 0463 90 11 05; www.libertyhotelmale.it; Piazza Garibaldi 33; s/d from €45/60) is one of a handful of atmospheric, shuttered places to kip in the village heart.

From **Peio Terme** (Pejo Terme; 1393m) in the **Valle di Peio**, chair lifts operate to the Rifugio Doss dei Cembri (2400m), from where expert mountaineers scale great heights to reach Monte Vioz (3645m) and the edge of the Forni glacier.

Ferrovia Trent–Malè buses connect Peio Terme with Madonna di Campiglio and with Malè in the Val di Sole. Malè is on the Trent–Malè train line (1½ hours, eight daily).

PALE DI SAN MARTINO
elevation 1467m

Hopping east across the Brenner motorway (A22), which brutally slices through the region, one comes up against the imposing **Pale di San Martino** – mountains so stark and grey-white they virtually glow in the dark. Noted for its Alpine vegetation and wildlife, including roe deer, chamois, marmots, wildfowl and birds of prey such as the golden eagle, this impressive mountain range is embraced by the **Parco Naturale Paneveggio-Pale di San Martino**. At its feet huddles San Martino di Castrozza, a small but popular Trentino ski resort and walking spot.

Equally well known, but for less fortunate reasons, is **Cavalese** (1000m), a small town wedged in the floor of the **Val di Fiemme** from where skiers cable car up to the Cermis ski area (2229m) and beyond. In 1998 the place made international headlines when a low-flying aircraft slashed straight through the cables of a full cable car, causing the skiers inside to plummet

to their deaths. The World Cup ski-jumping championships flew down its slopes in 2002, and the Nordic World Ski Championships returned for the second time to the valley in 2003.

Information
Cavalese Tourist Office (☎ 0462 24 11 11; www .aptfiemme.tn.it; Via Bronzetti 60; ⏱ 9am-noon & 3.30-7pm Mon-Sat, plus 9am-noon Sun late Jun–mid-Sep)
San Martino Tourist Office (☎ 0439 76 88 67; www.sanmartino.com; Via Passo Rolle 165; ⏱ 8.30am-12.30pm & 3-6pm Mon-Sat, 9.30am-12.30pm Sun)
Tourist Medical Service (San Martino ☎ 0439 76 87 39, Fiera di Primiero ☎ 0439 76 20 60)

Activities
San Martino is surrounded by excellent **ski runs** which, together with those in the Val di Fiemme, form part of the extensive Superski Dolomiti region. In winter ski buses connect the valley with the various runs. In summer a chair lift and cable car from San Martino whisk walkers to the Rifugio Rosetta (2600m), from where several trails (some easy, some requiring mountaineering skills) can be picked up.

Maps of the Pale di San Martino's well-marked **walking trails** are available at the tourist offices. Alternatively, try the Parco Naturale Paneveggio-Pale di San Martino's visitors centre (☎ 0439 76 88 59; parcopan.org; Via Laghetto, San Martino), or head 16km north to **Paneveggio** where the park also runs a **visitors centre**. A 1.2km trail leads from the cabin to the **Area Faunistica del Cervofauna**, a nature area where you can watch deer. At the park's impressive headquarters in the **Villa Welsperg** (⏱ 9.30am-12.30pm & 2-5pm) in Val Canali, suspended aquariums illustrate the park's water life and there are exhibitions dedicated to the flora and fauna. The villa itself was built in 1853 and is surrounded by stunning gardens. To get here, follow the southbound S50 from San Martino di Castrozza for 14km and in the village of Fiera di Primiero bear east along a narrow road for a couple of kilometres. After the hamlet of Tonadico, bear left (north) to the villa.

The tourist offices act as contact points for local Alpine guide groups which organise, among other things, **mountaineering ascents** on Pala di San Martino, Cima della Madonna and Sass Maor, a 120km-long, high-altitude skiing excursion.

TRENTINO-ALTO ADIGE

Sleeping & Eating

Local food is served at various *malghe* (alpine huts) around San Martino, since transformed into highly atmospheric little restaurants.

Malga Venegiota (☎ 0462 57 60 44; Via Rioni 1, Tonadico; ☼ Tue-Sun Jun-Sep) Typical dishes guaranteed to excite (see the boxed text p299) are dished up at this authentic mountain inn at 1824m in Tonadico, accessible in summertime by road or on foot (from Passo Rolle via a three-hour return trail from Malga Juribello or by a shorter trail incorporating the Baita Segantini chair lift).

Agritur Darial (☎ 0462 81 47 05; www.agritur darial.it; Via Cavada 61; B&B per person low/high season €28/31, half-board €31/44, single supplement per day €6) Perched high on a hill above the village, 4km east of Cavalese in Tresero, this inviting farmhouse dishes up stunning views of the Val di Fiemme and heart-warming local cuisine. Winter warmers include a sauna and roaring fire.

Hotel Madonna (☎ 0439 6 81 37; www.hotel madonna.it; Via Passo Rolle 72; d full board per person low/high season from €40/78) Kip overnight in San Martino's former post house dating to 1906. Run by the Poggi family from Bologna since the 1950s, the Madonna is a family-run affair with 25 comfortable rooms overlooking the main street. Half-board costs just €4 less per person a night.

Grand Hotel des Alpes (☎ 0439 76 90 69; www .hoteldesalpes.it; Via Passo Rolle 18; d low/high season €131/397; P ☒ ☐ ☒) San Martino's four-star wonder is wondrous no less. Breakfast in the chandelier-lit, wooden-clad Salle deglia Archi (Archer's Room), dine at Il Cervo (The Deer) or enjoy a less formal, heartier tucker at La Canisela (The Path).

Getting There & Away

Atesina buses run to San Martino from Trent and Canazei (via Predazzo).

CANAZEI & AROUND

This popular ski resort in the **Val di Fassa** is surrounded by the striking peaks of the Gruppo di Sella to the north, the Catinaccio (Rosengarten; 2981m) to the west and the Marmolada to the southeast. **Canazei** (population 1809, elevation 1465m) and the villages along the valley to **Moena** (population 2662, elevation 1114m), 15km south, are geared to summer and winter tourism,

although some locals still make a traditional living from dairy farming. Ladin culture is alive and kicking in Pozza di Fassa and neighbouring Vigo di Fass (see the boxed text, p314).

Those who'd rather flee the tourist flock can always head east from Moena, across the Passo San Pellegrino (1918m) into the **Valle del Biois**, where more rural pastures hold a couple of delicious places to sleep and eat. An eastbound journey from Canazei takes you across the breathtaking **Passo Pordoi** – complete with 27 hairpin bends, each considerably numbered for car-sick passengers – and into the Val Badia.

Information

Canazei Tourist Office (☎ 0462 60 11 13; www .fassa.com; Piazza Marconi 5; ☼ 8.30am-12.15pm & 3.30-7pm Mon-Sat, 10am-12.30pm Sun).

Information on the Valle del Biois (www .trevalli.com) is doled out by the tiny tourist offices in:

Caviola Tourist Office (☎ 0437 59 01 16; fax 0437 59 01 16; Via Lungo Tegosa 8; ☼ 10.30am-12.30pm & 4-5pm Mon-Fri)

Falcade Tourist Office (☎ 0437 59 92 41; falcade@ infodolomiti.ti; Corso Roma 1; ☼ 9am-12.30pm & 3.30-6.30pm)

Sights & Activities

Possibilities for **skiing** include 120km of downhill and cross-country runs, as well as challenging Alpine tours and the Sella Ronda ski circuit (see pp305–6). Dolomiti Superski passes are valid, alongside cheaper passes specific to the Val di Fassa which cost €70/121 for three/six days. The Tre Valli ski pass (from €80/145 for a three-/six-day pass) covers the Fassa, Biois and San Pellegrino valleys. In summer, you can ski down the Marmolada glacier.

Walkers can approach the Catinaccio group from Vigo di Fassa, 11km southwest of Canazei. The best approach to the Gruppo di Sella (see p305) is from Passo Pordoi, where a cable car goes to almost 3000m. Any forgotten gear can be picked up in Canazei at **Tecnica** (Via Roma 24) sport shop.

Canazei's green surrounds offer ample rambles for less-experienced walkers. Ask at the tourist office for a copy of the English-language brochure, *Low-level Walks in the*

Fassa Valley, which outlines 29 walks in the Val di Fassa (1.5km to 8km long). Of particular interest are those incorporating visits to old Ladin landmarks such as the **Molin de Pezol** (☎ 0462 76 40 89; Via Jumela 6; ☽ 10am-noon & 4-7pm Mon-Sat), a 19th-century mill 11km south of Canazei in Pera di Fassa; the **Botega da Pinter** (☎ 0462 57 35 74; Via Dolomiti 4; ☽ 10am-noon & 4-7pm Mon-Sat mid-Jun–mid-Sep), an authentic reconstruction of a cooper's workshop 17km south of Canazei in Moena; and 16th-century **La Sia** (☎ 0462 60 23 23; Via Pian Trevisan; ☽ 9am-noon & 3-6pm Mon-Fri mid-Mar–mid-Dec), a sawmill 3km east of Canazei in Penia along the narrow S641.

Staff at the tourist office can likewise advise on **mountain-bike trails**. In Canazei, **Detomas Fiorenzo** (☎ 0462 60 24 47; Via Pareda 31) is one of several sports shops to rent bicycles as well as skis and snowboards. In Falcade try **Tarcy Sport** (☎ 0437 50 70 79; Via Veneto 5; per hr/day around €5/15). The tourist office has several brochures detailing biking itineraries.

Sleeping & Eating
CANAZEI
Hotels and restaurants generally open mid-December to Easter and again for the short summer season from June to mid-September.

Camping Marmolada (☎ 0462 60 16 60; Via Pareda; person/tent & car €8/8) This site, strategically placed in the town centre almost opposite the cable car to Pecol (1926m), opens for both the winter and summer seasons.

Hotel Laurin (☎ /fax 0462 60 12 86; Via Dolomiti 91; d half-board per person from €47) One of the region's few hotels to open year-round, Hotel Laurin is a cosy wooden place with blooming flower boxes and a fun-loving clientele.

Stella Alpina (☎ 0462 60 11 27; www.stella-alpina.net; Via Antermont 4; B&B low/high season per person from €33/40) This charming shuttered place stares face-to-face at a traditional, Alpine wooden hut, traditionally for storing hay, and at a painted wooden shophouse. A vaulted cellar for tasting wine adjoins the seven-room hotel. A sauna and Jacuzzi are perks.

Osteria La Montanara (☎ 0462 60 13 52; Via Dolomiti 147-151; full meals €20) As well as full-blown meals, this cosy inn cooks up a tasty range of well-topped bruschette (€4.40) until 1am in season.

Canazei touts numerous **bars**, **cafés** and a **De Spar** (Via Dolomiti 53) supermarket.

VALLE DEL BIOIS
There is a trio of three-star hotels on Via Pineta (the S346) just west of Caviola in Falcade.

Pensione Rondinella (☎ 0437 59 01 22; fax 0437 59 01 22; Via Lungo Tegosa, Fedèr; s/d from €20/35; ☽ Jul-Apr) What you see is what you get at this simple, down-to-earth B&B with 11 rooms in the tiny hamlet of Fedèr, 2km from Caviola, signposted west of Canale d'Agordo off the S346. Rooms with balconies tout stunning views.

Tabià (☎ 0437 59 04 34; Fedèr; 1st/2nd courses from €5/7; ☽ Wed-Mon) Authentic, home-made cuisine is cooked up at this fabulous, family-run *tabià* (hay barn) which touts no menu but dishes up wholesome temptations like ravioli stuffed with pear and gorgonzola, and mushroom-laced *pansotti* (triangle-shaped ravioli) with fried cheese.

Getting There & Away
Canazei can be reached by Atesina bus from Trent and by SAD bus from Bolzano and the Val Gardena. Buses do not cross the high mountain passes (such as Passo di Sella) in winter.

GRUPPO DI SELLA
The Sella group, in the western Dolomites, straddles the border between Trentino and Alto Adige, close to Cortina d'Ampezzo in the Veneto and the spectacular Parco Naturale di Fanes-Sennes-Braies. To the west is the spiky Sasso Lungo (Langkofel; 3181m), which extends to the Alpe di Siusi in Alto Adige. To the east is the Val Badia and its main town, Corvara, while to the south lies the Val di Fassa.

Skiers can complete the tour of the Sella in a single day on the famous network of runs known as **Sella Ronda**. The long and challenging route (23.1km covered by runs and 13.5km by ski lifts) is only suitable for speedier skiers with some experience, a good level of fitness and lots of luck with the weather. Tourist offices have a leaflet that describes the clockwise and anticlockwise routes, kicking off from Selva (1565m; see p311) no later than 10am; Portavescovo, at 2495m, is the highest point. You'll need a Dolomiti Superski pass to complete the circuit.

For serious **walkers** there is a summer version of the same leaflet, which details the circular route that takes roughly eight hours to complete. Both the Sella and Sasso Lungo walking trails can be reached from Canazei or the Val Gardena resorts by bus to Passo di Sella or Passo di Pordoi. Passo di Sella (2244m) is a mountain pass laced with hairpin bends – a motorcyclist's paradise in summer – topped with the eye-sore hotel-restaurant **Albergo Maria Flora** (☎ 0462 60 11 16), which dishes up fantastic views. From the equally hair-raising Passo di Pordoi (2239m) a cable car takes you to Sasso Pordoi (2950m) – dubbed the 'panoramic terrace of the Dolomites'. Digest its breathtaking views from the café terrace of the **Rifugio Maria** (☎ 0462 60 11 78), then pick up the Alta Via No 2 trail which crosses the group, heads down to the Passo Gardena and continues into the breathtaking Parco Naturale Puez-Odle.

For more information on the Sella, see the Val Gardena (pp311–12) and the Val Badia (pp313–15).

ALTO ADIGE

This orderly Alpine fairyland owes more to its largely Austrian heritage than to its recent Italian history. Alto Adige (Südtirol) is a year-round attraction for skiers, climbers, walkers or those folk just looking to appreciate its natural splendour.

For local news, views and events, pick up a copy of the local Italian daily, *Alto Adige* (www.altoadige.it, Italian only); *Dolomitten*, published daily in German; or for culturally inquisitive souls, *La Usc di Ladins* (see the boxed text, p314).

BOLZANO (BOZEN)

pop 97,300 / elevation 265m

Provincial capital Bolzano is unmistakably Austrian. Forget your cappuccino and brioche and tuck into some *deutscher Kaffee* (German coffee) with *Sachertorte* (chocolate apricot cake). You'll hear Italian and German spoken (both languages are compulsory subjects in school) but, aside from concessions to the former in street, hotel and restaurant signs, there are precious few reminders of Italian rule here. The town's small historic centre, with its engaging Tirolean architecture and arcaded streets, harbours numerous outdoor cafés and restaurants, making it a very pleasant place to spend a few days.

Settled in the Middle Ages, Bolzano was an important market town that became a pawn in the power battles between the bishops of Trent and the counts of Tirolo. During the first decades of the 19th century it passed, with the rest of the Tirolo, from Bavaria to Austria to Napoleon's kingdom of Italy and, finally, again to Austria. Along with the rest of the Südtirol, Bolzano passed to Italy after WWI and was declared the capital of the province in 1927.

Bolzano is linked by a cable car to **San Genesio** (1087m), 10km northwest by a wiggly road; **Renon**, several kilometres east; and **Colle di Villa** (1181m), 4km south. The Colle di Villa cableway is the world's oldest – you can view the original gondola at the upper terminal. Numerous walking and biking trails can be picked up from all mountains and on clear days, Dolomite views are sublime.

Information

Banks riddle the centre and there's a currency exchange booth at the train station.

Green & Clean (Via Garibaldi 24; ☺ 6am-midnight) Self-service laundrette.

Hospital (☎ 0471 90 81 11; Via Lorenz Böhler) Out of the centre towards Merano.

Left Luggage (train station, Piazza Stazione; 1st 12 hrs €2, then €1 per 2-5 hrs; ☺ 8am-6.30pm)

Police Station (☎ 0471 97 60 00, ☎ 0471 94 76 80; Via Marconi 33)

Post Office (Via della Posta; ☺ 8am-6.30pm Mon-Fri, 8am-1pm Sat)

Tourist Office (☎ 0471 30 70 00; www.bolzano-bozen.it; Piazza Walther 8; ☺ 9am-6.30pm Mon-Fri, 9am-12.30pm Sat)

Sights & Activities

Start a sightseeing tour with the Gothic **cathedral** (Piazza Parrocchia; ☺ 9.45am-noon & 2-5pm Mon-Fri, 9.45am-noon Sat) and nearby **Chiesa dei Domenicani** (Piazza Domenicani; ☺ 9.30am-6pm Mon-Sat), with its cloisters and chapel featuring 14th-century frescoes of the Giotto school. Take a walk along the arcaded **Via Portici**, through the charming Piazza delle Erbe (the German name Obstplatz explains what this square is – the daily fresh-produce market), to reach the 14th-century **Chiesa di Francescani** (Via dei

BOLZANO (BOZEN)

Francescani). It features beautiful cloisters and a magnificent Gothic altarpiece carved by Hans Klocker in 1500 in the Cappella della Beata Vergine (Virgin's Chapel).

Museo Archeologico dell'Alto Adige (☎ 0471 98 20 98; www.archaelogiemuseum.it; Via Museo 43; adult/child €8/5.50; ☼ 10am-5pm Tue, Wed & Fri-Sun, 10am-7pm Thu) houses an important collection of regional treasures, including the mummified body of Ötzi (see the boxed text, p27). The body was discovered in the Similaun glacier in September 1991 and dates back about 5000 years. The so-called iceman's equipment is on display, accompanied by an exhaustive commentary.

The geological wonders of Alto Adige can be unearthed in the **Museo di Scienze Naturali Alto Adige** (☎ 0471 41 29 61; www.museonatura.it; Via dei Bottai 1; adult/child €5/3; ☼ 10am-6pm Tue-Sun).

Bolzano's surrounds sport several castles worth a peek, including 13th-century **Castel Mareccio** (☎ 0471 97 66 15; mareccio@comune.bolzan o.it; Via Claudia dé Medici 12; guided tours €4; ☼ tours 11.30am & 4.30pm Tue), north along Via della Roggia from Piazza delle Erbe. **Castel Roncolo** (☎ 0471 32 88 44; roncolo@comune.bolzano.it; Via San Antonio 15; adult/child €8/5.50; ☼ 10am-6pm Tue-Sun Oct-Jun, 10am-8pm Tue-Sun Jul-Sep), out of town on the road to Sarentino (Sarnthein), is renowned for its 14th-century frescoes; while **Castel Firmiano** (closed for restoration) was built on a military site dating back to AD 945. A bike is an invigorating means of getting around to all three; **shuttle buses** (☎ 0471 32 98 08) link Piazza Walther with Castel Roncolo between 10am and 6pm at weekends.

Bolzano's three cable cars whisk skiers and walkers into the mountains: **Funivia del Colle** (☎ 0471 97 85 45; Piazza Campiglio), **Funivia San Genesio** (☎ 0471 97 84 36; Via Sarentino) and **Funivia del Renon** (☎ 0471 97 84 79; Via Renon), 500m east of train station. Walkers and cyclists can buy gear at **Sportler Velo** (☎ 0471 97 77 19; Via Grappoli 56) or **Giacomelli Sports** (Via Museo 20a).

Tours

The tourist office (see p306) organises guided tours on foot of the old historic centre (€4, two hours, three times weekly).

The tourist office also organises guided expeditions of a gentle nature around Bolzano at weekends and during holidays

TRENTINO-ALTO ADIGE

from April to early November; a half/full-day walk costs €10/14 and places must be reserved in advance. For more serious hikes in Alto Adige, contact local walking club **Club Alpino Italiano** (☎ 0471 97 81 72; Piazza delle Erbe 46; ⏱ 11am-1pm & 5-7pm Tue-Fri).

Sleeping

Bolzano offers everything from camp sites to a techie art hotel. The tourist office has a list of surrounding farms offering B&B.

Croce Bianca/Weisses Kreuz (☎ 0471 97 75 52; Piazza del Grano 3; s/d without bathroom €28/52, d with bathroom €58) Breakfast is included in the rates charged by this cheap and cheerful, family-run place off Via dei Portici.

Hotel Feichter (☎ 0471 97 87 68; Via Grappoli 15; s/d/tr €52/80/95) The restaurant is on the ground floor and hotel reception on the first at this friendly, hectic and endearing family-run hotel.

Hotel Figl (☎ 0471 97 84 12; www.figl.net; Piazza del Grano 9; s/d from €75/106; P ⌘) Peering out across yet another pretty tourist-riddled square, Figl is a fine mid-range option for those seeking a tad more style and comfort.

Hotel Greif (☎ 0471 31 80 00; www.greif.it; Piazza Walther; s/d from €132/158; P ⌘ 🖳) Light and spacious with a PC in every room (each designed by a different artist), the highly innovative Griffin is an architect's or rich woman's dream.

Parkhotel Laurin (☎ 0471 31 30 00; www.laurin.it; Via Laurin 4; s/d from €105/158; P ⌘ 🖳 🐾) A wood-panelled beamed ceiling piano bar that hosts jazz concerts, vast grounds, a pool and highly acclaimed restaurant are but some of the highlights to be found at this beautiful Jugendstil hotel. Try to fit in a lunch on its sunny terrace if you can't stay here.

Eating

The best Bolzano restaurants specialise in Tirolean-style Austrian dishes such as *speckknödelsuppe* (bacon dumpling soup) washed down with a red Lagrein or St Magdalener wine.

Lounge Exil Cafe (☎ 0471 97 18 14; Piazza del Grano 2a) Young, fun and a funky place to hang out, this trendy industrial-style café is the place to sip cocktails, drink tea or sink your teeth into a brownie, salad or healthy bowl of yoghurt, fruit and muesli.

Nadamas (☎ 0471 98 06 84; Piazza delle Erbe; 1st/2nd courses €5/8) This is Bolzano's other happening place to hang out. Munch a lunch of couscous, salad or one of the other healthy options in a deep-red interior. Come dusk, drinkers spill on to the pavement outside.

Cavallino Bianco/Weiss Rössl (☎ 0471 97 32 67; Via dei Bottai 6; 1st/2nd courses €6/9; ⏱ 8am-1am Mon-Sat) Extremely popular and reasonably priced, the White Horse serves a wide choice of traditionally meaty treats (try the *testina di vitello* – lamb intestines) as well as less-gruesome dishes for vegetarians. It has a €11.90 fixed menu.

Hopfen & Co (☎ 0471 30 07 88; Piazza delle Erbe 17; 1st/2nd courses from €5/8) Hearty portions of traditional dishes – including a very memorable *gulasch* (stew) simmered with *canederli* in beer brewed on the premises – are served at this authentic brewery-cum-eating house.

Pick up fruit, vegetables, bread and cheese from the **morning market** (Piazza delle Erbe; ⏱ Mon-Sat) and wholesome breads topped or filled with grains galore at **Grandi** (Via dei Bottai 16a).

Getting There & Around

Bolzano airport (Aeroporto di Bolzano; ☎ 0471 25 52 55; info@abd-airport.it) is served by a couple of daily European flights.

Buses run by **SAD** (www.sad.it) leave from the **bus terminal** (toll-free ☎ 800 84 60 47; Via Perathoner) for destinations throughout the province, including Val Gardena (up to 12 daily), Brunico (up to 10 daily), Val Pusteria (four or five daily) and Merano (55 minutes, hourly between 6.10am and 11.25pm). SAD buses also head for resorts outside the province, including Cortina d'Ampezzo. Updated timetables are on the SAD website.

Bolzano **train station** (Piazza Stazione) is connected by hourly trains with Merano (40 minutes), Trent (30 minutes) and Verona (2½ hours), from where trains to dozens of other cities can be picked up. You can also catch a train from Bolzano to Brunico (€6.80, 1½ hours, six daily) in the Val Pusteria.

Bicycles can be picked up for free at the **open-air stall** (information ☎ 0471 99 75 78; Via della Stazione 2; ⏱ 7.30am-8pm Easter-Oct) near the train station or hired year-round from the Sportler Velo sports shop (see p307).

TRENTINO-ALTO ADIGE

MERANO (MERAN)

pop 34,235 / elevation 323m

Merano is a picturesque little place, although its typically Tirolean centre – clean, sedate and well tended – throngs with tourists in season. Its Terme di Merano, a complex of therapeutic baths and treatments, lures an elderly set, which flocks here to ease aches, pains and other bodily ills with a dose of self-pampering. The town neighbours the Parco Naturale del Gruppo di Tessa, the Parco Nazionale dello Stelvio and the spectacular Ortles mountain range, making Merano a handy stopover on the way to higher altitudes.

Orientation & Information

The train and bus stations are a 10-minute stroll from the centre. Exit the train station, turn right into Via Europa and at Piazza Mazzini take Corso Libertà – past the **tourist office** (☎ 0473 23 52 23; www.meraninfo.it; Corso Libertà 35; � 9am-12.30pm & 2-6pm Mon-Fri, 9.30am-12.30pm Sat) and several banks with ATMs – to reach the historic centre.

Pedestrianised Via dei Portici is the main shopping street. The **post office** (Via Roma 2) is on the other side of the River Passirio from the old town. For medical emergencies go to **Ospedale Civile Tappeiner** (☎ 0473 26 33 33; Via Rossini 5). In the mountains call **Emergency Mountain Rescue** (☎ 0473 22 23 33, ☎ 118).

Sights

The historic centre of town surrounds arcaded Via dei Portici and Piazza del Duomo – take any of the streets off Corso Libertà near the tourist office (leading away from the river). The **Terme di Merano** (Meraner Kurbad; ☎ 0473 23 77 24; Via Piave 9), under renovation until 2005, is a therapeutic bath dating to the 1930s and offering a full range of medical and relaxation treatments, including underwater massages and healthy radon baths in a small thermal pool.

The past two centuries are recaptured from a female perspective at the **Museo della Donna** (☎ 0473 23 12 16; Via dei Portici 68; adult/child €4/3; � 10am-6pm Mon-Fri, 10am-1pm Sat). Period costumes are among the exhibits displayed. Those seeking to buy their own traditional Tirolese costume to take home can buy one at **Haladi** (Via dei Porticiat 85). Local history is the focus of the **Museo Civico** (☎ 0473 23 60 15; Via delle Corse 42; adult/child €2/1.50; � 10am-5pm

Tue-Sat, 10am-1pm Sun Sep-Jun, 4-7pm Sun Jul & Aug). The third in the museum trio, the **Museo Ebraico** (☎ 0473 23 61 27; Via Schiller 14; admission free; � 3-6pm Tue & Wed, 9am-noon Thu, 3-5pm Fri) is housed in Merano's synagogue, dating to 1901. The museum recounts the history of the town's Jewish population from the early 19th century through to WWII.

Of Alto Adige's many castles **Castello Principesco** (☎ 0473 23 01 02; Via Galilei; adult/child €2/1.50; � 10am-1pm Sun Sep-Jun, 4-7pm Sun Jul & Aug) – home to the Tirol princes from 1470 – is one of the better-maintained. Lush Mediterranean foliage surrounds **Castel Trauttmansdorff** (Via San Valentino 51a), a 1850s castle surrounded by botanical gardens. Inside, the **Touriseum** (Tourist Museum; ☎ 0473 27 01 72; www.touriseum.it; garden & museum adult/child €9/free; � 9am-6pm mid-Mar–mid-Nov, 9am-9pm May-Sep) tells the historical tale of Alpine tourism. A 1½-hour guided visit/audioguide of the gardens costs €4/2.

Beer-lovers will enjoy a tour of the **Forst Brewery** (☎ 0473 26 01 11; Forst; advance reservations only), just outside Merano; the tourist office has details.

Activities

Some 6km east of town, the **Funivia Val di Nova** (adult half-/full-day ski pass €16/22; � 9am-noon & 1.15-5pm) cable car, operated by **Funivie Monte Ivigna** (☎ 0473 23 48 21; www.meran2000.com, Italian only; Via Val di Nova 37), carries winter sports enthusiasts up to Piffling in **Merano 2000**, a small ski station at 2000m, with 40km of slopes served by five chair lifts, a gondola and a couple of drag lifts. Skiing on the mountain is limited and best suited to beginners. Bus No 1A links Merano train station with the Val di Nova cable car.

Gentle walks abound in this neck of the woods. The tourist office runs guided walks between July and September, and distributes a free map, marked up with various parks and walks, including the popular Passeggiata Tappeiner which kicks off on Via Laurin and meanders for 4km around Monte Benedetto (514m) before dropping down to the banks of the River Passirio. The **chair lift** (☎ 0473 92 31 05; Via Laurin; � 9am-6pm Sep-Jun, 9am-7pm Jul & Aug), next to the start of the footpath, links Merano with the village of **Tirolo**, from where a **cable car** (☎ 0473 92 34 80) carries on up the mountain to **Muta**. Another itinerary, the **Passeggiata Gilf** makes for a pleasant riverside stroll – a different poem is carved on 24 wooden benches lining the footpath. Between July and September the tourist office organises walks with a mountain guide around Merano; places must be booked in advance and walkers must have hiking boots, wind and waterproof clothing, a small rucksack and sun cream.

Walking, cycling and other sports gear can be picked up at sports shop **Sportler** (☎ 0473 21 13 40; Via dei Portici 272).

Sleeping

Pension Tyrol (☎ 0473 44 97 19; Via XXX Aprile 8; B&B per person from €25; P) Most establishments in the centre are expensive, although Pension Tyrol, with its big garden off Corso della Libertà, has reasonable doubles to let.

Hotel West End (☎ 0473 23 23 76; www.westend.it; Via Speckbacher 9; d low/mid/high season €80/110/130, half-board per person €52/70/80; P ❀) At the western end of the riverside promenade, the regal facade of Hotel West End twinkles in all its mustard and gold loveliness, framed by a flowery garden. In summer dine by candlelight outside or borrow a bicycle (free) to razz around town.

Hotel Conte di Merano/Graf von Meran (☎ 0473 23 21 81; gapptouristik@dnet.it; Via delle Corse 78; d B&B/half-board per person low season €42/52, high season €50/60; P) This grandiose place is near Via dei Portici and has lovely rooms.

Hotel Aurora (☎ 0473 21 18 00; www.hotel-aurora -meran.com; Passerpromenade 38; B&B per person low/high season from €59/66; P ❀ ❀) Another fine spoil-yourself choice, the Aurora is splendidly placed on Merano's sunny riverside promenade. Its pavement terrace restaurant, La Terrazza, heaves day and night. Only south-facing rooms have air-conditioning.

Eating

Café Wolf (☎ 0473 23 33 49; Via delle Corse) The Wolf, an ideal spot for coffee and cake with its modern and minimalist interior, peers across at the Count of Merano (hotel).

Forsterbräu (☎ 0473 23 65 35; Corso della Libertà 90; 1st/2nd courses €6/10; ❀ Wed-Mon) Nestled in and around an atmospheric courtyard, this typically Tirolean restaurant cooks up a hot *gulaschsuppe* and a swimming choice of fresh trout dishes. The place is actually part of the Forst brewery, making a pint of Forst beer and a plate of *speck* (smoked cured ham; €8) a must.

Blaues Schift (Via delle Corse 28; 1st/2nd courses €6/7, pizzas €4.40-7) The Blue Ship lures the young and buoyant crowd out of the Merano woodwork with its pizzas (5pm to 11pm only) and hearty grills. Perch on a bar stool or lounge out back.

Rainer (☎ 0473 23 61 49; Via dei Portici 266-268; 1st/2nd courses €10/15) Rainer is another top spot to sample traditional Tirolese fodder in a wooden interior. The hand-written menu can be a trifle hard to decipher – one item says octopus salad.

Haisrainer (☎ 0473 23 79 44; Via dei Portici 100; 1st/2nd courses €6/10; ❀ Mon-Sat) Sink your teeth into a meaty Tirolese platter (€10) starring *wurstel* (sausage) and *crauti* (sauerkraut) at this traditional spot, notable for its cavernous feel.

Alto Adige's famed *speck* and other meats and sausages can be ogled at and bought at **Gögele** (Via dei Portici 77-83). Buy nutty brown breads riddled with every imaginable grain at **Preiss Chritine & Co** (☎ 0473 23 73 29; Via delle Corse 118 & 120) and anything else at the supermarket **De Spar** (Via delle Corse).

Getting There & Around

SAD buses connect Merano **bus station** (Piazza Stazione) with Monte San Caterina and other villages that give access to the Tessa group, as well as to Silandro and the valleys leading into the Ortles range and the Parco Nazionale dello Stelvio – see the next section for bus information.

Bolzano (€3.25, almost hourly) is an easy 40-minute journey from Merano **train station** (Piazza Stazione).

Pick up a free pair of wheels (small deposit required) from the open-air stand marked **'Noleggio Biciclette-Fahrradverleih'** (❀ 9am-7pm Mon-Sat Mar-Sep) next to the bus station.

PARCO NAZIONALE DELLO STELVIO

If you can tear yourself away from the Dolomites this national park offers even more fantastic walking possibilities, at low altitudes in the pretty valleys of Val d'Ultimo, Val Martello and Val di Solda, and at high altitudes on spectacular peaks such as the Gran Zebrù (3859m), Cevedale (3769m) and the breathtaking Ortles (3905m), all part of the Ortles range. There is a network of well-marked trails, including routes over some of the range's glaciers. The park incorporates one of Europe's largest glaciers, the Ghiacciaio dei Forni.

The glaciers permit year-round skiing and there are well-serviced runs at Solda and the **Passo della Stelvio** (2757m); the latter is the second-highest pass in the Alps and is approached from the north from the hamlet of **Trafoi** (1543m) on one of Europe's most spectacular roads, a series of tight switchbacks covering 15km with, at times, nerve-wrackingly steep gradients. The road is famous among cyclists, who flock to the park every summer to tackle the ascent.

Immediately south of the Passo della Stelvio is the little-known ski resort of **Bormio** (1125m), host to the 2005 Alpine World Skiing Championships. With the highest slopes at 3012m, good snow is assured season-long. Its **tourist office** (☎ 0342 90 33 00; www.bormioonline.com; Via Roma 131b) is an unbeatable source of information on the entire park; its website is exhaustive.

The Parco Nazionale dello Stelvio straddles both Alto Adige and Trentino and can be approached from Merano (from where you have easy access to the Val d'Ultimo, Val Martello, Val di Solda and the Passo Stelvio), or from the Val di Sole in Trentino, which gives easy access to the Valle di Peio and the Val di Rabbi.

Val di Solda
The village of **Solda** (1906m), at the head of the Val di Solda, is a small ski resort and a base for walkers and climbers in summer. Challenging trails lead you to high altitudes, including trail No 28, which crosses the Madriccio pass (3123m) into the Val Martello. Solda **tourist office** (☎ 0473 61 30 15) has information on accommodation and activities. Between October and Christmas the village all but shuts down.

SAD buses connect Solda with Merano Monday to Friday during the summer only; you need to change at Spondigna.

Val Martello
This picturesque valley is a good choice for relatively low-altitude walks, with spectacular views of some of the park's high peaks. The real beauty of the valley is that the environment is unspoiled by ski lifts and downhill ski runs. It is a popular base for tackling the glaciers (guided walks can be organised). In winter there is excellent

cross-country skiing, and climbers can crawl up the valley's frozen waterfalls from January to March. In spring the valley attracts ski mountaineers, since there is no danger of avalanches.

People with children might like to take trail No 20 up into the Val di Peder. It is an easy walk with some lovely picnic spots along the way and the chance to see animals, including chamois and deer. For accommodation inquire at the Pro Loco office.

The road into the valley is open year-round, and SAD bus 107 runs to **Martello** village from Silandro.

VAL GARDENA
An enchanting Alpine valley, Val Gardena is hemmed in by the towering peaks of the **Parco Naturale Puez-Odle**, the imposing Gruppo di Sella and Sasso Lungo, and the gentle slopes and pastures of the Alpe di Siusi, the largest high plain in the Alps. It is one of the most popular skiing areas in the Alps because of the relatively reasonable prices and excellent facilities proffered by the valley's main towns – **Ortisei** (population 4457, elevation 1236m), **Santa Cristina** (population 1768, elevation 1428m) and **Selva** (population 2502, elevation 1563m). Its ski runs throng with snow fiends in winter, while warmer months see walkers flock to trails at both high and low altitudes.

Along with Val Badia, the Val Gardena is an enclave that has managed to preserve the ancient Ladin language and culture, and a rich tradition in colourful legends (for more details see the boxed text, p314). The ancient tradition of woodcarving is likewise nurtured here and the valley's artisans are famed for their statues, figurines, altars and toys. Beware of mass-produced imitations.

Information
Tourism Val Gardena (www.valgardena.it)
Ortisei Tourist Office (☎ 0471 79 63 28; ortisei@ valgardena.it; Via Rezia 1; ☼ 8.30am-12.30pm & 2.30-6.30pm Mon-Sat, 8.30am or 10am-noon & 5-6.30pm Sun)
Santa Cristina Tourist Office (☎ 0471 79 30 46; s.cristina@valgardena.it; Via Chemun 9; ☼ 8am-noon & 2.30-6.30pm Mon-Sat, 8.30am or 9.30am-noon Sun)
Selva Tourist Office (☎ 0471 79 51 22; selva@ valgardena.it; Via Mëisules 213; ☼ 8am-noon & 3-6.30pm Mon-Sat, 8.30am or 9am-noon & 4.30pm or 5-6.30pm Sun)

TRENTINO-ALTO ADIGE

TRENTINO-ALTO ADIGE

Tourist Medical Service (Ortisei ☎ 0471 79 77 85, Selva ☎ 0471 79 42 66)

Activities

In addition to its own fine **downhill ski** runs, the valley forms part of the Sella Ronda, a network of runs connecting the Val Gardena, Val Badia, Livinallongo and Val di Fassa (for which you'll need a Dolomiti Superski pass). Ski passes covering the use of 81 lifts in the Val Gardena are cheaper – €22/62/108 for one/three/six days (high season €26/72/127). Areas such as the Vallunga, near Selva, offer **cross-country skiing**. There are stunning trails around Forcella Pordoi and Val Lasties in the Gruppo di Sella, and on the Sasso Lungo.

This is walkers' paradise with endless possibilities, from the challenging Alte Vie of the Gruppo di Sella and the magnificent Parco Naturale Puez-Odle, to picturesque family strolls in spots like the Vallunga. Those seeking guidance can contact the nearest office of the **Scuola di Alpinismo Catores** (www.catores.com) Ortisei (☎ 0471 79 82 23; Piazza della Chiesa; ☉ 5.30-7pm); Santa Cristina (☎ 0471 79 30 99; Piazza Dosses; ☉ 5.30-7pm). Both Alpine guide schools organise botanical walks as well as climbing courses, glacier excursions and treks.

In summer cable cars whisk walkers into the mountains from all three towns in the valley. From Ortisei you can ride a **cable car** to Seceda which, at 2456m, offers a memorable view – one of the most spectacular in the Alps – of the Gruppo di Odle, a series of spiky pinnacles. From Seceda trail No 2a passes through what most people would consider a typical Alpine environment – lush, green sloping pastures dotted with wooden *malghe*, used by herders as summer shelters.

Sleeping & Eating

Eat and sleep without sticking so much as your little toe outside the front door.

Alpenhotel Rainell (☎ 0471 79 61 45; www.rainell.com; Via Vidalong 19, Ortisei; d B&B per person low/high season from €44/61, d half-board from €55/72; P ⊠) Alpenhotel Rainell is, surprisingly, a quintessential Alpine pad surrounded by quintessential Alpine pastures. Warm up by the wood-burning ceramic stove in winter.

Hotel Hell (☎ 0471 79 67 85; www.hotelhell.it; Via Promenade 3, Ortisei; d half-board per person low/high season €56.80-64; P ⊠ 🖳) Never been to Hell? Then here is your chance. This four-star sports hotel is run by the highly accommodating Hell family who bend over backwards to make guests' stays as heavenly as possible – and they succeed.

Hotel Adler (☎ 0471 77 50 00; www.hotel-adler.com; Via Rezia 7, Ortisei; d low/high season from €91/152, breakfast €14; P ⊠ 🖳 🖼) A 'water world' with oriental and Turkish baths, and a Ladin farmstead where you can dip into a hay bath (see the boxed text, p313) are among the self-pampering novelties awaiting guests who stay at this stylish four-star wonder, housed in a frescoed 13th-century building. Much of the year, full-board seven-day packages are obligatory.

Getting There & Around

The Val Gardena is accessible from Bolzano by SAD bus, as well as from Canazei (summer only). Regular buses connect the towns along the valley and you can reach the Alpe di Siusi by either bus or cable car. Full timetables are available at the tourist offices.

In winter the Val Gardena Ski Express is a shuttle bus service linking the various villages and lifts in the valley; a €2 ticket covers a week's unlimited travel.

ALPE DI SIUSI & PARCO NATURALE DELLO SCILIAR

There's something magical about the view across the Alpe di Siusi to the Sciliar, as the green undulating pastures end dramatically at the foot of these towering peaks. It is a particularly spectacular scene in an area that certainly doesn't lack views. The Alpe di Siusi (1700m to 2200m), the largest plateau in Europe, forms part of what is known as the Altipiano dello Sciliar, which also incorporates the villages of **Castelrotto** and **Siusi**, lower down at about 1000m.

There is something for walkers of all ages and expertise in this area. The gentle slopes of the Alpe di Siusi are perfect for families with kids, and you won't need much more than average stamina to make it to the **Rifugio Bolzano** (☎ 0471 61 20 24) at 2457m, just under Monte Pez (2564m), the Sciliar's summit. If you're after more challenging walks, the jagged peaks of the Catinaccio group and the Sasso Lungo are nearby. These mountains are famous among climbers worldwide. There are also several *vie ferrate* and plenty of good trails for mountain bikers. The Catinaccio group can also be approached from the Val di Fassa.

Alpe di Siusi tourist offices in **Castelrotto** (☎ 0471 70 63 33; www.castelrotto.org; Piazza Kraus 1), **Siusi** (☎ 0471 70 70 24; Via Sciliar 8) and **Compaccio** (☎ 0471 72 79 04) have heaps of information on winter **downhill skiing**, **ski-mountaineering**, **cross-country skiing** and winter **walking** trails (with snow shoes) in the area – part of the Superski Dolomiti network.

The Altipiano dello Sciliar is accessible by SAD bus from Bolzano, the Val Gardena and Bressanone. By car exit the Brenner motorway (A22) at Bolzano Nord or Chiusa. May to October the roads of the Alpe di Siusi are closed to normal traffic. Tourists with a hotel booking in the zone can obtain a permit from the Compaccio tourist office, allowing them to drive between 4pm and 10am. Organise your pass before arriving in the area; ask your hotel for assistance. A regular bus service operates from Castelrotto and Siusi to Compaccio, and from there on to the Alpe di Siusi.

VAL BADIA

Along with the Val Gardena, Val Badia is one of the last strongholds of the ancient Ladin culture and language. Most local kids (as well as adults) are aware of the Ladin legends. Many are set on the nearby Fanes high plain, which forms part of the magnificent Parco Naturale di Fanes-Sennes-Braies. This is one of the most evocative places in the Dolomites and can be reached easily from the Val Badia, either on foot or by cable car from Passo Falzarego.

Towns in the valley – Colfosco (1645m), La Villa (1433m), San Cassiano (1537m) and Corvara (1568m) – together form the Alta Badia ski area.

Corvara
pop 1268 / elevation 1568m

The central town of the Ladin tribes, Corvara is a pleasant little place with plenty of accommodation. Primarily a ski resort it is also an excellent base for walkers wanting to tackle the peaks enclosing the Alta Badia. Of the Alta Badia's 130km of groomed slopes, it is the Gran Rosa ski slope, 4.5km north of Corvara in La Villa that is undoubtedly

---

HAY BATHS

A *bagno di fieno* (hay bath) is just that – a good old soak in hay. South Tiroleans have been doing it for centuries.

The grass that grows on the lower slopes of the Siusi Alps (1800m to 2200m) is reputed to make the best bath. In summer the mountain meadows' heady cocktail of green blades, aromatic plants and medicinal herbs, such as lavender and thyme, are cut when damp and left to ferment for several days. Then it's bath time.

Swaddled in a sheet, bathers immerse themselves in a 'trough' of hay, freshly watered and warmed, for about 15 minutes or so. As the bath hots up, so bathers sweat. Obesity, backache, gout, rheumatism and lumbago are among the rash of ills a hay bath is said to soothe. Spotty skins likewise benefit.

Hay baths are said to originate from the very simple concept of farmers taking a quick and refreshing kip on their freshly-cut hay. In 1901 great-grandfather Kompatscher of today's **Hotel Heubad** (Hotel Hay Bath; ☎ 0471 72 50 20; www.hotelheubad.com; Via Sciliar 12, Fiè di Sopra; d half-board per person low/mid/high season €66/74/82; ◷ Apr-Oct; P ☒ ☒), 12km northeast of Bolzano in the mountain hamlet of **Fiè allo Sciliar** (800m) opened South Tirol's first hay bathing station. Guests today can opt for one of several packages (a four-/seven-day stay with half-board and three/six hay baths and massages costs €370/770) but anyone can stroll in and place an order for a 20-minute hay bath (€28). Advance reservations ensure a successful soak.

In Trentino the slopes of Monte Bondone (1537m) yield the most soothing hay. Dip into one of 130 baths at the **Hotel Terme Bagni di Fieno** (☎ 0461 84 28 18; Via Bagni di Fieno 13; 1/12 baths €50/420; ◷ Jun–mid-Oct), a well-known spa 7km south of Trent in Garniga Terme. Bathers are obliged to undergo a medical examination (€40) before taking a plunge. Most other hotels in the spa resort offer hay-bath packages; the **tourist office** (☎ 0461 84 25 86; consorzio.bondone@trentino.to; Via Bagno di Fieno 18; ◷ 8am-12.30pm & 1.30-5pm Mon-Fri) has details.

THE LADIN TRADITION

Ladin language and culture can be traced back to around 15 BC, when the people of the Central Alps were forcibly united into the Roman province of Rhaetia. The Romans, of course, introduced Latin to the province but the original inhabitants of the area, with their diverse linguistic and cultural backgrounds, modified the language to such an extent that by around AD 450 it had evolved into an independent Romance language, known as Rhaeto-Romanic. At one point the entire Tirol was Ladin but today the language and culture are confined to the Val Gardena and the Val Badia where, in the 1981 census, about 90% of locals declared that they belonged to the Ladin language group. Along with German and Italian, Ladin is taught in schools, and the survival of the Ladin cultural and linguistic identity is protected by law. *La Usc di Ladins* (www.lauscdiladins.com, Ladin and Italian only) is the local Ladin-language newspaper, covering the Val Gardena and Val Badia.

Ladin culture is rich in vibrant poetry and legends, set amid the jagged peaks of the Dolomites and richly peopled by fairies, gnomes, elves, giants, princesses and heroes. Passed on by word-of-mouth for centuries, and often heavily influenced by Germanic myths, many of these legends were in danger of being lost. In the first decade of the 20th century journalist Carlo Felice Wolff, who had lived most of his life in Bolzano, undertook a major project: he spent 10 years gathering and researching the local legends, listening to the old folk, farmers and shepherds recount the legends and fairy tales. The legends he eventually published were reconstructed from the many different versions and recollections he gathered.

The magic of these many myths is rekindled in Ortisei's **Museo Ladin** (☎ 0471 79 75 54, Piazza San Antonio; admission free; ☺ 3-6.30pm Tue-Fri Jun, Sep & Oct, 10am-noon & 3-7pm Tue-Sun Jul & Aug, 3-6.30pm Tue & Fri Nov-Apr). The Ladin Museum has particularly good sections on flora and fauna specific to the Ladin lands, and local wood-carving. Ask here or at the tourist office for information on wood-carving courses run in the town in July and August. Of a similar ilk is the **Museo Ladin di Fascia** (☎ 0462 76 01 82; museo@istladin.net; Via Milano 5; admission free; ☺ 3-7pm Mon-Fri Sep-Jun, 10am-noon & 3-7pm Jul & Aug), in Pozza di Fassa in the Val di Fassa. The **Institut Cultural Ladin** (☎ 0462 76 42 67; Via della Chiesa 6), in neighbouring Vigo di Fassa, runs Ladin language courses.

True Ladin fiends should not miss the third in the trio, the state-of-the-art **Museo Ladin** (☎ 0474 52 40 20; www.museumladin.it, Ladin & Italian only; Via Tor 72; adult/child €5.50/2.75; ☺ 10am-6pm Sat Tue-Sat, 2-6pm Sun) inside 12th-century Tor Castle, some 15km south of Brunico in San Martino in Badia (S244). The largest of the three it is packed with informative and captivating multimedia displays.

the most legendary – bomb down it like the world's top skiers did during the 2003 Alpine Skiing World Cup Men's Giant Slalom!

Corvara **tourist office** (☎ 0471 83 61 76; www .altabadia.org; Via Col Alt 36; ☺ 8am-noon & 3-6pm Mon-Fri, 9am-noon & 3-6pm Sat, 10.30am-12.30pm Sun) distributes excellent activity information. For advice on **skiing**, **heli-skiing**, **ice climbing** and advanced **walking** trails, contact the **Associazione Guide Alpine Val Badia** (☎ 0471 83 68 98; guide.valbadia@rolmail.net; Via Burje; ☺ 6-7pm).

The closest public **hospital** (☎ 0474 58 11 11) is in Brunico; for helicopter mountain rescue call ☎ 0471 79 71 71 or ☎ 118.

ACTIVITIES

Corvara is on the much-vaunted **Sella Ronda** – a four-valley **downhill ski** circuit which, tackled from either direction, takes in 90 minutes of lifts and 120 minutes of

skiing – and is part of the Dolomiti Superski network (see p295). A cheaper Alta Badia ski pass, restricted to Alta Badia's 130km of slopes, costs €20/80/140 for one/three/six days (high season €23/91/159); passes are sold at the **ski pass office** (☎ 0471 83 63 66; Via Col Alt 88c). Ski schools are listed online at www.altabadiaski.com.

From the Passo Falzarego mountain pass (2105m), 20km east of Corvara, a **cable car** ascends into the Parco Naturale di Fanes-Sennes-Braies – see pp293–5. Alternatively, pick up trail No 12 from near La Villa or trail No 11, which joins Alta Via No 1 at the Capanna Alpina, a few kilometres off the main road between Passo Valparola and San Cassiano. Either trail takes you up to the Alpe di Fanes and the two *rifugi*, Lavarella and Fanes.

A combination of cable car and chair lift will take you from Corvara up into the

Gruppo di Sella at Vallon (2550m), where you'll get a spectacular view across to the Marmolada glacier. From Vallon you can traverse the Sella or follow the trail that winds around the valley at the top of the chair lift (about one hour). A good area for family walks is around Prelongià (2138m). Catch the cable car from La Villa and then take trail No 4 and trail No 23 to reach Prelongià. Trail No 23 takes you down to Corvara.

Horse riding, **mountain biking** and **hang-gliding** are other popular valley activities. A tandem flight with **paragliding** school **Centro Volo Libero Alta Badia** (☎ 0471 84 75 92; www.cvl-altabadia.com, Italian only; Via Bosc da Plan 46) in La Villa costs €75. Corvara tourist office has a list of places where you can hire mountain bikes and it distributes an excellent waterproof map detailing 10 mountain bike itineraries (with English explanations).

SLEEPING & EATING
Most hotels open early December to early April and mid-June to early October. All the places listed double as reasonable eating options.

Ciasa Blancia (☎ 0471 83 62 96; fax 0471 83 67 60; Via Sassongher 52; d half-board per person low/high season €40/65) Mountains and lots of fir trees make this something of a Heidi's hide-out, great for kids who like to roam wild.

Posta Zirm Hotel (☎ 0471 83 61 75; www.posta zirm.com; Via Col Alt 95; d half-board per person low/high season €80/139) Corvara's largest and most prominent hotel – at the top of the street next to the Sport Kostner shopping complex – is known among Brits for its zany tea dance in ski boots.

Hotel Marmolada (☎ 0471 83 61 39; www.hotel-marmolada.com; Via Col Alt 80; d half-board per person low/high season from €78/97; P) This large wooden structure, opposite the main ski pass office, is a charming place to stay in summer or winter. Its restaurant dishes up strictly regional, heart-warming fare.

La Perla (☎ 0471 83 61 32; www.romantikperla.it; Via Col Alt 105; d half-board per person low/high season from €115/185; P) Marketing itself as Corvara's 'romantik hotel', this oasis of luxury does indeed live up to its four stars. Excellent gourmet food and good wine dished up in a traditional, 18th-century Ladin-style restaurant are among its many sensory delights.

GETTING THERE & AWAY
From the bus stop in front of the Posta Zirm Hotel on Via Col Alt, **SAD buses** (toll-free ☎ 800 84 60 47; www.sii.bz.it) link Corvara with Bolzano (€6.50, 1¾ hours, up to five daily in season) and Brunico (€4.60, 1¼ hours, eight daily). Less-frequent services link Corvara with the Val Gardena, Passo Sella and Passo Pordoi, Canazei and the Passo Falzarego. Buses reroute in winter to avoid crossing high mountain passes.

CORTINA D'AMPEZZO
pop 6570 / elevation 1224m
Across the Fanes-Conturines range from the Val Badia is the queen of the Dolomites, Cortina d'Ampezzo. Italy's most famous, fashionable and expensive ski resort, Cortina is situated in the Veneto, but has been included here because of its central location. It is one of the best-equipped and most picturesque resorts in the Dolomites. Moreover, there is cheapish accommodation to be found if you know where to look and book well in advance.

Situated in the Ampezzo bowl Cortina is surrounded by some of the most stunning mountains in the Dolomites, including (in a clockwise direction) Cristallo, the Gruppo di Sorapiss-Marmarole, Antelao, Becco di Mezzodi-Croda da Lago, the Nuvolau-Averau-Cinque Torri and Tofane. To the south are the Pelmo and the Civetta. Facilities for both downhill and cross-country skiing are first class, and the small town's population swells dramatically during the ski season as the rich and famous pour in; equally great walking and climbing possibilities crowd out the town in summer too.

Information
Croce Bianca (☎ 0436 27 71) Emergency medical aid.
Multimedia Team Italia (☎ 0436 86 80 90; Largo Poste 59; ⊙ 9.30am-12.30pm & 3-7.30pm Mon-Fri; €9.30/hr)
Post Office (Largo Poste 20; ⊙ 8.30am-6.30pm Mon-Fri, 8.30am-1pm Sat)
Tourist Office (☎ 0436 32 31; www.infodolomiti.it; Piazzetta San Francesco 8; ⊙ 9am-12.30pm & 3.30-6.30pm)

Activities
Cortina offers some breathtaking **skiing**, especially for advanced skiers whose hearts

could well skip a beat when they stand at the top of the legendary Staunies black mogul run at 3000m. Of the resort's nine cable cars, two whisk walkers and skiers straight into the mountains from downtown Cortina: the two-stage **Funivia Cortina-Faloria** (☎ 0436 25 17; Via G Marconi; single/return €9.80/13) links the town with the Faloria ski area at 2123m, and the three-stage **Funivia Cortina-Tofana di Mezzo** (☎ 0436 50 52; Via dello Stadio; single/return €22/34) climbs to 3130m. Lifts generally run 9am to 5pm daily mid-December to early April, and from June to September or early October. Ski passes are sold at the **ski pass office** (☎ 0436 86 21 71; Via G Marconi 15); expect to pay from €80/ 140 for a three-/six-day Cortina d'Ampezzo ski pass. The pricier Dolomiti Superski ski pass also covers the resort. The tourist office has a list of sports shops which rent skis, poles and boots, and of ski schools.

Dog sledding, **scaling frozen waterfalls**, and **ice-skating** inside Cortina's **Olympic Ice Stadium** (☎ 0436 43 80; Via dello Stadio; admission/skate hire €3.60/6.70; ◷ 10.30am-12.30pm & 3.30-5.30pm mid-Dec–Mar) are among the other winter sports you can feast your muscles on. The **Gruppo Guide Alpine Cortina** (☎ 0436 86 85 05; www.guidecortina.com; Corso Italia 69a) organises the usual **rock-climbing** courses and guided **walks** for adults, as well as historical and naturalistic excursions and courses for kids. A particularly interesting half-day guided walk (€40) is around the artillery emplacements, fortified trenches and other WWI ruins in the mountains around Cortina – those interested in what happened here during WWI can pick up the English brochure *The Great War* at the tourist office. Of the area's many other spectacular walking trails, some are difficult and require special equipment.

Not far from Cortina, and accessible by Dolomiti Bus in summer, are the Tre Cime di Lavaredo, one of the world's most famous **climbing** locations and a panoramic place to walk. The fact that you can arrive by bus literally at the foot of the Tre Cime means the area is crawling with tourists in the high season.

Mountain bikers can hire bikes from the **Mountain Bike Center** (☎ 0436 86 38 61; Corso Italia 294; per 2 hrs/half-day/day €11/22/34) in town or from the **Centro Mountain Bike** (☎ 0436 86 22 01; per hr/4 hrs/day €6/15/25), 4km from Cortina in Fiames.

Sleeping
International Camping Olympia (☎ 0436 50 57; person/tent & car from €5/8; **P**) Pitch your tent at 1283m at this friendly site, 4km north of Cortina in Fiames, with space for 300 tents or book well ahead and snag one of 25 beds in a bungalow.

Pensione Fiames (☎ 0436 23 66; fax 0436 75 33; Via Fiames 13; s/d from €30/40) This *pensione*, 4km north of Cortina in Fiames, with garden and breakfast terrace is as cheap and basic as it gets.

Hotel Montana (☎ 0436 86 04 98; montana@cortina -hotel.com; Corso Italia 94; s/d from €35/45) Bang next to the church, central Montana is an unbeatable two-star deal.

Miramonti Majestic Grand Hotel (☎ 0436 42 01; www.geturhotels.com; Via Pezie 103; d low/high season €129/286; **P** 🛎 🖳 **P**) Its name alone reflects the grandeur of this five-star hotel, languishing in extensive fir tree–clad grounds just made for sleigh riding with jingle bells. Guests are regally spoilt.

Eating
Cortina boasts a couple of inspired places to eat in town and some inspiring lakeside choices, a short drive from the resort centre.

LP 26 (☎ 0436 86 22 84; Largo Poste 26; ◷ 11am-3pm & 5pm-2am Tue-Sun) Pork thighs hang up to dry at this hip *prosciutterie* where punters can savour mouth-melting *prosciutto* (ham) lounging on sofas around low tables or at shared bench-clad tables. The only *prosciutto* served is Dok Dall'Ava – seasoned for a minimum of 22 months. Piggie aside, you can also indulge in a platter of wild boar, deer, roe deer, chamois, turkey and…the list continues. *Prosciutto*-inspired pasta dishes are also cooked up.

Baita Fraina (☎ 0436 87 62 35; www.baitafraina.it; Via Fraina 1; d B&B/half-board per person low season €39/68, high season €60/88; ◷ Tue-Sun Jul-Sep & Dec–mid-Apr) This family-run B&B, 3km from the centre, is as popular for its kitchen as its seven homelike rooms with mountain views. Feast on beetroot-stuffed ravioli, followed by roe deer chops with onions and balsamic vinegar and – several hours later – a shot of one of 100 different grappas.

Ristorante Al Lago Ghedina (☎ 0436 86 08 76; Lago Ghedina; full meals around €25; ◷ Fri-Sun) This stunning chalet lake, 5km north of Cortina on the banks of Lake Ghedina, is a popular

TRENTINO-ALTO ADIGE

lunch spot with families (note that nearby playground kids!). Asparagus and truffles are among the fresh seasonal goodies that could well land on your plate.

Stock up on power snacks for the slopes at supermarket **Standa** (Via Franchetti).

Getting There & Away
From Cortina **bus station** (Via G Marconi), SAD buses run to Dobbiaco (45 minutes, twice daily), where you can change for Brunico and Bolzano. **Dolomiti Bus** (www.dolomitibus.it, Italian only) serves Pocol (€1.20, 15 minutes, nine daily), Passo Falzarego (€1.20, 20 minutes, nine daily) and Belluno (€4.70). There is also a bus service to Venice (€10.40, 3½ hours, one daily) run by **ATVO** (☎ 0436 86 79 21; www.atvo.it, Italian only). Local services connect the town with International Camping Olympia at Fiames and Pocol.

VALZOLDANA
Valzoldana lies a mere 20km south of Cortina, south of the imposing Civetta (3220m) and Pelmo (3168m) groups, yet it has none of the tourist trappings displayed by its more illustrious neighbour. Until the 19th century the Zoldani made their living by exploiting the local resources – metal deposits and water – to make nails for the Venetian Republic; until 1890, that is, when a flood destroyed their makeshift smithies. Many people left the region and emigrated to Munich and Vienna, setting up as travelling ice-cream and sorbet salesmen; today many of their descendants run famous ice-cream parlours the world over. Since the 1970s the profits from these commercial activities have fostered the growth of the tourism industry.

Modern **ski** runs hug the Civetta group at Zoldo Alto. Eighty kilometres of runs link the valley to the Dolomiti Superski network, allowing skiers to reach the Sella and Marmolada groups. In the lower valley around Forno di Zoldo, the landscape is unchanged, the prices and crowds have been kept under control and the food is authentic and excellent. On foot, take advantage of an extensive network of **walking** paths. Six days takes the more experienced on a round trip through unspoiled woodland beneath the peaks of less-famous mountains such as Sfornioi, Bosconero and Pramper. For more details of summer

and winter activities and accommodation, contact the Valzoldana tourist office in **Forno di Zoldo** (☎ 0437 78 73 49; fornodizoldo@infodo lomiti.it; Via Roma 1) or in **Zoldo Alto** (☎ 0437 78 91 45; zoldoalto@infodolomiti.it; Mareson).

Sleeping & Eating
There are numerous hotels and camp sites, where you can eat too, in the valley.

Rifugio Casera di Bosconero (☎ 0437 78 73 49; 🕑 Jun-Sep) Walkers can ask at the tourist office about this remote mountain hut, only accessible by foot. At 1457m, in the conifer forest at the foot of the mountain of the same name, it is accessible from Forno on the path marked 490A or from Lago di Pontesi on paths 490 or 485 – both are good half-day walks.

Casa Rosada (☎ 0437 79 42 26; casarosada@ dolomiti.it; Pralongo, Forno di Zoldo; 3- or 4-person apartments per week from €210) This beautiful mountain chalet, with flower boxes and green whichever way you turn, provides a real mountain getaway for those happy to cook themselves. Weekly forays in the forest are organised and a free shuttle bus runs guests year-round to and from the lifts.

Getting There & Away
The valley is served by the S251 that descends from the Forcella Staulanza pass (1789m) in the north to Longarone in the southeast. Coming from the south, leave the S51 at Longarone, following signs to Cortina, and then turn left onto the S251.

VAL PUSTERIA & THE SESTO DOLOMITES
On the Dolomites' northern edge, the Val Pusteria is bordered by the magnificent **Parco Naturale di Fanes-Sennes-Braies** and, further north, by the **Parco Naturale delle Dolomiti di Sesto**, which includes some of the area's most famous peaks – among them the Tre Cime di Lavaredo. The valley is easily reached from the Val Badia and Cortina d'Ampezzo along the spectacular Valle di Landro. Its main centre is **Brunico** (population 13,700, elevation 835m), a pleasant market town, which neighbours the tiny ski resort of **Plan de Corones** (2275m) and sports excellent transport connections for excursions into Parco Naturale di Fanes-Sennes-Braies. More picturesque options are extremely quaint **San Candido** (population 3112, elevation 1175m),

just 9km from Austria, or **Sesto** (population 1938, elevation 1311m) at the base of the Sesto Dolomites.

Information

Brunico Tourist Office (☎ 0474 55 57 22; www .bruneck.com; Via Europa 26; ☘ 9am-12.30pm & 3-6pm Mon-Fri, 9am-noon Sat)

Plan de Corones Tourist Office (☎ 0474 55 54 47; www.kronplatz.com; Via Michael Pacher 11a; ☘ 8am-noon & 2-6pm Mon-Sat, 10am-noon Sun)

San Candido Tourist Office (☎ 0474 91 31 49; Piazza del Magistrato; ☘ 8am-noon & 3.30-6.30pm Mon-Fri, 8am-noon Sat) Sells maps.

Sesto Tourist Office (☎ 0474 71 03 10; Via Dolomiti; ☘ 8am-noon & 2-6pm Mon-Sat, 10am-noon Sun)

Activities

Easy to get to from the Val Pusteria is beautiful Lago di Braies, a perfect spot for a picnic and a leisurely lakeside stroll. More serious walkers might like to tackle part of the Alta Via No 1, which starts here. Parco Naturale di Fanes-Sennes-Braies is more easily approached from the Val Badia or from Passo Falzarego.

At the other end of the valley, towards Austria, are the Sesto Dolomites, where there are some spectacular trails. The Valle Campo di Dentro, near San Candido, and the Val Fiscalina, near Sesto, are criss-crossed with trails – both **walking** and **cross-country skiing**. From the Val Fiscalina it's a long but easy walk along trail No 102 to Rifugio Locatelli (2405m), from where you will be able to get a great view of the Tre Cime di Lavaredo. Most trails around the Tre Cime are easy enough for first-time walkers and families, although they become rather like motorways in July and August when paths get packed with walkers on the tourist trail.

May to October, adventure seekers can take a spin on a raft with **Rafting Club Activ** (☎ 0474 67 84 22; Via Valle Aurina 22), 12km north of Brunico in Campo Tures. River **kayaking**, **canyoning** and **waterfall climbing** are among the wet activities run by the club. Count on paying about €40 per person for a half-day of **white-water rafting**; equivalent trips for kids along the tamer River Ahr cost from €15.

Plan de Corones (www.kronplatz.com), 4km south of Brunico, sports ample green and blue runs, making it ideal for beginners. The station is linked by cable car to Brunico. Ski passes cost up to €27/72/127 for

one/three/six days (high season €23/80/140), and the Dolomiti Superski pass can also be used. Gear can be hired in Brunico and Plan de Corones.

Mountain bikes can be hired at **Trojer Biciclette** (☎ 0474 91 32 16; Via Herzog Tassilo 2a) and **Papin Sport** (☎ 0474 91 34 50; Via Freising 9) in San Candido for around €13 a day. **Kronplatz Bike** (☎ 0474 55 21 86, ☎ 348 735 03 68; www.kronplatzbike .it; Via Ahmtaler 19) in Brunico charges €21/26 for a Hardtails/Fullys mountain bike. A fully fledged mountain biking club, Kronplatz should be the main contact for bikers seeking a mountain guide or organised expedition; a half-/full-day expedition typically costs €21/26 and the club organises biking and rafting trips (€31/49 half/full day). In Brunico, sports shop **Sportler** (☎ 0474 55 60 23; Via Centrale) sells cycling gear as well walking equipment, maps and guides.

Sleeping & Eating

The best places to nosh and nap are around Brunico or in sweet San Candido.

Gasthof-Albergo Oberraut (☎ 0474 55 99 77; d half-board per person €35, 1st/2nd courses from €8/12; ☘ Fri-Wed; **P**) Peace, perfect peace, is what this family-run farmhouse dishes up, 6km east of Brunico in Ameto. Snuggle under huge feather-filled bolsters, feast on deer goulash with polenta, breakfast on farm eggs and ham in the *stube* (cosy room with a fireplace) and remind yourself you're still in Italy. Locals flock from far and wide to eat here.

Hotel Amaten (☎ 0474 55 99 93; www.amaten.it; d half board low/mid/high season per person €29/30/37; **P**) Laze away on the flowery sun-drenched terrace of this lovely hotel-restaurant, a little up the lane from Oberraut and surrounded by green fields and a stunning panorama on the horizon. It's 6km east of Brunico in Ameto.

Cavallino Bianco/Weisses Roessl (☎ 0474 91 31 35; www.weissesroessl.com; Via Duca Tassilo 1, San Candido; d half-board per person low/high season from €94/160, 1st/2nd courses from €6/10; ☘ Wed-Mon; **P** ✗ ▢ ▣) This charming option, in a 16th-century house next to the village church, is a perfect place to eat then sleep. Feast on a *speck* platter (San Candido–based Senfter is the largest producer of *speck* in the valley) and pretend you're in heaven. A spa, fitness centre, pool and cinema for kids are perks.

Hotel Grauerbär (☎ 0474 91 31 15; www.hotel grauerbaer.com; Via Rainer 2, San Candido; d half-board per person low/mid/high season €45/67/92; P ⊠ ⊠) Four stars and a history dating to 1462 add up to one very lovely place to stay. The hotel is on a quiet pedestrian street in San Candido and guests have free use of the village swimming pool.

Le Sommelier (☎ 0474 91 61 22; Via Rainer 22a, San Candido; ⊙ Tue-Sun) Wine and pasta are the much-welcome mainstays of this stylish wine bar – an informal and friendly place to hang out and/or merry-make.

Entertainment

UFO (☎ 0474 55 57 70; www.ufobruneck.it, Italian only; Via Joseph Ferrari 20, Brunico; ⊙ café noon-midnight Tue-Thu, noon-1am Fri & Sat) UFO is without a doubt the most happening place found in the valley. A skate park, disco, café and arts centre all rolled into one, it hosts bands and concerts, plays and theatrical events, art exhibitions and various one-off hip happenings.

Shopping

Admirers of Sherlock Holmes' fine woollen cape can buy a moss-green lookalike at **Il Mondo del Loden** (The World of Loden; ☎ 0472 86 85 40; Via Val Pusteria 1; ⊙ 9am-6pm Mon-Sat), on the S49 in Vandoies, some 20km west of Brunico at the Val Pusteria's far western end. The shop is run by South Tirolean fashion house Oberrauch-Zitt, founded in 1846. The adjoining museum explains how sheepskins are turned into Loden – a prized (and pricey) woollen fabric, known for its warmth and waterproofing.

Getting There & Away

SAD buses head for Brunico (€4.50, 45 minutes, hourly) and Cortina (one hour, four daily) from San Candido. From Bolzano, there are buses to/from Merano, Val Badia, San Vigilio di Marebbe and Val Gardena (on the Innsbruck bus). From either town sporadic buses and trains go to Dobbiaco, from where buses go to Lago di Braies.

The Val Pusteria is reached by train from Bolzano via Fortezza (where a change is then necessary). Brunico and San Candido are 40 minutes and 1¼ hours from Fortezza respectively.

The Veneto

CONTENTS

Most travellers to the Veneto are so dazzled by Venice that they neglect the rest. Set aside a few days to behold Giotto's extraordinary frescoes in Padua and perhaps take in an opera at Verona's Roman Arena. Even without the opera, how can you pass up Verona, setting of *Romeo and Juliet* and every bit as romantic as it should be?

Vicenza, Palladio's home town and repository of some of his architecture, is well worth a stopover, perhaps on your way to the northern reaches of the Veneto and the slopes of Cortina d'Ampezzo, one of the world's most famous ski resorts. Strike out away from the big centres and you discover the pleasant city of Treviso, home of Benetton and a charming riverside medieval core, and Belluno, a great base for walks in the eastern Dolomites.

The region's cuisine is founded on rice and corn-based polenta. Risotto is cooked with almost everything the countryside and lagoon have to offer – from baby peas to shellfish. One of the Veneto's best-known contributions to the Italian table is tiramisù, a rich dessert of mascarpone cheese, coffee, Marsala, sponge and chocolate. The single most popular tipple is *prosecco*, a generic bubbly that flows freely in bars across the region. The Bellini, a cocktail of *prosecco* and peach nectar, has come a long way since Giuseppe Cipriani first mixed one at Harry's Bar in Venice in the 1950s, but most locals prefer a biting afternoon *spritz*.

HIGHLIGHTS

- **Modern Art**
  Peggy Guggenheim Collection (p337)
- **Glass & Old Lace**
  Murano (p344) and Burano (p344)
- **Seafood**
  A meal in one of Venice's *osterie* (pp350–3)
- **Palladio**
  A tour of his villas, from the Brenta (p357) to Vicenza (pp362–6)
- **Giotto**
  The frescoes of Padua's Cappella degli Scrovegni (p359)
- **Venice's Canals**
  Ride a gondola or just wander alongside them (p345)
- **Marvellous Mosaics**
  St Mark's Basilica in Venice (pp331–6) and the Santa Maria Assunta church on Torcello (pp344–5)
- **Walking**
  High mountain walks in the Alpine pastures of the Dolomites (p373)

★ Dolomites

★ Brenta Riviera

Vicenza ★ ★ Padua ★ Islands of the Laguna Veneta
Venice ★

THE VENETO

POPULATION: 4.54 MILLION   ■ AREA: 18,378 SQ KM

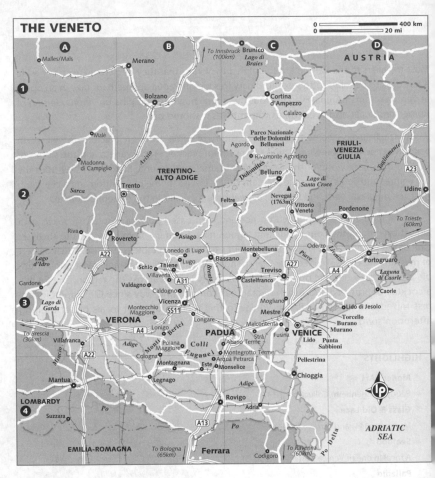

THE VENETO

VENICE (VENEZIA)

pop 63,000 (275,000 including mainland)

Perhaps no other city in the world has inspired the many superlatives heaped upon Venice by writers and travellers through the centuries.

Forget that Venice is no longer a great maritime republic and that its buildings are in serious decay and constantly threatened by rising tides. Today, Byron might be reluctant to take his daily swim along the now too-dirty Grand Canal (Canal Grande) but the thoughts of Henry James are as true as they were a century ago: 'Dear old Venice has lost her complexion, her figure, her reputation, her self-respect; and yet, with it all, has so puzzlingly not lost a shred of her distinction.' La Repubblica Serenissima (Most Serene Republic), remains a singular phenomenon.

The secret to seeing and discovering the real romance and beauty of Venice is to *walk*. Parts of Cannaregio, Dorsoduro and Castello are empty of tourists, even in the high season. You can become lost for hours in the narrow, winding streets between the Ponte dell'Accademia and Stazione di Santa Lucia (train station), where the signs that point towards San Marco and the Ponte di Rialto rarely seem to make sense (although in their own way they do) – but what a way to pass the time!

The city's busiest times are between May and September, Christmas and New Year, during Carnevale (February) and at Easter, but it is always a good idea to make a hotel booking.

HISTORY

The barbarian invasions of the 5th and 6th centuries saw the people from the Roman towns of the Veneto and along the Adriatic Sea flee to the marshy islands of the Venetian lagoon.

In the 6th century the islands began to form a loose federation, with each community electing representatives to a central authority, although its leaders were actually under the control of the Byzantine rulers in Ravenna. Byzantium's hold over Italy weakened in the early 8th century and in AD 726 the people of Venice elected their first *doge*, a type of magistrate, whose successors would lead the city for more than 1000 years.

By the late 11th century, Venice had become an important trading city and a great power in the Mediterranean, prospering out of the chaos caused by the First Crusade launched in 1095. The city continued to profit from the crusades during the 12th century and at the beginning of the 13th century, under Doge Enrico Dandolo, Venice led the Fourth Crusade on a devastating detour to Constantinople. Venice not only kept most of the treasures plundered from that great city, it also retained most of the territories won during the crusade, consolidating a maritime might in the Eastern Mediterranean that made it the envy of other powers. In 1271, the young Venetian merchant and explorer Marco Polo set out with his father and uncle on an overland trip to China, returning by sea over 20 years later.

During much of the 13th and 14th centuries the Venetians struggled with Genoa for maritime supremacy, a tussle that culminated in Genoa's defeat in 1380 during an epic siege at Chioggia. Their maritime power consolidated, the Venetians turned their attentions to dominating the mainland, capturing most of the Veneto and portions of what are now Lombardy and Emilia-Romagna.

However, events beyond Venetian control began to have a telling effect on the lagoon city. The increasing power of the Turks forced the Venetians to deploy forces to protect their Mediterranean interests. The fall of Constantinople in 1453 and the Venetian territory of Morea (in Greece) in

---

SAVING VENICE

Floods, neglect, pollution and many other factors have contributed to the degeneration of Venice's monuments and artworks. Since 1969, however, a group of private international organisations, under the aegis of Unesco, has worked to repair the damage.

The Joint Unesco-Private Committees Programme for the Safeguarding of Venice has raised millions of dollars for restoration work in the city; between 1969 and 2000 more than 100 monuments and 1000 works of art were restored.

Major restoration projects completed include the Chiesa di Madonna dell'Orto, the facade of the Chiesa di San Zulian, the Chiesa di San Francesco della Vigna, the Chiesa di Santa Maria Formosa and the Chiesa di San Nicolò dei Mendicoli, the Basilica di Santa Maria Assunta on Torcello and the old Jewish cemetery on the Lido. All sorts of projects continue all the time. One planned for the near future is the restoration of the bronze equestrian statue of Bartolomeo Colleoni.

Funding for the programme comes from 26 private and charitable organisations from Italy and a dozen other countries. Apart from restoration work, the programme also finances specialist courses for trainee restorers in Venice. Among the higher-profile groups involved in the effort are the UK's Venice in Peril Fund, whose honorary chairman is Lord Norwich, perhaps the greatest historian of Venice in English. For UK£50 a year you can join **Venice in Peril** (☎ 020-7957 8270; www.veniceinperil.org; 5 Stamford Bridge, Fulham Rd, London SW6 1HS). The fund is presently helping to restore the Emiliana chapel on San Michele (expected to cost UK£250,000).

Important though the work of these organisations is in keeping Venice's difficulties in the public eye, more than 90% of the finance for restoration and related projects in Venice since 1966 has come from the Italian government.

VENICE (VENEZIA)

A B C D

1

To Mestre (6km),
Venice Casino (10km)
& Marco Polo
Airport (10km)

Canale delle Sacche

Canale delle Navi

Parco
Groggia

43

See Cannaregio Map p340

22
45

CANNAREGIO

Sacca della
Misericordia

2

Ponte della Libertà

Isola del
Tronchetto

To Tronchetto Car Parks
(300m) & PalaFenice (600m)

Parco
Savorgnan

Grand Canal

See San Marco, San Polo & Santa Croce Map pp332-4

3

Stazione di
Santa Lucia
(Ferrovia)

Ponte dei
Scalzi

SANTA CROCE

Stazione
Merci

Stazione
Marittima
(Merci)

Garage
Comunale
37

7
33

Campo di
S Andrea

34

36

Piazzale
Roma

Giardini
Papadopoli

SAN POLO

Ponte di
Rialto

SAN MARCO

4

Canale Scomenzera

Grand Canal

Santa
Marta

St Mark's
Square

9

5

Stazione
Marittima

DORSODURO

Ponte dell'
Accademia

Punta
della
Dogana

Canale di Fusina

Fondamenta delle Zattere

41

46
24

28

38

Giudecca

Sacca Fisola

Fond San Biagio

Sant'Eufemia

Canale *della*

Zitelle

6

Sacca
San
Biagio

30

F Sant'Eufemia   F di Ponte Piccolo
11

23
1

40

27
29

Rio del Ponte Lungo

C San Giacomo

F di San

Giacomo
4

THE VENETO

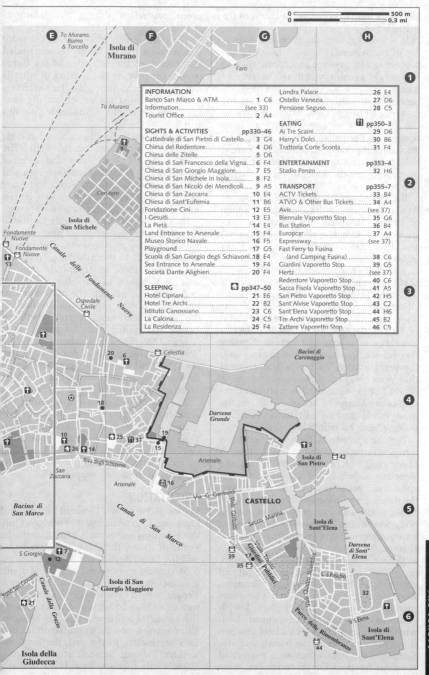

0 _____ 500 m
0 _____ 0.3 mi

INFORMATION
Banco San Marco & ATM.................. 1 C6
Information...................................(see 33)
Tourist Office............................... 2 A4

SIGHTS & ACTIVITIES pp330–46
Cattedrale di San Pietro di Castello.... 3 G4
Chiesa del Redentore..................... 4 D6
Chiesa delle Zitelle........................ 5 D6
Chiesa di San Francesco della Vigna.. 6 F4
Chiesa di San Giorgio Maggiore....... 7 E5
Chiesa di San Michele in Isola.......... 8 F2
Chiesa di San Nicolò dei Mendicoli... 9 A5
Chiesa di San Zaccaria................... 10 E4
Chiesa di Sant'Eufemia................... 11 B6
Fondazione Cini............................ 12 E5
I Gesuiti..................................... 13 E3
La Pietà...................................... 14 E4
Land Entrance to Arsenale.............. 15 F4
Museo Storico Navale..................... 16 F5
Playground.................................. 17 G5
Scuola di San Giorgio degli Schiavoni.18 E4
Sea Entrance to Arsenale................ 19 F4
Società Dante Alighieri................... 20 F4

SLEEPING pp347–50
Hotel Cipriani.............................. 21 E6
Hotel Tre Archi............................ 22 B2
Istituto Canossiano....................... 23 C6
La Calcina................................... 24 C5
La Residenza............................... 25 F4

Londra Palace.............................. 26 E4
Ostello Venezia............................. 27 D6
Pensione Seguso........................... 28 C5

EATING pp350–3
Ai Tre Scaini................................ 29 D6
Harry's Dolci............................... 30 B6
Trattoria Corte Sconta.................... 31 F4

ENTERTAINMENT pp353–4
Stadio Penzo............................... 32 H6

TRANSPORT pp355–7
ACTV Tickets................................ 33 B4
ATVO & Other Bus Tickets.............. 34 A4
Avis...(see 37)
Biennale Vaporetto Stop................. 35 G6
Bus Station................................. 36 B4
Europcar.................................... 37 A4
Expressway................................(see 37)
Fast Ferry to Fusina
(and Camping Fusina).................. 38 C6
Giardini Vaporetto Stop.................. 39 G5
Hertz......................................(see 37)
Redentore Vaporetto Stop............... 40 C6
Sacca Fisola Vaporetto Stop............. 41 A5
San Pietro Vaporetto Stop............... 42 H5
Sant'Alvise Vaporetto Stop.............. 43 C2
Sant'Elena Vaporetto Stop.............. 44 H6
Tre Archi Vaporetto Stop................ 45 B2
Zattere Vaporetto Stop................... 46 C5

1499 gave the Turks control of access to the Adriatic Sea.

Worse still in the long term, the discovery of the Americas in 1492 heralded the beginning of a new age in Atlantic trading that would eventually shift the balance of commercial power away from the Mediterranean. In the shorter term, the rounding of Africa's Cape of Good Hope in 1498 by the Portuguese explorer Vasco da Gama opened an alternative trade route to Asia, thus allowing European importers to avoid the Mediterranean and the taxes imposed on passing goods through intermediaries like Venice.

But Venice remained a formidable power. At home, the doges, the Signoria (a council of 10 high ministers that effectively constituted the executive arm of government) and, later, the much-feared judicial Consiglio dei Dieci (Council of Ten) ruled with an iron fist. They headed a complex system of councils and government committees, of which the Maggior Consiglio (Great Council) was the equivalent of parliament. The doge, an elected leader, was the figurehead of state and generally the most powerful individual in government, but the complex set of checks and balances put in place over the years limited his power and ensured that Venice was ruled by its aristocracy. A decree of 1297 virtually closed off membership of the Maggior Consiglio to all but the most established of patriarchal families, making Venice a tightly knit oligarchy.

For the security of the state, Venetians were encouraged to spy on each other in every city, port and country where the Venetian Republic had an interest. Acts considered detrimental to the interests of the state were punished swiftly and brutally. Public trials and executions were rare; a body would just turn up on the street as an example to other potentially wayward citizens.

Venice was remarkably cosmopolitan, its commerce attracting people of all nationalities, from Germans to Persians. And although Venice limited the commercial and social activities of its Jewish community, which is concentrated in what was one of Europe's earliest ghettos, it did nothing to stifle the Jewish religion. Similarly, the Armenians were permitted religious freedom for centuries and were given protection during the infamous Inquisition.

The city's wealth was made all the more conspicuous by the luxury goods traded and produced there. Venice had a European monopoly on the making of what is now known as Murano glass, its merchants had reintroduced the art of making mosaics, and Venetian artisans made fine silks and lace.

But even as her people wallowed in their well-being, Venice was on the wane. The Turks and the Vatican States made gains at the Republic's expense during the 16th and 17th centuries and in 1669 Venice lost Crete to the Turks after a 25-year battle – its last stronghold in the Mediterranean was gone.

Finally, in 1797 the Maggior Consiglio abolished the constitution and opened the city's gates to Napoleon, who in turn handed Venice to the Austrians. Napoleon returned in 1805, incorporating the city into his Kingdom of Italy, but it reverted to Austria after his fall. The movement for Italian unification spread quickly through the Veneto and, after several rebellions, Venice was united with the Kingdom of Italy in 1866. The city was bombed during WWI but suffered only minor damage during WWII, when most attacks were aimed at the neighbouring industrial zones of Mestre and Porto Marghera.

The city's prestige as a tourist destination grew during the 19th century as it was surpassed as a trade port by Trieste. Today, Venice's modest permanent population (less than half that of the 1950s) is swollen by up to 20 million visitors every year, the majority of them day-trippers.

ORIENTATION

Venice is built on 117 small islands and has some 150 canals and 409 bridges. Only three bridges cross the Grand Canal: the Ponte di Rialto, the Ponte dell'Accademia and the Ponte degli Scalzi.

Stretching away to the north and south are the shallow waters of the Laguna Veneta, dotted by what seems a crumbling mosaic of islands, islets and rocks. Among them, Murano, Burano and Torcello are all of interest and lie to the north. Acting as a breakwater to the east, the long and slender Lido di Venezia stretches some 10km south, followed by another similarly narrow island, Pellestrina, which reaches down to the sleepy town of Chioggia. The latter marks where the mainland closes off the lagoon to the south.

The city is divided into six *sestieri* (quarters): Cannaregio, Castello, San Marco, Dorsoduro, San Polo and Santa Croce. These town divisions date back to 1171. In the east, the islands of San Pietro and Sant' Elena, largely ignored by visitors, are attached to Castello by two and three bridges respectively.

You can drive your car to Venice and park it but there is nowhere to drive once you arrive. Ferries also transport cars to the Lido, where they can be driven (although buses are more than adequate there). In Venice itself all public transport is by *vaporetto* (small passenger boat/ferry) along the canals. To cross the Grand Canal between the bridges, use a *traghetto*, a cheap way to get a short gondola ride. Signs will direct you to the *traghetto* points.

The alternative is to go *a piedi* (on foot). To walk from the train station to St Mark's Square (Piazza San Marco) will take a good half-hour – follow the signs to San Marco.

From San Marco, the routes to other main areas, such as the Rialto, Accademia and the train station, are well signposted but can be confusing, particularly in the Dorsoduro and San Polo areas. For more information on local transport, see Getting Around (pp355–7).

A STREET BY ANY OTHER NAME

The names for the types of street in use today in Venice go back to the 11th century and bear little relationship to the terminology used in most mainland cities – Venice always did see itself as apart from the rest of Italy.

Of course, the waterways are not streets at all. The main ones are called *canale*, while the bulk of them are called *rio*. Where a *rio* has been filled in it becomes a *rio terrà* or *rio terà*.

What anywhere else in Italy would be called a *via* (street) is, in Venice, a *calle*. A street beside a canal is called a *fondamenta*. A *ruga* or *rughetta* is a smaller street flanked by houses and shops, while those called *salizzada* (sometimes spelled with one 'z') were among the first streets to be paved. A *ramo* is a tiny side lane, often connecting two bigger streets. A *corte* is a small dead-end street or courtyard. A quay is a *riva* and where a street passes under a building (something like an extended archway) it is called a *sotoportego*. A *piscina* is not a swimming pool but a one-time stagnant pool later filled in.

The only square in Venice called a *piazza* is San Marco (St Mark's Square), all the others are called *campo* (except for the bus station area, which is called Piazzale Roma). The small version is a *campiello*. Occasionally you come across a *campazzo*. On maps you may see the following abbreviations:

Calle – C, Cl

Campo – Cpo

Corte – Cte

Fondamenta – Fond, Fondam, F

Palazzo – Pal

Salizzada – Sal, Salizz

Street Numbering

Confused? You will be. Venice also has its own style of street numbering, introduced by the Austrians in 1841. Instead of a system based on individual streets, each *sestiere* (quarter) has a long series of numbers. A hotel might give its address as San Marco 4687, which doesn't seem to help much. Because the *sestieri* are fairly small, wandering around and searching out the number is technically feasible and sometimes doesn't take that long. But there is precious little apparent logic to the run of numbers – frustration is never far away. Most streets are named, so where possible we provide street names as well as the *sestiere* number throughout the guide.

For other suggestions on navigational aids, see p328.

INFORMATION
Bookshops
Libreria Demetra (Map p340; ☎ 041 275 01 52; Campo San Geremia, Cannaregio 282; ⏰ 9am-midnight Mon-Sat, 10am-midnight Sun) Late-night readers in need of a paperback (several languages catered for) should head here.

Studium (Map pp332–4; ☎ 041 522 23 82; Calle de la Canonica 337/a) A good selection of English-language guides and books on Venice.

Emergency
Police Station (Map pp324–5; ☎ 041 271 57 72; Fondamenta di San Lorenzo, Castello 5053) You can head here if you have been robbed.

Internet Access
Casanova (Map p328; ☎ 041 524 06 64; Rio Terrà Lista di Spagna, Cannaregio 158/a; €7/hr; ⏰ 9am-11.30pm) Here you go clubbing by night and online by day.

EasyContact (Map pp332–4; ☎ 041 71 10 97; www.easy-contact.it; Campo Nazario Sauro, Santa Croce 1005/a; €7.20/hr; ⏰ 10am-1.30pm & 3.30-8.30pm) You can get a four-hour card for €11.

Planet Internet (Map p340; ☎ 041 524 41 88; Rio Terrà San Leonardo, Cannaregio 1519; €8/hr; ⏰ 9am-midnight)

World House (Map pp332–4; ☎ 041 528 48 71; www .world-house.org; Calle della Chiesa, Castello 4502; €8/hr; ⏰ 10am-11pm)

Laundry
Self-service laundries are a rarity in Venice.
Bea Vita Lavanderia (Map pp332–4; Calle Chioverette, Santa Croce 665/b; 8kg wash/dry €3.50/2; ⏰ 8am-10pm)

Speedy Wash (Map p340; Rio Terrà San Leonardo, Cannaregio 1520; 8kg wash/dry €4.50/3; ⏰ 9am-11pm)

Lost Property
If you lose stuff in Venice it may well be gone forever but you could try the checking out the local **police station** (Map pp324–5; Vigili Urbani; ☎ 041 522 45 76) on Piazzale Roma. Otherwise the following numbers might be useful:
ACTV – buses (☎ 041 272 27 23)
Municipio (☎ 041 274 81 11)
Trenitalia (☎ 041 78 52 38)
Vaporetti (☎ 041 272 21 79)

Maps
Aside from Lonely Planet's *Venice* map, one of the best maps is the wine-red covered *Venezia*, produced by the Touring Club Italiano (scale 1:5000). If you plan to stay for the long haul, *Calli,* *Campielli e Canali* (Edizioni Helvetica) is for you (€17.50). This is the definitive street guide and will allow you to locate to within 100m any Venetian-style address you need.

Medical Services
Current information on late-night pharmacies is listed in *Un Ospite di Venezia* and daily newspapers such as *Il Gazzettino* or *La Nuova Venezia*.

Ospedale Civile (Map pp332–4; ☎ 041 529 41 11; Campo SS Giovanni e Paolo) This is the main hospital. For emergency treatment, go straight to the *pronto soccorso* (casualty) section, where you can also get emergency dental treatment.

Ospedale Umberto I (☎ 041 260 71 11; Via Circonvallazione 50) A modern mainland hospital.

Money
Most of the main banks are in the area around Ponte di Rialto and San Marco. There are numerous bureaux de change across the city and at the train station.

American Express (Map pp332–4; ☎ 041 520 08 44; Salizzada San Moisè, San Marco 1471; ⏰ 9am-5.30pm Mon-Fri, 9am-12.30pm Sat) It has an ATM for AmEx cards.

Travelex (Thomas Cook; Map pp332–4; ☎ 041 528 73 58; ⏰ 8.45am-8pm Mon-Sat, 9am-6pm Sun) St Mark's Square (St Mark's Square 142); Riva del Ferro (Riva del Ferro 5126)

Post
The **main post office** (Map pp332–4; Salizzada del Fondaco dei Tedeschi; ⏰ 8.10am-7pm Mon-Sat) is near the Ponte di Rialto. Stamps are available at windows No 1 to 4 in the central courtyard. There is something quite special about doing your postal business in this former trading house. Stand by the well in the middle and try to imagine the bustle as German traders and brokers shuffled their goods around on the ground floor or struck deals in their quarters on the upper levels back in the republic's trading heyday.

Telephone
There is a bank of **telephones** (Map pp332–4) near the post office on Calle Galeazza. Unstaffed phone offices can be found on Strada Nuova, Cannaregio (Map pp332–4); Ruga Vecchia San Giovanni 480, San Polo (Map pp332–4); and Calle San Luca 4585, San Marco (Map pp332–4). You will also find phones at the train station.

Tourist Information

The Azienda di Promozione Turistica (APT) tourist offices found in Venice have information on the town and the province. You could also try phoning the **central information line** (☎ 041 529 87 11; www.turismovenezia.it) available in Venice.

Infopoint (Map pp332–4; Venice Pavilion; ☼ 10am-6pm) Next to Giardini Ex Reali, a quick walk from St Mark's Square. Hires out My Venice audioguides that you can take around the city (from €3 an hour to €15 for two days).
Main tourist office (Map pp332–4; Piazza San Marco 71/f; ☼ 9am-3.30pm Mon-Sat) Staff will assist with information on hotels, transport and things to see and do in the city.

DISCOUNTS ON ADMISSION

Rolling Venice Concession Pass

If you are aged between 14 and 29, take your passport and a colour photograph to the **Assessorato alla Gioventù** (Map pp332–4; ☎ 041 274 76 50; fax 041 274 76 42; Corte Contarina, San Marco 1529; ☼ 9.30am-1pm Mon, Wed & Fri, 9.30am-1pm & 3-5pm Tue & Thu), and pick up the Rolling Venice card (€2.60), which offers significant discounts on food, accommodation, entertainment, public transport, museums and galleries.

You can also pick up the pass at the **Agenzia Arte e Storia** (Map pp332–4; ☎ 041 524 02 32; Corte Canal, Santa Croce 659), the **ACTV transport office** (Map pp332–4; Piazzale Roma) and outlets of the ACTV subsidiary, **Vela** (Map pp332–4; ☎ 041 24 24; www.velaspa.com). Two of these are located in front of the train station and one at Piazzale Roma. Pick up the *Rolling Venice* map, which lists all the hotels, restaurants, shops, museums, cinemas and theatres where the pass entitles you to reductions.

Other Discounts

In addition, admission to all state museums is free for EU citizens under 18 and over 65. In Venice this is only a handful of museums: the Gallerie dell'Accademia, the Ca' d'Oro and the Museo d'Arte Orientale. Admission to these museums is also free for non EU citizens 12 years old and under.

A handful of museums and galleries also offer reductions for students and seniors regardless of where they are from. It never hurts to ask.

Special Tickets

A **Museum Pass** covers entry to the Palazzo Ducale (Doge's Palace), Museo Correr, Museo Archeologico, Libreria Nazionale Marciana, La Torre dell'Orologio; Ca' Rezzonico, Museo Vetrario on Murano, Museo del Merletto on Burano, Palazzo Mocenigo, the Casa di Goldoni and Ca' Pesaro. The ticket costs €15.50 (students aged 15 to 29 pay €10) and can be purchased from any of these museums. It is valid for three months.

You can also buy a **Museum Card** for €11 (students aged 15 to 29 pay €5.50) that covers the Palazzo Ducale, Torre dell'Orologio, Museo Correr, Museo Archeologico and Libreria Nazionale Marciana only.

Further Museum Card options include a €8 (€4.50 for students) ticket for Ca' Rezzonico, Palazzo Mocenigo and the Casa di Goldoni, and a €6 (€4 for students) ticket for the Murano and Burano museums.

Another cumulative ticket groups the Gallerie dell'Accademia, the Ca' d'Oro and the Museo d'Arte Orientale (adult/child €11/5.50).

An organisation called **Chorus**, which is involved in the upkeep of Venice's most artistically significant churches, offers visitors a special ticket (adult/child and students €8/5) providing entry to 15 outstanding churches. The ticket is valid for a year. Entrance to individual churches is €2.

The churches from which you can choose are, in no particular order: Santa Maria Gloriosa dei Frari, Santa Maria del Giglio, Santo Stefano, Santa Maria Formosa, Santa Maria dei Miracoli, San Polo, I Gesuati, San Giovanni Elemosinario, San Giacomo dell'Orio, San Stae, Sant'Alvise, La Madonna dell'Orto, San Pietro di Castello, Redentore and San Sebastiano. The ticket, available from any of the churches, also includes the option of visiting the Tesoro (Treasury) of St Mark's Basilica. Among the more worthwhile churches to visit, if you don't want to see them all, are St Mark's (Tesoro), Santa Maria Gloriosa dei Frari, San Giacomo dell'Orio, Santo Stefano, San Polo and San Sebastiano.

Tourist Office Lido (Gran Viale Santa Maria Elisabetta 6/a; ☯ 9am-12.30pm & 3.30-6pm Jun-Sep only); Marco Polo airport (arrivals hall; 9.30am-7.30pm); Piazzale Roma (Map pp324-5; next to Garage Comunale; ☯ 9.30am-6.30pm); train station (Map pp332-4; ☯ 8am-8pm summer, 8am-6.30pm rest of year)

The useful monthly booklet *Un Ospite di Venezia* (A Guest in Venice), published by a group of Venetian hoteliers, is sometimes available from tourist offices. If not, you can find it in most of the larger hotels. Similar, but a little less informative, is *Pocket Venice*, sometimes available from tourist offices.

The APT operates a free 24-hour tourist helpline in case you have a complaint to make about services poorly rendered (from hotels, restaurants, water taxis and the like). Call ☎ 800 35 59 20 and follow the instructions. Alternatively you can contact the **Sportello di Conciliazione Turistica** (Map pp332-4; ☎ 041 529 87 23; complaint.apt@turismovenezia.it; Calle del Remedio, Castello 4421; ☯ 8.30am-1.30pm Mon-Fri).

Travel Agencies

Centro Turistico Studentesco e Giovanile (CTS; Map pp332-4; ☎ 041 520 56 60; www.cts.it; Calle Foscari 3252, Dorsoduro) The main Italian student and youth travel organisation.

Gran Canal Viaggi (Map pp332-4; ☎ 041 271 21 11; www.grancanal.it; Ponte dell'Ovo, San Marco 4759/4760)

SIGHTS

After wafting down the Grand Canal, you will want to organise yourself to see some of the cream of Venice's countless extraordinary sights. The following section is roughly divided up into the city's traditional *sestieri*, and together form a circuit through the city, starting in St Mark's Square and winding up there again at the end.

Grand Canal (Canal Grande)

Described by French writer Philippe de Commines in the 15th century as 'the finest street in the world, with the finest houses', the Grand Canal is a little dilapidated these days but still rivals the world's great boulevards. It weaves for 3.5km through the city like a huge, back-to-front 'S', with a depth of about 6m and a width ranging from 40m to 100m. Taking a *vaporetto* is the only way

to see the incredible parade of buildings, including more than 100 *palazzi*, which date from the 12th to the 18th centuries. Board *vaporetto* No 1 at Piazzale Roma and try to grab a seat on the deck at the back.

Not far past the train station and Canale di Cannaregio (the city's second-largest canal) and just after the Riva di Biasio stop (to the right) is one of the most celebrated Veneto-Byzantine buildings, the **Fondaco dei Turchi** (Map pp332-4). Once a Turkish warehouse and now the Museo Civico di Storia Naturale (Natural History Museum), it is recognisable by the three-storey towers on either side of its colonnade.

The canal continues past Rio di San Marcuola to **Palazzo Vendramin-Calergi** (Map p340) on the left. Richard Wagner died here in 1883 and it is now a fine Renaissance winter home for the casino. Further on and to the right, just after the San Stae stop, is the **Ca' Pesaro** (Map pp332-4), Baldassare Longhena's baroque masterpiece (built between 1679 and 1710). Longhena died worrying about the cost and the building was only completed after his death. It houses the Galleria d'Arte Moderna and Museo d'Arte Orientale.

Shortly after, to the left, is the **Ca' d'Oro** (Golden House; Map pp332-4), acclaimed as the most beautiful Gothic building in Venice. To the right, as the boat turns for the Ponte di Rialto, is the **pescaria** (fish market; Map pp332-4) on Campo della Pescaria, built in 1907.

On the right, just after the *pescaria*, are the **Fabbriche Nuove di Rialto** (Map pp332-4), built in 1555 by Jacopo Sansovino as a court house. Next door is the city's produce market and then the **Fabbriche Vecchie di Rialto** (Map pp332-4), built in 1522 to house markets and offices. Just before the Ponte di Rialto, on the left bank, the **Fondaco dei Tedeschi** (Map pp332-4) was once the most important trading house on the canal and now serves as the main post office. It was rebuilt after a fire in 1505 and frescoes by Titian and Giorgione (remnants on view in the Ca' d'Oro) once adorned its facade.

The stone **Ponte di Rialto** was built in the late 16th century by Antonio da Ponte, who won the commission over architects including Palladio. The Renaissance **Palazzo Grimani** (Map pp332-4), on the left after the bridge and just before the Rio di San Luca, was designed by Sanmicheli. Further along the same bank, the **Palazzo Corner-Spinelli** (Map pp332-4) was designed in the same period by Mauro Cordussi. Or the right, as the canal swings sharply to the left, is the late-Gothic **Ca' Foscari** (Map pp332–4), commissioned by Doge Francesco Foscari. One of the finest mansions in the city and seat of the university, it is followed on the left by the 18th century **Palazzo Grassi** (Map pp332–4). Now owned by FIAT, it is used as a cultural and exhibition centre. Opposite, the massive **Ca' Rezzonico** (Map pp332–4), designed by Baldassare Longhena, houses the city's collection of 18th-century art.

You are now approaching the last of the canal's three bridges, the wooden **Ponte dell' Accademia**, built in 1930 to replace a metal 19th-century structure. Past it and on the right is the unfinished **Palazzo Venier dei Leoni** (Map pp332–4), where American heiress Peggy Guggenheim lived until her death in 1979. It is home to her collection of modern art. Two buildings along is the delightful **Palazzo Dario** (Map pp332–4) built in 1487 and recognisable by the multicoloured marble facade and its many chimneys.

On the left bank, at the Santa Maria del Giglio stop, is **Palazzo Corner** (Map pp332–4), an imposing, ivy-covered residence also known as the Ca' Granda and designed in the mid-16th century by Jacopo Sansovino. On the right, before the canal broadens into the expanse facing San Marco, is Baldassare Longhena's magnificent **Chiesa di Santa Maria della Salute** (Map pp332–4), which takes central place in many a postcard of the city and its canal.

San Marco
Map pp332–4

Napoleon thought of **St Mark's Square** (Piazza San Marco) as the finest drawing room in Europe. Enclosed by the basilica and the arcaded Procuratie Vecchie and Nuove, the square plays host to competing flocks of pigeons and tourists. Stand and wait for the bronze *Mori* (Moors) to strike the bell of the 15th-century **Torre dell'Orologio**), which rises above the entrance to the Mercerie, the main thoroughfare from San Marco to the Rialto. Or sit and savour an expensive coffee at Florian or Quadri, 18th-century cafés across from each other on the piazza.

St Mark's Basilica (Basilica di San Marco; ☎ 041 522 52 05; Piazza San Marco; admission free; ☒ 9.45am-5pm Mon-Sat, 2-5pm Sun & holidays Apr-Oct, 9.30am-4pm Nov-Mar) embodies a magnificent blend of architectural and decorative styles, dominated by the Byzantine style and ranging through Romanesque to Renaissance. Note that modest dress is essential for visiting the basilica. This means covering your arms and skirts or pants at least down to the knees. The 'under-dressed' will be turned away, no matter how long they have queued.

The original church, a chapel built to house the purported remains of the evangelist St Mark (see the boxed text p336), was destroyed by fire in 932 and rebuilt, but in 1063 Doge Domenico Contarini decided it was poor in comparison to the splendid Romanesque churches being raised in mainland cities and had it demolished.

The new basilica, built on the plan of a Greek cross, with five bulbous domes, was modelled on Constantinople's (later destroyed) Church of the Twelve Apostles and consecrated in 1094. It was actually built as the doges' private chapel and remained so until it became Venice's cathedral in 1807.

For more than 500 years, the doges enlarged and embellished the church, adorning it with an incredible array of treasures plundered from the East, in particular Constantinople, during the crusades.

The arches above the doorways in the **facade** boast fine mosaics. The one on the left, depicting the arrival of St Mark's body in Venice, was completed in 1270. The three arches of the main doorway are decorated with Romanesque carvings, dating from around 1240.

On the loggia (balcony) above the main door are copies of four gilded bronze horses; the originals, on display inside, were stolen and brought to Venice when Constantinople was sacked in 1204, during the Fourth Crusade. Napoleon moved them to Paris in 1797 but they were returned following the collapse of the French Empire.

Through the doors is the **narthex**, or vestibule, its domes and arches decorated with mosaics, mainly dating from the 13th century. The oldest mosaics in the basilica, dating from around 1063, are in the niches of the bay in front of the main door from the narthex into the church proper. They feature the Madonna with the Apostles.

The **interior** of the basilica is dazzling; if you can take your eyes off the glitter of the mosaics, take time to admire the 12th-century marble pavement, a geometrical whimsy which has subsided in places, making the floor uneven.

THE VENETO

SAN MARCO, SAN POLO & SANTA CROCE

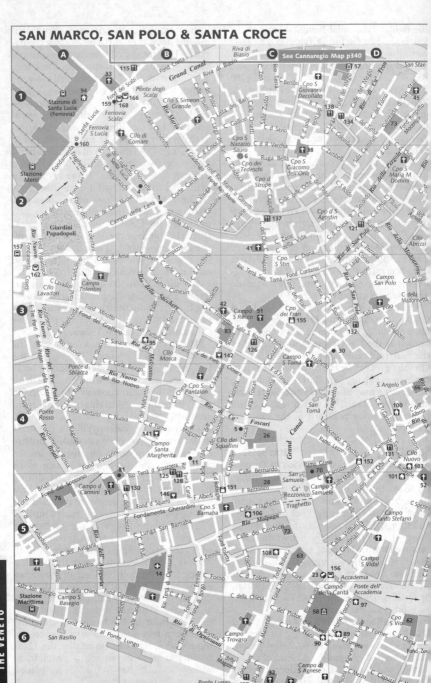

See Cannaregio Map p340

THE VENETO

THE VENETO

The lower level of the walls is lined with precious eastern marbles and above this decoration the extraordinary feast of gilded **mosaics** begins. Work started on the mosaics in the 11th century and continued until well into the 13th century. More were added in the 14th and 15th centuries in the baptistry and side chapels and, as late as the 18th century, still more mosaics were being added or restored.

To the right of the high altar is the entrance to the sanctuary. St Mark's body is contained in a sarcophagus beneath the altar. Behind the altar is the exquisite **Pala d'Oro** (adult/child €1.50/1), a gold, enamel and jewel-encrusted altarpiece made in Constantinople for Doge Pietro Orseolo I in 976. It was enriched and reworked in Constantinople in 1105, enlarged by Venetian goldsmiths in 1209 and reset again in the 14th century. Among the almost 2000 precious stones which adorn it are emeralds, rubies, amethysts, sapphires and pearls.

The **Tesoro** (treasury; adult/child €2/1), accessible from the right transept, contains most of the booty from the 1204 raid on Constantinople, including a thorn said to be from the crown worn by Christ.

Through a door at the far right end of the narthex is a stairway leading up to the **Galleria** (Museo di San Marco; ☎ 041 522 52 05; adult/child €1.50/1; ☺ 9.45am-5pm), which contains the original gilded bronze horses and the **Loggia dei Cavalli**. The *galleria* affords wonderful views of the church's interior, while the loggia offers equally splendid vistas of the square.

The basilica's 99m-tall **Campanile** (Bell Tower; adult/child €6/3; ☺ 9am-9pm late Jun–Aug, 9am-7pm Apr-Jun & Sep-Oct, 9am-4pm Nov-Mar), built in the 10th century, suddenly collapsed on 14 July 1902 and was rebuilt brick by brick. The views from the top are spectacular.

The former residence and offices of the Procurators of St Mark (who were responsible for the upkeep of the basilica), the **Procuratie Vecchie** were designed by Mauro Codussi and occupy the entire northern side of St Mark's Square.

On the southern side of the piazza are the **Procuratie Nuove**, planned by Jacopo Sansovino and completed by Vincenzo Scamozzi and Baldassare Longhena. Napoleon converted this building into his royal palace and demolished the church of San Geminiano at the western end of the piazza to build the wing commonly known as the Ala Napoleonica, which housed his ballroom.

The Ala Napoleonica is now home to the **Museo Correr** (☎ 041 240 52 11; Piazza San Marco; ☺ 9am-7pm Apr-Oct, 9am-5pm Nov-Mar), dedicated to the art and history of Venice. Through this museum you also access first the **Museo Archeologico**, which houses an impressive, if somewhat repetitive, selection of ancient sculptures, and then the **Libreria Nazionale Marciana**. Described by Palladio as the most sumptuous palace ever built, the Libreria was designed by Jacopo Sansovino in the 16th century. It takes up the entire western side of the Piazzetta di San Marco. Inside, the main reading hall is a sumptuous 16th-century creation. The ceiling was

decorated by a battalion of artists, including Veronese.

Stretching from St Mark's Square to the waterfront, **Piazzetta di San Marco** features two columns bearing statues of the Lion of St Mark and St Theodore (San Teodoro), the city's two emblems. Originally a marketplace, the area was also a preferred location for public executions and political meetings.

The **Palazzo Ducale** (Doges' Palace; ☎ 041 271 59 11; optional audioguide €5.50; ☺ 9am-7pm Apr-Oct, 9am-5pm Nov-Mar) was not only the doges' official residence, as the name suggests, but was also the seat of the Republic's government, housed bureaucrats and contained the prisons. Established in the 9th century, the palace began to assume its present form 500 years later with the decision to build the massive Sala del Maggior Consiglio for the council members, who ranged in number from 1200 to 1700. It was inaugurated in 1419.

The palace's two magnificent Gothic facades in white Istrian stone and pink Veronese marble face the water and Piazzetta di San Marco. Much of the building was damaged by fire in 1577 but it was successfully restored by Antonio da Ponte (who designed the Ponte di Rialto).

The former main entrance (and now exit), the 15th-century **Porta della Carta** (Paper Door), to which government decrees were fixed, was carved by Giovanni and Bartolomeo Bon. Leading from the courtyard, the **Scala dei Giganti** (Giants' Staircase) by Antonio Rizzo takes its name from the huge statues of Mars and Neptune, by Jacopo Sansovino, which flank the landing.

Past Sansovino's **Scala d'Oro** (Golden Staircase) are rooms dedicated to the various doges, including the **Sala delle Quattro Porte** (Hall of the Four Doors) on the 3rd floor, where ambassadors would be kindly requested to await their ducal audience. The room's ceiling was designed by Palladio and the frescoes are by Tintoretto. Off this room is the **Anticollegio** (College Antechamber), which features four Tintorettos and the *Ratto d'Europa* (Rape of Europa) by Paolo Veronese. Through here, the ceiling of the splendid **Sala del Collegio** (College Hall) features a series of artworks by Veronese. Next is the **Sala del Senato** (Senate Hall), graced by yet more Tintorettos.

The indicated route (you have no choice in the matter) then takes you to the immense **Sala del Maggior Consiglio** (Grand Council Hall) on the 2nd floor. It is dominated at one end by Tintoretto's *Paradiso* (Paradise), one of the world's largest oil paintings, measuring 22m by 7m. Among the many other paintings in the hall is a masterpiece, the *Apoteosi di Venezia* (Apotheosis of Venice) by Veronese, in one of the central ceiling panels. Note the black space in the frieze on the wall depicting the first 76 doges of Venice. Doge Marin Falier would have appeared there had he not been beheaded for treason in 1355.

Next, you find yourself crossing the small, enclosed **Ponte dei Sospiri** (Bridge of Sighs) to reach the prisons. The bridge is named because of the sighs prisoners tended to make on their way into the dungeons. The poor unfortunates to make this dismal crossing must have been well behaved indeed not to give more vigorous vent to their displeasure than a mere sigh.

The **Itinerari Segreti** (Secret Itineraries; ☎ 041 271 59 11; adult/child €12.50/7; tours ☉ 10am & 11.30am Apr-Oct) is a guided tour of lesser-known areas of the palace. The 1½-hour tour (also available in Italian and French) is an intriguing look at the underside of the palace. You pass from civil servants' offices to a torture chamber, the Inquisitor's office and upstairs to the **Piombi** (Leads; prison cells beneath the roof of the building). Here prisoners froze in winter and sweltered in summer. Giacomo Casanova got five years but managed to escape. You also get an explanation of the engineering behind the ceiling of the immense Sala del Maggior Consiglio below. Book a place on the tour in advance directly at the ticket office or by calling.

Around San Marco Map pp332–4

The **Mercerie**, a series of streets lined with shops, connects St Mark's Square and the Rialto in a rather tortuous manner. The **Chiesa di San Salvador** (☉ 9am-noon & 3-6pm Mon-Fri), built on a plan of three Greek crosses laid end to end, features Titian's *Annunciazione* (Annunciation), at the third altar on the right as you approach the main altar. Behind the main altar itself is another of his contributions, the *Trasfigurazione* (Transfiguration).

The area immediately west of St Mark's Square is a rabbit warren of streets and alleys lined with exclusive shops, where – if you search hard enough – you might pick up some interesting gifts and souvenirs

---

MAKING HIS MARK

The story goes that an angel appeared to the Evangelist Mark when his boat put in at Rialto while on his way to Rome from Aquileia. The winged fellow informed the future saint that his body would rest in Venice (which didn't exist at this point!). When he did die some years later, it was in Alexandria, Egypt. In 828, two Venetian merchants persuaded the guardians of his Alexandrian tomb to let them have the corpse, which they then smuggled down to their ship in port.

You've got to ask yourself why they would bother with such a strange cargo. Well, in those days, any city worthy of the name had a patron saint of stature. Venice had St Theodore (San Teodoro) but poor old Theodore didn't really cut the mustard in the Christian hierarchy. An Evangelist, though, would be something quite different. Did Doge Giustinian Partecipazio order this little body-snatching mission? We will never know. Whatever the truth of this tale, it seems that *someone's* putrid corpse was transported to Venice and that everyone rather liked to think St Mark was now in their midst. St Theodore was unceremoniously demoted and the doge ordered the construction of a chapel to house the newcomer. That church would later become the magnificent St Mark's Basilica. St Mark was symbolised in the Book of Revelation (the Apocalypse) as a winged lion and this image came to be synonymous with La Repubblica Serenissima (Most Serene Republic).

Legend also has it that, during the rebuilding of the basilica in 1063, the body of St Mark was hidden and then 'lost' when its hiding place was forgotten. In 1094, when the church was consecrated, the corpse (which must have been a picture of frailty by this time) broke through the column in which it had been enclosed. 'It's a miracle!' the Venetians cried. Or was it just incredibly dodgy plasterwork? St Mark had been lost and now was found. A grateful populace buried the remains in the church crypt where they now lie beneath the basilica's high altar.

such as watercolours of the city, marbled paper and carnival masks.

On the way to the Ponte dell'Accademia there are a couple of notable churches. The Renaissance **Chiesa di San Fantin** (Campo San Fantin) has a domed sanctuary and apse by Jacopo Sansovino. Also in Campo San Fantin stands the **Teatro la Fenice**, the opera house that opened in 1792 and was largely gutted by fire in January 1996. Several of Verdi's operas had their opening nights here and with a little luck Riccardo Muti will perform at the theatre's planned reopening at the end of 2003.

Before you go elsewhere, make sure you duck up just north of the Chiesa di San Fantin to admire the wonderful 15th-century external spiral staircase at the **Palazzo Contarini del Bovolo** (☎ 041 270 24 64; Corte del Bovolo, San Marco 4299; adult/child €2.50/2; ☼ 10am-6pm).

Return to Calle Larga XXII Marzo and turn right for the **Chiesa di Santa Maria del Giglio** (admission €2 or Chorus ticket; ☼ 10am-5pm Mon-Sat, 1-5pm Sun), also known as Santa Maria Zobenigo. Its baroque facade features maps of European cities as they were in 1678. Go on to Campo Francesco Morosini (Campo Santo Stefano) and the Gothic **Chiesa di Santo Stefano** (admission €2; ☼ 10am-5pm Mon-Sat, 1-5pm Sun) is on your right (the entry is on the western side). Of note are three paintings by Tintoretto in the little museum: *Ultima Cena* (Last Supper), *Lavanda dei Piedi* (Washing of the Feet) and *Orazione nell'Orto* (Agony in the Garden). Outside, the church's bell tower leans rather worryingly.

Dorsoduro

The **Gallerie dell'Accademia** (Map pp332–4; ☎ 041 522 22 47; adult/EU citizens 18-25 yrs/child under 12 & EU citizens under 18 & over 65 €6.50/3.25/free, audio guide 1-/2-person €3.50/5; ☼ 8.15am-2pm Mon, 8.15am-7.15pm Tue-Sun – hrs subject to frequent change) is a must for anyone with even a passing interest in art. The former church and convent of Santa Maria della Carità, with additions by Palladio, hosts a collection that follows the progression of Venetian art from the 14th to the 18th centuries.

Room 1 contains works by the early 14th-century painter Paolo Veneziano, including the *Incoronazione di Maria* (Coronation of Mary). The main feature of Room 2, which covers the late 15th and early 16th centuries, is Carpaccio's altarpiece *Crocifissione*

e Apoteosi dei 10,000 Martiri del Monte Ararat (Crucifixion and Apotheosis of the 10,000 Martyrs of Mt Ararat). It also contains works by Giovanni Bellini. Rooms 4 and 5 feature Andrea Mantegna's *San Giorgio* (St George), several paintings of the Madonna and Child by Giovanni Bellini and Giorgione's fabulous *La Tempesta* (The Storm). Rooms 6 to 10 contain works of the High Renaissance, including Tintoretto and Titian, but one of the highlights is Paolo Veronese's *Convito in Casa di Levi* (Feast in the House of Levi) in Room 10. Originally called *Ultima Cena* (Last Supper), the painting's name was changed because the Inquisition objected to its depiction of characters such as drunkards and dwarfs. The room also contains one of Titian's last works, a *Pietà*. In Room 13 are a number of works by the 18th-century painter Giambattista Tiepolo. Giovanni Bellini and Carpaccio appear again in subsequent rooms and the collection ends in Room 24 with Tiepolo's beautiful *Presentazione di Maria al Tempio* (Presentation of Mary at the Temple).

Peggy Guggenheim called the unfinished Palazzo Venier dei Leoni, a short stroll east of the Gallerie dell'Accademia, home for 30 years until she died in 1979. She left behind the **Peggy Guggenheim Collection** (Map pp332–4; ☎ 041 240 54 11; www.Guggenheim-venice.it; Palazzo Venier dei Leoni, Dorsoduro 701; adult/student & child €8/5; ☼ 10am-6pm Wed-Fri & Sun-Mon, 10am-10pm Sat) of works by her favourite modern artists, representing most of the major movements of the 20th century. Picasso, Mondrian, Kandinsky, Ernst, Chagall, Klee, Miró, Dalí, Pollock, Brancusi, Magritte and Bacon are all represented. Take a wander around the sculpture garden (which includes works by Moore, Giacometti and Ernst), where Miss Guggenheim and many of her pet dogs are buried.

Dominating the entrance to the Grand Canal, the beautiful **Chiesa di Santa Maria della Salute** (Map pp332–4; sacristy admission €1; ☼ 9am-noon & 3-6pm) was built in the 17th century in honour of the Virgin Mary, who was believed to have delivered the city from an outbreak of plague that had killed more than a third of the population. From inside Baldassare Longhena's octagonal main church you access the Great Sacristy, where Titian and Tintoretto left their mark. Every

THE VENETO

year, on 21 November, a procession takes place from St Mark's Square to the church to give thanks for the city's good health.

The Fondamenta delle Zattere, more simply known as the **Zattere** runs along the Canale della Giudecca from Punta della Salute to Stazione Marittima. It is a popular spot for the traditional evening *passeggiata* (stroll). The main sight is the 18th-century Santa Maria del Rosario, or **Chiesa dei Gesuati** (Map pp324–5; admission €2; ☺ 10am-5pm Mon-Sat, 1-5pm Sun), designed by Giorgio Massari. Tiepolo's ceiling frescoes tell the story of San Domenico. At the end of the Zattere, over Rio di San Basilio, the **Chiesa di San Sebastiano** (Map pp332–4; admission €2; ☺ 10am-5pm Mon-Sat, 1-5pm Sun) was the local church of Paolo Veronese, who provided most of the paintings and lies buried in the church.

The 17th- and 18th-century **Ca' Rezzonico** (Map pp332–4), which faces the Grand Canal, houses the **Museo del Settecento Veneziano** (Museum of the 18th Century; ☎ 041 241 01 00; Dorsoduro 3136; adult/student/child €6.50/4.50/2.50; ☺ 10am-6pm Wed-Mon Apr-Oct, 10am-5pm Wed-Mon Nov-Mar). Designed by Baldassare Longhena and completed by Massari, it was home to several notables over the years, including the poet Robert Browning, who died there. A broad staircase by Massari ascends from the ground floor to the main floor and on to the ballroom, a splendid hall dripping with frescoes and richly furnished with 18th-century couches, tables and statues in ebony. Particularly noteworthy is Tiepolo's ceiling fresco in the Sala del Trono (throne room), the *Allegoria del Merito tra Nobiltà e Virtù* (Allegory of Merit Between Nobility and Virtue).

Tiepolo also had a hand in the 16th-century **Scuola Grande dei Carmini** (Map pp332–4; ☎ 041 528 94 20; Campo Santa Margherita, Dorsoduro 2617; admission €5; ☺ 9am-6pm Mon-Sat, 9am-4pm Sun), near the church of the same name, just west of Campo Santa Margherita. Of its numerous works of art, the nine ceiling paintings by Tiepolo in the Salone Superiore (upstairs) depict the virtues surrounding the Virgin in Glory.

San Polo & Santa Croce   Map pp332–4

The massive Gothic **Chiesa di Santa Maria Gloriosa dei Frari** (Camp dei Frari; admission €2; ☺ 9am-6pm Mon-Sat, 1-6pm Sun), rich in art treasures, is one of the highlights of a visit to Venice.

It was built for the Franciscans in the 14th and 15th centuries and decorated by an illustrious array of artists. Titian, who is buried in the church, is the main attraction of the Frari. His dramatic *Assunta* (Assumption; 1518) over the high altar represents a key moment in his rise as one of the city's greatest artists, praised unreservedly by all and sundry as a work of inspired genius. Another of his masterpieces, the *Madonna di Ca' Pesaro* (Madonna of Ca' Pesaro) hangs above the Pesaro altar (in the left-hand aisle, near the choir stalls).

Just behind the bulk of the Frari is yet another Venetian treasure chest. Built for the Confraternity of St Roch in the 16th century and decorated with more than 50 paintings by Tintoretto, the **Scuola Grande di San Rocco** (☎ 041 523 48 64; Campo San Rocco, Dorsoduro 3052; adult/youth aged 18-26/child under 18 €5.50/4. 1.50; ☺ 9am-5.30pm Easter-Oct, 10am-4pm Nov-Easter) is one of Venice's great surprises.

After winning a competition (one of his competitors was Paolo Veronese), Tintoretto went on to devote 23 years of his life to decorating the school. The overwhelming concentration of paintings by the master is altogether too much for the average human to digest. Chronologically speaking, you should start upstairs (Scarpagnino designed the staircase) in the Sala Grande Superiore. Here you can pick up mirrors to carry around to avoid getting a sore neck while inspecting the ceiling paintings (which depict Old Testament episodes). Around the walls are scenes from the New Testament. A handful of works by other artists (such as Titian, Giorgione and Tiepolo) can also be seen. To give your eyes a rest from the paintings, inspect the woodwork below them – a marvel of curious and painstakingly executed designs, including a false book collection. Downstairs, the walls of the confraternity's assembly hall feature a serie on the life of the Virgin Mary, starting on the left wall with the *Annunciazione* (Annunciation) and ending with the *Assunzion* (Assumption) opposite.

A short walk east and across the Rio di San Tomà is the **Casa di Goldoni** (☎ 041 523 6 53; Calle Nomboli 2794; adult/child €2.50/1.50; ☺ 10am-5pm Mon-Sat Apr-Oct, 10am-4pm Mon-Sat Nov-Mar), home of Venice's greatest playwright, Carlo Goldoni, who was born here in 1707. The house is worth a visit and Goldoni fans will find a host of material on the playwright's life and works.

Heading for Ponte di Rialto from the Chiesa di Santa Maria Gloriosa dei Frari, you soon arrive in the vast **Campo San Polo**, the city's largest square after St Mark's. Locals bring their children here to play so if you are travelling with small kids they might appreciate some social contact while you take a cappuccino break.

The area around **Ponte di Rialto**, bursting with the life of the daily produce market, was one of the earliest settled locations in Venice. Rialto, or *rivo alto*, means high bank and the spot was considered one of the safest in the lagoon. There has been a market here for almost 1000 years – the **Fabbriche Vecchie** along the Ruga degli Orefici and the **Fabbriche Nuove**, running along the Grand Canal, were built by Scarpagnino after a fire destroyed the old markets in 1514.

Although there has been a bridge at the Rialto since the foundation of the city, the present stone construction by Antonio da Ponte was completed in 1592.

Virtually in the middle of the market, off the Ruga degli Orefici, is the **Chiesa di San Giacomo di Rialto**. According to local legend it was founded on 25 March 421, the same day as the city. Nearby is the recently restored **Chiesa di San Giovanni Elemosinario** (Ruga di San Giovanni; admission €2; ☼ 10am-5pm Mon-Sat, 1-5pm Sun), a beautiful little Renaissance church built on the site of an earlier one by Antonio Abbondi after a disastrous fire in 1514 destroyed much of the Rialto area. You would hardly know the church was here, crammed as it is into the surrounding housing. The frescoes inside the dome are by Pordenone, as is one of two altar pieces. Another, a depiction of the saint after which the church is named, is by Titian.

From Campo San Polo you could, instead of making for the Rialto, head north and then west in the general direction of the Santa Lucia train station. Several fine sights make this a worthwhile option and you can always double back towards the Rialto afterwards.

Tintoretto fans will want to visit the **Chiesa di San Cassiano** (Campo San Cassiano; ☼ 9am-noon Tue-Sat), northwest of the Rialto. The sanctuary is decorated with three of Tintoretto's paintings, *Crucifixion, Resurrection* and *Descent into Limbo*.

The Renaissance **Ca' Pesaro**, further north with its facade facing the Grand Canal, has housed the **Galleria d'Arte Moderna** (☎ 041 524 06 95; Santa Croce 2076; adult/child €5.50/3; ☼ 10am-6pm Tue-Sun Apr-Oct, 10am-5pm Tue-Sun Nov-Mar) on the ground floor since 1902. The collection lays a heavy emphasis on Italian and particularly Venetian art from the late 19th and 20th centuries, up until the 1950s. But these are interspersed with some engaging international collections covering a broad range. Many of the works were purchased from the Venezia Biennale art festival over the years and artists include De Chirico, Miró, Chagall, Kandinsky, Klee, Klimt, Moore and others. The **Museo d'Arte Orientale**, in the same building on the top floor, features a collection of Asian and Eastern oddments.

Continuing northwest past the Chiesa di San Stae, you'll find the **Fondaco dei Turchi** (☎ 041 524 08 85; Santa Croce 1730), a 12th-century building used as a warehouse by Turkish merchants and now housing the **Museo Civico di Storia Naturale** (Natural History Museum). The museum has been closed for years but is due to reopen in 2004 – if it does, take the kids there to see the impressive 12m-long crocodile.

South from the Fondaco dei Turchi in a broad leafy *campo* stands the 13th-century **Chiesa di San Giacomo dell'Orio** (Campo San Giacomo dell'Orio; admission €2; ☼ 10am-5pm Mon-Sat, 1-5pm Sun), which is worth a visit. It is one of the few good examples of Romanesque architecture (albeit somewhat disguised by later Gothic additions) in Venice. In front of the main altar is a wooden crucifix by Veronese and on the wall at the rear of the central apse a rare work by Lorenzo Lotto, *Madonna col Bambino e Santi* (Madonna with Child and Saints).

Cannaregio

The long pedestrian thoroughfare connecting the train station and St Mark's Square crawls with tourists – few venture off it into the peaceful back lanes.

The Carmelite **Chiesa dei Scalzi** (Map pp332–4; ☼ 7-11.45am & 4-6.45pm Mon-Sat, 7.45am-12.30pm & 4-7pm Sun & holidays) is next to the train station. There are damaged frescoes by Tiepolo in the vaults of two of the side chapels.

Along the Rio Terrà Lista di Spagna, the otherwise uninspiring 18th-century **Chiesa**

CANNAREGIO

0 -------- 200 m
0 -------- 0.1 mi

INFORMATION
Libreria Demetra.....................**1** A4
Planet Internet........................**2** B4
Speedy Wash..........................**3** B4

SIGHTS & ACTIVITIES pp330–46
Chiesa della Madonna dell'Orto...**4** D2
Chiesa di San Geremia.............**5** B4
Chiesa di Sant'Alvise................**6** C2
Museo Ebraico........................**7** B3
Palazzo Vendramin-Calergi......(see 20)
Schola Canton.........................**8** B3

Schola Italiana.........................**9** B3
Schola Levantina....................**10** B3
Schola Spagnola.....................**11** B3
Schola Tedesca.....................(see 7)

SLEEPING pp347–50
Alloggi Calderan & Casa
Gerotto...............................**12** A4

EATING pp350–3
Billa Supermarket....................**13** D4

Cantina Vecia Carbonera..........**14** D4
Gam Gam............................**15** B3
Paradiso Perduto....................**16** D3
Sahara................................**17** D3

DRINKING p353
Casanova..............................**18** A4
Osteria agli Ormesini..............**19** C3

ENTERTAINMENT pp353–4
Casinò Municipale di Venezia....**20** C4

---

di San Geremia (Map p340) holds the body of Santa Lucia, who was martyred in Syracuse in AD 304. Her body was stolen by Venetian merchants from Constantinople in 1204 and moved to San Geremia after the Palladian church of Santa Lucia was demolished to make way for the train station.

Venice has the dubious honour of having furnished the world with a new and sinister word after the area called the Ghetto. Most easily accessible from the Fondamenta Pescaria, next to the Canale di Cannaregio, through the **Sotoportego del Ghetto** (Map p340), this is often touted as the world's first ghetto, which is not wholly true. While the name was new, the concept of keeping Jews in one quarter of town was not (as Spanish Jews well knew). This area in Venice was once a *getto* (foundry), a word whose pronunciation later changed and took on a whole new meaning.

The city's Jews were ordered to move to the small island, the *Getto Novo* (Ghetto Nuovo, or New Foundry), in 1516. They were locked in at night by Christian soldiers and forced to follow a set of rules limiting their social and economic activities. They did retain full freedom of religious expression. Extreme overcrowding combined with building height restrictions meant that some apartment blocks have as many as seven storeys but with low ceilings. In 1797, after the fall of the Venetian Republic

Jews were allowed to leave the Ghetto to live wherever they chose.

The **Museo Ebraico** (Map p340; ☎ 041 71 53 59; Campo di Ghetto Nuovo, Cannaregio 2902/b; adult/student €3/2, guided tours of Ghetto & synagogues adult/student €8/6.50; ☟ 10am-7pm Sun-Fri except Jewish holidays Jun-Sep, 10am-5.30pm Sun-Thu, 10am-sunset Fri Oct-May; tours hourly 10.30am-5.30pm Sun-Fri) contains a modest collection of Jewish religious silverware. The guided tours of the Ghetto and three of its *scholas* (synagogues) that leave from the museum are highly recommended. Also inquire at the museum about guided tours to the old Jewish cemetery on the Lido.

Cross the iron bridge from Campo di Ghetto Nuovo to reach the Fondamenta degli Ormesini and turn right. This is a truly peaceful part of Venice, almost empty of tourists. There are some interesting bars and a couple of good restaurants along the *fondamenta*. Not far away, the 14th-century **Chiesa della Madonna dell'Orto** (Map p340; admission €2; ☟ 10am-5pm Mon-Sat, 1-5pm Sun) was Tintoretto's parish church and contains many of his works. Among them are the *Giudizio Finale* (Last Judgement), *Adorazione del Vitello d'Oro* (Adoration of the Golden Calf) and the *Apparizione della Croce a San Pietro* (Vision of the Cross to St Peter). On the wall at the end of the right aisle is the *Presentazione di Maria al Tempio* (Presentation of the Virgin Mary in the Temple). Tintoretto is buried with other family members in the church.

Further east the Jesuit church known popularly as **I Gesuiti** (Map pp324–5; ☟ 10am-noon & 4-6pm), and more properly as Santa Maria Assunta, dates from the early 18th century. Its baroque interior features walls with inlaid marble in imitation of curtains. Titian's *Martirio di San Lorenzo* (Martyrdom of St Lawrence) is first on the left as you enter the church, balanced by Tintoretto's *Assunzione della Vergine* (Assumption of the Virgin) in the northern transept.

From here you could head south towards the Grand Canal for the 15th century **Ca' d'Oro** (Golden House; Map pp332–4; ☎ 041 523 87 90; adult/student €3/1.50; ☟ 8.15am-2pm Mon, 8.15am-7.15pm Tue-Sun), so named for the gilding that originally decorated the sculptural details of the facade. Visible from the Grand Canal, the facade stands out from the remainder of the edifice, which is rather drab by comparison. Ca d'Oro houses the **Galleria Franchetti**

(Map pp332–4), an impressive collection of bronzes, tapestries and paintings. On the 2nd floor you can see a series of fragments of frescoes saved from the outside of the Fondaco dei Tedeschi. All but one are by Titian. The other, a nude by Giorgione, is the most striking, however.

As you move east, make the effort to stop by the utterly charming little **Chiesa di Santa Maria dei Miracoli** (Map pp332–4; admission €2; ☟ 10am-5pm Mon-Sat, 1-5pm Sun), a Renaissance chocolate box designed by Pietro Lombardo and boasting magnificent sculptures. Pietro and his son Tullio Lombardo executed the carvings on the choir. From here it is a quick hop eastwards over a couple of bridges into the neighbouring *sestiere* of Castello.

Castello
In Campo SS Giovanni e Paolo you are confronted by the proud equestrian bronze statue of Bartolomeo Colleoni, one of Venice's more loyal mercenary mainland commanders. It is as though he stands guard in front of the huge Gothic **Chiesa dei SS Giovanni e Paolo** (Map pp332–4; ☟ 7.30am-12.30pm & 3.30-7.30pm), founded by the Dominicans and built to rival the Franciscans' Frari in size and grandeur. Work started on the church, also known by its Venetian name of San Zanipolo, in 1333, but it was not consecrated until 1430. Its vast interior is divided simply into a nave and two aisles, separated by graceful, soaring arches. The beautiful stained-glass window (the largest in Venice) in the southern transept was made in Murano to designs by various artists, including Bartolomeo Vivarini and Girolamo Mocetto, in the 15th century.

Around the walls, many of the tombs of 25 doges were sculpted by prominent Gothic and Renaissance artists. Look out for Giovanni Bellini's polyptych of *San Vincenzo Ferreri* (St Vincent Ferrer) over the second altar of the right aisle. In the Cappella del Rosario, off the northern arm of the transept, is a series of paintings by Paolo Veronese, including ceiling panels and an *Adorazione dei Pastori* (Adoration of the Shepherds) on the western wall.

At right angles to the main facade of the church is the rather more eye-catching (well, not while the scaffolding stays up!) marble frontage of the former **Scuola Grande di San Marco** (Map pp332–4). Pietro Lombardo and his sons all worked on what was once one of the most important of Venice's religious confraternities. Codussi put the finishing touches on this Renaissance gem.

Almost directly south is another of Venice's most enchanting squares, full of life and chatter. It is presided over by the church that gives its name, the **Chiesa di Santa Maria Formosa** (Map pp332–4; Campo Santa Maria Formosa; admission €2; ☺ 10am-5pm Mon-Sat, 1-5pm Sun). Rebuilt in 1492 by Mauro Cordussi on the site of a 7th-century church, it contains an altarpiece by Palma Giovane depicting Santa Barbara. Just across a walkway off the southern end of the campo is the 16th-century **Palazzo Querini-Stampalia** (Map pp332–4). The mansion was donated to the city in 1868 by Count Gerolamo Querini. On its 2nd floor, the **Museo della Fondazione Querini-Stampalia** (Map pp332–4; ☎ 041 271 14 11; Castello 4778; adult/student & senior €6/4; ☺ 10am-1pm & 3-6pm Tue-Sun Oct-Apr, 10am-1pm & 3-6pm Tue-Thu & Sun, 10am-1pm & 3-10pm Fri & Sat May-Sep) has a collection of paintings and Venetian furniture.

East of Campo SS Giovanni e Paolo stands what to all intents and purposes seems the twin towers to the Campanile in St Mark's Square. It is in fact the bell tower of the **Chiesa di San Francesco della Vigna** (Map pp324–5; ☺ 8am-12.30pm & 3-7pm). Designed and built by Jacopo Sansovino, this 16th-century Franciscan church is named for the vineyard that once thrived on the site. Its facade was designed by Palladio and inside, just to the left of the main door, is a triptych of saints by Antonio Vivarini.

Not at all otherworldly is the site of **Arsenale** (Map pp324–5), the greatest medieval shipyards in all Europe and source of wonder to all who visited. The dockyards were founded in 1104 and at their peak were home to 300 shipping companies and employed up to 16,000 people, capable of turning out a new galley every 100 days. Covering 32 hectares and completely enclosed by fortifications, the Arsenale was a symbol of Venice's maritime supremacy. Napoleon wrecked it in 1797 but it was later rebuilt and remained in use until WWI as a shipyard for the Italian navy. The Renaissance gateway surmounted by the Lion of St Mark commemorates the Christian victory over the Turkish fleet in the Battle of Lepanto in 1571. You can enter the vestibule and peer through to the interior of the Arsenale. It can be open as early as 7am and is generally shut by 5pm. You get the chance to see more when temporary exhibitions are held.

The **Museo Storico Navale** (Map pp324–5; ☎ 041 520 02 76; Riva San Biagio, Castello 2148; admission €1.55; ☺ 8.45am-1.30pm Mon-Fri, 8.45am-1pm Sat), towards the Canale di San Marco on the far side of Rio dell'Arsenale, covers the Republic's maritime history with a huge exhibition of paraphernalia, model boats, costumes and weapons. Among the exhibits is Peggy Guggenheim's gondola, one of the oldest remaining in the city. The ticket also gets you entrance to the **Padiglione delle Navi** (Ships Pavilion; Map pp324–5), on Fondamenta della Madonna near the entrance to the Arsenale. Of the various boats on display, the most outstanding is the *Scalé Reale*, an early-19th-century ceremonial vessel last used in 1959 to bring the body of the Venetian Pope Pius X to rest at St Mark's Basilica.

At the eastern edge of Venice, the residential back lanes of Castello are worth walking through to see how the locals live. Beyond, the **Giardini Pubblici** (Map pp324–5), heart of the city's Biennale art festival, and the islands of **San Pietro** (Map pp324–5) and **Sant'Elena** (Map pp324–5) are pools of peace far removed from the busy heart of Venice.

From the Museo Storico Navale you can meander west towards San Marco along the waterside **Riva degli Schiavoni** (Map pp324–5), long the main landing stage of La Serenissima and still abuzz today. The exclusive hotels that line it have long been favourites for Venice's more affluent visitors. About halfway along is the Chiesa di Santa Maria della Pietà, known as **La Pietà** (Map pp324–5), where concerts are regularly held. Vivaldi was concert master here in the early 18th century. Look for the ceiling fresco by Tiepolo. If you attend a concert you will be able to visit a collection of original instruments used by Vivaldi's orchestra.

An unusual facade makes the 15th-century **Chiesa di Zaccaria** (Map pp324–5; ☺ 10am-noon & 4-6pm Mon-Sat, 4-6pm Sun) unique. Most of the Gothic facade is by Antonio Gambello, while the upper part, in Renaissance style, is by Codussi. On the second altar of the northern aisle is Giovanni Bellini's *La Vergine in Trono col Bambino, un Angelo Suonatore e Santi* (The Virgin Enthroned with Jesus, an Angel Musician and Saints).

Venice was known for its religious tolerance. Among those to find refuge here were Slavs, mostly from across the Adriatic. **Scuola di San Giorgio degli Schiavoni** (Map pp324–5; ☎ 041 522 88 28; Calle dei Furlani, Castello 3259/a; admission €3; ⏰ 10am-12.30pm & 3-6pm Tue-Sat, 10am-12.30pm Sun) was established by the Slavic community in the 15th century. The walls of the ground-floor hall are decorated with superb paintings by Vittore Carpaccio, depicting events in the lives of the three patron saints of Dalmatia: George, Tryphone and Jerome. The image of St George dispatching the dragon to the next life is a particularly graphic scene.

Giudecca

Originally known as the *spina longa* (long spine) because of its shape, Giudecca's present name probably derives from the word Zudega (from *giudicato*; the judged), which was applied to families of rebellious nobles at one time banished from Venice and later allowed to return. Some suggest the name refers to the Jews who lived here prior to the creation of the Ghetto. Rich Venetians later came of their own accord to build villas on the island. Its main attraction is the **Chiesa del Redentore** (Map pp324–5; admission €2; ⏰ 10am-5pm Mon-Sat, 1-5pm Sun), built by Palladio in 1577 after the city was saved from a savage outbreak of plague. On the third Saturday in July the doge would pay a visit to the church, crossing the canal from the Zattere on a pontoon bridge (the name Zattere means 'rafts'). The Festa del Redentore (Feast of the Redeemer) remains one

A SINKING CITY

Venice can be flooded by high tides during winter. Known as *acque alte,* these mainly occur between November and April (especially in November and December), flooding low-lying areas of the city such as St Mark's Square. The serious floods are announced several hours before they reach their high point by the sounding of 16 sirens throughout the city and islands. The wailing of the sirens is becoming an increasingly common part of the Venetian winter.

In some areas you can see the water rising up over the canal border, although most of the water actually bubbles up through drains. The best thing to do is buy a pair of *stivali di gomma* (Wellington boots; gumboots) and continue sightseeing. *Passarelle* (raised walkways) are set up in St Mark's Square and other major tourist areas of the city (you can pick up a brochure with a map of the *passarelle* at the tourist office) and the floods usually last only a few hours. If the flood level exceeds 1.2m, then you can be in trouble as even the walkways are no use at that level.

Since 1900, Venice has sunk by 23cm, partly due to rising sea levels and partly due to subsidence. Climate change could cause a general global rise in sea levels of 40cm to 60cm by 2100, which would make the city uninhabitable if no preventative measures are taken.

Another major concern is that the waters of the canals are incredibly polluted. Until the years after WWII, the Adriatic Sea's natural tidal currents flushed the lagoon and kept the canals relatively clean. But the dredging of a 14m-deep canal in the 1960s, to allow tankers access to the giant refinery at Porto Marghera, changed the currents. Work is now underway to clean the sludge from the city canals. In the wake of the *Prestige* oil tanker disaster off Spain in 2002, the Veneto regional government called on Rome to ban oil tankers from the lagoon – a tough demand. Fears of an oil spill in the lagoon remain ever-present but at least single hull tankers of the *Prestige* type *have* been banned.

As though all this was not enough, the salt water has also been corroding the city's foundations. Alarm bells have been ringing and eminent persons have warned that if efforts are not made to counteract the corrosion, canal-side buildings could start to collapse.

A plan to install mobile flood barriers at the main entrances to the lagoon, after decades of debate over their pros and cons, finally seems to be going ahead. In May 2003 the Italian prime minister launched the construction of the first barrier amid controversy (many fear the costly exercise will fail). The central government in Rome had approved the first phase around the Malamocco lagoon entrance (the main shipping lane into the lagoon) the year before. It will include a semi-circular breakwater to reduce the effect of high seas pushed up the Adriatic by southerly winds and a lock for waiting ships while the barriers are up. In all, 79 mobile barrier gates will be installed. They will be activated when floods of one metre or more above mean sea level threaten the lagoon.

THE VENETO

of the most important on Venice's calendar of events.

San Giorgio Maggiore

On the island of the same name, Palladio's **Chiesa di San Giorgio Maggiore** (Map pp324–5; bell-tower lift €3, church admission free; ☺ 9.30am-12.30pm & 2-6pm) has one of the most prominent positions in Venice and, although it inspired mixed reactions among the architect's contemporaries, it had a significant influence on architecture at the time. Built between 1565 and 1580, the church has an austere interior, an interesting contrast to its bold facade. Its art treasures include works by Tintoretto: an *Ultima Cena* (Last Supper) and the *Raccolta della Manna* (Shower of Manna) on the walls of the high altar, and a *Deposizione* (Deposition) in the Cappella dei Morti (Chapel of the Dead). Take the lift to the top of the 60m-high bell tower for an extraordinary view.

San Michele

The city's cemetery was established on **Isola di San Michele** (Map pp324–5) under Napoleon and is maintained by the Franciscans. The **Chiesa di San Michele in Isola**, begun by Codussi in 1469, was among the city's first Renaissance buildings.

Murano

The people of Venice have been making crystal and glass (the difference between the two lies in the amount of lead employed) since as early as the 10th century, when the secrets of the art were brought back from the East by merchants. The industry was moved to the island of Murano in the 13th century.

Venice had a virtual monopoly on the production of what is now known as Murano glass and the methods of the craft were such a well-guarded secret that it was considered treason for a glass-worker to leave the city. The incredibly elaborate pieces produced by the artisans can range from the beautiful to the grotesque – but, as the Italians would say, *i gusti son gusti* (there's no accounting for taste). Watching the glass-workers in action is certainly interesting. You can see them in several outlets along Fondamenta dei Vetrai and a couple on Viale Garibaldi. Look for the sign 'Fornace' (furnace).

The **Museo Vetrario** (☎ 041 73 95 86; Fondamenta Giustinian 8; adult/child €4/2.50; ☺ 10am-5pm Thu-Tue Apr-Oct, 10am-4pm Thu-Tue Nov-Mar) contains some exquisite pieces.

The nearby **Chiesa dei SS Maria e Donato** (☺ 9am-noon & 3.30-7pm Mon-Sat, 3.30-7pm Sun) is a fascinating example of Veneto-Byzantine architecture. Founded in the 7th century and rebuilt 500 years later, the church was first dedicated to the Virgin Mary. It was rededicated to San Donato after his bones were brought there from Cephalonia, along with those of a dragon he had supposedly killed (four of the 'dragon' bones are hung behind the altar). The church's magnificent mosaic pavement was laid in the 12th century and the impressive mosaic of the Virgin Mary in the apse dates from the same period.

The island is most easily reached by the regular *vaporetto* No 42 (41 the other way) from Fondamente Nuove, Ferrovia and other stops. Or take the No 5 from San Zaccaria or the DM from Tronchetto.

Burano

Famous for its lace industry, Burano is a pretty fishing village, its streets and canals lined with bright, pastel-coloured houses. The **Museo del Merletto** (☎ 041 73 00 34; Piazza Galuppi 187; adult/child €4/2.50; ☺ 10am-5pm Wed-Mon Apr-Oct, 10am-4pm Wed-Mon Nov-Mar) is a museum of lace making. If you plan to buy lace on the island, choose with care as these days not all of it is locally made.

Take an LN ferry from Fondamente Nuove to get to Burano.

Torcello

This delightful island, with its overgrown main square and sparse, scruffy-looking buildings and monuments, was at its peak from the mid-7th to the 13th century, when it was the seat of the Bishop of Altinum and home to some 20,000 people. Rivalry with Venice and a succession of malaria epidemics systematically reduced the island's splendour and its population. Today, fewer than 80 people call the island home.

The island's Veneto-Byzantine cathedral, **Santa Maria Assunta** (admission €3, bell tower €2, admission incl Museo di Torcello €6; ☺ 10.30am-5.30pm Mar-Oct, 10am-5pm Nov-Feb), shouldn't be missed. Founded in the 7th century and rebuilt in the 11th century, it was Venice's very first cathedral. On the cathedral's western wall is a vast mosaic depicting the Last Judgement but its great treasure would have to be the mosaic of the Madonna in the semi-dome of the apse. Starkly set on a pure gold background, the figure is one of the most stunning works of Byzantine art you will ever see in Italy.

The adjacent tiny **Chiesa di Santa Fosca** (☾ 10am-4.30pm) was founded in the 11th century to house the body of Santa Fosca. Across the square, in the Palazzo del Consiglio, is the **Museo di Torcello** (☎ 041 73 07 61; admission €2; ☾ 10.30am-5pm Tue-Sun Mar-Oct, 10am-4.30pm Tue-Sun Nov-Feb), which tells the history of the island. Part of the collection is in the adjacent **Palazzo dell'Archivio**. Both buildings date from the 13th century and together formed the nerve centre of temporal power in Torcello.

To reach the island take an LN ferry from Fondamente Nuove.

The Lido

The main draw here is the beach but the water can be polluted and the public areas are often unkempt. Some of the beaches at the southern end of the island, such as those at Alberoni, are an exception. If you want to stay closer to the northern end of the island (and the *vaporetto* stops), you will pay a small fortune (anything from €5 to €9 for a sun-lounger to €57 for a basic changing room per day) to hire a chair and umbrella in the more easily accessible and clearer areas of the beach.

The Lido forms a land barrier between the lagoon and the Adriatic Sea. For centuries the doges trekked out here to fulfil Venice's Marriage to the Sea ceremony by dropping a ring into the shallows, celebrating Venice's close relationship with the sea.

It became a fashionable seaside resort around the late 19th century and its more glorious days are depicted in Thomas Mann's novel *Death in Venice*. The rows of modern apartments and hotels ensure the beaches are crowded but the Lido is not quite the fashionable place that it once was.

The snappy **Palazzo del Cinema** hosts Venice's international film festival each September (see pp346–7). Apart from that, there is little to attract you here, unless you are passing through on your way to Chioggia. The Lido can be reached by various *vaporetti*, including the Nos 1, 51, 52, 61, 62, 82, N and the vehicle ferry from Tronchetto.

Chioggia

Chioggia lies at the southern end of the lagoon and is the second most important city in it after Venice. Invaded and destroyed by the Venetian Republic's maritime rival, Genoa, in the late 14th century, the medieval core of modern Chioggia is a crumbly but not uninteresting counterpoint to its more illustrious patron to the north. In no way cute like Murano or Burano, Chioggia is a firmly practical town, its big fishing fleet everywhere in evidence. If your time is limited in Venice, you can live without Chioggia – the trip can take about two hours each way. City bus No 1, 2, 6 or 7 connects Chioggia with the Sottomarina, saving you the 15-minute walk.

From the Lido, bus No 11 leaves from Gran Viale Santa Maria Elisabetta, outside the tourist office; it boards the car ferry at Alberoni and then connects with a steamer at Pellestrina that will take you to Chioggia (the whole trip costs €5 one way). Or you can take the more prosaic overland bus from Piazzale Roma (€3.90 one way, €7 return). The **tourist office** (☎ 041 40 10 68; www.chioggiatourism.it; Lungomare Adriatico 101) is on the waterfront at the Sottomarina.

ACTIVITIES
Gondola Rides

A gondola ride is the quintessence of romantic Venice, although at €62 for 50 minutes (€77.50 after 8pm) the official price is a rather hefty return from the clouds to reality. The rates are for a maximum of six people – less romantic but more affordable. After the first 50 minutes you pay in 25-minute increments (€31, or €38.75 after 8pm). Several travellers have reported successfully negotiating below the official rates (definitely possible if business is slow), so get your haggling skills in order! And don't let them haggle you above the official rates. These haven't changed since 1997.

Gondolas are available near main canals all over the city, or can be booked in the following areas: San Marco (☎ 041 520 06 85), Rialto (☎ 041 522 49 04), Piazzale Roma (☎ 041 522 11 51) and the train station (☎ 041 71 85 43).

THE VENETO

COURSES

Società Dante Alighieri (Map p324–5; ☎ 041 528 91 27; venicedantealighieri@libero.it; Istituto Paolo Sarpi, Fondamenta Santa Giusta, Castello 2821) The society offers courses in Italian at all levels.

Istituto Venezia (Map pp332–4 ☎ 041 522 43 31; www.istitutovenezia.com; Campo Santa Margherita, Dorsoduro 3116/a) The Venice Institute offers **language** and one- and two-week **cooking courses**. It also does a course in **Venetian history and art**, involving 12 guided tours of the city. Four weeks (80 hours) of intensive language classes cost €540.

Fondazione Cini (Map p324–5; ☎ 041 528 99 00, ☎ 041 271 02 29; www.cini.it; Isola di San Giorgio Maggiore) The foundation organises seminars on subjects relating to the city and its **culture**, in particular music and art.

VENICE FOR CHILDREN

Venice isn't for art-lovers and hopeless romantics alone. The city is varied enough to keep even the most recalcitrant juniors interested at least some of the time. Some of the stuff grown-ups like, such as gondola and *vaporetto* rides, taking time out on a beach or a good gelato, will also appeal to kids.

Understandably most of the museums and galleries will leave the little 'uns cold but some may work. Boys should get a kick out of the boats and model ships at the Museo Storico Navale (p342). The sculpture garden at the Peggy Guggenheim Museum (p337) may prove an educational distraction while you indulge your modern art needs.

Climbing towers is usually a winner. Try the Campanile in St Mark's Square (p331) or the bell tower at San Giorgio Maggiore (p344).

Parco Savorgnan (part of Palazzo Savorgnan) and the Giardini Pubblici (Map pp324–5) have swings and the like.

Discounts are available for children (usually aged under 12) on public transport and for admission to museums, galleries and other sights.

TOURS

You can join free tours for a biblical explanation of the mosaics in St Mark's Basilica. They are arranged by the Patriarcato (the church body in Venice) and take place in Italian at 11am Monday to Saturday, except on Wednesday, when it is at 3pm. English-language tours are at

11am on Monday, Thursday and Friday, and French-language tours are at the same time on Thursday. This timetable seems to be subject to regular change. Call ☎ 041 270 24 21 for details.

Consult *Un Ospite di Venezia* for details of other visits to churches and sights in the city. The tourist office has an updated list of authorised guides, who will take you on a walking tour of the city.

Travel agencies all over central Venice can put you onto all kinds of city tours, ranging from two-hour guided walks (€27) to gondola rides with serenade for €31 per person.

FESTIVALS & EVENTS

The major event of the year is **Carnevale**, when Venetians don spectacular masks and costumes for a 10-day street party in the run up to Ash Wednesday.

The APT publishes a list of annual events, including the many religious festivals staged by almost every church in the city. One is held in July at the Chiesa del Redentore (see p343) and another at the Chiesa di Santa Maria della Salute each November (see p331).

The city next hosts the **Palio delle Quattro Repubbliche Marinare** (Regatta of the Four Ancient Maritime Republics) in June 2007. The former maritime republics of Genoa, Pisa, Venice and Amalfi take turns to host this colourful event. The **Regata Storica** (Historic Regatta) is a gondola race along the Grand Canal preceded by a spectacular parade of boats decorated in 15th-century style. It is held on the first Sunday in September.

The **Venice Biennale**, a major exhibition of international visual arts, started in 1895 and was held every even-numbered year from the early 20th century onwards. However, the 1992 festival was postponed until 1993 so there would be a festival on the Biennale's 100th anniversary in 1995. It is held from June to October in permanent pavilions in the Giardini Pubblici (Map pp324–5), as well as in other locations throughout the city. The next one is in 2005. Major art exhibitions are held at the Palazzo Grassi (see p331) and you will find smaller exhibitions in various venues around the city throughout the year.

The **Venice International Film Festival** (Mostra del Cinema di Venezia), Italy's version of Cannes, is organised by the Biennale and held annually in August/September at the Palazzo del Cinema on the Lido (see p345).

In November in a procession over a bridge of boats to the Chiesa di Santa Maria della Salute, the **Festa della Madonna** gives thanks for the city's deliverance from plague in 1630.

SLEEPING

Venice is an expensive place to stay, it's as simple as that. Even in the depths of low season you won't find more than about half a dozen places offering singles/doubles without bathroom for less than €45/70. A decent budget double with private bathroom can easily cost from €100 up in high season. Most places include breakfast (often unsatisfactory) whether you like it or not.

Prices seem to rise inexorably and many other elements can make prices flux. Some hotels have the same prices year-round while others drop them when things are slow (as though that happens a lot). Low season for the average Venetian hotelier means November, early December and January. For some there's a dip in July and early August. Some of the more expensive hotels operate further price differentials: weekend rates can be higher than during the week. Rooms with views (especially of the Grand Canal) are generally dearer than those without. Finally, proprietors' whims can produce all sorts of results.

Most of the top hotels are around San Marco and along the Grand Canal but it is possible to find bargains tucked away in tiny streets and on side canals in the heart of the city. There are lots of hotels, and an especial concentration of relative cheapies, near the train station but it is a good 30-minute walk to San Marco. Several better-located budget options are spread across the city.

It's advisable to book well in advance year-round in Venice but particularly in May, September, during Carnevale and other holidays (such as Easter, Christmas and New Year) and at weekends.

The **Associazione Veneziana Albergatori** (Map pp324–5; ☎ 041 71 52 88; www.veniceinfo.it; ☯ 8am-10pm Easter-Oct, 8am-9pm Nov-Easter) has offices at the train station, in Piazzale Roma and at the Tronchetto car park. Staff here will book you a room but you must leave a

small deposit and pay a minimal booking fee. It has 'last-minute' booking numbers: from within Italy, the number is toll free ☎ 800 84 30 06; from abroad dial ☎ 041 522 22 64.

Budget travellers have the option of the youth hostel on Giudecca and a handful of other dormitory-style arrangements, some of them religious institutions. They mostly open in summer only. Camp sites on the mainland south of Mestre and along the Litorale del Cavallino coast at the north end of the lagoon are another option. The tourist office has a full list of camp sites in addition to those listed here.

Marina di Venezia (☎ 041 530 26 11; www.marina divenezia.it; Via Montello 6, Punta Sabbioni; site per person/tent €7.55/22.13; ☯ late Apr–Sep) On the Litorale de Cavallino, this place has just about everything, from a private beach to a shop, cinema and playground. It also has bungalows. You can get the *vaporetto* from Punta Sabbioni to Fondamente Nuove (Cannaregio) via Burano and Murano.

Campeggio Fusina (☎ 041 547 00 55; www.camping-fusina.com; Via Moranzani 79, Località Fusina; site per person/tent & car €7/14) Reasonably well equipped. You can eat at the restaurant; the bar hums on summer nights. The most direct link with Venice is on the LineaFusina *vaporetto* straight into Venice (Zattere), which costs €5/9 one way/return. A local bus (No 11) runs between the camp site and the train station in Mestre. Some travellers have reported being disturbed at night by summertime discos in the area.

San Marco   Map pp332–4
BUDGET

Locanda Casa Petrarca (☎ /fax 041 520 04 30; Calle Schiavone, San Marco 4386; s/d up to €60/93; d with toilet & shower up to €120) A family-run place in an ancient apartment building and one of the nicest budget places in the San Marco area. The cheerful owner speaks English. To get here, find Campo San Luca, follow Calle dei Fuseri, take the second left and then turn right into Calle Schiavone.

MID-RANGE

Hotel ai do Mori (☎ 041 520 48 17; www.hotel aidomori.com; Calle Larga, San Marco 658; d with/without bathroom €135/90; ☯) A higgledy-piggledy hotel just off St Mark's Square, with pleasant rooms, some of which offer close-up

THE VENETO

views of the Basilica. The pick of the crop is without doubt the cosy little double at the top that comes with a terrace attached.

Locanda Fiorita (☎ 041 523 47 54; www.locanda fiorita.com; Campiello Nuovo, San Marco 3457/a; s €80-130, d €100-145; ☒) A gem set on a little square a spit away from the broad Campo Santo Stefano. The rooms, some of which look on to the square, are simple but well maintained and it is hard to complain about the prices. With its greenery, timber beams and friendly service, it feels like home.

Locanda Antico Fiore (☎ 041 522 79 41; www .anticofiore.com; Corte Lucatello, San Marco 3486; s/d up to €125/145; ☒ ☖) This charming, completely restored hotel is located in an 18th-century *palazzo*. The front door is on a narrow *rio* just in from the Grand Canal, so you could arrive in style by water taxi at this modestly priced place. Inside you will find cosy lodgings over a couple of floors. All rooms are tastefully decorated (tapestries, timber furniture), each with a different colour scheme.

Locanda Art Deco (☎ 041 277 05 58; www.locanda artdeco.com; Calle delle Botteghe, San Marco 2966; d up to €135; ☒ ☖) Art Deco has bright, whitewashed rooms with exposed timber beam ceilings. Iron bedsteads are attached to particularly comfy beds with orthopaedic mattresses – no chance of backache in Venice if you stay in this enticing little hideaway.

Serenissima (☎ 041 520 00 11; www.hotelseren issima.it; Calle Goldoni, San Marco 4486; s/d up to €102/170; ☒ ☖) Bright, white rooms with parquet floors and simple, elegant furnishings, satellite TV and en suite bathrooms, make this a good choice, tucked away between San Marco and the Ponte di Rialto.

TOP END

Gritti Palace (☎ 041 79 46 11; www.starwood.com/ grittipalace; Campo Traghetto, San Marco 2467; s/d up to €587/1155; ☒) One of the grand old dames of Venetian living. This luxury property, the facade of which fronts the Grand Canal, is one of the most famous hotels in Venice. If you can afford to pay top rates, you'll be mixing with royalty and celebs.

Hotel Danieli (☎ 041 522 64 80; www.starwood italy.com; Riva degli Schiavoni, Castello 4196; s/d up to €500/1050; ☒) The Danieli opened as a hotel in 1822 in the 14th-century Palazzo Dandolo. Just wandering into the grand foyer – all arches, sweeping staircases and balconies, is a trip down through centuries

of splendour. Dining in the Terrazza Danieli rooftop restaurant is a feast for the eyes and palate.

Dorsoduro

There's a good spread of mid-range accommodation available in this area.

Hotel Galleria (Map pp332–4; ☎ 041 520 41 72; www .hotelgalleria.it; Accademia, Dorsoduro 878/a; s/d up to €88/145) The only one-star hotel right on the Grand Canal near the Ponte dell'Accademia. Space is a little tight, but the decor is welcoming in this 17th-century mansion. If you can get one of the rooms on the canal, how can you possibly complain?

Pensione Accademia Villa Maravege (Map pp332–4; ☎ 041 521 01 88; www.pensioneaccademia.it; Fondamenta Bollani, Dorsoduro 1058; s €80-122, d €128-180; ☒) Set in lovely gardens right on the Grand Canal and just a few steps away from the Gallerie dell'Accademia, this fine 17th-century villa has grand sitting and dining rooms, capped by splendid timber ceilings. Rooms are simple but elegant, some with four-poster beds and timber floors.

Albergo agli Alboretti (Map pp332–4; ☎ 041 523 00 58; www.aglialboretti.com; Rio Terrà Antonio Foscarini, Dorsoduro 884; s/d €104/180; ☒ ☖) It almost feels like an inviting mountain chalet when you step inside. In its price category, it is one of Venice's star choices. The management is friendly and the rooms tastefully arranged and mostly of a good size.

Ca' Pisani Hotel (Map pp332–4; ☎ 041 240 14 11; www.capisanihotel.it; Rio Terrà Antonio Foscarini, Dorsoduro 979/a; r €204-330; ☒) Named after the hero of the siege of Chioggia in 1310, this centuries-old building houses a curious departure in the Venetian hotel scene – a self-conscious design hotel, filled with 1930s and 1940s furnishings, as well as items specially made for the hotel. The rooms, some with exposed beam ceilings, are elegant, well equipped and full of pleasing decorative touches.

La Calcina (Map pp324–5; ☎ 041 520 64 66; www .lacalcina.com; Fondamenta Zattere ai Gesuati, Dorsoduro 780; s/d up to €106/182; ☒) John Ruskin stooped in here while he wrote *The Stones of Venice* in 1876. This charming little hotel has a smidgin of garden attached and looks across to Giudecca. The immaculate rooms with parquet floors and timber furnishings are sober but charming. Some have small terraces attached and others views over the

Canale della Giudecca. One has both views and a lovely terrace. Less expensive rooms come without the view while a few cheaper ones still are without private bathroom.

Pensione Seguso (Map pp324–5; ☎ 041 528 68 58; fax 041 522 23 40; Fondamenta Zattere ai Gesuati 779; s/d with bathroom up to €145/168; ☺ Mar-Nov; ☒) A typically Venetian russet-red *pension* in a lovely quiet position facing the Canale della Giudecca. Rooms are all nicely furnished and many enjoy lagoon views. It also has some cheaper rooms without private bathroom.

Locanda San Barnaba (Map pp332–4; ☎ 041 241 12 33; www.italian-shop.com/LSB; Calle del Traghetto, Dorsoduro 2785-6; s/d up to €110/170; ☒) is a charming 13-room hotel, elegantly carved out of a fine mansion. Rooms are well equipped and some face onto the canal. A small terrace graces the top of the building, as well as a small canal-side garden for breakfast or evening drinks.

San Polo & Santa Croce   Map pp332–4
BUDGET
Hotel dalla Mora (☎ 041 71 07 03; hoteldallamora@ libero.it; Salizzada San Pantalon, Santa Croce 42/a; s/d with bathroom up to €61/88) Dalla Mora sits on a small canal just off Salizzada San Pantalon. The hotel has clean, airy rooms, some with lovely canal views, and there is a terrace. Some, but not all, rooms are equipped with own shower and sink. It's a popular choice.

MID-RANGE
Locanda Sturion (☎ 041 523 62 43; www.locanda sturion.com; Calle Sturion, San Polo 679; s/d up to €150/250; ☒) Two minutes from the Ponte di Rialto, this place has been a hotel on and off since the 13th century (when it was the Hospitium Sturionis). The best of its 11 rooms are the two generous suites overlooking the canal. All rooms come with mod cons and are a deep, wine-red colour harking to the 18th century.

Hotel San Cassiano (☎ 041 524 17 68; www .sancassiano.it; Calle della Rosa, Santa Croce 2232; s/d up to €228/335; ☒ 🖵) The 14th-century Ca' Favretto houses a mixed selection of rooms (and an incredibly mixed range of prices), the better ones are high-ceilinged doubles overlooking the Grand Canal. The building is a wonderful old pile (which the managers continue to slowly refurbish), with stone doorways along the staircases. If you're up early, you can grab one of a couple of tables

for breakfast on the balcony on the Grand Canal.

Pensione Guerrato (☎ 041 522 71 31; web.tiscali .it/pensioneguerrato; Ruga due Mori, San Polo 240/a; d with/without bathroom €120/95) It is worth seeking out this place, hidden away amid the Rialto markets. It's housed in a former convent, which before had served as a hostel for knights heading off on the Third Crusade. From some of the spacious, light rooms you have at least glimpses of the Grand Canal.

Cannaregio
BUDGET
Alloggi Calderan and **Casa Gerotto** (Map p340; ☎ 041 71 53 61; Campo San Geremia, Cannaregio 283; dm €25, s/d with bathroom up to €80/150) The pick of the crop on this square for a simple, budget deal. They have combined to offer a whole range of rooms with a commensurately bewildering battery of prices. The singles are bright and hard to come by as they are generally occupied by long-term residents. The dorms are single sex. Triples are also available and most rooms have pleasing views over the square. Prices can drop by about a third in slow periods.

MID-RANGE
Hotel Tre Archi (Map pp324–5; ☎ 041 524 43 56; www.hoteltrearchi.com; Fondamenta di Cannaregio, Cannaregio 923; s/d €210/240; ☒) An attractive hotel of 24 rooms set away from the tourist rush in a bit of the 'real Venice'. The place is furnished and decorated in classical Venetian style. Many rooms have views over the canal and others over the internal garden.

Hotel Giorgione (Map pp332–4; ☎ 041 522 58 10; www.hotelgiorgione.com; Calle Larga dei Proverbi, Cannaregio 4587; s/d up to €173/400; ☒) A welcoming hotel with comfortable, if in some cases rather small, rooms mostly in a 15th-century mansion. At the centre of the hotel is a peaceful courtyard. You can take breakfast outside and sip drinks on the 1st-floor terrace. Some of the best top-floor rooms have little terraces.

Locanda Leon Bianco (Map pp332–4; ☎ 041 523 35 72; www.leonbianco.it; Corte Leon Bianco, Cannaregio 5629; d with Grand Canal view €165) Three wonderful rooms (out of eight) look right onto the Grand Canal. The undulating *terrazzo alla Veneziana* floors and heavy timber doors with their original locks lend the rooms real charm. There are no singles but the price drops in small rooms without canal views.

Castello

HOSTEL

Foresteria Valdese (Map pp332–4; ☎ /fax 041 528 67 97; www.diaconiavaldese.org/venezia; Castello 5170; dm €21, d €56-74) A rambling old mansion near Campo Santa Maria Formosa. Head east from the square on Calle Lunga, cross the small bridge and the Foresteria is in front of you. Double rates depend on the room and whether or not it has a bathroom. Breakfast is included. Book well ahead.

MID-RANGE

La Residenza (Map pp324–5; ☎ 041 528 53 15; www.venicelaresidenza.com; Campo Bandiera e Moro, Castello 3608; s/d up to €95/155; 🐾) This grand 15th-century mansion presides over a square in the Castello area. The main hall upstairs makes quite an impression with its candelabras, elaborate decoration and distinguished furniture. The rooms are rather more restrained but fine value.

Locanda Remedio (Map pp332–4; ☎ 041 520 62 32; fax 041 521 04 85; Calle del Remedio, Castello 4412; s/d up to €180/220; 🐾) Indeed something of a remedy...especially after the streaming, screaming masses of visitors thronging around San Marco, just a few minutes away. It's hard to imagine them so close to the tranquil little courtyard in which this inn is hidden. Try for the front double with the 16th-century fresco.

Londra Palace (Map pp324–5; ☎ 041 520 05 33; www.hotelondra.it; Riva degli Schiavoni, Castello 4171; s/d up to €275/585; 🐾) In a prime position overlooking the Canale di San Marco, most rooms in this four-star property have views over the water. They feature 19th-century period furniture, Jacuzzis and marble bathrooms. The colour of the brocades and other decorative touches vary from one room to the next. Cheaper rooms have views over the city rather than the lagoon.

Giudecca & the Lido

HOSTELS

Ostello Venezia (Map pp324–5; ☎ 041 523 82 11; vehostel@tin.it; Fondamenta delle Zitelle 86; dm with breakfast €16.50; ⏰ 7am-midnight) The one HI hostel in Venice is located in a peaceful spot on Giudecca. It's open to members only, although you can buy a card there. Evening

meals are available for €8. The hostel is on HI's computerised International Booking Network (IBN). Catch *vaporetto* No 41, 42 or 82 from the train station or Piazzale Roma to Zitelle.

Istituto Canossiano (Map pp324–5; ☎ /fax 041 522 21 57; Fondamenta di Ponte Piccolo 428; dm €15; ⏰ Jun-Sep) A good deal near the Ostello Venezia, this place takes in only women. *Vaporetto* No 41, 42 or 82 takes you to Sant'Eufemia on Giudecca.

BUDGET

Pensione La Pergola (☎ 041 526 07 84; Via Cipro 15, Lido; s/d with bathroom €42/83; 🐾) A homey little *pensione*, just off Gran Viale Santa Maria Elisabetta, and a good budget deal if you want to base yourself near the beach and commute in to Venice when it suits you. Prices can be halved in the low season and they have some cheaper rooms without private bathroom.

TOP END

Hotel Cipriani (Map pp324–5; ☎ 041 520 77 44; www .hotelcipriani.it; Giudecca 10; s €335-825, d €570-1370, ste €900-7000; 🐾) Set in the one-time villa of the Mocenigo family, surrounded by lavish grounds and pools, with unbeatable views across San Marco. It occupies virtually the whole eastern chunk of Giudecca and one UK newspaper declared recently that it 'may fairly lay claim to be the world's best hotel'.

Excelsior (☎ 041 526 02 01; www.starwood.com/ westin; Lungomare Guglielmo Marconi 41, Lido; d €450-775; 🐾 Ⓟ) A fanciful Moorish-style property that's long been the top address on the Lido. The Oriental theme continues in its luxurious rooms, many of which look out to sea or across the lagoon to Venice. Lounge about the outdoor and heated pools if the beach seems too far away!

EATING

Venice is about the most expensive city in Italy for eating out, so you may find yourself resorting to *tramezzini* (sandwiches) that cost up to €3 for lunch-time snacks.

Search out the little trattorie and *osterie* tucked away along side lanes and canals or dotted about squares away from the main tourist centres. Many bars serve filling snacks with lunch-time and pre-dinner drinks. A Venetian *osteria* is a cross between a bar and a trattoria, where you can sample *cicheti* (bar snacks), generally washed down with an *ombra* (small glass of wine). Some *osterie* also serve full meals.

Better areas to look for places to eat include the back streets of Cannaregio and San Polo, as well as around Campo Santa Margherita in Dorsoduro. A few good spots lurk about in Castello and in San Marco.

Cafés

If you can cope with the idea of paying from €4.50 for a coffee, spend an hour or so sitting at an outdoor table at the centuries-old Florian or Quadri and enjoy the atmosphere of St Mark's Square (an Irish coffee costs €13 and there is a €4.50 surcharge for the music).

Caffè Florian (Map pp332–4; ☎ 041 520 56 41; Piazza San Marco 56/59) The more famous of the two. Lord Byron and Henry James used to take breakfast (separately) here.

Caffè Quadri (Map pp332–4; ☎ 041 522 21 05; Piazza San Marco 120; ☺ Wed-Sun) In much the same league as Florian, and equally steeped in history.

Quick Eats

Brek (Map pp332–4; ☎ 041 244 01 58; Rio Terrà Lista di Spagna, Cannaregio 124; 1-/2-course meals €4/6; ☺ 7.30am-10.30pm) A much better place to do cheap fastish food than the average burger joint. You can get a decent full meal at lunch and dinner time and snacks throughout the day.

Spizzico (Map pp332–4; Campo San Luca, San Marco 4475-4476; pizza slices €3.50; ☺ 9am-11pm) Not bad for quick slices of pizza – the chain is quite popular across northern Italy.

Restaurants & Osterie
SAN MARCO   Map pp332–4

Ai Rusteghi (☎ 041 523 22 05; Campiello del Tentor 5513; snacks €1.50-3; ☺ Mon-Sat) The perfect stop for a great range in sandwiches. It also offers good wines. There's nothing better than an *ombra* (small glass of wine) or two and a couple of *panini* as a quick lunch-time snack.

Vino Vino (☎ 041 241 76 88; Ponte delle Veste 2007/a, San Marco; meals €20-25; ☺ Wed-Mon) A popular bar/*osteria* near Teatro La Fenice. The menu changes daily and the pre-prepared food is of a reasonable quality. Its *sarde in saor* (fried, marinated pilchards) is good.

Osteria al Bacareto (☎ 041 528 93 36; San Marco 3447; meals €30-50; ☺ Mon-Fri) This eatery brings the search for a good traditional trattoria in this corner of San Marco to an end. Since it doubles as an *osteria*, you can opt for a plateful of *cicheti* (snacks) with a glass of wine at the bar or outside. If you decide on a full sit-down meal you'll need to loosen the purse strings somewhat.

Ristorante da Ivo (☎ 041 528 50 04; San Marco 1809; meals €80-100; ☺ Mon-Sat) Da Ivo presents a selection of Venetian and Tuscan meat dishes, all washed down with a fine range of wines. Some seafood options are also available. The atmosphere is quietly elegant and your choice of dish and wine can easily send your bill into the deluxe category.

DORSODURO   Map pp332–4
Osteria ai Carmini (☎ 041 523 11 15; Rio Terrà Scoazzera, Dorsoduro 2894; meals €30-35; ☺ 9.30am-11pm Mon-Sat) A cosy haunt for fresh fish and seafood and one of the best in its genre around Campo Santa Margherita.

L'Incontro (☎ 041 522 24 04; Rio Terrà Canal 3062; meals €25-30; ☺ 12.30-3pm & 7.30pm-1am Wed-Sun, 7.30pm-1am Tue) A long-standing favourite in the busy Campo Santa Margherita area and for once the food mostly isn't Venetian. You can get some wonderful Sardinian specialities here, like suckling pig.

SAN POLO & SANTA CROCE   Map pp332–4
All'Arco (☎ 041 520 56 66; Calle Arco 436; snacks €1.50-3 ☺ Mon-Sat) The place for you if you are looking for a locals' spot for downing a few *cicheti* and a glass or two of wine.

Cantina do Mori (☎ 041 522 54 01; Sotoportego dei do Mori 429; ☺ Mon-Sat) Hidden away near the Ponte di Rialto is a traditional institution. Unfortunately, the local consensus is that the prices have gone up unreasonably. Shame, because it is an enticing place, oozing history and still attracting a lot of local custom for such items as its *francobolli* ('stamps'), tiny little stuffed bread snacks.

Cantina do Spade (☎ 041 521 05 74; Calle do Spade 860; meals €30-35; ☺ closed dinner Thu) Venice's oldest eating house invites more to sit down for a full meal than hang about the bar for snacks.

Vecio Fritolin (☎ 041 522 28 81; Calle della Regina 226; meals €35-45; ☺ Tue-Sat & lunch Sun) There's a touch of class to dining here. Fresh ingredients are unfailingly used to create a

THE VENETO

combination of classic and inventive local and more broadly Italian cuisine.

Trattoria al Ponte (☎ 041 71 97 77; Ponte del Megio 1666; meals €25-30; ♉ Mon-Fri & lunch Sat) They tend to specialise in meat dishes here but some fishy options are available. The food is reliable and the prices reasonable. Arrive early here and try to grab one of the few canal-side tables.

Osteria La Zucca (☎ 041 524 15 70; Calle del Tintor 1762; meals €30-35; ♉ Mon-Sat) Just over the bridge from Trattoria al Ponte, La Zucca is an excellent alternative. It seems like just another Venetian trattoria but the menu (which changes daily) is an enticing mix of Mediterranean themes. The vegetable side orders alone are inspired (try the *peperonata alle melanzane*, a cool stew of capsicum and aubergine) while the mains are substantial.

Shri Ganesh (☎ 041 71 90 84; Rio Marin 2426; set menus €22.50; ♉ Thu-Tue) A rare exotic flavour in Venice. Fancy a quick curry? Forget it. But a good slow one can be had on the pleasant little canal-side terrace of this place. It serves up authentic dishes at reasonable prices – pleased guests have scribbled their appreciation on the walls.

Da Fiore (☎ 041 72 13 08; Calle del Scaleter 2202; meals €85-110; ♉ Tue-Sat) This recipient of a Michelin star lurks behind an unprepossessing shop-front that belies the Art Deco interior. Traditional dishes, such as *risotto ai scampi* (prawn risotto) and *bigoli in salsa* (thick spaghetti with sauce), are prepared with optimum care. It has a good wine selection. Book ahead.

CANNAREGIO

Cantina Vecia Carbonera (Map p340; ☎ 041 71 03 76; Ponte Sant'Antonio 2329; meals €20-25; ♉ Tue-Sun) Here you get the option of propping up the bar and treating yourself to an *ombra* and a few *cicheti* in this ageless *osteria*.

Gam Gam (Map p340; ☎ 041 71 52 84; Ghetto Nuovo 2884; meals €25-30; ♉ noon-10pm Sun-Thu & lunch Fri) Great for your taste buds if you like Israeli-style falafels and other Middle Eastern delicacies, with the occasional variation on Italian food.

Osteria dalla Vedova (Map pp332-4; ☎ 041 528 53 24; Calle del Pistor 3912; meals €25-30; ♉ Mon-Wed & Fri-Sat) One of the oldest *osterie* in Venice. The 'Widow's Hostelry' (also known as Trattoria Ca d'Or) offers excellent and modestly

priced food, mostly from the sea. You can also wander in for the *cicheti*, a cornucopia of snacks from battered vegetables to little *folpeti* (deep-fried octopuses).

Paradiso Perduto (Map p340; ☎ 041 72 05 81; Fondamenta della Misericordia 2539; meals €25; ♉ Thu-Mon) A young crowd is attracted to the roisterous dining area here. Take up your place on a bench or sit outside in summer. An air of anarchy reigns, drink flows freely and live music sometimes fills the air. The *lasagne ai carciofi* (artichoke lasagne) is great but check out the *cicheti*.

Sahara (Map p340; ☎ 041 72 10 77; Fondamenta della Misericordia 2520; meals €20) Good Middle Eastern food is served here and you can even clap along to a display of belly dancing on a Saturday night.

CASTELLO

Al Vecio Penasa (Map pp332-4; ☎ 041 523 72 02; Calle delle Rasse 4587; sandwiches €1.50; ♉ 6.30am-11.30pm) An excellent selection of sandwiches and snacks at reasonable prices.

Alla Rivetta (Map pp332-4; ☎ 041 528 73 02; Ponte San Provolo 4625; meals €20-25; ♉ Tue-Sun) One of the few restaurants near St Mark's Square that can be recommended. It has long been on the tourist list of 'must' places to eat but you can still get edible seafood for not unreasonable prices. Even a few local gondoliers eat here.

La Mascareta (Map pp332-4; ☎ 041 523 07 44; Calle Lunga Santa Maria Formosa 5138; ♉ Mon-Sat) The 'little mask', is a perfectly genial tavern for the sipping of wine accompanied by a limited but tempting range of *cicheti*.

Trattoria Corte Sconta (Map pp324-5; ☎ 041 522 70 24; Calle Pestrin 3886; meals €50-60; ♉ Tue-Sat) This place is hidden well away off even the unbeaten track. The chefs prepare almost exclusively seafood, fresh from the market and served up to you in a charming little garden (or indoors). Try the *risotto ai scampi*.

GIUDECCA

Ai Tre Scaini (Map pp324-5; ☎ 041 522 47 90; Calle Michelangelo 53/c; meals €25; ♉ noon-2.30pm & 6pm-1am Mon-Sat) *The* popular local eatery. It's a no-nonsense place for seafood and other goodies, and you can dine in the garden out the back.

Harry's Dolci (Map pp324-5; ☎ 041 522 48 44; Fondamenta San Biagio 773; meals €90-110; ♉ Wed-Mon Apr-Oct), Associated with Harry's Bar and serving fantastic desserts (which is the main reason for dropping in) and expensive meals.

TORCELLO
Locanda Cipriani (☎ 041 73 01 50; Piazza Santa Fosca 29, Torcello; meals €50-80; ⊗ lunch Wed-Mon & dinner Sat, closed Jan) An exclusive, leafy culinary hideaway since 1946. Ernest Hemingway ate (and drank) here.

CHIOGGIA
Osteria Penzo (☎ 041 40 09 92; Calle Larga Bersaglio 526; Chioggia; meals €30; ⊗ Wed-Mon) One of several good-value restaurants specialising mostly in seafood in Chioggia, serving up piping-hot local dishes based entirely on the fleet's catch.

Gelaterie & Pasticcerie
Ice cream prices range from about €1 for a small cup to €2.50 for a big cone. Prices don't vary much but the generosity of serves can. The following are among some of the best *gelaterie* in Venice:

Gelateria il Doge (Map pp332–4; Campo Santa Margherita, Dorsoduro 2604)

Gelateria Millefoglie da Tarcisio (Map pp332–4; Salizzada San Rocco, San Polo 3034)

Gelateria Nico (Map pp324–5; Fondamenta delle Zattere, Dorsoduro 922)

Self-Catering
The best markets take place on the San Polo side of the Ponte di Rialto. Grocery shops, where you can buy salami, cheese and bread, are concentrated around Campo Beccarie, which happens to lie next to the city's main fish market.

Billa Supermarket (Map p340; Strada Nova, Cannaregio 3660; ⊗ 9am-7.30pm) is a reasonably well-stocked supermarket option for self-caterers.

DRINKING
Bars & Pubs
Caffè (Map pp332–4; ☎ 041 528 79 98; Campo Santa Margherita, Dorsoduro 2693; ⊗ Mon-Sat) A lively, hip student bar with snacks. It is known to locals as the *caffè rosso* because of the red sign. This square is one of the most happening in town with several good bars to choose from.

Café Noir (Map pp332–4; ☎ 041 71 09 25; Calle San Pantalon, Santa Croce 3805; ⊗ 7am-2am Mon-Sat) A

cool place to start the day with breakfast, or hang out into the night with a mixed crowd of Italian students and foreigners. The place has a laid-back, underground feel about it and gets pretty busy.

The Fiddler's Elbow (Map pp332–4; ☎ 041 523 99 30; Corte dei Pali, Cannaregio 3847; ⊗ 5pm-1am Thu-Tue) This representative of the Irish bar genre in Venice sets up a few tables outside on the square. Several others are dotted about town.

Osteria agli Ormesini (Map p340; ☎ 041 71 38 34; Fondamenta degli Ormesini, Cannaregio 2710; ⊗ to 2am Mon-Sat) Oodles of wine and 120 types of bottled beer in one knockabout little place. It's something of a student haunt and tipplers spill out on to the *fondamenta* to enjoy their ambers.

Harry's Bar (Map pp332–4; ☎ 041 528 57 77; Calle Vallaresso, San Marco 1323; cocktails €9.50-12; ⊗ noon-11pm) As well as being one of the city's more notable restaurants, Harry's is first and foremost known as a bar. Everyone who is anyone and passing through Venice usually ends up here sooner or later. The Aga Khan has lounged around here and characters as diverse as Orson Welles, Ernest Hemingway and Truman Capote have all sipped on a cocktail or two at Harry's.

Cavatappi (Map pp332–4; 041 296 02 52; Campo della Guerra, San Marco 3805; ⊗ 9am-midnight in summer, 9am-midnight Mon-Sat rest of year) A modern creamy white bar with halogen lighting and wines from all over Italy. In a rather daring departure for what is in many ways a small town, this place will appeal to all who miss a slightly metropolitan touch. Try cheeses from all over Italy, with a few French and Swiss additions, and if you want to eat inspect the untraditional menu.

ENTERTAINMENT
The Venice Carnevale (see Festivals & Events, p346) is one of Italy's best-known festivals but exhibitions, theatre and musical events continue throughout the year in Venice. Information is available in *Un Ospite di Venezia* and the tourist office also has brochures listing events and performances year-round. The monthly *Venezia News* magazine has extensive listings too.

Casinos
Casinò Municipale di Venezia (Map p340; ☎ 041 529 71 11; www.casinovenezia.it; Palazzo Vendramin-Calergi,

Cannaregio 2040; admission €5; ⏱ 3pm-3am) The elegant gambler's preferred haunt in the heart of Venice.

Venice Casino (☎ 041 529 71 11; www.casino venezia.it; Ca' Noghera, Via Triestina 222, Tessera; admission €5; ⏱ 11-4.45am Sun-Fri, 11-6am Sat) is Italy's premier mainland gambling house. It opened in 2001, near the airport. A free shuttle bus operates from Piazzale Roma.

Cinemas

Summer Arena (Campo San Polo) A cinema-under-the-stars during July and August. It often features British and American films but they are generally dubbed. About the only chance to catch cinema in the original language is during the September film festival (see pp346–7).

Nightclubs

Casanova (Map p340; ☎ 041 275 01 99; Lista di Spagna, Cannaregio 158/a; ⏱ 6pm-4am Tue & Thu-Sat) A quick stumble from the train station, this is about the only place in Venice that can vaguely call itself a club, complete with mirror balls. The music is mainstream and on occasion it can hop.

Round Midnight (Map pp332–4; ☎ 041 523 20 56; Fondamenta dello Squero, Dorsoduro 3102; ⏱ 7pm-4am Mon-Sat Sep-May) The dancing cove to head for after you've finished hanging about on Campo Santa Margherita. You can sip all sorts of cocktails and even get a snack. The music tends to be acid jazz and Latin.

Many young locals go to one of a handful of clubs on the mainland in and around Mestre. In summer, Jesolo and its beach (to the north of the lagoon) is where most of the action takes place.

Theatre, Opera & Classical Music

There are a number of options for more classical entertainment in Venice. Tickets for these places are available at the theatres or at ticketing agencies like **Vela** (☎ 041 24 24; www.velaspa.com).

Teatro La Fenice (Map pp332–4; ☎ 041 78 65 11; www.teatrolafenice.it; Campo San Fantin 1970, San Marco) It is hoped that this particular Phoenix, Venice's premier opera house since the late 18th century and a disaster area since its destruction by fire in 1996, will finally rise by the end of 2003. What the fate of its replacement since 1996, the big-top arrangement known as the **PalaFenice** (Map pp332–4; Isola del Tronchetto)

will be when the Fenice comes back to life is anyone's guess. Until then it continues to host the bulk of the city's grand opera performances. Tickets are available direct at the PalaFenice or at Vela outlets (such as those at Piazzale Roma and Ferrovia, just in front of the train station).

Teatro Malibran (Map pp332–4; ☎ 041 78 65 11; www.teatrolafenice.it; Calle del Teatro, San Marco 5870) Since its restoration, Teatro Malibran has shared some of the load with the PalaFenice. Prices range from €10 to €20 for poor spots at lower grade performances to €95 for a prime position for a grand night at the opera.

Teatro Goldoni (Map pp332–4; ☎ 041 240 20 11; www.teatrogoldonive.it; Calle Teatro Goldoni, San Marco 4650/b; tickets €15-42) Named after the city's greatest playwright, this is the main drama theatre in Venice. It's not unusual for Goldoni's plays to be performed here – after all, what more appropriate location?

SHOPPING

You can expect most shops hoping to sell to tourists to open all weekend during the high season (Easter to September).

The main shopping area for clothing, shoes, accessories and jewellery is in the narrow streets between San Marco and the Rialto, particularly the Mercerie and around Campo San Luca. The more up-market shopping area is west of St Mark's Square.

Classic gift options include Carnevale masks, *carta marmorizzata* (marbled paper), Murano glass and Burano lace.

Galleria Marina Barovier (Map pp332–4; ☎ 041 522 61 02; Calle delle Carrozze, San Marco 3216) It's damn expensive, but wander in to see the latest creations in glass by some of the most outstanding artists in Venice.

Ca' Macana (Map pp332–4; ☎ 041 520 32 29; Calle delle Botteghe, Dorsoduro 5176) One of the best stores and workshops in Venice producing Carnevale masks.

L'Arlecchino (Map pp332–4; ☎ 041 71 65 91; Calle dei Cristi, San Polo 1722-9) Staff say their masks are made only with papier-mâché (as they should be) to their own designs. The quality is indeed high.

Jesurum (Map pp332–4; ☎ 041 520 60 85; Merceria del Capitello, San Marco 4856) They've been in the lace business here since 1860, when Michelangelo Jesurum opened a lace school on the Isola di Burano to help resuscitate the island's centuries-old tradition.

Aliani (Map pp332–4; ☎ 041 522 49 13; Ruga Vecchia di San Giovanni, San Polo 654) An outstanding collection of cheeses and other delicatessen products have long made Aliani a favoured gastronomic stop in the Rialto area. You will also find a range of wines.

Legatoria Polliero (Map pp332–4; ☎ 041 528 51 30; Campo dei Frari, San Polo 2995) A traditional exponent of the art of Venetian bookbinding with (and without) marbled paper. You barely have room to stand when you penetrate this den, with piles of leather-bound books, paper-bound folders, and all sorts of other stationery piled higgledy-piggledy high to the rafters.

GETTING THERE & AWAY
Air
Venice's recently modernised **Marco Polo airport** (VCE; flight information ☎ 041 260 92 60; www.veniceairport.it) is 12km outside Venice and just east of Mestre (it also sometimes goes by the name of the nearby settlement of Tessera). Some flights, notably Ryanair's budget services from London and Brussels, use Treviso's minuscule **San Giuseppe airport** (TSF; ☎ 042 231 53 31), about 5km southwest of Treviso and 30km (about an hour's drive through traffic) from Venice. Airport bus services link both airports with Venice and Mestre, and the Alilaguna fast ferry runs from Marco Polo airport. For more details, see Getting Around following.

Boat
Apart from Mediterranean cruise ships that call in, a couple of companies run regular ferries to Venice from Greece. Contact **Minoan Lines** (www.minoan.gr) and **Blue Star Ferries** (www.bluestarferries.com).

Bus
ACTV (Map pp324–5; ☎ 041 528 78 86) local buses leave from Piazzale Roma for surrounding areas, including Mestre and Chioggia.

ATVO (Azienda Trasporti Veneto Orientale; ☎ 041 520 55 30) operates buses to destinations all over the eastern part of the Veneto. A handful of other companies have the occasional service to more distant locations but to get to most places in Italy the train is an easier option. Tickets and information are available at the ticket office on Piazzale Roma.

Car & Motorcycle
The A4 connects Trieste with Turin, passing through Mestre (and hence Venice). Take the Venice exit and follow the signs for the city. From the south, take the A13 from Bologna, which connects with the A4 at Padua.

Once you cross the bridge from Mestre, the **Ponte della Libertà** (Map p324–5), cars must be left at one of the huge car parks on Piazzale Roma or on the island of Tronchetto. Parking is not cheap and you will pay €18 or more for every 24 hours. Parking stations in Mestre are much cheaper.

In Piazzale Roma, **Avis** (Map pp324–5; ☎ 041 523 73 77, Italy-wide ☎ 199 10 01 33) has an office, as do **Europcar** (Map pp324–5; ☎ 041 523 86 16, toll free ☎ 800 82 80 50), **Hertz** (Map pp324–5; ☎ 041 528 35 24, Italy-wide ☎ 199 11 22 11) and **Expressway** (Map pp324–5; ☎ 041 522 58 25). They all have reps at Marco Polo airport too.

Train
The train station, **Stazione di Santa Lucia** (Map pp324–5), is directly linked by train to Padua (up to €4.44, 20 to 40 minutes), Verona (up to €12.65, one to 1½ hours), Milan, Trieste and Bologna, and is easily accessible from the cities of Florence and Rome. You can also reach Venice from major points in France, Germany, Austria, Switzerland, Slovenia and Croatia.

GETTING AROUND
To/From the Airport
The Alilaguna airport fast ferry costs €10 to/from Venice or the Lido and €5 to/from Murano. You can pick it up at the Zattere or near St Mark's Square, in front of the Giardini Ex Reali. The official rate (which hasn't changed in several years) for the water-taxi ride between Piazzetta di San Marco and the airport is €44.95. To/from the Lido costs €55.30.

ATVO (☎ 041 520 55 30) buses run to the airport from Piazzale Roma (€3, 20 minutes) via Mestre train station. Regular ACTV city bus No 5 also serves the airport from Piazzale Roma (€1.50, 30 minutes), however, it makes more stops.

Traghetto
The poor man's gondola, *traghetti* are used by locals to cross the Grand Canal where there is no nearby bridge. There is no

particular limit (except common sense) on the number of passengers who stand.

Traghetti operate from about 9am to 6pm between Campo del Traghetto (near Santa Maria del Giglio) and Calle de Lanza; Campo San Samuele, north of the Ponte dell'Accademia, and Calle Traghetto; Calle Mocenigo, further north, and Calle Traghetto; and Campo Santa Sofia and Campo della Pescaria.

Several other routes operate only from 9am to noon. They include the train station to Fondamenta San Simeon Piccolo; Campo San Marcuola to Salizzada del Fondaco dei Turchi; Fondamenta del Vin and Riva del Carbon; and Calle Vallaresso to Punta della Dogana. Some of these may on occasion not operate at all. The ride costs €0.40.

Vaporetto

The city's main mode of public transport are *vaporetti*. A car ferry (No 17) transports vehicles from Tronchetto, near Piazzale Roma, to the Lido. From Piazzale Roma, *vaporetto* No 1 zigzags up the Grand Canal to San Marco and then the Lido. It is a great introduction to Venice but there are faster lines if you are in a hurry.

Tickets can be purchased from the ticket booths at most landing stations and Vela outlets. Generally they are validated when sold to you, which means they are for immediate use. If they are not validated, or if you request them not to be (so you can use them later), you are supposed to validate them in the machines at each landing station before you get on the boat. You can also buy tickets when boarding (at a slightly higher price). You may be charged double if you have lots of luggage.

Catching these things can be confusing. Sometimes boats going both ways call at the same stop; occasionally boats are limited stops (for instance ferries heading down the Grand Canal from Piazzale Roma and Ferrovia only go as far as Rialto. At the bigger stops (like Ferrovia) different landings are set aside for the different routes *and* directions.

Single *vaporetto* tickets cost €3.50 (plus €3.50 for luggage!), even if you only ride to the next station. A 24-hour ticket is good value at €10.50 for unlimited travel. Better still are the three-day (€22) tickets. Rolling Venice passholders (see boxed text, p329)

can get the three-day ticket for €15. For information on the Venice Card, see following. Routes and route numbers can change, so the following list is a guide only.

DM (Diretto-Murano) Trochetto–Piazzale Roma–Ferrovia–Murano and back

LN (Laguna Nord) San Zaccaria–Lido–Litorale del Cavallino (Punta Sabbioni) and back OR Fondamenta Nuove–Murano–Burano–Torcello–Punta Sabbioni and back

T Torcello–Burano (hourly service) and back

1 Piazzale Roma–Ferrovia–Canal Grande–Lido and back

3 Fast Circular line: Tronchetto–Ferrovia–San Samuele–Accademia–San Marco–Tronchetto (summer only)

4 Fast Circular line in reverse direction to No 3 (summer only)

5 San Zaccaria–Murano and back

11 Lido-Pellestrina and back

13 Fondamenta Nuove–Murano–Vignole–Treporti and back

17 Car ferry: Tronchetto–Lido and back (extends to Punta Sabbioni in summer)

18 Murano–Vignole–Sant'Erasmo–Lido and back (summer only)

20 San Zaccaria–San Servolo–San Lazzaro and back

31 Pellestrina–Chioggia and back

41 Circular line: Piazzale Roma–Sacca Fisola–Giudecca–San Zaccaria–San Pietro–Fondamente Nuove–Murano–Ferrovia

42 Circular line in reverse direction to No 41

51 Circular line: Piazzale Roma–Zattere–San Zaccaria–Lido–San Pietro–Fondamente Nuove–Ferrovia

52 Circular line in reverse direction to No 51

61 Limited-stops circular line: Ferrovia– Piazzale Roma–Zattere–Arsenale–Sant'Elena–Lido

62 Limited-stops circular line in reverse direction to No 61

82 San Zaccaria–San Marco–Grand Canal–Ferrovia–Piazzale Roma–Tronchetto–Zattere–Giudecca–San Giorgio–Lido (summer only). A Limitato San Marco or Limitato Piazzale Roma sign means it will not go beyond those stops.

N All-stops night circuit: Lido–Giardini–San Zaccaria–Grand Canal–Ferrovia–Piazzale Roma–Tronchetto–Giudecca–San Giorgio–San Zaccaria (starts around 11.30pm; last service around 5am)

NMU (Notturno Murano) A night service between Fondamente Nuove – three or four runs from midnight

NLN (Notturno Laguna Nord) A night version of the Laguna Nord service – a handful of services between Fondamente Nuove and Burano, Mazzorbo, Torcello, Sant'Erasmo and Treporti.

Venice Card

Since late 2001 a new all-inclusive transport and sights card, **Venice Card** (☎ 041 24 24;

www.venicecard.it) has been in operation. It does *not* represent a financial saving over alternatives (indeed, can work out more costly), but with added potential discounts at certain restaurants, hotels and the like could prove handy. Having the card also removes some of the hassle of procuring individual museum tickets and *vaporetto* passes.

There are two types of Venice Card. The blue card gives you unlimited use of ferries and buses throughout the Venice municipality for one, three or seven days. It also gives you free access to the public pay toilets (otherwise €0.50 a go) scattered around town.

The orange version throws in the **Musei Civici** (City Museums) for free (see p329). The blue cards for people under 29 cost €9/22/49 for one/three/seven days, while the over 29 versions cost €14/29/51. The junior orange cards costs €18/35/61 and the senior versions €28/47/68.

Water Taxis

Water taxis are prohibitively expensive, with a set €13.95 charge for a maximum of seven minutes, an extra €4.15 if you order one by telephone, and various surcharges that make a gondola ride seem cheap.

AROUND THE VENETO

THE BRENTA RIVIERA

Dotted along River Brenta, which passes through Padua and spills into the Venetian lagoon, are more than 100 villas built over the centuries by wealthy Venetian families as summer homes; most are closed to the public. The most outstanding are the **Villa Foscari** (1571), built by Palladio at Malcontenta, and the **Villa Pisani**, also known as the Villa Nazionale, at Strà, which was built for Doge Alvise Pisani. It was used by Napoleon and was the site of the first meeting between Hitler and Mussolini. ACTV buses running between Padua and Venice stop at or near the villas. Those that open do so with widely varying timetables from May to the end of September. Ask at the tourist offices in Venice for the latest details on opening times and admission costs. See Around Vicenza later for information on other Venetian villas. You can do tours along the River Brenta.

The luxurious **Burchiello** (☎ 049 877 47 12; www.ilburchiello.it; adult/child one way €62/36; ☼ Mar-Oct) barge plied the River Brenta from Venice to Padua in the 17th and 18th centuries. Today's rather more modern version cruises up and down the river between Venice and Strà (price includes tours of Villa Foscari and Villa Barchessa Valmarana). Departures from Venice (Riva degli Schiavoni) are on Tuesday, Thursday and Saturday; those from Strà are Wednesday, Friday and Sunday. Shuttle buses connect Strà and Padua's main bus station. Other companies also operate tours along the Brenta, including **I Batelli del Brenta** (☎ 049 876 02 33; www.antoniana.it), offering similar tours at similar prices. Ask at the Venice or Padua tourist offices for more details.

PADUA (PADOVA)

pop 209,641

The city of St Anthony, home of Italy's second-oldest university, Padua is also the site of one of the most remarkable works of late Gothic art (prefiguring the Renaissance) in Northern Italy. At just 37km west of Venice, this dynamic student town, with its arcaded streets and fetching medieval centre, deserves at least a day trip from the lagoon city.

The Veneti tribes of the northeast established a town here even before the Romans arrived, but Patavium was then all but wiped off the map by Lombard invaders in AD 602. The city grew again as a powerful and wealthy city state in the 13th and 14th centuries under the Carrara clan, who set up the *studium* (university) but were also involved in incessant skirmishes with neighbours. Venice brought an end to this when it occupied Padua and its territories in 1405.

Information
BOOKSHOP
Feltrinelli International (Via San Francesco 14) For books in various languages.

EMERGENCY
Police Station (☎ 049 83 31 11; Riviera Ruzante 11)

INTERNET ACCESS
Internet Point In Collegio (☎ 049 65 84 84; Via Petrarca 9; membership fee €1.60, 1st hr €6, then €3/hr; ☼ 9am-2am)

THE VENETO

PADUA (PADOVA)

0 [_____] 400 m
0 [_____] 0.2 mi

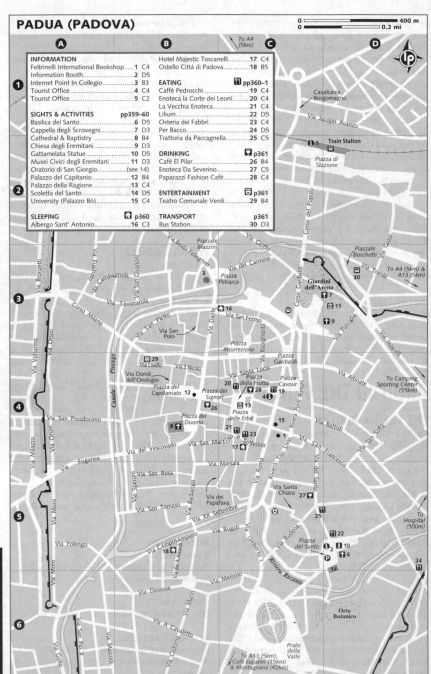

INFORMATION
Feltrinelli International Bookshop.....**1** C4
Information Booth..............................**2** D5
Internet Point In Collegio.................**3** B3
Tourist Office....................................**4** C4
Tourist Office....................................**5** C2

SIGHTS & ACTIVITIES pp359–60
Basilica del Santo.............................**6** D5
Cappella degli Scrovegni..................**7** D3
Cathedral & Baptistry.......................**8** B4
Chiesa degli Eremitani......................**9** D3
Gattamelata Statue...........................**10** D5
Musei Civici degli Eremitani...........**11** D3
Oratorio di San Giorgio...............(see 14)
Palazzo del Capitanio.......................**12** B4
Palazzo della Ragione.......................**13** C4
Scoletta del Santo.............................**14** D5
University (Palazzo Bò)......................**15** C4

SLEEPING p360
Albergo Sant' Antonio.....................**16** C3

Hotel Majestic Toscanelli...............**17** C4
Ostello Città di Padova...................**18** B5

EATING pp360–1
Caffè Pedrocchi................................**19** C4
Enoteca la Corte dei Leoni.............**20** C4
La Vecchia Enoteca..........................**21** C4
Lilium...**22** D5
Osteria dei Fabbri............................**23** C4
Per Bacco...**24** D5
Trattoria da Paccagnella..................**25** C5

DRINKING p361
Café El Pilar.....................................**26** B4
Enoteca Da Severino........................**27** C5
Paparazzi Fashion Café....................**28** C4

ENTERTAINMENT p361
Teatro Comunale Verdi....................**29** B4

TRANSPORT p361
Bus Station.......................................**30** D3

MEDICAL SERVICES
Complesso Clinico Ospedaliero (☎ 049 821 11 11; Via Giustiniani 1) Hospital.

POST
Post Office (Corso Garibaldi 33; ☉ 8.15am-7pm Mon-Sat, 8.30am-6.30pm Sun)

TOURIST INFORMATION
Information Booth (☎ 049 875 30 87; Piazza del Santo; ☉ high season variable times)
Tourist Office (www.apt.padova.it); train station (☎ 049 875 20 77; ☉ 9am-7pm Mon-Sat, 8.30am-12.30pm Sun Apr-Oct, 9.20am-5.45pm Mon-Sat, 9am-noon Sun Nov-Mar);
Vicolo Pedrocchi (☎ 049 876 79 27; ☉ 9am-12.30pm & 3-7pm Mon-Sat)

Sights
The **Padova Card** (€13; valid 48hrs) is a pass that allows you to visit the Cappella degli Scrovegni, Musei Civici agli Eremitani, Palazzo della Ragione, the first floor of Caffè Pedrocchi, a couple of minor chapels and Petrarch's House in Arquà Petrarca. It's available from tourist offices and the monuments concerned.

CAPPELLA DEGLI SCROVEGNI
Art lovers visit Padua just to see the lively Giotto frescoes in this **chapel** (phone or online booking 24hrs in advance ☎ 049 201 00 20; www.cappelladeglisc rovegni.it; Giardini dell'Arena; adult/child incl Musei Civici agli Eremitani €10/3, Musei Civici agli Eremitani closed Mon €6.50/3, booking fee €1; ☉ 9am-7pm; maximum 15min inside chapel) in the Giardini dell'Arena, just a five-minute walk from the train station. Enrico Scrovegni commissioned its construction in 1303 as a resting place for his father, who was denied a Christian burial because of his money-lending practices. Giotto's remarkable fresco cycle, probably completed between 1304 and 1306, illustrates the lives of Mary and Christ and is arranged in three bands. Among the most famous scenes in the cycle is the *Bacio di Giuda* (Kiss of Judas). The series ends with the *Ultima Cena* (Last Supper) on the entrance wall and the Vices and Virtues are depicted around the lower parts of the walls. Keep in mind the era when the frescoes were painted – Giotto was moving well away from the two-dimensional figures of his medieval contemporaries. He effectively was on the cusp between Gothic art and the remarkable explosion of new creativity that was still decades away – the

Renaissance. Booking ahead is obligatory. The admission ticket is also valid for the adjacent **Musei Civici agli Eremitani**, whose collection of 14th- to 18th-century Veneto art and largely forgettable archaeological artefacts includes a crucifix by Giotto.

CHIESA DEGLI EREMITANI
Completed in the early 14th century, this Augustinian **church** (Giardini dell'Arena; ☉ 8am-12.30pm & 4-6pm Mon-Sat, 9.30am-noon & 4-6pm Sun) was painstakingly rebuilt after bombing in WWII. The remains of frescoes created by Andrea Mantegna during his 20s are displayed in a chapel to the left of the apse. Most were wiped out in the bombing, the greatest single loss to Italian art during the war. The *Martirio di San Jacopo* (Martyrdom of St James), on the left, was pieced together from fragments found in the rubble of the church while the *Martirio di San Cristoforo* (Martyrdom of St Christopher), opposite, was saved because it had been removed before the war.

HISTORIC CENTRE
Via VIII Febbraio leads to the city's **university** (☎ 049 876 79 27; Via VIII Febbraio; ☉ 3 guided visits per day Mon-Sat), the main part of which is housed in the Palazzo Bò ('ox' in Veneto dialect – it's named after an inn that previously occupied the site). Established in 1222, the university is Italy's oldest after the one in Bologna. Europe's first anatomy theatre was opened here in 1594 and Galileo Galilei taught here from 1592 to 1610. The main courtyard and its halls are plastered with the coats of arms of the great and learned from across Europe.

Continue along to Piazza delle Erbe and Piazza della Frutta, which are separated by the grand Gothic **Palazzo della Ragione** (Piazza delle Erbe; adult/child €6/3; ☉ 9am-7pm Tue-Sun Feb-Oct, 9am-6pm Tue-Sun Nov-Jan), also known as the Salone for the grand hall on its upper floor.

West from here is the Piazza dei Signori, dominated by the 14th-century **Palazzo del Capitanio**, the former residence of the city's Venetian ruler. South of this is the city's **cathedral** (☎ 049 66 28 14; Piazza del Duomo; ☉ 7.30am-noon & 3.30-7.30pm Mon-Sat, 7.45am-1pm & 3.45-8.30pm Sun & holidays), built from a much-altered design by Michelangelo. The 13th-century Romanesque **baptistry** (adult/child €2.50/1; ☉ 10am-6pm) features a series of frescoes of

Old and New Testament scenes by Giusto de' Menabuoi, influenced by Giotto.

PIAZZA DEL SANTO

At the southern end of the old centre stands the majestic Basilica di Sant'Antonio, better known simply as the **Basilica del Santo** (⏰ 7.30am-7pm), which houses the corpse of the town's patron saint, St Anthony of Padua (1193–1232), and is an important place of pilgrimage. Construction of what is known to townspeople as Il Santo began in 1232. The saint's tomb, bedecked by requests for his intercession to cure illness and thanks for having done so, is in the Cappella del Santo, in the left transept. Look out for the saint's relics in the apse. The sculptures and reliefs of the high altar are by Donatello, master sculptor of the Florentine Renaissance. He remained in town long enough to carry out the Gattamelata equestrian statue that dominates Piazza del Santo in 1453. This magnificent representation of the 15th-century Venetian mercenary leader Erasmos da Narni (whose nickname, Gattamelata, translates as 'Honeyed Cat') is considered the first great bronze of the Italian Renaissance.

On the southern side of the piazza lies the **Oratorio di San Giorgio** (admission incl Scoletta del Santo €2; ⏰ 9am-12.30pm & 2.30-6pm Mar-Oct, 9am-12.30pm & 2.30-5pm Nov-Feb), the burial chapel of the Lupi di Soranga family of Parma, with 14th-century frescoes. Next door is the **Scoletta del Santo** (Scuola del Santo; admission with Oratorio di San Giorgio €2; ⏰ 9am-12.30pm & 2.30-7pm Mar-Oct, 9am-12.30pm & 2.30-5pm Nov-Feb), containing works believed to be by Titian.

Just south of Piazza del Santo, the **Orto Botanico** (⏰ 049 827 21 19; adult/child €2.58/1.55; ⏰ 9am-1pm & 3-6pm Apr-Oct, 9am-1pm Nov-Mar), laid out in 1545, is purportedly the oldest botanical garden in Europe.

Sleeping

Koko Nor Association (⏰ 049 864 33 94; www.band b-veneto.it/kokonor; Via Selva 5) For help in finding B&B-style accommodation in family homes (it has 15 places on the books) starting from around €36/55 for singles/doubles. The tourist office has a list of about 30 B&Bs.

Ostello Città di Padova (⏰ 049 65 42 10; www.ctgveneto.it/ostello; Via dei A Aleardi 30; dm with breakfast €15.50) Not bad as hostels go. To get there take bus No 3, 8 or 12 from the train station

to Prato della Valle and ask for directions. Dorms have 16 bunk beds and they have some family rooms too with four bunk beds and own bathroom attached.

Camping Sporting Center (⏰ 049 79 34 00; www .sportingcenter.it; Via Roma 123, Montegrotto Terme; site per person/tent €7.30/10; ⏰ Mar-Nov) The only camp site in the province of Padua, about 15km away from the city. It's big and boasts a swimming pool, access to spa facilities, shops and just about anything else your heart might desire. It can be reached by city bus M from the train station.

Albergo Sant'Antonio (⏰ 049 875 13 93; fax 049 875 25 08; Via San Fermo 118; s/d with bathroom €60/78; 🅿) Comfortable, airy rooms are a good deal on price. It has some cheaper ones with shared bathroom in the corridor.

Hotel Majestic Toscanelli (⏰ 049 66 32 44; www2.goldgate.it/hoteltoscanelli/; Via dell'Arco 2; s/d up to €124/161; 🅿 🅿) Hidden away in a leafy corner of one of the lanes that twist away from Piazza delle Erbe, the hotel boasts classy, newly renovated rooms, all in various styles (ranging from Imperial to what the owners call '19th-century English') and complete with all the usual mod cons. The place started in 1946 in what was once Padua's Jewish quarter.

Eating

Caffè Pedrocchi (⏰ 049 878 12 31; Via VIII Febbraio 15) Fronted by a spruced up neoclassical facade, this café has been in business since the 19th century. It was one of Stendhal's favourite haunts and remains a classy Padua coffee stop. You can also visit the grand 19th-century ballroom upstairs.

Lilium (⏰ 049 875 11 07; Via del Santo 181; ⏰ 7.30am-8pm winter, 7.30am-10pm Tue-Sun summer) A fine pastry shop that offers wonderful gelato and delicious sweet things.

Osteria dei Fabbri (⏰ 049 65 03 36; Via dei Fabbri 13; meals €20-25; ⏰ Mon-Sat) A roisterous traditional eatery, with lots of timber and bonhomie. Try the *ravioloni di magro* (exquisite, light ravioli with a butter and sage sauce).

La Vecchia Enoteca (⏰ 049 875 28 56; Via San Martino e Solferino 32; meals €40-45; ⏰ Tue-Sat & dinner Mon) An altogether swankier joint where mouthwatering meals can be had but with a greater impact on the wallet. It does a nice *filetto di manzo alla salsa bernese* (steak fillet in a Béarnaise sauce).

THE VENETO

Enoteca la Corte dei Leoni (☎ 049 875 00 83; Via Pietro d'Abano 1; meals €45; ☺ Tue-Sat & lunch Sun) A modern temple of wine, also offering a fine dining experience. In summer, book a table in the courtyard (where jazz concerts are also occasionally staged). The food is excellent if a little nouvelle in terms of portions and you can taste wine by the glass at the bar from a broad and well-selected wine list. The menu changes each week with such delights as *gnocchi di patate all'erba cipollina con ragout di funghi* (gnocchi in onion herbs and mushroom sauce).

Trattoria da Paccagnella (☎ 049 875 05 49; Via del Santo 113; meals €30; ☺ Mon-Sat) A comfortably elegant setting for fine Veneto cuisine, especially duck and game meats. How about *arrosto di coniglio disossato alle erbe* (boneless roast rabbit in herbs)?

Per Bacco (☎ 049 875 46 64; Piazzale Pontecorvo 10; meals €30-35; ☺ Tue-Sun) It's away from the centre but a visit repays the effort. Try the *tagliatelle alla norcina con tartufo nero* (tagliatelle with black truffles), a classic of Umbrian cuisine and a standing favourite here. The wine list is also strong.

Drinking

There are several traditional spots around Piazza delle Erbe for taking the evening *spritz* – the classic early evening aperitif in the Veneto, made of one part *prosecco* (local sparkling white), one part soda and one part bitters (such as Campari or the slightly sweeter Aperol). In summer especially, hundreds of people clutching their favourite tipples spread out across the square in the early evening. Much the same thing happens on a reduced scale on Piazza dei Signori.

Café El Pilar (☎ 049 65 75 65; Piazza dei Signori 8; ☺ 11am-3pm & 6pm-midnight) A mix of beautiful people and others converge here for the evening *spritz*. Often by 10pm people have scarpered – off to the disco perhaps? Nearby on Piazza del Duomo, a fair crowd of beautiful people, students and others hang about sipping cocktails and the like later on into the evening.

Enoteca Da Severino (☎ 049 65 06 97; Via del Santo 44; ☺ 11am-9pm) Wine-lovers are beckoned to come and taste tipples from around the region and beyond. The walls of this tiny wine bar are lined with bottles and appreciative drinkers spill out into the street in the warmer months.

Paparazzi Fashion Café (☎ 049 875 93 06; Via Marsilio da Padova 17; ☺ 6pm-1am Tue-Sun) A young cool crowd gathers here, all sunglasses at night and designer stubble, low red lights and dark drinking corners.

Entertainment

Teatro Comunale Verdi (☎ 049 877 70 11; www .teatroverdipd.it; Via Livello 32) Works of classic Italian and occasionally foreign theatre are staged here, ranging from the likes of local Veneto hero Goldoni through to Goethe or more modern playwrights such as Brecht. It's a grand old theatre in the round but clearly pretty much everything is performed in Italian.

Getting There & Away

BUS

Regular **SITA buses** (☎ 049 820 68 11) from Venice (€2.90, 45 to 60 minutes) arrive at Piazzale Boschetti, 200m south of the train station.

From Padua you can get buses to Montegrotto Terme, the Colli Euganei and as far afield as Genoa. Often you are better off with the train.

CAR & MOTORCYCLE

The A4 (Turin–Milan–Venice–Trieste) passes to the north, while the A13, which connects the city with Bologna, starts at the southern edge of town. The two motorways are connected by a ring road.

TRAIN

The easiest way to Padua from Venice is by train (up to €4.44, 20 to 40 minutes). Regular trains proceed from Padua to Bologna, Vicenza, Verona, Milan and beyond.

AROUND PADUA
Colli Euganei

Southwest of Padua, along the A13 or the SS16, the Colli Euganei (Euganean Hills) are dotted with vineyards and good walking trails: ask at the Padua tourist office for information about the trails and accommodation. As you move around, you will encounter numerous villages, along with the occasional castle and abbey scattered about the countryside.

If you are driving (which you pretty much have to as public transport is abysmal in the area), follow the signposted *Strada*

THE VENETO

dei Vini dei Colli Euganei (Euganean Hills Wine Road), which will take you on a tour of many vineyards. Pick up a map and itinerary from the tourist office in Padua.

The area is also famous for its hot springs or *terme*. The water passes underground from the low mountains of the Prealps north of Padova, where it is heated to more than 85°C and collects mineral salts. This water then bubbles up in the Colli Euganei area. The two main spa centres are Abano Terme and Montegrotto Terme. For information approach the tourist offices in **Abano** (☎ 049 866 90 55; Via Pietro d'Abano 18) and **Montegrotto** (☎ 049 79 33 84; Viale Stazione 60). Between the two towns, there are more than 100 hotels with hot springs facilities.

ARQUÀ PETRARCA
This quiet, hilly medieval village in the southern Colli Euganei was where Italy's great poet Petrarch (Petrarca) chose to spend the last five years of his life. You can visit his **house** (☎ 042 971 82 94, Via Valleselle 4, Arquà Petrarca; adult/child €5/3; ⌚ 9am-12.30pm & 3-7pm Tue-Sun Mar-Oct, 9am-12.30pm & 2.30-5.30pm Tue-Sun Nov-Feb), which is set in cheerful gardens and contains various bits and bobs that purportedly had something to do with the scribe. Buses run here from Este and Monselice, both a short distance to the south. Up to three daily buses from Padua (€2.35, 55 minutes) run a route to Este that takes them through here.

Monselice
pop 17,495
An easy train trip south from Padua, Monselice was once wrapped in no less than five protective layers of fortifications. The main point of interest here is the restored **castle** (☎ 049 729 31; adult/child €5.50/3; ⌚ 9-11am & 3-5pm Apr–mid-Nov; 1hr guided tour). The complex contains buildings raised between the 11th and 15th centuries. To get here, take the Padua–Montagnana train (20 minutes).

Este
pop 16,987
Heading west from Monselice along the road to Mantua (Mantova), this town is yet another in the chain of fortified strongholds in the area. Padua's Carrara clan were assiduous fortress builders – it seems they had a good number of enemies to keep at bay. Although the walls of their castle are in

reasonable shape, the inside is pretty much a ruin. On the bumpy lane that climbs northwards behind the castle is the **Villa Kunkler**, where Byron settled in for a year or so in 1817. Shelley also stayed here.

You'll find a couple of hotels here and the town is on the train line linking Montagnana (10 minutes), Monselice (10 minutes) and Padua (30 minutes).

Montagnana
pop 9417
About 12km west of Este rise the magnificent defensive perimeter walls, dating to the 13th and 14th centuries, of this fortified plains town. Of all the Veneto's walled towns, this is the most impressive – almost 2km studded with 24 towers and four gates. Once inside, however, there's not an awful lot to see.

Ostello Rocca degli Alberi (☎ /fax 042 98 10 76; fax 049 807 02 66; Castello degli Alberi, Montagnana; dm €9.50; ⌚ Apr–mid-Oct) is a unique HI youth hostel housed in a former watchtower of the town's extraordinary walls, and close to the town's train station.

The train from Padua (€2.90, 50 minutes) runs via Monselice and Este.

VICENZA
pop 110,454
Vicenza is the centre for Italian textile manufacture and a leader in the development and production of computer components, making it one of the country's wealthiest cities. Most tourists come to Vicenza to see the work of Palladio, who was particularly busy here.

Vicenza flourished as the Roman Vicentia. In 1404 it became part of the Venetian Republic. Testimony to the close ties between the lagoon city and Vicenza are the many Venetian Gothic mansions here.

Orientation
From the train station, in the gardens of Campo Marzo, Via Roma heads into Piazzale de Gasperi. From here, the main street, Corso Andrea Palladio, leads to the cathedral and the centre of town.

Information
EMERGENCY
Police Station (☎ 0444 54 33 33; Viale Giuseppe Mazzini 24)

VICENZA

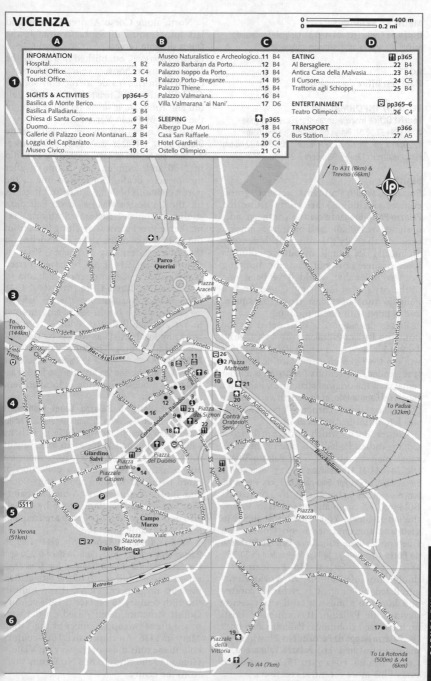

INFORMATION
Hospital...................................1 B2
Tourist Office..........................2 C4
Tourist Office..........................3 B4

SIGHTS & ACTIVITIES   pp364–5
Basilica di Monte Berico........4 C6
Basilica Palladiana.................5 B4
Chiesa di Santa Corona..........6 B4
Duomo...................................7 B4
Gallerie di Palazzo Leoni Montanari...8 B4
Loggia del Capitaniato............9 B4
Museo Civico.........................10 C4

Museo Naturalistico e Archeologico..11 B4
Palazzo Barbaran da Porto.......12 B4
Palazzo Isoppo da Porto..........13 B4
Palazzo Porto-Breganze...........14 B5
Palazzo Thiene.......................15 B4
Palazzo Valmarana..................16 B4
Villa Valmarana 'ai Nani'.........17 D6

SLEEPING   p365
Albergo Due Mori...................18 B4
Casa San Raffaele...................19 C6
Hotel Giardini.........................20 C4
Ostello Olimpico.....................21 C4

EATING   p365
Al Bersagliere........................22 B4
Antica Casa della Malvasia......23 B4
Il Cursore..............................24 C5
Trattoria agli Schioppi.............25 B4

ENTERTAINMENT   pp365–6
Teatro Olimpico.....................26 C4

TRANSPORT   p366
Bus Station.............................27 A5

MEDICAL SERVICES
Ospedale Civile (☎ 0444 99 31 11; Viale Ferdinando Rodolfi 37) Hospital for emergency treatment.

POST
Main Post Office (Contrà Garibaldi)

TOURIST INFORMATION
Tourist Office (www.vicenzae.org) Piazza dei Signori (☎ 0444 32 50 01; Piazza dei Signori 8; ✆ 10am-12.30pm & 3-6.30pm); Piazza Matteotti (☎ 0444 32 08 54; Piazza Matteotti 12; ✆ 9am-1pm & 2-6pm)

Sights
Piazza Castello contains several grand edifices, including the oddly truncated **Palazzo Porto-Breganze** on the southern side, designed by Palladio and built by Scamozzi (one of the city's leading 16th-century architects). Its couple of outsize columns look strange now but had the building been completed it would have been one of the city's most imposing. Corso Andrea Palladio runs northeast from the square and is lined with fine buildings.

Piazza dei Signori is dominated by the immense **Basilica Palladiana** (☎ 0444 32 36 81; ✆ 9am-5pm Tue-Sun), on which Palladio started work in 1549 over an earlier Gothic building (the slender 12th-century bell tower is all that remains of the original structure). Palladio's **Loggia del Capitaniato**, at the northwestern side of the piazza on the corner of Via del Monte, was left unfinished at his death.

Contrà Porti, which runs north from Corso Andrea Palladio, is one of the city's most majestic streets. The **Palazzo Thiene** (☎ 0444 54 21 31; admission free; ✆ 9am-noon & 3-6pm Tue-Wed Oct-Apr, 9am-noon & 3-6pm Wed & Fri, 9am-noon Sat May-Sep) at No 12, by Lorenzo da Bologna, was originally intended to occupy the entire block. You must book ahead to visit and the entrance is on Contrà San Gaetano Thiene. Palladio's **Palazzo Barbaran da Porto** (☎ 0444 32 30 14; adult/student €5.50/3.50; ✆ 10am-6pm Tue-Sun) at No 11 features a double row of columns. A World Heritage listed building, it is richly decorated and home to a museum and study centre devoted to Palladio. It frequently hosts architecture exhibitions. Palladio also built the **Palazzo Isoppo da Porto** at No 21, which remains unfinished. His **Palazzo Valmarana**, at Corso Antonio Fogazzaro 18, is considered one of his more eccentric creations.

North along Corso Andrea Palladio and left into Contrà di Santa Corona is the **Chiesa di Santa Corona** (✆ 8.30am-noon & 3-6pm Tue-Sun, 4-6pm Mon), established in 1261 by the Dominicans to house a relic from Christ's crown of thorns. Inside are the *Battesimo di Gesù* (Baptism of Christ) by Giovanni Bellini and *Adorazione dei Magi* (Adoration of the Magi) by Paolo Veronese.

Corso Andrea Palladio ends at the **Teatro Olimpico** (☎ 0444 22 28 00; ✆ 9am-5pm Tue-Sun Sep-Jun, 9am-7pm Tue-Sun Jul-Aug), started by Palladio in 1580 and completed by Scamozzi after the former's death. Considered one of the purest creations of Renaissance architecture, the theatre design was based on Palladio's studies of Roman structures. Scamozzi's remarkable street scene, stretching back from the main facade of the stage, is modelled on the ancient Greek city of Thebes. Since its restoration in 1934 it has become a prized performance space for opera and drama.

The nearby **Museo Civico** (☎ 0444 32 13 48; Palazzo Chiericati, Piazza Matteotti 37/39; ✆ 9am-5pm Tue-Sun Sep-Jun, 9am-7pm Tue-Sun Jul-Aug), housed in yet another Palladian edifice, contains works by local artists as well as by the Tiepolos and Veronese. The **Museo Naturalistico e Archeologico** (☎ 0444 32 04 40; Contrà di Santa Corona 4; ✆ 9am-5pm Tue-Sun Sep-Jun, 9am-7pm Tue-Sun Jul-Aug) has a modest collection of local ancient artefacts.

The **Gallerie di Palazzo Leoni Montanari** (☎ 800 57 88 75; Contrà di Santa Corona 25; adult/student €3.50/2.50; ✆ 10am-6pm Fri-Sun), with its sober baroque facade hides an extravagant interior. For a long time a private mansion and bank, it now contains a collection of more than 400 Russian icons (top floor) and mostly 18th-century Venetian paintings (1st floor), including some by Canaletto and Pietro Longhi. There are frequent temporary exhibitions too.

Basilica di Monte Bèrico (☎ 0444 32 09 98; Piazzale della Vittoria; ✆ 6.15am-12.30pm & 2.30-6pm Mon-Sat, 6.15am-12.30pm & 2.30-7pm Sun & holidays), set on top of a hill south of the city centre, presents magnificent views. It was built in the 18th century to replace a 15th-century Gothic structure, itself raised on the supposed site of two appearances by the Virgin Mary in 1426. An impressive 18th-century colonnade runs most of the way up Viale X Giugno to the church. Bus No 9 runs there from the centre.

Pass time the Venetian way on the island of **Burano** (p344)

JEFFREY N. BECOM

GLENN BEANLAND

Relax in style in a Venetian **gondola** (p345)

Wander the brightly coloured streets of the tiny fishing village of **Burano** (p344)

CHRISTOPHER GROENHOUT

DAMIEN

Take a (rare) quiet moment in **St Mark's Square** (p331), Venice

DAMIEN SIMONIS

Catch an opera at the
Roman arena, **Verona** (p366)

Walk, ski, mountain bike, hang glide or rock
climb (phew!) in the **Dolomites** (p293)

HANK

Enjoy the magnificent decoration of beautiful **St Mark's Basilica** (p331), Venice

GLENN BEANLAND

A 20-minute walk part of the way back down Viale X Giugno and then east along Via San Bastiano will take you to the **Villa Valmarana 'ai Nani'** (☎ 0444 54 39 76; Via dei Nani 2/8; admission €6; ☾ 10am-noon & 3-6pm Wed, Thu, Sat & Sun, 3-6pm Tue & Fri mid-Mar–early Nov), which features brilliant frescoes by Giambattista and Giandomenico Tiepolo. The 'ai Nani' (dwarfs) refers to the statues perched on top of the gates surrounding the property.

A path leads on to Palladio's Villa Capra, better known as **La Rotonda** (☎ 0444 32 17 93; Via Rotonda 29; admission La Rotonda €6, gardens only €3; ☾ villa 10am-noon & 3-6pm Wed Mar-Nov, gardens 10am-noon & 3-6pm Tue-Sun Mar-Nov). It is one of the architect's most admired (and copied) creations, having served as a model for buildings across Europe and the USA. The name comes from the low dome that caps this square based structure, each side fronted by the columns of a classical facade. Bus No 8 stops nearby.

Sleeping

Ostello Olimpico (☎ 0444 54 02 22; ostello.vicenza@tin.it; Viale Antonio Giuriolo 7-9; dm/s €14.50/18; ☾ 7.30am-9.30am & 3.30-11.30pm) An HI youth hostel in a fine building right by the Teatro Olimpico.

Albergo Due Mori (☎ 0444 32 18 86; fax 0444 32 61 27; Contrà do Rode 26; s/d up to €48/85) Located near Piazza dei Signori. It's a central cheapy with basic rooms but clean and reliable. It has a few cheaper doubles with shared bathroom in the corridor.

Casa San Raffaele (☎ 0444 54 57 67; albergosanraffaele@tin.it; Viale X Giugno 10; d with bathroom & breakfast €65; P) Located in a former convent behind the colonnade leading to Monte Bèrico, this is a charming spot to spend the night and the best choice in the lower budget range.

Hotel Giardini (☎ 0444 32 64 58; www.hotelgiardini.com; Viale Antonio Giuriolo 10; s/d with breakfast up to €103/129; ✂ P) A rather modern hotel (with decidedly little in the way of gardens), this is nevertheless a perfectly comfortable and handy choice for the heart of the town.

Eating

Antica Casa della Malvasia (☎ 0444 54 37 04; Contrà delle Morette 5; meals €20) This establishment has been around since 1200. In those days it was the local sales point for Malvasia wine imported from Greece by Venetian merchants, who usually gathered here in the evenings to

TICKETS PLEASE

Several combined ticket options are available. The Card Musei costs €7 (valid three days) and gives you entry to the Teatro Olimpico, Museo Civico (Palazzo Chiericati) and the Museo e Naturalistico Archeologico. For €8 you can also visit the obscure Museo del Risorgimento (3km south of the railway station), dedicated to Italian reunification. The Card Musei e Palazzi (€11) gets you entry to all these, the Gallerie di Palazzo Leoni Montanari and Palazzo Barbaran da Porto. The Card Vicenza e Ville (€22) adds La Rotonda and Villa Valmarana to the list.

sample the goods. Drinking is still a primary occupation in a locale that has changed little over the centuries – on offer is an array of 80 types of wine (especially Malvasia varieties) and around a hundred types of grappa (a grape-based liqueur)!

Al Bersagliere (☎ 0444 32 35 07; Contrà Pescheria 11; meals €30; ☾ Mon-Sat) A traditional *osteria* where you can eat *cicheti* at the bar or proceed to the cosy little tables for seasonal cooking (watch for the mushrooms in autumn). The *bigoli al ragù d'anatra* (thick spaghetti in duck sauce) is scrummy.

Il Cursore (☎ 0444 32 35 04; Stradella Pozzetto 10; meals €20-25; ☾ Wed-Mon) They've been serving up food here since the 19th century and although it's been given a face-lift, it remains a great spot for local dishes such as *spaghetti col baccalà mantecato* (spaghetti with salted cod prepared in garlic and parsley).

Trattoria agli Schioppi (☎ 0444 54 37 01; Contrà Castello 26; meals €25-30; ☾ Mon-Fri & lunch Sat) Hearty meat dishes are served up here, *fegato alla veneziano* (calf's liver with onions) and *baccalà alla vicentina* (a local cod favourite).

Drinking

On summer afternoons and evenings the central squares fill with people who gather for the *aperitivo*, that lingering evening tipple, and to chat. The tourist office has a list of bars and a few clubs, mostly well out of the centre.

Entertainment

Teatro Olimpico (☎ 800 323285, ☎ 0444 22 28 01; www.olimpico.vicenza.it; Corso Andrea Palladio) The stage for theatre, classical music concerts and other performances.

Concerts are held in summer at the **Villa Valmarana 'ai Nani'** – check at the tourist office for details.

Vicenza Jazz is an annual jazz festival held in May.

Getting There & Away
BUS
FTV (☎ 0444 22 31 15) buses leave from the bus station, just near the train station, for Thiene, Asiago (in the hilly north of the province), Bassano and towns throughout the nearby Monti Berici (Berici Hills).

CAR & MOTORCYCLE
The city is on the A4 connecting Milan with Venice. The SS11 connects Vicenza with Verona and Padua, and this is the best route if you want to hitchhike. There is a large car park near Piazza Castello and the train station.

TRAIN
Regular trains arrive from Venice (up to €5.58, 55 minutes) and Padua (up to €4.44, 20 to 30 minutes).

AROUND VICENZA
As Venice's maritime power waned in the 16th century, the city's wealthy inhabitants turned their attention inland, acquiring land to build sumptuous villas. Forbidden from building castles by the Venetian senate, which feared a landscape dotted with well-defended forts, Vicenza's patricians joined the villa construction spree. Many of the thousands that were built remain, albeit frequently run-down and closed to the public.

The tourist office in Vicenza can provide reams of information about the villas, including an illustrated map, *Ville dal 1400 al 1800*.

Drivers should have little trouble planning an itinerary. One possibility is to take the SS11 south of Vicenza to Montecchio Maggiore and then on to Lonigo and Pojana Maggiore. From there head north for Longare and back to Vicenza. A return trip of 100km, the route takes in about a dozen villas.

If you don't have a car, take the FTV bus north from Vicenza to Thiene, pass-ing through Caldogno and Villaverla, and then continue on to Lugo. The Villa Godi-Valmarana, now known as the **Malinverni**, at Lonedo di Lugo, was Palladio's first villa.

VERONA
pop 257,477
Wander the streets of Verona on a winter's night and you might believe the tragic love story of Romeo and Juliet to be true. Beyond the Shakespearean hyperbole, however, you'll find plenty to keep you occupied in one of Italy's most beautiful cities. Known as *piccola Roma* (little Rome) for its importance in imperial days, its truly golden era came during the 13th and 14th centuries under the Della Scala family (also known as the Scaligeri). The period was noted for the savage family feuding of which Shakespeare wrote in his play.

Orientation
Old Verona is small and easy to find your way around. Buses leave for the centre from outside the train station; otherwise, walk to the right, past the bus station, cross the river and walk along Corso Porta Nuova to Piazza Brà, 1.5km away. From the piazza, walk along Via G Mazzini and turn left at Via Cappello to reach Piazza delle Erbe.

Information
EMERGENCY
Police Station (☎ 045 809 04 11; Lungadige Porta Vittoria) Near Ponte Navi.

INTERNET ACCESS
Internet Train (☎ 045 801 33 94; www.internet train.it; Via Roma 17)
Internet Etc (☎ 045 800 02 22; Via Quattro Spade 3/b)

LAUNDRY
Onda Blu laundrette (Via XX Settembre 62a; ⊗ 8am-10pm)

MEDICAL SERVICES
Guardia Medica (☎ 045 807 56 27) Medical services from 8pm to 8am (the staff usually come to you).
Ospedale Civile Maggiore (☎ 045 807 11 11; Piazza A Stefani) Hospital; northwest from Ponte Vittoria.

MONEY
Banca Popolare di Bergamo (Piazza Brà) One of several banks with a currency exchange machine.

VERONA

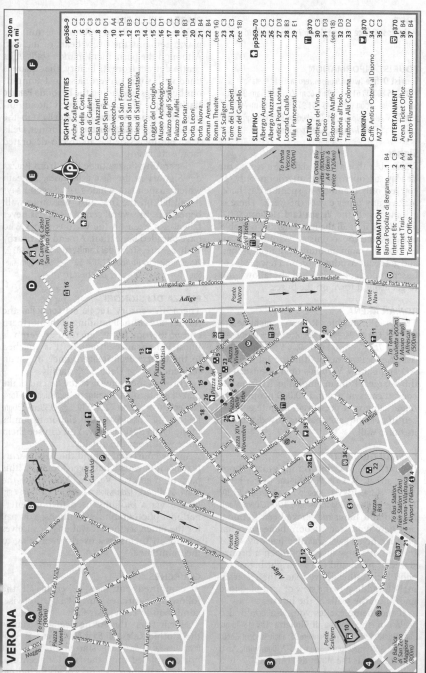

THE VENETO

POST

Main Post Office (Piazza Viviani 7; ✆ 8am-7pm Mon-Sat)

TOURIST INFORMATION

Tourist Office (www.tourism.verona.it); train station (☎ 045 800 08 61; ✆ 9am-6pm Mon-Sat, 9am-3pm Sun); Verona airport (☎ 045 861 91 63; ✆ to meet flights); Via degli Alpini (☎ 045 806 86 80; Via degli Alpini 9; ✆ 9am-7pm Mon-Sat, 9am-3pm Sun)

Sights

Remember that a lot of sights are closed on **Monday**, or open in the afternoon only. If you are only planning to spend a day here, make it any other day of the week. There is a joint ticket, the **Verona Card** (1-/3-days €8/12) for getting into all the main sights (available at sights and tobacconists). With it you can enter all the main monuments and churches, and get reduced admission on a few places of lesser importance. The card also allows you to get around town on the buses.

ROMAN ARENA

This pink marble Roman **amphitheatre** (☎ 045 800 32 04; Piazza Brà; adult/child €3.10/2.10; ✆ 9am-7pm Tue-Sun, 1.45-7.30pm Mon, 8am-3.30pm during opera season) was built in the 1st century AD and is now Verona's opera house. The third-largest Roman amphitheatre in existence, it can seat around 20,000 people. It is remarkably well preserved, despite a 12th-century earthquake that destroyed most of its outer wall.

CASA DI GIULIETTA

Just off Via G Mazzini, Verona's main shopping street, is **Casa di Giulietta** (Juliet's House; ☎ 045 803 43 03; Via Cappello 23; adult/child €3.10/2.10; ✆ 8.30am-7.30pm Tue-Sun, 1.30-7.30pm Mon). Romeo and Juliet may have been fictional but here you can swoon beneath what popular myth says was her balcony or, if in need of a new lover, approach a bronze statue of Juliet and rub her right breast for good luck. Others have made their eternal mark by adding to the slew of scribbled love graffiti on the walls of the house.

If the theme excites you, you could also seek out the **Tomba di Giulietta** (Juliet's Tomb; ☎ 045 800 03 61; Via del Pontiere 35; adult/student €2.60/1.50; ✆ 8.30am-7.30pm Tue-Sun, 1.45-7.30pm Mon). Also housed here is the **Museo degli Affreschi**, with a collection of frescoes of minor interest.

PIAZZA DELLE ERBE

Originally the site of a Roman forum, this piazza remains the lively heart of the city. Although the permanent market stalls in its centre detract from its beauty, the square is lined with some of Verona's most sumptuous buildings, including the baroque **Palazzo Maffei**, at the northern end, with the adjoining 14th-century **Torre del Gardello**. On the eastern side is **Casa Mazzanti**, a former Della Scala family residence. Its fresco-decorated facade stands out.

Separating Piazza delle Erbe from Piazza dei Signori is the **Arco della Costa**, beneath which suspends a whale's rib. Legend says it will fall on the first 'just' person to walk beneath it. In several centuries, it has never fallen, not even on the various popes who have paraded beneath it. Ascend the nearby 12th-century **Torre dei Lamberti** (☎ 045 803 27 26; admission by lift/foot €2.10/1.50; ✆ 9am-6pm Tue-Sun) for a great view of the city.

PIAZZA DEI SIGNORI

The 15th-century **Loggia del Consiglio**, the former city council building at the northern end of this square, is regarded as Verona's finest Renaissance structure. It is attached to the **Palazzo degli Scaligeri**, once the main residence of the Della Scala family.

Through the archway at the far end of the piazza are the **Arche Scaligere** (admission with Torre dei Lamberti by lift/foot €2.60/2.10; ✆ 9.30am-7.30pm Tue-Sun, 1.30-7.30pm Mon), the elaborate tombs of the Della Scala family. You can see them quite well from the outside.

In the courtyard behind the Arche, *scavi* (excavation work) has been done on this part of medieval Verona. You enter the **Scavi Scaligeri** (admission variable; ✆ 10am-6pm Tue-Sun) via a building used to host international photographic exhibitions. You pay for the latter, as the excavations themselves are not in themselves overly interesting to the uninitiated.

CHURCHES

A combined entrance ticket to all the following churches costs €5. Otherwise, admission to each costs €2.

North from the Arche Scaligere stands the Gothic **Chiesa di Sant'Anastasia** (✆ 9am-6pm Mon-Sat, 1-6pm Sun), started in 1290 but not completed until the late 15th century. Inside are numerous works of art including, in the sacristy, a lovely fresco by Pisanello of *San Giorgio che Parte per Liberare la Donzella dal Drago* (St George Setting out to Free the Princess from the Dragon).

The 12th-century **cathedral** (🕙 10am-5.30pm Mon-Sat, 1.30-5.30pm Sun) combines Romanesque (lower section) and Gothic (upper section) styles and has some intriguing features. Look for the sculpture of Jonah and the Whale on the southern porch and the statues of two of Charlemagne's paladins, Roland and Oliver, on the western porch.

At the river end of Via Leoni is the **Chiesa di San Fermo** (🕙 10am-6pm Mon-Sat, 1-6pm Sun), which is actually two churches: the Gothic church was built in the 13th century over the original 11th-century Romanesque structure. The **Chiesa di San Lorenzo** (🕙 10am-6pm Mon-Sat, 1-6pm Sun) is near the Castelvecchio and the **Basilica di San Zeno Maggiore** is further to the west.

CASTELVECCHIO

Southwest from Piazza delle Erbe, on the banks of the River Adige, is the 14th-century fortress of Cangrande II (of the Della Scala family). The fortress was damaged by bombing during WWII and restored in the 1960s. It now houses a **museum** (☎ 045 59 47 34; Corso Castelvecchio 2; adult/student €3.10/2.10; 🕙 9am-6.30pm Tue-Sun) with a diverse collection of paintings, frescoes, jewellery and medieval artefacts. Among the paintings are works by Pisanello, Giovanni Bellini, Tiepolo, Carpaccio and Veronese. Also of note is a 14th-century equestrian statue of Cangrande I. The **Ponte Scaligero**, spanning the River Adige, was rebuilt after being destroyed by WWII bombing.

BASILICA DI SAN ZENO MAGGIORE

A masterpiece of Romanesque architecture, this **church** (🕙 8.30am-6pm Mon-Sat, 1-6pm Sun), in honour of the city's patron saint, was built mainly in the 12th century, although its apse was rebuilt in the 14th century and its bell tower, a relic of an earlier structure on the site, was started in 1045. The basilica's magnificent rose window depicts the Wheel of Fortune. Before going inside, take a look at the sculptures on either side of the main doors. The doors themselves are decorated with bronze reliefs of biblical subjects. The highlight inside is Mantegna's triptych of the *Madonna col Bambino tra Angeli e*

Santi (Madonna and Child with Angels and Saints), above the high altar.

ACROSS THE RIVER

Across Ponte Pietra is a **Roman theatre**, built in the 1st century AD and still used today for concerts and plays. Take the lift at the back of the theatre to the convent above, which houses an interesting collection of Greek and Roman pieces in the **Museo Archeologico** (adult/student €2.60/1.50; 🕙 8.30am-7.30pm Tue-Sun, 1.30-7.30pm Mon). On a hill, behind the theatre and museum, is the **Castel San Pietro**, built by the Austrians on the site of an earlier castle.

Sleeping

If you are having problems finding a hotel room, you could try calling the **Cooperativa Albergatori Veronesi** (☎ 045 800 98 44; fax 045 800 93 72). It starts with two-star hotels and the service is free.

Villa Francescati (☎ 045 59 03 60; fax 045 800 91 27; Salita Fontana del Ferro 15; dm with breakfast €13.50; 🕙 7am-11.30pm) A beautifully restored HI youth hostel housed in a 16th-century villa not far from the camp site and should be your first choice of budget lodging. The gardens are gorgeous and it has family rooms too. Meals cost €8 but there are no cooking facilities.

Camping Castel San Pietro (☎ 045 59 20 37; www .campingcastelsanpietro.com; Via Castel San Pietro 2; site per car/person/tent €3.50/5.50/7; 🕙 mid-May–mid-Oct) Not a bad camp site, away from the bustle of the town below. Sites are leafy and you can relax on the two grand terraces. There's a minimarket, washing machines and other comforts. Catch bus No 41 or 95 from the train station. The staff can even help organise tickets for a night at the opera.

Locanda Catullo (☎ 045 800 27 86; locandacatu llo@tiscali.it; Via Valerio Catullo 1; s/d without bathroom €40/55, d with bathroom €65) A good cheaply with friendly management and clean, straightforward rooms. At these rates it's about the best value in town.

Albergo Aurora (☎ 045 59 47 17; fax 045 801 08 60; Piazza XIV Novembre 2; s/d with bathroom up to €104/117) A big, old, sprawling place where the better rooms are spacious and comfortable, although time is beginning to take its toll. The position is about as central as is possible.

Albergo Mazzanti (☎ 045 800 68 13; fax 045 801 12 62; Via Mazzanti 6; s/d up to €72/104) Just off Piazza dei Signori, Mazzanti is, if you can get one of the nicer rooms, probably marginally better value than the nearby Aurora. That said, some of the sleeping cubicles for singles are claustrophobic. In the low season, prices can reduce to less than half those listed for rooms without bathroom.

Antica Porta Leona (☎ 045 59 54 99; fax 045 59 52 14; Corticella Leoni 3; s/d up to €104/150) A reasonable three-star hotel located near Casa di Giulietta, whose rooms are full of character, if somewhat faded.

Eating

Trattoria Alla Colonna (☎ 045 59 67 18; Via Pescheria Vecchia 4; meals €25-30; ☺ Mon-Sat) A traditional dining experience at good prices in a family-run eatery. Several polenta dishes are on offer and the wine list isn't bad.

Bottega del Vino (☎ 045 800 45 35; Vicolo Scudo di Francia 3a; meals €45-55; ☺ Wed-Mon) A must if wine is your thing. In this age-old wine cellar the staff serve up some fine food too. The wine list is endless and your choice will be served with all the ceremony you might expect at a highbrow wine-tasting. The cost of your meal can vary wildly depending on your choice of tipple. If nothing else, wander in to this perennially busy dining hall – the frescoes, complemented by shelf loads of ancient bottles, are alone worth the effort.

Ristorante Maffei (☎ 045 801 00 15; Piazza delle Erbe 38; meals €60; ☺ closed lunch Mon winter) With the baroque splendour of the Palazzo Maffei, this is an elegant setting for dinner. Dining in the central courtyard is especially pleasant and you can dig into hearty meals – how about *filetto di maiale alle mele renette e senape di Dijon* (pork fillet with rennet apples and Dijon mustard)?

Trattoria all'Isolo (☎ 045 59 42 91; Via Seminario 4; meals €25; ☺ Thu-Tue) Across the river in what feels like a more genuine, less touristy Verona, all'Isolo offers good local cooking. In this tiny little eatery just about anything the staff does with *bigoli* is bound to please. They also do various things with horse and even donkey meat.

Il Desco (☎ 045 801 00 15; Via Dietro San Sebastiano 7; meals €80-100; ☺ Tue-Sat & lunch Sun) Rated one of the best restaurants in all of Italy and a Michelin-star winner. This is a refined dining option for meticulously prepared local cuisine.

Drinking

Caffè Antica Osteria al Duomo (Via Duomo 7; ☺ noon-2pm & 7-10pm Mon-Sat) A cosy tavern with mandolins, balalaikas and other stringed instruments hanging on the wall. Pop in for a drop of *fragolino* (the local sweet strawberry wine).

M27 (☎ 045 803 42 42; Via G Mazzini 27a; ☺ 10am-2am Tue-Sun) A young, hip Veronese crowd is attracted to this angular bar. Whether for morning coffee or evening cocktails they perch on designer stools in a squeaky-clean, polished ambience.

Entertainment

Roman Arena (☎ 045 800 51 51; www.arena.it; ticket office Ente Lirico Arena di Verona Via Dietro Anfiteatro 6/b; admission €15-150; ☺ opera season Jul-Sep) Tickets are available online and at travel agents around the country.

Teatro Filarmonico (☎ 045 800 28 80; Via dei Mutilati 4) This 18th-century theatre, just south of Piazza Brà, is also run by the Ente Lirico Arena di Verona. A winter programme of ballet and opera dominates the proceedings.

Getting There & Away
AIR
Verona-Villafranca airport (VRN; ☎ 045 809 56 66) is 16km outside the town and accessible by regular bus to/from the train station (20 minutes). Flights arrive from all over Italy and some European cities, including Amsterdam, Barcelona, Berlin, Brussels, Cologne, Frankfurt, Helsinki, London, Munich, Paris and Vienna.

BUS
The main intercity bus station is in front of the train station, in an area known as Porta Nuova. Although buses serve many big cities, they are generally only a useful option for those needing to reach provincial localities not served by train.

CAR & MOTORCYCLE
Verona is at the intersection of the Serenissima A4 (Turin–Trieste) and Brennero A22 motorways.

TRAIN
Verona has rail links with Milan, Mantua, Modena, Florence and Rome. There are also regular trains serving destinations

in Austria, Switzerland and Germany (10 daily to/from Munich).

The trip to/from Venice is easiest by train (up to €12.65, one to 1½ hours). Note that if you get the slow *regionale* train you could be travelling for up to 2½ hours!

Getting Around

AMT (city transport) bus Nos 11, 12, 13 and 72 (bus No 91 or 98 on Sunday and holidays) connect the train station with Piazza Brà and bus No 70 goes to Piazza delle Erbe (tickets cost €1 and are valid for an hour). Otherwise, it's a 20-minute walk along Corso Porta Nuova. Buy tickets (€0.85) before you board the bus from newsagents and tobacconists.

TREVISO

pop 82,450

A small, pleasant city with historical importance as a Roman centre, Treviso is well worth a day trip from Venice (easily accomplished by train) but you could also make a stopover if you are heading north for the Dolomites. Accommodation is limited in the city.

Treviso claims Luciano Benetton, the clothing manufacturer, as its favourite son. You will find a huge Benetton store in the centre of town but factory outlets around the outskirts of town are the strict preserve of Benetton employees.

Orientation

From the train station head north along Via Roma (over the canal), past the bus station and across the bridge (the nicely placed McDonald's on the river is an unmistakable landmark) and keep walking straight ahead along Corso del Popolo. At Piazza della Borsa veer left down Via XX Settembre and you arrive in the heart of the city, Piazza dei Signori.

Information

Tourist Office (☎ 0422 54 76 32; Piazzetta Monte di Pietà 8, adjacent to Piazza dei Signori; ☺ 9am-12.30pm & 2-6pm Tue-Fri, 9.30am-12.30pm & 3-6pm Sat-Sun, 9am-12.30pm Mon) From October to March, the afternoon hours shorten a little.

Sights & Activities

The tourist office promotes Treviso as the *città d'acqua* (city of water) and compares it

to Venice. While the River Sile, which weaves through the centre, and the handful of canals are quite beautiful in parts, the comparisons are more touching than realistic.

That said, it is delightful to wander around the city. Piazza dei Signori is dominated by the fine brick **Palazzo dei Trecento**, the one-time seat of city government beneath whose vaults you can now stop for coffee and a bite. The medieval main street is the porticoed Via Calmaggiore, which leads to the **cathedral** (Piazza del Duomo; ☺ 7.30am-noon & 3.30-7pm Mon-Fri, 7.30am-1pm & 3.30-8pm Sat-Sun), a massive structure whose main source of interest lies in the frescoes inside by Il Pordenone (1484–1539).

Backtrack to Piazza dei Signori and head east (around and behind the Palazzo dei Trecento) and you will soon find yourself in a warren of lanes that leads to five delightful bridges across the Canal Cagnan. This runs roughly north–south (you'll run into the fish market along the way) and spills into the River Sile at a particularly pleasant corner where part of the city walls remain intact. Treviso is a comparatively leafy town and this is particularly the case at some points along the canal. You can also see the occasional mill wheel (the one by Vicolo Molinetto still turns). While on the right bank of the canal you might pop into the deconsecrated **Chiesa di Santa Caterina** (☎ 0422 54 48 64; Via di Santa Caterina; admission €3; ☺ 9am-12.30pm & 2.30-6pm Tue-Sun). The church and its attached convent and cloisters are being developed as a museum to house the city's treasures. In the church itself are remarkable frescoes attributed to Gentile da Fabriano (who worked in the early 15th century). The beautiful Cappella degli Innocenti contains frescoes by other artists of the same period, depicting the lives of Christ and the Virgin Mary. To these have been added the extraordinary fresco cycle by Tomaso da Modena (1326–79) on the life and martyrdom of St Ursula (Santa Orsola or Orseola), recovered late in the 19th century from an already partly demolished church.

Tomaso also left frescoes in the imposing **Chiesa di San Nicolò** (Via San Nicolò; ☺ 7am-noon & 3.30-7pm), on the other side of town. Also over the other end of town is the **Museo Civico Luigi Bailo** (☎ 0422 65 84 42; Borgo Cavour 24; admission €3; ☺ 9am-12.30pm & 2.30-5pm Tue-Sat, 9am-noon Sun), named after the friar

THE VENETO

BUSTING WITH WINE

Sheltered beneath glass under the grand portico in front of the Palazzo dei Trecento is a weather-worn bust of a woman cupping voluminous breasts in her hands. This Fontana delle Tette (Tit Fountain) was erected in central Treviso by the town's governor (or *podestà*) in 1559. From the fountain's nipples sprang forth abundant water from the nearby Canal Cagnan but each year, when a new *podestà* took office, the water was replaced by wine, red from one breast and white from the other, for three festive days. This practice continued until the humourless Napoleon arrived and put an end to Venetian rule in 1797. A modern replica has been set up in a small courtyard just off Calle del Podestà, but alas the heady wine days are gone for good.

who in the late 19th century made it is his life work to collect ancient artefacts and artworks to preserve the memory of Treviso's past. At the time most townfolk thought him an eccentric. Today they owe him a debt of thanks. The museum hosts an archaeological section and a collection of mostly Veneto artists, including works by Tintoretto, Lorenzo Lotto, Titian and Cima da Conegliano. They are followed by local art of the early 20th century.

In summer, you can take a **boat cruise** (☎ 0422 78 86 63, ☎ 0422 78 86 71) on the *Silis* or *Altino* down the Sile to the Venetian lagoon and back. The tours are by reservation only; call or ask at the tourist office.

Sleeping

Albergo Campeol (☎ 0422 5 66 01; www.albergocampeol.it, Italian only; Piazza Ancilotto 4; s/d €52/83) A nicely maintained place in a restored building that spreads around a quiet little pedestrian square just off Piazza dei Signori. It's about the only decent central choice and three of the doubles have canal views.

Eating

Ristorante al Dante (☎ 0422 59 18 97; Piazza Garibaldi 6; meals €20-25; ☽ Mon-Sat) An excellent budget option where you can sidle up to the bar for a host of *cicheti* or dine at one of the teeny tables. In summer you can sit outside and gaze across to the river. Typically people

pop in for bar snacks and *prosecco*, or perhaps a crisp Friuli white.

Piola (☎ 0422 54 02 87; Via Carlo Alberto 11; pizzas €5-7; ☽ Tue-Sun) A hip little bar-cum-pizzeria, where you can sit outside on a little terrace or bury yourself in the dimly lit innards of the bar with Treviso's night crowd. The pizzas are good and you have a wide choice of toppings. This place has done well, opening branches as far away as Brazil – another local business success story!

Muscoli's (☎ 0422 58 33 90; Via Pescheria 23; dishes €6; ☽ Mon-Sat) This old-style no-nonsense *osteria* with timber beams and knockabout tables out the back, gets a mixed crowd of locals in for a glass or three of wine, a few snacks and the occasional dish in the dining area out the back, which looks over the Canal Cagnan. Dishes are simple affairs and sometimes little more than cold platters. There is no menu – the barman will just rattle off whatever is on for the day.

Ristorante Alle Becchiere (☎ 0422 54 08 71; Piazza Ancilotto 10; meals €20-25; ☽ Tue-Sat & lunch Sun) Offers a local menu with a few curve balls thrown in (like *trenette al pesto* from Liguria). Products are fresh and the end result is good in this historical eatery in the heart of the old town. The owners claim tiramisù was invented here!

Shopping

Benetton (☎ 0422 55 99 11; Piazza dell'Indipendenza 5; ☽ 9.15am-12.30pm & 3.30-7.30pm Tue-Sat, 3.30-7.30pm Sun-Mon) The temptation will, for many shoppers be too hard to resist. After all, this is where it all started.

Getting There & Away

The bus station is on Lungosile Mattei, near the train station in Piazzale Duca d'Aosta. ACTV buses connect Treviso with Venice and La Marca buses link it to other towns in the province, for example, Conegliano (45 minutes) and Vittorio Veneto (65 minutes).

It often makes better sense to get the train. The journey from Venice (€1.95) takes 25 to 30 minutes. Other trains connect the town with Belluno (via Conegliano and Vittorio Veneto), Padua and major cities to the south and west.

By car, take the SS53 for Venice and Padua.

BELLUNO

pop 35,079

Belluno is a beautiful little town at the foot of the Dolomites. If you start early enough, you could just about combine it with Treviso in a day trip from Venice, either by train or bus. Better still, hang around for a few days and use it as a base to explore the mountains. For further information on the Dolomites, see pp293–5.

Orientation

Buses arrive at Piazzale della Stazione, in front of the train station. From here take Via Dante (which becomes Via Loreto) and then turn left at the T-junction down Via Matteotti into the central Piazza dei Martiri.

Information

Tourist Office (☎ 0437 94 00 83; Piazza dei Martiri 8; ☑ 9am-12.30pm & 3.30-6.30pm) Produces a feast of information on walking, trekking, skiing and other sporting activities.

Sights

Although no notable monuments await inspection, a wander around the old town is pleasant. The main square (really a broad pedestrian avenue), **Piazza dei Martiri** (Martyrs' Square), takes its name from four partisans hanged here in the dying stages of WWII.

The heart of the old town is formed by **Piazza del Duomo**, dominated on one side by the early-16th-century Renaissance **Cattedrale di San Martino**, the **Palazzo Rosso**, from about the same period, and the **Palazzo dei Vescovi**. The latter's tower is one of three that belonged to the original 12th-century structure, which is long gone.

For most, the reason for reaching Belluno is as a starting point for activities in the mountains, from summertime **hiking** to **skiing** in winter. Stretching away to the northwest of Belluno is the **Parco Nazionale delle Dolomiti Bellunesi**, a beautiful national park laden with opportunities for those who want some mountain air.

Six **Alte Vie delle Dolomiti** (high altitude walking trails in the Dolomites) pass through the territory surrounding Belluno and along them you will find *rifugi* (mountain huts), on route No 1 in particular, where you can stay at the end of a day's hiking. Route No 1 stretches between Belluno and Lago di Braies.

Sleeping

Ostello Imperina (☎ 0437 6 24 51; coopsoc.lavia@tin.it; Località Le Miniere; B&B €13.50; ☑ 7am-10am & 3.30-11.30pm Apr-Sep) The nearest youth hostel, 35km northwest of Belluno at Rivamonte Agordino, within the Parco Nazionale delle Dolomiti Bellunesi. In this cabin there are some family rooms too. You must call ahead on April and May. You can get there on the Agordo bus (50 minutes) from Belluno.

A handful of hotels dot the town, as well as some B&Bs and *affittacamere* (rooms for rent). B&B amounts to a similar option as the latter but includes breakfast. Plenty more lodging options are scattered about the surrounding towns and villages.

Hotel Al Ponte della Vittoria (☎ 0437 92 52 70; fax 0437 92 75 10; Via Monte Grappa 1; s/d €31/49) Located just across the bridge from the centre of town. It is a reasonable deal with good sized, but rather plain, rooms.

Eating

La Taverna (☎ 0437 2 51 92; Via Cipro 7; meals €25; ☑ Mon-Sat) Here you have the option of snacking at the bar or proceeding through to the restaurant area, where you will be treated to hearty cooking. Around Christmas it serves a local speciality – a snail and eel combo that won't be to everyone's taste!

Getting There & Away

Autolinee Dolomiti (☎ 0437 94 12 37) buses depart from in front of the train station, on the western edge of town, for Agordo, Cortina d'Ampezzo, Feltre and smaller towns in the mountains and south of town.

Trains from Venice (€5.40, one hour 50 minutes) run here via Treviso.

By car you can take the A27 motorway from Venice (Mestre) or follow the state roads via Treviso. The latter can be time-consuming because of heavy traffic.

Friuli-Venezia Giulia

While the Adriatic coast is made up of little more than lagoons and flat wetlands, the Friulian plains and Giulian plateaus lead up to the pine-covered Alps in the north, bordered by the Veneto to the west, Austria to the north and Slovenia to the east.

Roman rule was followed by that of the Visigoths, Attila's Huns, the Lombards and Charlemagne's Franks. The Patriarchate of Aquileia, formed in the 10th century, unified the local church and remained autonomous for several centuries. By 1797 the region was under the control of Habsburg Austria. Most of Friuli joined Italy in 1866, but it was not until after WWI that Gorizia, Trieste, Istria and Dalmatia were included. The Latin-Germanic-Slav triangle found its bloodiest expression in WWI: many of Italy's 700,000 dead fell in Friuli-Venezia Giulia.

After WWII, Italy kept Trieste but in 1947 was obliged to cede Dalmatia and the Istrian peninsula to Tito's Yugoslavia. The Iron Curtain passed right through the fascinating frontier town of Gorizia. Udine in the south bears the marks of Venetian intervention, while Trieste is largely a neoclassical creation of Habsburg Austria.

In all, the region is relatively unexplored, and visitors can mix urban culture with gastronomy (discover some of Italy's best-known prosciutto) and nature (plunge into the Adriatic's coastal waters, ski down Il Carnia's northern resort slopes or hike along Alpine forest tracks). Those seeking the quirky face of Friuli can sleep in the epicentre of an earthquake.

HIGHLIGHTS

- **Priceless Gem**

  Extraordinary Roman sights in Aquileia (p385)

- **Gastronomic Orgasm**

  World-famous prosciutto (air-cured ham) from San Daniele (pp390–1)

- **Table Talk**

  Trieste's no-frill *buffets* (cheap restaurants) and Viennese-style cafés (p380)

- **Record Breakers**

  The world's largest Paleo-Christian mosaic floor in Aquileia (p385); the world's largest accessible cave, near Trieste (p382)

- **Green Peace**

  Nature reserves around the Grado and Murano Lagoons (pp386–7)

- **Fresh-air Frolics**

  Skiing, hiking & biking in the northern Il Carnia region (pp391–2)

- **POPULATION: 1.1 MILLION**
- **AREA: 7,845 SQ KM**

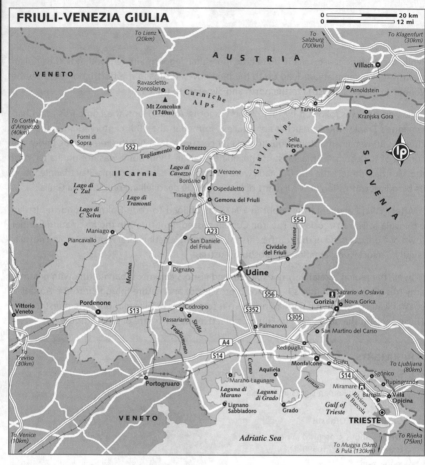

FRIULI-VENEZIA GIULIA

| 0 | 20 km |
| 0 | 12 mi |

To Lienz (20km)

To Salzburg (700km)

To Klagenfurt (30km)

AUSTRIA

VENETO

Villach

Ravascletto-Zoncolan

Carniche Alps

Arnoldstein

▲ Mt Zoncolan (1740m)

Tarvisio

Kranjska Gora

To Cortina d'Ampezzo (40km)

Forni di Sopra

Sella Nevea

S52

Tagliamento • Tolmezzo

Giulie Alps

SLOVENIA

Lago di Cavazzo

Venzone

Il Carnia

Bordano

Lago di C Zul

Trasaghis • Ospedaletto

Lago di Tramonti

Gemona del Friuli

Lago di C Selva

S13

S54

Maniago

Natisone

Piancavallo

A23

San Daniele del Friuli

Cividale del Friuli

Dignano

Udine

Medùna

S56

Pordenone

Gorizia

Sacrario di Oslavia

Vittorio Veneto

S13

Codroipo

S352

Nova Gorica

Stella

Passariano

S305

San Martino del Carso

Tagliamento

A4

Palmanova

S14

Redipuglia

To Treviso (30km)

Monfalcone

Duino

To Ljubljana (80km)

Cormor

Aquileia

S14

Sgonico

Portogruaro

Marano Lagunare

Isonzo

Miramare

Rupingrande

Laguna di Marano

Laguna di Grado

Barcola

Villa Opicina

VENETO

Lignano Sabbiadoro

Grado

Gulf of Trieste

Riviera di Barcola

TRIESTE

Adriatic Sea

To Venice (10km)

To Muggia (5km) & Pula (130km)

To Rijeka (75km)

TRIESTE

pop 215,100

Sitting snugly between the Adriatic Sea and Slovenia, Trieste (Trst in Slovenian) is an odd city. The faded grandeur of its largely homogenous architecture is owed entirely to its days as the great southern port of the Austro-Hungarian Empire during the 18th and 19th centuries. As the city developed, much of its medieval heart was levelled to make way for a new layer of neoclassical buildings. When Trieste became part of Italy in 1918, the government found the city no match for ports to the south, and it declined once more.

Czech-born Sigmund Freud came to the seaside town in 1876 to write a paper on the sexual organs of the eel. The poet and ultra-nationalist Gabriele d'Annunzio launched some of his madcap escapades into Yugoslavia from this city after WWI, and in 1945 the Allies occupied Trieste pending the settlement of Italy's border disputes with Belgrade. They remained here until 1954. Today, traffic through the port is growing, although its main purpose is as an unloading point for the massive oil tankers that supply a pipeline to Austria.

Strangely attractive, although hardly strong on specific tourist sights, Trieste is an interesting spot to end an Italian tour and embark on a foray into Slovenia and Croatia.

Information

EMERGENCY
Police Station (☎ 040 379 01 11; Via Tor Bandena 6)

INTERNET ACCESS
SmileNet (☎ 040 322 02 04; internetpoint@smiletech
.it; Piazza dello Squero Vecchio 1c; €2/15 mins; ☯ 10am-
1pm & 3-9pm Mon-Fri)

LEFT LUGGAGE
Bus Station (Piazza della Libertà; ☯ 6.15am-8.30pm
Mon-Fri, 6.30am-1pm Sat & Sun)
Train Station (Piazza della Libertà; ☯ 7am-8pm)

MEDICAL SERVICES
Hospital (☎ 040 399 11 11; Piazza dell'Ospedale)

MONEY
There are currency exchange booths at the
train and bus stations and ferry terminal,
and banks abound on Corso Italia.

POST
Post Office (Piazza Vittorio Veneto 1; ☯ 8am-7pm
Mon-Sat)

TOURIST INFORMATION
Regional Tourist Office (☎ 040 36 52 48;
www.regione.fvg.it, Italian only; Via Rossini 6;
☯ 9am-1pm Mon-Fri)
Trieste Tourist Office (☎ 040 347 83 12;
www.triestetourism.it; Piazza dell'Unità d'Italia 4b;
☯ 9am-7.30pm)

Sights

COLLE DI SAN GIUSTO
With commanding views across the city
and sea, this hill is topped by a rambling
15th-century **castello** (castle grounds €1; ☯ 9am-
6pm), largely built over earlier fortifications
by the city's Venetian rulers from 1470 onwards. Apart from wandering around the
walls, you can visit the **Museo del Castello di
San Giusto** (☎ 040 30 93 62; Piazza della Cattedrale 3;
adult/child €1.50/1; ☯ 9am-1pm Tue-Sun). It houses
a small collection of arms and period paraphernalia.

The **Basilica di San Giusto**, completed in
1400, is the synthesis of two earlier Christian basilicas, and blends northern Adriatic
and Byzantine styles. The interior contains
14th-century frescoes depicting San Justus,
the town's patron saint. Down the road, the
Civico Museo di Storia ed Arte ed Orto Lapidario
(History & Art Museum & Stone Garden Art; Via della

Cattedrale 15; adult/child €1.50/1; ☯ 9am-1pm Tue &
Thu-Sun, 9am-7pm Wed) displays religious artefacts and Egyptian oddments.

To get here, take bus No 24 from the
train station. Otherwise, walk up from the
waterfront area, following Via F Venezian,
Via San Michele and Via San Giusto.

AROUND BORGO TERESIANO
Winding back down Via Capitolina, you
come to Corso Italia, the main business
thoroughfare. The area of straight boulevards to the north, known as the Borgo
Teresiano, was designed by Austrian urban
planners in the 18th century for Empress
Maria Theresa. The boat-sprinkled **Canal
Grande**, which runs through this area,
marks the northern end of the harbour.
The striking Serbian-Orthodox **Chiesa di
Santo Spiridione**, on the street of the same
name, was completed in 1868 and sports
some glittering mosaics. The eastern end
of Piazza San Antonio Nuovo is dominated
by the enormous neoclassical Catholic
Chiesa di Sant'Antonio Taumaturgo (1842).

At its western end, Corso Italia spills into
elegant **Piazza dell'Unità d'Italia**, the result of
Austrian town-planning efforts. A stroll
south brings you to the waterfront **Acquario
Marino** (☎ 040 30 62 01; Riva Nazario Sauro 1; adult/
child €3/2; ☯ 9am-7pm Tue-Sun Apr-Sep, 8.30am-
1.30pm Tue-Sun Nov-Mar). The former **fish market**
(1913), which fills the southern half of the
building, is being transformed into a state-
of-the-art exhibition space. The waterfront
ends at a **lighthouse**.

Inland is the **Roman theatre** (Via del Teatro
Romano), built under Emperor Trajan in
the 1st century AD. Baroque **Chiesa di Santa
Maria Maggiore**, next door to the minute
Romanesque **Basilica di San Silvestro**, is one
of Trieste's finest churches.

MUSEUMS
The chief museum, the **Museo Revoltella**
(☎ 040 30 09 38; Via Diaz 27; adult/child €7/5; ☯ 9am-
7pm Wed-Mon), is a contemporary art gallery.
For oriental art, head to the **Museo d'Arte Orientale** (☎ 040 322 07 36; Via San Sebastiano 1; adult/child
€3/1.50; ☯ 9am-1pm Tue & Thu-Sun, 9am-7pm Wed).

Natural history comes to life at the
Museo Civico di Storia Naturale (☎ 040 30 18 21;
Piazza Hortis 4; adult/child €3/1.50; ☯ 8.30am-1.30pm
Tue-Sun), while animal life typical to Trieste's
unusual karstic terrain (see p382) can be

TRIESTE

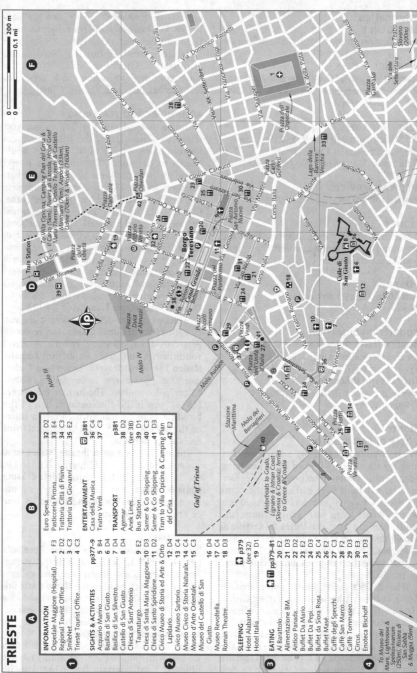

INFORMATION	
Ospedale Maggiore (Hospital)....1	F3
Regional Tourist Office...........2	D2
SmileNet.........................3	E4
Trieste Tourist Office............4	C3

SIGHTS & ACTIVITIES	pp377–9
Acquario Marino..................5	B4
Basilica di San Giusto...........6	D4
Basilica di San Silvestro........7	D4
Castello di San Giusto...........8	D4
Chiesa di Sant'Antonio	
Taumaturgo....................9	E2
Chiesa di Santa Maria Maggiore..10	D3
Chiesa di Santo Spiridione......11	D2
Civico Museo di Storia ed Arte & Orto	
Lapidario.....................12	D4
Civico Museo Sartorio...........13	C4
Museo Civico di Storia Naturale..14	C4
Museo d'Arte Orientale..........15	C3
Museo del Castello di San	
Giusto........................16	D4
Museo Revoltella................17	C4
Roman Theatre...................18	D3

SLEEPING	pp379
Hotel Alabarda............(see 32)	
Hotel Italia.....................19	D1

EATING	pp379–81
Al Barattolo.....................20	E2
Alimentazione BM................21	D3
Antico Panada...................22	D2
Buffet Da Mario.................23	D2
Buffet Da Pepi..................24	D3
Buffet da Siora Rosa............25	C4
Buffet Masé.....................26	E2
Caffè degli Specchi.............27	C3
Caffè San Marco.................28	F2
Caffè Tommaseo..................29	D3
Circus..........................30	E3
Enoteca Bischoff................31	D3

Euro Spesa......................32	D2
Pasticceria Pirona..............33	E4
Trattoria Città di Pisino.......34	C3
Trattoria Da Giovanni...........35	E2

ENTERTAINMENT	p381
Casa della Musica...............36	C4
Teatro Verdi....................37	C3

TRANSPORT	p381
Agemar.....................(see 38)	
Anek Lines......................38	D2
Bus Station.....................39	D1
Samer & Co Shipping.............40	C3
Samer & Co Shipping.............41	D3
Tram to Villa Opicina & Camping Pian	
del Grisa.....................42	E2

observed at the **Speleovivarium** (☎ 040 30 67 70; Via Guido Reni 2c; admission free; ☺ 10am-noon Sun mid-Oct–mid-Jun), a didactic science museum housed in an old air-raid shelter.

Nearby, on the waterfront in a restored wharf building (1874), is Trieste's **Museo del Mare** (Sea Museum; ☎ 040 30 49 87, Via Campo Marzio 5; adult/child €3/1.50; ☺ 9am-1pm Tue-Sun).

Tours

Trieste by Bus (adult/child €5.20/free, 2½ hours) city tours depart from in front of the train station at 2pm Saturday. Tours include a 30-minute stop at the Colle di San Giusto. The tourist office sells tickets.

The tourist office also runs thematic **walking tours** (adult/child €5.20/free, 2½ hours); advance bookings are obligatory.

Literary travellers can follow in the footsteps of James Joyce (1882–1941) with the English-language *Joyce: Triestine Itineraries* brochure, available for free at the tourist office. The Dublin-born writer lived in Trieste from 1905 to 1915, completing *A Portrait of the Artist as a Young Man* and kicking off *Ulysses* here. Fans of Trieste's rather lugubrious literary figure, Italo Svevo (1861–1928), can pick up the English-language *Svevo: Triestine Itineraries* brochure here.

Sleeping

Ask at the tourist office about 'T For You', a weekend discount deal involving many city hotels.

Ostello Tergeste (☎ 040 22 41 02; www.ostello tergeste.it; Viale Miramare 331; dm with breakfast €12, evening meal €8; reception ☺ 7am-11.30pm, check-in 1pm-11.30pm) This HI hostel by the sea, 7km northwest of town, is a stone's throw from Castello Miramare (see p382). Separate male and female dorms sport four to 20 beds. Guests must evacuate between 10am and 1pm, and curfew starts at 11.30pm.

Camping Pian del Grisa (☎ 040 21 31 42; www.piandelgrisa.it; Via Contovello 226, Opicina; person/tent/car from €4.70/3.70/2.80; Ⓟ ⛺) This large four-star site, 5km north of Trieste, has amenities galore. Bicycle enthusiasts can rent a mountain bike and seek advice on coastal itineraries. Take tram No 2 or bus No 4 from Piazza Oberdan.

Hotel Alabarda (☎ 040 63 02 69; www.hotelal abarda.it; Via Valdirivo 22; s/d with breakfast €34/49, with breakfast & bathroom €47/67; Ⓟ ▯) This

---

RISIERA DI SAN SABBA

This was once a rice-husking plant at the southern end of Trieste. In 1943 the Germans, with local Fascist help, built a crematorium here and turned it into Italy's only extermination camp. It is believed 20,000 people perished here, including 5000 of Trieste's 6000 Jews. Yugoslav partisans closed it when they liberated the city in 1945, and 20 years later it became a national monument and **museum** (☎ 040 82 62 02; Via Valmaura, Ratto della Pileria; admission free; ☺ 9am-6pm Mon-Fri & 9am-1pm Sat & Sun Apr–mid-May, 9am-1pm Tue-Sun mid-May–Oct). You can get there by bus No 10.

---

efficient and well-organised one-star hotel is on the 3rd floor of an attractive town house. Guests can access the Internet at reception.

Hotel Italia (☎ 040 36 99 00; hotelitalia@onenet.it; Via della Geppa 15; s/d low season €90/105, high season €105/125) The Italia is one of those could-be-anywhere-in-the-world places to stay, with free sweets at reception and a complimentary shower hat in the bathroom. It is conveniently close to the train station however, and is a sure bet when all you seek is a soft bed and inoffensive furnishings.

Hotel Grief Maria Theresia (☎ 040 41 01 15; Viale Miramare 109; s/d Mon-Thu €197/240, Fri-Sun €135/185; Ⓟ ✗ ▯) Polished wooden floors, exquisite rugs and various Greek-inspired busts with curly hair are part and parcel of this elegant seaside hotel, a few kilometres north along the coast. Ocean views from the roof-terrace restaurant tend to distract diners.

Eating
CAFÉS

Triestines take their coffee very seriously.

Caffè San Marco (☎ 040 36 35 38; Via Cesare Battisti 18; light lunch around €15) This café, rebuilt after WWI, is by far the most atmospheric – a favourite with students, chess players, newspaper readers and anyone in the mood for Austrian-style *kaffeeklatsch* (gossiping with friends over coffee).

Caffè Tommaseo (☎ 040 36 26 66; Riva III Novembre; 1st/2nd courses from €5.50/9.50) Languishing on the waterfront, this busy café – named after Tommaso Marcato who opened the place in 1830 – lures tourists in with a pricey-but-pleasing €20 lunch. Order a cappuccino and watch it arrive on a silver platter. Sculpted cherubs in the moulded ceiling and lots of mirrors add a Viennese feel.

Pasticceria Pirona (☎ 040 63 60 46; Largo della Barriera Vecchia 12) James Joyce sought inspiration at this cake shop and café, guaranteed to please the sweetest tooth.

Caffè degli Specchi (Piazza dell'Unità d'Italia 7; light lunch around €20) Caffè degli Specchi might well have opened its doors on the site of an old Greek café in 1839 but it still has a thing or two to learn about service – which is shockingly slow. Its prized terrace on Trieste's most regal square goes some way towards compensating.

BUFFETS
Fancy boiled meat and beer? To find out just what is in store for you and your tummy at Trieste's most traditional lunchtime haunts, see the boxed text, below. Once tried, never forgotten.

Buffet Da Pepi (☎ 040 36 68 58; Via Cassa di Risparmio 3; full meals around €10; ☺ Mon-Sat) Duck in here for the most authentic plate of boiled meat and beer in town – not recommended for those not into the smell (or sight) of meat. Various piggy cuts – tongue, trotter and intestine, to mention a few – have been cooked up here since 1897.

Buffet Da Mario (☎ 040 63 93 24; Via Torrebianca 41; 1st/2nd courses from €2.10/3.10; ☺ Mon-Sat) The menu, typed finger by finger on a manual typewriter, adds an authentic touch to this cheap buffet where you can fill up for as little as €5. The fried sardines (€5.20) and fried squid (€6.20) are lip-smacking.

Buffet Masé (☎ 040 63 94 28; Via Valdirivo 32; full meals around €10; ☺ Mon-Sat) Wash down a plate of German sausage with a huge mug of Munich lager in a Germanic atmosphere – perfect should you happen to be in Trieste on a freezing winter night.

Buffet da Siora Rosa (☎ 040 30 14 60; Piazza Hortis 3; 1st/2nd courses €4/7) Where else in Italy can you eat pasta with goulash spicy enough to make a Hungarian's hair curl? Fill up on a giant plate of gnocchi or *involtini* (light pastry filled with ham and several melted cheeses), followed by a sizzling platter of battered squid or sardines, at this friendly buffet – family-run and full of smiles!

RESTAURANTS
Al Barattolo (☎ 040 63 14 80; Piazza San Antonio Nuovo 2; pizzas from €6) This canal-side pizzeria with churchly views and a waterfront terrace is a good place to know about, especially on Sunday or mid-afternoon when most other places are closed.

Antico Panada (☎ 040 347 62 86; Via Rossini 8d; 1st/2nd courses from €6/8; ☺ Mon-Sat) Antico Panada dishes up a fantastic self-service buffet lunch for €7. Its terrace, smack-bang on the edge of the boat-filled canal, is the icing on the cake.

Trattoria Da Giovanni (☎ 040 63 93 96; Via San Lazzaro 14; full meals from €10; ☺ Mon-Sat Sep-Jul) This trattoria mixes old with new – ham legs dangling from the stark white ceiling add a dramatic touch. Dishes are traditional and generally pretty porky.

Circus (☎ 040 63 34 99; Via San Lazzaro 9b; courses €4.50; ☺ 8am-9pm Mon-Sat) 'Drinkjokecommunitypeoplefoodmusicjoyfriendlysnack' is the

---

WHERE TO FEAST ON FRIULIAN FODDER

Friulian cuisine has been influenced by many cultures but poverty has contributed the most. One typical dish, *brovada*, sees you eating turnips fermented with the dregs of pressed grapes. Otherwise, gnocchi (potato, pumpkin or bread dumplings) are popular, as are *cialzons* (a ravioli-gnocchi hybrid stuffed with everything from cheese to chocolate) or sausages and *bolliti* (boiled meats) dished up with polenta and *cren*, a rather strong horseradish. *Jota* is a thick soup of beans and sauerkraut.

Buffets (the local interpretation of a very basic Italian *osteria*) are the places to munch on all these dishes, and Trieste is particularly well endowed with them. Wines from the eastern hills of Friuli, stretching from near the city on the Slovene border up into the Alps, are considered the region's tastiest and are best sampled in a *frasca* or *locanda* (rustic, family-run wine bar).

Coffee, the finale to any Friulian feast, can be drunk *à la resentin* (coffee in a cup rinsed with grappa). A *gocciato* or *goccia* is a Triestine espresso or americano with a dash of foamed milk floating dead-centre on top. Stirring in sugar without disturbing the milk is an acquired art.

slogan of this fun-oriented café-restaurant, dressed up like a circus big top and flaunting a jazzy kind of feeling.

SELF-CATERING
Shop for basics at **Euro Spesa** (Via Valdirivo 13 & 22); fruit and veg at the daily **market** (Piazza del Ponterosso); pasta, pesto, honey and grappa at **Alimentazione BM** (Via San Nicolò 17); and wine at **Enoteca Bischoff** (☎ 040 63 14 22; Via Mazzini 21), a wine cellar dating from 1796.

Entertainment
Trieste's leading theatre and opera house is the **Teatro Verdi** (☎ 040 672 22 98; www.teatroverdi -trieste.com; Piazza Verdi 1). The Slovene side of Trieste life finds expression at the **Teatro Sloveno** (☎ 040 63 26 64; Via Petronio 4) just southeast of the centre, while the **Casa della Musica** (☎ 040 30 73 69; Via Capitelli 3) stages an eclectic mix of modern and traditional concerts/gigs.

Getting There & Away
AIR
Friuli-Venezia Giulia airport (TRS; ☎ 0481 77 32 24; www.aeroporto.fvg.it; Via Aquileia 46), also known as Ronchi dei Legionari or Trieste Airport, is 33km north of Trieste near Monfalcone. Direct flights to/from Munich, London Stansted (with no-frills airline Ryanair), Belgrade and Moscow arrive and depart from here, as well as domestic flights to/from Rome, Milan and Genoa.

BOAT
Ferries use the **Stazione Marittima** (ferry terminal; Molo del Bersaglieri 3) in town. Tickets year-round with **Anek Lines** (www.anek.gr) ferries to/from Corfu, Igoumenitsa and Patras in Greece are sold at **Agemar** (☎ 040 36 40 64; Piazza Duca degli Abruzzi 1a; deck seat one way low/high season €52/68, small car low/high season €66/98). Agemar also sells tickets for the car ferry that sails twice weekly to/from Durazzo (deck seat one way low/high season €50/65, small car low/high season €95/120).

For information and tickets for car ferries travelling to/from Pula (adult/child one way €9/4.50, two hours, five times weekly) and other towns in Croatia, go to **Samer & Co Shipping** (☎ 040 670 27 11; www .samer.com; Piazza dell'Unità d'Italia 7). It also has a **ticketing desk** (☎ 040 30 35 40; stazione.marittima @samer.com; Molo del Bersaglieri 3) located at the ferry terminal itself.

From mid-June to late September, Samer & Co also sells tickets for Adriatica motorboats along the coast to/from Grado (€6.45/12.90 one way/return, 55 minutes, one daily), Lignano (€7.25/14.45, 1¼ hours, one daily) and various points along the Istrian coast in Slovenia and Croatia. Tickets are sold at the terminal 45 minutes before departure.

BUS
National and international buses operate from the **bus station** (☎ 040 36 70 78; Via Fabio Severo 24). Services include to/from Udine (€4.30, 1¼ hours, at least hourly) and destinations in Slovenia and Croatia such as Ljubljana (€10.50, 2¾ hours, once daily Monday to Saturday), Zagreb (€11, five hours, once daily Monday to Saturday) and Dubrovnik (€55, 15 hours, once daily).

TRAIN
The **train station** (☎ 147 8 80 88; Piazza della Libertà 8) serves trains going to Gorizia (€3, 50 minutes, hourly), Udine (€5.60, 1½ hours, hourly), Venice (€10, two hours, at least hourly), Rome (€39.50, nine hours, twice daily) as well as Naples (€48.50, 12½ hours, twice daily).

Getting Around
Buses between Trieste bus station and Friuli-Venezia Giulia airport (€2.60, 50 minutes, once or twice hourly) are operated by Gorizia-based APT (Azienda Provinciale Trasporti Gorizia; see p384)

Bus No 30 connects the train station with Via Roma and the waterfront, bus No 24 goes to/from Castello di San Giusto, bus No 36 links Trieste bus station with Miramare, while Villa Opicina is served by tram No 2 or bus No 4. A single/double journey ticket costs €0.85/0.95 and a one-day ticket is available for €2.80.

Shuttle boats link the Stazione Marittima with Muggia year-round (one way/return €2.70/5, 30 minutes, six to 10 boats sail daily), and Barcola (€1.65, 20 minutes, five or six daily) and Grignano (€2.70, 55 minutes, five or six daily) from mid-April to mid-October. Transporting a bicycle on any route costs €0.55 one way. For more information, contact public transport company **Trieste Trasporti** (toll-free ☎ 800 016 675; www.trieste trasporti.it, Italian only).

AROUND TRIESTE

A short coastal trip northwest takes you to the **Riviera di Barcola**, a busy stretch of coast guarded by the **Faro della Vittorio** (☎ 040 41 04 61; Strada del Friuli 141; admission free; ☺ 3-7pm Apr-Sep, 10am-3pm Sun Oct-Mar), a lighthouse topped by a statue of Victory. The riviera's northern end, 7km north of Trieste, is crowned with **Castello Miramare** (☎ 040 22 41 43; adult/child €4/free, s/d audioguide €3.50/5; ☺ 9am-7pm Mon-Sat, 8.30am-7pm Sun Apr-Sep, 9am-6pm Mar & Oct, 9am-5pm Nov-Feb), a white castle set in 22 hectares of gardens on a rocky headland. Butterflies flutter in the greenhouses here, first established by Archduke Maximilian of Austria who had the castle built in 1855. After a brief stint as emperor of Mexico for Napoleon III, Maximilian was executed by the Mexicans in 1867. His widow Carlota, who remained at the castle, went mad.

The waters here are protected by the **Riserva Naturale Marina di Miramare** and swimming is forbidden. The reserve's **visitors centre** (☎ 040 22 41 47; www.riservamarinamiramare.it, Italian only; ☺ 10am-4.30pm Sat & Sun Sep-May, 9.30-11.30am & 2.30-4.30pm Jun-Aug), in the castle grounds, organises snorkelling and diving expeditions.

Aspiring scientists might enjoy a trip around the fascinating multimedia exhibitions at the **Science Centre Immaginario Scientifico** (☎ 040 22 44 24; www.immaginarioscientifico.it, Italian only; Riva Massimiliano e Carlotta 15; adult/child €4/3; ☺ 10am-8pm Sat & Sun Oct-May, 7-11pm Fri, 10am-9pm Sat & Sun Jun-Sep), an interactive science museum in Grignano Mare, next to Miramare. Bus No 36 links Trieste train station with Miramare and Grignano Mare (the last stop).

South along the coast, a 5km trip past Trieste's industrial outskirts (including the Illy coffee-roasting plant) and around the Baie de Muggia brings you to **Muggia** (population 13,299), a fortified fishing village with a 14th-century castle. Boats sail between Muggia and Trieste (see p381) and Slovenia is just 4km south from here.

Inland, the leggy strip of land between the coast and the Slovenian border is known as **Il Carso** (Carso Heights), a name pertaining to the geological make-up of this white calcareous tableland, potholed with caves and riddled with doline (sinkholes created when caves collapse).

Flora and fauna can be observed at close quarters at the **Carsiana Giardino Botanico** (☎ 040 22 95 73; adult/child €3/1.50; ☺ 10am-noon Tue-Fri Nov-Mar, 10am-noon Tue-Fri, 10am-1pm & 3-7pm Sat & Sun Apr-Oct) in Sgónico.

Near Villa Opicina, 5km northeast of Trieste, is the **Grotta Gigante** (☎ 040 32 73 12; adult/child €6.70/4.65; guided visits hourly 10am-noon & 2-4pm Nov-Feb, 10am-4pm Mar & Oct, every 30 minutes 10am-6pm Apr-Sep). At 107m high, 130m long and 65m wide, it is the world's largest accessible cave – the dome of St Peter's Cathedral could fit inside. Coloured globes light up the interior, accessible by 500 steps down (and up!). Take bus No 42 from Trieste's Piazza Oberdan, or tram No 2 – the scenic choice that has covered the 5.2km journey since 1902 – from the same square to Villa Opicina, then bus No 42 to the cave.

Karstic cave life can be observed at Trieste's Speleovivarium (see p379) , and local ethnographic tradition comes to life at the **Casa Carsico** (☎ 040 32 71 24; Rupingrande 31; admission free; ☺ 11am-12.30pm & 3.30-6pm Sun & holidays Apr-Nov) in **Rupingrande**, north of Villa Opicina. The plateau's most important folk festival, **Nozze Carsiche** (Karstic Wedding), is held every two years for four days at the end of August, 2km southeast of Rupingrande in a 16th-century fortress in **Monrupino**.

With the exception of Villa Opicina, you'll need your own transport to explore Il Carso.

GORIZIA

pop 37,072 / elevation 86m

That strangely un-Italian feeling common in Friuli-Venezia Giulia is no more evident than in Gorizia – bang on the frontier of the Latin and Slavic worlds, with a long history of Germanic Austrian tutelage. Most locals speak Italian and Slovenian, and road signs are in both languages. Austrian-style café culture (lots of rustling newspapers) rules and not a few of the GO licence plates are from Nova Gorica, that post-WWII creation over the border.

Only a short train or bus ride from Trieste or Udine, Gorizia is a quirky place and a stop worth making – not least from 2004 when the city's former Iron Curtain neighbour joins the European Union. The twin town of Gorizia-Nova Gorica will be the only town in the EU to be split by a manned border.

The city hosts a **jazz festival** each year in March.

History

Settled before the arrival of the Romans, the hilltop castle and surrounding town were always on the periphery of someone else's empire – Roman, Holy Roman and, from the early 16th century, that of the Austrian Habsburgs. Apart from a brief spell under Venice, Gorizia first came under Italian control after WWI. In the wake of WWII, Italy and Yugoslavia drew a line (in the form of a fence) through the city in 1947, leaving most of the old city in Italian hands, and spurring Tito's followers to erect the soulless Nova Gorica on the other side. In 1991, Gorizia became next-door neighbours to an independent Slovenia.

Even when Slovenia becomes part of the EU in 2004, the wire fence (topped with barbed-wire rolls until the 1990s) dividing the city will remain – border checkpoints and controls will continue to operate for as long as Slovenia is not party to the Schengen Convention (see p827).

Information

Cartlibreria Antonini (Via Mazzini 1316) Bookshop with maps and guides.

Post Office (cnr Corso Verdi & Via Oberdan)

Tourist Office (☎ 0481 38 62 25; giubileo11@ adriacom.it; Via Roma 5; ⏰ 9am-1pm & 3-5pm Mon-Fri)

Wash & Clean Laundrette (Via Mazzini 13b; €3/7kg; ⏰ 6am-10pm)

Borgo Castello

Gorizia's main sight is its **castle** (☎ 0481 53 51 46; Borgo Castello 58; adult/child €2.60/free, during exhibitions €4.20/free; ⏰ 9.30am-1pm & 3-7.30pm Tue-Sun Apr-Oct, 9.30am-6pm Tue-Sun Nov-Mar), the original nucleus of the town. It has undergone several transformations and was restored in the 1920s after suffering serious damage in WWI.

Beneath the main fortress, within the castle walls, is the **Museo della Grande Guerra** (☎ 0481 53 39 26; Borgo Castello 15; adult/child €3.10/ free; ⏰ 10am-7pm Tue-Sun Apr–mid-Sep, 10am-1pm & 2-7pm Tue-Sun mid-Sep–Mar), where the gory tale of WWI trench warfare is told.

Next door, the **Museo della Moda e delle Arti Applicate** (Museum of Fashion & Applied Arts; ☎ 0481 53 39 26; Borgo Castello 15; ⏰ 10am-7pm Tue-Sun Apr–mid-Sep, 10am-1pm & 2-7pm Tue-Sun mid-Sep–Mar) presents a far prettier picture. Admission to the war museum covers the fashion museum too.

THE ROUT OF CAPORETTO

The wanton spilling of young blood in the fight for centimetres of ground during WWI was not restricted to the killing fields of France and Russia. From May 1915 Italy decided to join the massacre, in the hope of ending the campaign for independence begun the century before by booting Austria off 'Italian' soil. The price of this folly, to a nation barely 50 years old, was 700,000 dead and more than a million wounded.

The main Italian front stretched from the Alps to the Adriatic Sea through Friuli and Giulia, and Italy made substantial gains in its first offensive – approaching Gorizia (which did not fall until the following year) and advancing as far as Caporetto in the north (in modern Slovenia).

From then on, typical trench warfare set in, with neither side making much progress. Some of the toughest fighting took place on the Carso plateau between Trieste and Gorizia, and the River Isonzo soon became to the Italians what the Somme was to the Allies in France.

In October 1917, disaster struck when the Austro-Hungarians (with the aid of crack German units) crushed the Italians at Caporetto, pretty much throwing them back to their 1915 starting lines, where they hung on grimly until the collapse of the Central Powers the following year. Italians don't meet their Waterloo, they 'have a Caporetto'.

Churches

The most outstanding of Gorizia's churches is **Chiesa di Sant'Ignazio** (Piazza della Vittoria), topped by onion-shaped domes (built 1654–1724). The 14th-century **Chiesa di Santo Spirito**, by the castle, is worth a peek, as is Gorizia's 18th-century **synagogue** (Via Ascoli 19; admission free; ⏰ 6pm-8pm Tue & Thu, 10am-1pm 2nd Sun of month Apr-Oct, 5pm-7pm Tue & Thu, 10am-1pm 2nd Sun of month Nov-Mar). Inside is a small exhibition dedicated to Jews in Gorizia and the Gorizian philosopher Carlo Michelstaedter (1887–1910), a 23-year-old writer who committed suicide after finishing his best-known work, *La persuasione e la rettorica* (Persuasion and Rhetoric).

Sleeping & Eating

Alla Transalpina (☎ 0481 53 02 91; Via Caprin 30; s/d from €44/68; P) This three-star hotel's unusual position, overlooking the infamous fence on one side and Nova Gorica train station on the other, makes it a fun place to stay. During special events, such as Gorizia's annual marathon, a couple of panels are removed from the fence here, allowing all and sundry to freely pass from one side to the other.

Cafés are plentiful on Corso Italia, the main street in the new part of town, while the old-town streets below the castle and around the covered **food market** (Via Verdi 30) are the best places to hunt down trattorie.

Caffè Morocco (☎ 0481 53 36 11; Corso Italia 106) Espresso-shooting locals cram the bar at this stylish and busy café that's decked out in glitzy Moroccan style. Sip a fruit tea or fruity cocktail and contemplate the icicle lights that drip from the blood-red ceiling. House music reigns Friday and Saturday evening.

Alla Luna (☎ 0481 53 03 74; Via Oberdan 13; full meals around €20; ⏰ Tue-Sun) Original ceramic tiles on the walls, a beamed ceiling and knick-knacks galore add a rustic touch to this historic trattoria, dating from 1876 and run by the same family for the last 40 years. The cushioned window seats are particularly cosy, and the choice of cold meat and cheese platters absolutely irresistible.

Getting There & Away

From the **bus station** (Via IX Agosto), off Corso Italia, buses operated by **Azienda Provinciale Trasporti Gorizia** (APT; toll-free ☎ 800 95 59 57; www.aptgorizia.it, Italian only) run to Nova Gorica, from where you can get buses to all over Slovenia. Check with the bus driver which border crossing he intends to make before hopping aboard – foreigners are only allowed to cross (on foot or by car) at the international Casa Rossa border crossing. Other bus services include to/from Aquileia (€3.05, two hours, six daily), Friuli-Venezia Giulia airport (€2.10, 35 minutes, 10 daily), Grado (€4.35, three hours, seven daily) and Palmanova (€2.60, 2½ hours, up to eight daily).

The **train station** (Piazzale Martiri Libertà d'Italia), about 1km southwest of the centre at the end of Corso Italia, has regular connections to/from Udine (€2.60, 30 minutes, at least hourly) and Trieste (€3.05, 50 minutes, hourly).

AROUND GORIZIA

The **Collio hills** around Gorizia produce some of Italy's finest white wines – among the

first in Italy to be awarded a *denominazione di origine controllata* (DOC; controlled origin denomination) in 1968 (see p71). The tourist office in Gorizia has a list of cellars where you can taste, buy and drink the local vintage.

More sobering are the monuments to WWI soldiers, built here during the 1930s. The remains of 57,200 soldiers who died during WWI rest inside the **Sacrario di Oslavia** (⏰ 8am-noon & 2-4.45pm Oct-Mar, 9am-12.30pm & 2.30-4.45pm Apr-Sep), 5km north of Gorizia.

The **Redipuglia Memorial**, beside the S305 near Redipuglia, 15km south of Gorizia, shelters the remains of 100,000 soldiers from the Italian Third Army. An on-site **museum** (☎ 0481 48 90 24; admission free; ⏰ 8.15am-12.15pm & 2-5.10pm Wed-Mon Oct-Mar, 8.30am-12.30pm & 2.30-5.45pm Wed-Mon Apr-Sep) relates the history of the Great War and there are fortified trenches and other warfare remnants to be seen at the foot of the monstrous 22-tier hillside memorial. Originally built on a much smaller scale next to the museum, the memorial was not deemed pompous enough by Mussolini who had the entire thing rebuilt (and 100,000 soldiers' remains shifted across the street) in 1937.

The area is sprinkled with other monuments, including one atop **Monte di San Michele**, 10km south of Gorizia near San Martino del Carso, the scene of particularly bloody encounters (you can wander through the battlefield today).

APT buses link Gorizia and Oslavia, and Redipuglia can be reached by train from Gorizia (€1.80, 15 minutes, at least hourly).

PALMANOVA

pop 5380 / elevation 26m

If you flew over it, you'd see what makes this town so special. Built 10km north of Aquileia in 1593 by the Venetians, Palmanova is a fortress in the form of a nine-pointed star – a fact that is hard to see once inside. Napoleon and the Austrians made later use of it, and to this day the Italian army maintains a garrison here.

From the hexagonal **Piazza Grande**, which sits at the centre of the star, six roads radiate out through the old town to the defensive walls, the city's real attraction. Head along one of the spokes, Borgo Udine, to uncover local history in the **Civico Museo Storico** (☎ 0432 92 91 06; propalma@libero.it; Borgo Udine 4; adult/child €1.05/0.50; ☯ 9.30am-12.30pm Thu-Tue), inside the Palazzo Trevisan. The museum also acts as a tourist office and has the lowdown on secret tunnel tours that wind beneath the city walls.

Military fiends should quick-march to the **Museo Storico Militare** (☎ 0432 92 35 35; Borgo Cividale Dongione di Porta Cividale; admission free; ☯ 9am-noon & 2-4pm Tue-Sat, 9am-noon Sun winter, 9am-noon & 4pm-6pm Tue-Sat, 9am-noon Sun summer) inside the Porta Cividale, one of three monumental entrances to the fortified town. The military museum traces the history of troops stationed in Palmanova from 1593 through to WWII.

The family-owned **Albergo Ristorante Roma Hotel** (☎ 0432 92 84 72; www.hotelromapalmanova.it; Borgo Cividale 27; s/d/tr with breakfast €36/52/66) is the only hotel fortunate enough to sit within the city walls.

Cafés stud central Piazza Grande, including **Caffè Torinese** (Piazza Grande 9; ☯ 7am-2am Thu-Tue) which cooks up some succulent salads and *panini* (bread roll with filling), as well as cheese and ham platters (€8), to be enjoyed with some local wine.

Palmanova is a bus ride from Gorizia, Udine and Aquileia.

AQUILEIA
pop 3351

Once the fourth city of the Roman Empire, Aquileia was founded in 181 BC. Within 100 years the city, dubbed the Second Rome, had become a major trading link between the imperial capital and the East. By the beginning of the Christian era, Aquileia was Italy's richest market town and subordinate only to Rome, Milan and Capua. A patriarchate was founded here as early as AD 4 and, in spite of repeated assaults by Huns, Lombards and others, Aquileia's religious importance ensured it a privileged position until as late as the 14th century.

Now comparably a tiny town – with Europe's largest Paleo-Christian mosaic floor – Aquileia lies at the eastern end of the Venetian plains. Guided tours of its extraordinary Roman sights are organised by the **tourist office** (☎ 0431 91 94 91; www.aquileiaturismo.info, Italian only; Piazza Capitolo 4; ☯ 9am-2.30pm Mon-Sat).

Sights

Head straight for the Latin cross-shaped **basilica** (Piazza Capitolo; admission free; ☯ 8.30am-6.30pm Mon-Sat, 8.30-10.30am & 11.15am-6.30pm Sun), rebuilt after the 1348 earthquake. Transparent walkways allow visitors to walk above the long-hidden 760-sq-m floor of the basilica's 4th-century predecessor – a precious and rare mosaic pictorial document of Christianity's early days, depicting episodes in Christ's life, Roman notables and animal scenes. Equally remarkable treasures fill the basilica's two crypts. The 9th-century **Cripta degli Affreschi** (Crypt of Frescoes; admission includes both crypts adult/child €2.60/free) boasts 12th-century frescoes depicting the heroics and tragic ends of martyrs, while the **Cripta degli Scavi** (Excavations Crypt) reveals 1st-century mosaics from a Roman house, a later 3rd-century mosaic, and the remains of a mosaic church floor from the 5th century. The basilica's 73m-tall **bell tower** (adult/child €1.10/0.55; ☯ 9.30am-12.30pm & 2.30-5pm Mon-Sat, 9.30am-1pm & 2.30-6pm Sun) was built in 1030 from stones from the old Roman amphitheatre. Sunday mass is celebrated in the basilica at 10.30am.

Scattered remnants of the **Roman town** include ruins of the one-time river port, houses, markets and the forum on Via Giulia Augusta. Hundreds of finds are displayed in the **Museo Archeologico Nazionale** (☎ 0431 9 10 16; Via Roma 1; adult/child €4/free; ☯ 8.30am-2pm Mon, 8.30am-7.30pm Tue-Sun).

Sleeping & Eating

Local chefs cook up Roman-inspired dishes during Aquileia's annual **Roman food festival**; ask at the tourist office for what's cooking where.

Ostello Domus Augusta (☎ 0431 9 10 24; www.ostelloaquileia.it; Via Roma 25; dm/d/tr with breakfast €13/34/46.50; reception ☯ 7.30am-12.30pm & 2-11.30pm, lock-out 10am-2pm; ☲) This gleaming new hostel is a real gem. Dorms sleep two to six people. There's a small garden out front where guests can lounge during the daily lock-out. Internet access costs €4 per hour and bicycle rental costs €2/8 for one/eight hours.

Camping Aquileia (☎ 0431 91 95 83; www.campingaquileia.it; Via Gemina 10; person/tent & car low season €4.20/6.50, high season €6/9; ☯ mid-May–mid-Sep; ℗) One of the most affordable camp sites in the area, Camping Aquileia is north of the centre near the river-port docks. It also rents three- and four-bed bungalows with kitchenette.

Hotel Restaurant Patriarchi (☎ 0431 91 95 95; www.hotelpatriarchi.it; Via Giulia Augusta 12; s/d €44/72.50; restaurant 🕑 Thu-Tue; **P**) This kitsch three-star choice is a stone's throw from the basilica and is as good as you'll get in small-town Aquileia. Its wine cellar is well stocked and the chef is a dab hand at fish dishes.

Getting There & Away
SAF buses link Aquileia with Grado (€1.35, 15 minutes, at least hourly), Palmanova (€1.75, 30 minutes, up to eight daily) and Udine (€2.55, 1¼ hours, up to eight daily). Daily buses to/from Gorizia (€3.05, two hours, six daily) are handled by Gorizia-based APT (see p384).

GRADO
pop 8926

Grado, 14km south of Aquileia, is your quintessential Adriatic beach resort, spread along a narrow island backed by lagoons. The small medieval centre, crisscrossed by narrow *calli* (lanes), is dominated by the Romanesque **Basilica di Sant'Eufemia** (Campo dei Parriarchi) and the nearby remains of a 4th- to 5th-century church **mosaic** (Piazza Biagio Marin). The beachfront – all the rage after Habsburg emperor Francis Joseph's visit in 1892 – is encrusted with *belle epoque* mansions, beach huts and thermal baths. From October to April the place is dead.

Small *casoni* (reed huts), built for fishermen during winter, dot the tiny islands surrounding Grado. In summer some can be visited by boat (2½ hours, adult/child €15/8); the **tourist office** (☎ 0431 87 71 11; www.gradoturismo.info, Italian only; Viale Dante Alighieri 72; 🕑 8.30am-1pm & 2.30-5pm Mon-Thu, 8.30am-1pm Fri) has details. Many of the islands are protected nature reserves and off limits to tourists.

Riserva Naturale Regionale della Valle Cavanata protects a 1920s fish-farming area and extraordinary birdlife in the eastern part of the lagoon. Further east, the final 15km-stretch of the River Isonzo's journey into the Adriatic flows through the **Riserva Naturale Regionale Foce dell'Isonzo**, a 2350-hectare nature reserve where visitors can bird-watch or horse-ride, cycle and walk around salt marshes and mud flats. Reserve

passes are sold at the **visitors centre** (adult/child €3/2; 🕑 9am-sunset Fri-Wed) in Isola della Cona.

Each year on the first Sunday in July a votive procession, with a statue of the Virgin Mary aboard, sails from Grado to the **Santuario di Barbana** (☎ 0431 8 04 53), an 8th-century church on an island 5km east. Grado fishermen have done this since 1237 when the Madonna of Barbana saved their town from the plague. Boats link the sanctuary with Grado (adult/child return €4/2.50, three to eight times daily from April to October, twice daily Sunday from November to March).

Sleeping & Eating
Albergo Alla Spiaggia (☎ 0431 8 48 41; www.alberg oallaspiaggia.it; Via Mazzini 2; s/d €59/108, half/full board per person from €63/68; 🕑 Apr-Oct; **P** 🐕) This late-1920s Art Deco hotel sports a quintessential seaside facade – sparkling white bar and blue tables and chairs adorning each balcony. It sits bang on the seafront and has a lovely garden out back.

Hotel Ville Bianchi (☎ 0431 8 01 69; www .villebianchi.it, Italian only; Viale Dante Alighieri 50; d full board per person low/high season €100/114; 🕑 Apr-Oct; **P** 🐕) Half-board yields such a small discount that you may as well go the whole hog at Grado's most historic hotel, dating from 1900. Look for the stunning white and gold mansion on the seashore.

Agli Artisti (☎ 0431 8 30 81; Campiello Porta Grande 2; 1st course €6.20, 2nd course €5-11; 🕑 Wed-Sun) On the old-town fringe, this pretty little spot cooks up seasonal market goodies, including asparagus-inspired dishes in season. Its terrace, strung with lamps beneath a pergola, is a highlight.

Getting There & Away
Grado is served by regular buses to/from Aquileia (€1.35, 15 minutes, at least hourly) and Udine (€3, 1¼ hours, 12 daily).

LAGUNA DI MARANO
The Marano Lagoon sprawls, in all its natural grandeur, immediately west of the Laguna di Grado. Frequented more by birdlife than human life, this wet spot is accessible by just a couple of gravel roads.

Pretty little **Marano Lagunare** (population 2100), a Roman fishing port later fortified, is the only settlement on the lagoon shore and a perfect hideaway. Peace and quiet is ensured by two nature reserves – the 1377-hectare **Riserva Naturale della Foci dello Stella**, which protects the marshy mouth of the River Stella, and the **Riserva Naturale della Valle Canal Nuovo**, a 121-hectare reserve in a former fishing valley. Bird-watching is the main activity at the **visitors centre** (☎ 0431 675 51; Via delle Valli 2), shared by the two reserves in a traditional fisherman's reed hut.

LIGNANO

The Lignano area is pure resort. Lying on the tip of a peninsula facing Laguna di Marano to the north and the Adriatic Sea to the south, **Lignano Sabbiadoro** (population 6543) sits at the northern head of three adjoining resorts. **Lignano Pineta,** 1km south, went up in the 1950s, while **Lignano Riviera**, the newest of the three at the mouth of the River Tagliamento, is marketed as the most nature-friendly.

The water, fronted by 8km of sandy beach, is the main attraction. Every imaginable water sport is available and there are a couple of funfairs, a zoo, water amusement parks and the Disney-style **Gulliverlandia** (☎ 0431 42 31 33; Lignano Sabbiadoro; adult/child low season €11/9, high season €13/10; ☺ 10am-6pm May–mid-Jul & Sep, 10am-11pm mid-Jul–Aug) to entertain kids.

The tourist offices in **Sabbiadoro** (☎ 0431 7 18 21; www.aptlignano.it; Via Latisana 42) and **Pineta** (☎ 0431 42 21 69; Via dei Pini 53; ☺ Jun-Sep) can help with reservations.

Lignano Sabbiadoro is linked by bus to Udine (€4.30, 1½ hours, nine to 11 daily).

UDINE

pop 95,320 / elevation 114m

The region's second-largest city, Udine has a topsy-turvy history that has left it heir to an odd mix of Italian, Slavic and Germanic culture. Some inhabitants still speak the local dialect, as dual street names (in dialect and Italian) testify.

The Romans founded Udine as a way-station. By the early 15th century, when it first came under Venetian control, Udine had grown into a city to rival nearby Cividale del Friuli and Aquileia. Napoleon's lieutenants briefly took control at the beginning of the 19th century, followed by the Austrians, until 1866 when the city joined the Italian kingdom. Udine survived WWII intact, but an earthquake in 1976 caused heavy damage and cost hundreds of lives –

see the boxed text, p391. The great Renaissance painter Giambattista Tiepolo lived here for many years, leaving a number of works behind.

Information

BOOKSHOPS

Libraria Carducci (Piazza XX Settembre 24; ☺ Mon-Sat) This bookshop stocks travel guides, as well as road and walking maps

EMERGENCY

Police Station (☎ 0432 59 41 11; Via della Prefettura 16)

INTERNET ACCESS

Internet Play (Via San Francesco d'Assisi 33; €4/hr; ☺ 9.30am-1pm & 3pm-midnight Mon-Fri, 9.30am-1pm & 3-8pm Sat, 3.30-7.30pm Sun)

MEDICAL SERVICES

Hospital (☎ 0432 55 21; Piazza Santa Maria della Misericordia 15) 2km north of the centre

MONEY

There is a bank and ATM opposite the train station at the southern foot of Via Roma, and plenty more on and around Piazza del Duomo.

POST

Main Post Office (Via Vittorio Veneto 42; ☺ 8.30am-7pm Mon-Sat)
Branch Post Office (Via Roma 25; ☺ 8.30am-2pm Mon-Fri, 8.30am-1pm Sat)

TOURIST INFORMATION

Tourist Office (☎ 0432 29 59 72; arpt1.ud@adria com.it; Piazza I Maggio 7; ☺ 9am-1pm & 3-5pm Mon-Fri, 9am-1pm & 3-6pm Sat)

Sights

PIAZZA DELLA LIBERTÀ & AROUND

A gem of the Renaissance, Piazza della Libertà lies at Udine's old-town heart. The 15th-century **Palazzo del Comune** (town hall), also known as the Loggia del Lionello after its architect, is a clear reminder of Venetian influence, as is the **Loggia di San Giovanni** opposite, which features a clock with Moorish figures that strike the hours.

The **Arco Bollani** (Bollani Arch), next to the Loggia di San Giovanni, was designed by Palladio in 1556 and leads up to the castle used by the Venetian governors. The **castle** (built in the mid-16th century after an

UDINE

0	500 m
0	0.3 mi

A **B** **C** **D**

INFORMATION
Internet Play......................................1 D4
Libraria Carducci...............................2 B4
Tourist Office....................................3 C4

SIGHTS & ACTIVITIES pp387–9
Arco Bollani.....................................4 B4
Castle...(see 4)
Cathedral...5 C4
Chiesa di San Francesco......................6 B5
Chiesa di Santa Maria del Castello.......7 C4
Galleria d'Arte Antica......................(see 4)
Galleria d'Arte Moderna.....................8 A2
Loggia di San Giovanni.......................9 B4

Museo Archeologico........................(see 4)
Oratorio della Purità........................10 D4
Palazzo del Comune
 (Loggia del Lionello)......................11 B4
Palazzo Patriarcale..........................12 C4

SLEEPING p389
Astoria Hotel Italia..........................13 B4
Hotel Europa..................................14 C5
Hotel Principe.................................15 C5

EATING pp389–90
Al Tutto Buono................................16 C5
Caffè Contarena..............................17 B4

Dimeglio Supermercato......................18 B4
Démar Caffè....................................19 B4
La Ciacarade..................................20 D4
Osteria con Cucina Sbarco dei Pirati..21 B3
Pane Vino e San Daniele 22 B4

DRINKING p390
Osteria al Barnabiti.........................23 B5
Pinocchio.......................................24 B4
Speziaria Pei Sani............................25 B4
Taverna dell'Angelo.........................26 D4

TRANSPORT p390
Bus Station....................................27 C5

earthquake in 1511 destroyed the previous castle) now houses the **Galleria d'Arte Antica** (☎ 0432 50 28 72; adult/child €2.60/1.80, admission free Sun am; 🕙 9.30am-12.30pm & 3-6pm Tue-Sun), with works by Caravaggio, Carpaccio and Tiepolo. Admission includes a visit to the **Museo Archeologico** (Archaeological Museum), also in the castle. The 12th-century **Chiesa di Santa Maria del Castello** on the hill used to stand within the medieval castle walls.

CATHEDRAL & AROUND
Heading south from Piazza della Libertà down Via Vittorio Veneto, you reach Piazza del Duomo and Udine's 13th-century Romanesque-Gothic **cathedral**, with several frescoes by Tiepolo displayed in the **Museo de Duomo** (☎ 0432 50 68 30; admission free; 🕙 9am-noon & 3pm-6pm Tue-Sun). Across the street is the **Oratorio della Purità**, with a beautiful ceiling painting of the Assumption by Tiepolo. Ask in the cathedral for a guided tour (free) of the oratory.

Northeast is the **Palazzo Patriarcale** (Patriarchal Palace; ☎ 0432 2 50 03; Piazza Patriarcato 1; admission €4/3; 🕙 10am-noon & 3.30-6.30pm Wed-Sun) where Tiepolo completed a remarkable series of frescoes in 1726 depicting Old Testament scenes.

South of Piazza del Duomo sits the 13th-century **Chiesa di San Francesco** (Largo Ospedale Vecchio; adult/child €5/3.50; exhibitions 🕙 9am-noon & 3.30-7pm Tue-Sun). Although once one of Udine's most striking churches, it is now used as a gallery and open only when exhibitions are on.

GALLERIA D'ARTE MODERNA
Udine's **Modern Art Gallery** (☎ 0432 29 58 91; Piazzale Paolo Diacono 22; adult/child €2.60/1.80; 🕙 9.30am-12.30pm & 3-6pm Tue-Sat, 9.30am-12.30pm Sun), just north of the centre, was established in 1885 after a rich Udinese merchant died and left his estate to the city. It features well-known 20th-century works by modern Friulian artists.

Sleeping
Those seeking farmhouse accommodation around Udine should contact the **Agriturismo del Friuli Venezia-Giulia** (☎ 0432 20 26 46; www.agriturismofvg.com; Via Gorghi 27).

Hotel Principe (☎ 0432 50 60 00; www.principe -hotel.it; Viale Europa Unita 51; s/d/tr Mon-Fri €69/99/119, Sat & Sun €59/79/99; P 🛠 🖳) Set back off the

road in a courtyard, Principe is a quiet and friendly 26-room option.

Hotel Europa (☎ 0432 29 44 46; fax 0432 51 26 54; Viale Europa Unita 47; s/d with breakfast from €44/68; P 🛠) This old-world place sits cheek-to-cheek with Hotel Principe.

Astoria Hotel Italia (☎ 0432 50 59 51; www.hotel astoria.udine.it; Piazza XX Settembre 24; s/d with breakfast Mon-Thu €126/184, Fri-Sun €86/108; P 🛠) This solid mid-range choice is the type of place local Rotarians would pick for their club meetings. Three-star comforts ensure no complaints are warranted.

Eating
Several open-air cafés and restaurants dot Piazza Matteotti and the surrounding pedestrian streets. Don't wait too late to eat out, as the city starts closing down for the night around 10pm.

Caffè Contarena (☎ 0432 51 27 41; Via Cavour 11; 🕙 Mon-Sat) An Art Deco interior offset by a wooden ceiling and weathered leather chairs lures a mixed Udinese crowd to this stunning café beneath the porticoes of Palazzo d'Aronco on Piazza della Libertà. An *enoteca* (wine bar) with knowledgeable staff adjoins the café and occasional live music entertains punters.

Démar Caffè (☎ 0432 50 40 80; Via Rialto 5; 🕙 Mon-Sat) Démar's minimalist and contemporary decor attracts a trendy crowd. The giant coffee beans on the walls add a comic touch to this predominantly coffee-and-cake place.

Osteria con Cucina Sbarco dei Pirati (☎ 0432 2 13 30; Riva Bartolini 12; full meals around €15) It might appear to be just another bar, but step inside and you emerge on a delightful wooden terrace above a stream, crammed with knick-knacks from another era.

La Ciacarade (☎ 0432 51 02 50; Via San Francesco d'Assisi 6; full meals around €20; 🕙 Mon-Fri) Ham hunks hung above the bar and giant bowls of fresh strawberries, cherries and other seasonal fruits entice diners into this authentic trattoria. Wash down a hearty meal with wine from the region.

Pane Vino e San Daniele (☎ 0432 29 99 34; Piazzetta Lionello 12; 1st/2nd courses from €6.50/11, monster-sized salads from €7) Bread, wine and the prosciutto from San Daniele (see pp390–1) make this an authentic lunch spot. Better still, its vast pavement terrace overlooking Palazzo d'Aronco buzzes on sunny days.

Bands set the joint jiving Friday and Saturday evening.

SELF-CATERING

Self-caterers can buy run-of-the-mill foodstuffs at **Dimeglio Supermercato** (Via Bonaldo Stringher) and regional cheese, meat and ready-made dishes from delicatessen **Al Tutto Buono** (☎ 0432 50 42 70; Via Roma 56).

Drinking

Pinocchio (Via Lovaria 3a; ☺ 8am-3pm & 6pm-2am Tue-Sat) Hip Pinocchio is a blues café and music bar with sprawling bar, low lights and thumping music.

Taverna dell'Angelo (Via Lovaria 3c; ☺ noon-3pm & 6pm-2am Mon-Fri, 6pm-2am Sat) Characterful Angelo pulls pints in this more traditional setting.

Speziaria Pei Sani (☎ 0432 50 50 51; Via Poscolle 13; ☺ 10am-9pm Mon-Sat) Walls are bottle-lined with wine after wine and grappa after grappa at this superb wine bar. Sit on the pavement terrace outside and taste the best of Friuli.

Osteria al Barnabiti (☎ 338 393 62 14; Piazza Garibaldi; ☺ Mon-Sat) Rough-cut around the edges it might be, but this typical *osteria* (wine bar) offers wine drinkers the quintessential drinking experience, day or night.

Getting There & Away

From the **bus station** (☎ 0432 50 69 41; Viale Europa Unita 31) services operated by **SAF** (toll-free ☎ 800 91 53 03, ☎ 0432 60 81 11; www.saf.ud.it) go to/from Trieste (€4.30, 1¼ hours, hourly), Aquileia (€2.55, 1¼ hours, up to eight daily), Lignano Sabbiadoro (€4.30, 1½ hours, nine to 11 daily) and Grado (€3, 1¼ hours, 12 daily). Buses also link Udine and Friuli-Venezia Giulia airport (€3.05, one hour, hourly).

Udine is on the main Trieste–Venice train line and services are regular in both directions.

VILLA MANIN

True contemporary art lovers will adore the exhibitions at **Villa Manin** (☎ 0432 90 47 21; wwww.villamanin.com; Piazzale Manin 10; adult/child €8/5; museum ☺ 9am-12.30pm & 3-6pm Tue-Sun, park ☺ 9am-5pm Tue-Fri, 9am-6pm Sat & Sun Easter-Oct), a villa in Passariano, 30km southwest of Udine. Home to the wealthy Manin family from the 1600s until as late as the 1990s

(when the last count died heirless), the vast mansion is surrounded by 19 hectares of manicured gardens. A victorious Napoleon Bonaparte turned it into his headquarters in 1797 and it was here that the Treaty of Campoformido (1797), that saw the Venetian empire swallowed up by the Habsburgs, was signed. Exhibition opening hours and admission fees vary, so call in advance.

CIVIDALE DEL FRIULI

pop 11,375 / elevation 138m

Lucky Cividale del Friuli, with its small medieval centre, has survived several devastating earthquakes. The town was founded by Julius Caesar in 50 BC and in AD 6 it became the seat of the first Lombard duchy.

Cividale, 15km northeast of Udine, is most picturesque where the 15th-century **Ponte del Diavolo** (Devil's Bridge), rebuilt in 1918, crosses the emerald-green River Natisone. Legend says the devil himself threw the 22m-high stone bridge into the river.

Walk through the cobbled lanes to the **Tempietto Longobardo** (Longobardo Temple; Borgo Brossano; adult/child €2/1; ☺ 10am-1pm & 3.30-5.30pm). Also known as the Oratorio di Santa Maria in Valle, this temple is an exquisite example of Lombard artwork. To the west, the 16th-century **cathedral** (Piazza del Duomo) houses the **Museo Cristiano** (Christian Museum; ☎ 0432 73 11 44; admission free; ☺ 9.30am-noon & 3-6pm Mon-Sat, 3-6pm Sun). Inside, the Altar of Ratchis is a magnificent example of 8th-century Lombard sculpture.

The **tourist office** (☎ 0432 73 14 61; arpt_cividale@regione.fvg.it; Corso Paolino d'Aquileia 10; ☺ 9am-1pm & 3-5pm Mon-Fri), near the Devil's Bridge, has plenty of information on walks around Cividale.

Trains connect Cividale with Udine (€1.50, 15 minutes, at least hourly) and Trieste (€3.60, 1½ hours, up to eight daily).

SAN DANIELE DEL FRIULI

pop 7750

So exquisitely sweet it practically melts in your mouth, *prosciutto San Daniele* is raw ham sliced off the hind leg of a slaughtered black pig and salted and cured for 12 to 18 months. Locals from San Daniele, the village from which it originates, 20km northwest of Udine, parade down the streets disguised as hams in August during the **Aria di Festa**, a four-day annual festival held to celebrate their world-famous ham. Almost 15% of all prosciutto consumed in Italy is from San Daniele.

A visit here is best suited to the culinary minded. There are no less than 27 *prosciuttifici* in the village, although the most you'll get to see of these large industrial ham-curing plants is a 30-minute tour of the curing room where the hams are hung to air. The **tourist office** (☎ 0432 94 07 65; www.infosandaniele.com; Via Roma 3; ☒ 9.30am-12.30pm Wed-Sat) has a list of *prosciuttifici* which accept visits; advance reservations are obligatory.

Touring the village's dozen or so *prosciutterie* (places to eat ham) is great fun; again, the tourist office has a list. For a light lunch of San Daniele wrapped around *grissini* (bread sticks), a San Daniele-filled sandwich or a no-frills platter of the wafer-thin sliced ham, look no further than **Bar Municipio** (☎ 0432 95 50 12; Via Garibaldi 21; ☒ Sun-Fri), a simple bar with tables and a fun-loving patron. **La Tavernaccia** (☎ 0432 94 16 94; Via Umberto I 18; ☒ Tue-Sun) is an upmarket choice. Prosciutto to eat on the move is sold at

Bottega del Prosciutto (☎ 0432 95 70 43; Via Umberto I 2), a divine delicatessen where you can also buy regional cheese and wine.

Gourmets will need their own wheels to get to San Daniele. Three cycling itineraries (each 22km) lead cyclists through the hills around the village.

IL CARNIA

North of Udine's earthquake zone, the lowlands give way to Alpine country on the way to Austria. Known generically as Il Carnia, after the people who settled here in around the 4th century BC, the region's attractions are walking, cycling and skiing.

The eastern half is characterised by forbidding and rocky bluffs along the valley to **Tarvisio** (population 5240, elevation 754m), an alpine walking and skiing resort 7km short of the Austrian border and 11km from Slovenia, also known for its Saturday market.

You can **ski** around Tarvisio but most Friuli-Venezia Giulia resorts lie in Il Carnia's more attractive, verdant western half. In a rough curve from west to east, names

---

THE EPICENTRE OF AN EARTHQUAKE

Somewhat surreal it might be, but a night spent in **Venzone** (population 2306) – one of a cluster of villages in Il Gemonese, a little-known pocket of land 30km north of Udine in the Tagliamento valley – is tantamount to a night spent in the epicentre of an earthquake.

On 6 May 1976 an earthquake measuring 6.5 on the Richter scale ripped through the village, a former Roman settlement with a medieval centre sufficiently prized to be declared a national monument in 1965. The strongest seismic shockwave lasted more than 90 seconds, killing 989 people and injuring another 3000 across an area of 5000 sq km in northern Friuli. For Venzone, at the centre of the quake, the final blow came on 15 September 1976 when a second earthquake struck. The second blast, 6.1 on the Richter scale, demolished what little remained of the shell-shocked village. That same year the village of rubble was re-declared an historic national monument.

With the exception of a ruined church on Via Alberton del Colle, which stands as a memorial to the 42 Venzone villagers who died, medieval Venzone has since been rebuilt stone by stone. Two churches, the city walls, gates and dozens of quaint town houses – such as the one housing the **tourist office** (☎ 0432 98 50 34; Via Glizoio di Mels 5/4; ☒ Apr-Sep) – have all been raised from the rubble.

The surrounding villages of **Trasaghis** (population 2550) and **Gemona del Friuli** (population 11,137) were also destroyed by the 1976 earthquakes. In **Gemona** (tourist office ☎ 0432 98 14 41; Piazza del Municipio 5; ☒ Apr-Sep) stubs of the outer walls and the steps leading up to the altar are all that remain of the once-stunning 15th-century **Chiesa di Santa Maria** (Via Cavour). Neighbouring **Bordano** (population 811), another victim, has since reinvented itself as one of Europe's largest butterfly centres. Some 1500 butterfly species (500 of which are nocturnal) flutter around **Monte San Simeone** (1505m), while in town, tropical butterflies are bred at the **Casa delle Farfalle** (☎ 0432 98 81 35; www.casaperlefarfalle.it; Via Canada 1; adult/child €6.50/3.50; ☒ 9.30am-12.30pm & 2-4pm Mar & Oct, 9.30am-12.30pm & 2-5.30pm Apr-Sep).

to watch out for include Piancavallo, Forni di Sopra, Ravascletto-Zoncolan and Sella Nevea. Downhill pistes best suited to beginners and intermediates start at 1700m.

Most towns have a couple of hotels; Udine's tourist office has a list (see p387). Those intent on **walking**, **cycling** or **biking** in the region should also pick up itinerary information there. Alternatively, contact the tourist offices in **Barcis** (☎ 0427 76 30 00; Piazza V Emanuele II 5), **Forni di Sopra** (☎ 0433 88 67 67; Via Cadore 1), **Piancavallo** (☎ 0434 65 51 91; Piazzale della Puppa) or **Tarvisio** (☎ 0428 21 35; www.tarvisiano.org; Via Roma 10).

Tarvisio is connected by train to Udine (€6.20, 1¾ hours, up to 10 daily).

Emilia-Romagna & San Marino

CONTENTS

The geography's simple: Emilia to the west, Romagna to the east and Bologna, the region's biggest town, bang in the middle.

Emilia-Romagna's architectural riches are mostly of the Renaissance. Its past is a family history: the Farnese in Parma and Piacenza, the Este in Ferrara and Modena, the Bentivoglio in Bologna, each leaving its legacy in stone and brick and patronising the finest artists of the day. In much earlier times, Ravenna, its breathtaking mosaics rivalled only by those of Istanbul, was capital of the Byzantine Empire's western regions.

Bologna, the regional capital, was one of Europe's most important medieval cities; its university is the continent's oldest and turned out the likes of Copernicus and Dante. Bologna is also Italy's food capital, drawing on fresh produce from the fertile Po valley and adding tortellini and lasagne to the Italian table and international cooking vocabulary. From Bologna you can make day trips to Ferrara, Modena and Parma, all once important Renaissance towns. Rimini, with its beaches and summer nightlife, is one of Italy's premier sun spots, while the tiny republic of San Marino, invaded daily by tourist armies, offers fine hilltop views.

Communications are excellent. Bologna is served by the A1 autostrada, sweeping south to Tuscany and north to the Veneto, and by the east-west Via Emilia (S9). Running in parallel to the Via Emilia is an efficient train line and, for much of its length, autostrada.

HIGHLIGHTS

- **Seeing Red**

  Bologna's magnificent red-brick monuments and over 40km of elegant arcades (p398)

- **Mighty Mosaics**

  Ravenna's shimmering early-Christian mosaics such as those found in the Basilica di San Vitale (p424)

- **Dream On**

  Galleria Ferrari's grand prix–winning racing cars in Maranello (p408)

- **Romanesque Splendour**

  The stone carvings of Modena's cathedral (p405)

- **The Big Cheese**

  Parmesan cheese factories (p412)

- **Culture Clash**

  Bologna's extensive arts programme (pp400–1)

Parma ★   ★ Modena   Maranello ★   ★ Bologna   Ravenna ★

POPULATION:	■ EMILIA-ROMAGNA 4 MILLION	■ SAN MARINO 27,730
AREA:	■ EMILIA-ROMAGNA 22,121 SQ KM	■ SAN MARINO 61 SQ KM

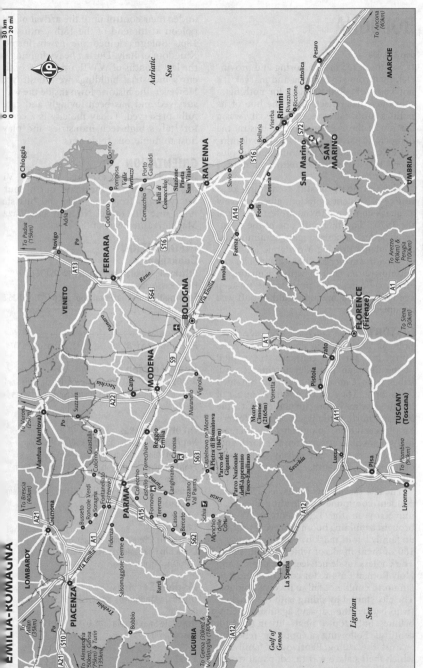

EMILIA-ROMAGNA & SAN MARINO

BOLOGNA

pop 380,000

If you think red brick's boring and provincial, then come to Bologna and marvel. It's not known as Red Bologna for nothing, a sobriquet that reflects both the hue of its politics (until fairly recently the city was a bastion of the Democratici di Sinistra, the democratic party of the left) and the dominant colour of its elegant monuments, plus over 40km – yes, that's 40km – of arcades and porticos.

The university is still something of a source of student agitation, albeit scarcely a squeak compared to the protest heyday of the 1970s. Together with one of the country's better organised gay communities, the students provide a dynamic air that's missing in smaller Emilian towns. The city administrators chip in with an unstinting and imaginative arts programme to keep even the most demanding culture-buff well occupied.

HISTORY

Bologna started life in the 6th century BC as Felsina, for two centuries the capital of the Etruscan Po valley territories until tribes from Gaul took over and renamed it Bononia. They lasted another couple of hundred years before surrendering to the Romans' northward march. As the Western Empire crumbled, Bologna became increasingly exposed to attack from the north and, for its pains, was successively sacked and occupied by Visigoths, Huns, Goths and Lombards.

The city reached its pinnacle as an independent commune and leading European university in the 12th century. Wealth brought a building boom and every well-to-do family left its mark by erecting a tower – 180 of them in all, of which 15 still stand. The endless tussle between the papacy and Holy Roman Empire for control of the Italian north could not fail to involve Bologna. The city started by siding with the Guelphs (who backed the papacy) against the Ghibellines, but adopted neutrality in the 14th century. Following a popular rebellion against the ruling Bentivoglio family, in which their palace was razed, papal troops took Bologna in 1506 and the city remained

under their control until the arrival of Napoleon at the end of the 18th century. In 1860 Bologna joined the newly formed Kingdom of Italy. During heavy fighting in the last months of WWII, up to 40% of the city's industrial buildings were destroyed. However, the historic town inside the wall survived and has been lovingly and carefully preserved. Today the city is a centre for Italy's high-tech industries and plays host to numerous trade fairs.

ORIENTATION

Bologna is easily explored on foot. Via dell'Indipendenza, the main north–south artery, leads from the train and bus stations into Piazza del Nettuno and Piazza Maggiore, the heart of the city.

INFORMATION

Bookshops

Feltrinelli – Italian bookshop (☎ 051 26 68 91; Piazza Ravegnana 1)
Feltrinelli – International bookshop (☎ 051 26 8 70; Via Zamboni 7b)

Emergency

Police Station (☎ 051 640 11 11; Piazza Galileo 7)

Gay & Lesbian

ArciGay (☎ 051 649 30 55; www.arcigay.it, Italian only; Via Don Minzoni 18) Provides information and arranges events.

Internet Access

Net Arena (Via de' Giudei 3d; €3.50/hr; 🕑 10am-midnight Mon-Fri, 10am-8pm Sat, 4-9pm Sun)
Fronte Retro (Via de' Chiari; €3.60/hr; 🕑 10.30am-8pm Mon-Sat, 2-7pm Sun)
Mousecafé (Via Belmeloro 3c; €2.75/hr; 🕑 8am-8pm Mon-Sat)

Laundry

iWash (Via G Petroni 38; 🕑 9am-9pm)
Onda Blu (Via Saragozza 34a/b; wash or dry €5.50; 🕑 6am-11pm)

Medical Services

Ospedale Maggiore (☎ 051 647 81 11; Via Emilia Ponente)
Ospedale Sant'Orsola (☎ 051 636 31 11; Via Massarenti 9)

Post

Main Post Office (Piazza Minghetti)

ALAN BENSON

Taste test Italy's exquisite proscuitto (cured ham) in **Parma** (p411)

The neverending vista of the **Alps** (p293)

NICK TAPP

DIANA MAYFIELD

Grado's famous 4th-century **mosaic** (p386)

DIANA MAYFIELD

Flex your Slovenian language skills in **Friuli-Venezia Giulia** (p374) near Slovenia

See red in the colourful streets of **Bologna** (p396)

NEIL SETCHFIELD

HA

Track down the shimmering early Christian mosiacs in **Ravenna** (p422)

JOHN HAY

Don't deny yourself the pleasure of one of Italy's best exports – **parmesan** (p68)

Dare to dream – grand prix–winning racing cars at **Galleria Ferrari** (p408) in Maranello

BOLOGNA

EMILIA-ROMAGNA & SAN MARINO

0 — 400 m
0 — 0.2 mi

INFORMATION
Branch Tourist Office.................(see 11)
Centro Servizi per i Turisti..............1 B1
CTS Travel Agency........................2 D2
Exchange Booth...........................3 B1
Feltrinelli (International Bookshop)......4 B1
Feltrinelli (Italian Bookshop)...........5 B1
Fronte Retro.............................6 C4
IWash Laundrette.........................7 D3
Mousecafé................................8 D3
Net Arena................................9 B1
Onda Blu Laundrette.....................10 B4
Tourist Office..........................11 A1

SIGHTS & ACTIVITIES pp398–400
Archiginnasio...........................12 C3
Basilica di San Domenico................13 C4
Basilica di San Petronio................14 A2
Basilica di Santa Maria dei Servi.......15 D3
Basilica di Santo Stefano...............16 C3
Cattedrale di San Pietro................17 A1
Chiesa di San Francesco.................18 B3
Chiesa di San Giacomo Maggiore..........19 D3
Le Due Torri............................20 B1
Museo Civico Archeologico...............21 A2
Museo Civico Medioevale e del
 Rinascimento...........................22 A1
Neptune's Fountain......................23 A1
Oratorio di Santa Cecilia...............24 D3
Palazzo Comunale (Palazzo
 D'Accursio)............................25 A1
Palazzo del Podestà...................(see 11)
Palazzo del Re Enzo.....................26 A1
Palazzo Poggi...........................27 D2
Pinacoteca Nazionale....................28 D2
University.............................(see 28)

SLEEPING p401
Albergo Garisenda.......................29 B1
Albergo Panorama........................30 B3
Hotel Commercianti......................31 A2
Hotel Orologio..........................32 A2
Hotel Roma..............................33 A2

Hotel Rossini...........................34 D3
Pensione Marconi........................35 B2

EATING pp401–3
Bass' Otto..............................36 B3
Diana...................................37 C2
Gelateria delle Moline..................38 C2
La Brace................................39 D3
La Sorbetteria Castiglione..............40 D4
Mercato delle Erbe......................41 B3
Osteria L'Infedele......................42 D3
Pizzeria Altero.........................43 B3
Pizzeria Emilia.........................44 D3
Tamburini...............................45 B1
Trattoria da Amedeo.....................46 A4
Trattoria da Danio......................47 A3
Trattoria da Gianni.....................48 B1

DRINKING pp401–3
Caffè al Teatro.........................49 D3
Café de Paris...........................50 B2
Cantina Bentivoglio.....................51 D2
Le Stanze...............................52 C2
Marsalino...............................53 C2
Osteria del Sole........................54 A1
Rosa Rose............................(see 48)

ENTERTAINMENT p403
Arena del Sole..........................55 C2
Cinema Capitol..........................56 C1
Cinema Odeon............................57 C2
Corto Maltese...........................58 C2
Kinki Disco.............................59 B1
Lumière Cinema..........................60 A3
Teatro Comunale.........................61 D2
Teatro Duse.............................62 D4

TRANSPORT p404
Aby-Car.................................63 C1
Europcar................................64 B1
Hertz...................................65 B1
Main Bus Station........................66 C1
Senzauto................................67 C1

Main Train Station

To Train Station (1km)

To Ostello Due Torri–San
Sisto (5km) & Centro Turistico
Città di Bologna (6km)

Via Stalingrado

Viale Angelo Masini

To Link Nightclub (750m);
AT3 & S64

To AcciGay (600m)

Parco
della
Montagnola

Piazza XX
Settembre

Piazza del
Otto Agosto

Piazza
dell'Indipendenza

Via delle Belle Arti

Via Zamboni

Via San Giacomo

To 39 &
A14

To S.
Giacomo

Piazza
Verdi

Via San Vitale

Via Irnerio

Via Oberdan

Via A. Righi

Via Marsala

Via delle Moline

Via Mascarella

Larga
Re-plenti

Piazza
Rossini

Via Castiglione

Strada Maggiore

To Ospedale
Sant'Orsola
(400m)

To A14
& Rimini
(120km)

To Centro
Europa Uno
(9km)

Via Santo Stefano

Piazza
Minghetti

Piazza
Maggiore

Piazza
Cavour

Via Rizzoli

Via Clavature

Via de' Poeti

Via Garibaldi

Via Luigi Carlo Farini

Via Farini

See Enlargement

Via Nazario Sauro

Via Ugo Bassi

Via Galliera

Via delle Mille

Via Cesare Boldrini

Via Milazzo

Via Marconi

Via Lame

Via Cesare Battisti

Via Testoni

Via Barberia

Piazza
Martello
Malpighi

Via del Pratello

Via Sant'Isaia

Via Nosadella

Viale Antonio Aldini

Via Pietralata

Via Costa

Via San Felice

Via Massimo d'Azeglio

Piazza
dei Tribunali

To Ospedale Maggiore (1.5km);
Airport (3km); A1, Modena (24km)
& Florence (93km)

To Villa
Serena Nightclub
(2km)

Via Sant'Isaia

Via Saragozza

Via Sangozza

Piazza
di Porta
Saragozza

Viale C Pepoli

Viale Giovanni Vicini

To Basilica Santuario
della Madonna di
San Luca (3.5km)

Piazza
del Nettuno

Piazza
Maggiore

Piazza
Galvani

Piazza di
Porta
Ravegnana

Via Clavature

Via Rizzoli

Vicolo
Mandria

Via D'Oro

Piazza
Minghetti

Piazza ED
Roosevelt

Via Marconi

Via Ugo Bassi

Tourist Information

Tourist Office (☎ 051 24 65 41; www.comune.bologna
.it/bolognaturismo) Main Office (Piazza Maggiore 1;
🕑 9am-8pm); Train Station (☎ 051 24 65 41;
🕑 8.30am-7.30pm Mon-Sat); Airport (🕑 8am-8pm
Mon-Sat, 9am-3pm Sun)
Centro Servizi per i Turisti (☎ 051 648 75 83,
☎ 800 85 60 65; www.bolognareservation.com;
🕑 10am-2pm daily & 3-7pm Mon-Sat) In the same
premises as the main tourist office, this service organises
hotel bookings free of charge.

Travel Agencies

CTS (☎ 051 23 75 01; Largo Respighi 2) Student travel
organisation.

DANGERS & ANNOYANCES

The city is starting to have problems with
street crime such as bag theft and pickpock-
eting. The area around the university, particularly Piazza Verdi, is a haunt for drug
addicts and can be unpleasant at night.

SIGHTS

The *Bologna dei Musei* card (one/three
days €6/8), purchased at any participating
museum, gets you admission to seven of
the city's major attractions. Children up to
14 go free.

Piazze Maggiore & Nettuno

Some of Bologna's most graceful medieval
and Renaissance monuments fringe Piazza
Maggiore and adjoining Piazza del Nettuno, to its north. At the centre of Bologna's
old city, this pair of bustling pedestrianised
squares are a focal point of city life, with
Bolognesi flocking to the cafés and gathered
around the mime artists and buskers who
perform on the uneven stone pavement.

Neptune's Fountain

Between the two piazze stands a mighty
bronze Neptune, sculpted in 1566 by a
Frenchman known to posterity as Giambologna. The four cherubs represent the winds
and the four sirens, water spouting from
every nipple, symbolise the four known
continents of this pre-Oceania world.

Palazzo Comunale (Palazzo D'Accursio)

The town hall lines the western flank of
the two piazze. Its immense central staircase, attributed to the Renaissance architect
Donato Bramante, was built wide enough

for horse-drawn carriages to chauffeur
their occupants up to the 1st floor. The
left side of the building was the residence
of the Accursio family and, from the 16th
to 19th centuries, home to the Papal Legate.
Above the main entrance is a bronze statue
of Pope Gregory XIII, a native of Bologna
and responsible for the Gregorian calendar.
Within are two art collections.

The **Collezioni Comunali d'Arte** (☎ 051 20 36 29,
admission €4; 🕑 9am-6.30pm Tue-Sat, 10am-6.30pm Sun)
includes paintings, sculpture and furniture
originally in private collections. You get a
magnificent view over Piazza Maggiore.

The splendid **Museo Morandi** (☎ 051 20 33
32; admission €4; 🕑 10am-6pm Tue-Sun) contains
over 200 paintings, watercolours, drawings
and prints spanning the career of the 20th-
century Bolognese artist, Giorgio Morandi.

Outside the *palazzo* are three large panels
bearing photos of hundreds of local partisans
killed in the resistance to German occupation. Such displays are relatively common in
the towns of Emilia-Romagna, which was a
centre of fierce partisan activity.

Palazzo del Re Enzo

Across from the Palazzo d'Accursio, this
palace is named after King Enzo of Sicily
who was confined here for 20 long years
in the 13th century. It's open only during
exhibitions.

Palazzo del Podestà

Beneath this fine example of Renaissance
architecture and behind the cafés facing
Piazza Maggiore, there is a whispering gallery where the two perpendicular passages
intersect. Stand diagonally opposite someone and whisper: the acoustics are amazing.
Notice how this medieval tower, a considerable feat of engineering, doesn't rest on the
ground but on the pillars of the vault. It too
is open only during exhibitions.

Basilica di San Petronio

Named after the city's patron saint, the
basilica (admission free; 🕑 7.30am-1pm & 2.30-6pm)
was started in 1392 but, for political reasons, never finished.

Originally intended to be larger than
the first St Peter's in Rome (the structure
destroyed to make way for Rome's present
basilica), San Petronio was effectively truncated by the papacy, which decreed it cou

not be larger than St Peter's and that much of the land should be used for a university. The facade is incomplete and if you walk along Via dell'Archiginnasio, on the eastern side of the basilica, you can see semiconstructed apses poking out oddly. Yet despite the papal intervention, the basilica is still the fifth largest in the world and an example of Gothic architecture at its best.

The central doorway, by Jacopo della Quercia, dates from 1425 and features a beautiful Madonna and Child and carvings from the Old and New Testaments. The chapels inside contain frescoes by Giovanni da Modena and Jacopo di Paolo. A giant brass sundial, designed by Cassini in 1656, stretches along the floor of the eastern aisle.

There are free guided tours of the basilica in Italian and English at 11.30am on Tuesday, Thursday and Saturday.

Museo Civico Archeologico

Just east of the basilica, the city's archaeological **museum** (☎ 051 23 38 49; Via dell' Archiginnasio 2; admission €4; ☺ 9am-6.30pm Tue-Sat, 10am-6.30pm Sun) has well-displayed and documented Egyptian and Roman artefacts and one of Italy's best Etruscan collections, less well presented. Highlights of the latter are two burial chambers unearthed near the city.

Archiginnasio

Site of the city's university from 1563 to 1805 and now its **library** (☎ 051 23 64 88; Piazza Galvani 1; admission free; ☺ 9am-1pm Mon-Sat), the Archiginnasio contains a 17th-century anatomy theatre, crafted entirely from wood. Note the lecturer's chair with its canopy supported by skinless nude figures. The theatre, together with many of the building's frescoes, was destroyed during WWII and completely rebuilt.

Museo Civico Medioevale e del Rinascimento

Housed in the Palazzo Ghilisardi-Fava, which has some fine frescoes by Jacopo della Quercia, this **museum** (☎ 051 20 39 30; Via Manzoni 4; admission €4; ☺ 9am-6.30pm Tue-Sat, 10am-6.30pm Sun) houses a collection of battle armour, bronze statues and medieval coffin slabs.

Le Due Torri

The two slender and seemingly precarious leaning towers that rise above Piazza di Porta Ravegnana are unmistakable landmarks. The taller one, all 97.6m of it, is the **Torre degli Asinelli** (admission €3; ☺ 9am-6pm, to 5pm winter). Built by the family of the same name in 1109, it has 498 steps that you can climb (despite the 1.3m lean) for a marvellous view over the city. The Garisenda family was even less cautious with foundations when erecting its own tower, originally designed to compete with its neighbour and later sized down to 48m because of its 3.2m lean. Wisely, given such a tilt, it's closed to the public.

University Quarter

Northeast of the towers, along Via Zamboni, is the **Chiesa di San Giacomo Maggiore** (Piazza Rossini; admission free; ☺ 7am-noon & 3.30-6pm). Built in the 13th century and remodelled in 1722, it's notable for the Bentivoglio chapel, with frescoes by Lorenzo Costa and an altarpiece by Francesco Raibolini (known as Il Francia).

The same pair were mainly responsible for the striking late-15th-century cycle of 10 frescoes describing the life of St Cecilia in the adjacent **Oratorio di Santa Cecilia** (☎ 051 22 59 70; Piazza Rossini; admission free; ☺ 10am-1pm & 3-7pm, to 6pm winter).

A little further up the road is the **Teatro Comunale**, where Wagner's works were heard for the first time in Italy.

The university has a whole range of museums (Ships and Old Maps, Military Architecture, Obstetrics, Anatomy of Domestic Animals and much more) open to the public and mostly within the **Palazzo Poggi** (☎ 051 209 96 02; www.unibo.it/musei-universitari, Italian only; Via Zamboni 33). Visit its website or call by the *palazzo* for a catalogue.

Pinacoteca Nazionale

North of the university, the **National Art Gallery** (☎ 051 421 19 84; Via delle Belle Arti 56; admission €4; ☺ 9am-7pm Tue-Sat) concentrates on works by Bolognese artists from the 14th century onwards. The extensive exhibits include several works by Giotto as well as Raphael's *Ecstasy of St Cecilia*. El Greco and Titian are also represented, but by comparatively little-known works.

Basilica di Santo Stefano

From the two towers, head southeast along Via Santo Stefano, long a residential area for Bologna's wealthy and lined with the elegant facades of their *palazzi*.

The **basilica** (☎ 051 22 32 56; Via Santo Stefano 24; admission free; ⏲ 9am-noon & 3.30-6pm) is actually a group of the four churches remaining from the original seven. On the right are the 11th-century Romanesque **Chiesa del Crocefisso** (Crucifix) and octagonal **Chiesa del Santo Sepolcro** (Holy Sepulchre), whose shape suggests it started life as a baptistry. The Chiesa del Crocefisso houses the bones of San Petronio, Bologna's patron saint. Tradition has it that the basin in the small courtyard is the one in which Pontius Pilate washed his hands after he condemned Christ to death. In fact it's an 8th-century Lombard artefact.

Santi Vitale e Agricola (☎ 051 22 05 70; Via San Vitale 50; admission free; ⏲ 8am-noon & 3.30-7.30pm) is the city's oldest church. Incorporating recycled Roman masonry and carvings, the bulk of the building dates from the 5th century and the tombs of the two saints, 100 years older still, once served as altars in the side aisles (today only one tomb remains). From the **Chiesa della Santa Trinità** you can pass to the modest medieval colonnaded cloister, off which there's a small **museum** with a limited collection of paintings and frescoes.

Basilica di San Domenico

The **basilica** (Piazza San Domenico 13; admssion free; ⏲ 9.30am-1pm & 3-6pm Tue-Sat, 3-5.30pm Sun) was erected in the early 16th century to house the remains of San Domenico, founder of the Dominican order, who died in 1221 soon after opening a convent on this very site.

The **Cappella di San Domenico** in the south aisle contains the saint's elaborate sarcophagus, incised with reliefs illustrating scenes from his life. Designed by Nicola Pisano in the late 13th century, the chapel was worked on by a host of artists over the following couple of centuries. Michelangelo carved the angel on the right of the altar when he was only 19. The chapel also has several paintings of the saint, whose skull lies in a reliquary behind the sarcophagus. Ask an attendant to let you see the small **museum** and the inlaid wood of the choir stalls behind the main altar.

When Mozart spent a month in the city's music academy, he occasionally played the church's organ.

Chiesa di San Francesco

Outside the east end of this **church** (Piazza San Francesco; admission free; ⏲ 6.30am-noon & 3-7pm) are the elaborate tombs of the *glossatori* (law teachers). The church, one of the first in Italy to be built in the French Gothic style, was completed in the 13th century and contains the tomb of Pope Alexander V.

Basilica Santuario della Madonna di San Luca

You can see the hilltop **Basilica Santuario della Madonna di San Luca** (46 Via di San Luca; admission free; ⏲ 7am-12.30pm & 2.30-7pm, to 5pm winter) from most parts of the city. Built in the mid-18th century, it houses a painting of the Virgin Mary, supposedly by Saint Luke (hence the place's name), which was transported from the Middle East to Bologna in the 12th century.

The sanctuary lies about 4km southwest of the city centre and is connected to the city walls by the world's longest portico, held aloft by 666 arches, beginning at Porta Saragozza, itself southwest of the centre. Each April a statue of the Virgin is carried along the portico. Take bus No 20 from the city centre to Villa Spada, from where you can get a minibus to the sanctuary (buy the €2.75 return ticket on the minibus). On a sunny day it's fun to get off at Meloncello and walk the remaining 2km under the arches.

TOURS

Three outfits offer guided walking tours of the city:

GAIA (☎ 051 24 65 41) Meets at 10.30am Wednesday, Saturday and Sunday outside the tourist office.
Le Guide d'Arte (☎ 349 575 64 03) Meets at 4pm Saturday and Sunday outside the tourist office.
Prima Classe (☎ 347 894 40 94) Meets at 11am, Monday and Sunday, 3pm Tuesday and Thursday beside Neptune's fountain.

You can just turn up on the day and are charge €13 per person.

Prima Classe also do two-hour **cycle tours** (€20 including bike rental) of the cultural high spots at 6pm on Friday and 4pm on Saturday. Ring to reserve.

FESTIVALS & EVENTS

Each summer the city sponsors a three-month **festival** of open-air events involving museums and galleries, the university, and local and national performers. Bologna's tourist offices carry programme details.

SLEEPING

Bologna's busy trade-fair calendar means that hotels are often heavily booked so it's prudent to reserve in advance. Budget hotels are in short supply and it is almost impossible to find a single room. The city's top-end hotels cater primarily to business people; when there are no fairs, some offer discounts of up to 50%.

Budget

Ostello Due Torri-San Sisto (☎ /fax 051 50 18 10; Via adagola 5; dm/d €13.50/15; 🖳) These two hostels, barely 100m apart, are in the country 4km from the heart of town. The older San Sisto annexe has more character. Take bus nos 93 (Monday to Saturday, daytime), 301 (Sunday) or 21B (daily, after 8.30pm) from Via Irnerio or Via Marconi.

Centro Europa Uno (☎ /fax 051 625 83 52; Via milia 297; s/d €12.50/31) Bookings are normally essential at this hostel, in San Lazzaro di Savena, about 9km southeast of Bologna. Take bus No 94 from central Bologna.

Centro Turistico Città di Bologna (☎ 051 32 50 www.hotelcamping.com, Italian only; Via Romita 12/ per person/tent site €7/11; 🏊) This very swish camp ground with all the creature comforts is on the north side of town, 6km from the main station. Take bus No 68 (€0.90, 15 minutes, seven daily) from Via dei Mille.

Mid-Range

Bologna has no shortage of hotels – though empty beds are sometimes at a premium.

Albergo Garisenda (☎ 051 22 43 69; fax 051 22 10 Galleria del Leone 1, Via Rizzoli 9; s/d/tr without bathroom €45/65/90) Decidedly the pick of the city's cheaper possibilities the Garisenda has seven rooms, some looking out over the leaning towers. Breakfast (included in the room rate) may be modest but – something too often absent from much grander establishments – the coffee is real and fresh expressed from the burbling machine. The entrance is within a covered shopping gallery.

Pensione Marconi (☎ 051 26 28 32; Via Marconi 22; s, s/d with bathroom €45/70) This *pensione* is a no-nonsense place where the price is right. Rooms are fairly basic; ask for one at the rear, away from traffic-ridden Via Marconi.

Albergo Panorama (☎ 051 22 18 02; panorama .hotel@libero.it; 4th fl, Via Livraghi 1; s/d/tr €50/65/89, d/tr with bathroom €80/90) Albergo Panorama is an altogether more welcoming option. Three generations play their part in the running of this family hotel, where rooms are large, airy and spotless. Some have great views if you crane your neck just slightly.

Hotel Rossini (☎ 051 23 77 16; fax 26 80 35; Via dei Bibiena 11; s/d €42/70, with bathroom €70/100; 🕐 mid-Aug–mid-Jul; 🞪) In the heart of the university area, this 21-room traditional family hotel is run to high standards by a charming elderly couple.

Hotel Roma (☎ 051 22 63 22; www.hotelroma.biz; Via Massimo d'Azeglio 9; s/d with breakfast €116/149; 🅿 🞪) Although the floral wallpaper and fabrics are a mite overpowering, the upmarket Roma offers superior comfort right in the heart of town, just off Piazza Maggiore. Parking costs €16.

Top End

Hotel Commercianti (☎ 051 23 30 52; www.bologna hotel.net; Via de' Pignattari 11; s €127-211, d €182-298; 🅿 🞪 🖳) Tucked away down an inconspicuous back alley, where the bas relief fresco figures on the walls of the Basilica di San Petronio gawp into the 1st-floor windows, lies one of Italy's finest small hotels. It occupies the restored 12th-century building that was Bologna's first town hall. A neat democratic touch: the hotel provides free bicycles for clients. Parking costs €26.

Hotel Orologio (☎ 051 23 12 53; www.bologna hotel.net; Via IV Novembre; s €120-211, d €173-326; 🅿 🞪 🖳 ❌) Belonging to the same company and just around the corner, Hotel Orologio occupies a lovely old *palazzo*. Rooms are exquisitely furnished and its eponymous clock, up in the tower, considerately doesn't strike during the night. Parking costs €26 here too.

EATING & DRINKING

Bologna the Red is also called La Grassa (The Fat), a term referring to the richness of the cuisine rather than the girth of its inhabitants, though the Bolognesi are indeed seriously serious about their food. Just look at the way all things edible, especially pasta, bread and cheeses, are displayed with style in shop windows.

The best pasta is *tirata a mano*, hand-stretched and rolled with a wooden pin, not a machine and a good many Bolognesi restaurants still roll their own. It is cooked in many ways and eaten with a multitude of sauces. Spaghetti bolognese, that favourite student culinary standby, originated here – though the Bolognesi call the meat sauce *ragù* and prefer to mix it with tagliatelli. *Mortadella*, known sometimes as Bologna sausage or baloney, also hails from the area. The hills nearby produce the light, fizzy Lambrusco red and a full, dry Sauvignon.

If you're after economical eating, the university district northeast of Via Rizzoli is well endowed with reasonable restaurants and trattorie.

Restaurants

Bass' Otto (Via Ugo Bassi 8; meals €10-15) Bass 8 styles itself 'Ristorante Free Flow', an apt description of this busy self-service joint, particularly popular with lunchtime crowds.

Tamburini (☎ 051 23 47 26; Via Caprarie 1; ☯ noon-3pm) Primarily a delicatessen, in business for over 70 years and selling some of Bologna's finest food products, Tamburini also offers a *very* classy version of the self-service genre with prices to match.

Pizzeria Altero (Via Ugo Bassi 10; pizza slice €0.60-1.20; ☯ 8am-11pm Mon-Sat) Elbow your way through the throng that regularly crams into this tiny pizzeria for a standup snack or takeaway. This is one of Bologna's best bets for tasty *pizza al taglio* (by the slice).

Pizzeria Emilia (Via Zamboni 27; pizza slice €1.55-2.60) Here's a deservedly popular student hangout with filling, tasty pizza slices.

Trattoria da Danio (☎ 051 55 52 02; Via San Felice 50a) Da Danio is full of locals who return time and again for delicious pasta, including tortellini stuffed with pumpkin, and mains such as grilled veal cutlets. The set

---

THE AUTHOR'S CHOICE

Trattoria da Gianni (☎ 051 22 94 34; Via Clavature 18; meals €25-33; ☯ lunch Tue-Sun) Down a side alley, its walls bedecked with testimonials and press cuttings and its tables adorned with fresh flowers, da Gianni is well worth seeking out, especially for its home-made pasta. Twirl their *tagliatelle al ragù* around your fork or stab the *tortellini al Trevigiano* (both €7).

---

menu at €11 is exceptional value and there a nonsmoking room.

Trattoria da Amedeo (☎ 051 58 50 60; V Saragozza 88; pasta €5.50-7.70, meals €20-30; ☯ Mo Sat) Traditional home-cooking is the dra here, with tagliatelle bolognese a specialit It too does a bargain lunch menu for €11

Diana (☎ 051 23 13 02; Via dell'Indipendenza 2 meals €20-25; ☯ Tue-Sun) Diana is famous fc its tortellini and infamous for its slight patronising white-jacketed waiters. Th said, you dine very well beneath cryst chandeliers at this long hall of a place. Ju give as good as you get.

Osteria L'Infedele (☎ 0335 669 23 61; Via Ge salemme 5a; snacks €5.15-6.50, wine by the glass from ☯ from 6.30pm Tue-Sun) L'Infedele is a co place to hang out with a glass of wine or fc a light meal; the friendly staff and excelle background jazz are bonuses.

La Brace (☎ 051 23 56 56; Via San Vitale 15; piz €4-7.50, mains €7-18) Wooden partitions bre up La Brace into intimate dining areas ar youthful portraits of James Dean, Brand Bardot and Mick Jagger gaze down though the years had never passed. T house strength, from antipasti through mains, is emphatically fish with a partic larly impressive range of starters; to samp a variety, go for their *antipasto di mc* (€9.50) a selection from the sea.

Gelaterias

La Sorbetteria Castiglione (☎ 051 23 32 57; Castiglione 44; ☯ Mon-Sun) If you don't belie us, take it from the Comitato Italiano Gelato, who awarded this place its Prem Speciale (special award) at the Concoi Internationale Gelatissimo 2003: it mal truly world-beating ice cream that you c see being churned at the rear of the sho

Gelateria delle Moline (Via delle Moline 13b) this primarily student hangout you c have your ice cream slapped between caccia (flatbread) or biscuits. Or just tak neat – and it doesn't come much neater

Cafés & Bars

Via del Pratello, just off Via Ugo Bassi, student and young people's haunt – und standably since it abounds in cheap bi *birrerie* (pubs), *osterie*, and trattorie.

Osteria del Sole (Vicolo Ranocchi 1d; ☯ 8am-7.30-9pm) This place first opened for busin in the 15th century and is the last busir

n Bologna that maintains the centuries-old
radition of the *osteria* strictly as watering
ole. If you want to eat, stock up from the
urrounding food shops. Hours, in princ-
ple as above, are erratic...

Rosa Rose (Via Clavature 18) This place, near
Trattoria da Gianni, simply buzzes. It's
pleasant for a cocktail or coffee, panini
(bread rolls with filling) or pasta – if you
an fight your way to a table amid the
throngs of regulars.

Cantina Bentivoglio (☎ 051 26 54 16; Via Mascarella
b; ☉ 8pm-2am) Call it wine bar (this bottle-
ned cellar has over 500 labels to choose
rom), restaurant (a good meal will set you
ack about €25, not including wine) or jazz
lub (there's live music nightly), snug Canna Bentivoglio makes for a great night out.

Caffè al Teatro (☎ 051 22 26 23; cnr Largo Respighi
Via Zamboni; meals €17-20) Modestly priced,
his is a relaxing place to hang out with a
rink or snack. There's plenty of student
fe at any time of the day and they also do
imple meals.

Marsalino (☎ 051 23 86 75; Via Marsala 13d) Tiny,
rty chameleon-like Marsalino is a tearoom
om 4pm, metamorphoses into a cocktail/
wine bar from 6pm, then, at 8pm, becomes
modest restaurant.

Le Stanze (☎ 051 22 87 67; Via Borgo San Pietro 1)
Here you'll find a cool, trendy, young clien-
ele. The frescoed walls and ceiling of this
ormer chapel of a patrician's *palazzo*, its
iendly staff and good music, sometimes
ve, give Le Stanze an agreeable ambience –
hough the drinks and company are more
ppealing than the food.

Café de Paris (☎ 051 23 49 80; Piazza Minghetti;
☉ 7-3am Mon-Sat, 10-3am Sun) One of the in-est
Bologna's many in places. With a small
rrace, shielded from the street, it has a
asonable selection of draught beers and
ixes some mean cocktails.

elf-Catering

or the freshest fruit and vegetables in
wn, drop into the **Mercato delle Erbe** (Via Ugo
ssi 27; ☉ Mon-Sat), Bologna's main covered
arket.

Just east of Piazza Maggiore, the area
ound Via Drapperie, Via Orefici, Via Pe-
herie Vecchie and Via Clavature is rich in
eciality food shops, including Tamburini
ee p402). There's an attractive daily pro-
ce market.

ENTERTAINMENT

A Guest of Bologna, available from some
hotels and tourist offices, is a useful, free bi-
monthly guide to what's on. *Bonews* (€2.50)
from newsstands is more comprehensive.

Cinemas

Lumière (☎ 051 52 38 12; www.cinetecadibologna.it,
Italian only; Via Pietralata 55a) An excellent public-
sector cinema, showing films few of which
would ever get a commercial release. Art-
house films are shown in their original
version, with Italian subtitles.

Cinema Odeon (☎ 051 22 79 16; Via Mascarella 3)
and **Cinema Capital** (☎ 051 24 10 02; Via Milazzo 1)
screen films in English one day per week.
The particular day varies, so phone ahead
to check.

Nightclubs

Bologna has one of Italy's liveliest night
scenes, bolstered by its active student population. Cantina Bentivoglio (see opposite) is
one of the best two jazz venues in town. The
other, the **Chet Baker Jazz Club** (☎ 051 22 37 95;
Via Polese 7a), has regular live music.

Link (☎ 051 37 09 71; Via Fioravanti 14) If techno,
hip-hop and the very latest music are your
thing, head for Link, north of the train station. This former social centre, now housed
in a municipal building, is a popular student hangout.

Kinki (☎ 0338 151 56 98; Via Zamboni 1a; cover
charge around €15.50; ☉ Thu-Sat) A long-time
favourite disco that welcomes lesbians
and gays.

Villa Serena (☎ 051 615 67 89; Via della Barca 1;
admission free; ☉ 9pm-3am Thu-Sat) Three floors
offer 1980s DJ music, film screenings and
live music. A comfortable garden offers
relaxed outdoor chilling areas.

Corto Maltese (☎ 051 22 97 46; Via Borgo San Pietro 9/2a; ☉ 9pm-3am Mon-Sat) A stylish popular
disco-bar.

Theatre, Opera & Live Music

Bologna has an active cultural scene around
the calendar. **Teatro Comunale** (☎ 051 52 99 99;
Piazza Verdi) is Bologna's main venue for
opera and concerts, with a year-round
programme. **Arena del Sole** (☎ 051 27 07 90;
Via dell' Indipendenza 44) puts on mainly modern
classics while **Teatro Duse** (☎ 051 23 18 36; Via
Cartoleria 42) has a varied programme of both
classical and contemporary theatre.

EMILIA-ROMAGNA &
SAN MARINO

SHOPPING

The main shopping streets are Via Ugo Bassi, Via Rizzoli, Via Marconi, Via dell' Indipendenza, Via Massimo d'Azeglio, Via Farini and Via San Felice. You can safely leave your wallet behind on Thursday afternoons, when all shops are shut.

On Friday and Saturday there's a flea and antique market at the Parco della Montagnola that seeps into Piazza del Otto Agosto.

GETTING THERE & AWAY

Air

International destinations from Bologna's Guglielmo Marconi **airport** (BLQ; ☎ 051 647 96 15), northwest of the city at Borgo Panigale, include London Gatwick (two to three daily; BA), London Stansted (two daily; Go and EasyJet), Paris (four daily; Alitalia and Air France), Frankfurt (four to five daily; Lufthansa) and Amsterdam (two to three daily; KLM).

Bus

Buses for regional destinations such as Ravenna, Ferrara and Modena leave from the **bus station** (☎ 051 29 02 90) off Piazza XX Settembre, just east of the train station. From here you can also catch buses to Ancona and Milan.

Car & Motorcycle

The city is linked to Milan, Florence and Rome by the A1 Autostrada del Sole. The A13 heads directly for Ferrara, Padua and Venice, and the A14 for Rimini and Ravenna. Bologna is also on the Via Emilia (S9), which connects Milan with the Adriatic coast. The S64 goes to Ferrara.

Most major car-hire companies are represented both at the airport and in town. Town offices include **Europcar** (☎ 051 24 71 01; Via G Amendola 12f) and **Hertz** (☎ 051 25 48 30; Via G Amendola 16a).

Train

A journey anywhere within 100km of Bologna will cost you a maximum of €3.60.

Bologna is a major transport junction for northern Italy and has many daily services to Rome and Milan.

GETTING AROUND

Aerobus (€4.50) connects the city with the airport. It leaves from the main train station roughly every 15 minutes from 5.30am to 11.10pm.

Bologna has a commendably efficient bus system, run by **ATC** (☎ 051 29 02 90; www.atc.bo.it, Italian only). It has information booths at the main train station and on Via Marconi. Buses No 30 and 21 are among several connecting the main train station with the city centre.

Much of the centre is off-limits to traffic – and is all the more visitor-friendly for it. If you're staying in the heart of town, your hotel can provide a permit (€7 per day) entitling you to 24 hours' parking within the *cordon sanitaire*.

Should you be footsore, the best way to get around the centre is by bike. You can hire one at the train station from **Aby-Car** (☎ 051 25 38 32; per hr/day/week €2/5.20/24) or with the largest selection of boneshakers you've ever seen, **Senzauto** (☎ 051 25 14 01 per day/week €6/40), under and beyond the arch beside Aby-Car.

To book a taxi, call ☎ 051 37 27 27 or ☎ 051 53 41 41.

PORRETTA

The tiny thermal spring town of Porretta Terme, known as Porretta, lies about 50km south of Bologna in the Apennines. Traditionally a sleepy resort for people wanting to take advantage of the therapeutic mineral waters, the town has in recent years become a draw for soul-music lovers from across Europe. Each year, during the third weekend in July, the town hosts the **Sweet Soul Music Festival**, a tribute to Otis Redding and a celebration of the Memphis sound. The festival is held over three nights in the town's Rufus Thomas Park.

Porretta's **tourist office** (☎ 0534 2 20 21; Piazza Libertà 11; ◷ 9am-1pm Mon-Sat, 4-6pm Mon & Thu-Sat) carries information about the festival.

Trains leave hourly for Porretta from Bologna. The town is also accessible by train from Florence.

Sleeping & Eating

Hotel Santoli (☎ 0534 2 32 06; www.hotelsantoli.com; Via Roma 3; s/d €77.50/119) This four-star, family-run hotel is comfortable, welcoming and green, blessed with both a roof garden and another secluded one at ground level. Il Bassetto, the hotel restaurant, serves a variety of imaginative dishes.

Trattoria Toscana (☎ 0534 2 22 08; Piazza della Libertà 7; s/d with bathroom €30/43, meals from €15; ☺ Tue-Sun) This is another good place to sample Emilian cuisine, and Tuscan too. It also rents rooms.

WEST OF BOLOGNA

MODENA
pop 177,000

Some 40km northwest of Bologna, Modena was one of a series of Roman garrison towns established along the Via Emilia in the 2nd century BC, in this case on the site of an already existing Etruscan settlement.

It was an obscure little place until it became a free city in the 12th century and then passed to the Este family late in the following century. Prosperity came when it was chosen as the capital of a much-reduced Este duchy in 1598, after the family lost Ferrara to the Papal States. Apart from a brief Napoleonic interlude, the Este family ran the town until Italian unification in the 19th century.

Modena is home to Luciano Pavarotti, Italy's favourite fat tenor, plus car manufacturers Ferrari, Maserati and De Tomaso, who all do their bit to make this town one of the most affluent in the country.

Orientation
Via Emilia, Modena's main drag, slices through the town from west to east. Flanking it to north and south are Piazza Grande and Piazza Mazzini, the town's principal squares.

Information
EMERGENCY
Police Station (☎ 059 41 04 11; Viale delle Rimembranze 12)

INTERNET ACCESS
Space Net (☎ 059 21 20 96; Piazza Grande 34; €4/hr; ☺ 10am-8pm)

MEDICAL SERVICES
Hospital (☎ 059 43 72 71/2; Piazzale Sant'Agostino)

POST
Main Post Office (Via Emilia 86)

TELEPHONE
Telecom Office (Via L C Farini 26)

TOURIST INFORMATION
Tourist Office (☎ 059 20 66 60; ☺ 9am-1pm Tue-Sun & 3-6pm Mon-Sat) Located just off Piazza Grande. Does a guide for disabled visitors, *Muoversi nella Città di Modena* – in Italian but with clear symbols indicating wheelchair access to the main sights.

ModenaTur (☎ 059 22 00 22; www.modenatur.net, Italian only; Via Scudari 8-10) Next door to the tourist office, ModenaTur can turn its hand to most things – booking accommodation without a fee, buying opera tickets, arranging a visit to a balsamic vinegar producer, private collection of vintage racing cars or *parmigiano reggiano* dairy.

Sights
CATHEDRAL
Started in 1099 and dedicated to Modena's patron saint, San Geminiano, the **cathedral** (Piazza Grande; admission free; ☺ 7am-noon & 3.30-7pm) is one of Italy's finest Romanesque places of worship. The facade is adorned with engagingly naive and vivid bas-reliefs depicting scenes from Genesis by the 12th-century sculptor Wiligelmo who – a rare practice in those times – autographed his work (see the panel to the left of the main door), as did the building's architect, Lanfranco (signing off in the main apse). Among the many vigorous carvings, both sacred and secular, are typical medieval themes depicting the months and agricultural scenes. Much of Wiligelmo's work has been removed to the **Musei del Duomo** (☎ 059 439 69 69; Via Lanfranco 6; admission €3; ☺ 9.30am-12.30pm & 3.30-6.30pm Tue-Sun), adjoining the north side of the cathedral. Here, you can hire an excellent audioguide (€1) covering both museum and cathedral.

The lurching early-13th-century **Torre Ghirlandina** (admission €1.50; ☺ 9.30am-12.30pm & 3-7pm Sun Apr-Jul & Sep-Oct) – another degree or two and it would outlean Pisa's – rises to 87m, culminating in a slender Gothic spire.

PALAZZO DEI MUSEI
Within the vast **Palazzo dei Musei** (☎ 059 439 57 11; Piazzale Sant'Agostino) are several galleries.

The **Galleria Estense** (admission €4; ☺ 8.30am-7.30pm Tue-Sun) features most of the Este family collection: a rich, well-displayed diachronic collection of the main schools of northern Italy from late medieval times to the 18th century. There are also some fine Flemish canvases and a canvas or two by Velázquez, Correggio and El Greco for good measure.

MODENA

0 _____ 400 m
0 _____ 0.2 mi

INFORMATION
Hospital...1 A2
ModenaTur.............................(see 4)
Space Net......................................2 B3
Telecom Office...........................3 C3
Tourist Office..............................4 B3

SIGHTS & ACTIVITIES pp405–6
Biblioteca Estense....................(see 8)
Cathedral.......................................5 B3
Chiesa di San Domenico..........6 C2
Galleria Estense.........................(see 8)
Musei del Duomo....................(see 5)
Museo Archeologico
  Etnologico...............................(see 8)
Museo Lapidario Estense......(see 8)
Palazzo Comunale......................7 B3
Palazzo dei Musei......................8 A2
Palazzo Ducale............................9 C2
Romanica.....................................10 B2
Torre Ghirlandina...................(see 5)
University.....................................11 C3

SLEEPING p407
Canalgrande Hotel..................12 B3
Hotel Centrale...........................13 B2
Hotel San Geminiano...............14 C4
Ostello San Filippo Neri........15 C2
Principe Hotel.............................16 D1

EATING pp407–8
Al Grottino...................................17 B2
Market..18 B3
Pasticceria Forno San Giorgio..19 C2
Ristorante Da Danilo...............20 B3
Ristorante Da Enzo...................21 B3
Trattoria da Omer.....................22 B3

ENTERTAINMENT p408
Teatro Comunale......................23 C3
Teatro Storchi............................24 C4

TRANSPORT p408
Bus Station..................................25 A1

The **Biblioteca Estense**, essentially a research library, has one of Italy's most valuable collections of books, letters and manuscripts including the *Bible of Borso d'Este*, its 1200 pages vividly illustrated by Ferrarese artists.

A *biglietto cumulativo* (combined ticket; €3.30) gives entry to the **Museo Archeologico Etnologico** and the **Museo Civico d'Arte** (both 9am-noon Tue-Sat, 4-7pm Tue, Sat, Sun, 10am-1pm Sun). In addition to well-displayed local finds from paleolithic to medieval, the museum has exhibits from Africa, Asia, Peru and New Guinea. Most interesting among the Museo Civico d'Arte's eclectic collection are the sections devoted to traditional paper making, textiles and musical instruments.

The **Museo Lapidario Estense** (admission free 8am-7pm) displays Roman and medieval stonework, including sarcophagi. It was partly closed for renovation at the time of writing.

PALAZZO DUCALE
Started in 1634 for the Este family, this heavy baroque edifice is now Modena's **military academy** (059 22 56 71; Piazza Rom admission €5; guided tours 10am-12.30pm Sun. Its scrubbed, fresh-faced, heel-clicking cadets in their trim hats and multicolou uniforms look as if they've marched righ off a Quality Street toffee tin. Fancy dres apart, they're considered Italy's crac soldiers.

Courses

Romanica (☎ 059 24 56 51; www.romanica.it; Via Caselmaraldo 45) runs courses in Italian language and culture for non-native speakers with a minimum enrolment of two weeks.

Festivals & Events

The **Settimana Estense** in late June is a week of banquets, jousts and other early Renaissance fun, an opportunity for the good folk of Modena to don period costume and let their hair down.

Modena celebrates balsamic vinegar, the product it gave to the world, with **Balsamica**, a series of **exhibitions**, events and tastings from mid-May to early June.

Pavarotti & Friends, held at the end of May, is a one-night megaconcert featuring the chubby tenor and a whole galaxy of international stars.

Sleeping

Modena is close enough to Bologna to make it a day trip, although the city does have a range of decent accommodation.

Ostello San Filippo Neri (☎ 059 23 45 98; hostel modena@hotmail.com; Via Santa Orsola 48-52; dm/d €14.50/15.50; 🖳) Modena's HI-affiliated hostel is conveniently central. The noise from neighbours above might lead to a sleepless night...

International Camping Modena (☎ 059 33 22 2; www.internationalcamping.org; Via Cave di Ramo 111, Bruciata; adult/tent site €6/11) Well endowed, this camp site is 5km west of the city in Bruciata. Take bus No 19.

Hotel San Geminiano (☎ 059 21 03 03; previdan@ iscali.net; Viale Moreali 41; d €55, s/d with bathroom €45/75; P 🖳) Southeast of the city centre, the San Geminiano, an easy 15-minute stroll from Piazza Grande, is run by a friendly young couple and offers free parking. Breakfast is included in the room rate.

Principe Hotel (☎ 059 21 86 70; hotprincipe@ irgilio.it; Corso Vittorio Emanuele 94; s/d/tr with breakfast €65/95/115; ✗ 🖳 🖳) Convenient for the train station, the Principe makes an excellent mid-range choice. Ask for a room overlooking the small park on the south side.

Hotel Centrale (☎ 059 21 88 08; fax 059 23 82 1; Via Rismondo 55; s/d €40/80, s/d/t with bathroom €80/130/175; ✗) In the very heart of town, the Centrale is a welcoming hotel that offers comfortable if somewhat pricey rooms. The bedroom wallpaper is a little gloomy

EMILIA-ROMAGNA & SAN MARINO

A TASTE WORTH WAITING FOR

Real *aceto balsamico* from Modena is a rare and beautiful thing. Commercial balsamic vinegar, as sold around the world, bears little relation to its upmarket cousin. Balsamic vinegar is made by boiling up vats of must (unfermented grape juice) from Trebbiano vines grown in a closely defined area around Modena. The must is filtered, placed in a large oak barrel, then over many years decanted and transferred into smaller barrels made of different woods that are stored in farmhouse lofts. The summer temperature in these lofts can reach 50°C, so the must condenses soon after evaporating. Modena's sharp winters are also essential for the process.

Aceto balsamico tradizionale di Modena is aged for at least 12 years, and *aceto balsamico tradizionale di Modena extravecchio* for at least 25. Compared with other vinegars, it's sweet and dense, complex and lingering. The older the vinegar, the thicker and more intensely flavoured it becomes.

Balsamic vinegar remains very much a boutique industry, monitored tightly by a consortium that maintains quality and controls the quantity produced.

ModenaTur (see p405) can arrange a free visit to a local producer – English-speaking if you're lucky.

and the illustrations of Dionysean romps may not be to everyone's taste...

Canalgrande Hotel (☎ 059 21 71 60; www.canal grandehotel.it; Corso Canalgrande 6; s/d/tr with breakfast €115/165/200; P ✗ ✗ 🖳) Despite its rather dowdy exterior, Hotel Canalgrande remains a venerable Modenese institution. It's a cosy place with antique furniture, frescoes overhead, stucco in plenty and a leafy, tranquil terrace giving onto a garden at the rear. Parking is €10.50.

Eating

Like Bologna and Parma, Modena produces excellent *prosciutto crudo* (cured ham). The city's gastronomic speciality is *zampone* (stuffed pig's trotter), something of an acquired taste that's well worth the effort. Modena also brews the bulk of Italy's prized balsamic vinegar, a rich aromatic condiment (see the boxed text, above). Tortellini

EMILIA-ROMAGNA &
SAN MARINO

is another speciality, as is Lambrusco, one of the more famous Italian sparkling reds, light and low in alcohol, which should be drunk chilled and with everything.

Al Grottino (☎ 059 22 39 85; Via Taglio 26; pizza €5.50-8, meals €25-30; ☯ Thu-Tue) This is a popular pizza joint and restaurant. It also does takeaways and has a non-smoking area.

Trattoria da Omer (☎ 059 21 80 50; Via Torre 33; pasta & mains all €7.50; ☯ Mon-Sat) Here's a friendly family trattoria serving wonderful Modenese and Ferrarese traditional pasta and mains. Just try their *tortellini fiocchi di neve* (snowflakes), which really do all but melt in the mouth.

Ristorante da Enzo (☎ 059 22 51 77; Via Coltellini 17; meals €20-30; ☯ Tue-Sun) Begin with something from the skeins of delicious fresh, home-made pasta that greet you as you enter this long-established restaurant. Da Enzo's other speciality is dishes featuring balsamic vinegar such as their *scaloppina all'aceto balsamico* (€8.25). The more adventurous might like to gnaw on another local and house speciality, *zampone di Modena con fagiolini* (pigs' trotters with beans).

Ristorante da Danilo (☎ 059 22 54 98; Via Coltellini 31; pasta €6.50, mains €11-16; ☯ Mon-Sat) Comfortable, cosy and just up the road, Danilo does good home-style cooking, with especially good lasagne.

Pasticceria Forno San Giorgio (☎ 059 22 35 14; Via Taglio 6) This place has been satisfying the sweet tooths of Modena with its cakes and pastries for well over a century. It's a great spot for coffee and cake or a snack.

There's a good fresh-produce **market** (☯ Mon-Sat), its main entrance is on Via Albinelli.

Entertainment
Several of the city's better bars line Via Emilia, near the cathedral. During July and August, the Piazza Grande makes a great venue for outdoor concerts and ballet.

Teatro Comunale (☎ 059 20 69 93; Corso Canalgrande 85) The opera season is in winter, with most performances at the Teatro Comunale.

Teatro Storchi (☎ 059 20 69 93; Largo Garibaldi 15) offers mainly drama.

Shopping
On the fourth Saturday and Sunday of every month, except for July and December, a giant antiques fair is held in Parco Nov Sad, 500m northwest of the city centre.

Getting There & Around
The **bus station** (☎ 059 22 22 20) is on Via Fabriani. **ATCM** (☎ 059 41 67 11; www.atcm.mo.it; Strada Sant'Anna 210) and other companies connect Modena with most towns in the region.

The main train station is in Piazza Dante. Destinations include Bologna (€2.40, 30 minutes), Parma (€5.45, 30 minutes) and Milan (€14.80, two hours).

The city is at the junction of the A1 Autostrada del Sole, which connects Rome with Milan, and the A22, which heads north for Mantua, Verona and the Brenner pass.

ATCM's bus No 7 connects the train station with the bus station and city centre.

At the train station you can hire a bike (6.30am to 8pm Mon-Fri) for a very reasonable €0.50 per hour or, if you don't fancy a little pedal-pushing, an electric bike at €1.30 per hour.

For a taxi, call ☎ 059 37 42 42.

AROUND MODENA
Galleria Ferrari
The legendary Enzo Ferrari died in 1988 but his factory in **Maranello**, 17km south of Modena continues to turn out world-beating racing and sports cars that we more mortal motorists can only dream of. **Galleria Ferrari** (☎ 0536 94 32 04; Via Dino Ferrari 43; adult/child €10/6; ☯ 9.30am-6pm) is essentially the Ferrari company's museum and historical archive. It boasts the largest collection of Ferraris on show in the world, including the ones in which Michael Schumacher won the 2000 and 2001 Formula One world championship (when we last passed the 2002 model, which completed his grand slam, was expected any day). There's also a host of memorabilia to satisfy the most avid Ferrari fan.

Carpi
Once the centre of the Pio family territories Carpi is an impressive Renaissance town constructed of the characteristic local red brick. A mere 20km north of Modena, it's easily reached by train. Elegant Palazzo Pio incorporates a medieval castle and dominates one of Italy's biggest squares which is closed in on one side by a rank of porticos. Ecclesiastical hotspots are found

in the 16th-century cathedral as well as the Romanesque Chiesa di Santa Maria del Castello.

Carpi's **tourist office** (☎ 059 64 95 40) is at Via III Febraio 2.

REGGIO EMILIA
pop 146,100

Also known as Reggio nell'Emilia, the town started life in the 2nd century BC as a Roman colony along the Via Emilia, which still cuts through it. Much of Reggio was built by the Este family during the 400 years it controlled the town, beginning in 1406.

The cheese we know in English as Parmesan ('of Parma'), is called more accurately in Italian *parmigiano reggiano*, reflecting the fact that production straddles both provinces.

Reggio's churches and museums are really only for ardent ecclesiastical and archaeological buffs. All the same, it has a pleasant enough centre and makes a good base for exploring the Apennines to the south.

Information
EMERGENCY
Police Station (☎ 0522 45 87 11; Via Dante Alighieri 6)

INTERNET ACCESS
Qui Qua (☎ 0522 40 61 72; Piazza Fontanesi 4a; €6/hr; ⏰ 9am-7.30pm Mon- Sat) Internet cafè.

MEDICAL SERVICES
Ospedale Santa Maria Nuova (☎ 0522 29 61 11; Viale Risorgimento 80)

POST
Post Office (Via Sessi 3)

TELEPHONE
Telecom Office (Galleria San Rocco 8f)

TOURIST INFORMATION
Tourist Office (☎ 0522 45 11 52; www.municipio.re.it turismo; Piazza Camillo Prampolini 5c; ⏰ 8.30am-1pm & 2.30-6pm Mon-Sat, 9am-noon Sun Sep-Jul, 8.30am-2pm Mon-Sat Aug) Located on the main square.

Sights
CHURCHES
The city's few sights are concentrated around Piazza del Monte (formerly Piazza Cesare Battisti), Piazza Camillo Prampolini and Piazza San Prospero.

Reggio's **cathedral** (Piazza Prampolini; ⏰ 7.30am-noon & 3.30-7pm) is wedged between the latter two piazze. Built in the 13th century in the Romanesque style, it was almost completely remodelled 300 years later.

The clean-lined facade of the 15th-century **Chiesa di San Prospero** (⏰ 7.30am-noon & 3.30-7pm), on the piazza of the same name, is guarded by a right royal pair of red marble lions and their four cubs. Its striking octagonal bell tower was built in 1537.

The baroque **Basilica della Ghiara** (Corso Garibaldi 44; ⏰ 10am-noon & 4-5.30pm Mon-Sat, 3.30-5.30pm Sun) has frescoes by 17th-century Emilian artists that merit more than a glance.

PALAZZO DEL MUNICIPIO
Within the 14th-century **town hall**, on the south side of Piazza Camillo Prampolini, is the **Sala del Tricolore**, the room where the Italian flag was devised during a conference that established Napoleon's short-lived Cispadane Republic in 1797.

TEATRO MUNICIPALE
On the north side of Piazza Martiri del VII Luglio, this imposing building with a bevy of muses and goddesses teetering on the edge of its roof, could almost be a royal palace. Built in 1857 as an opera house, it is now used for dance, opera and theatre performances.

MUSEUMS
The **Musei Civici** (☎ 0522 45 64 77; Via Secchi 2; admission free; ⏰ 9am-noon Tue-Fri, 9am-noon & 3-7pm Sat, 10am-1pm & 3-7pm Sun) houses a collection of 18th-century works of art and archaeological discoveries. The **Galleria Parmeggiani** (☎ 0522 45 64 76; Corso Cairoli 2; admission free; ⏰ 9am-noon Tue-Fri, 9am-noon & 3-7pm Sat, 10am-1pm & 3-7pm Sun) has some worthwhile Italian, Spanish and Flemish pieces, including an El Greco.

Sleeping
Ostello Basilica della Ghiara (☎ 0522 45 23 23; fax 0522 45 47 95; Via Guasco 6; dm/d with breakfast €13/14.50) Reggio's conveniently central, HI-affiliated and fairly disorganised hostel occupies an ex-monastery.

City Hotel (☎ 0522 45 53 76; fax 0522 45 53 79; Via Roma 37; s/d/tr €34/50/68, with bathroom €44/60/75) This hotel is in a quiet street near the Giardini Pubblici. Reception is a bit scruffy and dusty but rooms are clean and comfortable.

EMILIA-ROMAGNA & SAN MARINO

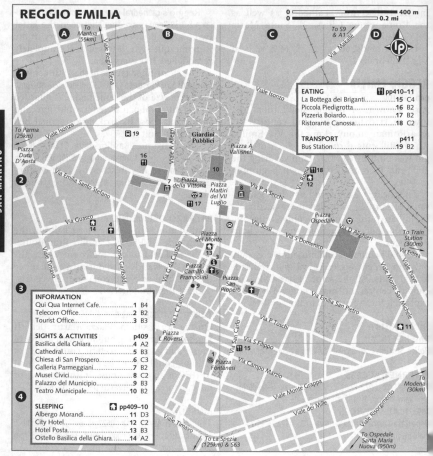

REGGIO EMILIA

0 ——————— 400 m
0 ——————— 0.2 mi

To Mantua (55km)

To S9 & A1

To Parma (25km)

Piazza Duca D'Aosta

Giardini Pubblici

Piazza A Vallisneri

Piazza della Vittoria

Piazza Martiri del VII Luglio

Piazza Ospedale

To Train Station (300m)

Piazza del Monte

Piazza Camillo Prampolini

Piazza San Prospero

Via Emilia San Pietro

Piazza L Roversi

Piazza Fontanesi

To Modena (30km)

To La Spezia (125km) & S63

To Ospedale Santa Maria Nuova (950m)

EATING	pp410–11
La Bottega dei Briganti	15 C4
Piccola Piedigrotta	16 B2
Pizzeria Boiardo	17 B2
Ristorante Canossa	18 C2
TRANSPORT	**p411**
Bus Station	19 B2

INFORMATION	
Qui Qua Internet Cafe	1 B4
Telecom Office	2 B2
Tourist Office	3 B3
SIGHTS & ACTIVITIES	**p409**
Basilica della Ghiara	4 A2
Cathedral	5 B3
Chiesa di San Prospero	6 C3
Galleria Parmeggiani	7 B2
Musei Civici	8 C2
Palazzo del Municipio	9 B3
Teatro Municipale	10 B2
SLEEPING	**pp409–10**
Albergo Morandi	11 D3
City Hotel	12 C2
Hotel Posta	13 B3
Ostello Basilica della Ghiara	14 A2

Street parking, with the local police station only 100m away, couldn't be safer...

Albergo Morandi (☎ 0522 45 43 97; www.albergo morandi.com, Italian only; Via Emilia San Pietro 64; s/d/tr with breakfast €67/95/123; P 🔀) Here's a friendly, family-run three-star hotel, handy for the train station.

Hotel Posta (☎ 0522 43 29 44; www.hotelposta.re.it; Piazza del Monte 2; s/d with breakfast from €135/175; P 🔀 🖳) Hotel Posta is a superb top-end choice, where each of the 32 rooms is individually decorated. Once residence of the Este family, then Palazzo del Capitano del Populo, or governor's residence, this venerable inn has been accommodating travellers for nearly five centuries. Ask for a room overlooking Piazza Prampolini.

Parking is €12. **Albergo Reggio** (s/d €75/95) also has rooms located nearby in its attractive nearby annexe.

Eating

There's a market, including fruit and veg, each Tuesday and Friday on Reggio's central squares. Typical local snacks include *erbazzone* (herb pie with cheese or bacon) and *gnocco fritto* (fried salted dough, the best as light as air).

Pizzeria Boiardo (☎ 0522 45 42 35; Galleria Cavour 3f; pizza €4.30-7.75; 🕑 Thu-Tue) For pizza or a straightforward meal, try this pizzeria in a covered gallery just south of Piazza della Vittoria. The wood-fired oven also burns away at lunchtime.

Piccola Piedigrotta (☎ 0522 43 49 22; Piazza XXV Aprile 1b; pizza €3.60-5.50, pasta from €5.35; ☻ Tue-Sun) This small pizzeria/trattoria makes tasty pizzas and simple pasta dishes in an informal setting. It also does takeaways.

La Bottega dei Briganti (☎ 0522 43 66 43; Via San Carlo 14b; pasta €6.70, mains €9.50-13.25; ☻ Mon-Sat) This *birreria/osteria* has a wonderful conspiratorial atmosphere and a small leafy courtyard. It serves up excellent pasta and risotto dishes.

Ristorante Canossa (☎ 0522 45 41 96; Via Roma 37; meals €25-30; ☻ Thu-Tue Sep-Jul) Ristorante Canossa, where the pasta is homemade, is one of few places in town serving excellent Reggiano cuisine. Dither between their *tortelli di zucca* (pumpkin tortelli) or *tortelli d'erba alla reggiana*.

Getting There & Around

Buse operator **ACT** (☎ 0522 43 16 67; www.actre.it, Italian only) serves the city and region from the bus station in Viale A Allegri. Destinations incude Carpi (see p408; €3.30, one hour, seven daily) and Castelnovo ne' Monti (see below; €4, 1¼ hours, at least 10 daily)

Frequent trains serve all stops on the Milan–Bologna line including Milan (€13.10, 1½ hours), Parma (€4.05, 15 minutes), Modena (€4.05, 15 minutes) and Bologna (€5.80, 45 minutes).

Reggio is on the Via Emilia (S9) and A1. The S63 is a tortuous but scenic route that takes you southwest across the Parma Apennines to La Spezia on the Ligurian coast.

For a taxi call ☎ 0522 45 25 45.

AROUND REGGIO EMILIA

Southwest of the city along the scenic S63 are the Apennines and the Parco del Gigante, now incorporated into the recently established **Parco Nazionale dell'Appennino Tosco-Emiliano** (www.appenninoreggiano.it). Among several signed walking trails, well served by *rifugi* (mountain huts), the most extensive is the Matilda Way, a four- to seven-day trek from Ciano, in the Enza valley near Canossa, to San Pellegrino in Alpe, just over the border in Tuscany.

The tourist office at **Castelnovo ne' Monti** (☎ 0522 81 04 30; Via Roma 33c; ☻ 9am-1pm Mon-Sat, 9.30am-12.30pm Sun, 3-6pm Tue & Sat) is well endowed with information about activities and accommodation and sells *Parco del*

Gigante, a handy map of the area at 1:25,000 with trails indicated. Its free *Ciclopista Ippovia del Gigante* is a good guide for cyclists. For a more gentle outing, ascend or walk around the **Pietra di Bismàntova** (1047m), a huge limestone outcrop 2.5km from town and a popular venue for climbers.

A pair of medieval castles once owned by Matilda, countess of Canossa, merit a detour, as much for their views as for their architectural interest. The castle of **Canossa** (☎ 0522 87 71 04; Via del Castello; admission free; ☻ 9am-12.30pm & 3-7pm Tue-Sun Apr-Oct, 9am-4.30pm Tue-Sun Nov-Mar) built in 940 and then rebuilt in the 13th century, is where Matilda famously reconciled the excommunicated Holy Roman Emperor Henry IV with Pope Gregory VII in 1077. May your visit be more pleasant than that of poor Henry who, as legend has it, stood outside, barefoot in the snow, for three days as penance for having insulted His Holiness. Largely ruined, the castle has a small museum.

From Canossa you can see across to the castle of **Rossena** (☎ 0522 24 20 27; admission €4.50; ☻ 3-7pm Sat, 11am-7pm Sun Mar-Oct, 2.30-5.30pm Sun Nov-Feb), better preserved but less accessible. By road 4.5km away, it's much nearer as the crow flies.

A good base for exploring the Po valley area north of Reggio Emilia is **Guastalla**, where there's an HI-affiliated youth hostel, **Ostello Quadrio Michelotti** (☎ /fax 0522 83 92 28; Via Lido Po 11; B&B €12). Both trains and buses run from Reggio Emilia.

PARMA

pop 170,000

Of the Emilian cities west of Bologna, Parma is the pick of the crop. Straddling the banks of Torrente Parma, a tributary of the Po, this well-off, orderly city should not be missed. The bicycle rules in the squares and cobbled lanes of the old town centre and the surrounding countryside is home not only to *parmigiano reggiano* (Parmesan) cheese and Parma ham (Italy's best prosciutto), but also to the massive Barilla pasta factory and a variety of castles and walking tracks. No doubt inspired by such plenty, Verdi composed many of his greatest works here and Stendhal immortalised the city in his classic French novel, *La Chartreuse de Parme*.

History

Originally Etruscan, Parma achieved importance as a Roman colony on what would become the Via Emilia. As Roman authority dwindled, the town passed to the Goths and later the Lombards and Franks. In the 11th century Parma threw in its lot with the Holy Roman Empire against the papacy and even furnished two antipopes. In the following centuries internal squabbling largely determined the city's turbulent fate, as it fell successively to the Visconti family, the Sforzas, the French and finally – sweet revenge – the papacy.

The Farnese family ruled Parma in the pope's name from 1545 to 1731, when the Bourbons took control, making Parma one of the pawns in European power games. Don Philip of Bourbon, son of Spain's Philip V, and his wife Louise Elisabeth, daughter of France's Louis XV, ushered in a period of peace and frenetic cultural activity. Following Napoleon's incursions into northern Italy at the beginning of the 19th century, Parma entered a period of instability that ended only with Italian unification.

Some 60 years later, the barricades went up as Parma became the only Emilian city to oppose the infamous 1922 march on Rome by Mussolini's blackshirts.

Orientation

From the train station Via Verdi leads south to the green turf of Piazza della Pace. Continue south along Via Garibaldi for Piazza Garibaldi, Parma's main square.

Information

EMERGENCY
Police Station (☎ 0521 21 94; Borgo della Posta 14)

INTERNET ACCESS
Aexis Telecom (☎ 0521 70 92 99; Piazzale Dalla Chiesa; €5/hr; ☼ 9am-10pm) Also offers cut-price phone calls.
PC Help Cyber Point, (☎ 0521 50 41 48; Via Massimo d'Azeglio 72d; €5/hr; ☼ 10am-8pm Mon-Sat)

LAUNDRY
Lavanderia Ad Acqua (Via Massimo d'Azeglio 108; ☼ 7.30am-10.30pm)

MEDICAL SERVICES
Hospital (☎ 0521 93 11 11; Via Gramsci 14)
Guardia Medica (☎ 0521 29 25 55) Emergency doctor.

POST
Main Post Office (Via Melloni) Off Via Garibaldi.

TELEPHONE
Telecom Office (Via Massimo d'Azeglio 66)

TOURIST INFORMATION
Tourist Office (☎ 0521 21 88 89; turismo.comune .parma.it/turismo; Via Melloni 1a; ☼ 9am-7pm Mon-Sat, 9am-1pm Sun) Just off Piazza della Pace.
InformaGiovani (☎ 0521 21 87 49) In the same building as the tourist office, this place has information for young people and disabled travellers.

Sights

PIAZZA DEL DUOMO

Externally, Parma's **cathedral** (Piazza Duomo; admission free; ☼ 9am-12.30pm & 3-7pm), consecrated in 1106, is classic Lombard-Romanesque. Internally, by contrast, the gross gilded pulpit and ornate lampholders clamped onto delicate pillars all shout high baroque bombast. You need to look up high for the baroque at its best – in the dome, Correggio's *Assumption of the Virgin* amid a swirl

---

THE BIG CHEESE

Imitated but never matched, *parmigiano reggiano* (Parmesan) is the king of Italy's cheeses. It has been made in the area around Parma for more than 700 years and is so valuable that wheels of the cheese were once accepted as currency.

The cheese is made with skimmed evening milk and full cream morning milk, which is poured into copper vats, cultured, heated and then stirred with a giant paddle. The cheesemakers delve into the vats – hairy arms and all – to check the consistency of the curd, then heave it out into cheesecloth. Each lump of curd is cut in two, shaped into a wheel form (which also imparts the distinctive parmigiano 'branding' on the rind) and left in brine for over a month before being aged for at least one and often two or more years. The regulating consortium checks every single cheese for quality before it is sold.

For a free two-hour visit to a Parmesan cheese factory, ring **Consorzio del Parmigiano Reggiano** (☎ 0521 29 27 00; www.parmigiano-reggiano.it; ☼ 8.30am Mon-Fri).

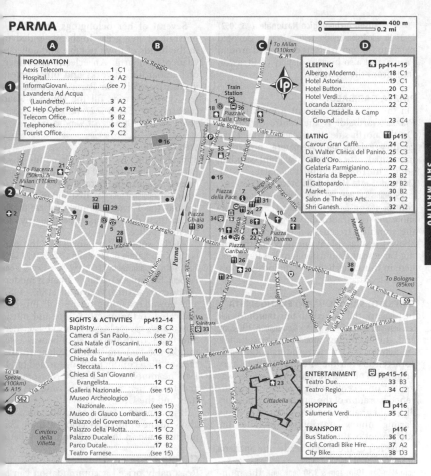

PARMA

EMILIA-ROMAGNA & SAN MARINO

---

f cherubims' limbs and, above the central ave, the Mannerist frescoes, attributed to attanzio Gambara. Take time to look at the estored wood inlay work in the sacristy nd, in the southern transept, Benedetto Antelami's highly stylised yet intensely noving sculpture, the *Descent from the Cross*, completed in 1178.

Antelami was also responsible for the triking pink marble **baptistry** (admission €2.70; 9am-12.30pm & 3-6.30pm) on the southern side f the piazza. Typically octagonal on the utside, it's divided into 16 segments with iothic architectural detail inside. Started in 196, it wasn't completed until 1307 after everal interruptions (notably when the upply of pink Verona marble ran out).

PALAZZO DELLA PILOTTA

The hulk of this immense **palazzo**, shattered by WWII air raids, looms over Piazza della Pace. Built for the Farnese family between 1583 and 1622, and supposedly named after the Spanish ball game of pelota which was played within its walls, it now houses several museums and galleries.

Galleria Nazionale (☎ 0521 23 33 09; admission incl Teatro Farnese €6; �% 8.30am-1.45pm Tue-Sun) includes works by local artists Antonio Correggio and Francesco Parmigianino plus Fra Angelico, Canaletto and El Greco. The **Teatro Farnese**, a copy of Andrea Palladio's Teatro Olimpico in Vicenza, is constructed entirely in wood and was almost completely rebuilt after WWII bombing.

The **Museo Archeologico Nazionale** (☎ 0521 23 37 18; admission €2; ☺ 8.30am-2pm) is devoted partly to Roman artefacts discovered around Parma and also hosts a display of Etruscan finds from the Po valley.

PIAZZA GARIBALDI

On the site of the ancient Roman forum, Piazza Garibaldi is the centre of Parma. On the north side, the facade of the 17th-century **Palazzo del Governatore**, nowadays municipal offices, sports a giant sundial, added in 1829. Behind the palace is the **Chiesa di Santa Maria della Steccata** (Piazza Steccata 9; admission free; ☺ 9am-noon & 3-6pm), which contains some of Francesco Parmigianino's most extraordinary work, especially the stunning frescoes on the arches, high above the altar. Many members of the ruling Farnese and Bourbon families lie buried here in this church, known to locals simply as La Steccata.

CHIESA DI SAN GIOVANNI EVANGELISTA

Just east of the cathedral, this **church** (Piazzale San Giovanni; admission free; ☺ 8am-noon & 3.30-6pm) and the adjoining **monastery** (admission free; ☺ 9am-noon & 3-5pm) were built in the early 16th century on the site of a 10th-century original. The ornate baroque facade was grafted on a century later and the magnificent decoration of the cupola – disgracefully ill-lit and unapproachable – is by Correggio. Parmigianino's contribution includes the adornment of the chapels.

Just left of the main facade, the **Spezieria di San Giovanni** (admission free; ☺ 8.30am-noon & 3-6pm Mon-Sat, 10am-1pm & 3.30-6pm Sun), the monastery's ancient pharmacy, sells all sorts of oils and unguents distilled by the monks.

For more Correggio, head for the **Camera di San Paolo** (☎ 0521 23 33 09; Via Melloni; admission €2; ☺ 8.30am-1.45pm), in the convent of the same name.

MUSEO DI GLAUCO LOMBARDI

Waterloo meant different things to different people. While Napoleon headed into miserable exile, his second wife, Marie-Louise of Austria, got off pretty lightly. After her heady few years as Empress of the French, she was left with the dukedom of Parma, Piacenza and Guastalla. She ruled until 1847, with a level of moderation and good sense uncommon for the time.

Several of her belongings, including a portrait of her great husband, ended up in the hands of town notable and collector Glauco Lombardi. An eclectic assortment of Lombardi's artworks and other objects illustrative of life in Parma over the past few centuries now fill the **Museo di Glauco Lombardi** (☎ 0521 23 37 27; Via Garibaldi 15; admission €4; ☺ 10am-3pm Tue-Sat, 9am-1pm Sun).

WEST BANK

Spread along the west bank of the River Parma (l'Oltretorrente) are the pleasant set-piece gardens of the **Parco Ducale** (☺ 7am-sunset winter, 6am-midnight summer), first laid out in 1560 around the Farnese family's **Palazzo Ducale**, which these days serves as headquarters for the local police.

At the southeastern corner of the park is the **Casa Natale di Toscanini** (☎ 0521 28 54 99; Via R Tanzi 13; admission €1.50; ☺ 9am-1pm & 2-6pm Tue-Sun), birthplace of Italy's greatest modern conductor, Arturo Toscanini (1867–1957) and nowadays home to a small museum dedicated to the maestro's life and music. Toscanini's career began almost by accident during a tour in Brazil, when he was asked to take the podium in Rio de Janeiro after the Brazilian conductor had stormed off. In 1908 he joined the New York Metropolitan and from then on split his time between Italy and the USA.

If in a musical frame of mind, you could also visit the tomb of Niccolò Paganini, 2km further south in the Cimitero della Villetta.

Sleeping

Reasonably priced accommodation can be difficult to find for most of the year so it is prudent to book.

Ostello Cittadella and camp ground (☎ 0521 96 14 34; Parco Cittadella 5; dm €9, person/tent site €6.50/1; ☺ Apr-Oct) The city's HI-affiliated youth hostel lies within the walls of a giant former fortress and accommodates 25 people in four-bed dorms. Take bus No 9 or 12 from the train station or city centre. The tiny camp ground also lies inside the fortress.

Locanda Lazzaro (☎ 0521 20 89 44; Via XX Marzo 14; s €38, s/d with bathroom from €40/52) Garret rooms with views over the Parma rooftops and an unbeatable position make Lazzaro a good bet, though don't expect to find anyone around outside restaurant hours. See p415 for details of its restaurant.

Albergo Moderno (☎ /fax 0521 77 26 47; Via A Cecchi s/d with bathroom €55/70) In a town that's short n economical accommodation, Albergo Moderno is a reasonable choice and couldn't e handier for the train station. Each bedroom's reproduction paintings in heavy gilt rames may, however, oppress a little.

Hotel Astoria (☎ 0521 27 27 17; www.piuhotels.com; la Trento 9; s/d/tr with breakfast €110/160/171; **P** **❄**) lso a stone's throw from the train station nd more upmarket, the Astoria, a bit on he bland side, is comfortable and especially opular with business visitors. Although eside a busy road, it's fully soundproofed. arking is €8.

Hotel Button (☎ 0521 20 80 39; fax 0521 23 87 83; d/tr €76/108/138; **P** **❄**) This hotel is right in ne heart of town, just off Piazza Garibaldi. edate and tranquil, it also has a 24-hour bar nd room service, should you fancy a little ite-night roistering. You can park for €13.

Hotel Verdi (☎ 0521 29 35 39; www.hotelverdi.it, lian only; Via Pasini 18; s/d €130/180; **❄** late-Aug– ristmas & mid-Jan–early Aug; **P** **❄** **▣**) Hotel erdi won't give you the warmest recep- on you've ever received. This apart, its 20 edrooms are tastefully furnished. All have arquet flooring, marble bathrooms and fes. Over the road is leafy Parco Ducale nd there's a decent separately managed estaurant next door.

ating

ou won't find it difficult to eat well in arma. If you're looking for a spot to sip ur Campari and read the paper, Piazza aribaldi is as good as any. The west bank so has its share of good restaurants.

Gallo d'Oro (☎ 0521 20 88 46; Borgo della Salina meals €20-25; **❄** Mon-Sat) Arty photos of ng-faded stars and 1950s covers from a *Gazzetta dello Sporto* and *Marie-France*: ch is the agreeably retro decor of Gallo Oro, where booking is essential. One of arma's best informal trattorie, it serves up nsistently good Emilian cuisine, includ- g delicious cold meats (just watch the countant-cum-meat slicer lovingly carve d set them out).

Locanda Lazzaro (☎ 0521 20 89 44; Via XX Marzo ; meals €22-28) Highly popular with locals ooking is normally essential), it does eat pasta and interesting meaty mains om all the major quadrupeds, including rse. See p414 for accomodation details.

Da Walter Clinica del Panino (☎ 0521 20 63 09; Borgo Palmia 2; **❄** Mon-Sat) It's small, tables are basic and the neon lights glare – yet the Cli- nica del Panino is just what a fast food joint should be. The staff is cheerful, there are over 100 varieties of snacks and sandwiches on offer (just tick/check the menu they pass to you) and prices are very reasonable.

Gelateria Parmigianino (☎ 0521 23 84 22; Via Cavour 39b) One of several tempting *gelaterie* in the centre.

Hostaria da Beppe (☎ 0521 20 65 08; Via Imbriani 51b; pasta €5.20-6.80, mains €7.50-13; **❄** Tue-Sat) For a classy meal tucked away from the main streets, search out Da Beppe. The pasta's homemade and the house speciality is risotto with *ossobuco* (veal shank marrow- bone; €10.50).

Il Gattopardo (☎ 0521 28 61 83; Via Massimo d'Azeglio 63a; pizza €5.15-7.75, mains €6.50-14 **❄** Tue- Sun) Il Gattopardo is both a pizzeria that serves huge portions, in-house and take- away, and a great restaurant offering a rich selection of fish mains.

Shri Ganesh (☎ 0521 20 01 69; Via Massimo d'Azeglio 79a; set menus €13-17) This place serves good Indian grub, to eat in or takeaway, and is a popular student haunt. Their lunchtime special menu (€8) is specially good value.

Salon de Thé des Arts (☎ 0521 20 60 06; Borgo del Parmigianino 5b; **❄** Tue-Sun) This stylish little place has a huge selection of teas to revive and refresh the weariest of travellers, ac- companied by crepes, sweet or savoury (€7) or a handful of their scrummy home-made chocolates.

Cavour Gran Caffè (☎ 0521 20 62 23; Via Cavour 30b; **❄** Mon-Sat) Whether on the terrace or inside beneath the colourful frescoes and glinting chandelier, you'll find Cavour Gran Caffè a pleasant drinks stop.

There's a **produce market** (Piazza Ghiaia; **❄** Mon-Sat) between the river and Piazza Garibaldi.

Entertainment

Parma's opera, concert and theatre season runs from about October to April. Inquire at the tourist office for details of current programmes.

Teatro Regio (☎ 0521 21 86 78; Via Garibaldi 16a) Offers a particularly rich programme of music and opera, even by exacting Italian standards.

Teatro Due (☎ 0521 23 02 42; Via Salnitrara 10) Presents the city's top drama.

In summer the city sponsors several outdoor music programmes.

Shopping

It would be a shame to leave Parma without a few local delicacies tucked away in your bag. **Salumeria Verdi** (Via Verdi 6c) is one of several great one-stop delicatessens with dangling sausages, shelves of Lambrusco wines, slabs of Parma ham and wheel upon wheel of *parmigiano reggiano* cheese.

Getting There & Around

TEP (☎ 800 97 79 66; www.tep.pr.it, Italian only) operates buses throughout the region, including into the Apennines. There are six buses daily to/from Busseto (€3.10, 1¼ hours) via Soragna (€2.60, one hour) – see following – leaving from Piazzale della Chiesa in front of the train station. A journey within the city costs €0.75.

Frequent trains connect Parma with Milan (€11.50, 1¼ hours), Bologna (€7.50, one hour), Brescia (€4.65, two hours), La Spezia (€5.75, 2½ hours), Modena (€5.45, 30 minutes) and Piacenza (€5.20, 30 minutes).

Parma is on the A1 connecting Bologna and Milan and just east of the A15, which runs to La Spezia. The Via Emilia (S9) passes right through town.

Leave your car at the underground car park in Viale Toschi or stick it beside one of the many meters near the station and along the main roads around the historic centre, from which motor traffic is banned.

For a taxi, call ☎ 0521 25 25 62.

Rent bikes from **City Bike** (☎ 0521 23 56 39; Viale Mentona 8a; per half day/day €6/10) or hire real old bargain-price spinejolters from **Cicli Corradi** (☎ 338 347 35 23; Via Massimo d'Azeglio 124a; per day €2.50).

AROUND PARMA
Verdi Country

If you have wheels you can make a pleasant day tour northwest of Parma, taking in a couple of the province's more than 20 castles and four buildings closely associated with Verdi, the city's most famous son.

Sitting in a murky moat and 19km northwest of Parma, the **Rocca Sanvitale di Fontanellato** (☎ 0521 82 90 55; adult/child €6.40/2.20; 9.30-11.30am & 3-6pm Apr-Oct, 9.30-11.30am

& 3-5pm Tue-Sun Nov-Mar) was built in the 16th century by the family of the same name. Conceived more as a pleasure dome than a military bastion, it has some vivid frescoes by Parmigianino. Admission is by guided tour (in Italian) only.

Nine kilometres further northwest is Soragna, site of the **Rocca Meli Lupi** (☎ 0524 59 7 64; admission €6.20; 9-11am & 3-6pm Tue-Sun Mar-Oct, 2.30-5.30pm Tue-Sun Nov-Feb). Constructed in 1385 and resembling more a stately home than a fortress, it's a fine example of early baroque and has retained its original period furniture. There are hourly guided tours.

The **Casa Natale di Giuseppe Verdi** (☎ 052 97 450; Roncole Verdi; admission €4; 9.30-11.45am 3-6.15pm Tue-Sun Mar-Oct, 9.30-11.45am & 2.30-4.45pm Tue-Sun Nov-Feb), site of the humble home where Giuseppe Verdi came into the world in 1813, is 5km further on.

Next stop is **Busseto**, with its splendidly ornate **Teatro Verdi** (admission €4; 9.30am-noon & 3-6.30pm Tue-Sun Mar-Oct, 9.30am-noon & 2.30-4.30pm Tue-Sun Nov-Feb) – admission is by guided tour only. Nearby is the **Casa Barezzi** (☎ 0524 9 11 17; Via Roma 119; admission €3; 10am-12.30pm 3-6.30pm Tue-Sun Mar-Oct, 10am-12.30pm & 2.30-5.30pm Tue-Sun Nov-Feb), home of the composer's patron and father-in-law, site of his first concert and packed with Verdi memorabilia.

Verdi's villa, **Sant'Agata** (☎ 0523 383 00 0; admission €6; Via Verdi 22; 9.30-11.40am & 3-6.40pm Mar-Sep, to 5.30pm Oct-Feb), where he composed many of his major works, sits in the countryside 5km northwest of Busseto.

A combined ticket for the first three Verdi venues costs €8. An alternative at €11 allows entry to all four. For more information on the Verdi sights, contact Busseto **tourist office** (☎ 0524 924 87; www.bussetolive.com Piazza Verdi 10; 9.30am-12.30pm & 3-7pm Apr-Sep 9.30am-12.30pm & 2.30-5.30pm Oct-Mar).

TEP buses from Parma run along this route up to six times a day, Monday to Saturday.

South into the Apennines

A pair of tempting routes lead south of Parma to cross the Apennines into northwest Tuscany. Alternatively, you could undertake either as a half-day outing from Parma.

The first roughly follows the River Parma towards **Langhirano**, famed for its high quality hams. About 5km short of the town and 18km from Parma rises the majestic **Castello** di Torrechiare (☎ 0521 35 52 55; admission €3; ☼ 8.30am-7.30pm Tue-Sun Apr-Sep, 8am-2pm Tue-Fri, 9am-5pm Sat-Sun Oct-Mar), which offers staggering views southwards towards the Apennines. It's one of many built or rebuilt by Pier Maria Rossi in the 15th century. Here, he romped with his lover Bianca Pellegrini in the exquisitely frescoed Camera d'Oro (Golden Room), where he (or more frequently she?) could look at a map of all his castles on the ceiling.

From Langhirano, follow the road down the west bank of the Parma, crossing the river at Pastorello and proceeding to **Tizzano Val Parma**, a charming Apennines village that offers pleasant walking in summer and reasonable winter skiing at **Schia**, 10km further on.

Further south still, the heights around **Monchio delle Corti** offer views to La Spezia on a good day. It's a possible base for exploring some of the 20 glacial lakes that dot the southern corner of the province, bordering Tuscany.

The mountains are crisscrossed with **walking** and **cycling** tracks and dotted with *rifugi*. An interesting **trekking** challenge is to follow a section of the signed **Romea**, or **Via Francigena**, an ancient pilgrim route heading south to Rome via the villages of Collecchio, Fornovo, Bardone, Terenzo, Cassio and Berceto, each with its small Romanesque church. The tourist office in Parma (p412) can advise on maps and accommodation.

Castello Bardi, about 60km southwest of Parma (not on the above route), also merits mention. Soaring above the surrounding town, it dates from 898, although most of the present structure was built in the 15th century.

PIACENZA
pop 98,400

In the northwestern corner of Emilia, just short of the Lombardy frontier, Piacenza, a prosperous town, is pleasant enough for a brief stop though short on arresting sites.

Orientation & Information
The train station is on the eastern edge of town, an easy 20-minute walk from the central square, Piazza dei Cavalli.

The **tourist office** (☎ 0523 32 93 24; Piazza dei Cavalli; ☼ 9am-12.30pm & 3-8pm Tue-Wed, Fri & Sat, 3pm Thu, 9am-12.30pm Sun) must be a serious contender for Italy's most complicated opening hours.

Sights
Piazza dei Cavalli (Square of the Horses) is dominated by the impressive brick and marble 13th-century town hall, also known as Il Gotico. The riders astride that pair of magnificent bronze horses that seem to stand guard over the square are the Farnese dukes Alessandro and his son Ranuccio. Cast by Francesco Mochi, these equestrian statues date from 1625.

The 12th-century Lombard-Romanesque **cathedral** (Via XX Settembre; ☼ 7.30am-noon & 3-7pm) harmoniously blends marble, white and pink, mellow sandstone and red brick. Some of the dome frescoes are by Guercino. The nearby **Basilica di Sant'Antonino** (Piazza Sant'Antonino; ☼ 8am-noon daily, 4-6.30pm Mon-Sat, 8-9.30pm Sun) was built in the 11th century on the site of an earlier church. Its peculiar octagonal tower is claimed to be the oldest of its type in Italy.

The **Palazzo Farnese** (☎ 0523 32 82 70; Piazza Citadella; combined ticket €5.25, Museo Civico €4.10, others €2.10-2.65; ☼ 8.30am-1pm Tue-Sat, 3-6.30pm Fri-Sun & 9.30am-1pm Sun), started in 1558, was never fully completed. It houses the Pinacoteca, an art gallery, and four little museums – of archaeology, carriages, Italian unification and the main one, the **Museo Civico** with its bizarre Etruscan Fegato di Piacenza, a sheep's liver in bronze that was used for divining the future.

A few blocks south of Piazza dei Cavalli, the **Galleria Ricci Oddi** (☎ 0523 32 07 42; Via San Siro 13; admission €2.60; ☼ 10am-noon & 3-6pm) contains a respectable collection of Italian art and sculpture from the 18th century onwards.

Sleeping & Eating
Astra (☎ 0523 45 43 64; Via Boselli 19; s/d €23.25/31) This is your best budget bet – but there's nothing fancy about it and it's about 1km south from the centre of town.

Hotel Nazionale (☎ 0523 71 20 00; www.hotel nazionale.it; Via Genova 35; s/d with breakfast from €68/75; P ⊠ ☐ ⊠) About 1km southwest of Piazza dei Cavalli (follow Corso Vittorio Emanuele II which becomes Via Genova), the 69-room Nazionale, over 70 years in business is clean and comfortable and makes a good mid-range option. Parking is €13.

EMILIA-ROMAGNA & SAN MARINO

Grande Albergo Roma (☎ 0523 32 32 01; Via Cittadella 14; s/d with breakfast €129/172; P ⊠ ⊠) Stylishly furnished, conveniently central and soundproofed, with a superb 7th-floor breakfast terrace. There's also a gym and sauna for fitness freaks. Parking is €15.50.

Santa Teresa (☎ 0523 32 57 86; Corso Vittorio Emanuele II 169b-c; mains €5.50-8) Excellent for modestly priced local cuisine including *pisarei e fasô* (€5.50), a satisfying fusion of red beans and the local pasta.

Antica Osteria del Teatro (☎ 0523 32 37 77; Via Verdi 16; mains €26-30; ☽ Tue-Sat) In an altogether different price bracket, this is one of Emilia's finest restaurants, set in a restored 15th-century palace. To avoid the agony of making difficult decisions from their enticing menu, you might want to go for their traditional menu (€55) or *menù degustazione* (€70). Or plump for the *treccia di branzino* (steamed, garnished sea bass; €26).

Getting There & Around

The bus station is on Piazza Citadella. Train, however, is more convenient for most destinations. There are direct train services to/from Milan (€6.55, 45 minutes), Turin (€14.15, two hours), Cremona (€2.50, 30 minutes), Parma (€5.20, 30 minutes) and Bologna (€11.40, 1½ hours).

Piacenza is just off both the A1 linking Milan and Bologna and the A21 joining Brescia and Turin. The Via Emilia (S9) runs past Piacenza on its way to Rimini and the Adriatic Sea.

Bus Nos 1, 2, 4, 6 and 8 run between the train station and Piazza dei Cavalli.

EAST OF BOLOGNA

FERRARA

pop 131,600

Lucrezia Borgia (see the boxed text, p35) found that marriage into the Este family brought several disadvantages, not least among them the move to this Po valley city, just south of the modern border with the Veneto. Close to the river and wetlands, Ferrara in winter can be cold, grey and shrouded in banks of fog. But winter doesn't last and Ferrara retains much of the austere splendour of its Renaissance heyday, when it was strong enough to keep both Rome and Venice at arm's length.

History

The Este dynasty ruled Ferrara from 1260 to 1598, its political and military prowess matched by intense cultural activity. Petrarch, Titian, Antonio Pisanello and poets Torquato Tasso and Ludovico Ariosto are just some of the luminaries who spent time here under the patronage of the Este dukes.

When the House of Este fell in 1598, Pope Clement VIII claimed the city, only to preside over its decline. Ferrara recovered importance during and after the Napoleonic period, when it was made chief city of the lower River Po. The local government has carefully restored much of the centre, which was battered during WWII.

Ferrara was the birthplace of Girolamo Savonarola (see the boxed text, p438), the fanatical Dominican monk whose statue with its manic eyes and posturing arms presides over the square that bears his name.

Orientation

Viale Cavour slices northwest–southeast from Porta Po near the train station to Piazza Medaglie d'Oro. It passes Ferrara's splendid castle, at whose feet spread old Ferrara's three principal piazze – Savonarola, del Castello and della Repubblica.

Information

EMERGENCY
Police station (☎ 0532 29 43 11; Corso Ercole I d'Este 26)

INTERNET ACCESS
Centro Servizi Link (☎ 0532 24 15 79; Via Aristo 57a €6.20/hr; ☽ 9am-1pm & 3.30-6.30pm)
Speedy Web (☎ 0532 24 80 92; Corso Porta Po 37; €6.20/hr; ☽ 9am-1pm & 3.30-7.30pm Mon-Fri, 10am-1pm Sat)

MEDICAL SERVICES
Ospedale Sant'Anna (☎ 0532 23 61 11; Corso della Giovecca 203)
Guardia Medica (☎ 0532 20 31 31) Emergency doctor

POST
Main Post Office (Viale Cavour 27)

TELEPHONE
Telecom Office (Largo Castello 30)

TOURIST INFORMATION
Tourist office (☎ 0532 20 93 70; www.ferrara info.com; ☽ 9am-1pm & 2-6pm Mon-Sat, 9.30am-1pm

FERRARA

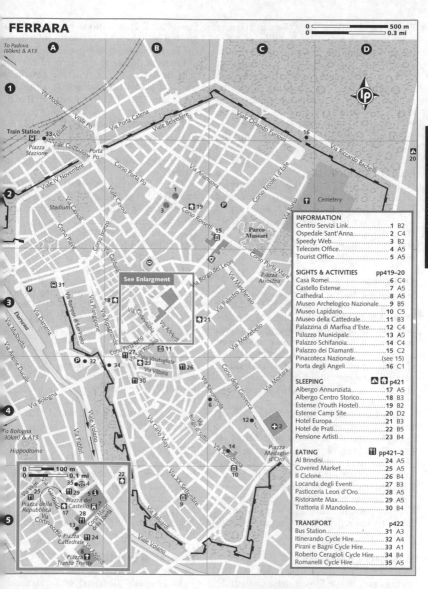

EMILIA-ROMAGNA &
SAN MARINO

2-5.30pm Sun) Located in the main courtyard of the
stello Estense.

ights
ASTELLO ESTENSE
he imposing **castle** (☎ 0532 29 92 33; Viale
vour; admission €6; ☺ 9.30am-5.30pm Tue-Sun)
as started in 1385 for Nicolò II d'Este,

primarily to defend the family from riot-
ous subjects who at one point rebelled over
tax increases. Later it became the dynasty's
permanent residence.

Although sections are now used as government offices, many of the rooms, including the royal suites, are open for viewing.
Highlights are the Sala dei Giganti (Giants'

Room) and Salone dei Giochi (Games Salon), with frescoes by Camillo and Sebastiano Filippi; the Cappella di Renée de France; and the claustrophobic dungeon. Here, in 1425, Duke Nicolò III d'Este had his young second wife, Parisina Malatesta, and his son, Ugo, beheaded after discovering they were lovers, providing the inspiration for Robert Browning's *My Last Duchess*.

For an extra €1 you can go up the tower.

PALAZZO MUNICIPALE

Linked to the castle, the 13th-century crenellated **town hall** once also contained Este family apartments. The entrance is watched over by copper statues of Nicolò III and his less wayward son, Borso – in fact 20th-century copies but none the less imposing for all that.

CATHEDRAL

Gaze long at the superb three-tiered marble facade of the **cathedral** (admission free; 7.30am-noon & 3-6.30pm Mon-Fri, 7.30am-12.30pm & 3.30-7.30pm Sat & Sun). Its upper part is a graphic representation of the final judgement and heaven and hell (just below, notice the four figures clambering out of their coffins). Astride a pair of handsome lions at the base squat an oddly secular duo, mouths agape at the effort of holding it all up.

Along the south side is an attractive colonnaded merchants' gallery.

Highlights of the **Museo della Cattedrale** (0532 76 12 99; Via San Romano; admission €4.20; 9.30am-1pm & 3-6pm Tue-Sun), just opposite, include a serene Madonna statue by Jacopo della Quercia, a couple of vigorous Cosimo Tura canvases of St George and the dragon and the Annunciation and some wonderful, witty bas reliefs illustrating the months of the year.

MUSEUMS & GALLERIES

You can buy a combined ticket (€6.70), giving entry to the Museo della Cattedrale, Palazzina di Marfisa d'Este and Museo Lapidario.

The **Palazzo dei Diamanti** (Palace of the Diamonds), named after the shaped stones decorating its facade, was built for Sigismondo d'Este late in the 15th century. Regarded as the family's finest palazzo, it's now home to the **Pinacoteca Nazionale** (0532 20 58 44; Corso Ercole I d'Este 17-21; admission €4; 9am-2pm Tue-Sat, 9am-1pm Sun), which houses works by artists of the Ferrarese and Bolognese schools.

Lucrezia Borgia spent many of her Ferrara days in what is now the **Casa Romei** (0532 24 03 41; Via Savonarola 30; admission €2; 8.30am-7.30pm Tue-Sun), a typical Renaissance house with a peaceful inner patio.

The **Palazzina di Marfisa d'Este** (0532 20 7 50; Corso Giovecca 170; admission €2; 9am-1pm & 3-6pm Tues-Sun), a patrician palace built in 1559 has ornate decorations and furnishings and a shady garden.

The 14th-century **Palazzo Schifanoi** (0532 20 99 88; Via Scandiana 23; admission €4.20 9am-7pm) is a sumptuous Este residence on Via Scandiana. The Salone dei Mesi (Room of the Months) is clad with vigorous, animated frescoes of the months and seasons by Francesco del Cossa. Sadly, all but one wall, illustrating September to December, are very deteriorated. A ticket also gives entry to the nearby **Museo Lapidario** (0532 20 99 88; Via Camposabbionario 23; 9am-6pm Tue-Sun), a small, undocumented collection of Roman and Etruscan stele, inscriptions and tombs.

The **Palazzo di Ludovico il Moro** is home to the **Museo Archeologico Nazionale** (0532 6 99; Via XX Settembre 124; admission €4; 9am-6pm Tue-Sun). The palazzo was built by Biagio Rossetti for the duke of Milan and the collection of Etruscan artefacts and Attic vases is well worth a look.

CITY WALLS

Although not terribly impressive, most of the 9km of ancient city walls are more of less intact and parts are walkable. Alternatively, hire a bike and cycle the perimeter (ask at the tourist office for its booklet, *Ten Bicycle Routes in the Province of Ferrara* Itinerary 1 describes the circuit).

Festivals & Events

On the last Sunday of May each year, the eight *contrade* (districts) of Ferrara compete in **Il Palio**, a horse race that momentarily turns Piazza Ariostea into medieval bedlam. Claimed to be the oldest such race in Italy, the first official competition was held in 1279.

The annual week-long **Ferrara Buskers Festival** (0532 24 93 37; www.ferrarabuskers.com) held in late August, attracts buskers from

round the globe, with the city paying travel
and accommodation expenses for a lucky
20 invited performers.

Sleeping

Accommodation is usually easy to find, although many hotels close during August.

Estense (☎ 0532 20 42 27; hostelferrara@hotmail.com; Corso Biagio Rossetti 24; dm/d €13/14.50) Confusingly also called Estense, Ferrara's HI-affiliated youth hostel is an easy walk from the centre.

Albergo Centro Storico (☎ /fax 0532 20 97 48; Via Vegri 15; s/d €26/36) This clean, comfortable, quiet place, located in a pretty medieval street, is excellent value.

Pensione Artisti (☎ 0532 76 10 38; Via Vittoria 66; s/d €21/38, d with bathroom €55) Also great value, cheery, and just a few minutes' walk south of the cathedral. There's a small cooking area for guest use on two of its three floors. If you want a room with bathroom (three out of twenty bedrooms), be sure to book.

Estense (☎ 0532 75 23 96; campeggio.estense@libero.it; Via Gramicia 76; person/tent site €6.50/6.50) Ferrara's only camp ground is just outside the city walls. Take bus No 1 or 5 from the train station to Piazzale San Giovanni and follow signs.

Albergo Annunziata (☎ 0532 20 11 11; www.annunziata.it; Piazza della Repubblica 5; s/d with breakfast from 120/175; 🅿 🖃) You won't be sharing the same bed but it's attested that no less a lover than Casanova slept –'spent the night' might be more accurate – here. At the time, this luxury hotel, bright with flowers and rich in all creature comforts (including free bicycle use) was but a simple locanda. Views are magnificent, whichever way your room faces. The hotel also has six recently and exquisitely restored apartments (€160 to €220 per day with breakfast).

Hotel de Prati (☎ 0532 24 19 05; www.hoteldeprati.com; Via Padiglioni 5; s €70-105, d €105-130; 🅿 🖃) In a quiet lane within a stone's throw of the castle, this is a splendid, tasteful, family place. Rooms have wrought-iron bedsteads and antique furniture and selected prints of works by Ferrara Renaissance painters hang in each. The corridors, by contrast, are enlivened by changing exhibitions of contemporary art. Breakfast is included in the price.

Hotel Europa (☎ 0532 20 54 56; www.hoteleuropaferrara.com; Corso Giovecca 49; s/d/tr with breakfast €72/112/136; 🅿 🖃 🖵) None of its successive renovations has deprived this 19th-century Ferrara institution of its period charm. Some rooms have disabled facilities while others still retain their original ceiling frescoes. Ask for a peep at the guest book, signed by luminaries including Benito Mussolini, the Khedive of Egypt, Emile Zola and Alexandre Dumas. Reserve room No 4 if you're in search of your musical muse; that's where Verdi slept. The hotel provides bicycles for free and parking costs €8.

Eating

Ferrara's cuisine is typical of the region, incorporating meats and cheeses. One local speciality is *cappellacci di zucca*, a pasta pouch filled with pumpkin that looks like a small, floppy hat. Another is *pampota*, a kind of gingerbread cake, stuffed with nuts and coated in dark chocolate.

Il Ciclone (☎ 0532 21 02 62; 1st fl, Via Vignatagliata 11; pizzas €3.50-7, meals €20-30; ☽ Tue-Sun) Il Ciclone is a bright, friendly pizzeria and restaurant that specialises in fish dishes. Dip your fork into their *risotto alla pescatore* (fisherman's risotto; €10.50). There's a non-smoking room.

Al Brindisi (☎ 0532 20 91 42; Via Adelardi 11; pasta from €6.50, wine per glass from €3.10; ☽ Tue-Sun) This splendid *osteria*-cum-*enoteca* (wine bar) is just the place for a glass of Romagna's finest wine and a hearty snack. Dating from 1435, its walls are lined with dusty vintage wine bottles and it claims among its past guests both Titian and Benvenuto Cellini.

Locanda degli Eventi (☎ 0532 76 13 47; Via Carlo Mayr 21; pasta €6.20-7.50, mains €10.50-13, menù turistico €15; ☽ Thu-Tue) *Tortelli verdi* with vegetables and truffles (€6.70) is one of the house specialities at this typical local trattoria; *scottaditto alle brace* (grilled lamb cutlets; €10.50) is another.

Trattoria il Mandolino (☎ 0532 76 00 80; Via Carlo Mayr 83; pasta €6.20-7, mains €10.50-16; ☽ lunch Wed-Mon) Lasagne so light that it melts in your mouth and *cappellacci di zucca* are two of the treats in store at this shrine of Ferrarese home-cooking.

Ristorante Max (☎ 0532 20 93 09; Piazza della Repubblica 16; meals €40-50; ☽ Tue-Sun) The menu at this warmly recommended place, staffed by a young, friendly team, is short, creative and particularly strong on fish dishes. The wine list is equally carefully selected. Service could be speedier but, despite the silver 'M' arches outside, this is no fast-food joint. Leave a cranny for dessert and their platter of made-on-the-premises rich dark chocolates. There's a non-smoking room.

Pasticceria Leon d'Oro (☎ 0532 20 93 18; Piazza Cattedrale 2-10; ☽ Thu-Tue) One of a trio of excellent *pasticcerie* facing the cathedral, the Leon d'Oro offers the best views.

Self caterers can stock up at Ferrara's **covered market** (Via Vegri; ☽ 7am-1.30pm Mon-Sat).

Getting There & Around

The bus station is on Via Rampari San Paolo. **ACFT** (☎ 0532 59 94 92; www.acft.it, Italian only) buses operate services within the city and to surrounding towns such as Comacchio (1¼ hours, 10 daily), as well as to the Adriatic beaches (some of these leave from the train station). There are also up to 19 buses daily to Bologna (one hour).

Most traffic is banned from the city centre. ACFT buses No 1, 2 and 9 run from the train station to the city centre.

For a taxi, call ☎ 0532 900 900.

Even better, get in the saddle and join the hundreds of other wheelers in Italy's most cycle-friendly city. There are four places where you can rent bikes (per hour/three hours/day around €2/6/10):

Roberto Ceragioli (Piazza Travaglio 4)
Itinerando (Piazzale Kennedy 6-8)
Pirani e Bagni (Piazzale Stazione)
Romanelli (Via de la Luna 10)

PO DELTA (FOCI DEL PO)

Considering the polluted state of the River Po, the Po delta, which straddles Emilia-Romagna and the Veneto, should be an unpleasant place. However, the stretch of coast where the river spills into the Adriatic Sea is strangely alluring, particularly because the wetlands surrounding its two large lagoons – the Valli di Comacchio in the south and the Valle Bertuzzi in the north – have been designated as nature reserves. The area provides some of Europe's best bird watching and, after years of neglect by tourist authorities, is now drawing quite a crowd. Despite this, many beaches have perennial problems with sludge-like algae caused by the dumping of phosphates upstream. Summertime mosquitoes are another irritation, so be sure to have insect repellent, if not mosquito nets, on hand.

Most towns in the area have tourist offices, though many open only in summer. They produce a wealth of information, including cycling itineraries, walking and horse-riding details, and tips on boat excursions, which are the best way to see the delta.

Sights & Activities

The **Abbazia di Pomposa** (☎ 0533 71 91 10 Codigoro; admission €4; ☽ 8.30am-7pm summer, to 4pm winter), 50km east of Ferrara, is one of Italy's oldest Benedictine abbeys, with a church dating from the 7th century. It is believed that the monk Guido d'Arezzo invented the musical scale here, and in its time the abbey was one of Italy's foremost cultural centres. Its decline began in the 14th century, and in 1652 it was closed. The church is adorned with frescoes from the 14th-century Rimini school and works by Vitale di Bologna. There's also a small museum.

The abbey stages a classical music festival, **Rassegna di Musica Clasica** (☎ 0533 72 9 71), each July.

Comacchio is a small fishing village that has one attraction – the Trepponti (Triple Bridge) built in 1635. The **tourist office** (☎ 0533 31 01 47) is at Via Buonafede 12.

The delta's main **information office** (☎ 054 44 68 66), north of Ravenna, is at Ca' Vecchia, a wildlife guardians' centre at Via Fossatone in the Stazione Pineta San Vitale park. It produces a bird map covering that part of the delta's nature reserve and in the sanctuaries at Punte Alberete and Valle Mandriole.

Sleeping

Albergo Luciana (☎ 0533 71 21 40; Via Roma 66 Codigoro; s without bathroom €26, d with bathroom €33 This place is about the best you'll find for cheap accommodation in the area.

RAVENNA

pop 139,750

Celebrated for the early Christian and Byzantine mosaics that adorn its churches and monuments, Ravenna was the capital of the Byzantine Empire's western region during the reign of Emperor Justinian and Empress Theodora.

The city had been the capital of the Western Roman Empire ever since 402, when the ineffectual Emperor Honorius moved his court from Rome because Ravenna

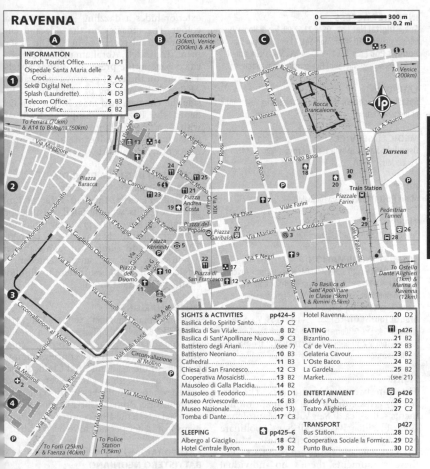

RAVENNA

0 — 300 m
0 — 0.2 mi

To Commacchio
(30km), Venice
(200km) & A14

To Venice
(200km)

To Ferrara (70km)
& A14 to Bologna (60km)

*Rocca
Brancaleone*

Darsena

Train Station

Piazzale
Farini

Pedestrian
Tunnel

To Ostello
Dante Alighieri
(1km) &
Marina di
Ravenna
(12km)

To Basilica di
Sant'Apollinare
in Classe (5km)
& Rimini (55km)

To Forlì (25km)
& Faenza (40km)

To Police
Station
(1.5km)

EMILIA-ROMAGNA & SAN MARINO

surrounding malarial swamps made it easier to defend from northern invaders. The barbarians, however, simply walked around him and marched into Rome in 410. Honorius was unable or unwilling to react, preferring to vegetate in Ravenna until his death in 423, and the city finally succumbed 50 years later.

The Byzantines arrived in 540 and ruled until the Lombards conquered the city in 752. Venetians controlled Ravenna from 1441 to 1509, when it was incorporated into the Papal States.

Under the Romans, Goths and Byzantines, Ravenna gradually rose to become one of the most splendid cities of the Mediterranean. Its mosaics, described by Dante in his *Divine Comedy* as a symphony of colour, are matched only by those of Istanbul. The city is close to Adriatic beaches, but they aren't the coast's most attractive.

Orientation

From the train station, on the eastern edge of town in Piazzale Farini, it's a short walk along Viale Farini and its continuation, Via Diaz, into the central Piazza del Popolo. From here, nearly everything of interest is within easy walking distance.

Information

EMERGENCY

Police Station (☎ 0544 29 91 11; Via Berlinguer 10-20)

INTERNET ACCESS
Sek@ Digital Net (☎ 0544 21 53 99; Via di Roma 79; €4/hr; ✆ 8am-10.30pm Mon-Sat, 11am-10.30pm Sun)
Buddy's Pub (☎ 0544 59 10 59; Via Magazzini Anteriori 31; €6/hr; ✆ Tue-Sun) Five computers available.

LAUNDRY
Splash (Via Candiano) Located over the tracks, just south of the train station.

MEDICAL SERVICES
Ospedale Santa Maria delle Croci (☎ 0544 28 51 11; Via Missiroli 10)

POST
Main Post Office (Piazza Garibaldi)

TELEPHONE
Telecom Office (Via G Rasponi 22)

TOURIST INFORMATION
Tourist Office (☎ 0544 3 54 04; www.turismo.ravenna .it; Via Salara 12; ✆ 8.30am-7pm Mon-Sat Apr-Sep, 8.30am-6pm Mon-Sat Oct-Mar, 10am-4pm Sun year-round) Located off Via Cavour.
Branch Tourist Office (☎ 0544 45 15 39; Via delle Industrie 14; ✆ 9.30am-12.30pm & 3-6pm Apr-Sep, 9.30am-1pm & 2.30-5pm Oct-Mar) Located at the Mausoleo di Teodorico.

Sights
There are two combined tickets. The first (€8.50) gives entry to the six main monuments – Basilica di San Vitale, Mausoleo di Galla Placidia, Basilica di Sant'Apollinare Nuovo, Basilica dello Spirito Santo, Museo Arcivescovile and Battistero Neoniano. For these monuments there's no individual admission price.

The second (€6.50) lets you into Mausoleo di Teodorico, the Museo Nazionale and, 5km southeast of town, Basilica di Sant'Apollinare in Classe, each of which has its own admission price.

The opening times we list are good for April to September and tend to be longer than those for the rest of the year.

The Basilica di San Vitale, Mausoleo di Galla Placidia and Museo Nazionale are all in the same complex, which has its main entrance on Via San Vitale.

BASILICA DI SAN VITALE
The **basilica** (✆ 9am-7pm) was consecrated in 547 by Archbishop Maximian. Its sombre exterior hides a dazzling internal feast of colour. The mosaics on the side and end walls represent scenes from the Old Testament. To the left, Abraham prepares to sacrifice Isaac in the presence of three angels. The one on the right portrays the death of Abel and the offering of Melchizedek. Inside the chancel, two magnificent mosaics depict the Byzantine Emperor Justinian with San Massimiano (left) and a particularly solemn and expressive Empress Theodora, his consort (right).

MAUSOLEO DI GALLA PLACIDIA
The **mausoleum** (✆ 9am-7pm) was constructed for Galla Placidia, the half-sister of Emperor Honorius, who initiated construction of many of Ravenna's grandest buildings, although it's unlikely that she ever lay here. The light inside, filtered through alabaster windows, is dim yet, supplemented by a single central lamp, is sufficient to illuminate the city's oldest mosaics.

MUSEO NAZIONALE
Ravenna's main **museum** (☎ 0544 3 12 41; admission €4; ✆ 8.30am-7.30pm Tue-Sun) has a wealth of accumulated pottery, bronzes, icons, vestments – and a greater concentration of portraits of the Madonna and Child, of very variable quality, than you're ever likely to see elsewhere. Monks began this collection of prehistoric, Roman, Christian and Byzantine artefacts in the 18th century and various items from later periods have been added.

CATHEDRAL, MUSEO ARCIVESCOVILE & BATTISTERO NEONIANO
The town's **cathedral** (Via G Rasponi) was built in 1733 after its 5th-century predecessor was destroyed by an earthquake. It's unremarkable but the small adjoining **Museo Arcivescovile** (Episcopal Museum; Piazza Arcivescovado ✆ 9am-7pm) contains an exquisite 6th-century ivory throne of Middle Eastern origin and some beautiful mosaics. Even more impressive, and still *in situ,* are the mosaics of the baptism of Christ and the apostles on the domed roof of neighbouring **Battistero Neoniano** (Via Battistero; ✆ 9am-7pm). Though to have started life as a Roman bath house (and there's a certain watery logic here since baptism at the time was by total immersion), it was converted into a baptistry in the 5th century.

OMBA DI DANTE

Much of Dante's *Divine Comedy* was written right here in Ravenna. Following his exile from Florence in 1302, Dante came to live in Ravenna, where he died in 1321. Florence still supplies the oil for the lamp that burns continually in his tomb, as a perpetual act of penance for having exiled him. The 18th-century **tomb** (Via Dante Alighieri admission free; ☯ 9am-7pm) is beside the **Chiesa di San Francesco**, which merits a detour to see the mosaic floor, shimmering beneath the flooded crypt. A mound placed over Dante's sarcophagus during WWII, to protect it from air raids, is proudly marked, and the area around the tomb has been declared a – much abused – *zona di silenzio* (area of silence).

Another literary great, Lord Byron, briefly lived in a house on nearby Piazza di San Francesco in 1819.

Near the tomb, pause briefly to admire the clean, neoclassical facade of the – inevitably named – **Teatro Alighieri**, Ravenna's main theatre, beside Piazza Garibaldi.

MAUSOLEO DI TEODORICO

This two-storey mausoleum, built in 520, is a considerable feat of construction with its huge blocks of stone, uncemented by any mortar, and broad dome, 11m in diameter. At its heart is a Roman basin of porphyry, for all the world like a giant bath, that was recycled as a sarcophagus.

OTHER CHURCHES

The **Basilica di Sant'Apollinare Nuovo** (Via di Roma; ☯ 9am-7pm), originally built by the Goths in the 6th century, is a must. The exquisite mosaic on the right (south) wall of the nave depicts a procession of 26 martyrs heading towards Christ in Majesty with his apostles. On the left wall is a complementary and equally expressive procession of virgins, bearing offerings to the Madonna.

The Gothic **Battistero degli Ariani** (Via degli Ani; admission free; ☯ 8.30am-7.30pm) is behind the **Basilica dello Spirito Santo**, just off Via Diaz. Like the Battistero Neoniano, the dome of this baptistry has a breathtaking mosaic depicting the baptism of Christ.

Five kilometres southeast of the city centre is the **Basilica di Sant'Apollinare in Classe** (☎ 0544 47 36 61; Via Romea Sud, Classe; admission , ☯ 8.30am-7.30pm Mon-Sat, 1-7pm Sun). The

basilica was built in the 6th century on the burial site of Ravenna's patron saint, who converted the city to Christianity in the 2nd century. The highlight of this harmonious construction is the brilliant, star-spangled mosaic in the apse. To get there take bus No 4 or the train to Classe.

Courses

The **Mosaic Art School** (☎ 335 561 84 85; www .mosaicschool.com; Via F Negri 14) has been running classes at all levels for over 30 years.

The **Centro Internazionale di Studi per l'Insegnamento del Mosaico** (Cisim; ☎ 0544 45 03 44; www.mosaico.ravenna.it; Via M Monti 32), 50 years in business, runs intensive one-week mosaic courses from late June to early September.

The **Cooperativa Mosaicisti** (Via Fiandrini 1), next to the Museo Nazionale, also runs courses.

Festivals & Events

Riccardo Muti, director of Milan's La Scala, has close ties with Ravenna and is intimately involved each year with the **Ravenna Festival** (☎ 0544 24 92 44; www.ravennafestival.org), one of Italy's top music festivals with recitals from mid-June to late July.

Stars of the jazz scene come to Ravenna in the second half of July for **Ravenna Jazz**. Year-round, check out www.crossroads -it.com (Italian only) for information about who's currently performing on Ravenna's active jazz scene.

Sleeping

The city is an easy day trip from Bologna but staying overnight is no problem except in high summer, when it's prudent to reserve. The closest camp grounds are at Marina di Ravenna on the beach (take ATM bus No 70 or follow the S67 from the town centre).

Ostello Dante Alighieri (☎ 0544 42 11 64; Via Aurelio Nicolodi 12; dm/d with breakfast €13/14) This HI youth hostel is in a modern building 1km from the train station. In an excellent initiative that ought to be copied by every hotel in the land, it has small box safes (€0.20) near reception where you can stash your valuables. Take bus No 1 or 70 from town or the train station.

Albergo al Giaciglio (☎/fax 0544 3 94 03; mmambo@racine.ra.it; Via Rocca Brancaleone 42; s/d/tr €30/42/55, with bathroom €36/51/65) This simple, family-run, 19-room hotel, one of the cheaper alternatives around and handy for the station, also has a decent restaurant (see following).

Hotel Ravenna (☎ 0544 21 22 04; fax 0544 21 20 77; Viale Maroncelli 12; s/d €38/52, s/d/tr with bathroom €45/65/88; **P**) Another family hotel and one that is even more convenient for the station, Hotel Ravenna is clean, pleasant and welcoming. It also has free parking for guests.

Hotel Centrale Byron (☎ 0544 3 34 79; fax 0544 3 41 14; Via IV Novembre 14; s/d from €54/85; **✻**) The Byron offers all the comforts you'd expect from a three-star hotel and more. Just off Piazza del Popolo, it couldn't be more central or nearer the action.

Camping Piomboni (☎ 0544 53 02 30; www.camping piombini.it; Viale della Pace 421; person/tent site €6.50/ 11.70; **✻** Easter–mid-Sep) Convenient for the beach and set in shady pinewood, this makes a good family camp ground, 8km from Ravenna.

Campeggio Rivaverde (☎ 0544 53 04 91; www .gestionecampeggi.it; Viale delle Nazioni 301; person/tent site €7.20/12; **✻** mid-Apr–mid-Sep) Equally shady with full facilities and a sandy beach, this camp site, 15km from Ravenna, is another attractive option.

Eating

Bizantino (Piazza Andrea Costa; set menus €6.20 & €7.50; **✻** lunch Mon-Fri) This popular self-service restaurant within the covered market is the place for a quick, economical lunchtime bite.

Al Giaciglio (☎ 0544 3 94 03; Via Rocca Brancaleone 42; pasta from €5.50, mains €5.50-9, tourist menu €13) Near the station and beneath the hotel of the same name, the Giaciglio makes its own pasta and specialises in Romagnan food, with fresh fish and seafood on Friday.

Ca' de Vèn (☎ 0544 3 01 63; Via Corrado Ricci 24; pasta €6.50-7.50, mains €8.50-13; **✻** Tue-Sun) As much *enoteca* as restaurant, it has a short but splendid menu that changes weekly. The vast, high-roofed eating area has been in turn lodging house, spice shop and wine cellar (just *look* at all those bottles of rarest Emiliagna wines on the shelves; you're unlikely to be able to afford to buy any of these but current best vintages are available at around €2.50 a glass). The non-smoking part isn't the usual poky, hived-off corner but a good 50% of the dining area. Highly recommended.

L'Oste Bacco (☎ 0544 3 53 63; Via Salara 20; mai €5.20-11.40, meals €20-28; **✻** Wed-Mon) Here's truly inventive little place, normally packe to the gunnels with discerning locals. Wel prepared regular dishes on the handwritte list of daily specials include *frittata ai por dolci* (omelette with leeks) and *tagliatelle a ragù* (tagliatelle with meat sauce).

La Gardela (☎ 0544 21 71 47; Via Ponte Marino meals €18-25; **✻** Fri-Wed) This is an elegant ye informal eatery whose specialities includ *cappalletti romagnoli al ragù* (hat-shape pasta with meat sauce; €5.20).

Gelateria Cavour (Via Cavour 42; gelati €1.5 2.75) For a sweet finale, head for Gelater Cavour.

Self-caterers and sandwich-fillers shoul stock up at the city's **covered market** (Piaz Andrea Costa).

Entertainment

You can see the mosaics by night (9pm 11pm) every Friday evening in July an August.

Buddy's Pub (☎ 0544 59 10 59; Via Magazz Anteriori 31; **✻** Tue-Sun) This place changes lil a chameleon according to the day of th week. Tuesday's Latino, Saturday is disc night and Thursday is student special. also has half a dozen computers for lat night surfing.

REMEMBERING IL DUCE

It might seem a little odd that Italy's great dictator, Benito Mussolini, should have been born and raised in the traditionally left-wing territory of the Romagna. Predappio, a village overloaded with monumental buildings erected by its most infamous son, is also the Fascist leader's final resting place; his remains were buried here in 1957. About 15km south of Forli (a dull town 45km northwest of Rimini along the Via Emilia), Predappio is the scene of pro-Fascist celebrations each year, when the faithful few mark 31 October, the anniversary of the day Mussolini became prime minister in 1922. Many of the young skinheads and older diehards probably forget that their beloved icon, before donning the black shirt, started his political life as a card-carrying socialist and journalist who rarely missed a chance to wave the red flag.

ietting There & Around

.TM buses depart from Piazzale Farini in ont of the train station for towns along he coast. **Punto Bus** (☎ 0544 68 99 00), on the iazza, is ATM's information and ticketing ffice. An in-town journey costs €0.75.

Frequent trains connect the city with Bo-)gna (€4.60), Ferrara (€4.15; change here or Venice), Faenza (€2.40), Rimini (€2.80) nd the south coast.

Ravenna is on a branch of the A14 Bologna-imini autostrada (motorway). The S16 (Via .driatica) heads south to Rimini and on own the coast. The main car parks are ast of the train station and north of the asilica di San Vitale.

To its immense credit, Ravenna runs a ee bicycle-hire service for visitors. Simply ick up a key from the main tourist office nd return the cycle half an hour before clos-ig time. Or else, just borrow a bike from ne of the several cycle parking stalls around •wn and return it there or to another. **Cooperativa Sociale la Formica** (☎ 0544 46 ` 30), operating from a shed just south of ie station, acts as a left-luggage office and :nts bikes (per hour/day €1/7.75).

ROUND RAVENNA

aenza

his Romagnola town has been producing igh-grade ceramics for hundreds of years nd gave us the word faïence (tin-glazed rthenware). A 30-minute train ride from avenna, the **Museo Internazionale delle Ceram-he** (☎ 0546 69 73 11; Via Baccarini 19; admission €6; ⌒ 9am-7pm Tue-Sat, 9.30am-1pm & 3-7pm Sun Apr-Oct, m-1.30pm Mon-Fri, 9.30am-1pm & 3-6pm Sat-Sun Nov-ar) is well worth a visit.

Faenza's **tourist office** (☎ 0546 2 52 31) is at iazza del Popolo 1.

IMINI

p 131,700

riginally Umbrian, then Etruscan and oman, Rimini sits at the centre of the iviera del Sole and is nowadays invaded nnually by beach lovers. The city contin-d to change hands through the Middle ges, knowing Byzantine, Lombard and ipal rule before ending up in the hands of ie Malatesta family in the 13th century. At e beginning of the 16th century, Cesare •rgia added the city to his list of short-ed conquests but it soon succumbed to

Venice, then the Papal States. Rimini joined the Kingdom of Italy in 1860.

The old city centre was badly damaged by 400 bombing raids in WWII but enough remains to warrant a quick look. The town's main attractions are the beach and its frenetic nightlife; young people flock here every weekend from as far as away as Rome. In summer, Rimini fills with Italian and, increasingly, foreign holidaymakers in search of a scrap of beach and nocturnal fun and games – they have more than 100 discos and clubs to choose from. In spite of all the frenzy, it remains a ritual family holiday destination for many Italians.

Rimini was the birthplace of Federico Fellini, Italy's most exuberant post-WWII film director. He and his wife and frequent star, Giulietta Masina are buried together in the town cemetery.

Orientation

The **main train station** (Piazzale Cesare Battisti) is at the northern edge of the old town. The old quarter is bounded by Corso Giovanni XXIII to the west and Corso d'Augusto, which is punctuated by old Rimini's two main squares, Piazza Tre Martiri and Piazza Ca-vour. Wherever you are, walk in an easterly direction and you can't fail to hit beach.

Information

EMERGENCY
Police station (☎ 0541 35 31 11; Corso d'Augusto 192)

INTERNET ACCESS
Bar Posto Pubblico (☎ 0541 2 98 28; Corso Giovanni 23; €3.50/hr; ⊗ 7.30-2am Mon-Sat, 11-2am Sun)

MEDICAL SERVICES
Hospital (☎ 0541 70 51 11; Viale Luigi Settembrini 2) Southeast of the centre.
Guardia Medica (☎ 0541 70 57 57) Emergency doctor.

POST
Main post office (Corso d'Augusto)

TOURIST INFORMATION
Tourist office (☎ 0541 5 69 02; www.turismo.provin cia.rimini.it; Piazzale Federico Fellini 3; ⊗ 8.30am-7pm Easter–mid-Sep, Mon-Sat mid-Sep–Easter)
Branch tourist office (☎ 0541 5 13 31; train station, Piazzale Cesare Battisti; ⊗ 8.30am-7pm Easter–mid-Sep, 10am-4pm Mon-Sat mid-Sep–Easter) Also three beach-front kiosks, summer only.

RIMINI

INFORMATION		
Bar Posto Pubblico	1	A3
Tourist Office Branch	2	C3
Tourist Office	3	C1

SIGHTS & ACTIVITIES	pp428–9	
Arco di Augusto	4	B4
Castel Sismondo	5	A4
Palazzo del Municipio	6	A4
Palazzo del Podestà	7	A4
Ponte di Tiberio	8	A3
Roman Amphitheatre	9	C4
Teatro Amintore Galli	10	A4
Tempio Malatestiano	11	B4

SLEEPING	pp429–30	
Associazione Italiana		
Albergatori	(see 3)	
Grand Hotel	12	C1

Hotel Aurora Centro	13	D3
Hotel Card	14	B3

EATING	p430	
Caffè Cavour	15	A4
Covered Market	16	B4
Osteria Saraghina	17	A4
Osteria della Piazzetta	18	A4
Osteria di Santacolomba	19	A4
Picnic	20	A4
Pizza da Nino	21	B4

ENTERTAINMENT	pp430–1	
Caffè Turismo	22	B4

TRANSPORT	p431	
Bicycle Hire	23	D2
Buses for San Marino & Rome	24	B3
Provincial Bus Station	25	C3

Adriatic Sea

Sights & Activities

CASTEL SISMONDO

At the southwestern corner of the old town, the **castle** (Piazza Malatesta; ☾ exhibitions only), also known as the Rocca Malatestiana, takes its name from Sigismondo, one of the Malatesta family, who ruled for a couple of centuries until Cesare Borgia took over in 1500. Sigismondo was hardly your ideal ruler; Pope Pius II – also no angel – burned his effigy in Rome and condemned him to hell for his crimes, which included rape, murder, incest, adultery and severe oppression of his people.

ROMAN REMAINS

The **Arco di Augusto** (Arch of Augustus) was built in 27 BC at the southeastern end of

Corso d'Augusto. At the Corso's wester end is the **Ponte di Tiberio** (Tiberius' Bridge slung across the creek in the 1st century A as testimony to the city's importance to th Empire. There are insubstantial remains a **Roman amphitheatre** (cnr Viale Roma & Via Bastio Orientali). The former Roman forum lies be neath Piazza Tre Martiri.

TEMPIO MALATESTIANO

The **temple** (Via IV Novembre 35; admission fr ☾ 8am-12.30pm & 3.30-6.30pm Mon-Sat, 9am-1p & 3.30-7pm Sun) of the Malatesta clan is th grandest monument in Rimini. Dedicate to St Francis, the church was transforme in the 15th-century to house the tomb Sigismondo Malatesta's beloved mistres

Isotta degli Atti. Most of the unfinished facade is by the Florentine Leon Battista Alberti, one of the period's great architects. The side chapels are separated from the single wide nave by pillared marble partitions, topped by tubby cherubs. The chapel nearest the altar on the south side has a fresco by Piero della Francesca.

PIAZZA CAVOUR

This central piazza is lined with the city's finest *palazzi*, including the **Palazzo del Municipio**, built in 1562 and rebuilt after being razed during WWII, and the 14th-century Gothic **Palazzo del Podestà**. The **Teatro Aminore Galli** only went up in 1857 in the feverish years leading to unification.

BEACHES

The Rimini riviera boasts a staggering 40km of mostly sandy beaches, in places 200m wide. Most are either rented to private companies, which in turn rent space to bathers, or are connected to hotels. Indeed, the only free sand you'll find is a stretch near the pier little larger than a couple of beach towels.

The typical daily charge for an umbrella and a pair of loungers is €12 (low season) and €14 (high season), including access to changing rooms and showers. These private areas are well worth it if you have children. All have bars and small playgrounds and most organise special activities. Several offer windsurfing courses and board hire.

Although the River Po pumps its polluted waters into the Adriatic north of town, all of Rimini town's beaches have been awarded the coveted EU blue flag.

THEME PARKS

Rimini isn't just for sun-lovers and socialites; the city abounds in theme parks at various points on the naffness scale for kids and their suffering parents. There's **Italia in Miniatura** (☎ 0541 73 20 04; www.italiainminiatur.com, Italian only; Via Popilia 239, Viserba SS16 km197; adult/child €13.50/10; ☼ 9am-7.30pm Apr-Jun & Sep, 9am-midnight Jul & Aug, 9am-sunset Sat & Sun Oct-Mar) in Viserba. It's an ambitious collection of reproductions of, well, bits of Italy, such as the area given over to scale models of some 120 buildings facing Venice's Grand Canal and Piazza San Marco. Take bus No 8 from the Rimini or Viserba train station.

Fiabilandia (☎ 0541 37 20 64; Via Cardano 15, Rivazzura di Rimini; adult/child €15/10; ☼ 10am-midnight Jul & Aug, 10am-7pm Apr-Jun & Sep) is a fantasy park full of weird and wonderful characters. It's not really suitable for very young children. Take bus No 9 from Rimini's train station.

There are also several dolphinariums in the area, including **Delfinario Rimini** (☎ 0541 5 02 98; www.delfinariorimini.it; Lungomare Tintori 2; adult/child €9/6; ☼ Easter-Sep), right on the beach at Rimini.

Those of an aeronautical bent will be flying high at the **Parco Tematico dell'Aviazione** (☎ 0541 75 66 96; Via S Aquilina 58; adult/child €8/6.50; ☼ 9am-7pm). With over 40 planes including MiGs, a DC3 once owned by Clark Gable and a Gloucester Javelin, plus a variety of weapons used to shoot them down, it's a great place for all those who've never quite grown up. Take bus No 7.

For altogether more harmless flying things, visit **Eden Park** (☎ 0541 72 06 38; Via Popilia 345-347; adult/child €4/3), a sanctuary for exotic birds at Torre Pedrera in the northern beach area.

Waterparks in and around Rimini include **Aquafàn** (☎ 0541 60 30 50; Via Pistoia, Riccione; adult/child €19/12; ☼ 10am-6.30pm mid-Jun–mid-Sep) at Riccione, about 15km south of town. Take bus No 42, 45, 46 or 53 from Rimini station.

Tours

In summer, there are free multilingual guided **tours** (☎ 0541 5 54 14; Tue, Jun–mid-Sep) of the old quarter. Just turn up at the town museum's **public relations office** (Corso d'Augusto 158).

Sleeping

In July and August accommodation can be difficult to find and very expensive since proprietors often make full board compulsory. In winter many of the 1500 hotels close and the city is dead. In summer touts, sanctioned by the tourist office, frequent intersections on the outskirts of the city and offer rooms at so-called bargain rates. A better alternative is to book through the **Associazione Italiana Albergatori** (☎ 0541 5 33 99; Piazzale Federico Fellini 3), beside the main tourist office, or by phoning **Adria Hotel Reservation** (☎ 0541 39 05 30).

The great majority of hotels close outside the main season. Those listed are open year-round. During August prices increase significantly.

EMILIA-ROMAGNA & SAN MARINO

Hotel Card (☎ 0541 2 64 12; www.hotelcard.it; Via Dante 50; s/d €25/39, with bathroom €35/49; P) With a 24-hour bar, breakfast thrown in and a mere 100m from the station, Hotel Card makes a good jumping off point for Rimini. Ask for a room facing the side street; Via Dante carries a lot of traffic.

Hotel Aurora Centro (☎ 0541 39 10 02; fax 0541 39 16 82; Via Tobruk 6; s/d €35/60; P) Run by an exuberant elderly couple, this hotel is another good choice, handier for the beach, with a downstairs bar.

Camping Maximum Internazionale (☎ 0541 37 26 02; Viale Principe di Piemonte 57; person/tent site €8/15; Y Jun-Sep) At Miramare, southeast of the city, this camp ground is near the water. Take bus No 11.

Camping Italia International (☎ 0541 73 28 82; fax 0541 73 23 22; Via Toscanelli 112, Viserba; adult/tent site €8.50/14.50; Y mid-May-Sep) Another possibility is Camping Italia International, northwest of the centre at Viserba. Take bus No 4.

Hotel Gasparini (☎ 0541 38 12 77; www.hotel gasparini.it; Via Boiardo 3; d/tr/q with breakfast €60/74/96) A couple of blocks back from the beach, Hotel Gasparini is exceptionally good value out of season and must rank high among Italy's friendliest hotels; those tiny bathrooms are more than counterbalanced by the great welcome from Manuela and Mauro and the lively bar.

Grand Hotel (☎ 0541 5 60 60; www.grandhotelrimini .com; Parco Federico Fellini; s/d with breakfast from €168/265; P   X   R) 'A fable of riches, luxury and oriental splendour': that's how Fellini regarded the Grand Hotel when he was a boy. Adolescent overstatement it might be but the Grand remains truly that with its private beach, shady garden and attentive service.

Eating

Rimini is not noted for its culinary contribution to the Italian table and many restaurants offer cheap tourist menus.

Picnic (☎ 0541 2 19 16; Via Tempio Malatestiano 3; mains €8.50-9.50; Y Tue-Sun) Unpretentious and reasonably priced, Picnic is one of the better budget deals. Try their *spaghetti allo scoglio* (with seafood; €8.30).

Pizza da Nino (Via IV Novembre 9) This is the place to drop by for tasty, instant, takeaway pizza by the slice (from €1.55).

Osteria Saraghina (☎ 0541 78 37 94; Via Poletti 32; pasta with seafood €7-10; Y Tue-Sun) It's fish and seafood all menu through at Osteria Saraghina,

another uncomplicated restaurant, just off the central Piazza Malatesta. The quality is excellent and friendly staff plus a view on Castel Sismondo are bonuses.

Osteria della Piazzetta (☎ 0541 78 39 86; Vicolo Pescheria 5; meals €25-35; Y Mon-Sat) Packed with locals, this *osteria* offers typical Romagna cuisine, served in hearty portions. Sample their *strozzapreti misto funghi e salsiccia* (Romagna's short-strand pasta with mushrooms and finely chopped sausage; €7).

Osteria di Santacolomba (☎ 0541 78 00 48; Via di Duccio 2-4; mains €11-14; Y lunch Mon-Sun) Off central Piazza Malatesta, this restaurant, which occupies a former church bell tower, serve traditional cuisine. The *zuppa di farro* (barley soup; €6.50) is a house speciality.

Osteria Tiresia (☎ 0541 78 18 96; Via XX Settembre 41; Y dinner Tue-Sun) You'll leave Teresia a least €100 the lighter but with a wonderful feeling in your tum after one of the finest meals you're ever likely to taste, consumed in agreeably – and paradoxically – peasant rustic surroundings.

Caffè Cavour (☎ 0541 78 51 23; Piazza Cavour 13 This is a good pitstop for cappuccino o panini throughout the day.

For self-catering or picnic provender load up at the **covered market** (Via Castelfidardo)

Entertainment

Barge (☎ 0541 12 26 85; Lungomare Tintori 13) A trendy place popular with locals and visitors alike, the Barge is a Romagnola version of the Irish pub. The tasteful decoration and good music (DJ or live), drinks and food are a magnet for all the fashionable twenty somethings.

Caffè Turismo (☎ 0541 2 27 15; Piazza Tre Mart 3) This is far from the tourist trap its name might imply. Designer cool, all glass and mellow olive-green, its *the* place for watching the beautiful people of Rimini strut their stuff. Drinks don't come cheap, however (cocktails around €5.50).

Discos and clubs come and go (in winter very few are open at all). Ask at the tourist office for your type of club and also about the special summer-service buses that service the discos. Most places are north and south of the town centre.

Le Cocoricò (☎ 0541 60 51 83; Via Chieti 44, Riccione; admission €26) The most famous club in the area is a mecca for Italian teenagers. Underground, techno and house music

ule. Go there with 2000 of your closest riends – you'll all fit in.

Paradiso Club (☎ 0541 75 11 32; Via Covignano 260; ☼ year-round) The music's eclectic and anyhing goes at Paradiso with its three dance oors, seven bars and restaurant.

etting There & Away

he city's **airport** (☎ 0541 71 57 11; Via Flaminia) aters only for charter flights.

There are regular buses to towns along e coast, including Riccione (No 11) and attolica (Nos 11 and 125). Buses run from imini's train station to San Marino (€6.20 eturn, 45 minutes, eight daily). There's so a daily direct bus to/from Rome 23.75, 5¼ hours).

Trains run frequently down the coast Ancona (€7.65), Bari (€28.75), Lecce 35.25) and Taranto (€31.50), and up the e through Bologna (€9.40) and on to ilan (€20.10).

You have a choice of the A14 (south into arche or northwest towards Bologna and ilan) or the toll-free (but often clogged) 6.

etting Around

RAM buses (€1) operate throughout the ty. Northwards, bus No 11 passes the ation and cathedral before heading for azzale di Federico Fellini. Southwards, s No 11 runs between the train station d Riccione.

In August, Blue Line are special lateght buses connecting the out-of-town ubs with the city centre, train station and mp sites. They run through the night til 6am.

For a taxi, ring ☎ 0541 5 00 20.

An open-air stall on Piazzale Kennedy nts city **bikes** (per hour €3) and mountain kes (€4).

AN MARINO

27,730

hat did King Arthur say of Camelot in onty Python's *The Holy Grail*? 'It is a y place.' Lying 657m above sea level and ly 10km from the Adriatic Ocean as the w flies, the 61-sq-km Repubblica di San arino, Europe's third smallest state after e Vatican and Monaco, seems a little silly

as well; one can only speculate as to what Mexico's consul does here – or, indeed, his homologue, the San Marino Honorary Consul in Honolulu – and you're unlikely to see a greater density of kitsch souvenir stands for quite a while. This said, the old town is pleasant enough and the views all around are quite spectacular.

If you're in Rimini, think of it as just another of the beach resort's theme parks. You can take pictures of the republic's soldiers, buy local coinage and send mail with San Marino stamps. Avoid weekends, especially in summer, when the town can be choked with visitors.

History

Several legends describe the founding of this hilly city-state, including one about a stonecutter who was given the land on top of Monte Titano by a rich Roman woman whose son he had cured. What's attested is that the inhabitants of the mountain republic are the inheritors of 1700 years of revolution-free liberty; 'Welcome to the Country of Freedom', the signs proclaim.

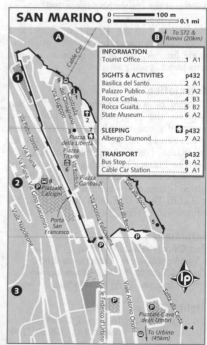

SAN MARINO		
INFORMATION		
Tourist Office	1	A1
SIGHTS & ACTIVITIES		p432
Basilica del Santo	2	A1
Palazzo Publico	3	A2
Rocca Cestia	4	B3
Rocca Guaita	5	B2
State Museum	6	A2
SLEEPING		p432
Albergo Diamond	7	A2
TRANSPORT		p432
Bus Stop	8	A2
Cable Car Station	9	A1

GOLD DIGGERS KEEP OUT

The Republic of San Marino has laws to stop foreign gold diggers snatching its supply of rich, elderly men. After several incidences of young foreigners marrying elderly San Marino residents for their money, regulations were introduced banning female domestic staff aged under 50. In the words of a spokesperson for the San Marino congress: 'It's a question of sovereignty and of the measures that a small state takes to protect itself.'

Everybody has left San Marino well alone. Well almost. Cesare Borgia took possession early in the 16th century, but his rule was short-lived as he died soon after. In 1739 one Cardinal Giulio Alberoni took over the republic but the pope backed San Marino's independence and he was sent packing.

During WWII the republic remained neutral and played host to 100,000 refugees until 1944, when the Allies marched into the town. San Marino joined the European Council in 1988 and the United Nations in 1992.

This tiny republic has some bizarre regulations (see the boxed text, above) and citizenship is passed on only through the male line. A 1999 referendum to change this law was not passed.

Orientation

Perched on a hilltop, the old part of San Marino, the only part of any interest, is essentially one main street. Enter via the Porta San Francesco, ascend Via Basilicius to Piazza Titano, keep climbing another 50m to Piazza Garibaldi, go to the end of parallel Contrada del Omagnano or Via Eugippo – then stop short or you'll fall over the cliff. That's it. You've done the capital of this nation state.

Information

Post Office (Viale Antonio Onofri 87; ⏲ 8.15am-4.30pm Mon-Fri) Sells the republic's special stamps.
Tourist Office (☎ 0549 88 29 98; www.omniway.sm; Contrada Omagnano 20; ⏲ 8.30am-6.30pm)

Sights

You might want to spend some time in the small **state museum** (☎ 0549 99 12 95;

Piazza Titano 1; adult/child €3/1.50; ⏲ 8am-8pm Apr–mid-Sep, 9am-5pm mid-Sep–Mar) even if most of the more interesting exhibits, which are impressively displayed, come from outside the republic. Or take a squint at the **Palazzo Pubblico** (admission €2.10). Or just wander along the well-kept city walls and perhaps poke around the two fortresses, **Rocca Guaita** and **Rocca Cestia** (admission for both €3; ⏲ 8am-8pm Apr–mid-Sep, 9am-5pm mid-Sep–Mar). Otherwise there are a several private minimuseums after your money – of modern weapons, instruments of torture, wax dummies and a reptilarium/aquarium.

Sleeping & Eating

There are several camp grounds signposted off the main road (S72) through the republic from Rimini.

Albergo Diamond (☎ /fax 0549 99 10 03; Contrada del Collegio 50; d with bathroom €54) has spacious rooms above a large, busy restaurant. It's a good choice if you miss the last bus out.

Food is not one of San Marino's strong points and the best thing about some of the cafés is the views. The city centre is well endowed with places offering set meals starting at €15.

Shopping

Nothing is probably the best advice. 'Welcome to Fred's Spirits: cheap booze and free drinks' proclaims one come-on. Fred and his fellow traders claim to sell cut-price alcohol but you'd want to be sure about what your poison is worth in Italy before buying here in the belief that you're getting duty-free bargains.

Getting There & Away

Buses run to/from Rimini (€6.20 return; 45 minutes; eight daily) and there's a once daily service travelling to Urbino. Buses arrive at the parking station in Piazzale Calcigni, better known as Piazzale dell' Autocorriere. The S72 leads into the city centre from Rimini.

If you arrive by car, leave it at one of the numerous car parks (Nos 6 and 7 are the highest up) and walk or take the series of stairs and elevators to the town. If all the town car parks fill up, you are obliged to park near the *funivia* (cable car; €3.10 return) and take it to the centre.

Tuscany (Toscana)

TUSCANY (TOSCANA)

Tuscany can rightly claim to have just about the best of everything – architecture, the country's greatest collection of art, soul-stirring countryside and some of Italy's finest fresh produce and best-known wines. It was from Tuscany, about 600 years ago, that the Renaissance rippled out across Europe.

The works of Michelangelo, Leonardo da Vinci and so many other 14th- to 16th-century Tuscan masters remain models for artists to this day. Tuscan architects such as Brunelleschi and Leon Battista Alberti have had an enduring influence on the course of architecture. Dante, Petrarch and Boccaccio planted the seeds for a unified Italian language with their vigorous literature.

Most people are drawn to Tuscany by the artistic splendours of Florence and Siena or to view the Leaning Tower of Pisa. But Tuscany features some of Italy's most impressive hill towns and has great scope for walking. In the south, Etruscan sites around Saturnia and Sovana take you away from the mainstream tourist itinerary. And southern Tuscany also boasts some pleasant beaches, especially on the Monte Argentario peninsula and Elba island.

Travelling in Tuscany is easy. The A1 and main train line ensure good north–south connections and major areas are easily accessible by public transport. A car does, however, give you greater flexibility.

TUSCANY (TOSCANA)

HIGHLIGHTS

- **Featuring Florence**
  The Uffizi Gallery, Palazzo Vecchio (pp447–9), cathedral (pp441–5) and baptistry (p444)

- **Lovely Boy**
  Michelangeo's *David*, posing in Florence's Galleria dell'Accademia (p452)

- **Tuscan Renaissance**
  The walled town of Lucca (pp474–8) and Pisa's Campo dei Miracoli (p481)

- **Siena's Local Derby**
  Il Palio, the world's shortest horse race (p496)

- **Fine Wines**
  Tickle the palate with fine Tuscan wines, from Chianti (pp489–91) to Montalcino (pp504–5)

- **Hilltop Towns**
  The medieval lanes and alleyways of San Gimignano (pp498–501), Volterra (pp501–4), Cortona (pp513–14) and Montepulciano (pp506–7)

- **Tuscany for Walkers**
  The challenge of the Apuane Alps, hiking in Garfagnana (p478), Mugello (p469) and Chianti (pp489–91)

★ Garfagnana
★ Mugello
★ Lucca   ★ Florence
Pisa ★
★ Chianti
San Gimignano ★
Volterra ★   Cortona ★
★ Siena
Montepulciano ★
★ Montalcino

■ POPULATION: 3.5 MILLION   ■ AREA: 22,991 SQ KM

FLORENCE (FIRENZE)

pop 374,500

Beside the banks of the River Arno and set among low hills clad in olive groves and vineyards, Florence is immediately captivating. Cradle of the Renaissance and home of Machiavelli, Michelangelo and the Medici, the city seems unfairly overblessed with art, culture and history.

Despite the relentless traffic and stifling summer heat, Florence attracts tourists by the millions each year. The French writer Stendhal was so dazzled by the magnificence of the Basilica di Santa Croce that he was barely able to walk for faintness. He's not the only one to have felt overwhelmed by the beauty of Florence – Florentine doctors reputedly treat a good dozen cases of 'Stendhalismo' a year.

You will need at least four or five days to do Florence any justice at all.

HISTORY

Controversy still reigns over who founded Florence. The commonly accepted story holds that Julius Caesar founded Florentia around 30 BC, making it a strategic garrison on the narrowest crossing of the Arno and by doing so controlling the Via Flaminia linking Rome to northern Italy and Gaul. But archaeological evidence suggests an earlier village, which was founded

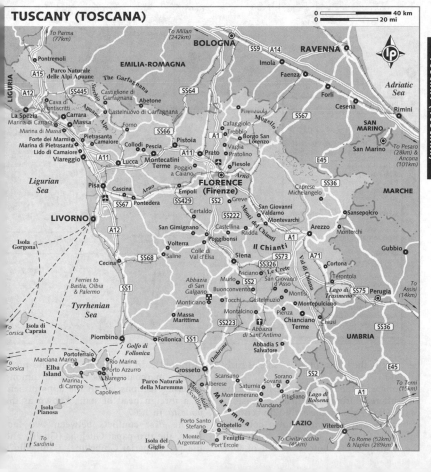

TUSCANY (TOSCANA)

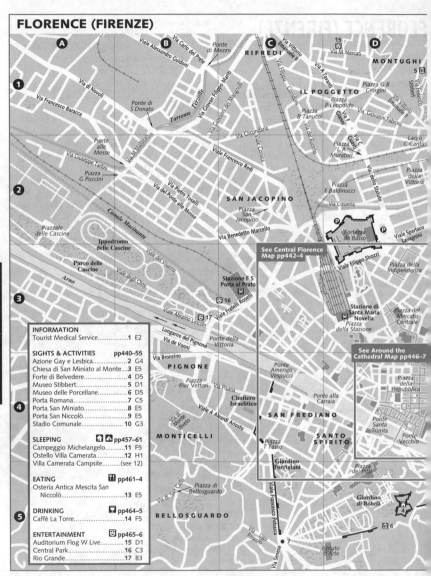

FLORENCE (FIRENZE)

perhaps by the Etruscans of Fiesole as early as 200 BC.

Along with the rest of northern Italy, the city suffered during the barbarian invasions of the Dark Ages. In the early 12th century, it became a free *comune* (town council), ruled by 12 *priori* (consuls), assisted by the Consiglio di Cento (Council of One Hundred), drawn mainly from the prosperous merchant class. Agitation among differing factions led to the appointment of a foreign head of state, known as the *podestà*, in 1207.

The first conflicts between two factions, the pro-papal Guelphs (Guelfi) and the pro-imperial Ghibellines (Ghibellini)

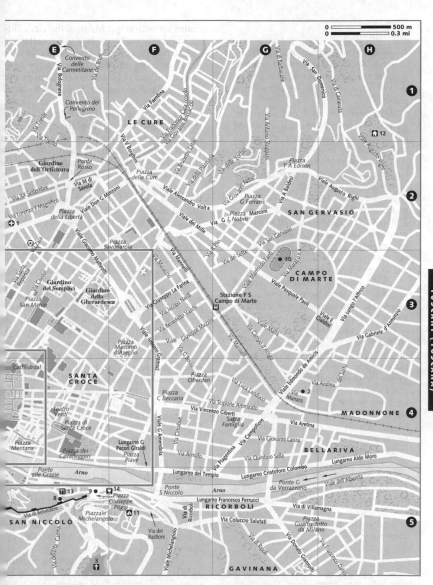

TUSCANY (TOSCANA)

started in the mid-13th century, with power passing from one to the other for almost a century.

In the 1290s the Guelphs split into two factions: the Neri (Blacks) and Bianchi (Whites). When the Bianchi were defeated, Dante was among those driven into exile in 1302. As the nobility lost ground the

Guelph merchant class took control, but trouble was never far away. The great plague of 1348 halved the city's population and the government was rocked by growing agitation from the lower classes.

In the late 14th century Florence was ruled by a caucus of Guelphs under the leadership of the Albizi family. Among the

TUSCANY (TOSCANA)

SAVONAROLA

The Renaissance was a time of extraordinary contrasts. Artists, writers and philosophers of great talent flourished against a backdrop of violence, war, plague and extreme poverty.

In Florence the court of Lorenzo de' Medici was among the most splendid and enlightened in Europe. Yet, in the streets and increasingly in Lorenzo's court itself, people had begun to listen intently to the fanatical preachings of a Dominican monk called Girolamo Savonarola.

Born in Ferrara in 1452, Savonarola moved to Florence in the last years of Lorenzo il Magnifico's rule. An inspired orator he preached against luxury, greed, corruption of the clergy and the Renaissance itself. To him the Church and the world were corrupt and its rulers, oppressors.

In 1494, when the Medici were expelled from Florence and a republic proclaimed, Savonarola was appointed its legislator. Under his severe, moralistic lead the city underwent a kind of religious reform.

His followers included some of the city's greatest humanist philosophers and artists but his enemies were many and powerful. Beside the exiled and much-miffed Medici stood the corrupt Pope Alexander VI who excommunicated Savonarola for preaching against him. Then, as the Florentine public turned cold on the evangelistic preacher, he came under attack from the Franciscan monks and began to lose the support of his dwindling political allies.

After refusing to undergo ordeal by fire, Savonarola was arrested. On 22 May 1498 in Piazza della Signoria (where today a plaque marks the spot), he was hanged and burned at the stake for heresy and his ashes were thrown into the Arno.

---

under his patronage. Many of the city's finest buildings are testimony to his tastes.

The rule of Lorenzo il Magnifico (1469–92), Cosimo's grandson, ushered in the most glorious period of Florentine civilisation and of the Italian Renaissance. His court fostered a great flowering of art, music and poetry, turning Florence into the cultural capital of Italy. Lorenzo favoured philosophers, but he kept up family tradition by sponsoring artists such as Botticelli and Domenico Ghirlandaio; he also encouraged Leonardo da Vinci and a young Michelangelo.

Not long before Lorenzo's death in 1492, the Medici bank failed and two years later the Medici were driven out of Florence. The city fell under the control of Girolamo Savonarola (see the boxed text, opposite), a Dominican monk, who led a puritanical republic until, after falling from public favour, he was tried as a heretic and executed in 1498.

After Florence's defeat by the Spanish in 1512, the Medici returned to the city only to be expelled five years later, this time by Emperor Charles V. But Charles not only allowed the Medici to return to Florence; he married his daughter to Lorenzo's great-grandson Alessandro de' Medici, whom he made duke of Florence in 1530. Seven years later one of the last truly capable Medici rulers, Cosimo I de Medici, took charge, becoming grand duke of Tuscany after Siena fell to Florence in 1569 and ushering in over 150 years of Medici domination of Tuscany.

In 1737 the grand duchy of Tuscany passed to the French House of Lorraine which retained control (apart from a brief interruption under Napoleon) until it was incorporated into the Kingdom of Italy in 1860. Florence briefly became the national capital but Rome assumed the mantle permanently in 1870.

Florence was badly damaged during WWII by the retreating Germans, who blew up all its bridges except the Ponte Vecchio. Devastating floods ravaged the city in 1966, causing inestimable damage to its buildings and artworks. However, the salvage operation led to the widespread use of modern restoration techniques that have subsequently saved artworks throughout the country. In 1993 the Mafia exploded a massive car bomb, killing five, injuring 3

---

families opposing them were the Medici, whose influence grew when they became the papal bankers.

In the 15th century Cosimo de' Medici emerged as head of the opposition to the Albizi and eventually became Florence's ruler. His eye for talent and his tact in dealing with artists saw the likes of Alberti, Brunelleschi, Lorenzo Ghiberti, Donatello, Fra Angelico and Fra Filippo Lippi flourish

and destroying a part of the Uffizi Gallery. Firenze Nuova, a large satellite town to the northwest, is being constructed in an effort to decrease the city's dependence upon tourism for its wealth.

ORIENTATION

Whether you arrive by train, bus or car, the central train station, Santa Maria Novella (Map pp442–4), is a good reference point. From it, a 10-minute walk along Via de' Panzani, then Via de' Cerretani brings you to the cathedral.

From Piazza di San Giovanni next to the cathedral (Map pp442–4), Via Roma leads to Piazza della Repubblica and continues as Via Calimala and Via Por Santa Maria to the Ponte Vecchio.

Take Via de' Calzaiuoli from the cathedral to get to Piazza della Signoria, the historic seat of government, and the Uffizi Gallery on its south side, overlooking the Arno.

Maps

If you want something that is more detailed than the tourist office's free sheet, its

Florence Map & Tour Itineraries (€0.50), covering the city centre, also has a street key. The green-covered *Firenze* (€5.50), produced by Litografia Artistica Cartografica and scaled at 1:9000 and including a cutaway of the centre at 1:5500, is one of the handiest commercial maps of the city available.

INFORMATION
Books

If you plan to spend time here, pick up Lonely Planet's *Florence*, which explores the city in much greater detail.

Bookshops

Paperback Exchange (Map pp442–4; ☎ 055 247 81 54; Via Fiesolana 31r) A vast range of new and second-hand books in English.

Feltrinelli International (Map pp446–7; ☎ 055 21 95 24; Via Cavour 12-20r) Books in English and major European languages.

Emergency

Police Station (Map pp436–7; ☎ 055 4 97 71; Via Zara 2) Has a foreigners office.

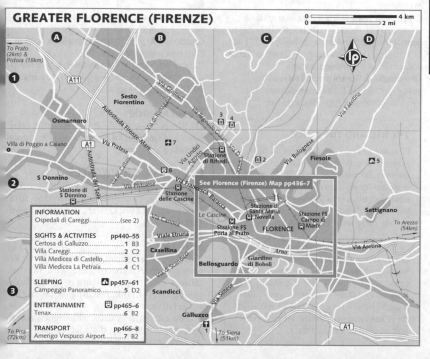

GREATER FLORENCE (FIRENZE)

0 ——— 4 km
0 ——— 2 mi

INFORMATION
Ospedali di Careggi....................(see 2)

SIGHTS & ACTIVITIES pp440–55
Certosa di Galluzzo....................1 B3
Villa Careggi............................2 C2
Villa Medicea di Castello.............3 C1
Villa Medicea La Petraia.............4 C1

SLEEPING pp457–61
Campeggio Panoramico.............5 D2

ENTERTAINMENT pp465–6
Tenax....................................6 B2

TRANSPORT pp466–8
Amerigo Vespucci Airport..........7 B2

Gay & Lesbian Travellers

Azione Gay e Lesbica (Map pp436–7; ☎ 055 67 12 98, www.azionegayelesbica.it, Italian only; Via Manara 12)

Libreria delle Donne (Map pp442–4; ☎ 055 24 03 84; Via Fiesolana 2b) For information to tune you into Florence's lesbian scene.

Internet Access

Il Cairo Phone Center (Map pp442–4; ☎ 055 263 83 36; Via de' Macci 90r; from €1.80/hr; 9.30am-9pm) Florence's cheapest log-on.

Internet Train (around €4/hr) Via dell'Oriuolo 40r (Map pp446–7; ☎ 055 263 89 68); Via Guelfa 24a (Map pp442–4; ☎ 055 21 47 94); Borgo San Jacopo 30r (Map pp446–7; ☎ 055 265 79 35); beneath Stazione di Santa Maria Novella (Map pp442–4; ☎ 055 239 97 20) Has over 15 branches.

Laundry

Wash & Dry (☎ 800 23 11 72; 8am-10pm) Via Nazionale 129r (Map pp442–4); Via del Sole 29r (Map p446-7); Via della Scala 52-54r (Map pp442–4); Via dei Servi 105r (Map p442-4); Via de' Serragli 87r (Map pp442–4).

Medical Services

Ospedali di Careggi (Map p439; ☎ 055 4 27 71; Viale Morgagni 8) Florence's main public hospital is north of the city centre.

Ospedale di Santa Maria Nuova (Map pp446–7; ☎ 055 2 75 81; Piazza Santa Maria Nuova 1)

Tourist Medical Service (Map pp436–7; ☎ 055 47 54 11; Via Lorenzo il Magnifico 59; 24 hrs) Has doctors who speak English, French and German.

Misericordia di Firenze medical service (Map pp446–7; ☎ 055 21 22 21; Vicolo degli Adimari 1; 1.30-5pm Mon-Fri) Runs a clinic for tourists.

THE RED AND THE BLACK

Florence has two parallel street-numbering systems; red or brown numbers indicate commercial premises while black or blue ones are for private residences. When written in full, black or blue addresses have only the number while red or brown addresses usually carry an 'r' for *rosso* (red) after the number.

To compound the confusion, black/blue numbers tend to denote whole buildings while each red/brown one refers to one commercial entity – and a building may have several of them. It can turn you purple if you're hunting in a hurry for a specific address: keep your eyes on both sets of numbers and be prepared to backtrack.

Farmacia Comunale (Map pp442–4; ☎ 055 21 67 61; inside Stazione di Santa Maria Novella; 24 hrs)

All'Insegna del Moro (Map pp446–7; ☎ 055 21 13 43; Piazza di San Giovanni 28; 24 hrs)

Money

Travelex (Map pp446–7; ☎ 055 28 97 81; Lungarno degli Acciaiuoli 6r)

American Express (Map pp446–7; ☎ 055 5 09 81; Via Dante Alighieri 22r)

Post

Main Post Office (Map pp446–7; Via Pellicceria)

Telephone & Fax

Telecom Office (Map pp442–4; Via Cavour 21r; 7am-11pm) Unstaffed.

Tourist Information

Main Tourist Office (Map pp442–4; ☎ 055 29 08 32; www.firenzeturismo.it; Via Cavour 1r; 8.30am-6.30pm Mon-Sat & 8.30am-1.30pm Sun)

Tourist Office (Map pp442–4; ☎ 055 21 22 45; Piazza Stazione 4; 8.30am-7pm Mon-Sat, 8.30am-2pm Sun)

Tourist Office (Map pp446–7; ☎ 055 234 04 44; Borgo Santa Croce 29r; 8.30am-7pm Mon-Sat, 8.30am-2pm Sun)

Amerigo Vespucci airport (Map p439; ☎ 055 31 58 74; 7.30am-11.30pm)

Consorzio ITA (p457; Stazione di Santa Maria Novella) Offers basic tourist information.

There are police **tourist help points** (in fact, small white vans) at the Ponte Vecchio (Map pp446–7) and Piazza della Repubblica (Map pp446–7).

Travel Agencies

CTS (Map pp442–4; ☎ 055 28 95 70; www.cts.it, Italian only; Via de' Ginori 25r) The Florence branch of this national youth-travel organisation.

DANGERS & ANNOYANCES

The most annoying aspect of Florence is the crowds, closely followed by the summer heat. Pickpockets are active in crowds and on buses.

SIGHTS

Florence can seriously overwhelm. We won't even *try* to compete with the battalions of litterati and other nobs who've spilled rivers of ink, reaching for an original superlative.

The city just swarms with sights, mostly within easy walking distance of each other. All we can do here is point and steer

TUSCANY (TOSCANA)

you through the most unmissable of the shouldn't-be-misseds. For sexier detail, pick up Lonely Planet's *Tuscany & Umbria*. To delve in even more depth, pack its *Florence*.

As everywhere in Italy, museums and monuments tend to close on Monday although since Florence is a year-round, week-through tourist destination, major monuments open daily. The tourist office has a comprehensive list of opening hours.

Piazza del Duomo & Around Map pp446–7

You'll probably already have glimpsed the sloping, brown-tiled dome to Florence's **Duomo** (☎ 055 230 28 85; admission free; ⏰ 10am-5pm Mon-Sat, 1.30-4.45pm Sun) as it peeks through the crowded streets around the square. All the same, the first glimpse of the cathedral's tiered pink, white and green marble facade will stop you in your tracks.

The cathedral was begun in 1296 by the Sienese architect Arnolfo di Cambio and took almost 150 years to complete. The facade, in fact, is neo-Gothic, built in the 19th century to replace Arnolfo di Cambio's uncompleted original, which was pulled down in the 16th century. Inside, the cathedral is decorated with frescoes by Vasari and Federico Zuccari and the stained-glass windows by Donatello, Andrea del Castagno, Paolo Uccello and Lorenzo Ghiberti positively glow.

The cathedral's vast interior, 155m long and 90m wide, and its sparse decoration comes as a surprise after the visually tumultuous facade. The sacristies on each side of the altar feature enamelled terracotta lunettes by Luca della Robbia over their doorways.

The two frescoes in the northern aisle commemorate the *condottieri* (mercenary leaders) Sir John Hawkwood and Niccolò da Tolentino, who fought for Florence in the 14th century. Also in the northern aisle is a painting of Dante, including a depiction of the *Divine Comedy*, by Domenico di Michelino.

A stairway near the main entrance of the cathedral leads to the **crypt** (admission €3; ⏰ 10am-5pm Mon-Fri, 10am-4.40pm Sat), with Brunelleschi's tomb and excavations that have unearthed parts of the 5th-century Basilica di Santa Reparata, which originally stood on the site.

Brunelleschi won a public competition to design the enormous **dome** (admission €6;

QUEUE JUMPING

If time is precious and money not a prime concern, you can skip (or at least shorten) some of the museum queues in Florence by booking ahead. In summer especially long queues can mean a sticky wait of up to four hours!

For a fee of €3 per museum you can book a ticket in advance to any of the state *musei statali* (museums) which include the Uffizi Gallery, Palazzo Pitti, Museo del Bargello, Galleria dell'Accademia, Museo Archeologico and Cappelle Medicee. Simply phone **Firenze Musei** (☎ 055 29 48 83; www.firenzemusei.it; ⏰ lines 8.30am-6.30pm Mon-Fri, 8.30am-12.30pm Sat) and when you arrive at the site go to the window for those with pre-booked tickets, quote your booking number, pay – and smile smugly at the perspiring hordes lined up.

For the Uffizi you can also buy tickets in advance at the gallery itself (also €3 per ticket).

If you prefer electronic methods, **Weekend a Firenze** (www.weekendafirenze.com) is an online service for booking museums, galleries, shows and tours. For this you pay €6.80 on top of the normal ticket price; reserve at least three days in advance. Print out the email confirmation they send and present it on the day of your visit. You can get tickets for the Uffizi, Galleria Palatina, Museo di San Marco, Museo del Bargello, Galleria dell'Accademia, Museo Archeologico, Cappelle Medicee and the Galleria d'Arte Moderna.

Many of the bigger hotels will also book entry tickets for you.

⏰ 8.30am-7pm Mon-Fri, 8.30am-4.45pm Sat, 1.30-5pm Sun), the first of its kind since antiquity. When Michelangelo went to work on St Peter's Basilica (Basilica di San Pietro) in Rome, he reportedly said: 'I go to build a greater dome, but not a fairer one'. You enter from outside the cathedral.

In 1334 Giotto designed and began building the graceful, 82m high **campanile** (bell tower; admission €6; ⏰ 8.30am-7.30pm Apr-Sep, 9am-5.30pm Oct, 9am-4.30pm Nov-Mar) with its 414 steps but died before it was completed. Andrea Pisano and Francesco Talenti continued the work. The first tier of bas-reliefs around the base, carved by Pisano but possibly designed by Giotto, depicts the Creation of

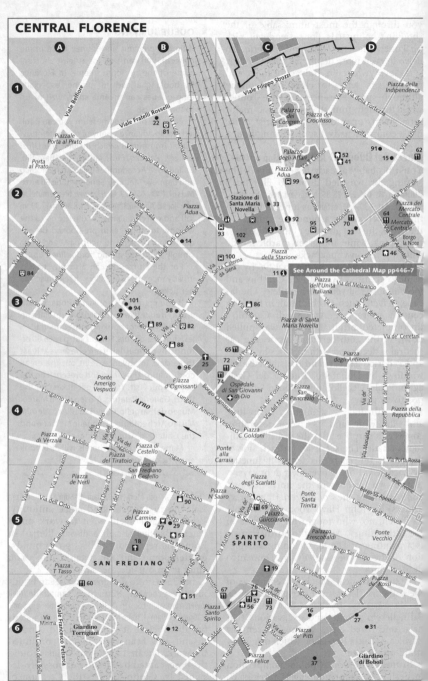

CENTRAL FLORENCE

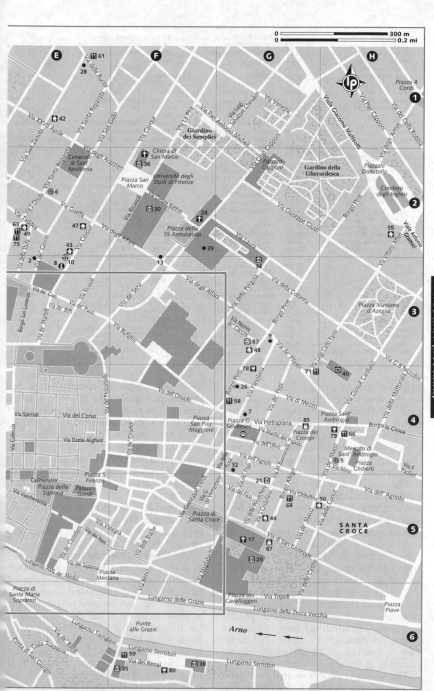

Man and the Arts and Industries. Those on the second tier illustrate the planets, cardinal virtues, the arts and seven sacraments. The sculptures of the Prophets and Sybils in the niches of the upper storeys are copies of works by Donatello and others – the originals are in the Museo dell'Opera del Duomo.

The mainly 11th-century Romanesque **baptistry** (battistero; admission €3; noon-6.30pm Mon-Sat, 8.30am-1.30pm Sun) may have been built as early as the 5th century on the site of a Roman temple. One of the oldest buildings in Florence, it's dedicated, like many baptistries in Italy, to St John the Baptist and counts Dante among the famous who have been dunked and baptised in its font.

The octagonal structure is chiefly famous for its gilded bronze doors, particularly the celebrated 15th-century eastern portals facing the cathedral, the *Gate of Paradise* (Porta del Paradiso) by Lorenzo Ghiberti. The bas-reliefs on its 10 panels depict scenes from the Old Testament.

The southern door, executed by Pisano and completed in 1330, is the oldest. The bas-reliefs on its 28 compartments deal predominantly with the life of St John the Baptist. The northern door is by Ghiberti, who won a public competition in 1401 for its design, and its main theme is also St John the Baptist.

Some of the doors are copies – the original panels are gradually being restored and placed in the Museo dell'Opera del Duomo.

Within, the vibrant 13th-century mosaics of the dome, created by artists from Venice, depict, among other themes, *Christ in Majesty* and the *Last Judgement*.

The **Museo dell'Opera del Duomo** (Map pp446–7; Piazza del Duomo 9; admission €6; 9am-7.30pm Mon-Sat, 9am-1.40pm Sun) features mostly sculptural treasures from the cathedral. Displays include the equipment used by Brunelleschi to build the dome, as well as his death mask. On the mezzanine floor is Michelangelo's *Pietà*, which he intended for his own tomb. Vasari recorded in his *Lives of the Artists* that, dissatisfied with both the quality of the marble and of his own work, Michelangelo broke up the unfinished sculpture

EUROPEANS DO IT CHEAPER

If you carry an EU passport (and you'll need to have it with you) and are under 18 or over 65, admission to all of Florence's state museums is free. EU citizens aged between 18 and 65 pay half-price.

destroying the arm and left leg of the figure of Christ. A student of Michelangelo later restored the arm and completed the figure of Mary Magdalene.

Eight of the original 10 panels from the baptistry's *Gates of Paradise* are also on display.

Most striking of Donatello's several carvings are the haunted gaze of his *Prophet Habakkuk*, originally in the bell tower, and his wooden carving of a gaunt, desolate *Mary Magdalene*. Also on the 1st floor, a pair of exquisitely carved *cantorie* (singing galleries) by Donatello and Luca della Robia face each other, musicians and children at play adding a refreshingly frivolous touch amid so much sombre piety.

From the Cathedral to Piazza della Signoria   Map pp446–7

Take Via de' Calzaiuoli from Piazza del Duomo to reach the **Chiesa di Orsanmichele** (Via Arte della Lana; closed for renovations). Originally a grain market, the church was formed in the 14th century when the arcades of the market building were walled in. Statues of the city guilds' patron saints adorn the exterior. Commissioned over a period of two centuries, they represent the work of many Renaissance artists. Some statues are now in the Museo del Bargello but many splendid pieces remain, including *John the Baptist* by Lorenzo Ghiberti and a copy of Donatello's *St George*.

Northwest is the **Piazza della Repubblica**, originally the site of a Roman forum and heart of the medieval city. Today's buildings, for the most part constructed in the late 19th century, are home to Florence's most fashionable and expensive cafés.

If you head east from the piazza and turn right into Via Santa Margherita, you'll find the **Casa di Dante** with a small **museum** (closed for renovations) tracing Dante's life. Continuing east on Via del Corso will bring you to the **Palazzo dei Pazzi**, which is attributed

to Brunelleschi. These days it's used as offices but you're free to wander into the courtyard.

The **Palazzo del Bargello** (1254), also known as the Palazzo del Podestà, was originally the residence of the chief magistrate. It then became a police station, during which time many unfortunates were tortured near the well in the centre of the medieval courtyard, site of the city's gallows. This gaunt building now enjoys a happier destiny as home to the excellent **Museo del Bargello** (☎ 055 238 86 06, Via del Proconsolo 4; admission €4; ☽ 8.15am-1.50pm Tue-Sat, 2nd & 4th Sun of the month, 1st, 3rd & 5th Mon of the month) with Italy's most comprehensive collection of Tuscan Renaissance sculpture.

Several works by Michelangelo grace the ground floor, notably his drunken *Bacchus* (executed when the artist was aged 22), a marble bust of *Brutus* and the *Tondo Pitti*, a large roundel of the Madonna and Child with the infant St John. Other works of particular interest are Benvenuto Cellini's rather camp marble *Ganimede* (Ganymede) and *Narciso* (Narcissus), along with Giambologna's *Mercurio Volante* (Winged Mercury).

Don't miss Donatello's stunning bronze *David* on the 1st floor, the first free-standing sculpture since antiquity to depict a fully nude man. Among many other works by Donatello are *San Giorgio* (St George), originally on the facade of the Chiesa di Orsanmichele, and the *Marzocco*, Florence's heraldic lion that once stood proud in the Piazza della Signoria.

The **Mercato Nuovo** (Via Porta Rossa), a loggia (open gallery) built in the mid-16th century to house the city's gold and silver trade has fallen on hard times and today is home to tacky souvenir and leather stalls. At its southern end is the Fontana del Porcellino (Piglet Fountain). Rub the porker's snout, throw a modest coin into the fountain and – so goes the legend – you're bound to return to Florence.

Return to Via de' Tornabuoni and head north for the **Palazzo Strozzi** (Piazza degli Strozzi), one of Florence's most impressive Renaissance palazzos. Although never completed, the three finished facades in heavy rusticated *pietra forte* (literally 'strong stone', a local sandstone), designed by Benedetto da Maiano, speak naked power. Inside is a

TUSCANY (TOSCANA)

grand if somewhat gloomy courtyard. The *palazzo* is today used for art exhibitions. Just along the road is the altogether more delicate **Palazzo dei Rucellai** (Via della Vigna Nuova), designed by Alberti, with its frieze and incised irregular blocks.

Piazza della Signoria   Map pp446–7

The hub of the city's political life through the centuries and surrounded by some of its most celebrated buildings, the piazza resembles an outdoor sculpture gallery. Ammannati's huge Fountain of Neptune spurts beside the Palazzo Vecchio, at whose entrance stand copies of Michelangelo's *David* (the original is in the Galleria dell'Accademia) and Donatello's *Marzocco*,

the heraldic Florentine lion (the original is in the Museo del Bargello). An equestrian statue of Cosimo I de' Medici by Giambologna prances in the centre of the piazza. Look on the ground for the bronze plaque marking the spot where Savonarola was hanged and burned at the stake in 1498.

Loggia della Signoria, built in the late 14th century as a platform for public ceremonies, eventually became a showcase for sculptures. To the left of the steps is Benvenuto Cellini's magnificent bronze statue of *Perseo* (Perseus) brandishing the head of Medusa. To the right is Giambologna's Mannerist *Rape of the Sabine Women*, his final work.

The **Palazzo Vecchio** (☎ 055 276 84 65; adult/child €5.70/4.30; 9am-7pm Fri-Wed, 9am-2pm Thu),

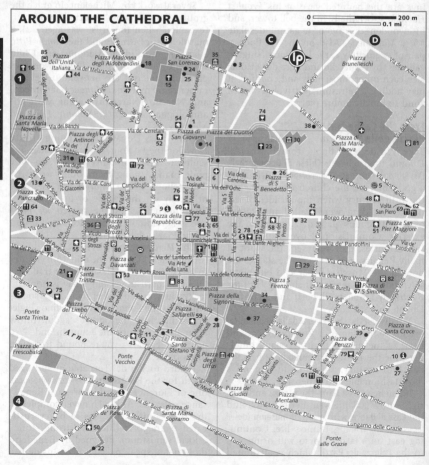

AROUND THE CATHEDRAL

built by Arnolfo di Cambio between 1298 and 1314, is the traditional seat of Florentine government. Its **Torre d'Arnolfo**, 94m high and crowned with striking crenellations, is as much a symbol of the city as the cathedral.

Created for the Signoria, the highest level of Florentine republican government, the Palazzo Vecchio became Cosimo I de' Medici's palace in the mid-16th century, before he moved to the Palazzo Pitti. The Medici commissioned Vasari to reorganise the interior and create a series of sumptuous rooms. Upstairs from Michelozzo's beautiful courtyard, just inside the entrance, the lavishly decorated apartments begin. The **Salone dei Cinquecento** was the meeting room of the 'parliament' during Savonarola's time. It was later used for banquets and festivities and features frescoes by Vasari and his apprentices, glorifying Florentine victories over archrivals Pisa and Siena. The monumental statuary includes a graphic series on the *Labours of Hercules* by Vincenzo de' Rossi and Michelangelo's *Genio della Vittoria* (Genius of Victory) statue, originally destined for Rome and Pope Julius II's tomb.

Vasari designed the intimate yet equally sumptuous little **studiolo** (Francesco I's study), decorated by a team of top Florentine Mannerist artists, that gives off the vast hall.

There follows a series of rooms, each dedicated to a senior member of the Medicis, whose decor blares their glory in heavy-handed manner until you reach, on the 2nd floor, the **Sala dei Gigli** (Room of the Lilies), named after its frieze of fleur de lys, symbol of the French monarchy. Look up at its remarkable coffered ceiling and enjoy Donatello's powerful carving of *Guiditta e Oloferne* (Judith & Holofernes). Just off this hall are the chancery, where Machiavelli plotted for a while, and the map room, intriguing for both cartophiles and the simply curious, its panels painted with maps, often very rudimentary, of the known world of the time.

From here you can climb to the battlements for fine views over the city.

Uffizi Gallery & Around   Map pp446–7

The Palazzo degli Uffizi, designed and built by Vasari in the second half of the 16th century at the request of Cosimo I de' Medici, originally housed the city's administrators, judiciary and guilds. It was, in effect, a government office building (*uffizi* meaning offices).

TUSCANY (TOSCANA)

INFORMATION		
All'Insegna del Moro (Pharmacy)	1	B1
American Express	2	C2
Feltrinelli International Bookshop	3	C1
Internet Train	4	D2
Internet Train	5	A4
Misericordia di Firenze Medical Service	6	B2
Ospedale di Santa Maria Nuova	7	D1
Tourist Help Point	8	B2
Tourist Help Point	9	B4
Tourist Office	10	D4
Travelex	11	B3
UK Consulate	12	A3
Wash & Dry Laundrette	13	A2

SIGHTS & ACTIVITIES	pp440–55	
Baptistry	14	B2
Basilica di San Lorenzo	15	B1
Basilica di Santa Maria Novella	16	A1
Campanile	17	B2
Cappelle Medicee	18	B1
Casa di Dante	19	C2
Chiesa di Orsanmichele	20	B3
Chiesa di Santa Trinità	21	A3
Corridoio Vasariano	22	A4
Duomo (Cathedral)	23	C2
Entrance to Basilica di San Lorenzo	24	B1
Entrance to Cloister & Biblioteca Laurenziana		
Medicea	25	C2
Istituto Europeo	26	C2
Istituto per l'Arte e il Restauro Palazzo		
Spinelli	27	D4
Loggia della Signoria		
(Loggia dei Lanzi)	28	B3
Museo del Bargello	29	C3

Museo dell'Opera Duomo	30	C2
Palazzo Antinori	31	A2
Palazzo dei Pazzi	32	C2
Palazzo dei Rucellai	33	A2
Palazzo del Bargello	(see 29)	
Palazzo Gondi	34	C3
Palazzo Medici-Riccardi	35	B1
Palazzo Strozzi	36	A2
Palazzo Vecchio	37	C3
Scuola Leonardo da Vinci	38	C1
Scuola Toscana	39	D3
Uffizi Gallery	40	C4
Walking Tours of Florence	41	B3

SLEEPING	🏠 pp457–61	
Albergo Bavaria	42	C2
Gallery Hotel Art	43	B3
Grand Hotel Baglioni	44	A1
Hotel Abaco	45	A2
Hotel Accademia	46	A1
Hotel Bellettini	47	B1
Hotel Dalí	48	D2
Hotel Helvetia & Bristol	49	B2
Hotel la Scaletta	50	A4
Hotel Orchidea	51	D2
Hotel Perseo	52	B2
Hotel Porta Rossa	53	B3
Hotel San Giovanni	54	B1
Hotel Scoti	55	A3
Pendini	56	B2
Pensione Ferretti	57	A2
Pensione Maria Luisa		
de' Medici	58	C2
Relais Uffizi	59	B3
Savoy	60	B2

EATING	🍴 pp461–4	
Angie's Pub	61	C4
Antico Noè	62	D2
Cantinetta Antinori	63	A2
Da il Latini	64	A2
Festival del Gelato	65	B2
Fiaschetteria Vecchio Casentino	66	C4
Gelateria Vivoli	67	D3
I Fratellini	68	B3
Il Nilo	69	D2
Osteria de' Benci	70	D4
Perchè No?	71	B3
Ristorante Self-Service Leonardo	72	B2
Trattoria Coco Lezzone	73	A3

DRINKING	🍷🍸 pp464–5	
Astor Caffè	74	C1
Capocaccia	75	A3
Gilli	76	B2
La Rinascente	77	B2
Mayday Lounge Café	78	C2
Red Garter House	79	D4
Rooftop Café	(see 77)	

ENTERTAINMENT	🎭 pp465–6	
Odeon Cinehall	80	B3
Teatro della Pergola	81	D2
Teatro Verdi	82	D3

SHOPPING	🛍 p466	
Mercato Nuovo	83	B3
Pusateri	84	B2

TRANSPORT	pp466–8	
ATAF Local Bus Stop	85	A1

Vasari also designed the Corridoio Vasariano, a long private corridor that links the Palazzo Vecchio and the Palazzo Pitti (Map p442-4), through the Uffizi and across the Ponte Vecchio. Cosimo's successor, Francesco I, commissioned the architect Buontalenti to modify the upper floor of the Palazzo to house the Medicis' growing art collection. Thus, indirectly, the first steps were taken to turn it into an art gallery.

The Uffizi Gallery houses the family's private collection, bequeathed to Florence in 1743 by the last of the Medici family, Anna Maria Ludovica, on condition that it never leave the city. The Uffizi, although by no means the biggest art gallery around, houses the world's single greatest collection of Italian and Florentine art.

Sadly, several of its artworks were destroyed and others badly damaged when a car bomb planted by the Mafia exploded outside the gallery's west wing in May 1993. Documents cataloguing the collection were also destroyed.

Partly in response to the bombing, but even more to the gallery's immense popularity (over 1.5 million visitors march through every year, compared to a mere trickle of 100,000 annually in the 1950s!), restoration and reorganisation will lead to what promoters refer to as the 'Nuovi Uffizi'. The floors below the present gallery have been largely cleared of state archives and, in a project estimated to cost about €60 million, it is intended to have a much bigger and modernised gallery open by the end of 2004. Until then and whenever you visit, you're likely to find several galleries closed. Check the illuminated signboard by the main entrance.

The gallery as it stands now is arranged to illustrate the evolving story of Italian and, in particular, Florentine art.

Given the crowds (you can easily find yourself queuing for up to four hours to get to the ticket window), consider booking ahead (see the boxed text, p441). Alternatively, plan to visit later in the day, when lines and waiting times tend to be shorter.

THE GALLERY

On the ground floor of the gallery (☎ 055 238 86 51; Piazza degli Uffizi 6; admission €6.50; ⏰ 8.15am-6.35pm Tue-Sun; ticket office closes 6.05pm) are the restored remains of the 11th-century **Chiesa di San Piero Scheraggio**, closed to the public at the time of writing.

Upstairs in the gallery proper, the first accessible rooms feature works by Tuscan masters of the 13th and early 14th centuries. Stars of Room 2 are three paintings of the *Madonna in Maestà* by Duccio di Buoninsegna, Cimabue and Giotto. All three were formerly altarpieces in Florentine churches. Looking at them in this order, you sense the transition from Gothic to the precursor of the Renaissance.

Room 3 traces the Sienese school of the 14th century. Of particular note is Simone Martini's shimmering *Annunciazione* (Annunciation), considered a masterpiece of the school.

Room 7 features works by painters of the early-15th-century Florentine school, which pioneered the Renaissance. There is one panel (the other two are in Paris' Louvre and London's National Gallery) from Paolo Uccello's striking *La Battaglia di San Romano* (Battle of San Romano). In his efforts to create perspective he directs the lances, horses and soldiers to a central disappearing point. Other works include Piero della Francesca's portraits of *Battista Sforza* and *Federico da Montefeltro*.

Room 9 is devoted largely to Antonio de Pollaiuolo. His series of six virtues is followed by an addition (*Fortezza* or Strength) by Botticelli. Here the clarity of line and light and the humanity in the face set it apart from Pollaiuolo's work, making the canvas a taster for the Botticelli Rooms, Nos 10 to 14 – considered the gallery's most spectacular. Highlights are the ethereal *La Nascita di Venere* (Birth of Venus) and *Allegoria della Primavera* (Allegory of Spring). Contrast these with his *Calunnia* (Calumny): for some a disturbing reflection of Botticelli's loss of faith in human potential as he aged, for others a deliberate reining in of his free spirit in order not to invite the attentions of the puritanical Savonarola.

Room 15 features Da Vinci's *Annunciazione*, painted when he was a student of Verrocchio. Quite different but equally arresting in its swirling composition is his unfinished *Adorazione dei Magi*.

Room 18, the Tribuna, houses the celebrated *Medici Venus*, a 1st-century-BC copy of a 4th-century-BC sculpture by the Greek sculptor, Praxiteles. The room also

TUSCANY (TOSCANA)

contains portraits of various members of the Medici family.

The great Umbrian painter Perugino, who studied under Piero della Francesca and later became Raphael's master, is represented in Room 19, as is Luca Signorelli. Piero di Cosimo's *Perseo Libera Andromeda* is full of fantastical whimsy with beasts and flying heroes. Room 20 features works from the German Renaissance, including Dürer's *Adorazione dei Magi*. His depictions of Adam and Eve are mirrored by those of Lucas Cranach. Room 21, with a heavily Venetian leaning, has works by Giovanni Bellini and his pupil Giorgione, along with a few by Vittorio Carpaccio.

The star of Room 25 is Michelangelo's dazzling *Tondo Doni*, which depicts the Holy Family. The composition is highly unusual, with Joseph holding Jesus on Mary's shoulder as she twists around to watch him. The colours are so vibrant, the lines so clear, it seems almost photographic. This masterpiece of the High Renaissance leaps out at you as you enter, demanding attention.

In Room 26 are works by Raphael, including his *Leo X* and *Madonna del Cardellino* (which may still be under restoration). The former is remarkable for the richness of colour (especially the reds) and detail. Also on display are works by Andrea del Sarto. Room 27 is dominated by the sometimes disquieting works of Florence's two main Mannerist masters, Pontormo and Rosso Fiorentino.

Room 28 boasts eight Titians, including *Venere d'Urbino* (Venus of Urbino). His presence signals a shift in the weighting to representatives of the Venetian school. Rooms 29 and 30 contain works by comparatively minor painters from northern Italy but Room 31 has some powerful paintings by Venice's Paolo Veronese, especially his *Sacra Famiglia e Santa Barbara* (Holy Family and St Barbara). In Room 32 it is Tintoretto's turn.

Room 35 comes as a bit of a shock as you are confronted with the enormous and sumptuous canvases of Federico Barocci (1535–1612) of Urbino. Rooms 36 and 37 are part of the exit while the adjoining Room 38 houses the extraordinary restored *Annunciazione* by Siena's Simone Martini and Lippo Memmi.

Room 41 is given over mostly to non-Italian masters such as Rubens, Van Dyck and Spain's Diego Velázquez. Pause before the two enormous tableaux by Rubens, sweeping with violence and power, representing the French King Henri IV at the Battle of Ivry and his triumphal march into Paris. The beautifully designed Room 42 (long closed but you can peek in), with its exquisite coffered ceiling and splendid dome, is filled with Roman statues.

Room 43 has a pair of contrasting canvases by Caravaggio, with his bold play of light and shade, notably in his *Il Sacrificio d'Isacco*. Rembrandt and other Dutch masters feature in Room 44 while Room 45 takes us back to Venice, with 18th-century works by Canaletto, Guardi, Tiepolo, Crespi and the two Longhi, along with a couple of stray pieces by the Spaniard Goya.

When Cosimo I de' Medici's wife bought the Palazzo Pitti and the family moved into their new digs, they wanted to maintain their link – literally – with what from now on would be known as the Palazzo Vecchio. So Cosimo commissioned Vasari to build the **Corridoio Vasariano** (Map p442-4 & p446-7), an enclosed walkway traversing the distance between the two palaces that would allow the Medicis to wander between each in privacy. At the time of writing, the passageway wasn't open to the public. For an update, contact Firenze Musei (see the boxed text, p441).

Santa Maria Novella & Around

West from the Uffizi is the **Ponte Santa Trinita** (Map pp446-7), rebuilt after being destroyed in WWII. Michelangelo is believed to have drawn the original plan of the bridge, which was executed by Ammannati. To its north is **Via de' Tornabuoni** (Map pp446-7), one of the city's most fashionable streets, lined with Renaissance mansions and classy shops including Ferragamo, Gucci and Armani.

The 14th-century **Chiesa di Santa Trinita** (Map pp446-7; Piazza Santa Trinita; ☮ 8am-noon Mon-Sat, 4-6pm daily) has eye-catching frescoes depicting the life of St Francis of Assisi by Domenico Ghirlandaio in Cappella Sassetti (in the south transept). Lorenzo Monaco, Fra Angelico's master, painted the altarpiece of the *Annunciation* in the fourth chapel of the south aisle and also the frescoes on the chapel walls.

Northwest from Ponte alla Carraia is the 13th-century **Chiesa di Ognissanti** (Map pp442-4; ☮ 9am-12.30pm & 4.30-5.30pm). The church with its typically baroque facade was much altered in the 17th century. Inside are older treasures: a pair of frescoes by Domenico Ghirlandaio and Botticelli's *San Augustin*. Seek out Ghirlandaio's fresco, above the second altar on the right, of the Madonna della Misericordia, protector of the Vespucci family. Amerigo Vespucci, the Florentine navigator who gave his name to the American continent, is supposed to be the young boy whose head peeks between the Madonna and the old man. Ghirlandaio's masterpiece, *Last Supper*, covers most of a wall in the former monastery's refectory.

The **Basilica di Santa Maria Novella** (Map pp446–7; ☎ 055 21 59 18; Piazza di Santa Maria Novella; adult/child €2.50/1.50; ☺ 9am-5pm Mon-Thu & Sat, 1-5pm Fri & Sun) was begun in the late 13th century as the Dominican order's Florentine base. It was largely completed by around 1360 but work on its facade and interior continued well into the 15th century. The lower section of the green and white marble facade is transitional from Romanesque to Gothic, while the upper section and the main doorway were designed by Alberti and completed around 1470. Halfway along the north aisle, the highlight of the Gothic interior is Masaccio's superb fresco of the Trinity (1428), one of the first artworks to use the then newly discovered techniques of perspective and proportion.

The first chapel to the right of the altar, the **Cappella di Filippo Strozzi**, features lively frescoes by Filippino Lippi depicting the lives of St John the Evangelist and St Philip. Another important work is Domenico Ghirlandaio's series of frescoes behind the main altar, painted with the help of artists who may have included the young Michelangelo. Relating the lives of the Virgin Mary, St John the Baptist (San Giovanni Battista) and others, the frescoes are notable for their depiction of Florentine life in the Renaissance. Brunelleschi's crucifix hangs above the altar in the **Cappella Gondi**, the first chapel left of the choir.

The cloisters (entrance on the left of the facade) feature some of the city's best frescoes. The **Chiostro Verde** (Green Cloister) is so named because green is the predominant colour of the fresco cycle by Paolo Uccello. The impressive **Cappellone degli Spagnuoli** (Spanish Chapel) contains frescoes by Andrea di Bonaiuto.

San Lorenzo Area
Map pp446–7

The Medici commissioned Brunelleschi to rebuild the **Basilica di San Lorenzo** (admission €2.50; ☺ 10am-5pm Mon-Sat) in 1425, on the site of a 4th-century basilica. Considered one of the most harmonious examples of Renaissance architecture, it was the Medici family church and many members are buried here. The two bronze pulpits are by Donatello, who died before they were completed. He is buried in the chapel featuring Fra Filippo Lippi's *Annunciation*. The church entrance is on Piazza San Lorenzo. Brunelleschi also designed the adjoining **Sagrestia Vecchia** (Old Sacristy), whose interior was decorated in the main by Donatello.

From another entrance off Piazza San Lorenzo, you enter the church's peaceful cloisters. A staircase leads from the first up to the **Biblioteca Laurenziana Medicea**, nowadays restricted to researchers burrowing through its 10,000 volumes. Commissioned by Cosimo de' Medici to house the Medici library, its real attraction is Michelangelo's magnificent vestibule and staircase, accessible to all.

Enter the **Cappelle Medicee** (☎ 055 238 86 02; admission €6; ☺ 8.15am-5pm Mon-Sat, 1st, 3rd & 5th Sun of the month, 2nd & 4th Mon of the month) via Piazza Madonna degli Aldobrandini. The **Cappella dei Principi** (Princes' Chapel), sumptuously decorated with precious marble and semiprecious stones, was the principal burial place of the Medici rulers. The graceful and simple **Sagrestia Nuova** (New Sacristy) was Michelangelo's first architectural work. His exquisite sculptures *Night and Day*, *Dawn and Dusk* and *Madonna with Child* adorn the Medici tombs.

Just off Piazza San Lorenzo is the extraordinary **Palazzo Medici-Riccardi** (☎ 055 276 03 40; Via Cavour 3; adult/child €4/2.50; ☺ 9am-7pm Thu-Tue). Since only seven visitors are allowed in at a time and for – you have to admire the symmetry – a maximum of seven minutes, it's essential to reserve your slot in advance.

Typical of the Florentine Renaissance style, it was designed by Michelozzo for Cosimo de' Medici in 1444. The principal Medici residence until 1540, it was the prototype for other buildings in the city, such as the Palazzo Pitti and Palazzo Strozzi, before being remodelled by its new owners, the Riccardi family, in the 17th century. The chapel upstairs has a series of wonderfully detailed, serene frescoes by Benozzo Gozzoli, whose ostensible theme of the *Journey of the Magi* is but a slender pretext for portraying members of the Medici clan in their best light. A couple of hundred years later, the Riccardis built the sumptuously decorated Sala di Luca Giordano, commissioning the eponymous artist to adorn the ceiling with his complex *Allegory of Divine Wisdom* (1685).

San Marco Area   Map pp442–4

Piazza San Marco is at the heart of the university area. Flanking it are the now deconsecrated Dominican convent and Chiesa di San Marco, where you'll find the **Museo di San Marco** (☎ 055 238 86 08; Piazza San Marco 1; admission €4; ☼ 8.15am-1.50pm Tue-Fri & 1st, 3rd & 5th Mon of the month, 8.30am-6.50pm Sat, 8.15am-7pm 2nd & 4th Sun of the month). Dip into the church, founded in 1299, rebuilt by Michelozzo in 1437 and again remodelled by Giambologna some years later. But you're really here for the splendours of the adjoining convent.

Famous Florentines who called the convent home include the painters Fra Angelico and Fra Bartolommeo, as well as Sant' Antoninus and Girolamo Savonarola (see the boxed text, p438). Fra Angelico, who painted the radiant frescoes on the convent walls, and Savonarola were of the same religious order – the latter arriving in Florence almost 30 years after the painter's death in 1455. The convent is a museum of Fra Angelico's works, many moved here in the 19th century. Among the better-known works are his *Deposizione di Cristo* and *Pala di San Marco*, an altarpiece for the church, paid for by the Medici family. The walls of the upstairs cells, painted *in situ* (if you're using a museum guide, look carefully for the faded numbers on each door) carry several masterpieces, including the magnificent *Madonna delle Ombre* (Virgin of the Shadows), on the external wall between cells No 25 and 26.

From Piazza San Marco, a right turn into Via Cesare Battisti brings you to the **Chiesa della SS Annunziata** (Piazza della SS Annunziata; admission free; ☼ 7.30am-12.30pm & 4-6.30pm), which was established in 1250 by the founders of the Servite order and rebuilt by Michelozzo and others in the mid-15th century. The church is dedicated to the Virgin Mary

and in the ornate tabernacle, to your left as you enter the church from the atrium, is a so-called miraculous painting of the Virgin. No longer on public view, the canvas is attributed to a 14th-century friar and legend says it was completed by an angel. Also of note are frescoes by Andrea del Castagno in the first two chapels on the left of the church, a fresco by Perugino in the fifth chapel, and the frescoes in Michelozzo's atrium, particularly the *Birth of the Virgin* by Andrea del Sarto and the *Visitation* by Jacopo Pontormo. Within the church's official opening hours, you'll need to time it right to squeeze yourself in between each morning's seven masses.

Also in the university district, the beautiful **Piazza della SS Annunziata**, where Giambologna's equestrian statue of Grand Duke Ferdinando I de' Medici commands the scene, usually teems with students rather than tourists. On its southeastern side, **Spedale degli Innocenti** (☎ 055 249 17 08; Piazza della SS Annunziata 12; admission €2.60; ☼ 8.30am-2pm Thu-Tue) was founded in 1421 as Europe's first orphanage (hence the 'innocents' in its name). Brunelleschi designed the portico, which Andrea della Robbia decorated with terracotta medallions of babies in swaddling clothes. At the north end of the portico, the false door surrounded by railings was once a revolving door where unwanted children were left. A good number of people in Florence with surnames such as degli Innocenti, Innocenti and Nocentini can trace their family tree only as far back as the orphanage. A small gallery inside features works by Florentine artists, including Luca della Robbia and Domenico Ghirlandaio, whose striking *Adorazione dei Magi* is at the right end of the hall.

About 200m southeast of the piazza is the **Museo Archeologico** (☎ 055 23 57 50; Via Colonna 38; admission €4.60; ☼ 2-7pm Mon, 8.30am-7pm Tue & Thu, 8.30am-2pm Wed & Fri-Sun). Its rich collection of finds, including most of the Medici hoard of antiquities, plunges you deeper into the past and offers an alternative to all that Renaissance splendour. On the 1st floor you can either head left into the ancient Egyptian collection or right for the smaller section on Etruscan and Greco-Roman art.

The former is an impressive collection of sculpture, tablets inscribed with hieroglyphics, various coffins and a remarkable array of everyday objects. The first two rooms of the Etruscan section hold funeral urns. Particularly noteworthy is the marble *Sarcofago delle Amazzoni* (Amazons' Sarcophagus; under restoration) from Tarquinia. Moving on you enter a gallery lined with cabinets positively stuffed with bronze statuettes and miniatures, dwarfed by the outstanding, growling *Chimera*, lionlike with a supplementary goat and snake head. Less allegorical and more literal, yet almost as compelling, is the life-size *Arringatore* (Orator).

The 2nd floor is rich in Greek sculpture and ceramics and Greek and Roman bronzes. Pause awhile to outstare the magnificent snorting *Medicci Riccardi* stallion's head in Room 1.

The **Galleria dell'Accademia** (☎ 055 238 86 09; Via Ricasoli 60; admission €6.50; 🕑 8.15am-6.50pm Tue-Sun) displays paintings by Florentine artists spanning the 13th to 16th centuries. Its main draw is Michelangelo's *David*, perhaps the world's most famous statue, which was carved from a single block of marble when the artist was only 29. Originally in the Piazza della Signoria, the colossal statue now stands in an alcove at the end of the main hall on the ground floor.

Santa Croce Area Map pp442–4

In Savonarola's day, **Piazza di Santa Croce**, today lined with souvenir shops, was used for the execution of heretics. Attributed to Arnolfo di Cambio, the Franciscan **Basilica di Santa Croce** (Piazza Santa Croce; admission incl museum €3; 🕑 9.30am-5pm Mon-Sat, 1-5pm Sun) was started in 1294 on the site of a Franciscan chapel; the facade and bell tower were added in the 19th century. The three-nave interior of the basilica is grand, if austere. The floor is paved with the tombstones of famous Florentines of the past 500 years, while monuments to the particularly notable were added along the walls from the mid-16th century.

TUSCANY (TOSCANA)

MACHIAVELLI'S MANOEUVRES

Born in 1469 into a poor offshoot of one of Florence's leading families, Niccolò Machiavelli got off to a bad start. His father, an impoverished small-time lawyer continually in debt, was at least rich in books, which his son devoured.

Somehow the young Machiavelli managed to swing a post in the city's second chancery at the age of 29 and so embarked on a colourful career as a Florentine public servant. Our man must have shown early promise, as by 1500 he was in France on his first diplomatic mission.

Impressed by the martial success of Cesare Borgia and the centralised state of France, Machiavelli came to the conclusion that Florence needed a standing army.

The city, like many others in the Italian peninsula, used to employ mercenaries to fight its wars. The problem was that mercenaries had few reasons to fight and die for anyone. They took their pay and often did their level best to avoid mortal combat. Machiavelli convinced his rulers of the advantages of a conscripted militia, which he formed in 1506. Three years later it was blooded in battle against the rebellious city of Pisa, whose fall was mainly attributed to the troops led by the wily statesman.

The return to power of the Medici family was a blow for Machiavelli, who was promptly removed from office. Suspected of plotting against the Medicis, he was even thrown into the dungeon in 1513 and tortured. He maintained his innocence and, once freed, retired to his little property outside Florence a poor man.

It was in these years that he produced his greatest writing. *Il Principe* (The Prince) is his classic treatise on the nature of power and its administration, a work reflecting the confusing and corrupt times in which he lived and a desire for strong and just rule in Florence and beyond.

He never got back into the mainstream of public life. He was commissioned to write an official history of Florence, the *Istorie Fiorentine*, and towards the end of his life he was appointed to a defence commission to improve the city walls and join a papal army in its ultimately futile fight against Imperial forces. By the time the latter had sacked Rome in 1527, Florence had again rid itself of the Medici. Machiavelli hoped that he would be restored to a position of dignity, but by now he was suspected almost as much by the Medicis' opponents as he had been years before by the Medici. He died frustrated and, as in his youth, on the brink of poverty in 1527.

Along the southern wall is Michelangelo's tomb, designed by Vasari, and a cenotaph dedicated to Dante, who is buried in Ravenna. Further along is a monument to the 18th-century dramatist and poet Vittorio Alfieri by Antonio Canova, a monument to Machiavelli and a gilded bas-relief *Annunciation* by Donatello.

The Cappella Castellani, a chapel to the right of the south transept, is completely covered with frescoes by Agnolo Gaddi. In the Cappella Baroncelli, at the end of the south transept, frescoes by his father, Taddeo Gaddi, depict the life of the Virgin. Agnolo Gaddi also painted the frescoes above and behind the altar.

Just west of the sacristy, the Capella dei Medici has a fine two-tone altarpiece in glazed terracotta by Andrea della Robbia. Between the two is Florence's Scuola del Cuoio (leatherwork school; see p466).

The Bardi and Peruzzi chapels, to the right of the chancel, are clad in rich frescoes by Giotto. In the central chapel of the northern transept (also a Bardi chapel) hangs a wooden crucifix by Donatello.

Brunelleschi designed the serene cloisters just before his death in 1446. His **Cappella dei Pazzi**, at the end of the first cloister, with its harmonious lines and restrained terracotta decoration, is a masterpiece of Renaissance architecture.

The **Museo dell'Opera di Santa Croce**, in the southwest corner of the first cloister, features a crucifix by Cimabue, restored to the degree possible after it was severely damaged during the disastrous 1966 flood, when more than 4m of water inundated the Santa Croce area.

Michelangelo owned the **Casa Buonarroti** (☎ 055 24 17 52; Via Ghibellina 70; admission €6.20; ☽ 9.30am-2pm Wed-Mon) but never lived in it. The Michelangelo memorabilia mostly consists of copies of his works and portraits of the master.

To the right of the ticket window is an archaeological display of items collected by the Buonarroti family, including some interesting Etruscan pieces. Beyond this room are some paintings done in imitation of Michelangelo's style, plus some glazed terracotta pieces by the della Robbia family.

Upstairs you can admire a detailed model of Michelangelo's design for the facade of the Basilica di San Lorenzo – as close as the church came to getting one. Also by Michelangelo are a couple of marble bas-reliefs and a crucifix. Of the reliefs, *Madonna della Scala* (Madonna of the Steps) is thought to be his earliest work.

The Oltrarno

Literally 'Beyond the Arno', the Oltrarno takes in all of Florence south of the river.

PONTE VECCHIO   Map pp446–7

The 14th-century structure has been draped in the glittering wares of jewellery merchants since the time Ferdinando I de' Medici ordered them here to replace the often malodorous presence of the town butchers who used to toss unwanted leftovers into the river. It was the only bridge not to be blown up by the Nazis in 1944; some say on Hitler's express orders, others that the German commander disobeyed those very orders (yet still wreaked havoc by razing the medieval quarters at either end). The views of and from the bridge are every bit as beguiling as you might expect.

PALAZZO PITTI   Map pp442–4

Begun in 1458 for the Pitti family, rivals of the Medici, the original nucleus of the **palace** (☎ 055 238 86 14) took up the space encompassing the seven sets of windows on the 2nd and 3rd storeys. Ironically, Cosimo I de' Medici and Eleonora de Toledo acquired the palace in 1549. It remained the official residence of Florence's rulers until 1919, when the Savoy royal family handed it over to the state. Combined entry to the palace and all galleries and museums costs €10.50 (€7.75 after 4pm) or you can pick and choose; quoted here are individual prices for each of the palace's five museums, of which the Galleria Palantina is by far the most significant.

The **Galleria Palatina** (Palatine Gallery; admission incl Royal Apartments before/after 4pm €8.50/4; ☽ 8.15am-6.50pm Tue-Sun) houses paintings from the 16th to 18th centuries, hung in lavishly decorated rooms and mostly collected by the Medici and their grand ducal successors.

As you pass through the resplendent **Sala Bianca** (White Room) with its ornate 18th-century stucco ceiling and crystal chandeliers, you enter the **Royal Apartments**, a series of rather sickeningly furnished and

TUSCANY (TOSCANA)

decorated rooms, where the Medici and their successors lived, slept and received their guests. The style and division of tasks assigned to each room is reminiscent of Spanish royal palaces, all heavily bedecked with drapes, silk and chandeliers. Each room has a colour theme, ranging from aqua green to deep wine red to dusty mellow yellow.

The paintings hanging in the gallery itself don't follow any particularly chronological or thematic sequence and canvases tend to hop about, so simply browse and stop and marvel where the fancy takes you.

Tuscan masters include Fra Filippo Lippi, Sandro Botticelli, Giorgio Vasari and Andrea del Sarto (well represented with a canvas in just about every room!). There are over 10 works by Raphael, fairly dispersed at the time of writing but expected to be concentrated in **Sala di Saturno** (Saturn Room) and a similar profusion by Titian (especially in the **Sala Venere**; Venus Room). Caravaggio features with his striking *Amore Dormiente* (Love Sleeping) in the **Sala dell'Educazione di Giove** (Education of Jupiter Room).

Other significant Italian and foreign painters represented include Tintoretto, Paolo Veronese, Jose Ribera, Bravo Murillo, Peter Paul Rubens, Velazquez and Van Dyck.

The palace's other galleries and museums are worth a look if you have plenty of time. The **Galleria d'Arte Moderna** and **Galleria del Costume** (admission €5; ⊙ 8.15am-1.50pm Tue-Sat, 1st, 3rd & 5th Sun, 2nd & 4th Mon of the month) have common opening hours and tariffs. The Modern Art Gallery covers mostly Tuscan works from the 18th to the mid-20th century while the Costume Museum has high-fashion apparel from the 18th and 19th centuries.

A *biglietto cumulativo* (combined ticket; €4) gives you entry to the palace's superb Renaissance **Giardino di Boboli** (Map pp436–7; Boboli Gardens; ⊙ 8.15am-7.30pm Jun-Aug; 8.15am-6.30pm Apr-May & Sep, 8.15am-5.30pm Mar & Oct, 8.15am-4.30pm Nov-Feb), laid out in the mid-16th century, and, observing the same hours, the **Museo delle Porcellane**. At the southern limit of the gardens and offering great views over the palace complex and Florentine countryside, it has a rich collection of Sèvres, Vincennes, Viennese and Meissen china and porcelain, gathered over the centuries by the illustrious tenants of Palazzo Pitti.

Entered from the garden courtyard, the **Museo degli Argenti** (Silver Museum; ⊙ 8.15am-4.20pm Tue-Sun, 2nd & 3rd Mon of the month) displays glassware, silver and semiprecious stones from the Medici collections.

Also within the gardens, which are occasionally a venue for summer classical music concerts, is the **Grotta del Buontalenti**, a fanciful artificial grotto designed by the eponymous artist. Within its recesses a fleshy *Venere* (Venus) by Giambologna rises from the waves.

FORTE DI BELVEDERE

The rambling fortifications of **Forte di Belvedere** (Map pp436–7; ☎ 055 200 14 86; admission €8; ⊙ 10am-sunset) were built by Grand Duke Ferdinando I towards the end of the 16th century to protect the Palazzo Pitti. Long closed for renovations, it has now reopened.

PIAZZALE MICHELANGELO   Map pp436–7

The breathtaking panorama from this vast esplanade, best approached via the wiggly road that climbs from the riverside and Piazza Guiseppe Poggi, rewards you in plenty for the steep climb. Here you can sit down at one of the cafés, catch your lost breath, rehydrate and marvel. An easier but less-rewarding alternative is to hop aboard bus No 13, which sets out from Stazione di Santa Maria Novella and crosses Ponte alle Grazie.

CHURCHES

The Oltrarno has three churches that are well worth seeking out.

The 13th-century **Basilica di Santa Maria del Carmine** (Map p442–4; Piazzle del Carmine) was all but destroyed by fire in the late 18th century. Fortunately the fire spared the magnificent frescoes by Masaccio in the **Cappella Brancacci** (☎ 055 238 21 95; admission €3.10; ⊙ 10am-5pm Wed-Mon, 1-5pm Sun), entered via the cloister to the right of the church. A maximum of 30 visitors are allowed into the chapel at a time so it's prudent to reserve in advance. Considered the painter's finest work, the frescoes had an enormous influence on 15th-century Florentine art. Masaccio painted them in his early 20s but interrupted the task to go to Rome, where he died when only 28. The cycle was completed some 60 years later by Filippino Lippi. Earlier frescoes in the cycle were painted by Masolino da Panicale. The frescoes' vibrant colours, combined with

Masaccio's vigorous style, create a strong visual impact. Masaccio's contribution includes the *Expulsion of Adam and Eve from Paradise* and *The Tribute Money* on the upper left wall.

Basilica di Santo Spirito (Map pp442–4; Piazza Santo Spirito; admission free; 10am-noon Mon-Fri & 4-5.30pm Thu-Tue), one of Brunelleschi's last commissions, is beautifully planned, with a colonnade of 35 columns and a series of sem-icircular chapels. The chapels' works of art include a *Madonna and Saints* by Filippino Lippi in the right transept. In the equally harmonious sacristy is a poignantly tender wooden crucifix (it's not often you see Christ with a penis) attributed to Michelangelo.

The austere **Chiesa di San Miniato al Monte** (Map pp436–7; 8am-7.30pm May-Oct, 8am-1pm & 2.30-6pm Nov-Apr), where building started in the 11th century, is a steep climb from Piazzale Michelangelo. Its green-and-white marble facade, depicting Christ between the Virgin and San Miniato and tacked on a couple of centuries later, is one of the finest examples of Tuscan Romanesque architecture.

Inside, you'll discover 13th- to 15th-century frescoes along the right wall, intricate inlaid marble designs down the length of the nave and a fine Romanesque crypt at the back, below the unusual raised presbytery with its fine marble pulpit crisscrossed with intriguing geometrical designs. The sacristy, to the right of the church, has some marvellously bright frescoes. The four figures in the cross vault are the Evangelists.

The **Cappella del Cardinale del Portogallo**, left of the church, features a tomb by Antonio Rossellino and a gorgeous terracotta ceiling by Luca della Robbia.

Bus No 13 stops nearby.

Certosa del Galluzzo   Map p439

From Porta Romana (Map pp436–7) at the southern tip of the Oltrarno area, follow Via Senese south about 3km to the village of Galluzzo, which is home to a quite remarkable 14th-century monastery, the **Certosa del Galluzzo** (055 204 92 26; admission by donation; accompanied visits 9.15am, 10.15am & 11.15am Tue-Sun, 3.15pm, 4.15pm, 5pm Tue-Sat, 3pm & 5pm Sun). The Carthusian order of monks once had 50 monasteries in Italy. Of these only two are now inhabited by monks of that order. The Certosa del Galluzzo passed into Cistercian hands in 1955.

The Certosa can only be visited with a guide (reckon on about 45 minutes). You will first be taken to the Gothic hall of the **Palazzo degli Studi**, now graced by a small collection of art, including five somewhat weathered frescoes by Pontormo. The **Basilica di San Lorenzo**, with 14th-century origins, has a Renaissance exterior. To one side of it is the **Colloquio**, a narrow hall with benches. Here the Carthusian monks were permitted to break their vow of silence once a week, though they got a second chance on Mondays when allowed to leave the monastery grounds for a gentle stroll. You end up in the **Chiostro Grande**, biggest of the complex's three cloisters and flanked by 18 monks' cells decorated with busts from the della Robbia workshop.

Bus No 37 from Stazione di Santa Maria Novella passes nearby.

COURSES

Florence has more than 30 schools offering courses in Italian language and culture. Others put on courses in art, including painting, drawing, sculpture and art history, and several offer cooking classes.

Language Courses

The tourist office in Via Cavour has a list of schools running language courses. Well established companies include those listed following:

Istituto Europeo (Map pp446–7; 055 238 10 71; www.istitutoeuropeo.it; Piazzale delle Pallottole 1, 50122)

Istituto di Lingua e Cultura Italiana per Stranieri Michelangelo (Map pp442–4; 055 24 09 75, www.michelangelo-edu.it; Via Ghibellina 88, 50122)

Centro Lingua Italiana Calvino (CLIC; Map pp442–4; 055 28 80 81; www.inter-med.net/clic; Viale Fratelli Rosselli 74, 50123)

Linguaviva (Map pp442–4; 055 29 43 59; www .linguaviva.it; Via Fiume 17, 50123) In the same building as Hotel Désirée.

Scuola Leonardo da Vinci (Map pp446–7; 055 29 44 20; www.scuolaleonardo.com; Via Bufalini 3, 50122)

Scuola Toscana (Map pp446–7; 058 494 22 46; www.scuolatoscana.com; Piazza Garibaldi 12, 55049)

Centro Lorenzo de' Medici (Map pp442–4; 055 28 73 60; Via Faenza 43, 50122)

Other Courses

Many of the above language schools also offer supplementary courses on things such as art, art history, cooking, fashion, music and the like. Some schools specialise in such courses.

Istituto per l'Arte e il Restauro Palazzo Spinelli (Map pp446–7; ☎ 055 24 60 01; www.spinelli.it; Borgo Santa Croce 10, 50122) Restoration (anything from paintings to ceramics), interior and graphic design, gilding and marquetry.

Accademia Italiana (Map pp442–4; ☎ 055 28 46 16; www.accademiaitaliana.com; Piazza de'Pitti 15, 50125) Language, culture and a wide range of design programmes in Italian including graphics, textile, fashion etc.

Cordon Bleu (Map pp442–4; ☎ 055 234 54 68; Via di Mezzo 55r, 50123) For gourmet cookery.

Florence Dance Center (Map pp442–4; ☎ 055 28 92 76; www.florencedance.org; Borgo della Stella 23r) Courses in classical, jazz and modern dance.

FLORENCE FOR CHILDREN

Buy each of the kids a copy of *Fun in Florence* by Nancy Shroyer Howard. With do-and-find sections for major sites such as the Cathedral and Uffizi courtyard, they can be happily employed while the grownups go round gawping at the boring bits.

There's a small **playground** in Piazza Massimo d'Azeglio (Map pp442–4), about 650m east of the cathedral. Beside the River Arno, about 1.2km west of Stazione di Santa Maria Novella, is the **Parco delle Cascine** (Map pp436–7), a massive public park.

Older children might find the **Museo Stibbert** (Map pp436–7; ☎ 055 47 55 20; Via Federico Stibbert 26; admission €5; ⏱ 10am-2pm Mon-Wed, 10am-6pm Fri-Sun) entertaining. The clothes, furnishings, and paintings from the 16th to the 19th centuries aren't that much of a pre-teen turn-on but the life-size figures of horses and their soldierly riders in all manner of suits of armour from Europe and the Middle East might raise a gasp.

TOURS
Bus
CAF Tours (Map pp446–7; ☎ 055 21 06 12; www .caftours .com; Via Roma 4) do coach tours of the city (€34 to €47) and nearby towns such as Lucca and Pisa.

Cycling
Florence by Bike (Map pp442–4; ☎ 055 48 89 92; www .florencebybike.it; Via San Zanobi 120-122r) does a day tour of the Chianti area (€35 including bike and equipment).

Bicycle Tuscany (☎ 055 22 25 80; www.bicycletus cany.com) does regular day tours in the Tuscan countryside (€60 with bike and equipment, including lunch and winery visit).

I Bike Italy (☎ 055 234 23 71; www.ibikeitaly.com) offers a 25km tour around Fiesole (€70) or a 50km circuit around Il Chianti (€80). Both are as much gastronomic as sporty and include shuttle bus, bike and gear hire, lunch and both wine and olive oil tastings.

The Accidental Tourist (☎ 055 69 93 76; www.ac cidentaltourist.com) offers fairly gentle half-day walking (€68) and cycling (€74) tours – plus cookery classes if you're interests are also gastronomic.

Walking
Walking Tours of Florence (Map pp446–7; ☎ 055 264 50 33; www.artviva.com; Piazza Santo Stefano 2) organises several excellent three-hour walks of the city (€20 to €35) led by specialists. They can also plot all sorts of specific walks to suit your personal needs and tastes – at a price – and offer half-day guided cycle tours.

The **Associazione Mercurio** (reservations ☎ 055 26 61 41; www.mercurio-italy.org) offers a similar range of visits within and beyond the city.

FESTIVALS & EVENTS

Florence is rich in festivals. One that always goes off with a bang is the **Scoppio del Carro** (Explosion of the Cart), in which a cart full of fireworks is exploded in front of the cathedral on Easter Saturday.

The **Festa di San Giovanni** (St John; Florence's patron saint) on 24 June is celebrated with the lively Calcio Storico medieval football matches which are played on Piazza di Santa Croce (Map pp442–4) and end with a firework display over Piazzale Michelangelo.

The **Festa delle Rificolone** (Festival of the Paper Lanterns), during which a procession of drummers, *sbandieratori* (flag-throwers), musicians and others in medieval dress winds its way from Piazza di Santa Croce to Piazza della SS Annunziata (Map pp442–4), celebrating the eve of Our Lady's birthday on 7 September.

Every two years Florence hosts the **Internazionale Antiquariato**, a major antiques fair attracting exhibitors from across Europe, held at the Palazzo Strozzi (Map pp446–7). The next fair will be in September/October 2005.

The **Maggio Musicale Fiorentino** in Florence is a major music festival (see p465).

SLEEPING

The city has hundreds of hotels in all categories and you'll find a good range of alternatives, including hostels and *affittacamere* (private rooms). There are more than 200 one- and two-star hotels alone in Florence, so even in the peak season it is generally possible, though not always easy, to find a room to stay in. All the same it's prudent to book ahead between mid-April and October.

Hotels and *pensioni* are concentrated in three main areas: near Stazione di Santa Maria Novella, near Piazza di Santa Maria Novella and in the old city between the cathedral and the Arno.

If you haven't reserved, shun the touts around Stazione di Santa Maria Novella and instead consult the **Consorzio ITA** (Informazione Turistiche Alberghiere; Map pp442–4; ☎ 055 28 28 93; fax 055 247 82 32; ☺ 8.45am-9pm) office who will make you a booking for a small fee (€2.30 to €7.75 according to the grade of hotel).

Tourist offices carry a list of *affittacamere*, where you can sometimes find rooms for around €25. Most fill with students during the academic year (October to June) but are a good option if you are staying for a week or longer.

When you arrive at a hotel ask for the full price of a room before putting your bags down; a minority of Florentine hotels and *pensioni* are adept at bill-padding, particularly in summer, requiring, for example, compulsory breakfast. Contact the main tourist office on Via Cavour if you have any problems.

Prices listed here are for the high season which, for those hotels that differentiate, starts on 15 April and fizzles out by mid-October (some dip a little in the hot months of July and August).

Accommodation Associations

These organisations can book you into member hotels. They usually offer a fair range of possibilities, but rarely drop below two stars.

Florence Promhotels (☎ 055 55 39 41 or 800 86 60 22; www.promhotels.it; Viale Volta 72)

Top Quark (☎ 055 33 40 41, toll free ☎ 800 60 88 22; www.familyhotels.com; Viale Fratelli Rossi 39r)

These two bodies specialise in *affittacamere* and short-stay apartments:

AGAP (Associazione Gestori Alloggi Privati; ☎ 055 505 10 12; www.agap.it; Viale Volta 127a)

Gente di Toscana (☎ 0575 52 92 75; www.gentedi toscana.it; Via S Michele, Scandicci) also covers Chianti country.

Camping

There are three camping options in and around Florence.

Campeggio Michelangelo (Map pp436–7; ☎ 055 681 19 77; www.ecvacanze.it; Viale Michelangelo 80; person/tent/car €8/5/4.50; ☺ Apr-Oct) This is the closest camp site to the city centre, just off Piazzale Michelangelo, south of the River Arno. Take bus No 13 from Stazione di Santa Maria Novella. Big and comparatively leafy, it's handy for the historic quarter though the steep walk back may have you panting.

Villa Camerata (Map pp436–7; ☎ 055 60 14 51; fax 055 61 03 00; Viale Augusto Righi 2-4; per person/tent €6/5) Beside the HI (Hostelling International) hostel of the same name (see p461), and in a green setting, space for tents is fairly limited but more generous for campervans.

See p468 for details of the third camp site, Campeggio Panoramico.

East of Stazione di Santa Maria Novella

BUDGET   Map pp442–4

Most of the hotels in this area are well run, clean and safe, but there are a few seedy establishments. Secure and salubrious places include those listed here:

Ostello Archi Rossi (☎ 055 29 08 04; fax 055 230 26 01; Via Faenza 94r; dm from €15.50, s €28.50) This private hostel, particularly popular with young Americans, is close to Stazione di Santa Maria Novella and a reasonable option though rooms are quite small. Decorated with guests' wall paintings and graffiti, it's generally full to the gills.

Pensione Bellavista (☎ 055 28 45 28; bellavista hotel@iol.it; 5th fl, Largo Alinari 15; s/d €60/75, with bathroom €70/87; ✖) Rooms are fairly small but a bargain if you can manage to book one of the two doubles with balconies and a view of the cathedral and Palazzo Vecchio. Breakfast, served in your room, costs €5.20.

Albergo Azzi (☎ /fax 055 21 38 06; Via Faenza 56; s/d with breakfast €40/65, with bathroom & breakfast €55/90) Rooms here are simple and comfortable – ask for one away from the noisy Via Faenza and enjoy breakfast on the hotel's terrace. The helpful management will arrange accommodation for you in other Italian cities.

MID-RANGE
This is the slightly upmarket hotel flank of the station. The bulk of the cheaper but frequently not so tempting options is over on the Via della Scala, west of the station.

Hotel Le Cascine (Map pp442–4; ☎ 055 21 10 66; fax 055 21 07 69; www.hotellecascine.it; 1st fl, Largo Alinari 15; s with breakfast 60-120, d with breakfast 90-170; (P) (X) (Q)) This three-star place with its young, friendly staff is one of the better choices in an area overburdened with hotels. Rooms are attractively furnished and some have balconies. Parking is €12.

Hotel Désirée (Map pp442–4; ☎ 055 238 23 82; www.desireehotel.com; Via Fiume 20; s/d €77/124; (P) (X)) A very personable hotel that offers fine rooms, many of which overlook a tranquil, leafy courtyard at the back. The spick-and-span high-ceilinged rooms are simply but tastefully furnished and have their own bathrooms. Parking is €20.

Hotel Accademia (Map pp446–7; ☎ 055 29 34 51; www.accademiahotel.net; Via Faenza 7; s/d/tr with breakfast €85/150/190; (X)) The hotel is within an 18th-century mansion with impressive stained-glass doors, carved wooden ceilings – and a marble staircase that tempts you to do your Ginger Rogers and Fred Astaire impersonation. Bedrooms are pleasant and parquet-floored.

Hotel Bellettini (Map pp446–7; ☎ 055 21 35 61; www.hotelbellettini.com; Via de' Conti 7; s/d/tr €95/130/ 160; (X) (Q)) This is a delightful, welcoming hotel with around 30 bright, well-furnished rooms – try for one with a view of the Basilica di San Lorenzo. It has an equally attractive, slightly more expensive annexe nearby.

Hotel San Lorenzo (Map pp442–4; ☎ 055 28 49 25; www.sanlorenzohotel.it; Via Rosina 4; s/d with shower €50/95, d/tr with bathroom & breakfast €105/130; (P) (Q)) With just eight rooms this two-star place is one of the city's many small family *pensioni*. In low season a double with bathroom can come down to €65.

Hotel Casci (Map pp442–4; ☎ 055 21 16 86; www.hotelcasci.com; Via Cavour 13; s/d/tr €100/140/180; (P) (X) (X) (Q)) This friendly family hotel with its attractive olive-green decor offers you the chance to stay in a 15th-century mansion on one of the city's main streets. Rooms all have minibar and safe. Look up

at the fresco as you scoff your buffet breakfast that includes fresh espresso coffee. Parking is between €23 and €27.

Hotel Globus (Map pp442–4; ☎ 055 21 10 62; www .hotelglobus.com; Via Sant'Antonino 24; s €60-100, d €70-180; (P) (X) (Q)) Stylishly and sensitively refurbished in 2002, this cosy, welcoming hotel, which once belonged to the composer Rossini, makes an excellent mid-range choice and comes recommended by several readers. All rooms have minibar, safe and free Internet access via the TV. Parking is €18.

TOP END   map pp442–4
Hotel Monna Lisa (☎ 055 247 97 51; www.monna lisa.it; Borgo Pinti 27; s/d/tr €201.50/284/413; (X) (P)) The Monna Lisa is in a fine Renaissance *palazzo*. Most of the furnishings and paintings are of the period, many of them family heirlooms. Nonchalantly on display are works by Giovanni Dupré, the 19th-century sculptor, whose relatives still own the hotel. The most attractive rooms look out over the bijou private garden, bedecked with flowers, where you can enjoy a buffet breakfast in summer.

Hotel Il Guelfo Bianco (☎ 055 28 83 30; www .ilguelfobianco.it; Via Cavour 57r; s €135, d from €180; (P) (X) (Q)) The 43 rooms here are attractively laid out and comfortable. Ask for room No 124, a charming double with its own private terrace. Alternatively, room Nos 42 and 56, at the same level, give great rooftop views. In addition to some fine antiques, a more original touch for Florence are the interesting contemporary paintings that adorn public areas and some bedrooms. Parking is €18.

Around Piazza di Santa Maria Novella   Map pp446–7
BUDGET
Just south of the Stazione di Santa Maria Novella, this area embraces Piazza di Santa Maria Novella, and the streets running south to the Arno and east to Via de' Tornabuoni.

Pensione Ferretti (☎ 055 238 13 28; www.emmeti.it/ Hferretti; Via delle Belle Donne 17; s/d/tr with breakfast €48/ 78/103, with bathroom & breakfast €60/98/123; (P) (X) (Q)) Hidden away on a tiny, quiet intersection, this modest hotel has a friendly, family feel to it. Rooms have ceiling fans and off-peak rates are substantially lower than the maximum. Parking is €21.

Hotel Abaco (☎ 055 238 19 19; www.abaco-hotel.it; 2nd fl, Via dei Banchi 1; d with/without bathroom €85/70; ❄ 🖳) It's quite a haul up to the 2nd floor with a heavy bag but well worth the effort. This simple, well-maintained establishment has just seven rooms, four without bathroom and all furnished in high baroque style. There are no singles, although in low season they will rent a double out for €60.

Hotel Scoti (☎ /fax 055 29 21 28; www.hotelscoti.com; Via de' Tornabuoni 7; s/d €65/85) This hotel within a 16th-century *palazzo* sits on Florence's smartest shopping strip. Renovated in 2003 it has resisted the temptation to bump up its prices excessively and is now an even more attractive choice. Rooms are full of character and have been refurnished with antique pieces and the common sitting room with its floor to ceiling frescoes is a little gem.

TOP END
Grand Hotel Baglioni (☎ 055 2 35 80; www.hotel baglioni.it; Piazza dell'Unità Italiana 6; d from €227; 🅿 ❄ 🖳) With its wooden beams and staircase and public areas of *pietra serena* (the soft grey stone typical of many Florentine monuments), the tone at the Baglioni is mellow. Some rooms fall into the 'superior' category and cost an extra €88. The rooftop terrace restaurant and garden have stirring views over the city.

Between the Cathedral & the Arno
BUDGET
This area is about 1km south from Stazione di Santa Maria Novella in the heart of old Florence.

Hotel Orchidea (Map pp446–7; ☎ 055 248 03 46; notelorchidea@yahoo.it; 1st fl, Borgo degli Albizi 11; s/d without bathroom €50/70) This is a fine, homely, old-fashioned *pensione* in a grand mansion. Rooms are simple, well maintained and full of character.

Hotels San Giovanni and Perseo, a pair of excellent choices, have the same Italian-Australian owners.

Hotel San Giovanni (Map pp446–7; ☎ 055 28 83 85; www.hotelsangiovanni.com; Via de' Cerretani 2; s/d/tr with breakfast €50/73/97, with bathroom & breakfast €70/93/120) Don't be deterred by the rather pokey stairwell up to the 2nd floor. This hotel, once part of the bishop's private residence (see the traces of fresco in several rooms), has charming, often spacious rooms with parquet flooring. Eight of the nine rooms

have views of the cathedral. You take breakfast in Hotel Perseo, where you also check in if no-one answers here.

Hotel Perseo (Map pp446–7; ☎ 055 21 25 04; www .hotelperseo.it; Via de'Cerretani 1; s/d/tr with breakfast €53/73/97, d/tr with bathroom & breakfast €93/120; 🅿 🖳) Offering greater comfort than its sister and but a well-lobbed stone away, Hotel Perseo has 19 rooms. The decor is befittingly arty with original canvases by the owner and one or two by long-forgotten, impecunious students who, in the harsh days after the Spanish Civil War, would leave a painting in lieu of rent. Valet parking is €24.

Hotel Dalí (Map pp442–4 ☎ 055 234 07 06; www .hoteldali.com; Via dell'Oriuolo 17; s/d €40/60, d with bathroom €75, extra bed €20; 🅿) A friendly, helpful young couple run this spruce, simple and warmly recommended hotel. Try for a room looking over the serene inner courtyard. One room can accommodate up to six so bring the gang. There's free parking, rare as icebergs in Florence.

MID-RANGE
Pensione Maria Luisa de' Medici (Map pp446–7; ☎ 055 28 00 48; Via del Corso 1; d/tr with breakfast €67/93, with bathroom & breakfast €80/113) This hotel, which occupies part of a 17th-century mansion, is tastefully furnished and rich in antiques. You can dip into the doctor owner's equally impressive collection of coffee table art volumes. You'll sleep soundly, protected by his superb collection of winged angels and cherubims that keep watch over the corridors. Rooms are enormous, most can easily accommodate four, even five.

Albergo Bavaria (Map pp446–7; ☎ /fax 055 234 03 13; Borgo degli Albizi 26; s/d €50/70, d/tr with bathroom €98/113) Albergo Bavaria is housed in the fine 16th-century Palazzo di Ramirez di Montalvo, built around a peaceful courtyard by Ammannati. Rooms are furnished with fine antique pieces. With its warm ochre colours, low wooden ceilings and flexible pricing, it makes an excellent choice in its category. Reservations, especially between May and July, are imperative.

Pendini (Map pp446–7; ☎ 055 211 170; www.florence italy.net; 4th fl, Via Strozzi 2; s €80-110, d €110-150; 🅿 ❄ 🖳) Another excellent choice, this family-owned place has rooms furnished with antiques and reproductions. In the off-season they are willing to come down quite a way in price. Parking is €24.

TUSCANY (TOSCANA)

Hotel Porta Rossa (Map pp446–7; ☎ 055 28 75 51; fax 055 28 21 79; Via Porta Rossa 19; s/d/tr with breakfast from €104/145/185; ⊠ ⊠) This old workhorse isn't as smart as many in its class but if you enjoy steeping yourself in history, check in. First functioning as an inn back in the 14th century, it nowadays exudes a fading 19th-century charm where rooms are huge and furnished in the antique style. Neither they nor the welcome is as fresh as it might be.

Relais Uffizi (Map pp446–7; ☎ 055 267 62 39; www .relaisuffizi.it; Chiasso del Buco 16, off Chiasso de' Baroncello; s/d/tr €120/180/220; P ⊠ ⊠ ⊔) This stylish small hotel, right in the heart of the action, is hidden away down an alley in a 16th-century building, a mere pigeon hop from Piazza della Signoria. From its breakfast room there are unparalleled views of the square; it's tempting to just sit there and watch life seethe below. Bedrooms are large and tastefully furnished and most have a bathtub. Parking is €30.

TOP END

Hotel Helvetia & Bristol (Map pp446–7; ☎ 055 2 66 51; www.hotelhelvetiabristolfirenze.it; Via dei Pescioni 2; s/d from €240/390; P ⊠ ⊔) Deservedly five-star, this hotel is one of Florence's most inviting top-level spots, distinguished by the elegance of its setting and the discreet yet warm charm of its staff. Each of its 56 rooms is individually and tastefully furnished in rich fabrics and fine antiques abound. Guests who've savoured its charm include Bertrand Russell, Pirandello and Stravinsky.

THE AUTHOR'S CHOICE

Gallery Hotel Art (Map pp446–7; ☎ 055 2 72 63; www.lungarnohotels.com; Vicolo dell'Oro 5; d with breakfast from €/315; P ⊠ ⊠) Should my Great Aunt Emily be generous in her will, I would set myself up in the Gallery Hotel Art. It is a very modish place indeed, unique in Florence and the perfect spot to retreat to if all that Renaissance begins to overwhelm. Strictly 21st-century, minimalist, edgy and soft hued, it earns the 'gallery' of its title for the contemporary art that decorates corridors and each of its 74 rooms. There's also a changing exhibition in its downstairs lounge/library and Japanese-style Fusion Bar. Parking is €29.

Savoy (Map pp446–7; ☎ 055 273 58 31; www.ro ccofortehotels.com; Piazza della Repubblica 7; s/d from €300/450; P ⊠ ⊔) Completely refurbished and modernised to mark the millennium, this stylish jewel in the Forte chain offers spacious living. It's a beguiling mix; all the rooms in this classic building have a fresh, contemporary feel. If you aren't on your knees after a day of sightseeing, its fitness centre offers exercise – with yet more heart-stopping views from its windows

Santa Croce & East of the Centre
Map pp442–4

BUDGET

Pensione Losanna (☎ 055 24 58 40; www.albergo losanna.com; Via Vittorio Alfieri 9; s/d/tr €39/52/70.50, d/tr with bathroom €68/92) This well-run establishment lies about 400m east of the Museo Archeologico as the crow flies. The lady here runs a tight, if small, ship and the place is frequently full. A couple of rooms can be made up as triples.

MID-RANGE

Hotel Wanda (☎ 055 234 44 84; www.hotelwanda.it; Via Ghibellina 51; s/d/tr with breakfast €70/88/119, d/tr with bathroom & breakfast €119/140; ⊠) This is a welcoming, tranquil, somewhat higgledy-piggledy place. Its large rooms, with ceiling frescoes, are much airier and lighter than the dowdy facade would suggest. For a fun night, request Room 13, which is lined with old mirrors.

Hotel Dante (☎ 055 24 17 72; www.hoteldante.it; Via S Cristofano 2; s/d €96/147; P ⊠) Tucked away in a quiet street right by the Basilica di Santa Croce, rooms are fine without being spectacular. All have smallish, recently renovated bathrooms. Hotel Dante's unique touch is that three out of the four rooms on each floor have a kitchen – ideal for families or if you fancy dining in rather than out. Parking is €10 to €15.

Oltrarno

BUDGET

Istituto Gould (Map pp442–4; ☎ 055 21 25 76; fax 055 21 25; gould.reception@dada.it; 2nd fl, Via de' Serragli 49; ⊙ 9am-1pm & 3-7pm Mon-Fri, 3-7pm Sat) Bunk beds in rooms of two, three or four at this Protestant youth centre are small but comfortable enough; the rooms are on the dingy side. Ask to be located in one overlooking the pleasant garden.

Ostello Santa Monaca (Map pp442–4; ☎ 055 26 83 38; www.ostello.it; Via Santa Monaca 6; dm €16; ☒ ▣) We warmly recommend this Oltrarno area hostel, a 15- to 20-minute walk south from Stazione di Santa Maria Novella. Friendly and run by a cooperative, it doesn't do meals but guests get a special deal at a nearby restaurant. There's a laundrette and also a guests' kitchen.

MID-RANGE

Hotel la Scaletta (Map pp446–7; ☎ 055 28 30 28; fax 055 28 95 62; www.lascaletta.com; top fl, Via de' Guicciardini 13; s/d with breakfast €93/135; ☒) La Scaletta is a delightfully friendly place, full of rambling corridors on three levels, within a 15th-century *palazzo*. Its worth the room rate simply for the great 360° roof terrace view and you're scarcely 100m from both the Ponte Vecchio and Palazzo Pitti.

Pensione Sorelle Bandini (Map pp442–4; ☎ 055 21 53 08; pensionebandini@tiscali.it; 3rd fl, Piazza S Spirito 9; d with/without bathroom €108/130) This rattling old *pensione* occupies the penultimate floor of yet another venerable old building which overlooks the hippest square around in Florence. Rooms aren't world class in comfort and are rather on the dowdy side, but the position and views from the balcony running its length compensate for any of the rough edges. All rates include breakfast.

Around Florence

BUDGET

Ostello Villa Camerata (Map pp436–7; ☎ 055 60 14 51; florenceaighostel@virgilio.net; Viale Augusto Righi 2-4; dm/d/tr with breakfast €15.50/38/49.50; ℗ ☒ ▣) This HI hostel, a converted 17th-century villa in extensive grounds, must rank as one of the most beautiful in Europe. Dinner costs €8 and there's a bar. Take bus No 17, 17B or 17C (€1, 30 minutes, every half-hour) from the southwest side of Stazione di Santa Maria Novella.

Renting Accommodation

Apartments in Florence aren't easy to come by and can be expensive. **Florence & Abroad** (Map pp442–4; ☎ 055 48 70 04; www.florenceandabroad .com; Via San Zanobi 58) specialises in short- and medium-term rental accommodation in Florence and the Fiesole area for those with a fairly liberal budget. See AGAP and Gente di Toscana (p457).

EATING

Simplicity and quality sum up Tuscany's cuisine and nowhere in the region will you find a wider choice than in Florence. Here, rich green Tuscan olive oil, fresh fruit and vegetables, tender meat and, of course, the classic wine, Chianti, are so often the basics of a good meal.

Meat eaters might want to take on the challenge of the local carnivore's classic, *bistecca alla fiorentina*, a huge slab of prime Florentine steak. It usually costs around €40 per kilogram, which is quite adequate for two.

Budget

EAST OF STAZIONE DI SANTA
MARIA NOVELLA   Map pp442–4

You can find some popular budget options in this area.

Nerbone (☎ 055 21 99 49; Mercato Centrale San Lorenzo; mains €5.20; ☺ lunch Mon-Sat) Nerbone, no airs and graces, simple as they come and just inside the central market's western entrance, has been serving steaming mid-day platters since 1872. The handwritten menu changes daily. If it's on, start with their particularly substantial *ribollita* (rich, chewy soup; €3.10) and round off your hearty lunch with *biscotti di Prato* (€2.50), a crunchy almond biscuit/cookie served with a shot of *vin santo*, a sweet dessert wine.

Mario (☎ 055 21 85 50; Via Rosina 2; mains €3.75-5, pasta €3.25-4.50; ☺ lunch Mon-Sat) In business for over 50 years, this bustling bar and trattoria near Piazza del Mercato Centrale attracts a mix of local workers and foreign strays.

Trattoria ZàZà (☎ 055 21 54 11; Piazza del Mercato Centrale 26r; lunch menu €13; ☺ Mon-Sat). Next door to Mario's, this place gets its produce fresh from the covered market, just across the square. It's a great spot for combining outdoor dining and a little people watching. The menu changes regularly and often sparkles with imaginative dishes.

I'Tozzo di Pane (☎ 055 47 57 53; Via Guelfa 94r; mains €8-13; ☺ closed Sun & lunch Mon) A young, friendly team run this simple neighbourhood place, where cool jazz warbles in the background. For starters, go for the *zuppa toscana*, a thick gruel of vegetables and barley. Although not to all tastes, the *trippa alla Fiorentina* (tripe) follows on a treat. The small rear garden is a pleasant retreat from the street in summer.

Il Vegetariano (☎ 055 47 50 30; Via delle Ruote 30r; meals around €15; ☾ lunch & dinner Tue-Fri, dinner Sat & Sun) One of the few veggie options in town, this is an unassuming locale with a great selection of fresh food, salads and mains.

BETWEEN THE CATHEDRAL & THE ARNO Map pp446-7

There are several good eateries for Tuscan treats around here, though you have to sift among the more standard tourist fare.

Ristorante Self-Service Leonardo (☎ 055 28 44 46; Via de' Pecori 35r; mains €3.50-4.50; ☾ 11.45am-2.45pm & 6.45-9.45pm Sun-Fri) When it comes to eating a full meal while you pinch pennies, it's hard to beat this refectory-style spot for simply filling an empty tum.

Angie's Pub (☎ 055 28 37 64; Via dei Neri 35r; snacks €2.50-5; ☾ noon-1am Mon-Sat, 6pm-1am Sun) Angie's offers a vast array of *panini* (bread rolls with filling) and focaccia, as well as hamburgers Italian-style, with mozzarella and spinach. Should nothing on that long *panini* menu tickle your palate, you can design your own from their range of juicy fillings.

AROUND OGNISSANTI

This area by the Arno has a trio of good spots.

Da il Latini (Map pp446-7; ☎ 055 21 09 16; Via dei Palchetti 6r; mains €10-18, pasta €6-7; ☾ Tue-Sat) This trattoria is a Florentine classic. There's been a tendency recently for it to rest a little too much on its laurels but the ambience, if a little contrived, is fine and the wine list remains impressive. And all those folk waiting in line can't be wrong...The food is largely Tuscan but the dining area speaks of Spain with all those legs of ham dangling from the ceiling.

Trattoria dei 13 Gobbi (Map pp442-4; ☎ 055 21 32 04; Via del Porcellana 9r; mains from €11, pasta from €5.50; ☾ Tue-Sun) The bucolic setting inside this trattoria also smacks a bit of the artificial but it's done tastefully enough with the low ceilings making their contribution and, in summer, the rear courtyard coming into play.

Sostanza (Map pp442-4; ☎ 055 21 26 91; Via del Porcellana 25r; mains €8.50-11.50; ☾ Mon-Fri) This authentic Tuscan eatery is a good spot for *bistecca alla fiorentina* and they simmer a mean minestrone (€5.50).

SANTA CROCE & EAST OF THE CENTRE

You can get inexpensive fare, from snacks to steaks, in this area.

Caffetteria Piansa (Map pp442-4; ☎ 055 234 23 62; Borgo Pinti 18r; set lunch €10.50; ☾ Mon-Sat) At this vaulted restaurant you basically point and choose from a limited number of cheap, tasty lunch-time dishes; for the rest of the day, it's more of a bar offering drinks and snacks. Don't leave lunch too late – the pots are whipped away by 2.30pm.

Osteria de' Benci (Map pp446-7; ☎ 055 234 49 23; Via de' Benci 13r; meals €25-30; ☾ Mon-Sat) Dining is a pleasure beneath this restaurant's vaulted ceiling. The young team changes the menu monthly and serves up honest slabs of *carbonata di chianina* – even more tender and succulent than the ubiquitous *bistecca alla fiorentina*. The food is well prepared, the atmosphere cosy and prices moderate.

Antico Noè (Map pp446-7; ☎ 055 234 08 38; Volta di San Piero 6r; panini €3.50-4, meals €25-30; ☾ Tue-Sun) This legendary sandwich bar, just off Piazza San Pier Maggiore, is another option for a light meal. They have two sections: the sandwich bar with its juicy cold cuts is takeaway only while next door they run a cosy restaurant.

Osteria Cibrèo (Map pp442-4; ☎ 055 234 11 00; Via de' Macci 124r; meals around €20; ☾ Tue-Sat) This is a true delight to the palate, located next door to the original and much more expensive restaurant of the same name (see p463). They offer no pasta at all but some enticing first courses such as *stormato di patate e ricotta* (€5; oven cooked potato and white cheese).

Ruth's (Map pp442-4; ☎ 055 248 08 88; Via Luigi Carto Farini 2a; meals around €12; ☾ Sun-Fri) For something a little different, try this place, at once kosher and vegetarian, beside Florence's synagogue. For a variety of savours, try Ruth's *pialto* (€8), a mixed platter including couscous, felafel, filo pastry pie and potato salad and quite filling in itself.

Ramraj (Map pp442-4; ☎ 055 24 09 99; Via Ghibellina 61r; set menu €8; ☾ Tue-Sun) Drop in here for takeaway tandoori and other Indian specialities or munch them at the long bench.

OLTRARNO

Borgo Antico (Map pp442-4; ☎ 055 21 04 37; Piazza Santo Spirito 6r; pizzas €6, mains €10-15) This pizzeria and restaurant is a great location in summer when you can sit at an outside table and enjoy the atmosphere in the piazza. Try one of their big, frondy salads at €6, just one of several vegetarian options. Servings in general are plentiful.

Il Tranvai (Map pp442–4; ☎ 055 22 51 97; Piazza Tasso 14r; meals up to €18.10; ۞ Mon-Fri) Whether you're eating elbow to elbow at the interior tables or out on the terrace, you're sure to savour the food at this wonderful, rustic Tuscan eatery. Since it's so deservedly popular, you'd be wise to reserve your small space.

Trattoria Casalinga (Map pp442–4; ☎ 055 21 86 24; Via de' Michelozzi 9r; mains around €5; ۞ Mon-Sat) The food at this popular, family-run eating place is great and a filling meal of pasta, meat or vegetables plus wine will come in at bargain-basement prices. Don't expect to linger over a meal as there's usually a queue of people eager to take over your table.

I Tarocchi (Map pp442–4; ☎ 055 234 39 12; Via dei Renai 16r; pizzas & 1st or 2nd courses €6-7; ۞ Tue-Fri & dinner Sat-Sun) This popular pizzeria/trattoria serves excellent pizzas. The first courses alone are enough to satisfy most people's hunger and the menu changes regularly.

Osteria Antica Mescita San Niccolò (Map pp436–7; ☎ 055 234 28 36; Via San Niccolò 62-64; meals €18-23; ۞ Mon-Sat) This is a fine little eating hideaway where the food is tasty and authentic. Throw in a good bottle from their impressive wine collection and you'll have a great meal.

Mid-Range
EAST OF STAZIONE DI SANTA MARIA NOVELLA
Ristorante Lobs (Map pp442–4; ☎ 055 21 24 78; Via Faenza 75-77r; mains around €25) This superb fish restaurant offers always fresh, exclusively Mediterranean fish and seafood. There's a non-smoking area at the rear and the setting is cosy with maritime frescoes and – appropriately – salmon-pink walls. At midday they do a selection of pasta specials (€7). Sluice it all down with their Soave wine from the country's northeast.

AROUND PIAZZA DI SANTA MARIA NOVELLA
Ostaria dei Centopoveri (Map pp442–4; ☎ 055 21 88 46; Via del Palazzuolo 31r; meals €35-40; ۞ Wed-Sun) A congenial spot in a not-so-congenial part of town, the 'hostel of the hundred poor people' is a quality dining option. It offers creative variations on traditional Tuscan food.

BETWEEN THE CATHEDRAL & THE ARNO   Map pp446–7
Trattoria Coco Lezzone (☎ 055 28 71 78; Via Parioncino 26r; meals €25-40; ۞ Mon-Sat) Appearances can deceive and what looks like your traditional Florentine people's trattoria is in fact an up-market re-creation with prices to match. No credit cards, no coffee, just very good food; this place knows its clients know it's good and doesn't make unnecessary concessions to them. *Ribollita* is the house speciality and Friday is fresh-fish day.

Cantinetta Antinori (☎ 055 29 22 34; Piazza degli Antinori 3; mains €13.50-15; ۞ Mon-Fri & dinner Sun) On the ground floor of 15th-century Palazzo Antinori, this place, more *enoteca* (wine bar) than restaurant, offers a reasonable meal accompanied by some fine wines – it is for the latter that most people come here.

OLTRARNO   Map pp442–4
Osteria Santo Spirito (☎ 055 238 23 83; Piazza S Spirito 16r; meals around €30). If you prefer a slightly higher quality meal than the bustling haunts across the square, this cosy restaurant, built on two floors and spilling onto the piazza in summer, is the place. Try the gnocchi with soft cheese *gratiné* and truffle oil (€9).

Ristorante Beccofino (☎ 055 29 00 76; Piazza degli Scarlatti 1r; 1st/2nd courses up to €10/20 ۞ Tue-Sun) Both restaurant and stylish *enoteca* (with over 50 wines on offer by the glass), Beccofino is decidedly nouvelle chic – no traditional bucolics in here, thank you. The stainless steel, floor-lit toilets are far from the least of its charms!

Top End
SANTA CROCE &
EAST OF THE CENTRE   Map pp442–4
Ristorante Cibrèo (☎ 055 234 11 00; Via de' Macci 118; meals up to €75 ; ۞ Tue-Sat) Next door to the fine

TUSCANY (TOSCANA)

THE AUTHOR'S CHOICE

I Fratellini (Map pp446–7; ☎ 055 239 60 96; Via dei Cimatori 38r; panini €2.10) It's little more than a hole in the wall and you eat in the street but my favourite quick snack place in all Europe is I Fratellini. You'll never see *panini*, fresh filled as you order, whipped up so quickly as at this wonderful, seething place, established in 1875. Just watch the deft backhand pass from maker to wine pourer. There's no seating and etiquette requires that you leave your empty glass on one of the two wooden shelves on the wall outside.

osteria of the same name (see p462), this highly regarded restaurant is the place for a special splurge. The decor is much the same as in the *osteria*, although the table settings are suitably more elegant.

Snacks

On the streets between the cathedral and the River Arno harbour are many pizzerie where you can buy takeaway pizza by the slice for €1 to €1.50.

Fiaschetteria Vecchio Casentino (Map pp446–7; ☎ 055 21 74 11; Via de Neri 17r; ✆ Tue-Sun) Casentino does a magnificent array of snacks and over 30 different kinds of *panini*, all under €6. It also keeps a good selection of wines by the glass.

Il Nilo (Map pp446–7; ☎ 055 24 16 99; Volta di San Piero 9r; ✆ noon-10pm) Zaki from Cairo, the man with the widest grin in town, does tasty shawarma and felafel sandwiches (€2.50 to €3.50) to takeaway or munch on the spot.

Gelaterias

Gelateria Vivoli (Map pp446–7; ☎ 055 29 23 34; Via dell'Isola delle Stinche 7) People queue outside this place, near Via Ghibellina, to delight in the gelati widely considered to be the city's best.

Festival del Gelato (Map pp446–7; ☎ 055 29 43 86; Via del Corso 75r) Just off Piazza della Repubblica, with over 70 flavours on offer, it can satisfy even the most demanding kid.

Perchè No? (Map pp446–7; ☎ 055 239 89 69; Via dei Tavolini 19r; ✆ Wed-Sun) This *gelateria* also does excellent ices.

Self-Catering

The **Mercato Centrale San Lorenzo** (central market; Map pp442-4; Piazza del Mercato Centrale; ✆ 7am-2pm Mon-Sat) is a cornucopia of delights for self-caterers and sandwich fillers.

DRINKING

Florence has a huge range of congenial places for a drink or two.

Cafés
Map pp446–7

Gilli (☎ 055 21 38 96; Piazza della Repubblica 39r; ✆ Wed-Sun) One of several historic cafés around the square, Gilli has been serving good coffee since 1733. It's very reasonably priced if you stand at the bar.

Sip a coffee (€2.60) at the rooftop café of the **Rinascente** (Via Speziali 13-23r) department

store, just off Piazza della Repubblica, and savour the stunning views of the square and cathedral.

Bars

Astor Caffè (Map pp446–7; ☎ 055 239 90 00; Piazza del Duomo 5r) You could take breakfast here, then return some 12 hours later to mix with the nocturnal crowd who gather around at night for loud music and cocktails both inside and out, right by the solemn walls of the cathedral.

Capoccaccia (Map pp446–7; ☎ 055 21 07 51; Lungarno Corsini 12-14r; ✆ Tue-Sun) The beautiful people of Florence gather here, especially on balmy spring and summer evenings, for a riverside nibble and cocktail. Tuesday night is sushi night and the DJ takes over at 11pm Wednesday to Sunday.

Red Garter House (Map pp446–7; ☎ 055 248 09 09; Via de Benci 33r; ✆ daily mid-Mar–mid-Jan, Tue-Sun mid-Jan–Mar) This satisfyingly raucous joint has cheap booze and live music nightly.

Mayday Lounge Café (Map pp446–7; ☎ 055 238 12 90; Via Dante Alighieri 16r) Altogether more stylish than Red Garter, there's often an art exhibition and the two *ragazzi* who run the place have an amazing collection of CDs, sometimes supplemented with live music.

Sant'Ambrogio Caffè (Map pp442–4; ☎ 055 24 10 35; Piazza Sant'Ambrogio 7r; cocktails €6; ✆ Mon-Sat) As well as being a place to get snacks, Sant'Ambrogio Caffè is especially dedicated to the sipping of cocktails. On summer nights they set up tables outside.

Rex Caffè (Map pp442–4; ☎ 055 248 03 31; Via Fiesolana 25r) Another stop on the cocktail circuit, this is a hip place to sip your favourite mixed concoction to a background of an illuminated world map. Take a martini at the luridly lit central bar or a quiet beer sitting at one of the shadowy metallic tables. Happy hour lasts from 5pm to 9.30pm.

Cabiria (Map pp442–4; ☎ 055 21 57 32; Piazza Santo Spirito 4r; ✆ Wed-Mon) This popular daytime café converts into a busy music bar at night. In summer the buzz extends on to Piazza Santo Spirito, which itself becomes a stage for an outdoor bar and regular free concerts.

La Dolce Vita (Map pp442–4; ☎ 055 28 45 95; Piazza del Carmine 6r; ✆ Mon-Thu, to 3am Fri-Sun) Just a piazza away from Santo Spirito, this place attracts a rather more self-consciously select crowd of self-appointed beautiful types.

Zoe (Map pp442–4; ☎ 055 24 31 11; Via dei Renai 13r; ❤ daily Apr-Oct, 6pm-2am Tue-Sun Nov-Mar) With its innards glowing red and bedecked with art exhibitions that change monthly, this bar heaves as its squadrons of punters, mostly young locals, end up spilling out onto the street.

Caffè La Torre (Map pp436–7; ☎ 055 68 06 43; Lungarno Benvenuto Cellini 65r; mixed drinks around €5.50) Hang out drinking until the wee hours, listening to all kinds of music from jazz to Latin rhythms.

ENTERTAINMENT

Several publications list the city's major festivals as well as theatrical and musical events.

Turismonotizie, nominally €0.50 but often available free, is a bimonthly published by the tourist office. *Informacittà* is a monthly freebie. Check their website, www.informac ittafirenze.it (Italian only), for the latest updates. *Eventi* is a free monthly flyer listing major events that's compiled by the tourist office, who also produce the annual brochure *Avventimenti*, covering major events in and around the city. *Florence Concierge Information* is a more compendious privately published free bimonthly.

Firenze Spettacolo, the city's definitive entertainment publication, is available monthly for €1.75 at bookstalls.

Box Office (Map pp442–4; ☎ 055 21 08 04; Via Luigi Alamanni 39; ❤ 10am-7.30pm Tue-Sat, 3.30-7.30pm Mon) is a handy centralised ticket outlet.

You can book tickets for the theatre, football matches and other events online through **Ticket One** (www.ticketone.it, Italian only).

Live Music & Clubs

Some of the bigger venues are well outside the town centre. Depending on who's playing, admission costs from nothing to over €10 – the drinks will cost you on top of that (at least €5 for a beer).

Jazz Club (Map pp442–4; ☎ 055 247 97 00; Via Nuova de' Caccini 3; 12-month compulsory membership €5, drinks around €6.50) This is Florence's top strictly jazz venue.

Tenax (Map pp442–4; ☎ 055 30 81 60; Via Pratese 46; admission free-€12; ❤ Tue-Sun) One of the city's more popular clubs, this place is well out to the northwest of town. It is one of Florence's biggest venues for Italian and international acts. Catch bus Nos 29 or 30 from Stazione

di Santa Maria Novella to get there. You'll need a taxi or a lift to get home.

Auditorium Flog W Live (Map pp436–7; ☎ 055 49 04 37, ☎ 055 21 08 04; Via M Mercati 24b; admission free-€12) Another venue for bands, this place is in the Rifredi area, also north of the centre but a little closer than Tenax. It's not as big (in any sense) as Tenax but has a reasonable stage and dance area. Catch bus Nos 8 or 14 from Stazione di Santa Maria Novella.

Central Park (Map pp436–7; ☎ 055 35 35 05; Via Fosso Macinante 2-6; admission €11-13; ❤ Tue-Sun) This is one of the city's most popular clubs. What music you hear will depend partly on the night, although as you wander from one dance area to another (there are four) you can expect a general range from Latin and pop through to house.

Rio Grande (Map pp436–7; ☎ 055 35 21 43; Viale degli Olmi; admission before/after 1am €16/20; ❤ Tue-Sat) Three dance spaces offer house, funk and mainstream commercial music to appeal to a fairly broad range of tastes. They put on regular theme nights; Thursday is usually salsa and Caribbean.

Cinemas

Surprisingly for such a cosmopolitan city, very few cinemas show films in their original version *(versione originale)*.

Odeon Cinehall (Map pp446–7; ☎ 055 21 40 68; www.cinehall.it, Italian only; Piazza Strozzi) This is the main location for seeing subtitled films, usually screened on Mondays, Tuesdays and Thursdays.

Cinema Fulgor (Map pp442–4; ☎ 055 238 18 81; Via Maso Finiguerra 22r) Screens English-language films on Thursday evenings.

Theatre & Classical Music

Teatro Comunale (Map pp442–4; ☎ 800 11 22 11; Corso Italia 16) A venue for concerts, opera and dance, organised by the **Maggio Musicale Fiorentino** (www.maggiofiorentino.com), which also runs an international concert festival at the theatre in May and June.

Teatro Verdi (Map pp446–7; ☎ 055 21 23 20; Via Ghibellina 99) Hosts drama, opera, concerts and dance from October to April.

Teatro della Pergola (Map pp446–7; ☎ 055 2 26 41; Via della Pergola 18) The **Amici della Musica** (☎ 055 60 74 40; www.amicimusica.fi.it) organises concerts here from September to April.

In summer especially, concerts of chamber music are held in churches across the

TUSCANY (TOSCANA)

city. The prestigious Orchestra da Camera Fiorentina (Florentine Chamber Orchestra) performance season runs from March to October.

SHOPPING

They say that Milan has the best clothes and Rome the best shoes, but Florence without doubt has the greatest variety of goods. It's also the city where some of the greats of fashion such as Gucci and Ferragamo first entered the rag trade. The main shopping area is between the cathedral and the Arno (Map pp446–7), with boutiques concentrated along Via Roma, Via de' Calzaiuoli and Via Por Santa Maria, leading to the goldsmiths lining the Ponte Vecchio. Window-shop along Via della Vigna Nuova and Via de' Tornabuoni, where the top designers, including Gucci, Yves Saint-Laurent, Ferragamo, Versace and Valentino, sell their wares.

At **Stockhouse Il Giglio** (Map pp442–4; ☎ 055 21 75 96; Borgo Ognissanti 86r) and **Stockhouse One Price** (Map pp442–4; ☎ 055 28 46 74; Borgo Ognissanti 74r), just along the road, labels are sold at tempting discount rates.

High fashion apart, Florence also has some very swanky specialist shops.

For gold and jewellery, browse the shops on either side of the Ponte Vecchio. Name locations include **Gherardi** (No 8r) and **Vettori** (No 37r).

Lovers of leather will enjoy the **Scuola del Cuoio** (Map pp442–4; ☎ 055 24 45 33; Via San Guiseppe 5r). At this training school, which you can also enter from the Basilica Santa Croce, you can both watch leatherworkers fashioning goods and buy the finished products. Elsewhere, Via de'Gondi and Borgo de' Greci (both Map pp446-7) are lined with leather shops.

Follow your nose to the **Oficina Profumo-Farmaceutica di Santa Maria Novella** (Map pp442–4; ☎ 055 21 62 76; Via della Scala 16), where you risk an olfactory orgasm. This pharmacy, originally established by the Dominicans, has been producing all manner of unguents, balms, soaps and scents ever since 1612. You may sniff at the prices when you see them...

Florence is also famous for its beautifully patterned paper, stocked in the many stationery and speciality shops throughout the city and at the markets. **Pineider** (☎ 055 28 46 55; Piazza della Signoria) is a particularly classy purveyor, in business since 1774.

Pusateri (Map pp446–7; ☎ 055 21 41 92; Via de'Calzaiuoli 25r) is a wonderful specialist shop that sells stylish gloves, and only gloves.

Jazz fiends really ought to pay a pilgrimage to **Twisted** (Map pp442–4; ☎ 055 28 20 11; Borgo S Frediano 21r), which has a quite outstanding collection of jazz recordings and posters.

Factory Outlets

Several outlet stores, offering discounts of 50% and more, ring Florence. The tourist office has a list. Some are single-brand, most bunch up several designers.

The Mall (Via Europa 8, Leccio Reggello; ☒ 10am-7pm Mon-Sat, 3-7pm Sun) is the handiest of the latter. It's about a 30-minute drive from downtown Florence, or a **shuttlebus** (☎ 055 865 77 75; return €25) can pick you up from your hotel or anywhere downtown.

Markets

Coming down to earth, in terms of both price and quality, the **open-air market** (9am-7.30pm Tue-Sun) that sprawls around the Piazza de San Lorenzo (Map pp446–7) and up towards the Mercato Centrale (Map pp436–7) offers leather goods, clothing and jewellery at low prices. Quality varies greatly. You can say the same for the goods being hawked at the similarly cheap and cheerful. **Mercato Nuovo** (Map pp446–7; Via Porta Rossa; ☒ 9am-7.30pm Tue-Sun).

The **Mercato dei Pulci** (flea market; Map pp442–4; Piazza dei Ciompi), off Borgo Allegri, is an amazing clutter of junk and bric-a-brac with the odd worthwhile antique waiting to be discovered. There's an especially big one that brings in vendors from all around on the last Sunday of the month.

GETTING THERE & AWAY
Air

Florence is served by two airports. **Amerigo Vespucci** (Map p439; ☎ 055 37 34 98; www.safnet.it) 5km northwest of the city centre at Via de Termine 11, caters for domestic and a handful of European flights.

Galileo Galilei (see p484), larger and one of northern Italy's main international and domestic airports, is about an hour away by car or regular train service.

Bus

The **SITA bus station** (Map pp442–4; ☎ 800 37 37 60; www.sita-on-line.it, Italian only; Via Santa Caterina da Sien

15) is just to the west of Piazza della Stazione. SITA and Tra-in share a direct, rapid service to/from Siena (€6.20, 1¼ hours, hourly) or you can change in Poggibonsi (50 minutes, half-hourly), where there are also connecting buses for San Gimignano (€5.40, 1¼ hours, 14 daily). Buses for Siena also run via Colle di Val d'Elsa (1¼ hours, hourly), where you change for Volterra (€6.45, 1½ hours, four daily).

Direct buses serve Arezzo, Castellina in Chianti, Faenza, Grosseto, Greve, Redda and other smaller cities throughout Tuscany.

Several bus companies, including **CAP** (Map pp442–4; ☎ 055 21 46 37) and **COPIT** (Map pp442–4; ☎ 800 57 05 30) operate from Largo Alinari, at the southern end of Via Nazionale. Services run to nearby towns including Prato (€2.20, 45 minutes, every 15 minutes), Pistoia (€2.60, 50 minutes, hourly).

Lazzi (Map pp442–4; ☎ 055 35 10 61; www.lazzi.it; Piazza Adua 1), next to Stazione di Santa Maria Novella, runs services to Rome, Prato (€2.20, 45 minutes, every half-hour), Pistoia (€2.70, 50 minutes, nine daily), Lucca (€4.70, 1½ hours, 18 daily) and Pisa (€6.20, two hours, hourly).

Lazzi forms part of the Eurolines network of international bus services. You can, for instance, catch a bus to Barcelona, Paris, Prague or London.

Car & Motorcycle

Florence is connected by the A1 northwards to Bologna and Milan and southwards to Rome and Naples. The Autostrada del Mare (A11) links Florence with Prato, Lucca, Pisa and the coast, and a *superstrada* (no tolls) joins the city to Siena.

The much more picturesque SS67 connects the city with Pisa to the west and Forlì and Ravenna to the east.

Train

Florence is on the Rome–Milan line. There are regular trains to/from Rome (€29.50 1½ to two hours), Bologna (€10.75, one hour), Milan (from €24.70, 2¾ to 3¼ hours) and Venice (€21.75, three hours). To get to Genoa and Turin, change in Pisa (€4.85, 1¼ hours, 40 daily).

The **train information office** (Map pp442-4; ☀ 7am-9pm) is in the southwest corner of the main foyer at Stazione di Santa Maria Novella.

GETTING AROUND
To/From the Airports

Vola in Bus (€4, every half-hour 6am to 11pm) is a bus service between the SITA bus station and Amerigo Vespucci.

Trains (€5.25; 1½ hours) leave Stazione di Santa Maria Novella for Galileo Galilei airport near Pisa about every hour until 5.18pm. If there's nothing direct, take a train to Pisa, from where there are more frequent connections. A taxi costs €15 to €18.

Bicycle

Alinari (Map pp442–4; ☎ 055 21 12 92; Via Guelfa 81r; ☀ daily Mar-Oct, Mon-Sat Nov-Feb) rents bikes from €2.50/7/45 per hour/five hours/week. They also hire scooters (€8/22/140) and motorbikes (from €12/55 per hour/day).

Florence by Bike (see p456) rents bikes from €2.50/7/30.50 per hour/five hours/three days.

Car & Motorcycle

Traffic is severely restricted in the city centre. If you've driven into Florence, dump your vehicle as soon as you can. A few hotels have private garages and many, including quite modest establishments, have a special arrangement with a nearby private garage. The fee for 24 hours varies from €15 to over twice this amount.

There are several car parks around the city centre fringe. If you are planning to spend the day in Florence, two options, both open round the clock, are beside Fortezza da Basso (Map pp436-7; €1.50 per hour) and beneath the Mercato Centrale (Map pp442–4; €1 for the first 90 minutes, then €1.40 per hour).

If you're unlucky enough to have your car towed away, phone ☎ 055 78 38 82.

A bunch of car-rental agencies (all Map pp442–4) cluster together in the Borgo Ognissanti area. Among the biggies are:

Avis (☎ 199 10 01 33; Borgo Ognissanti 128r)
Europcar (☎ 800 82 80 50; Borgo Ognissanti 53-57r)
Hertz (☎ 199 11 22 11; Via Maso Finiguerra 33r)

A couple of local competitors are **Happy Rent** (☎ 055 239 96 96; Borgo Ognissanti 153r), who also rent out motorbikes and scooters, and **Thrifty Rental** (☎ 055 28 71 61; Borgo Ognissanti 134r).

Public Transport

Buses of **ATAF** (Azienda Trasporti Area Fiorentina; ☎ 800 42 45 00; www.ataf.net) service the city centre, Fiesole and other areas on the city's periphery.

You'll find bus stops for several main routes around the Stazione di Santa Maria Novella (Map pp442-4). Some of the most useful lines operate from a stop just outside its southeastern exit. These include those listed here:

No 7 For Fiesole
No 13 For Piazzale Michelangelo
No 70 For the cathedral and the Uffizi (night bus)

A network of dinky little electric *bussini* (minibuses) operates around the centre of town. You can get a map of all bus routes, published by ATAF, from tourist offices.

Tickets for buses and *bussini* cost €1 and a handy *biglietto multiplo* (four-journey ticket) is €3.90; a day pass is €4. Stamp your ticket in the machine as you get on the bus. If you buy a ticket on board, it will cost you €1.50.

If you are hanging around Florence longer, you might want to invest in a *mensile* (monthly ticket) at €31.

Taxi
If you want to grab a taxi, call ☎ 055 42 42 or ☎ 055 43 90.

AROUND FLORENCE
Fiesole
Perched in hills about 8km northeast of Florence, between the valleys of the Arno and Mugnone rivers, Fiesole and its scattered villas have attracted the likes of Boccaccio, Marcel Proust, Gertrude Stein and Frank Lloyd Wright, all drawn by the lush olive groves and valleys – not to mention the spectacular view of Florence below.

Fiesole, for long the most important city in northern Etruria, was founded in the 7th century BC by the Etruscans. An easy half-day outing from Florence, it's a fabulous spot for a picnic and short walk. Avoid Sunday when half of Florence invades.

The **tourist office** (☎ 055 59 87 20; www.comune .fiesole.fi.it; Via Portigiani 3; ☽ 9am-6pm Mon-Sat, 10am-1pm & 2-6pm Sun Mar-Oct, 9am-5pm Mon-Sat, 10am-4pm Sun Nov-Feb) is just off Piazza Mino da Fiesole, the heart of the village.

SIGHTS & ACTIVITIES
A combined ticket (€6.50) gives you entry to Fiesole's main sights, the Museo Bandini and Zona Archeologica.

The **Museo Bandini** (☎ 055 5 94 77; Via Dupré; ☽ 10am-7pm Apr-Oct, 10am-5pm Wed-Mon Nov-Mar) has an impressive collection of early Tuscan Renaissance works, including Taddeo Gaddi's *Annunciation* and a beautifully illustrated copy of Petrarch's *Triumphs* (being restored).

Opposite the museum, the **Zona Archeologica** (☎ 055 5 94 77; Via Portigiani; ☽ 9.30am-7pm Apr-Oct, 9.30am-5pm Nov-Mar) features a 1st-century-BC Roman theatre, venue for the Estate Fiesolana, a series of concerts and performances held between June and August. Also in the complex are a small Etruscan temple and Roman baths, dating from the same period as the theatre. Its small archaeological museum, with exhibits from the Bronze Age to the Roman period, is worth a look.

Far in time and style from the Renaissance splendours of the valley below, the **Museo Primo Conti** (☎ 055 59 70 95; Via Dupré 18; admission €2.60; ☽ 9am-1pm Mon-Fri, 2nd & 3rd Sat of the month), about 300m north of the piazza, was the home of the eponymous avant-garde 20th-century artist and houses over 60 of his paintings.

For a five-star panorama, head 200m up steep Via S Francesco to a small viewpoint. If you are planning a picnic or just want a refreshing walk, pick up the tourist office brochure *Parco di Montefeceri*, which describes four easy walks from 1.5km to 3.5km.

SLEEPING & EATING
Campeggio Panoramico (☎ 055 59 90 69; www .florencecamping.com; Via Peramonda 1; per person/pitch €.9/14.50) If you have wheels this camp site, larger and cooler than the ones in Florence and with panoramic views of the city, makes a seductive alternative. It has bar, restaurant and pool.

There are a couple of decent restaurants right on Piazza Mino da Fiesole. For something more special, drop down to **Trattoria Le Cave di Maiano** (☎ 055 5 91 33; Via Cave di Maiano 16; meals around €25; ☽ Mon evening-Sun). In Maiano, a *frazione* (division) of Fiesole, this favourite with Florentines is a fine spot for traditional meat dishes and has a garden.

GETTING THERE & AWAY
Take ATAF bus No 7 from the Stazione di Santa Maria Novella in Florence. If you are driving, find your way to Piazza della Libertà in Florence and follow signs to Fiesole.

The Medici Villas

The Medicis built several opulent villas in the countryside around Florence as their wealth and prosperity grew during the 15th and 16th centuries. Most, nowadays enclosed by the city's suburbs and industrial sprawl, are easily reached by ATAF bus from Stazione di Santa Maria Novella. A combined ticket (€2) allows you to see two of the finest.

Villa Medicea La Petraia (☎ 055 45 26 91; Via della Petraia 40; ☽ 8.15am-sunset Tue-Sun, 1st & 4th Mon of the month) is about 3.5km north of the city. Commissioned by Cardinal Ferdinando de' Medici in 1576, this former castle was converted by Buontalenti and features a magnificent garden. Take ATAF bus No 28 from Stazione di Santa Maria Novella.

Villa Medicea di Castello (☎ 055 45 47 91; Via di Castello 47; ☽ park 8.15am-sunset Tue-Sun, 1st & 4th Mon of the month), further north, is Lorenzo il Magnifico's summer home. You can only visit the park. Again, take bus No 28.

Access to **Villa Medicea di Careggi** (☎ 055 427 97 55; Viale Pieraccini 17; admission free; ☽ 9am-6pm Mon-Fri, 9am-1pm Sat), where Lorenzo il Magnifico breathed his last in 1492, is limited as it is used as administrative offices for the local hospital. ATAF bus No 14C from Stazione di Santa Maria Novella runs past.

Another Medici getaway was the **Villa di Poggio a Caiano** (☎ 055 87 70 12; Piazza dei Medici 12; grounds/villa free/€2; ☽ tours hourly 8.15am-6.30pm Jun-Aug, 8.15am-5.30pm Sep-May). About 15km from Florence on the road to Pistoia, this mansion is set in magnificent sprawling gardens. Its interior is sumptuously decorated with frescoes and furnished much as it was when it was a royal residence of the Savoys. Take the COPIT bus (€3.75 return, 30 minutes) running between Florence and Pistoia – the bus stops right outside the villa.

The Mugello

The area northeast of Florence and leading up to the border with Emilia-Romagna is known as the Mugello. In it are some of Tuscany's most traditional villages, interspersed with elegant second homes for fortunate Florentines. The valley through which the River Sieve winds is one of Tuscany's premier wine areas.

In Borgo San Lorenzo the **Comunità Montana del Mugello** (☎ 055 849 53 46; Via P Togliatti 45), **Associazione Turismo Ambiente** (☎ 055 845 87 93; Piazza Dante 29) and **Borga Informa** (☎ 055 845 62 30; infoborgo@tin.it; Villa Pedori Giraldi) are all useful sources of information about the area. The latter two can arrange accommodation and excursions in the area.

The Medici originated from the Mugello and held extensive property in the area. Several Medici family castles, villas and palaces dot the area but most are closed to the public. Take the SS65 northwards from Florence. Near Vaglia, about 5km north of Pratolino, the **Parco della Villa Medici-Demidoff** (☎ 055 40 91 55; admission €2.60; ☽ 10am-8pm Thu-Sun Apr-Sep, 10am-6pm Sun Mar & Oct) is a lovely romantic garden, built around a long-demolished Medici villa. After about 12km turn right for glimpses of **Trebbio**, then **Cafaggiolo**, further along the same road. Originally a fortress, it was converted into a villa by Michelozzo in 1451. Neither are open to the public.

The area makes for pleasant walking. *Sorgenti Firenze Trekking* (SOFT; Florence Springs Trekking) are a network of signed day or half-day trails criss-crossing the area. *Mugello, Alto Mugello, Val di Sieve*, produced by SELCA, is a decent map for hikers at 1:70,000 (its trail No 8 is an easy 3½ hour round-trip walk, starting from the villa at Cafaggiolo and passing by Trebbio).

NORTHERN & WESTERN TUSCANY

PRATO

pop 174,500

Virtually enclosed within Florence's urban and industrial sprawl and a mere 17km to its northwest, Prato is one of Italy's main textile centres. Tuscany's second largest town after Florence, it has the country's largest concentration of Chinese immigrants, many now second-, or even third-generation Pratese. Founded by the Ligurians, the city fell to the Etruscans, then the Romans. As early as the 11th century it was an important centre for wool production. Continuing a tradition, textiles, together with leather working, are to this day Prato's main industries. It's worth dropping in on your way to the more picturesque cities of Pistoia, Lucca and Pisa or as a half-day trip from Florence.

TUSCANY (TOSCANA)

TUSCANY (TOSCANA)

Orientation

Prato's compact historical heart is girdled by near-intact city walls. Its nucleus is Piazza S Maria delle Carceri. The main train station (Prato Stazione Centrale) lies east of the city centre.

Information

The **tourist office** (☎ 0574 2 41 12; www.prato.turis mo.toscana.it; Piazza S. Maria delle Carceri; ☽ 9am-1.30pm & 2-7pm Mon-Sat, to 6pm in winter) has a secondary entrance at Via B. Cairoli 48.

A combined ticket (€5), bought at any of the three sites, gives entry to the Museo di Pittura Murale, Museo dell'Opera del Duomo and Castello dell'Imperatore.

Sights

MUSEO DI PITTURA MURALE

This small but impressive **museum** (☎ 0574 44 05 01; Piazza San Domenico; adult/child €5/3; ☽ 10am-6pm Mon & Wed-Sat, 10am-1pm Sun) houses a collection of largely Tuscan paintings. Among artists represented are Filippo Lippi, Paolo Uccello and Bernardo Daddi, with his touchingly naive polyptych of the miracle

of the Virgin's girdle (see the boxed text, p471). Enjoy too the 14th- to 17th-century frescoes and graffiti.

CATTEDRALE SANTO STEFANO

The 12th-century **cathedral** (Piazza del Duomo; ☽ 7am-noon & 3.30-7pm Mon-Sat, to 8pm Sun) has a typically Pisan-Romanesque facade. Unadorned but for a terracotta lunette by Andrea della Robbia, it's swathed in white and green Tuscan marble, a pattern you'll also come across in Siena, Pistoia and Lucca.

What's unique is its protruding exterior **Pulpito della Sacra Cintola**, jutting out over the piazza to the right of the main, western entrance. The original, much eroded panels of the pulpit, designed by Donatello and Michelozzo in the 1430s, are in the **Museo dell'Opera del Duomo** (☎ 0574 2 93 39; Piazza del Duomo 49; adult/child €5/3; ☽ 9.30am-12.30pm & 3-6.30pm Mon & Wed-Sat, 9.30am-12.30pm Sun).

CHIESA DI SANTA MARIA DELLE CARCERI

Built by Giuliano da Sangallo towards the end of the 15th century, the high, graceful interior of this **church** (Piazza Santa Maria delle

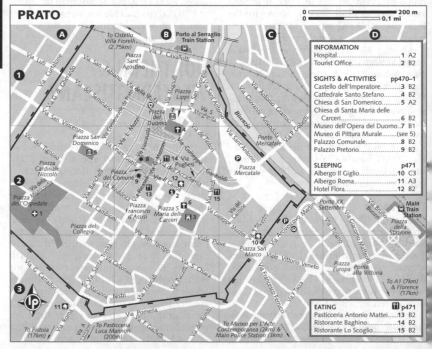

PRATO

0		200 m
0		0.1 mi

INFORMATION
Hospital..................................1 A2
Tourist Office........................2 B2

SIGHTS & ACTIVITIES   pp470-1
Castello dell'Imperatore..........3 B2
Cattedrale Santo Stefano........4 B2
Chiesa di San Domenico.........5 A2
Chiesa di Santa Maria delle
  Carceri...............................6 B2
Museo dell'Opera del Duomo..7 B1
Museo di Pittura Murale........(see 5)
Palazzo Comunale...................8 B2
Palazzo Pretorio.....................9 B2

SLEEPING   p471
Albergo Il Giglio....................10 C3
Albergo Roma.......................11 A3
Hotel Flora...........................12 B2

EATING   p471
Pasticceria Antonio Mattei....13 B2
Ristorante Baghino.................14 B2
Ristorante Lo Scoglio.............15 B2

Carceri; ☣ 7am-noon & 4-7pm) was a prototype for many a Renaissance church in Tuscany. The glazed terracotta frieze and, above it, medallions of the Evangelists are by Andrea della Robbia and his team.

CASTELLO DELL'IMPERATORE
On the same piazza, Prato's **castle** (☎ 0574 3 82 07; Piazza Santa Maria delle Carceri; admission €2; ☣ 9am-1pm) was built in the 13th century by the Holy Roman Emperor Frederick II. It's an interesting enough example of military architecture but, with its bare interior, only really worth dropping into if you're carrying a combined ticket.

Sleeping & Eating
Within easy reach of Florence, Prato is worth considering as an alternative base to the big city, especially in high season when prices rise and places can be booked solid.

Ostello Villa Fiorelli (☎ 0574 69 76 11; cspsrl@interfree.it; Parco di Galceti, Via di Galceti 64; dm €13) Prato's HI-affiliated youth hostel, served by bus No 13, is some 3km north of Piazza del Duomo.

Albergo Il Giglio (☎ 0574 3 70 49; albergoilgiglio@tin.it; Piazza San Marco 14; s/d €40/60, with bathroom €50/70) This is a friendly place with a cosy, could-be-home guest sitting room. The same family (who also own Albergo Roma) have run the place since 1969 so they've clearly got the mix right.

Albergo Roma (☎ 0574 3 17 77; fax 0574 60 43 51; Via G Carradori 1; s/d with bathroom €55/60) The 12 rooms at this one-star hotel are more modest but spruce, clean and excellent value for your euro. Ask for a room at the back as the hotel overlooks a busy road.

Hotel Flora (☎ 0574 3 35 21; www.prathotels.it; Via B Cairoli 31; s/d with breakfast €90/140; [P] [☒] [▢]) Here's an attractive three-star mid-range option in the heart of town. Bedrooms, most of them recently renovated, have attractive, polished parquet flooring. Parking is €10.

Ristorante Lo Scoglio (☎ 0574 2 27 60; Via Verdi 42; meals around €20, pizzas from €5.25; ☣ Tue-Sun) Lo Scoglio is a pleasant spot for a meal. The menu is wide-ranging, offering everything from pizza to fresh fish.

Ristorante Baghino (☎ 0574 2 79 20; Via dell'Accademia 9; meals €18-23; ☣ Mon-Sat) In much the same vein as Lo Scoglio, Ristorante Baghino offers more elegant surroundings and carries a decent wine list.

A GIRDLE FOR A VIRGIN
You don't often see a pulpit on the *outside* of a cathedral. But Prato's is rather special. It was grafted on so that the *sacra cintola* (sacred girdle), believed to be the Virgin Mary's, could be displayed five times a year (Easter, 1 May, 15 August, 8 September and 25 December). The Virgin, so goes the story, gave the girdle (or belt) to St Thomas. Generations later after the Second Crusade, a soldier brought it to Prato from Jerusalem. In medieval times huge importance was attached to such holy relics. But just how many girdles did Mary have? Another, declared the real thing in 1953 by the Orthodox Patriarch of Antioch, is stored in the Syrian city of Homs.

Among the magnificent frescoes inside the church, look for those behind the high altar by Filippo Lippi, depicting the martyrdom of St John the Baptist and St Stephen. Seek out too those by Agnolo Gaddi depicting the *Legend of the Holy Girdle*. They're in a chapel, bounded by intricate wrought iron screens, at the northwest corner of the nave.

Pick up a packet of *cantucci*, also called *biscotti di Prato*, a crunchy, rusk-like biscuit studded with almonds that you usually dip in wine. **Pasticceria Antonio Mattei** (☎ 0574 2 57 56; Via Bettino Ricasoli 20; ☣ Tue-Sat & morning Sun) makes them on the spot.

Pasticceria Luca Mannori (☎ 0574 2 16 28; Via Lazzarini 2; ☣ Wed-Mon), just outside the city walls, serves altogether more subtle cakes and pastries. On two occasions, Signor Mannori has been proclaimed world champion in international confectionery competitions – for his *torta sette veli* and *torta braccio di venere*.

Getting There & Around
CAP and Lazzi buses operate regular services to/from Florence (€2.20, 45 minutes, every 15 minutes) departing from the main Stazione Centrale train station.

By car, take the A1 Calenzano exit or the A11 Prato turnoff.

Prato is on the Florence–Bologna and Florence–Lucca train lines. Sample fares and destinations include to Florence (€1.50, 25 minutes, every 10 minutes), Bologna (€7.25, one hour, 20 daily), Lucca (€4, one hour, 20 daily) and Pistoia (€1.50, 20 minutes, half-hourly).

Several buses (€1), including Nos 3, 6 and 6A, connect the main train station with the cathedral.

PISTOIA
pop 85,900

Pistoia is a pleasant city that sits snugly at the foot of the Apennines. Only 45 minutes northwest of Florence by train, it deserves more attention than it normally gets. Although it has grown well beyond its medieval ramparts – and is now a world centre for the manufacture of trains – its historic centre is well preserved. Here in the 16th century, the city's metalworkers created the pistol, named after the city.

On Wednesday and Saturday mornings, Piazza del Duomo and surrounding streets become a sea of blue awnings and jostling shoppers as Pistoia hosts a lively market.

Orientation

From the train station, head north along Via XX Settembre, eventually turning right into Via Cavour. Via Roma, branching off the northern side of Via Cavour, takes you to the main square, Piazza del Duomo.

Information

Main Post Office (Via Roma 5)

Telecom Office (Corso Antonio Gramsci) Near Via della Madonna.

Tourist Office (☎ 0573 2 16 22; www.pistoia.turismo .toscana.it, Italian only; Piazza del Duomo 4; ⏲ 9am-1pm & 3-6pm Mon-Sat Sep-May, daily Jun-Aug) Occupies part of the Antico Palazzo dei Vescovi.

Sights

Most of Pistoia's visual wealth is concentrated on this central square. The Pisan-Romanesque facade of the **Cattedrale di San Zeno** (Piazza del Duomo; ⏲ 7am-12.30pm & 3.30-7pm) boasts a lunette of the Madonna and Child by Andrea della Robbia, who also made the terracotta tiles that line the barrel vault of the main porch. Inside, in the Cappella di San Jacopo, is the remarkable silver **Altarpiece of San Giacomo**. It was begun in the 13th century, with artisans adding to it over the ensuing two centuries until Brunelleschi contributed the final touch, the two half-figures on the left side. However, it's locked away in a gloomy **chapel**

(adult/child €2/0.50) off the north aisle. To visit you'll need to track down some church official.

The venerable building located between the cathedral and Via Roma is the **Antico Palazzo dei Vescovi** (Piazza del Duomo; admission €3.60; ⏲ 10am-1pm & 3-5pm Tue, Thu & Fri). There are guided tours (in Italian) four times a day through the wealth of artefacts, which were discovered during restoration work and dating as far back as Etruscan times. Across Via Roma is the **baptistry** (Piazza del Duomo; admission free; ⏲ 10am-6pm Jun-Aug, 7am-12.30pm & 3.30-7pm Tue-Sun Sep-May). Elegantly banded in green and white marble, it was started in 1337 to a design by Andrea Pisano.

Dominating the eastern flank of the piazza, the Gothic Palazzo Comunale houses the **Museo Civico** (Piazza del Duomo; ☎ 0573 37 12 96; adult/child €3.10/1.55; ⏲ 10am-7pm Tue-Sat, 9.30am-12.30pm Sun), with works by Tuscan artists from the 13th to 20th centuries.

The splendidly rich portico of the nearby **Ospedale del Ceppo** (Piazza Giovanni XXIII) will stop even the monument-weary in their tracks – the unique terracotta frieze by Giovanni della Robbia depicts the *Seven Works of Mercy* while the five medallions represent the *Virtues*.

Sleeping & Eating

Hotel Firenze (☎ 0573 2 31 41; www.hotel-firenze.it; Via Curtatone e Montanara 42; s/d with breakfast €60/80; Ⓟ Ⓧ Ⓠ) The rooms here are large and simple and have fridges. Although a little colourless and glum, their facilities are just fine. Parking is €5.20.

Hotel Leon Bianco (☎ 0573 2 66 75; www .hotelleonbianco.it; Via Panciatichi 2; s/d €65/95; Ⓟ Ⓧ Ⓠ) This friendly, family-owned hotel, by far the most venerable in town, has operated as an inn since the 15th century. Parking is €5.

Trattoria dell'Abbondanza (☎ 0573 36 80 37; Via dell'Abbondanza; meals €20-25; ⏲ Thu-Tue, closed Thu lunch) This little trattoria down a quiet passageway off Piazza Spirito Santo has a frequently changing menu and offers a good selection of soups and pasta.

Ristorante San Jacopo (☎ 0573 2 77 86; Via Crispi 15; meals around €20; ⏲ Tue-Sun, closed Tue lunch) Serving great Tuscan dishes, its house specialities include *baccalà alla Livornese* (salted cod; €3.50) and *pappardelle alle*

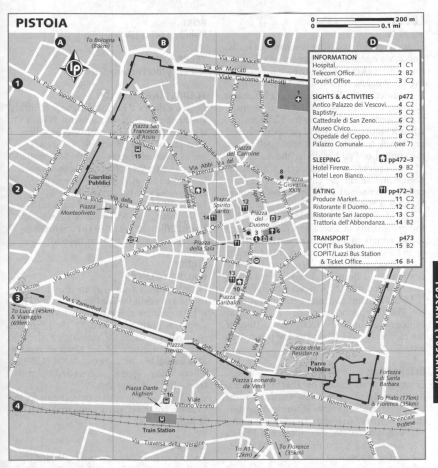

PISTOIA

INFORMATION
Hospital...1 C1
Telecom Office................................2 B2
Tourist Office..................................3 C2

SIGHTS & ACTIVITIES   p472
Antico Palazzo dei Vescovi...........4 C2
Baptistry..5 C2
Cattedrale di San Zeno.................6 C2
Museo Civico..................................7 C2
Ospedale del Ceppo......................8 C2
Palazzo Comunale.................(see 7)

SLEEPING   pp472–3
Hotel Firenze..................................9 B2
Hotel Leon Bianco.......................10 C3

EATING   pp472–3
Produce Market............................11 C2
Ristorante Il Duomo.....................12 C2
Ristorante San Jacopo.................13 C3
Trattoria dell'Abbondanza.......14 B2

TRANSPORT   p473
COPIT Bus Station.......................15 B2
COPIT/Lazzi Bus Station
  & Ticket Office............................16 B4

TUSCANY (TOSCANA)

lepre (wide flat pasta ribbons with stewed hare, red wine and tomato sauce; €3.20).

Ristorante Il Duomo (☎ 0573 3 19 48; Via Bracciolini 5; mains around €5; ☽ noon-3pm Mon-Sat) At this cheap, self-service, buffet-style place your plate can be heaped high with generous portions of pasta and salad. There's also a small selection of main dishes – if you've still a spare cranny.

There's a small **produce market** (Piazza della Sala), west of the cathedral.

Getting There & Around

Buses connect Pistoia with Florence and local towns in Tuscany. The main ticket office and departure point for COPIT and Lazzi buses is opposite the train station. However, Lazzi

buses to Florence (€2.70, 50 minutes, nine daily) depart from Piazza Treviso.

The city is on the A11 and the SS64 and SS66, which head northeast for Bologna and northwest for Parma respectively. Bus Nos 10 and 12 connect the train station with the cathedral.

The hotels we recommend can provide a pass entitling you to free street parking, 9pm to 9am, or can arrange private garage parking (around €5).

Trains link Pistoia with Florence (€2.55, 45 minutes, half hourly), Prato (€1.50, 20 minutes, every 30 minutes), Lucca (€3.10, 45 minutes, over 20 per day), Pisa (€4, 1¼ hours, five direct daily) and Viareggio (€4, one hour, hourly).

LUCCA

pop 85,500

Hidden behind imposing Renaissance walls, Lucca, an essential stopover on any Tuscan tour, also makes a charming base for exploring the Apuane Alps and the Garfagnana.

Founded by the Etruscans, Lucca became a Roman colony in 180 BC and a free *comune* (self-governing city) during the 12th century, when it enjoyed a period of prosperity based on the silk trade. In 1314 it briefly fell under the control of Pisa but under the leadership of local adventurer Castruccio Castracani degli Antelminelli, the city regained its freedom and remained an independent republic for almost 500 years.

Napoleon ended this in 1805. He created the principality of Lucca and placed one of the seemingly countless members of his family in need of an Italian fiefdom (this time his sister Elisa) in control. Twelve years later the city became a Bourbon duchy, before being incorporated into the Kingdom of Italy.

Lucca remains a strong agricultural centre. The long periods of peace it has enjoyed explain the almost perfect preservation of the city walls, which were rarely put to the test.

Orientation

From the train station on Piazza Ricasoli, just outside the city walls to the south, walk westwards to Piazza Risorgimento and through Porta San Pietro. Head north along Via Vittorio Veneto, over immense Piazza Napoleone and on to Piazza San Michele, the centre of town.

Information

EMERGENCY

Police Station (☎ 0583 5 89 01; Viale Cavour 38)

INTERNET ACCESS

Rinascimento (☎ 0583 46 98 73; Via Cesare Battisti 50-54; €2.50/hr; ☿ 11am-8pm Mon-Sat) Cheap but slightly shambolic.

Mondochiocciola (☎ 0583 44 05 10; Via del Gonfalone 12; €5.50/hr; ☿ 9.30am-1.30pm & 4-8pm Mon-Sat)

LAUNDRY

Niagara (☎ 335 6 29 20 55; Via Michele Rosi 26; ☿ 8am-10pm)

MEDICAL SERVICES

Hospital (☎ 0583 97 01; Via dell'Ospedale)

POST

Main Post Office (Via Vallisneri 2)

TELEPHONE

Telecom Office (Via Cenami 19)

TOURIST INFORMATION

Look for the local English-language monthly, *Grapevine* (€1.80), with a useful What's On section. It's stocked at most tourist offices.

Main Tourist Office (☎ 0583 44 29 44; www.in -lucca.it, Italian only; Piazzale Verdi; ☿ 9am-7pm Mar-Oct, 9am-5.30pm Nov-Feb) Definitely the best informed. Rents bicycles (see p478) and stocks an excellent city audioguide in English (1/2 persons €9/12).

Tourist Office (☎ 0583 91 99 31; Piazza Santa Maria 35; ☿ 9am-8pm Apr-Oct, 9am-1pm & 3-7pm Nov-Mar)

Tourist Office (☎ 0583 91 99 41; Piazza Napoleone; ☿ 10am-7pm Apr-Oct, 10am-1pm Nov-Mar)

Sights

BIRDS-EYE LUCCA

Huff and puff your way up the 207 steps of the **Torre delle Ore** (Via Fillungo; admission €3.50), a 13th-century clock tower whose possession was hotly contested by rival families in medieval days. Or else attack the 230 equally steep stairs of the tower of the **Palazzo Guinigi** (Via Sant'Andrea; adult/child €3.50/2.50), where a tiny copse of self-seeded holm oak trees offer welcome shade.

Whichever one you choose, the sweeping overview of the city, once you make the top, is stunning.

CATHEDRAL

Lucca's mainly Romanesque **cathedral** (Piazza San Martino; admission free; ☿ 9.30am-5.45pm Sun-Fri, 9.30am-6.45pm Sat, 1-5.45pm Sun), dedicated to San Martino, dates from the 11th century. The exquisite facade was constructed in the prevailing Lucca-Pisan style. Each of the columns in its upper part is carved by a local artisan and every one is different. The reliefs over the left doorway of the portico are believed to be by Nicola Pisano.

The interior was rebuilt in the 14th and 15th centuries with a Gothic flourish. Matteo Civitali designed the pulpit and, in the north aisle, the 15th-century *tempietto* (small temple) that contains the **Volto Santo**. Legend has it that this simply fashioned image of Christ on a wooden crucifix, dated to the 11th century, was carved by Nicodemus, who witnessed the crucifixion.

TUSCANY (TOSCANA)

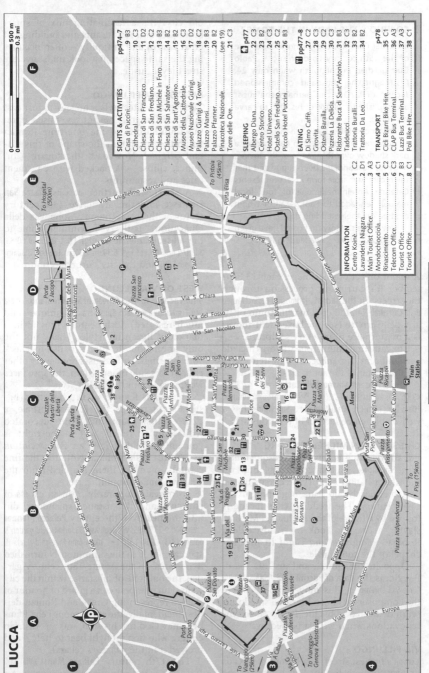

LUCCA

0 500 m
0 0.3 mi

TUSCANY (TOSCANA)

TUSCANY (TOSCANA)

SO WHO'S THE LADY IN THE TOMB?

Ilaria del Carretto, the young second wife of the 15th-century Lord of Lucca, Paolo Guinigi, died in childbirth when only 24. Distraught, her husband commissioned Jacopo della Quercia, perhaps the most accomplished sculptor of his day, to carve her tomb.

So, for centuries, has gone the story...

However, recent research has thrown a dark shadow over this image of the loving, grieving husband. It's been suggested that the reclining marble form in fact represents Caterina Antelminelli, one of four local maidens engaged to Paolo – all of whom died before their wedding day.

Now *there's* a story that could have given the tabloids of the day a feeding frenzy.

A major object of pilgrimage, each 13 September it's carried in procession through the streets. In the **sacristy** (admission €2, incl Museo della Cattedrale €4), the cool marble tomb of Ilaria del Carretto (see the boxed text above) is a masterpiece of funerary sculpture.

The cathedral's numerous artworks include a magnificent *Last Supper* by Tintoretto, over the third altar of the south aisle.

The adjacent **Museo della Cattedrale** (☎ 0583 49 05 30; adult/child €3.50/2; ☉ 10am-6pm summer, 10am-2pm Mon-Fri, 10am-5pm Sat & Sun winter) has a well-displayed collection of religious art.

CHIESA DI SAN MICHELE IN FORO

Equally dazzling is this Romanesque **church** (Piazza San Michele; ☉ 8am-noon & 3-6pm), built on the site of its 8th-century precursor over a period of nearly 300 years, beginning in the 11th century. The wedding-cake facade is topped by a figure of the Archangel Michael slaying a dragon. Look for Andrea della Robbia's *Madonna and Child* in the first chapel of the south aisle.

Opposite the church and just off Via di Poggio, is the **Casa di Puccini** (☎ 0583 58 40 28; Corte San Lorenzo 9). This modest house where the composer was born houses a small museum dedicated to his life. It was closed for renovations when we last passed by.

VIA FILLUNGO

Lucca's busiest street, Via Fillungo, threads its way through the medieval heart of the old city. It's a fascinating mix of smart boutiques and restaurants and buildings of great charm and antiquity – often occupying the same space; just look up, above the street level bustle.

EAST OF VIA FILLUNGO

The **Piazza Anfiteatro** is a huge oval just east of Via Fillungo. The houses, raised upon the foundations of the one-time Roman amphitheatre, retain the shape of this distant original. Nowadays, the square – or, rather, ellipse – is packed with pavement cafés and restaurants.

A short walk further east is **Piazza San Francesco** and the attractive 13th-century **church** of the same name. Along Via della Quarquonia is the Villa Guinigi, home to the **Museo Nazionale Guinigi** (☎ 0583 49 60 33; adult/child €4/free; ☉ 8.30am-7.30pm Tue-Sat, 8.30am-1.30pm Sun) and the city's art collection.

WEST OF VIA FILLUNGO

The facade of the **Chiesa di San Frediano** (Piazza San Frediano; ☉ 7am-5pm) has a unique (and much-restored) 13th-century mosaic in a markedly Byzantine style. That's not the only anomalous feature – pause to check your bearings. Unlike just about every other church this side of Jerusalem, the apse faces *west*, away from the Holy City.

The main feature of the beautiful basilica's interior is the **Fontana Lustrale**, a 12th-century baptismal font decorated with sculpted reliefs, just to the right as you enter. Behind it is an *Annunciation* by Andrea della Robbia. Note too the fine capitals, many of them recycled from the nearby Roman amphitheatre.

To retreat temporarily from an excess of churches and Renaissance splendour, dip into the nearby 17th-century **Palazzo Pfanner** (☎ 340 9 23 30 85; Via degli Asili 33; adult/child garden & palace €4/3, €2.50/1.50; ☉ 10am-6pm Mar–mid-Nov). A staircase leads to the sumptuously furnished living area. In the ornate 18th-century garden, the only one of substance within the city walls, you pass between a guard of honour of statues representing Greek and Roman deities (incidentally, the eponymous Felix Pfanner, may God rest his soul, was an Austrian émigré who first brought beer to Italy – and brewed it in the *palazzo's* cellars).

The 17th-century **Palazzo Mansi** (Via Galli Tassi 43), a wonderful piece of rococo excess (that elaborate, gilded bridal suite must have inspired such high jinks in its time), houses the smallish **Pinacoteca Nazionale** (☎ 0583 5 55 70; admission €4; ✆ 8.30am-7pm Tue-Sat, 8.30am-1.30pm Sun) with paintings of the same period and some lively frescoes.

CITY WALLS
Take time out from monument bashing to walk, jog or cycle all 3km of the rim of the city's walls. You'll be far from alone and you'll get some great Peeping Tom glimpses into the lives of those below.

Courses
Centro Koinè (☎ 0583 49 30 40; www.koinecenter.com; Via A Mordini 60) is a language school offering **Italian courses** for foreigners.

Festivals & Events
The city that gave birth to both Puccini and Boccherini has admirably catholic musical tastes. For more than 50 years the nearby village of Torre del Lago has been holding its annual **Puccini festival**, spanning July and August, while Lucca's annual **Summer Festival**, held in July, pulls in top performers such as Oasis, David Bowie, Jamiroquai, Rod Stewart and George Benson.

Sleeping
In this popular tourist town where accommodation options are fairly limited, it's always prudent to book ahead, except in the doldrum winter months.

Ostello San Frediano (☎ 0583 46 99 57; info@ostello lucca.it; Via della Cavalerizza 12; dm with/without bathroom €16/15, 2-/4-/6-person family room €39/78/117; ✗ ⬜) This excellent HI-affiliated hostel with its 148 beds in voluminous rooms occupies a vast former schoolhouse. It has a bar, intermittently staffed, and an indifferent restaurant.

Centro Storico (☎ 0583 49 07 48; www.affittacame recentrostorico.com; Corte Portici 16; d with/without bathroom €90/80) Here's a B&B with aspirations. Friendliness itself, it's a great option smack in the heart of town. There's no curfew (you get your own front-door key), all rooms are equipped with a small fridge and safe and breakfast is included in the price. In slack periods, they may discount for singles.

Albergo Diana (☎ 0583 49 22 02; www.albergo diana.com; Via del Molinetto 11; s/d €36/47, d with bathroom €67; Ⓟ ⬜) This family-run two-star

hotel has nine slightly chintzy but satisfying rooms. If you fancy a little more comfort, consider their **annexe** (s/d €75/95; ✗), once the family home and recently converted. Here all bedrooms have a safe and the two ground floor ones are equipped for the handicapped. Parking is €4.

Piccolo Hotel Puccini (☎ 0583 5 54 21; www.hotel puccini.com; Via di Poggio 9; s/d with bathroom €55/80) Smart, friendly, centrally located and within spitting distance of Piazza San Michele, Hotel Puccini, while not spectacular, has a lot going for it.

Hotel Universo (☎ 0583 49 36 78; Piazza del Giglio 1; www.universolucca.com; s/d/tr €95/140/180) Built in 1857 and facing Lucca's equally venerable Teatro del Giglio, the Universo sits on an attractive square and offers old-fashioned charm with modern service.

Eating
Ristorante Buca di Sant'Antonio (☎ 0583 5 58 81; Via della Cervia 3; meals from €35; ✆ Tue-Sun, closed Sun dinner) This stylish restaurant is a favourite with discerning locals so do book ahead. While expensive, it's well worth splashing out for. The menu includes such treats as veal and guinea-fowl.

Trattoria Buralli (☎ 0583 95 06 11; Piazza Sant'Agostino 9; ✆ Thu-Tue) This intimate local favourite makes few concessions to outsiders. You can play easy and go for the à la carte menu with English translation, better, however, to throw a wild card and pluck one of their eight different menus, mostly €16 to €18. Friday night is veggie night, when they offer a four-course meat-free menu for €15.

Trattoria da Leo (☎ 0583 49 22 36; Via Tegrimi 1; mains €8-9.50; ✆ Mon-Sat) A popular, noisy trattoria, Da Leo is always a good bet. In summer the shaded outside seating is a bonus and an excellent little corner for people watching.

Di Simo Caffè (☎ 0583 49 62 34; Via Fillungo 58) This grand bar and *gelateria* was once patronised by Puccini and his coterie (the maestro would tickle the ivories of the piano at the entrance to the dining area). In season it spoons out some mean ice creams. Year-round, go for their leafy salads and mains (both €7.80). And hey, you'll never come across a more subtly camouflaged toilet door, indistinguishable from the wooden panelling that surrounds it. Take your leave early...

Osteria Baralla (☎ 0583 44 02 40; Via Anfiteatro 5-9; meals €25-30; 🕑 Mon-Sat) With its pleasing pink brick vaulting, Baralla is rich in Tuscan specialities and carries a good range of wines by the glass. Service is swift and needs to be; the place is a firm Lucchese favourite.

Girovita (☎ 0583 46 94 12; Piazza Antelminelli 2; salads & pastas €6.50; 🕑 Tue-Sun) A pleasant, predominantly veggie place from whose piazza seating you get a picture-postcard view of the cathedral's facade.

For pizza by the slice, join lots of others for a quick fillup at **Pizzeria La Delicia** (☎ 0583 44 05 22; Via Fillungo 5).

You shouldn't leave town without sampling a slice of *buccellato*, a cross between a biscuit and a bun, typical of Lucca. You won't find it fresher than at **Taddeucci** (Piazza San Michele 34; 🕑 Fri-Wed), a fine *pasticceria* where it's made on the premises.

Getting There & Away
CLAP buses (☎ 0583 58 78 97) serve the region, including destinations in the Garfagnana such as Castelnuovo (€3.30, 1½ hours, 11 daily).

Lazzi (☎ 0583 58 48 76) runs hourly buses to Florence (€4.70, 1½ hours) and Pisa (€2.20, 45 minutes). It has four daily services to La Spezia (€5.20, three hours) and six to Marina di Carrara (€3.20, two hours) via Marina di Massa (€3.20, 1¾ hours). Both companies operate from Piazzale Verdi.

The A11 runs westwards to Pisa and Viareggio and eastwards to Florence. The SS12, then the SS445 from Forno, links the city with the Garfagnana.

Lucca is on the Florence–Pisa–Viareggio train line and there are also services into the Garfagnana. There are frequent trains to/from Pisa (€2, 25 minutes) and Florence (€4.45, 1¼ to 1½ hours) via Pistoia (€3.10, 45 minutes) and Prato (€4, one hour).

Getting Around
Most cars are banned within the city walls and you can expect a few hard stares if you attempt to drive in. This said, many hotels will give you a permit entitling you to park in spaces for residents (indicated by yellow lines). Ask at the tourist office for *Easy Parking*, a map showing both intra- and extramural parking areas.

Small CLAP electric buses connect the train station, Piazza del Giglio (near Piazza

Napoleone) and Piazzale Verdi, but it is just as easy, and much more pleasurable, to walk.

Lucca is a very bike-friendly town. You can hire cycles from **Poli** (☎ 0583 49 37 87; Piazza Santa Maria 42), nearby **Cicli Bizzarri** ☎ 0583 49 60 31; Piazza Santa Maria 32) and the main tourist office. Rates are about €2.25 per hour, €10.50 per day.

For a taxi, call ☎ 0583 49 49 89.

AROUND LUCCA
The **Parco de Pinocchio** (☎ 0572 42 93 42; adult/child €8.50/6.50; 🕑 8.30am-dusk), a tribute to Italy's naughtiest and best-selling fictional character, is in a pinewood just outside the village of **Collodi**, 15km east of Lucca. With a series of mosaics recounting the main episodes in the puppet's life, statues and tableaux, it's as much a treat for grownups as it is for the kids.

THE GARFAGNANA
The heart of the Garfagnana is in the valley formed by the River Serchio and its tributaries. It's an excellent area for walking, horse riding and a host of other outdoor pursuits and the region is well geared for tourism. The **Consorzio Garfagnana Turistica** (☎ 0583 64 44 73; Comunità Montana, Via Vittorio Emanuele 9; 🕑 9am-1pm & 2.30-7pm Mon-Sat, hrs can vary) in Castelnuovo di Garfagnana can reserve accommodation and sells maps.

Walkers should pick up a copy of *Garfagnana Trekking*, which details a 10-day walk. Another booklet, *Garfagnana a Cavallo*, details guided horse treks.

Apuane Alps
This mountain range rears up between the coastal Versilia Riviera and, inland, the vast valley of the Garfagnana. Altitudes are relatively low, compared to the real Alps further north, but the Apuane Alps offer great walking possibilities, often with spectacular views of the coastline and Ligurian Sea. Lonely Planet's *Walking in Italy* describes a couple of fun multiday routes. You'll find a good network of marked walking trails and *rifugi* (mountain huts). To guide your steps, pick up *Alpi Apuane Settentrionali*, published by the Massa and Carrara tourist offices with trails and *rifugi* marked up, or *Alpi Apuane*, from Edizione Multigraphic of Florence. Both are at 1:25,000.

MASSA & CARRARA

The province of Massa and Carrara stretches towards Tuscany's northwestern limit. Massa, its administrative centre, has little to entice you. Both towns' beachfront extensions, Marina di Massa and Marina di Carrara, are popular with holidaying Italians.

Just look at the snow-capped mountains dominating Carrara (even in high summer), at the foothills of the Apuane Alps – but it's all illusion and really marble, field upon field of it, in vast quarries that eat into the hills. The texture and purity of Carrara's white marble is unrivalled. Michelangelo selected blocks from here for many of his masterpieces. More recently Henry Moore would pick his way through the jumble of rocks and cutoffs in search of the perfect piece.

There's a **tourist office** (☎ 0585 63 25 19; Piazza Menconi 6; ☼ 9am-12.30pm & 4-6pm Mon-Sat year-round, 9am-noon Sun Jul-Aug) in Marina di Carrara.

Ostello Apuano (☎ 0585 78 00 34; ostelloapuano@hotmail.com; Viale delle Pinete 237, Marina di Massa; dm €8.25; ☼ mid-Mar–Sep) is an attractive HI-affiliated youth hostel right on the seafront at Partaccia, just north of Marina di Massa. From Carrara train station catch bus No 53, marked Via Avenza Mare.

Both Massa and Carrara are accessible from the A12 and the SS1 Via Aurelia; signs direct you to the quarries and other attractions.

PISA
pop 92,000

Once, if briefly, a maritime power to rival Genoa and Venice, Pisa now draws its fame from an architectural project gone terribly wrong: its Leaning Tower (Torre Pendente). But the world-famous tower is only one of a trio of Romanesque splendours on the green carpet of the Campo dei Miracoli, a serious rival to Venice's Piazza San Marco for the title of Italy's most memorable square.

Pisa has a centuries-old tradition as a university town and today too swarms with students.

History

Possibly of Greek origin, Pisa became an important naval base under Rome and

---

CARRARA'S MARBLE

For centuries, marble (derived from the Greek *marmaros*, meaning shining stone) has been hewn, shaped and fashioned as a luxury material for sculpture and prestige construction. Carrara has long been the world's largest extractor and shaper of marble.

It's amazing that there's any mountain left in the hinterland behind the town. The Romans, harnessing team of both slaves and free men, first hacked into the hillside (look for the quarrymen's initials, chiselled into the rock to indicate stakes and claims). Their tools and extraction techniques remained scarcely unchanged until the 19th century, when gunpowder blasted away even more of the mountainside.

Wasteful and destructive, gunpowder was eventually replaced by the helicoidal thread, a thick hawser, guided by pulleys, that ground its way through the rock like a cheese wire paring off Parmesan. Nowadays towering cranes operate diamond-cutting chains that slice off huge cubes, which litter the mountain like some giant kid's building blocks.

The workshops of Carrara still turn out their share of *putti* (winsome cherubs), Madonnas, tombstones and the like, but most marble nowadays is shipped abroad in giant blocks, to be worked elsewhere. Then again, several international sculptors we might name have had a chip knocked off the old block and a corner or two rounded in order to fashion their next oeuvre into rough shape and take the drudgery out of the task.

The **Museo del Marmo** (☎ 0585 84 5746; Viale XX Settembre; admission €3.10; ☼ 10am-6pm Mon-Sat May-Jun & Sep, 10am-8pm Mon-Sat Jul-Aug, 8.30am-1.30pm Oct-Apr) is opposite the stadium, halfway between Carrara and Marina di Carrara. With descriptive panels in English, it has more marble in more varieties than you'll ever have seen before and describes extraction from chisel-and-hammer days to the 21st century's high-powered industrial quarrying.

Head 5km north of town to visit the **Cava di Fontiscritti**, a working quarry, where the guy who runs the souvenir shop has a small private **marble museum** (☎ 0585 7 09 81; admission free; ☼ 9am-7pm Easter-Nov).

remained a significant port for many centuries. The city's so-called Golden Days began late in the 9th century when it became an independent maritime republic and a rival of Genoa and Venice. The good times rolled on into the 12th and 13th centuries, by which time Pisa controlled Corsica, Sardinia and most of the mainland coast as far south as Civitavecchia. Most of the city's finest buildings date from this period, when the distinctive Pisan-Romanesque architectural style flourished.

Pisa's support for the Ghibellines during the tussles between the Holy Roman Emperor and the pope brought the city into conflict with its mostly Guelph Tuscan neighbours, including Siena, Lucca and Flor-

ence. The real blow came when Genoa's fleet inflicted a devastating defeat on Pisa at the Battle of Meloria in 1284. After the city fell to Florence in 1406, the Medici encouraged great artistic, literary and scientific endeavours and re-established Pisa's university. The city's most famous son, Galileo Galilei, later taught at the university.

Orientation

Stazione Pisa Centrale, the main train station, is at the southern edge of town. The main intercity bus station is on nearby Piazza San Antonio. The medieval centre is about 800m north, across the River Arno. Campo dei Miracoli (also known as Piazza del Duomo) is about another 650m north.

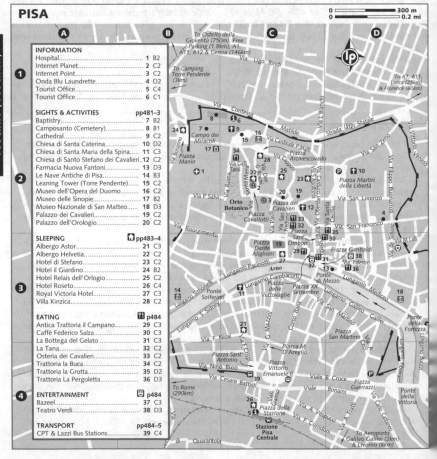

PISA

```
0          300 m
0          0.2 mi
```

INFORMATION
Hospital..1 B2
Internet Planet...................................2 C2
Internet Point....................................3 C2
Onda Blu Laundrette..........................4 D2
Tourist Office.....................................5 C4
Tourist Office.....................................6 C1

SIGHTS & ACTIVITIES   pp481–3
Baptistry...7 B2
Camposanto (Cemetery)....................8 B1
Cathedral...9 C2
Chiesa di Santa Caterina.................10 D2
Chiesa di Santa Maria della Spina...11 C3
Chiesa di Santo Stefano dei Cavalieri..12 C2
Farmacia Nuova Fantoni..................13 D3
Le Nave Antiche di Pisa...................14 B3
Leaning Tower (Torre Pendente).....15 C2
Museo dell'Opera del Duomo..........16 C2
Museo delle Sinopie.........................17 B2
Museo Nazionale di San Matteo......18 D3
Palazzo dei Cavalieri........................19 C2
Palazzo dell'Orologio.......................20 C2

SLEEPING   pp483–4
Albergo Astor....................................21 C3
Albergo Helvetia..............................22 C3
Hotel di Stefano...............................23 C2
Hotel il Giardino...............................24 B2
Hotel Relais dell'Orlogio..................25 C2
Hotel Roseto.....................................26 C4
Royal Victoria Hotel.........................27 C3
Villa Kinzica......................................28 C2

EATING   p484
Antica Trattoria il Campano............29 C3
Caffè Federico Salza.........................30 C3
La Bottega del Gelato.......................31 C3
La Tana..32 C2
Osteria dei Cavalieri.........................33 C2
Trattoria la Buca..............................34 B2
Trattoria la Grotta............................35 D2
Trattoria La Pergoletta.....................36 D3

ENTERTAINMENT   p484
Bazeel...37 C3
Teatro Verdi......................................38 D3

TRANSPORT   pp484–5
CPT & Lazzi Bus Stations..................39 C4

Information

EMERGENCY
Police Station (☎ 050 58 35 11; Via Mario Lalli)

INTERNET ACCESS
Internet Point (☎ 050 50 37 00; Via dei Mille 3/5; €3.10/hr; ⏰ 10.30am-midnight Mon-Fri, 1pm-midnight Sat & Sun)
Internet Planet (☎ 050 83 07 02; Piazza Cavallotti 3-4; €3.10/hr; ⏰ 10am-midnight Mon-Sat, 2pm-midnight Sun)

LAUNDRY
Onda Blu (☎ 800 86 13 46; Via San Francesco 8a; ⏰ 8am-10pm)

MEDICAL SERVICES
Hospital (☎ 050 99 21 11; Via Roma 67)
Farmacia Nuova Fantoni (Lungarno Mediceo 51; ⏰ 24 hrs) All-night pharmacy.

POST
Main Post Office (Piazza Vittorio Emanuele II)

TOURIST INFORMATION
Tourist Office (☎ 050 56 04 64; www.pisa.turismo .toscana.it; Piazza del Duomo; ⏰ 9am-6pm Mon-Sat, 10.30am-4.30pm Sun) Just north of the Leaning Tower.
Train Station Office (☎ 050 4 22 91; Piazza della Stazione; ⏰ 9am-7pm Mon-Sat, 9.30am-3.30pm Sun)
Airport Office (☎ 050 50 37 00)

Campo dei Miracoli

The Campo dei Miracoli ranks as one of the world's most beautiful squares. Set among its sprawling lawns is one of Europe's most extraordinary concentrations of Romanesque splendour – the cathedral, the baptistry and the Leaning Tower, all financed with the loot and booty brought back to the city after Pisa whupped the Arabs in Sicily. The piazza teems with people – students studying or at play, local workers eating lunch and tourists, many (a fun one, this) getting snapped as they extend their arms Tai-Chi-like so the shot suggests they're heaving the tower over.

There's a staggered pricing system. One option (€6) admits you to two monuments or museums. Another (€8.50) – which we recommend as it can eliminate a lot of queuing – gives entry to four (the two museums, baptistry and Campo Santo cemetery).

The cathedral itself – an absolute must – costs an extra €2 and the Leaning Tower

WHY THE LEANING TOWER LEANS

Welcome to one of the world's great cock-ups. The cathedral's *campanile* (bell tower) was in trouble from the start. Its architect, Bonanno Pisano, managed to complete only three tiers before the tower started to lean on the south side. Shifting soil is the most favoured explanation and the 'leaning tower' continued to lean by an average of 1mm every year. Over the years several solutions to stop the lean were tried without success and occasionally with some opposition: the controversial Italian art historian, Vittorio Sgarbi, once said it would be 'better to see it fall and remember it leaning than see it straightened by mistake'.

In 1998 cables were wrapped around the 3rd storey and attached to A-frames. This held the tower in place while workers removed small portions of soil on the northern side to create a counter-subsidence. It did the trick: the famous lean has lost 40cm and experts reckon that the tower is safe for at least the next 300 years. The lean is now 4.1m off the perpendicular (at one stage it was 5m) but more importantly the slippage that caused the tower to lean in the first place has finally been arrested.

a hefty €15. Bring the kids while they're small; under 10s go free everywhere except the tower, from which they're excluded for safety reasons.

Opening times are of Machiavellian complexity. In some cases there are summer, autumn and winter times, plus weekday and weekend variants. We quote below summer and winter 'extremes'. For the pattern of the day, call ☎ 050 56 05 47, a number covering all monuments and museums.

Cathedral

The majesty of Pisa's **cathedral** (admission €2; ⏰ 10am-7.40pm Mon-Sat, 1-7.40pm Sun summer, 10am-12.45pm & 3-4.45pm Mon-Sat, 3-4.45pm Sun winter) made it a model for Romanesque churches throughout Tuscany and even on Sardinia. Begun in 1064 it's clad inside and out with alternating bands of dark green and cream marble that were to become characteristic of the Pisan-Romanesque style.

The main facade has four exquisite tiers of columns diminishing skywards. The vast interior has 68 columns in classical style. The bronze doors of the transept, facing the Leaning Tower, are by Bonanno Pisano. The 16th-century bronze doors of the main entrance were designed by the school of Giambologna to replace the wooden originals, destroyed in a fire in 1596, after which the interior was also mostly redecorated. Enjoy the depth of detail that Giovanni Pisano imparted to the vibrant early-14th-century marble pulpit in the north aisle, on which he spent 10 years of his life. Above the altar, a striking mosaic of *Christ in Majesty*, completed by Cimabue in 1302, stares down upon visitors.

Leaning Tower (Torre Pendente)

Only a limited number of visitors are allowed to go up the **tower** (www.opapisa.it; admission €15; ☽ 8am-8pm summer, 9am-7pm winter) each day. To be sure you're one of them, reserve well in advance, either via the website or in person.

See the boxed text, p481.

Baptistry (Battistero)

The unusual round **baptistry** (admission €5; ☽ 8am-7.40pm summer, 9am-4.40pm winter) was started in 1153 by Diotisalvi, remodelled and continued by Nicola and Giovanni Pisano more than a century later and finally completed in the 14th century – which explains the mix of architectural styles. The lower level of arcades is in the Pisan-Romanesque style and the pinnacled upper section and dome are Gothic. Inside, Nicola Pisano carved the beautiful pulpit (compare it with the one that his son, Giovanni, made for the cathedral) while in 1246 Guido da Como chiselled the octagonal white marble font, big as a moderate swimming pool and used in its time for baptism by total immersion. The acoustics beneath the dome are remarkable; risk a low whisper and hear it resound. Climb the stairs to the gallery for a great overview.

Cemetery (Camposanto)

They say that behind the white wall of this exquisite **cemetery** (admission €5; ☽ 8am-7.40pm summer, 9am-4.40pm winter) is soil shipped from Calvary during the crusades – and reputed to reduce cadavers to skeletons within days. During WWII allied artillery badly damaged or destroyed many of the cloisters' precious frescoes. Among those saved and displayed in the Fresco Room were the *Triumph of Death* and *Last Judgement*, attributed to an anonymous 14th-century painter known as 'The Master of the Triumph of Death'. Many of the more interesting sarcophagi are of Greco-Roman origin, recycled for prominent Pisans in the Middle Ages.

Museo delle Sinopie

This **museum** (admission €5; ☽ 8am-7.40pm summer, 9am-4.40pm winter) houses vast reddish-brown sketches drawn onto walls as the base for frescoes – and revealed in the cemetery after the WWII artillery raids. Now restored to the degree possible, these *sinopie* give a fascinating insight into the process of creating a fresco.

Museo dell'Opera del Duomo

This **museum** (☽ 8am-7.20pm summer, 9am-4.20pm winter) has a profusion of artworks from the cathedral, tower and baptistry, including a magnificent ivory carving of the *Madonna and Child* by Giovanni Pisano (room 11).

The City

From Campo dei Miracoli, head south along Via Santa Maria and turn left at Piazza Cavallotti for the splendid **Piazza dei Cavalieri**, remodelled by Vasari in the 16th century. The **Palazzo dell'Orologio**, on the northern side of the piazza, occupies the site of a tower where, in 1288, Count Ugolino della Gherardesca, along with his sons and grandsons, were starved to death on suspicion of having helped the Genovese enemy at the Battle of Meloria, an incident recorded in Dante's *Inferno*. The **Palazzo dei Cavalieri**, on the northeastern side of the piazza, was redesigned by Vasari and features remarkable graffiti decoration. The piazza and *palazzo* are named for the Knights of Santo Stefano, a religious and military order founded by Cosimo de' Medici. Their church, **Chiesa di Santo Stefano dei Cavalieri**, was also designed by Vasari. The **Chiesa di Santa Caterina** (Piazza Martiri della Libertà; admission free; ☽ 10.30am-6.30pm Mon-Sat, 1-6.30pm Sun), north of Via San Lorenzo, is a fine example of Pisan-Gothic architecture and contains works by Nino Pisano.

Wander south to the area around **Borgo Stretto**, the city's medieval heart. East along the waterfront boulevard, the Lungarno

Mediceo, is the **Museo Nazionale di San Matteo** (☎ 050 54 18 65; Lungarno Medicei; admission €4; ☺ 8.30am-7.30pm Tue-Sat, 8.30am-1.30pm Sun), a fine gallery featuring, in particular, works by Giovanni and Nicola Pisano, Masaccio and Donatello.

Cross the Ponte di Mezzo and head west to reach the **Chiesa di Santa Maria della Spina** (Lungarno Gambacorti; admission €1.10; ☺ 11am-1.30pm & 2.30-6pm Tue-Fri, 11am-1.30pm & 2.30-8pm Sat & Sun summer, 10am-2pm Tue-Sun winter). Built in the early 14th century to house a thorn from Christ's crown, this tiny church beside the Arno is refreshingly intimate after the megaweights of the Campo dei Miracoli.

Return to the north bank via Ponte Solferino and walk westwards to the Arsenale, Pisa's one-time shipyards. Nowadays, they house **Le Nave Antiche di Pisa** (The Ancient Ships of Pisa; ☎ 050 2 14 41; Lungarno Simonelli; adult/child €3/free; ☺ 10am-1pm & 2-6pm Tue-Sun), a display of everyday and more exotic objects (there's even a lion's tooth) recovered from a veritable graveyard of shipwrecked vessels that foundered between the 3rd century BC and the 4th century AD and were discovered in 1998.

Festivals & Events

The **Palio delle Quattro Antiche Repubbliche Marinare** (Regatta of the Four Ancient Maritime Republics) sees a procession of boats and a dramatic race between the four historical maritime rivals – Pisa, Venice, Amalfi and Genoa. The event rotates between the four towns: Genoa in 2004, Amalfi in 2005, Pisa again in 2006 and Venice in 2007. Although usually held in June, it has on occasion been delayed as late as September.

Other cultural and historical events include the **Gioco del Ponte**, a festival of traditional costume held on the last Sunday in June. On 17 June, the River Arno comes to life with the **Regata Storica di San Ranieri**, a rowing competition commemorating the city's patron saint.

Sleeping

Pisa has a reasonable number of budget hotels but many double as residences for students during the school year so it can be difficult to find a cheap room.

Camping Torre Pendente (☎ 050 56 17 04; www.campingtoscana.it/torrependente; Via delle Cascine 86; person/tent/car €7.25/6.20/4.50; ☺ Apr–mid-Oct; ☒)

This large camp site, west of the cathedral, isn't Tuscany's most attractive but it does boast a supermarket, restaurant and small pool.

Ostello della Gioventù (☎ /fax 050 89 06 22; Via Pietrasantina 15; dm €21) This is a rambling non-HI hostel beside a murky stream. Take bus No 3 from the train station or town centre.

Albergo Helvetia (☎ 050 55 30 84; Via Don Gaetano Boschi 31; s/d €35/45, d with bathroom €62) South of and handy for the cathedral, this is a welcoming, unkempt family place with a tousled garden. It offers pleasant rooms on a quiet street.

Hotel Roseto (☎ 050 4 25 96; www.hotelroseto.it; Via Mascagni 24; s/d/tr €53/67/87; ☒) This hotel is the handiest of all for the train station and a late-night arrival. With cosy if unspectacular rooms and a small garden, it's great value for your euro.

Hotel di Stefano (☎ 050 55 35 59; www.hoteldistefano.pisa.it; Via Sant'Apollonia 35; s/d €50/70, s/d/tr with bathroom €80/95/120; P ☒ 🖳) This hotel has good modern rooms and a small private bar. You can glimpse the Leaning Tower from the hotel's roof terrace. Parking is €15.

Hotel il Giardino (☎ 050 56 21 01; www.pisaonline.it/giardino; Piazza Manin 1; s/d with bathroom & breakfast €70/110; P ☒) You'll find sparkling, well-maintained rooms and friendly staff. Enjoy breakfast on their tranquil upstairs terrace with the city walls and dome of the Baptistry in full view.

Villa Kinzica (☎ 050 56 04 19; fax 050 55 12 04; Piazza Arcivescovado 2; s/d/tr with breakfast €77/103/123; ☒) One of Pisa's more attractive options, Villa Kinzica has 34 attractive rooms, bags of character – and views of the Leaning Tower as a bonus.

Albergo Astor (☎ 050 4 45 51; www.hotel-astor.com; Via Manzoni 22; d with/without bathroom €65/53) An easy walk from the train station, this two-star family hotel has 'small, comfortable modern rooms and a particularly helpful receptionist.

Royal Victoria Hotel (☎ 050 94 01 11; www.royalvictoria.it; Lungarno Pacinotti 12; s/d with breakfast €62/72; with bathroom & breakfast €95/115; P ☒ 🖳) For old-world luxury accompanied by attentive service, this doyen of Pisan hotels represents excellent value for money. Rooms overlooking the river come no more expensive. Ecologically friendly, it rents bicycles to guests for €5 per day and whizzy little Smart cars for €40. Parking is €16.

Hotel Relais dell'Orlogio (☎ 050 83 03 61; www .hotelrelaisorologio.com; Via della Faggiola 12-14; s €225; d with breakfast from €286; P X X) Pisa's newest and only five-star hotel is tucked away in a quiet street. Each of the 21 rooms in this tastefully restored 14th-century noble tower house is decorated differently, flowers cascade in public areas and there's a tranquil rear patio. Parking is €20.

Eating

Being a university town, Pisa has a good range of eating places, especially around Borgo Stretto and the university.

La Tana (☎ 050 58 05 40; Via San Frediano 6; meals €10-14; ☯ Sat-Thu) With friendly service and affordable prices, it's not surprising that La Tana is so popular, especially with students and staff from the nearby university. The food, mainly pizza and pasta, is served up on rustic wooden tables and you can snuggle down in the booths. If you're in a rush to get back to some serious monument bashing, go for their *pasta veloce* (speedy pasta; €6.70).

Trattoria La Buca (☎ 050 56 06 60; Via Galli Tassi 6; mains €6.25-9.30, pizzas €4.65-6.20; ☯ Sat-Thu) This friendly, popular trattoria comes with strong reader endorsement. Convenient for the Campo di Miracoli, its rear garden lets you to switch off from a temporary excess of the Romanesque.

Osteria dei Cavalieri (☎ 050 58 08 58; Via San Frediano 16; ☯ Mon-Fri & dinner Sat) Try their high-speed, one-dish only – but what a dish – lunch-time special (€11). Highly regarded by locals in the know, it also offers a selection of original menus (€25 to €30), including dishes such as *carpaccio pulpo* (octopus carpaccio).

Antica Trattoria il Campano (☎ 050 58 05 85; Via Cavalca 19; mains €9-13; ☯ Thu-Tue) Campano has an adventurous Tuscan menu. For starters (though it's almost a complete meal in itself) go for their *Tagliere del Re* (€12, minimum two people): 'It's a surprise', says the menu but we'll let you into the secret – you get a wonderfully rich platter of 12 kinds of Tuscan antipasti. You can dine downstairs beneath vaulted arches or upstairs under the bare rafters.

Trattoria La Pergoletta (☎ 050 54 24 58; Via delle Belle Torri 40; meals around €25; ☯ Tue-Sun) This is a wonderful sprawling place, tucked away out of sight just north of the river.

Trattoria La Grotta (☎ 050 57 81 05; Via San Francesco 103; meals around €25; ☯ Mon-Sat) As the name suggests, La Grotta (The Cave) is a cavernous place that serves up good portions of Tuscan fare. One highlight is their creative gastronomic menu (€26), which changes monthly, reflecting what's in season.

Caffè Federico Salza (☎ 050 58 02 44; Borgo Stretto 46) A tantalising selection of cakes and chocolates at this bar, one of the city's finest.

La Bottega del Gelato (Piazza Garibaldi) For great ice cream head for this place near the river and join the constant queue, winter and summer alike.

There's an open-air morning **food market** (Piazza delle Vettovaglie), off Borgo Stretto.

Entertainment

If it's nightlife you're after, your best bet is – as the lady in the tourist office herself recommended – to head for the nearby coast.

Bazeel (☎ 050 9 71 10 52; Piazza Garibaldi; ☯ 6pm-2.30am Tue-Sun) Rings the changes with its DJs and often has live music.

Teatro Verdi (☎ 050 94 11 11; Via Palestro 40) Regularly stages opera and ballet.

Getting There & Away

AIR

The city's **Aeroporto Galileo Galilei** (☎ 050 50 07 07; www.pisa-airport.com), about 2km south of the city centre, is Tuscany's main international airport and handles flights to major cities in Europe.

Daily destinations include London Gatwick (British Airways), London Stansted (Ryanair), Birmingham (My TravelLite), East Midlands (BMI Baby), Paris Charles de Gaulle (Air France) and Frankfurt (Ryanair).

BUS

Lazzi (☎ 050 4 62 88; Piazza Vittorio Emanuele II) operates hourly services to Lucca (€2.20, 45 minutes, 30 daily) and Florence (€6.20, two hours, hourly). Change at Lucca for services to Prato, Pistoia, Massa and Carrara. **CPT** (☎ 050 50 55 11; Piazza Sant'Antonio) has services to Volterra (€5.05, two hours, 10 daily) and Livorno (€2.20, 50 minutes, half-hourly).

CAR & MOTORCYCLE

Pisa is close to both the A11 and A12. The SS67 runs to Florence, while the north-south SS1, the Via Aurelia, connects the city with La Spezia and Rome.

TUSCANY (TOSCANA)

TRAIN

Pisa is connected to Florence and is also on the Rome–La Spezia train line. Destinations include Florence (€4.85, 1¼ hours, 40 daily), Rome (€15.45 to €23.05, three to four hours, 20 daily), Livorno (€1.50, 15 minutes, hourly), Pistoia (€4, 1¼ hours, five direct daily) and Lucca (€2, 25 minutes, 24 daily).

Getting Around

To get to the airport take a train from the station (€1, five minutes, 15 per day), or CPT bus No 3 (€0.80), which passes through the city centre on its way to the airport. For a taxi, call ☎ 050 54 16 00.

CPT bus Nos 3 and 4 (€0.80) runs between the station and cathedral.

Large car parks abound in Pisa. The one just northwest of the cathedral (€1 per hour Monday to Saturday, €1.50 Sunday) is handy. There's a huge free carpark about 2km north of Campo dei Miracoli with frequent shuttle buses to the centre (€1.10 return).

Trattoria La Buca (see p484) hires out bicycles.

LIVORNO

pop 161,300

Livorno, still occasionally called by its bizarre anglicised name, Leghorn, was hammered hard in WWII. Its postwar building programme may be charitably described as unimaginative. Frankly, it's a bit of a dump, a place to pass through if you're catching a boat for Sardinia or Corsica.

Orientation

From the main train station on Piazza Dante walk westwards along Viale Carducci, Via de Larderel, then Via Grande into central Piazza Grande, Livorno's main square.

Information

EMERGENCY

Police Station (☎ 0586 23 51 11; Piazza Unità d'Italia)

INTERNET ACCESS

Caffè Grande (Via Grande 59; €5/hr; ✆ 7am-11pm Wed-Mon) Has three machines.

MEDICAL SERVICES

Hospital (☎ 0586 22 31 11; Viale Alfieri 36)

POST

Main Post Office (Via Cairoli 46)

TELEPHONE

Telecom Office (Largo Duomo 14)

TOURIST INFORMATION

Tourist Kiosk (☎ 0586 20 46 11; www.livorno.turismo .toscana.it; Piazza del Municipio ✆ 10am-1pm & 3-6pm Mon-Sat)

Tourist Office (☎ 0586 89 53 20; ✆ Jun-Sep) Near the main ferry terminal, Stazione Marittima.

Sights

The **Fortezza Nuova** (admission free), in the area known because of its small canals as Piccola Venezia (Little Venice – oh please!), was built for the Medici in the late 16th century. The interior is now a park and little remains except the sturdy outer walls.

Close to the waterfront is the city's other fort, the **Fortezza Vecchia**, built 60 years earlier on the site of an 11th-century building and currently undergoing renovation. The **Mercato Centrale**, Livorno's magnificent late-19th-century neoclassical food market, 95m long, miraculously survived allied WWII bombing intact. For us, it's the finest site in town.

At the **Museo di Storia Naturale del Mediterraneo** (☎ 0586 80 22 94; Via Roma 234; admission €5.20; ✆ 9am-1pm Tue-Sat, 3-7pm Tue, Thu & Sun) you can see the 20m-long skeleton of 'Annie', a common whale and the highlight of the *sala del mare* (sea room), and specimens of Mediterranean creatures, all, alas, stuffed or skeletal.

The **Museo Civico Giovanni Fattori** (☎ 0586 80 80 01; Via San Jacopo in Acquaviva 65; admission €4.15; ✆ 10am-1pm & 4-7pm Tue-Sun), in a pretty park, features works by the 19th-century Livorno-based artistic movement led by Giovanni Fattori and often has temporary exhibitions. The city's unspectacular **cathedral** is just off Piazza Grande.

Sleeping & Eating

Albergo L'Amico Fritz (☎ 0586 40 11 49; fax 0586 42 94 66; Viale Carducci 180; s/d €40/55, with bathroom €50/72) Near the train station, this is a good value, if unspectacular choice.

Pensione Dante (☎ 0586 89 43 70; Via degli Scali d'Azeglio 28; s/d €28/40) Dante offers a friendly welcome. With clean, whitewashed rooms, it's on the 1st floor of a large peeling mansion near the port.

Hotel Gran Duca (☎ 0586 89 10 24; www.granduca.it, Italian only; Piazza Micheli; s/d with breakfast €93/119; Ⓟ Ⓧ) For considerably greater comfort and more character, check into this three-star hotel, built into the old protective walls of the port. Rooms are fully equipped and, for fitness freaks, there's the added bonus of a Jacuzzi, Turkish bath and fitness centre.

Hotel Città (☎ 0586 88 34 95; www.hotelcitta.it, Italian only; Via di Franco 32; s/d/tr with breakfast €85/105/148; **P** 🍴 🖥) Here's another tempting three-star option in the heart of town. Family owned, it looks unprepossessing from the outside but rooms, though small-ish, are just fine and come equipped with fridge and safe. Parking costs €13.

Ristorante Aragosta (☎ 0586 89 53 95; Piazza dell'Arsenale 6; meals €20-30; 🕑 Mon-Sat) For seafood, try this restaurant right on the waterfront – it's another place whose nondescript exterior masks inner pleasures.

Cantina Senese (☎ 0586 89 02 39; Borgo dei Cappuccini 95; meals from €25; 🕑 Mon-Sat) This popular, unpretentious local eatery is also fabulous for seafood. Squeeze onto one of the long wooden tables and, if you pass by on a Friday, try the Livornese speciality *cacciucco di pesce*, a rich fish soup served with garlic bread.

Load up with fresh produce for the boat at Livorno's magnificent **Mercato Centrale** (Via Buontalenti). The area around Piazza XX Settembre is the place for bars and cafés.

Getting There & Away
BOAT
Livorno is a major port. Regular departures for Sardinia and Corsica leave from Calata Carrara, beside the Stazione Marittima.

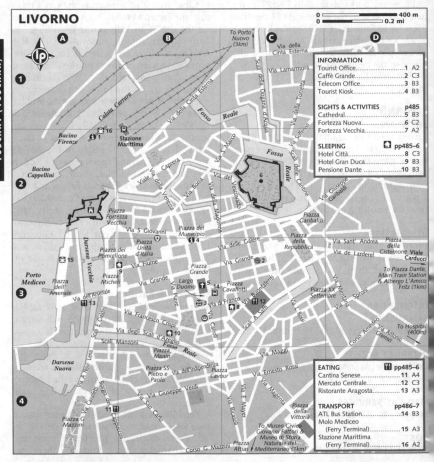

LIVORNO

TUSCANY (TOSCANA)

INFORMATION	
Tourist Office	1 A2
Caffè Grande	2 C3
Telecom Office	3 B3
Tourist Kiosk	4 B3

SIGHTS & ACTIVITIES	p485
Cathedral	5 B3
Fortezza Nuova	6 C2
Fortezza Vecchia	7 A2

SLEEPING	pp485–6
Hotel Città	8 C3
Hotel Gran Duca	9 B3
Pensione Dante	10 B3

EATING	pp485–6
Cantina Senese	11 A4
Mercato Centrale	12 C3
Ristorante Aragosta	13 A3

TRANSPORT	pp486–7
ATL Bus Station	14 B3
Molo Mediceo (Ferry Terminal)	15 A3
Stazione Marittima (Ferry Terminal)	16 A2

Some ferries depart from Porto Mediceo, a smaller terminal near Piazza dell'Arsenale, and also from Porto Nuovo, about 3km north of the city along Via Sant'Orlando.

Ferry companies operating from Livorno include those listed here:

Corsica Ferries and **Sardinia Ferries** (☎ 019 21 55 11; www.corsicaferries.com, www.sardiniaferries.com; Stazione Marittima) Corsica (deck-class €23-30, four hours, two or three services per week, daily in summer), Sardinia (deck-class to Golfo Aranci, near Olbia €23-36, nine hours, four services per week, daily in summer).

Grandi Navi Veloci (☎ 0586 40 98 04; Porto Nuovo) Sicily (Palermo; deck class €62 to €94; 17 hours, three weekly).

Lloyd Sardegna (☎ 0565 22 23 00; www.lloydsar degna.it; Porto Nuovo) Sardinia (Olbia; €26, 11 hours, daily).

Moby Lines (☎ 0565 93 61, ☎ 0586 82 68 23; www.mobylines.it; Stazione Marittima) Corsica (Bastia €15 to €28, three to four hours) and Sardinia (Olbia; deck class €25 to €52, eight to 12 hours).

Toremar (☎ 0586 89 61 13; www.toremar.it, Italian only; Porto Mediceo) Isola di Capraia (€10.40, 2½ hours, once or twice daily).

BUS
ATL buses (☎ 0586 88 42 62) depart from Largo Duomo for Cecina (€2.85, one hour, every half-hour), Piombino (€5.75, 2¼ hours, up to 10 daily) and Pisa (€2.20, 45 minutes, hourly).

CAR & MOTORCYCLE
The A12 runs past the city and the S1 connects Livorno with Rome.

TRAIN
Livorno is on the Rome–La Spezia line and is also connected to Florence and Pisa. Sample destinations and fares include Rome (€14.30 to €23.90, three to four hours, 12 daily), Florence (€5.60, 1½ hours, 16 daily) and Pisa (€1.50, 15 minutes, 11 daily).

Trains are a lot less frequent to Stazione Marittima, the station for the ports, but buses to/from the main station run quite regularly.

Getting Around
ATL bus No 1 runs from the main train station to Porto Mediceo. To reach Stazione Marittima, take bus No 7 or electric bus No PB1, PB2 or PB3. All pass through Piazza Grande and a journey costs €0.80.

ELBA ISLAND (ISOLA D'ELBA)
pop 30,400

Napoleon should have considered himself lucky to be exiled to such a pretty spot. Arriving in May 1814, he escaped within the year and went on to meet his Waterloo. Nowadays more than a million tourists a year willingly allow themselves to be marooned here. They come to swim in its glorious blue waters, lie on the beaches and eat fine food. Others are drawn by Elba's mountainous terrain, which offers challenging treks and staggering views.

If you can, avoid August when the island gets unpleasantly crowded and reservations are essential.

Just 28km long and 19km across at its widest point, Elba is well equipped for tourists, with plenty of hotels and camp sites. The main towns are Portoferraio on the northern side and Marina di Campo in the south.

Before tourism, Elba's main industry was iron-ore mining. The hordes have only arrived in recent years, so the island is not yet overdeveloped. Which is not to say the people of Elba haven't learned a few tricks of the trade – don't expect to eat well and cheaply here. Also, in the height of summer many hotels operate a compulsory half-board policy.

Orientation & Information
INTERNET RESOURCES
Elba Link (www.elbalink.it) Carries lots of useful information about the island.

TOURIST INFORMATION
Portoferraio (☎ 0565 91 46 71; www.aptelba.it; Calata Italia 43; 🕒 8am-8pm Mon-Sat, 8am-2pm Sun Easter-Oct, 8am-2pm & 3-6pm Mon-Sat Oct-Easter) Called the Agenzia per il Turismo Archipelago Toscano.
Marina di Campo (☎ 0565 97 79 69; Piazza dei Granatieri; 🕒 Jun-Sep)
Associazione Albergatori Isola d'Elba (☎ 0565 91 55 55; www.albergatorielbani.it; Calata Italia 20, Portoferraio) Reserves accommodation.

Activities
If you're here for an active time, pick up the tourist office leaflet *Elba: Isola Multisport*. In Italian, it has a useful map and lists walking and cycling trails plus opportunities for scuba diving, windsurfing and other watersports.

TUSCANY (TOSCANA)

Isola d'Elba, at 1:25,000 and published by Edizioni Multigraphic, and *Isola d'Elba*, at 1:35,000 from Vivaldi Editori, both have recommended routes for walkers and cyclists overprinted. The latter also has descriptions in English of 10 walks and six around mountain bike routes around the island. **Il Libraio** (☎ 0565 91 71 35; Calata Mazzini 9), on the waterfront beside the old town, stocks both.

Portoferraio

From the ferry terminal the old town, enclosed by a medieval wall and protected by a pair of brooding fortresses, is a bit less than a kilometre along the foreshore. Here you'll encounter the **Villa dei Mulini** (☎ 0565 91 58 46; Piazzale Napoleone; admission €3; ☼ 9am-7pm Mon & Wed-Sat, 9am-1pm Sun), Napoleon's home while he was emperor of this small isle. During his brief Elban exile, he certainly didn't want for creature comforts – contrast his Elba lifestyle with the simplicity of his camp bed and travelling trunk when he was on the campaign trail.

The **Villa Napoleonica di San Martino** (☎ 0565 91 46 88; admission €3; admission & times as Villa dei Mulini; admission €3; ☼ 9am-7pm Tue-Sat, 9am-1pm Sun), where Napoleon occasionally dropped in, is set in hills about 5km southwest of town. The villa, modest by Napoleonic standards, is dominated by the overbearing mid-19th-century gallery at its base, built to house his memorabilia.

A combined ticket for both museums costs €5.

SLEEPING & EATING

Acquaviva (☎ 0565 91 55 92; www.campingacquaviva.it; person/tent/car €11/12/2.50; ☼ mid-Apr–mid-Oct) About 4km west of town, Acquaviva, right on the beach with its own shop, bar and restaurant, is Portoferraio's nearest camp site.

Ape Elbana (☎ 0565 91 42 45; apelbana@elba2000.it; Salita de' Medici 2; r per person with breakfast €33-47; P ✷) In the old town this is the island's oldest hotel, where guests of Napoleon are reputed to have stayed. Rooms are comfortable enough though the furniture feels more second-hand than antique. Ask for one of the larger rooms overlooking Piazza della Repubblica.

Villa Ombrosa (☎ 0565 91 43 63; www.villaombrosa.it; Via De Gasperi 3; r per person with breakfast from €43; P) Villa Ombrosa is another of the very few hotels on the island that open year round.

It has a great location overlooking the sea and Spiaggia delle Ghiaie and a small private stretch of beach. The restaurant serves good Tuscan dishes.

Emanuel (☎ 0565 93 90 03; Località Enfola; set menu from €25) Out on a headland a few kilometres west of town, Emanuel has been serving up consistently good Elban dishes for years – probably the best way to go is the *menù di degustazione*, which gives you a rounded experience of the local cuisine.

Stella Marina (☎ 0565 91 59 83; Banchina Alto Fondale; meals €20-35) This is a justifiably popular fish and seafood restaurant. Stuck in a carpark beside the Toremar ferry jetty and unpromising from the exterior, its cuisine is fine and imaginative though the drinks are overpriced. There's a nonsmoking area.

Marciana Marina

Almost 20km west of Portoferraio, Marciana Marina, unlike so many brash, modern marinas, is a place with roots and character. Fronted by some pleasant pebble beaches, it makes a fine base for attacking the island's best walking trails.

Casa Lupi (☎ /fax 0565 9 91 43; Località Ontanelli; d with bathroom €70; ☼ Jun-Sep) This is one of the cheapest alternatives to Portoferraio. About half a kilometre inland on the road to Marciana, it has good views.

Ristorante Loris (☎ 0565 9 94 96; Via XX Settembre 29; pizzas €4.70-7.50, mains €4.50-13.50) This is a promising fish and seafood venue; all pastas are homemade. Try, for something special, their *ravioli all'astice*, lobster ravioli in a pepper and parmesan sauce.

Osteria del Piano (☎ 0565 90 72 92; Via Provinciale 24; meals around €25) About halfway between Portoferraio and Marciana Marina, on the road just outside Procchio, is the unassuming Osteria del Piano. Looks aren't everything – they make all their own pasta and serve up some astonishing concoctions, such as black-and-white spaghetti in a lobster sauce.

Around Marciana Marina

A winding 4km ascent brings you to the attractive inland village of **Poggio**, with its steep, cobbled alleys and stunning views of Marciana Marina and the coast.

Albergo Monte Capanne (☎ /fax 0565 9 90 83; Via dei Pini 13; s/d €26/46, d with bathroom €52; ☼ Apr-Oct) If it gets too warm for you on the coast, chill out at this great little mountain retreat where you're assured of a robust, cheery welcome.

Some 750m south of the nearby village of **Marciana**, a **cable lift** with open, barred cabins like parrot cages operates in summer and whisks you almost to the summit of Monte Capanne with views, on a clear day, as far as Corsica.

Marina di Campo

Marina di Campo, on the south side of island, is Elba's second-largest town. Set in a picturesque bay, its small fishing harbour adds character to what is otherwise very much a holiday town. Its beach of bright, white sand pulls in holidaymakers by the thousands; coves further west, though less spectacular, are more tranquil.

Albergo Thomas (☎ 0565 97 77 32; www.elba thomashotel.com; Viale degli Etruschi 32; per person with breakfast €38-55; ☒ mid-Mar–Oct). This three-star hotel, attractively set among pine trees and a short walk from the beach, is one of the more affordable options in the town itself.

Porto Azzurro & Capoliveri

Dominated by its fort, built in 1603 by Philip III of Spain and now a prison, Porto Azzurro is quite a pleasant resort town close to some excellent beaches.

Albergo Villa Italia (☎/fax 0565 9 51 19; villaitalia@infoelba.it; Viale Italia 41; d/tr/q with break-fast €80/90/105) The 12 recently renovated bedrooms at this clean, friendly place are small but adequate and about the cheapest in town. It's on a fairly noisy road but only about 200m from the beach.

Ristorante Cutty Sark (☎ 0565 95 78 21; Piazza del Mercato 25; meals €25-35) The *ravioloni all'Ammiraglia* are big ravioli filled with courgettes (zucchini) and shrimp meat and bathed in a shrimp and tomato sauce.

From Porto Azzurro, take a short trip south to **Capoliveri**, one of the island's little hilltop surprise packets. Wander its narrow streets and enjoy the giddy views before trying out one of the nearby beaches – Barabarca, accessible only by a steep track that winds down a cliff, and Zuccale, more easily accessible and perfect for families.

Getting There & Away

AIR

There's a small **airport** (☎ 0565 97 60 11) just outside Marina di Campo. **Elbafly** (☎ 0565

97 68 71; www.elbafly.it) offers twice-daily flights to/from Pisa and Milan (Linate), June to October.

BOAT

Elba is an agreeable hour's ferry journey from Piombino. Services travelling to Portoferraio are most frequent, while some call in at Rio Marina and Porto Azzurro. Boats are run by **Moby Lines** (☎ 0565 93 61; www.mobylines.it) and **Toremar** (☎ 0565 3 11 00; www.toremar.it, Italian only). Unless it's a summer weekend or the middle of August, when queues can form, simply buy a ticket at the port. Prices (€6.50 to €9.50 per person, €28 to €50 per small car) vary according to season.

Getting Around

BUS

The island's bus company, **ATL** (☎ 0565 91 43 92), runs an efficient trans-island service. From Portoferraio (the terminal is almost opposite the Toremar jetty), there are over 10 runs daily (all €1.80) to/from Marciana Marina, Marina di Campo, Capoliveri and Porto Azzurro.

CAR, MOTORCYCLE & BICYCLE

Alternatively, you can steam around Elba by mountain bike or scooter. Typical high season daily rates are city bikes €10, mountain bikes €12 to €15, mopeds (50cc) €23 to €30, scooters (100 to 125cc) €35 to €40 – and small cars €45 to €55.

Two Wheels Network (TWN; ☎ 0565 91 46 66; www.twn-rent.it; Viale Elba 32, Portoferraio), one of several car-rental outlets, rents bikes, scooters – even kayaks.

CENTRAL TUSCANY

IL CHIANTI

Il Chianti, as the gentle hills and valleys between Florence and Siena are called, produces some of the country's best-marketed wines; it's not called Chiantishire for nothing. The best known is Chianti Classico, a blend of white and red grapes which is sold under the Gallo Nero (Black Cockerel) symbol.

Il Chianti is split between the provinces of Florence (Chianti Fiorentino) and Siena (Chianti Sienese). The lovely Monti del

Chianti rising into the Apennines mark the area's eastern boundary.

It's a land of rolling hills, olive groves and vineyards. Among them stand Romanesque churches known as *pievi* and the many castles of Florentine and Sienese warlords. But perhaps the hype has been just a trifle overdone. In other areas of Tuscany there's plenty of more spectacular country to be seen (around Pitigliano or up in the Apuane Alps, for instance). Let's not put you off, but the Tuscan countryside by no means begins and ends in Il Chianti.

The picturesque SS222, known as the Strada Chiantigiana, runs between Florence and Siena. You can get around by bus but your own wheels make exploration very much easier. Many explore Il Chianti by bicycle and it's also gentle walking country. Pack a copy of *Chianti Clasico: Val di Pesa-Val d'Elsa*, a map at 1:25,000 with hiking trails superimposed. Lonely Planet's *Walking in Italy* describes a three-day classic of its own that passes through Greve and Radda in Chianti

Budget accommodation is limited. You'll need to book well ahead since this is a popular area for tourists year-round.

For some useful links, call up www.chiantionline.com.

Greve

About 20km south of Florence on the Chiantigiana, Greve is the first good base for exploring the area. You can get there easily from Florence by SITA bus. Its unusual, triangular Piazza Matteotti, surrounded by porticoes, is an interesting provincial version of a Florentine piazza. At its heart stands a statue of Giovanni da Verrazano, local boy made good and discoverer of New York harbour. He's commemorated there by the Verrazano Narrows (the good captain lost a 'z' from his name somewhere in the mid-Atlantic) bridge, linking Staten Island to Brooklyn and indelibly printed in the soul and on the soles of every runner who's done the New York marathon.

If good wines tickle your palate, hit town for Greve's annual wine fair, held during the first or second week of September.

The **tourist office** (☎ 055 854 52 43; Via L Cini 1) is 500m east of the piazza. When it's closed, call by **Slow Travel** (☎ 055 854 62 87; Via Verrazzano 33).

If you're looking for a place to stay there are a couple of good choices, both with quality restaurants.

Albergo Giovanni da Verrazzano (☎ 055 85 31 89; verrazzano@ftbcc.tin.it; Piazza Matteotti 28; s/d €60/77, with bathroom €77/89; ▯) With some of its 10 rooms overlooking the main square, this is a pleasant three-star family hotel.

Albergo Del Chianti (☎ 055 85 37 63; www.albergodelchianti.it; Piazza Matteotti 86; s/d with breakfast €80/98; ✄ ✆) This is another three-star hotel, also sitting on Greve's central piazza. It has a pool, garden and attractive breakfast bar.

Macelleria Falorni (☎ 055 85 30 29; Piazza Matteotti 69-71) This place is renowned throughout Tuscany for its prime quality meat and salamis. The two huge chopping tables outside its door give a clue...

Le Cantine di Greve in Chianti (☎ 055 854 64 04; Piazza delle Cantine; ✆ 10am-1pm & 3.30-7.30pm) This vast *enoteca*, with over 1200 varieties of chianti and other wines on sale, blends tradition and 21st-century technology. Buy yourself a pre-paid wine-card (from €10), stick it into one of the taps that dispense more than 100 different wines and your tipple trickles out. Follow signs from the square.

Castellina

The huge cylindrical silos at the entry to town may make you think you've hit the industrial zone by mistake. In fact, they're brimming with Chianti Classico, the wine that, together with tourism, brings wealth to this small community, long ago a frontier town between warring Siena and Florence. From the car park walk into town beneath the tunnel-like Via del Volte. This medieval street, originally open to the elements, then encroached upon by shops and houses is now a long, vaulted, shady tunnel, particularly welcome in summer.

Pick up a bottle or two of the classic nectar at **Botega del Vino** (Via della Roca 11-13), which carries an impressive range.

Radda

Radda, 11km east of Castellina, retains much of its charm despite the tourist influx and makes a good base for a couple of days' walking. The **tourist office** (☎ 0577 73 84 94; Piazza Castello 6; ✆ 10am-12.30pm & 3-6.30pm Mon-Sat Feb-Oct, 10am-noon & 4-6pm Mon-Sat Nov-Jan, 10am-12.30pm Sun May-Sep) occupies an ex-convent.

It has a couple of route descriptions (in English) of half-day walks.

The nucleus of the village is Piazza Ferrucci, where the 16th-century **Palazzo del Podestà**, its facade emblazoned with shields and escutcheons, faces the village church, whose *Christ in Majesty* over the main portal is now sadly all but effaced by the elements.

Getting Around

SITA buses connect Florence and Greve (55 minutes, half-hourly), two daily continuing to Radda (1½ hours) and one to Castellina (1½ hours).

SIENA

pop 54,350

Siena is one of Italy's most enchanting cities. While Florence, its historical rival, saw its greatest flourishing during the Renaissance, Siena's artistic glories are Gothic.

The medieval centre bristles with majestic Gothic buildings, such as Palazzo Comunale on Il Campo, the main square, while its profusion of churches and small museums harbour a wealth of artwork. Budget in a couple of days to savour the city and its rich treasures. Or make it more than two; Siena also makes a great base for exploring central Tuscany – especially the five-star medieval towns of San Gimignano and Volterra. One problem: accommodation of any kind is difficult to find in summer, unless you book ahead, and well nigh impossible during the city's famous twice-yearly festival, Il Palio.

History

According to legend Siena was founded by the son of Remus, and the symbol of the wolf feeding the twins Romulus and Remus is as ubiquitous in Siena as in Rome. In reality the city was probably of Etruscan origin, although it wasn't until the 1st century BC, when the Romans established a military colony there called Sena Julia, that it began to grow into a proper town.

In the 12th century, Siena's wealth, size and power grew with its involvement in commerce and trade. Consequently its rivalry with neighbouring Florence also grew, leading to numerous wars during the first half of the 13th century between Guelph Florence and Ghibelline Siena. In 1230 Florence besieged Siena and catapulted dung and donkeys over its walls. Siena's revenge came at the Battle of Montaperti in 1260 but victory was short-lived. Only 10 years later the Tuscan Ghibellines were defeated by Charles of Anjou and for almost a century Siena was allied to Florence, chief town of the Tuscan Guelph League (supporters of the pope).

This was when Siena, ruled by the Council of Nine (a bourgeois group constantly bickering with the aristocracy) enjoyed its greatest prosperity. It was the Council that directed the construction of so many of the fine buildings in the Sienese-Gothic style that give the city its striking appearance; lasting monuments such as the cathedral, the Palazzo Comunale and Il Campo itself.

The Sienese school of painting had its origins at this time with Guido da Siena and reached its peak in the early 14th century with the works of artists such as Duccio di Buoninsegna and Ambrogio Lorenzetti.

A plague outbreak in 1348 killed two-thirds of the city's 100,000 inhabitants and led to a period of decline for Siena.

At the end of the 14th century, Siena came under the control of Milan's Visconti family, followed in the next century by the autocratic patrician Pandolfo Petrucci. Under Petrucci the city's fortunes improved until the Holy Roman Emperor Charles V conquered Siena in 1555 after a two-year siege that left thousands dead. He handed the city over to Cosimo I de' Medici who barred the inhabitants from operating banks and thus severely curtailed Siena's power.

Siena was home to Santa Caterina, one of Italy's most famous saints. But saints don't make money. Siena today relies on tourism for its prosperity and success of its Monte dei Paschi di Siena bank, founded in 1472 and now one of the city's largest employers.

In 1966 Siena was the first European city to banish motor traffic from its heart. To stroll its arteries, unclogged by carbon monoxide and unthreatened by speeding vehicles is not the least of the town's pleasures.

Orientation

Historic Siena, still largely surrounded by its medieval walls punctuated by the eight original city gates, is small and easily tackled on foot, although the way streets swirl in semicircles around Il Campo may confuse you. At the city's heart is this gently sloping square, around which curve its main streets: Banchi di Sopra, Via di Città and Banchi di Sotto.

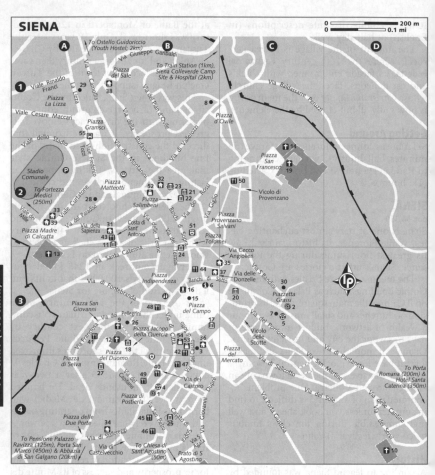

Information

EMERGENCY
Police Station (☎ 0577 20 11 11; Via del Castoro)

INTERNET ACCESS
Internet Train (Via di Pantaneto 57)
Internet Train (Via di Città 121)

LAUNDRY
Siena has a couple of self-service laundrettes around town:
Laundrette (Via del Casato di Sotto 17; wash & dry 7kg €6)
Wash & Dry (Via di Pantaneto 38; ☯ 8am-10pm)

MEDICAL SERVICES
Hospital (☎ 0577 58 51 11; Viale Bracci) Just north of Siena at Le Scotte.

POST
Main Post Office (Piazza Matteotti 1)

TELEPHONE
Telecom Office (Via dei Termini 40)
Telecom Office (Via di Pantaneto 44)

TOURIST INFORMATION
Tourist Office (☎ 0577 28 05 51; www.terresiena.it; Piazza del Campo 56; 9am-7pm) Impressively well informed; can help to reserve accommodation (see p496)

Sights
IL CAMPO
The magnificent, scallop-shaped, slanting Piazza del Campo has been the town's civic centre ever since the Council of Nine staked

it out in the mid-14th century. Tourists gather to take a break from sightseeing – backpackers lounge on the pavement in the square's centre, while the better-heeled drink expensive coffees or beers at the outdoor cafés around the periphery.

The square's paving is divided into nine sectors, representing the members of the Council of Nine. In the upper part of the square is the 15th-century **Fonte Gaia** (Gay Fountain). The original panels by Jacopo della Quercia are severely weathered and those which clad the fountain are reproductions (for more about their restoration and 'reconstruction', see p494).

At the lowest point of the piazza, the spare, elegant **Palazzo Comunale** is also known as the Palazzo Pubblico, or town hall. Entry to the ground-floor central courtyard is free. From the *palazzo* soars its graceful bell tower, the **Torre del Mangia** (admission €5.50; 🕙 10am-7pm mid-Mar–Oct, 10am-4pm Nov–mid-Mar), 102m high, completed in 1297.

The lower level of the *palazzo's* facade features a characteristic Sienese-Gothic arcade. Inside is the **Museo Civico** (☎ 0577 29 22 63; adult/student €6.50/4; 🕙 10am-7pm mid-Mar–Oct, 10am-5.30pm Nov–mid-Mar), occupying rooms richly decorated by artists of the Sienese school.

Of particular note is Simone Martini's famous *Maestà* (Virgin Mary in Majesty) in the Sala del Mappamondo. Completed and signed in 1315, it features the Madonna beneath a canopy, surrounded by saints and angels and is his first known canvas. In the Sala dei Nove are Ambrogio Lorenzetti's didactic frescoes, depicting *Allegories of Good and Bad Government*, contrasting the harmony

of good government with the – alas, much deteriorated and maybe there's a message there – privations and trials of those subject to bad rule, headed by the Devil himself. The chapel has delightful frescoes by Taddeo di Bartolo depicting the life of the Virgin.

CATHEDRAL

Although it has some Romanesque elements, the **cathedral** (☎ 0577 4 73 21; Piazza del Duomo; admission free; 🕙 7.30am-7.30pm Mon-Sat, 2-7.30pm Sun mid-Mar–Oct, 7.30am-5pm Mon-Sat, 2-7.30pm Sun Nov–mid-Mar) is one of Italy's great Gothic churches. Begun in 1196, it was completed by 1215, although work continued on features such as the apse and dome well into the 13th century. Work then began on enlarging and embellishing the structure. The magnificent facade of white, green and red polychrome marble was begun by Giovanni Pisano – who completed only the lower section before his death – and finished towards the end of the 14th century. The mosaics in the gables are 19th-century additions. The statues of philosophers and prophets by Pisano above the lower section are copies; the originals are in the adjacent Museo dell'Opera Metropolitana.

In 1339 the city's leaders planned to enlarge the cathedral and create one of Italy's biggest churches. Known as the Nuovo Duomo (New Cathedral), the remains of this project can be seen on Piazza Jacopo della Quercia, at the eastern side of the cathedral. The daring plan, to build an immense new nave with the present church becoming the transept, was scotched by the plague of 1348.

The most precious feature of the cathedral's interior is the inlaid marble floor,

TUSCANY (TOSCANA)

SAFE COMBINATIONS

Siena has a bewildering permutation of combined tickets. The distribution when we last visited was as follows:

- Museo Civico & Torre del Mangia (€9.50)
- Museo dell'Opera Metropolitana, Libreria Piccolomini, Battistero di San Giovanni (€7.50)
- Museo Civico, Santa Maria della Scala, Centro di Arte Contemporaneo (€9)
- Museo dell'Opera Metropolitana, Libreria Piccolomini, Battistero di San Giovanni, Oratorio de San Bernadino, Museo Diocesano (€9.50)
- Museo Civico, Santa Maria della Scala, Centro di Arte Contemporaneo, Museo dell'Opera Metropolitana, Libreria Piccolomini, Battistero di San Giovanni – the bumper bundle though not including Torre del Mangia (€16)

---

decorated with 56 panels depicting historical and biblical subjects. The earliest ones are graffiti designs in simple black and white marble, dating from the mid-14th century. The latest, marquetry panels in coloured marble were created in the 16th century. The most valuable are kept covered and revealed only from 7 to 22 August each year.

Other highlights include the exquisitely crafted marble and porphyry pulpit by Nicola Pisano, aided by his equally talented son, Giovanni. Seek out too the bronze statue of St John the Baptist by Donatello, in a chapel off the north transept.

Through a door from the north aisle is another of the cathedral's jewels, the **Libreria Piccolomini** (admission €1.50; ☉ 9am-7.30pm Mon-Sat, 2-7.30pm Sun mid-Mar–Oct, 10am-1pm & 2-5pm Mon-Sat, 2-7.30pm Sun Nov–mid-Mar), built to house the books of Enea Silvio Piccolomini, better known as Pius II. The walls of the small hall are covered with vividly coloured narrative frescoes by Bernardino Pinturicchio, depicting events in the life of Piccolomini.

MUSEO DELL'OPERA METROPOLITANA

This **museum** (☎ 0577 28 30 48; Piazza del Duomo 8; admission €5.50; ☉ 9am-7.30pm mid-Mar–Sep, 9am-6pm Oct, 9am-1.30pm Nov–mid-Mar) is in what would have been the southern aisle of the nave of the Nuovo Duomo. Among its great artworks, which formerly adorned the cathedral, are the 12 statues of prophets and philosophers by Giovanni Pisano that decorated the facade. The museum's main draw is Duccio di Buoninsegna's striking early-14th-century *Maestà*, which is painted on both sides as a screen for the cathedral's high altar. The front and back have now been separated and the panels depicting the story of the Passion hang opposite the Maestà. Other artists represented in the museum are Ambrogio Lorenzetti, Simone Martini and Taddeo di Bartolo and there's also a rich collection of tapestries and manuscripts. For a great panoramic view – and a touch of physical exertion to counterbalance so much aesthetic exercise – haul yourself up the 131 steps that lead, via a very narrow, corkscrew stairway, to the top of the facade of the putative Nuovo Duomo.

BAPTISTRY

Just north of the cathedral and down a flight of stairs is the **baptistry** (Battistero di San Giovanni; Piazza San Giovanni; admission €2.50; ☉ 9am-7.30pm mid-Mar–Sep, 9am-6pm Oct, 10am-1pm & 2-5pm Nov–mid-Mar).

While the baptistry's Gothic facade has remained unfinished, the interior is richly decorated with frescoes. The centrepiece, literally and figuratively, is a marble font by Jacopo della Quercia, decorated with bronze panels in relief and depicting the life of St John the Baptist. Artists include Lorenzo Ghiberti (*Baptism of Christ* and *St John in Prison*) and Donatello (*Herod's Feast*).

SANTA MARIA DELLA SCALA

In the basement of this former **pilgrims' hospital** (☎ 0577 22 48 11; Piazza del Duomo 2; admission €5.20; ☉ 10am-6pm mid-Mar–Oct, 10.30am-4.30pm Nov–mid-Mar) are copies and touched-up reproductions of Jacopo della Quercia's magnificent frescoes for Il Campo's Fonte Gaia. The Sala dei Pellegrinaio is clad in vivid, secular frescoes (quite a relief after so much spirituality all around town) by Domenico di Bartolo, lauding the good works of the hospital and its patrons. There's also a collection of Roman and Etruscan remains.

PINACOTECA NAZIONALE

The 15th-century **Palazzo Buonsignori** (☎ 0577 28 11 61; Via San Pietro 29; adult/student €4/2; ☉ 8.30am-1.30pm Mon, 8.15am-7.15pm Tue-Sat, 8.15am-1.15pm

Sun) is, above all, a showcase for the greatest of Sienese artists. Look for Duccio di Buoninsegna's *Madonna dei Francescani*, the *Madonna col Bambino* (Madonna with Child) by Simone Martini, and a series of Madonnas by Ambrogio Lorenzetti.

CHIESA DI SAN DOMENICO

This imposing Gothic **church** (Piazza San Domenico; admission free; 7.30am-1pm & 3-6.30pm), much altered over the centuries, is associated with Santa Caterina di Siena, who took her vows in its Cappella delle Volte (the only known portrait of the saint to be painted during her lifetime is above the altar in the raised chapel at the west end). In the **Cappella di Santa Caterina**, off the south aisle, are frescoes by Sodoma depicting events in her life – and her head, in a 15th-century tabernacle above the altar. She died in Rome, where most of her body is preserved, but, in line with the bizarre practice of collecting relics of dead saints, her head was returned to Siena. In a small window box to the right of the chapel are her desiccated thumb and the nasty-looking whip that she flogged herself with for the well being of the souls of the faithful.

For more of Santa Caterina – figuratively speaking – visit **Casa di Santa Caterina** (0577 4 41 77; Costa di Sant'Antonio 6; admission free; 9am-12.30pm & 3-6pm), where the saint was born. The rooms of the house, converted into small chapels in the 15th century, are decorated with frescoes and paintings by Sienese artists, including Sodoma.

OTHER CHURCHES & PALAZZI

The 15th-century **Loggia dei Mercanti**, where merchants used to plot deals, is just northwest of Il Campo. From here, strike east along Banchi di Sotto to pass **Palazzo Piccolomini**, a Renaissance *palazzo* housing the city's archives. Further east are the 13th-century **Basilica di Santa Maria dei Servi**, with frescoes by Pietro Lorenzetti in a chapel off the north transept, and 14th-century **Porta Romana**. Also on the south side and worth a detour is **Chiesa di Sant'Agostino** (Prato di Sant'Agostino; admission €2; 10.30am-1.30pm & 3-5.30pm mid-Mar–Oct). The second altar on the south aisle has a superb *Adoration of the Crucifix* by Perugino while the Piccolomini chapel's jewel is Sodoma's *Adoration of the Magi*.

Return to Loggia dei Mercanti and head north on Banchi di Sopra, past Piazza Tolomei,

dominated by the 13th-century **Palazzo Tolomei**. Further along, Piazza Salimbeni is bounded to the north by **Palazzo Tantucci**, Gothic **Palazzo Salimbeni**, (prestige head office of Monte dei Paschi di Siena bank) to the east and Renaissance **Palazzo Spannocchi** on the third flank. Northeast of here, along Via dei Rossi, is **Chiesa di San Francesco**, with its vast single nave. It's suffered over the years – from a devastating 17th-century fire and its use as army barracks. Beside it is **Oratorio di San Bernardino** (0577 28 30 48; Piazza San Francesco; admission €2.50; 10.30am-1.30pm & 3-5.30pm mid-Mar–Oct) with its small museum of religious artworks.

Courses

LANGUAGE

Università per Stranieri (University for Foreigners; 0577 24 01 15; www.unistrasi.it; Piazzetta Grassi 2) offers various courses in Italian language and culture.

Other reputable Italian language schools that also offer supplementary cultural – and even culinary – options:

Scuola Leonardo da Vinci (0577 24 90 97; www.scuolaleonardo.com; Via del Paradiso 16)

Società Dante Alighieri (0577 4 95 33; www.dantealighieri.com; Piazza la Lizza 10)

Saena Iulia (0577 4 41 55; www.saenaiulia.it; Via Monna Agnese 20)

MUSIC

The **Accademia Musicale Chigiana** (0577 2 20 91; www.chigiana.it; Via di Città 89) offers classical music courses every summer as well as seminars and concerts performed by visiting musicians, teachers and students as part of the Settimana Musicale Senese.

The **Associazione Siena Jazz** (0577 27 14 01; fax 0577 28 14 04; Via Vallerozzi 77), one of Europe's foremost institutions of its type, offers courses in jazz.

Tours

Treno Natura (0577 20 74 13; May, early Jun, Sep & Oct) is a great way to see the stunning scenery of the Crete Senese, south of Siena. The train line loops from Siena, through Asciano, across to the Val d'Orcia and Stazione di Monte Antico and back to Siena. The line, which opened in the 19th century, was closed in 1994 and trains are now run exclusively for tourists and staffed by volunteers. There are usually three per day, stopping at Asciano and Monte

---

IL PALIO

This spectacular event, held twice yearly on 2 July and 16 August, in honour of the Virgin Mary, dates from the Middle Ages and features a series of colourful pageants, a wild horse race around Il Campo and much eating, drinking and celebrating in the streets.

Ten of Siena's 17 *contrade* (town districts) compete for the coveted *palio* (silk banner). Each *contrada* has its own traditions, symbol and colours plus its own church and *palio* museum – rivalry is razor keen.

On festival days, Il Campo becomes a racetrack, with a ring of packed dirt around its perimeter serving as the course. From about 5pm representatives of each *contrada* parade in historical costume, each bearing their individual banners.

The race is run at 7.45pm in July and 7pm in August. For scarcely one exhilarating minute, the 10 horses and their bareback riders tear three times around Il Campo with a speed and violence that make your hair stand on end.

Even if a horse loses its rider, it is still eligible to win, and since many riders fall each year, it is the horses in the end who are the focus of the event. There is only one rule: riders are not to interfere with the reins of other horses.

Book well in advance if you want to stay in Siena at this time and join the crowds in the centre of Il Campo at least four hours before the start, or even earlier, if you want a place on the barrier lining the track. If you can't find a good vantage point, don't despair – the race is televised live (the Sienese exact a huge fee from the national TV network, RAI, for screening rights), then repeated throughout the evening on TV.

If you're in town a day or two before the race, you may get to see the jockeys and horses trying out in Il Campo – almost as good as the real thing. Between May and October, **Cinema Moderno** (☎ 0577 28 92 01; Piazza Tolomei; admission €5.25; ☼ 9.30am-5.30pm) runs a mini-epic 20-minute film of Siena and Il Palio that will take your breath away. Show this guide for a 20% reduction.

TUSCANY (TOSCANA)

Antico, and there are connecting trains from Florence. Round-trip tickets cost €15.

Festivals & Events

The Accademia Musicale Chigiana (see p495) mounts the **Settimana Musicale Senese** in July and the **Estate Musicale Chigiana** in July, August and September. Concerts in these series are frequently held at the Abbazia di San Galgano (p504), about 20km southwest of the city and at Sant'Antimo (p505), near Montalcino. For information, call ☎ 0577 2 20 91.

In July and August, the city hosts **Siena Jazz** (☎ 0577 27 14 01; www.sienajazz.it), an international festival with concerts at the Fortezza Medici and various sites throughout the city.

In November, the **Festa di Santa Cecilia**, a series of concerts and exhibitions, takes place to honour Cecilia, patron saint of musicians.

Sleeping

Siena offers a good range of accommodation but budget hotels generally fill quickly so it's always advisable to make a reservation. If you haven't one, forget about finding a room during Il Palio.

The tourist office has lists of accommodation and will also make reservations free of charge for *affitacamere* (rooms for rent) and hotels of three stars and above. You can also book in person or online through **Siena Hotels Promotion** (☎ 0577 28 80 84; www.hotelsiena.com; Piazza Madre di Calcutta 5; ☼ 9am-8pm Mon-Sat summer, 9am-7pm winter).

Siena Colleverde (☎ 0577 28 00 44; fax 0577 33 32 98; Via Scacciapensieri 47; per person/pitch €7.75/7.75; ☼ late-Mar–early Nov) This site is 2km north of the historical centre. Take bus No 3 or No 8 from Piazza Gramsci or Viale Tozzi.

Ostello Guidoriccio (☎ 0577 5 22 12; Via Fiorentina 89, Località Stellino; dm €13, meals €8.80) This HI-affiliated youth hostel is about 2km northwest of the city centre. Take bus No 10, 15 or 35 from Piazza Gramsci, No 4 or 77 from the train station.

Hotel Le Tre Donzelle (☎ /fax 0577 22 39 33, Via delle Donzelle 5; s/d €33/46, d with bathroom €60) This central, friendly, popular choice was originally constructed as a tavern in the 13th century. Rooms are clean and simple and the shared bathrooms are spotless.

Piccolo Hotel Etruria (☎ 0577 28 80 88; hetruria@ tin.it; Via delle Donzelle 3; s/d €50/80) Another family hotel off Il Campo, it's equally central and welcoming with pleasant, large rooms with full facilities.

Both of these fine hotels observe a 12.30am curfew, which shouldn't be too much of a drawback. Many other hotels don't, however, so the street outside can be noisy in summer.

Locanda Garibaldi (☎ 0577 28 42 04; Via Giovanni Dupré 18; d with bathroom €60) Directly above a restaurant, Garibaldi can get a bit noisy. The communal areas are on the gloomy side but the seven bedrooms are big and bright.

Albergo Bernini (☎ 0577 28 90 47; www.albergo bernini.com; Via della Sapienza 15; s with bathroom €78, d with/without bathroom €82/62) This welcoming, family-run hotel (the owner is a professional accordion player who often squeezes his box for guests) has a wonderful roof terrace with views across to the cathedral and the Chiesa di San Domenico. There's a midnight curfew and reservations are essential, April to October.

Cannon d'Oro (☎ 0577 4 43 21; www.cannon doro.com, Via dei Montanini 28 s/d €70/86; P) Don't be deterred by the golden cannon (the very one that gave the place its name) trained upon you as you debouch from a narrow alley to face the otherwise amicable reception desk of this trim, attractive, excellent value hotel. Parking is €13.

Piccolo Hotel il Palio (☎ 0577 28 11 31; phiphuno@ tin.it; Piazza del Sale 19; s/d €69/96) This hotel is on a quiet piazza about 1km on foot from Il Campo. Reception's slightly scatty but rooms are cosy and many have beamed ceilings, imparting a farmhouse feel.

Chiusarelli (☎ 0577 28 05 62; www.chiusarelli.com; Viale Curtatone 15; s/d with breakfast €75.50/112.50; P 🞩 💻) This hotel has been functioning continuously since its construction in 1870. Chiusarelli has a pleasant, spacious breakfast room and bedrooms are attractive. Those at the rear are for lovers of quiet and lucky football fans – they overlook the stadium where Siena, promoted to Serie A in 2003, play home matches on alternate Sundays.

Pensione Palazzo Ravizza (☎ 0577 28 04 62; www.palazzoravizza.it; Pian dei Mantellini 34; s/d/tr with breakfast from €80/100/190; P 🞩 💻) At the tip-top end of the market is a delightful Renaissance *palazzo* with frescoed ceilings and carefully selected antique furniture. Service is courteous and efficient and there's a small, leafy garden.

Hotel Duomo (☎ 0577 28 90 88; www.hotelduomo.it; Via Stalloreggi 38; s/d/tr with breakfast €104/130/171; P 🞩) This attractive, renovated 17th-century *palazzo* has tastefully decorated rooms, several offering views of the cathedral.

Hotel Santa Caterina (☎ 0577 22 11 05; www .hscsiena.it; Via Piccolomini 7; s/d with breakfast up to €98/ 144; P 🞩) This elegantly renovated 18th-century villa, just outside the city walls and a stone's throw beyond the Porta Romana, is a tranquil haven. Rooms are tastefully furnished, the breakfast room is light and airy and there's a lovely garden with open views to the surrounding hills. Parking is €12.

Eating

According to the Sienese, most Tuscan cuisine has its origins here. Among the many traditional dishes are *ribollita* (bean soup), *panzanella* (summer salad of soaked bread, basil, onion and tomatoes), *pappardelle con la lepre* (ribbon pasta with hare) and the juicy charcoal-grilled beef steaks of the Chianina. *Panforte*, a rich cake of almonds, honey and candied fruit, was originally created as tuck for crusaders to the Holy Land.

RESTAURANTS
La Chiacchera (☎ 0577 28 06 31; Costa di Sant'Antonio 4; pasta €3.70-4.50, meals €11-15; 🕑 Wed-Mon) This tiny, informal restaurant run by a young staff has a great menu of local specialities. The wooden tables on a quiet pedestrian street make it a good lunch venue. You'd be wise to reserve.

Osteria da Cice (☎ 0577 28 80 26; Via San Pietro 32; mains €7-11.50, tourist menu €12; 🕑 Tue-Sun) This place is also in the hands of a friendly team, reflecting its mainly youthful clientele. It's the place for an informal, relaxed meal and the menu has plenty of vegetarian options.

Il Carroccio (☎ 0577 4 11 65; Via del Casato di Sotto 32; pasta €6.50-7, mains €12-15; 🕑 Thu-Tue) It does excellent pasta in attractive rustic surroundings. Try their *pici*, a kind of thick spaghetti typical of Siena, and select something a little special from their long and carefully nurtured wine list.

Trattoria Tullio ai Tre Cristi (☎ 0577 28 06 08; Vicolo Provenzano 1; meals €20-27; 🕑 Thu-Tue) This has been a place for hungry Sienese for nigh on 170 years – so the service is perhaps understandably sometimes on the slow side. This apart, it's a delightful place: wood-panelled, brick-vaulted and tucked away down a clearly signed side alley.

Taverna del Capitano (☎ 0577 28 80 94; Via del Capitano 6-8; meals €18-25; Ⓨ Wed-Mon) Here's a grand little spot for local food with friendly service. Specialities include *zuppa di farro* (barley soup) and *ossobuco al sienese* (marrowbone stew). The tables outdoors are pleasant in summer.

Osteria del Castelvecchio (☎ 0577 4 95 86; Via di Castelvecchio 65; mains €9.50, meals €23; Ⓨ Wed-Mon) Highly regarded by locals, Osteria del Castelvecchio's menu changes daily. It is also a good spot for veggies, with at least four vegetarian dishes normally on offer.

Al Marsili (☎ 0577 4 71 54; Via del Castoro 3; meals from €25; Ⓨ Tue-Sun) This is one of the city's better-known restaurants, where booking is essential. The vaulted dining rooms are smart and the menu features lots of meaty mains and fruity desserts.

Ristorante da Mugolone (☎ 0577 28 32 35; Via dei Pellegrini 8; meals €30-35; Ⓨ Fri-Wed, closed dinner Sun) Here's another excellent Sienese restaurant with attentive service that offers local specialities in an attractive setting.

Antica Osteria da Divo (☎ 0577 28 43 81; Via Franciosa 29; mains €17.50-20, meals €35-40; Ⓨ Mon-Sat) The background jazz is as mellow as the walls are rough-hewn. At the lower, cellar level you're dining amid Etruscan tombs. If the budget's tight you can still have an enjoyable eating experience by eschewing their rather pricey mains.

SELF-CATERING

Nannini (Banchi di Sopra 22) Always crowded, Nannini is something of a Sienese institution, baking its finest cakes and serving good coffee with speed and panache.

Pizzicheria de Miccoli (☎ 0577 28 91 84; Via di Città 93-95) Richly scented, de Miccoli's windows are festooned with sausages, piled-up cheeses and porcini mushrooms by the sackful. It is the place to stock up on great picnic fodder.

Shopping

Ricama (☎ 0577 28 83 38; Via di Città 61) This shop promotes the crafts of Siena, in particular embroidery.

La Cantina in Piazza (Via Casato di Sotto 24; Ⓨ closed afternoon Wed) A specialist wine shop, it is ideal for a picnic special or a case to lug home.

Consorzio Agrario Siena (Via Pianagini 13) A rich emporium of local food and wines.

Getting There & Away

BUS

From Piazza Gramsci, regular Tra-in or SITA buses leave for Florence (€6, 1¼ hours, half-hourly), San Gimignano (€5, 1½ hours, hourly; directly or changing in Poggibonsi), Poggibonsi (€3.60, one hour, up to 10 daily) and Colle di Val d'Elsa (€2.30, 30 minutes, hourly) with connections for Volterra (€4.45).

Sena buses also leave from Piazza Gramsci for Rome (€16, three hours, 10 daily) and there are six buses daily to Arezzo (€4.60, 1½ hours). Both **Tra-in** (☎ 0577 20 42 46) and **Sena** (☎ 0577 28 32 03; www.sena.it) have offices underneath the piazza.

Buses to Montalcino (€3, 1½ hours, six daily), Montepulciano (€4.35, 1¾ hours, four to five daily) and other destinations in the Crete Senese and Chianti area leave from Piazza Stazione.

CAR & MOTORCYCLE

From Florence take the SS2, the *superstrada*, or the more attractive SS222, also known as the Chiantigiana, which meanders its way through the hills of Chianti.

TRAIN

Siena isn't on a major train line. From Rome change at Chiusi, from Florence at Empoli; buses are a better alternative.

Getting Around

Tra-in operates city bus services (€0.90). Buses No 8, 9 and 10 run between the train station and Piazza Gramsci. Cars are banned from the town centre. There are large car parks at the Stadio Communale and around the Fortezza Medici; both just north of Piazza San Domenico.

For a taxi, call ☎ 0577 4 92 22.

SAN GIMIGNANO
pop 7000

As you crest the hill coming from the east, the 13 towers of this walled town look like a medieval Manhattan. And when you arrive you might well feel that half of Manhattan's population has moved in. Within easy reach of both Siena and Florence, San Gimignano is a tourist magnet. Come in winter or early spring to indulge your imagination a little; in summer you'll spend your time dodging fellow visitors. Even then though, you'll discover a different, almost peaceful San Gimignano, once the last bus has pulled out.

There's a good reason for such popularity. The towers, which once numbered 72, were symbols of the power and wealth of the city's medieval families. San Gimignano delle Belle Torri (meaning 'of the Fine Towers' – though they're actually almost devoid of design and rather dull unless sheer height impresses you) is surrounded by lush, productive land and the setting is altogether enchanting.

Originally an Etruscan village, the town was named after the bishop of Modena, San Gimignano, who is said to have saved the city from Attila the Hun. It became a *comune* in 1199, but continually fought with Volterra. Internal battles between Ardinghelli (Guelph)

and Salvucci (Ghibelline) families over the next two centuries caused divisions. Most towers were built during this period – in the 13th century, one *podestà* (town chief) forbade the building of towers higher than his own 51m pile. In 1348 plague wiped out much of the population and weakened the nobles' power, leading to the town's submission to Florence in 1353. Today, not even the plague would deter the summer swarms!

Orientation

From the main gate, Porta San Giovanni, at the southern end of the town, Via San Giovanni heads north to Piazza della Cisterna and the connecting Piazza del Duomo. From here the other major thoroughfare,

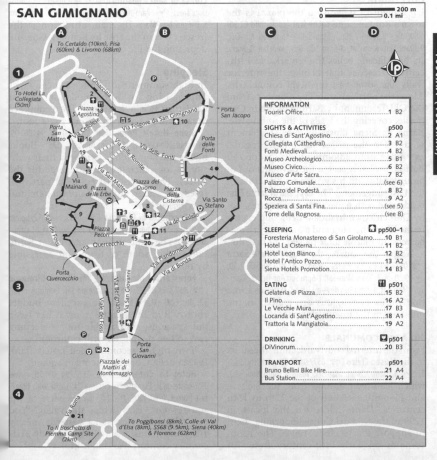

Via San Matteo extends to the principal northern gate, Porta San Matteo.

Information

Tourist office (☎ 0577 94 00 08; www.sangimignano .com; Piazza del Duomo 1; ⏰ 9am-1pm & 3-7pm Mar-Oct, 9am-1pm & 2-6pm Nov-Feb)

Sights

If you're an assiduous sightseer, two combined tickets can save you money. One (adult/child €7.50/5.50) gives admission to the Palazzo Comunale complex and the archaeological museum. The other (adult/child €5.50/2.50) gets you into the Collegiata and nearby Museo d'Arte Sacra.

COLLEGIATA

Up a flight of steps from the piazza is the town's Romanesque **cathedral** (adult/child €3.50/ 1.50; ⏰ 9.30am-7.30pm Mon-Sat, 1-5pm Sun Apr-Oct, 9.30am-5pm Mon-Sat, 1-5pm Sun Nov–mid-Jan & Mar). Its bare facade belies the remarkable 14th-century frescoes that blanket the interior walls like some vast medieval comic strip. Along the north aisle are key moments from the Old Testament by Bartolo di Fredi. Opposite, covering the walls of the south aisle, Barna da Siena illustrates New Testament scenes. On the inside wall of the facade, extending onto adjoining walls, Taddeo di Bartolo probably scared the daylights out of pious locals with his gruesome depiction of the Last Judgement. The **Cappella di Santa Fina** is adorned with naive and touching frescoes by Domenico Ghirlandaio depicting events in the life of the saint and a quite superb alabaster and marble altar picked out in gold.

Across the square, the **Museo d'Arte Sacra** (☎ 0577 94 03 16; Piazza Pecori 1; adult/child €3/1.50; ⏰ 9.30am-7.30pm Mon-Sat, 1-5pm Sun Apr-Oct, 9.30am-5pm Mon-Sat, 1-5pm Sun Nov–mid-Jan & Mar) has some fine works of religious art, culled, in the main, from the town's churches.

PALAZZO COMUNALE

From the internal courtyard, climb the stairs to the **Museo Civico** (☎ 0577 94 00 08; adult/child €5/ 4; ⏰ 9.30am-7.20pm Mar-Oct, 10am-5.50pm Nov-Feb), which features paintings from the Sienese and Florentine schools of the 12th to 15th centuries. Dante addressed the locals in 1299 in the Sala del Consiglio, urging them to support the Guelphs' cause. The room contains an early-14th-century fresco of the *Maestà* by Lippo Memmi. Climb up the *palazzo's* **Torre Grossa** for a spectacular view of the town and surrounding countryside.

MUSEO ARCHEOLOGICO

This recently opened **complex** (☎ 0577 94 03 48; Via Fologore da San Gimignano 11; adult/child €3.50/ 2.50; ⏰ 11am-6pm Apr-Oct, Sat-Thu Nov-Dec) is home to the town's small archaeological museum and the **Speziera di Santa Fina**, a reconstructed 16th-century pharmacy and herb garden.

OTHER SIGHTS

From the **Rocca**, what remains of the town's fortress, there are great views over the surrounding countryside.

At the northern end of the town is the **Chiesa di Sant'Agostino** (Piazza Sant'Agostino; admission free; ⏰ 7am-noon & 3-7pm Apr-Oct, 7am-noon & 3-6pm Nov-Mar). Its main attraction is the fresco cycle in the apse by Benozzo Gozzoli, depicting the life of Sant'Agostino.

Sleeping

In high summer San Gimignano can be as unpromising for accommodation as that Christmas Eve in Bethlehem. But a couple of organisations will help to find you a roof.

Siena Hotels Promotion (☎ 0577 94 08 09; www.hotelsiena.com; Via San Giovanni 125) Books hotels and some *affitacamere* via their website or for callers-in (€2 surcharge for the latter). The tourist office, for its part, will reserve a wider range of *affitacamere* and also *agriturismi*.

Il Boschetto di Piemma (☎ 0577 94 03 52; bpiem ma@tiscalinet.it; person/tent/car €5.30/5.50/4; ⏰ Easter–mid-Oct) The nearest camp site, it's at Santa Lucia, 2km south of town and accessible by bus

Foresteria Monastereo di San Girolamo (☎ 0577 94 05 73; Via Fologore da San Gimignano 26-32; dm €23; Ⓟ) This is an excellent budget choice. Run by friendly nuns, it has basic but spacious, comfortable rooms sleeping two to five people, all with bathroom.

Two highly recommended hotels flank Piazza della Cisterna, the main square.

Hotel La Cisterna (☎ 0577 94 03 28; www .hotelcisterna.it; Piazza della Cisterna 24; s/d/tr with breakfast from €70/90/120; Ⓟ ⌧ ⛳) A view of the square? Or vistas across the valley? You can take your pick at La Cisterna, nearly 100 years in business yet offering truly 21st-century comfort. Parking is €15.

Hotel Leon Bianco (☎ 0577 94 12 94; Piazza della Cisterna 13; www.leonbianco.com; s/d/tr with breakfast from €80/100/135; 🕱 🖵) Leon Bianco faces La Cisterna across the square. It's equally welcoming and friendly, occupies a 14th-century mansion and has a great breakfast patio.

Hotel l'Antico Pozzo (☎ 0577 94 20 14; www .anticopozzo.com; Via San Matteo 87; s/d/tr with breakfast from €90/130/160; P 🕱 🖵) This hotel occupies an elegant 15th-century town house. Rooms with high ceilings and wrought-iron beds are comfort itself and come equipped with fridge and safe. Parking is €15.

Eating

Locanda di Sant'Agostino (☎ 0577 94 31 41; Piazza Sant'Agostino 15; bruschetta from €4; 🕑 closed Mon Dec-Feb) This is a pleasant spot for a relatively quiet drink, crispy salad and sampling from their repertoire of 49 *bruschette*.

Trattoria La Mangiatoia (☎ 0577 94 15 28; Via Mainardi 5; meals around €25; 🕑 closed Mon Oct-Jun) This trattoria serves tempting fare. With candles flickering and classical music in the background, share it with that special someone.

Le Vecchie Mura (☎ 0577 94 02 70; Via Piandornella 15; meals €22-28; 🕑 dinner Wed-Mon) This is a wonderful spot, especially if you snap up a terrace table on a warm summer's night. The food competes with the view of rolling green hills. Book ahead to avoid queuing.

Il Pino (☎ 0577 94 04 15; Via Cellolese 8-10; meals €35-40; 🕑 Fri-Wed) Spruce and airy, Il Pino has fresh flowers on the tables, friendly; attentive service; and a menu that can rival any in town, including several truffle-based specialities. Save a cranny for one of their tempting desserts, all confectioned on the premises.

Gelateria di Piazza (☎ 0577 94 22 44; Piazza della Cisterna 4; 🕑 Mar–mid-Nov) As the pictures around the wall attest, many celebrities have closed their lips around one of Gelateria di Piazza's rich ice creams ('all the family thought the ice cream was delicious' attested one Tony Blair). There's even a variant based on Vernaccia, the local wine.

Each Thursday morning there's a **produce market** (Piazza della Cisterna & Piazza del Duomo).

Entertainment

DiVinorum (☎ 0577 90 71 92; Piazza della Cisterna 30; 🕑 11.30am-1am Fri-Wed Mar-Oct, 6pm-1am Fri-Wed Nov-Feb) Housed in former stables, DiVinorum is a cool wine bar run by local lads. There's live music or a DJ weekends.

Getting There & Around

Buses arrive in Piazzale dei Martiri di Montemaggio beside the Porto San Giovanni. The tourist office carries timetables. For Florence (€5.40, 1¼ hours, 14 daily), change in Poggibonsi. Regular Tra-in buses run to Siena (€5, one to 1½ hours, hourly) directly or with a change at Poggibonsi.

There's also a service to Volterra (€4.25, 1½ hours, four daily) with a change in Colle di Val d'Elsa. The closest train station is in Poggibonsi.

To reach San Gimignano by car, take the SS68 from Colle di Val d'Elsa, which is on the SS2 between Florence and Siena. There's a large car park outside the Porta San Giovanni.

Bruno Bellini (☎ 0577 94 02 01; Via Roma 41) rents mountain bikes (€15/25/34 for 1/2/3 days) and scooters (from €31 per day).

VOLTERRA

pop 11,600

The Etruscan settlement of Velathri was an important trading centre and remained so under the Romans, who renamed it Volaterrae. A long period of conflict with Florence started in the 12th century and ended only when the Medici took possession of the city in the 15th century.

Perched high on a rocky plateau, 29km southwest of San Gimignano, the town's well-preserved medieval ramparts give Volterra a forbidding air, while the gentle Tuscan countryside rolling out for miles around provides the perfect contrast. The city has long had a strong alabaster industry, a legacy from the Etruscans.

Orientation

Whichever of the four main gates you enter through, the road will lead you to central Piazza dei Priori.

Information

Tourist office (☎ 0588 8 72 57; www.volterratur.it; Piazza dei Priori 19-20; 🕑 9am-1pm & 2-7pm Apr-Oct, 10am-1pm & 2-6pm Nov-Mar) Offers a free hotel booking service and rents out town audioguides (€ 7/10 for 1/2 persons).

Sights

PIAZZA DEI PRIORI & AROUND

Piazza dei Priori is ringed by austere medieval mansions. The 13th-century **Palazzo dei Priori** (admission €1; 🕑 10am-6pm Sat & Sun),

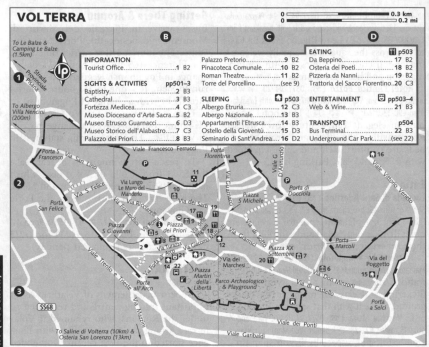

VOLTERRA

INFORMATION
Tourist Office..............................1 B2

SIGHTS & ACTIVITIES   pp501-3
Baptistry......................................2 B3
Cathedral.....................................3 B3
Fortezza Medicea........................4 C3
Museo Diocesano d'Arte Sacra...5 B2
Museo Etrusco Guarnacci...........6 D3
Museo Storico dell'Alabastro......7 C3
Palazzo dei Priori........................8 B3

Palazzo Pretorio..........................9 B2
Pinacoteca Comunale.................10 B2
Roman Theatre...........................11 B2
Torre del Porcellino..............(see 9)

SLEEPING   p503
Albergo Etruria..........................12 C3
Albergo Nazionale.....................13 B3
Appartamenti l'Etrusca..............14 B3
Ostello della Gioventù................15 D3
Seminario di Sant'Andrea..........16 D2

EATING   p503
Da Beppino................................17 B2
Osteria dei Poeti........................18 B2
Pizzeria da Nanni.......................19 B2
Trattoria del Sacco Fiorentino...20 C3

ENTERTAINMENT   pp503-4
Web & Wine................................21 B3

TRANSPORT   p504
Bus Terminal...............................22 B3
Underground Car Park...........(see 22)

the oldest seat of local government in Tuscany, is believed to have been a model for Florence's Palazzo Vecchio. Highlights are a fresco of the Crucifixion by Piero Francesco Fiorentino on the staircase, the magnificent cross-vaulted council hall and a small antechamber on the 1st floor giving a bird's-eye view of the piazza below.

From the **Palazzo Pretorio**, also from the 13th-century, thrusts the **Torre del Porcellino** (Piglet's Tower), so named because of the wild boar protruding from its upper section.

The **cathedral** (Piazza San Giovanni; admission free; 8am-12.30pm & 3-6pm) was built in the 12th and 13th centuries. Highlights include a small fresco, the *Procession of the Magi* by Benozzo Gozzoli, behind a terracotta nativity group, tucked away in the oratory at the beginning of the north aisle. Note too the exquisite 15th-century tabernacle by Mino da Fiesole that rises above the high altar. Just west of the cathedral, the 13th-century **baptistry** features a small marble font by Andrea Sansovino.

Nearby, the **Museo Diocesano d'Arte Sacra** (0588 8 62 90; Via Roma 1; admission incl Pinacoteca Comunale & Museo Etrusco Guaranacci €7; 9.30am-1pm & 3-6.30pm mid-Mar–Oct, 9am-1pm Nov–mid-Mar) merits a peek for its collection of ecclesiastical vestments, gold reliquaries and works by Andrea della Robbia and Rosso Fiorentino. The **Pinacoteca Comunale** (0588 8 75 80; Via dei Sarti 1; admission incl Museo Etrusco Guaranacci & Museo Diocesano d'Arte Sacra €7; 9am-7pm mid-Mar–Oct, 9am-2pm Nov–mid-Mar) houses a modest collection of local art.

MUSEO ETRUSCO GUARANACCI

All the exhibits at this, one of Italy's finest Etruscan **museums** (0588 8 63 47; Via Don Minzoni 15; admission incl Pinacoteca Comunale & Museo Diocesano d'Arte Sacra €7; 9am-7pm mid-Mar–Oct, 9am-2pm Nov–mid-Mar) were unearthed locally. They include a vast collection of some 600 funerary urns carved mainly from alabaster and tufa. The best examples (those dating from later periods) are on the 2nd and 3rd floors. Original touches are the Ombra della Sera bronze ex-voto, a strange, elongated nude figure that would fit harmoniously in any museum of modern art, and the urn of the Sposi, a terracotta rendering of an elderly couple, their faces depicted in portrait fashion rather than the usual stylised manner. It's well worth investing €3 in their audioguide.

MUSEO STORICO DELL'ALABASTRO
As befits a town that has hewn the rock from nearby quarries ever since Etruscan times, Volterra has its own alabaster **museum** (☎ 0558 8 68 68; Piazza XX Settembre 3; admission €2.60; ☽ 9am-7pm mid-Mar–Oct, 9am-1pm Nov–mid-Mar).

OTHER SIGHTS
On the city's northern edge is a **Roman theatre** (admission €2; ☽ 10am-6pm Sat & Sun), a well-preserved complex, complete with Roman bath house.

The **Fortezza Medicea**, built in the 14th century and altered by Lorenzo il Magnifico, is nowadays a prison. To its west is the pleasant **Parco Archeologico**; little of archaeological interest has survived but it's a good place for a picnic.

Le Balze, a deep eroded limestone ravine about 2km northwest of the city centre, has claimed several churches since the Middle Ages as the buildings tumbled into its deep gullies. A 14th-century monastery, perched close to the precipice, seems in danger of continuing the tradition.

Sleeping
Camping le Balze (☎ 0558 8 78 80; Via di Mandringa 15; person/tent/car €6/4/2; ☽ Easter-Sep; ☒) The closest camp site to town has a pool and sits right on Le Balze.

Ostello della Gioventù (☎ /fax 0588 8 55 77; Via del Poggetto; dm €11; ☽ Jun-Sep) Large and airy, if ramshackled, this privately run hostel is the cheapest deal around – but don't expect much of the food.

Seminario di Sant'Andrea (☎ 0588 8 60 28; fax 0588 9 07 91; Viale Vittorio Veneto 2; d with/without bathroom €36/28) This active church retreat (there are still eight priests in residence) is a peaceful place with vaulted ceilings and 60 large, clean rooms. Open to all comers, it's a mere 600m or so from Piazza dei Priori.

Albergo Etruria (☎ /fax 0588 8 73 77; Via Giacomo Matteotti 32; s/d with bathroom €46/67) Here's a pleasant, cosy family hotel. Look for the remains of an Etruscan wall upstairs in this 18th-century building and savour the fine views from the roof garden – a real garden with lawns and bushes.

Albergo Nazionale (☎ 0588 8 62 84; Via dei Marchesi 11; s/d/tr €50/68/80) The Nazionale is a little overpriced for what are quite small rooms. It counts DH Lawrence as a former guest.

Albergo Villa Nencini (☎ 0588 8 63 86; www .villanencini.it; Borgo S. Stefano 55; s/d with breakfast €60/80; ⓟ ☒) This is a tranquil family hotel a mere 200m beyond Porta S Francesco yet a world away from the town's summer bustle. Choose the original 17th-century mansion or the recently constructed new wing. With access to its restaurant and impressive collection of wines, you're fully self-sufficient.

Appartamenti l'Etrusca (☎ 0588 8 40 73; Via Porta all'Arco 37-41; apartments for 1/2/3 €40/69/72) Unlike most such rental companies, L'Etrusca is happy to take you on for even a single night. The exterior of this late Renaissance building gives no hint of all the mod cons within.

Eating
Da Beppino (☎ 0588 8 60 51; Via delle Prigioni 13; meals around €25; ☽ Thu-Tue) This place serves good pizza, baked in a wood-fired oven, pasta plus a range of Tuscan dishes. At lunchtime the tables outside are highly coveted.

Trattoria del Sacco Fiorentino (☎ 0588 8 85 37; Piazza XX Settembre 18; mains around €10; ☽ Thu-Tue) This modest little eatery serves up fine Tuscan food with a happy selection of local wines. Try the *coniglio in salsa di aglio e Vin Santo* (rabbit simmered in a garlic dessertwine sauce) or choose from one of the several dishes of wild boar.

Osteria dei Poeti (☎ 0588 8 60 29; Via Giacomo Matteotti 55; tourist menu €12, mains €8-16; ☽ Fri-Wed) Extremely popular with locals, this is another typical Tuscan rustic restaurant, all pleasing mellow brickwork and golden arches. The cuisine, however, is delightfully out of the ordinary. For starters opt for the *antipasto del poeta* (€10), a rich assortment of canapes, cheeses and cold cuts.

Pizzeria da Nanni (☎ 0588 18 40 87; Via delle Pregioni 40; pizzas €5.25-6.25; ☽ Mon-Sat) A hole-in-the-wall-plus – plus being the excellent pizzas that Nanni spatulas from his oven, while sustaining a vivid line in backchat, notably with his long-suffering wife. You can eat at low wooden tables or take away.

Entertainment
Web & Wine (☎ 0588 8 15 31; Via Porta all'Arco 11/13; ☽ 7am-1am Tue-Sun) is one of those splendid places that defy guidebook characterisation. It's at once Internet Point (web access €5 per hour), a stylish *enoteca* (it carries a

good selection of tipples), a snack stop and hip designer café (it's not everyday you step across a glass floor, revealing underlit Etruscan remains and a 5m deep Renaissance grain silo).

Getting There & Around

Driving and parking inside the walled town are more or less prohibited. Park in one of the designated parking areas around the circumference, most of which are free. Your best bet is at the four-storey paying underground car park at Piazza Martiri della Libertà, which is also the bus terminal.

The tourist office carries timetables. **CPT buses** (☎ 0588 8 61 86) connect the town with Saline (€1.55, 20 minutes, over 15 per day) and its train station. From Saline, 9km to the southwest, there are bus connections for Pisa (€5.05), and Cecina (€3.20). For San Gimignano (€4.30), Siena (€4.45) and Florence (€6.45), change at Colle di Val d'Elsa (€2.25).

From Saline's small train station, a train runs to Cecina, on the Rome–Pisa line. By car, take the SS68, which runs between Cecina and Colle di Val d'Elsa.

ABBAZIA DI SAN GALGANO

About 20km southwest of Siena on the SS73 is the ruined 13th-century **San Galgano abbey** (☎ 0577 75 67 00; admission free; ✆ 8am-7.30pm), one of the country's finest Gothic buildings in its day and now a ruin that still speaks strongly of its past. The monks of this former Cistercian abbey were among Tuscany's most powerful, forming the judiciary and acting as accountants for the *comuni* of Volterra and Siena. They presided over disputes between the cities, played a significant role in the construction of the cathedral in Siena and built themselves an opulent church.

By the 16th century the monks' wealth and importance had declined and the church had deteriorated to the point of ruin. The walls remain standing but the roof collapsed long ago. The Accademia Musicale Chigiana in Siena sponsors concerts at the abbey during summer (see p496).

On a hill overlooking the abbey is the tiny, round Romanesque **Cappella di Monte Siepi**, built for local soldier and saint, San Galgano, who lived his last years here as a hermit. A real-life 'sword in the stone'

is under glass in the floor of the chapel, plunged there, legend has it, by San Galgano to indicate his renunciation of worldly life.

The bus service between Siena and Massa Marittima passes nearby to the southwest.

LE CRETE

Southeast of Siena, this area of rolling clay hills is a feast of classic Tuscan images – bare ridges topped by a solitary cypress tree, hills silhouetted one against another as they fade into the misty distance, their gently undulating flanks scored here and there by steep ravines, as scarred and eroded as any cowboy badlands. Hire a car or bike in Florence or Siena and spend a few days pottering around Le Crete, a Tuscan dialect word meaning clay. Should you be around on a Sunday in summer, book your passage on the Treno Natura (see Tours, pp495–6).

Staggering scenery apart, one of Le Crete's main draws is the **Abbazia di Monte Oliveto Maggiore** (☎ 0577 70 76 11; admission free; ✆ 9.15am-noon & 3.15-6pm Apr-Oct, to 5pm Nov-Mar), a 14th-century monastery, still home to around 40 monks. It's famous for the frescoes by Signorelli and Sodoma that decorate its Great Cloister, illustrating events in the life of the ascetic St Benedict. The embellishments on some of the pillars are among the earliest examples of 'grotesque' art, copied from decorations found in the then newly excavated Domus Aurea created by Nero in Rome.

MONTALCINO

pop 5100

A pretty town, perched high above the Orcia valley, Montalcino is best known for its wine, the Brunello. One of Italy's best reds, it has gained considerable international fame. There are plenty of wine cellars around town where you can taste and buy Brunello (a bottle costs a minimum of €20; we did say it was special!) as well as other local wines such as Rosso di Montalcino.

If you're a jazz-loving oenophile, you'll savour the town's annual *Jazz & Wine* festival, held in the 2nd and 3rd weeks of July.

The **tourist office** (☎ 0577 84 93 31; www.prolocomontalcino.it; Costa Municipio 1; ✆ 10am-1pm & 5.40pm Apr-Oct, Tue-Sun Nov-Mar) is just off Piazza del Popolo, the main square. It can reserve accommodation and tell you which vineyards are open for tastings.

The **Museo Civico e Diocesano d'Arte Sacra** (☎ 0577 84 60 14; Via Ricasoli; adult/child €4.50/3; ☼ 10am-1pm & 2-5.40pm Tue-Sun) occupies a former monastery. Off Piazza Sant'Agostino, it's also the site of Montalcino's future archaeological museum. In addition to canvases by Andrea di Bartolo, Sano di Pietro and others, it has a fine collection of painted wooden sculptures by the Sienese school.

The 14th-century **fortress** (☎ 0577 84 92 11; admission free; ☼ 9am-8pm Apr-Oct, to 6pm Nov-Mar) dominates the town. Within its fortifications is an *enoteca* where you can both sample and buy the local wines. To walk the ramparts (though the view is almost as magnificent as from the courtyard) buy a ticket (adult/child €3/1.50) at the bar.

Sleeping & Eating

Il Giardino (☎ /fax 0577 84 82 57; Piazza Cavour 4; s/d €45/53) All 10 rooms are doubles and excellent value at this friendly, family-run, two-star hotel. Occupying a venerable building overlooking Piazza Cavour, its decor has a distinct 1970s feel.

Hotel Il Giglio (☎ 0577 84 81 67; hotelgiglio@tin.it; Via S Saloni 5; s/d/tr €53/75/85; P) Montalcino's oldest hotel, substantially renovated in 2002, is another family concern. Rooms have comfortable wrought-iron beds – each gilded with a painted *giglio*, a lily – and all doubles have panoramic views. Il Giglio also has a small **annexe** (s/d/tr €42/58/68), just up the street, which also has an **apartment** (2-/3-/4-people €63/72/80).

Both hotels have restaurants that are well worth a visit.

Hotel Vecchia Oliviera (☎ 0577 84 60 28; www.vecchiaoliviera.com; Angolo Via Landi 1; d with breakfast from €165; P ☼ ☎) Just beside the Porta Cerbaia, this is a wonderful top-end choice. Tastefully furnished and tranquil – it's at the very limit of the town – each of its rooms is individually decorated.

Trattoria Sciame (☎ 0577 84 80 17; Via Ricasoli 9; meals about €20; ☼ Wed-Mon) Small and popular, this unassuming place serves good home-made pasta dishes and straightforward, well-prepared meals.

Taverna Il Grappolo Blu (☎ 0577 84 71 50; Scale di Via Moglio 1; meals €17-25; ☼ Sat-Thu) The chef here does ingenious things with local ingredients – try their juicy *coniglio al brunello* (rabbit cooked in Brunello wine; €11).

Getting There & Away

Regular Tra-in buses (€3, 1½ hours, six daily) run to/from Siena.

ABBAZIA DI SANT'ANTIMO

This strikingly beautiful isolated Romanesque **church** (☎ 0577 83 56 59; Castelnuovo dell'Abate; admission free; ☼ 10.30am-12.30pm & 3-6.30pm Mon-Sat, 9am-10.30am & 3-6pm Sun) lies just below the village of Castelnuovo dell'Abate. Set in a broad valley it's best visited in the morning, when the sun streaming through the east windows creates an almost surreal atmosphere.

The exterior, built in pale travertine stone, is simple but for the stone carvings of the bell tower and apse windows, which include a Madonna and Child and various fantastical animals. Inside take time to study the capitals of the columns lining the nave, especially the one representing Daniel in the lion's den (second on the right as you enter).

The sacristy, with its monochrome frescoes depicting the life of St Benedict, is in what is known as the Carolingian Chapel, probably constructed in the 8th century.

Three daily buses connect Montalcino with the village of Castelnuovo dell'Abate (€1, 15 minutes). From here, it's an easy walk to the church.

PIENZA

pop 2250

Pienza, too often dismissed as Montepulciano's little sister, is well worth visiting for its own sake.

Orientation & Information

The heart of this tiny village is Piazza Pio II. The **tourist office** (☎ /fax 0578 74 90 71; ☼ 9.30am-1pm & 3-6.30pm) is on this central square, within the Palazzo Comunale.

Sights

Spin 360° and you've already taken in Pienza's major monuments. Gems of the Renaissance and all constructed between 1459 and 1462 (a mere three years), they're grouped around Piazza Pio II. This, the main square, is named after the Pope who, in one of the earliest examples of town planning, commissioned the architect Bernardo Rossellino to rebuild the little town of his birth.

TUSCANY (TOSCANA)

Highlights of the **cathedral** (⏲ 8.30am-1pm & 2-6pm) with its ober Renaissance facade are a superb marble tabernacle by Rossellino and five altarpieces, all by Sienese artists.

The **Palazzo Piccolomini** (☎ 0578 74 85 03; adult/child €3/2; ⏲ 10am-12.30pm & 3-6pm Tue-Sun), Pio II's country residence and considered Rossellino's masterpiece, can be visited by guided tour (last tours 11.45am and 5.25pm). From its loggia, there's a spectacular panorama over the Val d'Orcia below.

Palazzo Borgia, also called the Palazzo Vescovile, houses Pienza' small **Museo Diocesano** (☎ 0578 74 99 05; adult/child €4.10/2.60; ⏲ 10am-1pm & 3-6pm Wed-Mon mid-Mar–Oct, Sat & Sun Nov–mid-Mar) with paintings of the Sienese school and some striking 16th-century Flemish tapestries.

Almost a monument in its own right, the pungent **Bottega del Naturalista** (Corso Rossellino 16) has a truly mouthwatering choice of cheeses, in particular the renowned *Pecorino di Pienza*, made from ewe's milk.

MONTEPULCIANO
pop 13,900

Set atop a narrow ridge of volcanic rock, Montepulciano looks down upon the superb countryside of the Valdichiana. Producer of some of the region's finest wines, including the highly reputed *Vino Nobile*, it's the perfect place to spend a quiet day or two.

Orientation & Information

The town sheers off to left and right from the main street, which rises equally steeply southwards from Porta al Prato to the Piazza Grande. The 750m walk may leave you breathless but, bordered by the town's finest buildings, is well worth the exercise.

The **tourist office** (☎ 0578 75 73 41; proloco mp@bccmp.com; Via di Gracciano nel Corso 59) is decidedly short on information but can reserve accommodation without charge.

The **Strada del Vino Nobile Information Office** (☎ 0578 71 74 84; www.stradavinonobile.it; Piazza Grande 7; ⏲ 10am-1.30pm & 3-7pm Mon-Sat Mar-Oct, 10am-1pm & 3-6.30pm Mon-Fri, 10am-1pm Sat Nov-Feb) is much more user friendly. It books accommodation, plus restaurants, and, between May and October, arranges wine tours and tastings.

Sights

Most of the main sights are clustered around Piazza Grande, although the town's streets

harbour a wealth of *palazzi*, fine buildings and churches (unfortunately, the sheer number of churches and dearth of priests means that many remain locked up).

From the **Porta al Prato**, designed by the Florentine Antonio da Sangallo the Elder, walk southwards along Via di Gracciano nel Corso. At the upper end of Piazza Savonarola is the **Colonna del Marzocca**, erected in 1511 to confirm Montepulciano's allegiance to Florence. The splendid stone lion, squat as a pussycat atop this column is, in fact, a copy; the original is in the Museo Civico.

Among several noble residences lining the main street is the **Palazzo Bucelli** at No 73, the lower courses of whose facade are recycled Etruscan and Latin inscriptions and reliefs. The **Palazzo Cocconi**, nearly opposite at No. 70, was also designed by Sangallo.

Continuing up Via di Gracciano nel Corso, you'll find Michelozzo's **Chiesa di Sant' Agostino** (Piazza Michelozzo; admission free; ⏲ 9am-noon & 3-6pm) with its lunette above the entrance holding a terracotta Madonna and Child, John the Baptist and St Augustine. Opposite, a medieval **tower house** is topped by the town clock and the bizarre figure of **Pulcinella** (Punch of Punch & Judy fame), which strikes the hours.

Continue up the hill and turn right at the Loggia di Mercato, first left into Via del Poggiolo, then left again into Via Ricci. In the Gothic Palazzo Neri-Orselli is the **Museo Civico** (☎ 0578 71 73 00; Via Ricci 10; adult/child €4.15/2.60; ⏲ 10am-7pm Aug, 10am-1pm & 3-6pm Tue-Sun Sep-Jul). The small collection features terracotta reliefs by the della Robbia family and Gothic and Renaissance paintings.

Over **Piazza Grande**, the town's highest point, broods the austere **Palazzo Comunale** (☎ 0578 71 22 43; admission free; ⏲ 9.30am-12.30pm Mon-Fri). Built in the 13th-century Gothic style and remodelled in the 15th century by Michelozzo, it still functions as the town hall. From the top of its **tower** (admission €1.50) on a clear day, you can see as far as the Monti Sibillini to the east and the Gran Sasso to the southeast.

Opposite is the **Palazzo Contucci**, and its extensive wine cellar **Cantine Contucci** (☎ 0578 75 70 06; ⏲ 8am-12.30pm & 2.30-6.30pm), open for visiting and sampling.

The 16th-century **cathedral** (Piazza Grande, admission free; ⏲ 9am-noon & 4-6pm) has an unfinished facade. Above the high altar is a lovely triptych by Taddeo da Bartolo depicting the Assumption.

To the west and prominent in the valley below is domed **Chiesa di San Biagio** (Via di San Biagio; admission free; 🕑 9am-12.30pm & 3-7pm, to 6pm winter), a fine Renaissance church built by Antonio da Sangallo the Elder, its highlight an impressive marble altar piece.

Sleeping & Eating

Bellavista (🕾 0578 75 73 48, 🕾 0347 823 23 14; bellavista@bccmp.com; Via Ricci 25; d €49-60) Nearly all of the 10 double rooms in this house, warmly recommended by readers, have fantastic views. No-one else lives here so phone ahead in order to be met and given a key (if you've omitted this stage, there's a phone in the entrance lobby from where you can call).

Meublé Il Riccio (🕾 0578 75 77 13; www.ilriccio.net; Via Talosa 21; s/d €75/85; P 🚫 🚭 🖳) This gorgeous tiny hotel, with only six bedrooms, occupies a Renaissance *palazzo* just off Piazza Grande. Rooms all have a safe and fridge, the communal areas are a delight in themselves, as is the porticoed courtyard.

Albergo Il Marzocco (🕾 0578 75 72 62; fax 0578 75 75 30; Piazza Savonarola 18; s/d €60/88) This 16th-century building has been run as a hotel by the same family for over a century. Rooms are large, comfortable and well furnished. Ask for a room with balcony.

Trattoria Diva e Maceo (🕾 0578 71 69 51; Via di Gracciano nel Corso 90; meals €20-28; 🕑 Wed-Mon) This simple, uncomplicated trattoria, a favourite with locals, carries a good selection of wines of the area.

Borgo Buio (🕾 0578 71 74 97; Via Borgo Buio 10; meals €30-40; 🕑 Sat-Thu) The menu could scarcely be shorter. But then the quality of the cuisine could hardly be higher at this rustic, low-lit restaurant that also functions as an *enoteca*.

La Grotta (🕾 0578 75 74 79; Via San Biagio 2; meals €40-50; 🕑 Thu-Tue) Opposite the church of San Bagio, La Grotta is Montepulciano's finest restaurant. Inside this 15th-century building the dining is appropriately elegant while the tables in the garden are tempting for a summer lunch.

Caffè Poliziano (🕾 0578 75 86 15; Via di Voltaia nel Corso 27) Established as a café in 1868, Poliziano has had a chequered past – at times café-cabaret, minicinema, grocery and, once again since 1990, an elegant café,

lovingly restored to its original form by the current owners.

Getting There & Around

Tra-in runs five buses daily travelling between Montepulciano and Siena (€4.35, 1¾ hours) via Pienza. Regular LFE buses connect with Chiusi (€2, 50 minutes, half-hourly).

Chiusi-Chianciano Terme (rather than Stazione di Montepulciano, which has very infrequent services), 10km southeast, is the most convenient train station. It's on the main Rome–Florence line and buses for Montepulciano meet each train.

By car, take the Chianciano Terme exit from the A1 and follow the SS146 for the 19km trip to Montepulciano. Cars are banned from the town centre. There are car parks near the Porta al Prato, from where minibuses weave their way to Piazza Grande.

SOUTHERN TUSCANY

MAREMMA & ETRUSCAN SITES

The area known as the Maremma extends along the Tuscan coast from just north of Grosseto to the southern border with Lazio, embracing the Parco Regionale della Maremma and Monte Argentario. Inland are the extraordinary hill towns of Sovana, Sorana and Pitigliano, each rich in Etruscan remains.

Parco Regionale della Maremma

This spectacular **nature park** (admission €6-8) includes the Monti dell'Uccellina, which drop to a magnificent stretch of unspoiled coastline. The friendly **visitors centre** (🕾 0564 40 70 98; 🕑 7.30am-6.30pm Jul-Sep, 8.30am-2pm Oct–mid-Mar, 8.30am-4pm mid-Mar–Jun) is in Alberese, on the park's northern edge. Access is limited to nine signed walking trails, varying from 2.5km to 12km. Entry (by ticket bought at the visitors centre) varies depending upon whether a minibus transports you to your chosen route. Depending upon your trail, you stand a chance of spotting deer, wild boar, foxes and hawks.

The **Centro Turismo Equestre Il Rialto** (🕾 0564 40 71 02), 300m north of the visitors centre, offers canoe and horse-riding outings and also rents mountain bikes.

Between July and September, when the park gets very crowded, a couple of routes are closed and two more can only be undertaken in a guided group because of the high risk of forest fire.

Terme di Saturnia

This **thermal spa** (☎ 0564 60 08 00; www.terme disaturnia.it; admission Mon-Fri €12.50, Sat & Sun €14) is about 2.5km south of the village of Saturnia. You can happily spend a whole day dunking yourself in the hot pools and signing on for some of the ancillary activities such as – we swear it – 'mud therapy on water bed' or 'micromassage of the gums'.

On the other hand, if you just fancy a quick dip, head left down a dirt lane some 500m south of the Terme turnoff and have fun for free in the warm waters that cascade down a gentle waterfall.

Pitigliano

Pitigliano seems to grow organically from the high rocky outcrop that towers over the surrounding countryside. The main monuments are within a stone's throw of Piazza Garibaldi, where you'll find the **tourist office** (☎ 0564 61 71 11; Piazza Garibaldi 51; ⏰ 9.30am-1pm Tue-Sat, 3.30-7pm Mon-Sat).

Just off the square are an imposing 16th-century viaduct and the 13th-century **Palazzo Orsini** (☎ 0564 61 44 19; adult/child €3/2; ⏰ 10am-1pm & 3pm-dusk Tue-Sun). Its small museum houses a cluttered collection of ecclesiastical objects, assembled, you get the feeling, as much to fill the vast empty space as for any aesthetic merit.

Opposite the *palazzo* is the altogether more organised **Museo Etrusco** (adult/child €2.60/1.55; ⏰ 10am-1pm & 4-7pm Tue-Sun Apr-Sep, 10am-1pm & 3-6pm Tue-Sun Oct-Mar). Descriptive panels, however, are only in Italian.

Only the tall bell tower remains as a reminder of the Romanesque original of Pitigliano's **cathedral** with its baroque facade and unexceptional interior. The town's medieval lanes and steep alleys are a delight to wander, particularly around the small **Ghetto** quarter. The tiny, richly adorned **synagogue** (☎ 0339 701 30 20, ☎ 0564 61 60 06; Vicolo Manin; adult/child €2.50/1.50; ⏰ 10am-12.30pm & 4-7pm Tue-Fri, 4-7pm Sun, hours can vary) fell into disrepair with the demise of Pitigliano's Jewish community at the end of WWII and was practically rebuilt from scratch in 1995.

A visit includes the synagogue, a small Museum of Jewish Culture and the old bakery, butcher's and dyeing shops.

There are some spectacular walks around Pitigliano. The base of the rocky outcrop is stippled with Etruscan tomb caves carved into the soft tufa, many of them recycled as storage cellars. You can follow the Vie Cave, indicated on the tourist office map, then continue along a signed trail (about 6km) to Sovana. For more challenging hikes, ask for their free 1:50,000 map *Dolce Maremma*.

Talking of things *dolce* (sweet), pick up a stick of two of *sfratto*, a gorgeously sticky local confection of honey and walnuts from **Il Forno** (Via Roma 16). Counterbalance the sweetness with a glass or two of the town's excellent dryish Bianco di Pitigliano wine.

Albergo Guastini (☎ 0564 61 60 65; www.laltramaremma.it/guastini, Italian only; Piazza Petruccioli 16 & 34 s/d/tr €34/57/71; ⏰ mid-Feb–mid-Jan) Pitigliano's only hotel is particularly friendly and welcoming. Perched on the edge of the cliff face, many of its rooms have marvellous views. Its highly regarded **restaurant** (meals around €25) also merits a visit.

Osteria Il Tufo Allegro (☎ 0564 61 61 92; Vico della Costituzione 2; meals around €20; ⏰ lunch & dinner Thu-Mon, dinner Tue & Wed) Just off Via Roma, the aromas emanating from its kitchen should be enough to draw you into the cavernous chamber, carved out of the tufa rock foundations.

GETTING AROUND

Rama buses (☎ 0564 61 60 40) leave from the train station at Grosseto for Pitigliano (€5, two hours, four daily). They also connect Pitigliano with Sorano (€2.15, 15 minutes, four daily) and Sovana (€2.10, 30 minutes, two daily).

Sovana

Sovana is really little more than a one-street village of butterscotch sandstone – but, gosh, it's pretty. The **tourist office** (☎ 0564 61 40 74, ⏰ 9am-1pm & 3-7pm mid-Mar–Oct, 10am-1pm & 2-5pm Nov–mid-Mar) is in the Palazzetto dell'Archivio on the main Piazza del Pretorio.

The **Chiesa di Santa Maria** (Piazza del Pretorio ⏰ 10am-7pm) is a starkly simple Romanesque church with a magnificent 9th-century ciborium, or canopy, in white marble, one of the last remaining pre-Romanesque works

Spare some time for Florence's **Duomo** (p441) – 150 years in the making!

Check out Florence's grand **Palazzo Vecchio** (p447)

DALLAS STRIBLEY

JEFFREY N. BECOM

Explore the local village life of **Lucca** (p474), but stay away from that crazy Italian traffic!

JON DAVISON

Brave the climb up the slightly less leaning tower of **Pisa** (p479)

NICK TAPP

Drink in the spectacular views, or embark on some breathtaking walks in the **Apuane Alps** (p478)

Stay in one of the picturesque villas studding the hills around rural **Tuscany** (p433)

JEFF CAN

BETHUNE CARMICHAEL

Superb Tuscan **wines** from the local winemaker ...

DAVID TOMLINSON

... to the finished **product** (p464)

left in Tuscany and some rich Renaissance frescoes.

Walk east along Via del Duomo to reach the imposing Gothic-Romanesque **cathedral** (🕐 10am-1pm & 2.30-7pm Apr-Sep, to 6pm Oct-Mar). Although largely rebuilt in the 12th and 13th centuries, the original construction dates back to the 9th century. The striking portal on the north wall is composed of fragments from this earlier building – or, as some would maintain, from a pagan temple. Sovana was the birthplace of Pope Gregory VII; at this eastern end of the village are a cluster of medieval mansions and the remains of a fortress that belonged to his family.

Within the **Necropoli di Sovana** (admission €5.50; 🕐 9am-7pm summer, 10am-5pm winter), 1.5km south of the village, are Tuscany's most significant Etruscan tombs, the grandest of which is the **Tomba Ildebranda**, the only surviving temple-style tomb.

The area is famous for its *vie cave*, deep, narrow sunken walkways carved into the rock by the Etruscans. Drovers' roads? Ceremonial passages? Trenches for safe movement in time of attack? To this day no-one knows their purpose. The most spectacular can be as much as 20m deep and run for up to 1km. You'll pass a typical one 500m west of Pitigliano on the road to Sovana.

Taverna Etrusca (☎ 0564 61 61 83; fax 0564 61 41 93; Piazza Pretorio 16; s or d €49-80; 🕐 Feb-Dec) This three-star hotel has simple but attractive rooms with stripped wooden floors and a good restaurant downstairs.

Albergo Scilla (☎ 0564 61 65 31; www.scilla -sovana.it; Via R Siviero 1-3; d €92; ⓟ 🐾) Tastefully renovated, Scilla has comfortable rooms with attractive wrought-iron beds, mosaics in the bathrooms and a quiet garden. Across the road you can enjoy fine fare at its attractively glassed-in restaurant, **Ristorante dei Merli** (meals around €35; 🕐 Tue-Sun).

Sorano

Sorano is something of the poor relation of the three hill towns. High on a rocky spur, its houses, many nowadays unoccupied, seem to huddle together in an effort not to shove one another off their precarious perch. The town's main attraction is the partly renovated **Fortezza Orsini** (Piazza Cairoli; admission €2; 🕐 10am-1pm & 3-7pm Apr-Sep, 10am-1pm & 2-5pm Fri-Sun Oct-Mar).

A few kilometres out of Sorano, on the road to Sovana, is the **Necropoli di San Rocco**, another Etruscan burial area.

MONTE ARGENTARIO

Once an island but long ago linked to the mainland by a couple of extensive sand bars, rugged Monte Argentario is popular with holidaying Romans and almost neglected by the rest of the world.

Orbetello

Sitting in the middle of three isthmuses, Orbetello speaks of Mediterranean lands further west. The main attraction is its **cathedral** (Piazza della Repubblica; 🕐 9am-noon & 3-6pm), which has retained its 14th-century Gothic facade despite being remodelled in the Spanish style in the 16th century. Other reminders of the Spanish garrison that was stationed in the city for nigh on 150 years include the Viceroy's residence on Piazza Eroe dei Due Mondi, the fort and city walls, parts of which are the original Etruscan fortification.

Porto Santo Stefano

This one-time fishing port, like its neighbour, Port'Ercole, just along the coast, now devotes itself in the main to tourism, much of it up-market.

Information

Tourist office (☎ 0564 81 42 08; 1st fl, Lungomare dei Navigatori 33; 🕐 9am-1pm & 4-7pm Mon-Sat Apr-Sep, mornings only Oct-Mar) Scheduled to move to premises in Piazzale Sant'Andrea.

Zéb (☎ 0564 81 48 60; Viale Marconi 23; €4.20/hr; 🕐 9am-1pm & 4-8pm Mon-Sat, 10am-1pm Sun) Internet access.

ACTIVITIES

If you've wheels, follow signs for the Via Panoramica, a circular route offering great coastal views across to the hazy whaleback of the Isola de Giglio across the water. For another spectacular drive, take a right turn 6km east of Porto Santo Stefano, up the signed road leading to **Convento dei Frati Passionisti**, a convent with sensational views across to the mainland.

There are plenty of reasonable pebbly beaches, one of the most popular being the long strip of **Feniglia**, northeast of Port'Ercole.

Toremar and SRL sail regularly (€6.20 one way) to the **Isola de Giglio**, Tuscany's second-largest island after Elba, which makes a pleasant day trip.

SLEEPING

Accommodation on the peninsula is generally expensive.

Camping Feniglia (☎ 0564 83 10 90; camping.fe niglia@virgilio.it; per person/tent €8/7; ☺ Apr-Oct) In Feniglia, about 1.5km north of Port'Ercole, this camp site is just 50m from the sea. Trouble is, most of it is occupied by permanently planted caravans and family tents.

Pensione Weekend (☎ /fax 0564 81 25 80; Via Martiri d'Ungheria 3; d with bathroom from €51.65) This little gem is excellent value for money. Ask for the top room, No 19, which has its own terrace and wonderful sea views. The friendly, polyglot owner can give you a voucher entitling you to a 20% reduction at Lo Sfizio (see below).

Albergo Belvedere (☎ /fax 0564 81 26 34; Via del Fortino 51; s/d with breakfast €70/95) This luxury complex, 1km east of the harbour, overlooks the water and has its own private beach.

Hotel Torre di Cala Piccola (☎ 0564 82 51 11; www.torredicalapiccola.com; Cala Piccola; s/d/tr with breakfast from €201/268/330; ☺ Apr-Oct; P ✕ ♒ 🖳) To leave the crowds in your wake and enjoy spectacular seascapes, take a bungalow at this self-contained complex, built around an old Spanish watchtower, 8km southwest of Porto Santo Stefano. A minibus transports you down the hillside to the hotel's private beach.

EATING

Porto Santo Stefano has a good selection of restaurants, most of them fairly pricey.

Lo Sfizio (☎ 0564 81 25 92; Lungomare dei Navigatori 26; pizzas from €5.50, meals €22-30; ☺ Wed-Mon) The decor, with its corny fish theme and bar of blinking lights doesn't do much for Lo Sfizio. What draws in diners are their very reasonably priced fish and seafood dishes and the friendly informality of its youthful staff.

Il Veliero (☎ 0564 81 22 26; Via Panoramica 149-151; meals €30-35; ☺ Tue-Sun Feb-Dec) Expect to find the freshest of fare from the sea on the menu of this excellent restaurant, high above the port – the owner's father runs a fish shop in town. It's a steep climb (head up the steps, guarded by a terracotta lion,

just above Pensione Weekend) but well worth the exertion – especially if you've reserved a table at their small terrace with its plunging view.

Trattoria Da Siro (☎ 0564 81 25 38; Corso Umberto 100; meals €30-35; ☺ Tue-Sun) Overlooking the waterfront, Da Siro also manages that same mix of well-prepared fish and seafood, spiced with an impressive seascape.

For a great view without paying panoramic prices, grab a pizza from **Pizzeria da Gigetto** (☎ 0564 81 44 95; Via del Molo 9) and munch it on their waterfront terrace, then finish off with an ice cream from **Bar Gelateria Chioda**, right next door.

Getting There & Away

Frequent **Rama buses** (☎ 0564 85 00 00) connect most towns on the Monte Argentario with downtown Orbetello (€1.50, 15 minutes) and continue to the train station. They also run to Grosseto (€3.25, one hour, up to five daily).

By car follow signs for Monte Argentario from the SS1, which connects Grosseto with Rome.

EASTERN TUSCANY

AREZZO
pop 92,300

Heavily bombed during WWII, Arezzo isn't one of Tuscany's prettiest cities. That said, the small medieval centre packs some inspiring highlights: the sloping Piazza Grande, the Pieve di Santa Maria and, of course, the five-star frescoes by Piero della Francesca in the Chiesa di San Francesco. The setting for much of Roberto Benigni's Oscar-winning film *Life is Beautiful*, it's well worth a visit, easily accomplished as a day trip from Florence.

Arezzo, in its time an important Etruscan town, was later absorbed into the Roman Empire. A free republic as early as the 10th century, it supported the Ghibelline cause in the violent battles between pope and emperor and was eventually subjugated by Florence in 1384. It's the birthplace of the Renaissance poet Petrarch, who popularised the sonnet format, penning his verses in both Latin and Italian.

Arezzo stages a huge and highly reputed antiques fair, pulling over 500 exhibitors, in

AREZZO

0 ———————— 200 m
0 ———————— 0.1 mi

INFORMATION
Tourist Office.................................1 A4

SIGHTS & ACTIVITIES   pp511–12
Casa di Petrarca..............................2 C3
Casa di Vasari................................3 B2
Cathedral......................................4 C2
Chiesa di San Domenico....................5 B2
Chiesa di San Francesco....................6 B3
Museo Archeologico.........................7 B4
Museo Statale d'Arte Medioevale e
   Moderna....................................8 B2

Palazzo della Fraternità dei Laici.........9 C3
Palazzo delle Logge Vasariane..........10 C3
Pieve di Santa Maria.......................11 C3
Roman Amphitheatre.......................12 B4

SLEEPING   p512
Cavaliere Palace Hotel.....................13 B3
Cecco..14 B4
La Terrazza...................................15 B3

EATING   pp512–13
Antica Trattoria da Guido.................16 B3
La Buca di San Francesco.................17 B3
La Torre di Gnicche........................18 C3
Ristorante Vasari...........................19 C3
Trattoria Lancia dell'Oro.................20 C3

TRANSPORT   p513
Bus Station..................................21 A3

TUSCANY (TOSCANA)

the Piazza Grande and surrounding streets on the first Saturday and Sunday of every month.

Orientation
From the train station on the southern edge of the walled city, pedestrianised Corso Italia leads to the Piazza Grande, Arezzo's nucleus.

Information
Hospital (Via A de Gasperi) Outside the city walls.
Police station (☎ 0575 2 36 00; Via Fra Guittone)
Post office (Via Guido Monaco 34)
Tourist office (☎ /fax 0575 2 08 39; Piazza della Repubblica 28; ☺ 9am-1pm & 3-6.30pm Mon-Sat, 9am-1pm Sun) Beside the train station.

Sights
CHIESA DI SAN FRANCESCO
The apse of this 14th-century **church** (Piazza San Francesco; ☺ 8.30am-noon & 2-6.30pm) houses one of the greatest works of Italian art, Piero della Francesca's fresco cycle of the *Legend of the True Cross*. This masterpiece, painted between 1452 and 1466, relates in 10 episodes the story of Christ's death. You can get some sense of the frescoes from beyond the cordon in front of the altar but to really appreciate them up close you need to plan ahead for a **visit with audio guide** (reservations ☎ 0575 90 04 04; www.pierodellafrancesca.it; admission €5; every 30 mins 9am-7pm Mon-Sat, 1-6pm Sun Apr-Sep, 9am-6pm Mon-Sat, 1-5.30pm Sun Oct-Mar). Since only 25 people are allowed in every half-hour, it's

essential to pre-book. The ticket office is to the right of the church's main entrance.

PIEVE DI SANTA MARIA

This 12th-century **church** (Corso Italia; ☯ 8am-1pm & 3-6.30pm) has a magnificent Romanesque arcaded facade, in form reminiscent of the cathedral at Pisa, yet without the glorious marble facing. Over the central doorway are lively carved reliefs, representing the months of the year. The 14th-century bell tower with its 40 windows is something of an emblem for the city. The monochrome of the interior's warm, grey stone is relieved by Pietro Lorenzetti's fine polyptych, *Madonna and Saints*, beneath the semidome of the apse.

PIAZZA GRANDE & AROUND

The galleries of the **Palazzo delle Logge Vasariane**, completed in 1573, overlook this sloping piazza. The **Palazzo della Fraternità dei Laici**, in the northwest corner, was started in 1375 in the Gothic style and finished after the onset of the Renaissance. Via dei Pileati leads to the **Casa di Petrarca** (☎ 0575 2 47 00; Via dell'Orto 28; admission free; ☯ 10am-noon Mon-Sat & 3-5pm Mon-Fri), the former home of the poet, which contains a small museum and the Accademia Petrarca.

THE CATHEDRAL

Arezzo's **cathedral** (Via Ricasoli; ☯ 7am-12.30pm & 3-6.30pm) was started in the 13th century yet not completed until well into the 15th. At the entrance to the north transept, an exquisite small fresco of *Mary Magdalene* by Piero della Francesca is dwarfed in size, but not beauty, by the rich marble reliefs of the tomb of Bishop Guido Tarlati.

CHIESA DI SAN DOMENICO & AROUND

The short detour to the **Chiesa di San Domenico** (Piazza San Domenico; ☯ 9am-1pm & 3.30-7pm) is a must in order to see its haunting *Crucifixion*, one of Cimabue's earliest works, painted around 1265, which rears above the main altar. To the west, the **Casa di Vasari** (☎ 0575 40 90 40; Via XX Settembre 55; adult/child €2/1; ☯ 9am-7pm Mon & Wed-Sat, 9am-1pm Sun) was built and sumptuously decorated by the architect himself. The gardens have been recreated in geometrical Renaissance style.

Down the hill, the **Museo Statale d'Arte Medioevale e Moderna** (☎ 0575 40 90 50; Via San Lorentino 8; adult/child €2/1; ☯ 8.30am-7pm Tue-Sun) houses works by local artists, including Luca Signorelli and Vasari, spanning the 13th to 18th centuries.

MUSEO ARCHEOLOGICO & ROMAN AMPHITHEATRE

East of the train station, the **museum** (☎ 0575 2 08 82; Via Margaritone 10; admission €4; ☯ 8.30am-7.30pm) is in a convent overlooking the remains of the **Roman amphitheatre**. It houses an interesting collection of Etruscan and Roman artefacts, including locally produced craftwork.

Sleeping

Villa Severi (☎ 0575 29 90 47; www.peterpan.it; Via F Redi 13; dm/d €15/35; ☯ Apr-Sep) This non-HI youth hostel is out of town in a wonderfully restored and spacious villa overlooking the countryside.

La Terrazza (☎ 0575 2 83 87; la_terrazza@tiscali.it; Via Guido Monaco 25; s/d with bathroom & breakfast €30/45) La Terrazza is excellent value. Essentially a couple of stylish apartments with five rooms, it's so new they hadn't even got the sign up when we passed. There's a kitchen for guest use. Go down the passage beside Blockbuster and up to the 5th floor.

La Toscana (☎ /fax 0575 2 16 92; Via M Perennio 56; s/d €31/47) A little away from the action, La Toscana is also great value. Rooms are bright and clean as a new pin and there's a small garden at the rear.

Cecco (☎ 0575 2 09 86; fax 0575 35 67 30; Corso Italia 215; s/d €40/60) This Soviet-style building, handy for the train station, has 42 soulless but clean and convenient rooms and a ground-floor restaurant.

Cavaliere Palace Hotel (☎ 0575 2 68 36; www.cavalierehotels.com; Via Madonna del Prato 83; s/d with breakfast €93/135; Ⓟ Ⓧ) Arezzo's top hotel will give you a friendly welcome and a comfortable experience in rooms that, while unexciting, are well soundproofed and more than adequate. Parking is €13.

Eating & Drinking

Antica Trattoria da Guido (☎ 0575 2 37 60; Via della Madonna del Prato 85; meals from €18; ☯ Mon-Sat) This economical trattoria serves up excellent, home-style food.

La Buca di San Francesco (☎ 0575 2 32 71; Via San Francesco 1; meals €25-30; ☯ Wed-Sun & lunch Mon) Facing the church of San Francesco, La

Buca di San Francesco's walls are decorated with alluring frescoes. It is one of the city's more enticing restaurants.

La Torre di Gnicche (☎ 0575 35 20 35; Piaggia San Martino 8; meals €25-30; Thu-Tue) This fine old *osteria* offers a rich variety of antipasti. Choose from their rich range of local *pecorino* cheeses, accompanied by a choice red from its extensive wine list.

Trattoria Lancia dell'Oro (☎ 0575 2 10 33; Piazza Grande 18-19; meals €30-35; ☽ Tue-Sun) The food is fine here and it's hard to beat its commanding position looking over Piazza Grande.

Ristorante Vasari (☎ 0575 2 19 45; Logge Vasariane 19; meals €30-35; ☽ Mon-Sat) Overlooking the piazza, this is a pleasant spot, whether for a fully-fledged meal or simply a relaxing drink.

Piazza Sant'Agostino comes alive each Tuesday, Thursday and Saturday with the city's **produce market**.

Getting There & Away

Bus services from Piazza della Repubblica include Cortona (€2.50, one hour, 11 daily), Sansepolcro (€3, one hour, hourly) and Siena (€4.60, 1½ hours, seven daily). For Florence, you're better off hopping on the train.

Arezzo is on the Florence–Rome train line with frequent services to Rome (€12 to €19.40, 1½ to 2½ hours) and Florence (€4.85, 35 minutes to 1½ hours). Arezzo is a few kilometres east of the A1 and the SS73 heads east to Sansepolcro.

SANSEPOLCRO
pop 15,750

Sansepolcro, like Arezzo, is an important stop on an itinerary of Piero della Francesca's work. Between the two, make a brief stop in **Monterchi** to see the artist's famous fresco **Madonna del Parto** (Pregnant Madonna; ☎ 0575 7 07 13; Via della Reglia 1; adult/child €3.10/1.80; ☽ 9am-1pm & 2-7pm Tue-Sun Apr-Sep, to 6pm Oct-Mar).

Sansepolcro is the birthplace of Piero della Francesca. The artist left town when quite young and returned in his 70s to work on his treatises, including his seminal *On Perspective in Painting*.

Sansepulcro has a small **tourist office** (☎ /fax 0575 74 05 36; Piazza Garibaldi 2; ☽ 9.30am-1pm & 3.30-6.30pm).

The **Museo Civico** (☎ 0575 73 22 18; Via Aggiunti 65; adult/child €6.20/3; ☽ 9am-1.30pm & 2.30-7.30pm

Jun-Sep, 9.30am-1pm & 2.30-6pm Oct-May), 100m west of the tourist office, is the pride of Sansepolcro and features Piero della Francesca's masterpiece, *Resurrection*.

Albergo Fiorentino (☎ 0575 74 03 50; fax 0575 74 03 70; Via L Pacioli 60; s/d/tr with breakfast €50/70/90, meals €20-25; Ⓟ) This exceptionally friendly central hotel also runs a highly recommended restaurant where the imaginative menu changes with the seasons (the cheerful owner tells you with pride that there'll never be a freezer in *his* kitchen). Parking is €9.

SITA buses link Sansepolcro with Arezzo (€3, one hour, hourly) and there are nine trains daily to Perugia (€4.20, 1¾ hours).

CORTONA
pop 22,500

Set high on a hillside cloaked in olive groves, Cortona offers stunning views across the Tuscan countryside. In the late 14th century it attracted the likes of Fra Angelico, who lived and worked here for about 10 years. Artists Luca Signorelli (1450–1523) and Pietro da Cortona (1596–1669) were both born here.

On the first Sunday in June, the town hosts the **Archidado games**, a crossbow competition. Among other festivities, contestants from the city's traditional neighbourhoods dress up in medieval garb to compete for the *verretta d'oro* (golden arrow).

Orientation & Information

Piazzale Garibaldi, on the southern edge of the walled city, is where buses arrive. From it there are sensational views across the plain to Lago di Trasimeno. From the piazzale, walk straight up Via Nazionale – about the only flat street in the whole town – to Piazza della Repubblica, the main square.

The **tourist office** (☎ 0575 63 03 52; Via Nazionale 42; ☽ 9am-1pm & 3-7pm Mon-Sat, 9am-1pm Sun May-Sep, 9am-1pm Mon-Sat & 3-6pm Mon-Tue & Thu-Fri Oct-Apr) is on Via Nazionale.

Sights

Start in Piazza della Repubblica with the **Palazzo Comunale**, built in the 13th century, renovated in the 16th and again, infelicitously, in the 19th. To the north is attractive **Piazza Signorelli** and, on its north side, 13th-century **Palazzo Casali**, whose rather plain facade was added in the 17th century. Inside is the **Museo dell'Accademia Etrusca** (☎ 0575 63 04 15; Piazza Signorelli 9; admission €4.20; ☼ 10am-7pm Tue-Sun Apr-Oct, to 5pm Nov-Mar), which displays substantial local Etruscan finds, including an elaborate 5th-century BC oil lamp.

Little is left of the Romanesque character of the **cathedral**, northwest of Piazza Signorelli. It was completely rebuilt late in the Renaissance and again, indifferently in the 18th century. Its true wealth lies in the **Museo Diocesano** (☎ 0575 6 28 30; Piazza del Duomo 1; adult/child €5/1; ☼ 10am-7pm Tue-Sun Apr-Oct, to 5pm Nov-Mar) in the former church of Gesù. Its fine collection includes works by Luca Signorelli and a beautiful *Annunciation* and *Madonna* by Fra Angelico.

At the eastern edge of the city centre is the 19th-century **Chiesa di Santa Margherita** (Piazza Santa Margherita; ☼ 7.30am-noon & 3-7pm), constructed around the Gothic tomb of Santa Margherita. Further up the hill is the 16th-century **Fortezza** (☎ 0575 60 37 93; adult/child €3/1.50; ☼ 10am-6pm May-Sep), built for the Medici by Laparelli, who designed the fortress city of Valletta in Malta.

Sleeping & Eating

Ostello San Marco (☎ /fax 0575 60 13 92; ostellocorto na@libero.it; Via Maffei 57; dm B&B €10.50; ☼ mid-Mar-mid-Oct) A short, steep walk east of Piazzale Garibaldi, this attractive HI hostel occupies a former monastery. Dinner, compared to the usual hostel fare, is quite a treat.

Hotel Italia (☎ 0575 63 02 54; hotel.italia@technet.it; Via Ghibellina 5; s with breakfast €65 d with breakfast €87-97) This three-star family hotel (just look at the array of cycling and football trophies in the lobby, amassed by father and son) is just off Piazza della Repubblica, in a 17th-century *palazzo*. Well-appointed rooms have traditional cross-beamed ceilings and tiled floors and the views from the roof terrace are breathtaking.

Hotel San Michele (☎ 0575 60 43 48; www.hotel sanmichele.net; Via Guelfa 15; s/d from with breakfast €83/134; P ☒) Also just off Piazza della Repubblica, this is Cortona's finest *albergo* (hotel). Primarily Renaissance but with elements dating from the 12th century and modifications over subsequent centuries, it's like a little history of Cortona in stone. Rooms are airy, spacious and exquisitely furnished. Parking is €11.

Trattoria Dardano (☎ 0575 60 19 44; Via Dardano 24; meals €15-20; ☼ Thu-Tue) This is just one of half a dozen reliable, no-nonsense trattorie that line Via Dardano.

Ristorante Tonino (☎ 0575 63 05 00; Piazza Garibaldi 1; meals about €30-35; ☼ closed Tue & Mon dinner) This restaurant specialises in antipasti and has magnificent views as far as Lago di Trasimeno from its summer terrace.

Pan e Vino (☎ 0575 63 10 10; Piazza Signorelli 27; ☼ Tue-Sun) This is a huge and hugely popular dining hall, right in the heart of town. For a quick snack of regional specialities, go for the *piatto del cacciatore*, the hunter's platter of wild boar, deer, goose and turkey. There are over 500 wines to choose from and most of the pasta (€5.20 to €6.25) is homemade.

Osteria del Teatro (☎ 0575 63 05 56; Via Maffei 2; meals €25-30; ☼ Thu-Tue) Although this Cortona classic has recently moved from its modest premises to a grand converted *palazzo*, the menu and the quality of its cuisine have remained constant. In summer, try their *ravioli ai fiori di zucca* (pumpkin-flower ravioli; €7.50).

There's a Saturday **market,** including farmers' products, in Piazza Signorelli.

Getting There & Around

For bicycle and scooter hire go to **Axofidis** (☎ /fax 0575 60 42 44; Piazza Signorelli 26). Bikes are €10 per day and scooters from €34.

From Piazzale Garibaldi, regular LFI buses connect the city with Arezzo (€2.50, one hour, 11 daily). The town is served by two train stations, both on the main Rome–Florence line. Camucia–Cortona, 6km away, is handier for Arezzo (€2, 20 minutes, hourly) and Florence (€6.30, two hours, hourly), while Terontola, about 5km south of Camucia-Cortona, is the best bet for Rome (€9, 2¼ hours, every two hours) and Perugia (€3.25, 40 minutes, 16 per day).

Shuttle buses, running at least hourly, connect Cortona's Piazzale Garibaldi with the stations at Camucia (€1, 15 minutes) and Terontola (€1.50, 20 minutes). The tourist office has schedules.

By car the city is on the north–south SS71 that runs to Arezzo. It's also close to the SS75 that connects Perugia to the A1.

Umbria & Marche

515

A magical landscape of mountains, dotted with olive trees, draped by grape vines, its summits studded with hilltowns, Umbria and Marche offers superb art and architectural treasures that reflect thousands of years of history and culture. The Etruscans and Romans left their mark as did the popes, who conquered the independent city *comuni* (town councils) that grew out of the Middle Ages and ruled a network of Papal States across central Italy.

Despite the network of roads, the area has not yet bowed to the tyranny of tourism and an astonishing amount of the landscape appears to have remained unchanged for centuries.

In Umbria, which gave birth to more than its fair share of saints and painters, the beautifully preserved medieval towns of Perugia and Gubbio, St Francis' home town of Assisi and the extraordinary cathedral in Orvieto seem to hover under the same hazy light that inspired the medieval masters. Marche has long stretches of coast, the still thriving port city of Ancona, beach resorts with medieval hearts, exquisite towns such as Macerata and the Renaissance jewel in its crown – Urbino, World Heritage Site and a pinnacle of Italian artistic achievement.

When you're tired of the Romans and bored by the Renaissance, head for the hills – to walk or wander, to glide or ski, ride bikes or horses along deserted tracks, climb rocks or spy rare species of bird and flower in the superbly maintained national parks.

HIGHLIGHTS

- **Modern Music**

  Swing to cool Umbria Jazz (p526) in the heat and heart of cultured Perugia

- **Latin Lazing**

  Sip anisette in the sun with the locals at historic Antico Caffe Meletti (p570) on Ascoli Piceno's glorious Piazza del Popolo

- **Gastronomic Guides**

  Take a taster's tour of wines, oils and truffles; try Lago Trasimeno (pp529–30)

- **Magnificence & Mysticism**

  Meditate on the intense blue pervading Giotto's stunning fresco-cycle in the Basilica di San Francesco in Assisi (pp533–4)

- **Gothic Splendour**

  Gasp at Orvieto's grand Gothic cathedral and Signorelli's prophetic frescoes (pp546–7)

- **Renaissance Man**

  Marvel at the Duke Motefeltro's Ideal City – Urbino – the Renaissance in microcosm (pp557–61)

POPULATION:	■ UMBRIA 840,482	■ MARCHE 1.4 MILLION
AREA:	■ UMBRIA 8,456 SQ KM	■ MARCHE 9,691 SQ KM

UMBRIA

Umbria is rich in natural beauties, but also in great and ancient civilisations, based on a system of independent towns, firmly established in antiquity. One of the few landlocked Italian regions, Umbria is *il cuore verde dell'Italia* (Italy's green heart). In spring the countryside is splashed with the red, pink, yellow, purple and blue of wild flowers and in summer it explodes with the vibrant yellow of the sunflowers harvested to make cooking oil. The rolling mountains of the Apennines in the north and east descend into hills, many capped by medieval towns, and eventually flatten out into lush valleys along the River Tiber.

Perugia, a short distance west and the region's capital, is a stunning city of great cultural traditions that enjoys a lively nightlife fired by the city's two universities, including a University for Foreigners. Spoleto's internationally renowned arts festival, the beauty of the Valnerina area in Umbria's southeast, and the Italian peninsula's largest lake, Lago Trasimeno, are all powerful attractions.

This is a land of tastes and flavours. Nature is fundamental to the Umbrian. Umbria even has a special department – l'Assessorato alle Politiche Agricole e Forestali della Regione dell'Umbria – to protect and promote products typical of the area. Umbrian cuisine is simple but delicious and based on locally grown ingredients, perfected over centuries. Tartufo (truffle) is used in sauces, pasta and rice dishes. Umbria's porcini (a type of mushroom) can be added to pasta or rice, but are best eaten as `steaks'. Orvieto's golden wines and the Sagrantino of Montefalco are respected throughout Europe.

HISTORY

Prehistoric remains, conserved largely in the Archaeological Museum in Perugia, reveal a human presence here as far back as the Palaeolithic and Neolithic periods. Around 1000 BC the Oscan-Umbrians swept into the region. Later, the Etruscans settled the western bank of the Tiber, founding the towns of Perugia and Orvieto, eventually creating 12 powerful city-states. But Umbrian civilisation really began to decline when it came into contact with Rome. By the end of the 2nd century BC Rome had all the towns of Umbria under its control and had initiated great public works such as the Via Flaminia, which joined Rome with the upper Adriatic. Remains of the Roman period can still be seen in Perugia, Assisi, Foligno, Gubbio, Todi, Spoleto, Narni and Terni.

The Saracen invasions of the 5th and 6th centuries ended Roman rule and caused the Umbrians to retreat to fortified medieval hill towns such as Gubbio and Todi.

With the barbarian hordes constantly at the gates, Christianity found fertile terrain and began to flourish. One of the first religious buildings, the church of Sant'Angelo, was built in Perugia between the 5th and 6th century.

St Benedict was born in Norcia in 480 and, a few centuries later, the Benedictine monastic order was founded at San Pietro in Perugia. From the first centuries of the late medieval period and throughout the 13th and 14th centuries, monasticism spread throughout Umbria.

By the 11th century the main cities in the region had become independent city-republics, united in a strong spiritual current generated by the religious movements. But domination by the Goths, the Lombards and various ruling families, as well as centuries of Guelph–Ghibelline rivalry, led to a long decline that left Umbria ripe for papal rule from the early 16th century.

In the 14th century, *signorie*, or dominions ruled by powerful noble families, flourished. But eventually all of Umbria came to be controlled as part of the Papal States, and remained so until the 19th century.

PARKS & RESERVES

Umbria shares the beautiful Monti Sibillini national park with Marche (see Monti Sibillini, p544). The park has various information centres, called Case del Parco. Check their website www.sibillini.net.

East of Gubbio, the Parco Regionale del Monte Cucco is dotted with caves, many of which can be explored, and is well set up for walkers, rock climbers and horse riders. For more information on the park visit http://parchi.provincia.perugia.it (Italian only) or www.parks.it.

GETTING AROUND

Extensive bus routes, state train services and the private Ferrovia Centrale Umbra

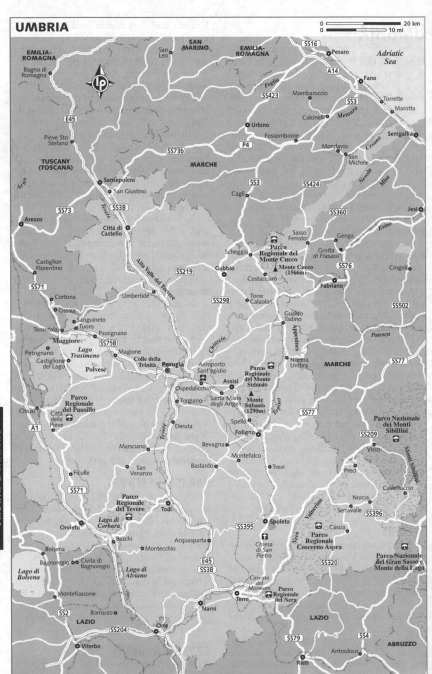

(Umbrian Central Railway) make most areas of the region easily accessible. For general Umbria transport information call ☎ 800 51 21 41 or check the website: www.umbriatrasporti.it. Perugia's local transport service is run by Azienda Perugino della Mobilità (APM). For information or complaints, call ☎ 800 51 21 41, free in Italy. For information and ticket sales for local and out of town services call: Stazione Fontivegge ☎ 075 506 78 91, Piazza dei Partigiani ☎ 075 506 78 94, Piazza Italia ☎ 075 506 78 92.

PERUGIA
pop 158,282

One of Italy's best-preserved medieval hill towns, Perugia has a lively and bloody past. The Umbrii tribe inhabited the surrounding area but it was the Etruscans who founded the city, which reached its zenith in the 6th century BC. It fell to the Romans in 310 BC and was given the name Perusia. During the Middle Ages the city was racked by the internal feuding of the Baglioni and Oddi families and violent wars against its neighbours. In the mid-13th century Perugia was home to the Flagellants, a curious sect who whipped themselves as a religious penance. In 1538 the city was incorporated into the Papal States under Pope Paul III, remaining under papal control for almost three centuries.

Perugia has a strong artistic and cultural tradition. Its university, founded in the 13th century, is one of the oldest in the world. It was home in the 15th century to fresco painters Bernardino Pinturicchio and his master Pietro Vannucci (known as Il Perugino), who was to teach Raphael, and also attracted the great Tuscan masters Fra Angelico and Piero della Francesca. The Università per Stranieri, established in 1925, offers courses in Italian and attracts thousands of students from all over the world.

Orientation

Like many towns found in Umbria, the historical centre of Perugia is a steep climb/drive up from the more modern sections of the town below. Several decades ago, city authorities began major excavations to provide four *scala mobile* (escalators). The main two are from Piazza Partigiani to Piazza Italia (☽ 6.30am to 1.45am) and from Via P

Pellini to Via dei Priori (☽ 6.45am to 1.15am). Much of the historical centre of town is closed to traffic. Drivers should follow the Centro signs and park in one of the well-signposted car parks, then take a escalator up to the city centre (for more details, see p527).

If you arrive at Perugia's main train station, Stazione Fontivegge, you'll need to catch a bus to Piazza Italia.

Intercity buses arrive and leave from Piazza dei Partigiani.

Old Perugia's main strip, Corso Vannucci, runs south to north from Piazza Italia through Piazza della Repubblica and finally ends in the heart of the old city at Piazza IV Novembre, bounded by the cathedral and the Palazzo dei Priori.

Information
BOOKSHOPS
Simonelli (Corso Vanucci 80)
Libreria Betti (Corso Vanucci 107)
Libreria Novecento (Via dei Priori)
Grimana Libri (book@grimanalibri.com; Piazza Fortebraccio 1c)

EMERGENCY
Police Station (☎ 075 506 21, emergencies ☎ 112, ☎ 113; Piazza dei Partigiani) Down the *scala mobile* that starts in the Rocca Paolina at Piazza Italia.
Posto di Guardia (Palazzo dei Priori, Corso Vanucci) In the historic centre.

INTERNET ACCESS
Expect to pay around €2 per hour, less for students or those with subscriptions.
Tele Net Internet Point (☎ 075 573 20 54; Via Bartolo 35; ☽ 9.30am-11pm, 2-11pm Sun)
Internet Point Perugia (Via A Fabretti; ☽ 9am-7pm)
Internet Point (☎ 0339 269 17 28; Via Ulisse Rocchi 4; ☽ 9am-7pm Mon-Fri, noon-2.30pm & 4-7pm Sat)
Internet Point (Corso Cavour 150)

LAUNDRY
Onda Blu (Corso dei Bersaglieri 4; ☽ 9am-10pm)

LEFT LUGGAGE
Train Station (€3 per bag for the 1st 12 hrs, €2 every 12 hrs thereafter)

MEDIA
The monthly publication *Viva Perugia – What, Where, When* (€0.80 from newsstands) lists events and useful information.

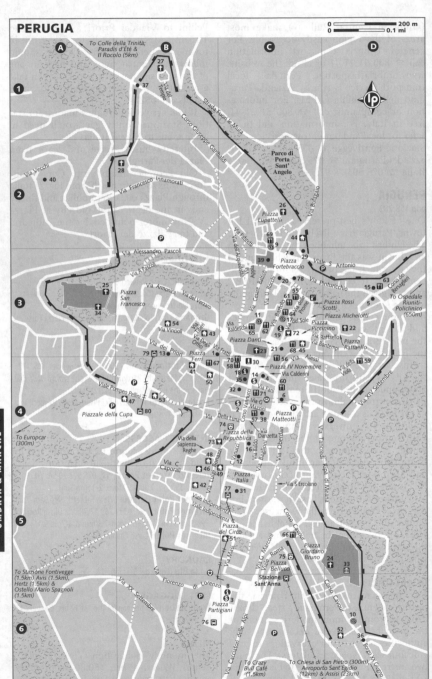

PERUGIA

MEDICAL SERVICES

Ospedale Riuniti-Policlinico (☎ 075 57 81; Viale Bonacci Brunamonti) Hospital northeast of the city centre.

Emergency Doctor (☎ 075 340 24)

Farmacia San Martino (Piazza Matteotti 26; ⊗ 24 hrs) Pharmacy.

MONEY

Currency Exchange Booth (Stazione Fontivegge; ⊗ 7.30am-8.30pm)

Bancomat (Piazza dei Partigiani) Next to the Infotourist point; accepts Visa, MasterCard, Cirrus cards.

Money Exchange Agency (Corso Vanucci) Just before Piazza IV Novembre; they may try to charge as much as 10% for exchange of a euro travellers cheque.

Banca del Umbria (Corso Vanucci 39) Currency-exchange machine.

POST

Main Post Office (Piazza Matteotti; ⊗ 8.10am-6pm Mon-Sat)

TOURIST INFORMATION

Tourist Office (☎ 075 572 33 27; Palazzo dei Priori, Piazza IV Novembre 3; ⊗ 8.30am-1.30pm & 3.30-6.30pm Mon-Sat, 9am-1pm Sun)

Welcome Point (☎ 075 573 08 08; www.periscopio.it; Via del Sole 6; ⊗ 9am-8pm) Privately run tourist information service. Information on private courses in cooking, Italian language, painting and ceramics.

InfoUmbria (☎ 075 57 57; www.infoumbria.com; Largo Cacciatori delle Alpi 3b) An independent tourist office. The staff, most of whom speak English, will make hotel reservations for free. They provide an excellent free map with sights, museums, hotels, services and activities in the area. Also offer excursions and guided tours in conjunction with **Guide in Umbria** (☎ 075 573 29 33; www.guideinumbria.com, Italian only).

TRAVEL AGENCIES

CIT (☎ 075 572 60 61; Corso Vannucci 2)

CTS (☎ 075 572 70 50; Via del Roscetto 21) Specialises in budget and student travel; sells ISIC cards to foreign students.

Sights
AROUND PIAZZA IV NOVEMBRE

The imposing facades identify Piazza IV Novembre as the old city's main square. The austere **cathedral** (☎ 075 572 38 32; Piazza IV Novembre; admission free; ⊗ 8am-noon & 4pm-sunset) was started in 1345 and completed in 1430. The magnificent 16th-century doorway, facing the Fontana Maggiore in the square, is by Galeazzo Alessi. On 30 July, you can witness the annual unveiling of the city's prized relic: the Virgin Mary's wedding ring, usually locked inside 15 boxes.

Fra Bevignate designed the **Fontana Maggiore** (Great Fountain) in 1278, but it was left to Nicola and Giovanni Pisano to execute the plan. The bas-relief statues represent scenes from the Old Testament and the 12 months of the year. A female figure on the upper basin (facing Corso Vannucci) bears fruit representing fertility, the city's symbol.

Most eye-catching of all in the square is the 13th-century Palazzo dei Priori. Long the seat of secular power in Perugia, it still houses the municipal offices. Annexed to these is the **Galleria Nazionale dell'Umbria** (☎ /fax 075 572 10 09; bookings & information ☎ 199 101 330; www.gallerianazionaledellumbria.it, Italian only; Corso Vannucci 19; adults/18-25 yr olds/EU citizens under 18 or over 65 €6.50/3.25/free; ☼ 8.30am-7.30pm), which contains a collection of paintings by Umbrian artists, including Pinturicchio and Perugino.

The vaulted **Sala dei Notari** (Notaries' Hall; ☎ 075 577 23 39; Palazzo dei Priori, Piazza IV Novembre 3; admission free; ☼ 9am-1pm & 3-7pm Tue-Sun year-round plus Mon Jun-Sep), on the 1st floor of the *palazzo*, was built in 1296 for the city council. Its walls are decorated with colourful frescoes. To reach it, climb the flight of steps from Piazza IV Novembre.

In the Corso Vannucci side of the *palazzo* is the **Collegio della Mercanzia** (Merchants' Guild; ☎ 075 573 03 66; Corso Vannucci 15; admission €1.05; ☼ 9am-1pm & 2.30-5.30pm Mon-Sat & 9am-1pm Sun & holidays Mar-Oct; 8am-2pm Tue, Thu & Fri; 8am-4.30pm Wed & Sat & 9am-1pm Sun & holidays Nov-Feb). This was the seat of the city's powerful Renaissance-era merchants who formed one of several *arti* (guilds) that still exist today. Reflecting their one-time prestige is the impressive early-15th-century carved-wood panelling inside.

A few doors up in the same building is the **Collegio del Cambio** (Exchange Guild; ☎ 075 572 85 99; Corso Vannucci 25; admission €2.60; ☼ 9am-12.30pm & 2.30-5.30pm Tue-Sun, 9am-12.30pm Sun Mar-Oct, 8am-2pm Tue-Sat, 9am-12.30pm Sun & holidays Nov-Feb), constructed in 1450 and decorated with magnificent frescoes by Perugino. A combined ticket for both guilds costs €3.10.

WEST OF CORSO VANNUCCI

West along Via dei Priori leads to Piazza San Francesco. The 15th-century **Oratorio di San Bernardino** has a facade decorated with bas-reliefs by early Renaissance sculptor Agostino di Duccio. Next to it is the ruined **Chiesa di San Francesco al Prato**, destroyed over the centuries by various natural disasters. It is used as an atmospheric location for concerts.

TOWARDS THE UNIVERSITÀ PER STRANIERI

You can venture down into 3rd-century BC **Pozzo Etrusco** (Etruscan Well; ☎ 075 573 36 69; Piazza

Danti 18; adult/child €1.80/1.05, incl Cappella di San Severo; ☼ 10.30am-1.30pm & 2.30-6.30pm Apr-Sep, 10.30am-1.30pm daily, 2.30-4.30pm Mon-Fri & 2.30-5.30pm Sat & Sun Oct-Mar). From here take Via del Sole to **Cappella di San Severo** (☎ 075 573 38 64; Piazza Raffaello; admission incl Pozzo Etrusco €1.80; ☼ 10.30am-1.30pm & 2.30-6.30pm Apr-Sep, 10.30am-1.30pm daily, 2.30-4.30pm Mon-Fri & 2.30-5.30pm Sat & Sun Oct-Mar), which is decorated with Raphael's *Trinity with Saints* (thought by many to be his first fresco) as well as frescoes by Perugino.

From the *cappella*, walk back to Piazza Michelotti and turn north into the small Piazza Rossi Scotti, from where you can enjoy a lovely view. Take the steps down to Piazza Fortebraccio and the Università per Stranieri, housed in the baroque Palazzo Gallenga. To the southeast is the **Arco d'Augusto**, one of the ancient city gates. Its lower section is Etruscan, dating from the 3rd century BC; the upper part is Roman and bears the inscription 'Augusta Perusia'.

AROUND CORSO GIUSEPPE GARIBALDI

North along Corso Giuseppe Garibaldi is the **Chiesa di Sant'Agostino** (Piazza Lupattelli; admission free; ☼ 8am-noon & 4pm-sunset), which houses a beautiful 16th-century choir by famed sculptor and architect Baccio d'Agnolo. Further north along the same thoroughfare, Via del Tempio branches off to the Romanesque **Chiesa di Sant'Angelo** (☎ 075 57 22 64; Via Sant'Angelo; admission free; ☼ 9.30am-noon & 3.30pm-sunset), which is said to stand on the site of an ancient temple. Corso Giuseppe Garibaldi continues through the 14th-century wall by way of the **Porta Sant'Angelo**. A 10-minute walk south of the gate along Via Zefferino Faina takes you to the former Chiesa di San Francesco delle Donne and the headquarters of the **Giuditta Brozzetti fabric company** (☎ 075 4 02 36; www.brozzetti.com; Via T Berardi 5; ☼ 9am-1pm & 3-6pm Mon-Fri), where you can purchase hand-woven linens.

SOUTH OF THE CENTRE

At the southern end of Corso Vannucci are the tiny **Giardini Carducci**, with lovely views of the countryside. The gardens stand atop a once-massive 16th-century fortress, now known as the **Rocca Paolina**, which was built by Pope Paul III. The ruins remain a symbol of defiance against oppression for Perugia's people. A series of *scala mobili* run through

UMBRIA & MARCHE

the Rocca so that you can wander through the ancient medieval streets.

Along Corso Cavour, the early-14th-century **Chiesa di San Domenico** (☎ 075 573 16 35; Piazza Giordano Bruno; admission free; ❧ 8am-noon & 4pm-sunset) is the city's largest church. Sadly, its Romanesque interior, lightened by the immense stained-glass windows, was replaced by austere Gothic fittings in the 16th century. Pope Benedict XI, who died in 1325 after eating poisoned figs, lies buried here. The adjoining convent is the home of the **Museo Archeologico Nazionale dell'Umbria** (☎ 075 57 27 14; Piazza Giordano Bruno 10; admission €2.05, free to EU citizens under 18 & over 65; ❧ 8.30am-7.30pm Tue-Sun, 2.30-7.30pm Mon), which has an excellent collection of Etruscan pieces and a section on prehistory.

Continuing along Corso Cavour, you come to the **Porta San Pietro**, the Roman gateway built to commemorate the addition of Rome to unified Italy. Keep going along Borgo XX Giugno to reach the 10th-century **Chiesa di San Pietro** (☎ 075 3 47 70; Borgo XX Giugno; admission free; ❧ 8am-noon & 4pm-sunset), entered through a frescoed doorway in the first courtyard. The interior is an incredible mix of gilt and marble and contains a *Pietà* by Perugino.

Courses

Università per Stranieri (☎ 075 574 61; www.unistrapg.it; Palazzo Gallenga, Piazza Fortebraccio 4, Perugia 06122) Offers courses in language, literature, history, art and other subjects. It runs degree courses as well as one-, two- and three-month intensive courses. The basic language course costs €233 per month.

Istituto Europea di Arti Operative (☎ 075 650 22; Via dei Priori 14) This arts institute runs courses in fashion, graphic design, industrial and interior design, drawing and painting.

Tours

InfoUmbria (see Tourist Information, p521) organises guided tours of the city, leaving the Fontana Maggiore each day, and other sightseeing tours on request.

Festivals & Events

Umbria Jazz (www.umbriajazz.com) attracts international performers for 10 days each July. Check with the tourist office for details. Tickets cost from €7.75 to €25.80 and can be bought in advance from **Associazione Umbria**

Jazz (☎ 075 573 24 32; info@umbriajazz.com; Piazza Danti 28) or from **Sala Borsa Merci** (☎ 075 573 02 71; Via Mazzini 9). InfoUmbria can also help.

Sagra Musicale Umbra, the Festival of Sacred Music, in September comprises classical and religious music. In January and June, the **Amici della Musica** (☎ 075 572 52 64; www.amicimusicapg.it, Italian only; Corso Vanucci 63) organise a series of classical music concerts in some of Perugia's most atmospheric venues.

For ballet lovers, there are performances in Perugia and around from January to April, organised by the **Fondazione Umbria Spettacolo** (☎ 075 572 67 64; www.ballettumbria.com, Italian only; Via Bontempi 25).

Sleeping

Perugia has a good selection of reasonably priced hotels, but it's a good idea to book during the Umbria Jazz festival or in August and May. The **Agenzia di Promozione Turistica dell'Umbria** (☎ 075 57 59 51; www.umbria2000.it, Italian only) publishes an excellent annually updated booklet of hotels with facilities and prices, available at most tourist offices in Umbria. The Perugia tourist office can give you a list of hotels and *agriturismo* (farm-stay) options in and around Perugia. For reservations and options for B&B, *agriturismo*, short-term apartments or rooms as well as hotels, InfoUmbria and Welcome Point/Il Periscopio are both helpful.

About 10 religious institutions offer accommodation in Perugia. Generally, rates are cheap and a stay must last at least two days. They have a curfew of 9pm (10pm in summer). The tourist office can provide a list.

BUDGET

Centro Internazionale per la Gioventù (☎ 075 572 28 80; www.ostello.perugia.it; Via Bontempi 13; dm €10.35, sheets €1.05; ❧ mid-Jan–mid-Dec) A non-HI; the common room has a fresco-decorated ceiling and the views from the terrace are fantastic. The large kitchen is another bonus but the midnight curfew is strictly enforced.

Ostella Internazionale per la Gioventù Mario Spagnoli (☎ 075 501 13 66; perugiahostel@tiscali.it; Via Cortonese 14, Pian di Massiano) A newish hostel near the stadium.

Albergo Anna (☎ /fax 075 573 63 04; www.albergoanna.it; Via dei Priori 48; s €26-30, with bathroom €36.15, d €42-46, with bathroom €50-62) This quirky little *pensione*, on the 2nd floor of a 17th-century town house, has basic rooms with

UMBRIA & MARCHE

THE AUTHOR'S CHOICE

Hotel Rosalba (☎ 075 572 82 85/06 26; Piazza del Circo 7; s/d with bathroom €50/65) Conveniently located on a quiet piazza just up the hill from the Piazza dei Partigiani bus station and close to the *scala mobile* that leads up to Piazza Italia. All rooms have been beautifully decorated and include modern facilities, including TV and direct-dial phones and there is parking available nearby. Highly recommended.

direct-dial phones and TV. Its major attraction is its kind and jovial owners – the place is full of paintings, drawings and period paraphernalia.

Pensione Paola (☎ 075 572 38 16; Via della Canapina 5; s/d/tr €31/48/60) This modern house is five minutes' walk from the town centre, in a quiet spot near a pretty park, down the *scala mobile* from Via dei Priori. There are eight rooms with shared bath and you have use of the kitchen.

Albergo Aurora (☎ /fax 075 572 48 19; Viale Indipendenza 21; s without bathroom €29-37, d with bathroom €62) This two-star hotel has a great view, though its rooms are nothing special.

Albergo Morlacchi (☎ 075 572 03 19; morlacchi@ tiscalinet.it; Via L Tiberi 2; s/d/tr with bathroom €38/60/70) This friendly, slightly ramshackle family-run two-star hotel is basic but popular, so book ahead. It's a bit hard to find – follow Via Vincioli right to the end and into Via degli Offici, then turn left.

The city has two camp sites, both in Colle della Trinità, 5km northwest of the city and reached by taking bus No 9 from Piazza Italia (ask the driver to drop you off at the Superal supermarket, from where it's a 300m walk to the camp sites).

Paradis d'Été (☎ 075 517 97 14, ☎ 338 267 82 71; Via del Mercato 29a; Colle della Trinità; site per person/tent €5.15/4.15) Camp site has 50 well-shaded sites with good facilities and a swimming pool.

Il Rocolo (☎ /fax 075 517 85 50; jnlagu@tin.it; Str Fontana Trinità 1n, Colle della Trinità; sites per person/tent €4.65/3.85; ⌛ 15 Jun–15 Sep) Il Rocolo has over 100 sites with a bit of shade and all the standard facilities.

MID-RANGE

Primavera Mini Hotel (☎ 075 572 16 57; www.pr imaveraminihotel.com; Via Vincioli 8; s/d €41/57) This

quiet cosy hotel in the centre of Perugia offers spectacular views and has been recently refurbished. All rooms include bathroom and direct-dial telephone. There's a bright communal TV room and coffee machine. Excellent value.

Hotel Signa (☎ /fax 075 572 41 80; www.hotel signa.com; Via del Grillo 9; s €42-48, d/tr €60/90, breakfast €6; 🖳) Situated in a quiet part of the old town, off Corso Cavour, close to the Archaeological Museum this attractive little family-run two-star hotel has been renovated to provide bright, clean rooms. There's a bar, breakfast room and pretty garden terrace.

Hotel Eden (☎ 075 572 81 02; fax 075 572 03 42; Via C Caporali 9; s/d €36/57) This place has 12 light-filled, beautifully clean rooms and a very nice communal area. Reception can be a bit grumpy but it's quiet and central.

Hotel Priori (☎ 075 572 33 78; hotelpriori@ perugia.com; Via Vermiglioli 3; s/d with bathroom €60/91) This pleasant hotel, another two-star, is in a great location on the corner of Via dei Priori. The rooms are large (rooms with three and four beds are available) and breakfast is served on a terrace.

Hotel Fortuna (☎ 075 572 28 45; fortuna@umbriah otels.com; Via Luigi Bonazzi 19; s without bathroom €35-68, s with bathroom €40-72, d €55-133; 🖳) This hotel has rooms with all the trimmings, price depends on season. It's very comfortable and there is even the odd fresco.

Hotel Europa (☎ 075 572 68 83; www.hoteleuropa -pg.com; Via P Pellini 19; r with bathroom €54-64) Two-star hotel down the scala mobile from the historic centre.

TOP END

Hotel la Rosetta (☎ /fax 075 572 08 41; www.perugia online.com/larosetta; Piazza Italia 19; s €77.50, d €117.50-168) This is one of Perugia's better hotels with exquisite individually designed rooms.

RENTAL ACCOMMODATION

If you plan to stay in Perugia for at least a month, **Atena Service** (☎ 075 573 29 92; www .atenaservice.com; Via del Bulagaio 38) can help you organise accommodation costing from €206.60 (for a single room in a group apartment) to €1030 (for four people) per month. The tourist offices listed earlier can also help you find holiday houses and *af-fittacamere* (rooms rented on a weekly or monthly basis).

Appartamenti Vacanze Signa Paolo (☎ 075 572 66 67; hotelsigna@tin.it; Borgo XX Giugno 38) The same people who run the Hotel Signa have some apartments for weekly rental. Prices range from €345 per week for two people to €390 per week for a three-person apartment, plus €25 for final cleanup. Linen and crockery for three people is provided. Credit cards are not accepted.

Eating
CAFÉS
Perugia offers many cafés where you can sit and chat as you snack without having to pay a huge supplement to get off your feet.

Sandri (Corso Vannucci 32) The city's finest café retains a medieval air. There's a delicious selection of pastries and it's popular for breakfast. There are stools for perching, but it can get a bit crowded.

Caffè di Perugia (Via Mazzini 10) Judged one of the best cafés in Italy by the prestigious Italian *Gambero Rosso* guide, this elegant place serves fine coffee, tea or hot chocolate and delicious pastries; in the *enacoteca* you can sample Italian and foreign vintage wine accompanied by cheeses, hors d'oeuvres and live piano music.

RESTAURANTS
Ristorante dal Mi'Cocco (☎ 075 573 25 11; Corso Giuseppe Garibaldi 12; set menu €13; ☼ Tue-Sun) This place, popular with students, serves up local specialities on rustic tables. The menu changes daily, so basically you eat what you're given.

Pizzeria Mediterranea (☎ 075 572 63 12; Piazza Piccinino 11/12; pizzas from €4.15; ☼ Wed-Mon) Pizza is made in the traditional wood-fired oven. This place is popular and can get fairly busy at times so be prepared to queue.

La Vecchia Perusia (☎ 075 572 59 00; Via Ulisse Rocchi 9; meals €20) Serves Umbrian dishes. It can fill quickly.

Ristorante Victoria (☎ 075 572 59 00; Piazza IV Novembre 7) An intimate little restaurant, serving local and national dishes and wines. You'll dine comfortably and pay around €15 for a glass of wine and a plate of risotto with cheese and truffles. A full meal costs a little more.

Cesarino (☎ 075 572 89 74; Piazza IV Novembre 4-5) One of the few places that still serves good Umbrian food, this attractive place is well situated opposite Fontana Maggiore.

The home-made pasta with porcini mushrooms or truffles are definitely worth trying at around €25.

Aladino (☎ 075 572 09 38; Via delle Prome 11; full meal €35; ☼ closed Mon & lunch) Near Porta Sole, this wine bar serves great antipasti, a large selection of wines and cheeses and gets top marks for atmosphere. Dishes include quail with Calvados and ginger.

Civico 25 (☎ 075 571 63 76; Via della Viola 25) Here you'll find great wines, local sausage and cheese, seasonal local dishes, great home-made desserts and a casual, young crowd. Expect to spend around €20 for the full Monty.

Osteria Tre Archi (☎ 075 572 60 41; Via Marconi 16; meals €18; ☼ Mon-Sat) Right beside the three arches not far from Piazza dei Partigiani, this simple and cheap place serves interesting, filling dishes and great home-made pasta.

Lumera (☎ 075 572 61 81; Corso dei Bersagliere 22; meals €25) In the heart of the university area, this little place serves antipasti like tzatziki and Arab bread along with chunks of cheese. Try the apple and nut tart.

Osteria del Bartolo (☎ 075 5731561; Via Bartolo 30; meals €40-60) This elegant place specialises in Umbrian dishes, but with its own creative input. It uses no cream or butter in its dishes which are based on truffles, oil, wild herbs, cereals, vegetables, pork and cheese.

Osteria del Gambero (☎ 075 573 54 61; Via Baldeschi 17; meals €30) One of the best restaurants in town, with great atmosphere and dishes that combine tradition and creativity. Menus include ravioli with potatoes, nuts and asparagus; lamb cooked in herbs, chocolate fondue with coffee sauce. Wines are excellent too.

Il Falchetto (☎ 075 573 17 75; Via Bartolo 20; meals €25-30) Serves Umbrian dishes and regional and national wines, in a friendly and warm atmosphere.

QUICK EATS
Papaia (Via dei Priori) Cheap and cheerful bar with a *sala interna* – smoking and non-smoking – where you can eat a plateful of delicious crepes – savoury (including one with truffles for around €4.70) and sweet, or other snacks.

SELF-CATERING
There is a **covered market** (☼ 7am-1.30pm Mon-Sat) down the stairs from Piazza Matteotti,

UMBRIA & MARCHE

where you can buy fresh produce, bread, cheese and meat.

Drinking

Bottega del Vino (☎ 075 571 61 81; Via del Sole 1; €25; ⊗ Mon-Sat) If you love jazz and good wine, this friendly place just around the corner from the Fontana Maggiore offers more than 400 local and foreign wines, excellent cheese, liver terrine and salads. Don't miss the home-made desserts and chocolate. Credit cards accepted.

If you just fancy a pint or two, there are a few good pubs to choose from. Here are some of the stayers.

Shamrock Pub (☎ 075 573 66 25; Piazza Danti 18) For a late-night drink pulled by an Irish lass with a Guinness certificate, follow the crowd down a dank but atmospheric alley towards the Pozzo Etrusco off Piazza Danti.

Joyce's Pub (☎ 075 573 46 95; Via Luigi Bonazzi 15; ⊗ noon-3pm & 7.30pm-2.30am Mon-Fri) Irish drinks, tasty bar snacks and televised sport.

Bar Centrale (Piazza IV Novembre 35) It's smoky inside and is a popular meeting place for students. Outside, under the umbrellas you can sit and watch the students on the cathedral steps.

Entertainment

You don't have to wander very far in search of Perugia's nightlife. Just stroll down to Piazza IV Novembre in the early evening. There's plenty of organised activity and it's easy to find live music. Keep an eye on the notice boards at the Università per Stranieri, which often organises free concerts and excursions and check the monthly *Viva Perugia* for up-to-date listings.

Contrappunto Jazz Club (☎ 075 573 36 67; Via Scortici 4) This is one of Perugia's best clubs, and regularly features top-notch Italian and international jazz musicians. The beer garden is a blessing on summer evenings.

Other clubs include: **Web Arena Music Café** (☎ 075 584 51 43; Via Vecchi 30g) Karaoke on Friday and Saturday nights, happy hour every Tuesday night when a medium beer will cost you just €2.50.

Crazy Bull Café (☎ 075 353 46; Via Palermo 21b) and the discobar **Velvet** (☎ 075 572 13 21; www.velvetfashioncafe.com; Via Roma 20) offer live music, usually disco.

Cinema Teatro del Pavone (☎ 075 572 49 11; cinegatti@libero.it; Corso Vanucci) shows films in the original language, many in English, every Monday.

Getting There & Away

AIR

Aeroporto Sant'Egidio (☎ 075 59 21 41, tickets ☎ 075 592 14 33), 12km east of the city, has flights to/from Milan with many international connections. An airbus runs between the airport and Piazza Italia (€2.60, 30 minutes, three per day) to coincide with flights.

BUS

Buses depart from Piazza dei Partigiani for Siena (€9, 1½ hours, twice daily, once on Sunday), and cities throughout Umbria, including Assisi (€2.80, 50 minutes, five daily), Gubbio (€4, one hour 10 minutes, 11 daily), Orvieto (€6, two hours, at 2pm Monday to Saturday) and Spoleto (€5, 1½ hours, at 2pm and 3.45pm Monday to Friday, at 2pm only on Saturday). Current bus routes, company details and timetables are listed in the monthly booklet *Viva Perugia – What, Where, When* (€0.80), available from newsstands, but it's best to check with the transport companies. The APM information office in the bus station will give you a free copy of the *orario* (timetable) for buses to Assisi, Gubbio, Todi, Deruta. Buy tickets at the APM office before you get on the bus, otherwise you will have to pay a supplement. For more information, call ☎ 800 51 21 41, or check their website www.apmperugia.it (Italian only).

The Perugia–Rome service is operated by **Sulga** (☎ 075 500 96 41, toll-free ☎ 800 099 661; www.sulga.it, Italian only); there are roughly five buses daily (€14.45, 2½ hours) in each direction and three continue on to Fiumicino airport (€18.10, 3¾ hours). Sulga also operates the Assisi–Perugia–Florence service (€10.35, two hours), which runs daily in each direction, leaving Perugia at 7.30am and Florence at 6.40pm

SENA (☎ 800 930 960, from cell phones ☎ 199 730 760; www.sena.it) operates a bus to Siena and Florence every Wednesday, leaving from the train station at noon, arriving Siena 1.15pm and Florence 2.15pm. The bus leaves Florence at 4pm, arrives Siena 5pm and Perugia 6.15pm.

SIMET (www.simetspa.it, Italian only) has buses to Siena, Florence, Livorno and Pisa.

Autolinea Ruocco (☎ 800 901 591) has a daily (except Wednesday) bus service from Perugia to Urbino (€10, leaving at 2pm, arriving 4pm, except Sunday when it leaves 6pm and arrives 8pm).

From mid-June to early September, there are regular connections between Perugia and the Adriatic Riviera, book at the Piazza Partigiani **APM office** (☎ 075 506 78 94).

CAR & MOTORCYCLE
From Rome, leave the A1 at the Orte exit and follow the sign for Perugia, which will take you to the SS3B-E45. From the north, exit the A1 at Valdichiana and take dual carriageway S75b for Perugia. The S75 to the east connects the city with Assisi. From the south or from Ancona, exit Motorway A14 Adriatic at Ancona Nord and follow the signs for Gubbio.

If you arrive in Perugia by car, follow the Centro signs up the hill to Piazza Italia. You can leave your car here in a metered parking spot (€1.55), either on the piazza or on the hill immediately preceding it. You are only allowed to stay for one hour, but on Sunday parking is free all day.

TRAIN
The main train station, **Stazione Fontivegge** (☎ 075 500 74 67; Piazza Vittorio Veneto), is a few kilometres west of the city centre and easily accessible by frequent buses from Piazza Italia. The ticket office is open between 6am-8pm, at other times you can buy from machines. For information on train timetables and connections call ☎ 848 88 808 between 7am and 9pm (not available from cell phones) or visit the Trenitalia website (www.trenitalia.com). There is also a train timetable posted at the bottom of the *scala mobile* just before Piazza dei Partigiani.

There are nine daily direct services to Rome (two to 2½ hours), including two fast Eurostar services (€17.50), otherwise change at Terontola (€3.25, 40 minutes, at 5.35am, 6.46am, 11.53am then every two hours) or Foligno (€2.15, 40 minutes, hourly). From Foligno you can reach Spoleto (55 minutes), Terni and Orte. Trains to Florence via Arezzo run about every two hours (€6-7, two hours) and connect with trains to Bologna and Milan. Other destinations and fares include Assisi (€1.60, 20 minutes, hourly), Spello (€1.95, 30 minutes, hourly), Arezzo (€3.80,

one hour 10 minutes, every two hours) To get to Orvieto (€6) is rather complicated, as you have to travel via Torontola and Chiusi, often with up to an hour's wait for a connection. The private **Ferrovia Centrale Umbra railway** (☎ 075 572 39 47) runs from Stazione Sant'Anna on Piazzale Bellucci and serves Deruta (€1.30, 20 minutes, seven daily), Sansepolcro (€3.80, one hour 20 minutes, 12 daily), Terni (€4.25, 1½ hours, hourly) and Todi (€2.80, one hour, hourly).

Getting Around
BUS
From Stazione Fontivegge, catch any bus heading for Piazza Italia. Tickets (€0.80, valid for 70 minutes from time they are validated) must be bought from a small kiosk in front of the station entrance, or from the newspaper shop inside. A 24-hour ticket will cost you €3, or if you're going to use buses frequently, you can buy 10 tickets for €7.20. There's another **APM** (☎ 800 51 21 41, ☎ 075 50 67 81; www.apmperugia.it) kiosk on Piazza Italia in front of Hotel Rossetti, where you can buy tickets from 7am. You can also buy tickets at *tabacchi*. If you buy tickets on the bus, you will have to pay a hefty supplement.

CAR & MOTORCYLE
Much of the historic city centre is closed to normal, nonresident traffic until 1pm, although tourists may drive to their hotels. Parking is permitted from 1pm to 10pm. There are supervised, fee-paying car parks at Piazza dei Partigiani (☹ 24 hours), Viale Pellini (☹ 6am to 2am), Mercato Coperto (Covered Market – ☹ 24 hours), Briglie-Ripa di Meana near Piazza Matteotti (☹ 6am to 2am), Piazza Antonio near the Cathedral (☹ 6am to 2am), Piazzale Europa near Tre Arche and S Anna Station (☹ 6am to 2am). There are free, unsupervised car parks at Piazzale del Bove in the Campo di Marte area, not far from the railway station and at Cupa (Via A Cecchi).

If you intend to use the car parks a lot, buy an *abbonamento* (unlimited parking ticket pass; cost per day/week €8.25/43.65), from the ticket office at the car park. There's an English-speaking number ☎ 075 573 25 06.

For further information on parking, phone ☎ 075 577 53 78. If you park illegally and return to find your car gone, chances are

UMBRIA & MARCHE

it has been towed away. Call the Deposito Veicoli Rimossi (☎ 075 577 53 75) to check; be prepared to pay around €103.30 to retrieve your car.

The following companies are recommended for local car hire:

Avis Stazione Fontivegge (☎ 075 575 000 95; Piazza Vittorio Veneto 7) Sant'Egidio Airport (☎ 075 692 93 46; fax 0756 92 97 96)

Hertz (☎ 075 500 24 39; Piazza Vittorio Veneto 4)

Europcar (☎ 075 573 17 04; fax 075 573 42 01) City (Via R Andreotto 7); airport (Sant'Egidio Airport)

Maggiore Stazione Fontivegge (☎ 075 500 74 99) Sant'Egidio Airport (☎ 075 692 92 76)

For scooter hire, there's **Scooty Rent** (☎ 075 572 07 10; cell ☎ 333 102 65 05; www.scootyrent.com; Via della Volpe), just off Via Pinturicchio, where you can hire scooters for any period from one hour to one month, starting from €6.

For a taxi, call ☎ 075 500 48 88.

TORGIANO

To really appreciate Umbria it's worth making a trip to Torgiano, south from Perugia, to discover the secrets of wine and olive oil production. Torgiano is famous throughout the world for its wine and you can expect the best in hospitality here. You'll also find one of Umbria's finest hotel restaurants, run by the Lungarotti family, whose passion for all things to do with wine led to the establishment of a museum of wine. If you're celebrating a five-star occasion, then you can eat, drink and be very merry and then bed down in great style and comfort.

Sights & Activities

Museo del Vino (☎ 075 988 02 00; Corso Vittorio Emanuele 11; admission €4, incl Museo dell'Olivo e dell'Olio €7; ☯ 9am-1pm & 3-7pm summer, 9am-1pm & 3-6pm winter) Established by the Lungarotti Foundation the museum traces the history of the production of wine in the region from Etruscan time. Displays of utensils, graphic art, wine containers and production techniques fill 20 rooms in the 16th-century *palazzo*. Guided tours in English can be arranged for groups but must be booked ahead. There are discounts for students or large groups. You can also visit the Lungarotti cellars, but bookings (☎ 075 988 661; fax 075 988 66 50) are necessary.

Museo dell'Olivo e dell'Olio (☎ 075 988 03 00; www.lungarotti.it; admission €4; ☯ 10am-1pm & 3-7pm summer, 10am-1pm & 3-6pm winter) With support from research institutes in Italy and abroad, the Lungarotti family helped organise this museum, which opened in 2000. Housed in a series of medieval houses, the museum traces the production cycle of the olive, outlines its biology, and documents the culture and use of olives and how they relate to the economy, the landscape, religion, medicine, diet, sport, crafts and traditions.

Festivals & Events

In the second half of November, the **Banco d'Assaggio dei Vini** – wine tasting demonstration – is an important event on the international calendar. For more details about this event, contact the Umbria Tourist Board in Perugia (p521).

Sleeping & Eating

Tre Vaselle (☎ 075 988 04 47; www.3vaselle.it; Via Garibaldi 48; s €105-145, d €129-245) This hotel and restaurant is run by the Lungarotti family and the ambience is warm and tasteful, while the superb rooms are delightful in every detail, with beautiful views from all angles. Food and service is of excellent quality. Try the *fiori di zucca farciti e gratinati con ricotta e timo*, or ravioli stuffed with ricotta and herbs with truffle sauce. For a full meal at the restaurant, expect to pay around €60.

DERUTA

pop 7400

About 15km south of Perugia, on the SS3B-E45 to Terni, Deruta is famed for its richly coloured and intensely patterned pottery. The Etruscans and Romans worked the clay around Deruta but it was not until the bright blue and yellow metallic-oxide majolica glazing technique was imported from Majorca in the 15th century that the ceramics industry took off.

Deruta is a good place to buy ceramics as prices are lower than in Perugia and other towns, but watch out for low-quality, mass-produced stuff.

You can get a taste for the genuine article at the **Museo della Ceramica** (☎ fax 075 971 10 00; Largo San Francesco; adult/under 6s €3/free, discounts for large groups or children 7-14; ☯ Wed-Mon 10.30am-1pm, 2.30-5pm Oct-Mar, 10.30am-1pm, 3-6pm Apr-Sep) in the former Franciscan convent. The history of the production of pottery in Deruta from the 14th century until the beginning of the 20th century is presented, along with an explanation of the development of the special glaze, including some splendid examples.

APM buses connect the town with Perugia (€1.95, 30 minutes, six daily) and it has a handful of hotels.

LAGO TRASIMENO

The fourth-largest lake in Italy, Lago Trasimeno offers swimming, fishing and other water sports. The surrounding area also offers some great opportunities to sample delicious local wines and produce.

In 217 BC this area witnessed one of the bloodiest battles in Roman history as Hannibal's Carthaginians ambushed and almost annihilated Roman army troops led by Consul Flaminius, killing 15,000 soldiers. The battlefield extended from Cortona and Ossaia (Place of Bones), in Tuscany, to the small town of Sanguineto (The Bloody), just north of the lake.

Passignano & Castiglione del Lago

This is a popular spot for holidaying Italians, so book accommodation in advance for the summer months. Castiglione del Lago, up on a chalky promontory on the lake's western side, is dotted with olive trees and dominated by a 14th-century fortress.

INFORMATION

Tourist Office (☎ 075 965 24 84; info@iat.castiglione -del-lago-pg.it; Piazza Mazzini 10, Castiglione del Lago; ☒ 8.30am-1pm & 3.30-7pm Mon-Sat & 9am-1pm Sun) Staff can advise on the many *agriturismo* options and good walking tracks in the area.

SIGHTS & ACTIVITIES

Many people visit this lake district to indulge in water sports, walking and horse riding. But many also go for the culinary delights. The locals are very proud of their excellent produce – most notably their high-quality DOC wines (see p71) and DOP olive oils. If you are interested in following the Strade del Vino (Wine Route) of the Colli del Trasimeno (Trasimeno Hill district), the **Associazione Strada del Vino Colli del Trasimeno** (☎ 075 58 29 41; www.montit rasimeno.umbria.it, Italian only; Comunità Montana, Via S Bonaventura 10, Perugia) produces a brochure with suggested itineraries. You can also pick up this brochure at the tourist office

in Castiglione del Lago. Look out, too, for the guide to local restaurants, *Trasimeno a Tavola,* which includes sample menus and price guides, also available from the tourist office.

The main specialities of the Trasimeno area are fish dishes, such as *regina in porchetta* – carp cooked in a wood oven; and *regamaccio,* a kind of soupy stew of the best varieties of local fish, cooked in olive oil, white wine and herbs.

Castiglione del Lago's attractions include the **Palazzo della Corgna** (☎ 075 965 82 10; Piazza Gramsci; admission incl Rocca del Leone €2.60; ☒ 10am-1pm & 4-7.30pm summer, 9.30am-4.30pm Sat & Sun winter), an ancient ducal palace. A covered passageway connects the palace with the 13th-century **Rocca del Leone**, an excellent example of medieval military architecture.

The lake's main inhabited island, **Isola Maggiore**, near Passignano, was reputedly a favourite with St Francis. The hilltop **Chiesa di San Michele Arcangelo** contains a Crucifixion painted by Bartolomeo Caporali around 1460. The island is famed for its lace and embroidery production and you can see examples in the **Museo del Merletto** (Lace Museum; ☎ 075 825 42 33; Via Gugliemi, near the port, Isola Maggiore; admission €2.60; ☒ 10am-1pm & 2.30-6pm).

Ask at one of the tourist offices for a booklet of walking and horse-riding tracks. Horse-riding centres include the **Poggio del Belveduto** (☎ 075 82 90 76; www.poggiodelbelveduto .it; Via San Donato 65, Loc Campori di Sopra in Passignano).

You can hire bicycles at these outlets: **Cicli Valentini** (☎ /fax 075 95 16 63; Via Firenze 68b, Castiglione del Lago)
Marinelli Ferrettini Fabio (☎ /fax 075 95 31 26; Via B Buozzi 26, Castiglione del Lago)
Eta Beta modelissmo (☎ 075 82 94 01; infor@etbeta modellismo.com; Via della Vittoria 58, Passignano)
Rognoni Brunello (☎ 075 82 92 39; Via Pompili 61, Passignano)

SLEEPING & EATING

For a full list of places to stay in this area, pick up a brochure from the local tourist office, check www.umbria2000.it or consult the Umbria Infotourist Map available from the **InfoUmbria office** (p519; ☎ 075 572 72 18, Perugia), where they will also help you make reservations.

Kursaal (☎ 075 82 80 85; www.camping.it/umbria/ kursaal; Viale Europa 41, Passignano; site per person/tent

UMBRIA & MARCHE

€6.20/8.25; ☿ Apr-Oct) This camp site is on the lake shore but there's not much privacy. There's also a three-star **hotel** (www.kursaalhotel.net; s with bathroom €62-70, d €76-86; ⚑).

Pensione del Pescatore (☎ 075 829 60 63; delpescatore@libero.it; Via San Bernardino 5, Passignano; s/d €28.50/47.50) This family-run *pensione* has 11 simple but appealing rooms above a charming local trattoria.

In Castiglione del Lago you can choose between lakeside camping or town centre luxury, or investigate some *agriturismo* options through the tourist offices listed earlier.

Listro (☎ 075 95 11 93; fax 965 82 00; Via Lungolago; site per person/tent €4.15/4.15; ☿ Apr-Sep) This camp site is on the lake shore and has about 100 pitches, various leisure activities (including table tennis and volleyball) and facilities for the disabled.

Hotel Miralago (☎ 075 95 11 57; www.hotel miralago.com; Piazza Mazzini 5; s €52-76, d €62-93; ☿ Apr-Oct) The Miralago is very central and top-floor rooms have magnificent lake views. There's also a good restaurant downstairs.

Acquario (☎ 075 965 24 32; www.castiglionedel lago.it/acquario; Via Vittoria Emanuele 69; r €24-30; ☿ Thu-Tue Apr-Oct, Thu-Mon Nov-Mar) This is a great place to try out the local carp *in porchetta*, fresh from the lake. The tagliatelle are great too. Credit cards are accepted.

Locanda del Principato (☎ 075 968 02 20; Via Badiali 34; meals €20-25; ☿ dinner Thu, Fri & Sat) The friendly proprietor of this little place will advise you what's hot today – porcini mushrooms, fresh truffles, cheeses.

On the island of Isola Maggiore try **Hotel Da Sauro** (☎ 075 82 61 68; fax 075 82 51 30; Via Guglielmi 1; s/d €60/65), a family-run establishment with just 10 rooms in a rustic stone building at the northern end of the village. The restaurant downstairs is very popular.

Getting There & Around
APM buses connect Perugia with Passignano (€2.60, one hour, five daily) and Castiglione del Lago (€4.15, one hour 20 minutes, eight daily). Passignano is also served by regular trains from Perugia (€1.95, 25 minutes, hourly) via Terontola (€1.30, 10 minutes, hourly), making it the most accessible part of the lake.

Castiglione del Lago is on the Florence–Rome train line, but the Intercity trains don't stop here and local trains are slow and stop at every station.

APM also operates a regular ferry service (☎ 075 82 71 57). The company has information offices on the waterfront at each town, where you can pick up a timetable. The return trip to Isola Maggiore from Passignano costs €5.15 and takes 20 minutes each way. Hourly ferries connect Passignano with Castiglione del Lago (€6.70 return, one hour).

TODI
pop 17,000
Originally an Etruscan frontier settlement, Todi ended up as a prosperous commune in the early Middle Ages – a prosperity reflected in the grandness of its central Piazza del Popolo. Set atop a craggy hill, it seems to have ignored the 21st century. Getting there by public transport can be quite a slog.

Information
Tourist Office (☎ 075 894 33 95; info@iat.todi.pg.it; Piazza Umberto I 6; ☿ 9am-1pm & 4-7pm Mon-Sat, 9.30am-12.30pm Sun, 3.30-6.30pm Mon-Sat winter)
Banco Populare di Todi (Piazza del Popolo 27)
Internet Access (Piazza Umberto 1/17)

Sights
The 13th-century **Palazzo del Capitano del Popolo** (☎ 075 895 62 16; Piazza del Popolo; admission €3.10; ☿ 10.30am-1pm & 2-6pm Apr-Aug, 10.30am-1pm & 2-5pm Tue-Sun Mar & Sep, 10.30-1pm, 2-4.30pm Tue-Sun Oct-Feb) features an elegant triple window and houses the city's recently restored *pinacoteca* (picture gallery) and archaeological museum. There's a room covered in frescoes which is devoted to ceramics and the collection also spills over into the 13th-century **Palazzo del Popolo**, which faces the square.

The **cathedral** (☎ 075 894 30 41; Piazza del Popolo; admission free; ☿ 8.30am-12.30pm & 2.30-6.30pm), at the northwestern end of the square, has a magnificent rose window and intricately decorated doorway. The 8th-century crypt is worth visiting for the inlaid wooden stalls in the chancel. Wander through Todi's medieval labyrinth and pop into some of the other churches, including the lofty **Tempio di San Fortunato** (Piazza Umberto 1; admission free; ☿ 9.30am-12.30pm & 3-6pm), with frescoes by Masolino da Panicale and the tomb of San Jacopone, Todi's beloved patron saint. Just outside the city walls is the late Renaissance **Chiesa di Santa Maria della Consolazione**, designed by Donato Bramante in 1508 but not completed until 99 years later.

Festivals & Events

The **Todi Festival**, held for 10 days each July/August, is a mixture of classical and jazz concerts, theatre, ballet and cinema.

Sleeping & Eating

Prices are fairly steep in the centre of town.

Villa Luisa (☎ 075 894 85 71; www.villaluisa.com; Via A Cortesi 147; s €50-75, d €70-104; 🖭) This place is well outside the city walls but it's set in its own park-like grounds.

Ristorante Umbria (☎ 075 89 42 737; Via Santa Bonaventura 13; meals €35) This restaurant, as its name suggests, serves local dishes. It's reasonably expensive but worth it for the view from the terrace.

Ristorante Cavour (☎ 075 894 37 30; Corso Cavour 21/23; meals €15.50) There's pizza and pasta and good views if you snaffle the right tables.

Te Moenga (☎ 075 894 50 22; liz@webparadisse.it; r per person €18-29, per week €110-176) This converted farmhouse, about 4km from Todi has been restored by an hospitable architect. A self-contained flat with self catering facilities is also available.

Getting There & Away

APM buses from Perugia (€4.75, 1½ hours, four daily) terminate in Piazza Jacopone, just south of Piazza del Popolo. Several other buses terminate in Piazza Consolazione (from here take city bus A or B or walk uphill 2km to the centre). There is one daily service to Orvieto (€4.15, 1½ hours) at 5.50am, which returns at 1.55pm.

Todi is on the **Ferrovia Centrale Umbra** (☎ 075 894 20 92) train line but the train station is inconveniently located 3km east of the town centre at Porte Rio in the valley below. City bus C runs there (€0.60, 20 minutes). By road, Todi is easily reached on the SS3B-E45, which runs between Perugia and Terni, or take the Orvieto turnoff from A1 Milano-Roma-Napoli.

ASSISI

pop 25,000

Despite the millions of tourists and pilgrims it attracts every year, the home town of St Francis remains a tranquil refuge. Since Roman times, its inhabitants have been aware of the

visual impact of their city, perched halfway up Monte Subasio (1290m).

St Francis was born here in 1182 and his spirit hovers over every aspect of the city's life. He renounced his father's wealth to pursue a life of chastity and poverty, founding the order of mendicant friars known as the Frati Minori (Order of Minors; they became known as the Franciscans after St Francis' death). The order attracted a huge following. With one of his disciples, St Clare (Santa Chiara), born in 1193, St Francis co-founded the Franciscans' female Ordine delle Clarisse (Order of the Poor Clares).

The Basilica di San Francesco is the city's, and possibly Umbria's, main draw, but do check before coming that your trip doesn't coincide with a religious celebration, when hotels are likely to be booked out, see p534.

Orientation

Piazza del Comune is the centre of Assisi. At the northwestern edge of this square, Via San Paolo and Via Portica both eventually lead to the Basilica di San Francesco. Via Portica also leads to the Porta San Pietro and the Piazzale dell'Unità d'Italia, where most intercity buses stop, although APM buses from smaller towns in the area terminate at Piazza Matteotti. The train station is 4km southwest of the city in Santa Maria degli Angeli (use the shuttle bus).

Information

EMERGENCY

Police Station (☎ 075 81 22 15; Piazza del Comune)

INTERNET ACCESS

Internet World ☎ /fax 075 81 23 27; Via S Gabriele dell'Addolorata 25; 🕑 11am-1pm & 3-9pm Mon-Sat, 4-9pm Sun)

MONEY

Cassa di Risparmio di Perugia (Piazza del Comune) ATM and currency-exchange machine.

POST

Post Office (🕑 8.10am-6.25pm Mon-Fri, 8.10am-1pm Sat & Sun) Just inside Porta San Pietro and next to Porta Nuova.

TOURIST INFORMATION

Tourist Information (☎ 075 81 25 34; info@ iat.assisi.pg.it; Via S Croce; 🕑 8am-6.30pm Mon-Sat, 10am-1pm & 2-5pm Sun summer, 8am-2pm & 3-6pm Mon-Sat, 9am-1pm Sun winter)

ASSISI

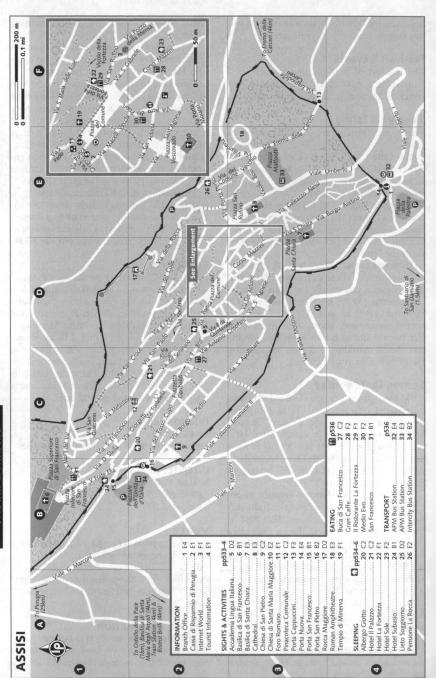

UMBRIA & MARCHE

INFORMATION
Branch Office....................................1	E4
Cassa di Risparmio di Perugia.........2	E1
Internet World...................................3	F1
Tourist Information............................4	E1

SIGHTS & ACTIVITIES pp533–4
Accademia Lingua Italiana................5	D2
Basilica di San Francesco.................6	B1
Basilica di Santa Chiara....................7	E3
Cathedral..8	B3
Chiesa di San Pietro.........................9	C2
Chiesa di Santa Maria Maggiore.....10	E2
Foro Romano....................................11	E1
Pinacoteca Comunale.......................12	C2
Porta Cappuccini...............................13	F3
Porta Nuova......................................14	E4
Porta San Francesco.........................15	B1
Porta San Pietro................................16	B2
Rocca Maggiore.................................17	D2
Roman Amphitheatre.......................18	E3
Tempio di Minerva...........................19	F1

SLEEPING pp534–6
Albergo Giotto..................................20	C2
Hotel Il Palazzo.................................21	C2
Hotel La Fortezza..............................22	F1
Hotel Sole..23	F2
Hotel Subasio...................................24	B1
Lieto Soggiorno................................25	D2
Pensione La Rocca...........................26	E2

EATING p536
Buca di San Francesco....................27	C2
Gran Caffe.......................................28	F2
Il Ristorante La Fortezza..................29	F1
Medio Evo.......................................30	F2
San Francesco..................................31	B1

TRANSPORT p536
APM Bus Station...............................32	E4
APM Bus Station...............................33	E3
Intercity Bus Station.........................34	B2

Branch Office (☎ 075 81 67 66; just outside Porta Nuova; ☻ Easter-Nov)

MEDICAL SERVICES
Ospedale di Assisi (☎ 075 813 92 27) About 1km southeast of Porta Nuova in Fuori Porta.

Sights
BASILICA DI SAN FRANCESCO
This **basilica** (☎ 075 81 90 01; Piazza di San Francesco; admission free; ☻ 7am-7pm Apr-Sep, to 5pm Oct-Mar), comprising two churches, one built on top of the other, suffered extensively when two earthquakes struck Umbria in September 1997. During restoration, new technology was used to make the basilica as earthquake-proof as possible.

The lower church was started in 1228, two years after St Francis' death. Two years later, work began on the upper church on a patch of land known as the Hill of Hell because death sentences were carried out there, but later renamed Paradise Hill.

The **upper church** (enter from Piazza Superiore di San Francesco) contains a sequence of 28 frescoes depicting the life of St Francis. It has long been claimed that these frescoes were painted by Giotto. However, the latest theories indicate at least three major artists were at work here: Pietro Cavallini, an (as yet) unidentified colleague and, it appears, a young Giotto – possibly the author of the final six scenes.

The **lower church** has walls also covered with frescoes. Those by Simone Martini showing the life of St Martin, in the first chapel on the left as you face the altar, are the highlights.

Along the left wall of the left transept are celebrated frescoes by Pietro Lorenzetti, depicting scenes of the Crucifixion and the life of St Francis. In the right transept are works by Cimabue and, below, more scenes by Simone Martini. A small chapel, reached by stairs on the right-hand side of the church, contains various mementos of St Francis' life, including his shirt and sandals, and fragments of his celebrated 'Canticle of the Creatures'. Descend the stairs in the middle of the lower church to reach the crypt containing St Francis' tomb. The crypt was rediscovered in 1818; the coffin had been hidden in the 15th century for fear of desecration.

ST FRANCIS OF ASSISI

Of all the Catholic saints, one of the best known and most loved is St Francis (San Francesco). Born in Assisi in 1182, the son of Pietro di Bernardone, a wealthy cloth merchant, St Francis' early years were a sharp contrast to the humble life that he became so famous for. A witty and reckless youth, he showed little aptitude for study, preferring instead to hang out with the other wealthy young men of Assisi, feasting, singing and squandering his father's money.

During a skirmish with the rival city of Perugia, Francis (aged about 20) was captured and held prisoner for a year. Laid low by an illness (probably contracted in a Perugian jail), he started to regret his idle youth and on recovery decided to become a knight, before a voice in a dream told him to go back to Assisi.

On his return, Francis took up an increasingly nomadic and eccentric lifestyle. But when he impulsively sold a large stock of his father's cloth to raise money to rebuild the church of St Damian, Bernardone's patience finally snapped. Fleeing his father's wrath, Francis hid in a cave, emerging a month later dirty, emaciated and the laughing stock of Assisi, who pelted him with mud and stones as he walked through town.

Exasperated, his father disinherited him and dragged him before the city council, whereupon Francis pointed out that since he had entered the service of God he was no longer under civil jurisdiction. Francis set forth into the hills behind Assisi, where he renounced all worldly goods, flung himself into charitable works and improvised hymns of praise.

It wasn't long before Francis started to build up a following and the foundations of the Franciscan order were established. In 1212 he co-founded a second order for women, called the Poor Clares. He continued with charitable works throughout his life and went on to preach in market places throughout Italy. In 1224, he received the stigmata on the hill at La Verna but by now the years of unremitting toil had taken their toll on his body. Weakened, exhausted and practically blind, St Francis died on the dirt floor of a small hut in Assisi on 3 October 1226 at the age of 44.

The basilica's **Tesoreria** (treasury; ☎ 075 81 90 01; Basilica di San Francesco; admission €1.55; ⏲ 9.30am-noon & 2.30-6.30pm Mon-Sat Apr-Oct), accessible from the lower church, contains a rich collection of relics given to the Franciscans over the years.

Dress rules are applied rigidly in both churches – absolutely no shorts, miniskirts or low-cut dresses.

OTHER SIGHTS

From the basilica, take Via San Francesco back to Piazza del Comune, once the site of a partially excavated **Foro Romano** (Roman Forum; ☎ 075 81 30 53, entrance Via Portica; admission €2.05; ⏲ 10am-1pm & 3-7pm, 2-5pm winter). The **Tempio di Minerva**, facing the same square, is now a church. Some of the shops on the piazza open their basements to reveal Roman ruins. The city's **Pinacoteca Comunale** (☎ 075 81 20 33; Via San Francesco 10; adult/child €2.05/1.55; ⏲ 10am-1pm & 3-7pm summer, 10am-1pm & 3-5pm winter) displays Umbrian Renaissance art and frescoes from Giotto's school.

Off Via San Antonio is Piazza Vescovado and the Romanesque **Chiesa di Santa Maria Maggiore**. South of Piazza del Comune, along Corso Mazzini and Via Santa Chiara, is the pink and white 13th-century Romanesque **Basilica di Santa Chiara** (☎ 075 81 22 82; Piazza Santa Chiara; admission free; ⏲ 7am-noon & 2-7pm), with a deteriorating but nonetheless striking facade. The body of Santa Chiara is in the crypt. Cast a glance at the Byzantine crucifix that is said to have told St Francis to re-establish the moral foundations of the Church. Part of the Basilica di Santa Chiara remains closed for repairs due to earthquake damage.

Northeast of the Basilica di Santa Chiara, the 13th-century Romanesque **cathedral** (☎ 075 81 60 16; Piazza San Rufino; admission free; ⏲ 7am-noon & 2-7pm), remodelled by Galeazzo Alessi in the 16th century, contains the font at which St Francis was baptised. Dominating the city is the massive 14th-century **Rocca Maggiore** (☎ 075 81 52 92; Via della Rocca; admission €2.60; ⏲ 10am-sunset), a hill fortress offering fabulous views over the valley and across to Perugia. Most of the fortress is closed for a long restoration that will see it converted into an immense art gallery.

A 30-minute walk south from Porta Nuova, the **Santuario di San Damiano** (☎ 075 81 22 73; admission free; ⏲ 10am-12.30pm & 2-6pm summer, 10am-12.30pm & 2-4pm winter) was built on the spot where the crucifix spoke to St Francis and where he wrote his 'Canticle of the Creatures'.

About 4km east of the city, reached via the Porta Cappuccini, is the **Eremo delle Carceri** (☎ 075 81 23 01; admission free; ⏲ 6.30am -7.15pm Easter-Nov, 6.30am-5.30pm winter), to which St Francis retreated after hearing the word of God. The *carceri* (prisons) are the caves that functioned as hermits' retreats for St Francis and his followers. In the valley southwest of the city, near the train station, the imposing **Basilica di Santa Maria degli Angeli** (☎ 075 8 05 11; Santa Maria degli Angeli; admission free; ⏲ 6.30am-8pm) was built around the first Franciscan monastery. St Francis died in its **Cappella del Transito** on 3 October 1226.

Activities

Local bookstores sell maps (€7.75) of walks on nearby Monte Subasio, produced by the Club Alpino Italiano (CAI). None of them are too demanding and the smattering of religious shrines and camp sites could make for an enjoyable two-day excursion.

Courses

Some people may favour Assisi over Perugia as a place to live and learn Italian. **Accademia Lingua Italiana** (☎ /fax 075 81 52 81; www.krenet.it/alia; Via Giotto 5) runs a variety of language and culture courses and can arrange accommodation.

Festivals & Events

The **Festa di San Francesco** falls on 3 and 4 October and is the main religious event of the city's calendar. **Easter week** is celebrated with processions and performances. The **Ars Nova Musica** festival, held from late August to mid-September, features local and national performers. The colourful **Festa di Calendimaggio** celebrates the coming of spring in perky medieval fashion and is normally held over several days at the end of the first week of May.

Sleeping

Assisi is well-appointed for tourists but in peak periods, such as Easter, August and September, and the Festa di San Francesco, you will need to book accommodation well in advance. Even outside these times, many of the hotels will often be full. The tourist office has a complete list of private rooms, religious institutions (of which there are 17), flats and *agriturismo* options in and around Assisi and they will help with bookings. Otherwise, keep an eye out for *camere* (rooms for rent) signs as you wander the streets. Outside Assisi, consider staying in Santa Maria degli Angeli, 4km southwest, near the train station with a half-hourly shuttle bus to the city centre. Petrignano is also on the bus route.

BUDGET

Pensione La Rocca (☎ /fax 075 81 22 84; www.hotel arocca.it; Via Porta Perlici 27; s/d €35/43) All 24 rooms at this popular one-star hotel have private baths, but try and nab one with sweeping views of the valley.

Hotel Sole (☎ 075 81 23 73/81 29 22; fax 075 81 37 06; Corso Mazzini 35; s/d/tr with bathroom €42/62/83, breakfast €6) This comfortable little hotel has 35 rooms, in renovated 15th-century buildings, now on both sides of the street. There are direct-dial phones in every room, a TV room and lounge, restaurant, lift and bar.

Lieto Soggiorno (☎ 075 81 61 91; Via A Fortini 26; s/d from €24/39, d with bathroom €36-55) This two-star hotel is a short walk west of Piazza del Comune. Staff can be testy when there's a crowd.

MID-RANGE

Hotel Il Palazzo (☎ 075 81 68 41/42; www.hotelil palazzo.it; Via San Francesco 8; s with bathroom & breakfast €60-77, d with breakfast €90-120) The rooms in this lovely 15th-century palazzo, half of which is occupied by the owners, have been restored in the simple elegance that Italians are famous for – white walls, terracotta floors, a few pieces of fine old furniture in splendidly carved wood, beautiful carpets. Despite its central position the hotel is also very quiet and filled with light. The only disadvantage is that there are a lot of stairs to negotiate.

Hotel La Fortezza (☎ 075 81 24 18; www.lafor tezzahotel.com; Vicolo della Fortezza 2b; s/d with bathroom €52) Comfortable, charming and intimate hotel run by the Ciocchetti family behind their restaurant just off Piazza del Comune.

TOP END

Albergo Giotto (☎ 075 81 22 09; htlgiotto@tin.it; Via Fontebella 41; s/d €94/142; P) This modern

three-star hotel, just metres away from the Basilica di San Francesco, has 70 rooms, and often caters for groups. It has a restaurant and bar which gives onto a large balcony overlooking the beautiful surrounding countryside.

Hotel Subasio (☎ 075 81 22 06; www.umbria.org/ hotel/subasio; Via Frate Elia 2; s/d/tr with breakfast €114/ 181/207) The Subasio is a truly gorgeous but pricey hotel, so it's best for splash-out occasions. All the rooms are furnished in Florentine Renaissance style, and distinguished former guests include Greta Garbo and Charlie Chaplin.

AROUND ASSISI

If you are looking to get away from the main tourist hub of Assisi there are some nice budget options as well as a couple of mid-range hotels. Most are located in lovely, quiet surrounds.

Ostello della Pace (☎ 075 81 67 67; www.assisi hostel.com; Via Valecchie 177; B&B €12.90, f €15.50; 🕐 1 Mar–10 Jan) Assisi's HI youth hostel is spotless and has great pillows. It's on the shuttle-bus route between Santa Maria degli Angeli and Assisi.

Victor (☎ 075 806 45 26; fax 075 806 55 62; www .victorhostel.com; Via Sacro Tugurio, Rivotorto; r with bathroom €10-12) and **Victor Center** (Via Romana 31, Capodacqua; r with bathroom €10-12) These establishments in the countryside surrounding Assisi have small rooms in a large garden. There's a large kitchen which makes them ideal for family groups.

In the Santa Maria degli Angeli area near the railway station, try **Hotel Villa Elda** (☎ 075 804 17 56; www.villaelda.com; S Pietro Campagna 139; s with bathroom €36-41, d with bathroom €55-75); there's a restaurant and bar, garden and access for disabled.

Near Petrignano, **La Torretta** (☎ 075 803 87 78; Via del Ponte 1, s with bathroom €46-62, d with

UMBRIA & MARCHE

THE AUTHOR'S CHOICE

San Francesco (☎ 075 81 23 29; Via San Francesco 52; meals €35) Right in the heart of the tourist action, this is nevertheless a peaceful place to eat fine food and drink fine wine without breaking the bank. Admire the Basilica as you eat fresh pasta, delicious local meat and seasonal specialities, including porcini mushrooms and fresh herbs.

bathroom €72-90) is set in a lovely garden and has its own bar.

Eating

CAFÉS

Gran Caffe (☎ 075 815 51 44; Corso Mazzini 16) This elegant place has the most fabulous gelati and mouth-watering pastries and cakes and a great selection of drinks. Try the *tè freddo alla pesca* (iced tea with peach) on a hot day, choose from a selection of delicious hot chocolates and coffee when the weather is cool. Remember it costs much more to sit.

RESTAURANTS

Assisi offers a good selection of traditional Italian and Umbrian delicacies, including two of Umbria's best restaurants (San Francesco and Cavalieri).

La Fortezza (☎ 075 81 24 18; Via della Fortezza 2b; meals €20; ☿ dinner Fri-Wed Mar-Jan) This family-run restaurant off Piazza del Comune serves traditional Umbrian dishes, as well as those from Trentino, and a good selection of local wines. Credit cards are accepted.

Buca di San Francesco (☎ 075 81 22 04; Via Brizi 1 – Via Cristofani 26; meals €18-25; ☿ Tue-Sun) Sample traditional Umbrian dishes and specialities of the house in a medieval setting. Choose bruschette, local sausage, *spaghetti alla buca*, gnocchi and home-made desserts. Credit cards are accepted.

Bistrot Brilli (☎ 075 804 34 33; Via Los Angeles 83; meals €30; closed lunch Tue & Sat) Not far from the railway station and the Santa Maria degli Angeli church, downhill from the main historic centre. Popular with Italians for its ambience and the quality of its food, this little place offers an interesting selection of salads, raw fish and cold meats as well as soups, risottos and pasta.

Cavalieri (☎ 075 803 00 11; Via Matteotti 47; meals €40; ☿ Tue-Sun) This elegant restaurant, set in a beautiful garden in the atmospheric Petrignano countryside a few kilometres away from the main town, is the ideal place if you are not in any hurry.

Medio Evo (☎ 075 81 30 68; Via Arco dei Priori 4; meals €45; ☿ Thu-Tue) Traditional Umbrian dishes are served in fabulous vaulted 13th-century surroundings.

Getting There & Away

APM buses connect Assisi with Perugia (€2.90, 50 minutes, 10 daily) and other local towns, leaving from the bus station on Piazza Matteotti. Most APM buses also stop on Largo Properzio, just outside the Porta Nuova. Piazzale dell'Unità d'Italia is the terminus for **SULGA buses** (☎ 075 500 96 41) for Rome (€16.55, three hours, three daily), Florence (€11.65, 2¾ hours, one per day at 6.45am, returning at 5pm) and other major cities.

Although Assisi's train station is 4km away at Santa Maria degli Angeli, the train is still the best way to get to many places as the services are more frequent than the buses. It is on the Foligno–Terontola line with regular services to Perugia (€1.55, 30 minutes, hourly). You can change at Terontola for Florence (€9, two hours, 10 daily) and at Foligno for Rome (€11.20, two hours, 11 daily).

To reach Assisi from Perugia by road, take the SS75, exit at Ospedalicchio and follow the signs.

Getting Around

A shuttle bus (€0.60) operates every half-hour between Piazza Matteotti and the train station. Normal traffic is subject to restrictions in the city centre and daytime parking is all but banned. Several car parks dot the city walls (connected to the centre by orange shuttle buses), or head for Via della Rocca, the road that leads up to Rocca Maggiore. There are no restrictions beyond the P (parking) sign. This leaves a short, if steep, walk to the cathedral and Piazza del Comune.

SPELLO

pop 7600

Spello's proximity to Perugia and Assisi makes it well worth a brief trip. Emperor Augustus developed much of the land in the valley, but the Roman ruins are some distance from the town and your time could be better spent wandering Spello's narrow cobbled streets.

The local **tourist information office** (☎ 0742 30 10 09; Piazza Matteotti 3; ☿ 9.30am-12.30pm & 3.30-5.30pm) can provide you with a list of accommodation and they have maps of walks in the surrounding area, including an 8km walk across the hills to Assisi. For more information, contact the main **regional tourist office** (☎ 074 235 44 59; info@iat.foligno.pg.it) at Foligno.

The Augustan **Porta Venere** leads to the gloomy **Chiesa di Sant'Andrea** (Piazza Matteotti; admission free; 🕒 8am-7pm) where you can admire a fresco by Bernardino Pinturicchio. A few doors down is the 12th-century **Chiesa di Santa Maria Maggiore** (Piazza Matteotti; admission free; 🕒 8.30am-12.30pm & 3-7pm summer, 8.30am-12.30pm & 3-6pm winter) and the town's real treat, Pinturicchio's beautiful frescoes in the **Cappella Baglioni**. Also of note is the chapel's exquisite floor (dating from 1566). The people of Spello celebrate the feast of Corpus Domini in June (the date changes each year) by skilfully decorating stretches of the main street with fresh flowers in colourful designs. Come on the Saturday evening before the Sunday procession to see the floral fantasies being laid out (from about 8.30pm) and participate in the festive atmosphere. The Corpus procession begins at 11am Sunday.

Sleeping

Hotels are expensive and there are cheaper options in Assisi and Perugia. Even better, try *agriturismo* or B&B options.

Il Cacciatore (☎ 0742 65 11 41; fax 0742 30 16 03; Via Giulia 42; s with bathroom €47-52, d with bathroom 75-90) This place has a great restaurant (closed Monday) with a large terrace, perfect for a summer lunch, and traditional rooms.

Hotel Palazzo Bocci (☎ 0742 30 10 21; www.emmeti .it; Via Cavour 17; s from €70-90, d from €130-150) This exquisite four-star 18th-century hotel is a classy option with a walled garden and frescoes in the sitting room.

Getting There & Away

APM buses connect Spello with Perugia (€2.90, one hour, five daily) and Foligno (€0.60, 15 minutes, nine daily), and there are also connections to Assisi (€1.30, 15 minutes, six daily, Monday to Saturday). Trains are a better option, with almost hourly connections linking Spello with Perugia (€2, 30 minutes), Assisi (€1.10, 10 minutes) and Foligno (€0.80, 15 minutes). Spello is on the SS75 between Perugia and Foligno.

AROUND SPELLO

Bevagna, about 8km southwest of Foligno (through which you'll pass if you're on public transport), is a charming, medieval hamlet with a couple of Romanesque churches on the central Piazza Silvestri. It

comes to life in the last week of June for the Mercato delle Gaite, where olde-worlde taverns open up and medieval-era handicrafts are brought back to life.

Seven kilometres to the southeast, **Montefalco** is also known as the Ringhiera dell'Umbria (Balcony of Umbria) for its expansive views. Again, the town is a pleasant medieval backwater graced with several churches. Don't leave here without trying the local Sagrantino wine.

GUBBIO
pop 32,000

Seated on the steep slopes of Monte Ingino overlooking a picturesque valley, the centuries-old *palazzi* of Gubbio exude a warm ochre glow.

Gubbio is famous for its Eugubian Tablets, which date from 300 to 100 BC and constitute the best existing example of ancient Umbrian script. An important ally of the Roman Empire and a key stop on the Via Flaminia, the town declined during the Saracen invasions. In the 14th century it fell into the hands of the Montefeltro family of Urbino and was later incorporated into the Papal States.

Orientation

The classic hill town is small and easy to explore, especially if you use the **lifts** (☎ 075 922 1291 25; Via XX Settembre; 🕒 10am-1pm & 3-7pm Mon-Sat, 9.30am-7.30pm Sun & holidays) that have been built into excavated rocks. You'll find them just off Piazza Grande and they will take you to the Duomo (cathedral) and the Palazzo Ducale and the Diocesan Museum. The immense traffic circle known as Piazza Quaranta Martiri, at the base of the hill, is where buses to the city arrive, and there's a large car park there. From here it is a short, if somewhat steep, walk up Via della Repubblica to the main square, Piazza Grande, also known as the Piazza della Signoria. Corso Garibaldi and Piazza Oderisi are to your right as you head up the hill.

Information
EMERGENCY
Police Station (emergencies ☎ 113; Via XX Settembre 97)

MEDICAL
Hospital (☎ 075 9 23 91; Piazza Quaranta Martiri)

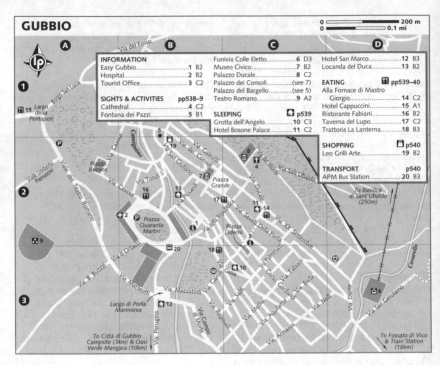

GUBBIO

INFORMATION		Funivia Colle Eletto........6 D3	Hotel San Marco........12 B3
Easy Gubbio........1 B2		Museo Civico........7 B2	Locanda del Duca........13 B2
Hospital........2 B2		Palazzo Ducale........8 C2	
Tourist Office........3 C2		Palazzo dei Consoli........(see 7)	**EATING** pp539–40
		Palazzo del Bargello........(see 5)	Alla Fornace di Mastro
SIGHTS & ACTIVITIES pp538–9		Teatro Romano........9 A2	Giorgio........14 C2
Cathedral........4 C2			Hotel Cappuccini........15 A1
Fontana dei Pazzi........5 B1		**SLEEPING** p539	Ristorante Fabiani........16 C2
		Grotta dell'Angelo........10 C3	Taverna del Lupo........17 C2
		Hotel Bosone Palace........11 C2	Trattoria La Lanterna........18 B3
			SHOPPING p540
			Leo Grilli Arte........19 B2
			TRANSPORT p540
			APM Bus Station........20 B3

POST

Post Office (Via Cairoli 11; ☻ 8.10am-5pm Mon-Sat)

TOURIST INFORMATION

Tourist Office (☎ 075 922 06 93; info@iat.gubbio
.pg.it; Piazza Oderisi; ☻ 8.30am-1.45pm & 3.30-6.30pm
Mon-Fri, 9am-1pm & 3.30-6.30pm Sat, 9.30am-12.30pm
& 3.30-6.30pm Sun, 3-6pm Mon-Fri winter, 3-6pm Sat
winter)

Easy Gubbio (☎ 075 922 00 66; Via della Repubblica
13) Run by a consortium of local traders.

Sights

PIAZZA GRANDE

Gubbio's most impressive buildings look
out over Piazza Grande, dominated above
all by the 14th-century **Palazzo dei Consoli**,
attributed to Gattapone. The crenellated
facade and tower can be seen from all over
the town. Though the building is currently
undergoing restoration, you can enter
the **Museo Civico** (☎ 075 927 42 98; Piazza Grande;
adult/under-25s incl gallery €3.60/2.05; ☻ 10am-1pm &
3-6pm Apr-Sep, 10am-1pm & 2-5pm Oct-Mar) through
the door below the main entrance. This
displays the Eugubian Tablets, discovered

in 1444 near the Teatro Romano (Roman
Theatre) southwest of Piazza Quaranta
Martiri (see p539). The seven bronze tablets are the main source for research into
the ancient Umbrian language. Upstairs is
a picture gallery featuring works from the
Gubbian school.

CATHEDRAL & PALAZZO DUCALE

Via Ducale leads up to the 13th-century
pink **cathedral** (Via Federico da Montefeltro; donations
welcome; ☻ 9am-5pm Mon-Sat, 9am-1pm Sun), with a
fine 12th-century stained-glass window and
a fresco attributed to Bernardino Pinturicchio. Opposite, the 15th-century **Palazzo
Ducale** (☎ 075 927 58 72; Via Federico da Montefeltro;
adult/child €2.05/free; ☻ 9am-7.30pm Tue-Fri, 9am-
10.30pm Sat & Sun) was built by the Montefeltro family as a scaled-down version of their
grand *palazzo* in Urbino.

OTHER SIGHTS

From Piazza Grande, Via dei Consoli
leads west to the 13th-century **Palazzo del
Bargello**, the city's medieval police station
and prison. In front of it is the **Fontana dei**

UMBRIA & MARCHE

Pazzi (Fountain of Lunatics), so named because of a belief that if you walk around it three times, you will go mad – on summer weekends the number of tourists carrying out this ritual is indeed cause for concern about their collective sanity.

Southwest of Piazza Quaranta Martiri, off Viale del Teatro Romano, are the overgrown remains of a 1st-century AD **Teatro Romano** (☎ 075 922 09 22; admission free; ☾ 8.30am-7.30pm Apr-Sep, 8am-1.30pm Oct-Mar). Most of what you see is reconstructed.

From Via San Gerolamo you can ride the curious birdcage funicular **Funivia Colle Eletto** (☎ 075 927 38 81; return €5) to the **Basilica di Sant'Ubaldo** that houses the three huge 'candles' used during the Festa dei Ceri (see below) and the preserved body of Sant'Ubaldo in a glass coffin above the altar.

Festivals & Events

The **Festa dei Ceri** (Candles Festival) is held each year on 15 May to commemorate the city's patron saint, Sant'Ubaldo. The event starts at 5.30am and involves three teams, each carrying a *cero* (these 'candles' are massive wooden pillars weighing about 400kg, each bearing a statue of a 'rival' saint) who race through the city's streets. This is one of Italy's liveliest festivals

Also in May, on the last Sunday of the month, there's the annual **Palio della Balestra**, an archery competition involving medieval crossbows, in which Gubbio competes with its neighbour, Sansepolcro.

Sleeping

BUDGET

Many locals rent rooms to tourists, so ask at the tourist office about *affittacamere*. You can also get a brochure there which lists hotels, camp sites and restaurants in the area with current prices.

Locanda del Duca (☎ /fax 075 927 77 53; locandadelducaditraversi@tin.it; Via Piccardi 1; s €37-45, d €52-60, tr from €65) One of the cheapest hotels in town, Locanda del Duca has just seven rooms, all with pleasant polished wood interiors.

Grotta dell'Angelo (☎ 075 927 17 47; grottadellangelo@jumpy.it; Via Gioia 47; s/d from €35/50; ☾ closed 7 Jan–7 Feb) Clean and welcoming, this two-star hotel has modern rooms and a charming garden restaurant.

Città di Gubbio (☎ 075 927 20 37; fax 075 92 76 20; Loc Ortoguidone; site per person/tent €7.75/8.25;

☾ Apr-Sep) For camping, try this site in Ortoguidone, a southern suburb of Gubbio, about 3km south of Piazza Quaranta Martiri along the SS298 (Via Perugina).

MID-RANGE

Hotel San Marco (☎ 075 922 02 34; www.hotelsanmarcogubbio.com; Via Perugina 5; s €55-65, d €68-88) There are 60 rooms in this large converted monastery. Many of the rooms have traditional cross-beamed ceilings, a few have private balconies and there's a pleasant garden.

Hotel Bosone Palace (☎ 075 922 06 88; hotel bosone@libero.it; Via XX Settembre 22; s €61-73, d €70-80) This chic three-star hotel has 17th-century frescoes in the breakfast room.

Oasi Verde Mengara (☎ 075 922 70 04; www.gubbio.com/oasiverdemengara; Loc Mengara Vallingegno 1; half-board per person up to €50) Just 10km south of the city is the *agriturismo* Oasi Verde Mengara. Its fine restaurant offers a memorable and very filling meal for around €20. It also organises horse riding (€12.90 per hour). Oasi Verdi Mengara is easily accessible from Gubbio using the regular APM bus to Perugia, which stops right outside (ask the driver to tell you when to get off).

Agenzia Agrituristica Cigliano (☎ 075 92 53 33; cell ☎ 03 392 16 11 11, Giovanni.DeAgazio@infoservice.it; B&B per person around €20, evening meals €8) A large farmhouse on the outskirts of Gubbio, has been recommended by readers. The owners, the De Agazio family, can arrange to pick you up.

Eating

Ristorante Fabiani (☎ 075 927 46 39; Piazza Quaranta Martiri 26; meals €20; ☾ Wed-Mon) This place is a large traditional trattoria with garden seating.

Trattoria La Lanterna (☎ 075 927 66 94; Via Gioia 23; meals €20; ☾ Fri-Wed) Many meals feature local specialities like the delicious *tartufi* (truffles).

Taverna del Lupo (☎ 075 927 43 68; fax 075 927 12 69; Via Ansidei 21; meals €35-47; ☾ Tue-Sun) Stylish, yet not too extravagant, this restaurant serves very good Umbrian dishes in lovely 13th-century surrounds. There's an emphasis on truffles in season, and there's a good wine list.

Hotel Cappuccini (☎ 075 92 34; info@parkhotelaicappuccini.it; Via Tifernate; meals €35-40) This delightful hotel restaurant in a former convent, serves great food at quite reasonable prices. Risotto and tortelli are very good here. You can stay the night too, at their four-star hotel.

Villa Montegranelli Hotel (☎ 075 922 01 85; fax 075 927 33 72; meals €40-45) In the Monteluiano district, this is another fabulous place to eat and drink. The restaurant is set in a lovely park overlooking Gubbio and the biggest Christmas tree in the world. Try the swordfish stuffed with *mozzarella di buffalo* and tiny tomatoes. This is also a great place to sample local oils.

Alla Fornace di Mastro Giorgio (☎ 075 922 18 36; Via Mastro Giorgio 2; meals €50; ☺ Wed-Mon). One of the best restaurants in Umbria, this is also one of the more expensive. But you'll dine in what was once the workshop of the painter, elegantly refurbished. All credit cards are accepted.

Shopping
Leo Grilli Arte (☎ 075 922 22 72; Via dei Consoli 78; ☺ 9.30am-1pm & 3-7pm Tue-Sun) In the Middle Ages, ceramics were one of Gubbio's main sources of income and there are some fabulous contemporary samples on sale in this crumbly 15th-century mansion.

Getting There & Around
APM buses run to Perugia (€3.80, one hour 10 minutes, six daily), Gualdo Tadino (€2.25, 50 minutes, 10 daily) and Umbertide (€2.60, 50 minutes, three daily) and the company operates a service to Rome (€14.45, four hours) leaving daily at 5.50am. Buses depart from Piazza Quaranta Martiri. You can buy tickets at Easy Gubbio, Via della Repubblica 13.

The closest train station is at Fossato di Vico, about 18km southeast of the city. Trains run from Fossato to Rome (€10.10, 2½ hours, eight daily), Ancona (€4.20, one hour 20 minutes, nine daily) and Foligno (€2.40, 40 minutes, roughly hourly) where you can pick up connections to Arezzo, Perugia and Florence. Hourly APM buses connect the station with Gubbio (€1.95, 30 minutes), although there are delays of up to an hour between train and bus connections.

By car or motorcycle, take the SS298 from Perugia or the SS76 from Ancona, and follow the signs. Parking in the large car park in Piazza Quaranta Martiri costs €0.50 per hour.

Walking is the best way to get around, but ASP buses connect Piazza Quaranta Martiri with the funicular station and most main sights.

AROUND GUBBIO
Parco Regionale del Monte Cucco
East of Gubbio, this park is dotted with caves, many of which can be explored. It is well set up for walkers, rock climbers and horse riders, and has many hotels and *rifugi* (mountain huts). **Costacciaro**, accessible by bus from Gubbio (€1.95, 30 minutes) via Scheggia or Fossato di Vico, is a good base and the starting point for a walk to the summit of Monte Cucco (1566m). For more information contact parco.montecucco@tiscalinet.it or check http://parchi.provincia.perugia.it.

Other options include cross-country skiing, archery and rafting, hang-gliding and parachuting. Ask for details at the tourist office in Gubbio.

The **Centro Escursionistico Naturalistico Speleologico** (☎ 075 917 04 00; www.infoservice.it; Via Galeazzi 5, Costacciaro) can help with information about exploring local caves, walking and mountain-bike routes. **Club Alpino Italiano** (CAI) produces a walking map, Carta dei Sentieri Massiccio del Monte Cucco, for sale in local bookshops and newsagents (€4.65).

Those interested in horse riding should try the **Campeggio Rio Verde** (☎ 075 917 01 38) camp site 3km west of Costacciaro. They charge €12.90 per hour, but horses are only available for hire during July and August.

Many agriturismo establishments in the area can also arrange horse riding; the Tourist office in Gubbio has further details and the Umbria APT office publishes information. Check www.umbria2000.it or ask for their booklet on hotels in Umbria, which also lists horse-riding options. It is possible to hire mountain bikes at the **Coop Arte e Natura** (☎ 075 917 07 40; Via Stazione 2) in the village of Fossato di Vico, about 8km southeast of Costacciaro.

SPOLETO
pop 37,360
Each June and July, this otherwise quiet town takes centre stage for an international parade of drama, music, opera and dance (see p543). If you plan to visit Spoleto during

There are plenty of sights surround Orvieto's **cathedral** (p546); the piazza is a popular meeting place for locals

An imposing welcome from Orvieto's **cathedral** (p546)

Man's best friend and champion **truffle** (p221) hunter!

Trek in the **Corno Grande** (p574), the Apennine's highest peak

Spend some time wandering the ancient ruins of **Pompeii** (p623) and **Vesuvius** (p622)

Visit the **Parco Nazionale d'Abruzzo** (p580), an important part of Italy's conservation movement protecting endangered species such as the Marsican brown bear and Apennine wolf

the festival, book accommodation and tickets months in advance. When the festival ends, Spoleto goes back to sleep, but it's nonetheless an enchanting town to spend a day or two exploring.

Orientation

The old part of the city is about 1km south of the main train station – take the orange shuttle bus marked A, B or C for Piazza della Libertà in the centre, where you'll find the tourist office and the Roman-era theatre. Piazza del Mercato, a short walk northeast of Piazza della Libertà, marks the engaging heart of old Spoleto. Between here and Piazza del Duomo you'll find the bulk of the city's monuments and some fine shops.

Information

EMERGENCY
Ambulance (☎ 0743 4 48 88)
Police (☎ 0743 403 24: Viale Trento e Trieste)

INTERNET ACCESS
Tuta Birra (Via di Fontesecca 7)

MEDICAL SERVICES
Hospital (☎ 0743 21 01; Via Madonna di Loreto)

POST
Post Office (entrance off Viale Giacomo Matteotti; ☺ 8.15am-7pm Mon-Sat)

TOURIST INFORMATION
Tourist Office (☎ 0743 22 03 11, ☎ 0473 23 89 11; info@iat.spoleto.pg.it; Piazza della Libertà 7; ☺ 9am-1pm & 4-7pm Mon-Fri, 9am-1pm & 3.30-6.30pm Mon-Fri winter, 10am-1pm & 4-7pm Sat year-round)

Sights

ROMAN SPOLETO
Make your first stop the **Teatro Romano** (☎ 0743 22 32 77; Via S Agata; adult/child incl museum €2.05/1; ☺ 9am-7pm) on the western edge of Piazza della Libertà. The 1st-century theatre is currently used for performances during the summer. Have a quick look at the ceramics collection in the **Museo Archeologico** next to the theatre.

East of Piazza della Libertà, around Piazza Fontana, are more Roman remains, including the **Arco di Druso e Germanico** (Arch of Drusus and Germanicus; sons of the Emperor Tiberius), which marks the entrance to the old forum. The excavated

Casa Romana (Roman house; ☎ /fax 0743 464 34; Via di Visiale; adult/child €2.05/1; ☺ 10am-1pm & 3-6pm Wed-Mon 16 Oct–15 Mar, 10am-8pm daily 16 Mar–15 Oct) dates from the 1st century.

The city boasts an **Anfiteatro Romano** (Roman Amphitheatre), one of the country's largest. Unfortunately it is within military barracks and closed to the public.

CHURCHES
A short walk north through Piazza del Municipio takes you to the 12th-century **Chiesa di Sant'Eufemia** (☎ 0743 23 10 22; Via A Saffi; adult/child incl Museo Diocesano €3.10/1.55; ☺ 10am-12.30pm & 3.30-7pm summer, 10am-12.30pm & 3.30-6pm winter). Set within the grounds of the Archbishop's *palazzo*, it is notable for its *matronei* – galleries set high above the main body of the church to segregate the female congregation.

From here, it is a quick stroll northeast to the **cathedral** (☎ 0743 443 07; Piazza del Duomo; admission free; ☺ 7.30am-12.30pm & 3-6pm summer, 7.30am-12.30pm & 3-5pm winter), consecrated in 1198 and remodelled in the 17th century. Inside, the first chapel to the right of the nave was decorated by Bernardino Pinturicchio, and Annibale Carracci completed an impressive fresco in the right transept. The frescoes in the domed apse were executed by Filippo Lippi and his assistants. Lippi died before completing the work and Lorenzo de Medici travelled to Spoleto from Florence and ordered Lippi's son, Filippino, to build a mausoleum for the artist. This now stands in the right transept of the cathedral. The spectacular closing concert of the Spoleto Festival is held on the piazza.

OTHER SIGHTS
Inside the town hall on Piazza del Municipio is the **Pinacoteca Comunale** (☎ 0743 21 81; Piazza Comunale 1; adult/child €2.05/1; ☺ 10am-1pm & 3-6pm Tue-Sun, guided tour only). It is a sumptuous building, with some impressive works by Umbrian artists.

Dominating the city is the **Rocca Albornoziana** (☎ /fax 0743 22 30 55; Piazza Campello; adult/child €4.65/3.60; ☺ 10am-8pm 11 Jun–15 Sep, 2.30-5pm Mon-Fri, 10am-5pm Sat & Sun, closed noon-3pm Mon-Fri Mar–10 Jun, 16 Sep–31 Oct, 1 Nov–14 Mar; entrance is by guided tour only, reservations essential), a former papal fortress that until 1982 was a high-security prison housing such notables as Pope John Paul II's attempted assassin, Ali Agca.

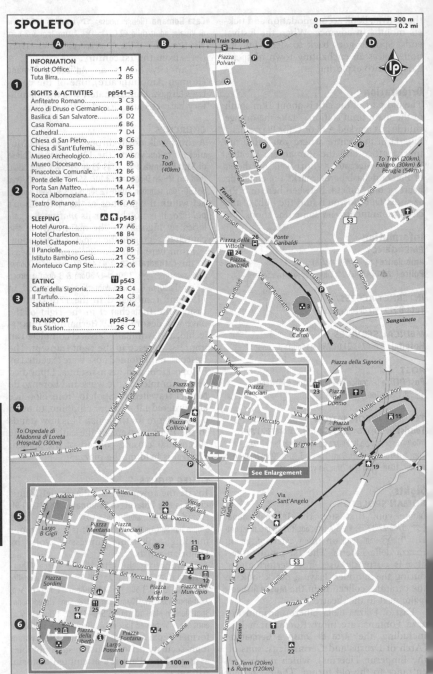

SPOLETO

0 ——— 300 m
0 ——— 0.2 mi

To Todi
(40km)

Main Train Station

Piazza
Polvani

To Trevi (20km),
Foligno (30km) &
Perugia (54km)

Piazza della
Vittoria

Ponte
Garibaldi

Piazza
Garibaldi

Sanguineto

Piazza
Cairoli

Piazza della Signoria

Piazza S
Domenico

Piazza
Pianciani

Piazza
del
Duomo

Via del Mercato

Piazza
Collicola

Piazza
Campello

Via del Ponte

To Ospedale di
Madonna di Loreta
(Hospital) (300m)

See Enlargement

S. Andrea

Via Filitteria

Vicolo
degli Eroli

Via
Sant'Angelo

Largo
B Gigli

Piazza
Mentana

Piazza
Pianciani

Via del Duomo

Piazza
Sordini

Via del Mercato

Piazza
del
Mercato

Piazza del
Municipio

Piazza
della
Libertà

Piazza
Fontana

Largo
Possenti

0 ——— 100 m

To Terni (20km)
& Rome (120km)

UMBRIA & MARCHE

Along Via del Ponte is the **Ponte delle Torri**, erected in the 14th century on the foundations of a Roman aqueduct. Cross the bridge and follow the lower path, Strada di Monteluco, to reach the **Chiesa di San Pietro** (☎ 0743 448 82; Loc San Pietro; admission free; ⏰ 9.30am-11am & 3.30-6.30pm). The 13th-century facade, the church's main attraction, is liberally bedecked with sculpted animals.

Festivals & Events
The Italian-American composer Gian Carlo Menotti conceived the **Festival dei Due Mondi** (Festival of Two Worlds) in 1958. Now known simply as the Spoleto Festival, it has given the city a worldwide reputation. However, the festival is not what it once was. Funding crises have affected both the quality and quantity of events, and cutting-edge performances, for which the festival gained its reputation, are now rarely seen.

Events at the festival, held over three weeks from late June to mid-July, range from opera and theatre to ballet and art exhibitions. Tickets cost from €5.15 to €103.30 and generally sell out by March or April. There are usually several free concerts in various churches.

For information, call ☎ 0743 4 47 00, fax 0743 4 05 46, or write to The Box Office, Piazza della Libertà 12, 06049 Spoleto, Italy. You can find further details and book tickets online at www.spoletofestival.it.

Sleeping
The city is well served by cheap hotels, *affittacamere*, hostels and camp sites, although if you're coming for the festival you will need to book a room months in advance.

Monteluco (☎ /fax 0743 22 03 58; Loc San Pietro; site per person/tent €4.10/4.10; ⏰ Apr-Sep) This leafy, quiet camp site is just behind the Chiesa di San Pietro, in easy walking distance of the town centre.

If you want to try living like the natives in a tiny medieval town around 10km from Spoleto, you can find a sweet little self-contained B&B right underneath the ancient castle that gives the town, Castel Ritaldi, its name. The friendly proprietor speaks some English and is an expert on all things Umbrian. You can have plenty of privacy, but he will gladly share his knowledge (and his home-made oil and sausages, as well as

his wife's excellent cakes.) He can also arrange pool access. Contact **Giuseppe Fantaulli** (☎ 0743 51180; cell ☎ 349 579 30 47; Viale Martiri del Resistenza 7, Castel Ritaldi 06044).

Istituto Bambino Gesù (☎ 0743 402 32; Via Sant'Angelo 4; s/d with breakfast €25.80/51.65) The nuns at this religious institution, just off Via Monterone, are incredibly welcoming. What's more, the perfect silence means you're guaranteed to sleep like a log.

Hotel Aurora (☎ 0743 22 03 15; www.hotelauroraspoleto.it; Via Apollinare 3; s/d €51.40/80) Just off Piazza della Libertà, the Aurora is very central. Some rooms have pleasant balconies and breakfast is excellent.

Il Panciolle (☎ /fax 0743 456 77; Via del Duomo 3; s/d with bathroom from €36.15/51.65) This sweet, comfortable hotel near the cathedral has its own restaurant downstairs and is a reliable bet.

Hotel Charleston (☎ 0743 22 00 52; www.hotelcharleston.it; Piazza Collicola 10; s/d €64/105) The Charleston has a relaxing chalet feel with an open fireplace in the hall and a great little terrace outside for breakfast.

Hotel Gattapone (☎ 0743 22 34 47; www.hotelgattapone.it; Via del Ponte 6; s €85-170, d €140-230). This place is in a top location and the interiors are suitably chic.

Eating
Spoleto is one of Umbria's main centres for the *tartufo nero* (black truffle), used in a variety of dishes. Trying them can be a costly exercise – so check the price before digging in.

Il Tartufo (☎ 0743 402 36; truffles@libero.it; Piazza Garibaldi 24; meals €25; ⏰ Tue-Sat) With such a name, obviously this place specialises in truffles, black and white. Try a glass of the excellent Sagrantino Montefalco or Arquato Rosso.

Sabatini (☎ 0743 221831; Corso Mazzini 52-54; ⏰ Tue-Sun Sep-Dec & Feb-Jun) Another good place to eat local specialities made with local products.

Caffe della Signoria (☎ 0743 463 33; Piazza della Signoria 5; meals €35; ⏰ Thu-Tue) This welcoming, rustic place has a beautiful garden with a fabulous view where you can eat bruschette, delicious home-made pasta and desserts.

Getting There & Around
Most **Società Spoletina di Imprese Trasporti** (SSIT; ☎ 0743 21 22 08/9; www.spoletina.com) buses depart from Piazza della Vittoria and some

also make a stop at the train station. Buses to Perugia (€5.15, one hour) leave daily at 6.20am and 7.10am. There are also services to Bastardo (€2.60, 40 minutes, five daily), Norcia (€4.15, one hour, six daily) and dozens of other small towns. Buses to Monteluco run in summer only (€0.60, 15 minutes, every two hours).

Trains from the main **station** (☎ 0743 485 16; Piazza Polvani) connect with Rome (€6.80-13.20, one to 2½ hours, hourly), Ancona (€7.75, two hours, 10 daily), Perugia (€3.40, one hour, hourly) and Assisi (€2.40, 30 minutes, hourly). The Eurostar train service from Rome to Perugia stops at Spoleto (about one hour 20 minutes from Rome). Cost to Perugia from Rome is €17.

The city is easily explored on foot. Orange shuttle buses A, B and C run between the train station, Piazza Garibaldi and Piazza della Libertà (€0.60).

THE VALNERINA

The Valnerina is a beautiful area, on the Umbrian side of the Parco Nazionale dei Monti Sibillini, which takes in much of Marche.

If you plan to spend a few quiet days wandering the valley, the pretty medieval village of Preci is a good place to stay. The area is criss-crossed by walking trails and you might try to pick up a copy of the aptly titled *20 Sentieri Ragionati in Valnerina* (20 Well-Thought-Out Routes in Valnerina), in Italian, available for free from local tourist offices.

Information

Tourist agencies have erected road signs with suggested itinerary maps on them.

Valnerina-Cascia (☎ 0743 711 47; Piazza Garibaldi 1, Cascia) is a good place to go to get local information.

Sleeping

Agli Scacchi (☎ /fax 0743 992 21; Q.re Scacchi 12, Preci; s/d from €25.80/41.30, half-board per person from €36.15) Small but pleasant two-star hotel.

Bed & Breakfast Nonna Rosa (☎ 0743 93 81 23, cell ☎ 3393799727; www.nonna-rosa.it; r per person with breakfast €25) In tranquil Fiano d'Abeto, between Preci and Norcia, lovely Federica can offer you cosy and luxurious accommodation. Nonna Rosa, Federica's grandmother has lived in this lovely farmhouse for decades and is delighted to welcome guests. If you don't have a car, Federica can arrange to pick you up from the bus drop-off point.

Getting There & Away

Spoleto is the best point from which to head into the Valnerina. **SSIT** (☎ 0743 21 22 11) operates buses from Piazza Stazione to the terminal at Via della Stazione in Norcia (€4.15, one hour, six daily), from where connecting buses run along the Valnerina to Preci (€1.95, 40 minutes, Monday to Saturday at 1.25pm) and Cascia (€1.95, 30 minutes, nine daily). Getting to Castelluccio is not so easy, as there are only two services from Norcia, both on Thursday at 6.25am and 1.30pm (€2.60, 50 minutes).

The SS395 from Spoleto and the SS209 from Terni join with the SS320 and then the SS396, which passes through Norcia. The area is also accessible from Ascoli Piceno in Marche.

Norcia

This fortified medieval village is the valley's main town and a transport hub of sorts. Like the rest of the Valnerina, Norcia has suffered from earthquakes over the centuries; several buildings were damaged in 1997. For tourist information, visit the **Casa del Parco** (☎ 0743 81 70 90; Via Solferino 22; 9.30am-12.30pm & 3-6pm Mon-Fri, 9.30am-12.30pm & 3.30-6.30pm Sat & Sun).

FESTIVALS & EVENTS

The last weekend in February is dedicated to a **market** and display of black truffles, with lots of music and folkloric festivities.

ACTIVITIES

The Casa del Parco has information on walking and other activities in the surrounding area. To hang-glide or para-glide head for Castelluccio.

The area forms part of the **Parco Nazionale dei Monti Sibillini**. Buy Kompass map No 666 (scale 1:50,000) of walking trails, available from the Casa del Parco.

To learn **hang-gliding**, contact **Pro Delta** (☎ 0743 82 11 56; www.prodelta.it/eng/main.htm; Via delle Fate 3) in Castelluccio; it opens in summer only. No credit cards accepted, but readers have enthused about the courses. Another school is **Fly Castelluccio** (☎ 0736 25 56 30; Via Iannella 32, Ascoli Piceno, Marche) A

UMBRIA & MARCHE

beginners course of five days will cost about €361.50.

To hire bikes you could try the **Associazione Pian Grande** (☎ 0743 81 72 79, ☎ 0743 81 70 22; Pian Grande di Castelluccio di Norcia), which is open mostly in the afternoons from Easter to October. They can also arrange horse riding.

SLEEPING & EATING

Norcia produces the country's best salami – in fact the word Norceria signifies sausage products in Italy. This is also a stronghold of the elusive black truffle.

Da Benito (☎ 0743 81 66 70; ristorante.benito@ libero.it; Via Marconi 5; s €27-40, d €30-55) This is a friendly one-star hotel within the city walls. There are eight modest rooms above a family-run restaurant.

Hotel Grotta Azzura (☎ 0743 81 65 13; www .bianconi.com; Via Alfieri 12; s €35-85, d €45-120) An 18th-century palazzo with suits of armour in the reception, this hotel boasts a vast medieval-style banquet hall and one of Norcia's better restaurants.

Around Norcia

If you have a car, don't miss the vast **Piano Grande**, a high plateau east of Norcia, under Monte Vettore (2476m). It becomes a sea of colour as flowers bloom in early spring.

Perched above the Piano Grande is the tiny, hilltop village of **Castelluccio**, famous for its lentils and *pecorino* and *ricotta* cheeses.

You can camp just about anywhere on the Piano Grande, but if you want to stay in town overnight, Castelluccio does have one hotel.

Albergo Sibilla (☎ /fax 0743 82 11 13; Via Piano Grande 2; s/d from €29-34/45-55) This hotel has just 11 rooms, some with a view, and a good restaurant downstairs.

ORVIETO

pop 21,600

Tourists in Orvieto are drawn first and foremost by the magnificent cathedral, one of Italy's finest Gothic buildings. The town rests on top of a craggy cliff, and although medieval Orvieto is the main tourist magnet, Etruscan tombs and the city's underground chambers testify to the area's antiquity.

Orientation

Trains pull in at Orvieto Scalo and from here you can catch bus No 1 up to the old town or board the funicular to take you up the steep hill to Piazza Cahen. But call in first at the small ATC tourist office near the station, where you can get maps and the Orvieto Carta Unica (see the boxed text, below) which allows you limited free parking or bus and funicular transport. From the funicular and bus station at the top of the hill, walk straight along Corso Cavour, turning left into Via del Duomo to reach the cathedral. There's plenty of parking space in Piazza Cahen and in several designated areas outside the old city walls.

Information

EMERGENCY

Police Station (☎ 0763 39 21 11; Piazza Cahen)

INTERNET ACCESS

Caffè Montanucci (0763 34 12 61; Corso Cavour 21; ☯ Thu-Tue)

MEDICAL SERVICES

Doctor (☎ 0763 301 884)
Hospital (☎ 0763 30 71) In the Ciconia area, east of the railway station.
Emergency (☎ 118)

POST

Post Office (Via Cesare Nebbia; ☯ 8.10am-6pm Mon-Sat)

TOURIST INFORMATION

ATC (beside the railway station; ☯ 8am-1.15pm & 4-6pm except Sat) Tourist office.

CARTA UNICA

Orvieto Carta Unica card (€12.50) entitles you to five hours' free car parking at the train station or a return trip on the funicular and city buses, plus admission (only once) to the Cappella di San Brizio in the cathedral, the Museo Claudio Faina e Civico, the Torre del Moro (Moor's Tower) and Orvieto Underground in Parco delle Grotte (see p547). Buy it at the museums and monuments, at the main tourist office, just outside the railway station and at the funicular station.

ORVIETO

INFORMATION
ATC................................(see 2)
Caffè Montanucci.....................**1** B2
Carta Unica.........................**2** F1
Tourist Office.......................**3** C3

SIGHTS & ACTIVITIES   pp546–8
Bottega Michelangeli...............**4** B2
Cathedral...........................**5** C3
Chiesa di San Francesco............**6** C3
Chiesa di San Giovenale............**7** A2
Chiesa di Sant'Andrea..............**8** B2

Consorzio Tutela Vini di Orvieto....**9** C2
La Rocca...........................**10** E1
Museo Archeologico.................**11** D3
Museo Claudio Faina e Civico......**12** C3
Museo dell'Opera del Duomo....(see 15)
Museo di Emilio Greco.............(see 15)
Orvieto Underground...............**13** C3

Palazzo del Popolo................**14** C2
Palazzo Papale....................(see 11)
Palazzo Soliano...................**15** C3
Parco delle Grotte...............(see 13)
Porta Maggiore....................**16** A2
Pozzo di San Patrizio.............**17** E1
Torre del Moro....................**18** C2

Carta Unica (beside the railway station; 9am-4pm) Tourist office.

Tourist Office (0763 34 17 72; info@iat.orvieto.tr.it; Piazza del Duomo 24; 8.15am-1.50pm & 4-7pm Mon-Fri, 10am-1pm & 4-7pm Sat, 10am-noon & 4-6pm Sun & holidays)

Sights

CATHEDRAL

Little can prepare you for the visual feast that is the **cathedral** (0763 34 11 67; Piazza del Duomo; admission free; 7.30am-12.45pm year-round plus 2.30-7.15pm Apr-Sep, 2.30-6.15pm Mar & Oct & 2.30-5.15pm Nov-Feb). Started in 1290, this remarkable edifice was originally planned in the Romanesque style but, as work proceeded and architects changed, Gothic features were incorporated into the structure. The black-and-white marble banding of the main body of the church is overshadowed by the rich rainbow colours of the facade. A harmonious blend of mosaic and sculpture, plain stone and dazzling colour, it has been likened to a giant outdoor altar screen.

Pope Urban IV ordered that the cathedral be built, following the Miracle of Bolsena in 1263, when a priest who was passing through the town of Bolsena (near Orvieto) had his doubts about transubstantiation dispelled when blood began to drip from the Host onto the altar linen while he celebrated mass. The linen was presented to Pope Urban IV, in Orvieto. He also declared the new feast day of Corpus Domini.

The building took 30 years to plan and three centuries to complete. It was probably started by Fra Bevignate and later additions were made by Lorenzo Maitani (responsible for Florence's cathedral), Andrea Pisano, his son Nino Pisano, Andrea Orcagna and Michele Sanicheli. The great bronze doors, the work of Emilio Greco, were added in the 1960s.

Inside, Luca Signorelli's fresco cycle *The Last Judgement* shimmers with life. Look for it to the right of the altar in the **Cappella di San Brizio** (admission €3; 10am-12.45pm daily, plus 2.30-7.15pm Apr-Sep, 2.30pm-6.15pm Mar & Oct & 2.30pm-5.15pm Mon-Sat & 2.30pm-5.45pm Sun Nov-Feb, closed during Mass). Signorelli began work on the series in 1499, and Michelangelo is said to have taken inspiration from it. Indeed,

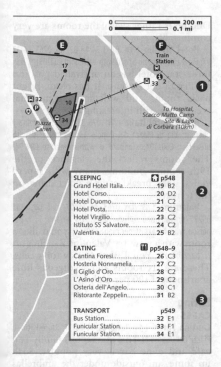

to some, Michelangelo's masterpiece runs a close second to Signorelli's work. The **Cappella del Corporale** (admission free; 🕙 7.30am-12.45pm & 2.30pm-7.15pm summer, shorter hrs winter; closed during Mass) houses the blood-stained altar linen of the miracle, preserved in a silver reliquary decorated by artists of the Sienese school. The walls feature frescoes depicting the miracle, painted by Ugolino di Prete Ilario.

AROUND THE CATHEDRAL

Next to the cathedral is the **Museo dell'Opera del Duomo** (☎ 0763 34 24 77; Palazzo Soliano, Piazza del Duomo), which houses a clutter of religious relics from the cathedral, as well as Etruscan antiquities and works by artists such as Simone Martini and the three Pisanos: Andrea, Nino and Giovanni. It has been closer for renovation, so check at the tourist office to see if it has reopened.

Museo di Emilio Greco (☎ 0763 34 46 05; fax 0763 34 46 64; Palazzo Soliano, Piazza del Duomo; adult/child €2.50/1.50; 🕙 10.30am-1pm & 2-6.30pm Tue-Sun Apr-Sep, 10.30am-1pm & 2-5.30pm Tue-Sun Oct-Mar) displays a collection of modern pieces

donated by the creator of the cathedral's bronze doors. A €4.50 combined ticket includes admission to the Pozzo di San Patrizio (see following).

Around the corner in the Palazzo Papale, you can see Etruscan antiquities in the **Museo Archeologico Nazionale** (☎ /fax 0763 34 10 39; Palazzo Papale, Piazza del Duomo; admission €2; 🕙 8.30am-7.30pm)

The **Museo Claudio Faina e Civico** (☎ 0763 34 15 11; www.museofaina.it; Piazza del Duomo 29; adult/child or elderly €4.50/3; 🕙 9.30am-6pm Apr-Sep, 10am-5pm Tue-Sun Oct-Mar) opposite the cathedral, houses one of Italy's most important collection of Etruscan archaeological artefacts, as well as some significant Greek ceramic works, mostly found near Piazza Cahen in tombs dating back to the 6th century BC. There are guided tours at 11am and 4pm (3pm October to March) and an interactive trip for kids.

Other Sights & Activities

Head northwest along Via del Duomo to Corso Cavour to **Torre del Moro** (Moor's Tower; ☎ 0763 34 45 67; Corso Cavour; adult/child €2.60/1.85; 🕙 10am-8pm May-Aug, 10am-7pm Mar, Apr, Sep & Oct, 10.30am-1pm & 2.30pm-7pm Nov-Feb). Climb all 250 steps for sweeping views of the city. Back on ground level, continue west to Piazza della Repubblica, and to the 12th-century **Chiesa di Sant'Andrea** (Piazza della Repubblica; free; 🕙 8.30am-12.30pm & 3.30pm-7.30pm) and its curious decagonal bell tower. The piazza, once Orvieto's Roman forum, is at the heart of what remains of the medieval city.

North of Corso Cavour, the 12th-century Romanesque-Gothic **Palazzo del Popolo** presides over the piazza of the same name. At the northwestern end of town is the 11th-century **Chiesa di San Giovenale** (Piazza Giovenale; admission free; 🕙 8am-12.30pm & 3.30-6pm), its interior brightened by 13th- and 14th-century frescoes.

Standing watch at the town's easternmost tip is the 14th-century **La Rocca** (rock fortress), part of which is now a public garden. To the north of the fortress, the **Pozzo di San Patrizio** (St Patrick's Well; ☎ 0763 34 37 68; fax 0763 34 46 64; Viale Sangallo; adult/concession €3.50/2.50; 🕙 10am-6.45pm Apr-Sep, 10am-5.45pm Oct-Mar) is a well, which was sunk in 1527 on the orders of Pope Clement VII. More than 60m deep, it is lined by two spiral staircases for water-bearing mules.

UMBRIA & MARCHE

For a trip back in time, **Orvieto Underground** (☎ 0763 34 48 91, cell ☎ 339 733 27 64; speleotecnici@libero.it; Parco delle Grotte; admission €5.50; ☼ 11am-6pm) is a fascinating tour of the city's underground caves. These were still in use well into last century: the cool air meant that food could be safely stored before the advent of the fridge. They even doubled up as air-raid shelters in WWII. Tours (with English-speaking guides) leave from in front of the tourist office on Piazza del Duomo at 11am, 12.15pm, 4pm and 5.15pm.

Festivals & Events

Umbria Jazz Winter takes place from the end of December to early January, with a great feast and party on New Year's Eve. Ask at the tourist office for a programme. See Festivals & Special Events in the Perugia section earlier in this chapter for details of the summer jazz festival (p523).

Sleeping

It is always a good idea to book ahead in summer or at the weekend or if you're planning to come over New Year when the Umbria Jazz Winter festival is in full swing.

Istituto SS Salvatore (☎/fax 0763 34 29 10; www.argoweb.it/orvieto/ospitalita/case.uk.html; Via del Popolo 1; s/d €31/51.65) The nuns prefer it if you stay a minimum of two nights at this simple but spotless religious hostel. There's a 10pm curfew.

Hotel Posta (☎ 0763 34 19 09; fax 07 633 40 909 Via L Signorelli 18; s/d without bathroom €31/44, with bathroom €37/56, breakfast €6) Rooms in this stolid, rather ramshackle but impressive 16th-century building are simple but have a quirky edge and the owners are friendly and helpful.

Scacco Matto (☎ 0744 95 01 63; fax 0744 95 03 73; Lago di Cobra; site per person/tent €4.15/4.65) The closest camp sites are about 10km east of the town, on Lago di Corbara near Baschi. Scacco Matto is tiny (just 12 pitches) and fairly basic but it stays open year-round.

Corso (☎/fax 0763 34 20 20; hotelcorso@libero.it; Corso Cavour 343; s/d €41-59/62-80; ✖) This attractive three-star hotel near Piazza Cahen has 16 bright rooms all with bathroom.

Hotel Duomo (☎ 0763 34 18 87; hotelduomo@tiscalinet.it; Vicolo di Maurizio 7, entrance around the cnr; s/d €55-70/80-100; ☐) On a quiet side street, just a few steps away from the cathedral,

Duomo is rather swish; the rooms are very comfortable.

Hotel Virgilio (☎ 0763 34 18 82; fax 0763 34 37 97; Piazza del Duomo 5; s/d with bathroom €62/85) This three-star hotel has an unrivalled position on Piazza del Duomo. It has clean, bright basic rooms and welcoming communal areas hung with interesting art.

Grand Hotel Italia (☎ 076 334 32 75; hotelita@libero.it; Via di Piazza del Popolo 13; s/superior d with breakfast €60/104, standard d with breakfast €89-94) The rooms reflect the elegance of the 19th-century building, many with superb views. Take breakfast or a quiet drink on the terrace.

Valentina (☎/fax 0763 34 16 07, cell ☎ 347 6527779; valentina.z@tiscalinet.it; Via Vivaria 7; r per person with breakfast per night €60) If you'd like a room with a view, try Valentina Zanchi's *affittacamere*. You'll want to stay for weeks. There are six rooms and a gorgeous little apartment (€100 per night).

Eating

CAFÉS

Cantina Foresi (☎/fax 0763 34 16 11; itforesi@tin.it; Piazza del Duomo 2) This marvellous family-run café and wine bar is very popular. Soak up some sun outside under the umbrellas facing the cathedral. Here you can get delicious, and cheap snacks made with the finest local products – salads and *panini* with the excellent local sausages and *porcetto*, and local cheeses, for just a few euros. Wash it down with a selection of great wines from the ancient cellar.

Caffè Montanucci (☎ 0763 34 12 61; Corso Cavour 21; hot dishes from €3.60; ☼ Thu-Tue; ☐) This is a not a bad place for a sandwich or pasta. There's plenty of space to sit. They make their own chocolates, which shouldn't be missed, and of course there's gelato too.

RESTAURANTS

Osteria dell'Angelo (☎ 0763 341 805; Piazza XXIX Marzo 8/A; €40; ☼ Tue-Sun) Judged by local food writers to be one of the best restaurants in Umbria, this is certainly an elegant place. The banana soufflé with a rum-and-cream sauce is recommended and the wine list is extensive.

Hosteria Nonnamelia (☎ 0763 34 24 02; Via del Duomo 25) This place, just opposite Piazza Luigi Barzini, offers excellent lunch dishes served on beautifully carved wooden tables, surrounded by a carved wooden forest and other fantastic and evocative wooden sculpture, produced in Orvieto's world famous Bottega Michelangeli (see following).

L'Asino d'Oro (☎ 0763 34 44 06; Vicolo del Popolo 9; mains around €7.75; ✆ Tue-Sun Apr-mid Oct). Despite its modest appearance, the food at this place is superb. Meals are served outside under an arbour and the menu changes daily.

Antica Trattoria Del'Orso (☎ 0763 34 16 42; Via della Misericordia 18; meals €25; ✆ Wed-Sun) This little place serves good national and local dishes and central Italian wines.

Il Giglio d'Oro (☎ 0763 341903; Piazza Duomo 8; €45) This place has a creative way with traditional local dishes and international fare. The desserts are particularly splendid.

Ristorante Zeppelin (☎ 0763 34 14 47; Via G Garibaldi 28; meals from €24; ✆ closed dinner Sun) This natty place has a cool 1920s atmosphere and serves traditional Umbrian food with generous servings and a creative twist.

Shopping

Despite being a tourist town, Orvieto still has plenty of shops selling high quality ceramics, lace and delicious sample packs of local wines, sausage, olive oil, cheeses and *funghi* (mushroom) products. Explore and enjoy.

Bottega Michelangeli (☎ 0763 34 26 60; www .michelangeli.it; Via Gualverio Michelangeli 3b) This workshop in Orvieto sells cherubic wooden dolls (€250 to €600) and puppets as well as tables, beds, cupboards, bookcases. The Michelangeli sisters design interiors and exteriors for homes, bars, shop windows, banks, gardens.

Getting There & Away

Buses depart from the station on Piazza Cahen and make a stop at the train station as well. Cotral buses connect the city with Viterbo in Lazio (€2.80, 1½ hours, seven daily) and Bagnoregio (€1.55, one hour, seven daily). ATC buses (☎ 0763 34 22 65) travel on to Baschi (€1.75, 40 minutes, seven daily), Bolsena (€2.60, 40 minutes, twice daily), Perugia (€8.70, two hours, one daily at 5.45am) and Todi (€4.15, one hour, at 1.55pm returning at 5.50am). SIRA (☎ 0763 417 30 053) runs a daily service to Rome at 8.10am, and at 7.10am on Sunday (€4.65, 1½ hours).

Trains travel to Rome (€6.80, one hour 20 minutes, hourly) and Florence (€9.30, 2¼ hours, every two hours). To get to/from Perugia, you'll need to go via Chiusi and then change at Terontola, where you may need to wait for an hour or so (€5.90, 1¼ hours, every two hours). The city is on the A1, and the SS71 heads north to Lago Trasimeno.

Getting Around

A century-old funicular connects Piazza Cahen with the train station, with carriages leaving every 15 minutes from 7.15am to 8.30pm daily (€0.65 or €0.85 including the bus from Piazza Cahen to Piazza del Duomo). Bus No 1 also runs up to the old town from the train station (€0.65). Once in Orvieto, the easiest way to see the city is on foot, although ATC bus A connects Piazza Cahen with Piazza del Duomo and bus B runs to Piazza della Repubblica.

AROUND ORVIETO

The Etruscans produced wine in the district, the Romans continued the tradition, and today the Orvieto Classico wines are among the country's most popular. There are 17 vineyards to visit but you need a car, as ATC bus services are irregular at best.

Pick up a copy of the free pamphlet *Andar per Vigne* (in Italian) from the tourist office or pop into the **Consorzio Tutela Vini di Orvieto** (☎ 0763 34 37 90; Corso Cavour 36) in Orvieto for details of its driving tour of the local vineyards.

MARCHE

Marche is 31% undulating hills and 69% mountains. It also has 180km of beautiful coast though, oddly, the hills seem to precipitate abruptly into the sea, like nightfall with no dusk. This narrow band between the Apennines and the Adriatic Sea, like Umbria, is a seismic region. But the hundreds of enchanting towns that cling to the hill tops are still crammed with an astonishing heritage of ancient churches, splendid monuments and priceless art treasures, that oddly, have been largely ignored by travellers. The capital, Ancona, has been a maritime port since the Greeks discovered it centuries ago and is still Italy's link with the East, with a

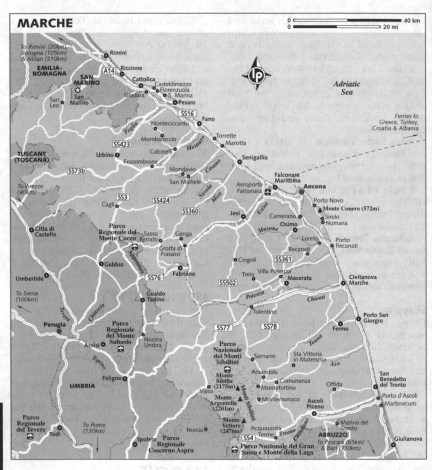

MARCHE

0 — 40 km
0 — 20 mi

To Rimini (20km),
Bologna (105km)
& Milan (310km)

EMILIA-
ROMAGNA

SAN MARINO

San Leo

San Marino

Rimini
Riccione
Cattolica
Casteldimezzo
Fiorenzuola
S. Marina
Gradara
Pesaro

Adriatic
Sea

Ferries to
Greece, Turkey,
Croatia & Albania

SS16
Fano

Montecciccardo

Mombaroccio

TUSCANY
(TOSCANA)

SS423

Calcinelli

Urbino

Fossombrone

Torrette
Marotta

Metauro

Senigallia

SS73b

Mondavio
San Michele

Cesano

Falconara
Marittima

Ancona

To Arezzo
(40km)

SS3

Cagli

SS424

SS360

Nevola

Aeroporto
Falconara

Misa

Jesi

Esino

Porto Novo

Monte Conero (572m)

Sirolo
Numana

Parco
Regionale del
Monte Cucco

Sasso
Ferrato

Genga

Grotta di
Frasassi

Camerano

Osimo

Musone

Loreto

Porto
Recanati

Recanati

Citta di
Castello

Umbertide

SS76

Fabriano

Cingoli

SS502

Treia

Villa Potenza

Macerata

Civitanova
Marche

To Siena
(100km)

Gubbio

Gualdo
Tadino

Potenza

Chienti

Porto San
Giorgio

Tevere

Chiascio

Perugia

Parco
Regionale
del Monte
Subasio

Tolentino

SS77

SS78

Fermo

Assisi

Nocera
Umbra

Topino

Foligno

Parco
Nazionale
dei Monti
Sibillini

Sarnano

Tenna

Aso

Sta Vittoria
in Matenano

San
Benedetto
del Tronto

UMBRIA

Monte
Sibilla
(2175m)

Amandola

Comunanza

Montefortino

Offida

Porto d'Ascoli
Martinsicuro

Visso

Monte
Argentella
(2201m)

Montemonaco

Ascoli
Piceno

Parco
Regionale
del Tevere

Todi

To Rome
(130km)

Monte
Vettore
(2476m)

Monti Sibillini

Acquasanta
Terme

Tronto

Castellano

Marino del
Tronto

ABRUZZO

Giulianova

Spoleto

Norcia

Parco
Regionale
Coscerno Aspra

SS4

Parco Nazionale del Gran
Sasso e Monte della Laga

To Pescara (65km)
& Bari (310km)

large university population and an interesting modern artistic agenda. Further inland you can visit some of Italy's most splendid ancient cities: Urbino, the Renaissance in microcosm; the stunningly beautiful Ascoli Piceno and lovely little Macerata. In Pesaro you'll find the sea, the opera, new cinema and ancient archaeology.

HISTORY

The Piceni, one of Italy's earliest tribes, were the first inhabitants but the Romans reached what was later to become known as Marche in the middle of the 4th century BC. Pesaro and Ancona along the coast, Urbino and Cagli towards the Appenines – became part of the Byzantine empire, while

the rest of the territory was taken by the Lombards.

By the 12th century many towns had established themselves as independent self-ruling *comuni* but the struggle between the Guelphs and the Ghibellines was fierce. And as powerful families battled to extend their dominions, in 1356 the Church of Rome claimed power over 75 cities and territories, through a statute that remained in force until 1816.

In 1860, in one of the Risorgimento's most decisive battles, general Cialdini triumphed over the pontifical army at Castelfidardo. and a year later the administrative region now know as Marche was part of unified Italy.

PARKS & RESERVES

In the 1980s and 90s as seaside tourism expanded and local industries continued to develop, several protected nature reserves were established. These included the treeless, impressive and, in parts, forbidding national park of Monti Sibillini in the southwest, and four regional parks – the superb Monte Cònero park around Ancona, Sasso Simone e Simoncello, Monte San Bartolo, Gola della Rossa e di Frasassi.

The Marche Regional Office of Tourism publishes some excellent free brochures and booklets on camping, *agriturismo* and other accommodation options as well as details on the various parks themselves. You can pick up this information (though most is in Italian) at the main tourist office in Ancona or check www.turismo.marche.it.

TRANSPORT

The A14 and S16 (Via Adriatica) hug the coastline, while the inland roads provide easy access to all towns. Inland bus services are quite frequent and regular trains ply the coast on the Bologna-Lecce line. Getting from the coastal towns to places further inland by public transport is a little more complicated and you need to carefully study bus and train timetables for connections.

ANCONA

pop 100,000

Ancona, a major point of trade with the east since the Middle Ages, remains the mid-Adriatic's largest port, doing a healthy business in tourism as well as road freight. The old centre of Ancona was heavily bombed in WWII but today the provincial capital, which supports a major university, is a fascinating mixture of ancient and modern and is also a very congenial base for exploring the national park and nearby towns.

Orientation

There are two distinct parts to Ancona – the modern sprawl around the train station, and the old centre further up the hill. All trains arrive at the main station on Piazza Nello e Carlo Rosselli, though a few continue 1.5km north to the ferry terminal. There are several hotels near Piazza Roma and a cluster around the main train station. What remains of the old town stretches in an arc around the waterfront.

If you arrive by ferry, walk from Largo Dogana, near the ferry terminal uphill southeast to the central Piazza Roma and east to the city's grand Piazza Cavour.

A taxi from the station to the town centre will cost around €10.

Before you leave Platform One, buy a ticket from the *tabacchi*, just before the door that leads to the station's entrance/exit. It opens 6am to 11pm and a ticket will cost around €0.88 and is valid for an hour after you have validated it on the bus.

When you exit the station, bus Nos 1 and 4 will take you to the Port and the centre of town. But to make sure you get on the bus that goes in the right direction, cross the first bus stop to the stop in front of it, where you'll see a big sign that says Porto/Centro.

If you are travelling from the port or the city centre towards the train station, you need to wait for the 1/4 bus in Piazza della Repubblica, outside the Teatro delle Muse.

MAPS

You'll find plenty of maps of Ancona and surrounds at the excellent newsstand at the main train station or at bookshops and newsstands around town. Ancona Port Authority publishes an interesting map of the port. See tourist offices under Information, pp552–3.

Information

EMERGENCY

Police (☎ 071 2 28 81, emergency ☎ 112, ☎ 113; Via Giovanni Gervasoni 19) South of the city cente.

INTERNET ACCESS

Internet Centre (☎ 071 280 08 56; Corso Carlo Alberto 82; ☼ 9.30am-12.30pm & 4pm-late Tue-Sat)
Internet Point (Opposite the train station; €3.50/hr, €0.50 to print a page)

INTERNET RESOURCES

Comune di Ancon Online (www.comune.ancona.it, Italian only) A rich information source covering transport, accommodation, restaurants, events and much more.
Regione Marche (www.turismo.marche.it, Italian only) The official tourist office website; also has useful information on Ancona, including accomodation and sights.

LAUNDRY

Laundrette (Corso Carlo Alberto 76)

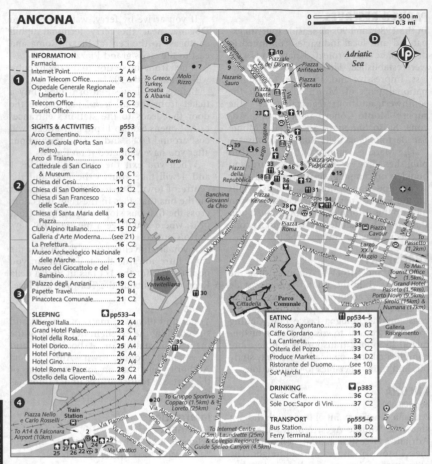

ANCONA

0 — 500 m
0 — 0.3 mi

INFORMATION
Farmacia.....................................1 C2
Internet Point............................2 A4
Main Telecom Office.................3 A4
Ospedale Generale Regionale
 Umberto I................................4 D2
Telecom Office..........................5 C2
Tourist Office............................6 C2

SIGHTS & ACTIVITIES p553
Arco Clementino........................7 B1
Arco di Garola (Porta San
 Pietro).....................................8 C2
Arco di Traiano.........................9 C1
Cattedrale di San Ciriaco
 & Museum..............................10 C1
Chiesa del Gesù........................11 C1
Chiesa di San Domenico..........12 C2
Chiesa di San Francesco
 delle Scale..............................13 C2
Chiesa di Santa Maria della
 Piazza......................................14 C2
Club Alpino Italiano.................15 D2
Galleria d'Arte Moderna......(see 21)
La Prefettura............................16 C2
Museo Archeologico Nazionale
 delle Marche..........................17 C1
Museo del Giocattolo e del
 Bambino.................................18 C2
Palazzo degli Anziani...............19 C1
Papette Travel..........................20 B4
Pinacoteca Comunale..............21 C2

SLEEPING pp533–4
Albergo Italia...........................22 A4
Grand Hotel Palace..................23 C1
Hotel della Rosa.......................24 A4
Hotel Dorico.............................25 A4
Hotel Fortuna...........................26 A4
Hotel Gino................................27 A4
Hotel Roma e Pace...................28 A4
Ostello della Gioventù.............29 A4

EATING pp534–5
Al Rosso Agontano..................30 B3
Caffe Giordano........................31 C2
La Cantineta.............................32 C2
Osteria del Pozzo.....................33 C2
Produce Market........................34 D2
Ristorante del Duomo..........(see 10)
Sot'Ajarchi...............................35 B3

DRINKING p383
Classic Caffe.............................36 C2
Sole Doc:Sapor di Vini............37 C2

TRANSPORT pp555–6
Bus Station...............................38 D2
Ferry Terminal..........................39 C2

Adriatic Sea

To Greece,
Turkey,
Croatia
& Albania

Molo
Rizzo

Nazario
Sauro

Porto

Piazzale
del Duomo

Piazza
Anfiteatro

Piazza
del Senato

Piazza
Dante
Alighieri

Piazza
della
Repubblica

Banchina
Giovanni
da Chio

Piazza
Kennedy

Piazza
Roma

Piazza del
Plebiscito

Piazza
Cavour

Largo
XXIV
Maggio

Galleria
Risorgimento

Stamira

Mole
Vanvitelliana

La
Cittadella

Parco
Comunale

To Main
Tourist Office
(1.5km);
Grand Hotel
Passeto (1.5km);
Porto Novo (9.5km);
Sirolo (15km) &
Numana (17km)

To
Passetto
(1.2km)

Vittorio Veneto

Piazza Nello
e Carlo Rosselli

Train
Station

To A14 & Falconara
Airport (10km)

To Gruppo Sportivo
Copparo (1.5km) &
Loreto (25km)

To Internet Centre
(25m); Laundrette (25m)
& Collegio Regionale
Guide Speleo Canyon (4.5km)

LEFT LUGGAGE
Train Station (end of platform one; €3 per bag
for the first 12 hrs, €2 for each successive 12 hrs;
24 hrs)
Ferry Terminal (free for the first two days)

MEDICAL SERVICES
Ospedale Generale Regionale Umberto I (☎ 071
596 40 16; Via Conca-Torrette) For urgent cardiological
attention call ☎ 071 596 50 16.
Farmacia Notturne (☎ 071 20 22 746; Corso G Mazzini 1; to 11pm, on call 11pm-7.45am) Another branch
at Piazza U Bassi 7 (☎ 071 89 42 08).

POST
Main Post Office (Largo XXIV Maggio; 8.15am-7pm
Mon-Sat)

Branch Post Office (cnr Via Ciriaco Pizzecolli & Via della
Catena)
Branch Post Office (ferry terminal)
Telecom Office (Piazza Roma 26; ☎ 8am-9.45pm)
Opposite the main train station.

TOILETS
Train Station (€0.52; a shower with towel and soap
included €5.16)
Ferry Terminal (free)

TOURIST INFORMATION
Main Tourist Office (☎ 071 35 89 91; www.turismo
.marche.it; Via Thaon de Revel 4; 9am-2pm & 3-6pm
Mon-Fri summer, 9am-1pm & 3-6pm Sat, & 9am-1pm
Sun; shorter hours in winter) Inconveniently placed at the
eastern end of town. Take bus 1/4 to Piazze IV Novembre.

UMBRIA & MARCHE

You'll need to buy a ticket (€0.88, valid one hour) from a *tabacchi*. The tourist office is just past the Grand Hotel Passetto. By bus from Piazza Cavour it's about five minutes, otherwise it's a pleasant 20 minute walk.
Ferry Terminal (☎ 071 20 11 83; ☽ 8am-8pm Tue-Sat & 2-8pm Sun & Mon 1 Jun-15 Sep)

Sights

The elegant Piazza del Plebiscito was medieval Ancona's main square, which has since been overtaken by grander, if less atmospheric, piazzas in the modern town. **La Prefettura**, the former police station, is in a 15th-century palace dominating the piazza and is noted for its beautiful courtyard. At its eastern end stands the baroque **Chiesa di San Domenico** (Piazza del Plebiscito; admission free; ☽ 7.15am-12.30pm & 4-7pm), containing the superb *Crucifixion* by Titian and *Annunciation* by Guercino. Near the church is the 13th-century city gate, the **Arco di Garola** (Garola's Arch), also known as Porta San Pietro.

MUSEUMS & CHURCHES

From La Prefettura, head north along Via Ciriaco Pizzecolli through the old city's ramparts to Palazzo Bosdari, which houses the **Pinacoteca Comunale** and **Galleria d'Arte Moderna** (☎ 071 222 50 45; Via Ciriaco Pizzecolli 17; adult/discounts €4/3; ☽ 9am-7pm Tue-Fri, 9am-1pm Mon, 8.30am-6.30pm Sat, 3-7pm Sun). The gallery displays works spanning six centuries, from artists including Guercino, Carlo Crivelli, Lorenzo Lotto and Titian. If you also wish to visit the Pinacotecas in nearby Loreto and Recanati, you can buy a combined entrance ticket for €7.80.

A bit further north along Via Ciriaco Pizzecolli and off to the right is **Chiesa di San Francesco delle Scale**, noteworthy for its 15th-century Venetian-Gothic doorway by Orsini. Beyond the church is Vanvitelli's **Chiesa del Gesù** (Church of Jesus), which is nearly always closed. Nearby is the economics faculty of the city's 13th-century university in the **Palazzo degli Anziani**.

The **Museo Archeologico Nazionale delle Marche** (☎ 071 20 26 02; Via Ferretti 1; adult/child €4.15/free; ☽ 8.30am-7.30pm Tue-Sun summer) is in the Palazzo Ferretti, which includes impressive collections of Greek vases and artefacts from the Iron Age as well as Celtic and Roman remnants.

Museo del Giocattolo e del Bambino (☎ 071 565 67; Via della Loggia Ancona Antica; ☽ 9am-1pm &

4-8pm) is a museum devoted to children and their games.

CATTEDRALE DI SAN CIRIACO

Via Giovanni XXIII leads up Monte Guasco to Piazzale del Duomo where there are sweeping views of the city and the port. Here, the Romanesque **cathedral** (☎ 071 20 03 91; Piazzale del Duomo; admission free; ☽ 8.30am-noon & 3-7pm, closes 6pm winter) has Byzantine and Gothic features. The small **museum** (☎ 071 5 26 88; Piazzale del Duomo 9; admission free, donations welcome; ☽ 4pm-6pm in summer, book at other times) by the cathedral, holds the 4th-century sarcophagus of Flavius Gorgonius, a masterpiece of early Christian art. You can take Bus 11 which runs from Piazza Roma to Piazza Repubblica. There's also a handy bar/restaurant which sells drinks, gelati and snacks at the top of the hill. **Ristorante del Duomo** (☽ 10am-midnight Tues-Sun).

WATERFRONT

North of Piazza Dante Alighieri, along the esplanade Lungomare Luigi Vanvitelli, is the **Arco di Traiano** (Trajan's Arch), erected in 115 BC. Luigi Vanvitelli's **Arco Clementino** (Clementine's Arch), inspired by the former and dedicated to Pope Clement XII, is further on, near Molo Rizzo. South of Piazza Dante Alighieri you'll find the small Piazza Santa Maria and the disused, tumbledown **Chiesa di Santa Maria della Piazza**, which retains scraps of 5th- and 6th-century pavement mosaics. Heading southwest along Via XXIX Settembre, the large building is the **Mole Vanvitelliana**, Designed by Luigi Vanitelli in 1733 for Pope Clementine. It is now the magnificent venue for some major exhibitions. Call ☎ 071 207 23 48 for details.

Festivals & Events

Ancona Jazz takes place in October. The **Premio Marche**, an international exhibition of contemporary art is held in November and December, and the festival of the city's patron saint, San Ciriaco takes place in May. Check with the tourist office for details.

Sleeping
BUDGET

Ostello della Gioventù (☎ /fax 071 422 57; Via Lama-ticci 7; B&B €11.90; ☽ closed 11pm-4.30pm) Ancona's HI-youth hostel has clean and sunny dorms in a rather ugly-looking building a block from the train station.

Hotel Gino (☎ /fax 071 421 79; hotel.gino@tiscalinet .it; Via Flaminia 4; s/d with breakfast €31/47) The best thing going for this place is that it's cheap and close to the railway station and bus stop. You get TV and shower in every room.

Hotel Dorico (☎ 071 430 09; fax 071 427 61; Via Flaminia 8; s/d/tr with breakfast 35/45/55) This is the nicest of the downmarket places on the outskirts of Ancona. Despite its position on the busy road, it's reasonably quiet, clean and comfortable. Reception staff are young, polite and accommodating and there are showers, telephone and TV in every room. Credit cards accepted.

Albergo Italia (☎ 097 426 07; fax 071 442 21; Piazza Rosselli 9; s/d/tr €39/66/89) The rooms are a little shabbier than the spotlessly clean and bright foyer might suggest, but all have shower, toilet and TV.

MID RANGE

Hotel Roma e Pace (☎ 071 20 20 07, ☎ 20 73 742; fax 207 47 36; Via G Leopardi 1; s/d/tr €58.94/112/124; 🔀 P) This delightful hotel, right in the centre of the historic town, manages to retain the charm which has made it popular for the last couple of centuries at the same time providing the comforts necessary for 21st-century visitors. All rooms have bathroom, direct-dial telephone and TV.

Hotel Fortuna (☎ 0714 26 63; www.hotelfortuna.it; Piazza Rosselli 15; s/d/tr with breakfast 52/83/98; 🔀) Though not situated in the most picturesque part of town, this three-star hotel is nevertheless convenient and provides modern, tastefully furnished rooms, which include en suites, TV and direct-dial phones. Telex and fax services are also available.

Hotel della Rosa (☎ /fax 071 413 88, ☎ 071 426 51; www.hoteldellarosa.it, Italian only; Piazza Rosselli 3; s/d/ tr with breakfast €55/88/98; 🔀 🖳) This comfortable hotel has been completely refurbished and reopened in 2001. Close to the train station and the exhibition centre (Lazzaretto), it is also convenient for the A14 autostrada exit for Ancona North. The 38 light-filled rooms are nicely decorated and have en suites, direct-dial phones and satellite TV. Wheelchair access is also available.

TOP END

Grand Hotel Palace (☎ 071 20 18 13; palace.anco na@tiscalinet.it; Lungomare Luigi Vanvitelli 24; s/d from

€110/120; 🕑 closed Christmas; 🔀 P) Luxurious, light rooms, with beautiful sea views. The hotel is five minutes from the historic centre and within walking distance of Ancona's major shops and most popular restaurants, yet is quiet and tranquil. All rooms have their own bath, telephone and satellite TV. Weekend rates are Friday to Sunday.

Grand Hotel Passetto (☎ 071 313 07/8/9; fax 071 328 56; Via Thaon de Revel 1; s/d €115/175, d for single use €140; 🔊) At the newer and quiet end of town near the tourist office, this gorgeous hotel with wonderful views over the sea is situated just above the scenic route that leads into the Parco Naturale de Cònero and some lovely beaches. There's a good restaurant just across the road and the beach is not far down the hill.

Eating
RESTAURANTS

Osteria del Pozzo (☎ 071 207 39 96; Via Bonda 2; meals €15.50) This small place is just off Piazza del Plebiscito and serves good, reasonably priced food in a convivial atmosphere.

La Cantineta (☎ 071 20 11 07; Via Gramsci 1c; meals €14) This is a simple trattoria near the old town centre. They'll recite the menu rather than give you a list, but have faith, for a huge plate of pasta, a side dish of salad or vegetables, a glass of wine, some bread will be a bargain. For mains, the house speciality is *stoccafisso*.

Passetto (☎ 071 332 14; Piazza 1V Novembre 1; meals €45; 🕑 closed Mon, dinner Sun & Aug) This elegant place at the far post-war end of Ancona overlooks the sparkling Adriatic, and serves traditional dishes, home-made desserts and good wines.

Heading towards the train station you'll find two good eating options.

Sot'Ajarchi (☎ 071 20 24 41; Via Gugliemo Marconi 93; meals €25-50; 🕑 Mon-Sat) This small restaurant under the *portici* in front of the port specialises, not surprisingly, in fish. For *primo* try *pasta alla marinaro* or *minestra di seppie*, follow it up with a main course such as the recommended *guazzetto*, and finish off with a simple home-made dessert like *zuppa inglese* and some *biscottini* dipped in *vin santo*.

Al Rosso Agontano (☎ 071 207 52 79; www .allrossoagontano.it; Via Marconi 3; meals €40; 🕑 closed Sun, Sat lunch, Christmas holidays & mid-Aug) This delightful simple, modern restaurant/wine bar

UMBRIA & MARCHE

under the *portici* of the *lungoporto* has great service and a terrific selection of wines. Try lamb cutlets with artichokes fried in soya sauce; a *terrina pescatrice*; swordfish garnished with *riso croccante*; *baccalà* with potatoes and black olive sauce.

QUICK EATS
Caffè Giordano (Corso Mazzini 53; ☺ 7am-9pm Mon-Sat) Giordano, who speaks English, is more than happy to give tourist information to visitors. There is a *sala interna* with four tables for coffee (€0.80) and snacks (*primi* from €4, *insalata*, €3.50, baguette €3.50. *tramezzini* €2). This is also a good place for an evening *aperitivo*.

SELF-CATERING
The **produce market** (Corso Giuseppe Mazzini 130; ☺ 7.30am-12.45pm & 5-8pm, 4.30-7.30pm winter) sells fresh fruit, vegetables and other food.

Drinking
Solo Doc: SapordiVini (☎ 339 241 34 16; Corso Giuseppe Mazzini 106) Right on the corner of Piazza Roma (opposite the fountain of the 13 Cannelle), this cosy little *enoteca* pipes beautiful classical music out onto the street. It opens 8am to 2pm for coffee and snacks and from 5pm to midnight for aperitifs and nightcaps.

Classic Caffe (☎ 071 20 30 00; Corso Giuseppe Mazzini 19) This café bar is very popular with the hip crowd in the evening between 7pm and 10pm. You can sip champagne for €6.20, cocktails for €5.50 and other drinks for €4.20. A beer here costs €4.20 and wine €3.10.

Getting There & Away
AIR
Scheduled flights from London, Rome, Milan and Turin, as well as some charter flights, land at **Falconara airport** (☎ 071 282 71), 10km west of Ancona. In summer there are also flights to Olbia on Sardinia.

BOAT
Ferry operators have booths at the ferry terminal. Timetables are subject to change, prices fluctuate with the season, some lines come and go – your best bet is to check with the tourist office or at the terminal. Most lines offer discounts on return fares, and boats are generally roll-on, roll-off car ferries.

BUS
Most provincial and regional buses depart from Piazza Cavour, where you'll find timetables displayed at the ticket offices. **Conero Bus** (☎ 071 280 20 92, ☎ 800 21 88 20 for information and timetables) and **Reni** (☎ 071 804 65 04) run buses to provincial towns such as Loreto (€1.70, one hour, five daily), Recanati (€1.90, 1¼ hours, five daily), Osimo (€1.30, 40 minutes, half-hourly), Sirolo (€1.25, 35 minutes, hourly) and Numana (€1.25, 40 minutes, hourly). Other companies run buses to Macerata (€2.60, 1½ hours, 10 daily), Senigallia (€1.50, 35 minutes, four daily) and Pesaro (€2.95, one hour 20 minutes, four daily) – the last two are run by **Bucci** (☎ 071 792 27 37) which also has a service to Urbino (€5.15, 2½ hours) at 2pm Monday to Saturday.

CAR & MOTORCYCLE
Ancona is on the A14, which links Bologna with Bari. The SS16 coastal road runs parallel to the autostrada and is a more pleasant (toll-free) alternative. The DS76 connects Ancona with Perugia and Rome.

TRAIN
Ancona is on the Bologna–Lecce line and regular services link it with Milan (from €19.35, 5½ hours, every two hours or €31, 3½ hours with ES/Intercity), Turin (from €24.65, 6½ hours, four direct daily), Rome (€13, three hours 10 minutes, five ES daily), Bologna (from €10.10, 2¾ hours, 20 daily), Lecce (from €24.65, seven hours, eight daily) and most main stops in between, such as Pesaro (€5.35, 50 minutes, hourly) Senigallia (€1.75, 25 minutes, hourly) and Fano (€4.05, 40 minutes, hourly). For information, call ☎ 848 88 80 88 (not available from cell phones) between 7am-9pm.

Getting Around
Conero Bus' service J runs roughly every hour from the train station to the airport, from 6.05am to 8.30pm Monday to Saturday and seven times a day on Sunday (€1.10, 25 to 45 minutes). The bus labelled 'Ancona-Aeroporto' does the trip during August and on Sunday and public holidays.

There are about six Conero Bus services, including No 1/4 which connects the main train station with the ferry terminal and Piazza Cavour (€0.65) – look for the bus

UMBRIA & MARCHE

stop with the big sign displaying Centro and Porto.

For a taxi, call ☎ 071 4 33 21.

You can hire a car at the train station, where you'll find **Europcar** (☎ 071 20 31 00), **Maggiore** (☎ 071 4 26 24), or at the airport, where you'll also find Hertz.

AROUND ANCONA
Parco Naturale del Monte Cònero

This park extends 5800 hectares around **Monte Cònero** in the province of Ancona and takes in the beautiful coastal towns of **Portonovo** (9.5km south of Ancona), **Sirolo** (22km from Ancona) and **Numana** (a further 2km south east) as well as **Camerano**, further inland. With its mountains and rolling hills, many species of birds and well maintained walking tracks, it offers wonderful opportunities for all sorts of seaside and rural activities (as well as some great places for eating and drinking).

For more information on suggested itineraries within the park and areas especially equipped for camping and caravanning, contact **Campeggio Club Adriatico** (☎ /fax 071 13 43 71; Viale della Vittoria 37; Ancona). For information on the park itself and to arrange guided tours, contact **Consorzio del Parco del Conero** (☎ 0719 33 11 61; www.parks.it/parco.conero, Italian only; Via Vivaldi 1/3, Sirolo) or the **Visitors Centre** (☎ /fax 071 933 18 79; Via Peschiera 30/a, Sirolo).

Eating

There are a few rather good restaurants in Conero Park.

PORTONOVO
Laghetto (☎ 071 801 11 83; Via Portonovo; meals €30-35; ☯ closed Mon winter & Jan-Mar) Situated in a wooden chalet a few steps away from the sea, Laghetto provides great meals and great service.

Susci Bar al Clandestino (☎ 071 80 14 22; Via Portonovo, Loc Poggio; ☯ mid-May–mid-Sep) Susci Bar Al Clandestino serves food that is highly recommended by Italy's food critics. There's no formality here and after a swim in the beautiful Baia di Portonove, you can drop in for a taste of its Mediterranean sushi or some 'cool' tapas.

Giacchetti (☎ 071 80 13 84; Via Portonove 171; meals €40; ☯ closed Mon winter & Nov-Mar) Serves great seafood dishes and has been doing so for years.

Hotel Fortino Napoleonico (☎ 071 80 14 54; Via Poggio 1; meals €50; ☯ Tue-Sun, closed Jan) An upmarket place where you can dine elegantly on dishes comprising good, fresh seafood.

SIROLO
Rocco (☎ /fax 071 933 05 58; Via Torrione 1; meals €45-55; ☯ Wed-Mon, closed mid-Oct–Easter) Lovely place run by passionate young cooks who base their excellent dishes on local fresh fish.

Hostaria Il Grottino (☎ 071 933 12 18; Via dell'Ospedale 9; ☯ Fri-Mon & Wed, closed Nov & 15-30 Jan) Comfortable and popular – you'd be wise to book.

NUMANA
Saraghino (☎ /fax 071 739 15 96; Via Litoranea 209, Loc. Martelli; meals €45; ☯ Tue-Sun, closed Feb) Gaze out to sea with a glass of excellent wine and one of the superb and creative dishes (artichokes with gorgonzola, *tagliatelle con scampetti*, *vongole e pomodoro fresco*) prepared by one of Italy's celebrated up-and-coming young chefs, Roberto Fiorini.

Costarella (☎ 071 736 02 97; Via IV Novembre 35; meals €55; ☯ Wed-Mon, closed Dec-Easter) You'll find this delightful little place at the top of a steep flight of steps in the middle of the town. The dishes are based on local produce, fish of course, and seasonable vegetables. The antipasti are definitely worth sampling.

Loreto

Thousands of Catholic pilgrims travel here every year because they believe that angels transferred the house of the Virgin Mary from Palestine to this spot towards the end of the 13th century. The basilica that was built over the site was begun in 1468, on Gothic lines, and later expanded and added to by some of the luminaries of the Renaissance, including Bramante, to become today's **Santuario della Santa Casa** (☎ 071 97 01 04, ☎ 071 97 68 37; Piazza della Madonna; admission free; ☯ 6.15am-12.30pm & 2.30-8pm).

For a meal, try **Andreina** (☎ 071 97 01 24; Via Buffolareccia 14; meals €30; ☯ Wed-Mon, closed Jul). This rustic little restaurant has a certain elegance. Meat dishes and local wines are a specialty, though other dishes like its omelettes with black truffles are definitely worth trying too.

Loreto lies about 28km south of Ancona and can be reached easily by bus. Loreto train station (Bologna–Lecce line) is a few

OUT & ABOUT IN ANCONA

There's plenty to keep active people happy around Ancona.

Trekking

Escursioni Parco del Conero (☎ 071 933 03 76; Via Vivaldi 1/3) in Sirolo specialises, as its name suggests, in walking trips through the park.

Horse Riding

Around Ancona:

Agriturism II Corbezzolo (☎ 071 213 90 39; Contrada Piancarda 124)
Circolo Ippico Le Torrette (☎ 071 80 22 27; Via Paterno 249)
Centro Ippico Cittadella (☎ 071 280 28 80; Via Circonvallazione 2)
Gruppo Ippico Anconetano (☎ 330 88 08 01; Via Piantate Lunghe, Ancona-Candia)
Club Ippico del Conero (☎ 071 80 45 69; Via Buranico 199, Varano di Ancona)

In Sirolo:

Circolo Ippico Sirolo/Agriturismo II Ritorno (☎ 071 933 15 44; Via Piani d'Aspio 12)
Circolo Ippico II Cerfoglio (☎ 348 335 80 78; Via Mulinello)

Cycling & Mountain Biking

If you're into mountain biking you might like to contact Mr Ramazzotti at **Crazy Bike** (☎ 071 73 10 21; Via Loretana 146), in Camerano. For cycling, contact **Papette Travel** (☎ 071 20 41 65; Via Marconi 46, Ancona) or **Gruppo Sportivo Copparo** (☎ 071 89 68 01; Via Gigli 38, Ancona).

Caving & Rock Climbing

A useful contact for rock climbers is **Club Alpino Italiano** (☎ 071 207 06 96; Via Cataldo 3, Ancona). Caving fans could try **Collegio Regionale Delle Guide Speleo Canyon** (☎ 071 28 67 74, ☎ 338 990 54 81; Via Crocioni 33, Ancona) or **GSM** (Gruppo Speleologia Marche; ☎ 071 207 06 96; Via Cialdini 29) of the CAI in Ancona.

Water Sports

The eastern boundary of the Conero Park is a stretch of beaches. If you want to sail into summer, there are a number of useful contacts in Ancona. The **Centro Nautico** (☎ 071 208 08 31; Via Mattei 42); **Comunque Vela** (☎ 071 286 13 17, Via Ginelli 19); or there's **Sef Stamura** (☎ 071 207 53 24; Via M Vanvitelliana).

Golf

Contact **Conero Golf Club** (☎ 071 736 06 13; Via Betelico 6, Sirolo).

kilometres away, but shuttle buses connect it with the town centre.

Falconara Marittima

Known mostly for its airport, modern-day **Falconara Marittima,** 13.5km northwest of Ancona is an industrial seaside town. Nevertheless, the town still has some interesting traces of its medieval past at Falconara Alta, high above the modern town. These include a 13th-century castle, former home of the Cortesi counts, the 13th-century **Santa Maria delle Grazie** church, and the impressive Rocca Priora, constructed in 1198.

For an excellent meal, head for **Villa Amalia** (☎ 071 916 05 50; www.villa-amalia.it; Via degli Spagnoli 4; meals €50; ☺ Wed-Sun lunch, Mon, closed Jan & Jul). Not only is it a great place to eat, but you can sleep here too.

URBINO

pop 6000

Urbino is the jewel of Marche and one of the best-preserved and most beautiful hill towns in Italy. It enjoyed a period of great splendour under the Montefeltro family from the 12th century onwards, and reached its zenith under Duca Federico da Montefeltro.

UMBRIA & MARCHE

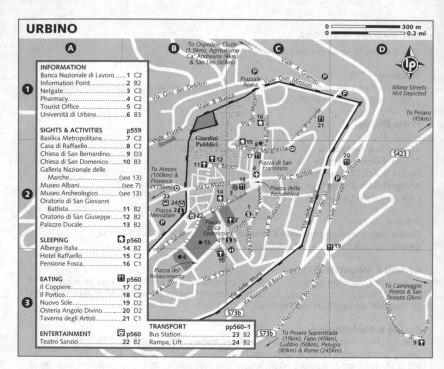

URBINO

Artists in particularly good grace with the duke included Piero della Francesca, Paolo Uccello, Justus of Ghent and Giovanni Santi (the father of Raffaello Sanzio, the great Raphael, who was born in the city).

By the mid 16th century, central Italy was ruled by the pope; only the duchy of Urbino remained autonomous. The city and its territories were now reigned over by the Della Rovere family, since the Montefeltro family had been left without heirs. The family was, however, linked to the papacy. Two of its members were elected popes (Sisto IV and Giulio II), and Francesco Maria I Della Rovere became commander of the pontifical army. The town can be a pain to reach by public transport, but should not be missed. The area to the north, particularly the winding road to San Marino and on into Emilia-Romagna, is a treat and there are plenty of hotels in the small towns along the way.

Orientation

Buses arrive at Piazza Mercatale at the walled city's western edge, where you'll find a couple of bars, a restaurant, some offices and the police station. From this piazza it's a short steep walk up Via G Mazzini to Piazza della Repubblica. From there you head back south along Via Vittorio Veneto for Piazza Duca Federico and the sprawling Piazza del Rinascimento. However, if you cross Piazza Mercatale to the Rampa, for €0.25 you can take a *ascensore* (lift) to the Teatro Sanzio at the end of Via Garibaldi and a short walk from the town's main attraction, the Palazzo Ducale. Drivers are most likely to arrive at Piazzale Roma at the city's northern edge, where cars can be parked free of charge. Via Raffaello connects Piazzale Roma with Piazza della Repubblica.

MAPS

You can buy the useful *Urbino Mini-guide con pianta* (in English) for €2 from the Piazza Mercatale information point, or from various newspaper and magazine shops in the old town.

The Comune di Urbino (www.comune .urbino.ps.it, Italian only) also issues a free map of the town which lists the principal monuments. It's available from the main tourist office.

Information

EMERGENCY
Police Station (emergencies ☎ 112, ☎ 113; Piazza Mercatale)

INTERNET ACCESS
Netgate (☎ 0722 24 62; Via G Mazzini 17) Operates on a subscription system, but you can log on as a guest.

MEDICAL SERVICES
Ospedale Civile (☎ 0722 30 11; Via Bonconte da Montefeltro) Hospital located about 1.5km north of the city centre.
Pharmacy (Piazza della Repubblica 9)

MONEY
Banca Nazionale di Lavoro (Via Vittorio Veneto 53) ATM and exchange facilities.

POST
Post Office (☎ 0722 37 79 17; Via Bramante 18; � 8.30am-6.30pm Mon-Sat)

TOILETS
There are public toilets (free) just around the corner from the main tourist office, opposite the Chiesa di San Domenico.

TOURIST INFORMATION
Information Point (� 6.30am-8.30pm) at the entrance to the lift that takes you from the main car park and bus station in Piazza Mercatale to the old town uphill.
Tourist Office (☎ 0722 26 13; fax 0722 24 41; Via Puccinotti 3, � 9am-1pm Mon-Sat, also 3-6pm & 9am-1pm on Sun & holidays from May-Sep)

Sights

PALAZZO DUCALE
The grand residence of Urbino's ruling dynasty was completed in 1482 and is one of Italy's most complete early Renaissance **palaces** (☎ 0722 32 90 57; Piazza Duca Federico; adult/child incl Galleria Nazionale delle Marche €4.15/free; ☸ 8.30am-7.15pm Tue-Sun, 8.30am-2pm Mon).

From Corso Garibaldi you get the best view of the complex with its unusual **Facciata dei Torricini**, a three-storey loggia in the form of a triumphal arch, flanked by circular towers. The palazzo now houses the **Galleria Nazionale delle Marche**, a formidable art collection, and the less inspiring **Museo Archeologico**.

A monumental staircase, one of Italy's first, leads to the *piano nobile* (literally 'noble floor') and the Ducal Apartments. The best-preserved room is Duca Federico's **Studiolo**. Most famous of the paintings on display is Piero della Francesca's masterpiece, *The Flagellation*. Another highlight is the remarkable portrait of Federico and his son Guidobaldo, attributed to the Spanish artist Pedro Berruguete. The collection also includes a large number of drawings by Federico Barocci.

BASILICA METROPOLITANA
Rebuilt in the early 19th century in neoclassical style, the interior of Urbino's basilica (Piazza Duca Federico; admission €1.55; ☸ 9.30am-noon & 2.30-6pm) commands greater interest than its austere facade. Particularly memorable is Federico Barocci's *Last Supper*. The basilica's **Museo Albani** contains further paintings, including Andrea da Bologna's *Madonna del Latte* (Madonna Breastfeeding).

CHURCHES & ORATORIES
Opposite the Palazzo Ducale, the medieval **Chiesa di San Domenico** is notable for its lunette, the panel above the 15th-century doorway, by Luca della Robbia.

The 14th-century **Oratorio di San Giovanni Battista** (☎ 0347 671 11 81; Via Barocci; admission €1.55; ☸ 10am-12.30pm & 3-5.30pm Mon-Sat, 10am-12.30pm Sun) features brightly coloured frescoes by Lorenzo and Giacomo Salimbeni. A few steps away, the **Oratorio di San Giuseppe** (☎ 0347 61 11 81, Via Barocci; admission €1.55; ☸ same as above) boasts a stucco *Nativity* by Federico Brandani.

The **Chiesa di San Bernardino** (☎ 0722 32 05 39; Viale Giuseppe di Vittorio; admission free; ☸ 8am-6pm), 2km southeast of the city walls, houses the mausoleum of the dukes of Urbino.

CASA DI RAFFAELLO
North of the Piazza della Repubblica you'll find the 15th-century **house** (☎ 0722 32 01 05; Via Raffaello 57; admission €2.60; ☸ 9am-1pm & 3-7pm Mon-Sat, 10am-1pm Sun, spring & summer, mornings only Nov-early Mar) where Raphael spent his first 16 years. On the first floor is possibly one of Raphael's first frescoes, a Madonna with child.

Courses
Università di Urbino (☎ 0722 30 52 50; fax 0722 30 52 87; www.uniurb.it; Via Saffi 2, Urbino 61029)

UMBRIA & MARCHE

Offers an intensive course in language and culture for foreigners during August for €380 and it can arrange accommodation for €210 for the month. Details and booking from March to 19 July. Write to the Segreteria dell' Università, or call their toll-free number within Italy ☎ 800 46 24 46.

Festivals & Events

In May, Urbino decks itself in flowers for the **Urbino Città Fiorita** festival. The **Urbino Jazz Festival** takes place in June, the **International Festival of Ancient Music** in July and there's an antique fair on the fourth Sunday of every month. The **Festa dell' Duca** takes place on the third Sunday in August, when the town's streets become the setting for a costume procession and the re-enactment of a tournament on horseback. Check with the tourist office for up-to-date details.

Sleeping

The tourist office can provide a full list of private rooms and other accommodation options.

Pensione Fosca (☎ 0722 254 2l; fax 0722 26 00; Via Raffaello 67; s/d €21/35) This charming but tiny *pensione*, on the top floor of an ancient building, just up from the Casa di Raffaello, has simple but appealing rooms with shared bath.

Campeggio Pineta (☎ 0722 47 10; fax 0722 47 34; Via San Donato, Loc. Cesana; site per person/tent up to €5.50/12) Urbino's only camp site is 2km east of the city in San Donato and has all the standard facilities.

Albergo Italia (☎ 0722 27 01; www.albergo-italia -urbino.it; Corso Garibaldi 32; s/d €41-67/62-114) This thoroughly refurbished place is clean and enjoys a good position behind the Palazzo Ducale.

Hotel Raffaello (☎ 0722 47 84; www.albergoraff aello.com; Via Santa Margherita 40; s/d €52-87.80/88-114) Despite the rather austere marbled entrance, the three-star Raffaello has comfortable rooms and serves a good breakfast.

Eating

Don't miss the *strozzapreti al pesto*, available in most restaurants. These worm-like shreds of pasta were designed to choke priests, but they're delicious.

Nuovo Sole (☎ 0722 32 87 78; Via Nazionale 73; meals from €12.90) Just east of the city walls,

this affordable Chinese restaurant makes a good change for those who can't face another plate of pasta.

Il Portico (☎ 0722 27 22; Via G Mazzini 7; snacks from €1.55; ☽ Mon-Sat) For bruschetta, salads and light meals, try this bookshop *osteria*.

Taverna degli Artisti (☎ 0722 26 76; Via Bramante 52; meals €15.50; ☽ closed Tue winter) This restaurant serves good pasta and meat dishes. Their giant pizzas are served on huge wooden slabs.

Il Coppiere (☎ 0722 32 23 26; Via Santa Margherita 1; meals €25.80) This 1st-floor restaurant has elegant dining.

Agriturismo Ca' Andreana (☎ 0722 32 78 45; Via Padana 119; meals €25; ☽ Tue-Sun, closed mid-Jan & beginning Oct) Start with the *norcineria* – that's the local sausage – and Montefeltro cheeses with a crisp glass of white wine. Try the *capellace* with olives and herbs before you check out the delicious homemade sweets.

Osteria Angolo Divino (☎ 0722 32 75 59; Via Sant'Andrea 14; ☽ Thu-Mon, closed Oct) This is another great place where you'll eat and drink good local fare.

Entertainment

The arts come alive in Urbino during the summer season.

Teatro Sanzio (☎ 0722 22 81; Corso Garibaldi) hosts plays and concerts, particularly from July to September. Pick up a brochure at the main tourist office.

Getting There & Around

The Pesaro-based company **Soget** (☎ /fax 0721 37 13 18) runs up to 10 services daily between Urbino and Pesaro (€2.50, 55 minutes). Pick up a timetable at their ticket office on Piazza Matteotti, Pesaro. Bucci (☎ 0721 3 24 01) runs two buses per day to Rome (€18.10, five hours) at 6am and 4pm, has one service to Ancona (€5.15, 2½ hours) at 4.40pm and goes to Arezzo (€5.15, two hours 40 minutes) at 7am.

Take the bus to Pesaro to pick up trains (see p563).

An autostrada and the S423 connect Urbino with Pesaro, and the S73b connects the town with the SS3 for Rome. Most motor vehicles are banned from the walled city. **Taxis** (☎ 0722 25 50) and shuttle buses operate from Piazza della Repubblica and Piazza Mercatale. There are car parks outside the city gates. Note that there's no parking on Piazzale Roma on Saturday morning as it's market day.

PESARO

pop 90,000

Pesaro offers an expanse of beach as well as the remains of a medieval centre, though in midsummer you can't move for the crowds. Most of the population seems to amble around on bicycles. This, and the fact that the town is blessed with lots of avenues of wide shady trees, gives it a relaxed holiday air, even though it is quite a busy and prosperous provincial capital.

Orientation

The train station is southwest of the centre, away from the beach. From the station, walk along Viale del Risorgimento, through Piazza Lazzarini and continue to Piazza del Popolo, the town's main square. Via Rossini takes you to Piazzale della Libertà and the waterfront.

Information

EMERGENCY

Police Station (☎ 0721 38 61 11; Via Giordano Bruno 5)

INTERNET ACCESS

Biblioteca Centrale Comunale (☎ 0721 38 74 96; Via Rossini 37) Free but you must make a reservation in person the day before you want to use it.

INTERNET RESOURCES

Pesaro Urbino Tourism (www.turismo.pesarourbino.it) Has excellent information, with maps, hotels and sights.

LEFT LUGGAGE

Train Station €3 per bag for the first 12 hours, €2 for every 12 hours thereafter.

MEDICAL SERVICES

Pronto soccorso (emergency ☎ 118, casualty ☎ 0721 3 29 57).
Ospedale San Salvatore (hospital; ☎ 0721 36 11; Piazzale Albani)

POST

Post Office (Piazza del Popolo; ☒ 8.15am-7.40pm Mon-Sat)

TELEPHONE & FAX

Telecom Office (Piazza Matteotti; ☒ 7am-11pm summer, reduced hrs low season) Southeast of Piazza del Popolo.

TOURIST INFORMATION

Tourist Office (☎ 0721 6 93 41; www.comune .pesaro.ps.it; Piazzale della Libertà 11; ☒ 9am-1pm & 3.30-6.30pm Mon-Sat; 9am-1pm Sun) Pick up its free *Handy Guide*, in English.

Sights & Activities

The 15th-century **Palazzo Ducale**, dominating Piazza del Popolo, housed the ruling Della Rovere family. Today it houses bureaucracy and is closed to the public. The splendid windows that grace its facade are by Domenico Rosselli.

Head northwest along Corso XI Settembre to reach Via Toschi Mosca and the town's combined **Musei Civici**, **Museo delle Ceramiche** and **Pinacoteca** (☎ 0721 38 75 41; Piazza Toschi Mosca 29; adult/under 25s €2.60/free; ☒ 9.30am-12.30pm Tue-Sun year-round, plus 4-7pm Thu & Sun Sep-Jun, 5-8pm Wed & Fri-Sun, 5-11pm Tue & Thu Jul & Aug). The production of ceramics has long been a speciality of Pesaro and the museum has a worthy collection, while the Pinacoteca houses Giovanni Bellini's magnificent altarpiece depicting the coronation of the Virgin.

In 1792 the composer Rossini was born in what is now known as the **Casa Natale di Rossini** (☎ 0721 38 73 57; Via Rossini 34; adults/under 25s €2.60/free; ☒ 9.30am-12.30pm Tue-Sun & 4-7pm Thu-Sun). Here, a small museum contains various personal effects and his spinet. You can purchase a joint ticket for the Musei Civici and the Casa Natale di Rossini for €4.15.

Avid Rossini fans may also want to visit the Conservatorio di Musica, which includes the **Museo Rossini** (also called Tempietto Rossiniano; ☎ 0721 3 00 53; Piazza Olivieri; ☒ guided tours only), which is off Via Branca. To organise a tour, phone ahead or contact the tourist office.

The **Chiesa di Sant'Agostino** (Corso XI Settembre; free; ☒ 8am-7pm) features some intricate 15th-century inlaid-wood choir stalls. The modest **Museo Oliveriano** (☎ 0721 3 33 44; Via Mazza 97; admission free; ☒ 4-7pm Mon-Sat Jul & Aug, 9.30am-12.30pm Mon-Sat the rest of the year on request) contains archaeological finds from the area, including a child's tomb from the Iron Age. Apply for admission at the adjoining library.

Festivals & Events

Pesaro is quite a cultural hub. In June, it hosts the **International Festival of New Cinema**.

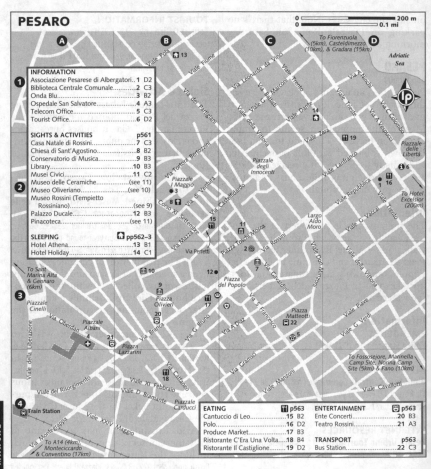

PESARO

0 ___ 200 m
0 ___ 0.1 mi

To Fiorenzuola
(5km), Casteldimezzo
(10km), & Gradara (15km)

Adriatic
Sea

INFORMATION
Associazione Pesarese di Albergatori.. **1** D2
Biblioteca Centrale Comunale............**2** C3
Onda Blu......................................**3** B2
Ospedale San Salvatore.....................**4** A3
Telecom Office...............................**5** C3
Tourist Office.................................**6** D2

SIGHTS & ACTIVITIES p561
Casa Natale di Rossini........................**7** C3
Chiesa di Sant'Agostino......................**8** B2
Conservatorio di Musica.....................**9** B3
Library...**10** B3
Musei Civici...................................**11** C2
Museo delle Ceramiche..................(see **11**)
Museo Oliveriano........................(see **10**)
Museo Rossini (Tempietto
Rossiniano)..............................(see **9**)
Palazzo Ducale.............................**12** B3
Pinacoteca.................................(see **11**)

SLEEPING pp562–3
Hotel Athena................................**13** B1
Hotel Holiday...............................**14** C1

EATING p563
Cantuccio di Leo..................**15** B2
Polo.................................**16** D2
Produce Market...................**17** B3
Ristorante C'Era Una Volta....**18** B4
Ristorante Il Castiglione.........**19** D2

ENTERTAINMENT p563
Ente Concerti......................**20** B3
Teatro Rossini.....................**21** A3

TRANSPORT p563
Bus Station........................**22** C3

In honour of its most famous son, the town also hosts the **Rossini Opera Festival** (0721 3 80 01; fax 0721 380 02 20; www.rossinioperafestiva.it; Via Rossini 24; 10am-1pm & 3-5pm Mon-Fri) at the Teatro in Piazza Lazzarini.

Sleeping

Many hotels close from October to April and the camp sites may well do the same, so go to the tourist office when you first arrive to find out what's open.

The town's local hotel association, the **Associazione Pesarese di Albergatori** (0721 679 59; www.apahotel.it; Viale della Repubblica 46) will help you locate a room. The tourist office can also provide a lengthy list of apartments which can be handy if you are stuck.

The closest camp sites are about 5km south of the town centre at Fossosejore on the coast.

Hotel Athena (0721 3 01 14; fax 0721 3 38 78; Viale Pola 18; s/d from €25.80/36.15) On a leafy street at the northwest end of town, the Athena is a good two-star choice. The conservatory-style entrance is welcoming and the rooms are clean and bright.

Hotel Holiday (0721 3 48 51; fax 0721 37 03 10; Viale Trento 159; s/d €39/59) It may lack charm, but all rooms in this concrete block have private balconies and fairly large bathrooms.

Hotel Excelsior (0721 3 27 20; excelsior@ pesaro.com; Lungomare Nazario Sauro; full board s/d starting at €70/90;) The Excelsior is right on the beach;

UMBRIA & MARCHE

Marinella (☎ 072155795; www.campingmarinella.it; Loc. Fossosejore; sites per person/tent up to €7.50/9; ✆ Apr-Sep) This camp site is on the SS16 at the 244km mark. You can get here from Pesaro on one of the regular AMI buses to Fossosejore.

Norina (☎ 0721 5 57 92; fax 0721 5 51 65; Via Marina Ardizia 181; Loc. Fossosejore; site per person/tent up to €6.51/12.14; ✆ Apr–mid-Oct) This place is close to the Marinella camp site.

Eating

This resort town offers up a few tasty options.

Ristorante C'Era Una Volta (☎ 0721 3 09 11; Via Cattaneo 26; pizzas from €2.60) This is a good pizzeria with a great atmosphere – diners share long wooden tables and are watched over by a tank of piranha.

Polo (☎ 0721 37 59 02; Viale Trieste 231; meals €12.90-18.10) Polo's a fairly hip and popular establishment which serves a good mix of Italian and international food (and an extraordinary variety of grappa).

Ristorante Il Castiglione (☎ 0721 649 34; Viale Trento 149; meals €31; ✆ Tue-Sun) Try this swish place which is like a small castle set in rambling gardens. Fresh fish is a speciality.

Cantuccio di Leo (☎ 0721 680 88; Via Perfetti 18; meals €30) A great *enoteca* in the heart of Pesaro with some excellent wines and dishes served in a warm and romantic atmosphere.

Conventino (☎ 0721 91 05 88; Via Conventino 1; meals €30) Sample the best of seasonal food in this converted convent.

Gennaro (☎ 0721 273 21; fax 0721 273 21; Via S Marina Alta 30; meals €25) The trattoria specialises in seafood.

There are food shops and a **produce market** on Via Branca, behind the post office.

Entertainment

Teatro Rossini (☎ 0721 331 84; Piazza Lazzarini) hosts a series of symphony concerts throughout the year. For information contact the **Ente Concerti** (☎ 0721 324 82; enteconcerti@libero.it; Via Branca 93).

Getting There & Around

The main bus station is on Piazza Matteotti. **AMI** (☎ 0721 28 91 45, ☎ 0721 37 48 62) buses connect Pesaro with Cattolica (€1.10, 45 minutes, hourly), Fossosejore (€0.60, 15 minutes, half-hourly), and most small towns in the region. **Bucci** (☎ 0721 3 24 01) operates a service to Ancona (€2.95, one hour 20

minutes, four daily) and to Rome at 6am daily (€19.35, four hours 40 minutes). Buses make the return journey from Rome at 4pm. **Soget** (☎ 0721 37 13 18) runs up to 10 buses daily to Urbino (€1.90, 55 minutes).

Pesaro is on the Bologna–Lecce train line and you can reach Rome (€15.45, four hours) by changing trains at Falconara Marittima, just before Ancona. There are hourly services to Ancona (€5.35, 50 minutes), Rimini (€2.25, 30 minutes) and Bologna (€7.25, two hours). Catch the Ancona-bound train for Fano (€1.30, 10 minutes) and Senigallia (€2.20, 25 minutes). By car, Pesaro is on the A14 and the SS16.

AMI buses connect the train station with Piazza Matteotti, including bus Nos 1, 3, 4, 5, CD and CS. For a taxi in the centre, call ☎ 0721 3 14 30; at the train station, call ☎ 0721 3 11 11.

AROUND PESARO

If you want slightly more secluded beaches than the Pesaro waterfront, take the Strada Panoramica Adriatica coast road heading north from Pesaro to Cattolica in Emilia-Romagna. The walled, hilltop town of **Gradara** boasts an impressive 14th-century castle. The smaller fishing towns of **Casteldimezzo** and **Fiorenzuola** are appealing and quieter, even during the summer. Fighting in WWII was heavy around here, and 2km east of Gradara just off the SS16, there is a **British war cemetery** (✆ 24 hrs).

Regular AMI buses link Pesaro with Casteldimezzo (€1.10, 30 minutes, five daily), Fiorenzuola (€0.85, 25 minutes, five daily) and Gradara (€1.10, one hour, hourly).

SENIGALLIA

pop 30,000

Senigallia's aptly named **Spiaggia di Velluto** (Velvet Beach) is reputedly one of the best lidos (bathing beaches) on the Adriatic coast.

The **tourist office** (☎ 071 792 27 25; iat.senigallia@regione.marche.it; Piazzale Morandi 2; ✆ 9am-1pm & 3.30-6.30pm Mon-Sat, plus Sun mornings summer) is between the beach and the train station.

Apart from sun, sea and sand, the main draw is the **Rocca Roveresca** (☎ 071 632 58; Piazza del Duca; admission €2.05; ✆ 8.30am-7.30pm Tue-Sun), whose four stout, crenellated towers make it hard to miss. Its plush Renaissance interior makes a visit well worthwhile.

Sleeping & Eating

If you're having trouble finding a room, try the **Associazione Alberghi e Turismo** (☎ 071 6 53 43; Viale IV Novembre 2).

Spiaggia di Velluto (☎ /fax 071 6 48 73; Lungomare Leonardo da Vinci; site per person/tent from €4.40/13.45) This camp site is about 3km south of Senigallia, right on the beach.

Liana (☎ 071 6 52 06; fax 071 792 17 50; Lungomare Leonardo da Vinci 54; site per person/tent from €4.65/13.45) This camp site, just north of Spiaggia di Velluto, has slightly better facilities.

Albergo Eleonora (☎ 071 792 73 73; fax 071 65 94 82; Lungomare G Marconi 2; s/d from €20.65/41.30, compulsory full board in Aug €46.50 per person) This fairly anonymous red high-rise is on the waterfront, close to the train station. It's friendly, open year-round, and has a handy bar and restaurant downstairs.

Getting There & Away

All buses stop at the main train station which is in the town centre on Via Rafaele Sanzio. Bucci buses operate along the SS16 coastal road to Ancona (€1.50, 35 minutes, 25 daily), Fano (€1.50, 30 minutes, five daily) and Pesaro (€1.70, 50 minutes, four daily). Plenty of trains also service the same stretch.

GROTTE DI FRASASSI

In September 1971 a team of climbers stumbled across an aperture in the hill country around Genga, about 50km southwest of Ancona, which tuned out to be the biggest known caves in Europe, containing a spectacle of stalactites and stalagmites, some of them 1.4 million years old.

There's now a 1.5km-long trail laid through five chambers. **Ancona Abyss**, the first chamber, is almost 200m high, 180m wide and 120m long. Tour groups are taken through the caves every couple of hours. Tours last about an hour and cost €10.35. The ticket area and car park are just outside San Vittore Terme, and the entrance to the caves is 600m further west. For €25.80, you can get rigged up in caving gear to explore the remaining chambers, while for €36.15 you can have a more challenging experience that lasts for three hours and involves passing across 30m chasms and crawling on your hands and knees along narrow passages and tunnels. It has to be booked well in advance. Call the **Consorzio Grotte di Frasassi** (☎ 0732 900 80). To stay overnight,

there are a couple of hotels in San Vittore Terme and Genga.

To reach the caves from Ancona, take the SS76 or catch the train for Genga (€2.95, 45 minutes, four daily), about 2km from the caves' ticket area; a shuttle bus runs from the train station in summer.

MACERATA

42,000

This bustling provincial capital is one of Italy's better kept secrets. Macerata was established in the 10th century. It is as impressive as many Umbrian and Tuscan hill towns but without hordes of tourists.

Orientation

Piazza della Libertà is the focal point of the medieval city, contained within the 14th-century walls above the sprawl of the more modern development. Intercity buses arrive at the huge Giardini Diaz below. An underground pass leads to a *ascensore* (lift) that takes you to the bottom of Via XX Settembre in the old town. Follow this road through Piazza Oberdan and along Via Gramsci to reach Piazza della Libertà and the tourist office. If you arrive by train, bus 6 links the train station, which is south of the city centre, to Piazza della Libertà. Other buses climb up Viale Leopardi. If you get off at the Rampa Zara you'll find another lift to take you up and into the centre of the old town.

There is parking virtually right around the walls and you may even find a space on one of the main squares inside the old city.

Information

EMERGENCY

Police Station (emergency ☎ 112, ☎ 113; Piazza della Libertà 14)

INTERNET ACCESS

Internet centre (☎ 0733 26 44 04; Piazza Mazzini 51)
Mercurio Net (☎ /fax 0733 23 5209; Via B Gigli 14)

INTERNET RESOURCES

Comune di Macerata (www.comune.macerata.it, Italian only) Has some useful information on the area.
Provincia di Macerata (www.provincia.macerata.it, Italian only) Website of the provincial government.

MEDICAL SERVICES

Ospedale Civile (casualty ☎ 0733 25 72 13, emergency ☎ 118; Via S Lucia)

UMBRIA & MARCHE

MACERATA

	0	——————	200 m
	0	——————	0.1 mi

A	**B**	**C**	**D**
INFORMATION	Palazzo Ricci........................7 B3		**EATING** 🍴 p560
Internet Centre.......................1 C3	Palazzo del Comune...............8 C2		Da Secondo..........................14 C2
Telecom Office........................2 C2	Pinacoteca.........................(see 6)		Pizzeria da Luciano................15 C2
Tourist Office.........................3 C2			Rosa....................................16 B2
	SLEEPING 🛏 p566		
SIGHTS & ACTIVITIES pp565–6	Arcadia Hotel........................9 D3		**TRANSPORT** p560
Arena Sferisterio......................4 D3	Hotel Arena.........................10 D3		APM Buses............................17 D2
Loggia dei Mercanti..................5 C2	Hotel Claudiani.....................11 B2		Bus Station...........................18 A2
Museo Civico...........................6 B3	Hotel Lauri...........................12 B2		
Museo delle Carrozze.............(see 6)	Ostello Asilo Ricci..................13 D3		

POST

Post Office (Piazza Oberdan 1-3; ⏰ 8.15am-7.30pm Mon-Sat)

TELEPHONE & FAX

Telecom Office (Galleria del Commercio 24; ⏰ 9am-1pm & 4-7pm)

TOURIST INFORMATION

Tourist Office (☎ 0733 23 48 07; iat.macerata@regione.marche.it; Piazza della Libertà 11; ⏰ 9am-1pm & 3-7pm Mon-Sat summer, 9am-1pm & 3-6pm Mon-Fri, 9am-1pm Sat winter, & 9am-1pm Sun year-round)

Sights & Activities

One of the city's finest buildings, the 16th-century Renaissance open-air **Loggia dei Mercanti**, in Piazza della Libertà was built by the Farnese pope, Paul III. In the courtyard of the **Palazzo del Comune** are archaeological remains from Helvia Recina, a Roman town 5km north of Macerata, which was destroyed by the Goths.

In Piazza Vittorio Veneto, at the end of the main boulevard Corso della Repubblica, you will find three museums in the one building: the **Museo Civico**, the **Museo delle Carrozze** and the **Pinacoteca** (☎ 0733 25 63 61; Piazza Vittorio Veneto 2; admission free; ⏰ 9am-1pm & 4-7.30pm Tue-Sat, 4-7.30pm Mon, 9am-1pm Sun). The latter has a good collection of early Renaissance works, including a 15th-century Madonna by Carlo Crivelli. The Museo delle Carrozze houses an extensive collection of 18th- to 20th-century coaches (the horse-drawn kind). The Museo Civico contains Roman and Piceni archaeological remains.

The 16th-century **Palazzo Ricci** (☎ 0733 261 484; Via D Ricci 1; admission free; ⏰ 4-6pm Tue & Thu, 10am-12am Sat) houses a collection of 20th-century Italian masters such as Giorgio De Chirico, Giacomo Balla, Gino Severini, Fortunato Depero and Renato Guttoso. In July and August it is the venue for a national exhibition of 20th-century Italian art.

The superb open-air **Arena Sferisterio**, (☎ 0733 23 07 35; macerataopera@mercurio.it; Piazza Mazzini 10; ⏰ 9.30am-1pm & 4-8pm summer, 10.30am-1pm & 5-8pm Mon-Sat winter), which resembles an ancient Roman arena, was built between 1819–29. Between 15 July and 15 August every year it is the venue for the **Stagione**

Lirica (Opera Festival; www.macerataopera.org) one of Italy's most prestigious musical events, which attracts big operatic names, For more information check the website or contact the **Associazione Arena Sferisterio** (☎ 0733 26 13 34; Macerata Opera, Via S Maria della Porta 65).

Sleeping

Ostello Asilo Ricci (☎ /fax 0733 23 25 15; ostelloasiloricci@cssg.it; Via dell'Asilo 36; B&B per person €14.50) This youth hostel, housed in a former but much-restored school, is clean and airy. What's more, there's no lockout and no curfew.

Hotel Lauri (☎ /fax 0733 23 23 76; Via T Lauri 6; s/d up to €45/75) There are 30 spacious and comfortable rooms at this very central hotel, which has a polished air.

Hotel Arena (☎ 0733 23 09 31; albergoarenamc@libero.it; Vicolo Sferisterio 16; s/d €42/70) This two-star hotel does a great breakfast (included in the price). The rooms are clean, with all the mod cons of a more expensive hotel, yet it manages to retain an intimate feel.

Arcadia Hotel (☎ 0733 23 59 61; Via P Matteo Ricci 134; s/d/tr €60/90/110; **P**) This pleasant little hotel in a quiet street not far from the cathedral gives three-star comfort at very reasonable prices. There's room for just six cars in their garage so book ahead.

Hotel Claudiani (☎ 0733 26 14 00; www.hotelclaudiani.it; Via Ulissi 8; s €65-90, d €95-125; **P**) The rooms have a modern elegance in a completely refurbished old *palazzo*. There's a garage at Via Armaroli 98 for use of clients. Parking costs €8.

Le Case (☎ 0733 23 18 97; www.ristorantelecase.it; Locanda Mozzavicini 16; s/d incl breakfast €75/100, meals €30-60; **⌘**) In a restored monastery, a few kilometres from the centre, is a marvellous place to eat fantastic food and drink great wine without breaking the bank. You can then sleep it off in delightful 'country house' rooms in the middle of the verdant Marche countryside. This is a kind of health resort – a swim in the pool, a massage and sauna are free for house guests. You can also fish, cycle in the lovely open spaces, go horse riding or just chat to the friendly staff.

Eating

Da Secondo (☎ 0733 26 09 12; Via Pescheria Vecchia 26; meals €30; ☽ Tue-Sun) This is one of the better restaurants in town, with dining on a shaded terrace

Rosa (☎ 0733 26 01 24; Via Armaroli 17; meals €30; ☽ Mon-Sat) A traditional Italian trattoria in the centre of town, Rosa's is full of bustle and bottles of excellent local wine, paintings and photos on the walls, friendly and welcoming staff and great, inexpensive food as well. Try *frittattine al tartufo* or *alla coratella*. The home-made pasta is great too.

Several pizzerias, such as **Pizzeria da Luciano** (☎ 0733 26 01 29; Vicolo Ferrari 12), serve quick takeaway food.

Getting There & Around

If you're using public transport you'll need to plan carefully to make connections to Macerata. The **train station** (☎ 0733 24 03 54) is at Piazza XXV Aprile 8/10. There's one direct train daily to Ancona (€3.72, one hour) at 6.35am (from Ancona, the direct train leaves at 8.01am), otherwise you'll need to change at Civitanova Marche (€1.75, 25 minutes, half-hourly).

The orange buses are the **APM buses** (☎ 0733 23 23 92) that operate within the town of Macerata from Piazza della Libertà and from Rampa Zara. The blue buses will take you out of Macerata. Several bus companies (Contram, Crognaletti, Farabollini) operate services to Rome (€17.55, four hours, three daily), Ancona (€2.60, 1½ hours, 10 daily), Foligno (€3.60, two hours, two daily) and Civitanova Marche (€1.05, 50 minutes, hourly), where you can get connections to Ascoli Piceno. Ask at the tourist office for timetables, also available at the bus terminal in **Giardini Diaz** (☎ 0733 23 09 06).

You'll find taxis for hire at Piazza della Libertà (☎ 0733 23 35 70); at the train station (☎ 0733 24 03 53) as well as at Giardini Diaz (☎ 07333 23 13 39).

The SS77 connects the city with the A14 to the east and roads for Rome in the west.

AROUND MACERATA

On 1 August, in **Treia**, you can witness the annual **Disfida del Bracciale**, a festival that revives the tradition and folklore that surround the 19th-century game, which involves players hitting leather balls with spiked wooden hand guards.

ASCOLI PICENO
pop 55,000
Dominated by nearby mountains leading into the Apennines, Ascoli Piceno's art

history and traditions rival many of the better-known towns in Italy. Its old centre is extensive. Largely constructed in local travertine stone and laid out according to the traditional Roman model, it reached its zenith during the Renaissance, but has many interesting reminders of its medieval and more ancient past.

Ascoli Piceno was probably settled by the Piceni tribe in the 6th century BC. The salt trade eventually brought the city into contact with the Romans, to whom it finally fell in 268 BC. By the 6th century AD, the Goths and then the Lombards were in control. The city flourished in the Middle Ages, despite being ransacked by the troops of Holy Roman Emperor Frederick II after a long siege in 1242.

Orientation

The old town and its modern extension are separated by the Castellano River. The train station is in the new town, east of the river. From the station, turn right into Viale Indipendenza and head west across Ponte Maggiore, along Corso Vittorio Emanuele

and past the cathedral. Head for Piazza Giudea, then Piazza Viola which takes you to Piazza Fausto Simonetti just behind Piazza del Popolo, the heart of the medieval city. The walk takes around 15 minutes.

MAPS

The Provincia di Ascoli Piceno, in conjunction with the Istituto Geografico D'Agostini, publishes a useful road map for the province, with information in English. Parco Piceno publishes a free map (available at the tourist office) of the historical centre of Ascoli, with an index of monuments and streets. You can also pick up a copy of the *Pianta della Città* (Map of the City) published by the *comune*, at the main tourist office which indicates places of interest, parking areas and hotels within the city.

Information
BOOKSHOPS

Rinascita (☎ 0736 25 96 53; www.rinascita.it, Italian only; Piazza Roma 7; 🖳) This lovely bookshop has it all: a few books in English, lots of maps, a café, and a lovely

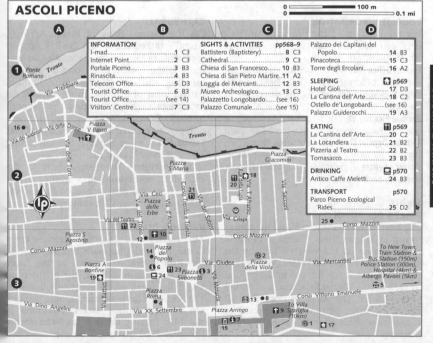

area where you can just sit about reading newspapers and books with lots of *simpatico* people.

EMERGENCY
Police Station (☎ 0736 35 51 11; Viale della Repubblica 8)

INTERNET ACCESS
Internet point (Piazza della Viola 14)
I-mad (☎ 0736 26 31 79; fax 0736 24 72 74; Viale De Gaspari 2; €3 an hour)

INTERNET RESOURCES
Parco Piceno (www.parcopiceno.com) A consortium interested in promoting the area.
City of Ascoli Pisceno (www.comune.ascoli-piceno.it) Information on events and festivals.

MEDICAL SERVICES
Hospital (☎ 0736 35 81; Monticello) Located 4km east of town.

POST
Post Office (Via Crispi; ☯ 8.15am-7.40pm Mon-Sat)

TOILETS
There are public toilets in Piazza della Viola.

TOURIST INFORMATION
For information on the province, (in Italian) you can also call the free number ☎ 1670 197 60.
Tourist Office (☎ 0736 25 30 45; iat.ascolipiceno@regione.marche.it; Piazza del Popolo; ☯ 8.30am-1.30pm & 3-7pm Mon-Fri, 9am-1pm Sat & Sun) The main *comune*-run office.
Portale Piceno (☎ 0736 277 539; portalepiceno@provincia.ap.it.; Piazza Simonetti; ☯ 9am-1pm & 3.30-7pm)
Tourism Dept of the Province of Ascoli Piceno (☎ 0763 277; fax 0736 277 547) Has an information centre.
Visitor's Centre (Piazza Arringo) Inaccessible at the time of research due to building works.

Sights
PIAZZA DEL POPOLO
The heart of medieval Ascoli and the town's forum in Roman times, Piazza del Popolo is dominated on the western side by the 13th-century **Palazzo del Popolo**. The seat of Ascoli's rulers, it was burned to the ground in 1535 during a bitter local feud and rebuilt 10 years later. The statue of Pope Paul III above the main entrance was erected in recognition of his efforts to bring peace to the town.

The beautiful **Chiesa di San Francesco** (☎ 0736 25 94 46; Piazza del Popolo; admission free; ☯ 7am-12.30pm & 3.30-8pm) was started in 1262 and features a 15th-century wooden crucifix and 16th-century works by Cola dell'Amatrice. Virtually annexed to the church is **Loggia dei Mercanti** built in the 16th century by the powerful guild of wool merchants, who displayed their products here.

PINACOTECA
The second-largest art gallery in Marche is inside the 17th-century Palazzo Comunale on Piazza Arringo, southeast of Piazza del Popolo. The **Pinacoteca** (☎ 0736 29 82 13, ☎ 0736 29 82 04; Piazza Arringo; adult/child €3.10/1.55; ☯ 9am-1pm, plus 3-7pm summer) boasts 400 works, including paintings by van Dyck, Titian, Carlo Crivelli and even an etching by Rembrandt. The gallery was founded in 1861 with works taken from churches and religious orders that were suppressed in the wake of Italian unification. Across Piazza Arringo, the **Museo Archeologico** (☎ 0736 25 35 62; Piazza Arringo; adults/under-18s €2.05/free; ☯ 8.30am-7.30pm Tue-Sun) has a collection of implements used by the ancient Piceni tribe.

CATHEDRAL
On the eastern flank of Piazza Arringo, Ascoli's **cathedral** (☎ 0736 25 97 74; Piazza Arringo; admission free; ☯ 7am-12.30pm & 4-8pm) was built in the 15th century over a medieval building and dedicated to Saint Emidio, patron saint of the city. In the **Cappella del Sacramento** is what is considered by critics to be Carlo Crivelli's best work, the *Polittico*, a polyptych executed in 1473. The **crypt of Sant Emidio** has a more modern but interesting series of mosaic tableaux.

The **battistero** (baptistry), next to the cathedral, something of a traffic barrier today, has remained unchanged since it was constructed in the 11th century.

VECCHIO QUARTIERE
The town's Old Quarter stretches from Corso Mazzini (the main thoroughfare of the Roman-era settlement) to the River Tronto. Its main street is the picturesque Via delle Torri, which eventually becomes Via Solestà. This is a perfect spot to wander. On Via delle Donne (Street of Women) is the 14th-century **Chiesa di San Pietro Martire** (☎ 0736 25 52 14; Piazza V Basso; admission free

UMBRIA & MARCHE

☼ 7.30am-12.30pm & 3.30-7pm), dedicated to the saint who founded the Dominican community at Ascoli. The chunky Gothic structure houses the Reliquario della Santa Spina, containing what is said to be a thorn from Christ's crown.

The 40m-high **Torre degli Ercolani** located on Via dei Soderini, west of the Chiesa di San Pietro Martire, is the tallest of the town's medieval towers. Abutting it is the **Palazzetto Longobardo**, a 12th-century Lombard-Romanesque defensive position and now the Ostello dei Longobardi, a youth hostel (see Sleeping for details). Just to the north is the well-preserved **Ponte Romano**, a single-arched Roman bridge.

Festivals & Events

The town's big festival is the **Quintana**, a medieval pageant that includes jousting on horseback, held on the first Sunday of August. Hundreds of locals dressed in traditional costume fill the town centre for parades and other medieval doings continue during July and August. For more information contact the **Ente Quintana** (☎ 0736 29 82 23; quintanaascoli@rinascita.it). Between October and February, the city also comes alive with shows, concerts and opera during the city's **Stagione Lirica**.

Sleeping

There are not a lot of hotel options in the historical centre of Ascoli, but it's wise to book ahead during festival times. Tourist offices have lists of other accommodation options including rooms and apartments, *agriturismo* and B&B options in outlying districts.

Ostello dei Longobardi (☎ 0736 26 18 62; fax 0736 25 91 91; Via dei Soderini 26; B&B €11) An HI-card is obligatory at this hostel inside a 12th-century castle, but thankfully there's no curfew. It's certainly not the cleanest of places, and the hot water system is decidedly dodgy, but they don't get much more atmospheric than this.

La Cantina dell'Arte (☎ 0736 25 56 20; fax 0736 25 57 44; Rua della Lupa 8; s/d €30/40) The rooms here are simple but clean and all have private bath. The owners also run a very cheap restaurant opposite.

Albergo Pavoni (☎ /fax 0736 34 25 75; Via Navicella 135/b; s/d €26/42, without bathroom €21/36) This place is 5km out of town in Marino del Tronto. Take bus No 3 from Piazza Arringo.

Hotel Gioli (☎ 0736 25 55 50; fax 0736 25 21 45; Viale De Gaspari 14; s/d €65/100; **P**) This efficient, modern hotel is one of the few in the centre of town close to the autostrada exit and with its own garage (€11 per night). Naturally all rooms have TV, direct-dial phones, shower or bath. There's a bar and a lift too.

Palazzo Guiderocchi (☎ 0736 24 40 11; Via C Battisti 3; info@palazzoguidorocchi.com; s €80-130, d €90-210) This stunningly beautiful *palazzo* combines 21st-century comfort and style with the ancient traditions of craftsmanship. If you want the ultimate in romance and luxury, this is the place to stay, if only so you can boast that you spent a night in the bedroom of Flavia Guiderocchi, 12th-century dame of war. There's a roof garden, a lovely breakfast area and restaurant.

There are several hotels and *agriturismo* options outside the main city, which are listed on the *comune*'s map, with details. Ask the tourist office about the **Villa Sgariglia** (☎ 0736 423 68; Localita Piagge; s/d €39/57) a lovely place in the rolling hills run by the tourist office itself.

Eating
RESTAURANTS

Ascoli is responsible for a delicious idea for a starter. *Olive all'ascolana* are olives stuffed with meat and deep-fried. You'll find them in most of these places. And after your meal try their *mistra*, an after-dinner drink made with aniseed, licorice and distilled secrets.

La Cantina dell'Arte (☎ 0736 25 56 20; Rua della Lupa 5; meals €7.75; ☼ Mon-Sat) For a really cheap meal, try this restaurant; the service is lightning and the decor's fun, with copper pans and musical instruments covering the walls.

La Locandiera (☎ 0736 26 25 09; Via Goldoni 2; meals €20; ☼ Tue-Sat) This friendly trattoria, with vaulted brick ceilings, is popular with locals and great value for money. Sample the antipasti – the dishes just keep coming, and are always linked to seasonal produce.

Pizzeria al Teatro (☎ 0736 25 35 49; Via del Teatro 3; pizzas from €3.10, mains from €5.15; ☼ Tue-Sun) This place near the theatres has a good garden restaurant.

Tornasacco (☎ 0736 25 41 51; Piazza del Popolo 36; meals €23.25) A spiffy establishment in the heart of town.

Drinking

Antico Caffè Meletti (☎ 0736 25 96 26; Piazza della Repubblica; ☼ 8am-late) This is the perfect place to gaze at one of the most beautiful, and tranquil piazzas in Italy. From the shade of the ancient portico you can sip a coffee or the famous anisette – a speciality of the house. It was once a popular spot for the likes of Ernest Hemingway, Jean-Paul Sartre and the painter Renato Guttuso. The café, founded in 1907, fell into disrepair but has been completely restored to its former glory.

Getting There & Away

Buses leave from Piazzale della Stazione, in front of the train station in the new part of town, east of the Castellano river. **Start** (☎ 0736 34 22 43) runs four buses daily to Rome (€10.85, three hours). In Rome, Start buses leave from Viale Castro Pretorio 84, near Stazione Termini. **Mazzuca** (☎ 0736 40 22 67) serves Montemonaco (€2.60, 1½ hours, three daily), Amandola (€2.20, one hour 10 minutes, three daily) and other towns near the Monti Sibillini range. At 6.30am daily, **Amadio** (☎ 0736 34 23 40) runs a service to Florence (€22.70, 6¼ hours) via Perugia (€15, 4¼ hours) and Siena (€20.15, 5½ hours).

A spur train line connects Ascoli Piceno with Porto d'Ascoli (€1.70, 35 minutes) every hour and San Benedetto del Tronto (€2.20, 40 minutes), both of which are on the Bologna–Lecce line. From San Benedetto there are half-hourly trains to Ancona (€4.15, one hour 10 minutes). Ask at the train station for a free timetable brochure (*orario*) for Marche trains.

From the A14 motorway exit at San Benedetto del Tronto and follow the superstrada (expressway) for Ascoli Piceno. From Rome, take the Antique Salaria or A2 motorway L'Aquila-Teramo. Follow the state road Piceno–Aprutina for Ascoli Piceno.

Getting Around

Most of the tranquil historic centre of Ascoli Piceno is closed to motor traffic. Locals walk or cycle and visitors can have free use of a bicycle for the duration of their stay if they present an ID document to **Parco Piceno Ecological Rides** (☎ 0736 26 32 61; Corso Mazzini 224).

MONTI SIBILLINI

Rising bare and forbidding in the lower southwest of Marche, the stark Monti Sibillini range is one of the most beautiful stretches of the Apennines. Dotted with caves and lined with **walking** trails, it is also the scene of more energetic activities such

---

UMBRIA & MARCHE

MAGIC MOUNTAINS

Sibylline – the very word has come to mean occult and mysterious and for centuries the rugged, wild world of Monti Sibillini has stirred the imagination of writers. In the Middle Ages, this mountain range of 20 summits was know as a realm of demons, necromancers and fairies. The name derives from the famous legend of Sibyl (who was an oracle), thought to be able to foresee the future and said to live in a cave below one of the three highest peaks of the range – Mt Sibylla.

Whether or not you believe these ancient stories, you can't help but be entranced by the magic of these mountains that straddle Umbria and Marche. As you climb, the vegetation changes – woods of oak, European hop and flowering ash, then the beechwoods predominate. Higher still you find rough grazing land and rare, precious species of flowers like Apennine edelweiss. In the summer, the northernmost part of the park is filled with blooming orchids, liliacease, narcissus and alpine aster. The creatures that live in the mountains are wild spirits too. There are wolves, wild cats, roe deer and porcupines, and golden eagles, goshawk, sparrowhawk and peregrine falcon soar overhead.

The 70,000 hectares set aside in 1993 as a national park also contain other evocative reminders of an ancient world. There are abbeys and medieval towns nestling at the bottom of the mountains, and churches with late-Gothic frescoes, castles and lookout towers erected by valley dwellers to defend themselves against Saracen raids. In the valley of the Fiastroe River is the Grotta dei Fratti – the friars cave, an impressive ravine hollowed out by water which served as a refuge in the 11th century for the Clareno monks. Norcia, the birthplace of Saint Benedict, the patron saint of Europe, is the starting point for many excursions including to the Abbey of Sant Eutizio, in the *comune* of Preci, founded at the end of the 5th century and famous for the skills the monks developed in healing the sick with medicinal herbs from the Sibillini Mountains.

as **hang-gliding** and **horse riding**. The range is littered with *rifugi* and offers reasonable **skiing** in winter. You can follow **trekking** paths that encircle the whole park and can be covered in nine stages. There are paths especially designed for families, others go through interesting old town centres, others can be followed on horseback or mountain bike.

Amandola is one of the prettiest villages in Marche. Though there is no cheap accommodation, there are quite a few options in surrounding localities. Just south is **Montefortino**, a good base for accessing Montemonaco, at the base of Monte Sibilla, a place for serious walkers.

Although **Montemonaco** is not easily reached by public transport, you'll be surprised by the number of tourists. Many come here for the **Gola dell'Infernaccio** (Gorge of Hell), one of the easiest and most spectacular walks in Marche.

To reach the range, take the SS4 from Ascoli Piceno and follow the signs. Buses connect the area with Ascoli Piceno and various cities throughout Marche. See also p544 for details about hang-gliding and how to get to the mountains from Umbria.

Information

The **tourist office** (☎ 0733 65 71 44; iat.sarnanon@ regione.marche.it; Largo Ricciardi 1) in Sarnano has walking and climbing information and details of accommodation in the park. The CAI publishes a detailed guide to the mountains (in Italian), complete with maps: *Parco Nazionale dei Sibillini – Le Più Belle Escursioni*, by Alberico Alesi and Maurizio Calibani. Information on organised tours is also available from the various town branches of **Case del Parco** Amàndola (☎ /fax 0736 848 598, Via Indipendenza 73); Montefortino (☎ /fax 0736 85 94 14; Via Roma 8); Montemonaco (☎ /fax 0736 85 94 14; Via Roma). The park has a website: www.sibillini.net (Italian only) and further information is available if you email informazioni@sibillini.net.

To fully appreciate the local specialities like *tartufe* and *funghi*, chestnuts, pecorino cheese, *salumi*, honey, and the very fragrant *mela rosa*, pick up a brochure from the **Comunita Montana dei Sibillini** (☎ 0736 84 43 79, ☎ 0736 84 45 26; cmsibillini@provincia.ap.it; Piazza IV Novembre w, Comunanza, Ascoli Piceno 63044).

Activities

Il Maneggio Le Querce (☎ /fax 0733 65 82 11; C da Bisio, Sarnano) found in the province of Macerata can arrange horse rides and courses in equitation.

Sleeping

There is a camp site just south of Montefortino at Cerretana and one near Sarnano as well.

Montespino (☎ /fax 0736 85 92 38; Locanda Cerretana; site per person/tent €3.60/6.20; ☺ 1 Jun-30 Sep) There are over 100 sites here, a restaurant and supermarket.

Quattro Stagioni (☎ 0733 65 11 47; fax 65 11 04; C da Forseneta) Sites available all year for €4 to €5 per person per night, and bungalows for €37 to €73.

Montemonaco offers accommodation at good rates.

Albergo Sibilla (☎ 0736 85 61 44; Via Roma 52; r per person with breakfast €38.75-43.90) This friendly, family-run place has 10 rooms, all with private bathrooms.

Rifugio della Montagna (☎ 0736 85 63 27; fax 0736 856 327; Loc. Foce; r per person €20.65) Just outside Montemonaco, it's not a typical mountain refuge as its name would suggest. There's also a good restaurant here.

Cittadella (☎ 0736 84 42 61; www.cittadelladesibillini.it; d per person €25-35) Offers B&B in a fabulous farmhouse. It produces nuts and cheese, mushrooms and sausages. Walking, cycling and horse riding excursions can also be arranged.

In the Montefortino area **Casa Rosi** (☎ 0763 85 00 23; www.casarosi.it; Montazzolini 8, Montefortino 63047; d per person €30) English couple Judi and Richard Hill offer B&B and marvellous views.

Abruzzo & Molise

CONTENTS

Abruzzo, along with neighbouring Molise, is a predominantly mountainous area of spectacular scenery and wild beauty. With a history of poverty and neglect, neither region is as rich in artistic and cultural heritage as its more illustrious neighbours, but to overlook them would be to miss a world apart. The medieval hilltop towns here remain as they've always been, while the countryside is often untamed and sometimes almost creepy. Wolves and bears roam at will and the tradition of witches and wizards is all too believable.

But tourism is moving in, particularly in Abruzzo where the national parks straddle the Apennines and offer fantastic hiking opportunities in summer. From easy strolls through the green valley floors to heavy-duty climbs in the mountains, there is something for all tastes. In winter the skiing facilities, although not world class, are still popular. For less strenuous activities, sun-seekers can head to the ever-popular Adriatic resorts and fight for space with the beach crowds.

The two regions (known collectively as the Abruzzi until divided in 1963) are among Italy's most earthquake-prone. In 2002 Molise hit the headlines when a quake measuring 5.4 on the Richter scale destroyed a primary school in the hilltop town of San Giuliano di Puglia, killing 29 people, including a class of 26 children and their teacher. One of the area's worst disasters struck in 1915 when a massive jolt left 30,000 people dead.

HIGHLIGHTS

■ **Trekking**

Trek beneath the magnificent peak of Corno Grande, the Apennines' highest peak (p578)

■ **Wildlife**

Eyeball a wolf or bear in the wild at the popular Parco Nazionale d'Abruzzo (pp580–1)

■ **Festival**

Squirm like the snakes in Cocullo's Processione dei Serpari (Snake-Charmers' Procession; p579), one of Italy's strangest festivals

■ **Ancient Site**

Savour the Roman ruins at Saepinum (p583) near Campobasso

■ **Literary Homage**

Visit the classical poet Ovid's birthplace at Sulmona (p579)

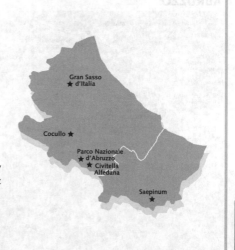

POPULATION:	■ ABRUZZO 1.2 MILLION	■ MOLISE 316,548
AREA:	■ ABRUZZO 10,794 SQ KM	■ MOLISE 4,438 SQ KM

ABRUZZO

Abruzzo's wild mountainous terrain is breathtaking – from the forests of the Parco Nazionale d'Abruzzo in the south, to the Gran Sasso d'Italia, a massif of stark peaks and 1000m-high precipices capped by the Apennines' highest mountain, the Corno Grande (2914m).

The medieval towns of L'Aquila and Sulmona are also well worth visiting and the countryside is speckled with an array of castles and isolated hilltop *borghi* (cluttered towns and villages little changed over the centuries).

In antiquity, Abruzzo was famed for its witches, wizards and snake-charmers – members of a tribe known as the Marsi, who lived around modern-day Avezzano. Even today, snakes feature in a bizarre annual festival in the mountain village of Cocullo, near Sulmona (see p579).

Traditionally, Abruzzo is grazing territory and its sheep farmers still play an important role in the local economy. A key agricultural area is the Piana del Fucino (Fucino Plain), east of Avezzano, which was created by draining the vast Lago Fucino in the late 19th century. The ancient Romans had an earlier shot at draining the lake in what proved a remarkable, yet disastrous, feat of engineering. Having built a tunnel about 10km long to drain the lake into a neighbouring valley, they opened the sluice gates, only to find the tunnel too small for the massive volume of water. Thousands of spectators, including Emperor Claudius, almost drowned.

L'AQUILA
pop 70,005 / elevation 720m

Sitting in the shadow of the Gran Sasso d'Italia, L'Aquila isn't a city that is easy to warm to. It's the coldest regional capital in Italy and its position and dour architecture give it a distinctly gloomy appearance. But it is worth a little exploration, and as the evening sun casts an opaque rose light over the surrounding mountains you'll probably find your spirits rising.

Legend has it that the city was founded by Emperor Frederick II in 1240 by drawing

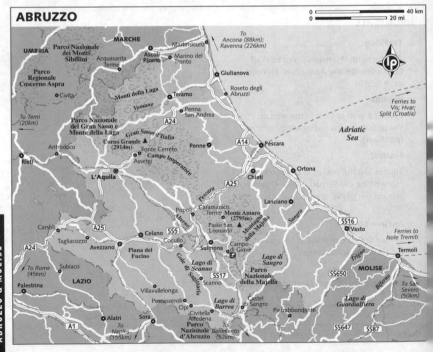

together the citizens of 99 villages. The new citizens of L'Aquila (meaning 'The Eagle' – a reference to the eagle in the imperial coat of arms) established 99 churches and 99 piazzas, as well as a fountain with (almost) 99 spouts. Earthquakes have destroyed most of the churches and piazzas but the medieval fountain, Fontana delle 99 Cannelle, survives. As does the town hall bell, which chimes 99 times every evening.

L'Aquila's people have a rebellious spirit but have frequently backed the wrong horse. The Swabian King Manfred sacked the city in 1266 because the people sided with the pope against him. The city then endured a 13-month siege by the Aragonese for supporting the House of Anjou in the fight for mastery of the Kingdom of Naples. L'Aquila rose against Spanish rule twice in the 16th and 17th centuries and both times the city was crushed. The 1703 earthquake all but finished off L'Aquila. Revolt finally proved fruitful when, in 1860, the city was made regional capital for its efforts towards national unity.

Orientation

L'Aquila's train station is west and downhill from the old centre. Bus Nos 5, 8, M11 and 30 will take you into town. Get off in Via XX Settembre, from where it's a short walk up Corso Federico II to Piazza del Duomo and the elegant old boulevard Corso Vittorio Emanuele. The main bus station is south of the town centre and linked to Piazza del Duomo by an escalator.

Information

Hospital (☎ 0862 36 81; Località Coppito)
Internet Games (Via Garibaldi 27; €3/30 min; ☻ 10am-1pm & 4pm-midnight Mon-Sat) For Internet access.
L'Aquila City (www.laquila.com, Italian only) Internet resource.
Police Station (☎ 0862 43 01; Via Strinella 2)
Post Office (☎ 0862 63 73 10; Piazza del Duomo; ☻ 8am-6.30pm Mon-Sat)
Telephone Office (Via Patini 48)

TOURIST INFORMATION

Main Tourist Office (☎ 0862 41 08 08; Piazza Santa Maria Paganica 5; ☻ 9am-1pm & 4-7pm Mon-Sat, 9am-1pm Sun Jun-Sep, 9am-1pm & 3-6pm Mon-Fri, 9am-1pm Sat Oct-May)
Branch Tourist Office (☎ 0862 2 23 06; Via XX Settembre 8; ☻ 9am-1pm & 4-7pm Mon-Sat, 9am-1pm Sun Jun-Sep, 9am-1pm & 3-6pm Mon-Fri, 9am-1pm Sat Oct-May)
Centro Turistico Gran Sasso (☎ 0862 2 21 47; Corso Vittorio Emanuele 49; ☻ 9am-1pm & 4-7pm Mon-Fri) Operates as a travel agency with a hotel reservation service and is a good source of information about the town and the Gran Sasso area.

Sights

CASTLE

This massive edifice of steep, blanched battlements sunk deep into a now-empty moat is L'Aquila's most impressive monument. Known as the **forte spagnolo**, it was built by the Spanish to overawe the locals after they'd unsuccessfully rebelled. Offering wonderful views over the Gran Sasso d'Italia, it today houses the **Museo Nazionale d'Abruzzo** (☎ 0862 63 31; Castello Cinquecentesco; admission €4; ☻ 9am-8pm Tue-Sun), home to a collection of mainly local religious artworks and, bizarrely enough, the skeleton of a mammoth, found near the town in the early 1950s.

CHURCHES

The **Basilica di San Bernardino** (☎ 0862 2 22 55; Piazza San Bernardino; admission free; ☻ 7am-noon & 4-6pm Mon-Sat, 4-6.30pm Sun) is fronted by a magnificent three-tiered, cream-coloured classical facade. Inside, peer up at the exquisite baroque ceiling and savour the intricately detailed relief decoration of San Bernardino's mausoleum, the work of local artisan Silvestro dell'Aquila. San Bernardino, originally of Siena, spent his last years in L'Aquila.

The Romanesque **Basilica di Santa Maria di Collemaggio** (☎ 0862 2 63 92; Viale di Collemaggio; admission free; ☻ 8.30am-1pm & 3-8pm Mon-Sat, 8.30am-8pm Sun) has an equally imposing facade, its rose windows encased by a quilt pattern of pink and white marble. The basilica was built at the instigation of a hermit, Pietro da Morrone, who was elected pope at the age of 80 in 1294. Pietro took the name Celestine V, but this unworldly, trusting man was no match for the machinations of courtiers and politicians and he was eventually forced to abdicate. His successor, Pope Boniface VIII, saw Celestine as a threat and threw him into prison, where he died. As founder of the Celestine order, he was canonised seven years later and his tomb lies inside the basilica.

In contrast to these two splendid basilicas, L'Aquila's **cathedral** (Piazza del Duomo),

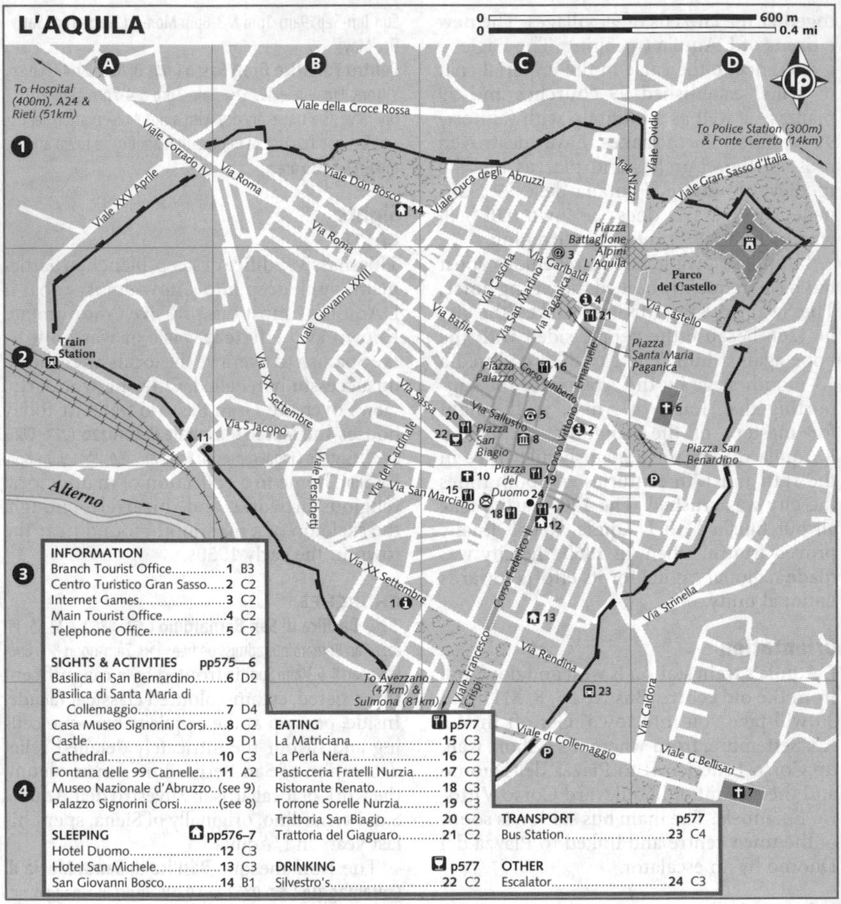

L'AQUILA
0 600 m
0 0.4 mi
To Hospital (400m), A24 & Rieti (51km)
To Police Station (300m) & Fonte Cerreto (14km)
To Avezzano (47km) & Sulmona (81km)
Viale della Croce Rossa
Viale Corrado IV
Via Roma
Viale XXV Aprile
Viale Don Bosco
Viale Duca degli Abruzzi
Viale Nizza
Viale Ovidio
Viale Gran Sasso d'Italia
Piazza Battaglione Alpini L'Aquila
Parco del Castello
Via Garibaldi
Via Cascina
Via San Martino
Via Paganica
Via Bafile
Viale Giovanni XXIII
Via Castello
Piazza Santa Maria Paganica
Train Station
Via XX Settembre
Piazza Palazzo
Corso Umberto
Corso Vittorio Emanuele
Via Sassa
Via Sallustio
Piazza San Biagio
Via S Jacopo
Piazza San Bernardino
Viale Persichetti
Via del Cardinale
Via San Marciano
Piazza del Duomo
Alterno
Corso Federico II
Via Strinella
Via Rendina
Viale Francesco Crispi
Via Caldora
Viale di Collemaggio
Viale G Bellisari
INFORMATION
Branch Tourist Office 1 B3
Centro Turistico Gran Sasso 2 C2
Internet Games 3 C2
Main Tourist Office 4 C2
Telephone Office 5 C2
SIGHTS & ACTIVITIES pp575–6
Basilica di San Bernardino 6 D2
Basilica di Santa Maria di Collemaggio 7 D4
Casa Museo Signorini Corsi 8 C2
Castle 9 D1
Cathedral 10 C3
Fontana delle 99 Cannelle 11 A2
Museo Nazionale d'Abruzzo (see 9)
Palazzo Signorini Corsi (see 8)
SLEEPING pp576–7
Hotel Duomo 12 C3
Hotel San Michele 13 C3
San Giovanni Bosco 14 B1
EATING p577
La Matriciana 15 C3
La Perla Nera 16 C2
Pasticceria Fratelli Nurzia 17 C3
Ristorante Renato 18 C3
Torrone Sorelle Nurzia 19 C3
Trattoria San Biagio 20 C2
Trattoria del Giaguaro 21 C2
DRINKING p577
Silvestro's 22 C2
TRANSPORT p577
Bus Station 23 C4
OTHER
Escalator 24 C3

shattered more than once by earthquakes, can boast only an unexceptional neoclassical facade.

CASA MUSEO SIGNORINI CORSI

This **museum** (☎ 0862 41 09 00; Via Patini 42; adult/child €3.10/2.10; 🕑 4pm-7pm Tue-Fri, 10am-1pm & 4-7pm Sat & Sun) occupies the Palazzo Signorini Corsi, ancestral home of the Corsi family who bequeathed all of their considerable collection to the town. The museum houses a particularly fine collection of religious art and period furniture.

FONTANA DELLE 99 CANNELLE

A symbol of the city, the 'Fountain of the 99 Spouts', just west of the centre, was constructed in the late 13th century. The source of the constant supply of fresh water remains a mystery, but throughout the city's turbulent history it has often proved a lifesaver. Count the various stone faces, gargoyles and the like – they don't seem to add up to the magic number!

Sleeping

San Giovanni Bosco (☎ 0862 6 3931; Viale Don Bosco 6; s/d/tr with bathroom €26/46/50) This religious institution is the nearest L'Aquila has to a youth hostel. The rooms are basic and clean and the cheapest in town. There is an 11pm curfew.

Hotel Duomo (☎ 0862 41 08 93; duomo@worldtel.it; Via Dragonetti 6; s/d with bathroom €57/78) Within a stone's throw of Piazza del Duomo, this hotel offers a warm welcome and quiet charm. All rooms have TV and telephone.

Hotel San Michele (☎ 0862 42 02 60; www .stmichelehotel.it; Via dei Giardini 6; s/d/tr with bathroom & breakfast €60/86/105; **P**) The parquet floors, plants and airy rooms make a good first impression. Rooms are comfortable and have the usual creature comforts.

Eating
CAFÉS
For a quick bite or a cappuccino, try one of these options.

Torrone Sorelle Nurzia (Corso Vittorio Emanuele 38) This elegant parlour specialises in a chocolate variety of *torrone*, a nougat confection guaranteed to bring out the child in everyone.

Pasticceria Fratelli Nurzia (Piazza del Duomo 50-51) This cake shop is Torrone Sorelle Nurzia's competition and a breakaway from the same family business, which dates back to 1835.

RESTAURANTS
Traditional specialities include *maccheroni alla chitarra* (thick homemade macaroni) and *agnello* (fresh lamb). Fruit and veg is sold at the **market** (Piazza del Duomo), which is held most days.

La Perla Nera (☎ 0862 41 34 79; Piazza Palazzo 5; pizza slice €1.50) A great little takeaway that does a brisk lunchtime trade in calzone and a variety of original pizzas.

La Matriciana (☎ 0862 2 60 65; Via Arcivescovado 5/a; tourist menu €13, full meal €17; ☼ Mon-Sat) This basic trattoria, off Piazza del Duomo, serves filling fare at reasonable prices. The bowl of chillies offered with some of its pasta dishes adds a piquant kick to the simple but tasty ingredients used.

Trattoria San Biagio (☎ 0862 2 21 39; Piazza San Biagio 4; full meals around €20; ☼ Mon-Sat) After 150 years in business serving Abruzzese dishes, this local institution remains as popular as ever. You'll need to get in early for a lunchtime table.

Trattoria del Giaguaro (☎ 0862 2 40 01; Piazza Santa Maria Paganica 4; full meals €18-20; ☼ Wed-Sun & lunch Mon) Well established and popular, this is another good option for a medium-priced meal.

Ristorante Renato (☎ 0862 2 55 96; Via dell' Indipendenza 9; full meals around €20; ☼ Mon-Sat)

LA PERDONANZA

Tempted by the thought of a little extra indulgence in L'Aquila?

L'Aquila's festival *par excellence* goes back to 1294 and the day when Celestine V, on his inauguration as pope in the Basilica di Santa Maria di Collemaggio, established **La Perdonanza** (the 'forgiveness' or 'pardoning'). Since that time, every evening of 28th August, the Porta Santa (Holy Door) of the church where he lies buried is swung open. The faithful stream through in their thousands for the next 24 hours, confident that all who cross the threshold will be absolved of their sins.

Nowadays La Perdonanza is as much a lay as a spiritual celebration and the whole town gives itself over to partying throughout the week leading up to the opening of the portal.

This restaurant specialises in regional cuisine, and its lamb dishes are particularly good.

Drinking
There are plenty of bars around Piazza del Duomo, but for a pub head to Via Sassa. The ever-present Irish pub is **Silvestro's** (Via Sassa 24; ☼ 7pm-2am Tue-Sun), where the service is friendly and the beer is on tap.

Entertainment
An annual season of weekly concerts is held between October and May by, among others, the **Società Aquilana dei Concerti** (☎ 0862 41 41 61). If you're in town during the summer, ask about the special open-air concert, ballet and drama performances.

Getting There & Away
L'Aquila is not well served by train, but bus connections are efficient and comprehensive.

ARPA (☎ 0862 41 28 08, Rome ☎ 06 442 33 928) buses run to Rome's Stazione Tiburtina (€8.70, frequent). They also connect L'Aquila with Avezzano (€4.70, frequent), Sulmona (€5.10, seven daily) and Pescara (€7.20, seven daily). All leave from the main **bus station** (Viale di Collemaggio).

By train, the town is accessible from Rome (€10.20, four hours) via Sulmona or

ABRUZZO & MOLISE

Terni, and from Pescara (€6, two to three hours) via Sulmona.

PARCO NAZIONALE DEL GRAN SASSO E MONTI DELLA LAGA

The bulk of this park's 1500 sq km lies within Abruzzo, but it also spills over into Lazio and Le Marche.

The **park office** (☎ 0862 6 05 21; www.gransasso lagapark.it, Italian only; Via del Convento 1; ☺ 10.30am-1pm & 4-6pm Mon-Fri) is in Assergi, some 10km northeast of L'Aquila. It carries information and a park map in English. For walking, pick up the IGN map *Parco Nazionale del Gran Sasso* at 1:25,000.

There's a cable car (€9.50/11.50 weekdays/weekends and holidays) leaving **Fonte Cerreto** every 30 minutes for **Campo Imperatore** (2117m), a desolate highland plain where Mussolini was briefly imprisoned in 1943. There are walking trails and a small but popular ski area.

The 9km *via normale* (normal route) to the top of Corno Grande is rated moderate–demanding. The popular ascent starts in the main parking area at Campo Imperatore and follows an impressive and surprisingly straightforward route to the summit at 2914m. The route should be relatively free of snow from early June to late September/early October. For more details, see Lonely Planet's *Walking in Italy*.

The park has a network of *rifugi* (mountain huts) for walkers. Hotel accommodation is limited and expensive, but there is a camp site and a hostel.

Camping Funivia del Gran Sasso (☎ 0862 60 61 63; Fonte Cerreto; person/tent/car high season €6.20/4.70/1; ☺ mid-May–mid-Sep) is a handy base for walking, and is also the nearest camp site to L'Aquila. Or tumble out of the cable car into **Ostello Campo Imperatore** (☎ 0862 40 00 11; Campo Imperatore; per person €15; ☺ year-round), a hostel offering basic accommodation in rooms for two or four.

From L'Aquila, take bus No 6 (€1, 10 daily) from Via Castello to Fonte Cerreto.

SULMONA

pop 25,000 / elevation 400m

Birthplace of the classical poet Ovid, whose statue stands proud in the main square, Sulmona is a charming little town, hemmed in by mountains. The medieval centre is pristine and perfect for a stroll. Easily covered

in a day, the town makes a good base for exploring southern Abruzzo.

Sulmona's modern claim to fame is the *confetti* industry – the production of sugar almonds, which are presented to guests at Italian weddings. The shops along Corso Ovidio stock plenty of elaborate examples.

Orientation

The town's main street, Corso Ovidio, runs from the Via Communale, a small park beside Piazzale Tresca, to the impressive Piazza Garibaldi, a five-minute walk. It's closed to traffic outside business hours.

Information

3D Sistemi (☎ 0864 21 20 47; Piazza Plebiscito 2; €1.50/15 min; ☺ 9am-1pm & 4-7.30pm Fri-Wed, 9am-1pm Thu) For Internet access.

Tourist Office (☎ 0864 5 32 76; Corso Ovidio 208; ☺ 9am-1pm Mon-Fri, 3-6pm Tue, Wed & Thu winter, 9am-1pm & 4-7pm Mon-Sat, 9am-1pm Sun summer)

Sights

The **Palazzo dell'Annunziata** (Corso Ovidio), a harmonious blend of Gothic and Renaissance architecture, houses a small **municipal museum** (☎ 0864 21 02 16; Corso Ovidio; admission €1; ☺ 10am-1pm Tue-Sat, 10am-1pm & 4-7pm Sun). Beside the palazzo is a baroque church of the same name, rebuilt after the 1703 earthquake. On Piazza XX Settembre beside Corso Ovidio is a statue of Ovid. See the boxed text, p579.

Piazza Garibaldi is the scene of a colourful market every Wednesday and Saturday morning. In one corner is the austere Renaissance **Fontana del Vecchio** (Fountain of the Old One) and the 13th-century **aqueduct** which borders the piazza on two sides. The most interesting feature of the **Chiesa di San Filippo Neri**, also on the piazza, is its Gothic entrance. On the adjacent Piazza de Carmine, the Romanesque portal is all that remains of **Chiesa di San Francesco della Scarpa** destroyed in the 1703 earthquake.

In Sulmona, sweet-making become art at the Fabbrica Confetti Pelino, largest of the sugared-almond manufacturers. Housed in the egg-blue factory is the **Museo dell'Arte Confettiera** (☎ 0864 21 00 47; Via Stazion Introdacqua 55; admission free; ☺ 9am-12.30pm & 3.30-6.30pm Mon-Sat), a 15-minute walk from Port Napoli (signposted), at the southern end of Corso Ovidio.

Sleeping & Eating

Albergo Ristorante Stella (☎ 0864 5 26 53; www.albergostellaristorante.com, Italian only; Via Panfilo Mazara 18; s/d with bathroom & breakfast €35/50) A friendly welcome is extended at this simple hotel, where the rooms are large and light.

Hotel Italia (☎ 0864 5 23 08; Piazza Salvatore Tommasi 3; s/d with bathroom €32/52) Just west of central Piazza XX Settembre, this elegant building has rooms which, although a little tatty, are full of character.

Ristorante Italia (☎ 0864 3 30 70; Piazza XX Settembre 23; full meals €20; Tue-Sun) Tuck into delicious local dishes like those your gran would have prepared. Helpings are large and the maternal patrons enjoy seeing people eat well.

Ristorante Mafalda (☎ 0864 3 45 38; Via Solimo 20; full meals around €20; Mon-Sat) Some 50m east of Corso Ovidio, this place has a pleasant summertime garden and an equally agreeable indoor vaulted dining room.

Gran Caffé (Piazza XX Settembre 12-14) A café popular with locals, young and old.

Getting There & Away

ARPA (☎ 0864 20 19 33) buses leave from a confusing variety of points, including Via Communale, the train station and beneath the Ponte Capograssi. To find out which stop you need, ask at the tobacconist at Piazza XX Settembre 18, the official ticket sales point.

Buses link Sulmona to L'Aquila (€5.50, nine daily), Pescara (€7, seven daily), Naples (€12, five daily), Scanno (€2.70, 10 daily) and other nearby towns.

The train station is about 2km downhill from the historic centre, and the half-hourly bus No A runs between the two. Trains link the town with L'Aquila (€3.50, one hour), Pescara (€3.50, 1¼ hours), Rome (€9, 2½ hours) and Naples (€12.40, four hours).

AROUND SULMONA

Skiing

Some modest ski slopes lie east of Sulmona. About 18km of tortuous driving brings you to **Campo di Giove**, around which you'll find 15km of downhill runs and also some cross-country trails. It is the first in a series of small ski areas (the next is at **Passo San Leonardo**, about 10km north of Campo di Giove) leading up into the Montagna della Majella and the Parco Nazionale della Majella.

OVID

The Augustan poet, considered by some as being second only to Virgil, has a mixed, and not altogether flattering, reputation. Born in Sulmona in 43 BC and sent at an early age to Rome to study rhetoric and make himself a comfortable career in politics, Ovid preferred to write poetry instead. His early erotic verse, such as *Amores* and *Ars Amatoria* (The Art of Love), gained him quick popularity in Roman high society. Possibly his most ambitious work was *Metamorphosis*, a kind of extended cover version of a whole gamut of Greek myths which culminated in descriptions of Caesar's transformation into a star and the apotheosis of Augustus, ruler at the time. This last piece of sycophancy did not stop the emperor from banishing him to the Black Sea in AD 8. He died in Tomi, in modern Romania, 10 years later.

Parco Nazionale della Majella

This 750-sq-km national park stretches to the east of Sulmona. Within it are Monte Amaro (2795m), the second-highest summit in the Apennines, and 30 other peaks that exceed 2000m. For further information contact the **park headquarters** (☎ 0871 80 07 13; www.parks.it/parco.nazionale.majella; Via Occidentale 6) in Guardiagrele.

Cocullo

Cocullo stages one of Italy's strangest festivals. On the first Thursday in May, villagers celebrate the feast of San Domenico by adorning a statue of the saint with jewels, banknotes and live snakes. The statue is then carried through the village by fearless bearers, themselves also bedecked with writhing reptiles. The festival, said to have pagan origins, is known as the **Processione dei Serpari** (Snake-Charmers' Procession). Festivities start around 10am, the procession begins at noon and the fun continues throughout the afternoon.

Cocullo has no accommodation but is accessible by ARPA bus from Sulmona (€2.20, 40 minutes) and Scanno. You can also reach Cocullo by train from Celano (€1.80, 35 minutes, five daily). Ask at the tourist offices in Sulmona and Scanno for details, as the usually scant transport services are increased for the festival.

Scanno

elevation 1050m

Much of the reward in visiting Scanno is in the getting there. The exhilarating drive up from Sulmona takes you through the Gole di Sagittaro (Sagittarius Gorges) and past the tranquil Lago di Scanno, while continuing south of the village takes you into the heart of the Parco Nazionale d'Abruzzo. The medieval village itself is increasingly being swamped by hotels built to serve the tourist trade. Out of season, however, you can still get a sense of how this remote community must once have been.

Long a centre of wool production and for centuries an exclusive supplier to the Franciscan order, Scanno was 'discovered' by photographers after WWII who, fascinated by the use of traditional costume, heralded the village as an example of traditionalism in a modern world. Even today it's still possible to see a handful of elderly women in costume.

Above the village, a chair lift leads to a small ski area.

The **tourist office** (☎ 0864 7 43 17; Piazza Santa Maria della Valle 12) is on the edge of the medieval town centre.

SLEEPING

There are plenty of hotels, most of which insist on at least half-board in high season (August). Many close in winter.

Pensione Nilde (☎ 0864 7 43 59; Viale del Lago 101; d with bathroom high season €45, half/full board per person €40/45) On the road rising up to the village, this, Scanno's cheapest option. Low-key modesty is the style at this simple lodge, which offers views across to the medieval centre.

Pensione Grotta dei Colombi (☎ 0864 7 43 93; Viale dei Caduti 64; d with bathroom €48, half/full board per person high season €43/50) It's worth staying at this friendly hotel for the views and food. It serves a robust daily menu for €18.

Also recommended are **Albergo Margherita** (☎ 0864 7 43 53; Via Domenico Tanturri 100; half/full board per person high season €52/56) and the more expensive **Hotel Vittoria** (☎ 0864 7 43 98; hotelvittoria@hotmail.com; Via Domenico di Rienzo 46; half/full board per person €70/75).

EATING

Trattoria Lo Sgabello (☎ 0864 74 74 76; Via dei Pescatori 45; full meals around €18) Down the stairs from the historic centre, this welcoming trattoria serves tasty regional dishes. As you tuck in, check out the photos of the locals in their traditional gear.

Ristorante Gli Archetti (☎ 0864 7 46 45; Via Silla 8; full meals around €28; Wed-Mon) Within the medieval town, this much-vaunted restaurant serves high-quality cuisine in an unpretentious setting.

GETTING THERE & AWAY

ARPA (☎ 0864 21 04 69) buses connect Scanno with Sulmona.

Autolinee Schiappa (☎ 0864 7 43 62) bus services depart Stazione Tiburtina in Rome for Scanno (2½ hours) at noon, 3pm, 5.45pm and 9.15pm.

PARCO NAZIONALE D'ABRUZZO

Established by royal decree in 1923, the Parco Nazionale d'Abruzzo is the most popular of the region's national parks, attracting about two million visitors annually. Incorporating 1100 sq km of the Apennines, it is ringed by an external protected area of 1500 sq km. Since its inception, the park has been at the forefront of Italy's conservation movement and, along with the neighbouring Parco Nazionale della Majella, is the last refuge of the native Marsican brown bear and Apennine wolf. At last count there were around 80 bears, 40 wolves, 600 indigenous Abruzzo chamois and 10 lynx living wild. You might also spot a golden eagle, preying on the chamois kids.

Orientation & Information

A convenient base is the lively town of Pescasseroli or, if you prefer somewhere more low-key, nearby Civitella Alfedena.

In Pescasseroli (1167m) the **park information office** (☎ 0863 9 19 55; Via Consultore 1; 10am-2pm & 3-5.30pm Tue-Sun) has loads of useful information, including a Carta Turistica map (€6) where walking routes and *rifugi* are highlighted. There is also a **tourist office** (☎ 0863 91 04 61; Via Piave 2; 9am-1pm & 3-6pm Mon-Sat, 9am-1pm Sun).

The **Centro di Visita** (☎ 0863 91 04 05; Viale Colli D'Oro; admission €6; 10am-2pm & 3-5.30pm Tue-Sun) has a small natural history museum and zoo.

Less hectic than Pescasseroli, Civitella Alfedena (1121m) lies on the park's eastern edge above Lago di Barrea. There you'll find a combined park information and visitors centre, the **Centro Lupo** (☎ 0864 89 01 41; information centre free, wolf museum €3; ☷ 10am-1pm & 3-5.30pm Tue-Sun). At the small wolf museum you can view the open-air corral where a few wolves still prowl in semi-captivity. In a smaller enclosure lurks a family of lynx. There's also a **tourist office** (☎ 0349 213 23 94), which is open the same hours as the Centro Lupo.

Activities

This is trekking territory, with well-marked trails ranging from easy family jaunts to serious hikes. Information is readily available from the park information offices, which also organise guided tours. Lonely Planet's *Walking in Italy* also has details about walking opportunities in Abruzzo.

Sleeping & Eating

Albergo Prato Rosso (☎ 0836 91 05 42; Via della Chiesa 14, Pescasseroli; d with bathroom €35-50, extra bed €10) This snug family hotel has comfortable rooms. The walls, however, are paper-thin, so hope for quiet neighbours.

Campeggio dell'Orso (☎ 0863 9 19 55; person with tent €7; ☷ year-round) About 1km south of Pescasseroli, this camp site also has a **rifugio** (per bed €9).

Albergo La Torre (☎ 0864 89 01 21; www.albergo latorre.com; Via Castello 3, Civitella Alfedena; d with bathroom €39-52, half-board per person €35-42, full meals around €18) This walkers' favourite extends a warm welcome and serves hearty local cuisine.

Campeggio Wolf (☎ 0864 89 03 60; Via Nazionale, Civitella Alfedena; person/tent/car high season €5/5/3; ☷ Apr-Oct) This camp site is conveniently situated in the heart of town.

Pizzeria San Francisco (☎ 0863 91 06 50; Via Isonzo 1, Pescasseroli; pizzas about €5) A popular joint in Pescasseroli where pizzas are prepared as they should be: in a wood-burning oven.

Getting There & Away

Pescasseroli, Civitella Alfedena and other villages in the park are linked by five daily **ARPA** (☎ 0864 21 04 96) buses to Avezzano (and from there to L'Aquila) and to Castel di Sangro (with onward travel to Sulmona by bus or train). Between mid-June and mid-September, a daily Roma Tiburtina bus runs between Rome and Pescasseroli, departing at 8am.

PESCARA

pop 115,448

Pescara is a heavily developed seaside resort and commercial centre that in winter offers little and in summer is packed to the gills. However, it's the main regional transport hub so you might find yourself passing through.

Jazz fans should take in the annual international **jazz festival** (☎ 085 37 41 98), held in the second half of July at the Teatro D'Annunzio.

Orientation & Information

From the train and intercity bus stations on Piazzale della Repubblica, the beach is just a short walk northeast down Corso Umberto I.

The **tourist office** (☎ 0854 21 01 88; Piazza Primo Maggiore 5; ☷ 9am-1pm & 4-7pm Mon-Sat, 9am-1pm Sun summer, 9am-1pm Mon-Fri winter) is situated at the sea end of Corso Umberto 1.

Sights

If you've a little time on your hands, the **Museo delle Genti d'Abruzzo** (☎ 0854 28 35 17; Via delle Caserme 22; admission €4; ☷ 9am-1pm Mon-Sat, 3.30-6pm Tue & Thu, 9am-1pm & 9pm-12.30am Mon-Fri, 9am-1pm Sat Jul-Aug) tells the story of local peasant culture.

Sleeping & Eating

Albergo Planet (☎ 0854 21 16 57; Via Piave 142; s/d €23/42, with bathroom €28/52) Check out the punk pink wallpaper at this basic but central, excellent-value hotel.

Hotel Natale (☎ 0854 22 28 85; Via del Circuito 175; s/d €29/37.50, s/d/tr with bathroom €32/48/65) This hotel is a little way out from the centre and the rooms are basic and somewhat tired, but it's still a sound choice.

Hotel Alba (☎ 0853 8 91 45; www.hotelalba.pesca ra.it; Via Michelangelo Forti 14; s/d with bathroom €52/74) This place is convenient for the train station and has decent enough rooms, but the service can be a little snooty at times.

Pinguino (☎ 085 6 28 69; Corso Manthonè 36; full meal €15-20, pizzas from €4.20) Across the River Pescara, this reasonably priced restaurant also functions as a pizzeria.

Cantina di Jozz (☎ 0854 51 88 00; Via delle Caserme 61; set menu €22; ☷ Tue-Sat & lunch Sun) The locals rate this place and the food here is good, if unexceptional, and the atmosphere convivial.

Getting There & Away

AIR
Pescara airport (PSR; ☎ 0854 32 42 00) is 4km out of town and easily reached by bus from the train station. **Ryanair** (www.ryanair.com) has regular flights to/from London Stansted.

BOAT
A catamaran (passengers only) runs four times weekly to Croatia's Dalmatian islands of Vis and Hvar and on to Split (called Spalato in Italian; one way €89-114, about six hours) between mid-June and late September. For information, contact **Agencia Sanmar** (☎ 0854 51 08 73) at the port.

BUS
ARPA buses leave from Piazzale della Repubblica for L'Aquila (€7.20, two hours, 10 daily), Sulmona (€5, 1¼ hours, five daily) and many other destinations in Abruzzo. They also run to Naples (Piazza Garibaldi, €17, 4½ hours, three daily) and Rome's Stazione Tiburtina (€15, 2¾ hours, two daily). Timetables are posted at the ARPA **ticket office** (☎ 0854 21 50 99) on the piazza.

CAR & MOTORCYCLE
Heading along the coast, you can choose between the A14 and the often-busy SS16; the latter hugs the coast more closely. Both the A25 and SS5 lead toward Rome, L'Aquila and Sulmona.

TRAIN
Pescara is on the main train line along the Adriatic coast, which runs to Bologna (€17.40, 3½ hours, frequent), Ancona (€6.90, 1¾ hours, frequent), Foggia (€9, about two hours, 10 daily) and points further south, as well as to L'Aquila (€6.90, change at Sulmona), Sulmona (€3.40, 1¼ hours, frequent) and Rome (€11.30, 3½ hours, six daily).

AROUND PESCARA
Hidden away in **Chieti**, a fairly typical hilltop town 18km south of Pescara, lies the region's most important museum. Housed in a 19th-century villa, the **Museo Archeologico Nazionale** (☎ 0871 33 16 68; admission €4; ☼ 9am-7pm) displays a fantastic collection of local finds. The ground floor is dominated by stupendous Roman sculpture, but also contains a collection of 15,000 coins dating from the 4th century BC to the 19th

century. On the first floor the so-called 'Warrior of Capestrano' steals the show. This 6th-century BC funerary statue sports some fine curves and natty headgear.

To get to the museum take a train to Chieti Scalo and then bus No 1 to the historic centre, some 5km uphill.

MOLISE

The second-smallest region in Italy, Molise is one of the country's forgotten areas. Over much of the countryside lies a palpable air of abandon and the towns are largely unexciting. A kind of cultural bridge from north to south, it doesn't merit a long stay.

But it's not all bad news. You can wander through the Roman ruins of Saepinum, southwest of Campobasso, and there are good walking opportunities in the Monti del Matese. Excavations in Isernia have unearthed what is believed to be the oldest village in Europe, and the small beach resort of Termoli is a jumping-off point for the Isole Tremiti, bunched together off the coast of northern Puglia (see pp656–7).

CAMPOBASSO
pop 51,297 / elevation 701m
There is very little reason to come to Campobasso, Molise's regional capital, unless you're trying to get to nearby Saepinum. Modern and basically unappealing, Campobasso is a regional transport hub. The national *carabinieri* (military police) training school is here, as is a high-security prison.

The **tourist office** (☎ 0874 41 56 62; Piazza della Vittoria 14; ☼ 8am-2pm Mon-Sat) tries to help. To reach it from the train station, turn left into Via Cavour, right into Corso Bucci and left again into Corso Vittorio Emanuele.

You can kill a couple of hours wandering up into the older part of town to take a look at the Romanesque churches of **San Bartolomeo** (13th century) and **San Giorgio** (12th century). The castle, now a military weather station, is striking from a distance but less impressive close up. More worthwhile is the **Museo Samnitico** (Samnite Museum; ☎ 0874 41 22 65; Via Chiarizia 12; admission free; ☼ 9am-1pm & 3-7pm Tue-Sun), which displays items from local sites.

Campobasso is connected by bus to Termoli, Isernia and Pescara. Local trains run

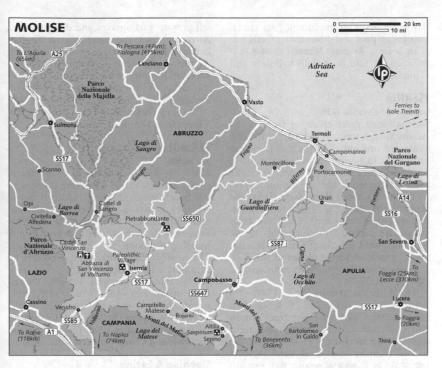

MOLISE

to Isernia (10 daily), Benevento (five daily) and Termoli (nine daily). Long-distance buses service Rome (€12.40, 3½ hours, five daily) and Naples (€9, 3½ hours, three daily).

AROUND CAMPOBASSO

One of Italy's least-visited Roman ruins, **Saepinum** (admission free), is a tough destination if you're without wheels, but more than merits the effort. An unimportant provincial town, it survived into the 9th century before being sacked by Arab invaders. The well-preserved ruins include most of the town walls and bastion towers, a temple, a triumphal arch and the foundations of numerous houses. You're free to wander at will.

To reach Saepinum by public transport, take one of the infrequent Mosca buses from Campobasso to the hamlet of Altilia, right beside the site, or to Sepino, a 3km walk away.

The **Monti del Matese**, southwest of Campobasso, offer good walking in summer and good skiing in winter. Take a bus from Campobasso to Campitello Matese or a train from Campobasso or Isernia to Bojano (Boiano). From either point trails lead into the mountains.

Campitello Matese (1430m) is a small winter and summer sports resort where, according to season, you can hire mountain bikes (€2 per half-hour) or ski equipment from **Galeassi Sport** (☎ 0874 78 41 80). Around this upland valley there's some fine walking through pine and beech woods and above the tree line.

The resort has several hotels, but they're not for the budget-conscious.

Rifugio Jezza (☎ 0874 78 41 88; full board per person €50-70, full meals around €18; ☺ year-round) This is the pick of the possibilities. This friendly, family-run place has character and is considerably less spartan than its name might imply. Accommodation is in cosy double rooms with full facilities and the restaurant serves filling local fare.

Albergo Kristiania (☎ 0874 78 41 07; r with breakfast from €60; ☺ Dec-Apr & Jun-Sep; ☻) At the entrance to the resort, the Kristiania is a comfortable place to relax in after a hard

ABRUZZO & MOLISE

day outdoors. You might enjoy its sauna, swimming pool and other sports facilities.

In season, **Autolinee Micone** (☎ 0874 78 01 20) buses run four times daily to Bojano and Campobasso.

ISERNIA

pop 21,192 / elevation 423m

Isernia's one great claim to fame is the nearby village, thought to be up to 700,000 years old and possibly the most ancient settlement in Europe. It was discovered in 1979, and excavations are ongoing. Stone tools discovered at the site are on display at the town's small **Museo Santa Maria delle Monache** (☎ 0865 41 51 79; Corso Marcelli 48; admission €2; ☽ 8.30am-7.30pm). From the train station it's a good 20-minute walk to the museum; head left along Corso Garibaldi and continue under the cathedral arch into the old quarter. To visit the excavations call ☎ 0865 41 35 26.

The dusty **tourist office** (☎ 0865 39 92; 6th fl Palazzo della Regione, Via Farinacci 9; ☽ 8am-2pm Mon-Sat) is a 200m walk from the train station (turn left into Corso Garibaldi and right into Via Farinacci).

The recently renovated **Hotel Sayonara** (☎ 0865 5 09 92; www.sayonara.is.it; Via G Berta 131; s/d with bathroom & breakfast €45/60, lunch & dinner €10) is centrally located and has cool, relaxing rooms. Go straight (north) from the train station, turn right onto Via Berta and follow this for four blocks.

Isernia is reached by bus from Campobasso and Termoli (information is posted in Piazza della Repubblica in front of the train station) and by train from Sulmona (€6.90), Pescara (€9) and Campobasso (€2.80).

AROUND ISERNIA

Just outside **Pietrabbondante**, about 30km northeast of Isernia, are the remains of a pre-Roman village, including a Greek-style theatre. It was originally settled by the Samnites, who controlled the area before Roman domination. Six buses a day connect Isernia and Pietrabbondante.

Near Castel San Vincenzo, about 25km northwest of Isernia, is the **Abbazia di San Vincenzo al Volturno** (☎ 0865 95 52 46; admission free; ☽ 9am-noon & 3-5pm daily summer, Sat & Sun only rest of year). This Benedictine abbey was one of the foremost monastic and cultural centres in 9th-century Europe before it

fell prey to earthquakes and Arab raiders. After centuries, the contemplative life has been resumed, bizarrely in the form of a community of American nuns from Connecticut. But they're not what draw the visitor; rather, it's the magnificently preserved Byzantine frescoes lying deep in the crypt.

Buses run between Isernia and Castel San Vincenzo, a 1km walk from the abbey.

TERMOLI

pop 30,590

More low-key than some of its northern rivals, Termoli makes a relaxing if unexciting beach stop. The tiny medieval *borgo* (village) boasts a 12th-century **cathedral** and 13th-century Swabian **castle**, built by Frederick II. Termoli is also a year-round jumping-off point for the Isole Tremiti. The town is filled with holiday-makers in summer, and accommodation, especially for the budget-conscious, is tight. Things don't improve in winter – most of Termoli simply shuts down.

The **tourist office** (☎ 0875 70 39 13; Piazza Bega; ☽ 8am-noon Mon-Sat) is 100m east of the train station along Corso Umberto I.

Sleeping & Eating

Cala Saracena (☎ 0875 5 21 93; SS Europa 2, 174; person/tent/car high season €7/6.50/3.40; ☽ Jun–mid-Sep) There are camping facilities at Cala Saracena, located on the SS16 Adriatica to Pescara road (also known as Europa 2). It can be reached by local bus from the train station.

Pensione Villa Ida (☎ 0875 70 66 66; Via Mario Milano 27; s/d with bathroom & breakfast low season €37/52, high season €42/62, full board €48-62; ☽ Easter-Nov) A short 150m walk from the train station and two blocks from the sea, this place represents good value in all but the highest season. Full board is compulsory in August.

Hotel Meridiano (☎ 0875 70 59 46; www.hotelmeridiano.com; Lungomare Cristoforo Colombo 524; s/d with bathroom low season €57/67, high season €62/72) Overlooking the beach, this place has large rooms and friendly service.

Da Antonio (☎ 0875 70 51 58; Corso Umberto I 59; full meals around €20) Locals like to lunch on the seafood here, which is particularly good.

Getting There & Away

BOAT

Termoli is the only port with a year-round daily ferry service to the Isole Tremiti (see

TERMOLI TIME

The role of Greenwich (London) in the history of time is well chronicled, but that of Termoli remains obscure. Sitting at 42° longitude and 15° latitude, as confirmed by the calculations of Francesco Porro on 1 April 1898, it is on Termoli that Italian and Central European Time is set. The actual line of measurement, the 15th meridian, passes through a crumbling tower known as the Mulino a Vento, which today forms the centrepiece of a hideous block of flats on the Rio Vivo.

The idea of international time zones was formally accepted in Washington DC in 1884 – prior to this each country operated on its own time – and adopted a year later. Taking the Greenwich meridian as the central axis, zones were established at intervals of 15°. The Italian government accepted this system on 1 November 1893 and Termoli found itself the timekeeper for the entire peninsula and beyond.

pp656–7). The service is operated by **Adriatica Navigazione** (☎ 0875 70 53 43) and leaves Termoli at 9am; it sets back from the Isole Tremiti at 2.30pm or 4.20pm. Between June and August, Navigazione Libera del Golfo and Navigargano also operate services. Buy your ticket at each company's kiosk at the ferry terminal. The fare is €14.50 return by boat or about €28.50 return for the faster hydrofoil trip.

BUS
The intercity bus station is beside Via Martiri della Resistenza. **SATI buses** (☎ 0874 6 50 50) link Termoli with Campobasso (hourly) and Pescara (three daily). **Cerella** (☎ 0873 39 11 68) has two early-morning buses daily to/from Isernia and is one of several companies to service Rome and Naples.

CAR & MOTORCYCLE
Termoli is on the A14 and SS16, which follow the coast north to Pescara and beyond and south to Bari. The SS87 links Termoli with the Campobasso area overlooking the Cigno river valley.

TRAIN
Termoli is on the main Bologna–Lecce train line along the Adriatic coast.

ALBANIAN TOWNS
Several villages to the south of Termoli form an Albanian enclave dating to the 15th century. These include Campomarino, Portocannone, Ururi and Montecilfone. Although inhabitants shrugged off their Orthodox religion in the 18th century, locals still use (as their first language) a version of Albanian incomprehensible to outsiders. Each year Ururi (3 May) and Portocannone (Monday after Whit Sunday) stage a bizarre chariot race. The chariots (more like carts) are pulled by bulls and hurtle round a traditional course urged on by youngsters on horseback.

All the villages can be reached by bus from Termoli.

Campania

The best known of Italy's southern regions, Campania is a bewildering mix of dramatic coastal scenery and forgotten mountains, ancient sites and modern sprawl. Presiding over all of this is Naples, the one true metropolis of the Mezzogiorno (literally 'midday', the evocative name for Italy's sunny south) and one of Europe's most densely populated cities. About three million people live in the shadow of Mt Vesuvius, which is still, 2000 years after the destruction of Pompeii and Herculaneum, a constant threat.

Further down the coast the Greek temples of Paestum are among the best preserved in the world while to the west of Naples the Lago d'Averno (Lake Avernus), in the Campi Flegrei, was believed to be the entrance to the ancient underworld.

Legend abounds in Campania. Homer and Ulysses, Virgil and other characters of classical mythology have all left their mark. Stories tell how sirens lured sailors to their deaths off Sorrento and of islands inhabited by mermaids. Travel down the bewitching Amalfi Coast or out to these magical islands, Capri among them, and maybe all this will start to make more sense.

The reality, however, can often be more prosaic as the summer hordes pile in, blocking roads and pushing prices sky-high. Still, console yourself with a *limoncello*, and head back to Naples for a pizza. They're the best in the world.

HIGHLIGHTS

- **Panorama**
  Gaze down at the sparkling Amalfi Coast from hill-top Ravello (pp637–8)

- **Ancient Ruins**
  See how the Romans lived and died at perfectly preserved Pompeii (pp623–7) and Herculaneum (pp620–2)

- **Volcano**
  Peer into the crater of Mt Vesuvius (pp622–3)

- **Blue Sea**
  Stare into the shimmering waters of Capri's Grotta Azzurra (pp613–14)

- **Museum**
  Marvel at the Graeco-Roman wonders in Naples' Museo Archeologico Nazionale (p595)

- **Eating**
  Bite into a *pizza margherita* anywhere in downtown Naples (p602)

- **Timeless Temples**
  Wander among the wild flowers that colour the remarkable Greek temples at Paestum (pp641–3)

Naples ★   ★ Mt. Vesuvius
            ★ Pompeii
              Ravello
Capri ★   ★
      Amalfi Coast

- POPULATION: 5,652,492 | - AREA: 13,595 SQ KM

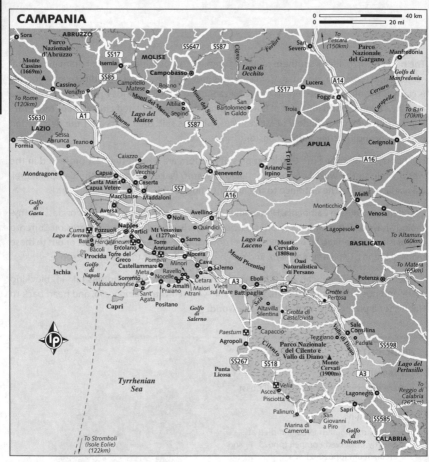

CAMPANIA

NAPLES (NAPOLI)

pop 1,000,470

It's impossible to approach Naples without preconceptions. No other city in Italy arouses such passion and it's rare to meet an Italian indifferent to the subject. But this adds to the city's distinct edge, to the vibrant sense of self that is disarmingly infectious and utterly irresistible. The fact is, Naples is fun.

Raucous, polluted, unruly, anarchic, deafening and with many of its majestic historical buildings grubby and crumbling, Naples has at least as much in common with Casablanca in Morocco or Egypt's

Alexandria on the other side of the Mediterranean as with fellow European ports such as Genoa, Marseilles or Barcelona. And, like these cities, it's glued together by the sheer zest and vitality of its inhabitants.

Beautifully positioned on the bay that bears its name, Naples has a little – and often a lot – of everything. The old centre, once the heart of ancient Neapolis and now bristling with ancient churches, a medieval university and countless eateries and cafés, pulsates to the beat of noisy street markets, swarms of people buzzing around on Vespas and the general chaos of a city at work.

Nothing is orderly and regulation is observed with absolute discretion. Traffic lights are routinely ignored, as are one-way signs and just about every other road rule. It's not unusual to see a whole family aboard a single Vespa or children careening about on mopeds.

But while this is all relatively harmless, there is a nasty side. The Neapolitan Mafia, the Camorra, thrives, specialising in bank hold-ups, controlling the local fruit and vegetable markets, prostitution and the massive *toto nero* (illegal football pools). The families also have hands in the booming black market in fake designer clothes and CDs.

The city has, however, undergone something of a facelift in the last decade. Since the left-wing mayor Antonio Bassolino instigated a massive drive to clean up the city for the 1994 G7 summit, many churches, museums and monuments that had been off-limits to the public for decades were reopened and tourist areas made safer. It was a good time and led, in 2000, to Bassolino being booted upstairs to the presidency of the Campania region. His shoes were filled by Naples' first ever female mayor, Rosa Iervolino, who, continuing the centre-left politics of her predecessor, has inevitably suffered the fate of those who follow big personalities. She is, however, a determined operator keen to make her mark.

HISTORY

Soon after founding Cumae in 1000 BC, colonists from Rhodes established a settlement on the western side of Mt Vesuvius. Many centuries later Phoenician traders from present-day Lebanon and Greeks from Athens were attracted by the splendour of the coast and so expanded the settlement, christening it Neapolis (New City). It thrived as a centre of Greek culture and later, under Roman rule, became something of a VIP resort, a favourite of emperors Pompey, Caesar and Tiberius.

After successive waves of invasion by the wild Goths and a couple of spells associated with Byzantium, Naples remained an independent dukedom for about 400 years until captured by the Normans in AD 1139. They, in turn, were replaced by the German Hohenstaufens, whose Swabian dynasty lasted until 1266 and gave the city many new institutions, including its university. After the defeat and death of Manfred, king of Sicily, at the battle of Benevento in 1266, Charles I of Anjou took control of the Kingdom of Sicily and turned Naples into its de facto capital. Following a period of disorder, the Angevins were succeeded in 1442 by the Spanish house of Aragón, under whom the city came to prosper. Alfonso I of Aragón, in particular, introduced new laws and promoted the arts and sciences.

In 1503 Naples and the Kingdom of Sicily were absorbed by Spain, which sent viceroys to the area to rule as virtual dictators. Despite their heavy-handed rule Naples flourished artistically and acquired much of its splendour during this period. Indeed it continued to flower when the Spanish Bourbons re-established Naples as capital of the Kingdom of the Two Sicilies in 1734 (which encompassed part of the Italian peninsula and Sicily from the mid-15th to mid-19th centuries). Aside from a Napoleonic interlude under Joachim Murat (1806–15), the Bourbons remained until unseated by Garibaldi and the Kingdom of Italy in 1860, when Naples was a serious but unsuccessful contender for capital of the new nation.

The city was heavily damaged during more than 100 bombing raids in WWII and marks can still be seen on many monuments. The Allies subsequently presided over a fairly disastrous period of transition from war to peace – many observers have since attributed the initial boom in the city's organised crime, at least in part, to members of the occupying forces. A severe earthquake in 1980 and the dormant Vesuvius looming to the east remind Neapolitans of their city's vulnerability.

ORIENTATION

Naples stretches along the waterfront and is divided into *quartieri* (districts). Stazione Centrale and the bus station are off Piazza Garibaldi, east of Spaccanapoli, the ancient heart of Naples. Piazza Garibaldi and its side streets form an enormous, unwelcoming transport terminus and street market. The area is distinctly seedy and quite a few of the cheaper hotels, some of which double as brothels, are here.

A wide shopping street, Corso Umberto I, skirts the southern edge of Spaccanapoli, aligned southwest from Piazza Garibaldi to Piazza Bovio. From here Via A Depretis runs to the huge Piazza Municipio, dominated

CAMPANIA

NAPLES (NAPOLI)

INFORMATION		
ANM Bus Information Office............1	G2
ANM Information Kiosk....................2	G2
CTS Travel Agency..........................3	F3
Every Tour (American Express)........4	E4
Feltrinelli.......................................5	D5
Internet Café di Napoli...................6	H2
Internetbar.....................................7	E3
Main Tourist Office.........................8	D5
Multimedia......................................9	F3
My Beautiful Laundrette................10	E3
Ospedale Loreto-Mare (Hospital)....11	H3
Pharmacy......................................12	H2
Tourist Information Office.............13	E4
Tourist Information Office.............14	H2
Tourist Information Office.............15	E3
Tourist Information Office.............16	A5

SIGHTS & ACTIVITIES	**pp593–8**
Acquario.......................................17	C5
Basilica del Carmine Maggiore......18	G3
Basilica di San Giorgio Maggiore...19	F3
Basilica di Santa Chiara.........(see 15)
Biblioteca Nazionale......................20	E5
Cappella di San Severo..................21	F3
Castel dell'Ovo.............................22	E6
Castel Nuovo................................23	E4
Castel Sant'Elmo..........................24	D4
Cathedral......................................25	F2
Certosa di San Martino..................26	D4
Chiesa dei Girolamini....................27	F2
Chiesa del Gesù Nuovo..................28	E3

Chiesa di San Domenico		
Maggiore.....................................29	F3
Chiesa di San Francesco di Paola..30	E5
Chiesa di San Lorenzo Maggiore....31	F2
Chiesa di San Paolo Maggiore........32	F2
Chiesa di Sant'Angelo a Nilo.........33	F3
Chiesa di Sant'Anna dei Lombardi.34	E3
Chiesa di SS Filippo e Giacomo.....35	F3
Cima Tours...................................36	G2
Fontana dell'Immacolatella...........37	E6
Fontana di Nettuno.......................38	E4
Museo Archeologico Nazionale......39	E2
Museo Civico Gaetano Filangieri....40	F3
Museo Civico.........................(see 23)
Museo del Palazzo Reale........(see 20)
Museo di Antropologia..................41	F3
Museo di Mineralogia.............(see 41)
Museo di Zoologia.................(see 41)
Museo Nazionale della Ceramica Duca di	
Martina.......................................42	C4
Museo Nazionale di San	
Martino...............................(see 26)
Museo Pignatelli...........................43	C5
Napoli Sotterranea........................44	F2
Ospedale delle Bambole................45	F3
Palazzo Cuomo.....................(see 40)
Palazzo di Carafa di Maddaloni.....46	F3
Palazzo Filomarino........................47	E3
Palazzo Marigliano........................48	F3
Port'Alba (City Gate)....................49	E3
Tourcar...50	E4
University.....................................51	F3

SLEEPING	**pp600–2**
6 Small Rooms..............................52	E3
Albergo Duomo.............................53	F3
Albergo Sansevero (Degas)............54	E3
Albergo Sansevero.........................55	E3
Ginevra 2......................................56	H2
Grand Hotel Oriente......................57	E4
Grand Hotel Santa Lucia................58	E6
Hostel of the Sun..........................59	F4
Hostel Pensione Mancini................60	G2
Hotel Bellini..................................61	F2
Hotel Belvedere............................62	D3
Hotel Casanova.............................63	G2
Hotel Gallo...................................64	G2
Hotel Le Orchidee.........................65	F4
Hotel Pinto-Storey.........................66	C5
Hotel Prati....................................67	G2
Hotel Rex.....................................68	E6
Hotel Zara....................................69	G2
Napolit'amo..................................70	E4
Ostello Mergellina........................71	A5
Parteno..72	D5
Pensione Astoria...........................73	E5
Pensione Margherita......................74	C4
Pensione Ruggiero.................(see 66)
Sansevero D'Angri.........................75	E3
Soggiorno Sansevero.....................76	E3

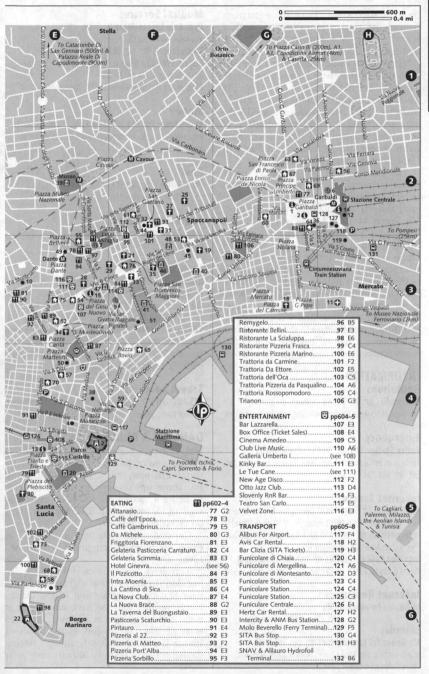

CAMPANIA

by the Castel Nuovo. From the waterfront behind the castle, ferries sail to the bay islands, Palermo and other long-distance destinations.

The Palazzo Reale (the former royal palace), next to the castle, stands over Piazza Trento e Trieste. Naples' main street, Via Toledo, leads north from the square, briefly becomes Via Roma, passes alongside Piazza Dante, on the western boundary of Spaccanapoli, then undergoes three more name changes before reaching the Parco di Capodimonte, north of the centre.

The extensions of two of Naples' more original streets, Via San Biagio dei Librai (which becomes Via B Croce at its western end) and Via dei Tribunali, eventually meet Via Roma. Much of Naples' street life, artisans and a host of good, cheap restaurants can be found in this area. Via San Biagio dei Librai is part of an almost straight run from near Stazione Centrale through Spaccanapoli to the foot of the hill-top Vomero district.

To the south and west extend broad boulevards and majestic squares leading to Santa Lucia and Mergellina. Above it all sits Naples' upper-middle class in the relative calm of Vomero, a natural balcony with grand views across the city and bay to Vesuvius.

INFORMATION
Bookshops
Feltrinelli (☎ 081 240 54 11; Piazza dei Martiri) For a selection of books in English, including Lonely Planet titles.

Emergency
Police Station (☎ 081 794 11 11; Via Medina 75) There is an office for foreigners here. To report a stolen car, call ☎ 081 794 14 35.

Internet Access
Multimedia (☎ 081 551 47 08; Via San Giovanni Maggiore Pignatelli 34; €0.50/20 mins; ☯ 9.30am-9.30pm)
Internetbar (☎ 081 29 52 37; Piazza Bellini 74; €3/hr; ☯ 9-2am Mon-Sat, 8pm-2am Sun)
Internet Café di Napoli (☎ 081 563 48 36; 2nd fl, Piazza Garibaldi 73; €1.50/15 mins; ☯ 9am-9pm Mon-Sat)

Internet Resources
In Naples (www.inaples.it)

Laundry
My Beautiful Laundrette (☎ 081 542 21 62; Via Montesanto 2; 6kg load €7; ☯ 9am-8.30pm Mon-Sat) There's also an Internet point (€3/hr).

Medical Services
Ospedale Loreto-Mare (hospital; ☎ 081 254 27 01; Via Amerigo Vespucci)
Ambulance (☎ 112, 081 752 06 96)
Guardia Medica (doctor; ☯ 24 hrs) Phone numbers are in listings guide *Qui Napoli*.
Pharmacy (Stazione Centrale; ☯ 8am-8pm)

Money
Every Tour (☎ 081 551 85 64; Piazza Municipio 5-6) Represents American Express, changes money and is an agent for Western Union.

Post
Post Office (☎ 081 551 14 56; Piazza Matteotti; ☯ 8.15am-7pm Mon-Sat)

Tourist Information
Main Tourist Office (☎ 081 40 53 11; Piazza dei Martiri 58; ☯ 8.30am-2.30pm Mon-Fri)

More useful, however, are:
Information Offices Stazione Centrale (☎ 081 20 66 66; ☯ 9am-7.30pm Mon-Sat, 9am-1.30pm Sun); Mergellina train station (☎ 081 761 21 02; ☯ 9am-7.30pm Mon-Sat, 9am-1.30pm Sun); Piazza del Gesù Nuovo (☎ 081 552 33 28; ☯ 9am-8pm Mon-Sat, 9am-3pm Sun); Via San Carlo 7 (☎ 081 40 23 94; ☯ 9am-8pm Mon-Sat, 9am-3pm Sun) Stocks the essential tourist brochure *Qui Napoli* plus a city map and guides to major monuments.

Travel Agencies
CTS (☎ 081 552 79 60; Via Mezzocannone 25) An efficient student travel centre.

DANGERS & ANNOYANCES
Naples has a certain reputation and, although you're unlikely to encounter Mafia shootouts, petty crime can be a problem. For some tips on how to reduce the risk of being a victim, see p814. Be especially vigilant for moped bandits and pickpockets on crowded transport.

Car and motorcycle theft is also rife, so think twice before bringing a vehicle into town.

Travellers should be careful about walking alone in the streets at night, particularly near Stazione Centrale and Piazza Dante. Never venture into the dark side streets at night unless you are in a group. The area west of Via Toledo and as far north as Piazza Carità, though safe enough during daylight hours, can be threatening after dark.

SIGHTS

To make the best of your time and money in Naples (and indeed the entire Campania region) an excellent investment is the **Campania artecard** (toll free ☎ 800 600 601; www.campaniartecard.it). A cumulative ticket that covers museum admission and transport, it comes in various forms. In Naples itself a three-day ticket (€13) gives free admission to two participating sites, a 50% discount on others and free transport in Naples and the Campi Flegrei. Other options range from €25 to €28 and cover sites as far afield as Pompeii and Paestum. They can be bought at train stations, newsagents, participating museums, via the Internet or through the call centre.

It's also worth noting that in most museums the ticket office closes an hour before the stated closing time of the museum.

Spaccanapoli
CATHEDRAL
Built on the site of earlier churches, which were themselves preceded by a temple to the pre-Christian god Neptune, this grand cathedral (☎ 081 44 90 97; Via Duomo; ☺ 8am-12.30pm & 4.30-7.30pm Mon-Sat, 8.30am-1pm & 5-8pm Sun) was begun by Charles I of Anjou in 1272. Largely destroyed in 1456 by an earthquake, it's undergone numerous alterations. The neogothic facade is the result of late-19th-century cosmetic surgery. Inside, above the wide central nave, is an ornately decorated coffered ceiling.

Central to Naples' religious (some would say superstitious) life is the 17th-century baroque **Cappella di San Gennaro** (Chapel of St Januarius; also known as Cappella del Tesoro or the Chapel of the Treasury). Housed within the chapel are the skull and a couple of phials of the congealed blood taken from San Gennaro, the city's patron saint. He was martyred at Pozzuoli, west of Naples, in AD 305 and tradition holds that these phials of his blood liquefied when his body was transferred back to Naples. Every year in May and September thousands gather here to pray for a miracle – that the blood will again liquefy and save Naples from any potential disaster. The saint is said to have saved the city from calamity on numerous occasions – although the miracle unspectacularly failed

to occur in 1941 when Vesuvius erupted. For further details of this mysterious festival see p600.

The next chapel eastwards contains an urn with the saint's bones, cupboards full of femurs, tibias and fibulas and a stash of other relics. Below the high altar is the **Cappella Carafa**, also known as the Crypt of San Gennaro, a Renaissance chapel built to house the saint's relics.

Halfway down the north aisle and beyond the mainly 17th-century **Basilica di Santa Restituta** is the so-called 'archaeological zone' (admission €3; ☺ 9am-noon & 4.30-7pm Mon-Sat, 9am-noon Sun). The tunnels beneath lead you deep into the remains of the site's original Greek and Roman buildings. Here too is the **baptistry**, the oldest in Western Europe, with its remarkably fresh 4th-century mosaics.

AROUND THE CATHEDRAL
Opposite the cathedral is the entrance to the **Chiesa dei Girolamini** (☎ 081 44 91 39; ☺ 9.30am-12.30pm & 2-5.30pm Mon-Sat, 9.30am-12.30pm Sun), also called San Filippo Neri, which is a rich baroque church with two facades. The more imposing 18th-century facade, facing Via dei Tribunali, is now closed. A small picture gallery in the adjoining convent features works from the 16th to 18th centuries.

Duck around the corner into Via dei Tribunali and to the left in Piazza San Gaetano you'll come across **Chiesa di San Lorenzo Maggiore** (☎ 081 29 05 80; Via dei Tribunali 316; excavations €2.58; ☺ 9am-5pm Mon-Sat, 9.30am-1pm Sun). The interior of the church, begun in the 13th century, is French Gothic. Catherine of Austria, who died in 1323, is buried here and her mosaic-covered tomb is among the most eye-catching of the church's adornments. You can pass through to the cloisters of the neighbouring convent, where Petrarch stayed in 1345. Beneath the complex are some excavations of the original Graeco-Roman city.

Across Via dei Tribunali is **Chiesa di San Paolo Maggiore** (Piazza San Gaetano 76; ☺ 9am-1pm). It was built in the late 16th century on the site of a Roman temple and the opulent interior houses the Sanctuary of San Gaetano. For details of Napoli Sotterranea (Underground Naples; entrance just beside the church), see p599.

While you're in the area check out the **Basilica di San Giorgio Maggiore** (Via Duomo 237; ☒ 8am-noon & 5-7pm Mon-Sat, 8am-1pm Sun). It's situated where Via San Biagio dei Librai meets Via Duomo and is worth a quick look for its classical and relatively austere – by Neapolitan standards – interior.

Across the road is the 15th-century **Palazzo Cuomo**, built by Tuscan artists. The building was moved several metres in 1881 when the street was widened. It now contains the **Museo Civico Gaetano Filangieri** (☎ 081 20 31 75; Via Duomo; ☒ closed at the time of writing).

VIA SAN BIAGIO DEI LIBRAI

Pass the **Ospedale delle Bambole** (Dolls' Hospital; Via San Biagio dei Librai 81), a famous landmark and one of the many artisan shops on this street and its continuation, Via B Croce, the parallel Via dei Tribunali to the north and the labyrinth of side alleys. You'll come across not only goldsmiths and other jewellers, but also makers of the famously elaborate Neapolitan *presepi* (nativity scenes).

At No 39, two blocks west of the Dolls' Hospital, is **Palazzo Marigliano**, behind whose grubby facade is a magnificent Renaissance entrance hall. Carrying on westwards you pass **Palazzo di Carafa di Maddaloni** and **Chiesa di SS Filippo e Giacomo** with their contrasting baroque and classical styles.

CHIESA DI SANT'ANGELO A NILO

This **church** (☎ 081 420 12 22; entrance at Vico Donnaromita 15; ☒ 10am-noon & 2-4pm Mon-Fri) sits beside Via San Biagio dei Librai, its facade benignly presided over by a quartet of tubby gilt cherubs. Built in 1385 and remodelled in the 18th century, it contains the monumental Renaissance tomb of one Cardinal Brancaccio, to which Donatello contributed.

Where Via San Biagio dei Librai becomes Via B Croce, in the piazza bearing its name, stands the Gothic **Chiesa di San Domenico Maggiore** (Piazza San Domenico Maggiore 8a; ☒ 8am-noon & 5-7pm), which was completed in 1324 by the Dominican order and much favoured by the Aragonese nobility. The church's interior, a cross between baroque and 19th-century neogothic, features some fine examples of Renaissance sculpture. In the sacristy are 45 coffins of the princes of Aragón and other nobles.

The deceptive simplicity of **Cappella di San Severo** (Via de Sanctis 19; admission €5; ☒ 10am-7pm

Mon & Wed-Sat, 10am-1.30pm Sun May-Oct, 10am-5pm Mon & Wed-Sat, 10am-1pm Sun Nov-April), on a narrow lane east of the church, is a dazzling contrast to the treasure chest of sculpture inside. Giuseppe Sanmartino's *Cristo Velato* (Veiled Christ), for instance, still confounds experts who cannot agree on how he created the apparently translucent veil. Also baffling is Corradini's *Pudicizia* (Modesty), which makes no attempt to hide the erotic. Also known as the Cappella di Santa Maria della Pietà dei Sangro, the chapel is the tomb of the princes of Sangro di San Severo.

AROUND PIAZZA DEL GESÙ NUOVO

From Piazza San Domenico Maggiore, Via B Croce continues west, following the course of the old Roman main street. Croce, Italy's foremost philosopher and historian in the first half of the 20th century, lived and died in **Palazzo Filomarino**, a grand Renaissance building on the right at No 12 just before you reach Via S Sebastiano.

Across Via S Sebastiano is **Basilica di Santa Chiara** (☎ 081 552 62 09; Via B Croce; ☒ 7am-12.30pm & 4.30-7pm), one of Naples' principal medieval monuments, and its adjacent convent. Built by the Angevins in the 14th century it suffered from subsequent earthquakes and baroque alterations. Since WWII, when incendiary bombs burned out the church and destroyed many works of art, it has been returned more or less to its original Gothic appearance. Within the **nuns' cloisters** (admission €4; ☒ 9.30am-1pm & 2.30-5.30pm Mon-Sat, 9.30am-1pm Sun), behind the church, is a long parapet entirely covered in decorative ceramic tiles, depicting landscapes and scenes from the nuns' lives.

A few steps west, Piazza del Gesù Nuovo opens before you with its ornate freestanding *guglia* (obelisk). The 16th-century **Chiesa del Gesù Nuovo** (☎ 081 551 86 13; Piazza del Gesù Nuovo; ☒ 6.45am-1pm & 4-7.30pm), on the northern side of the piazza, is one of the city's greatest examples of Renaissance architecture. The interior was redecorated in Neapolitan baroque style after a fire in 1639.

The 15th-century **Chiesa di Sant'Anna dei Lombardi** (☎ 081 551 33 33; Piazza Monteoliveto; ☒ 8.30am-12.30pm Tue-Sat), southwest of Piazza del Gesù Nuovo, features fine Renaissance sculpture, including a superb terracotta *Pietà* (1492) by Guido Mazzoni.

AROUND PIAZZA DEL CARMINE

On the waterfront in Piazza del Carmine, the **Basilica del Carmine Maggiore** was the scene of the 1647 Neapolitan Revolution led by Masaniello. Each year on 16 July a fireworks display celebrates the festival of the Madonna by simulating the burning of the bell tower.

Museo Archeologico Nazionale

Considered the most important **archaeological museum** (☎ 081 44 01 66; Piazza Museo Nazionale; admission €6.50; ♥ 9am-7.30pm Wed-Mon) in Europe, this place displays treasures forming one of the most comprehensive collections of Graeco-Roman artefacts in the world. Originally a cavalry barracks and later the seat of the city's university, the museum was established by Charles of Bourbon in the late 18th century to house the rich collection of antiquities he had inherited from his mother, Elizabeth Farnese, as well as the treasures that had been discovered at Pompeii and Herculaneum. It also contains the Borgia collection of Etruscan and Egyptian relics.

To avoid getting lost in its rambling galleries – numbered in Roman numerals – invest €7.50 in the bilingual *Guida di Orientamento* or, to concentrate upon the highlights, €4 for an audioguide in English.

Many items from the Farnese collection of classical sculpture, including the famous *Toro Farnese* (Farnese Bull), are displayed on the ground floor. Sculpted in the early 3rd century AD, the *Toro Farnese*, probably a Roman copy of a Greek original, is an enormous group of figures depicting the death of Dirce, Queen of Thebes, who in Greek mythology was tied to a bull and torn apart over rocks. Carved from a single block of marble, it was later restored by Michelangelo.

On the mezzanine floor are mosaics, mostly from Pompeii, including the Battle of Alexander, the best-known depiction of the great Macedonian emperor. It once paved the floor in the Casa del Fauno at Pompeii and is just one of a series of remarkably detailed and lifelike pieces.

The 1st floor is largely devoted to a treasure trove of discoveries from Pompeii, Herculaneum, Stabiae and Cumae. Items range from huge murals and frescoes to a pair of gladiator helmets, household items, ceramics and glassware – even eggcups. Galleries 86 and 87 house an extraordinary collection of vases of mixed origins, many carefully reassembled from fragments. In the basement is a smaller Egyptian collection.

The **Gabinetto Segreto** (Secret Room) reopened to the public in 2000 after decades of being accessible only to the seriously scientific. The ancient smut on display includes an intriguing statue of Pan up to no good with a nanny goat and nine paintings depicting erotic positions, which served as a menu for brothel clients.

South of Spaccanapoli
CASTEL NUOVO

When Charles I of Anjou took over Naples and the Swabians' Sicilian kingdom, he found himself in control not only of his new southern Italian acquisitions, but also of possessions in Tuscany, northern Italy and Provence (France). It made sense to base the new dynasty in Naples, rather than Palermo in Sicily, and Charles launched an ambitious construction program to expand the port and city walls. His plans included converting a Franciscan convent into the castle that still stands in Piazza Municipio. Also called the Maschio Angioino, it has crenellated round towers that make it one of the most striking buildings in Naples.

The 'New Castle' was erected in three years from 1279 but what you see today is the result of renovations by the Aragonese two centuries later, as well as a meticulous restoration effort prior to WWII. The heavy grey stone that dominates the castle was imported from Mallorca. The two-storey Renaissance triumphal arch at the entrance, the Torre della Guardia, commemorates the triumphal entry of Alfonso I of Aragón into Naples in 1443.

Spread across several halls on three floors is the **Museo Civico** (☎ 081 795 58 77; admission €5; ♥ 9am-7pm Mon-Sat, 9am-2pm Sun). The 14th- and 15th-century frescoes and sculptures on the ground floor are of the most interest. The other two floors display paintings, either by Neapolitan artists or with Naples or Campania as subjects, covering the 17th to the early 20th centuries.

Nearby on Via Medina is Bernini's **Fontana di Nettuno**, dating from 1601. Originally situated on Piazza Bovio, it has been moved to allow construction of the Metropolitana to continue on its former site.

PIAZZA TRENTO E TRIESTE

One of Naples' more elegant squares, Piazza Trento e Trieste, is fronted on the north-eastern side by Italy's largest opera house, the sumptuous **Teatro San Carlo** (☎ 081 797 21 11; Via San Carlo 98), famed for its perfect acoustics. Locals proudly boast that it was built in 1737 – 40 years before Milan's La Scala. True in a way; but San Carlo, nowadays home to one of Italy's oldest ballet schools, was destroyed by fire in 1816 and later restored. To book a guided tour call the San Carlo shop (☎ 081 40 03 00; admission €5).

Across Via San Carlo is one of the four entrances to the imposing glass atrium of the **Galleria Umberto I**, opened in 1900.

PALAZZO REALE

Facing the grand Piazza del Plebiscito, this magnificent **palace** (☎ 081 794 40 21; entrance on Piazza Trento e Trieste; admission €4; ⏰ 9am-8pm Thu-Tue), was built around 1600. It was completely renovated in 1841 and suffered extensive damage during WWII. The statues of the eight most important kings of Naples were inserted into niches in the facade in 1888.

From the courtyard a huge double staircase leads to the royal apartments, which house the **Museo del Palazzo Reale**, a rich collection of furnishings, porcelain, tapestries, statues and paintings.

The palace has also, since 1925, been home to the **Biblioteca Nazionale** (☎ 081 40 12 73; admission free; ⏰ 9am-7.30pm Mon-Fri, 9am-1.30pm Sat), which includes the vast Farnese collection brought to Naples by Charles of Bourbon, with at least 2000 papyruses discovered at Herculaneum and fragments of a 5th-century Coptic Bible. Visitors should bring ID as staff check it as a security measure.

CHIESA DI SAN FRANCESCO DI PAOLA

At the eastern end of Piazza del Plebiscito, this dominating church was begun by Ferdinand I in 1817 to celebrate the restoration of his kingdom after the Napoleonic interlude. Flanked by semicircular colonnades, the church is based on the Pantheon and is a popular wedding spot.

Santa Lucia

CASTEL DELL'OVO

The so-called **Castle of the Egg** (☎ 081 764 05 90; Borgo Marinaro; admission free; ⏰ 9am-6pm Mon-Fri,

9am-1pm Sat & Sun) is on the small rocky island off Santa Lucia, known as Borgo Marinaro. Built in the 12th century by the Normans on the site of a Roman villa, the castle became a key fortress in the defence of Campania. You can wander through the island's small lanes, which are mostly occupied by restaurants.

The **Fontana dell'Immacolatella**, at the end of Via Partenope, dates from the 17th century and features statues by Bernini and Naccherini.

Lungomare Caracciolo

West of Santa Lucia, Via Partenope spills into Piazza della Vittoria, marking the beginning of the Riviera di Chiaia. This boulevard runs beside **Villa Comunale**, a large park marked on its seaward side by Via Francesco Caracciolo, closed to traffic on Sunday mornings and taken over by strollers, skaters, scooters and joggers.

Within the park is the city's **aquarium** (☎ 081 583 32 63; Villa Comunale; adult/child €1.50/1; ⏰ 9am-6pm Mon-Sat, 9.30am-7pm Sun summer, 9am-5pm Mon-Sat, 9am-2pm Sun winter). Founded in the late 19th century by German naturalist Anton Dohrn, this is Europe's oldest aquarium. Its 30 tanks contain some 200 species of sea life exclusively from the Gulf of Naples.

Close by is **Museo Pignatelli** (☎ 081 761 23 56; Riviera di Chiaia 200; admission €2.10; ⏰ 9am-2pm Tue-Sun), an old patrician residence containing mostly 19th-century furnishings, china and other knick-knacks. A pavilion set in the villa's gardens houses a coach museum.

Vomero

Visible from all over the city, Vomero (*vom*-e-ro) hill is a serene and well-to-do residential quarter that rises above the chaos below. Three funicular railways connect the two (p607).

CASTEL SANT'ELMO

Commanding spectacular views across the city and bay, this austere, star-shaped **castle** (☎ 081 578 40 30; Largo San Martino; admission €1; ⏰ 8.30am-7.30pm Tue-Sun) was built into the tufa rock of the hill by the Spanish in 1538. Impressive though it is, the castle has seen little real action, serving more often than not as a prison. Admission times and price can vary when the castle is used for exhibitions.

CERTOSA DI SAN MARTINO

Barely 100m from the castle lies this Carthusian monastery, established in the 14th century and rebuilt in the 17th century in Neapolitan baroque style. It houses the **Museo Nazionale di San Martino** (☎ 081 578 17 69; Via Tito Angelini; admission €6; ☉ 8.30am-7.30pm Tue-Sun), which features a section on naval history, an area dedicated to the history of the Kingdom of Naples and an extensive art collection. Of particular interest is the Sezione Presepiale, several rooms devoted to a collection of Neapolitan *presepi* carved in the 18th and 19th centuries. Not all of the monastery is open to the public but you can enjoy the tranquil baroque Chiostro Grande (Main Cloister), whose manicured gardens are ringed by elegant porticoes.

Adjacent is the monastery's church, with exquisite marblework and a good number of frescoes and paintings, particularly by 17th-century Neapolitan artists. There is a magnificent view from the terraced gardens and from Largo San Martino, the square outside its main entrance.

VILLA FLORIDIANA

In a city decidedly short of green space, this public **park** (admission free; ☉ 9am-1 hr before sunset Tue-Sun) is a tonic, spreading down the slopes from Via D Cimarosa in Vomero to Mergellina. The stately home at its lower, southern end was built in 1817 by Ferdinand I for his wife, the Duchess of Floridia. Today it contains the **Museo Nazionale della Ceramica Duca di Martina** (☎ 081 578 84 18; admission €2.50; ☉ 8.30am-2pm Tue-Fri, 9am-2pm Sat & Sun), which has an extensive collection of European, Chinese and Japanese china, ivory, enamels and Italian majolica.

Capodimonte
PALAZZO REALE DI CAPODIMONTE

Work on a new palace for Charles of Bourbon started in 1738 and took almost a century to complete. On the northern edge of the city, the distinctive pinky-orange and grey palace is set in extensive **parklands** (admission free; ☉ 8am-1 hr before sunset) that were once aristocratic hunting grounds. Extensively restored, the palace houses the **Museo e Gallerie di Capodimonte** (☎ 081 749 91 11; Parco di Capodimonte; admission €7.50; ☉ 8.30am-7.30pm Tue-Sun), which displays the important Farnese collection (see the boxed text below). The paintings hang in the royal galleries on the 1st floor and are divided into periods and schools. The extensive collection boasts works by, among many others, Bellini, Botticelli, Caravaggio, Correggio, Masaccio and Titian. One of its most famous paintings is Masaccio's *Crocifissione* (Crucifixion). Other highlights are Bellini's *Trasfigurazione* (Transfiguration), and nine canvases by Titian.

Also on the 1st floor are the **royal apartments** with an extensive collection of armour, ivories, bronzes, porcelain and majolica, tapestries and other works of art.

VORACIOUS COLLECTING, FARNESE STYLE

It was Cardinal Alessandro Farnese who founded the Farnese collection. On becoming Pope Paul III in 1534, he began by gathering art treasures for the Vatican, then turned his attention to embellishing the family seat, Palazzo Farnese, in Rome. Through papal influence, the Farnese family monopolised excavations around the city. In 1540 the *Toro Farnese* (Farnese Bull) was discovered near the Terme di Caracalla and installed in the gardens of Palazzo Farnese. It remained there until 1787, when it was moved to Naples' Museo Archeologico Nazionale, now the home of other famous Farnese treasures such as *Venere Callipigia* and *Ercole a riposo*.

This particular pope's vow of celibacy didn't prevent him from fathering four children. One of the most interesting paintings at the Palazzo Reale di Capodimonte is an unfinished portrait by Titian of Paul III with his two grandsons – Ottavio, who became the Duke of Parma and Piacenza, and Gran Cardinale Alessandro, who later became a serious collector in his own right. Alessandro continued the collection, commissioning works from Michelangelo, El Greco and other contemporary painters of renown.

The collection was transferred to Capodimonte from the Farnese family's power base in Parma and Piacenza in 1759. Many paintings were sold off in the 19th century, when the entire remaining collection was transferred to what is now the Museo Archeologico Nazionale. The paintings were returned to Capodimonte in 1957.

The 2nd-floor galleries display work by Neapolitan artists from the 13th to 19th centuries.

CATACOMBE DI SAN GENNARO

Dating from the 2nd century, the **catacombs** (☎ 081 741 10 71; Via di Capodimonte 16; admission €2.60; ☺ closed for restoration) house a mix of tombs, corridors and broad vestibules held up by columns and arches, and are decorated with early Christian frescoes and mosaics. Tradition has it that San Gennaro was originally buried here.

WALKING TOUR

You'll never walk all of Naples in a day but the itinerary we describe here will take you

through the heart of the city and give you a good overview.

Starting from Piazza Garibaldi, head a short way down Corso Umberto I before veering right into Via Egiziaca a Forcella. After crossing Via P Colletta, follow the street as it veers left and merges into Via Vicaria Vecchia. Where it meets the busy cross-street, Via Duomo, stands the **Basilica di San Giorgio Maggiore (1)** on your left and, two blocks northwest up Via Duomo, the **cathedral (2)**. Opposite the cathedral is the entrance to **Chiesa dei Girolamini (3)**.

Walk back southeast to where you emerged onto Via Duomo. Turn right off Via Duomo into Via San Biagio dei Librai, one of the liveliest roads in Spaccanapoli

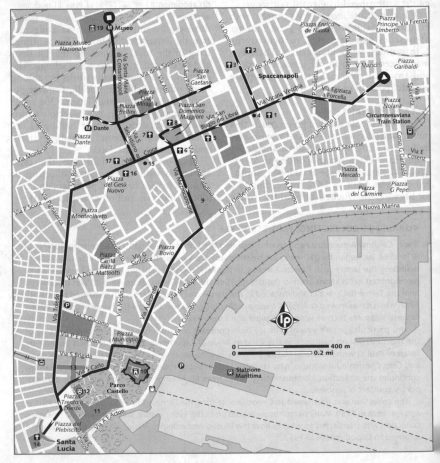

and one of the original Roman streets. You'll pass the **Ospedale delle Bambole (4)**, or Dolls' Hospital, **Chiesa di SS Filippo e Giacomo (5)** and **Chiesa di Sant'Angelo a Nilo (6)**.

The rear of the imposing **Chiesa di San Domenico Maggiore (7)** abuts onto the café-fringed, pedestrianised piazza of the same name. At the heart of the square is a *guglia*, a kind of ground-level, richly carved baroque steeple or obelisk, topped by a statue of the good saint himself. The not-to-be-missed **Cappella di San Severo (8)** is just off this square in a lane east of the church.

From the square you have a choice. You could head south along Via Mezzocannone past the **university (9)**, then rejoin Corso Umberto I, turning right and following it into Piazza Bovio. From this square, Via A Depretis leads southwest to Piazza Municipio and the round-towered **Castel Nuovo (10)**. Continue southwest from the square and you'll come to **Palazzo Reale (11)**, **Teatro San Carlo (12)**, **Galleria Umberto I (13)** and **Chiesa di San Francesco di Paola (14)**. From here you could follow the waterside around to Santa Lucia and beyond to Mergellina, or turn north from Piazza Trento e Trieste up Via Toledo back into the heart of Spaccanapoli.

The other option from Piazza San Domenico Maggiore is to continue westwards along Via B Croce, past **Palazzo Filomarino (15)**, then **Basilica di Santa Chiara (16)** as far as Piazza del Gesù Nuovo and **Chiesa del Gesù Nuovo (17)**. Backtrack from the square to the first intersection and turn left along Via S Sebastiano. At the next intersection on your left a short street leads down to **Port'Alba (18)**, a city gate built in 1625, then to Piazza Dante. Back on route and ahead of you is Piazza Bellini and, to the right, Piazza Luigi Miraglia, from which Via dei Tribunali leads east. You're now walking along the **decumanus**, or main street, of the original Greek, and later Roman, town. Two-thirds of the way along Via dei Tribunali stood the Greek **agora**, or central market and meeting place, in what is now Piazza San Gaetano.

A great place to rest your weary feet is in one of Piazza Bellini's several cafés. While you're at it you could inspect the remains of the ancient Greek city walls under the square. From the square, an easy walk north along Via Santa Maria di Costantinopoli brings you to the unmissable **Museo Archeologico Nazionale (19)**.

NAPLES FOR CHILDREN

Other than the castles and catacombs, the aquarium and the never-dull street life, there are a number of attractions which might appeal to children.

Within the university is a museum complex, the **Museo di Mineralogia, Zoologia e Antropologia** (☎ 081 253 51 62; Via Mezzocannone 8; admission to each €0.70; 9am-1.30pm & 3-5pm Mon, 9am-1.30pm Tue-Sun Sep-Jul). Museo della Mineralogia features minerals, meteorites and quartz crystals collected from the Vesuvius region. Museo della Zoologia is the most child-friendly of the three while Museo della Antropologia, across the courtyard, is also worth peeking into.

Città della Scienza (Science City; ☎ 081 372 37 28; www.cittadellascienza.it; Via Coroglio 104; adult/child €7/6; 9am-5pm Tue-Sat, 10am-7pm Sun, 5pm-midnight Fri, Sat & Sun 21 Jun–1 Sep) takes visitors on an interactive exploration of the world around us. Features examine natural phenomena, the science behind modern communication and, in the planetarium (€1.50), the night sky. Take the underground to Bagnoli and then bus No C9 or C10.

Edenlandia (☎ 081 239 40 90; www.edenlandia.it, Italian only; Viale Kennedy 76; adult/child under 1.1m €2/free, single tickets/all day pass €1/10; varies, call ahead), Naples' historic amusement park, has more than 200 attractions. Take the Ferrovia Cumana from Stazione Cumana, westbound, and get off at Edenlandia station.

TOURS

Cima Tours (☎ 081 20 10 52; cimatour@tin.it; Piazza Garibaldi 114) and **Tourcar** (☎ 081 552 04 29; Piazza Matteotti 1) organise excursions to the Gulf of Naples islands, the Amalfi Coast and Pompeii, Herculaneum and Vesuvius. A half-day tour to Pompeii costs about €40, including admission costs.

Napoli Sotterranea (Underground Naples; ☎ 081 29 69 44; www.napolisotterranea.com; Piazza San Gaetano 68; admission €9.30; 1½ hr tours noon, 2pm & 4pm) For something completely different, dip underground for a guided tour that takes you 40m below the city to explore the network of passages and caves. They were originally hewn by the Greeks to extract the soft tufa stone for construction, then extended by the Romans as water conduits. Clogged up with illegally dumped refuse over centuries, they were used as air-raid shelters in WWII.

FESTIVALS & EVENTS

Naples' main festivals honour San Gennaro. On the first Sunday in May, 19 September and 16 December each year, thousands gather in the cathedral for the **Festa di San Gennaro**, to witness the saint's blood, held in two phials, liquefy: a miracle said to save the city from potential disasters (p593).

Other important festivals include the **Madonna del Carmine**, held on 16 July in Piazza del Carmine, which culminates in a fireworks display, and the **Madonna di Piedigrotta** (5 to 12 September). At Christmas, thousands of elaborate *presepi* are erected around the city.

Neapolis Rock Festival, held at the height of summer, attracts top international acts. It's held west of town, down by the beach at Arenile di Bagnoli (p605).

SLEEPING

Accommodation in Naples is plentiful and relatively inexpensive, and can be charming. But quality varies and some of the budget hotels, particularly around Stazione Centrale, can be decidedly seedy. The places we list, however, are clean, safe and reliable.

If you want to stay in the heart of historic Naples head for Spaccanapoli. The atmosphere here, although not exactly peaceful, is fun and you'll have many of the city's sights within easy walking distance. For a more relaxing stay the Mergellina, Vomero and Santa Lucia areas are considerably less hectic and offer a completely different view of the city.

While room prices should always be read as a guide rather than gospel truth in Italy, this is even more the case in Naples. The following prices are a fair indication. Unfortunately some hotels only have doubles and often are not willing to offer lower prices for solo travellers.

The closest camp sites are in Pozzuoli (pp608–9) to the west and Pompeii (pp623–7) to the east.

Budget

AROUND STAZIONE CENTRALE

Hostel Pensione Mancini (☎ 081 553 67 31; www .hostelpensionemancini.com; Via Mancini 33; dm/s/d with breakfast €18/35/45, s/d/tr with bathroom & breakfast €55/ 80/90) Space is tight at this welcoming place, meaning that it can become something of a squeeze, but the atmosphere makes it a pleasant haven from the bedlam outside.

Hotel Ginevra (☎ 081 28 32 10; www.hotelginevra.it; Via Genova 116; s/d/tr €30/50/65, d/tr with bathroom €60/80) This long-time travellers' favourite remains a solid choice. The exuberant owners have also opened a slightly pricier option on the same floor with the brilliant name **Ginevra 2** (d with bathroom €70; 🔀), where rooms are plusher.

Hotel Casanova (☎ 081 26 82 87; www.hotelcasa nova.com; Corso G Garibaldi 333; s/d high season €18/39, with bathroom €26/51.50) With a name like a brothel this is, in fact, a small family hotel boasting a roof terrace and recently renovated rooms. Use the safer Corso G Garibaldi entrance rather than the main one located on Via Venezia.

Hotel Zara (☎ 081 28 71 25; hotelzar@tin.it; 2nd fl, Via Firenze 81; s/d €26/40, with bathroom €35/55; 🖳) Run by the same family as the Casanova, this place has attentive service and the book exchange is a welcome source of reading material.

Hotel Gallo (☎ 081 20 05 12; fax 081 20 18 49; Via S Spaventa 11; s/d with breakfast €50/60, with bathroom & breakfast €57/83) This is a bustling little no-nonsense hotel and the rooms are clean and comfortable, in sharp contrast to the surrounding streets.

SPACCANAPOLI & CITY CENTRE

Many hotels in this area are near Piazza Dante, which you can reach by bus No R2 from Stazione Centrale. Alternatively, Piazza Dante is on line one of the Metropolitana.

Hostel of the Sun (☎ 081 420 63 93; www.hostel napoli.com; Via Melisurgo 15; dm/s/d €18/45/50, d with bathroom €70; 🖳) Handy for the ferry terminal, this is fast becoming a backpacker favourite thanks, in part, to the ultrahelpful young staff. There is a kitchen, no curfew, and Internet access costs €1.50 for 30 minutes.

6 Small Rooms (☎ 081 790 13 78; www.at6small rooms.com; Via Diodata Lioy 18; dm/d €17/55) On the top floor of a venerable old building, this popular hostel is a cheerful choice. Should the lady downstairs be in the mood there's an evening plate of pasta (€3.50), otherwise it's the kitchen stove. They only accept same-day phone reservations.

Hotel Bellini (☎ 081 45 69 96; fax 081 29 22 56; Via San Paolo 44; s with bathroom €51, d with bathroom €67-77)

Tucked away in the heart of Spaccanapoli, this small hotel is full of Neapolitan charm. The rooms are decorated in unique style – check out some of the wall paintings – and the welcoming owner is a font of city lore.

Albergo Duomo (☎ 081 26 59 88; hotelduomo@ libero.it; Via Duomo 228; s/d with bathroom high season €40/65) As the name suggests this is situated not 100m from the cathedral. Rooms here are a warm pink and comfortable and airy, if a little anonymous.

MERGELLINA, VOMERO & SANTA LUCIA
Ostello Mergellina (☎ 081 761 23 46; fax 081 761 23 91; Salita della Grotta 23; dm/d B&B per person €14/16; ☼ year-round) This HI hostel is a reliable choice, although it gets busy in peak periods and some readers complain that the entrance can be seedy after dark. Laundry facilities are a plus but the 12.30am curfew less so. There's a maximum stay of three nights in July and August.

Pensione Margherita (☎ 081 556 70 44; Via D Cimarosa 29; s/d/tr €35/62/87) This place, just a few doors from the funicular station in Vomero, has views over Capri and Sorrento. The welcome is motherly and the no-frills rooms are large and simple.

Pensione Astoria (☎ 081 764 99 03; Via Santa Lucia 90; s/d/tr €26/50/60) Basic and clean, this place is in a lovely part of town, near the sea. All rooms come with a washbasin, bidet and TV.

Mid-Range
AROUND STAZIONE CENTRALE
Hotel Prati (☎ 081 26 88 98; www.hotelprati.it; Via C Rosaroll 4; s/d with bathroom & breakfast high season €80/110, full meals €20-25) With an attractive roof-garden restaurant and rooms with all the creature comforts, this is a decent option either as a hotel or dining venue.

SPACCANAPOLI & CITY CENTRE
Napolit'amo (☎ 081 552 36 26; www.napolitamo.it; Via Toledo 148; s with bathroom & breakfast €62, d with bathroom & breakfast €78-83; ☐) Live like nobility in this 16th-century palace, which retains much of the atmosphere of its former glory days. Magnificent 18th-century mirrors reflect the stylish palatial decor in this highly recommended palatial hideaway.

Hotel Le Orchidee (☎ 081 551 07 21; fax 081 251 40 88; Corso Umberto I 7; s/d with bathroom €70/88) Rooms here are large, functional and clean

and the hotel is well positioned for the ferry terminal. It's on the 5th floor, and you'll need a €0.50 coin for the lift.

Sansevero D'Angri (☎ 081 21 09 07; www.albergo sansevero.it; Piazza VII Settembre 28; d/suites with bathroom high season €110/150; ☒) Staying here is like sleeping in a genuine palace – not surprising given that Vanvitelli, the original architect, also designed the royal palace at Caserta. Some of the huge rooms have frescoes, the parquet is genuine 17th century and Garibaldi was an early guest.

The following three hotels (under the same ownership) represent excellent value for money. Each is situated in an historical building, similarly decorated with simple, tasteful wicker furniture. The buildings are protected so the owners can't erect signs, making it a tad tricky to find them. Doubles with bathroom and breakfast at all three places cost €88 to €95 and each has a couple of rooms without bath for €68 to €75.

Albergo Sansevero (☎ 081 21 09 07; www.albergo sansevero.it; Via Santa Maria di Costantinopoli 101) Look for the two fine marble pillars flanking the courtyard entrance as you head north from Piazza Bellini.

Albergo Sansevero Degas (☎ 081 551 12 76; Calata Trinità Maggiore 53) This hotel is so named because the building once belonged to Edgar Degas, the French impressionist. Enter the courtyard opposite Caffè Novocento and take the lift to the third floor.

Soggiorno Sansevero (☎ 081 551 57 42; Piazza San Domenico Maggiore 9) You'll find this place just around the corner from the Cappella di San Severo on the eastern side of the piazza.

MERGELLINA, VOMERO & SANTA LUCIA
Hotel Rex (☎ 081 764 93 89; www.hotel-rex.it; Via Palepoli 12; d with bathroom & breakfast €120; ☒) Handy for the seafront is this relaxed three-star pad. There's no dining room, meaning that breakfast has to be served in your room. Shame.

Pensione Ruggiero (☎ 081 66 35 36; hotelrug@ libero.it; 3rd fl, Via Martucci 72; s/d with bathroom & breakfast €70/90) As you enter the grand old building near Amedeo Metro station, you'll need sharp eyes to spot the lift hidden in the corner. Rooms here are bright and inviting and the owners extend a warm welcome.

Hotel Pinto-Storey (☎ 081 68 12 60; www.pinto storey.it; 4th-5th fl, Via Martucci 72; s/d with bathroom & breakfast €80/122) Facilities are fine and the rooms are cosily furnished at this laid-back, some might say sleepy, hotel, in the same building as the Ruggiero.

Top End

SPACCANAPOLI & CITY CENTRE

Grand Hotel Oriente (☎ 081 551 21 33; www.oriente.it; Via A Diaz 44; s/d with bathroom & breakfast €155/220; ❷ ℗) A fairly charmless hotel catering to the business trade, the Orient is nevertheless smack-bang in the centre of town and offers all the requisite creature comforts.

MERGELLINA, VOMERO & SANTA LUCIA

Hotel Belvedere (☎ 081 578 81 69; fax 081 578 54 17; Via Tito Angelini 51-59; s/d with bathroom €100/120) No other hotel in Naples can offer guests such a magnificent panorama. Right beside the Certosa di San Martino monastery, the aptly named Hotel Belvedere stands at Naples' highest point.

Parteno (☎ 081 245 20 95; www.parteno.it, Italian only; Via Partenope 1; s/d/tr with bathroom & breakfast €110/137/165; 🖵) Discretion and style are the bywords for this intimate and elegant hotel. Hidden in a seafront building, its six rooms are exquisitely furnished and guests can use a nearby gym and sauna.

Grand Hotel Santa Lucia (☎ 081 764 06 66; www.santalucia.it; Via Partenope 46; s/d with bathroom & breakfast high season €210/322; 🖵 ❷) This grand hotel overlooks the marina and Borgo Marinaro. All the mod cons are elegantly incorporated into the tasteful rooms and there is even – something rare in Italy – a nonsmoking floor.

EATING

Neapolitan food is among Italy's (and therefore the world's) best. The pizza was created here and nowhere on earth will you eat it better. Topped with mozzarella cheese and fresh tomato sauce, it's standard fare, as is the related calzone, a puffed-up version with the topping becoming a filling instead. *Misto di frittura* – deep-fried potato, aubergine (eggplant) and courgette (zucchini) flowers – tempts from tiny stalls in tiny streets, as does mozzarella *in carozza* (deep-fried in bread). Seafood, particularly clams and mussels, is a speciality (although it's best to avoid uncooked shellfish as the bay is very polluted). The cakes are simply unbeatable and even the coffee tastes better in Naples.

THE PERFECT PIZZA

Naples and Rome vie for pizza supremacy yet their two products could scarcely be more different. Pizzas in Naples have a soft doughy base while your true Roman pizza usually has a very thin crust.

Neapolitans regard their version as the authentic one – after all, they will argue, their forefathers actually invented pizza in the 18th century. Pizzerie in Naples serving the 'real thing' have a sign on the door: *la vera pizza napolitana* (the real Neapolitan pizza). It's not just for show – to merit the seal of approval a pizza-maker has to conform to strict requirements. For a Margherita, named after Queen Margherita (1851–1926, wife of King Umberto of Savoy), the cheese must be mozzarella (preferably made from buffalo milk), the olive oil extra virgin and the salt from the sea. Rolling pins are banned (the dough must be tossed by hand) and the pizza has to be cooked in a wood-fired oven at a temperature of between 215°C and 250°C.

Do your own research. For about the best pizza in Naples, head for Da Michele (p603) near Stazione Centrale. In Rome, try Pizzeria Remo (p141) in Testaccio. Buon appetito!

Cafés

Intra Moenia (☎ 081 29 07 20; Piazza Bellini 70) Arty, literary, left-leaning with a mixed gay and hetero clientele, Intra Moenia is a great place to pass an hour or two pondering one of Naples' more beautiful piazzas. It has a small bookshop and publishing house too.

Caffè dell'Epoca (☎ 081 29 17 22; Via Santa Maria di Costantinopoli 81-82; ❷ Mon-Sat) Virtually across the road from Intra Moenia, this stylish café has been serving its wonderful coffee since 1886.

Caffè Gambrinus (☎ 081 41 41 33; Via Chiaia 12) A veritable institution, Naples' oldest and most stylish café remains the haunt of artists, intellectuals and musicians – including saxophonist and ex-president of the US, Bill Clinton. Hordes of tourists are not unknown either.

Quick Eats

Pizzeria al 22 (☎ 081 552 27 26; Via Pignasecca 22; pizza slices from €1) Off Piazza Carità, this place serves excellent pizza by the slice.

Friggitoria Fiorenzano (☎ 081 551 27 88; Piazza Montesanto 6; fried snacks each €0.15) Visit for deep-fried vegetables – the aubergine slices and courgette flowers are especially good.

For ice cream and cakes the possibilities are limitless, but the places listed below have all been rigorously tested.

Gelateria Scimmia (☎ 081 552 02 72; Piazza Carità 4) One of the city's best-known *gelaterie*, and temptingly positioned for those on their evening stroll along Via Toledo.

Remygelo (☎ 081 66 73 04; Via F Galliani 29a) Remygelo in Mergellina draws the sweet-toothed from all over the city – all prepared to go out of their way to pick up a tub or two of ice cream or some figure-wrecking pastries.

Attanasio (☎ 081 28 56 75; Vico Ferroviario 2-4) Convenient for a snack if you're passing through Stazione Centrale, this place is deservedly famous throughout Italy for its *sfogliatelle* – the great Neapolitan pastry, a vaguely sweet ricotta-filled number that tastes best straight from the oven.

Pintauro (☎ 081 41 73 39; Via Toledo 275) You can smell the *sfogliatelle*, served fresh from the oven throughout the day, as you approach.

Pasticceria Scaturchio (☎ 081 551 38 50; Via Pignasecca 22-24) The Neapolitans come here to order their cakes – read into this what you will.

Gelateria Pasticceria Carraturo (Via C Bernini 9-11) This ice-cream chain has five popular outlets around town, including one up in Vomero.

Restaurants
SPACCANAPOLI & STAZIONE CENTRALE
Da Michele (☎ 081 553 92 04; Via Cesare Sersale 1; pizzas €5-7) If the pizzas here are not the best in the world, they're up there. There are only two types – margherita (mozzarella and tomato) or marinara (mozzarella and garlic), so it's pointless asking for a menu. It's always crowded, so take a ticket and wait.

Trianon (☎ 081 553 94 26; Via P Colletta 42-6; pizzas €5-10) An institution in Neapolitan circles – film director Vittorio de Sica and comic actor Totò were regulars – this historic pizzeria does its city proud. On the dough since 1923, it's still tossing the pizzas with the best of them.

Pizzeria Sorbillo (☎ 081 44 66 43; Via dei Tribunali 32; pizzas from €5) Another popular pizza parlour

that vies for the city's No 1 spot. There are now three generations of the Sorbillo family, all in the pizza business in Italy or the US.

Pizzeria di Matteo (☎ 081 45 52 62; Via dei Tribunali 94; pizzas from €3) Come Saturday night you won't be able to get near this place. It's distinctly dingy on the outside, but its fried nibbles are great and the pizzas huge, bubbling and delicious.

Il Pizzicotto (☎ 081 551 62 91; Via Mezzocannone 129; pasta from €4, pizza & beer €5) This snug little eatery, right in the heart of student-land, is a popular lunchtime choice. Try it and you'll see why. Worth the money is its three-course lunch menu (€7.20).

Trattoria da Carmine (☎ 081 29 43 83; Via dei Tribunali 330; full meals around €11) One of dozens of small family trattorie in this area, it offers good basic grub in a simple, no-frills environment. Helpings are large and the wine's dangerously cheap.

Ristorante Bellini (☎ 081 45 97 74; Via Santa Maria di Costantinopoli 79-80; full meals €25) The fish trolley by the entrance will alert you to the house speciality – seafood. Pasta portions are served on a grand scale and the fish is as fresh as the morning catch. If you're pushed for time, grab a mini-pizza (€1.10) from their street-side stall.

Pizzeria Port'Alba (☎ 081 45 97 13; Via Port'Alba 18; pizzas around €5; ☽ Thu-Tue) Just around the corner from Ristorante Bellini and founded in 1830, this is one of Naples' oldest and most characterful pizzerie.

La Nuova Brace (☎ 081 26 12 60; Via S Spaventa 14-16; tourist menu €8.30, full meals around €17; ☽ Mon-Sat) A no-nonsense eatery, this handy bolt hole provides a welcome refuge from the mayhem of nearby Piazza Garibaldi and Stazione Centrale. There's poetry on the walls and the food's not bad either.

La Nova Club (☎ 081 551 48 94; Via Santa Maria La Nova 9; full meals around €23; ☽ lunchtime Mon-Fri, dinner Sat) Near the main post office, this place offers excellent food at reasonable prices – you can even tell the waiter your upper spending limit and he will help you order accordingly. You might need to ring the bell to get in.

La Taverna del Buongustaio (☎ 081 551 26 26; Vico Basilico Puoti 8; full meals around €13) The sign in the window says: 'You don't waste time here, you eat'. Tucked away off the western side of Via Toledo, this simple place serves excellent seafood and filling local fare.

CAMPANIA

SANTA LUCIA

Ristorante La Scialuppa (☎ 081 764 53 33; Via Lucilliana; full meals around €30; ⊙ Tue-Sun) On Borgo Marinaro, you can either eat on the terrace overhanging the marina or on the pretty little piazza on the other side. This, not surprisingly, inflates the prices of the reasonable food.

Ristorante Pizzeria Marino (☎ 081 764 02 80; Via Santa Lucia 118-120; pizzas from €3.65, full meals around €20; ⊙ Tue-Sun) A popular local joint, this long-established place serves great pizzas. First, however, whet your appetite by delving into the huge antipasto spread of fishy wonders.

Trattoria Da Ettore (☎ 081 764 04 98; Via Santa Lucia 56; pizzas from €4.30; ⊙ Mon-Sat) Further along from Marino is Da Ettore, renowned for its delicious *pagnotiello*, a sort of calzone stuffed with mozzarella, ham and mushrooms. It's often busy so be prepared to queue.

MERGELLINA & VOMERO

Trattoria Pizzeria da Pasqualino (☎ 081 68 15 24; Piazza Sannazzaro 77-79; full meals around €18; ⊙ Wed-Mon) Just round the corner from Mergellina train station, this trattoria is the business. Sit on the frenetic square and taste the *insalata caprese* (mozzarella and tomatoes soaked in olive oil) and you'll know everything's right with the world.

Trattoria dell'Oca (☎ 081 41 48 65; Via Santa Teresa a Chiaia 11; full meals around €20; ⊙ Mon-Sat Sep-Jul) This snug place near Piazza Amedeo comes highly recommended. The menu changes daily and the cooking is as appealing as the wood decor.

La Cantina di Sica (☎ 081 556 75 20; Via C Bernini 17; full meals around €25; ⊙ Tue-Sun) In Vomero, this trattoria with its high, vaulted roof serves excellent Neapolitan dishes. The *spaghetti alle vongole e pomodorini* (with clams and cherry tomatoes) and the *pasta genovese* (pasta with onion sauce) are highly recommended.

Ristorante Pizzeria Frasca (☎ 081 556 51 98; Via Raffaele Morghen 12; pizzas around €5; ⊙ Wed-Mon) Also in Vomero, and less stylish than Trattoria dell'Oca, Frasca has a pleasant garden for alfresco dining in summer and also does home/hotel deliveries.

Trattoria Rossopomodoro (☎ 081 556 81 69; Via D Cimarosa 144; daily menu around €10) This place looks like an Andy Warhol Neapolitan theme restaurant. But don't let the giant cans of tomato painted on the walls put you off the food, which is simple and tasty.

ENTERTAINMENT

The monthly *Qui Napoli* and local newspapers are the best guides to what's on when. You can buy tickets for most sporting and cultural events at **Box Office** (☎ 081 551 91 88; Galleria Umberto I 15-16). Ask here or at the tourist office about what's happening during your stay.

Each May the city authorities organise Maggio dei Monumenti, a month of concerts and cultural activities in various museums and monuments around town; most of these are free. From May until September there are open-air concerts in various locations. Ask at the tourist offices for details.

Nightclubs & Live Music

Neapolitan nightlife is very street-oriented. Young, hip Neapolitans tend to loaf around the piazzas, particularly Piazza del Gesù Nuovo and Piazza San Domenico Maggiore, before moving on late-ish to jazz joints or trendy (some might say tacky) clubs. In these areas it is, however, perfectly possible to enjoy a night out by simply buying your beers from the nearest bar and hanging out. If you want club action, be aware that some of the smarter clubs charge hefty admission or membership fees (up to €40).

Bar Lazzarella (☎ 081 551 00 05; Calata Trinità Maggiore 7-8) A popular watering hole just off Piazza del Gesù Nuovo, this is an ideal spot to watch the night-time crowds drift by.

Slovenly RnR Bar (Vico San Geronimo 24) In a former life this underground cellar was known as Echos Club. It's had a change of name but it's the same scene where new talent is given a chance. The emphasis is on live rock music with an international flavour. It has, in the past, promoted groups from Turkey, Ireland and the Balkans.

Operating from cellars which abut each other, neighbouring **Le Tue Cane** (Via Cisterna dell'Olio 14-15) and **Kinky Bar** (☎ 081 552 15 71; Via Cisterna dell'Olio 13) both attract a lively, mainly student crowd. Kinky Bar is a reggae joint; Le Tue Cane is more versatile.

Velvet Zone (☎ 347 810 73 28; Via Cisterna dell'Olio 11; admission & 1st drink around €10; ⊙ 11pm-6am) Different night, different sound; you'll hear an eclectic mix of hip-hop, rock, techno, pop and more here.

New Age Disco (☎ 081 29 58 08; Via Atri 36; admission €8; ☺ 10pm-2am Tue-Sun) Something of a gay favourite, this place bangs out everything from 80s revival music to industrial and techno.

Club Live Music (Salita della Grotta 10) In Mergellina, right on the youth hostel's doorstep and burrowed into the hillside, this club generally lives up to its name. It heats up early for Naples and a queue usually starts forming by 9.30pm.

Otto Jazz Club (☎ 081 552 43 73; Piazzetta Cariati 23) West of Piazza Trento e Trieste, this is a long-established place that primarily features Neapolitan jazz.

Biggest of the venues for live music concerts is **Palapartenope** (☎ 081 570 68 06; Via Barbagallo 115). It seats over 8000 and pulls in both Italian and international acts.

In summer consider heading out of town for the relative evening cool of the beach.

Arenile di Bagnoli (☎ 081 230 30 50; Via Nuova Bagnoli 10; admission €10; ☺ 10pm-5am May-Sep) This huge complex has several bars and cabanas where you can dance. It's also the venue for the annual Neapolis Rock Festival (p600).

Cinema

Finding undubbed films in English is not easy but try the **Cinema Amedeo** (☎ 081 68 02 66; Via Martucci 69; tickets €6.70), which shows original-language films on Thursday nights.

Theatre

There are year-round concerts and performances of opera and ballet at **Teatro San Carlo** (☎ 081 797 21 11; Via San Carlo 98). Unfortunately for visitors, most tickets are sold on a seasonal, subscription basis and relatively few are left over for individual purchase. These start at around €20 then spiral steeply upwards, always selling like hot *sfogliatelle*.

Sport

It's now a long time since Napoli (the local football team), led by the genius of Maradona, won the national championship. Currently fighting to avoid relegation from Serie B (the Italian second division), the team still attracts crowds of up to 70,000. Home matches are played at the **Stadio San Paolo** (ticket information ☎ 081 593 23 23; Piazzale Vincenzo Tecchio) in

the western suburb of Mostra d'Oltremare, usually on Sunday. If the opposition's any good tickets are very hard to come by.

To get there take the Metropolitana to Campi Flegrei.

SHOPPING

They say you can buy anything in Naples, and you'll see why after even a short wander around the city centre. From designer stores to improvised stalls with goods straight off the back of a truck, Naples certainly seems to have it all.

In particular Naples is renowned for its gold and Christmas items such as *presepi* and *pastori* (shepherds). The nativity scenes can take on huge proportions, becoming fantastic models of the whole of Bethlehem. Most artisans are in Spaccanapoli, in particular along Via dei Tribunali, Via B Croce and the side streets and lanes. Many goldsmiths and jewellery shops are clustered around Via San Biagio dei Librai.

If you like old dolls, head for **Ospedale delle Bambole** (p594).

The city's more exclusive shops are in Santa Lucia, behind Piazza del Plebiscito, along Via Chiaia to Piazza dei Martiri and down towards the waterfront. Young people shop along Via Roma and Via Toledo.

Street markets, where you can buy just about everything, are scattered across the city centre, including Piazza Garibaldi and along Via Pignasecca, off Piazza Carità.

GETTING THERE & AWAY
Air

Capodichino airport (NAP; ☎ 081 789 62 59), about 8km northeast of the city centre, is southern Italy's main airport, linking Naples with most Italian and several major European cities.

Airlines represented include:

Alitalia (☎ 081 709 33 33, international flights ☎ 848 86 56 42) Internal flights and international connections via Rome and Milan.

Air France (☎ 848 88 44 66) Daily to Paris.

British Airways (☎ 848 81 22 66) Daily to London Gatwick.

Go (☎ 848 88 77 66) Daily to London Stansted.

Boat

Ferries and hydrofoils leave for Capri, Sorrento, Ischia, Procida and Forio from Molo Beverello in front of the Castel Nuovo.

Longer-distance ferries for Palermo, Cagliari, Milazzo, the Aeolian Islands (Isole Eolie) and Tunisia leave from the Stazione Marittima, next to Molo Beverello.

Alilauro and SNAV also operate hydrofoils to Ischia, Procida and Capri from Mergellina.

Qui Napoli lists current timetables for Gulf of Naples services.

Tickets for shorter journeys can be bought at the ticket booths on Molo Beverello and at Mergellina. For longer journeys try the offices of the ferry companies or travel agents.

A list of the routes serviced follows. The fares, unless otherwise quoted, are for a high-season, deck-class single. The reduction for a return journey isn't significant.

Alilauro (☎ 081 761 10 04) Operates hydrofoils to Ischia (€13) and Forio (€14).

Caremar (☎ 081 551 38 82) Serves Capri (ferry/hydrofoil €5.50/10.40), Ischia (€5.50/10.40) and Procida (€4.40/7.70).

Linee Lauro (☎ 081 552 28 38) Linked with Alilauro, it has ferries to Ischia (€7) and a year-round service at least weekly to Tunis (deck class €80 to €120; *poltrona* or airline-style seat €85 to €125; bed in shared cabin €90 to €130). It also has direct runs to/from Sardinia and Corsica in summer. Fares for both destinations are: deck class €35 to €70; bed in shared cabin €48 to €85.

Navigazione Libera Del Golfo (NLG; ☎ 199 44 66 44) Runs hydrofoils to/from Capri (€12) year-round and ferries to/from Amalfi (€10; summer only).

Siremar (☎ 081 580 03 40) Part of the Tirrenia group, Siremar operates boats to the Aeolian Islands and Milazzo (€40.90). The service is up to six times a week in summer, dropping by 50% in the low season.

SNAV (☎ 081 428 51 11) Runs hydrofoils to Capri (€12), Procida (€ 8.80) and Ischia (€12). In summer there are daily services to the Aeolian Islands. SNAV also operates Sicilia Jet (€57 to €80), which foams down the coast to Palermo daily mid-April to September.

Tirrenia (☎ 199 12 31 99) Has a weekly boat to/from Cagliari (deck class €26 to €32; shared cabin €39 to €52) and one to/from Palermo (deck class €34 to €40; shared cabin €36 to €45). The service increases to twice weekly in summer. From Palermo and Cagliari there are connections to Tunisia, directly or via Trapani (Sicily).

Bus

Most buses for Italian and some European cities leave from Piazza Garibaldi in front of Stazione Centrale. Check destinations carefully or ask at the information kiosk in the centre of the piazza because there are no signs. Regular buses serve, for example, Caserta, Benevento and Avellino from here. See those towns for more information.

Maco (☎ 080 310 51 85) has buses to Bari (€19, three hours). **Miccolis** (☎ 099 735 37 54) runs to Taranto (€13.45, four hours), Lecce (€23.25, 5½ hours) and Brindisi (€21.20, five hours), while **CLP** (☎ 081 531 17 07) serves Foggia (€9, two hours), Perugia (€27.40, 3¾ hours) and Assisi (€29, 4¾ hours).

You can buy tickets and catch **SITA** (☎ 081 552 21 76; www.sita-on-line.it, Italian only) buses either from the port, Varco Immacolatella, or from Via G Ferraris, near Stazione Centrale; you can also buy tickets at **Bar Clizia** (Corso Arnaldo Lucci 173).

Within Campania, SITA runs buses to Pompeii (€2.20, 40 minutes) and several other towns on the Amalfi Coast, and Salerno (by motorway). Casting wider, it also links Naples with Bari (€19.20, three hours) and operates a service to Germany, including Dortmund (€109) via Munich (€87), Stuttgart (€87), Frankfurt (€95) and Dusseldorf (€109). You can connect from this service for Berlin (€115) and Hamburg (€115).

Car & Motorcycle

Naples is on the major north–south Autostrada del Sole, numbered A1 (north to Rome and Milan) and A3 (south to Salerno and Reggio di Calabria). The A30 skirts Naples to the northeast, while the A16 heads northeast to Bari.

When approaching the city, the motorways meet the Tangenziale di Napoli, a major ring road around the city. The ring road hugs the city's northern fringe, meeting the A1 for Rome and the A2 to Capodichino airport in the east and continuing towards Campi Flegrei and Pozzuoli and the west.

Train

Naples is the rail hub for the south. For information, call ☎ 89 20 21. The city is served by *regionale, diretto*, Intercity and the superfast Eurostar trains. They arrive and depart from **Stazione Centrale** (☎ 081 554 31 88) or Stazione Garibaldi (on the lower level). There are up to 30 trains daily to/from Rome.

The Ferrovia Cumana and the **Circumflegrea** (☎ 800 00 16 16), based at Stazione Cumana on Piazza Montesanto, 500m southwest of Piazza Dante, operate services to Pozzuoli (€1.40, every 22 minutes) and Cuma (€1.40, 40 minutes, six per day). Giranapoli tickets (see following) are not valid as far as Pozzuoli.

The **Circumvesuviana** (☎ 081 772 24 44; Corso G Garibaldi), about 400m southwest of Stazione Centrale (take the underpass from Stazione Centrale), operates trains to Sorrento via Ercolano, Pompeii and other towns along the coast. There are about 40 trains daily running between 5am and 10.30pm (reduced services on Sunday). A ticket to Pompeii costs €2.20.

GETTING AROUND
To/From the Airport
For the airport there are two possibilities: **ANM** (☎ 800 63 95 25) bus No 3S (€0.77, 30 minutes, every 15 minutes) from Piazza Garibaldi, or the Alibus airport bus (€3, 20 minutes, at least hourly) from Piazza Municipio.

A taxi will set you back about €21.

Car & Motorcycle
The constant honk of impatient motorists, the blue lights of ambulances and police cars flashing, the car behind a constant 10cm from your rear end, one-way streets and traffic lights that nobody observes – forget driving in town unless you have a death wish. Park your car at one of the several car parks, most of which are staffed, and walk around the city centre.

In addition to the anarchic driving, car theft is a major problem in Naples.

Both **Avis** (☎ 081 761 13 65; Corso Arnaldo Lucci 203) and **Hertz** (☎ 081 20 62 28; Piazza Garibaldi 91b) have offices at the airport and near Stazione Centrale. Or try the national company **Maggiore** (☎ 081 552 19 00), which has branches within both the station and the airport.

It's impossible to hire a moped in Naples because of the high incidence of theft.

Public Transport
You can buy 'Giranapoli' tickets at stations, ANM booths and tobacconists. A ticket costs €0.77 and is valid for 90 minutes of unlimited travel by bus, tram, Metropolitana, funicular, Ferrovia Cumana or Circumflegrea. A daily ticket is good value at €2.32. These tickets are not valid to Pompeii or Ercolano on the Circumvesuviana train line.

Bus
Most city ANM buses operating in the central area depart from and terminate in Piazza Garibaldi. To locate your stop you'll probably need to ask at the information kiosk in the centre of the square.

There are four frequent routes (R1, R2, R3 and R4) that connect to other (less frequent) buses running out of the centre. Useful services include:

R1 From Piazza Medaglie d'Oro to Piazza Carità, Piazza Dante and Piazza Bovio.

R2 From Stazione Centrale, along Corso Umberto I, to Piazza Bovio, Piazza Municipio and Piazza Trento e Trieste.

R3 From Mergellina along the Riviera di Chiaia to Piazza Municipio, Piazza Bovio, Piazza Dante and Piazza Carità.

No 3S From Piazza Municipio along Corso Umberto 1 to Piazza Garibaldi and on to the airport.

No 24 From the Parco Castello and Piazza Trento e Trieste along Via Toledo, Via Roma to Capodimonte.

No 137R From Piazza Dante north to Capodimonte, further north and then back to Piazza Dante.

No 201 From Stazione Centrale to the Museo Archeologico Nazionale and on to Piazza Municipio and Via San Carlo.

No 404 destra A night bus operates from midnight to 5am (hourly departures) from Stazione Centrale through the city centre to the Riviera di Chiaia and on to Pozzuoli, returning to Stazione Centrale.

Tram No 1 Operates from east of Stazione Centrale, through Piazza Garibaldi, the city centre and along the waterfront to Piazza Vittoria.

Tram No 29 Travels from Piazza Garibaldi to the city centre along Corso G Garibaldi.

Funicular Railway
Three of Naples' four funicular railways connect downtown with Vomero:

Funicolare Centrale ascends from Via Toledo to Piazza Fuga.

Funicolare di Chiaia travels from Via del Parco Margherita to Via D Cimarosa.

Funicolare di Montesanto climbs from Piazza Montesanto to Via Raffaele Morghen.

The fourth, Funicolare di Mergellina, connects the waterfront at Via Mergellina with Via Manzoni. Giranapoli tickets are valid for one trip only on the funicular railways.

Train
The Metropolitana (Underground) is, in fact, mostly above ground.

Line one runs north from Piazza Dante stopping at Museo (for Piazza Cavour and line two), Salvator Rosa, Cilea, Piazza Vanvitelli, Piazza Medaglie d'Oro and seven stops beyond.

CAMPANIA

Line two runs from Gianturco, just east of Stazione Centrale, with stops at Piazza Garibaldi (for Stazione Centrale), Piazza Cavour, Montesanto, Piazza Amedeo, Mergellina, Piazza Leopardi, Campi Flegrei, Cavaleggeri d'Aosta, Bagnoli and Pozzuoli.

Taxi

Official taxis are white, metered and bear the Naples symbol on their front doors. They generally ignore kerbside arm-wavers. There are taxi stands at most of the city's main piazzas or you can call one of the five taxi cooperatives such as **Napoli** (☎ 081 556 44 44) or **Consortaxi** (☎ 081 552 52 52). There's also a baffling range of supplements: €2.10 flag fee, €1.60 extra on Sundays and holidays, €2.10 more between 10pm and 7am, €0.80 for a radio taxi, €2.60 for an airport run, €0.50 per piece of luggage in the boot (trunk) and €1.60 for transporting a small animal (so leave the gerbil at home). Because of traffic delays, even a short trip may end up costing more than you anticipated.

Taxi drivers may tell you that the meter's kaput. However, you can, and should, insist that they switch it on.

AROUND NAPLES

CAMPI FLEGREI

The area west of Naples is called the Campi Flegrei (Phlegraean – 'Fiery' – Fields), a classical term for the volcanic activity that has made it one of the globe's most geologically unstable areas. It was partly through the Campi Flegrei, which include the long-settled towns of Pozzuoli, Baia and Cuma, that Greek civilisation arrived in Italy. Homer believed the area to be the entrance to Hades, fiery Hell, and Virgil wrote of it in *The Aeneid*. St Paul also briefly put in and found time to give a sermon here. Now part of suburban Naples, it retains several reminders of the ancient Greeks and Romans. Easily accessible by public transport or car, it makes a worthwhile half-day visit.

Pozzuoli

Now a dreary suburb southwest of Naples, Pozzuoli is the birthplace of Sofia Loren – oh, and there are some impressive Roman ruins too. Established by the Greeks in 530 BC and renamed Puteoli (Little Wells) by the Romans, it was once one of the Mediterranean's most important ports.

The **tourist office** (☎ 081 526 66 39; Piazza Matteotti 1a; ☘ 9am-3.30pm) is beside the Porta Napoli gate, a five-minute walk downhill from the train station. Ask for the information-heavy brochure, *Welcome to Campi Flegrei*. It's also worth investing €4 in a cumulative ticket that covers the Tempio di Serapide, the Solfatara crater and the archaeological sites of Baia and Cuma.

Just east of the port, you can gaze down upon the **Tempio di Serapide** (Temple of Serapis), so named because a statue of the Egyptian god Serapis was found among its ruins. In fact it was the town market which, archaeologists reckon, skilfully designed toilets at either side of the eastern apse. It has been badly damaged over the centuries by seismic activity, which raises and lowers the ground level over long periods. The church of **Santa Maria delle Grazie**, some 400m away, is sinking at a rate of about 2cm a year because of this.

Head northeast along Via Rosini to the substantial ruins of the **Anfiteatro Flavio** (☎ 081 526 60 07; Via Rosini; admission €4; ☘ 8.30am-2 hrs before sunset Wed-Mon), dating from the 1st century BC. This is Italy's third-largest amphitheatre, with seating for over 20,000 spectators, and it could be flooded, like many amphitheatres, for mock naval battles. In AD 305 seven Christian martyrs were thrown to the wild beasts here. They survived only to be beheaded later.

Continue northeast up Via Rosini, which becomes Via Solfatara and leads to the desolate **Solfatara Crater** (☎ 081 526 23 41; Via Solfatara 161; admission €5; ☘ 8.30am-1 hr before sunset) after about 2km. You can catch any city bus heading uphill. Known to the Romans as the Forum Vulcani (home of the god of fire), its acrid steam, sulphurous waters and mineral-rich mud were famed as a health cure from classical times until the 20th century. With the whiff of brimstone in your nostrils, pass beside the pool of glooping mud as steam jets squirt and burp from the ground. The entire crater is a layer of rock supported by the steam pressure beneath.

Pozzuoli has several camp sites which are the nearest ones to Naples (the alternatives are in Pompeii, east of the city). They're much of a muchness and full to the gills in summer. One that stands out from the usual tented villages is **Camping Vulcano Solfatara** (☎ 081 526 74 13; vulcano.solfatara@iol.it; Via Solfatara 161; person/tent/car €8.80/5.40/6.50; ☻ Apr-Oct; ☒), shrouded in greenery and with excellent facilities. It's 750m from the Pozzuoli Metropolitana station.

Baia & Cuma

About 7km west of Pozzuoli is **Baia**, once a fashionable Roman bathing resort known for its debauchery. Its extensive remains are now submerged some 100m from the shore. At weekends between April and September you can view them from a glass-bottomed boat run by the **Associazione Aliseo** (☎ 081 526 57 80; admission €7.75). Year-round, however, you can see the elaborate Nymphaeum, dredged up and reassembled in the small **Museo Archeologico dei Campi Flegrei** (☎ 081 523 37 97; Via Castello; admission €4; ☻ 9am-1 hr before sunset Tue-Sun). The vast castle that houses the museum was constructed in the late 15th century by the house of Aragón as a defence against possible French invasion. It served as a military orphanage during most of the 20th century.

Cuma (known to the Greeks as Cumae), some 10km northwest of Pozzuoli, was the earliest Greek colony on the Italian mainland. If Sybil the oracle, one of the ancient world's greatest prophets, speaks to you, you should pay a visit to the **Antro della Sibilla Cumana** (Cave of the Cumaean Sybil) within the **Acropoli di Cuma** (☎ 081 854 30 60; Via Montecuma; admission €4; ☻ 9am-2 hrs before sunset).

Inland and 5km from Pozzuoli is the **Lago d'Averno** (Lake Avernus), one of three crater lakes and the mythical entrance to the underworld where Aeneas descended to meet his father. It makes a good spot for a picnic!

Portici

Southeast out of Naples in the unlovely suburb of Portici is the **Museo Nazionale Ferroviario Pietrarsa** (☎ 081 567 21 77; Via Pietrarsa, Portici; admission free; closed at time of writing), Europe's largest railway museum. Covering 36,000 sq metres, exhibits tell the fascinating story of the construction of Italy's railway network. Take a Trenitalia train from Stazione Centrale to Pietrarsa-San Giorgio a Cremano.

Getting There & Away

BOAT

There are frequent car and passenger ferries from Pozzuoli to the islands of Ischia

and Procida, run by a variety of companies. Typical prices are €2.50 to Procida and €5.50 to Ischia – more if you take the hydrofoil option.

CAR & MOTORCYCLE

Take the Tangenziale ring road and hop off at the Pozzuoli exit. Less swift, more scenic and infinitely more frustrating, take Via Francesco Caracciolo along the Naples waterfront to Posillipo, then on to Pozzuoli.

TRAIN

Ferrovia Cumana serves Pozzuoli, Baia and Cuma while the Metropolitana runs as far as Pozzuoli. For details of both, see pp607–8.

CASERTA

pop 74,801

Dominating this otherwise nondescript town is the gigantic Palazzo Reale (Royal Palace), and this is the only reason to come to Caserta.

Probably founded in the 8th century by the Lombards on the site of a Roman emplacement atop Monte Tifata, Caserta, a mere 22km north of Naples, spread onto the plains below from the 12th century onwards. The construction of the Bourbons' grand palace assured the town an importance it would otherwise never have known.

Star Wars fans will also, of course, know that George Lucas used the palace for the interior shots of Queen Amidala's royal residence in *Star Wars Episode 1: The Phantom Menace*.

Caserta's **tourist office** (☎ 0823 32 11 37; Palazzo Reale; ☻ 8.30am-3.40pm Mon-Sat) is near the entrance to the palace gardens.

Palazzo Reale

This vast **palace** (☎ 0823 44 74 47; admission €6; ☻ 8.30am-7pm Tue-Sun), more commonly known as the Reggia di Caserta, is one of Italy's most visited historical sites. Invaded by tourists in the holidays and by school groups during term time, a visit can become a trial of patience.

Work started in 1752 after Charles III of Bourbon, ruler of Naples, decided to build himself a palace that would emulate Versailles. Neapolitan Luigi Vanvitelli was commissioned for the job and established his reputation as one of the leading architects of the era after working on the palace.

The building, with a facade stretching 250m and containing 1200 rooms, 1790 windows and 34 staircases, is homage to a vanity of massive proportions. You enter by Vanvitelli's immense staircase and follow a route through the royal apartments, elaborately decorated with tapestries, furniture and crystal. Beyond the library is a room containing a vast collection of *presepi*, composed of hundreds of hand-carved characters.

To clear the head afterwards, a walk in the elegant landscaped **grounds** (🕒 8.30am-2 hrs before sunset, last entry 1 hr before closing) has a curative effect. They stretch out for some 3km to a waterfall and fountain of Diana and, most famously, to the **Giardino Inglese** (English Garden; tours every hr) with its intricate pathways, exotic plants, little lakes and fake Roman ruins – all very much in fashion at the time it was laid out. To cut down on walking you can cover the same ground in a pony and trap (from €5) or for €1 you can bring a bike into the park.

Your ticket gives entry to the royal apartments, grounds, Giardino Inglese, and a **museum** (🕒 8.30am-12.30pm) of local archaeological finds. Within the palace there's also the **Mostra Terrea Motus** (admission free with palace ticket; 🕒 9am-6pm) illustrating the 1980 earthquake that devastated the region. At the end of all this you can restore your energy in the palace's cafeteria and restaurant.

There's a good guidebook, *The Royal Palace of Caserta and the Old Town* (€1 to €5, depending on your bargaining prowess), which the persistent vendors will thrust upon you.

Getting There & Away

CPTC buses connect Caserta with Naples' Piazza Garibaldi (€2.70) about every 30 minutes between 8am and 8pm. Some Benevento services also stop in Caserta. The town is on the main train line between Rome (€10.15) and Naples (€2.80). Both bus and train stations are near the Palazzo Reale entrance, which is signposted from each. If you're driving, follow the signs for 'Reggia'.

AROUND CASERTA

In the surrounding urban spread there are a few historic gems.

In San Leucio, about 2km northwest of Caserta, the Complesso Monumentale

Belvedere houses **Museo di Archeologia Industriale** (☎ 0823 30 18 17; admission €2.60; 🕒 5 guided tours a day Mon-Sat). Dating from the late 18th century, this industrial complex was a pet project of King Ferdinando to house the poor and employ them in a silk factory. Take bus No 107 from the Caserta train station.

About 10km to the northeast of Caserta (take CPTC bus No 10) lies **Caserta Vecchia**, the original medieval hill town, which includes the remains of a 9th-century castle and a 13th-century cathedral.

The modern city of **Santa Maria Capua Vetere** (ancient Capua), about 12km west of Caserta, was populated by the Etruscans, the Samnites and later the Romans. The ruins include an **amphitheatre** (☎ 0823 79 88 64; admission €2.50; 🕒 9am-5.30pm Tue-Sun) from the 1st century AD. The largest in Italy after the Colosseum in Rome, it is famous as the starting point for the gladiators' revolt led by Spartacus. There are also remains of the **Arco d'Adriano** (Hadrian's Arch), under which passed the Via Appia, and a **Mithraic temple**. Most of the artefacts from the area are now in the **Museo Provinciale Campano** (☎ 0823 96 14 02; Via Roma 68; admission €4.30; 🕒 9am-1.30pm Tue-Sun) in the modern town of Capua.

Regular CPTC buses run from the Caserta train station to Santa Maria Capua Vetere (€1, 30 minutes).

BENEVENTO
pop 63,230

Surrounded by the green hills of the Apennines, Benevento is a provincial capital about 60km northeast of Naples. After a period as a Lombard duchy, when it controlled much of southern Italy, the town was transferred to the control of the papacy in the 11th century and remained mostly under papal rule until 1860.

The **tourist office** (☎ 0824 31 99 38; Piazza Roma 11; 🕒 8.30am-1.45pm & 2.45-6pm) is centrally located and well stocked with useful information.

Sights

The town was heavily bombed in WWII and the Romanesque **cathedral** with its elaborate facade had to be largely rebuilt. Southwest of the cathedral is a restored Roman theatre dating from Hadrian's time. The **Arco di Traiano** (Trajan's Arch), built in AD 114, commemorates the opening of the

Via Traiana while the **obelisk** (Piazza Matteotti) marks the Napoleonic invasion of Italy.

Chiesa di Santa Sofia, near the piazza, adjoins what was once a Benedictine abbey. Founded in AD 762, its main entrance dates from the 12th century. The abbey contains the **Museo del Sannio** (☎ 0824 2 18 18; Piazza Santa Sofia; admission €3; ☽ 9am-1pm Tue-Sun), which houses remnants of a temple dedicated to Isis, dating from AD 88, along with a gallery of mainly medieval paintings.

Sleeping

At these prices you can't expect much, but the rooms at **Albergo Genova** (☎ 0824 4 29 26; Via Principe di Napoli 103; s/d €15.50/25.85), the cheapest place in town, are clean and simple. The hotel is well situated for the train station.

Getting There & Away

FBN buses (☎ 0824 2 49 61) and **Ferrovia Benevento trains** (☎ 0824 32 07 11) both operate direct services between Benevento and Naples. FS is slower, since you have to change trains in Caserta, but has direct trains to/from Rome. Buses also link Benevento with Rome and Campobasso. Benevento is on the SS7 (Via Appia) and close to the A16.

AVELLINO & AROUND

About 50km east of Naples is the town of Avellino. The **tourist office** (☎ 0825 7 47 32; www.eptavellino.it, Italian only; Piazza Libertá 50) is helpful, although a day in town is enough, especially as accommodation options are poor.

The mountainous area southwest of Avellino, particularly around the towns of Quindici and Sarno, was the scene of horrific mud slides in 1998, in which over 130 people died. The immediate cause was excessive rainfall but irresponsible deforestation and unauthorised building on the surrounding hills also contributed to the disaster.

The area's main attraction is the vertiginous summit of **Monte Vergine** and the **sanctuary** devoted to the Virgin Mary, north of the city. A young pilgrim, Guglielmo di Vercelli, erected a church here in the 12th century and so began a tradition of pilgrimage that continues to the present day. His remains were finally laid to rest in the crypt of the modern basilica in 1807.

From the summit (1493m) you can see Naples on a clear day and the twisting drive up from Avellino is quite thrilling. In winter

---

THE BATTLE OF BENEVENTO

It was on the green fields north of Benevento that the short but glorious Italian adventure of the Swabians came to a bloody halt.

In 1250 Emperor Frederick II died in Puglia, leaving his southern Italian kingdom to his son Conrad. For the next eight years Conrad fought the papacy for control of the kingdom until Manfred, Frederick's illegitimate son, stepped into the breach and grabbed the reins. But Rome was prepared to fight dirty and in 1265 offered the kingdom to Charles I of Anjou in exchange for the removal of Manfred and his Swabians. The scene was set for battle.

Manfred assembled a 15,000-strong army which, on 25 February 1265, he positioned on the Grandella plain to wait for the French. Charles and his 30,000 troops, exhausted by the long march, opted to stop short of the Swabian positions. Manfred then made his big mistake. Reasoning that he was outnumbered two to one, he decided to throw caution to the wind and attack.

At dawn the following day, Manfred's Saracen archers and German cavalry stormed Charles' camp. Things went fine at first but as soon as the French cavalry entered the fray things began to go awry. Thousands of Manfred's men simply upped swords and scarpered, leaving their boss and a band of die-hards to face the music. Every one of them fell. Manfred was 34, and with him passed the short, but illustrious, Swabian line.

---

there's limited skiing at Lago di Laceno, about 30km southeast of Avellino.

Avellino has buses to Naples every 20 minutes. There are summer buses from Avellino to Monte Vergine and the sanctuary.

GULF OF NAPLES (GOLFO DI NAPOLI)

CAPRI
pop 7,270

Capri, as well as being a legendary idyll, is probably the most mispronounced island in Italy. Unlike the car, the stress is on the first syllable (*ca*-pri), not the second.

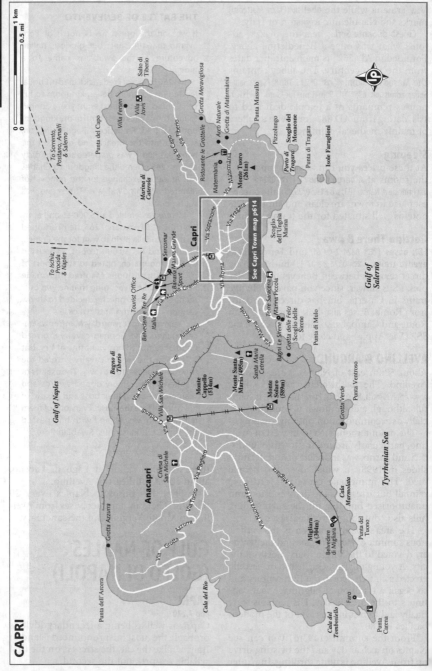

CAMPANIA

CAPRI

0 ─── 1 km
0 ─── 0.5 mi

Gulf of Naples

To Ischia,
Procida & Naples

To Sorrento,
Positano, Amalfi
& Salerno

Salto di Tiberio
Villa Jovis
Villa Fersen
Punta del Capo
Grotta Meravigliosa
Arco Naturale
Grotta di Matermania
Punta Massullo
Ristorante le Grottelle
Matermania
Monte Tuoro (261m)
Pizzolungo
Scoglio del Monacone
Porto di Tragara
Punta di Tragara
Isole Faraglioni

Marina di Caterola

Via di Capo
Via Tiberio
Via Sopramonte
Capri
Sercomar
Banana Maina Grande Sport
Via Roma
Via Tragara
Via Matermania

Belvedere il Te Re
Italia
Tourist Office
Via Marina Grande
Anacapri

See Capri Town map p614

Scoglio dell'Unghia Marina

Bagno di Tiberio

Torre Saracena
Marina Piccola
Bagni Le Sirene
Grotta delle Felci
Scoglio delle Sirene
Punta di Mulo

Gulf of Salerno

Via Provinciale
Via Orlandi
Villa San Michele
Monte Cappello (514m)
Monte Santa Maria (485m)
Santa Maria a Cetrella
Monte Solaro (589m)
Via Migliara
Punta Ventroso

Grotta Verde

Anacapri
Chiesa di San Michele
Via Tuoro
Via Pagliaro
Via Migliara
Via Nuova del Faro
Via Axzurra
Via Grotta

Cala Marmolata

Tyrrhenian Sea

Punta dell'Arcera
Grotta Azzurra
Migliara (304m)
Belvedere di Migliara
Punta del Tuono
Cala del Rio
Cala del Tombosiello
Faro
Punta Carena

A day-tripper's paradise, Capri is heavily geared to tourism (read: industrial doses of tasteless tat) with up to 5000 visitors a day stepping off the boats in summer. It's also a confirmed spot on the Mediterranean celebrity circuit, which means prices are high and economy virtually impossible. But the fact remains, Capri is fantastically beautiful. Breathtaking caves, luxuriant vegetation and the charming narrow lanes of its small towns have attracted visitors for centuries.

The best time to visit is spring or October, once the summer crowds have ebbed away.

History

Already inhabited in the Palaeolithic age, Capri was subsequently occupied by the Greeks. The Romans, for their part, had taste; Emperor Augustus made the island his private playground and Tiberius retired there in AD 27. Augustus is believed to have founded the world's first palaeontological museum, in the Villa Augustus, to house fossils and Stone Age artefacts unearthed by his workers.

Tiberius, a victim of Tacitus' pen, has gone down in history as something of a fiend on the island, although there is little evidence to back the lurid claims concerning the emperor's sexual shenanigans. The mud stuck, however, and until modern times his name has been equated by the islanders with evil. When the eccentric Swedish doctor Axel Munthe first began picking about the ruins of Roman palaces and villas on the island in the late 19th century, locals would observe that it was all '*roba di Tiberio*' – Tiberius' stuff.

Throughout history the people of Capri and Anacapri have been at loggerheads and are always ready to trot out their respective patron saints to ward off the *malocchio* (evil eye) of their rivals.

Orientation

About 5km from the mainland at its nearest point, Capri is a mere 6km long and 2.7km wide. As you approach, you get a lovely view of the town of Capri with the dramatic slopes of Monte Solaro (589m) to the west, hiding the village of Anacapri.

All hydrofoils and ferries arrive at Marina Grande, a small settlement that is essentially an extension of Capri town. Buses connect the port with the towns of Capri and Anacapri and a cable car links the marina with Capri town (p617). Otherwise, follow Via Marina Grande for a twisting 2.25km uphill walk. Turn left (east) at the junction with Via Roma for the centre of Capri town or right (west) for Via Provinciale di Anacapri, which eventually becomes Via G Orlandi as it reaches Anacapri.

Information

Capri Internet Point (☎ 081 837 32 83; Viale De Tommaso 1, Anacapri; €5/1 hr) For Internet access.
Hospital (☎ 081 838 12 05; Via Padre R Giuliani 17)
Police Station (☎ 081 837 72 45; Via Roma 70, Capri)
Post Offices Capri (☎ 081 837 58 29; Via Roma 50); Anacapri (☎ 081 837 1015; Viale De Tommaso 8)
Telephone Office (☎ 081 837 54 47; Piazza Umberto 1, Capri)

INTERNET RESOURCES
Capri Island (www.capri.net)
Capri Tourism (www.capritourism.com)

TOURIST INFORMATION
Tourist Offices Marina Grande (☎ 081 837 06 34; 🕑 8.30am-8.30pm Jun-Sep, 9am-1pm & 3.30-6.45pm Mon-Sat Oct-May); Capri town (☎ 081 837 06 86; Piazza Umberto I; 🕑 8.30am-8.30pm Jun-Sep, 9am-1pm & 3.30-6.45pm Mon-Sat Oct-May); Anacapri (☎ 081 837 15 24; Piazza Vittoria; 🕑 8.30am-8.30pm Jun-Sep, 9am-1pm & 3.30-6.45pm Mon-Sat Oct-Dec & Mar-May) Each office can provide a free stylised map of the island and a more detailed one (€0.80) that also has town plans of Capri and Anacapri. For hotel listings and other useful information ask for a copy of *Capri È* (free) or buy *Capri Exclusive* (€6.20). Audioguides (€2.50) are also available at the Marina Grande office.

Sights
GROTTA AZZURRA

Capri's craggy coast is studded with more than a dozen sea caves, most of them accessible and spectacular but none as stunning, or as famous, as the **Blue Grotto** (admission €4; 🕑 visits 9am-1hr before sunset). Two Germans, writer Augustus Kopisch and painter Ernst Fries, are credited with discovering the grotto in 1826 but in fact they merely renamed what the locals had long called Grotta Gradola. Remains of Roman work, including a carved ledge towards the rear of the cave, were found later.

At some time, geologists believe, the cave sank to its present height, about 15m to 20m below sea level, blocking every opening except the 1.3m-high entrance. This causes the refraction of sunlight off the sides of the cavity, creating the magical blue colour, and a reflection of light off the white sandy bottom, giving anything below the surface a silvery glow.

Boats leave to visit the cave from the Marina Grande and a return trip will cost €15.30, which comprises return motorboat to the cave (€7), rowing boat in (€4.30) and admission fee (€4); allow a good hour. You only save a little money and lose a lot of time by catching a bus from Anacapri or Capri since you still have to pay for the rowing boat and admission fee. The singing 'captains' are included in the price, so if they push for a tip, it's up to you.

The grotto is closed if the sea is too choppy, so before embarking check that it's open with the Marina Grande tourist office, no more than 25m from the motorboat ticket booth.

It's possible to swim into the grotto before 9am and after 5pm, but do so only in company and if the sea is completely calm.

CAPRI TOWN

From Piazza Umberto I in the centre of Capri, you can contentedly while away an afternoon wandering through the narrow lanes. In the square itself is the 17th-century **Chiesa di Santo Stefano**. Note the pair of languidly reclining patricians in the chapel to the south of the main altar and the well-preserved Roman tiling in the northern one. Beside the latter is a reliquary with some saintly bone that reputedly saved Capri from the plague in the 19th century.

Head down Via D Birago or Via V Emanuele for **Certosa di San Giacomo** (☎ 081 837 62 18; Viale Certosa; admission free; ☺ 9am-2pm Tue-Sat, 9am-1pm Sun), a rather stark 14th-century Carthusian monastery with cloisters and a painted chapel. The nearby **Giardini di Augusto** (Gardens of Augustus) are altogether more colourful and command a good view of the **Isole Faraglioni**, the rock stacks along the southern coast.

The **Museo del Centro Caprese i Cerio** (☎ 081 837 66 81; Piazzetta Cerio 5; admission €2.50; ☺ 10am-1pm Tue, Wed, Fri & Sat, 3-7pm Thu) has a library of books and journals about the island and a

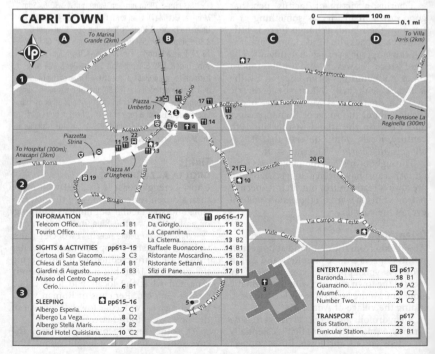

CAPRI TOWN

INFORMATION		EATING	🍴 pp616–17
Telecom Office.....................1 B1		Da Giorgio...........................11 B2	
Tourist Office......................2 B1		La Capannina......................12 C1	
		La Cisterna..........................13 B2	
SIGHTS & ACTIVITIES pp613–15		Raffaele Buonacore............14 B1	
Certosa di San Giacomo.......3 C3		Ristorante Moscardino........15 B2	
Chiesa di Santa Stefano........4 B1		Ristorante Settanni.............16 B1	
Giardini di Augusto..............5 B3		Sfizi di Pane.......................17 B1	
Museo del Centro Caprese i			
Cerio..............................6 B1		**ENTERTAINMENT** 🎭 p617	
		Baraonda............................18 B1	
SLEEPING 🛏 pp615–16		Guarracino.........................19 A2	
Albergo Esperia....................7 C1		Musmé................................20 C2	
Albergo La Vega...................8 D2		Number Two.......................21 C2	
Albergo Stella Maris..............9 B2			
Grand Hotel Quisisiana.........10 C2		**TRANSPORT** p617	
		Bus Station.........................22 B2	
		Funicular Station.................23 B1	

collection of Neolithic and Palaeolithic fossils found locally.

VILLA JOVIS & AROUND

East of the town centre, a comfortable hour's walk along Via Tiberio leads to the one-time residence of Emperor Tiberius, **Villa Jovis** (Jupiter's Villa; ☎ 081 837 06 34; Via Tiberio; admission €2; 🕑 9am-1 hr before sunset), also known as the Palazzo di Tiberio. The largest and best preserved of the island's Roman villas, it was a vast pleasure complex in its heyday and included imperial quarters, entertainment areas, grand halls, gardens and woodland.

The stairway behind the villa leads to **Salto di Tiberio** (Tiberius' Leap), a cliff from where, says the story, Tiberius had out-of-favour subjects hurled into the sea.

A pleasant walk down Via Matermania leads to the **Arco Naturale**, a rock arch formed by the pounding sea. Doubling back to the first crossroads, you can turn left to drop down a long series of steps and follow the path south, then west, back into town, enjoying good views of Punta di Tragara and Isole Faraglioni on the way.

ANACAPRI & AROUND

Many visitors are lured to **Villa San Michele** by the words of its most-famous inhabitant, Swedish doctor and dog-lover Dr Axel Munthe. The eclectic house he built on the ruined site of a Roman villa remains immortalised in his book *The Story of San Michele*. The **villa** (☎ 081 837 14 01; Viale Axel Munthe; admission €5; 🕑 9am-6pm May-Sep, 10.30am-3.30pm Nov-Feb, 9.30am-4.30pm Mar, 9.30am-5pm April & Oct), a short walk north of Piazza Vittoria, houses Roman sculptures from the period of Tiberius' rule. The pathway behind offers superb views over Capri. The (often closed) stairway of 800 steps leading from the town was the only link between Anacapri and the rest of the island until the mountain road was built in the 1950s.

From Piazza Vittoria, you can take a **chair lift** (€5.50; 🕑 9.30am-sunset Mar-Oct, 10.30am-3pm Nov-Feb) to the top of **Monte Solaro** where, on a (rare) clear day, you can see for miles. From Anacapri a bus runs to **Faro**, less-crowded and boasting one of Italy's tallest lighthouses.

Activities

Capri, obviously, is ideal for water sports. For scuba diving contact **Sercomar** (☎ 081 837 87 81; www.caprisub.com; Via Colombo 64, Marina Grande). **Bagni Le Sirene** (☎ 081 837 69 70; Marina Piccola) hires out canoes and motorised dinghies and can take you water-skiing. For sailboards and catamarans contact **Banana Sport** (☎ 081 837 51 88; Via Marina Grande 12). Expect to pay around €185 for a motorised dinghy for the day and €100 for a three-dive package.

The main places to swim are Bagno di Tiberio, a small inlet west of Marina Grande, where the emperor himself dipped; a rocky area at Marina Piccola; at Faro; off concrete ledges at the Grotta Azzurra (only before 9am or after 5pm); and further west of the grotto below the restaurants.

There are also plenty of hiking opportunities. Contact the tourist offices for details of routes, which are mostly classed as moderate to easy.

Festivals & Events

The main secular festival is from 1 to 6 January, when local folk groups perform in Piazza Diaz, Anacapri and in Capri's Piazza Umberto I.

Sleeping

Hotel space is at a premium during the summer and many places close in winter. There are few really cheap rooms at any time of the year and beware of the compulsory breakfast in summer.

Camping is forbidden and offenders are either prosecuted or 'asked' to relocate to a hotel. You might want to inquire at the tourist offices about renting a room in a private home.

MARINA GRANDE

On the road going up from the port there are two options.

Belvedere e Tre Re (☎ 081 837 03 45; www.belvedere-tre-re.com; Via Marina Grande 238; s with bathroom high season €80-110, d €100-130; Ⓟ) This place, which is under five minutes' walk from the port, is handy for those who like messing about in boats. It also affords some good views.

Italia (☎ 081 837 06 02; fax 081 837 03 78; Via Marina Grande 204; s/d with bathroom high season €87.50/106.50) The views here, up the hill beyond Belvedere e Tre Re, are even better and the quality is pretty much the same despite the slightly cheaper rates.

CAMPANIA

CAPRI

Albergo Stella Maris (☎ 081 837 04 52; fax 081 837 86 62; Via Roma 27; s/d with bathroom €45/80; year-round) Right in the noisy heart of town, opposite the bus station and just off Piazza Umberto I, this place has small but functional rooms. Watch out for the single room under the stairs – it's a tight squeeze even for one.

Albergo Esperia (☎ 081 837 02 62; fax 081 837 09 33; Via Sopramonte 41; d with bathroom & breakfast €115-170; year-round; 🕮) An understated old-style elegance pervades this charming 19th-century villa. It's tranquil and intimate and most rooms enjoy spectacular views. It also has a small restaurant.

Pensione La Reginella (☎ 081 837 05 00; lareginella@libero.it; Via Matermania 36; s/d with bathroom high season €70/130; 🕮) Vistas here, up the hill and east of Albergo Esperia, are just as breathtaking, though the prices are more modest. It's a reliable choice and also has a decent restaurant.

Albergo La Vega (☎ 081 837 04 81; fax 081 837 03 42; Via Occhio Marino 10; d with bathroom & breakfast €200-280; 🕮 🛁) In the pricey part of town, upmarket La Vega is immensely proud of the spectacular views from its terraced swimming pool.

Grand Hotel Quisisiana (☎ 081 837 07 88; www.quisi.com; Via Camerelle 2; s/d with bathroom & breakfast high season €350/500; 🕮 🛁) Capri's historic five-star hotel offers its guests a more comfortable stay than 150 years ago, when it started life as a sanatorium. Set in a gracious garden, it provides luxury at prestigious prices.

ANACAPRI

Anacapri and its hotels virtually close during the winter.

Loreley (☎ 081 837 14 40; fax 081 837 13 99; Via G Orlandi 16; s/d with bathroom & breakfast high season €75/115; Mar-Nov; Ⓟ) Situated on the road rising up from Capri, this above-average hotel has decent rooms, some with views across to Naples.

Eating

The island's culinary gift to the world is *insalata caprese*, a salad of fresh tomato, basil and mozzarella bathed in olive oil. Look out for *caprese* cheese, a cross between mozzarella and ricotta, and *ravioli caprese*, ravioli stuffed with ricotta and herbs.

Many restaurants, like the hotels, close over winter.

RESTAURANTS – CAPRI

Ristorante Settanni (☎ 081 837 01 05; Via Longano 5; full meals around €20; Fri-Wed mid-Mar–Jan) Up an alley, this friendly place serves unspectacular local dishes. However, the cheerful service and sweeping panorama make it a nice place to dine.

La Cisterna (☎ 081 837 56 20; Via M Serafina 5; pizza from €5, full meals €20) Ignore the menu (half-written in Japanese) and you'll enjoy the island fare prepared at this family-run eatery in the lanes off Piazza Umberto I.

Ristorante Le Grottelle (☎ 081 837 57 19; Via Arco Naturale 13; full meals around €25; Apr-Oct) For a touch of grotto dining, Le Grottelle is the place. Tucked inside a couple of small caves 200m before the Arco Naturale (p615), the menu offers no surprises, but dishes are simple and tasty.

La Capannina (☎ 081 837 07 32; Via Le Botteghe 12; full meals around €45; mid-Mar–mid-Nov) Favoured by the visiting Hollywood aristocracy, La Capannina is one of the island's longest established and best traditional restaurants. Its prices reflect this.

Also worth considering are:

Da Giorgio (☎ 081 837 0898; Via Roma 34; full meals around €22) Here's yet another place with a great panorama.

Ristorante Moscardino (☎ 081 837 06 87; Via Roma 28; full meals around €25) A stone's throw from Da Giorgio, this place offers good food at standard island prices.

RESTAURANTS – ANACAPRI

Il Solitario (☎ 081 837 13 82; Via G Orlandi 96; pasta from €5) The leafy garden provides a wonderful backdrop to the hearty plates of homemade pasta they dish out here, hidden away down a side street.

La Giara (☎ 081 837 38 60; Via G Orlandi 67; pizzas around €5) There's nothing intimate or particularly scenic about this place near the bus stop. However, the pizzas are good and there's also a full menu on offer.

Trattoria Il Saraceno (☎ 081 837 20 99; Via Trento e Trieste 18; full meals around €15) A homely little restaurant, just off Via Orlando. The *ravioli caprese* is excellent and the proprietor's own wine slips down a treat.

Two other recommendations are **Pizzeria Materita** (☎ 081 837 33 75; Via G Orlandi 140; pizzas from €4.50), serving reliable pizzas to eat in or take away, and **Mamma Giovanna** (☎ 081 837 20 57; Via Boffe 3-5; full meals around €25), which dishes up family fare from its spot overlooking Piazza Diaz.

QUICK EATS

Locals do their shopping at the **market** underneath the Capri bus station. For a quick bite, **Sfizi di Pane** (Via Le Botteghe 15) has a rich selection of local breads and cakes. **Raffaele Buonacore** (Via Vittorio Emanuele 35) does fantastic takeaway pizzas and savoury tarts (€3.50), to be chased down by a dollop of their tempting ice cream.

Entertainment

CAPRI

The scene in Capri tends to be expensive, often tacky, and the natural domain of football stars and beauty queens. Your best hope is to hang out in the central piazzas or take a drink at any one of the numerous watering holes in town. **Guarracino** (☎ 081 837 05 14; Via Castello 7; ☹ 8pm-4am) is among the more pleasant spots for a drink.

To shake a leg try the clubs **Musmé** (☎ 081 837 60 11; Via Camerelle 61b), **Number Two** (☎ 081 837 70 78; Via Camerelle 1), a short stroll down the street and a fave of VIPs including Naomi Campbell, or **Baraonda** (Via Roma 6).

ANACAPRI

Sit around in one of the cafés on Piazza Diaz or shoot pool at **Bar Materita** (Via G Orlandi 140). For nightlife, clubs **Zeus** (☎ 081 837 11 69; Via G Orlandi 103; ☹ 10pm-5am), with its commercial music and famous faces, and **Underground** (Via G Orlandi 259), playing dance music and cabaret, might get your blood rushing. Typical cover charges hover around €20 (they accept credit cards).

Shopping

Ceramic tiles and everything lemony are the big sellers. Shops abound, but always make sure to check the quality.

On the lemon front, the island is famous for its perfume and *limoncello*. The former smells like lemons and the latter tastes like sweet lemon vodka. Visit **Limoncello Capri** (Via Capodimonte 27, Anacapri) to taste the liqueur. The perfumeries are everywhere.

If your ship has come in, you might like to pick up a little number from one of the designer shops on Via Cammarelle

in Capri, which is like walking into a page from *Vogue* magazine.

Getting There & Away

See Naples (pp605–6) and Sorrento (p631) for details of year-round ferries and hydrofoils. In summer there's also a service to/from Salerno (hydrofoil €13.50), Positano (hydrofoil €13) and Amalfi (hydrofoil €13.50).

Getting Around

There is no vehicle-hire service on the island and few roads wide enough for a car. Between March and October you can only bring a vehicle to the island if it's either registered outside Italy or hired at an international airport – but there's really no need as buses are regular and taxis plentiful.

The best way to get around is by **SIPPIC bus** (☎ 081 837 04 20). A ticket costs €1.30 on the main routes between Marina Grande (departing from just west of the pier), Capri, Anacapri, Grotta Azzurra and Faro. Buses run between Capri and Anacapri until past midnight. A cable car links Marina Grande with Capri. It is swifter than the bus and costs €1.30.

From Marina Grande a taxi ride costs around €15 to Capri and about €20 to Anacapri; from Capri to Anacapri costs about €10. For a taxi in and around Capri call ☎ 081 837 05 43 and if you are in Anacapri ☎ 081 837 11 75.

ISCHIA

pop 18,009

Ischia is the most developed of the islands in the Gulf of Naples and a major tourist destination. Yet, away from its few towns, the islanders continue to live and work the land as they always have, seemingly indifferent to the annual onslaught of tourists.

Although nowadays Ischia is especially loved by Germans, it was the Greeks who first colonised the island in the 8th century BC, calling it Pithecusa. Largely volcanic, it has long been noted for its thermal springs, which pull in the punters as much as the beaches.

The main centres are the touristy towns of Ischia and Ischia Porto, Casamicciola Terme, Forio and Lacco Ameno, all fairly unattractive and overcrowded compared with picturesque Ischia Ponte, Serrara,

Fontana, Barano d'Ischia and Sant'Angelo. Sant' Angelo is, in addition, tranquil; no cars are allowed in town.

Orientation
Ferries dock at Ischia Porto, the main tourist centre. It's about a 2km walk from the pier to Ischia Ponte, an attractive older centre.

Information
Ischia Online (www.ischiaonline.it) This Internet resource is considerably more useful than the tourist office.
Tourist Office (☎ 081 507 42 31; Via Iasolino, Banchina Porto Salvo; ☽ 9am-2pm & 3-8pm Mon-Sat)

Sights & Activities
In Ischia Ponte you'll find the remains of **Castello d'Ischia** (☎ 081 99 28 34; admission €8; ☽ 9.30am-1hr before sunset Apr-Oct). Within this Aragonese castle complex, joined to the mainland by a causeway, are a 14th-century cathedral, several smaller churches and a weapons museum.

Keen gardeners, and indeed anyone who loves plants, should visit **La Mortella** (☎ 081 98 62 20; Via F Calese 35, Forio; admission €8; ☽ 9am-7pm Tue, Thu, Sat & Sun Apr-Nov). More than 300 species from all over the world thrive here in one of Italy's finest landscaped gardens. The gardens were established by Sir William Walton, the late British composer, and his wife, who made La Mortella their home in 1949.

A fairly strenuous uphill walk from the village of Fontana brings you to the top of **Monte Epomeo** (788m), the island's highest point, with superb views of the Gulf of Naples.

Among the better beaches is Lido dei Maronti, south of Barano. If you're interested in diving, **Gator Sub** (☎ 081 90 08 93; Casamicciola Terme), **Ischia Diving Center** (☎ 081 98 50 08; Ischia Porto) and **Roja Diving Center** (☎ 081 99 92 14; Sant' Angelo) all have equipment for hire and run courses. A single dive will typically cost from €30.

Tours
Between April and October **Ischia Direct Tours** (☎ 081 507 40 50; www.ischiadirecttours.com; Via Porto 5-9) offers a three-hour tour of the island with an English-speaking guide for €44 (including lunch). If you're only on the island for the day, it's not a bad idea.

Sleeping
Most hotels close in winter, and prices normally drop considerably in those that stay open. In summer call the tourist office in advance to establish room availability. During the peak period, watch for the compulsory breakfast or half board and extra charges for the showers.

Il Gabbiano (☎/fax 081 90 94 22; SS Forio-Panza 162, Forio; B&B per person €16; ☒) This hostel is one of the best around. Near to the beach, it has bedrooms sleeping two, four or six, all with balconies and great sea views.

Locanda Sul Mare (☎ 081 98 14 70; Via Iasolino 90; s/d with bathroom €28/58; ☽ Mar-Nov) This agreeably eccentric place, a 400m walk from the port, is full of character. The corridors are lined with works of modern art that compensate for the bare simplicity of the rooms.

Albergo Macrì (☎/fax 081 99 26 03; Via Iasolino 96; s/d with bathroom Aug €40/70, Jul & Sep €36/69) Next to Locanda Sul Mare, down a blind alley, this place offers more comfort for greater outlay. Rooms are light and airy and bamboo bedsteads add to the sunny feel.

Villa Antonio (☎ 081 98 26 60; www.villantonio.com; Via San Giuseppe della Croce 77; s/d with bathroom & breakfast €49/80; ☽ Apr-Sep) This place, a 1.5km walk from the port, is a good option, with some rooms overlooking the sea and the Castello d'Ischia.

Conchiglia (☎ 081 99 92 70; Via Chiaia delle Rose; B&B per person Aug €62, Sep-Jul €33.60, full meals around €25) In Sant'Angelo, friendly Conchiglia, perched over the water, offers recently renovated rooms and a good restaurant.

Casa Francesco (☎ 081 99 93 76; fax 081 99 91 50; Via Nazario Sauro 62; d with bathroom & breakfast €65-70) Also in Sant'Angelo, Casa Francesco is across a small causeway leading to the tip of the promontory. The atmosphere is homely and the owners extend a warm greeting to their guests.

Da Franceschina (☎/fax 081 99 01 09; Via Corrado Buono 51; s/d with bathroom €26/46; ☽ Easter-Oct) This place in Barano is good value for money. Half board is compulsory in August.

There are also three camp sites on the island.

Mirage (☎/fax 081 99 05 51; Lido dei Maronti 37; person/tent/car €7.50/4/4.50; ☽ year-round) This is perhaps the best-placed site, on the beach south of Barano.

Camping Internazionale (☎ 081 99 14 49; fax 081 99 14 72; Via Foschini; person/tent/car €7/6/4; ☽ May-Sep)

Not far from Ischia Porto, this camp site is handy for the ferry terminal. There are also bungalow options from €18.

Eurocamping dei Pini (☎ 081 98 20 69; fax 081 98 41 20; Via delle Ginestre 28; person/tent high season €8.30/7.25; ☯ year-round) This camp site is also near Ischia Porto and offers a bungalow option.

Eating

La Bitta (☎ 081 98 40 73; Rive Droite; full meals around €20) A reliable choice among the restaurants strung along the seafront in Ischia Porto. Decorated with the usual marine accoutrements, it has cheerful and friendly service. The food, although not spectacular, is fish-based and filling.

Lo Scoglio (☎ 081 99 95 29; Sant'Angelo; full meals around €25; ☯ Apr-Nov) As the name (The Rock) suggests, Lo Scoglio overlooks a small cove and specialises in well-prepared seafood. Warmly recommended.

Pirozzi (☎ 081 99 11 21; Via Seminario 47, Ischia Ponte; full meals around €18) The terrace overlooking the sea is a great place to mull over the evening's big decision: pasta or pizza. The menu here is fairly standard, as is the food.

Getting There & Away

See p605 for details. You can catch ferries direct to Capri (€12) and Procida (€2.50) from Ischia.

Getting Around

The main bus station is in Ischia Porto. There are two principle lines: the CS (Circo Sinistra; Left Circle) and CD (Circo Destra; Right Circle), which circle the island in opposite directions, passing through each town and leaving every 30 minutes. Buses pass near all hotels and camp sites. A single ticket, valid for 90 minutes, costs €1.20, while a ticket valid from 6am to 6pm is €4. Taxis and micro-taxis (Ape three-wheelers) are also available.

You can do this small island a favour by not bringing your car. If you want to hire a car or scooter for a day, there are plenty of rental firms. **Fratelli del Franco** (☎ 081 99 13 34; Via A De Luca 133), in addition to hiring out cars (from €30 per day) and mopeds (€21 to €32), also has mountain bikes (around €10 per day). You can't take a rented vehicle off the island.

PROCIDA
pop 10,770

The pastel pinks, whites and yellows of Procida's tiny cubic houses, cluttered along the waterfront, make for a colourful introduction to the island. In fact so ideal is the setting that the island has often been used as the celluloid image of Mediterranean paradise. The international hit *Il Postino* was partly filmed here, as was the sinister tale of *The Talented Mr Ripley* (along with Ischia).

Procida is the smallest of the islands in the Gulf of Naples and makes an attractive alternative to its more famous neighbours.

Orientation & Information

Marina Grande is the hop-off point for ferries and hydrofoils and forms most of the tourist showcase. Procida's **tourist office** (☎ 081 810 19 68; Via Roma; ☯ 9.30am-1pm & 3.30-7pm Mon-Sat May-Sep, 9.30am-1pm Mon-Sat Oct-Apr) is next to the Caremar ticket office. However, infinitely more useful is the **website** (www.procida.net).

Sights & Activities

The best way to explore the island is on foot – it's only about 4 sq km – or by bike (p620). However, the island's narrow roads can be clogged with cars – one of the island's few drawbacks.

The 16th-century **Palazzo Reale d'Avalos**, recently used as a prison, dominates the island but is now all but abandoned. More interesting is the **Abbazia San Michele Arcangelo** (☎ 081 896 76 12; Via Terra Murata 89; admission €2; ☯ 9.45am-12.45pm year-round, plus 3-5.30pm May-Oct), about a 1km uphill walk from Marina Grande. Within the complex are a church, a small museum with some arresting paintings and a honeycomb of catacombs.

You have to be up and about fairly early to visit the **nature reserve** (admission free; ☯ 8.30am-noon Mon-Sat, last entry 10am) on the tiny satellite island of Vivara. Linked to Procida by a bridge, it's an excellent place for birdwatching or strolling.

The **Procida Diving Centre** (☎ 081 896 83 85; www.vacanzeaprocida.it) runs diving courses and hires out equipment. Budget €30 for a single dive, €57 for a full day.

Festivals & Events

On Good Friday there's a colourful procession of the Misteri. A wooden statue

CAMPANIA

of Christ and the *Madonna Addolorata*, along with life-size tableaux of plaster and papier mâché illustrating events leading to Christ's crucifixion, are carted across the island. Men dress in blue tunics with white hoods while many of the young girls dress as the Madonna.

Sleeping & Eating
Hotel Casa Gentile (☎ 081 896 77 99; www.casa gentile.it; Via Marina Corricella 88; s/d with bathroom €60/80, full meals €25-30) You really couldn't be nearer the water at this pastel-pink hotel overlooking the delightfully scruffy sea-front. Rooms are cool and spacious and the restaurant serves a mean grilled fish.

Crescenzo (☎ 081 896 72 55; info@hotelcrescenzo.it; Via Marina di Chiaolella 33; s & d with bathroom & breakfast high season €93, full meals around €30; ☯ year-round) Overlooking the yachts moored in the marina, this hotel offers a warm welcome and decent rooms. As is common in these parts it also has a decent fish restaurant.

Hotel Riviera (☎/fax 081 896 71 97; Via G da Procida 36; s/d with bathroom & breakfast €45/60, half/full board per person €70/75; ☯ Apr-Oct) Set a little back from the village of Marina di Chiaolella, the rooms at this pretty hotel are pleasant enough. They also have the added bonus of being more peaceful than many on the island.

La Rosa dei Venti (☎/fax 081 896 83 85; www .vacanzeaprocida.it/frameres01-uk.htm; Via Vincenzo Rin-aldi 32; per person €24-35; ☯ year-round) This is a cluster of self-contained cottages that sleep up to six people. They're set in a large, lush garden on a cliff top overlooking the sea; the charge depends on the season and how many people you pack in.

Camp sites are dotted around the island. Typical prices are €7.75 per site plus €8 per person. On the eastern side of the island try **Vivara** (☎ 081 896 92 42; Via IV Novembre) or, on the same road, **La Caravella** (☎ 081 896 92 30; Via IV Novembre). Near the better beaches of Ciraccio on the western side are **Privato Lubrano** (☎ 081 896 94 01; Via Salette 14) and its neighbour **Graziella** (☎ 081 896 77 47; Via Salette 15).

There are several good restaurants along the waterfront near the port, including **L'Approdo** (☎ 081 896 99 30; Via Roma 76; full meals around €20) serving magnificent and reason-ably priced seafood. Try the grilled cuttle-fish, which really does melt in the mouth. Just a few feet away, **Il Cantinone** (☎ 081

896 88 11; Via Roma 55; full meals around €18) offers similar fare.

Getting There & Around
Procida is linked by boat and hydrofoil to Ischia (€2.50, 45 minutes), Pozzuoli and Naples (see p609 for more details). SEPTSA runs a limited bus service (€0.80), with four lines radiating from Marina Grande. Bus No L1 connects the port and Chiaolella. The small open micro-taxis can be hired for two to three hours for about €20, depending on your bargaining prowess. You can hire boats from **Barcheggiando** (☎ 081 810 19 34) and local fishermen may be willing to take you out for between €5 and €10 per person, depending on the size of your group.

Perhaps the best – and certainly the most ecologically friendly – way to move around the island is by bike. **Associazione Azione Verde** (☎ 081 896 73 95) might rent you one. At the time of writing they were unable to provide any useful information or prices, but a typi-cal price would be about €10 per day.

SOUTH OF NAPLES

HERCULANEUM & ERCOLANO
Ercolano is today a pretty awful Nea-politan suburb 12km southeast of the city proper. Classical Herculaneum, by contrast, was a peaceful fishing and port town of about 4000 and something of a re-sort for wealthy Romans and Campanians. According to legend, Herculaneum was a Greek settlement founded by Hercules. Whatever the truth of this, it later passed to the Samnites before becoming a Roman town in 89 BC.

History
The fate of Herculaneum paralleled that of nearby Pompeii. Destroyed by an earthquake in AD 63, it was completely submerged in the AD 79 eruption of Mt Vesuvius. The difference was that Herculaneum was buried by a river of volcanic mud, not the *lapilli* (burning fragments of pumice stone) and ash that rained on Pompeii. The mud helped preserve it for posterity. The town was rediscovered in 1709 and amateur excavations were carried out intermittently until 1874, with many finds being carted

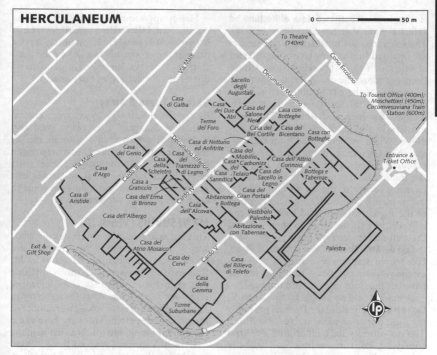

HERCULANEUM

0 —— 50 m

To Theatre (140m)

Cono Ercolano

Via Mare

Decumano Massimo

Sacello degli Augustali

Casa di Galba

To Tourist Office (400m); Moschettieri (450m); Circumvesuviana Train Station (600m)

Casa dei Due Atri

Casa del Salone Nero

Casa con Botteghe

Terme del Foro

Casa del Bel Cortile

Casa del Bicentario

Casa con Botteghe

Decumano Inferiore

Casa di Nettuno ed Anfitrite

Casa del Mobilio Carbonizz

Entrance & Ticket Office

Via Mare

Casa del Genio

Casa della Scheletro

Casa del Tramezzo di Legno

Casa del Telaio

Casa dell'Attrio Corinzio

Cardo III

Casa d'Argo

Casa Sannitica

Casa del Sacello in Legno

Bottega e Taberne

Casa a Graticcio

Cardo IV

Casa del Gran Portale

Casa di Aristide

Casa dell'Erma di Bronzo

Casa dell'Alcova

Abitazione e Bottega

Casa dell'Albergo

Vestibolo Palestra

Abitazione con Tabernae

Exit & Gift Shop

Casa del Atrio Mosaico

Casa dei Cervi

Cardo V

Casa del Rilievo di Telefo

Palestra

Casa della Gemma

Terme Suburbane

LP

off to Naples to decorate the houses of the well-to-do or to end up in museums. Serious archaeological work began in 1927 and excavation continues today.

Orientation & Information

Modern Ercolano's main street, Via IV Novembre, leads from the Circumvesuviana train station, at the town's eastern edge, to Piazza Scavi and the main ticket office for the excavations – an easy 600m walk.

At the **tourist office** (☎ /fax 081 788 12 43; Via IV Novembre 82; ☺ 9am-2pm Mon-Sat) you can pick up a brochure with an inadequate map of the ruined city and very little else.

On sale at the bookshop beside the exit point at Herculaneum there is the useful guidebook in English translation: *Pompeii, Herculaneum & Vesuvius* (€7.25), published by Edizioni Kina.

The Ruins

At the **ruins** (☎ 081 739 09 63; admission €10, combined ticket incl Pompeii & 3 minor sites €18; ☺ 8.30am-7.30pm Apr-Oct, 8.30am-5pm Nov-Mar) be prepared for some of the houses to be closed,

although an attendant may be around to open them.

Beside the main entrance and ticket office you may be gently assailed by guides – if you do take one on, make sure both of you understand what kind of fee is expected at the end.

Follow the path running above and around the site, then descend through a short tunnel to emerge beside the **Terme Suburbane** (Suburban Baths) in the site's southernmost corner. These baths make a great introduction to the site with their deep pools, stucco friezes and bas-reliefs looking down upon marble floors and wall cladding.

The site is divided into 11 *insulae* (islands) carved up in a classic Roman grid pattern. The two main streets, Decumano Massimo and Decumano Inferiore, are crossed by Cardo III, IV and V.

The **Casa d'Argo** (Argus House) is a well-preserved example of a Roman noble family's house, complete with a porticoed garden and *triclinium* (dining area).

The most extraordinary mosaic to have survived intact is in the *nyphaeum* (fountain and bath) of **Casa di Nettuno ed Anfitrite** (House of Neptune & Amphitrite; Cardo IV). The warm colours in which the two deities are depicted hint at how lavish the interior of other well-to-do households must have been. For more fine mosaics make your way to another of the city's public baths, **Terme del Foro** (Central Baths), with its separate sections for men and women. The floor mosaics in the latter are in pristine condition. While women passed from the *apodyterium* (changing rooms; note the finely executed naked figure of Triton adorning the mosaic floor) through the *tepidarium* (warm room) to the *caldarium* (steam bath), men had the added bracing option of the *frigidarium* – a cold bath. You can still see the benches where bathers sat and the wall shelves for clothing.

Casa del Atrio Mosaico (House of the Mosaic Atrium; Cardo IV), an impressive mansion, also has extensive floor mosaics – time and nature have left the floor buckled and uneven.

Behind it, and accessible from Cardo V, **Casa dei Cervi** (House of the Deer) is probably the most imposing of the nobles' dwellings. The two-storey villa, built around a central courtyard, contains murals and still-life paintings. In the courtyard is a diminutive pair of marble deer assailed by dogs and an engaging statue of a drunken Hercules peeing.

Casa del Gran Portale (cnr Decumano Inferiore & Cardo V) is named after the elegant brick Corinthian columns that flank its main entrance. Inside are some well-preserved wall paintings.

Sacello degli Augustali, in its time a school, retains a pair of lively, well-preserved murals.

Off the main street is **Casa del Bicentenario** (Bicentenary House; Decumano Massimo), so named because it was excavated 200 years after digging at Herculaneum first began. A crucifix found in an upstairs room is evidence that there might have been Christians in the town before AD 79.

Northwest of the ruins are the remains of a **theatre** (Corso Ercolano), dating from the Augustan period.

Sleeping & Eating
You'll do better staying in Naples or Sorrento and making the easy rail journey to Herculaneum than staying in Ercolano.

Handy for a quick bite before heading out of town, **I Moschettieri** (☎ 081 777 48 61; Via IV Novembre 90-92; pasta €4.50-8) is a quick-service place at the crossroads just before the train station. It serves surprisingly good pasta dishes and a selection of tasty snacks.

Getting There & Away
By far the easiest way to get from central Naples or Sorrento to Ercolano (and also to Pompeii, which many visitors cover in the same day) is by the Circumvesuviana train (p607). A return ticket to Naples costs €3.40. By car take the A3 from Naples, exit at Ercolano Portico and follow the signs to car parks near the site's entrance.

MT VESUVIUS (VESUVIO)
This legendary volcano dominates the landscape, looming ominously over Naples and its environs. Although not as active as Mt Etna in Sicily, Vesuvius (1281m) is anything but extinct and scientists consider more eruptions a sure thing. After the last blow in 1944 its plume of smoke, long a reminder of the peril, disappeared. This may have eased the minds of some, but for those living in the shadow of Vesuvius (as about three million people do), the question is not if, but when.

Vesuvius' name is probably derived from the Greek *besubios* or *besbios*, meaning 'fire'. The volcano erupted with such ferocity on 24 August AD 79 that it all but destroyed the towns of Pompeii and Herculaneum and pushed the coastline out several kilometres. Subsequent years have witnessed regular displays of the mountain's wrath, the more destructive being those of 1631, 1794 (when the town of Torre del Greco was destroyed), 1906 and, most recently, 1944.

Trasporti Vesuviani (☎ 081 559 31 73) buses run from Ercolano train station to Vesuvius car park (€3.10 return, buy your ticket on the bus). There's then a 1.5km walk (allow 30 to 45 minutes) to the **summit area** (admission €6) and the rim of the crater. Buses depart from Ercolano train station at 9.30am, 10.30am, 11.50am, 12.50pm and 1.50pm. They return at 11.35am, 1pm, 1.55pm, 3pm and 4.10pm. All services leave Pompeii 30 minutes earlier. Be warned, however, that when weather conditions are bad they do shut the summit path and suspend bus departures. By car exit the A3 at Ercolano

Portico and follow signs for Parco Nazionale de Vesuvio. A licensed taxi should cost about €31 for four people.

Watch out for a couple of scams. Readers have reported independent bus owners in Ercolano lying about public transport times and charging ludicrous sums to get you up and down. And the little old couple who thrust walking sticks at visitors to help them on the push to the summit aren't doing it for charity, as they will make very clear when you descend.

Pack a sweater since it can be chilly up top, even in summer. Sunglasses are useful against the swirling ash and trainers or walking shoes are more practical than sandals or flip-flops (thongs).

On the winding route up to the crest, check out the **Museo dell'Osservatorio Vesuviano** (Museum of the Vesuvian Observatory; ☎ 081 6 10 84 83; www.ov.ingv.it, Italian only; admission free; 🕑 10am-2pm Sat & Sun), which tells of 2000 years of Vesuvius-watching.

POMPEII
pop 25,891

Victim of the world's most famous volcano disaster, Pompeii is Italy's top tourist attraction. About 2.3 million people pile in every year, making the magnificent ruins seem as crowded as the ancient streets must once have been. Ever since Pliny the Younger described the eruption of Vesuvius in AD 79, the city has been the stuff of books, scholarly and frivolous, and a perfect subject for the big screen. It offers the richest insight into the daily life of the Romans; most of it is open to the public and requires at least three or four hours to visit.

Less than a kilometre down the road from the ruins, the depressingly grim modern town of Pompeii boasts a second big crowd-puller: the Santuario della Madonna del Rosario (Sanctuary of Our Lady of the Rosary), a famous place of miracles that attracts pilgrims from all over Italy.

History

The eruption of Vesuvius wasn't the first disaster to strike the Roman port of Pompeii. In AD 63 it was devastated by an earthquake. Following a rapid rebuild, it was just beginning to get back in the swing when lightning struck for the second time. On 24 August AD 79 Vesuvius blew its top, burying the city under a layer of *lapilli* (burning fragments of pumice stone) and killing some 2000 of the city's 20,000 inhabitants.

This, some might suggest, was a tragically appropriate destiny for a town that had been founded on prehistoric lava from the very same Vesuvius. The origins of Pompeii are uncertain, but it seems likely that it was founded in the 7th century BC by the Campanian Oscans. Over the next seven centuries the city fell to the Greeks and the Samnites before, in 80 BC, becoming a Roman colony.

After its catastrophic demise some 160 years later, the city gradually receded from the public eye until 1594, when the architect Domenico Fontana stumbled across the ruins while digging a canal. However, short of recording the find, he took no further action.

Exploration proper finally began in 1748 under the king of Naples, Charles III of Bourbon, and continued systematically into the 19th century. Giuseppe Fiorelli, who worked for the Italian government from 1858, is credited with most of the major discoveries.

Most of the ancient city has now been unearthed but work continues and new finds are still being made. In 2000, for example, road works on the nearby A3 revealed a whole frescoed leisure area.

Today, many of the more spectacular mosaics and murals sit in the Museo Archeologico Nazionale in Naples (p595) and other museums around the world. This is an unfortunate by-product of overtourism and underfunding, which have been eroding the original 66-hectare site. To counter this, hopes are resting on inclusion on Unesco's World Heritage List and a law giving the site management company commercial autonomy.

Orientation

The Circumvesuviana drops you at Pompeii-Scavi-Villa dei Misteri station, beside the main Porta Marina entrance. By car, signs – and energetic touts – direct you from the A3 to the *scavi* (excavations) and car parks. There are several camp sites, hotels and restaurants in the vicinity, although the choice is better in the adjacent modern town of Pompeii.

Information

First Aid Post (Via T Ravallese)
Police Booth (Piazza Esedra)
Post Office (Piazza Esedra)

TOURIST INFORMATION

Tourist Offices Porta Marina (☎ 081 850 72 55; Piazza Porta Marina Inferiore 12; ☽ 8am-3.30pm Mon-Sat); Pompeii town (☎ 081 850 72 55; Via Sacra 1; ☽ 8am-3.30pm Mon-Sat Oct-Mar, 8am-7pm Mon-Sat Apr-Sep)

The Ruins

The Porta Marina is nowadays the principle entrance to the **ruins** (☎ 081 857 53 47; www.pompeiisites.org; admission €10, combined ticket incl Herculaneum & 3 minor sites €18; ☽ 8.30am-7.30pm Apr-Oct, last entry 6pm; 8.30am-5pm daily Nov-Mar, last entry 3.30pm). Audioguides (€6) are available but a

good guidebook (see p621) is still a useful tool since it's easy to miss some of the more important sites.

The original town was encircled by a wall punctuated by towers and eight gates. Entering by the southwestern sea gate, **Porta Marina**, which was considerably closer to the water before the eruption, you pass on the right the **Tempio di Venere** (Temple of Venus). Originally one of town's most lavish temples, its position made it the target of repeated pillaging, leaving it in the abandoned state you see today.

Further along Via Marina, on the left, you pass the striking **Tempio di Apollo** (Temple of Apollo), the oldest of Pompeii's religious buildings, to enter the **foro** (forum), the centre of the city's life. South of this,

---

ASHES, FIRE & BRIMSTONE

One of the most vivid accounts of the eruption of Vesuvius is by Pliny the Younger, writing to the historian Tacitus. In it Pliny describes how his uncle, Pliny the Elder, renowned as an early naturalist, met his death:

'He embraced his terrified friend, cheered and encouraged him and, thinking he could calm the latter's fears by showing his own composure, gave orders that he was to be carried to the bathroom. After his bath he lay down and dined; he was quite cheerful, or at any rate pretended he was, which was no less courageous.

Meanwhile on Mt Vesuvius broad sheets of fire and leaping flames blazed at several points, their bright glare emphasised by the darkness of the night. My uncle tried to allay the fears of his companions by repeatedly declaring that these were nothing but bonfires left by the peasants in their terror, or else empty houses on fire in the districts they had abandoned. Then he went to rest and certainly slept, for as he was a stout man his breathing was rather loud and heavy and could be heard by people coming and going outside his door. By this time the courtyard leading to his room was full of ashes mixed with pumice stones so that its level had risen; if he had stayed in the room any longer he would never have got out. He was wakened and came out to join Pomponianus and the rest of the household who had sat up all night. They debated whether to stay indoors or take their chance in the open, for the buildings were now shaking with violent shocks and seemed to be swaying to and fro as if torn from their foundations. Outside on the other hand, there was the danger of falling pumice stones, even though these were light and porous; however, after comparing the risks they chose the latter. As a protection against falling objects they put pillows on their heads tied down with cloths.

Elsewhere there was daylight by this time but they were still in darkness, blacker and denser than any ordinary night, which they relieved by lighting torches and various kinds of lamp. My uncle decided to go down to the shore and investigate on the spot the possibility of escape by sea but he found the waves still wild and dangerous. They spread a sheet on the ground for him to lie down and he repeatedly asked for cold water to drink. Then the flames and smell of sulphur, giving warning of the approaching fire, drove his companions to flight and roused him to stand up. He stood leaning on two slaves and then suddenly collapsed, I imagine because the dense fumes choked his breathing by blocking his windpipe, which was constitutionally weak and narrow and often inflamed. When daylight returned on the 26th – two days after he had last been seen – his body was found intact, uninjured and still fully clothed as though he were in sleep rather than in death.'

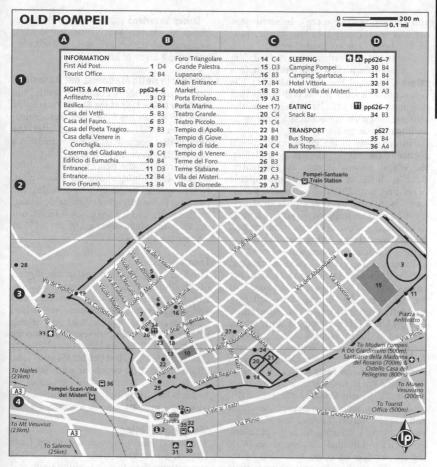

OLD POMPEII

0 _____ 200 m
0 _____ 0.1 mi

INFORMATION	
First Aid Post.....................**1** D4	
Tourist Office......................**2** B4	

SIGHTS & ACTIVITIES	pp624–6
Anfiteatro............................**3** D3	
Basilica................................**4** B4	
Casa dei Vettii.....................**5** B3	
Casa del Fauno....................**6** B3	
Casa del Poeta Tragico.......**7** B3	
Casa della Venere in	
Conchiglia.........................**8** D3	
Caserma dei Gladiatori.......**9** C4	
Edificio di Eumachia..........**10** B4	
Entrance.............................**11** D3	
Entrance.............................**12** B4	
Foro (Forum)......................**13** B4	

Foro Triangolare................**14** C4	
Grande Palestra..................**15** D3	
Lupanaro............................**16** B3	
Main Entrance....................**17** B4	
Market................................**18** B3	
Porta Ercolano...................**19** A3	
Porta Marina..................(see 17)	
Teatro Grande....................**20** C4	
Teatro Piccolo....................**21** C4	
Tempio di Apollo...............**22** B3	
Tempio di Giove.................**23** B3	
Tempio di Iside...................**24** C4	
Tempio di Venere...............**25** B4	
Terme del Foro....................**26** B3	
Terme Stabiane..................**27** C3	
Villa dei Misteri.................**28** A3	
Villa di Diomede................**29** A3	

SLEEPING	pp626–7
Camping Pompei................**30** B4	
Camping Spartacus............**31** B4	
Hotel Vittoria....................**32** B4	
Motel Villa dei Misteri.......**33** A3	

EATING	pp626–7
Snack Bar...........................**34** B3	

TRANSPORT	p627
Bus Stop.............................**35** B4	
Bus Stops...........................**36** A4	

opposite Tempio di Apollo, is the **basilica**, the city's law courts and exchange. Dating back to the 2nd century BC, it was one of Pompeii's greatest buildings. Among the fenced-off ruins to the left as you enter are some delightfully gruesome body casts.

The forum, which incidentally was closed to cart traffic, is surrounded by the **Tempio di Giove** (Temple of Jupiter), one of whose two flanking triumphal arches remains, the **market**, where you can see the remains of a series of shops, and the **Edificio di Eumachia**, which features an imposing marble doorway.

Continue down Via Marina which, after the Edificio, becomes Via dell'Abbondanza, until you reach Via dei Teatri on the right.

This leads to the **Foro Triangolare** and the city's theatre district. To your left is the entrance to **Teatro Grande**, originally built in the 2nd century AD and capable of seating 5000 spectators. Adjoining it is the more recent **Teatro Piccolo**, also known as the Odeion. The **Caserma dei Gladiatori** (Gladiators' Barracks), behind the theatres, is surrounded by a portico of about 70 columns.

From the pre-Roman **Tempio di Iside** (Temple of Isis), rebuilt after the AD 63 earthquake and dedicated to the Egyptian goddess, turn left back to Via dell'Abbondanza, which intersects with Via Stabiana. **Terme Stabiane** is a 2nd-century BC bath complex complete with *frigidarium* (cold room), *apodyterium* (changing room), *tepidarium* (warm room)

CAMPANIA

and *caldarium* (hot room). In some you can still see the original tiling and murals. Several body casts are located here.

Towards the northeastern end of Via dell'Abbondanza, **Casa della Venere in Conchiglia** (House of the Venus Marina) has recovered well from the WWII bomb that damaged it in 1943. Its highlight is the striking fresco of the goddess lounging in an unusually large conch shell.

Hidden away in the green northeastern corner of the city lies the grassy **anfiteatro**, the oldest known Roman amphitheatre. Built in 70 BC, it was at one time capable of holding up to 20,000 bloodthirsty spectators. The nearby **Grande Palestra** is an athletics field with an impressive portico and, at its centre, the remains of a swimming pool. It was here that the young men of the emperor's youth associations worked out.

Return along Via dell'Abbondanza and turn right into Via Stabiana (which becomes Via del Vesuvio) to see some of Pompeii's grandest houses. Turn left into Via della Fortuna to meet, on your right, **Casa del Fauno** (House of the Faun), which featured a magnificent mosaic, now in Naples' Museo Archeologico Nazionale. A couple of blocks further along Via della Fortuna is **Casa del Poeta Tragico** (House of the Tragic Poet), with some decent mosaics still *in situ*. Nearby **Casa dei Vettii** (Vicolo di Mercurio) sports some well-preserved paintings and statues. Across the road from Casa del Fauno, along Vicolo Storto, is the **Lupanaro**, Pompeii's top brothel with murals indicating the services on offer. And what better place for the young rakes to wash away their sins than the **Terme del Foro** (Forum Baths), a short walk away on Via Terme.

From the Terme del Foro you can continue to the end of Via Terme and turn right into Via Consolare, which takes you out of the town through Porta Ercolano at Pompeii's northwestern edge. Once past the gate you pass **Villa di Diomede**, then turn right and you'll come to **Villa dei Misteri**, one of the most complete structures left standing in Pompeii. The Dionysiac Frieze, the most important fresco still on site, spans the walls of the large dining room. One of the largest paintings from the ancient world, it depicts the initiation of a bride-to-be into the cult of Dionysus, the Greek god of wine.

Museo Vesuviano (☎ 081 8 50 72 55; Via Bartolomeo 12; admission free; ☮ 8am-2pm Mon-Sat), southeast of the excavations, contains an interesting array of artefacts.

Santuario della Madonna del Rosario

Dominating modern Pompeii's centre, the **Sanctuary of Our Lady of the Rosary** (Piazza Bartolo Longo; ☮ 6.30am-2pm & 3-6.30pm) was consecrated in 1891, some 15 years after the miracle that guaranteed its fame. In 1876 a young girl was cured of epilepsy after praying in front of the painting, *Virgin of the Rosary with Child*, above the main altar. News rapidly spread and to this day the painting is the subject of popular devotion.

The Santuario is flanked by a freestanding 80m **campanile** (bell tower; ☎ 081 850 70 00; ☮ 9am-1pm & 3-5pm).

Tours

The tourist offices warn against the dozens of unauthorised guides who swoop on tourists, charging exorbitant prices for brief and generally inaccurate tours. Authorised guides wear identification tags and belong to one of four cooperatives: **Promo Touring** (☎ 081 850 88 55), **Casting** (☎ 081 850 07 49), **Gata** (☎ 081 861 56 61) and **Cast** (☎ 081 856 42 21). The official price for a two-hour tour, whether you're alone, a couple or in a group of up to 25, is €94. Be wary if visiting out-of-the-way ruins unless you're in a group.

Sleeping & Eating

Pompeii is best visited on a day trip from Naples, Sorrento or Salerno, as once the excavations close there's nothing to do and the area around the site becomes decidedly seedy.

Ostello Casa del Pellegrino (☎ /fax 081 850 86 44; Via Duca D'Aosta 4; dm with breakfast €13) Situated a stone's throw from the Santuario in the town centre, this HI youth hostel has good, basic facilities in dormitories or rooms for five or six people.

Camping Spartacus (☎ 081 862 40 78; www .campingspartacus.it; Via Plinio 117; person/tent/car high season €6/3/3) Situated at the beginning of Via Plinio, the main road into town, this large camp site is a reliable place to put up for the night.

Camping Pompei (☎ 081 862 28 82; www.camping pompei.com; Via Plinio 113; person/tent/car high season €5/ 6/6, d with bathroom €56, bungalow from €35) Next to

Spartacus, this has similar facilities and is conveniently placed for a quick motorway getaway the morning after.

Motel Villa dei Misteri (☎ 081 861 35 93; www.villadeimisteri.it; Via Villa dei Misteri 11; d/tr with bathroom high season €60/80; 🅿 🐾) With well-fitted rooms overlooking the central swimming pool, this place offers the perfect place to recharge the batteries after some serious sightseeing. There's also a pretty good restaurant.

Hotel Vittoria (☎ 081 536 90 16; www.pompeihotel vittoria.com; Piazza Porta Marina Inferiore 2; s/d with bathroom & breakfast €45/85) Hotel Vittoria sits just outside the Porta Marina entrance to the ruins. A popular place for the lunching hordes, it becomes much quieter at the end of the day, enabling you to enjoy the characterful old building.

Pompeii is not an ideal place in which to dine well of an evening. There's a **snack bar** (Via di Mercurio; pasta from €4.70) within the ruins, but if you want something more substantial, try the restaurant at Hotel Vittoria or Motel Villa dei Misteri. Alternatively, head for modern Pompeii, where busy Via Roma, the continuation of Via Plinio, has several options. **Á Dó Giardiniello** (Via Roma 89; pizzas from €5), for example, is a no-nonsense pizzeria.

Getting There & Away
BUS
SITA (p606) operates regular bus services between Naples and Pompeii, while CSTP (p641) runs buses from Salerno. Marozzi offers services between Pompeii and Rome.

SITA buses depart from in front of the post office outside Porta Marina, while CTSP and Marozzi buses leave from in front of Hotel Vittoria.

CAR & MOTORCYCLE
Take the A3 from Naples, a trip of about 23km, otherwise you could spend hours weaving through narrow streets and traffic snarls. Use the Pompeii exit and follow signs to Pompei Scavi. Car parks are clearly marked and vigorously touted.

TRAIN
From Naples, take the Circumvesuviana train (€2.20) for Sorrento and get off at Pompei-Scavi-Villa dei Misteri station.

SORRENTO
pop 17,429

An unashamed resort town, Sorrento lines the cliffs that look over the water to Naples and Mt Vesuvius. According to Greek legend, the Sirens, mythical provocateurs of pure voice and dodgy intent, lurked in these parts. Sailors of antiquity were powerless to resist the beautiful song of these maidens-cum-monsters who would lure them and their ships to their doom. Homer's Ulysses escaped their deadly lure by having his oarsmen plug their ears and by strapping himself to the mast of his ship as he sailed past.

Less dangerous now, Sorrento is packed to the gills in high summer, predominantly with British and German holiday-makers. However, there is still just enough southern Italian charm to make a stay here enjoyable, and it's handy for Capri (15 minutes away) and the Amalfi Coast.

Orientation
Piazza Tasso, bisected by Sorrento's main street, Corso Italia, is the centre of town, having supplanted Piazza Angelina Lauro as its nucleus. It's about a 300m walk northwest of the train station, along Corso Italia. If you arrive at Marina Piccola, where ferries and hydrofoils dock, walk south along Via Marina Piccola then climb about 200 steps to reach the piazza. Corso Italia becomes the SS145 on the way east to Naples and, heading west, changes its name to Via Capo.

Information
EMERGENCY
Police Station (☎ 081 807 44 33; Corso Italia 236)

INTERNET ACCESS
Sorrento Info (☎ 081 807 40 00; Via Tasso 19; €3/30 mins; 🕑 10am-1.30pm & 4-8pm Mon-Sat Nov-Apr, 10am-1.30pm & 5-10.30pm Mon-Sat May-Oct)

INTERNET RESOURCES
Sorrento Tourism (www.sorrentotourism.it)

MEDICAL SERVICES
Hospital (☎ 081 533 11 11; Corso Italia 1)

MONEY
Acampora Travel (☎ 081 878 48 00; Piazza Angelina Lauro12) Represents American Express.
Deutsche Bank (Piazza Angelina Lauro 22-29) The bank has an ATM.

SORRENTO

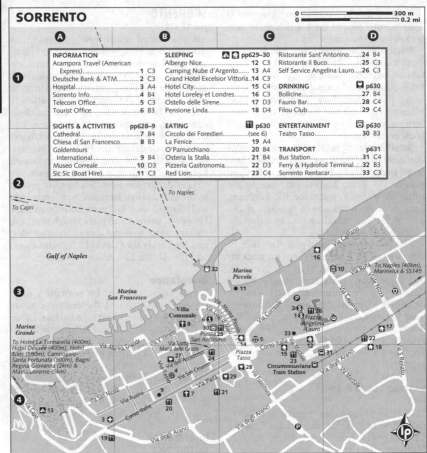

0 _____ 300 m
0 _____ 0.2 mi

INFORMATION		
Acampora Travel (American		
Express)...........................	1	C3
Deutsche Bank & ATM............	2	C3
Hospital..................................	3	A4
Sorrento Info.........................	4	B4
Telecom Office......................	5	C3
Tourist Office........................	6	B3

SIGHTS & ACTIVITIES	pp628–9	
Cathedral...............................	7	B4
Chiesa di San Francesco.........	8	B3
Goldentours		
International..........................	9	A4
Museo Correale.....................	10	D3
Sic Sic (Boat Hire)..................	11	C3

SLEEPING	pp629–30	
Albergo Nice.........................	12	C3
Camping Nube d'Argento.......	13	A4
Grand Hotel Excelsior Vittoria..	14	C3
Hotel City..............................	15	C4
Hotel Loreley et Londres........	16	C3
Ostello delle Sirene...............	17	D3
Pensione Linda......................	18	D4

EATING	p630	
Circolo dei Forestieri..............	(see 6)	
La Fenice...............................	19	A4
O'Parrucchiano......................	20	B4
Osteria la Stalla.....................	21	B4
Pizzeria Gastronomia.............	22	D3
Red Lion................................	23	C4

Ristorante Sant'Antonino.......	24	B4
Ristorante il Buco...................	25	C3
Self Service Angelina Lauro....	26	C3

DRINKING	p630	
Bollicine...............................	27	B4
Fauno Bar.............................	28	C4
Filou Club.............................	29	C4

ENTERTAINMENT	p630	
Teatro Tasso.........................	30	B3

TRANSPORT	p631	
Bus Station...........................	31	A4
Ferry & Hydrofoil Terminal.....	32	B3
Sorrento Rentacar.................	33	C3

POST

Post Office (☎ 081 878 14 95; Corso Italia 210;
🕑 8am-6.30pm Mon-Fri, 8am-12.30pm Sat)

TELEPHONE

Telephone Office (☎ 081 807 33 17; Piazza Tasso 37)

TOURIST INFORMATION

Tourist Office (☎ 081 807 40 33; Via Luigi De Maio 35;
🕑 8.45am-6.15pm Mon-Sat) In the Circolo dei Forestieri
(Foreigners' Club), it provides the excellent information
magazine *Surrentum*.

Sights & Activities

The gleaming white facade of the **cathedral**
(Corso Italia) gives no hint of the exuberance
housed within. There's a particularly striking

crucifixion above the main altar. The triple-
tiered bell tower rests on an archway
into which three classical columns and a
number of other fragments have been set.

Within the 18th-century **Palazzo Correale**,
which has some interesting murals, is the
Museo Correale (☎ 081 878 18 46; Via Correale; admission €6; 🕑 9am-2pm Wed-Mon), containing a small
collection of 17th- and 18th-century Neapolitan art and an assortment of Greek and
Roman artefacts. The gardens offer views of
the bay and steps lead down to the shore.

Views up and down the coast from **Villa
Comunale park** are breathtaking, and equally
impressive from the gardens of the beautiful, if modest, cloister of **Chiesa di San Francesco**, just beside the park.

Stroll along **Corso Italia**, which is closed to traffic in the centre between 10am and 1pm and 7pm to 7am, and through the narrow streets of the old town. At the time of writing the town council was set to introduce a fee of €1 for cars or mopeds entering the centre; whether this lasts remains to be seen.

If you're after a beach, head for **Marina Grande**, a 700m walk west from Piazza Tasso, which has small strips of sand. The jetties nearby sport ubiquitous umbrellas and deck chairs which cost up to €15 a day. **Bagni Regina Giovanna**, a 2km walk west along Via Capo (or take the bus for Massalubrense), is more picturesque, set among the ruins of the Roman Villa Pollio Felix. To the east is a small beach at Marinella. See below for boat-hiring information.

Tours

Sic Sic (☎ 081 807 22 83; Marina Piccola; ◷ May-Oct) hires out a variety of boats (starting at around €20 an hour) and organises boat cruises.

Goldentours International (☎ 081 878 10 42; Corso Italia 38e) offers tours to the Amalfi Coast (€25), Pompeii (€34), Capri (€40) and other destinations.

Festivals & Events

The **Sorrento Film Festival**, regarded as the most important in the country for Italian-produced cinema, is held annually, usually in November.

The city's patron saint, Sant'Antonio, is remembered on 5 February each year with processions and huge markets. The saint is credited with having saved Sorrento during WWII when Salerno and Naples were heavily bombed.

Sleeping

Most accommodation is in the town centre or clustered along Via Capo, the coastal road west of the centre. To reach this area catch a SITA bus for Sant'Agata or Massalubrense from the train station. Book early for the summer season.

BUDGET

Hotel Elios (☎ 081 878 18 12; Via Capo 33; s/d with bathroom high season €30/55; ◷ Apr-Oct) Even if the rooms here are basic the views are absolutely five-star, looking out over the water towards Naples. An excellent option for no-frills budget accommodation.

Pensione Linda (☎ /fax 081 878 29 16; Via degli Aranci 125; s/d with bathroom high season €35/70) This modest hotel offers a warm welcome and old fashioned courtesy, as well as good value for money. Rooms are spacious and decorated with furniture seemingly selected at random.

Hotel City (☎ /fax 081 877 22 10; hotel_city@libero.it; Corso Italia 221; s/d with bathroom & breakfast high season €50/68; 💻) A clean and friendly place on Sorrento's main drag, with its only downside being the intrusive traffic noise from the street. Internet access for guests costs €2.60 per half-hour.

Albergo Nice (☎ 081 878 16 50; fax 081 878 30 86; Corso Italia 257; s/d with bathroom high season €50/75; ◷ Mar-Nov; ✗) This central hotel shares its entrance with a newsagent, so you can pop down and pick up the paper on the way for breakfast. Traffic noise can also be a problem here.

Ostello delle Sirene (☎ /fax 081 877 13 71; Via degli Aranci 160; dm with breakfast €16, s/d with breakfast high season €50/64; ◷ year-round) This private hostel is a cheap bet for a dorm bed, but for a single or double room you can do better elsewhere. Some readers complain of a less-than-friendly welcome.

Camping Nube d'Argento (☎ 081 878 13 44; www.nubedargento.com; Via Capo 21; person/tent high season €7/10; ◷ Mar-Dec; 🐾) Hidden in a sea of olive trees, this site has good facilities and is only 200m from the beach.

Campogaio-Santa Fortunata (☎ 081 807 35 79; Via Capo 41; person/tent high season €8.50/6.50; ◷ Apr-Sep) Not far from the Nube D'Argento on the same road, this camp site offers very similar services.

MID-RANGE

Hotel Désirée (☎ /fax 081 878 15 63; Via Capo 31b; s/d with bathroom & breakfast high season €55/85; ◷ Mar-Dec) Overlooking the sea, this relaxed hotel has tastefully decorated rooms, a panoramic roof terrace and its very own lift down to the beach. At these prices that can't be bad.

Hotel La Tonnarella (☎ 081 878 11 53; www.latonnarella.com; Via Capo 31; d with bathroom €140, with bathroom & sea view €145; ◷ Mar-Oct) Next door to Désirée, La Tonnarella is elegantly decorated with antique lemon and blue tiles and is a great spot from which to enjoy sweeping views. It has a private lift down to the beach.

Hotel Loreley et Londres (☎ 081 807 31 87; fax 081 532 90 01; Via Califano 12; d with bathroom high season €79; ☙ Mar-Nov) A stylish old building looking directly on to Mt Vesuvius, this hotel occupies one of the best sites in town. The ambience here is relaxing and calm, an escape from the bustle of the centre.

TOP END
Grand Hotel Excelsior Vittoria (☎ 081 807 10 44; www.exvitt.it; Piazza Tasso 34; s/d from €231/268) The Grand Dame of Sorrento, this grand old hotel sits aloof in its extensive, carefully tended gardens, once the site of a villa belonging to Emperor Augustus. It offers the luxury of a bygone age at 21st-century prices.

Eating
Ristorante Sant'Antonino (☎ 081 877 12 00; Via Santa Maria delle Grazie 6; full meals around €20, pizzas from €4.60) This unpretentious restaurant in the heart of town has something for most budgets with three different set menus on offer. Its pasta dishes are tasty and filling and the grilled meat is particularly good.

Osteria La Stalla (☎ 081 807 41 45; Via Pietà 30; full meals around €18; ☙ dinner Thu-Tue) Set among orange trees in a converted stable, this is one of the rare restaurants in Italy to offer an optional gluten-free menu. In summer meals are served in its delightful garden.

La Fenice (☎ 081 878 16 52; Via degli Aranci 11; full meals from €18, pizzas from €4; ☙ Tue-Sun) You'll be met by the day's fish catch as you enter this green and floral restaurant. But they'll be as happy to serve you a pizza as seafood pasta at this popular spot.

O'Parrucchiano (☎ 081 878 13 21; Corso Italia 67; full meals around €20; ☙ Thu-Tue) This isn't the restaurant for you if you're looking for intimacy. A tour-group favourite, it resembles a massive and lush greenhouse. But don't be put off by it – the food is good and the service efficient.

Ristorante il Buco (☎ 081 878 23 54; Rampa Marina Piccola 5; full meals around €40) Despite its original name (The Hole), this is one of Sorrento's most lauded restaurants. Specialising in *nouvelle cuisine*, this place has an atmosphere well suited to serious dining, being a former monastic wine cellar.

Circolo dei Forestieri (Foreigners' Club; ☎ 081 877 32 63; Via Luigi de Maio 35; full meals around €20; ☙ lunch & dinner) A home-away-from-home for expats, Circolo dei Forestieri enjoys one of Sorrento's most spectacular views. Drop by for a snack or meal, or just sip a drink on the broad terrace.

Self Service Angelina Lauro (☎ 081 807 40 97; Piazza Angelina Lauro 39-40; pasta around €3; ☙ Wed-Mon) One of several economical snack venues ringing this far-from-picturesque square, this place also functions as a café and bar. Vegetarians will welcome its wide buffet range of non-meat dishes.

Red Lion (☎ 081 807 30 89; Via Marziale 25; pasta from €5, set menu €10) Not as bad as the name might suggest, this place is still the land of the pizza and pint. It's popular with the hostel crew, and you can catch up on the sports channel while munching on the decent pasta.

Pizzeria Gastronomia (☎ 081 807 47 08; Via degli Aranci 138; pizzas from €3) This cheap and cheerful place is bang opposite Pensione Linda and handy for the hostel too.

Drinking
There is no shortage of English-style pubs in the town centre, but for something a little more Mediterranean you can choose from a number of bars and cafés.

Bollicine (☎ 081 878 46 16; Via dell' Accademia 9) You can sample Campanian and other wines by the glass at this snug wine buffs' bar. Nibble on the local specialities, cheeses or cold meats.

Filou Club (☎ 081 878 20 83; Via Pietà 12; ☙ Thu-Tue) This popular piano bar, where the ivories are tickled until 4am, makes a great place to round off a night on the town.

For locals, whether perched at the bar or on the terrace, **Fauno Bar** (Piazza Tasso) is the late-evening place to see and be seen.

Entertainment
Outdoor concerts are held during the summer months in the cloisters of Chiesa di San Francesco.

Teatro Tasso (☎ 081 807 55 25; Piazza San Antonino) If you thrill to the Sound of Music, you might enjoy Sorrento Musical (€21), which plays here at 9.30pm Monday to Saturday from March to October. It's a potpourri of Neapolitan songs, including a sing-along with *O Sole Mio* and *Torna a Sorrento*, plus many other less-overworked Neapolitan numbers.

Shopping

Shoppers will enjoy browsing the small, nominally pedestrian alleys north of Corso Italia and west of Piazza Tasso. Look out for the local embroidery and lace and, peculiar to Sorrento, the elaborate marquetry (compositions of inlaid wood).

Getting There & Away

SITA buses serve the Amalfi Coast and Sant'Agata, leaving from outside the Circumvesuviana train station. Buy tickets at the station bar or from shops bearing the blue SITA sign. At least 12 buses a day run between Sorrento and Amalfi (€2.30), looping around Positano (€1.30); more than 10 buses also run to Ravello (€1).

Circumvesuviana trains run every half-hour between Sorrento and Naples via Pompeii and Ercolano (€1.80 to each).

Linee Marittime Partenopee (☎ 081 807 18 12) runs up to 10 hydrofoils daily to/from Capri (€17 return, 20 minutes) and at least six to/from Naples (€14 return, 35 minutes), while **Caremar** (☎ 081 807 30 77) has three fast-ferry sailings daily to/from Capri (€11.40 return, 25 minutes). All depart from the port at Marina Piccola, where you can buy your tickets.

Getting Around

Bus Line C runs from Piazza Tasso to the port at Marina Piccola. Tickets (€1 for 90 minutes) are available at tobacconists, newsagents and bars.

Sorrento Rentacar (☎ 081 878 13 86; Corso Italia 210a) is one of several rental companies hiring out scooters (€38) and cars (from €60 a day).

For a taxi call ☎ 081 878 22 04.

AMALFI COAST (COSTIERA AMALFITANA)

One of the most breathtaking coastlines in Europe, the Amalfi Coast stretches 50km east from Sorrento to Salerno. A narrow asphalt ribbon, itself a feat of road-building as spectacular as the views, winds along cliffs that drop to crystal-clear blue waters and passes through the beautiful towns of Positano and Amalfi. Peering down from its lofty lookout is the stunning hillside village of Ravello.

In summer the coast is jam-packed with wealthy tourists, prices are inflated and finding a room is next to impossible; you're much better off coming during spring and autumn. The Amalfi Coast all but shuts down in winter but you can still find places to stay. The area is also famous for its ceramics.

When planning your itinerary, you'll find www.amalfiscoast.com a useful Web source.

Walking

In the hills, dozens of small paths and stairways connect the coastal towns with mountainside villages. Useful information can be found in Lonely Planet's *Walking in Italy,* which has a chapter featuring the best walks around the Amalfi Coast and Sorrento peninsula; *Landscapes of Sorrento and the Amalfi Coast* by Julian Tippett with clear descriptions of over 60 mainly short walks in the area; and *Strade e Sentieri* (€6.50; in Italian only), a worthwhile general guide. The most reliable map to walk by is the Club Alpino Italiano's *Monti Lattari, Peninsola Sorrentina, Costiera Amalfitana: Carta dei Sentieri* (€7.75) at 1:30,000.

Getting There & Away
BOAT

Linee Marittime Partenopee (☎ 081 807 18 12) operates year-round ferries and hydrofoils between Sorrento and both Naples and Capri. **Caremar** (☎ 081 807 30 77) also serves the Sorrento–Capri route. Otherwise, most other routes operate only in summer, when a variety of companies operate hydrofoils between Sorrento, Amalfi, Positano and Capri.

BUS

SITA (☎ 081 552 21 76) operates a service along the SS163 between Sorrento and Salerno with buses leaving about every hour. Buses also connect Rome and the Amalfi Coast, terminating in Salerno (see p641).

CAR & MOTORCYCLE

The coastal road is magnificent – as a passenger. To drive it can be something of a white-knuckle ride, as bus drivers nonchalantly edge their way round hairpin bends, jauntily tooting at every turn. In summer it becomes a 50km-long traffic jam and can take hours to navigate.

From Naples take the A3, just after Pompeii branch off for Castellammare and follow signs for Sorrento. At Meta you can continue to Sorrento or, if your destination's further east, bypass the town by taking a short cut over the hills, thus saving yourself a good 30 minutes. To join the coastal road from Salerno, follow signs for Vietri sul Mare or Amalfi.

TRAIN

From Naples you can either take the Circumvesuviana to Sorrento or a Trenitalia train to Salerno, then continue along the Amalfi Coast, either eastwards or westwards, by SITA bus.

POSITANO

Positano is arguably the most picturesque and photographed of the coastal towns. What is not in question, however, is that you'll need a sturdy set of knees, for where most towns have streets, Positano has steps. Lots of them. Chock-a-block with expensive boutiques and cute houses, this is very much the town of a thousand postcards.

Orientation

Positano is split in two by a cliff bearing the Torre Trasita (tower). West of this is the smaller, less-crowded Spiaggia del Fornillo beach area and the less-expensive side of town; east is Spiaggia Grande, backing up to the town centre.

Navigating is easy, if steep. Via G Marconi, part of the SS163 Amalfitana, forms a huge hairpin around and above the town, which cascades down to the sea. From it, one-way Viale Pasitea makes a second, lower loop, ribboning off Via G Marconi from the west towards the town centre then climbing back up as Via Cristoforo Colombo to rejoin Via G Marconi and the SS163.

Information

Banca dei Paschi di Siena (Via dei Mulini) Has an ATM.
Banco di Napoli (Via dei Mulini) Also with ATM .
Il Brigantino (Via del Saracino 35; €5/30 mins) For Internet access at a central location.
Police Station (☎ 089 87 50 11; cnr Via G Marconi & Viale Pasitea)
Post Office (cnr Via G Marconi & Viale Pasitea)

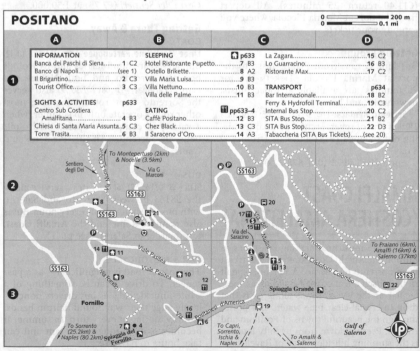

POSITANO

| | | 0 | 200 m |
| | | 0 | 0.1 mi |

INFORMATION		SLEEPING	🏠 p633	La Zagara.....................................15 C2
Banca dei Paschi di Siena......... 1 C2		Hotel Ristorante Pupetto.........7 B3		Lo Guarracino...........................16 B3
Banco di Napoli.....................(see 1)		Ostello Brikette..........................8 A2		Ristorante Max..........................17 C2
Il Brigantino............................... 2 C3		Villa Maria Luisa.........................9 B3		
Tourist Office............................ 3 C3		Villa Nettuno...........................10 B3		TRANSPORT p634
		Villa delle Palme.....................11 B3		Bar Internazionale...................18 B3
SIGHTS & ACTIVITIES p633				Ferry & Hydrofoil Terminal.....19 C3
Centro Sub Costiera		EATING	🍴 pp633–4	Internal Bus Stop.....................20 C2
Amalfitana............................ 4 B3		Caffè Positano.........................12 B3		SITA Bus Stop..........................21 B2
Chiesa di Santa Maria Assunta..5 C3		Chez Black...............................13 C3		SITA Bus Stop..........................22 D3
Torre Trasita............................ 6 B3		Il Saraceno d'Oro....................14 A3		Tabaccheria (SITA Bus Tickets)......(see 20)

Tourist Office (☎ 089 87 50 67; Via del Saracino 4;
☻ 8am-2pm & 3.30-8pm Mon-Sat year-round, 3.30-8pm
Jul & Aug) At the foot of the Chiesa di Santa Maria Assunta
steps.

Sights & Activities

Positano's most famous, and pretty much only, sight is **Chiesa di Santa Maria Assunta** (Piazza Flavio Gioia), its ceramic dome gleaming under the sun. Inside, regular classical lines are broken by pillars topped by gilded Ionic capitals, while winged cherubs peek from above every arch. Above the main altar is a 13th-century Byzantine Black Madonna and Child.

With the church done it's time to head for the nearby beach. Hiring a chair and umbrella on the fenced-off areas of the **beaches** costs around €15 per day but the crowded public areas are free. **Boating** isn't cheap either. On Spiaggia Grande expect to pay from €12 an hour for a rowing boat or €22 for a small motor boat (cheaper rates are offered for half- or full-day rental).

For **diving** enthusiasts, **Centro Sub Costiera Amalfitana** (☎ 089 81 21 48) operates from Spiaggia del Fornillo.

Lovers of classical music may want to coincide their visit with Positano's **'Summer Music'**, an annual international chamber music festival held at the end of August or early September.

If you're a keen walker and reasonably fit, set aside a day for the classic **Sentiero degli Dei** (Path of the Gods; five to 5½ hours). It follows the steep, well-defined paths linking Positano and Praiano, from where you can catch a bus back along the coastal road. See also p634.

For staggering views with much less effort, stroll the Via Positanesi d'America, the cliffside path which links the two beaches. Reward yourself with a cold drink on the terrace of Hotel Ristorante Pupetto.

Sleeping

Positano has several one-star hotels, which are usually booked well in advance for summer. Ask at the tourist office about rooms in private houses, which are generally expensive, or apartments.

Ostello Brikette (☎ 089 87 58 57; www.brikette .com; Via G Marconi 358; dm €22; ☻ Apr-Nov) About 200m west of the bus stop by Bar Internazionale, this little jewel is friendly and full of

character. And to top it off, the price drops to €20 if you stay for two or more nights.

Villa Maria Luisa (☎ 089 87 50 23; www.pensione marialuisa.com, Italian only; Via Fornillo 42; s/d with bathroom €40/65; ☻ Mar-Nov) A lovely little hotel, the Maria Luisa offers modest rooms, some with balconies, and a small terrace with magnificent views of the bay. The Falstaffian owner, Carlo, also gives a wonderful welcome speech.

Villa Nettuno (☎ 089 87 54 01; www.villanettuno positano.it; Viale Pasitea 208; d with bathroom high season €70-80; ☻ year-round) It's worth tackling the last few steps to find this charming hotel hidden among the foliage. The welcome is warm and most rooms have balconies or open onto a communal terrace.

Villa delle Palme (☎ /fax 089 87 51 62; Viale Pasitea 252; d with bathroom high season €80; ☻ Mar-Dec; **P**) The parking on offer here is not to be sniffed at, in a zone where flat space is highly sought-after. The owners also run the excellent Saraceno d'Oro restaurant, just below (see below).

Hotel Ristorante Pupetto (☎ 089 87 50 87; fax 089 81 15 17; pupetto@starnet.it; Via Fornillo 37; s/d with bathroom & breakfast high season €90/150; ☻ Apr-Dec) This is right beside Spiaggia del Fornillo, and you can just about tumble onto the beach from all its rooms (which have sea views). You can also eat at the restaurant (see p634).

Eating

Most restaurants are overpriced and many close over winter, making a brief reappearance for Christmas and New Year.

Il Saraceno d'Oro (☎ 089 81 20 50; Viale Pasitea 254; pizzas around €6, full meals €24) This highly popular eatery scores well on all counts – food, service and decor. The menu is unexceptional but the profiteroles are not. Try them in chocolate sauce or in a local lemon concoction and be happy.

Lo Guarracino (☎ 089 87 57 94; Via Positanesi d'America; full meals from €30) Here you pay for location. On the cliffside path connecting Positano's two beaches, the panorama is unfettered by niggly little eyesores like houses or cars. The food is simple and popular, so booking ahead is a good idea.

Chez Black (☎ 089 87 50 36; Via del Brigantino 19; full meals around €30) A favourite with the smart sweater-over-the-shoulders set, this recommended spot overlooking Spiaggia Grande specialises in seafood. Much sought-after is the *spaghetti a la Black* cooked in cuttlefish ink and, for a blowout, the mixed seafood grill.

Ristorante Max (☎ 089 87 50 56; Via dei Mulini 22; full meals around €35) In much the same price bracket and also specialising in creatures pulled from the sea, this chic restaurant offers elegant, intimate dining within a contemporary art gallery.

For good value fish and seafood with the briny almost at your feet, dine on the vast terrace of **Hotel Ristorante Pupetto** (p633), where restaurant prices are much more reasonable than hotel rates.

For a quick bite or an aperitif, **La Zagara** (☎ 089 87 59 64; Via dei Mulini 6) has overpriced snacks – but when you're sitting on the terrace in the shade of lemon trees, the high prices don't seem to matter so much.

The terrace of **Caffé Positano** (Viale Pasitea 170), with its commanding views of town and sea, makes a great place for a relaxing drink or ice cream (€1.50).

Getting There & Around

To take a SITA bus (services to Amalfi, Sorrento and towns in-between) at the top (northern end) of Viale Pasitea, buy your ticket at Bar Internazionale, just opposite the stop. For the easternmost bus stop get the bus in town from the tobaccinist at the bottom of Via Cristoforo Colombo. If you forget you're in for a long descent and climb back up.

Positano is a snakes-and-ladders town. If your knees can take a steep ascent or drop there are dozens of narrow alleys and stairways that make walking relatively easy and joyously traffic-free. Otherwise a small orange bus follows the lower ring road every half-hour, passing along Viale Pasitea, Via Cristoforo Colombo and Via G Marconi. Stops are clearly marked and you buy your ticket (€0.80) on board. It passes by both SITA bus stops.

Between Easter and October ferries link Positano with Capri, Naples and other towns along the Amalfi Coast.

AROUND POSITANO
Nocelle

This tiny, still relatively isolated village (450m) lies east of Positano. It's accessible by road or, more interestingly, by a short walking track from the end of Positano's Via Mons S Clinque. Before heading back have lunch at **Trattoria Santa Croce** (☎ 089 81 12 60; meals around €20) and enjoy the panoramic views from its terrace. In summer the place is open for both lunch and dinner; at other times of the year it's best to phone and check in advance. Buses link Nocelle and Positano, running roughly every half-hour in summer.

Praiano

The coastal town of Praiano is less scenic than Amalfi but has more budget accommodation options, including the only camp site on the Amalfi Coast.

Along the coastal road east of Praiano, **La Tranquillità** (☎ 089 87 40 84; www.continental.praiano .it; Via Roma 21; 2 people & tent €39, bungalows €90, s/d with bathroom per person from €60/45), also known as Continental, has an option to suit most tastes. The complex has a restaurant and the SITA bus stops outside.

AMALFI
pop 5527

Amalfi might no longer be a maritime superpower but its name lives on in tourist brochures across the world. In summer you cannot move here and even out of season the coaches pour in with metronomic regularity. At its peak in the 11th century, Amalfi, which in those days had a population of around 70,000, was a supreme naval power and a bitter enemy of the northern maritime republics Pisa and Genoa. Its navigation tables, the Tavole Amalfitane, formed the world's first maritime code and governed all shipping in the Mediterranean for centuries.

The town was founded in the 9th century. Through its connections with the Orient, the city, so it claims, introduced to Italy such modern wonders as paper, coffee and carpets.

Orientation

Most of Amalfi's hotels and restaurants are around Piazza Duomo or along Via Lorenzo d'Amalfi and its continuation, Via Capuano, which snakes north from the cathedral.

Information

Deutsche Bank (Corso Repubbliche Marinare) Next door to the tourist office; has an ATM.

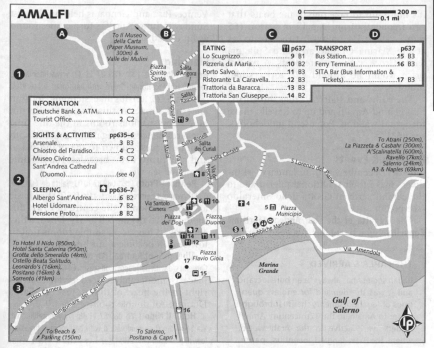

AMALFI

0 _____ 200 m
0 _____ 0.1 mi

INFORMATION
Deutsche Bank & ATM...........**1** C2
Tourist Office.....................**2** C2

SIGHTS & ACTIVITIES   pp635–6
Arsenale.............................**3** B3
Chiostro del Paradiso..........**4** C2
Museo Civico......................**5** C2
Sant'Andrea Cathedral
   (Duomo)......................(see 4)

SLEEPING   pp636–7
Albergo Sant'Andrea.............**6** B2
Hotel Lidomare.....................**7** B2
Pensione Proto.....................**8** B2

EATING   p637
Lo Scugnizzo.....................**9** B1
Pizzeria da Maria................**10** B2
Porto Salvo.......................**11** B3
Ristorante La Caravella.........**12** B3
Trattoria da Baracca............**13** B3
Trattoria San Giuseppe.........**14** B2

TRANSPORT   p637
Bus Station........................**15** B3
Ferry Terminal.....................**16** B3
SITA Bar (Bus Information &
   Tickets)..........................**17** B3

To Il Museo della Carta (Paper Museum, 300m) & Valle dei Mulini

To Atrani (250m), La Piazzeta & Casbahr (300m), A'Scalinatella (600m), Ravello (7km), Salerno (24km), A3 & Naples (69km)

To Hotel Il Nido (850m), Hotel Santa Caterina (950m), Grotta dello Smeraldo (4km), Ostello Beata Solitudo, Leonardo's (16km), Positano (16km) & Sorrento (41km)

To Beach & Parking (150m)

To Salerno, Positano & Capri

Gulf of Salerno

Marina Grande

Post Office (Corso Repubbliche Marinare) Next door to the tourist office.

Public Toilet (€0.50) Next door to the tourist office.

Tourist Office (☎ 089 87 11 07; 19 Corso Repubbliche Marinare; ☺ 8.30am-1.30pm & 3-5.15pm Mon-Fri, 8.30am-12.30pm Sat) Has little useful information but some pretty brochures.

Sights & Activities

The **Sant'Andrea cathedral** (☎ 089 87 10 59; Piazza del Duomo) makes an imposing sight at the top of its sweeping flight of stairs. The cathedral dates in part from the early 10th century, and its ornate facade has been rebuilt twice, most recently at the end of the 19th century. Although the building is a hybrid, the Arabic-Norman style of Sicily predominates, particularly in the two-tone masonry and bell tower. The interior is mainly baroque and the altar features some fine statues together with 12th- and 13th-century mosaics.

The adjoining 13th-century **Chiostro del Paradiso** (admission €2.50; ☺ 9.30am-7pm Jun-Oct, 9.30am-5.15pm Nov-May) was built in Arabic style to house the tombs of prominent citizens.

The small, one-room **Museo Civico** (☎ 089 87 10 66; Piazza Municipio; admission free; ☺ 8.30am-1pm Mon-Fri), behind Corso Republicche Marinare in the town hall building, contains the Tavole Amalfitane and other historical documents. Ask at the window halfway up the entry stairs for a guide sheet in English. The former republic's restored **Arsenale** (Via Matteo Camera; admission free; ☺ 9am-8pm Easter-Sep) is the only ship-building depot of its kind in Italy.

Up in Valle dei Mulini, an easy walk from town, is **Il Museo della Carta** (paper museum; ☎ 0328 318 86 26; Via delle Cartiere; admission €3.10; ☺ 10am-6pm), set up in a paper mill dating from the 13th century (see the boxed text p636).

The ceramics shops that you'll see mostly clustered around Piazza Duomo reflect Amalfi's traditional promotion of this craft.

In Conca dei Marini, about 4km along the coast towards Positano, is the **Grotta dello Smeraldo** (admission €5; ☺ 9am-4pm), a grotto so named for the emerald colour of its sandy floor. SITA buses pass by but it's more fun to take one of the boats that run frequently from Amalfi in season (€5 return; allow 1½ hours). At the grotto, as at the Marina Grande area and Spiaggia Santa Croce, you can hire boats. A typical price would be around €22 for a small motor boat.

The paths and stairways that thread the hills behind Amalfi and up to Ravello make for grand walking. For useful guidebooks, see p631.

Festivals & Events

On 24 December and 6 January, skin-divers make their traditional pilgrimage to the ceramic crib in Grotta dello Smeraldo (see p635).

The **Regatta of the Four Ancient Maritime Republics**, which rotates between Amalfi,

---

THE PAPER'S ARRIVED

Italian society has always been bureaucratic and it was the demand for endless quantities of legal documents that first brought paper to Amalfi. In the 12th century Amalfi traders were active in the Arab world, where the new-fangled invention, paper, was already proving more practical than heavy parchment. The merchants learned the paper-making techniques and brought them back to Amalfi, where the ready supply of water from the surrounding mountains was a crucial ingredient.

The basic process for making paper was simple. In the first stage, rags of linen, cotton and hemp were beaten by heavy wooden mallets, powered by a hydraulic wheel, to form a pulp. This pulp was then diluted with water and spread thinly over wire frames. The water was drained off and the resulting sheet placed on a bed of woollen felt. An operator would then build up a 'lasagne' of felt and pulp sheets before placing the whole lot under a press. The squashed paper sheets were placed directly on top of each other to create a 'post', which was left to dry before treatment with animal gelatin and smoothing by hand.

Refinements in the process arrived with more sophisticated machinery but the fundamental process remained unchanged for centuries, much to the joy of the region's army of bureaucrats, lawyers and notaries.

Venice, Pisa and Genoa, is held on the first Sunday in June. Amalfi's turn comes round again in 2005.

Sleeping

Hotel Lidomare (☎ 089 87 13 32; www.lidomare.it; Largo Duchi Piccolomini 9; s/d with bathroom & breakfast high season €45/100) It's like stepping into an ancestral home at this lovely family-run hotel. The spacious rooms in the one-time ducal residence are elegantly furnished with antique pieces – down to the grand piano and map prints in the breakfast room. Some also have sea views.

Pensione Proto (☎ 089 87 10 03; Salita dei Curiali 4; d with/without bathroom high season €85/75) For basic accommodation in the centre of town this modest hotel fits the bill nicely. Down a tiny alleyway, it has clean, simple rooms that in low season become a fair bit cheaper.

Albergo Sant'Andrea (☎ 089 87 11 45; Via Santolo Camera; s/d with bathroom high season €44/75; 🕮) This place is moderately priced given that it's right in the heart of things, just off Piazza Duomo. All double rooms have a TV.

Hotel Il Nido (☎ 089 87 11 48; www.hotelilnido.it; Via Salvatore Quasimodo 30; d with bathroom & breakfast low/high season €85/110; 🕮) Less than 1km west of the centre, this roadside hotel offers uncluttered, attractive rooms with balconies affording staggering views over the sea.

Hotel Santa Caterina (☎ 089 87 10 12; www.hotel santacaterina.it; Strada Amalfitana 9; d high season from €330; 🕮) Lounge by the saltwater pool, work out in the gym or simply enjoy the extensive grounds at one of Italy's top hotels. When you need to eat, try one of its two restaurants. The guest book reads like an international Who's Who and includes the ex-First Lady Hilary Clinton.

The following three options are outside Amalfi.

Ostello Beata Solitudo (☎ /fax 089 82 50 48; beatasol@tiscalinet.it; Piazza G Avitabile 5; dm €9.50; year-round; 🖳) This small, friendly 16-bed HI hostel in the San Lazzaro district of Agerola lies up in the hills 16km north of Amalfi. It offers self-catering facilities and also has a small camp site. SITA buses connect Agerola (p637).

Leonardo's (☎ /fax 081 802 50 02; v.pisacane@tin.it; Via Miramare 17; d/tr with bathroom from €35/50) Just down the road from Ostello Beata Solitudo, Leonardo's is a bit of everything – restaurant, pizzeria and *pensione*, offering a more comfortable, yet still economical, alternative to the hostel.

A'Scalinatella (☎ 089 87 14 92; www.hostelscali natella.com; Piazza Umberto I; dm with breakfast €10-21, d €36-83) A backpacker favourite, this hostel has a range of accommodation options, all of which have self-catering facilities. The brothers who run the place are also a mine of information about local walking possibilities. The hostel is in Atrani, a 15-minute walk northeast of Amalfi.

Eating

Trattoria San Giuseppe (☎ 089 87 26 40; Salita Ruggiero II 4; pizzas from €5, full meals around €25; ☻ Fri-Wed) This family-run restaurant serving homestyle cooking is a good bet. It's hidden away in Amalfi's labyrinthine alleyways – fortunately it's clearly signed from Via Lorenzo d'Amalfi.

Pizzeria da Maria (☎ 089 87 18 80; Via Lorenzo d'Amalfi 16; pizzas €8, full meals around €30) Easy to find, this cavernous place sits on Amalfi's main thoroughfare and is often full of lunching tour-groups. The food is good, if not exceptional. Evenings are much quieter.

Trattoria da Baracca (☎ 089 87 12 85; Piazza dei Dogi; full meals around €20, tourist menu €15.50; ☻ Thu-Tue) It's plonked in the middle of a piazza. Though the blue fishing decor is enough to put most people off, you'll eat pretty well at prices that (for Amalfi) are quite reasonable.

Ristorante La Caravella (☎ 089 87 10 29; Via Matteo Camera 12; full meals around €45; ☻ Wed-Mon) There's nothing remotely reasonable about the prices at La Caravella, but you shouldn't visit one of Amalfi's finest restaurants looking to economise. The food and service is top-notch.

Porto Salvo (☎ 089 87 24 45; Piazza Duomo; pizzas & panini €2.50) In the southwestern corner of the square and primarily a takeaway place, Porto Salvo does gorgeous pizza, *panini* and *panozzo* (pizza stuffed with mozzarella and tomatoes). Try its bag of mixed fried goodies for €3. You can also enjoy lunch at outside tables for no extra charge.

For great pastries drop in to **Lo Scugnizzo** (Via Capuano 16).

Down the road, in Atrani, you can stuff yourself silly at **La Piazzeta**, the restaurant belonging to A'Scalinatella (see above) for about €10.

Casbahr (☎ 089 87 10 87; Piazza Umberto 1) is highly recommended as a friendly place for a coffee and a chat.

Getting There & Away

SITA buses run from Piazza Flavio Gioia to Sorrento (€2.30, more than 12 daily) via Positano (€1.30) and also to Salerno (€1.80, at least hourly), Agerola (€1.30, more than 12 daily) and Naples (€3.10, eight daily, various routes). You can buy tickets and check current schedules at SITA Bar.

Between Easter and mid-September there are daily ferry sailings to Salerno (€4), Naples (€10), Positano (€6) and the islands of Capri (€22 return) and Ischia (€16).

RAVELLO

pop 2524 / elevation 350m

Ravello is a stylish town affording views that even by local standards are spectacular. Former playground of Jackie Kennedy and current home to Gore Vidal, Ravello sits like a natural balcony overhanging Amalfi and the nearby towns of Minori and Maiori. The 7km drive from Amalfi up the Valle del Dragone passes through the soaring mountains and deep ravines that characterise the area. From Ravello you can continue inland across the mountains to link up with the A3 to Naples and Salerno near Nocera.

Ravello's **tourist office** (☎ 089 85 79 77; Piazza Duomo 10; ☻ 8am-8pm Mon-Sat Jun-Sep, 8am-7pm Oct-May) has lots of practical information.

Sights & Activities

The **cathedral** (Piazza Duomo) dates from the 11th century and features an impressive marble pulpit with six lions crouched at its base. The free museum in the crypt contains religious artefacts.

Overlooking the piazza is **Villa Rufolo**. Its last resident was the German composer Wagner, who wrote the third act of *Parsifal* here. The villa was built in the 13th century for the wealthy Rufolos and was home to several popes as well as Charles I of Anjou. The villa's **gardens** (☎ 800 21 32 89; admission €4; ☻ 9am-6pm) are the inspirational setting for the town's impressive program of classical music (p638).

Some way east of Piazza Duomo is the 20th-century **Villa Cimbrone** (admission €4.50; ☻ 9am-6pm), set in magnificent gardens.

Worth the admission price just for the views, Villa Cimbrone is said to have been used by Greta Garbo as a hideaway.

You can also visit the town's vineyards: the small **Casa Vinicola Caruso** (Via della Marra), **Vini Episcopio** (Hotel Palumbo, Via Toro) and **Vini Sammarco** (Via Nazionale). If you prefer a touch of the hard stuff, visit **Giardini di Ravello** (Via Nazionale), beside Vini Sammarco, or **Profumi di Ravello** (Via Trinità), where *limoncello* is produced. Whatever tickles your palate, don't forget that it's a hairy, hairpin ride back to the coast.

Festivals & Events

Ravello's program of classical music begins in March and continues until late October. It reaches its crescendo in the **Festivale Musicale di Ravello**, held in the second half of July, when international orchestras and special guests play a repertoire that always features Wagner. Tickets start at €20 and can go as high as €130 for some performances. For information and reservations, contact the **Ravello Concert Society** (☎ 089 85 81 49; www.ravelloarts.org). The concerts are held in the gardens of the Villa Rufolo (p637).

Ravello's patron saint, San Pantaleon, is recalled with fun and fireworks in late July.

Sleeping & Eating

Book well ahead for summer – especially if you're planning a visit during the Festivale Musicale in July.

Parsifal (☎ 089 85 71 44; www.hotelparsifal.com; Viale d'Anna 5; s/d with bathroom & breakfast high season €60/120, half board per person €80) The flowery entrance to this former convent, parts of which date back to the 13th century, is a joy. Situated in a tranquil corner of Ravello, the hotel offers decent rooms and fantastic views. Half board is compulsory from June to September. It also has a fine restaurant.

Hotel Toro (☎ /fax 089 85 72 11; www.hoteltoro.it; Via Wagner 3; s/d with bathroom & breakfast €72/103; ☻ Easter-Nov) Just off central Piazza Duomo, Hotel Toro is a tasteful place where your only problem might be the clang of the cathedral bells disturbing your beauty sleep. The colourful walled garden is a delightful place in which to sip your sun-downer.

Albergo Ristorante Garden (☎ 089 85 72 26; www.starnet.it/hgarden/welcome.html; Via Boccaccio 4; d with bathroom & breakfast high season €95; ☻ mid-Mar–late Oct)

This welcoming hotel has faded a little since Jackie Kennedy passed by with her young kids in tow, but it's still a good option for a place to stay. You'll also save on lugging your bags around if you come by bus, as it's right by the stop.

Cumpà Cosimo (☎ 089 85 71 56; Via Roma 44-6; full meals around €30) It's very much a family affair at this intimate, almost self-sufficient place. Meat comes fresh from the family butchers shop, vegetables and fruit are homegrown and even the house wine is homebrew.

Ristorante Palazzo della Marra (☎ 089 85 83 02; Via della Marra 7; full meals €35-40) Splash out and you may possibly enjoy the best meal of your trip here. The food is a snip above the competition, both in quality and price, and you can't really fault the 12th-century building for style.

If you're pushed for time or simply want to chew on a pizza, drop in to **Take Away Pizza** (☎ 089 85 76 05; 41 Viale Parco della Rimembranza).

Getting There & Away

SITA operates about 15 buses daily between Ravello and Amalfi (€1, 25 minutes). By car, turn left (north) about 2km east of Amalfi. Vehicles, thankfully, are not permitted in Ravello's town centre but there's plenty of space in supervised car parks on the perimeter.

FROM AMALFI TO SALERNO

The 20km drive to Salerno, although marginally less exciting than the 16km stretch westwards to Positano, is exhilarating and dotted with a series of little towns, each worth a brief look around and each a potential base.

Atrani, just round a headland, is a pretty extension of Amalfi with a little beach. Further on are the towns of **Minori** and **Maiori**. Although lacking much of the charm of their better-known partners up the road, both have plenty of hotels and Maiori has a fairly decent-sized beach. Perhaps most attractive is the fishing village of **Cetara**.

Shortly before you reach Salerno, you pass through **Vietri sul Mare**, set on a rise commanding views over its larger neighbour and a good place to buy local ceramics. The town has plenty of workshops and showrooms and there are some good buys if you shop around.

SALERNO

pop 141,724

After visiting the oh-so-pretty little towns of the Amalfi Coast, the urban sweep of Salerno might come as a bit of a shock. One of southern Italy's many victims of earth tremors and landslides, it was also left in tatters by the heavy fighting that followed the 1943 landings of the American 5th Army, which were just to the south of the city. With the exception of a charming, tumbledown medieval quarter and a pleasant seafront promenade, the city doesn't offer much. It is, however, an important transport junction and an excellent base for exploring the Amalfi Coast to the west and Paestum and the Costiera Cilentana to the southeast.

Originally an Etruscan and later a Roman colony, Salerno flourished with the arrival of the Normans in the 11th century. Robert Guiscard made it the capital of his dukedom in 1076 and under his patronage the Scuola Medica Salernitana was renowned as one of medieval Europe's greatest medical institutes.

Orientation

Salerno's train station is on Piazza Vittorio Veneto, at the eastern end of town. Most intercity buses stop here and there are a number of hotels nearby. Salerno's main shopping strip, the car-free Corso Vittorio Emanuele, leads off northwest to the medieval part of town. Running parallel is Corso Garibaldi, which becomes Via Roma as it heads out of the city for the Amalfi Coast. Tree-lined Lungomare Trieste, on the waterfront, changes its name to Lungomare Marconi at the massive Piazza della Concordia on its way out of town, southeast towards Paestum.

Information

EMERGENCY

Police Station (☎ 089 61 31 11; Piazza Amendola)

INTERNET ACCESS

Mail Box (Via Diaz 19; €1.50/25 mins; ☉ 9am-1.30pm & 5.30-8pm Mon-Sat)

Interlanguage Point (☎ 089 75 35 81; 1st fl, Corso Vittorio Emanuele 14; ☉ 9am-1pm & 3.30-9pm Mon-Sat)

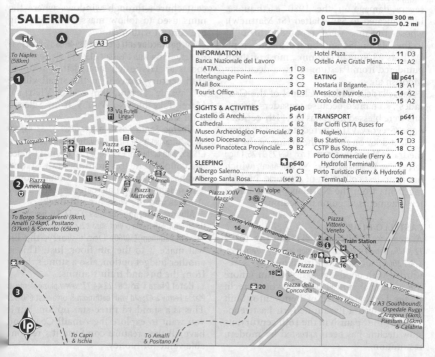

SALERNO

0 — 300 m
0 — 0.2 mi

INFORMATION
Banca Nazionale del Lavoro
  ATM.. 1 D3
Interlanguage Point................... 2 C3
Mail Box... 3 C2
Tourist Office................................. 4 D3

SIGHTS & ACTIVITIES   p640
Castello di Arechi...................... 5 A1
Cathedral.. 6 B2
Museo Archeologico Provinciale.7 B2
Museo Diocesano.......................... 8 B2
Museo Pinacoteca Provinciale.... 9 B2

SLEEPING   p640
Albergo Salerno.......................... 10 C3
Albergo Santa Rosa................(see 2)

Hotel Plaza..................................... 11 D3
Ostello Ave Gratia Plena.......... 12 A2

EATING   p641
Hostaria il Brigante................... 13 A1
Messico e Nuvole....................... 14 A2
Vicolo della Neve....................... 15 A2

TRANSPORT   p641
Bar Cioffi (SITA Buses for
  Naples).. 16 C2
Bus Station.................................... 17 D3
CSTP Bus Stops............................ 18 C3
Porto Commerciale (Ferry &
  Hydrofoil Terminal)............. 19 A3
Porto Turistico (Ferry & Hydrofoil
  Terminal)................................. 20 C3

To Naples (58km)
Via Risorgimento
Via Fratelli Linguiti
Via M Vernier
Via Torquato Tasso
Via delle Canali
Piazza Alfano
Via S Michele
Via Mercanti
Via Tannelli
Piazza Matteotti
Via Velia
Via Cilento
Piazza XXIV Maggio
Via Diaz
Via Volpe
Piazza Amendola
Via Roma
Corso Vittorio Emanuele
Piazza Vittorio Veneto
Corso Garibaldi
Train Station
Lungomare Trieste
Piazza Mazzini
Piazza della Concordia
Lungomare Marconi
Irno
Via Torrione
To Borgo Scacciaventi (8km), Amalfi (24km), Positano (37km) & Sorrento (65km)
To Capri & Ischia
To Amalfi & Positano
To A3 (Southbound), Ospedale Ruggi d'Aragona (6km), Paestum (36km) & Calabria

INTERNET RESOURCES
Salerno City (www.salernocity.com, Italian only)
Salerno Memo (www.salernomemo.com, Italian only)

MEDICAL SERVICES
Ospedale Ruggi D'Aragona (hospital; ☎ 089 67 11 11; Via San Leonardo)

MONEY
There's a Banca Nazionale del Lavoro ATM at the train station. You'll find several banks with ATMs on Corso Vittorio Emanuele.

POST
Post Office (Corso Garibaldi 203)

TOURIST OFFICES
Tourist Office (☎ 089 23 14 32; Piazza Vittorio Veneto; 9am-8pm Mon-Sat)

Sights
CATHEDRAL
The city's **cathedral** (☎ 089 23 13 87; Piazza Alfano; 10am-6pm), built by the Normans under Robert Guiscard in the 11th century and remodelled in the 18th century, sustained severe damage in the 1980 earthquake. It's dedicated to San Matteo (St Matthew), whose remains were reputedly brought to the city in 954 and buried in the crypt. With its 28 Roman columns, most of them plundered from Paestum, it has a decidedly Moorish air.

Cappella delle Crociate (Chapel of the Crusades), so named because crusaders' weapons were blessed here, has the 11th-century pope Gregory VII interred under the altar.

Next door on the northern side of the cathedral is **Museo Diocesano** (☎ 089 23 91 26; Largo del Plebiscito 12; admission free; 9am-6pm), which has a modest collection of artworks including items from the Norman period and a few fragments of Lombard sculpture.

CASTELLO DI ARECHI
A steep walk to **Castello di Arechi** (☎ 089 22 72 37; Via Benedetto Croce; admission free; 7am-noon & 4-7.30pm) along Via Risorgimento is rewarded with good views, if you can ignore the industrial sprawl beneath you. Arechi II, the Lombard duke of Benevento, built the castle over a Byzantine fort. Last renovated by the Spanish in the 16th century, its slow decline has been arrested by modern restoration.

MUSEO ARCHEOLOGICO PROVINCIALE
This **museum** (☎ 089 23 11 35; Via San Benedetto 28; admission free; 9am-8pm Mon-Sat) contains archaeological finds from around the region, including some particularly fine classical pieces.

MUSEO PINACOTECA PROVINCIALE
Deep in the heart of the medieval quarter, this small **gallery** (☎ 089 258 30 73; Via Mercanti 63; admission free; 8am-2pm & 3-8pm Tue-Sat, 9am-1pm Sun, 1-8pm Mon) houses an interesting collection dating from the Renaissance right up to the first half of the 19th century. There are some fine canvases by local boy Andrea Sabatini da Salerno and an assortment of works by foreign artists living in the area.

Sleeping
Ostello Ave Gratia Plena (☎ 089 79 02 51; fax 089 40 57 92; Via dei Canali; dm with breakfast €14, d B&B per person €15.50; year-round) This highly recommended HI hostel is light, airy and pristine. It's in a former 16th-century convent, and you can look directly down into the adjacent church through windows where the nuns used to follow mass, thus avoiding eye contact with men.

Borgo Scacciaventi (☎ /fax 089 46 66 31; Piazza San Francesco 1; dm with breakfast €13; Apr-Sep) This too is an HI hostel, located in a restored 16th-century convent in the small village of Cava de' Tirreni, 3km east of Vietri sul Mare. Take bus No 4 or 9 from Salerno train station.

Albergo Santa Rosa (☎ /fax 089 22 53 46; alb .srosa@tiscalinet.it; 2nd fl, Corso Vittorio Emanuele 14; s/d €25/35, with bathroom €35/55) This friendly place is a couple of metres from the train station and has anonymous and functional rooms. The neighbouring flats can be pretty noisy at times and the walls are not thick.

Albergo Salerno (☎ 089 22 42 11; paviansas@ tiscalinet.it; 5th fl, Via G Vicinanza 42; s/d high season €36/ 42, with bathroom €50/60) Don't worry, the lift will make it to the 5th floor. Just. This is another budget option, also a stone's throw from the bus and train stations.

Hotel Plaza (☎ 089 22 44 77; www.plazasalerno.it; Piazza Ferrovia 42; s/d with bathroom & breakfast €60/92) This is a standard three-star option, but if you want to explore the Amalfi Coast and have all the creature comforts it's reasonable value for money.

Eating

The medieval quarter is the place to head for. It's a lively area full of trattorie and bars, ideal for food followed by a spot of people-watching.

Messico e Nuvole (☎ 347 089 87 27; Larghetto Fra Giovanni da Salerno; full meals around €17) Take a break from pasta at this Mexican joint. The decor is all orange, yellow and dim lighting and the food considerably better than your average Tex-Mex concoction. It's also a good place for tequila.

Vicolo della Neve (☎ 089 22 57 05; Vicolo della Neve 24; full meals around €20; ☾ dinner Thu-Tue) You might have to queue to get a table at this Salerno institution. The owners have been in the restaurant business for about five centuries so they've had plenty of time to perfect the traditional fare they dish out so efficiently.

Hostaria il Brigante (☎ 089 22 65 92; Via Fratelli Linguiti 2; full meals around €18; ☾ Tue-Sun) This is a cheerful little trattoria right in the heart of the medieval quarter. It makes for a fun meal out but it fills quickly at the weekend.

Entertainment

There are numerous bars and pubs along Via Roma and dotted throughout the medieval quarter. You could do worse than join the locals in their *passeggiata* (evening stroll) and stop off for a drink when the urge arises.

Getting There & Away

BOAT

Ferries run from Salerno's Porto Turistico to Positano and Amalfi from April through October, while departures for Capri and Ischia leave from Porto Commerciale. Hydrofoils to these destinations also run in summer. Contact the tourist office for current schedules.

BUS

Most **SITA buses** (☎ 089 40 51 45) set out from Piazza Vittorio Veneto, beside the train station. Those that follow the Amalfi Coast leave about every hour. The exception is the Naples service, which departs every 25 minutes from outside **Bar Cioffi** (Corso Garibaldi 134), where you buy your ticket.

CSTP (☎ 089 48 70 01) operates bus Nos 4 and 50 to Pompeii from Piazza Vittorio

Veneto. For Paestum and other towns along the southern coast take bus No 34 from Piazza della Concordia.

Buonotourist runs an express weekday service to Rome's Fiumicino airport, departing from the train station. The bus also passes by the EUR-Fermi Metropolitana stop in Rome. However, if central Rome (rather than the airport) is your destination, it probably makes more sense to take the train.

CAR & MOTORCYCLE

Salerno is on the A3 between Naples and Reggio di Calabria, which is toll free from Salerno southwards.

TRAIN

Salerno is a major stop between Rome (€20), Naples (€2.90) and Reggio di Calabria (€28.60), and is served by all types of trains. It also has good train links with inland towns and the Adriatic coast.

Getting Around

Walking is the most sensible option if you're staying in the heart of Salerno. Bus No 41 runs from the train station to the cathedral.

PAESTUM

One of the enduring images of southern Italy is that of three Greek temples standing in fields of wild red poppies. The trio are among the best-preserved monuments of Magna Graecia, as the Greeks called their colonies in southern Italy and Sicily. The small town nearby is close to some of Italy's better beaches and just south of where US forces landed in 1943.

Paestum, or Poseidonia as the city was originally called (in honour of Poseidon, the Greek god of the sea), was founded in the 6th century BC by Greek settlers and fell under Roman control in 273 BC, becoming an important trading port. The town was hit by the successive blows of the retreat of the Roman Empire, periodic outbreaks of malaria and savage raids by the Saracens, and was gradually and understandably abandoned. Its temples were rediscovered in the late 18th century by road-builders – who proceeded to plough their way right through the ruins. However, the road did little to alter the state of the surrounding area, which remained full of malarial swamps, teeming with snakes and scorpions, until well into the 20th century.

Such days are long past and the site is these days a Unesco World Heritage Site. It is easily covered on foot. The **tourist office** (☎ 0828 81 10 16; Via Magnia Grecia 887; ◷ 9am-5pm May-Jul, 9am-8pm Aug, 9am-4pm Mon-Sat, 9am-1pm Sun Sep-Apr) has a lot of useful information.

The most economical way to enjoy Paestum is to buy a combined entrance ticket (€6.50), covering both temples and museum.

The Ruins

At the ruins (admission €4; ◷ 9am-1 hr before sunset), the first temple you meet on entering the site from the northern end, near the tourist office, is the 6th-century-BC **Tempio di Cerere** (Temple of Ceres). Smallest of the three temples, it served for a time as a Christian church.

As you head south you can pick out the basic outline of the large rectangular **forum**, heart of the ancient city. Among the partially standing buildings are the vast domestic housing area, an Italic temple, the Greek theatre, Bouleuterion (where the Roman senate met) and, further south, the amphitheatre – through which that infamous road was ploughed.

Tempio di Nettuno (Temple of Neptune), dating from about 450 BC, is the largest and best preserved of the three temples; only parts of its inside walls and roof are missing. Almost next door, the so-called **basilica** (in fact, a temple to the goddess Hera) is Paestum's oldest surviving monument. Dating from the middle of the 6th century BC and with nine columns across and 18 along the sides, it's indeed a majestic building. Just to its east you can, with a touch of imagination, make out remains of the temple's sacrificial altar.

In its time the city was ringed by an impressive 4.7km of walls, subsequently built and rebuilt by both Lucanians and Romans. The most intact section is south of the ruins themselves.

Tickets are sold at the main entry point or, during winter, from the museum. Here you can also pick up an audioguide (€4).

Museo di Paestum

This well-appointed **museum** (☎ 0828 81 10 23; admission €4; ◷ 9am-7pm, closed 1st & 3rd Mon of the month), just east of the site, houses a collection of much weathered metopes (bas-relief friezes), including 33 of the original 36 from Tempio di Argive Hera (Temple of Argive Hera), 9km north of Paestum, of which virtually nothing else remains.

Sleeping & Eating

Accommodation tends to be pricey and in summer is absolutely heaving. Think about Salerno or Agropoli as alternatives.

Camping Villaggio dei Pini (☎ 0828 81 10 30; Via Torre; 2 people & tent €18; ◷ year-round) The price charged here varies according to season; bungalows (from €42) are also available.

Albergo Villa Rita (☎ /fax 0828 81 10 81; hotelvillar ita@tiscalinet.com; Zona Archeologico 5; d with bathroom & breakfast high season €83; ◷ Mar-Oct; ⊠) Set back from the main road in its own grounds, this place is a tranquil haven in the midst of the summer holiday chaos. It's also conveniently close to the ruins.

As with accommodation, restaurants tend to inflate their prices. There are a few cafés and snack bars and a couple of restaurants along Via Magnia Grecia, which slices between the temples and the museum.

For something more special at prices to suit every budget, just outside the southern walls you'll find **Ristorante Nettuno** (☎ 0828 81 10 28; Via Principe di Piemonte; full meals around €20). Guarding the southeastern entry to the ruins, Nettuno offers elegant dining at prices neither cheap nor ludicrous. The mozzarella here is particularly good and you know it's fresh as the sweet smell of buffalo wafts in from the farm just down the road.

Getting There & Away

CSTP (toll free ☎ 800 01 66 59) and **SCAT** (☎ 0974 83 84 15) buses run hourly from Salerno's Piazza della Concordia to Paestum and on to Agropoli.

If you're driving you could take the A3 from Salerno and exit for the SS18 at Battipaglia. Better, however, and altogether more pleasant is the Litoranea, the minor road that hugs the coast. From the A3 take the earlier exit for Pontecagnano and follow signs for Agropoli and Paestum, which is 36km from Salerno.

Paestum is on the train line from Naples through Salerno to Reggio di Calabria. Most trains stop at Stazione di Capaccio, nearer the new town (about 6km from the site) and less frequently at Stazione di Paestum, less than 1km from the temples. Trains are less frequent than CSTP buses. Ask at the tourist office for the current timetables.

PARCO NAZIONALE DEL CILENTO E VALLO DI DIANO

The wild and empty highlands of the Parco Nazionale del Cilento e Vallo di Diano are the perfect antidote to the holiday mayhem along the coast. Occupying the area southeast of Salerno up to the regional borders with Basilicata and Calabria, it is a little-explored area that boasts barren beauty and a number of worthwhile sights. The only problem is transport; without your own you'll need plenty of time. For information ask at the tourist office in Paestum (p642).

The World Wide Fund for Nature has a wildlife sanctuary, **Oasi Naturalistica di Persano** (☎ 0828 97 46 84; ☿ Sep-Apr), about 20km northeast of Paestum on the River Sele. It's mainly wetlands and is home to a wide variety of birds, both resident and seasonal. Signs direct you there from the SS18.

There are also two cave systems well worth exploring. **Grotte di Pertosa** (☎ 0975 39 70 37; short/long tour €5/8; ☿ 9am-7pm Apr-Oct, 9am-4pm Nov-Mar), 40km northeast of Paestum, were discovered in the late 19th century. The tour takes you through 1700m of caves bristling with stalagmites and stalactites. A SITA bus leaves at about 9am from Salerno's Piazza della Concordia; another will take you back in the afternoon. By car take the A3 southbound from Salerno. The caves are 9km from the Petina exit.

Nearer to Paestum, the **Grotte di Castelcivita** (☎ 0828 97 50 09; tour €6.70; tours depart 10am, 11am, noon & every hr 2.30-6.30pm) is where Spartacus is said to have taken refuge following his slave rebellion in 71 BC. There is a De Rosa **bus** (☎ 0828 94 10 65) that departs from Capaccio Scalo at 9.30am and returns at 4.30pm. From Paestum it's about 20km; take the SS18 towards Salerno and follow the signs.

In the opposite direction, down the A3 towards Calabria just beneath the village of Padula, is the **Certosa di San Lorenzo** (☎ 0975 77 85 49; admission €4; ☿ 9am-7.30pm) which merits a detour. Also known as Certosa di Padula, this vast monastery has had a turbulent history. Begun in the 14th century

and much modified over the centuries, it was abandoned in the 19th century, then suffered further degradation as a children's holiday home and later a concentration camp. Many of the monks who lived here were from wealthy aristocratic families and no expense was spared in its construction – as the restored elaborate chapels, huge central courtyard and the wood-panelled library reveal.

Mafia junkies might find **Museo Joe Petrosino** (☎ 0975 773 95; Via Guiseppe Petrosino; admission free; ☿ 10am-1pm & 3-6pm mid-Mar–Sep) particularly interesting. Up in Padula the unexceptional village house where this early fighter against the US mafia was born contains a small museum recording 'la vita e morte di un detective' who was gunned down in 1909 by the leader of the local clan as he returned to his native country. For a guided tour by the great man's great-grandson Nino Melito, call the **Joe Petrosino Association** (☎ 348 332 50 96).

Lamanna buses run from Salerno to Padula and (less frequently) to Teggiano.

COSTIERA CILENTANA (CILENTO COAST)

Southeast of the Gulf of Salerno, the coastal plains begin to give way to more rugged territory, a foretaste of what lies further on in the stark hills and mountains of Basilicata and the more heavily wooded peaks of Calabria. This southernmost tract of the Campania littoral doesn't lend itself to summer seaside frolics (with some exceptions) – snorkellers will appreciate some of the rocky points. Despite an irregular splattering of camp sites and holiday accommodation, the beaches are not as popular as those further northwest or southeast in Basilicata and Calabria. CSTP buses leave Salerno for Sapri, on the regional boundary between Campania and Basilicata. Trains heading south from Salerno also stop at most towns on the Costiera Cilentana. By car take the SS18, which connects Agropoli with Velia via the inland route, or the SS267, which hugs the coast.

Agropoli

This charming coastal town has a small, ramshackle medieval core, perched on a high promontory overlooking the sea and topped by a crumbling old castle. A rewarding stop, it makes an excellent base for Paestum and the beaches to the northwest.

There is a **tourist office** (☎ 0329 622 77 54; Corso Garibaldi 38; ☽ 10.30am-1pm & 3.30-7.30pm Mon-Sat) on the main shopping street.

Ostello La Lanterna (☎ /fax 0974 83 83 64; lanterna@cilento.it; Via Lanterna 8; dm with breakfast €10.50; ☽ mid-Mar–Oct) At Agropoli's northern extremity, this friendly HI hostel is homely and relaxed. There are also beds available in family rooms (€11) and an evening meal for €7.

Camping Torino (☎ /fax 0828 81 18 51; Via Litoranea Linora; 2 person sites high season €31.50; ☽ Mar-Sep) About 6km north of Agropoli along the Litoranea road, this camp site beside the beach has all the facilities and is a short drive from Paestum.

Hotel Carola (☎ 0974 82 64 22; fax 0974 82 64 25; Via Pisacane 1; s/d with bathroom & breakfast high season €63/82, full meals around €25; ✂ Ⓟ) Not far from the tourist harbour, this welcoming hotel has big, well-appointed rooms with all the creature comforts. You can also eat at its highly rated restaurant.

Pizzeria U'Sghiz (☎ 0974 82 45 82; Piazza Umberto I; pizzas from €2.50) Purists will blanch but the pizzas here are made with wholemeal flour – an original touch that works. Served ready-cut, the pizzas come with the topping specified and nothing else, so if you want tomato or mozzarella you'll have to ask for them.

Velia

The **ruins** (☎ 0974 97 23 96; admission €2; ☽ 9am-6pm Mon-Sat) of the Greek settlement of Elea, founded in the mid-6th century BC and later a popular spot for wealthy Romans, are worth a visit only if you have the time. The ruins here are considerably smaller than those at Paestum, and in a far worse state.

Prices at **Albergo Elea** (☎ /fax 0974 97 15 77; Via Elea 69; s/d with bathroom €35/70, half board per person €35) in nearby Ascea, conveniently near the water, are negotiable outside summer.

The train station for Ascea is at Marina di Ascea. To get to the ruins from there, wait for a local bus to Castellamare di Velia.

South to Sapri

From Ascea to Sapri, a dowdy seaside town a few kilometres short of Basilicata, the road climbs, dips and curves its way through country that, while not Italy's prettiest, is rarely dull and at times is spectacular. The beaches along this part of the coast are good and the water usually crystal-clear.

Pisciotta, 12km southeast of Ascea, is an attractive medieval village that clings to the mountainside.

Agriturismo San Carlo (☎ /fax 0974 97 61 77; Via Noce 8; B&B per person €30, half/full board per person €35/40) is a bargain place to stay and eat. It also produces a remarkable olive oil from the unique local Pisciotta olive trees.

Another 25km or so further on, southeast of the resort town of Palinuro (in and around which are camp sites and several hotels), are some striking white-sand **beaches**. A little further still, where the road turns steeply inland to pass through San Giovanni a Piro, is Marina di Camerota, which has a small medieval centre. From there it's another 25km to Sapri. If you get this far you should really make the effort to continue the short distance into Basilicata (p686).

Puglia, Basilicata & Calabria

CONTENTS

Italy's deep south is little known to foreign visitors. But venture into these parts and you'll be rewarded with an unforgettable experience, for no other regions so clearly reveal the contradictory nature of Italy and the Italians. Uplifting natural beauty and a near-tropical sea are often minutes from soul-destroying urban sprawl; architectural gems sit beside illegal construction on a rampant scale; and a generosity of spirit goes hand in hand with a mean-minded suspicion of outsiders.

These southern regions are Italy's poorest but also the least populated – a decided advantage for travellers wanting to get off the beaten track. However, don't expect to be alone by the sea in summer – this is where Italians take their August holidays.

While you won't find the sumptuous artistic treasures of Rome or Florence, the architecture in these regions is of particular interest. It was along the Ionian coast that the Greeks first established the colonies of Magna Graecia and evidence of this is everywhere. Successive eras of Norman, Swabian, Angevin and Spanish rule all left a diverse heritage of churches, fortresses and other monuments. No-one, however, is able to place the strange conical-roofed stone houses, the *trulli,* unique to Puglia. Of the three regions, history has dealt Puglia the better hand. Basilicata and Calabria have often been left to their own devices and still today a sense of weary resignation is a pervasive reality.

HIGHLIGHTS

■ **Coastline**

The magnificent Promontorio del Gargano (pp651–6)

■ **Architecture**

Lecce's over-the-top baroque palaces (pp671–5)

■ **Rock Life**

Matera's *sassi,* hewn from rock (pp683–4)

■ **Original Design**

The *trulli* dotted around Puglia's Valle d'Itria (pp664–8)

■ **Hiking**

Calabria's Sila Massif mountain range (pp695–6)

■ **Greek Sculpture**

The perfect form of the Bronzi di Riace sculptures in Reggio di Calabria (pp696–9)

■ **Underground**

The incredible cave system, the Grotte di Castellana (pp665–6)

(map labels: Promontorio del Gargano; Valle d'Itria; Grotte di Castellana; Matera; Lecce; Sila Massif; Reggio di Calabria)

POPULATION:	■ PUGLIA 3,983,487	■ BASILICATA 595,727	■ CALABRIA 1,993,274
AREA:	■ PUGLIA 19,348 SQ KM	■ BASILICATA 9,992 SQ KM	■ CALABRIA 15,080 SQ KM

PUGLIA

Puglia, the 'heel' of Italy's boot, is bordered by two seas, the Adriatic to the east and Ionian to the south. This strategic position, combined with more than 800km of difficult-to-defend coastline, has shaped the region's history. As today illegal immigrants and smugglers bypass the coast's defences, so in the past foreign invaders stormed in.

The first were the Greeks who in the 8th-century BC founded Magna Graecia, a string of settlements along the Ionian coast. The major city was Taras (Taranto), which was settled by Spartan exiles and dominated the region until defeat by the Romans in 272 BC.

Less than 100 years later, in 190 BC, the Romans completed Via Appia, which ran from Rome to Brindisi, as it still does. The Norman legacy is seen in magnificent Romanesque churches across the region; Foggia and its province were favoured by the great Swabian king, Frederick II, several of whose castles remain; and Lecce, richly baroque, bears the architectural mark of its Spanish colonisers.

Highlights include the sanctuary dedicated to St Michael the Archangel (San Michele Arcangelo) at Monte Sant'Angelo; the mysterious octagonal Castel del Monte near Andria; and the extraordinary floor mosaic in Otranto's cathedral.

Natural wonders also abound. The stark Isole Tremiti, the ancient Foresta Umbra on the Promontorio del Gargano and the beautiful beaches of the Penisola Salentina (Salentine Peninsula) are all magnificent places to visit. And that's not even mentioning the food.

To get the best out of Puglia, and indeed the whole of the south, your own transport is an advantage and, at times, essential.

FOGGIA
pop 154,760

Foggia is an unfortunate example of what earthquakes, WWII bombs and modern construction can do to a city. Shabby and largely charmless, it sits amid the patchwork landscape of the broad Tavoliere plain. An important transport junction, it has little to offer the visitor other than connections with San Giovanni Rotondo and the forests and beaches of the Promontorio del Gargano. The nearby towns of Troia and Lucera are also worth a visit; the former for its Romanesque cathedral and Lucera for its Swabian-Angevin castle.

A TASTE OF PUGLIA

Puglia is a food- and wine-lover's paradise – no matter how hard you try, it's difficult to eat badly here. One reason is that the fresh produce is of such high quality. Indeed, many of the basic elements of the Italian kitchen originate from Puglia – a huge proportion of Italy's fish is caught off the extensive Puglian coast, 80% of Europe's pasta is produced here and up to 80% of Italy's olive oil originates in Puglia and Calabria.

Tomatoes, broccoli, chicory, fennel, figs, melons, cherries and grapes are just some of the choice fruits and vegetables you'll find. Almonds, grown near Ruvo di Puglia, are used in many traditional cakes and pastries.

Like their Greek forbears, the folk of Puglia eat a lot of *agnello* (lamb) and *capretto* (kid). The meat is usually roasted or grilled with aromatic herbs, or served in tomato-based sauces.

Fish and seafood are abundant. Raw fish (such as anchovies or baby squid) marinated in olive oil and lemon juice is not uncommon. *Cozze* (mussels) are prepared in a variety of ways. One recipe from the Bari area, *tiella alla barese*, has mussels baked with rice and potatoes.

Bread and pasta are both fundamental to the Puglian diet, with per-capita consumption at least double that of the USA. The best bread comes from Altamura. You'll find *orecchiette* (small ear-shaped pasta, sometimes called *strascinati*) in most places, often served with vegetable toppings. Other common Puglian pasta shapes are *cavatelli* and *capunti*.

Many quality wines are produced on the Penisola Salentina (the Salice Salentino is one of the best reds), in the *trulli* area around Locorotondo (home to a cool dry white of the same name), and in the plains around Foggia and Lucera. Some of Italy's best rosé wines hail from Puglia and perfectly complement the local cuisine.

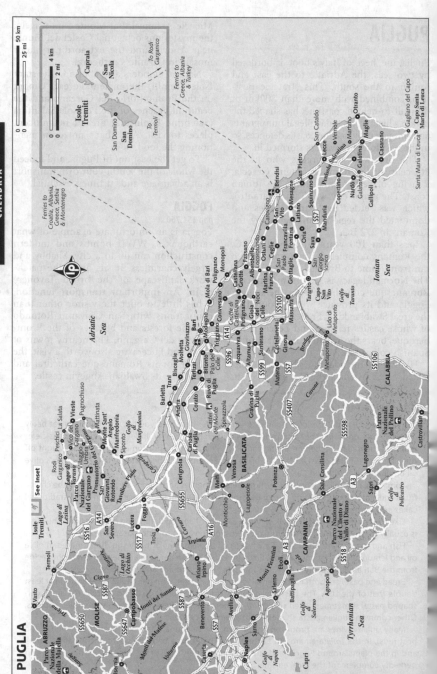

In the 12th century the town was one of Swabian king Frederick II's favourites, but it later declined under the rule of the Spanish house of Aragon.

Orientation

Train and bus stations face Piazza Vittorio Veneto, on the north rim of the town. Viale XXIV Maggio leads south into Piazza Cavour. On or around the Viale are several hotels, restaurants and shops, as well as the post and telephone offices. From Piazza Cavour, Via Lanza leads to Corso Vittorio Emanuele II and what remains of the old quarter.

Information

EMERGENCY
Police Station (☎ 0881 66 81 11; Via Gramsci Antonio 1)

POST
Post Office (Viale XXIV Maggio)

TELEPHONE & FAX
Telecom Office (Via Piave 29; ☺ 8am-9pm)

TOURIST INFORMATION
Tourist Office (☎ 0881 72 36 50; 1st fl, Via Senatore Emilio Perrone 17; ☺ 8am-1.30pm Mon-Fri) From Piazza Cavour, head south along Corso P Giannone. Take the third turning left into Via Cirillo and go straight on until Piazzale Puglia – Via Perrone is on the right.

Sights

The **cathedral** (☎ 0881 77 34 82; off Corso Vittorio Emanuele; ☺ 7am-12.30pm & 5-8pm) is Foggia's only noteworthy sight. Built in the 12th century, the lower section remains true to the original Romanesque style. The top half, exuberantly baroque, was grafted on after an earthquake. Most of the cathedral's treasures were lost in the quake but you can see a Byzantine icon preserved in a chapel inside the church. Legend has it that in the 11th century shepherds discovered the icon lying in a pond over which burned three flames. These flames are now the symbol of the city.

The **Museo Civico** (☎ 0881 72 62 45; Piazza Nigri; admission free; ☺ 8am-2pm Sun- Fri & 3.30pm-7pm Tue & Thu) houses archaeological finds from the province. At the time of writing the museum was closed for restoration.

Sleeping & Eating

Albergo Venezia (☎ 0881 77 09 03; Via Piave 40; s/d with bathroom & breakfast €43/60). Rooms at this conveniently central hotel have all the charm of a doctor's waiting room. However, they're functional and reasonable value for money.

Hotel Europa (☎ 0881 72 10 57; www.hoteleuropa fgtin.it; Via Monfalcone 52; s/d/ste with bathroom & breakfast €57/83/124; ✗) About 50m from the train station, this place has nicely fitted rooms. For a few euros more you can enjoy their suites, which are considerably larger and decked out in some style.

Hotel Cicolella (☎ 0881 56 61 11; www.hotelcicole lla.isnet.it; Viale XXIV Maggio 60; s/d with bathroom €110/170; ✗) Founded more than 100 years ago, this Foggia landmark is a delightful blend of old-world charm spiced with contemporary efficiency. Rooms come with all the requisite mod cons.

There are several trattorie in the side streets west of Viale XXIV Maggio.

Ristorante L'Angolo Preferito (☎ 0881 70 85 90; Via Trieste 21; meals from €15) The menu, which changes daily and is announced by the waiter, makes heavy use of local produce – good news as Foggia is in the middle of farm country. Dishes are simple, well cooked and tasty.

Ristorante Margutta (☎ 0881 70 80 60; Via Piave 33; meals €25) This friendly family restaurant near Albergo Venezia is very popular and often full. It specialises in fish dishes and offers a small but select menu.

Getting There & Around

BUS
Buses depart from Piazzale Vittorio Veneto, in front of the train station, for towns throughout the province of Foggia.

SITA (☎ 0881 77 31 17; www.sita-on-line.it, Italian only) runs buses to Vieste (€4.65, 2¾ hours, five daily) via Manfredonia (€1.80, 50 minutes), Monte Sant'Angelo (€3.65, 1½ hours, seven daily), San Giovanni Rotondo (€2.60, one hour, frequent), Lucera (€1.30, 30 minutes, eight daily) and Campobasso in Molise (€5.70, 1½ hours, two daily).

Ferrovie del Gargano (☎ 0881 72 51 88; www .ferroviedelgargano.com, Italian only) serves Manfredonia (€1.80, 45 minutes, frequent), Troia (€1.50, 50 minutes, frequent) and Barletta (€4.10, two hours, 11 daily).

Tickets for both companies are available from the tobacconist at the train station or the bar opposite under the Cinema Ariston sign.

CLP (☎ 081 531 17 06 in Naples) runs six direct autostrada (motorway) buses daily, connecting Foggia with Naples (€9) – they're a faster option than the train. Buy your ticket on board.

CAR & MOTORCYCLE
Take the SS16 south for Bari or north for the Adriatic coast, Termoli and Pescara. The Bologna-Bari A14 also passes Foggia. For Naples, take the SS655, which links with the east–west A16.

TRAIN
There's a frequent service from Foggia to Bari (€14.50, 1¼ hours) and on to Brindisi (€24, 2½ hours) and Lecce (€25, 2½ hours). Northwards, up to 10 trains daily head for Pescara, Ancona (€29, 3½ hours) and Bologna (€42, 5½ hours), from where three trains daily continue to Milan (€53, 7½ hours).

LUCERA
pop 35,940 / elevation 219m
Like many towns in the south, Lucera does its best to surround its charms with scruffy suburbs. Less than 20km west of Foggia, it's worth a visit for its Swabian castle and unusual history.

The site was first settled in the 4th century BC by the Romans, who named it Luceria Augusta. The fall of the Empire meant decay for the town but Frederick II resuscitated it in the 13th century. Arab bandits had become a growing problem in Sicily, so Frederick decided to remove the thorn from his side by relocating all of them to Puglia. Some 20,000 were dispatched to Lucera, where the emperor allowed them to build mosques and practise Islam freely. From the Arabs of Lucera he recruited his famous Saracen bodyguard, who accompanied him on his journeys between castles and even to the Crusades against their fellow Saracens.

The French occupiers replaced many of the town's mosques with Gothic churches when Charles I of Anjou conquered Lucera in 1269, and in 1300 his successor, Charles II, had all the Arabs slaughtered.

Sights
The imposing **castle** (admission free; ☯ 8am-2.30pm & 4-8pm Tue-Sun), which stands on the town's highest point, was built by Frederick II in 1233. Charles II of Anjou added its external walls, which form a pentagon guarded by 24 towers. The remains stand in the northeastern corner of the enclosure. Excavations have also revealed the remains of Roman buildings.

In the centre of the old town, the **cathedral** (☯ 8am-noon & 4-7pm) was begun by Charles II in 1300 to celebrate the defeat of the Saracens. It is considered the best example of Angevin architecture in southern Italy. The Gothic **Chiesa di San Francesco** (☯ 8am-noon & 4-7pm) was also erected by the prolific Charles II.

On the eastern outskirts of town is a poorly maintained 1st-century-BC **Roman amphitheatre** (admission free; ☯ 8am-2.30pm & 4-8pm Tue-Sun).

Sleeping
Hotel La Balconata 2 (☎ 0881 52 09 98; www.labalconata.it; Via Ferrovia 15; s/d with bathroom & breakfast €35/60; 🅿) Just outside the old city gate, this friendly place offers rooms decorated with an eye to style. The views over the seemingly endless plains of the Tavoliere are also impressive.

The hotel also owns and acts as reception for the more economical **Albergo Al Passetto** (Piazza del Popolo; s/d with bathroom & breakfast €26/45), on the inside of the city gate and great value for money.

Getting There & Away
Lucera is easily accessible from Foggia by SITA buses (€2.30, 30 minutes, five daily), which terminate in Piazza del Popolo, or by Ferrovia del Gargano buses, which cover the same route.

TROIA
The village of Troia, 18km south of Lucera, has nothing to do with the Troy of legend. However, its beautiful Puglian-Romanesque **cathedral** (Piazza Episcopio) merits a visit. Set into the main facade is a splendid 13th-century rose window, while beneath it is a pair of richly wrought 12th-century bronze portals. Gargoyles and other creatures adorn the exterior, and there are hints of Oriental influence. Once inside, seek out the superbly sculpted pulpit. At the time of writing the cathedral was closed for restoration.

Albergo Alba d'Oro (☎ 0881 97 04 25; Viale Kennedy 28; s/d with bathroom €30/46; 🅿) From the outside this place seems not to exist, but ring the bell and you'll find that the welcome is warm and rooms are simple without frills. It's about 10 minutes' walk to the centre.

Regular Ferrovie del Gargano buses link Troia and Foggia.

MANFREDONIA

pop 57,884

Founded by the Swabian king Manfred, Frederick II's illegitimate son, this port town has little to attract tourists other than a majestic castle and transport connections to the Promontorio del Gargano.

Intercity buses and trains both terminate in central Piazza Marconi. From there, semipedestrianised Corso Manfredi leads to Piazza del Popolo after 300m and to the tourist office (☎ 0884 58 19 98; Piazza del Popolo 11; ☼ 8.30am-1.30pm Mon-Fri).

Sights

Guarding the far end of Corso Manfredi is the town's **castle** (admission €2.50; ☼ 8.30am-7.30pm daily except 1st & last Mon of month). The building was started by Manfred and completed by Charles of Anjou. Within it, the **Museo Archeologico Nazionale del Gargano** displays local finds.

About 2km south of town is **Siponto**, an important port from Roman to medieval times, when it was abandoned in favour of Manfredonia because of earthquakes and malaria. Apart from the **beaches**, the only thing of interest is the distinctly Byzantine-looking 11th-century Romanesque **Chiesa di Santa Maria di Siponto**.

Sleeping & Eating

Hotel Sipontum (☎ /fax 0884 54 29 16; Viale di Vittorio 229; s/d with bathroom €26/41) This hotel won't win any marks for glamour, but the rooms are clean. To get here take bus No 2 from the centre and it's virtually the last building on the left before you leave town.

Ristorante Coppolarossa (☎ 0884 58 25 22; Via dei Celestini 13; meals €26-31) This jovial family-run restaurant comes highly recommended. Specialising in seafood, it grills, fries and boils with panache, producing dishes of high quality. As a starter the seafood buffet (€7) is difficult to top.

Getting There & Away

Regular trains and both **SITA** (☎ 0881 77 31 17) and **Ferrovie del Gargano** (☎ 0881 72 51 88) buses

connect Manfredonia with Foggia and Bari, while SITA has seven buses daily to/from Vieste (1¾ hours). There are also frequent buses daily to/from Monte Sant'Angelo. Get tickets and timetable information from Bar Impero on Piazza Marconi, from where all services leave.

PROMONTORIO DEL GARGANO (GARGANO PROMONTORY)

The Promontorio del Gargano is one of the most beautiful areas in southern Italy. Characterised by white limestone cliffs, a crystal-clear green sea, beautiful beaches and ancient forests, the 'spur' of the Italian boot has something for everyone. The magnificent flora and fauna of the **Parco Nazionale del Gargano** is an obvious attraction, but there's also two historic pilgrim destinations, Monte Sant'Angelo and San Giovanni Rotondo.

Nowadays a popular tourist playground, the Gargano's beach resorts, especially around Vieste and Peschici, are developing rapidly to accommodate the annual influx of sun- and fun-seekers.

Foresta Umbra

The ancient beeches and oaks of the Foresta Umbra, in the promontory's mountainous interior, make up one of Italy's last remaining original forests. Walkers and mountain-bikers will find plenty of well-marked trails within the forest's 15,000 hectares and there are several picnic areas.

At the Villaggio Umbra, in the heart of the forest, the Corpo Forestale dello Stato runs a **visitors centre** housing a small **museum and nature centre** (☎ 0884 56 09 44; admission €1; ☼ 9am-5pm Jun-Sep). The main **park office** is, however, in Monte Sant'Angelo (☎ 0884 56 89 01; Via Abate 121). Here they can organise guided walks and tours in the forest and throughout the peninsula.

Specialist tour operators within the Gargano Promontory zone also organise excursions throughout the parkland. Based in Foggia, **Blue Animation Team** (☎ 0881 70 86 66; Vico Cervo 3) leads five-hour night-time walks (€20) and four-hour mountain-bike rides (€18). Prices include minibus transfer, equipment hire and picnic. From Vieste, **Agenzia Kelian** (☎ 0884 70 23 44; Via Firenze 3) and **Agenzia Sol** (☎ 0884 70 15 58; Via Trepiccioni 5) both lead trekking and biking excursions.

PUGLIA, BASILICATA & CALABRIA

Monte Sant'Angelo
pop 14,184 / elevation 796m

You know as soon as you arrive in Monte Sant'Angelo that it's important. You know because the hustlers move in, pushing everything from car-parking space to kitsch religious souvenirs. But these rogues have been operating for centuries, for as long as pilgrims have been coming to this isolated mountain town overlooking the south coast of the Gargano. The object of devotion is the Santuario di San Michele. Here, in AD 490, St Michael the Archangel is said to have appeared in a grotto before the Bishop of Siponto.

During the Middle Ages, the sanctuary marked the end of the pilgrims' Route of the Angel, which began in Normandy and passed through Rome. In AD 999, Holy Roman Emperor Otto III made a pilgrimage to the sanctuary to pray that prophecies of the end of the world in the year 1000 would not be fulfilled. The sanctuary's fame grew after the widely predicted apocalypse proved to be a damp squib.

SIGHTS

As you descend the steps to the **Santuario di San Michele** (admission free; ⏰ 7.30am-7.30pm Mon-Sat, 6.30am-7.30pm Sun Jul-Sep; shorter hours in winter) note the graffiti, some of it the work of 17th-century pilgrims. St Michael is said to have left a footprint in stone inside the grotto, so it became customary for pilgrims to carve outlines of their feet and hands and leave accompanying messages.

Finely etched Byzantine bronze and silver doors open into the grotto itself. Inside, a 16th-century statue of the archangel covers the site of his footprint. To its left is an imposing marble bishop's chair resting on two lions, while behind the main altar is a small fountain of legendary 'healing' waters, now sealed.

Once outside, head down the short flight of steps opposite the sanctuary to the **Tomba di Rotari** (admission €0.60), which is, in fact, not a tomb but a 12th-century baptistry. Notice the deep basin sunk into the floor for total immersion, US Southern Baptist style. You enter the baptistry through the facade of the **Chiesa di San Pietro**, with its intricate rose window all that remains of the church, destroyed by a 19th-century earthquake. The Romanesque portal of the adjacent

11th-century **Chiesa di Santa Maria Maggiore** has some fine bas-reliefs. Within are some well-preserved medieval frescoes.

The serpentine alleyways and jumbled houses of this town are perfect for a little aimless ambling. Commanding the highest point is a Norman **castle** (admission €1.55; ⏰ 8am-7pm summer, 9am-1pm & 2.30-6pm winter) with Swabian and Aragonese additions. Take time too to head for the **belvedere**, a specially situated building that gives visitors sweeping views of the coast.

SLEEPING & EATING

You're better off staying elsewhere. Surprisingly, in a place that teems with visitors, accommodation is limited.

In a complex 1km downhill from the historic centre are two hotels offering similar facilities at identical prices.

Rotary Hotel (☎ 0884 56 21 46; Via Pulsano; s/d with bathroom & breakfast high season €52/73; 🏊) Rooms are standard but the views over the rock-strewn landscape are anything but. The hotel also has a decent restaurant (tourist menu €15).

Hotel Sant'Angelo (☎ 0884 56 55 36; www.hotel santangelo.com; Via Pulsano; s/d with bathroom & breakfast high season €52/73) The recent addition to the duo, this hotel has a wonderful panoramic balcony where its restaurant meals are served.

La Jalantuúmene (☎ 0884 56 54 84; Piazza de Galganis 5; set menu €25) This restaurant is justifiably recommended by everyone. It serves excellent fare, accompanied by a long, select wine list, in picturesque surroundings. In summer, tables spill into the petite piazza.

Don't leave town without tasting the local sweets, *ostie ripiene* (literally, 'stuffed hosts'; two wafers like the hosts used at Mass with a filling of caramelised almonds).

GETTING THERE & AWAY

Monte Sant'Angelo is accessible by **SITA** (☎ 0881 77 31 17) bus from Foggia, Manfredonia, Vieste and San Giovanni Rotondo. Buy tickets from Bar Esperia next to the sanctuary.

Vieste
pop 13,514

The most popular seaside resort on the promontory and the best equipped with tourist facilities, Vieste is a bright little place in summer. In winter it more or less closes down, which is handy for getting away from things, less so for finding places to sleep and eat.

The better beaches are to the south, between Vieste and Pugnochiuso, and to the north towards Peschici, particularly in the area known as La Salata.

ORIENTATION & INFORMATION

From Piazzale Manzoni, where intercity buses terminate, a 10-minute walk east along Via XXIV Maggio, which becomes Corso Fazzini, brings you to the old town and the attractive promenade of the Marina Piccola. The pink **tourist office** (☎ 0884 70 88 06; Piazza Kennedy; ☉ 8am-1.30pm Mon-Fri & 4pm-7pm Tue-Thu Nov-Mar, 8am-1.30pm & 3-9pm Mon-Sat Apr-Oct) is at the south end of the Marina. The post office is on Piazza Vittorio Veneto, where there are also several public telephones.

SIGHTS & ACTIVITIES

The old town, with its whitewashed houses and winding medieval streets, offers a couple of sights of interest, although tourists come here for the beaches rather than the history. The **cathedral** is Puglian-Romanesque but underwent alterations in the 18th century.

Head up to the **Chianca Amara** (Bitter Stone; Via Cimaglia), on which thousands of citizens were beheaded when the Turks sacked Vieste in the 16th century. Nearby, at the town's highest point, is a **castle**, built by Frederick II. It's now occupied by the military and closed to the public although the tourist office can organise guided tours.

The **Museo Malacologico** (Mollusc Museum; ☎ 0884 70 55 12; Via Pola 8; admission free; ☉ 9.30am-noon & 5pm-midnight) contains a huge collection of seashells from all over the world.

At the port, **Centro Ormeggi e Sub** (☎ 0884 70 79 83; May-Sep) offers diving courses in English and rents out sailing and motorboats.

If you're just after a beach and don't have your own transport, **Spiaggia del Castello** is 1km south of town.

SLEEPING

Most of Vieste's many hotels and *pensioni* are scattered along the beachfront roads north and south of town. Camp sites (as many as 80) abound, particularly along Lungomare E Mattei to the south.

THE WORLD'S MOST MARKETED MONK

On 16 June 2002 the most recognisable monk in Italy took his place in the pantheon of saints. Before an estimated 300,000 devotees, Padre Pio (1887–1968) became the 457th saint to be canonised by Pope John Paul II.

To permit this, the Church had, of course, to have a proven miracle; reputation doesn't cut it with the Vatican. Step forward a seven-year-old boy who in February 2000 had defied medical opinion and made a miraculous recovery from meningitis. It was all thanks to Padre Pio, the boy told his mum. Apparently, the good father had appeared to the comatose boy telling him he'd be cured. No sooner said than done. Pio's long reputation as a miracle-worker was thus rubber-stamped.

But for his millions of fans worldwide the proof already existed. The evidence was overwhelming – the way he literally came out smelling of roses; the stigmata which appeared on his hands; and his reputed wrestling with the devil, who appeared before him sometimes in the guise of a black cat, sometimes as a naked woman.

Padre Pio spent most of his life in **San Giovanni Rotondo** where he arrived in 1916 as an ailing Capuchin priest in need of a cooler climate. San Giovanni Rotondo was then a tiny, isolated medieval village in the heart of the Gargano, but as Pio's fame grew so the village underwent something of a miraculous transformation, expanding well beyond its original limits. These days, about eight million pilgrims a year pile into town.

The tomb of Padre Pio lies in the modern **sanctuary** (admission free; ☉ 5.30am-8pm), within which is his **cell** (☉ 7.30am-noon & 3.30-6.30pm). The sanctuary is at the heart of a vast complex that also includes the Home for the Relief of Suffering, one of Italy's premier hospitals (established by Pio), and a new church, still under construction, which will seat over 7000 faithful.

SITA buses run five times daily to/from Monte Sant'Angelo and over 10 buses daily serve both Manfredonia and Foggia.

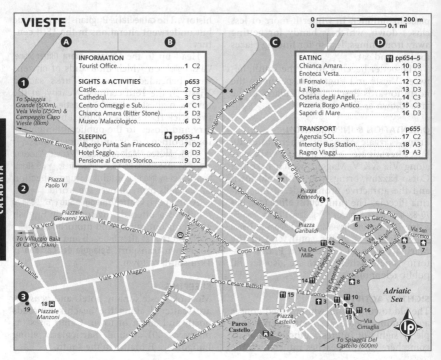

VIESTE

Albergo Punta San Francesco (☎ 0884 70 14 22; www.viestedoc.it/hotelpuntasanfrancesco.htm; Via San Francesco 2; s/d with bathroom & breakfast high season €70/55; ❄) One of the few places in town to remain open in winter, this tasteful hotel occupies a one-time olive-oil factory. The welcome is warm and the rooms are decorated in a simple, understated style.

Vela Velo (☎ 0884 70 63 03; velavelo@viesteonline.it; Lungomare Europa 19; s/d with bathroom & breakfast high season from €40/65; ☾ Easter–mid-Oct) Vela Velo is ideal for water-sports enthusiasts as the hotel has its own windsurfing school. It's situated some 600m north of the old town; prices include access to a private beach and free mountain-bike use.

Pensione al Centro Storico (☎ 0884 70 70 30; cstorico@viesteonline.it; Via Mafrolla 32; s/d with bathroom & breakfast high season €35/55; ☾ Easter–Oct) Old-fashioned hospitality is offered at this historic *pensione*. In a former convent in the old quarter, it has large, high-ceilinged rooms. The terrace, where breakfast is served, offers magnificent views over the port.

Hotel Seggio (☎ 0884 70 81 23; hotel.seggio@ tiscalinet.it; Via Veste 7; d with bathroom & breakfast from €65, full board per person €45-78; ☾ Apr-Oct; ❄ ⊘) Occupying a 17th-century *palazzo* where the town council once sat, this comfortable hotel has a private pool, beach and sunbathing terraces – everything you need for the Puglian summer.

Campeggio Capo Vieste (☎ 0884 70 63 26; Litoranea Vieste Peschici Km 8; person/tent/car high season €9/ 12/4; ☾ Apr-Oct) This camp site is at La Salata, between Vieste and Peschici, and accessible by Ferrovie del Gargano bus.

Villaggio Baia di Campi (☎ 0884 70 00 00; person/tent/car high season €8.30/9.30/3.10; ☾ Apr-Oct) Here's another good camping option, near Pugnochiuso on the coast road between Vieste and Mattinata.

EATING

Pizzeria Borgo Antico (☎ 0884 70 24 82; Corso Cesare Battisti 11; pizza & beer €11) This unpretentious place has the decided advantage of being open in winter when most other places are not. Its pizzas are made the proper way – in a wood oven – and taste as they should.

Sapori di Mare (☎ 0884 70 79 79; Via Judeca 30; meals €22; ☾ Jun-Sep) At the end of Via

Cimaglia in the old town, this is a panoramic spot for a fish dinner or just a cool drink while savouring the glorious view of sea and coastline.

Osteria degli Angeli (☎ 0884 70 11 12; Via Celestino V 50; meals €20; ☯ late-May–Sep) Near the cathedral, this is a friendly restaurant offering fine cooking. A house speciality worth trying is *troccoli dell'angeli* (pasta with prawns).

Enoteca Vesta (☎ 0884 70 64 11; Via Duomo 14; meals €25) If your wine is as important as your food this is the place for you. This restaurant, housed in a cave, maintains a magnificent selection of Puglian wines to tickle the palate.

La Ripa (☎ 0884 70 80 48; Via Cimaglia 16; meals from €25; ☯ Mar-Oct) This is an atmospheric place to sample some live seafood, the house speciality. The Ripa, dating mostly from the 16th century, resembles a minimuseum of objects collected by the owner over the years.

For a snack on the go, head to **Il Fornaio** (Via Fazzini 1) near the entrance to the old town, which serves tasty pizza by the slice, or **Chianca Amara** (Via Cimaglia 4) for typical local cakes and pastries.

GETTING THERE & AROUND
Vieste's port is just north of the old town, about a five-minute walk from the tourist office. In summer, several companies with ticket offices at the port, including Adriatica and Motonave, run boats to the Isole Tremiti. There's at least one boat daily from June to September and a return trip costs €26.

Many companies also offer tours of the caves that pock the Gargano coast. A typical three-hour tour costs around €10.

Buses operated by **SITA** (☎ 0881 77 31 17) run between Vieste and Foggia (€4.75, 2¾ hours, five daily) via Manfredonia, while the **Ferrovie del Gargano** (☎ 0881 72 51 88) bus and train network connects the town with Peschici, Rodi Garganico and other towns on the promontory. Buses terminate at Piazzale Manzoni and timetables are posted outside **Ragno Viaggi** (☎ 0884 70 15 28) on the square. Services connecting coastal towns are frequent in summer and almost nonexistent at other times of the year.

Agenzia SOL (☎ 0884 70 15 58; sol@solvieste.it; Via Trepiccioni 5) sells bus and boat tickets and can provide information on walking and cycling opportunities, plus boat hire. They also hire out mountain bikes (per day/week from €10/50) and cars (per day from €46).

Peschici

On a rocky outcrop above a sparkling bay, Peschici is a lovely little town which, while a fast-developing resort, remains relatively unspoiled.

Whitewashed houses reminiscent of Greek island villages line cobbled alleyways with suggestive names – Vico Purgatorio (Purgatory Lane), Via Malconsiglio and Via Buonconsiglio (Bad Advice and Good Advice Streets). Their origins are anyone's guess; Vico Stretto (Narrow Lane) is more straightforward.

Peschici's sandy beaches and hotels fill up in summer, so book well in advance.

ORIENTATION & INFORMATION
The medieval and more interesting part of town clings to the cliff top at the point of the bay, while the newer parts extend inland and around the bay. In winter, buses terminate beside Chiesa di San Antonio. For the rest of the year, the terminal is beside the sports ground, uphill from the town's main street, Corso Garibaldi. Turn right into the corso and walk straight ahead to reach the old town.

There is a small **tourist office** (☎ 0884 96 27 97; Corso Garibaldi 57; ☯ 10.30am-12.30pm & 5.30-7.30pm Mon-Fri, 10.30am-12.30pm Sat) with useful accommodation information.

SLEEPING & EATING
Peschici has several hotels and *pensioni* but prices tend to be expensive and many insist upon a minimum of half board. Numerous camp sites dot the coast east and west of Peschici.

Locanda al Castello (☎ 0884 96 40 38; Piazza Castello 29; d with bathroom & breakfast from €60, half/full board per person high season €55/70) Arriving at this cheerful place is like entering a family home. The welcome is genuine and the atmosphere unstuffy. Situated right by the cliffs, it is definitely the pick of the old quarter, with fine sea views. It also runs a decent restaurant (full meal about €18) and neighbouring pizzeria (evenings only).

Hotel Timiana (☎ /fax 0884 96 43 21; Viale Libeta 73; full board per person €42-73; ☯ mid-Apr-mid-Sep;

⊠ ⓐ) Set in its own pine-rich grounds 800m from the sea, Hotel Timiana has cool white rooms ideal for an afternoon siesta. It offers a free shuttle bus to the beach and serves delicious local dishes in its restaurant.

Pensione La Torretta (☎ /fax 0884 96 29 35; Via Torretta 13; full board per person €38-80) A relative newcomer, this *pensione* offers simple, un-cluttered rooms, some with sea views. There is a large panoramic balcony where meals are served and drinks taken. A bargain out of season.

Baia San Nicola (☎ /fax 0884 96 42 31; person/ tent/car high season €8.60/8/3.50; ☷ mid-May–mid-Oct) Situated on one of the most beautiful bays in the Gargano, this camp site is 2km out of town on the road towards Vieste. It of-fers all the usual facilities and can organise windsurfing lessons and equipment hire.

Camping Parco degli Ulivi (☎ 0884 96 34 04; person/tent/car high season €9.90/8.50/2.90; ⓐ) Sites here are shaded by the olive trees so char-acteristic of these parts. It's a few kilometres west on the road to Rodi Garganico and boasts a pool and private beach.

Ristorante La Taverna (☎ 0884 96 41 97; Traversa di Via Castello 6; meals from €20) If you're tall you'll need to mind your head as you stoop into this cosy, characterful place just off Via Castello, in the heart of the old town. The old boys who cook here like to see their customers eat well.

GETTING THERE & AWAY

Ferrovie del Gargano serves Peschici. It runs buses to/from Vieste (seven daily) and has five trains daily to/from San Severo (with connections to/from Foggia) via Rodi Garganico. From April to September (daily from June), boats leave Peschici's port for the Isole Tremiti. For boat information and tickets, go to **Agrifoglio Tour** (☎ 0884 96 27 21; Piazza Sant'Antonio 3) or **CTM Compagnia de Navigazione** (☎ 0884 96 42 34; Corso Umberto I).

ISOLE TREMITI

Tell an Italian you're going to the Isole Tremiti and chances are they'll look at you enviously and start wistfully enthus-ing about the islands' beauty. It's no ex-aggeration either as the three islands that make up this small archipelago, 36km north of the Promontorio del Gargano, are stunning.

A convict station until the 1930s, San Domino, San Nicola and Capraia are now a popular summer day trip from the main-land. Out of season, most tourist facilities close down and the few permanent resi-dents resume their quiet, isolated lives.

Legend says that Diomedes, a Greek hero of the Trojan War, was buried here. A rare species of bird (the Diomedee) found on the islands are said to be his faithful warriors who continue to lament his death with their mournful cries. Early in the 11th century, Benedictine monks founded the Abbazia e Chiesa di Santa Maria (Abbey of St Maria) on San Nicola. The Bourbon King Ferdinand IV used the abbey as a jail, a tradition continued by the Fascists, who sent political exiles to the islands in the 1920s and 1930s.

Easily defensible, San Nicola was always the administrative and residential centre of the islands, while the lusher San Domino was used to grow crops. Nowadays, most of the islands' accommodation and other facilities are on San Domino.

Your boat will arrive at either San Dom-ino or San Nicola. Don't panic if you've been dropped off on the wrong island; small boats regularly make the brief cross-ing (€1.50 one way).

Sights & Activities
SAN NICOLA
Within the abbey complex is the **Abbazia e Chiesa di Santa Maria**, which features an 11th-century floor mosaic, a painted wooden Byzantine crucifix brought to the island in AD 747 and a black Madonna, probably transported here from Constantinople in the Middle Ages.

SAN DOMINO
San Domino has the islands' only sandy beach, which becomes extremely crowded in summer. However, there are several small coves where you can **swim** in the amazingly clear water off the rocks.

If you're feeling energetic, a **walking** track around the island starts at the far end of San Domino village, beyond Pensione Nassa. Alternatively, you could hire a bicycle from Jimmy Bike at Piazzetta San Domino. To hire a motorised rubber dinghy call ☎ 347 938 70 51 and expect to pay about €70 a day. Boats leave from San Domino's small port to visit the island's sea caves (€10) or to tour all three islands (€16).

CAPRAIA
The third of the islands, Capraia is completely uninhabited – by humans at least. Birdlife is plentiful and the flocks of seagulls make an impressive spectacle. There is no organised transport to the island as there's nothing to do once you get there, but if your curiosity gets the better of you, ask a local fisherman for a ride. You'll have to negotiate a rate and agree a time to return as otherwise you're in for a long night.

Sleeping & Eating
In summer you'll need to reserve well in advance. Out of season, phone to check that your chosen hotel is open. In the high season most hotels insist on full board – no bad idea, since eating options are limited.

Al Faro (☎ 0882 46 34 24; annalisalisci@tin.it; Via della Cantina Sperimentale, San Domino; half board per person €44-60; ☺ year-round) To get to this colourful place follow the only road up from the port and go straight for about 1km. Rooms here are decorated with paintings of sea life, so you might wake up face to face with a giant red fish.

Hotel Gabbiano (☎ 0882 46 34 10; www.hotel -gabbiano.com; Piazza Belvedere, San Domino; half/full board per person high season €88/99; ☺ year-round) Situated on the tiny piazza in San Domino, this hotel offers decent rooms with the usual three-star trappings and a terrace restaurant overlooking San Nicola.

To stock up on picnic fodder, **La Bottega dei Sapori** mini-market, opposite Al Faro, makes hearty *panini* (bread rolls with filling).

Getting There & Away
See Getting There & Away under Peschici (p656) and Vieste (p655), and under the Termoli (Molise) section (pp584–5 in the Abruzzo & Molise chapter.

TRANI
pop 53,923
Known as the 'Pearl of Puglia' Trani's magnificent port-side cathedral is one of the region's most photographed churches and a seriously good reason for visiting this charming town. Some 40km north-west along the coast from Bari, it makes an ideal base for exploring this part of Puglia – Barletta, Molfetta and Castel del Monte are all within easy reach.

Trani was important in the Middle Ages – the modern world's earliest written maritime code, the Ordinamenta Maris, was drawn up here in 1063 – and was at its height during the reign of Frederick II.

Orientation & Information
The **train station** (Piazza XX Settembre) is also the point of departure for most provincial buses. From it, Via Cavour leads through tree-lined Piazza della Repubblica, the main square, to Piazza Plebiscito and the public gardens. Turn left for the small picturesque harbour and the cathedral, spectacularly located on a rise at its northern end.

The helpful **tourist office** (☎ 0883 58 88 30; 1st fl, Palazzo Palmieri, Piazza Trieste; ☺ 8.30am-1.30pm Mon-Fri & 3-6pm Tue & Thu) is about 200m south of the cathedral.

Sights
CATHEDRAL
Started in 1097 on the site of a Byzantine church, the **cathedral** (☎ 0883 58 24 70; ☺ 8am-noon & 5-8pm Jun-Sep, 8.15am-12.15pm & 3.15-6.30pm Mon-Sat, 9am-12.45pm & 4-7pm Sun Oct-May), dedicated to St Nicholas the Pilgrim, was not completed until the 13th century. Its simple but imposing facade is decorated with blind arches. The original bronze doors of the main portal (now on display inside the church for conservation reasons) were cast by Barisano da Trani, an accomplished 12th-century artisan who also cast the bronze doors of the cathedral at Ravello and the side doors of the cathedral at Monreale.

The grand interior of the cathedral is stunningly simple in Norman style. Near the main altar, take a look at the remains of a 12th-century floor mosaic, similar in style to the one at Otranto. Below the church is the crypt, a forest of ancient columns, where the bones of St Nicholas are kept beneath the altar.

The crypt opens onto the Byzantine Chiesa di Santa Maria della Scala which itself sits on the **Ipogèo San Leucio**, a chamber believed to date from the 6th century.

CASTLE
The spiritual and the secular each powerfully announce their presence in Trani.

Some 200m north of the cathedral, the vast 13th-century **castle** (☎ 0883 50 66 03; Via Lionelli; admission €2; ⏰ 8.30am-7.30pm Sun-Fri & 8.30am-10.30pm Sat mid-Jun–mid-Sep) sits squat. and Built by Frederick II, then altered by the Angevins, it served until recently as a prison.

AROUND THE PORT

There are several interesting *palazzi* and churches around the picturesque port area. The 15th-century Gothic **Palazzo Caccetta** and nearby 12th-century **Chiesa di Ognissanti** (All Saints' Church) are both on Via Ognissanti, close to the cathedral. The Templars built the church as part of a hospital complex for knights injured in the crusades. From a different era, the 18th-century **Palazzo Palumbo-Quercia**, facing Piazza Quercia on the south side of the harbour, is also worth searching out.

Sleeping

Albergo Lucy (☎ 0883 48 10 22; Piazza Plebiscito 11; s/d with bathroom €36/42) This charming hotel in a restored 17th-century *palazzo* offers huge rooms full of character. The vaulted ceilings are high, letting in plenty of light, and the decor is unobtrusive. It's also ideally located close to the port.

Hotel Capirro (☎ 0883 58 07 12; Via Corato; s/d with bathroom €26/46.50) A concrete block of a building about 3km south of town, this huge hostelry is popular with Italian coach parties (for which read cheerful chaos). But at these prices you can't really ask for more. Take the bus for Corato at the train station.

Hotel Regia (☎ /fax 0883 58 44 44; Piazza Duomo 2; s/d with bathroom from €110/120) Magnificently located just across the road from the cathedral in the 18th-century Palazzo Filisio, this is style with a capital 'S'. Rooms are large with parquet flooring and the elegant furniture is perfectly suited. What's more, there's a good restaurant.

Eating

Pizza l'Ancora (☎ 0347 803 46 18; Via Banchina al Porto 10; pizzas about €4, meals €15-18; ⏰ Thu-Tue). The food at this easy-going seaside venue is plentiful and tasty. Given the location, much of the menu is given over to fish, which is cheerfully grilled, boiled or fried with appetising efficiency. The seafood salad as an antipasto makes a great meal opener.

Pizzeria Al Faro (☎ 0883 48 72 55; Via Statuti Marittimi 48; meals €15; ⏰ Thu-Tue) Another waterfront eatery, this is a good choice for a no-nonsense snack or *tavola calda* (cheap pre-prepared meal). The setting is wonderful, perfect for whiling away those heavy lunchtime hours.

La Darsena (☎ 0883 48 73 33; Via Statuti Marittimi 98; meals €25; ⏰ Tue-Sun) This is a stylish restaurant lined with pictures of Puglia in former days and occupying part of Palazzo Palumbo-Quercia. No prizes for guessing that the fish and seafood are particularly good.

Ristorante La Nicchia (☎ 0883 48 20 20; Via S Gervasio 69; meals €18; ⏰ Fri-Wed) This friendly town-centre trattoria is popular with locals who come for good food, convivial atmosphere and reasonable prices. Dishes make much use of high-quality Puglian produce.

There's a produce **market** (Piazza della Libertà; ⏰ mornings Mon-Sat) about 150m north of Piazza della Repubblica.

Getting There & Away

Buses operated by **STP** (☎ 0883 49 18 00) connect Trani with points along the coast and inland, including Barletta, Andria and Altamura. Services depart from in front of **Bar Desirée** (☎ 0883 49 10 30; Piazza XX Settembre), where timetables and tickets are available.

In July and August, at least one early-morning bus from Trani leaves in time to connect with the 8.30am service from Andria to Castel del Monte (pp659–60). The first return run to Andria leaves the castle at 3pm.

The SS16 runs through Trani, linking it to Bari and Foggia, or you can hook up with the A14 Bologna–Bari autostrada.

Trani is on the main train line between Bari and Foggia and is easily reached from towns along the coast.

AROUND TRANI
Barletta

About 13km northwest along the coast from Trani, Barletta is a fairly nondescript port town. Even so, it merits a quick visit for its cathedral, castle and the so-called Colossus, a Roman-era bronze statue in the town centre.

ORIENTATION & INFORMATION

From the train station, go down Via Giannone and through the municipal gardens. Turn right along Corso Garibaldi to reach

Barletta's centre. From the bus station on Via Manfredi, walk to Piazza Plebiscito and turn right to meet Corso Vittorio Emanuele.

There is a **tourist office** (☎ 0883 33 13 31; Corso Garibaldi 208; ☽ 8.30am-2pm & 5-7pm Tue & Thu) in the town centre.

SIGHTS

The 12th-century Puglian-Romanesque **cathedral** (Corso Garibaldi; ☽ open during church services) is among the region's better-preserved examples of this architectural style.

The imposing waterside **castle** (☎ 0883 57 83 20; Piazza Corvi; admission €4; ☽ 9am-1pm & 3-7pm Tue-Sun), one of Italy's largest, was initially built by the Normans, then rebuilt by Frederick II and fortified by Charles II of Anjou. Whisper sotto voce in the cannon room, impressive in itself, and enjoy its strange stereophonic echo. Enjoy too the display of Sicilian puppets and the castle's art collection, which includes over 90 works by Barletta's famous son, Giuseppe De Nittis.

Back in the town centre, just off Corso Garibaldi on Corso Vittorio Emanuele, is the **Colossus**, a chubby bronze Roman statue over 5m tall, which is believed to be of Emperor Valentinian I. It was plundered during the sacking of Constantinople in 1203 and then snapped up by Barletta after the ship carrying it sank off the Puglian coast. Green with verdigris, it stands stolidly before the 12th-century **Basilica del Santo Sepolcro** (not usually open to the public). Originally Romanesque, this church subsequently underwent Gothic and baroque face-lifts.

FESTIVALS & EVENTS

The **Disfida (Challenge) of Barletta**, held on the last Sunday in July, is one of Italy's best-known medieval pageants. It re-enacts a duel between 13 Italian and 13 French knights on 13 February 1503, when the town was besieged by the French. The homeside won and the chivalrous French decamped.

GETTING THERE & AWAY

From the bus station on Via Manfredi, **Ferrovie del Gargano** (☎ 0881 72 51 88) buses link Barletta with Foggia (€4.20, two hours, frequent); there are regular **STP** (☎ 0883 49 18 00) buses to Trani and Molfetta; **SITA**

(☎ 080 5790 11 11) serves Manfredonia, San Giovanni Rotondo and Bari; and **Ferrotramviaria** (☎ 080 523 22 02) goes to Andria.

Barletta is on both the Bari–Foggia Trenitalia coastal train line and the Bari-Nord train line. It's easily accessible from Trani and other points along the coast, as well as inland towns.

Castel del Monte

Castel del Monte (☎ 0883 56 99 97; admission adult/child €3/free; ☽ 9am-6pm) is one of southern Italy's most prominent and talked-about landmarks. Rising from a hill-top, it's visible for miles around and is nowadays a Unesco World Heritage Site.

Nobody really knows why Frederick II built it (see the boxed text, below) or why he adopted such a peculiar octagonal design. Some theories claim that according to the geometric-symbolic beliefs of the mid-13th century, the octagon represented the union of the circle and square, of God-perfection (the infinite) and man-perfection (the finite). The castle was therefore nothing less than a celebration of the relationship between man and God. Others claim it was a simple

---

THE CASTLE THAT FREDERICK BUILT

Legend has it that during the construction of Castel del Monte, Frederick II dispatched one of his courtiers to Puglia to check progress. However, the courtier was distracted in Melfi, Basilicata, where he fell in love with a beautiful woman 'whose eyes caused him to forget Castel del Monte and his sovereign'. He dallied in Melfi until a messenger from Naples arrived with orders for him to submit his report at once. Rather than admit that he'd been negligent, the courtier told Frederick that the castle was 'a total failure, neither beautiful nor practical' and that the architect was 'an impostor'. The architect, hearing of Frederick's anger at the courtier's assessment, threw himself to his death from one of the castle's towers. When news of the architect's death reached Frederick, he set out for Castel del Monte with the dishonest courtier. Seeing the magnificent building and again enraged, this time at the death of its architect, Frederick hauled the courtier up one of the towers and threw him, in turn, to his death.

hunting lodge – in Frederick's day, the surrounding country was heavily forested and teeming with game. The absence of a moat or other system of defence certainly suggests that it was not built primarily to withstand attack.

The castle is built on an octagonal base, each corner equipped with an octagonal tower. Completely restored, its interconnecting rooms have decorative marble columns and fireplaces, and the doorways and windows are framed in corallite stone, which once covered the entire lower floor.

The car park (€2.60; open April to September) is over 1km from the castle entrance. A free shuttle bus runs between the two.

GETTING THERE & AWAY

Without wheels, travelling to Castel del Monte is a pain. The least difficult way is via Andria. From July to mid-September, there are three buses daily except Sunday from Piazza Municipio in Andria to the castle. They depart at 8.30am, 1.45pm and 4.30pm. The first return is at 3pm. Andria is within easy reach of Trani by bus, or of Bari via the Bari-Nord train. The Andria–Spinazzola bus (several per day) passes close to the castle – ask the driver to let you off. See also the Getting There & Away section under Trani (p658).

BARI

pop 332,143

Bari has a reputation as a grim port town best avoided unless you're taking a ferry to Greece. This is not entirely fair. In recent years considerable effort has been made to smarten up the centre, and while this hasn't exactly transformed the city it has definitely improved things. However, this doesn't mean that you'll want to spend much time here, simply that you can have more fun while waiting for your ferry.

Capital of Puglia and the south's most important city after Naples, Bari is a frenetic place that offers a handful of interesting sights and can make a good base for exploring neighbouring towns. Once an important Byzantine town, it continued to flourish under the Normans and later under Frederick II. And what's more, it's here that San Nicola di Myra, better known as Father Christmas, is buried. His remains,

embalmed in manna, a liquid said to have miraculous powers, were stolen from what is now present-day Turkey in 1087. They were interred in Bari's Basilica di San Nicola, built especially for the purpose, which remains an important place of pilgrimage.

Occupied by the Allies during WWII, the port city endured heavy German bombing.

Orientation

Orient yourself from Piazza Aldo Moro in front of the main train station in the newer, 19th-century section of the city. From the square, it's about 1km northwards to Bari Vecchia, the old town.

The newer part of Bari is on a grid plan. Any of the streets heading north from Piazza Aldo Moro will take you to Corso Vittorio Emanuele II, separating old and new cities, and on to the ferry terminal. Wide and imposing Corso Cavour is a popular shopping strip.

Information

EMERGENCY
Police Station (☎ 080 529 11 11; Via Gioacchino Murat 4)

INTERNET ACCESS
Netcafè (☎ 080 524 17 56; Via Andrea da Bari 11; €4/hr; ☽ 8.30am-11pm)

INTERNET RESOURCES
Puglia Turismo (www.pugliaturismo.com)

MEDICAL SERVICES
Hospital (☎ 080 547 31 11; Piazza Giulio Cesare)
Guardia Medica (☎ 080 543 70 04) 24-hour doctor.

MONEY
There are plenty of banks, including one with an ATM at the station. There's a currency exchange booth at the ferry terminal, but you may well find that exchange rates are better in town.
Morfimare Travel Agency (☎ 080 578 98 11; Corso Antonio de Tullio 36-40) Represents American Express.

POST
Post Office (Piazza Cesare Battisti; ☽ 8am-6.30pm Mon-Fri, 8am-12.30pm Sat)

TELEPHONE & FAX
Telecom Office (Via Marchese di Montrone 123; ☽ 8am-10pm)

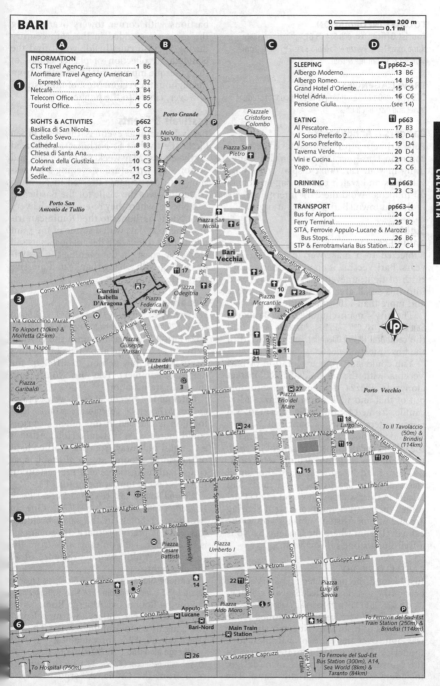

BARI

0 ————— 200 m
0 ————— 0.1 mi

Ⓐ

INFORMATION
CTS Travel Agency.............................**1** B6
Morfimare Travel Agency (American
  Express).....................................**2** B2
Netcafè..**3** B4
Telecom Office................................**4** B5
Tourist Office..................................**5** C6

SIGHTS & ACTIVITIES p662
Basilica di San Nicola......................**6** C2
Castello Svevo................................**7** B3
Cathedral.......................................**8** B3
Chiesa di Santa Ana........................**9** C3
Colonna della Giustizia..................**10** C3
Market...**11** C3
Sedile..**12** C3

SLEEPING pp662–3
Albergo Moderno..........................**13** B6
Albergo Romeo.............................**14** B6
Grand Hotel d'Oriente...................**15** C5
Hotel Adria....................................**16** C6
Pensione Giulia.....................(see **14**)

EATING p663
Al Pescatore..................................**17** B3
Al Sorso Preferito 2.......................**18** D4
Al Sorso Preferito..........................**19** D4
Taverna Verde...............................**20** D4
Vini e Cucina................................**21** C3
Yogo...**22** C6

DRINKING p663
La Bitta...**23** C3

TRANSPORT pp663–4
Bus for Airport..............................**24** C4
Ferry Terminal...............................**25** B2
SITA, Ferrovie Appulo-Lucane & Marozzi
  Bus Stops...................................**26** B6
STP & Ferrotramviaria Bus Station....**27** C4

Porto Grande

Molo
San Vito

Piazzale
Cristoforo
Colombo

Piazza San
Pietro

Porto San
Antonio de Tullio

Piazza San
Nicola

Bari
Vecchia

Corso Vittorio Veneto

Giardini
Isabella
D'Aragona

Piazza
Odegitria

Piazza
Federica II
di Svevia

Piazza
Mercantile

Via Gioacchino Murat
To Airport (10km) &
Molfetta (25km)

Via Napoli

Piazza
Giuseppe
Massari

Piazza della
Libertà

Corso Vittorio Emanuele II

Piazza
Garibaldi

Via Piccinni

Via Piccinni

Via Abate Gimma

Piazza
Erio del
Mare

Porto Vecchio

Via Calefati

Via Calefati

Via XXIV Maggio

Largo
Adua

To Il Tavolaccio
(50m) &
Brindisi
(114km)

Via Principe Amedeo

Via Dante Alighieri

Via Nicolai Beatillo

University

Piazza
Umberto I

Via Imbriani

Piazza
Cesare
Battisti

Via Crisanzio

Via Petroni

Piazza
Luigi di
Savoia

Piazza G Guiseppe Carulli

Corso Italia

Appulo-
Lucane

Piazza
Aldo Moro

Via Zuppetta

To Ferrovie del Sud-Est
Train Station (250m) &
Brindisi (114km)

Bari-Nord

Main Train
Station

To Hospital (750m)

Via Giuseppe Capruzzi

To Ferrovie del Sud-Est
Bus Station (300m), A14,
Sea World (8km) &
Taranto (84km)

Viale Unità d'Italia

TOURIST INFORMATION
Tourist Office (☎ 080 524 23 61; aptbari@pugliatu
rismo.com; 1st fl, Piazza Aldo Moro 33a; ☼ 8am-2pm
Mon-Fri & 3-6pm Tue & Thu)

TRAVEL AGENCIES
CTS (☎ 080 521 32 44; Via Fornari 7) Good for student
travel and discount flights.

Dangers & Annoyances
Petty crime is a problem, so take the usual
common-sense precautions. Don't leave anything in your car, don't display money or
valuables and watch out for bag-snatchers
on mopeds. Avoid the dark internal streets
of the old town (Bari Vecchia) at night.

Sights
BARI VECCHIA
Subjected to a makeover in the last few
years, Bari Vecchia is an atmospheric labyrinth of tight, uneven alleyways. Squeezed
into this small area are some 40 churches
and more than 120 little shrines.

The city's main churches, the **Basilica di
San Nicola** (☎ 080 573 71 11; Piazza San Nicola) and
the **cathedral** (Piazza Odegitria), are discussed in
the boxed text on p665.

You could start your exploration of Bari
Vecchia with the no-holds-barred **market**
alongside Piazza del Ferrarese. Stumble
out of that and walk north to Piazza Mercantile, fronted by the **Sedile**, the medieval
headquarters of Bari's Council of Nobles.
Set aside in the square's northeast corner is
the **Colonna della Giustizia** (Column of Justice),
to which, says tradition, debtors were tied.

Then head northwest past the small
Chiesa di Santa Ana to the Basilica di San
Nicola. A brief walk south via Strada D Carmine – both street and monument signing
are all but non-existent – brings you to the
cathedral, from where the Castello Svevo is
a well-flung stone's throw west.

CASTELLO SVEVO
Just beyond the perimeter of Bari Vecchia
broods the so-called **Castello Svevo** (Swabian Castle; ☎ 080 528 61 11; Piazza Isabella d'Aragona; admission
€2; ☼ 8.30am-7.30pm Tue-Sun). Its stones relate
four levels of history. A Norman structure
was built over the ruins of a Roman fort.
Frederick II then incorporated parts of
the Norman castle into his own design,
including two towers that still stand. The

bastions with corner towers overhanging
the moat were added in the 16th century
during Spanish rule. Inside you'll find the
Gipsoteca, a collection of plaster copies of
Romanesque monumental decoration from
throughout the region. Most of the castle is,
however, closed to the public.

Festivals & Events
Bari's big annual event is the **Festa di San
Nicola** (Festival of St Nicholas), celebrated
on the closest May weekend to the 2nd and
3rd of May. On Saturday evening a procession with participants dressed in Norman
costume leaves the castle for the Basilica di
San Nicola, where they re-enact the delivery
of St Nicholas' bones to the Dominican friars. The next day, with a statue of the saint
taking pride of place, a fleet of boats sets sail
along the coast. In the evening the festivities go out with a bang thanks to a massive
fireworks competition.

Sleeping
Sea World (☎ 080 549 11 75; fax 080 549 12 02; Strada
Adriatica 78; person/tent/car high season €8/7/3, s/d high
season €30/66) This seaside camp site is some
8km out of town and also offers bungalows
(from €28 in low season to €168 in the
height of summer). Take bus No 12 from
the main train station.

Hotel Adria (☎ 080 524 66 99; www.adriahotel
bari.com; Via Zuppetta 10; s/d with bathroom €42/68) Restoration is planned at this hotel, so prices
could increase. As it stands, Hotel Adria is
a tranquil hideaway from the traffic chaos
of the centre. Rooms are comfortably spacious, bathrooms large and the restaurant
serves a decent tourist menu for €13.

Albergo Romeo (☎ 080 523 72 53; Via Crisanzio
12; s/d/tr/q with bathroom €37/56/75/95) One of
two modest hotels in the same building,
this place is pretty ordinary. Its advantage
is its location – it's an easy walk from the
station and within walking distance of all
the city sights.

Pensione Giulia (☎ 080 521 66 30; Via Crisanzio
12; s/d €42/52, with bathroom €52/65, all with breakfast)
On the 1st floor above Albergo Romeo, this
family-run concern offers a warm welcome
and a highly useful ironing service. There is
also a safe available for valuables.

Albergo Moderno (☎ 080 521 33 13; Via Crisanzio
60; s/d with bathroom €42/65; ☒) Just down the
road from the Giulia, Albergo Moderno

offers trim, airy rooms, complete with TV and kitchen stove. The air-con is a definite plus in a city where summer temperatures can top 40°C.

Grand Hotel d'Oriente (☎ 080 524 40 11; Corso Cavour 32; s/d with bathroom & breakfast from €68/104) Originally this grand old hotel catered to wealthy merchants from the Balkans and Far East, hence the name. An imposing building on busy Corso Cavour, it combines modern efficiency with the elegance of the Titanic era.

Eating

Vini e Cucina (☎ 338 212 03 91; Strada Vallisa 23; meals €10) Grab a seat at this cult eatery in Bari Vecchia and mix with fishermen and students alike. The food is basic and filling and served by the one indefatigable waiter, who more or less remembers every order without writing a word. You'll remember your meal here!

Il Tavolaccio (☎ 080 558 86 36; Via Petroni 53; meals €15-20; ❤ Wed-Mon) The waiter will propose a little antipasto to start you off. Say yes and you'll still be eating half an hour later. Portions are huge at this modest trattoria and if you make it to the pasta dishes, the seafood options are good. Excellent value for money.

Al Pescatore (☎ 080 523 70 39; Piazza Federico di Svevia 6-8; meals from €25) As the name might suggest, Al Pescatore specialises in seafood and grilled fish. With the fish market not far away you can rest assured that what's on your plate was probably swimming free the day before. The grilled squid in particular is memorable.

Taverna Verde (☎ 080 554 08 70; Largo Adua 19; meals from €18; ❤ Mon-Sat) This low-ceilinged and stylish place is popular with business folk who bring their clients here. The food, as you'd expect, is good, if not exceptional and the prices reasonable.

Al Sorso Preferito (☎ 080 523 57 47; Via de Nicolò 42; full meal about €20; ❤ Wed-Mon) Look out for the yellow signs outside this long-established restaurant. In the same price and quality range as Taverna Verde, this roomy old hotel has loads of character. A block away is its originally named sister restaurant, **Al Sorso Preferito 2** (☎ 080 524 00 22; ❤ Tue-Sun).

Chill out with great frozen yoghurt at **Yogo** (☎ 0347 807 20 77; Via Nicolo dell'Arca 5).

If you're self-catering or stocking up for a ferry journey, pass by the **market** (Piazza del Ferrarese).

Drinking

Of an evening Piazza Mercantile in Bari Vecchia is the centre of the pub scene. Every night Bari's young and beautiful congregate in the square; some drinking at the various pubs, others just hanging out. Your best bet is to grab a beer wherever and join them. A popular pub with the English in town is **La Bitta** (Via Re Manfredi).

Getting There & Away

AIR

Bari's **airport** (BRI; ☎ 080 583 52 04) is 10km west of the city in Palese. There are domestic flights to/from Bologna, Catania (Sicily), Florence, Milan, Palermo, Rome and Venice.

BOAT

Unlike ferry traffic to/from Brindisi, it's busy year-round in Bari, especially to Greece but also to Albania and Serbia and Montenegro. All boat companies have offices at the ferry terminal, accessible from the main train station by bus No 20. Fares to Greece from Bari are generally more expensive than from Brindisi; the trip takes much the same time. Once you have bought your ticket and paid the embarkation tax (per person or car to Greece or Yugoslavia €7, per person or car to Albania €2.84), you get a boarding card, which must be stamped by the police at the ferry terminal.

The main companies and the routes they served at the time of writing are listed. We quote one-way fares and, where there's a seasonal variation, the high summer price. Tariffs can be as much as one-third cheaper outside the peak period of mid-July to late August. Bicycles normally travel free.

Adriatica (☎ 080 523 58 25; www.adriatica.it) To/from Durrës (Durazzo, eight hours) in Albania. Deck class €59.40; poltrona (airline-type seat) €64.60; cabin berth from €82.70; car €93. Daily departure at 11pm year-round.

Superfast (☎ 080 528 28 28; www.superfast.com) To Igoumenitsa (9½ hours) and Patras (Patrassa, 15½ hours) in Greece. Deck class €57; poltrona €70; dm bed €88; cabin berth from €112. Daily departure at 8pm year-round. Superfast is the only company that accepts Eurail, Euro-domino and Inter-Rail passes (you have to pay only port taxes and a high-season supplement, if applicable).

Ventouris Ferries (☎ 080 521 76 09; www.ventouris .gr) To Igoumenitsa, Patras and Corfu. Deck class €45; *poltrona* €56; cabin berth from €72; car €56. Regular ferries. Also daily ferries to/from Durrës (Albania).

Montenegro Lines (☎ 080 578 98 27; reservations via Morfimare travel agency (see Money, p660). To Bar in Montenegro. Deck class €47; cabin berth €62; car €69. Six ferries per week.

BUS

Intercity buses leave from several locations around town.

From Via Giuseppe Capruzzi, on the southern side of the main train station, **SITA** (☎ 080 579 01 11) covers local destinations. This is also the departure point for **Ferrovie Appulo-Lucane** (☎ 080 72 52 28) serving Altamura, Gravina di Puglia and Matera, plus **Marozzi** (☎ 080 505 82 80) buses for Rome (day departures only; the overnight bus departs from Piazza Aldo Moro) and other long-distance destinations.

Piazza Eroi del Mare is the terminal for **STP** (☎ 080 555 93 05) buses serving Andria (€3.35, seven daily), Barletta (€3.35, frequent), Molfetta (€1.80, frequent) and Trani (€2.85, frequent). **Ferrotramviaria** (☎ 080 523 22 02) buses also leave from here for Andria, Barletta and Ruvo di Puglia.

Buses operated by **Ferrovie del Sud-Est** (FSE; ☎ 080 542 65 52) leave from Largo Ciaia, south of Piazza Aldo Moro, for Brindisi (€6.20, 2½ hours, four daily) and Taranto (€4.60, 1½ hours, six daily). They run frequently to Alberobello (€3.10, 1½ hours), Grotte di Castellana (€2.10, one hour; also FSE trains), Locorotondo (€3.10, 1¼ hours), Martina Franca (€3.60, 1½ hours), Polignano (€2, 45 minutes) and Ostuni (€4.10, two hours).

CAR & MOTORCYCLE

Bari is on the A14 autostrada, which heads northwest to Foggia, south to Taranto and connects with the A16 to Naples at Canosa di Puglia. Exit at Bari-Nord to reach the centre of town.

TRAIN

Like buses, a whole network of train lines connects Bari with the wider world.

From the main **train station** (☎ 89 20 21), national Trenitalia trains go to Milan (€37.70, 8½ hours) and Rome (€36, five hours). There are frequent services to cities across Puglia, including Foggia (€6.50, 1½ hours), Brindisi (€6.50, 1¼ hours), Lecce (€7.50, 2¼ hours) and Taranto (€6.50, 1¼ hours).

Of the private train services, the **Ferrovia Bari-Nord** (☎ 080 578 95 11) connects the city with the airport (€0.80, at least 20 daily), continuing to Bitonto, Andria and Barletta.

The **Ferrovie Appulo-Lucane** (☎ 080 572 52 28) line links Bari with Altamura (€2.60), Matera (€3.60, 10 trains and six buses daily), Gravina (€3.20) and Potenza (€7.80, four trains and one bus daily).

FSE trains (☎ 080 542 65 52) head for Alberobello, Castellana, Locorotondo, Martina Franca and Taranto, leaving from the station in Via Oberdan – cross under the train tracks south of Piazza Luigi di Savoia and head east along Via Giuseppe Capruzzi for about 500m.

Getting Around

To get to the airport take the Alitalia bus (€4.13), which leaves the main train station, calling by the airline's office at Via Calefati 37, 80 minutes before most flight departures.

Central Bari is quite compact – a 15-minute walk will take you from Piazza Aldo Moro to the old town. For the ferry terminal take bus No 20 from Piazza Aldo Moro. A single journey costs €0.80 and a day pass is €1.80.

Street parking is hell. There's a large free parking area just south of the main port entrance and a paying multistorey car park between the main and Ferrovie del Sud-Est train stations.

THE TRULLI AREA

Puglia's unique *trulli* are circular, conical-roofed whitewashed houses built of stone without a single trowelful of mortar. This, it is said, was a tax-dodging device. In the past when the tax collector passed, the *trulli* inhabitants simply dismantled their houses, leaving them free from any house duties. Once the collector was safely distant, up the houses would go again.

The distinctive roofs, topped with pinnacles, are tiled with concentric rows of grey slate and often painted with astrological or religious symbols. Designed to be warm in winter and cool in summer, their origin is obscure but few of these solid-looking

PUGLIA, BASILICATA & CALABRIA

THE ROMANESQUE CATHEDRALS OF PUGLIA

Of over 15 significant Romanesque religious buildings in Puglia, only nine have been preserved in the original style. These include the cathedrals at Bari, Altamura, Barletta, Bitonto, Molfetta, Ruvo di Puglia and Trani. Although considered to be merely a church, the Basilica di San Nicola in **Bari**, of exceptional architectural value, served as a model for many of the churches built in the Puglian-Romanesque style.

The 12th-century Basilica di San Nicola was built on the ruins of a Byzantine *palazzo* to house the reputedly miracle-working bones of St Nicholas, stolen by Bari sailors from their resting-place in Myra (in what is now Turkey). The basilica has a stark, imposing facade, simply decorated with blind arches and mullioned windows and flanked by two bell towers. On the north side, look for the Lion's Doorway with its beautiful sculptures and bas-reliefs depicting chivalric scenes. Inside, below the richly gilded 17th-century ceiling, are a splendid 12th-century altar canopy and bishop's chair, known as the throne of Elias. The remains of St Nicholas are down in the crypt, where there is also, and uniquely for a Catholic basilica, an Orthodox chapel. This was built to cater to the pilgrims from Russia, Greece and the Balkans, to whom St Nicholas is of particularly value.

Bari's cathedral, from the same era, was built on the remains of a Byzantine original. Although retaining its elegant Romanesque shape and bell tower, it's been much altered over the centuries.

The cathedrals of Bitonto, Ruvo di Puglia and Molfetta lie west of Bari. The cathedral of **Bitonto** is a particularly stunning example of Puglian-Romanesque architecture. Built in the late 12th century on the model of the Basilica di San Nicola in Bari, it is dedicated to St Valentine. Note the carved animals and plants that decorate the capitals on the side walls. Nearby is the 17th-century Chiesa di Purgatorio. Above its main door are sinners burning in purgatory, flanked by two large figures of Death dancing with delight at their fate. You can get to Bitonto from Bari on the private Bari-Nord train line.

The graceful cathedral in **Ruvo di Puglia** has a striking facade with a fine rose window and three portals. The delicately carved central portal features columns supported by griffins, resting on (now very worn) lions, themselves supported by squashed human figures. Ruvo too is on the Bari-Nord train line.

Molfetta is worth a stop not only for its impressively simple cathedral but also for its tumbledown medieval centre. Known as the Duomo Vecchio, the cathedral, started in 1150, was completed at the end of the 13th century. Its stark, undecorated white facade is flanked by two bell towers. The interior is a mix of Romanesque, Byzantine and even Islamic architecture. The Borgo Vecchio, the medieval quarter behind the cathedral, is crumbling although parts are being restored. Molfetta is on the main Bari–Foggia train line, about 20 minutes from Bari.

Altamura is about 45 minutes southwest of Bari and easily accessible on the Appulo-Lucane train line. Its 13th-century cathedral, constructed during the reign of Frederick II, was badly damaged by an earthquake in 1316. It later suffered some unfortunate baroque renovations, when the elegant medieval main portal and rose window were moved from their original position to what had been the apse. The cathedral is in the old town's main street, Via Federico II di Svevia.

constructions date back more than a couple of centuries.

The *trulli* area is the Valle d'Itria, extending from Conversano and Gioia del Colle in the west to Ostuni and Martina Franca in the east. The greatest concentration of *trulli* is in and around Alberobello.

Grotte di Castellana

Definitely worth the hassle of getting to, these spectacular limestone **caves** (☎ 800 21 39 76, ☎ 080 499 82 11; Piazzale Anelli; long tour €13, short tour €8; ☽ 8.30am-7pm, guided tours in English long tour 11am & 4pm, short tour 1pm & 6pm Mar-Oct, rest of the year on request), 40km southeast of Bari, are Italy's longest natural subterranean network. The interlinked galleries, first discovered in 1938 by Franco Anelli, contain incredible stalactite and stalagmite formations – look out for the jellyfish, the bacon and the stocking. The highlight, however, is the **Grotta Bianca**, an incredible cave of eerie white beauty.

There are two tours: a 1km, 50-minute trip that does not include the Grotta Bianca; and the full 3km, two-hour trip that does. Visit too the **Museo Speleologico Franco Anelli** (admission free; 🕐 9am-noon & 3-6pm) or book a visit to the **osservatorio astronomico** (☎ 080 499 82 11; admission €2).

By rail, head for Castellana Grotte on the FSE Bari–Taranto train line. From the station there are local buses to the caves 2km away.

Alberobello

The *trulli* capital of the world, Alberobello is becoming something of a theme park these days, virtually entirely given over to tourism. Still, this Unesco World Heritage Site is a pretty enough place and, tourist tat notwithstanding, well worth a visit.

To check your emails head to **Internet** (☎ 080 432 29 42; Corso Trieste; 30; €1.50/15 mins), while the **tourist office** (☎ 080 432 51 71; Piazza del Popolo; 🕐 9.30am-1pm Mon-Sat & 3.30-5.30pm Mon-Fri) is in the Casa d'Amore, just off the main square.

There are not many sights as such in town, it's more a case of walking around and admiring the eccentricity of it all. Within the quarter of **Rione Monti**, on the south side of town, over 1000 *trulli* cascade down the hillside. To its east, on the other side of Via Indipendenza, is **Rione Aia Piccola**. It's much less commercialised, with a respectable 400 *trulli*, many of which are still used as family dwellings.

In the modern part of town, the 16th-century **Trullo Sovrano** (☎ 080 432 60 30; Piazza Sacramento; admission €1.30; 🕐 10am-7pm Apr-Oct, shorter Sun hours in winter) has been converted into a museum illustrating the history of the *trulli*.

SLEEPING & EATING

Hotel Lanzillotta (☎ 080 432 15 11; fax 080 432 53 55; Piazza Ferdinando IV 31; s/d with bathroom & breakfast €38.70/56.80) This recently restructured hotel just off Piazza del Popolo is an excellent choice. A friendly welcome awaits and the rooms, eight of which have bathtubs, are decent. It also serves a mean three-course dinner of local specialities for about €13.

Hotel dei Trulli (☎ 080 432 35 55; hoteldeitrulli@in media.it; Via Cadore 32; s/d with bathroom & breakfast from €72.30/118.80) If you've ever wondered what it's like to sleep in a genuine *trullo*, you won't get much idea here. What you will get is the town's top hotel set in a wonderful shady garden of pine, juniper and cypress.

Camping dei Trulli (☎ 080 432 36 99; www.camp ingdeitrulli.com; person/tent/car €5/4/1.50) This well-equipped camp site is just out of town on Via Castellana Grotte.

Ristorante Trullo d'Oro (☎ 080 432 18 20; Via Felice Cavallotti 29; meals €25) You won't find many locals eating at this (you guessed it) converted *trullo*, hidden away behind Piazza del Popolo. Still, the food isn't bad and the setting original – at least it would be if it wasn't in Alberobello.

GETTING THERE & AWAY

The easiest way to get to Alberobello is on the FSE Bari–Taranto train line. From the station, walk straight ahead along Via Mazzini, which becomes Via Garibaldi, to reach Piazza del Popolo.

Locorotondo

Just down the road from Alberobello, Locorotondo makes a great lunchtime stop. Perched on a hill overlooking the Valle dei Trulli, it offers fine views, a pristine historic centre and a renowned white wine. Easily reachable on the FSE Bari–Taranto train line, the town is, as its name suggests, completely circular (Locorotondo translates as Round Place).

U'Curdunn (☎ 0804 31 70 70; Via Dura 19; meals €20; 🕐 Tue-Sun) Lose yourself in the alleyways of the historic centre, and if you're lucky you'll come across this charming trattoria. Pride of place is given to organically grown local vegetables, which really do taste as they should.

La Taverna del Duca (☎ 0804 31 30 07; Via Papatodero 3; meals from €18; 🕐 Tue-Sun) Near the Piazza Vittorio Emanuele II entrance to the old town, this place serves up no surprises, simply delicious home-style food. You will, of course, want to wash this down with a carafe or two of the local white wine.

Martina Franca

Martina has one of the finest old quarters in Puglia. Baroque balconies decorated with ornate wrought iron look down on narrow alleyways little changed in centuries.

Founded in the 10th century by refugees fleeing the Arab invasion of Taranto Martina Franca flourished from the 14th century, when it was granted tax exemptions (*franchigie*, hence the name Franca) by Philip of Anjou.

ORIENTATION & INFORMATION
The FSE train station is downhill from the historic centre. Go right along Viale della Stazione, continuing along Via Alessandro Fighera to Corso Italia; continue to the left along Corso Italia to Piazza XX Settembre.

The **tourist office** (☎ 080 480 57 02; Piazza Roma 37; ◷ 9am-1pm & 5-7.30pm Mon-Fri, 9am-12.30pm Sat) occupies a couple of rooms within the enormous Palazzo Ducale.

SIGHTS
Passing under the baroque **Arco di Sant'Antonio** at the western end of pedestrianised Piazza XX Settembre, you emerge into Piazza Roma, flanked by the 17th-century **Palazzo Ducale**, a vast edifice now used as municipal offices.

From the piazza, follow Corso Vittorio Emanuele into Piazza Plebiscito, at the heart of the historic centre and dominated by the exuberant baroque facade of the 18th-century **Basilica di San Martino**, its centrepiece the good St Martin himself, swinging a sword and sharing his cloak with a beggar.

FESTIVALS & EVENTS
In the second half of July and early August, the town stages the annual **Festival della Valle d'Itria**, a feast for opera-lovers. For information call the **Centro Artistico Musicale Paolo Grassi** (☎ 080 480 51 00), in the Palazzo Ducale.

SLEEPING & EATING
Hotel Da Luigi (☎ /fax 080 485 61 24; Via Taranto; s/d with bathroom €31/48) This hotel is 2km from Martina Franca, on the left as you head towards Taranto. One of Martina's cheapest options, rooms are more than OK and the meals served at the hotel restaurant are pretty good. FSE buses for Taranto pass the hotel.

La Cremaillere (☎ 080 449 00 52; Via Orimini 1; d with bathroom €46.50-56.80) The second of the out-of-town budget choices is La Cremaillere, 5.5km beyond Da Luigi. Comfort at this place pretty much corresponds to the prices, so don't arrive expecting luxury. It also has its own restaurant.

Park Hotel San Michele (☎ 080 480 70 53; www.parkhotelsm.it; Viale Carella 9; s/d with bathroom & breakfast €65/93; ✖ P ⬚) Set in a lovely, leafy garden, this is Martina's top hotel and the

decor is stylish, the service slick and, given the comfort, the prices reasonable. It's a popular spot for wedding receptions.

Rosticceria Ricci (☎ 080 480 55 34; Piazza Plebiscito 10-12; meals €18) This is the joint for roasts. Situated within a stone's throw of the Basilica di San Martino, it specialises in roast meats, pleasantly accompanied by salad and wine.

Trattoria La Tavernetta (☎ 080 430 63 23; Corso Vittorio Emanuele 30; meals from €18) Another simple trattoria ideally placed in the old town. There is nothing spectacular about the cooking but just serving average food in these parts means you'll eat well.

Villaggio In (☎ 080 480 5021; Via Arco Grassi 8; meals €20) This is a decidedly classy joint where you can dine downstairs then clamber up to the rooftop piano bar, which often has live music at weekends.

GETTING THERE & AROUND
Take the **FSE** (☎ 080 480 80 20) train from Bari or Taranto. FSE buses also connect Martina Franca with Taranto, Alberobello, Castellana Grotte and Bari, arriving in Viale Europa and Corso Italia.

Bus Nos III and IV connect the FSE train station, down on the plain, with Piazza XX Settembre.

Ostuni
This stunning town sits like a white beacon on three hills east of Martina Franca and about 40km northwest of Brindisi. The seemingly disordered tangle of narrow cobblestone streets, many little more than arched stairways between the houses, recalls a North African Arab medina. Rising above it all in sombre brown stone is the 15th-century Gothic **cathedral**.

Ostuni makes an ideal day trip from either Brindisi or Bari.

ORIENTATION & INFORMATION
From Piazza della Libertà, where new town meets old, take Via Cattedrale to the cathedral. From the piazza in front of the cathedral, turn right for a view across the olive groves to the Adriatic – or turn left to get agreeably lost in Ostuni's whitewashed lanes.

Ostuni's **tourist office** (☎ 0831 30 12 68; Corso Mazzini 8; ◷ 8.30am-1.30pm & 5.30-8.30pm Mon-Fri, 8.30am-1.30pm & 6.30-8.30pm Sat, shorter hrs winter) is just off Piazza della Libertà.

SLEEPING & EATING

Albergo Tre Torri (☎ 0831 33 11 14; Corso Vittorio Emanuele II 298; s/d €34/45, with bathroom €38/51) A 10-minute walk from Ostuni's busy old town is this cheerful, homely little hotel. The owners offer a warm welcome and rooms are unobtrusively decorated. You can also enjoy the panoramic views of the town.

Hotel Orchidea Nera (☎ 0831 30 13 66; Via Mazzini 118; s with bathroom €30.50-36.50, d with bathroom €52-62) Closer to the action than Tre Torri, this slightly wacky place is excellent value for money. The huge, high-ceilinged doubles with views over plain and sea are especially good value at €62.

To eat, head for the old town where there are a number of trattorie, all of a good quality and mostly reasonably priced.

Osteria del Tempo Perso (☎ 0831 30 33 20; Gaetano Tanzarella Vitale 47; meals from €28) A self-styled rustic restaurant (which some might call twee), this place serves great Puglian food. Face the cathedral's south wall, turn right through an archway into Largo Giuseppe Spennati and follow signs to the restaurant.

GETTING THERE & AROUND

STP buses run between Ostuni and Brindisi about every two hours, arriving in Piazza Italia in the newer part of Ostuni. They also connect the town with Martina Franca. Trains run more regularly to/from Lecce (via Brindisi) and Bari. A local bus covers the 2.5km between the station and town, running every half-hour.

You can rent a bike from **Alba Travel Agency** (☎ 339 866 43 66; Largo Bianchieri 2; per day/week €13/35).

BRINDISI

pop 90,010

For most travellers Brindisi represents little more than a point of departure or arrival. And only a tiny minority will not have heard the horror stories about thieves waiting to rip you off the moment you step foot in town or of touts ready to whip you off to dodgy hotels. The fact is Brindisi is not that bad; there is simply very little to do other than wait – more boring than dangerous.

The major embarkation point for ferries between Italy and Greece, Brindisi swarms with people in transit. Most backpackers gather at the train station, ferry terminal

or in pedestrianised Piazza Cairoli or Piazza del Popolo.

Settled in ancient times and occupied by Rome in 3 BC, Brindisi is a natural safe harbour that prospered under the Romans and retained its importance until after the crusades. Invasion, plague and earthquake brought about decline but today it is a busy merchant and passenger port with, if you care to linger, a small historic heart.

Orientation

The new port is east of town, across the Seno di Levante at Costa Morena, in a bleak industrial wilderness.

The old port is about 1km from the train station along Corso Umberto I, which leads into Corso Garibaldi. There are numerous takeaway food outlets and places to eat along the route, as well as a bewildering array of ferry companies and travel agencies.

Information

EMERGENCY

Police Station (☎ 0831 54 31 11; Via Perrino 1)

INTERNET ACCESS

Internet (Via Bastione S Giorgio; €5/hr)
Photocenter (Corso Umberto I 114; €5/hr)

INTERNET RESOURCES

Ferries (www.ferries.gr) Details of ferry fares and timetables.

MEDICAL SERVICES

Hospital (☎ 0831 53 71 11; SS7 for Mesagne) Southwest of the centre.

MONEY

Corso Umberto I and Corso Garibaldi bristle with currency exchange offices, and good old-fashioned banks also abound.

POST

Post Office (☎ 0831 47 11 11; Piazza Vittoria; ☑ 8am-6.30pm Mon-Fri, 8am-12.30pm Sat)

TOURIST INFORMATION

Tourist Office (☎ 0831 52 30 72; Viale Regina Margherita 44; ☑ 8.30am-2pm & 3.30-7pm Mon-Fri, 8.30am-1pm Sat)

Dangers & Annoyances

We have received a disturbing report of racial harassment by authorities. This is no

BRINDISI

INFORMATION
Internet...................................... 1 B4
Photocenter Internet.................. 2 B4
Tourist Office............................. 3 C2

SIGHTS & ACTIVITIES   pp669–70
Castello Svevo............................ 4 A2
Cathedral................................... 5 C2
Museo Archeologico.................. 6 C2
Palazzo Balsamo......................... 7 C2
Roman Column........................... 8 C2

SLEEPING
Grande Albergo Internazionale.......... 9 C2
Hotel Altair................................ 10 D3
Hotel Majestic........................... 11 B4
Hotel Regina.............................. 12 B4
Hotel Venezia............................ 13 C3

EATING
Iaccato....................................... 14 B2
La Lanterna................................ 15 C2
Market....................................... 16 C3
Supermarket.............................. 17 D3

TRANSPORT   pp670–1
Appia Travel.............................. 18 C2
Blue Star Ferries........................ 19 D3
Buses for Costa Morena (Ferry
 Terminal)................................. 20 D2
FSE & STP Bus Stops.................. 21 B4
Hellenic Mediterranean Lines Office. 22 C3
Italian Ferries............................ 23 D3
Med Link Lines.......................... 24 C3
Old Ferry Terminal.................... 25 D2

Seno di Ponente

Viale dei Mille

To Carpe Diem (2km)
& Chiesa di Santa
Maria del Casale (4km)

Viale Regina Margherita

*Piazza
Vittorio
Emanuele*

**Porto
Interno**

Via Colonne

*Piazza
del
Duomo*

Via Tarantini

Via Fornari

*Piazza
Vittoria*

Corso Garibaldi

Via Picanelli

*Piazza
del
Popolo*

Via XX Settembre

Via Cristoforo Colombo

Via Mazzini

*Piazza
Cairoli*

Umberto I

Corso Roma

Via Lata

Via del Mare

To Hospital
(2km)

*Piazza
Francesco
Crispi*

Via Bastioni San Giorgio

Corso

Via Cavour

Via Sapone a

*Largo
Palumbo*

Via Porta Lecce

**Seno di
Levante**

Via Tor Pisana

**Train
Station**

Via Bastioni Carlo V

Via Indipendenza

To Superstrada,
Airport (7km),
Lecce (38km),
Taranto (70km)
& Bari (100km)

To Fragline
Ferry Company
(150m) & Costa
Morena (7km)

To Police
Station (200m)

0 — 200 m
0 — 0.1 mi

---

the norm but racial tensions have increased as illegal immigration continues.

In summer thieves can be a problem with so many inviting backpacks and bags lying around. Keep tabs on your valuables and nothing of the remotest interest should be left unattended. Women are advised to be careful alone at night.

With regards to ticket scams, the safest strategy is to deal directly with a reputable ferry company. Don't take the word of anyone you meet by chance on the street and if any offer sounds too good to be true, it probably isn't true. Readers also report that some less-scrupulous travel agents will assure you that your Eurail or Inter-Rail pass is invalid or that the quota's full in order to

sell you a full-price ticket. Check with the ferry company.

Sights

For the Romans, as for travellers today, Brindisi was the end of the line or, more specifically, of Via Appia, which stretched cross-country from Rome. For centuries, two great **columns** marked the end of the imperial highway. One was presented to the town of Lecce back in 1666 as thanks to San Oronzo, that town's patron saint, for having relieved Brindisi of the plague. The other is *in situ* but swathed in scaffolding. Tradition has it that the Roman poet Virgil died in a house near here after returning from a voyage to Greece.

In the small historic quarter, the modest **cathedral** (Piazza del Duomo) was originally built in the 11th century but substantially remodelled about 700 years later. Abutting it on the north side is the small **Museo Archeologico** (☎ 0831 22 14 01; Piazza del Duomo 8; admission free; ☺ 9am-1pm & 3-7pm Mon-Fri, mornings only Sat & Sun). Across the tranquil square is **Palazzo Balsamo**, which has a fine loggia.

The town's main sight is the **Chiesa di Santa Maria del Casale**, 4km north of the centre towards the airport. Built by Prince Philip of Taranto around 1300, this originally Romanesque church has both Gothic and Byzantine touches. To get there, follow Via Provinciale San Vito round the Seno di Ponente bay. Alternatively, take the airport bus.

Brindisi's other site of consequence is the stocky **Castello Svevo**, another of Frederick II's monuments to militarism. Unfortunately, like its counterpart in Taranto, it's occupied by the military and bristles with 'keep out' signs.

Sleeping

Carpe Diem (☎ 0831 59 79 54; Via N Brandi 2; dm €14) This cheerful private hostel, about 2km out of town, is the cheapest option around. There are welcome laundry facilities and for €7 they'll do you an evening meal. Take bus No 3 or 4 from Via Cristoforo Colombo near the train station or call and they'll come and pick you up.

Hotel Venezia (☎ 0831 52 75 11; Via Pisanelli 4; s/d from €13/25) Another cheap option, this friendly lodge is in the centre of town; turn north at the eastern end of Via Carmine. The 11 rooms here are fine and represent excellent value for money.

Hotel Altair (☎ 0831 56 22 89; Via Giudea 4; s/d €20/37, with bathroom €30/50) Hidden away in a side street off Corso Garibaldi, this modest hotel has old-style high-ceilinged rooms. It's ideal for early-morning departures as the port bus stop is less than five minutes' walk away.

Hotel Regina (☎ 0831 56 20 01; fax 0831 56 38 83; Via Cavour 5; s/d with bathroom & breakfast €51.70/77; ☒ P) Ignore the crass 1980s black and chrome decor in the reception and you'll find the Regina a comfortable enough place to pass the night. The private garage is also not to be sniffed at.

There are two top-end hotels, quite different in character from each other.

Hotel Majestic (☎ 0831 59 79 41; www.ht-majestic.it; Corso Umberto I 151; s/d with bathroom & breakfast €88/125; ☒ P) It's all military-style efficiency at this convenient hotel. Opposite the train station, it's altogether more comfortable than the dreary concrete exterior would suggest and a particularly good deal at weekends, when rates fall by 20%.

Grande Albergo Internazionale (☎ 0831 52 34 73; www.albergointernazionale.it; Viale Regina Margherita 23; s/d with bathroom from €110/130; ☒ P) Brindisi's top hotel, this early 19th-century seafront palace was built for English merchants on their way to and from Bombay and the Raj. Other than an excellent restaurant and great views over the inner harbour, this luxury hotel also offers a playroom for children.

Eating

Iaccato (☎ 0831 52 40 84; Via Lenio Flacco 32; meals €15, pizzas from €3.60; ☺ Thu-Tue) About 400m beyond the tourist office, this is a popular restaurant named in honour of its founder, a noted local fisherman. Seafood is a speciality and they do a mean seafood, saffron and asparagus risotto (€6.20). Laid-back and cheerful, they'll just as happily serve you a pizza and a beer.

La Lanterna (☎ 0831 22 40 26; Via Tarantini 14-18; meals from €25) For a touch more sophistication head to La Lanterna. Established over 40 years ago in a restored 15th-century *palazzo*, it has a delightful garden and boasts an impressive list of local wines.

For supplies for the boat trip, stock up at the colourful fresh-food **market** (Piazza Mercato; ☺ mornings Mon-Sat), just behind the post office, or at the **supermarket** (Corso Garibaldi 106).

Getting There & Away
AIR

From Papola Casale (BDS), Brindisi's small airport, there are internal flights to/from Rome, Naples, Milan, Bologna and Pisa.

BOAT

Ferries, all of which take vehicles and have snack bars or restaurants, leave Brindisi for Greek destinations including Corfu (10 to 15 hours), Igoumenitsa (nine to 12 hours), Patras (15 to 20 hours) and the Ionian Islands. From Patras there is a bus to Athens. Boats also service Albania (daily) and Turkey (seasonal).

Most ferry companies operate only in summer. All have offices at Costa Morena (the new port), and the major ones also have offices in town. There's a €6 port tax. Fares generally increase by up to 40% on peak travel days in July and August (we list low-season, one-way fares).

Hellenic Mediterranean Lines (☎ 0831 52 85 31; www.hml.gr; Corso Garibaldi 8) To Corfu, Igoumenitsa and Patras (April to October) and the Ionian Islands (July and August). Deck class €22; *poltrona* (airline-type seat) €28; cabin berth €40. The largest and most reliable of the lines, Hellenic Mediterranean accepts Eurail and Inter-Rail passes, entitling you to travel free in deck class (paying a €15 supplement during Jul & Aug). If you intend to use your pass, it is best to reserve in advance in high summer. Out of season, use the town office.

Blue Star Ferries (☎ 0831 56 22 00; www.blue starferries.com; Corso Garibaldi 65) To/from Igoumenitsa, mostly via Corfu. Deck class from €30; cabin berth from €64.60. Sailing is possible year-round (Wednesday to Monday).

Fragline (☎ 0831 54 85 40; www.fragline.gr; Via Spalato 31) To Corfu and Igoumenitsa. Deck class €24; *poltrona* €34; cabin berth €44. Ferries run April to September.

Italian Ferries (☎ 0831 59 08 40; www.italian ferries.it; Corso Garibaldi 96-98) To/from Vlore (Valona; in Albania). *Poltrona* €41. Daily ferries. Also to/from Corfu/ Paxos. Deck class €57/73. Italian Ferries accepts Eurail and Inter-Rail passes for tickets bought at their town centre office, entitling you to pay €21 for a *poltrona*; €31 for a cabin berth. For Eurail holders there is a €20 surcharge for July and August sailings.

Med Link Lines (☎ 0831 52 76 67; www.ferries.gr/ medlink; Corso Garibaldi 49) To Greece and to Cesme (Turkey; bi-weekly car ferry, summer only). Deck class €61; *poltrona* €72; cabin berth €102.

Check in at least two hours before departure or you risk losing your reservation (a strong possibility in the high season).

At the time of writing, Hellenic Mediterranean Line's low-/high-season fares for vehicles to Greece were motorcycles €9/20, cars €20/50, minibuses €44 to €75 and caravans €89 to €157. Bicycles go free.

BUS
Buses operated by **STP** (☎ 0831 54 92 45) connect Brindisi with Ostuni (€2.30) and towns throughout the Penisola Salentina. Most leave from Via Bastioni Carlo V, in front of the train station. **FSE** (☎ 099 477 6 27) buses serving local towns also leave from here.

Marozzi runs to Rome (Stazione Tiburtina; €32.55, nine hours, four daily) and Pisa and Florence (€52, 14 hours, one daily) leaving from Viale Arno. **Appia Travel** (☎ 0831 52 16 84; Viale Regina Margherita 8-9) sells tickets.

CAR & MOTORCYCLE
For the new ferry terminal, follow signs for Costa Morena from the autostrada. Allow plenty of time to board your ferry.

TRAIN
Brindisi is on the main Trenitalia train line. It has regular local services to Bari (€6.20, Eurostar one hour, *regionale* one hour 40 minutes), Lecce (€2.40, 40 minutes) and Taranto (€3.62, one hour 10 minutes). Other destinations include Bologna (€42.30, 8¼ hours), Milan (€51.10, 9½ hours), Naples (€29, 6¼ hours) and Rome (€35.10, six hours).

Getting Around
A free minibus operated by Portabagagli connects the train station and old ferry terminal with Costa Morena. It departs two hours before boat departures. You'll need a valid ferry ticket.

To reach the airport take the shuttle bus (€3) from the old ferry terminal.

LECCE
pop 97,458
As you stare open-mouthed at the madcap baroque architecture in the city centre, it's almost difficult not to laugh. So joyously extravagant is the stonework that cynics might speak of over-the-top folly. Less-grumpy critics will simply admire what is known to Italians as *barocco leccese* (Lecce baroque). The local stone actually encourages extravagance; it's particularly malleable yet soon after being quarried it hardens, making it the perfect building and sculpting material.

A centre of learning, Lecce, sometimes referred to as 'the Florence of the south', is a university town with deep roots, style, grace – and plenty of student cafés and bars. Convenient for both the Adriatic and Ionian Seas, it makes a great base for exploring the Penisola Salentina.

History
The original settlement was overrun in the 3rd century BC by the Romans, who named

PUGLIA, BASILICATA & CALABRIA

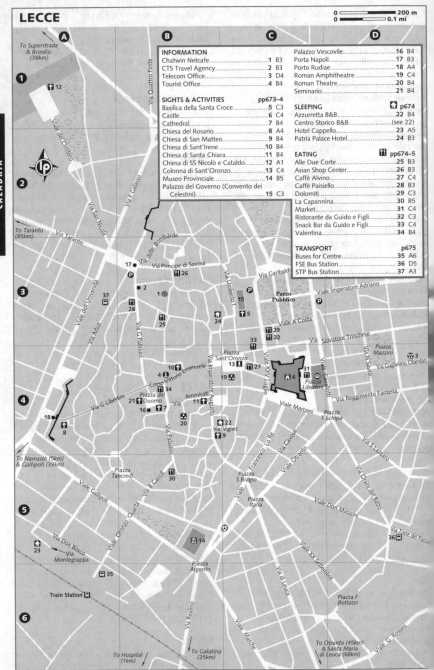

LECCE

0 — 200 m
0 — 0.1 mi

INFORMATION

Chatwin Netcafe	1 B3
CTS Travel Agency	2 B3
Telecom Office	3 D4
Tourist Office	4 B3

SIGHTS & ACTIVITIES pp673–4

Basilica della Santa Croce	5 C3
Castle	6 C4
Cathedral	7 B4
Chiesa del Rosario	8 A4
Chiesa di San Matteo	9 B4
Chiesa di Sant'Irene	10 B4
Chiesa di Santa Chiara	11 B4
Chiesa di SS Nicolò e Cataldo	12 A1
Colonna di Sant'Oronzo	13 C4
Museo Provinciale	14 B5
Palazzo del Governo (Convento dei Celestini)	15 C3

Palazzo Vescovile	16 B4
Porta Napoli	17 B3
Porto Rudiae	18 A4
Roman Amphitheatre	19 C4
Roman Theatre	20 B4
Seminario	21 B4

SLEEPING p674

Azzurretta B&B	22 B4
Centro Storico B&B	(see 22)
Hotel Cappello	23 A5
Patria Palace Hotel	24 B3

EATING pp674–5

Alle Due Corte	25 B3
Asian Shop Center	26 B3
Caffè Alvino	27 C4
Caffè Paisiello	28 B3
Dolomiti	29 C3
La Capannina	30 B5
Market	31 C4
Ristorante da Guido e Figli	32 C3
Snack Bar da Guido e Figli	33 C4
Valentina	34 B4

TRANSPORT p675

Buses for Centre	35 A6
FSE Bus Station	36 D5
STP Bus Station	37 A3

To Superstrada & Brindisi (38km)

To Taranto (85km)

To Namastè (5km) & Gallipoli (39km)

To Hospital (1km)

To Galatina (25km)

To Otranto (45km) & Santa Maria di Leuca (68km)

Parco Pubblico

Piazza Sant'Oronzo

Piazza del Duomo

Piazza Vignes

Piazza Mazzini

Piazza Libertini

Piazza T Schipa

Piazza Tancredi

Piazza S Biagio

Piazza Italia

Piazza Argento

Piazza F Bottazzi

Train Station

it Lupiae. From this period are the remains of an imposing amphitheatre, in Piazza Sant'Oronzo, and a Roman theatre. Ruled in turn by Byzantines, Normans and Swabians, the city came into its own between the 16th and 18th centuries, when it was embellished with splendid religious buildings and secular palaces.

Orientation

The train station is about 1km southwest of Lecce's historic centre. The town centre's twin main squares are Piazza Sant'Oronzo and Piazza del Duomo, linked by pedestrian Corso Vittorio Emanuele. From the station, walk straight ahead along Viale Oronzo Quarta, which becomes Via B Cairoli, then bear left into Viale Paladini.

Information

EMERGENCY
Ambulance (☎ 0832 22 86 30)
Police Station (☎ 0832 69 11 11; Viale Otranto 1)

INTERNET ACCESS
Chatwin Netcafe (☎ 0832 27 78 59; Via Isabella Castriota 8; €3/hr; ☼ 10am-1.30pm & 5-10pm Mon-Sat)

MEDICAL SERVICES
Hospital (☎ 0832 66 11 11; Via San Cesario) Situated 2km south of the centre on the road to Gallipoli.

MONEY
You'll find several banks on and around Piazza Sant'Oronzo.

POST
Post Office (☎ 0832 24 35 36; Piazza Libertini)

TELEPHONE & FAX
Telecom Office (Via Guglielmo Oberdan 13)

TOURIST INFORMATION
Tourist Office (☎ 0832 24 80 92; Corso Vittorio Emanuele 24; ☼ 9am-1pm & 3-8pm Mon-Sat Jun-Sep, 9am-1pm Mon-Fri & 3-5pm Tue & Thu Oct-May)

TRAVEL AGENCIES
CTS Travel Agency (☎ 0832 30 18 62; Via G Palmieri 39) For youth bargain fares.

Sights

BASILICA DELLA SANTA CROCE
Little can prepare you for the opulence of the most celebrated example of Lecce baroque,

the **Basilica della Santa Croce** (☎ 0832 24 19 57; Via Umberto I; ☼ 8am-1pm & 4-7.30pm). Throughout the 16th and 17th centuries, a team of artists worked to decorate the building and its extraordinarily ornate facade. The interior is more conventionally Renaissance and definitely deserves a look if you can recover from the impact of the exterior. Giuseppe Zimbalo also left his mark in the former Convento dei Celestini, just north of the basilica, which is nowadays the **Palazzo del Governo**, the headquarters of local government.

PIAZZA DEL DUOMO
Although it fails to rival the splendour of the Basilica della Santa Croce, the baroque feast continues in Piazza del Duomo. The almost unassuming 12th-century **cathedral** (☎ 0832 30 85 57; ☼ 6.30am-noon & 5-7.30pm) was completely restored in baroque style by Giuseppe Zimbalo, who was also responsible for the 70m-high **bell tower**. Also in the piazza is the 15th-century **Palazzo Vescovile** (Episcopal Palace), reconstructed in 1632, with a beautiful 1st-floor loggia. On the western side of the square is the **Seminario**, designed by Giuseppe Cino and completed in 1709. At the time of writing it was closed for restoration.

CHURCHES & OTHER SIGHTS
On Corso Vittorio Emanuele, the interior of 17th-century **Chiesa di Sant'Irene** (☼ 8am-11am & 4-6pm Mon-Sat) boasts a magnificent pair of mirror-image baroque altarpieces, squaring up to each other across the transept. Other baroque churches of interest include the last work of Giuseppe Zimbalo, **Chiesa del Rosario** (Via G Libertini); **Santa Chiara** (Piazza Vittorio Emanuele), its every niche a swirl of twisting columns and ornate statuary; and, 200m to its south, the **Chiesa di San Matteo** (Via dei Perroni 29). The **Chiesa di SS Nicolò e Cataldo** (Via San Nicola), along from the Porta Napoli, was built by the Normans in 1180 and rebuilt in 1716 by the prolific Cino, who retained the Romanesque rose window and portal.

Lecce's 16th-century **castle**, which was built around a 12th-century Norman tower, is closed to the public unless there is a temporary exhibition.

The **Museo Provinciale** (☎ 0832 24 70 25; Viale Gallipoli) is still undergoing extensive renovations.

ROMAN REMAINS

Well below the level of Piazza Sant'Oronzo is the 2nd-century-AD **Roman amphitheatre**, discovered in the 1930s. Nearby rises the **Colonna di Sant'Oronzo**, one of the two columns that marked the end of the Via Appia at Brindisi. Donated to the city by the burghers of Brindisi in thanks to Lecce's patron saint for relieving the town of the plague in 1666, it was subsequently topped by a disproportionately small statue of the good St Oronzo himself.

Within the small **Roman theatre** (☎ 0832 24 61 09; Via Ammirati; admission €2.60; ◷ 10am-1pm), also uncovered in the 1930s, is an equally small museum, with some wonderfully preserved frescoes and mosaics, transferred from local sites.

Sleeping

Bed and breakfast is becoming the best accommodation option in town as budget hotels continue to close.

Centro Storico B&B (☎ 0832 24 28 2; www.bed andbreakfast.lecce.it; Via Vignes 2b; s/d with bathroom & breakfast high season €31/52; ⚒) Mind your head as you stoop to enter this 16th-century *palazzo*. Rooms in this charming hideaway are more comfortable than the price would suggest and all have a private balcony. There's also a nifty terrace for sunbathing.

Azzurretta B&B (☎ 338 258 59 58; www.bblecce.it; Via Vignes 2; s/d with bathroom & breakfast high season €35/52) Run by the same family as the Centro Storico and on the same floor in the same building, this place offers similar rooms at similar prices. It is an excellent city-centre option.

Hotel Cappello (☎ 0832 30 88 81; fax 0832 30 15 35; Via Montegrappa 4; s/d with bathroom €30/45; P) Overlooking the railway tracks, this place is mighty handy for the train station. Its rates are bargain-basement and the rooms are more than adequate. It also offers off-road parking (€8 per night).

Camping Namasté (☎ 0832 32 96 47; www.camp ing-lecce.it; Via Novoli; person/tent & car €5/16) Just over 4km out of town is this 35,000-sq-metre camp site. It's a sound environmental option, as it forms part of an organic farming concern. You might also take one of the yoga courses run on-site. To get to Namasté take bus No 26 from the train station.

Patria Palace Hotel (☎ 083 224 51 11; fax 0832 24 51 11; Piazzetta Riccardi; s/d with bathroom & breakfast

€130/180) Right in the middle of barmy baroque territory, this top-range option has all the requisite comforts. Each room is decorated differently and some boast views over the Basilica della Santa Croce.

Eating

CAFÉS

There are many fine cafés to choose from around town.

Caffè Alvino (☎ 0832 24 74 36; Piazza Sant'Oronzo 30) Sip your cappuccino and watch the world pass by in the beautiful piazza. The café also serves a decent *rustica*, a confection of puff pastry, mozzarella cheese and tomato.

Caffè Paisiello (☎ 0832 30 14 04; Via G Palmieri 72) Sample the pastries or ice cream here as you sip your chosen drink.

Valentina (Via Petronelli 3) This well-known delicatessen has a dazzling array of multicoloured pasta, cheeses and local specialities on offer.

RESTAURANTS

Asian Shop Center (☎ 0832 24 07 24; Via Principe di Savoia 35; curries from €5.50) It's worth visiting this genuine Indian eatery for novelty value alone. After all that pasta and pizza, what could be better than a good old curry, to eat in or take away?

Ristorante Da Guido e Figli (☎ 0832 30 58 68; Via XXV Luglio 14; meals about €15) This is one branch of two family eateries. A deep cavernous restaurant, it offers antipasto fans a mouthwatering buffet. Located just around the corner at Via Trinchese 10, the same family runs a self-service pizza takeaway

---

THE AUTHOR'S CHOICE

Alle due Corti (☎ 0832 24 22 23; www.alledue corti.com; Corte dei Giugni 1; meals €15-20) For a taste of the sunny Salentina, this elegant yet laid-back restaurant stands out. The menu is classical Puglian with plenty of fresh fruit, vegetables and home-made pasta. It really is Mediterranean cooking at its simple best. Don't worry if you don't understand the menu (written in dialect, not Italian) as the waiter explains everything. And if all else fails, ask for whatever – it's all excellent.

The restaurant also has a shop selling local produce.

which is open 11.30am to 3.30pm Monday to Saturday.

La Capannina (☎ 0832 30 41 59; Via B Cairoli 13; pizzas from €3.10, meals €16) Halfway between the train station and the centre, this is another friendly, family place. And yet again the antipasto buffet of over 20 items is too good to resist.

Dolomiti (☎ 0832 24 63 84; Viale A Costa 5; meals €10) A brash self-styled everyman of a restaurant, this is the place to indulge that very Italian of habits, the late-night croissant. They'll also do for you pizza, snacks or a plateful of pasta.

SELF-CATERING

Pick up your own ingredients at the fresh-produce **market** (Piazza Libertini; ☾ mornings Mon-Sat).

Getting There & Away

STP (☎ 0832 35 91 42) runs buses connecting Lecce with towns throughout the Penisola Salentina, including Galatina and Santa Maria di Leuca, leaving from Via Adua.

FSE (☎ 0832 34 76 34) runs buses to towns including Gallipoli (€2.10, one hour, four daily), Otranto (€2.10, one hour, two daily) and Taranto (€4.60, two hours, frequent), leaving from Via Torre del Parco.

Brindisi is 30 minutes away from Lecce by motorway and the SS7 leads to Taranto.

There are frequent trains to Bari (€7.50, 2¼ hours) via Brindisi (€2.40, 40 minutes), and daily services to Rome (€35.55, seven hours) and Bologna (€42.30, 8½ hours). For Naples (€29.96, six hours), change in Caserta. FSE trains also depart from the main station for Taranto, Bari, Otranto, Gallipoli and Martina Franca.

Getting Around

The historic centre of Lecce is best seen on foot. Among others, bus Nos 1, 2 and 4 run from the train station to Viale Marconi.

AROUND LECCE

The small town of **Galatina**, 18km south of Lecce, was a Greek colony up until the Middle Ages, and the Greek language and customs were sustained until the early 20th century. It is almost the only place where the ritual of *tarantulism* (a frenzied dance reminiscent of a voodoo frenzy and meant to rid the body tarantula bite poison)

is still practised. The tarantella folk dance evolved from it and, each year on the feast day of St Peter and St Paul (29 June), the ritual is performed at the (now deconsecrated) church dedicated to the saints.

The town's gem is its late-14th-century **Basilica di Santa Caterina d'Alessandria** (☾ 7am-noon & 4.30-8pm summer, 7am-noon & 3.30-6pm winter), one of Puglia's rare examples of Gothic architecture. The earlier Romanesque facade has three intricate portals and a lovely rose window. But hold your breath for the interior: its five naves and Gothic pointed arches are almost entirely covered in frescoes – scenes from the Old and New Testaments and the lives of the Madonna and Santa Caterina d'Alessandria.

STP buses run between Galatina and Lecce.

OTRANTO

Otranto's fame is rather grisly. In 1480 the town was besieged by the Turks and on surrendering some 800 inhabitants were massacred in what became known as the Sack of Otranto. Perhaps it was this that inspired Horace Walpole to write his 1764 Gothic horror story *The Castle of Otranto.*

Italy's easternmost port and long a base of Byzantine power, Otranto was, in its time, a major point of departure for merchants, pilgrims and crusaders heading for the Orient and the Holy Land. Today it is a summer resort town that is packed in summer and a pretty location out of season. Worth a visit in its own right, it also makes a good base for a coastal tour of the Penisola Salentina.

The **tourist office** (☎ 0836 80 14 36; Piazza Castello; ☾ 9am-1pm & 3-8pm Mon-Fri Jun-Sep, 9am-1pm Mon-Fri Oct-May) faces the castle.

Sights

Otranto's premier attraction is the brilliant mosaic in the Romanesque **cathedral** (☾ 8am-noon & 3-7pm Apr-Sep, 8am-noon & 3-5pm Oct-Mar). First built by the Normans in the 11th century and subsequently subjected to a face-lift or two, the magnificent cathedral is a forest of slender pillars and carved capitals. The walls bear well-preserved Byzantine frescoes, while underfoot is the vast restored 12th-century floor mosaic occupying the whole of the nave. It's a vibrant masterpiece depicting the tree of life and other scenes of myth and legend, both Christian and pagan. Rex Arturis (King Arthur) is depicted on horseback near the top of the tree.

In the chapel to the right of the altar is a bizarre sight. Its walls are lined with glass cases packed tight with skulls and bones, the remains of the victims of the Sack of Otranto.

Just south of the cathedral is a small **diocesan museum** (10am-noon & 4-8pm Apr-Sep, 10am-noon & 3-6pm Oct-Mar) where you can see segments of a 4th-century Roman mosaic, recently discovered under the cathedral's 12th-century floor.

Within tiny **Chiesa di San Pietro** are more vivid Byzantine frescoes. If, as is probable, you find the church closed, call by the guardian's house at Piazza del Popolo 1, some 30m away.

The Aragonese **castle** (Piazza Castello; admission free except during exhibitions; 9am-1pm Mon-Fri), at the eastern edge of town beside the port, is typical of the squat, thick-walled forts you'll find in coastal towns throughout Puglia. Built in the late 15th century after the Turkish massacre, it is characterised by cylindrical towers that widen towards the base.

Sleeping & Eating

Hotel Meublé (/fax 0836 80 19 52; Porto Craulo 13; d with bathroom high season €60-78) Situated within five minutes' walk of the beach, this modest place is ideally suited for a summer stay. Its patio is shrouded in greenery and makes for a lovely spot to sample their pizza, scrupulously prepared in a wood oven.

Hotel Bellavista (/fax 0836 80 10 58; Via Vittorio Emanuele 18; s/d with bathroom & breakfast high season €85/114) Recently renovated, this bright hotel has some rooms with balconies overlooking the seafront – take one of these and you can watch the world go by on the long summer evenings. It's not the quietest of spots though.

Hydrusa (0836 80 12 55; Via del Porto; person/ tent/car high season €6/6/1.50) This camp site near the port is fairly basic, but try to find anywhere cheaper!

La Duchesca (0836 80 12 04; Piazza Castello; meals from €18) At this pretty little trattoria you can ponder the hidden horrors of the castle lurking opposite. The menu (which includes pizza) is basic and the food fine.

Alternatively, simply sip a drink while sitting on the square.

Getting There & Away

Otranto can be reached from Lecce by FSE train (€2.50, one hour) or bus (€3.10, 50 minutes).

A Marozzi buses run daily to/from Rome. There are three daily departures from the port and calling at Lecce and Brindisi.

For travel information and reservations, go to **Ellade Viaggi** (0836 80 15 78; www.elladeviaggi.it, Italian only; Via Guglielmotto d'Otr 33) at the port.

AROUND OTRANTO

The road south from Otranto takes you along a wild coastline. The land here is rocky, and when the wind is up you can see why it is largely treeless. Many of the towns here started life as Greek settlements and a few of the older folk still speak Greek. There are few monuments to be seen but the occasional solitary tower appears, facing out to sea. When you reach **Santa Maria di Leuca**, you've hit the bottom of the heel of Italy and the dividing line between the Adriatic and Ionian Seas. The Ionian side of the Penisola Salentina in particular is spattered with reasonable beaches. There are few cheap hotels in the area but camp sites abound along the coast.

GALLIPOLI
pop 21,089

The name of this picturesque old town is appropriate; deriving from Greek, it means 'beautiful city'. Jutting into the Ionian Sea 39km southwest of Lecce, Gallipoli is actually an island connected to the mainland and modern city by a bridge. An important fishing centre, it has a history of strong-willed independence, being the last Salentine settlement to succumb to the Normans in the 11th century.

The **tourist office** (0833 26 25 29; Piazza Imbriani 8; 9am-1pm & 5-9pm Jul-Aug, 9am-1pm Mon-Fri & 4-6pm Tue & Thu Sep-Jun) is just over the bridge.

The entrance to the medieval island town is guarded by an Angevin **castle**. Just opposite, below the ramp leading to the island, is a fish market that makes up for its small size with great variety.

Right in the heart of the old town is the 17th-century baroque **cathedral** (083

26 19 87; Via Antonietta de Pace; ⊙ open only during services), adorned with paintings by local artists. A little further west, the small **Museo Civico** (☎ 0833 26 42 24; Via Antonietta de Pace) was closed for renovations at the time of writing.

Back over the bridge and just in the modern part of town is the **Fontana Antica**. Reconstructed in the 16th century from a Greek original, this fountain's much-weathered sculptured figures tell a steamy tale of incest and bestiality.

Hotel Al Pescatore (☎/fax 0833 26 36 56; Riviera Colombo 39; s/d with bathroom & breakfast from €44/67, half board compulsory in Aug €67) In the old town, Al Pescatore has 16 spacious rooms available, some with views of the port. To enter the hotel you pass through a lovely light atrium full of vegetation. There's also a good restaurant, specialising in the freshest of fish, where a full meal costs from €20.

Trattoria La Tonnara (☎ 0833 26 10 58; Via Garibaldi 7; pizza from €6, full meal from €18; ⊙ Tue-Sun) Near the cathedral, La Tonnara is one of several restaurants in the old town where you can eat well. In addition to the a la carte menu, it does pizza over wood (in the evenings only).

FSE buses and trains link Gallipoli to Lecce.

TARANTO
pop 207,199

Break through the industrial horror-show that Taranto presents its visitors and you'll find a vivacious historic city. Founded in the 7th century BC by exiles from Sparta, it was christened Taras and grew to become one of the wealthiest and most important colonies of Magna Graecia, with a peak population of 300,000. The fun finished, however, in the 3rd century BC when the Romans marched in, changed its name to Tarentum and set off a two-millennia decline in fortunes.

Taranto, along with La Spezia, is Italy's major naval base and the presence of young sailors is emblematic of a city that has always looked to the sea. In fact, one of the city's more esoteric claims to fame is that it is alleged to be the point where the first cat landed on European shores.

Worth a quick visit, Taranto is unlikely to keep you busy for long.

Orientation

Taranto neatly splits into three. The old town is on a tiny island, lodged between the port and train station to the northwest and the new city to the southeast. The more expensive hotels, tourist office and banks are in the grid-patterned new city.

Information

EMERGENCY
Police Station (☎ 099 454 51 11; Via Anfiteatro 8)

INTERNET ACCESS
Chiocciolin@it (☎ 099 453 80 51; Corso Umberto I 85; €5.16/hr; ⊙ 9am-1pm & 4.30-9pm Tue-Sat, Mon 4.30-9pm)

MEDICAL SERVICES
Hospital (☎ 099 453 24 07; Via Bruno)

POST
Post Office (☎ 099 470 75 91; Lungomare Vittorio Emanuele III)

TOURIST INFORMATION
Tourist Office (☎ 099 453 23 97; Corso Umberto I 113; ⊙ 9am-1pm & 5-7pm Mon-Fri, 9am-noon Sat)

Dangers & Annoyances

Ironically in a town that welcomed Europe's first cat, stray dogs can be a nuisance. This is particularly true around the old town, which itself can be dodgy after dark.

Sights

CITTÀ VECCHIA

Despite efforts to clean up the old town, it obstinately remains run-down and dilapidated. This isn't good news as most of the city's sights are in the old town.

Guarding the swing bridge that joins the old and new town, the **Castello Aragonese**, at the island's southern extreme, is an interesting enough structure that was completed in 1492. Unfortunately it's occupied by the Italian navy and inaccessible to visitors.

The 11th-century **cathedral** (Via del Duomo) is one of Puglia's oldest Romanesque buildings. Remodelled in the 18th century, its three-nave interior is divided by 16 marble columns supporting Romanesque and Byzantine capitals. Its baroque Cappella di San Cataldo is decorated with frescoes and inlaid marble. The whole cathedral is dedicated to San Cataldo, Taranto's patron saint.

PUGLIA, BASILICATA & CALABRIA

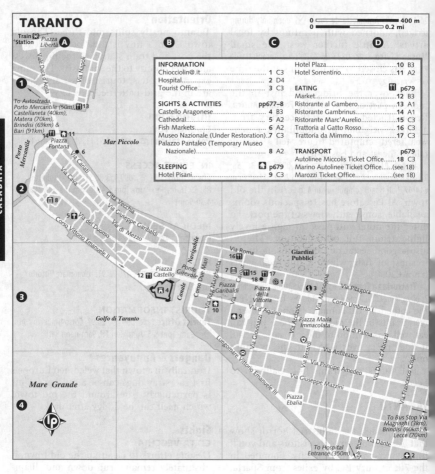

TARANTO

0 ———————— 400 m
0 ———————— 0.2 mi

INFORMATION	
Chiocciolin@.it..................................	1 C3
Hospital...	2 D4
Tourist Office....................................	3 C3

SIGHTS & ACTIVITIES	pp677–8
Castello Aragonese...........................	4 B3
Cathedral..	5 A2
Fish Markets.....................................	6 A2
Museo Nazionale (Under Restoration)..7 C3	
Palazzo Pantaleo (Temporary Museo	
Nazionale)......................................	8 A2

SLEEPING	🛏 p679
Hotel Pisani......................................	9 C3

Hotel Plaza.......................................	10 B3
Hotel Sorrentino...............................	11 A2

EATING	🍴 p679
Market..	12 B3
Ristorante al Gambero......................	13 A1
Ristorante Gambrinus........................	14 A1
Ristorante Marc'Aurelio.....................	15 C3
Trattoria al Gatto Rosso...................	16 C3
Trattoria da Mimmo..........................	17 C3

TRANSPORT	p679
Autolinee Miccolis Ticket Office........	18 C3
Marino Autolinee Ticket Office......(see 18)	
Marozzi Ticket Office....................(see 18)	

Visit Via Cariati's **fish markets**, where all the rich variety of the morning's catch is on display. Taranto has been famous since antiquity for what it draws from the sea, in particular its shellfish and its gorgeously fleshy oysters.

MUSEO NAZIONALE

Renovation work on Taranto's premier museum is still ongoing. At least that's what the sign says; evidence of work in progress is noticeably absent. A shame, as this archaeological **museum** (☎ 099 453 21 12; Corso Umberto I 41) is one of the most important in Italy and houses, among other ancient artefacts, an impressive collection of antique gold jewellery. You can

get some idea of its scandalously hidden treasures by visiting the temporary display in **Palazzo Pantaleo** (☎ 099 471 84 92; Corso Vittorio Emanuele II; admission €2; 🕒 8.30am-7.30pm) in the old town.

Festivals & Events

Le Feste di Pasqua (Holy Week) in Taranto is a time of high emotion and huge crowds. Thousands of people come to witness the processions – on Holy Thursday the Procession of the *Addolorata* (Sorrowful and on Good Friday the Procession of the Mysteries – when sinister bearers clad in Ku Klux Klan–like robes carry statues representing the Passion of Christ around town.

Sleeping

Hotel Sorrentino (☎ 099 470 74 56; Piazza Fontana 7; s/d €20/27, with bathroom €25/38) This is a simple, no-frills budget hotel where rooms are basic and cheap. And at this price the restaurants that surround the square outside might seem all the more appealing.

Hotel Pisani (☎ 099 453 40 87; fax 099 470 75 93; Via Cavour 43; s/d with bathroom & breakfast €25/46) In the new town, this is another value-for-money budget option. Rooms are a good size but can be a bit gloomy. That's the price to pay for the quiet location down a shaded side street.

Hotel Plaza (☎ 099 459 07 75; www.hotelplazataranto.com, Italian only; Via d'Aquino 46; s/d with bathroom & breakfast €55/78) The decor at this big commercial hotel looks as if it got stuck in a time warp somewhere around the 1960s. However, rooms are well equipped and the hotel is conveniently central.

Eating

The food is generally excellent in Taranto. Mussels are a speciality and are usually fantastically cheap.

Ristorante Marc'Aurelio (☎ 099 4 52 78 93; Via Cavour 17; meals €15-18) Popular with the locals, this excellent restaurant serves fantastic and abundant antipasto. You can either follow this with pizza prepared in a wood-fired oven or with one of the tempting pasta dishes.

Trattoria da Mimmo (☎ 099 459 37 33; Via Giovinazzi 18; meals €15; ☿ Thu-Tue) Another city-centre trattoria that pulls in the punters, especially at the weekend. The menu throws up no surprises, but that's OK; it simply means the cooks prepare what they know in a way they've long since perfected.

Trattoria al Gatto Rosso (☎ 099 452 98 75; Via Cavour 2; meals €15; ☿ Tue-Sun) For a reasonably priced meal, this place fits the bill as well as the others. Relaxed and unpretentious, it can get very busy, so be prepared to wait.

Ristorante Gambrinus (☎ 099 471 65 52; Via Fontana 61; meals €18; ☿ Thu-Tue) Seafood is what this bustling restaurant is all about. Not far away from the fish market, you know that what you're eating is as fresh as the morning's catch. The house menu also has the added bonus of including an unspecified quantity of wine in the price.

Ristorante al Gambero (☎ 099 471 11 90; Piazzale Democrate; meals €25) There are some who say Al Gambero, the grand old master of Tarantino dining, isn't what it once was. No matter, it's still pretty good. So near to the sea you can almost point to the fish you want, it is slightly more elegant than Gambrinus.

There's a fresh-produce **market** (Piazza Castello; ☿ mornings Mon-Sat) just west of the Ponte Girevole.

Getting There & Around

Buses heading north and west depart from Porto Mercantile; those going south and east from Via Magnaghi in the new city.

FSE (☎ 099 477 46 27) buses connect Taranto with Martina Franca and Bari (leaving from Porto Mercantile), as well as Ostuni (leaving from Via Magnaghi) and smaller towns in the area. Infrequent **SITA** (☎ 099 829 50 86) buses leave from Porto Mercantile for Matera and Metaponto. Chiruzzi buses also serve Metaponto. **STP** (☎ 0832 31 69 51) and FSE buses connect Taranto with Lecce.

Marozzi (☎ 099 459 40 89) has express services to/from Rome's Stazione Tiburtina (€36.60, six hours, four daily), leaving from Porto Mercantile. **Marino Autolinee** (☎ 080 311 23 35) does a run through the night to Turin (€49) via Milan (€43). **Autolinee Miccolis** (☎ 099 735 37 54) runs three buses daily to/from Naples (€13.45, four hours) via Potenza (€7.25, two hours) and Salerno (€11.90, 3¼ hours). The ticket office for all three companies is at Corso Umberto I 67.

Both **Trenitalia** (☎ 89 20 21) and **FSE** (☎ 099 471 59 01) trains connect Taranto with Brindisi (€3.65, 1¼ hours, frequent), Bari (€6.20, 1¼ hours, frequent), Martina Franca (€2.30, 45 minutes, eight daily) and Alberobello, as well as the cities of Potenza (€7.90, two hours, four daily), Naples (€22.40, 4½ hours, four daily) and Rome (€36, 6½ hours, five daily).

AMAT (☎ 099 4 52 67 32) bus Nos 1/2, 3 and 8 run between the station and the new city.

For a taxi call ☎ 099 7 30 47 34.

BASILICATA

Basilicata is one of Italy's least-explored regions. A land of rock and mountains, of forests and upland meadows, this dramatic territory spans Italy's 'instep' with brief strips of coastline touching the Tyrrhenian and Ionian Seas. While no longer the desolate, malaria-ridden land of poverty-stricken peasants so powerfully described by Carlo Levi in his novel *Christ Stopped at Eboli*, it retains a strong sense of isolation and remains one of Italy's poorest regions. This despite the continued development of mainland Western Europe's largest oil field, discovered in 1996 in the mountainous area 30km south of Potenza.

Known to the Romans as Lucania (a name still heard today), Basilicata was a favoured hunting ground of bandits in the late 19th century. Against a backdrop of unification, bands of outlaws were often sponsored by Bourbon loyalists to oppose political change and earned a reputation for ferocity.

Much has, of course, changed since those times. Government subsidies and development programs have improved communications but economic progress has been slow. Peasants still farm this ungiving land as their ancestors did, using techniques unchanged for centuries. They do, however, produce marvels – excellent bread, really flavoursome fruit and vegetables and arguably the best ricotta cheese in the country.

Italy's favourite after-dinner tipple *amaro*, a bitter liqueur, is also a historic product of Basilicata.

Don't come to Basilicata expecting to find a treasure chest of art, architecture and ancient history. The region's dramatic landscape, particularly the Tyrrhenian coast, and its close connection with the culture that Levi recorded, along with the fascinating city of Matera, are the main attractions.

POTENZA
pop 69,655 / elevation 819m

The best way to see Potenza is quickly and by night. That way you'll avoid the sight of some of the most brutal housing blocks you're ever likely to see. In addition, Basilicata's regional capital is the highest in the land, making it cloyingly hot in summer and bitterly cold in winter. There really is very little reason to come here but you may find yourself passing through or even overnighting. Badly damaged in repeated earthquakes, Potenza has lost most of its medieval buildings.

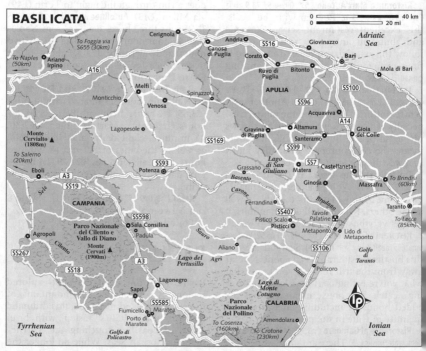

BASILICATA

The centre of town straggles east to west across a high ridge. To the south lie the main Trenitalia and Ferrovie Appulo-Lucane train stations, connected to the centre by bus Nos 1 or 10.

The **tourist office** (☎ 0971 27 44 80; www.apt basilicata.it; Piazza XVIII Agosto; ☼ 8am-2pm Mon-Fri & 4-7pm Tue & Thu) is central.

Sights

Potenza's sights, such as they are, are in the old centre of town, which is at the very top of the hill – take the elevators from Piazza Vittorio Emanuele II. The ecclesiastical highlight is the **cathedral**, originally erected in the 12th century but rebuilt in the 18th. Elegant Via Pretoria, flanked by a boutique or two, makes a pleasant traffic-free stroll. North of the town centre is the **Museo Archeologico Provinciale** (☎ 0971 44 48 33; Via Ciccotti; admission free; ☼ 9am-1pm Tue-Sun & 4-7pm Tue-Thu), which houses a collection of artefacts discovered in the region.

Sleeping & Eating

Pensione Europa (☎ 0971 3 40 14; Via Giacinto Albini 3; s €16, d with bathroom €31) At the western end of Via Pretoria in the old centre, this place is really basic. Rooms are clean and functional, and at these prices you can't really ask for much more.

Grande Albergo Potenza (☎ 0971 41 02 20; albergo@libero.it; Corso XVIII Agosto 46; s/d with bathroom €73/100) If you have to overnight in Potenza, this is the place to console yourself. A quality hotel with all the creature comforts, it adds a much-needed touch of style to the town.

Monticchio (☎ 0971 2 48 80; Via Caserma Lucana 30; meals €15; ☼ Mon-Sat) Up in the old centre, this simple trattoria isn't the place for adventurous dining. However, the food is hearty and well cooked and the service is friendly, even if rather lugubrious.

Getting There & Away

BUS

Various companies operate out of several places; the tourist office has a comprehensive list of destinations and services.

Grassani (☎ 0835 72 14 43) has two buses daily to Matera (€5.32, one hour). **SITA** (☎ 0971 50 68 11) has daily services to Melfi, Venosa and Maratea. Buses leave from Via Appia 185 and also stop near the Scalo Inferiore Trenitalia train station.

Liscio (☎ 0971 5 46 73) serves destinations including Rome (€17, 4½ hours, one daily) and Naples (€7.50, two hours, three daily) via Salerno (€5.40, 1½ hours).

CAR & MOTORCYCLE

Potenza is connected to Salerno in the west by the A3. Metaponto lies southeast along the SS407, the Basentana. For Matera, take the SS407 and then turn north onto the SS7 at Ferrandina.

TRAIN

To pick up a train on the main Trenitalia line from Taranto to Naples, go to **Potenza Inferiore** (☎ 0971 20 21). There are regular services to/from Taranto (€7.90, two hours), Salerno (€5.75, 2¼ hours) and Foggia (€5.75, two hours). Trains also travel to Metaponto (€5.75, 1½ hours) and occasionally direct to Naples (€7.90, two hours). To get to Matera (€3.35, one hour, frequent), change to an **FAL** (☎ 0971 41 15 61) bus at Ferrandina on the Metaponto line. For Bari (€12.35, three hours, three daily), use the **Ferrovie Appulo-Lucane** (☎ 0971 41 15 61) at Potenza Superiore station.

NORTH OF POTENZA

It's perfectly possible to explore this area of green valleys and rolling hills and be the only foreigner in sight. Dotted with several interesting sites, it is best explored by car as public transport is sporadic at best. Here is the home of Basilicata's best wine, Aglianico del Vulture, a robust red that complements the region's hearty cuisine.

Lagopesole, 28km from Potenza, boasts Frederick II's largest **castle** (donations welcome; ☼ 9.30am-1pm & 4-7pm Mar-Sep, 3-5pm Oct-Feb), a stark barrack-like structure heaped over a Norman fortress.

Melfi, 53km north of Potenza, was an important medieval town and a favourite residence of Frederick II. Surrounded by 4km of Norman walls and dominated by a solid castle, it was largely refashioned by Frederick. The castle houses the **Museo Nazionale del Melfese** (☎ 0972 23 87 26; admission €2.50; ☼ 9am-8pm Tue-Sun, 2-8pm Mon), which has an excellent collection of artefacts found in the area, some dating from the 8th century BC. Seek out the impressive 2nd-century-AD Roman sarcophagus, housed in a small room within the southeast tower. Melfi's

cathedral, repeatedly shaken by earthquakes, has a fine gilded wooden ceiling and maintains its 12th-century bell tower.

Some 15km southwest of Melfi, the lakes at **Monticchio** are a popular summer recreation spot.

The pick of the area's towns, **Venosa**, about 25km east of Melfi, was once a thriving Roman colony and is the birthplace of the poet Horace. Tourist information is available at **Minutiello Viaggi** (☎ 0972 3 25 69; Largo Baliaggio 5). At the northeastern end of town, you can wander around the sparse remains of the original **Roman settlement** (admission free; ☙ 9am-1 hr before sunset Wed-Mon), which includes a bath complex and an amphitheatre. Next to the ruins is the **Abbazia della Santissima Trinità** (☎ 0972 3 42 11), the most impressive Norman legacy in Basilicata. Within the complex are the abbey *palazzo* and a pair of churches, one never completed.

Venosa's 15th-century Aragonese castle, entered from Piazza Umberto I, the town's main square, contains a small **archaeological museum** (☎ 0972 3 60 95; admission €2.50; ☙ 9am-8pm Wed-Mon, 3-8pm Tue).

Hotel Orazio (☎ /fax 0972 3 11 35; Vittorio Emanuele 142; s/d with bathroom €36/50) This hotel in Venosa is a veritable palace. The high-ceilinged, graciously decorated rooms are overseen by a pair of grandmotherly ladies who do all they can to make your stay comfortable. Well worth a stop.

Melfi and Venosa can both be reached by a daily bus from Potenza (see p681).

MATERA

pop 57,311 / elevation 405m

Matera is absolutely unique. In no other city do you come face to face with such powerful images of Italy's lost peasant culture. Its famous *sassi* – stone houses carved out of and into the twin ravines that slice through town – tell of a poverty now difficult to imagine in a developed European country.

Today a Unesco World Heritage Site, the *sassi* were home to more than half of Matera's populace until well after WWII. People and animals slept together and, despite an infant mortality rate of over 50%, a typical family cave sheltered an average of six children. Change only came in the late 1950s when the local government built new

housing and forcefully relocated the 15,000 inhabitants of the *sassi*.

It took half a century and vast amounts of development money to eradicate malaria and starvation in Basilicata. Today people are returning to live in the *sassi* – but as a trend rather than a necessity.

Orientation

A short walk down Via Roma from the train and bus stations off Piazza Matteotti brings you to the Piazza Vittorio Veneto, the pedestrianised heart of town. The two *sassi* ravines open up to its east and southeast.

MAPS

It's easy enough to find your own way around the *sassi*. Arm yourself with the map *Matera: Percorsi Turistici* (€1.30), which describes in English four well-signposted itineraries. It's explicit enough to allow you to roam off-route and is available from **Libreria dell'Arco** (Via Ridola 37).

Information

EMERGENCY
Police Station (☎ 0835 33 46 27; Piazza Vittorio Veneto)

INTERNET ACCESS
Internet Point (☎ 0835 34 61 12; Piazza Vittorio Veneto 49; €4/hr)

INTERNET RESOURCES
Basilicata Turistica (www.aptbasilicata.it)

MEDICAL SERVICES
Guardia Medica (☎ 0835 24 35 38) 24-hour doctor.
Hospital (☎ 0835 24 32 12; Via Montesaglioso) 1km southeast of the centre.

POST
Post Office (☎ 0835 33 05 74; Via del Corso 1; ☙ 8am-6.30pm Mon-Fri, 8am-12.30pm Sat)

TELEPHONE & FAX
Telecom Office (Via del Corso)

TOURIST IFORMATION
Tourist Office (☎ 0835 33 19 83; Via De Viti De Marco 9; ☙ 9am-1pm Mon-Sat & 4-6.30pm Mon & Thu)
Information Kiosks (☎ 0835 24 12 60; Via Madonna delle Virtù; ☙ 9.30am-12.30pm & 4-7pm summer) In the *sassi*. Run by the Comune di Matera, there are also kiosks on Piazza Matteotti and Via Lucana.

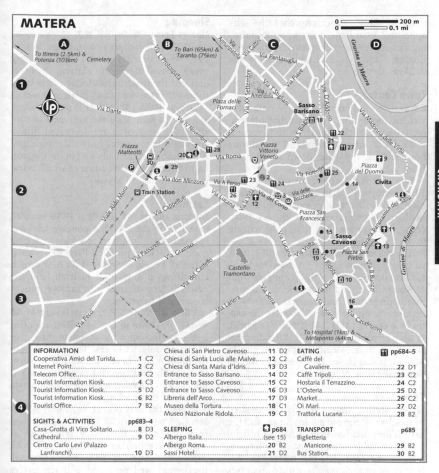

MATERA

INFORMATION		
Cooperativa Amici del Turista	1	C2
Internet Point	2	C2
Telecom Office	3	C2
Tourist Information Kiosk	4	C3
Tourist Information Kiosk	5	D2
Tourist Information Kiosk	6	B2
Tourist Office	7	B2

SIGHTS & ACTIVITIES	pp683–4	
Casa-Grotta di Vico Solitario	8	D3
Cathedral	9	D2
Centro Carlo Levi (Palazzo Lanfranchi)	10	D3

Chiesa di San Pietro Caveoso	11	D2
Chiesa di Santa Lucia alle Malve	12	C2
Chiesa di Santa Maria d'Idris	13	D3
Entrance to Sasso Barisano	14	C2
Entrance to Sasso Caveoso	15	C2
Entrance to Sasso Caveoso	16	C2
Libreria dell'Arco	17	D3
Museo della Tortura	18	C1
Museo Nazionale Ridola	19	C3

SLEEPING	⌂ p684	
Albergo Italia	(see 15)	
Albergo Roma	20	B2
Sassi Hotel	21	D2

EATING	🍴 pp684–5	
Caffè del Cavaliere	22	D1
Caffè Tripoli	23	C2
Hostaria il Terrazzino	24	C2
L'Osteria	25	D2
Market	26	C2
Oi Marì	27	D2
Trattoria Lucana	28	B2

TRANSPORT	p685	
Biglietteria Manicone	29	B2
Bus Station	30	B2

The Sassi

The two *sassi* areas, **Barisano** and **Caveoso**, had no electricity, running water or sewerage system until well into the 20th century. The oldest *sassi* (dating from medieval times or earlier) are at the top of the ravine and the dwellings in the lower sections of the ravine, which seem the oldest, were in fact established this century.

The *sassi* zones are accessible from several points around the centre of Matera. There is an entrance just off Piazza Vittorio Veneto. Alternatively, take Via delle Beccherie to Piazza del Duomo and follow the tourist itinerary signs to enter either Barisano or Caveoso. Sasso Caveoso is also accessible from Via Ridola by the stairs next to Albergo Italia.

Caveoso is the more picturesque of the two *sassi* areas. Highlights include the **Chiesa di San Pietro Caveoso** (Piazza San Pietro, Sasso Caveoso), plus the rock churches of **Santa Maria d'Idris** and **Santa Lucia alle Malve**, both with well-preserved Byzantine frescoes.

A couple of *sassi* have been refurnished as they were when the last inhabitants occupied them. The more interesting of the two is the **Casa-Grotta di Vico Solitario** (off Via B Buozzi; admission €1.50), which has a guide sheet in English.

For the morbid, the **Museo della Tortura** (Torture Museum; Via S Biagio; admission adult/child €3/1.50; 🕑 9am-1pm & 4-7.30pm Tue-Sun) has all manner of monstrous devices, including a genuine guillotine.

In the outlying rock churches, the self-appointed guardians insist upon declaiming an automaton spiel in severely fractured English – and expect a backhander for this dubious service.

Town Centre

Excavations in Piazza Vittorio Veneto have yielded more ruins of Byzantine Matera, including a rock church with frescoes, a castle, a large cistern and numerous houses. You can gaze down to the site from the piazza.

The relatively sedate exterior of the 13th-century Puglian-Romanesque **cathedral** (Piazza del Duomo) ill-prepares you for the neobaroque excess within, a clumsy 19th-century aberration. At the time of writing it was closed for renovation.

The **Museo Nazionale Ridola** (☎ 0835 31 00 58; Via Ridola 24; admission €2.50; ⏰ 9am-8pm Tue-Sun, 2-8pm Mon) occupies the 17th-century convent of Santa Chiara and has a collection of primarily prehistoric and classical artefacts. A little south, on Piazzetta Pascoli, is the **Centro Carlo Levi** (☎ 0835 31 42 35; Palazzo Lanfranchi). It houses paintings by Levi, including an enormous mural depicting peasant life in Matera. It was closed for extensive renovation at the time of writing.

Tours

Upon entering Matera you will be assailed by hustlers offering to guide you around the *sassi*. There are, however, plenty of official guides available – the tourist office has details. Alternatively, contact **Itinera** (☎ 0835 26 32 59; www.guideitinera.too.it), which organises guided tours in English, or **Cooperativa Amici del Turista** (☎ 0835 33 03 01; www.materaturistica.it; Via Fiorentini 28-30).

Festivals & Events

Matera celebrates the feast day of **Santa Maria della Bruna** (the city's patron saint) on 2 July. The high point of the festival is a colourful procession from the cathedral when a statue of the Madonna is carried along in a cart ornately decorated in papier-mâché. When the procession ends (and once the statue has been removed), it's time for the *assalto al carro*, when the crowd descends on the cart and its contents and tears them to pieces in order to take away what the faithful regard as precious relics.

Sleeping

Albergo Roma (☎ /fax 0835 33 39 12; Via Roma 62; s/d €22/32) This budget option dates back to 1927 when tourists weren't exactly falling over themselves to get to Matera. The hotel outlived the malaria and today offers basic rooms at prices you can't better in town.

Albergo Italia (☎ 0835 33 35 61; www.albergo italia.com; Via Ridola 5; s/d with bathroom & breakfast €75/98) All 46 rooms are decorated differently at this *sasso*-side hotel. The furniture is old-fashioned and sits well in the elegant, high-ceilinged rooms, some of which boast views over Sasso Caveoso.

Eating

Trattoria Lucana (☎ 0835 33 61 17; Via Lucana 48; meals €20; ⏰ Mon-Sat) This popular trattoria specialises in regional cooking, making good use of local produce. Particularly good is the all-veggie *antipasto della casa*, which constitutes a mini-meal in itself, and the *cavatelli lucana*, pasta with sausage, mushrooms and tomatoes.

L'Osteria (☎ 0835 33 33 95; Via Fiorentini 58; full meal €15-18) Down in the Sasso Barisano, this is the perfect spot for intimate dining as there are only six tables. The cuisine is of the home-made, hearty school and the service friendly and cheerful. A typical dish is the *capunti e fagioli*, white beans and pasta simmered in a pork stock.

Oi Marí (☎ 0835 34 61 21; Via Fiorentini 66; pizza from €3.50, pasta from €6.50) Just down the road from L'Osteria, this place sells itself as a stylish Neapolitan pizzeria – and with some justification as the setting is original, the pizzas well prepared and the prices reasonable.

Hostaria il Terrazzino (☎ 0835 33 25 03; Vico San Giuseppe 7; tourist menu €13) The food is what

---

SOMETHING SPECIAL

Sassi Hotel (☎ 0835 33 10 09; www.hotelsassi.it; Via San Giovanni Vecchio 89; dm/s/d with bathroom & breakfast €16/52/90) Matera's *sassi* are unique, which means that the Sassi Hotel is also unique. After all, where else can you bed down in a Unesco World Heritage Site?

Actually built into the rocky landscape that makes up the Sasso Barisano, the hotel offers a special atmosphere complemented by the friendliness of the owners.

you'd expect from a city-centre restaurant catering to tourists, but the cave-like interior and terrace overlooking Sasso Barisano make this a decent spot to eat. It's signposted from Piazza Vittorio Veneto.

For a light snack, coffee or a liqueur (strictly *Amaro Lucano*, of course) try **Caffè del Cavaliere** (off Via Fiorentini in Sasso Barisano) or **Caffè Tripoli** (Piazza Vittorio Veneto 17).

There's a daily fresh-produce **market** (Via A Persio) just south of Piazza Vittorio Veneto.

Getting There & Away
BUS
The bus station is just north of Piazza Matteotti, near the train station. **SITA** (☎ 0835 33 28 62) runs buses connecting Matera with Taranto (€4.40, 1½ hours, six daily) and Metaponto (€2.70, one hour, up to five daily), as well as many small towns in the province. **Grassani** (☎ 0835 72 14 43) has two buses per day to Potenza (€5.35).

Marozzi (Rome ☎ 06 225 21 47) runs three buses daily between Rome and Matera. A joint SITA/Marozzi service leaves at 10.35pm for the northern cities of Siena, Florence and Pisa via Potenza. Advance booking is essential.

Buy your ticket for all services except Grassani (pay on the bus) at **Biglietteria Manicone** (☎ 0835 33 28 62; Piazza Matteotti 3-4).

CAR & MOTORCYCLE
Matera's narrow alleys and steep contours are no place for a vehicle. It's better to leave your car north of the *sassi* area and continue on foot. Central Piazza Vittorio Veneto is pedestrianised.

TRAIN
Ferrovie Appulo-Lucane (FAL; ☎ 0835 33 28 61) runs regular trains (€3.65, 1½ hours, at least 12 daily) and buses (€3.70, four to six daily) to/from Bari. For Potenza, take a FAL bus to Ferrandina and connect with a Trenitalia train, or go to Altamura to link up with FAL's Bari–Potenza run.

ALIANO
Not one of Italy's – or even Basilicata's – great tourist stopovers, this tiny hill-top village southwest of Matera might attract Carlo Levi groupies who have their own transport. When he was exiled to Basilicata between 1935 and 1936, he lived for a time in Aliano (formerly Gagliano) where little has changed in the past 75 years. Wander to the edge of the old village to see the house where he stayed. Two **museums** have been established in the town, one devoted to Levi (who is buried in the village) and another to the peasant tradition of the area.

Aliano is accessible by SITA bus from Matera, with a change in Pisticci Scalo.

METAPONTO
Metaponto's Greek ruins might not be as picturesque as those of Paestum in neighbouring Campania, but they are impressive and warrant a visit. Founded by Greek colonisers between the 8th and 7th centuries BC, the city of Metaponto prospered as a commercial and grain-producing centre. One of its most famous residents was Pythagoras, who established a school here after being banished from Crotone (in what is now Calabria) towards the end of the 6th century BC.

After Pythagoras died, his house and school were incorporated into a Temple of Hera. The remains of the temple – 15 columns and sections of pavement – are known as the Tavole Palatine (Palatine Tables), since knights, or paladins, are said to have gathered there before heading to the crusades.

Overtaken politically and economically by Rome, Metaponto met its end in the Second Punic War of 207 BC.

Modern Metaponto's only real attraction is a sandy beach, Lido di Metaponto, which is not the coast's best and in summer is completely swamped. It's about 3km east of the train station.

Sights
From the train station, go straight ahead for 500m to a roundabout. To your right (east) is the **Parco Archeologico** (about 1.5km from the roundabout; admission free) and to the left, the **Museo Archeologico Nazionale** (☎ 0835 74 53 27; Via Aristea 21; admission €2.50; ⏰ 9am-7pm). In the park, the site of ancient Metapontum, you can see what remains of a **Greek theatre** and the Doric **Tempio di Apollo Licio**. The museum houses artefacts from Metapontum and other sites. If it's at home (it's often on tour), the accompanying exhibition on wine, 'Il Vino di Dionisio', is fun to visit.

To walk in the footsteps of Pythagoras, head to the **Tavole Palatine**. Follow the slip road for Taranto onto the SS106 and it's a little way north, just off the highway.

Sleeping

Accommodation in Metaponto is not great; most places close in winter, prices are high and in summer everything is usually booked out.

Hotel Turismo (☎ 0835 74 19 18; Viale delle Ninfe 5; d with bathroom €68, half board per person €56; ❄) One of a number of large, bog-standard summer hotels by the sea, this place is one of the cheaper options. To get a room in high summer, you'll need to book ahead.

Camping Magna Grecia (☎ 0835 74 18 55; Via Liolo; person/tent/car high season €6.75/7.25/2.60; ☼) This seven-hectare camp site is an easy 800m from the sea. Facilities are comprehensive and should you get fed up with the saltwater of the sea, you can always cool off in the pool.

Getting There & Away

SITA buses run to Metaponto from Matera and from Taranto's Porto Mercantile. The town is on the Taranto–Reggio di Calabria line, and trains connect with Potenza, Salerno and occasionally Naples. The station is 3km west of the Lido di Metaponto. If you don't want to walk, wait for one of the regular **SITA** (☎ 0835 38 50 07) or **Chiruzzi** (☎ 0835 54 40 35) buses to pass by on the way to the beach.

AROUND METAPONTO

If you get as far as Metaponto, consider continuing about 21km southwest along the coast to **Policoro**, originally the Greek settlement of Eraclea. The ruins are no more impressive than those of Metapontum but the **museum** (☎ 0835 97 21 54; Via Colombo 8; admission €2.50; ☼ 9am-8pm Wed-Mon, 2-8pm Tue) is worth the visit alone. It has a fabulous display of artefacts excavated in the area, including two complete tombs with skeletons surrounded by the objects and jewellery with which they were buried.

SITA buses run down the coast from Metaponto to Policoro but are frequent only in summer.

TYRRHENIAN COAST (COSTA TIRRENICA)

Basilicata's Tyrrhenian coast is short (about 20km) but sweet. The SS18 coastal road threads its way between craggy mountains and cliffs that drop away to the sea. This makes for one of the prettiest stretches of the whole Tyrrhenian coast – but one that peters out virtually as soon as you leave Basilicata in either direction.

About halfway between the Campanian and Calabrian borders, and a short, steep ride up from the coast, lies the small town of **Maratea**. Watched over by a 22m-tall statue of Christ at the Santuario di San Biagio, Maratea has been done no harm by tourism. The high part of town, as so often along the south Tyrrhenian coast, forms the historic core. The new town has spread out below, although so far it's unobtrusive.

Maratea is the administrative centre of a series of coastal villages, the prettiest of which are **Fiumicello** and **Porto di Maratea**, which has plenty of bars and restaurants, and buzzes until the early hours in summer. Most of the accommodation is down in these coastal settlements and each has at least one small, protected beach.

The **tourist office** (☎ 0973 87 69 08; Piazza Gesù 40; ☼ 8am-8pm Mon-Sat, 9am-1pm & 5-8pm Sun Jul-Aug, shorter hrs Sep-Jun) is in Fiumicello.

Centro Sub Maratea (☎ 0973 87 00 13; Via Santa Caterina 28; Maratea) offers diving courses for all levels, while **Maratea Mare Service** (☎ 0973 87 69 76; Porto di Maratea) rents boats. Ask for Franco.

Albergo Fiorella (☎ 0973 87 65 14; fax 0973 87 69 21; Via Santa Veneri 21; s/d €35/50, d with bathroom €60) In Fiumicello, this simple place has the longest corridor of any hotel in southern Italy. Rooms are minimally decorated with facilities comprising a bedside lamp. Still, it's friendly and one of the cheapest options in this charming little village.

Villa degli Aranci (☎ /fax 0973 87 63 44; Via Profiti 7; s/d with bathroom €70/110, half board per person €95) Also in Fiumicello, this place is considerably more attractive than Albergo Fiorella as its higher prices reflect. A lovely villa surrounded by orange trees, it makes for a great stay.

La Bussola (☎ 0973 87 68 63; Via Santavenere 43; pizza meal about €10; ☼ Tue-Sun) A small and welcoming pizzeria in Fiumicello, this is where the locals come for their takeaways. The young *pizzaiolo* (pizza cook) knows his trade and prepares pizzas that are cooked just long enough to acquire that wonderful smoked flavour.

SITA (☎ 0971 50 68 11) buses link Maratea to Potenza. They also run up the coast to Sapri in Campania and south to Praia a Mare in Calabria. Local buses connect the coastal towns and Maratea train station with the old centre of Maratea, running frequently in summer. Intercity and regional trains on the Rome–Reggio di Calabria line stop at Maratea train station, below the town. Local trains run infrequently between Praia a Mare, Maratea's various coastal settlements and Sapri.

CALABRIA

With some of the country's better beaches and a brooding, mountainous interior, the toe of the Italian boot represents for many travellers little more than a train ride down the Tyrrhenian coast on the way to/from Sicily. Calabria does, however, merit a little more.

A tough ancient land, it offers visitors two faces. On the one hand there is its natural beauty – its beaches are among Italy's best and the mountain scenery is stunning; on the other, there is the appalling eyesore of the urban landscape. The number of half-finished buildings is all too evident, even if not all of them are uninhabited. In fact, they often mask well-furnished flats where families live happily untroubled by invasive house taxes.

Calabria's history dates back to Palaeolithic times, although it was the Greeks from Sicily who first settled, founding a colony at what is now Reggio di Calabria. Remnants of this colonisation, which spread along the Ionian coast and featured Sibari and Crotone as the star settlements, are still visible today. The fun didn't last though and in 202 BC the cities of Magna Graecia came under Rome's permanent sway. Later, as Rome declined, the Byzantines took superficial control. Their ineffectual rule and the appearance of Saracen (Arab) raiders off the coast prompted a decline that was never really arrested; Calabria continued to be a backwater for a succession of Norman, Swabian, Aragonese, Spanish and Bourbon rulers based in Naples. Although the brief Napoleonic incursion at the end of the 18th century, and the arrival of Garibaldi and Italian unification, inspired hope for change, Calabria remained virtually feudal.

One of the by-products of this history of misery was the growth of banditry and later pervasive organised crime. Calabria's mafia, known as the 'ndrangheta, incites fear in much of the region's population, although tourists are rarely the target of its aggression. For many, the only answer has been to get out and, for at least a century, Calabria has seen its young people emigrate to the north or abroad in search of work.

You can get pretty much anywhere by public transport but it is not always fast or easy.

Getting There & Away

Lamezia Terme (Sant'Eufemia Lamezia) airport (SUF; ☎ 0968 41 41 11), 63km south of Cosenza and 36km west of Catanzaro, serves Calabria as a whole. At the junction of the A3 and SS280 motorways, it links the region with major Italian cities and is also a destination for charters from northern Europe.

CATANZARO

pop 97,252 / elevation 320m

The best view of Catanzaro is of it fading into the distance as you leave town. A grim mountain-top city 12km inland from the Ionian coast, it replaced Reggio di Calabria as the regional capital in the early 1970s. Scarcely anything remains of its Byzantine origins or medieval architecture thanks to the usual combination of earthquakes and WWII bombs. Other than transport connections, there's precious little to draw you here.

Orientation

The train station for the Ferrovie della Calabria (FC) is just north of the city centre. Walk south along Via Indipendenza for Piazza Matteotti, the main square, from where Corso Mazzini takes you further south. The main Trenitalia train station is about 2km south and downhill from the centre – you can take a local bus or the cable car from Piazza Roma.

Information

CTS (☎ 0961 72 45 30; Via Indipendenza 26) Travel agency for budget journeys.
Hospital (☎ 0961 88 31 11; Viale Pio X) North of town.
Police Station (☎ 0961 88 91 11; Piazza Cavour)
Post Office (Piazza Prefettura; ⏰ 8.10am-6pm Mon-Sat)

PUGLIA, BASILICATA & CALABRIA

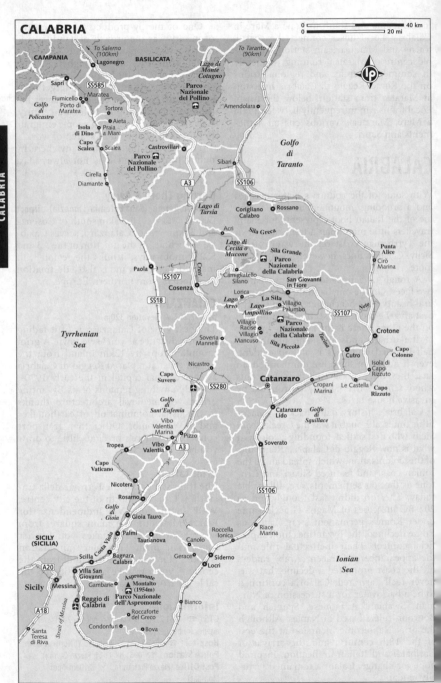

CALABRIA

0 — 40 km
0 — 20 mi

CAMPANIA

To Salerno (100km)
Lagonegro
BASILICATA

To Taranto (90km)

Lago di Monte Cotugno

Parco Nazionale del Pollino

Sapri

Fiumicello
Porto di Maratea
Maratea
SS585
Tortora

Golfo di Policastro

Aieta

Isola di Dino
Praia a Mare
Capo Scalea
Scalea

Amendolara

Castrovillari

Parco Nazionale del Pollino

Sibari

Golfo di Taranto

Cirella
Diamante

A3

SS106

Lago di Tarsia

Corigliano Calabro
Rossano

Acri
Sila Greca

Lago di Cecita o Mucone

Sila Grande
Parco Nazionale della Calabria

Punta Alice
Cirò Marina

Paola

SS107

Cosenza

Camigliatello Silano

San Giovanni in Fiore

SS18

Lorica
Lago Arvo
Lago Ampollino
La Sila
Villagio Palumbo

SS107

Neto

Crotone

Tyrrhenian Sea

Soveria Mannelli

Villagio Racise
Villagio Mancuso

Parco Nazionale della Calabria
Sila Piccola

Tacina

Cutro

Capo Colonne

Nicastro

Capo Suvero

SS280

Catanzaro

Cropani Marina
Le Castella

Isola di Capo Rizzuto
Capo Rizzuto

Golfo di Sant'Eufemia

Vibo Valentia Marina
Pizzo

Catanzaro Lido

Golfo di Squillace

Tropea

Vibo Valentia

A3

Soverato

Capo Vaticano

Nicotera

Rosarno

SS106

Golfo di Gioia
Gioia Tauro

SICILY (SICILIA)

Palmi
Taurianova

Roccella Ionica
Riace Marina

Scilla
Costa Viola
Bagnara Calabra

Canolo
Gerace

Siderno
Locri

Ionian Sea

A20

Villa San Giovanni
Messina

Gambarie
Aspromonte
Montalto (1954m)
Parco Nazionale dell'Aspromonte

Sicily

Reggio di Calabria

Roccaforte del Greco
Bianco

A18

Condofuri
Bova

Santa Teresa di Riva

Strait of Messina

Tourist Office (☎ 0961 74 17 64; 2nd fl, Galleria Mancuso, Via Spasari 3; ☼ 8.30am-1pm Mon-Fri & 3-5pm Mon & Wed)

Sights

CITY CENTRE

There really isn't a lot to see. The **cathedral** was almost completely rebuilt after the last war and is quite ordinary. Nearby, the **Chiesa di San Domenico del Rosario** contains several attractive Renaissance paintings by comparative unknowns but is rarely open. More impressive, at least externally, is the baroque **Basilica dell'Immacolata** with its marble-clad columns. Unfortunately, at the time of writing it was covered in scaffolding.

The city's **Museo Provinciale** (☎ 0961 72 00 19; Villa Margherita; admission free; ☼ 10am-1.30pm & 3.30-5.30pm Tue-Fri, 10am-1.30pm Sat, 9am-12.30pm Sun) has finally re-opened after years of restoration. Situated just inside the Villa Trieste, a green oasis worth a stroll in its own right, it houses a large collection of Greek and Roman coins, some local archaeological finds and various modern works by Calabrian artists.

CATANZARO LIDO

To soak up the sun head for Catanzaro Lido (previously known as Catanzaro Marina), 12km away down on the coast. One of the Ionian coast's major resorts, it's heavily developed but less tacky than many others and the beaches stretching off in both directions are among the best on this coast.

Sleeping & Eating

Albergo Belvedere (☎ /fax 0961 72 05 91; Via Italia 33; s/d €24/40, with bathroom €33/54) Looking out over the surrounding hills, this is a friendly enough stopover. Rooms are functional and clean, as the pervading smell of industrial-strength floor-cleaner suggests.

Grand Hotel (☎ 0961 70 12 56; fax 0961 74 16 21; Piazza Matteotti; s/d with bathroom & breakfast from €67/93) If it's all about location, this characterless hotel standing in the middle of a road junction wins zero points. Rooms, however, are comfortable and fitted with all the mod cons.

Da Salvatore (☎ 0961 72 43 18; Via Salita del Rosario 28; meals €11, pizzas from €3) Hidden down a narrow side street, this unpretentious restaurant serves excellent local dishes as well as tempting pizza. Try the *salsiccia alla Palanca* (sausage with greens), a unique dish

named in honour of a local football hero who ate this every time he passed by.

Il Mahé (☎ 0961 74 60 34; Via Indipendenza 55; meals €18; ☼ Mon-Sat & Sun evening) Il Mahé is all things to all people. Downstairs, there's a good *rosticceria*. Upstairs functions as pizzeria and restaurant. Also on the 1st floor (evenings only) is a bar with nightly entertainment, including live music at weekends.

Lo Stuzzichino (☎ 0961 72 44 87; Piazza Matteotti 5; meals €10) If you need a feed and aren't too worried about the finer aspects of dining, this self-service, no-nonsense, plonk-it-on-the-plate joint is the place for you. It offers excellent value for your euro.

Caffé Imperiale (☎ 0961 74 32 31; Corso Mazzini 159) A belle epoque–style café on Catanzaro's main thoroughfare, this place is a favoured spot for a weekend ice cream. The coffee and cakes aren't bad either.

Getting There & Away

BUS

Buses run by **Ferrovie della Calabria** (FC; ☎ 0961 89 61 11) terminate beside the FC train station. They serve Catanzaro Lido, other cities on the Ionian coast, La Sila and towns throughout the province – notably Cosenza (€4.15, 1½ hours, eight daily) and Vibo Valentia (€3.15, two hours, four daily).

TRAIN

FC runs trains between the city and Catanzaro Lido, where you can pick up a Trenitalia train for Reggio di Calabria or head northeast along the Ionian coast.

From the Catanzaro city Trenitalia station, trains connect with Lamezia Terme, Reggio di Calabria and Cosenza, as well as Naples, Rome, Milan and Turin.

Getting Around

Catanzaro's cable car (tickets €0.75) rises from the Trenitalia train station to Piazza Roma near the city centre. Otherwise, take city bus Nos 11, 12, 40 or 41. The Circolare Lido bus connects the city centre, the Trenitalia train station and Catanzaro Lido.

IONIAN COAST

Less crowded than the Tyrrhenian shores, the Ionian coast nevertheless has its fair share of unappealing tourist villages. This territory can seem brooding and resistant to outsiders, especially if you venture into the hills and valleys away from the coast.

Most of the tourist villages, hotels and camp sites close for up to eight months of the year, so finding accommodation can be tricky. Add to that the woes of travelling on slow trains or infrequent buses and the area might start to seem unappealing. Don't despair. There are dozens of small hill towns to explore and some of the beaches are quite good.

Gerace

A stunning example of a medieval hill town, Gerace is worth a detour for the views alone – on the one side the Ionian Sea, on the other the dark, silent mountains of the interior. About 10km inland from Locri on the SS111, it is becoming something of a routine stop on the tourist circuit. It boasts Calabria's largest Romanesque **cathedral**, high up in the town. First laid out in 1045, later alterations have robbed it of none of its majesty.

Ristorante a Squella (☎ 0964 35 60 86; Viale della Resistenza 8; meals €13) For a taste of traditional Calabrian cooking, this trattoria is the place. Modest and welcoming, it makes for a great lunchtime stop – afterwards you can wander down the road admiring the views.

Further inland is **Canolo**, a small hamlet seemingly untouched by the 20th century. Buses connect Gerace with Locri and Canolo with Sidernia.

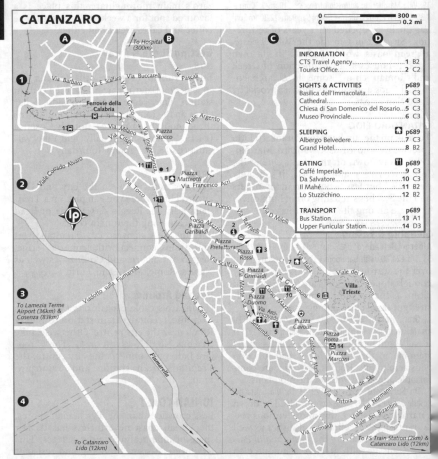

CATANZARO

INFORMATION
CTS Travel Agency...........................**1** B2
Tourist Office...................................**2** C2

SIGHTS & ACTIVITIES   p689
Basilica dell'Immacolata..................**3** C3
Cathedral...**4** C3
Chiesa di San Domenico del Rosario...**5** C3
Museo Provinciale............................**6** C3

SLEEPING   p689
Albergo Belvedere............................**7** C3
Grand Hotel......................................**8** B2

EATING   p689
Caffè Imperiale.................................**9** C3
Da Salvatore...................................**10** C3
Il Mahé..**11** B2
Lo Stuzzichino.................................**12** B2

TRANSPORT   p689
Bus Station.....................................**13** A1
Upper Funicular Station...................**14** D3

Isola di Capo Rizzuto
pop 13,175

About 40km northeast of Catanzaro Lido, Isola di Capo Rizzuto is rich in Greek history as well as nature with its shoreline a protected marine reserve.

At **Le Castella**, about 10km southwest of Isola, the impressive 16th-century Aragonese castle was built on the site of an ancient Greek fort (Il Phrourion). Constructed in the 3rd century BC, it was designed to protect Crotone in the wars against Pyrrhus. Unfortunately, at the time of writing the castle was closed to visitors. For further information check out www.riservamarina caporizzuto.it.

At the northern tip of this zone is **Capo Colonne**, marking the site of the Greek fortress complex of Hera Lacinia. Only a solitary column belonging to a Doric temple remains to testify to the spot's former splendour.

Albergo L'Aragonese (☎ 0962 79 50 13; Via Discesa Marina; half/full board per person high season €47/58) This place at Le Castella looks over the Aragonese castle, which is linked to the mainland by a short causeway. A decent place to stay, it also has a restaurant where a full meal costs about €20.

The area offers some of the best camping along the Ionian coast. There are around 15 camp sites near Isola. A good choice is **La Fattoria** (☎ 0962 79 11 65; fax 0962 95 78 95; Via del Faro; person/tent €8/8; ✆ Jun-Sep), about 1.5km from the sea.

Crotone
pop 59,757

Calabria's major industrial centre and the region's only Ionian port, Crotone is an ancient city. About 10km north of Isola di Capo Rizzuto, it was founded by the Greeks in 710 BC and reached its zenith in the following century, when it was a major power famed for the beauty of its women and the metaphysics of Pythagoras. Today, unfortunately there remains precious little to see.

There is a **tourist office** (☎ 0962 2 31 85; Via Torino 148; ✆ 8.30am-1pm Mon-Sat, 3-7pm Mon & Wed) in the city centre.

The **Museo Archeologico Statale** (☎ 0962 90 56 25; Via Risorgimento 120; admission €2 ✆ 9am-7.30pm, closed 1st & 3rd Mon of month) is one of Calabria's better museums. Nearby is a restored 16th-century **castle** (☎ 0962 92 15 35; Via Risorgimento; admission €2; ✆ 9am-1pm & 3-7pm

Tue-Sat, 9am-12.45pm Sun). Typical of the cylindrically towered fortresses erected by the Aragonese in southern Italy, it nowadays houses a small **museum**.

Albergo Concordia (☎ 0962 2 39 10; Piazza Vittoria 12; s/d €22/42, with bathroom €30/52) One of Crotone's few accommodation options, this place has basic rooms which, if not especially inviting, are perfectly adequate. The initial welcome can be a little frosty.

Hotel Capitol (☎ 0962 2 55 20; Piazza Umberto I; s/d with bathroom & breakfast €46/65) With no evident signs, this place can be difficult to find, hidden as it is behind a crumbling facade. But the hotel has plenty of character. The reception area is gigantic and the rooms have high ceilings and simple decor.

North of Crotone

The coastline from Crotone to Basilicata is the region's least developed, partly because the beaches are not terribly good. Public transport is generally irregular, although the coast road is decent and is slowly being upgraded.

CIRÒ MARINA

About 30km north of Crotone, Cirò Marina is a decent-sized town with plenty of hotel rooms and good beaches marred only by the ugly offshore concrete breakwaters.

Hotel Atena (☎ 0962 3 18 21; Piazza Municipio; s/d with bathroom €35/49, half/full board per person €57/67) Plastic and chipboard are the dominant materials here but the beds are comfortable and a bargain outside peak season.

ROSSANO

Rossano, 56km northwest of Cirò, is really two towns – Lido Sant'Angelo, a standard beach resort and coastal extension of the town of Rossano Scalo, and the more interesting original hill town, 6km inland.

The transformation over such a short climb is remarkable. The snaking road takes you through green countryside and seemingly back in time to the atmospheric old town, once an important Italian link in the Byzantine Empire's chain.

Various reminders of Rossano's ties to the ancient city of Constantinople remain. In the central aisle of the **cathedral** is a 9th-century Byzantine fresco of the Madonna and Child, nowadays encased within an ornate polychrome baroque structure. For more proof, visit the **Museo Diocesano** (☎ 0983 52 52 63; admission €3.10; ☒ 9.30am-12.30pm & 4-7pm Tue-Sun) next door, which houses a precious 6th-century codex containing the gospels of St Matthew and St Mark in Greek. If it's closed, ask at **Cooperativa Neilos**, beside the phone kiosk.

Hotel Scigliano (☎ 0983 51 18 46; www.hotel scigliano.it; Viale Margherita 257; s/d with bathroom & breakfast €54/85, €13.50 extra in Jul & Aug; ☒ **P**) Near the train station in the modern town, this hotel is big, brash and comfortable. It's also friendly and runs a good restaurant where you'll pay about €18 for a meal.

Camping Torino (☎ 0983 51 23 94; Località Frasso; person/tent/car €8/8/3) This camp site is 50m from the sea at Marina di Rossano. With all the requisite facilities it's a good option for sun-seekers.

Rossano is on the Taranto–Reggio di Calabria train line. From town, the SS177 is a pretty drive across La Sila to Cosenza.

SIBARI

About 4km south of Sibari is what's left of what was once the seat of the ancient Sybarites, the people of the short-lived Greek city-state renowned for its wealth and love of comfort. You can visit the **remains** (admission free; ☒ 9am-1 hr before sunset daily) – 90% of them beneath reclaimed farmland and bisected by the highway. It was destroyed by a jealous Crotone in the 6th century BC, and excavations since the 1960s have brought only a glimmer of its glory to light. The small **Museo Archeologico della Sibaritide** (admission €2; ☒ 9am-7.30pm except 1st & 3rd Mon of month) is 7km from the site and can't compare with the riches at Metaponto and Policoro further north.

COSENZA

pop 73,341 / elevation 238m

Passing the cheek-by-jowl high-rises as you enter Cosenza it looks like the same old story – an ancient city redeveloped on the cheap and in a rush. So to discover its medieval core in the otherwise charmless city centre is a welcome surprise. Rising above the confluence of two rivers, the Crati and Busento, its narrow alleyways, some no more than steep stairways, wind past once-elegant mansions up to the hill-top castle.

A university town since 1968, Cosenza is the most attractive of Calabria's three

provincial capitals. What's more, it's a transportation hub and a gateway into the mountains of La Sila.

Orientation

The main drag, Corso Mazzini, runs south from Piazza Fera (near the bus station) and intersects Viale Trieste before meeting Piazza dei Bruzi. What little there is of accommodation, food, banks and tourist assistance is all within about a 10-minute walking radius of this intersection. Head further south and cross the Busento River to reach the medieval part of town.

Information

EMERGENCY

Police Station (☎ 0984 89 11 11; Via Frugiuele 10)

INTERNET ACCESS

Casa della Cultura (☎ 0984 79 02 71; Corso Telesio Bernardino 98; 1 hr free; ☒ 8am-8pm Mon-Sat)

MEDICAL SERVICES

Hospital (☎ 0984 68 11; Via F Migliori)

POST

Post Office (☎ 0984 2 24 03; Via V Veneto)

TELEPHONE & FAX

Telecom Office (at the bus station off Piazza Fera)

TOURIST INFORMATION

Tourist Office (☎ 0984 2 74 85; 1st fl, Corso Mazzini 92; ☒ 8am-1.30pm Mon-Fri & 2-5pm Mon-Wed)

Sights

Cosenza isn't blessed with a huge number of must-see sights but those that exist are up in the old town.

The 12th-century **cathedral**, rebuilt in a restrained baroque style in the 18th century, is fairly unexceptional except for a copy of an exquisite 13th-century Byzantine Madonna in a chapel off the north aisle.

From the cathedral, you can take the steps up Via del Seggio through a little medieval quarter before turning right to reach the 13th-century **Convento di San Francesco d'Assisi**, which retains a chapel from the original structure behind the south transept.

Up high and reached by Corso Vittorio Emanuele is the **castle**, built by the Normans, rearranged by Frederick II, then the

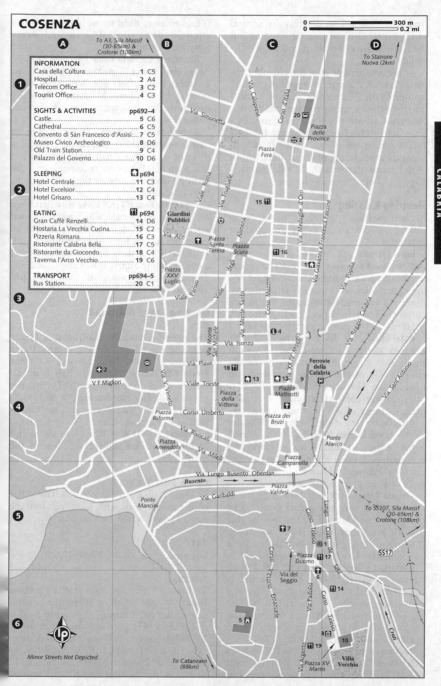

COSENZA

INFORMATION	
Casa della Cultura	1 C5
Hospital	2 A4
Telecom Office	3 C2
Tourist Office	4 C3

SIGHTS & ACTIVITIES	pp692–4
Castle	5 C6
Cathedral	6 C5
Convento di San Francesco d'Assisi	7 C5
Museo Civico Archeologico	8 D6
Old Train Station	9 C4
Palazzo del Governo	10 D6

SLEEPING	p694
Hotel Centrale	11 C3
Hotel Excelsior	12 C4
Hotel Grisaro	13 C4

EATING	p694
Gran Caffè Renzelli	14 D6
Hostaria La Vecchia Cucina	15 C2
Pizzeria Romana	16 C3
Ristorante Calabria Bella	17 C5
Ristorante da Giocondo	18 C4
Taverna l'Arco Vecchio	19 C6

TRANSPORT	pp694–5
Bus Station	20 C1

0 — 300 m
0 — 0.2 mi

To A3, Sila Massif (30-65km) & Crotone (108km)

To Stazione Nuova (2km)

To SS107, Sila Massif (30-65km) & Crotone (108km)

To Catanzaro (88km)

Minor Streets Not Depicted

Angevins, and left in disarray by several earthquakes. Little of interest remains but the view makes the steep ascent worthwhile.

At the southern edge of the old city centre is Piazza XV Marzo, an appealing square fronted by the Palazzo del Governo. Tucked into the piazza's northwest corner is the Accademia Cosentina and, within it, the city's one-room **Museo Civico Archeologico** (☎ 0984 81 33 24; admission free; ☿ 9am-1pm Mon-Fri), which contains a scattering of local finds. South of the piazza stretches shady **Villa Vecchia**, a huge and welcome oasis of green.

Sleeping & Eating

Accommodation can be a problem in Cosenza, as the city isn't exactly geared for tourism.

Hotel Excelsior (☎ /fax 0984 7 43 83; Piazza Matteotti 14; s/d with bathroom €34/52; **P**) The reception of this once-grand station hotel retains the dimensions of its more illustrious past. About to undergo restoration, rooms are currently large, practical and, above all, good value. The private garage costs €5.

Hotel Grisaro (☎ 0984 2 79 52; fax 0984 2 78 38; Viale Trieste 38; s/d with bathroom €36/52) This well-signposted city-centre hotel is a reliable choice. Well positioned for everywhere in town, it has 26 rooms that, although characterless, are comfortable and clean. The main entrance is on Via Monte Santo.

Hotel Centrale (☎ 0984 7 57 50; fax 0984 7 36 84; Viale Mancini; s/d with bathroom & breakfast €78/115) Aimed at the business market, rooms are bland and well equipped. What is not bland is the eye-catching Dalì-inspired sofa, the orange centrepiece of a reception designed to strike.

Pizzeria Romana (☎ 0984 2 69 91; Corso Mazzini 190; pasta €3) Ignore the garish plastic and neon decor and you'll find the food at this popular lunchtime haunt is not bad at all. It won't win any gourmet awards but for a quick midday snack it fits the bill nicely.

Hostaria La Vecchia Cucina (☎ 0984 2 94 39; Via Miceli 21; meals €25) Given that Cosenza is not on the sea, it's pretty amazing what the cooks here manage to do with fish. The grilled swordfish goes down a treat and the spaghetti alle vongole (spaghetti with clams) is given a unique twist. Try it!

Taverna l'Arco Vecchio (☎ 0984 7 25 64; Piazza Archi di Ciaccio 21; meals €25) The sister restaurant of La Vecchia Cucina, this family concern is tucked away deep in the old town. It has attractive, low-ceilinged rooms and serves tasty local dishes.

Ristorante Calabria Bella (☎ 0984 79 35 31; Piazza Duomo; meals €20) Also in the old town, Calabria Bella offers excellent food in an intimate atmosphere. Much patronised by discerning locals, it specialises in Calabrian cuisine.

Ristorante da Giocondo (☎ 0984 2 98 10; Via Piave 53; meals from €15; ☿ Mon-Sat) For a no-frills plate of pasta this small family restaurant is a good bet. Prices are reasonable and the location is very handy for the hotels around the old station.

Gran Caffè Renzelli (☎ 0984 2 68 14; Corso Telesio 46) This venerable café, which bakes its own gooey cakes and desserts, has been run by the same family for five generations. Sink your teeth into their torroncino torrefacto, a confection of sugar, spices and hazelnuts, or varchiglia alla monocale (chocolate and almond cake).

Getting There & Around
BUS

The main bus station is northeast of Piazza Fera. Services leave for Catanzaro, Paola and towns throughout La Sila. **Autolinee Preite** (☎ 0984 41 30 01) has half a dozen buses daily along the north Tyrrhenian coast, while **Autolinee Romano** (☎ 0962 2 17 09) serves Crotone and Reggio di Calabria, as well as Rome and Milan.

Amaco (☎ 0984 30 80 11) bus Nos 15, 16 and 28 link the centre and Stazione Nuova, the main train station.

CAR & MOTORCYCLE
Cosenza is off the A3 autostrada. The SS107 connects the city with Crotone and the Ionian coast, across La Sila.

TAXI
For a taxi, call ☎ 0984 2 88 77.

TRAIN
The main Trenitalia train station, **Stazione Nuova** (☎ 0984 2 70 59), is about 2km northeast of the city centre. Trains go to Reggio di Calabria (€11.20, two hours 40 minutes, 15 daily), Salerno (€17, two hours 40 minutes, 16 daily), Naples (€20, 3¼ hours, 13 daily) and Rome (€32.80, 5¼ hours, 12 daily), as well as most destinations around

the Calabrian coast. The Ferrovie della Calabria line, which has its terminal beside the old train station, serves La Sila and other small towns around Cosenza.

LA SILA

Though less spectacular than many of the mountain ranges further up the peninsula, La Sila (the Sila Massif) is still impressive and offers good walking. The highest peaks, many covered in thick forest, reach 2000m. Here the dominant tree is the tall Corsican pine, found in Italy only in Calabria and on the slopes of Mt Etna (Sicily). There is some winter skiing in the central Sila Grande, over 7000 hectares of which are national park. The other two areas are the Sila Greca, north of the Grande, and the Sila Piccola to the south. Sadly, there are few *rifugi* (mountain huts) and camping in the national parks is forbidden.

The main towns are Camigliatello Silano and San Giovanni in Fiore, both accessible by Ferrovie della Calabria buses (about 10 daily) along the SS107, which links Cosenza and Crotone, or by the twice-daily train running between Cosenza and San Giovanni in Fiore. You will find accommodation in various towns throughout La Sila and at several tourist resorts, including Villaggio Palumbo and Villaggio Mancuso. Skiers can use lifts around Camigliatello Silano and near Lorica, on Lago Arvo.

Information

Good quality information in English is a scarce commodity in these parts. As good a starting point as any is the **Calabrian National Park office** (☎ 0984 57 97 57) in Camigliatello Silano while, for what they're worth, there are **tourist offices** (Camigliatello Silano ☎ 0984 57 80 91; Lorica ☎ 0984 99 70 69).

More useful, at least for hard facts on walking opportunities, is the website www.museoditaverna.org/relaz_eng.htm, which details eight popular nature trails.

Camigliatello Silano

Ordinary enough in summer, Camigliatello looks quite cute under snow. It is a popular local skiing resort but won't host any international competitions. A few lifts operate on Monte Curcio, about 3km to the south.

The forests of La Sila yield a wondrous variety of wild mushrooms, both edible and poisonous. Sniff around **Antica Salumeria Campanaro** (Piazza Misasi 5); it's a temple to things fungoid, an emporium of rich odours, fine meats, cheeses, pickles and wines, rivalled in richness, if not in size, by its neighbour, **La Casa del Fungho**.

The town has about 15 hotels, including the following.

Hotel Miramonti (☎ 0984 57 90 67; haquila@ fitad.it; Via Forgitelle 87; d with bathroom high season €40, full board per person €45) Up in the heart of the village, Miramonti offers impeccable accommodation at budget prices.

Hotel Aquila & Edelweiss (☎ 0984 57 80 44; fax 0984 57 87 53; Viale Stazione 11; full board s/d with bathroom per person high season €98/82) This three-star hotel, wood-panelled, cosy and welcoming behind a rather stark facade, also runs a good restaurant specialising in Calabrian cuisine.

San Giovanni in Fiore

Although this is the biggest town in La Sila, it has little to recommend it. The provincial accommodation guide lists a lot of hotels here but most are scattered around the nearby small villages – some as far away as Lorica, 20km to the west.

Lorica

A peaceful little spot on Lago Arvo, Lorica is a minor ski resort, with a lift operating nearby. Accommodation is generally of a good standard. Recommended is **Albergo La Trota** (☎ 0984 53 71 66; fax 0984 53 71 67; Via Nazionale; full board d with bathroom per person high season €45), or for camping try **Villaggio Turistico Lago Arvo** (☎ /fax 0984 53 70 60; Passo della Cornacchia; site per person €4) and **Camping Lorica** (☎ 0984 53 70 18; site per person €5), beside the lake.

Villaggio Palumbo

About 10km south of San Giovanni in Fiore, this is a tourist village **resort** (☎ 0962 49 30 17) on Lago Ampollino. There are two similar ventures further south on the road to Catanzaro: **Villaggio Racise** and **Villaggio Mancuso**. Hotels within the resort all offer weekend package deals including food and accommodation and are set up for outdoor activities such as cross-country skiing and horse riding.

Soveria Mannelli

Set deep in pine woodland, **La Pineta** (☎ /fax 0968 66 60 79; Bivio Bonacci; dm €10) is on the SS19 inland Catanzaro–Cosenza road, 43km north of Catanzaro. It's 4km from the nearest train station but buses running between Cosenza and Catanzaro can drop you nearby. An evening meal costs €8.

REGGIO DI CALABRIA

pop 179,509

There are two reasons to follow the long, long road that leads to Reggio, the last stop on the mainland. The first is to get a boat to Sicily, the second to see the world-famous Greek statues, the Bronzi di Riace. Neither of these activities will take you far from the waterfront, which is good news because it's the only part of town worth seeing.

In fact, Reggio's seafront pedestrian promenade is a lovely place to wander, as the orange lights of Sicily sparkle so close, coyly tempting you to visit. Unfortunately, any romance in the air is lost the moment you turn away from the sea and hit the concrete slum tenements.

Rocked repeatedly by earthquakes, the most recent devastation in 1908, this once-proud ancient Greek city has plenty of other woes, including organised crime. You may notice an unusually large police presence, especially around the law courts in Piazza Castello.

Orientation

Stazione Centrale, the main train station, is at the southern edge of town on Piazza Garibaldi, where most buses also terminate. Walk north along Corso Giuseppe Garibaldi, the city's main street, for the tourist office and other services. The corso has long been a kind of de facto pedestrian zone in the evening, as streams of locals parade in the ritual *passeggiata* (evening stroll). Nowadays, however, it faces strong competition from the promenade running parallel to it along the shoreline.

Information

EMERGENCY

Police Station (☎ 0965 41 11 11; Corso Giuseppe Garibaldi 442)

MEDICAL SERVICES

Hospital (☎ 0965 39 71 11; Via Melacrino)

POST

Post Office (☎ 0965 31 51 11; Via Miraglia 14)

TOURIST INFORMATION

Tourist Office (☎ 0965 2 11 71; Via Roma 3; 🕓 8am-1.30pm Mon-Fri & 3-5pm Mon & Wed)
Branch Tourist Offices (🕓 8am-1.30pm Mon-Fri & 3-5pm Mon & Wed) Stazione Centrale (☎ 0965 2 71 20); airport (☎ 0965 64 32 91); city centre (☎ 0965 89 20 12; Corso Giuseppe Garibaldi 329)

Sights

Reggio was virtually rebuilt after the 1908 earthquake that devastated southern Calabria, leaving few historic buildings. Consequently, there's little to see or do.

The one major exception is Reggio's **Museo Nazionale** (☎ 0965 81 22 55; Piazza de Nava; admission €4; 🕓 9am-7.30pm except 1st & 3rd Mon of month). This museum alone, with its wealth of finds from Magna Graecia, makes a visit to Reggio worthwhile. Its greatest glory and one of the world's finest examples of ancient Greek sculpture are the Bronzi di Riace, two bronze statues hauled up off the Ionian coast near Riace in 1972. Housed in a special room and set on earthquake-proof stands, the larger-than-lifesize sculptures depict that favourite of ancient Greek subjects, naked and muscular soldiers. The artist remains unknown but probably lived in the 5th century BC. On the top floor are canvases, primarily by southern Italian artists, in one of the Mezzogiorno's best collections. It's well worthwhile investing in an audioguide (€3.60, available in English).

The gleaming white **cathedral** (Piazza del Duomo, just off Corso Garibaldi) was rebuilt in Romanesque style from the rubble of the 1908 earthquake. Just to its northeast, on Piazza Castello, are a pair of stolid towers, virtually all that remains of a 15th-century Aragonese **castle**.

Sleeping

Prices in town are reasonable and finding a room should be easy, even in summer, since most visitors to Reggio pass straight through on their way to Sicily.

Albergo Noël (☎ 0965 33 00 44; Viale Genoese Zerbi 13; s/d with bathroom €27/37) This place has the feel of an army barracks with rooms uniformly lining the corridor and the majority of customers being young men on the move. But rooms all have a TV, of sorts, and are excellent value.

Hotel Diana (☎ 0965 89 15 22; fax 0965 2 40 61; Via Vitrioli 12; s/d/tr with bathroom €27.50/55/74) It's

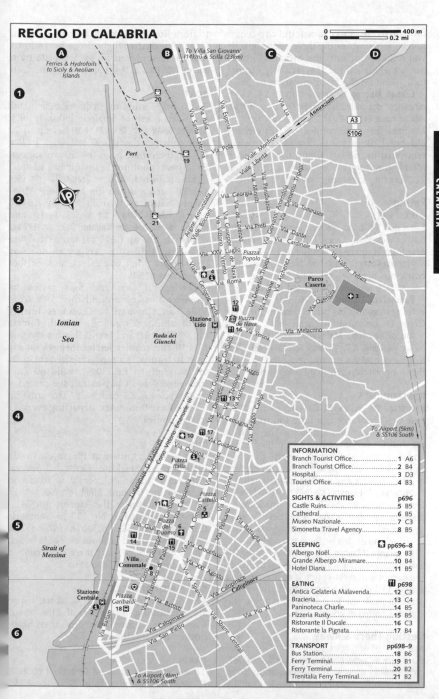

REGGIO DI CALABRIA

0 — 400 m
0 — 0.2 mi

A · **B** · **C** · **D**

Ferries & Hydrofoils to Sicily & Aeolian Islands

To Villa San Giovanni (14km) & Scilla (23km)

A3
S106
Annunciata

Port

Ionian Sea

Rada dei Giunchi

Stazione Lido

Piazza Popolo
Piazza de Nava

Parco Caserta

Via Melacrino

Strait of Messina

Villa Comunale

Piazza Italia

Piazza Castello

Piazza del Duomo

Stazione Centrale

Piazza Garibaldi

To Airport (5km) & SS106 South

To Airport (4km) & SS106 South

INFORMATION	
Branch Tourist Office	1 A6
Branch Tourist Office	2 B4
Hospital	3 D3
Tourist Office	4 B3

SIGHTS & ACTIVITIES	p696
Castle Ruins	5 B5
Cathedral	6 B5
Museo Nazionale	7 C3
Simonetta Travel Agency	8 B5

SLEEPING	pp696–8
Albergo Noël	9 B3
Grande Albergo Miramare	10 B4
Hotel Diana	11 B5

EATING	p698
Antica Gelateria Malavenda	12 C3
Bracieria	13 C4
Paninoteca Charlie	14 B5
Pizzeria Rusty	15 B5
Ristorante Il Ducale	16 C3
Ristorante la Pignata	17 B4

TRANSPORT	pp698–9
Bus Station	18 B6
Ferry Terminal	19 B1
Ferry Terminal	20 B2
Trenitalia Ferry Terminal	21 B2

difficult to miss this characterful city-centre hotel – look out for the three neon signs. If you're lucky (or not) the owner will bash out a melody on the spectacularly out-of-tune piano on the vast downstairs patio.

Grande Albergo Miramare (☎ 0965 81 24 44; miramare@reggiocalabriahotels.it; Via Fata Morgana 1; s/d with bathroom €115/150; ✵) Enjoy the view of Mt Etna from the comfort of this elegant old hotel. Built in 1929 and completely renovated in the late 1980s, the Miramare offers sumptuous hospitality with all the 21st-century creature comforts.

Eating
QUICK EATS
For a quick bite, there are plenty of places to buy a snack along Corso Giuseppe Garibaldi. The following are recommended.

Pizzeria Rusty (Via Crocefisso) Next to the cathedral, this pizzeria serves pizza by the slice from €1.10 and tempting fried nibbles.

Paninoteca Charlie (☎ 0965 2 28 05; Via Generale Tommasini 10) This place, next to the Red Cross, is also good for cheap snacks.

Antica Gelateria Malavenda (☎ 0965 89 14 49; cnr Via Romeo & Via Giovanni Amendola) For the town's richest ice cream, you can't surpass this long-established Reggio favourite.

RESTAURANTS
Bracieria (☎ 0965 2 93 61; Via Demetrio Tripepi 81-83; meals €18) This place is a little too rustic for it to be the genuine article but the food is the real thing. Specialising in grilled meat and fish, it also serves an amazingly good *sapori della Calabria* antipasto comprising brilliant ricotta and chilli-hot bruschetta.

Ristorante la Pignata (☎ 0965 2 78 41; Via Demetrio Tripepi 122; full meal about €25) Home-made pasta dishes are the house specialities here. Try the *strozzapreti al ragù di carne selvaggina* (pasta in game sauce). It's really very good.

Ristorante Il Ducale (☎ 0965 89 15 20; Corso Vittorio Emanuele III 13; meals from €30) Go up the regal red carpet and treat yourself to dinner with a view. Overlooking the seafront, this is the place to push the boat out and enjoy some stylish Calabrian cooking.

Getting There & Away
AIR
The city's **airport** (Aeroporto Civile Minniti; REG; ☎ 0965 64 05 17) is at Ravagnese, about 5km to the south. Alitalia and/or Air One fly

to/from Rome, Milan and Bergamo, and the occasional charter flight drops by. In town, Alitalia is represented by **Simonetta travel agency** (☎ 0965 33 14 44; Corso Giuseppe Garibaldi 521).

BOAT
Boats for Messina in Sicily leave from the port (just north of Stazione Lido). In high season, **SNAV** (☎ 081 4 28 51 11) has up to 20 hydrofoils per day (€2.90 one way). In low season, there may be as few as two sailings. Some boats continue to the Aeolian Islands.

The national railway **Trenitalia** (☎ 0965 89 20 21) runs a dozen big hydrofoils Monday to Saturday to/from Messina (€4.20 return). **Meridiano** (☎ 0965 81 04 14) and **Navigazione Generale Italiana** (NGI; ☎ 335 842 77 84) each run up to 12 car ferries daily on this route. Prices for cars are €8 one way (passengers don't pay extra), and for foot passengers €1.50.

Ferries for cars and foot passengers cross to Messina around the clock from Villa San Giovanni, 20 minutes further north along the rail line. Both **Caronte** (☎ 0965 79 31 31) and **Tourist Shipping** (☎ 0965 75 14 13) run regular ferries throughout the year; to transport a medium-sized car costs one-way/return €17/30.50, valid 60 days (passengers don't pay extra); the price for motorcycles is €5 each way. The crossing takes 20 to 30 minutes, departing every 15 to 20 minutes.

BUS
Most buses terminate at Piazza Garibaldi, in front of Stazione Centrale. Several different companies operate to towns in Calabria and beyond. **ATAM** (☎ 0965 62 01 29, ☎ 800 43 33 10) serves the Aspromonte Massif, with regular bus No 127 to Gambarie (1½ hours, three daily). **Salzone** (☎ 0965 75 15 86) has buses to Scilla about every 1½ hours. **Lirosi** (☎ 0965 5 75 52) has three daily runs to Rome and three to Catanzaro.

CAR & MOTORCYCLE
The A3 ends at Reggio di Calabria. If you are continuing further south, the SS106 hugs the coast round the 'toe', then heads north along the Ionian Sea.

TRAIN
Trains stop at **Stazione Centrale** (☎ 89 20 21) and less frequently at Stazione Lido

near the museum. Reggio is the terminus for daily trains to/from Milan (€60, nine daily), Rome (€40, eight daily) and Naples (€32, two daily). There are also services for Turin, Florence and Venice but for a wider choice change at Paola (at least 15 daily). Regional services run daily to Catanzaro and Sapri and, less frequently, to Cosenza, Taranto, Nicotera and Bari.

Getting Around

Orange local buses run by **ATAM** (☎ 0965 62 01 29 ☎ 800 43 33 10) cover most of the city. For the port, take bus Nos 13 or 125 from Piazza Garibaldi outside Stazione Centrale. The Porto–Aeroporto bus (No 125) runs from the port via Piazza Garibaldi to the airport and vice-versa (€0.52 per trip or €0.80 for up to 90 minutes of travel). Buy tickets at ATAM offices, tobacconists or newsstands.

ASPROMONTE MASSIF

Notorious as the hiding-place used by kidnappers, the Aspromonte Massif rises inland from Reggio di Calabria. Its highest peak, **Montalto** (1955m), is dominated by a huge bronze statue of Christ and offers sweeping views across to Sicily.

The Montalto area, now a national park, has some walking trails, albeit not quite as spectacular or demanding as La Sila. Centred on the area's main town of Gambarie, trails cover some 70km of parkland and are colour-coded for ease of navigation. For more information call at the **Gambarie tourist office** (☎ 0965 74 32 95; Piazza Carmelo Mangeruca).

To reach Gambarie, take ATAM city bus No 127 or 128 from Reggio di Calabria (€1.90, 1½ hours, three daily). Most of the roads inland from Reggio eventually hit the main SS183 road that runs north to the town.

TYRRHENIAN COAST (COSTA TIRRENICA)

The region's western seashore is a mixture of the good, the bad and the ugly. Certain stretches are crammed with tacky package resorts that attract holidaying Italians by the thousand each summer. But there are several small towns that are pleasant to stay in and the odd cove with a protected sandy beach.

TO BRIDGE OR NOT TO BRIDGE

While wooing the nation on his way to victory in the 2001 general elections, Silvio Berlusconi made many promises. One of the more modest was to sweep aside thousands of years of geography and bridge the 3km strait that divides Sicily from the Italian mainland.

To do this planners have come up with a €4.6 billion project to build the world's longest suspension bridge between Reggio di Calabria and Messina. With a total length of 3.7km it will require two 382m towers to support the record-breaking 3,300m span. Currently, the Akashi Kaikyo bridge in Japan holds the title with a span of 1,991m.

Construction is set to start in spring 2005 with completion due by 2011. That's assuming all concerned agree on the money, 60% of which is to come from the private sector.

A plan, it seems, that doesn't convince everyone. Environmentalists, in particular, are outraged. The Strait of Messina, they say, supports a finely balanced marine ecosystem that will be completely destroyed; migratory birds will have to find another flight path; and where on earth will workers dump the estimated eight million tons of soil they'll dig up?

Add to this the fact that the area is seriously earthquake prone and you begin to see why previous governments have quietly let the idea drift away.

The Mafia, of course, will have nothing to do with the partitioning of some of the biggest construction contracts ever awarded in Italy.

The journey along the Costa Viola, from Rosarno to Scilla and on towards Reggio di Calabria, is one of Italy's great coastal drives, with breathtaking views of Sicily.

For information about the coast, try the main tourist office in Reggio di Calabria (p696) or if you're coming from the north, the one in Cosenza (p692). Out of season, most hotels, camp sites and tourist villages close. In summer many of the hotels are full, although you should have an easier time with the camp sites.

Most coastal towns are on the main train line between Reggio and Naples, and the SS18 road hugs the coast for much of the way. The A3 from Reggio di Calabria to Salerno runs further inland.

Scilla

Scilla comes as a breath of fresh air after the urban mayhem of Reggio and Villa San Giovanni. A picturesque and lively summer town, it marks the beginning (or end if you're travelling southwards) of a striking stretch of coastline. The highlands of the Aspromonte extend to the coast and the views from the cliffs across to Sicily fuel the imagination.

Scilla's highpoint is a rock at the northern end of town that was said to be the lair of Scylla, the mythical six-headed sea monster who drowned sailors as they tried to navigate the Strait of Messina (and if she didn't get them, the whirlpool Charybdis, across in Sicily, would). Swimming off the town's beach is today somewhat safer, as is life for the fisherfolk who operate out of the small port.

Albergo le Sirene (☎ 0965 75 40 19; Via Nazionale 55; s/d with bathroom €26/46) A friendly and homely *pensione*, le Sirene offers fairly plain rooms. In recompense some of them are illuminated by great views over the water to Sicily. There is also a large terrace, which boasts the same views and is ideal for observing the evening *passeggiata* along the promenade.

Promontorio di Tropea

The Promontorio di Tropea, 50km north of Scilla, stretches from Nicotera in the south to Pizzo at the northern end. Boasting some of Italy's best sandy beaches and aquamarine seas, it is a regular summer destination for thousands of Italian holiday-makers.

About 20km northwest of Nicotera at **Capo Vaticano** are dozens of tourist villages and hotels, most of which are open from May to October and impose a full-board arrangement and, frequently, a one-week minimum stay in high season.

Hotel Villaggio Stromboli (☎ 0963 66 90 93; hotel.stromboli@tiscalinet.it; full board per person €44-81) Situated on a beautiful bay 4km northeast of Capo Vaticano, this stylish holiday village looks towards the island of Stromboli (complete with volcano). It also has villas from €38 to high season €95.

Hotel Residence Costa Azzurra (☎ 0963 66 31 09; www.hotelcostazzurra.com; full board per person €44-73; ❷) This smallish, family-run hotel offers

beach access and the full gamut of facilities, including its own swimming pool.

Around 10km northeast of Capo Vaticano, **Tropea** is a beautiful little town perched high above the coast. Particularly popular with German tourists, it's probably the prettiest spot on Calabria's Tyrrhenian coast with several long sandy beaches within walking distance. There is a useful **tourist office** (☎ 0963 6 14 75; Piazza Ercole; ❷ 9am-1pm & 4-8pm) in the centre of the old town. Most of the 10 or so hotels are in the higher price bracket and many close for winter.

Hotel Virgilio (☎ 0963 6 19 78; fax 0963 6 23 20; Viale Tondo 27; s/d with bathroom low season €39/62, high season €62/93; ❷ P) This friendly family hotel offers a warm welcome in season or out. Rooms are decorated in a cool, light summer fashion with TV and creature comforts. It's a particular bargain out of season.

Ristorante Pizzeria Don Rocco (☎ 0963 60 70 67; Largo Duomo; meals €15) A short walk from the centre leads you to this buzzing pizzeria-cum-trattoria. Frequented by locals and visitors alike, the atmosphere is convivial and the food excellent. In particular, they do exciting things with tomatoes and octopuses.

About 8km south of Pizzo, up high and slightly inland, is the long-established town of **Vibo Valentia**, good for a brief roam and a useful transport hub. The **tourist office** (☎ 0963 4 20 08; Via Forgiari; ❷ 7.30am-1.30pm Mon-Fri & 2.30-5pm Mon & Wed) is just off Corso Vittorio Emanuele (behind the Galleria Vecchia). Above the town is its castle, built by the Normans and later extended and reinforced by both Frederick II and the Angevins. From it, there's a sweeping panorama of coast, inland hills and, on a clear day, the volcanic island of Stromboli. It houses an excellent small **museum** (☎ 0963 4 33 50; admission €2; ❷ 9am-7pm), which has a wealth of well-displayed artefacts from Hipponion, the original Greek settlement and Roman Valentia, which superseded it.

A coastal railway runs around the promontory from Rosarno and Nicotera to Vibo Valentia Marina and Pizzo. **SAV** (☎ 0963 61 29) buses also connect most resorts with Tropea and Pizzo.

Pizzo

In the bars of Pizzo, you will find possibly Italy's best *tartufo*, a type of chocolate ice cream ball.

Inside the town's 16th-century **Chiesa Matrice di San Giorgio** (Via Marconi) lies the tomb of Joachim Murat, king of Naples from 1808 until 1815, when he was defeated by the Austrians and the Bourbons were restored to the Neapolitan throne. Although he was the architect of various enlightened reforms, the locals showed no great concern when Murat was imprisoned and executed here. To witness a re-enactment of his trial and death, head to the 15th-century **Castello Murat** (☎ 0963 53 25 23; admission €1; ☼ 9am-1pm & 3-10pm Jun-Sep) south of Piazza della Repubblica.

Immediately north of town, almost on the beach, the tiny **Chiesa di Piedigrotta** was literally carved into the tufa rock by Neapolitan shipwreck survivors in the 17th century. The church was later added to (the statue of Fidel Castro kneeling before a medallion of Pope John XXIII is an obvious recent addition) but the place is crumbling away and there is no move afoot to stop the rot.

Wander through Piazza della Repubblica, at the heart of the picturesque old centre of Pizzo, before settling in at one of the square's many **gelateria** terraces for a cold drink or ice-cream fix.

Paola

The 80km of coast from Pizzo northwards to Paola is mostly overdeveloped and ugly. Paola is the main train hub for Cosenza, about 25km inland, and is a large, comparatively nondescript place. Watched over by a crumbling castle, its main attraction is the **Santuario di San Francesco di Paola** (☎ 0982 58 25 18; admission free; ☼ 6am-1pm & 2-6pm). The saint lived and died in Paola in the 15th century, and the sanctuary that he and his followers carved out of the bare rock has for centuries been the object of pilgrimage. More interesting, however, is the pleasant cloister of the monastery (still in use today), planted with roses and surrounded by naive wall paintings depicting the saint's truly incredible miracles. The original church contains an ornate reliquary of the saint. Also within the complex is a modern basilica, built to mark the second millennium.

In town you can get a decent *panini* (€3.20) and a pint at the **Old Square** (Piazza IV Novembre 4), a pub bizarrely decorated with such typical Calabrian sports clobber as an MS Jumbo cricket bat!

There are several hotels near the station but it might be preferable to stay in towns further north along the coast.

Diamante to Praia a Mare

Diamante and Cirella mark the southern end of a largely uninterrupted stretch of wide, grey pebbly beach that continues for about 30km to Praia a Mare, just short of Basilicata. Backed by rows of camp sites and growing development projects, the coast lacks much of the scenic splendour to the north in Basilicata or indeed south towards Reggio di Calabria.

If you're finding the coast a little flat, head for the hills and old Scalea. About 15km south of Praia, it's one of the more eye-catching towns along the northern coast. Climb the stairway lanes past the muddle of tumbledown houses, or stop in Piazza de Palma for a beer at the Tarì Bar.

Praia a Mare

A couple of kilometres short of the border with Basilicata, Praia a Mare is a modern and drab resort town.

There is a **tourist office** (☎ 0985 7 25 85; Via Amerigo Vespucci 6; ☼ 8am-1pm Mon-Sat) with information on the **Isola di Dino**, just off the coast and famed for its sea caves. To visit the caves expect to pay around €5 for a guided tour from the old boys who operate off the beach. Alternatively ask at the tourist office.

La Mantinera (☎ 0985 77 90 23; www.lamantinera.it; 2 people, tent & car €13-33.50; ☼ mid-Apr–Sep) This slick tourist village at the southern end of town offers a range of accommodation options. Full board in a double with bathroom costs €38.50 to €87 per day, while bungalows range from €260 to €795 per week. Situated 300m from the beach, La Mantinera is comfortable, well equipped and lively.

As an alternative place to stay, consider Maratea, across the regional frontier in Basilicata (see Maratea p686), which has considerably more charm.

Autolinee Preite (☎ 0984 41 30 01) operates five or six buses daily in each direction between Cosenza and Praia a Mare. **SITA** (☎ 0971 50 68 11) goes north to Maratea and Potenza. Regular trains also pass for Paola and Reggio di Calabria.

PUGLIA, BASILICATA &
CALABRIA

Aieta & Tortora

The hill villages of **Aieta** and **Tortora**, about 12km and 6km inland, respectively, from Praia, belong to another world. About three daily **Rocco** (☎ 0985 76 53 12) buses serve both villages. The towns are precariously perched upon ridges that must have been hard going before asphalt days. Aieta is higher than Tortora and the journey constitutes much of the reward for going there. When you arrive, walk up to the 16th-century **Palazzo Spinello** at the end of the road and take a look into the ravine behind it.

Sicily

SICILY

Afloat in the centre of the Mediterranean, commanding the narrow straits between mainland Italy and Cap Bon in Tunisia, Sicily and its turbulent history is a lesson in geopolitics. As the axis between north and south, east and west, Sicily has been involved in nearly every major Mediterranean war, the ebb and flow of invasion depositing fragments of language, art, architecture, religion and social habits that have made the island the one true mirror of Mediterranean history and culture over the centuries.

Here history has been preserved for posterity, from the coolly classic architecture of Hellenistic Greece and the startling artistic fusion of Arab craftsmanship and Norman austerity, to the pomp and extravagance of Spanish baroque and the Byzantine corruption of modern-day politics. Complexity of culture is only matched by stunning natural beauty and an incredible diversity of landscape, rolling hills and valleys swathed in olive trees and grape vines, brooding Etna with its steep volcanic escarpments covered in citrus orchards, over a thousand kilometres of aquamarine coastline and a necklace of encircling islands.

Goethe rhapsodised that 'to have seen Italy without seeing Sicily, is not to have seen Italy at all – for Sicily is the key to everything', but in truth the island is remote and, far from providing the key to modern Italy, it illustrates the vital, and often violent, struggle between Eastern and Western ideology that is still being played out on the world stage today.

SICILY

HIGHLIGHTS

■ **Culture Vulture**

A night at the opera in Palermo (p719) or Catania (p745)

■ **Adrenaline Rush**

Hiking up the Stromboli at night (p733)

■ **Artistic Treasure**

The 6,340 sq m of golden mosaic at Monreale (p721) and stunning Villa Romana del Casale (pp756–7)

■ **Religious Feast**

The exultant Easter rituals in Trapani (p765) or the veneration of Catania's patron saint, Agata, in February (p743)

■ **Classic Sicily**

Wander through 2500-year-old ruins at Selinunte (pp760–1), Agrigento (pp757–60), Segesta (p767) and Syracuse (pp747–53)

■ **Indulgence**

Soaking in the *acquacalda* (hot springs) at Gadir, Pantelleria (p770) or sunning yourself on the deck of Hotel Raya overlooking Stromboli (p732)

■ POPULATION: 5 MILLION (5,076,700) | ■ AREA: 25,709 SQ KM

HISTORY

All Mediterranean nations have contributed to Sicily's hotchpotch history, but ultimately the island's deep-rooted cultural reference points are Magna Graecia (south and east Sicily) and Moorish north Africa (north and west). This fundamentally cultural divide originates from the island's first inhabitants – the Sicani who came from Libya and settled in northern Sicily, the Siculi from Latium who settled the east and the Elymni from Greece in the south. The subsequent colonisation of the island by Carthaginians from north Africa and Greeks (in the 8th to 6th centuries BC) only compounded this cultural divide with the establishment of powerful cities such as Syracuse, Catania, Messina, Agrigento, Trapani and Palermo.

Although inevitably part of the Roman Empire, it was not until the Arab invasions of AD 831 that Sicily truly came into its own. Arabic became the common language and churches were converted to mosques, but with these exceptions Arab rule was benign and benefited the island and its economy. Trade, farming and mining were all fostered under Arab influence and Sicily soon became an enviable prize for European opportunists. Capturing Messina in 1060, Robert Guiscard and his brother Roger I of Hauteville were just such men. Carving up the island between them, they began what was soon to become Sicily's most magnificent era.

Impressed by the cultured Arab lifestyle, Roger shamelessly borrowed and improved on it, spending vast amounts of money on palaces and churches and encouraging a cosmopolitan atmosphere in his court. But such prosperity – and decadence (Roger's grandson, William II, even had a harem) – inevitably gave rise to envy and resentment, and after 400 years of pleasure and profit the Norman line was extinguished and the kingdom passed to the German House of Hohenstaufen. In the centuries that followed, Sicily passed to the Holy Roman Emperors, the French, the Aragonese and the Austrians in a turmoil of rebellion and revolution until the Spanish Bourbons united Sicily with Naples in 1734 as the Kingdom of the Two Sicilies. Barely 100 years later, on 11 May 1860, Giuseppe Garibaldi, recognising Sicily as a hotbed of revolution, planned his daring and dramatic unification of Italy from Marsala.

Reeling from this staggering catalogue of colonisers, everyday Sicilians struggled to live in poverty-stricken conditions. Unified with Italy, but no better off, nearly one million men and women emigrated to the USA between 1871 and 1914, before the outbreak of WWI. Ironically, the Allies (seeking Mafia help in America for the reinvasion of Italy) helped in establishing the Mafia's stranglehold on Sicily that was to plague the country right up until the 1990s. In the absence of suitable administrators they invited Don Calógero Vizzini to do the job – under Mussolini the same man had been locked up as one of the most undesirable *mafiosi*. When in 1948 Sicily became a semi-autonomous region with its own parliament and legislative powers, Mafia control extended right to the heart of politics with subversive support of the Christian Democrat Party, and the country plunged into a 50-year silent civil war from which it is only now emerging, following the anti-Mafia maxi-trials of the late 1990s.

CLIMATE

The climate brings mild weather in winter, but summer is relentlessly hot and the beaches swarm with holiday-makers. The best times to visit are April to early June (spring) and September to October (autumn), when it is warm enough for the beach but not too hot for sightseeing.

DANGERS & ANNOYANCES

Sicilians are generally welcoming and sociable, but women might find the local men a little too friendly. Female tourists

---

THE SICILIAN CONNECTION

- One million Sicilians left the island between 1950 & 1970
- 500,000 Sicilians live in Europe
- 5 million Sicilians live outside Italy
- 18 million Italians of Sicilian origin live in the USA
- Yet the current population of the island is only 5 million

should take a hint from local women and avoid walking around at night alone in the bigger cities.

You won't have to worry about confronting the Godfather, but there are the usual problems of petty crime that any big city faces. Pickpockets and bag-snatchers are most prevalent in the marketplaces although, having said that, you only need a little common sense and street savvy to enjoy yourself without any problems. Car theft is a problem in Palermo, so using private, guarded car parks is advisable.

SHOPPING

As in Spain and Portugal, the Arabs brought a rich tradition of ceramic production to Sicily. Major ceramics centres include Caltagirone and Santo Stefano di Camastra. A love of coral and turquoise jewellery reflects another north African tradition, most strongly in evidence on the west coast and in particular in Trapani and Cefalù. Old-fashioned European traditions of lace-making and embroidery can be found in Palermo and small towns inland.

But perhaps the best shopping to be done in Sicily centres on its food and wine. The Aeolian Islands, along with Taormina and Cefalù, have a substantial number of gourmet delicatessens. Sicilian wines are also beginning to make an impression on the international market. Long used as a base for French wine due to their full-bodied strength, many are now being produced under their own labels. Some of the best include Donnafugata's Inzolia, almost any Nero d'Avola from Pachino, Regaleali, Passito di Pantelleria (a sweet dessert wine with the heady taste of apricots), Malvasia from Salina and, of course, Marsala.

For the ultimate memento, however, you could always purchase one of Palermo's paladin puppets, although they stand up to 1.5m tall so you may have trouble finding a place for it at home.

GETTING THERE & AWAY
Air
Flights from all over mainland Italy and from major European cities land at Palermo and Catania. Palermo's airport (PMO),

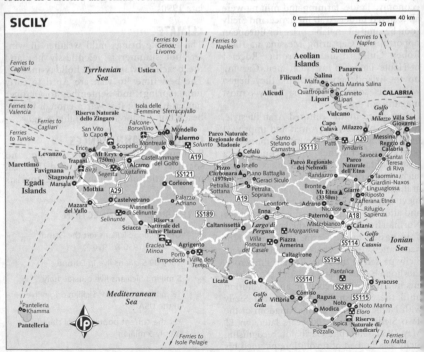

renamed Falcone-Borsellino after the two anti-Mafia judges assassinated in the city in 1992, is at Punta Raisi, about 31km west of the city, while Catania's airport (CTA), Fontanarossa, is 7km south of that city. Buses run from both airports into the respective city centres. See the transport sections of Palermo (pp719–20) and Catania (p745) for further details. To obtain information on flights to/from Sicily, contact **Alitalia** (☎ 00 39 06 65 641; www.alitalia.com) offices.

Boat

Regular car and passenger ferries cross the strait between Villa San Giovanni (Calabria) and Messina. Hydrofoils run by the railways and snappier jobs run by SNAV connect Messina directly with Reggio di Calabria. See Messina in this chapter (p736) and Reggio di Calabria (p698) for details.

Sicily is also accessible by ferry from Genoa, Livorno, Naples and Cagliari, and from Valencia (Spain), Malta and Tunisia. The main company servicing the Mediterranean is **Tirrenia** (call centre ☎ 199 12 31 99; www.tirrenia.it) and its services to/from Sicily include Palermo–Cagliari, Palermo–Naples, Trapani–Cagliari and Trapani–Tunisia.

Grandi Navi Veloci (Livorno ☎ 058 640 98 94, Genoa ☎ 010 58 93 31, Palermo ☎ 091 58 74 04; www.grimaldi.it), run by the Grimaldi group, has more upmarket and luxury ferries from Valencia (once weekly), Livorno (three per week) and Genoa (daily) to Palermo.

TTT Lines (☎ 095 746 21 87; www.tttlines.it, Italian only) has a daily ferry from Naples to Catania leaving at midnight while **Virtu Ferries** (☎ 356 31 88 54; 8 Princess St, Ta'Xbiex, Malta) has ferries from Malta to Catania between March and October.

Ustica Lines (☎ 0923 2 22 00; www.usticalines.it, Italian only) runs summer ferries from Trapani to Naples via Ustica, and from Trapani to Pantelleria.

SNAV (Naples ☎ 081 761 23 48, Palermo ☎ 091 58 60 66; www.snavali.com) runs a summer ferry between Palermo and Naples (four hours). See p719 for details.

Ferry prices are determined by the season and tend to increase considerably in summer (Tirrenia's high season varies according to destination, but is generally from July to September). Timetables can change dramatically each year. Tirrenia publishes an annual booklet listing all routes and prices, available at Tirrenia offices, agencies and the tourist information booth at the port.

In summer, all routes are busy and you need to book several weeks in advance. Tickets can be booked through the company concerned or at travel agencies throughout Italy. Offices and telephone numbers for the ferry companies are listed in the Getting There & Away sections for the relevant cities.

The following is only a guide to fares, based on high-season travel at the time of writing. For a *poltrona* (airline-type seat), fares were: Genoa–Palermo (€109, 20 hours) and Livorno–Palermo (€96, 17 hours) on Grandi Navi Veloci; Naples–Palermo (€38.75, 11 hours), Palermo–Cagliari (€26.10, 14 hours) and Trapani–Tunisia (€51.40, 11 hours) on Tirrenia; Naples–Catania on TTT Lines (€50, 7½ hours).

Fares for cars vary according to the size of the vehicle. High-season charges for the Palermo–Cagliari route range from €93 to €105.

There are also ferry and hydrofoil services, mainly operated by **Siremar** (☎ 091 749 31 11, general information ☎ 199 123 199; www.siremar.it, Italian only), from Sicily to the small groups of islands off the coast: Aeolian Islands (pp725–34), Egadi Islands (pp769–70), Pantelleria (p770) and Ustica (pp721–2).

Bus

Direct bus services between Rome and Sicily are operated by several companies, including **SAIS** (☎ 091 616 60 28; www.saistrasporti.it; Via P Balsamo 20, Palermo) and **Segesta** (☎ 091 616 90 39, ☎ 091 616 79 19; Via P Balsamo 26, Palermo). In Rome, the buses leave from Stazione Tiburtina.

Interbus (☎ 090 66 17 54) runs from Rome direct to Messina (€29 one way, nine hours).

SAIS runs two services between Rome and Catania (€35.60, 14 hours), continuing to Agrigento. You have to change at Messina to continue to Palermo. In Catania the bus connects with others to Syracuse, Ragusa and Enna.

In Rome, you can get tickets and information at the **Eurojet agency** (☎ 06 474 28 01; Piazza della Repubblica 54), or go to the bus station at Piazzale Tiburtina. Booking is obligatory.

SICILY

Train

Direct trains run from Milan, Florence, Rome, Naples and Reggio di Calabria to Messina and on to Palermo, Catania and other provincial capitals – the trains are transported from the mainland by ferry from Villa San Giovanni. Be prepared for long delays on Intercity trains on this route. Ticket prices depend on distance travelled. For example, one-way fares on Intercity trains are: Rome–Palermo (1st/2nd class €76.65/55.63, 11 hours, nine daily); Rome–Catania (€66.21/48.14, 9½ hours, three daily); Milan–Palermo (€100.24/72.14, 19 hours, one daily); Milan–Messina (€121.59/96.80, 14 hours, two daily).

For train information, call ☎ 147 88 80 88 (7am to 9pm) or go to the information office at any train station.

GETTING AROUND
Air

Boat connections to Sicily's off-shore islands are frequent and reliable, but you may want to catch a plane for Pantelleria (PNL). Tickets can be bought at the airport or booked through any travel agent, including **Sestante CIT** (☎ 091 58 63 33; Via della Libertà 12, Palermo). **Gandalf Air** (toll free ☎ 848 84 88 80; www.gandalfair.it) has flights for Pantelleria (€80) from Birgi airport, south of Trapani.

Bus

The best mode of public transport on Sicily is the bus. Numerous companies run services connecting the main towns around the coast. Services also connect these cities with the smaller towns along the coast and in the interior. You might be able to get bus timetables from local tourist offices although this very much varies from town to town, otherwise just ask for a timetable at the ticket office. The companies with the most extensive networks are SAIS and AST. See the Getting There & Away and Getting Around sections for each town.

Car & Motorcycle

There is no substitute for the freedom your own vehicle can give you, especially for getting to places not well served by public transport. Roads are generally good and autostrade (motorways) connect most major cities. It is possible to hitchhike on Sicily, but don't expect a ride in a hurry.

Single women should not hitchhike under any circumstances.

Train

The coastal train service between Messina and Palermo and between Messina and Syracuse is efficient, and the run between Palermo and Agrigento is also generally OK. However, train services to other places in the interior can be infrequent and slow, and it is best to do some research before deciding between train and bus. The service from Noto to Ragusa, for instance, is picturesque but very slow.

Trenitalia (toll free ☎ 848 88 80 88, Italian only, not accessible from mobiles; www.trenitalia.com) is the partially privatised train system, previously known as the Ferrovie dello Stato (FS). Intercity (IC) trains are the fastest and most expensive, while the *regionale* is the slowest. All tickets must be validated before you board your train. There are left-luggage facilities at all train stations and charges are from €2.60 per day per piece of luggage.

PALERMO

pop 750,000

Dignified and decrepit, Palermo wears its 3000-year history with long-suffering indifference. Colonised since the 8th century BC, first by the Phoenicians, Palermo only truly flourished under Arab and later Norman rule, when the synthesis of Arab culture and Norman ambition brought about the city's golden age in the 12th century. After 400 years of enlightened living the city fell to a succession of rulers (German, French, Spanish and English), none of whom could revive the city's previous grandeur. The only notable change, under the Spaniards, was the imposition of a rational baroque city-plan that succeeded in disguising the true Moorish character of the city.

Heavily bombed during WWII, the city has been much neglected since. In recent years its only fame has originated from headline-grabbing assassinations and the notorious anti-Mafia maxi-trials of the 1990s, when the then Italian prime minister, Giulio Andreotti, was summoned to Palermo to stand trial for alleged government involvement with the Mafia. Since the climax of the trials and the exposure and imprisonment of many of the Mafia's most influential henchmen, Palermo has been emerging from its troubled past. The city mayor, Leoluca Orlando, has made it his mission to root out corruption and restore the city to some of its former glory. His inspired vision is already being felt in the extensive restoration work throughout the city and in the determined optimism of young Palermitans.

ORIENTATION

Palermo is a large but manageable city. Via Maqueda is the central street, extending from the train station in the south to the grand Piazza Castelnuovo, the location of Teatro Politeama Garibaldi (Politeama Garibaldi Theatre), in the north. Here it turns into Via della Libertà, a wide leafy boulevard lined with late-19th-century apartment blocks, which marks the beginnings of the modern half of the city. Via Maqueda is bisected by Corso Vittorio Emanuele, running east to west from the port of La Cala to the great Arab-Norman nucleus of the cathedral and Palazzo dei Normanni. This intersection, known famously as the Quattro Canti (Four Corners), divides historic Palermo into four traditional quarters that contain the majority of Palermo's sights. Parallel to Via Maqueda runs the slightly more modern Via Roma, the second main street of the old town and a cheap and popular high street. A one-way system rotates traffic north up Via Roma from the train station and south down Via Maqueda.

INFORMATION
Bookshops
Feltrinelli (Via Maqueda 395) A good selection of English books and maps.
Flaccovio (Via Maqueda 35)
Mondadori (Via Roma on Piazza San Domenico) Also has two computers for Internet access (€5/hr).

Emergencies
Police Station (theft & lost documents ☎ 091 21 01 11, foreigners office ☎ 091 651 43 30; Piazza della Vittoria)

Internet Access
Internet cafés come and go rapidly. Prices are around €5 per hour.
Aboriginal Cafe (☎ 091 662 2229; Via Spinuzza 51)
Crazy Village (☎ 091 33 12 72; Via Roma 182/188)

Left Luggage
Ferry Terminal (🕙 7am-8pm; from €1) Baggage deposit.
Train Station (€2.58 per bag/12 hrs)

Medical Services
Lo Cascio (☎ 091 616 21 17; Via Roma 1; 🕙 4.30pm-8.30am) Late-night pharmacy near the train station.
Ospedale Civico (☎ 091 666 11 11; Via Carmelo Lazzaro) The main hospital.

Money
Banks are open from 8.20am to 1.20pm. Most of them have ATMs although the newer Bancomat 3-plus machines are more reliable. ATMs are scattered throughout the city.
Cambio Exchange Offices Airport (🕙 8am-7pm Mon-Sat); Train Station (🕙 8am-8pm)
Ruggieri & Figli (☎ 091 58 71 44; Via Enrico Amari 40; 🕙 9am-1pm & 4-7pm Mon-Fri, 9am-1pm Sat) Representatives for American Express. They will cash travellers cheques for cardholders only.

Post & Telephone
Palazzo delle Poste (Via Roma 322; 🕙 8.30am-6.30pm Mon-Fri, 8.30am-12.30pm Sat) This monolithic post office is one of the few Fascist buildings in Palermo and it dominates Via Roma. Smaller branch offices can be found at the train station, to the right of the tracks, and on Piazza Verdi. They have the same opening hours.
Telecom Office (Piazza Giulio Cesare; 🕙 8am-9pm)
Telecom Office (Piazzale Ungheria; 🕙 8am-8pm)

Tourist Information
Tourist Office (☎ 091 605 81 11; Piazza Castelnuovo 35; www.palermotourism.com, Italian only; 🕙 8.30am-2pm & 2.30-6pm Mon-Fri, 8.30am-2pm Sat) Plenty of brochures on the major sights in Palermo and the surrounding areas, the most useful of these being the bi-monthly *Agenda*.
Tourist Office Branch Train Station (☎ 091 616 59 14; 🕙 8.30am-2pm & 2.30-6pm Mon-Fri, 8.30am-2pm Sat); Airport (☎ 091 59 16 98; 🕙 8am-noon)
Information Booths Molo Piave; Via Cavour; Piazza Bellini; Piazza Marina; Piazza della Vittoria; Piazza Giulio Cesare, in front of the train station (🕙 9am-2pm & 3-8pm Mon-Thu, 8.30am-8.30pm Fri & Sat, 9am-1pm & 3-7pm Sun)

Travel Agencies
The following agencies book train, ferry and air tickets:
CTS (☎ 091 611 07 13; Via Nicoló Garzilli 28g) Also offers tours of the island.

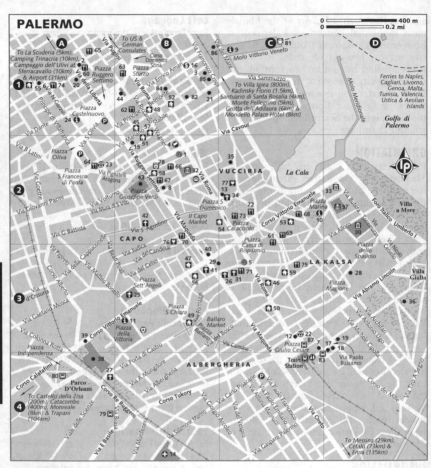

PALERMO

Record Viaggi (☎ 091 611 09 10; Via Marino Stabile 168)

Sestante (☎ 091 58 63 33; Via della Libertà 12)

SIGHTS
Around the Quattro Canti

The busy intersection of Corso Vittorio Emanuele and Via Maqueda marks the **Quattro Canti** (Four Corners), the centre of the oldest part of town. Known locally as *il teatro*, this intersection is the actual and ideal centre of the town, with a perfect circle of curvilinear facades that disappear vertiginously up to the blue vault of the sky. The 17th-century Spanish baroque facades are now clearly visible after an extensive clean.

Across Via Maqueda is Piazza Pretoria, a crowd of imposing churches and buildings that surround the ornate **Fontana Pretoria** (currently beneath scaffolding for restoration, although it can still be viewed through windows). The huge scale of the fountain dominates the piazza with its tiered basins and host of nude statues depicting tritons, nymphs and river-gods. Originally intended for a Tuscan villa, the cavorting statues proved a bit much for Sicilian churchgoers attending the grandly formal **San Giuseppe dei Teatini**, and they prudishly dubbed it the Fountain of Shame.

Just around the corner in Piazza Bellini is the red-domed **Chiesa di San Cataldo**. It is no longer possible to enter this small church, however its main interest lies in the Arab-Norman style of its exterior – the imam's *mihrab* (the alcove where he stands to lead the prayers) is clearly visible on the western end. Just next door is the famous **Chiesa di Santa Maria dell'Ammiraglio**, (Piazza Bellini 3; admission free; ☾ 8am-1pm & 3.30-5.30pm Mon-Sat, 8.30am-1pm Sun), known more commonly as La Martorana. One of Palermo's foremost churches, it is constantly busy with the business of weddings. This 12th-century structure was the brainchild of King Roger's Syrian Emir, George of Antioch. Originally planned as a mosque (it too has a *mihrab* visible from the outside), the Greek craftsmen employed to decorate it brought their own Christian vision to the stunning mosaic interior. Delicate Fatimid capitals endlessly repeating the name of Allah support a domed cupola depicting Christ enthroned amid his archangels, and in a stunning show of arrogance King Roger II receives his crown from Christ himself.

Albergheria

West along Corso Vittorio Emanuele, past the waving palms in Piazza delle Vittoria, rises the fortress palace of **Palazzo dei Normanni**, once the centre of a magnificent medieval court and now the seat of the Sicilian parliament. Guided tours of the

Palazzo Reale (☎ 091 705 43 17; fax 091 705 47 37; Piazza Indipendenza 1; admission free; ☾ 9am-noon Mon, Fri & Sat; group visits must be pre-booked by fax) take you through the Sicilian parliamentary assembly and the sumptuous **Sala di Ruggero II**, King Roger's former bedroom.

Downstairs, just off the three-tiered loggia, is Palermo's premier tourist attraction, the **Cappella Palatina** (☎ 091 705 48 79; admission free; ☾ 9-11.45am & 3-4.45pm Mon-Fri, 9-11.45am Sat, 9-10am & noon-1pm Sun), designed by Roger II in 1130. As the richest king in Christendom, Roger was able to indulge his love of Arab art and culture, employing the best Byzantine craftsmen to adorn his royal chapel. The exquisite mosaics (coloured glass onto which gold leaf has been applied) that cover the interior of the chapel glitter in the gloom, recounting the stories of the Old Testament. Other scenes recall Palermo's pivotal role in the Crusades, an ironic reference given the fact that the chapel was decorated by Muslim artists. The wooden *muqarnas* ceiling – unique in a Christian church – is a masterpiece of honeycomb carving, where Persian octagonal stars vie with intricate scenes of hunting and dancing and dark-eyed beauties. Set against the back wall is the royal throne (also inlaid with mosaic) with Christ Pantocrator (the All-Powerful) above, pointedly entrusting

SICILY

the Norman kings with the Holy Law. This is one of the busiest tourist sites in Palermo so be prepared to queue.

South of the *palazzo*, you can find a tranquil refuge from the crowds in the peaceful Norman cloisters of the **Chiesa di San Giovanni degli Eremiti** (Via dei Benedettini; admission €4.50; 9am-1pm & 3-7pm Mon-Sat, 9am-12.30pm Sun & hols).

Behind the splendours of the Palazzo dei Normanni lies the run-down district of Albergheria. A poor and ramshackle quarter once inhabited by the Norman court officials, it has so far escaped the redeeming attention of the restoration programme.

CUMULATIVE TICKETS & DISCOUNTS

It is possible to obtain cumulative tickets to visit some of Palermo's sites, making them a fraction cheaper. There are discounts (listed below) available to students and pensioners who are residents of the European Union (EU). Similar tickets can be obtained to visit the sites in Syracuse. Ask at the tourist office for details.

- €8 Museo Archeologico Regionale, Galleria Regionale di Palazzo Abatellis, Palazzo Mirto

- €8 Castello della Zisa, La Cuba, the cloisters of Monreale, Chiesa di San Giovanni degli Eremiti

- €6 Galleria Regionale di Palazzo Abatellis, Museo Archeologico Regionale

- €5 Galleria Regionale di Palazzo Abatellis, Palazzo Mirto

- €5 Museo Archeologico Regionale, Palazzo Mirto

Free entry for all EU citizens under the age of 18 and over the age of 65 to Galleria Regionale di Palazzo Abatellis, Museo Archeologico Regionale, Palazzo Mirto, the cloisters of Monreale, Castello della Zisa, La Cuba and Chiesa di San Giovanni degli Eremiti.

Discounted entry for EU citizens between 18 and 25 to Galleria Regionale di Palazzo Abatellis, Museo Archeologico Regionale, Palazzo Mirto, the cloisters of Monreale, Castello della Zisa, La Cuba and Chiesa di San Giovanni degli Eremiti. Entrance to each costs €2 and you will need to produce proof of age.

Home to a growing population of illegal immigrants, Albergheria is the location of Palermo's busiest street market, the **Ballaro market** (Piazza Ballaro). The bustling atmosphere, mounting rubbish and community spirit, although initially intimidating, are a good insight into a poorer Palermo that is not such a distant memory.

TOURS

Excellent guided tours run by **Associazione Sicilia e Dintorni** (☎ 091 21 83 44; Piazza Principe di Camporeale 27) show visitors the underside of Albergheria's streets, visiting craftsmen's workshops and sampling street snacks in the local market.

Il Capo

On 5 May 1072, the Norman 'wolf' Robert Guiscard seized Palermo, thus beginning the city's most prosperous and prodigious era. Ambitious builders, the Normans converted mosques and palaces, giving rise to the extraordinary Arab-Norman style unique to Sicily. Chief among these is the **cathedral** (☎ 091 33 43 76; Corso Vittorio Emanuele; admission free; 7am-7pm Mon-Sat, 8am-1.30pm & 4-7pm Sun & hols), an extraordinary feast of ziggurat crenellations, majolica cupolas, geometric patterns and blind arches. The later addition of the three-arched portico, a masterpiece of Catalan-inspired architecture with its slender pillars and spiral motif, only adds to the extraordinary decorative effect. Set back from the street, the foreground planted with palms, the oriental impact is enough to skew one's compass. The interior, although impressive in scale, is a marble shell, a sadly unexotic resting place for the royal Norman tombs. The **crypt** and **treasury** (admission €1.55; 9.30am-5.30pm Mon-Sat) contain various jewels belonging to Queen Costanza of Aragon, a bejewelled Norman crown and, most bizarrely, a tooth extracted from Santa Rosalia, the patron saint of Palermo.

Bordering Albergheria, Il Capo is another web of interconnected streets and blind alleys. Impoverished like its neighbour, it too has its own street market, **Il Capo**, running the length of Via Sant'Agostino.

The centrepiece of the quarter is the imposing monastery of **Sant'Agostino** (admission free; 8am-noon & 4-5.30pm), which ran the region in medieval times. Redecorated by the rich Scláfani family, the interior sports putti statues by Giacomo Serpotta, one of Palermo's foremost stucco workers in the 17th century, while the older cloister is decorated in a similar style to that of Monreale (p721). Northwards the alleys of Il Capo lead to Piazza Giuseppe Verdi and the grand neoclassical **Teatro Massimo** (☎ 091 605 35 15, toll free ☎ 800 65 58 58; www.teatromassimo.it; guided tours €3; ⊙ 10am-4pm Tue-Sun). Built between 1875 and 1897 by Giovanni Battista Basile and subsequently his son Ernesto, to celebrate the unification of Italy, the theatre has become a symbol of the triumph and tragedy of Palermo itself. Its long history is symptomatic of the conflicting powers that struggle for supremacy in Palermitan society – civic pride and cultural creativity pitted against the sinister shadows of Pirandellian bureaucracy and Mafia control, which is said to have been responsible for the extraordinary 24 years it took to restore. Appropriately, the closing scene of *The Godfather III*, with its visually stunning juxtaposition of high culture and low crime, drama and death, was filmed here.

Vucciria

Plunge into the streets heading towards the old harbour of La Cala from the Quattro Canti and you'll find a few more architectural gems of a completely different nature. The **Oratorio del Rosario di Santa Zita** (Via Valverde 3; admission free; ⊙ 9am-1pm & 3-6pm Mon-Fri, 9am-1pm Sat) and the **Oratorio del Rosario di San Domenico** (Via dei Bambinai 2; admission free; ⊙ 9am-1pm Mon-Fri, 2-5.30pm Sat) were used by nobles as social clubs and are a showy display of 17th-century status and wealth. Covered in a preposterous riot of stuccowork by Giacomo Serpotta, they represent the excessive love of ornamentation favoured by Palermitan nobles. Santa Zita is the undisputed jewel in Serpotta's crown, with the entire altarpiece a writhing mass of allegorical statues and capering cherubs leering out in all their three-dimensional glory.

In stark contrast the shabby streets of Vucciria mark the almost medieval chasm between rich and poor that existed in Sicily right up until the 1950s. Amid the alleys is Palermo's most notorious street market, **Vucciria** (Piazza Caracciolo), once the heart of poverty-stricken Palermo. A den of crime and filth, the Vucciria used to be a bustling place filled with shrieking vendors, swaying carcasses and every imaginable fruit and vegetable – a scene of bounty immortalised by Renato Guttuso (1912–87), Sicily's most famous modern artist. However, as his contemporary, Leonardo Sciascia (novelist; 1921–89), pointed out, the painting more aptly illustrates the longings of a hungry man. Vucciria has now ceded its preeminent place to the more popular Ballaro market (p712), but the real essence of Guttuso's painting is only to be found in the huge street market of Catania (p743).

Walking north and crossing Via Roma will bring you to the **Museo Archeologico Regionale** (☎ 091 611 68 05; Via Bara all'Olivella 24; admission €4.50; ⊙ 8.30am-6pm Mon & Fri, 8.30am-1.30pm Sat, Sun & hols). Housed in a pretty Renaissance monastery, the galleries of this museum surround a lovely inner courtyard and display some of Sicily's most valuable Greek and Roman artefacts. The most important rooms are ranged around the courtyard and display numerous treasures from Selinunte, most notably a series of metopes (decorative friezes) illustrating familiar stories such as Perseus and Medusa, Hercules and the Amazons and the metamorphosis of Actaeon.

La Kalsa

Due to its proximity to the port, La Kalsa was subjected to carpet-bombing during WWII, leaving it derelict and run-down. Mother Teresa considered it no better than the Third World and established a mission here. Thankfully, this galvanised the authorities into action and the quarter is now the main beneficiary of the restoration project. Wandering through the narrow cobbled streets is an experience in itself, reminiscent as they are of the north African souks in Tripoli and Fez. Flashes of blue sea are visible between the tightly-packed houses, while balconies overhead are within touching distance of each other.

The arterial Via Alloro hides Palermo's best museum, the wonderful **Galleria Regionale di Palazzo Abatellis** (☎ 091 623 00 11; Via Alloro 4; admission €4.50; ⊙ 9am-2pm Mon-Fri & 3-8pm Tue, Wed & Thu, 9.30am-1.30pm Sat & Sun), full of treasures and paintings from the Middle Ages to the 18th century. The interior was designed by Carlo Scarpa, one of Italy's leading interior designers, and displays each piece thoughtfully. The gallery gives a great insight into

Sicilian painting – something sadly lacking in more recent years – and numbers among its treasures the famously terrifying *Trionfo della Morta* (Triumph of Death). Room 4 houses the gallery's most famous piece, the exquisite white marble bust of Eleonora d'Aragona by Francesco Laurana. The gallery holds a range of constantly changing temporary exhibitions.

Behind the gallery is the **Complessa di Santa Maria dello Spasimo** (☎ 091 616 14 86; Via Spasimo; admission free; ☼ 9am-midnight), originally a church and convent and the only example of Northern Gothic in Sicily, with its elegant polygonal apse and tall slender nave that has stood for centuries without a roof. Throughout the years it has done duty as a fortress, theatre, hospital and poor house, and more recently it has been converted into an exhibition space and concert venue. It's sensational to visit at night.

Striking out from Palazzo Abatellis in the opposite direction up Via IV Aprile will bring you to the gentrified **Piazza Marina** with its small but perfect **Giardino Garibaldi**. Surrounded on all sides by elegant *palazzi*, this is Palermo's prettiest and quietest piazza. The largest *palazzo* on the square is the imposing 14th-century **Palazzo Chiaramonte Steri** (☎ 091 33 41 39; Piazza Marina; ☼ open for exhibitions only). Built as the fortified residence of the Chiaramonte family (one of the most powerful families of the Aragonese period), the *palazzo* subsequently became the headquarters of the Inquisition in the 17th century and miserable heretics were burnt to death outside. It's now part of the University of Palermo and is only open for special exhibitions.

On a lighter note, just around the corner from Piazza Marina you will find the **Museo Internazionale delle Marionette** (☎ 091 32 80 60; Via Butera 1; adult/concession €3/1.50; ☼ 9am-1pm & 4-7pm Sun-Fri), set up by the Association for the Conservation of Popular Traditions. The museum houses over three thousand puppets, marionettes, glove puppets and shadow figures collected from Palermo, Catania and Naples, as well as many from far-flung countries such as China, India, southern Asia, Turkey and Africa. A show is staged every Friday at 5.30pm; the museum has a detailed programme.

If you just fancy getting away from it all and want to give the kids a break, head for **Villa Giulia** (Via Lincoln; admission free; ☼ 8am-8pm)

in the far southeastern corner of the quarter fronting the sea. This formal Italian garden, complete with geometric planting and symmetrical paths, is a welcome relief from the claustrophobic streets of the historic centre and it includes a play area for children. The adjoining **Orto Botanico** (☼ 9am-6pm Mon-Fri, 8.30am-1.30pm Sat & Sun) is an added bonus for plant enthusiasts.

The Suburbs

A short bus or car journey west from Piazza Castelnuovo leads to **Castello della Zisa** (☎ 091 652 02 69; Piazza Guglielmo il Buono; admission €2.60; ☼ 9am-6.30pm Mon-Fri, 9am-1pm Sat & Sun), one of the only remaining monuments to the decadence of Moorish Palermo. With stalactite vaults, latticework windows, fountains and even a wind chamber to protect the Emir from the hot African sirocco, the villa deserves its name, which comes from the Arabic *al aziz*, meaning magnificent. Today it houses a museum of Arab crafts of where main features are superbly crafted screens and a gorgeous 12th-century bronze basin. Take bus No 124 from Piazza Ruggero Settimo.

South of the *castello* is the morbid and peculiarly Sicilian **Catacombe dei Cappuccini** (☎ 091 21 21 17; Via Cappuccini 1; admission €1.50; ☼ 9am-noon & 3-5pm), where the mummified bodies and skeletons of some 8000 Palermitans, who died between the 17th and 19th centuries, are on show! Earthly power, sex, religion and professional status are still rigidly distinguished: men and women occupy separate corridors and within the women's area there is a first-class section for virgins. The sight is nothing short of bizarre, with corridors of courtly Palermitans still dressed in their best, if faded, velvets and silks.

FESTIVALS & EVENTS

Sicily is rightly famous for its festivals and Palermo has its fair share. It's also worth investigating the festivals of small villages and towns surrounding major cities as many of these preserve ancient traditions, each unique to its town. Information about local festivals can be found on the tourist information websites.

February

Carnevale Sicily's oldest carnival is held in Termini Imerese, a suburb of Palermo. Decorated floats and enormous papier-mâché figures parade the streets.

April
Easter Holy Week This major religious festival is celebrated virtually all over the island. In Palermo there are Greek Orthodox celebrations at La Martorana.

July
U Fistinu (10-15 July) Mountain procession to celebrate Santa Rosalia, the patron saint of Palermo.
Palermo di Scena Music, theatre, cinema and ballet programs throughout summer.

December
Festival di Morgana Puppeteers from all over the world gather at Museo Internazionale delle Marionette.
Opera Season Teatro Massimo commences its opera season, which ends in May.

SLEEPING
All the mid-range hotels and some of the more atmospheric restaurants are located in the historic centre around the Quattro Canti, while most of the budget options can be found on Via Roma towards the train station. The better hotels are clustered around Piazza Verdi at the northern end of town. Prices in Sicily, and especially in Palermo, fluctuate depending on season and demand. It is always better to call and book in advance.

Budget
Albergo Ariston (☎ 091 33 24 34; Via Marino Stabile 139; s/d €40/55; 🗱) A rather run-down apartment block disguises Palermo's best budget hotel and this place cannot be recommended highly enough. It has a great location at the top end of town between Piazza Castelnuovo and Piazza Verdi, and the rooms are sparklingly clean. Although no English is spoken the staff are extremely polite and try to be as helpful as possible.

Ambasciatori Hotel (☎ 091 610 66 881; fax 091 610 01 05; Via Roma 111; s/d €47/67; P 🗱) Previously known as the Hotel Azzuro di Lampedusa (the sign still hangs outside), the Ambasciatori has been completely renovated and is good value for money. The reception staff are efficient and polite and the hotel, located on the 5th floor of an old *palazzo*, is one of the quieter options on Via Roma.

Hotel Regina (☎ 091 611 42 16; htregina@libero.it; Corso Vittorio Emanuele 316; s/d €21/40 without bathroom, d with shower €50; P) The best thing about this hotel is its location, situated just off the Quattro Canti and within easy walking

distance of all the major sights. The interior is a jumble of cheap but adequate furnishings but the lack of air-conditioning is a drawback in summer.

Hotel Cortese (☎ 091 33 17 22; htcortese@iol.it; Via Scarparelli 16; s/d €35/60; 🗱) For an old town experience try this hotel, tucked behind the Ballaro market in Albergheria. The dim vaulted entrance is gloomy although the rooms are comfortable enough. A stay here, surrounded by crumbling apartment blocks, gives you a real insight into old Palermo, where life is played out on the streets. Don't over-romanticise this option – old Palermo can be dirty, noisy and busy as well as atmospheric!

Trinacria (☎ 091 53 05 90; Via Barcarello 25, Sferracavallo; person/tent/car €4.60/4/2.70) Palermo's best camp site is by the sea at Sferracavallo, an area noted for its fish restaurants. Catch bus No 616 from Piazzale A de Gaspari (which can be reached by bus No 101 from the train station).

Campeggio dell'Ulivi (☎ 091 53 30 21; Via Pegaso, Sferracavallo; person €7.55) This camp site is open year-round and the reception can supply you with bus tickets, timetables and city maps. Take bus No 615 from Piazza Vittorio Veneto at the top of Via delle Libertà, which drops you outside the camp site. Price is inclusive of shower and electricity.

Mid-Range
Hotel Tonic (☎ 091 605 53 38; www.hoteltonic.com; Via Marino Stabile 126; s/d €75/95; 🗱) This friendly and efficient hotel deserves its good reputation. All staff speak good English and the hotel is well equipped and comfortable with two rooms reserved for the disabled. Although the hotel does not have its own garage there is parking 75m down the road at a cost of €13 per day. Room prices remain the same year-round.

Hotel Elite (☎ 091 32 93 18; elitehotel@tin.it; Via Mariano Stabile 136; s/d €70/90; P 🗱 💻) Completely renovated in 2002, Hotel Elite is now one of the best value-for-money options in Palermo and offers a range of services, including laundry. The staff are friendly and speak English and the carpeted halls and bedrooms are a blessing in the winter.

Residence d'Aragon (☎ 091 662 22 22; fax 091 662 22 73; Via Ottavio D'Aragona 25; s/d €90/130; 🗱) This discreet and classy hotel is located in a surprisingly quiet side street just off the raucous Via Roma. It has an exceptional range of services including laundry, room service and satellite TV and it also caters for the disabled.

Hotel del Centro (☎ 091 617 03 76; hoteldelcentro@libero.it; Via Roma 72; s/d €70/85; P ☒ ☐) This friendly and busy hotel on Via Roma is good value for money and is tastefully decorated throughout, with wrought-iron beds and spotlessly clean bathrooms. The hotel's proximity to the station is useful for those with onward journeys.

Hotel Letizia (☎ 091 58 91 10; hotel-letizia@neomedie.it; Via dei Bottai 30; s/d €63/83; ☒) A lovely little hotel and one of the few off the quaint Piazza Marina. Each of the 16 bedrooms is individually decorated and the wooden floors and low ceilings give it a cosy feel. There is also a small terrace on which you can enjoy your breakfast (€5). Some of the bathrooms include a bath.

Hotel Joli (☎ 091 611 17 65; www.hoteljoli.com; Via Michele Amari 11; s/d €70/90; ☒) Another comfortable hotel in the same area as Tonic and Elite. Although very efficient, it seems to lack soul and some of the huge rooms appear cavernous rather than luxurious. Some do have nice balconies over Piazza Florio and there is convenient parking down the road (€13 per day).

Hotel Moderno (☎ 091 58 86 83; fax 091 58 86 83; Via Roma 276; s/d €70/90; ☒) Like most hotels in Italy with the name 'Moderno', it's not, but the rooms are comfortable and it's within spitting distance of La Vucciria.

Top End

Hotel Principe di Villafranca (☎ 091 611 85 23; www.principedivillafranca.it; Via G Turrisi Colonna 4; s/d €126/180; P ☒ ☐) This hotel is situated just off Via della Libertà in what is one of the most exclusive areas of Palermo. It's furnished throughout with Sicilian antiques and expensive linens and the suites have whirlpool baths. All bedrooms have satellite TV, minibars and Internet access. The excellent restaurant Il Firriato (p718), the cosy library with its huge fireplace and the cutting-edge gym make this the ultimate in luxury.

Grand Hotel e des Palmes (☎ 091 602 81 11; www.despalmes.thi.it; Via Roma 398; s/d €121/185; P ☒) Opened in 1874, the Grand Hotel is one of Palermo's most historic hotels. Classical musicians such as Wagner, painters

(Renato Guttuso), writers, actors and politicians (most recently Giulio Andreotti) have all passed through its doors. Like a royal court it has been the scene of intrigue, double-dealings and liaisons throughout Palermo's history, although it was abandoned by the elite in the 1970s in favour of the even more ostentatious Villa Igiea. The grand salons still impress with their chandeliers and gigantic mirrors while the rooms are sumptuously decked out.

Centrale Palace Hotel (☎ 091 33 66 66; www.centralepalacehotel.it; Corso Vittorio Emanuele 327; s/d €120/206; P ☒) This renovated 18th-century *palazzo* is one of Palermo's most elegant hotels, with luxurious rooms (two have facilities for disabled travellers) and a high level of service which it prides itself on. It also has a wonderful rooftop restaurant with views over Palermo.

Massimo Plaza Hotel (☎ 091 32 56 57; www.massimoplazahotel.com; Via Maqueda 437; s/d €120/185; P ☒) Scoring 10 out of 10 for position (directly opposite Teatro Massimo), this is one of Palermo's more intimate hotels. Extremely comfortable, if a little overpriced, the hotel also runs a very useful shuttle service to Mondello (p720). **Villa Igiea** (☎ 091 54 76 54; www.villaigiea.thi.it; Salita Belmonte 43; s/d €164/256; P ☒ ☒) This is Palermo's luxury hotel *par excellence*, attracting Italy's most illustrious names as well as the international jet set. Designed by Ernesto Basile, the villa takes its cue from the palatial architecture of the 15th century. The hotel is stunningly situated in its own terraced gardens at the foot of Monte Pellegrino overlooking the sea.

EATING

One of Sicily's best-kept secrets is its ancient cuisine, a mixture of spicy and sweet flavours – no doubt part of the island's long contact with Arab colonisers. A reflection of Sicily's proximity to north Africa is the presence of couscous on menus and there is a strong tradition of street food such as *panelle* (chickpea fritters). Palermo's most famous dish is the tasty *pasta con le sarde*, with sardines, fennel, peppers, capers and pine nuts. Cakes and pastries are works of art – try the *cannoli*, tubes of pastry filled with cream, ricotta or chocolate – and like the Spaniards, Sicilians have a penchant for marzipan. Traditional Sicilian cuisine is currently enjoying something of a revival and there is a growing number of quality restaurants and some excellent wine bars. Sicilians are late eaters and restaurants rarely open for dinner before 8pm, and only start to fill up around 10pm.

Quick Eats

Antica Focacceria di San Francesco (☎ 091 32 02 64; Via A Paternostro 58; mains €7; ⓨ 9am-midnight) A Palermitan institution popular with working men and families, this atmospheric place is one of the city's oldest eating houses and is worth seeking out. It serves calzone, pizza slices and an age-old Palermitan snack – a *panino* (filled roll) with *milza* (veal innards) and ricotta cheese. It also has a lovely outdoor area in Piazza San Francesco.

Trattoria Shanghai (☎ 091 58 97 02; Vicolo dei Mezzani 34; meals €13; ⓨ noon-11pm Mon-Sat Mar-Jan) A raffish, rough-and-tumble place in a crumbling house, Shanghai has simple food at good prices and as a result is always packed. It's the right place for a quick lunch after visiting the Vucciria market, from where the food is hauled up in baskets.

Foccaceria del Massimo (☎ 091 33 56 28; Via Bara all'Olivella 76; mains €4; ⓨ noon-4pm Mon-Sat) This place just off Piazza Verdi is a popular workman's restaurant. Slices of pizza, sandwiches and daily pasta dishes provide simple but filling fare.

El-Maghreb (Via Bara all'Olivella 75; shwerma €3; ⓨ noon-late Tue-Sun) An extremely cheap Tunisian kebab house, El-Maghreb is always open and serves massive *shwerma* (pitta breads filled with lamb and salad) for a few euros. You can also order *mezze* and *tagine*. Situated just on the corner of Piazza Olivella and playing loud Arabic music, this is one of the more lively spots in Palermo.

Restaurants
MID-RANGE
Mi Manda Picone (☎ 091 616 06 60; Via A Paternostro 59; meals €20; ⓨ 8pm-1am) In a fabulous 13th-century building and with summer seating in the beautiful Piazza San Francesco, this excellent restaurant serves *nouvelle cuisine* as well as hearty platters of cheese and *charcuterie* (cooked cold meats). It's also a wine bar – the walls are lined with an extensive selection of Sicilian wine and the staff are knowledgeable and helpful.

Osteria dei Cucùnci (☎ 091 612 47 54; Via dei Candelai 35; meals €20; ⓨ 8pm-late; ✗) This elegant

wine bar/grill room is one of a growing number of fashionable eateries serving Sicilian cuisine with a modern twist. The decor is atmospheric with a galleried eating area upstairs. The bar specialises in Sicilian reds – try the gorgeously smooth merlot by La Planeta. Close to the club I Candelai (p718), this place fills up at the weekends, but it will seem strangely empty until the witching hour of 10pm.

La Cambusa (☎ 091 58 45 74; Piazza Marina 17; meals €12; ⓨ 12.30-3pm & 8pm-midnight Mon-Sat) Almost exclusively devoted to fish, La Cambusa is a favourite with the locals and its proximity to the old port of La Cala makes it a serious fish restaurant. You select the fish of your choice from the cold counter and they whisk it off to be cooked in the kitchen. Although it has a great atmosphere in the evenings, the busier it is, the ropier the service.

Trattoria Stella (☎ 091 616 11 36; Via Alloro 104; meals €23; ⓨ noon-midnight Tue-Sun, closed for 2 weeks Aug) Situated in the courtyard of the old Hotel Patria, Stella is another popular local restaurant. In summer the tables fill the old courtyard and the food is hearty Sicilian fare.

Pizzeria Bellini (☎ 091 616 56 91; Piazza Bellini 6; ⓨ 7-1am Wed-Mon) Overshadowed by La Martorana, this popular pizzeria is an attractive spot for lunch and dinner when the churches are atmospherically floodlit. Its claim to fame is Marlon Brando's autograph, which is suitably praiseworthy.

Capricci di Sicilia (☎ 091 32 77 77; Via Instituto Pignatelli 6; meals €18; ⓨ 1-3.30pm & 8pm-midnight Jul-Sep, 8pm-midnight Aug) Tucked behind the colonnade on the left of Piazza Sturzo, this intimate little restaurant takes great pride in the typical Sicilian dishes it serves up. Pastas are flavoured with sardines, broccoli and sea urchins and there is a good selection of antipasto. Its atmosphere is slightly formal and it is advisable to make a reservation in summer.

TOP END
Most of the upmarket restaurants are on the outskirts of Palermo or in nearby towns. The locals head for beachside Mondello (p720) to eat seafood.

La Scuderia (☎ 091 52 03 23; Viale del Fante 9; mains €12-20; ⓨ 12.30-3pm & 8.30pm-midnight Mon-Sat, closed 2 weeks Aug) The imaginative cuisine in this highly regarded restaurant is complemented by its pretty flower-filled terrace.

SICILY

Despite being 5km outside Palermo, tables here are sought after and reservations are essential, as is appropriate attire. The menu has a surprisingly good selection of meat dishes, less common in Sicily in general.

Sant'Andrea (☎ 091 33 49 99; Piazza Sant'Andrea 4; meals €26; ☷ 1-3pm & 8pm-midnight Wed-Mon Feb-Dec) Right in the heart of Vucciria, this good restaurant serving fresh food from the market was the regular haunt of Peter Robb whilst he researched his excellent book about the Mafia, *Midnight in Sicily*. The restaurant, in the old atmospheric piazza, mirrors the brooding atmosphere of the book; the pasta dishes are superb.

Il Firriato (☎ 091 53 02 82; Via G Turrisi Colonna 4; meals €30; ☷ noon-3pm & 8-11pm Tue-Sat) Although Il Firriato is the restaurant for Hotel Principe di Villafranca (p716) it is also open to the public and can be accessed from the street. Its limited menu is a sign of the care they take over each dish – the roast lamb is particularly delicious and the desserts are to die for.

Cucina Papoff (☎ 091 58 64 60; Via Isidoro La Lumia 32; ☷ 12.30-3.30pm & 8.30-11pm Mon-Sat Sep-Jul) This lovely Art Nouveau restaurant in the newer part of town serves imaginative Sicilian dishes such as *u maccu* (broad beans in fennel) to a trendy young crowd.

Charleston (☎ 091 32 13 66; Piazzale Ungheria 30; ☷ noon-3pm & 8-11pm Mon-Sat Oct-May) Charleston is one of Palermo's classiest, most formal restaurants. Its main establishment is in Palermo, not far from Teatro Massimo, but from June to early October it moves to its Mondello branch (☎ 091 45 01 71, Viale Regina Elena), inside the Stabilimento Balneare (a private beach). Most Sicilians view eating here as a real event and diners spend their time people-watching – if you don't want to look out of place put on your best gear and make a reservation.

DRINKING
CAFÉS
There are numerous cafés with outdoor tables where you can linger over breakfast or lunch; the following are just a handful of the better ones.

Antico Café Spinnato (☎ 091 58 32 31; Via P di Belmonte 107-15; ☷ 8am-11pm) This sophisticated tea salon has shady outdoor tables and cakes that are too beautiful to eat. The gelato is pretty popular too.

Il Baretto (☎ 091 32 96 40; Via XX Settembre 43; ☷ 11am-11pm Tue-Sat) This little café with its besuited waiters gives a good insight into how the other half lives. Rich young Palermitans dressed head to toe in designer labels, ladies with serious hairdos and eccentric old men with panama hats and shades all congregate here for their light lunch. Aperitifs come accompanied by nuts and crisps, and tasty finger food is served at lunchtime.

Andrea di Martino (☎ 091 58 59 90; Via Mazzini 54; ☷ 8am-late) A very busy, large café just off Via della Libertà serving cocktails and fast food. It is amazing how good hot chips can taste after one too many cocktails. In the evenings its outdoor tables are swamped.

BARS AND NIGHTCLUBS
Compared with the rest of Italy, Sicilian nightlife is somewhat sedate and introverted, centred more on restaurants and private parties. However, there are a growing number of bars, especially in summer resorts. Most good bars and dance venues are in the newer part of Palermo and in summer everyone decamps to **Mondello Lido** by the sea. On weeknights almost nothing moves in Palermo.

I Candelai (☎ 091 32 71 51; Via dei Candelai 65; €5; ☷ 11pm-late Fri-Sun) Mainstream rock pumps throughout this popular nightclub as teens and 20-somethings shake their thing and engage in some serious flirting.

Kadinsky-Florio (☎ 091 637 53 38; Discesa Tonnara; ☷ 8pm-late) On the beach at Arenella, this is a great place to come to while away the night dancing and drinking. It's stylish and gets a good rap from the locals. However, it is a bit of a hike from the centre of town.

I Grilli Giù (☎ 091 58 47 47; Piazza Cavalieri di Malta 11; ☷ from 8pm) A popular cocktail bar (and restaurant) northeast of the Vucciria market, where you can sip a cocktail and listen to the latest DJ tricks.

Mondello Palace Hotel (☎ 091 45 00 01; Via Principe di Scalea 12; ☷ 7.30pm-late) This bar out at Mondello is popular with Palermitans in summer when the heat in town gets oppressive. In summer an express bus (No 6) leaves for Mondello from the central train station, otherwise use the buses listed on p720.

ENTERTAINMENT
The daily paper *Il Giornale di Sicilia* has a listing of what's on. Tourist information booths also have programs and listings.

Teatro Massimo (☎ 091 605 31 11; Piazza Verdi 9) Ernesto Basile's Art Nouveau masterpiece, restored to its former glory, stages opera, ballet and music concerts. Its program runs from October to May.

Teatro Politeama Garibaldi (☎ 091 605 32 49; Piazza Ruggero Settimo) This is the main venue for music and ballet.

Opera dei Pupi (☎ 091 32 34 00; Via Bara all'Olivella 52) A good break for young kids, and the elaborate old puppets will endear themselves to adults too. Shows are generally staged at 5.30pm weekends. Tickets cost €5.15 (children €2.60). At No 40 in the same street is one of several artisans who makes and repairs the puppets.

GETTING THERE & AWAY
Air
Falcone-Borsellino airport (PMO) is at Punta Raisi, 31km west of Palermo. For 24-hour information on domestic flights call **Alitalia** (airport ☎ 091 601 92 50, office ☎ 091 601 93 33, Via della Libertà 39), and for international flights call the main airport number ☎ 091 702 01 11. At any time of year, it's usually possible to find charter flights between Palermo and major European cities. **Ryanair** (UK ☎ 0871 246 0000; www.ryanair.com) has a daily direct flights between Stansted (in the UK) and Palermo.

Boat
Ferries leave from Molo Vittorio Veneto, off Via Francesco Crispi, for Cagliari (Sardinia), Valencia (Spain), Naples, Livorno and Genoa (see p707).

Tirrenia (call centre ☎ 199 12 31 99, ☎ 091 602 11 11; www.tirrenia.it; Calata Marinai d'Italia; ☺ 8.30am-12.30pm & 3.30-8.45pm Mon-Fri, 3.30-8.45pm Sat, 5-8.45pm Sun) has an office at the port, to the right of the main entrance.

Siremar (☎ 091 58 24 03; www.siremar.it, Italian only; Via Francesco Crispi 118) runs ferries and hydrofoils (July to August only) to Ustica (€9.90 ferry, €16.10 hydrofoil foot passenger).

SNAV (www.snavali.com) is represented in Palermo by the **Pietro Barbaro agency** (☎ 091 33 33 33; Via P di Belmonte 55). It also has an office inside the port gates near Molo S Lucia, where the hydrofoils depart. SNAV runs a summer-only hydrofoil service to the Aeolian Islands. It also operates a daily ferry service between Palermo and Naples from April

IL TEATRO DEI PUPI

For generations puppet shows entertained workers and children with their chivalric tales of intrigue and derring-do. Tales centred around the legends of Charlemagne's heroic knights, Orlando and Rinaldo, while the extended cast included the fair Angelica, the treacherous Gano di Magonza and forbidding Saracen warriors. A host of magicians and monsters created constant diversions and distractions that kept storylines running for weeks at a time. Good puppeteers are judged on the dramatic effect they can create – lots of stamping feet and a gripping running commentary – and on their speed and skill in directing the battle scenes.

to October, departing 9am and arriving at 1pm. Tickets cost €49.60 each way (€62 in July, August and September).

Grandi Navi Veloci (☎ 091 58 79 39; www.grimaldi .it; Calata Marina d'Italia), part of the Grimaldi Group, is also at the port, to the left of the main entrance. There is another office in town on Via Mariano Stabile. The company runs ferries from Palermo to Genoa (daily), Livorno (three weekly) and Valencia (once weekly).

Bus
The main intercity bus station is around Via P Balsamo east of the train station. See p707 for details of national services. In addition to these, **SAIS Trasporti** (☎ 091 617 11 41; www.saistrasporti.it; Via P Balsamo 20) runs services to Cefalù (€4.65, one hour, two daily). **SAIS Autolinee** (☎ 091 616 60 28; www.saisautolinee.it; Via P Balsamo 16) also services Catania (€11.72, 2½ hours, hourly Monday to Saturday), Enna (€5.95, 1¾ hours, six daily), Piazza Armerina (€9.55, 1½ hours, eight daily) and Messina (€12.39, 3¼ hours, hourly). **Segesta** (☎ 091 616 90 39; www.segesta.it; Via P Balsamo 26) runs very frequent services to Trapani (€7, two per hour Monday to Friday) and Interbus runs to Syracuse (€13.40, four hours, six daily Monday to Saturday). **Cuffaro** (☎ 091 616 15 10; www.cuffaro.it; Via P Balsamo 13) has buses to Agrigento (€6.70, 2½ hours, seven daily Monday to Saturday).

AST (☎ 091 680 00 11; Corso Ruggero), away from the main terminal near Piazza Indipendenza

SICILY

and the university, runs four daily buses to Ragusa. It also operates services travelling to Corleone, Cefalù, Palazzo Adriano and Montelepre.

Numerous other companies service points throughout Sicily and most have offices in the Via P Balsamo area. Their addresses and telephone numbers, as well as destinations, are listed in the tourist information booklet *Agenda*, available at the tourist office.

Car & Motorcycle

Palermo is accessible by autostrada from Messina (only partially completed) and from Catania (A19) via Enna (this route is quicker). Trapani and Marsala are also easily accessible from Palermo by autostrada (A29), while Agrigento and Palermo are linked by a good state road (S121) through the interior of the island.

To rent a car try **Avis** (☎ 091 58 69 40; Via Francesco Crispi 115) near the port, as well as an office at the airport (☎ 091 59 16 84), or **Sicily by Car** (☎ 091 58 10 45; Via Marino Stabile 6/a), which also rents out scooters. All major rental companies are represented in Palermo and are listed in *Agenda*.

Train

Regular trains leave from the train station for Milazzo, Messina, Catania, Trapani, Syracuse and Agrigento, as well as nearby towns such as Cefalù. There are also Intercity trains to Reggio di Calabria, Naples and Rome. Train timetable information is available in English at the station. There is a Transalpino office inside the station, as well as left luggage and very clean toilet facilities (€0.20). In summer the **ticket office** (☎ 091 603 30 88; ⏲ 7am-8.45pm) gets very busy, so allow enough time before departure for purchasing tickets.

GETTING AROUND
To/From the Airport

A half-hourly bus service operated by **Prestìa e Comandè** (☎ 091 58 04 57) runs from the airport to the centre of town, where it stops outside the Teatro Politeama Garibaldi and the train station. Tickets for the 45-minute journey cost €4.65 and are available on the bus. Journeys to the airport run with similar frequency and pick up at the same points. This is by far the best way to travel from the airport to Palermo.

An hourly train service, the Trinacria Express, runs from the airport to the central station (€4.50). There are plenty of taxis outside the airport and the fare for the same trip is about €35. All the major car hire companies are represented at the airport, including Hertz, Avis and Sicily by Car.

Bus

Palermo's city **buses** (AMAT; ☎ 091 35 01 11; www .amat.pa.it, Italian only) are efficient and regular, and most stop in front of the train station. Ask at the information booths around town for a leaflet detailing the different lines. Tickets must be purchased before you board and are available from tobacconists or the booths at the terminal. They cost €0.80 and are valid for two hours. A day pass is €2.60.

There are two small buses – Linea Gialla and Linea Rossa (the yellow line and red line) – that operate in the narrow streets of the old part of town and can be useful if you are moving between tourist sights and your feet need a rest.

Car & Motorcycle

If you have dealt with Rome or Naples in your own vehicle, Palermo will present no difficulties. Theft of, and from, vehicles is a problem, however, and you are advised to use one of the attended car parks around town if your hotel has no parking space. You'll be looking at around €13 per day. Some hotels have small car parks, but they are often full; check with your hotel proprietor.

AROUND PALERMO

Northwest of the city is the popular beach of **Mondello**. In summer beachfront Viale Regina Elena is crowded with tourists and Palermitans taking a break from the city. All but two of the beaches charge an admission fee of €8, but there is an official free tourist beach and the Charleston beach. All registered hotels in Palermo can give you tickets for these. There are numerous seafood restaurants and snack stalls along the avenue and in the evening Mondello is lit up with bars and nightclubs.

Between Palermo and Mondello is Monte Pellegrino and the **Santuario di Santa Rosalia** (☎ 091 54 03 26; Monte Pellegrino; admission free; ⏲ 7am-7pm). Palermo's patron saint, Santa Rosalia, lived as a hermit in a cave on the mountain, now the site of a 17th-century shrine. The water, channelled from the roof of the cave into a large font, is said to have miraculous powers. Whatever your beliefs, this is a fascinating place to visit, but remember that it is a shrine, not a tourist haunt. The road to the sanctuary suffers from landslides and is often closed for repairs.

Monreale

Inspired by a heavenly vision of the Virgin and driven by earthy ambition, William II set about building the magnificent **Monreale Cathedral** (☎ 091 640 44 13; admission free; ☽ 8am-6pm, treasury 9.30am-noon & 3.30-5.30pm), 8km southwest of Palermo and accessible by frequent city buses from Palermo's Piazza Indipendenza. Living in the shadow of his grandfather (Roger II, who was responsible for the cathedral in Cefalù and the Cappella Palatina in Palermo), and vying with his rival Walter of the Mill (the Palermitan archbishop), William was determined to build a cathedral greater than anything that had gone before. The result was Monreale, considered the finest example of Norman architecture in Sicily, incorporating Norman, Arab, Byzantine and classical elements.

Although the exterior is both graceful and elegant, nothing can quite prepare you for the dazzling interior, one of the most impressive creations of the Italian Middle Ages. The shimmering mosaics represent a poor man's Bible with all Old Testament stories laid out in tender detail from the Creation of Man and the act of Original Sin to the birth of Christ and man's redemption, a total of 42 different episodes. For €1 lights will illuminate the walls in dazzling detail. The artists were local and Venetian mosaicists, but the influence of the Byzantine style is all-pervasive. Completed in 1184 after only 10 years' work, the mosaics are the apogee of Norman-Arab art, an articulate and fitting tribute to the sophistication of Sicilian culture at the time.

In the central apse, made up of 130 panels, is the dominating half-figure of Christ Pantocrator giving benediction, and below him the Virgin Mary and child. Beneath them again are the ranks of saints, each identified by name (look out for St Thomas à Becket between Silvester and Laurence; he was canonised in 1173, just before the mosaics were started). The side apses are dedicated to the martyrdoms of St Paul (east) and St Peter (west). Other impressive elements include the massive bronze doors by Bonanno Pisano, pagan capitals featuring Roman gods, and a gilded ceiling.

Outside the cathedral is the entrance to the **cloisters** (admission €4.50; ☽ 9am-7pm Mon-Sat, 9am-1.30pm Sun), which illustrate William's own love of Arab artistry. This tranquil courtyard is pure Orientalism, with elegant Romanesque arches supported by an exquisite array of slender columns alternately decorated with shimmering mosaic patterns. Each capital is different and taken together they represent a unique sculptural record of medieval Sicily – musicians playing instruments, Oriental characters wearing turbans surrounded by snakes, acrobats, cherubs and a host of writhing animals and foliage. The capital of the 19th column on the west aisle depicts William II offering the cathedral to the Madonna.

William II lies entombed in a white marble sarcophagus in the cathedral.

Ustica

Almost 60km north of Palermo lies the lonely island of Ustica, a haven for serious divers and an easy day trip from Palermo. This tiny island (8.7 sq km) is actually the tip of a submerged volcano sitting on the seabed, and as a result the waters around the island are a feast of fish and coral. The limpid waters are kept sparkling clean by an Atlantic current through the Straits of Gibraltar and are ideal for snorkelling, diving and underwater photography.

As Sicily's oldest marine reserve (established in 1986), Ustica has a well-organised tourist infrastructure catering specifically for divers. There are a number of dive outfits on the island open from April to October. There is a **tourist office** (☎ 091 844 94 56; Piazza Umberto 1; ☽ 8am-1pm & 4-6pm Mon-Fri, 8am-2pm Sat & Sun) for the marine reserve in the centre of the village. Emergency numbers include **casualty** (☎ 091 844 92 48) and the **police station** (☎ 091 844 90 49).

ACTIVITIES

Among the most rewarding dive sites are the **Secca Colombara** to the north of the island and the **Scoglio del Medico** to the west. Note that Zone A of the marine reserve, taking in a good stretch of the western coast north of Punta dello Spalmatore, is protected. Fishing, diving and even swimming are forbidden in this area without permission. The reserve's information office can organise sea-watch diving excursions into the zone.

Two recommended diving centres are **Profundo Blu Ustica** (☎ 091 844 96 09; www.ustica -diving.it; Via C Colombo), which offers a range of itineraries including a deep-sea archaeological tour that explores wrecks and amphora in their original sites; and **Katuma Scuola Sub** (☎ 091 844 9216; www.katuma.it, Italian only; Via Petriera 7). The cost of dives ranges from around €38 for a single dive to €340 for a fully-fledged open water course. Both outfits also rent wetsuits and equipment. You can also hire a boat and cruise around the island, visiting its many grottoes and tiny beaches. **Hotel Ariston** (☎ 091 844 90 42; Via della Vittoria 5) organises boat trips and diving (it also rents motorcycles).

The rugged coastline is partly accessible along coastal paths and hides a series of grottoes and caverns. It is possible to hike or cycle along these mountain trails, the most scenic passing through pine woods up to the summit of Guardia di Mezzo at 248m, before descending to the to the best part of the coast at **Spalmatore**, where you can swim in natural rock pools.

SLEEPING & EATING

There are eight hotels and several *affitta-camere* (rooms for rent) on Ustica.

Pensione Clelia (☎ 091 844 90 39; www.hotel clelia.it; Via Sindaco 29; s/d €75/130; ⚡) is a good little hotel and it also has a good **restaurant**. Off-peak prices drop significantly.

GETTING THERE & AROUND

Siremar operates a car ferry daily (2½ hours) year-round. From June to September there are at least two Siremar hydrofoils per day from Palermo (1¼ hours). One-way passenger fares are €16 (hydrofoil) and €10.85 (ferry) in the high season. The **Siremar** (☎ 091 874 93 111; www.siremar.it, Italian only; Piazza Capitano Longo 9) office is in the centre of Ustica.

During summer you can also pick up the Trapani–Favignana–Ustica–Naples hydrofoil, run by Ustica Lines three days per week. The journey from Naples to Ustica takes four hours and costs €64.55 one way.

Orange minibuses run around the island from the village, or you can hire a moped (around €26) at Hotel Ariston in town (see this page).

NORTHERN COAST

PARCO NATURALE REGIONALE DELLE MADONIE

This 40,000 hectare park between Palermo and Cefalù incorporates the Madonie mountain range and some of the highest mountains on Sicily after Mt Etna. The highest peak in the range is Pizzo Carbonara (1979m) and the wilder wooded slopes are home to wolves, wild cats and eagles. Forests cover vast areas of the mountains: holm oak, pines, eucalyptus, holly trees and the near-extinct Ancient Nebrodi fir that has survived since the last Ice Age. Wood was cut from these slopes to make the roof of Monreale Cathedral. In summer, *agriturismo* (farm stays) is a good way of exploring the area and its cuisine, which is significantly different from that of the coast. Specialities include roasted lamb and goat, cheeses, grilled mushrooms and aromatic pasta with *sugo* (wild fennel).

Instituted in 1989 by the Region of Sicily, the park also takes in several small towns and villages and plenty of farms and vineyards. It is an inhabited area, rather than simply a nature reserve – so you can combine walking with visits to some of the more interesting towns in the park, such as Geraci Siculo, Isnello, Castelbuono, Petralia Soprana and Petralia Sottana. In winter, **Piano Battaglia** is the only place in Sicily, other than Etna, where you can **ski**. Equipment can be rented at Rifugio Giuliano Marini (see Sleeping, p723, for details). Skis and boots cost around €28 per day.

There are information offices of the Ente Parco delle Madonie (the body responsible for the park) in Petralia Sottana (☎ 0921 68 40 11; Corso Paolo Agliata 16) with information about the park and several one-day **walks**, as well as transport and accommodation.

Sleeping

There are several *rifugi* (mountain huts) in the park and some good *agriturismo* possibilities. Due to the nature of the area most hotels have their own restaurants and many only offer half-board accommodation.

Rifugio Giuliano Marini (☎ 0921 64 99 94; Località Piano Battaglia; full board per person €28; ☼ winter; **P**) Right at the peak of the Madonie range at Pizzo Carbonara, this *rifugio* has chalet-style rooms and good facilities. You can also rent your ski equipment here.

Madonie (☎ /fax 0921 64 11 06; Corso Paolo Agliata 81, Petralia Sottana; half board s/d €55/85; **P**) Country comfort in a late-19th-century building. The Madonie has good facilities and access for the disabled.

Tenuta Gangivecchio (☎ /fax 0921 68 91 91; Contrada Gangi Vecchia; half board per person €56.80; ☼ closed Jul & Aug; **P**) This place, run by the Tornabene family, is in a former Benedictine convent dating from the 14th century, just out of the town of Gangi towards the interior of Sicily. Children under 10 aren't accepted at Easter or New Year.

Transport could be a problem in the Madonie unless you have a car. The towns within the park are serviced by SAIS and AST buses from Palermo, Cefalù, Castelbuono and Petralia, but if you want to reach some of the more secluded parts of the park, you might find that hitching a ride is the only option. To return to the coast by car take the A19 or the more scenic winding route via Piano Battaglia.

CEFALÙ
pop 26,000

This quaint little fishing village sitting in the shadow of La Rocca (the Rock) has long been the north coast's favourite holiday spot. Its popularity is reflected in the number of tour buses that hit town daily during summer and fill the streets long into the night. However, despite the crowds, the winding medieval streets, stunning setting, sandy beaches, good nightlife and great shopping continue to lure a steady stream of beautiful people.

From the train station, turn right into Via Moro to reach Via Matteotti and the old town. If you're heading for the beach, turn left and walk along Via Gramsci, which becomes Via V Martoglio.

Information
EMERGENCIES
Ambulance (☎ 0921 42 45 44)
Police Station (☎ 0921 42 11 04; Via S Cannizzaro 4)

INTERNET ACCESS
Prices are from €5 per hour.
All Around Sicily (Via Umberto 1)
Bacco on Line (Corso Ruggero 38)

MEDICAL SERVICES
Hospital (☎ 0921 92 01 11)

MONEY
There are plenty of ATMs in town.
Banco di Sicilia (Piazza Garibaldi; ☼ 8.30am-1.30pm & 2.35-3.45pm Mon-Fri)
Banca S Angelo (Via Roma; ☼ 8.30am-1.30pm & 2.45-3.45pm Mon-Fri) This branch has an exchange office.

POST & TELEPHONE
Agenzia S Mauro (Via Vazzana 7; ☼ 8am-1.30pm & 4-6pm Mon-Fri, mornings Sat) Serves as the town's telephone exchange.
Post Office (Via Vazzana 2; ☼ 8.30am-6.30pm Mon-Fri, 8.30am-12.30pm Sat) Right down the *lungomare* (beachfront road).

TOURIST INFORMATION
Tourist Office (☎ 0921 42 10 50; www.cefalu-tour .pa.it; Corso Ruggero 77; ☼ 8am-2.30pm Mon-Fri, 9am-1pm Sat) The staff running the tourist office are not particularly helpful, but they have plenty of leaflets to hand out.

Sights
Looming over the town, the craggy mass of **La Rocca** appears a suitable home for the race of Giants that are said to have been the first inhabitants of Sicily. It was here that the Arab's built their citadel until the Norman conquest in 1063 brought the people down from the mountain to the port below. This dramatic backdrop, combined with the narrow Moorish streets of the town, has made Cefalù a popular film set, most notably for *Cinema Paradiso*. An enormous staircase, the **Salita Saraceno**, winds up through three tiers of city walls in a 30-minute climb nearly to the summit. From here you have stunning views of the town below, while nearby the 4th-century **Tempio di Diana** (☼ 24 hrs) provides a quiet and romantic getaway for young lovers.

Cefalù's **cathedral** (☎ 0921 92 20 21; Piazza del Duomo; admission free; ☼ 8am-noon & 3.30-7pm) is the final jewel in the Arab-Norman crown alongside the Cappella Palatina and Monreale. It was built by Roger II in the 12th century to fulfil a vow to God after his fleet was saved during a violent storm off Cefalù. Inside, a towering figure of Christ Pantocrator is the focal point of the elaborate Byzantine mosaics. Framed by the steep cliff, the twin pyramid towers of the cathedral stand out over the **Piazza del Duomo**, making this an enjoyable place for a morning coffee or evening aperitif (it's crowded in summer).

Off Piazza del Duomo is the private **Museo Mandralisca** (☎ 0921 42 15 47; Via Mandralisca 13; adult/student €4.15/1.05; ☒ 9am-7pm). It has a rather faded collection of Greek ceramics and Arab pottery with the one standout being *The Portrait of an Unknown Man* by Antonello da Messina.

Sleeping & Eating

Hotels and restaurants tend to be overpriced in Cefalù due to the high demand, although there are some good camp sites in the area. The food is also rather disappointing, suffering from slapdash cooking – which is hardly surprising given the number of people queuing for seats in summer.

Cangelosi Rosaria (☎ 0921 42 15 91; Via Umberto I 26; s/d €20/36) A private house, this is the only really cheap option in town and with just four rooms you will have to book in advance. There are communal bathrooms and a shared TV room.

La Giara (☎ 0921 42 15 62; fax 0921 42 25 18; Via Veterani 40; s/d €60/75; ☒) This comfortable hotel is tucked down one of the tiny cobbled streets close to all the action in town. It also has a lovely sun terrace and the reception staff are efficient and helpful.

Hotel Riva del Sole (☎ 0921 42 12 30; fax 0921 42 19 84; Via Lungomare 25; d half board €85; ☒) Situated right on the beachfront next to a string of restaurants, this modern hotel offers a good standard of accommodation and great views. There is also a garden and a swinging nightclub.

Costa Ponente Internazionale (☎ 0921 42 00 85; Località Contrada Ogliastrillo; person/tent €5.50/4.50; ☒) Situated 4km west of the town, this is one of the best-maintained camping sites in Sicily. It has a tennis court and a swimming pool and is in a lovely scenic and shady spot. To reach it take the bus (€1) from the train station heading for La Spisa.

You won't have trouble finding a place to eat – there are dozens of restaurants and several bars along Via Vittorio Emanuele –

but the food can be surprisingly mundane and the ubiquitous tourist menus unimaginative.

Trattoria La Botte (☎ 0921 42 43 15; Via Veterani 6; pasta €7; ☒ 12.30-3pm & 7-11.30pm Tue-Sun) Despite not having a sexy beachfront location, this eatery just off Corso Ruggero continues to send out good food in a town where it is in short supply. It offers excellent antipasto and pasta dishes and its house speciality, *casarecce alla botte* (pasta with a meat sauce), is a tasty change from fish.

Pizzeria Trappitu (☎ 0921 92 19 72; Via di Bordonaro 96; mains €10; ☒ 7.30pm-midnight) This restaurant has a lovely seafront terrace and is hugely popular with the locals. Pizza is the favourite and there's a good selection of wines to go with it.

Getting There & Away

SAIS buses leave Palermo for Cefalù (€4.65, one hour, twice daily), arriving at Cefalù's train station.

Trains from Palermo leave every 30 minutes (€3.60, one hour) and the journey right along the coastline is wonderfully scenic. Trains also connect Cefalù to Milazzo (€9.55, two hours, seven daily) and Messina (€10.45, three hours, 11 daily). From mid-June to September, hydrofoils link Cefalù with the Aeolian Islands (€15.50 one way, twice daily).

TINDARI

At Capo Tindari, further along the coast towards Milazzo, are the ruins of **ancient Tyndaris** (☎ 0941 36 90 23; admission €2.05; ☒ 9am-1 hr before sunset), a Greek settlement founded on a rocky promontory in 396 BC by Dionysus the Elder. The site has unparalleled views over the Oliveri lagoon. Today, a Greek theatre, Roman buildings (including a well-preserved house with mosaic floors) and fragments of the city's ramparts remain in a pleasingly wild setting. A **museum** houses a collection of Hellenistic statues as well as Greek and Roman pottery. From mid-July to early-September the theatre hosts a festival of Greek drama, opera and music. For information ask at the **tourist office** (☎ 0941 36 91 84; Via Teatro Greco 15) at the entrance to the site, which also has maps and brochures about Tyndaris.

Nearby is the **Santuario della Madonna Nera** (admission free; ☒ 8am-noon & 3-7pm). Built in the 1960s, this enormous, ostentatiously decorated church houses a statue of a black Madonna thought to have been made in Asia Minor and washed ashore in Sicily. Believed to have miraculous powers and bearing the inscription *Nigra sum, sed hermosa* ('I am black, but beautiful'), the statue has been revered since Byzantine times and is a place of pilgrimage.

To get to Tindari, catch a train to Patti (6km away on the Palermo–Messina line) and then a take a bus (20 minutes) to the site from outside the station (€1.30, three daily, with increased services in summer). From the Oliveri beach you can reach the **Laghetti di Marinello Riserva Naturale**, a series of capricious sandbanks that provide a natural haven for migrating birds.

MILAZZO

pop 33,000

Most people aiming for the Aeolian Islands pass through here, and as a result Milazzo has the feel of a staging-post to somewhere better. Although once an area of great natural beauty with its rocky coves and sandy beaches (some of the few in Sicily), modern Milazzo is marred by oil refineries and light industry.

The **tourist office** (☎ 090 922 28 65; Piazza C Duilio 10; ☑ 8am-2pm & 4-7pm Mon-Fri year-round, 8am-2pm Sat, Sun Jul-Sep) is behind Via Crispi and the staff here are used to dealing with tourists. All the ferry company offices are directly opposite the port, along Via Rizzo.

The town does have a nice Spanish quarter, however, and a number of Renaissance churches, as well as a huge **Spanish castle** (☎ 090 922 12 91; Via Impallomeni; admission free; guided tours on the hr 10am-noon & 3-5pm Tue-Sun Sep-May, 10am-noon & 5-7pm Tue-Sun Jun-Aug) perched atop a vertiginous cliff. There is good **swimming** to be had at Capo Milazzo (6km north of the city) at the tip of the spit of land that stretches out towards the Aeolian Islands, but the most accessible pebble beach is at the end of Via Colombo.

Sleeping & Eating

Hotels in Milazzo are not great value for money as most people only stay for one or two nights.

Hotel Capitol (☎ 090 928 32 89; Via Giorgio Rizzo 91; s/d €34/60; ☒) The Capitol is close to the hydrofoil dock and although the rooms are quite plain, the hotel is kept scrupulously clean throughout. Credit cards are not accepted.

Petit Hotel (☎ 090 928 67 84; www.petithotel.it; Via dei Mille; s/d €70/100; ☒) Highly recommended by the tourist office, this new establishment brings a little class and comfort to Milazzo. The top-floor terrace is given over to a restaurant serving organic food.

Al Pescatore (☎ 090 928 65 95; Via Marina Garibaldi 176; mains €10) Delicious seafood dishes and swift service. The staff are efficient and used to dealing with people about to catch boats.

Il Covo del Pirata (☎ 090 928 44 37; Via San Francesco 1; pizzas €7; ☑ noon-3pm & 8-11pm Mon-Tue & Thu-Sat) The ground floor of this very good restaurant is a popular pizzeria at night. As it's one of Milazzo's best restaurants it is advisable to make a reservation.

Getting There & Away

Milazzo is easy to reach by bus or train. **Giuntabus** (☎ 090 67 37 82) runs a half-hourly service from Messina (€3.10, 45 minutes; 14 daily, one Sunday). All intercity buses run from Piazza della Repubblica along the quayside. Trains run from Palermo (€12.40, three hours) and Messina (€2.60, 45 minutes). The train station is very far away on Piazza Marconi, connected to the port by AST buses (€0.77, every 30 minutes). See p726 for details of travel to and from the Aeolian Islands.

AEOLIAN ISLANDS

Stunning cobalt sea, wild windswept mountains swathed in flowers and steaming volcanoes go some way to explaining why the Aeolians (Isole Eolie) are the European holy grail for island-lovers. Part of a huge volcanic ridge stretching 200km north from the coast of Sicily near Milazzo, the seven islands of Lipari, Vulcano, Salina, Panarea, Stromboli, Alicudi and Filicudi represent the very pinnacle of this 3000m-high outcrop that was formed a million years ago. The islands were created by successive explosions – Panarea, Filicudi and Alicudi first, then Lipari and Salina, and finally Vulcano and Stromboli (which are still boiling). They exhibit an extraordinary variety of landscape, from hillsides of silver-grey pumice and lush green vineyards to jagged veins of black obsidian used to make tools that provided the mainstay of the islands' economy over 5000 years ago. The rich volcanic soil fosters a wilderness of flowers and plants, as well as an abundance of sea life, making the islands a paradise for naturalists and scuba divers alike.

The beauty of the islands and their unpredictable nature have tempted and repelled men throughout the centuries. Myths ascribe the islands to the god of the winds, Aeolus, and they were also thought to be home to the monster Polyphemus and the god of fire, Vulcan. Modern hedonists, including film stars – notably Robert de Niro and Madonna – and the international jet set, arrive in droves in summer to swim, hike, dive and party in this floating playground. The best time to come is in May and early June or late September and October. Prices soar in July and August due to the weight of people on the islands.

Getting There & Away

Ferries and hydrofoils leave regularly from Milazzo and Messina (in summer). In Milazzo, all the ticket offices are along Via L Rizzo, at the port; in Messina the office is halfway up Via Vittorio Emanuele II. You have to purchase your tickets at the port ticket offices before boarding; telephone bookings are not accepted unless they are done weeks in advance. Hydrofoils are twice as frequent and faster than the ferries although more expensive. Peak season is from June to September and, although ferries and hydrofoils operate year-round, the winter services are much reduced and sometimes cancelled – to the outer islands at any rate – due to heavy seas. All the following prices were one-way high-season fares at the time of writing.

Both SNAV and Siremar run hydrofoils to Lipari (€10.10) and on to the other islands. SNAV hydrofoils also connect the islands with Messina (€19.15, 1½ hours from Lipari, one service daily) and Reggio di Calabria (€21.70, two hours from Lipari, one service daily, year-round), as well as Naples and Palermo (summer only).

Siremar runs car ferries from Milazzo to the islands (€7.50, two hours, small cars €24), but they are slower and less regular. NGI Traghetti runs a limited car-ferry service for around the same rates.

Siremar also runs ferries from Lipari to Naples (three per week).

Lipari's two ports are separated by the citadel – hydrofoils arrive at and depart from Marina Corta, while ferries service use Marina Lunga. Siremar and SNAV have ticket offices in the same building at Marina Corta. Siremar also has a ticket office at Marina Lunga. Full tariff and timetable information is available at all offices. On the other islands, ticket offices are at or close to the docks.

Examples of one-way fares with SNAV hydrofoils and Siremar ferries, and sailing times from Lipari, are:

Hydrofoils/Ferries from Lipari to	cost (€)	duration
Alicudi	14/8.60	1½/3¾ hours
Panarea	6.20/3.90	1/2 hours
Salina	5.45/2.90	20/45 minutes
Stromboli	12.15/7.50	1½/3¾ hours
Vulcano	2.10/1.30	10/25 minutes

LIPARI

pop 11,000

The 'capital' of the islands, Lipari has a quaint harbour and the town is a delightful maze of pastel-coloured houses. Everyone seems to know everyone else and the streets are full of shops selling beachwear and surf gear. The fortified castle that looms over Marina Corta is a reminder of more turbulent times when this little harbour place was the regular victim of pirates and brigands eager to get their hands on the revenue from lucrative obsidian and pumice mining. North of Lipari town are the popular pebble beaches of Canneto and Porticello, while naturalists determinedly set out to hike around the island in search of private coves and bays. At the centre of the archipelago and with a good variety of hotels and restaurants, Lipari remains the best-equipped base for island-hopping.

Orientation

Lipari's two harbours, Marina Lunga and Marina Corta, are on either side of the cliff-top citadel, which is surrounded by 16th-century walls. The town centre extends between them. The main street, Corso Vittorio Emanuele, runs roughly north–south to the west of the castle. From Marina Corta, walk across the piazza to Via Garibaldi; follow the 'centro' signs for Corso Vittorio Emanuele.

Information

EMERGENCIES
Police Station (☎ 090 981 13 33)

INTERNET ACCESS
Prices are from €5 per hour.
Internet Point (Via Corso Vittorio Emanuele 53)
Net C@fe (☎ 090 981 3527; Via Garibaldi 61) Open all day, this café serves snacks and regularly screens football matches.

INTERNET RESOURCES
Eolie on Line (www.isole-eolie.com) Numerous useful links, some in Italian only.

MEDICAL SERVICES
Emergency Doctor (☎ 090 988 52 26; Via Garibaldi) Just 50m up from the waterfront.
Farmacia Internationale (Corso Vittorio Emanuele 128; ☽ 9am-1pm & 5-9pm Mon-Fri) Pharmacy.
Ospedale Civile di Lipari Centralino (☎ 090 98 851, ambulance ☎ 090 989 52 67; Via Santana)

MONEY
Corso Vittorio Emanuele is lined with ATMs to help relieve you of your money. The other islands do not have such good facilities so it is best to sort out your finances here before moving on. You can change cash at the post office, otherwise try:
Banco Antonveneta (Corso Vittorio Emanuele; ☽ 8.20am-1.20pm & 2.35-3.35pm Mon-Fri)
Banco di Roma (Corso Vittorio Emanuele; ☽ 8.25am-1.35pm & 2.10-4.10pm Mon-Fri, 8.25am-1.35pm Sat)

POST
Post Office (Corso Vittorio Emanuele 207; ☽ 8.30am-6.30pm Mon-Fri, 8.30am-1.20pm Sat)

TOURIST INFORMATION
Tourist Office (☎ 090 988 00 95; www.netnet.it /aasteolie; Corso Vittorio Emanuele 202; ☽ 8am-2pm & 4-10pm Mon-Sat, 8am-2pm Sun Jul-Aug, 8am-2pm & 4.30-7.30pm Mon-Fri, 8am-2pm Sat Sep-Jun) This office provides information for all the islands and can assist you with finding accommodation. Pick up a free copy of *Ospitalità in blu*, which contains details of accommodation and services on all the islands. In the off-peak season the office is randomly closed in the afternoon.

Sights
After the mercenary Barbarossa rampaged through the town in 1544 murdering most of the citizens, enslaving the women and desecrating the relics of St Bartholomew,

the Spaniards rebuilt and fortified Lipari in the **citadel** (☽ 9am-7pm) at the top of the small cliff between the town's harbours. Within these fortifications you will find the fabulous **Museo Archeologico Eoliano** (☎ 090 988 01 74; Castello di Lipari; admission €4.50; ☽ 9am-1.30pm & 3-7pm Mon-Sat) – one of the very best museums in Sicily – which traces the volcanic and human history of the islands. It is divided into three sections: an archaeological section devoted to artefacts found on Lipari, from the Neolithic and Bronze Ages to the Roman era; a classical section with finds from Lipari's necropolis (including the most complete collection of sensational miniature Greek theatrical masks in the world); and a section on finds from the other islands.

Nearby is the **Chiesa di San Bartolo** (admission free; ☽ 9am-1pm & 4-7pm), built in 1654 to replace the Norman church that Barbarossa destroyed. The only part of the original structure to survive the raids was the 12th-century Benedictine **cloisters** (admission €0.50; ☽ 9am-1pm & 4-7pm).

The southern part of the citadel contains viewable **archaeological ruins** dating from the Neolithic period to the Roman era, which have given archaeologists valuable clues to the prehistoric civilisations that flourished in the Mediterranean. These have yielded many of the exhibits now in the museum.

Activities
Snorkelling and scuba diving are incredibly popular given the crystal-clear waters. For details of courses or to rent equipment, contact **Diving Center La Gorgonia** (☎ 090 981 20 60; www.lagorgoniadiving.it; Salita San Giuseppe, Marina Corta). The basic beginners course costs €93. Masks and fins can also be rented for €9.

You can rent boats from **Da Massimo** (☎ 090 981 1714, ☎ 338 369 4404; Marina Corta, same office as Gruppo di Navigazione), which is a great way to view the islands and have a taste of the jet set. Prices range from €70 to €250 depending on size of the boat and if crew are required.

Sunbathers and swimmers head for Canneto, a few kilometres north of Lipari town, to bask on **Spiaggia Bianca**. Further north are the **pumice mines** of Pomiciazzo and Porticello, where there is another beach, **Spiaggia della Papesca**, dusted white by the fine pumice dust that gives the sea its limpid turquoise colour.

The western side of the island is greener and wilder, with Lipari's largest vineyards at **Pianoconte**. On this side of the island great views of Salina, Alicudi and Filicudi can be enjoyed from the rugged, windy cliff tops – **Quattropani** is a pretty spot to stop for a drink.

Tours

Gruppo di Navigazione (☎ 090 981 25 84; www.nav igazioniregina.com; ticket booth at Marina Corta) conducts boat tours of all the islands from March to October, including one to Stromboli by night (€25) to see the Sciara del Fuoco (Trail of Fire; p733). There are also tours to Alicudi and Filicudi (€30).

Festivals & Events

On 24th August the island celebrates the **Feast of St Bartholomew** with parties, processions and a burst of fireworks.

The **Wine & Bread Festival**, held in mid-November in the Pianoconte district, gives a great opportunity to sample some of the island's liquid delights.

Sleeping

Lipari provides plenty of options for a comfortable stay. However, prices soar in summer (increasing on average by 30%), particularly in August, due to very high demand. In peak season, if all else fails, the staff at the tourist office will billet new arrivals in private homes on the island. Don't dismiss outright offers by touts when you arrive, as they usually have decent rooms in private houses. To rent an apartment, contact the tourist office for a list of establishments.

BUDGET

The various *affittacamere* operators renting furnished rooms offer a good deal, as you usually have use of a kitchen.

Diana Brown (☎ 090 981 25 84; dbrown@netnet.it; Vico Himera 3; d low/high season €35/90; 🞲) Diana Brown's spotless, comfortable rooms (some with small kitchens) are tucked behind Corso Vittorio Emanuele in a small alleyway. South African-born Diana is a fount of local information. She also does laundry and operates a book exchange (leave one, take as many as you like) and, together with her husband Salvatore, runs Gruppo di Navigazione (see Tours, above).

Casa Vittorio (☎ 090 981 15 23; casavittorio@ netnet.it; Vico Sparviero 15; d low/high season €31/62) These comfortable furnished rooms are off Via Garibaldi near Marina Corta. You'll find the owner (unless he finds you first) at Via Garibaldi 78, on the way from Marina Corta to the town centre. Some rooms sleep up to five people and there is a communal kitchen and two terraces with views.

Baia Unci (☎ 090 981 19 09; fax 090 981 17 15; Marina Garibaldi 2, Località Canneto; person/tent high season €7.75/13.95; 🕒 15 Mar-15 Oct) This camp site is the only one on the island. It has sites underneath shady eucalyptus trees and there is self-service restaurant. Reserve for August. To get here take the bus from the Esso service station at Marina Lunga.

MID-RANGE

Casajanca (☎ 090 988 02 22; www.casajanca.it; Marina Garibaldi 115, Località Canneto; d low/high season €93/165; 🞲) This wonderful small hotel is situated just behind the waterfront at Canneto. The attractively decorated rooms are comfortable, and the dappled courtyard is a relaxing place to enjoy breakfast. Way above the other mid-range hotels in Lipari. Reservations are advised.

Pensione Neri (☎ 090 981 14 13; htlneri@netnet.it; Via G Marconi 43; d low/high season €62/124; 🞲) This lovely old renovated villa is conveniently located right in the historic centre. If you have to catch an early ferry, they'll provide brekkie for you to take away.

Hotel Oriente (☎ 090 981 14 93; hoteloriente@ netnet.it; Via G Marconi 35; s/d €70/119; 🞲) Next to Pensione Neri, this hotel has a bar, garden and very comfortable rooms – great value in low season. Rooms for up to four people are also available.

Hotel Rocce Azzure (☎ 090 981 32 48; rocceaz zure@interfree.it; Via Maddalena 69, Porto delle Genti: r low/high season per person €37/57; 🞲) This large hotel is located right on the beach in a nice bay. The comfortable rooms all have balconies. In July and August a minimum of half board is required.

TOP END

Villa Meligunis (☎ 090 981 24 26; www.villameli gunis.it; Via Marte 7; d low/high season €120/290; 🞲) Meligunis is Lipari's top hotel, housed in a converted 18th-century villa on a hill overlooking Marina Corta. Luxurious accommodation, great facilities and a scenic rooftop terrace make this place the height of luxury. Diving and water sports can also be arranged at reception.

Carasco (☎ 090 981 16 05; www.carasco.it; Porto Delle Genti; d low/high season €70/105; 🛇 🗩) Carasco's got the works – private swimming jetty, lovely pool and terrace and a decent restaurant. Run by the same people for 25 years, it exudes a homely atmosphere.

Eating & Drinking

Fish abound in the waters of the archipelago and include tuna, mullet, cuttlefish and sole, all of which end up on restaurant tables at the end of the day. Alternatively, try pasta prepared with the island's excellent capers. Reservations are recommended in summer.

Filippino (☎ 090 981 10 02; Piazza Municipio; mains €20-30; 🕑 noon-2.30pm & 7.30-10.30pm, closed Mon Oct-Mar) Occupying nearly half the piazza, Filippino remains Lipari's classiest restaurant. The menu is based on old-fashioned Sicilian cooking and is full of surprising tastes – veal in sweet Malvasia wine or bass with salsa. Dress appropriately and reserve a table in advance.

Also recommended is Filippino's summer restaurant, **E Pulera** (☎ 090 981 11 58; Via Diana; mains €18-20; 🕑 7.30pm-2am Jun-Oct), set on a terrace in the middle of a garden.

Kasbah (☎ 090 981 10 75; Via Maurolico 25; pizzas €8, mains €14; 🕑 7pm-3am Mar-Oct) Boasting the most attractive decor and atmosphere of any of Lipari's eateries, the Kasbah, with its north African theme, is a relaxed place for an aperitif and an excellent place for a quality meal – the pizzas are simply delicious. The Kasbah operates on a first-come, first-served basis so it's best to get in early.

La Cambusa (☎ 349 476 60 61; Via Garibaldi 72; fish €12; 🕑 7-11pm) This tiny restaurant has a great reputation. Although it specialises in fish it also does a mean pasta and the atmosphere is relaxed and unpretentious.

La Piazzetta (☎ 090 981 25 22; off Corso Vittorio Emanuele, behind Pasticceria Subba; pizza €4-7; 🕑 noon-2pm, 7.30pm-midnight, closed lunch Sep-Jun) Another great pizza restaurant that has served the likes of Audrey Hepburn. Always popular, with tables that extend into the small piazza. Great location and lively atmosphere.

La Nassa (☎ 090 981 13 19; Via G Franza; mains €7-15; 🕑 8.30am-3pm & 6pm-midnight Jul-Oct, closed Nov-Easter, Thu Apr-Jun) Genuine Aeolian cuisine is served in this family-run trattoria. Favourites include fish such as *cernia*, *sarago* and *dentice*, or try the Aeolian sausages (a house speciality).

People with access to a kitchen can shop for supplies at the **grocery shops** and **SISA supermarket** on Corso Vittorio Emanuele.

If you fancy a late-night drink or want to be in the right place for crowd-gazing during *passeggiata*, **Bar La Precchia** (☎ 090 981 13 03; Corso Vittorio Emanuele 191) is a local favourite. It has an enormous menu of drinks from caffe frappé and fruit milkshakes to cocktails and wine. In summer it's open until 3am and often has live music.

Getting There & Around

See p726 for ferry and hydrofoil details.

Autobus Urso Guglielmo (☎ 090 981 12 62) has buses leaving from the Esso service station at Marina Lunga for Canneto (nine daily, more frequently in summer), Porticello (seven daily) and Quattropani (at least nine daily). The tourist office has timetables. The company also offers special sightseeing trips around the island at 9.30am, 11.30am and 5pm daily.

Boats and scooters are available for hire from **Roberto Foti** (☎ 090 981 23 52; Via F Crispi 31), to the right as you leave Marina Lunga, and several other establishments (the tourist office has a list). A moped costs low/high season €15/30 per day, a rubber dinghy is around €60.

VULCANO
pop 800
Vulcano is the least attractive of the Aeolian Islands but is worshipped for its therapeutic mud baths and hot springs. Its weird steaming landscape, with its oozing psychedelic minerals, black beaches and a noticeable absence of greenery, makes the island an interesting day trip if you can overcome the vile smell of sulphurous gases that wafts over everything.

Of Vulcano's three volcanoes, the oldest lies on the island's southern tip and was already extinct in ancient times. The youngest, Vulcanello, next to the mud baths at the island's northeastern end, rose from the sea in the 2nd century BC. The only active volcano, Fossa di Vulcano, has a number of fumaroles; its broad, smoking crater broods over the port. A tranquil place, Gran Cratere hasn't blown for more than four centuries, but with the recent activity on Stromboli and Etna and a predicted explosion in the next 20 years, the future may well be less peaceful.

Orientation

Boats dock at Porto di Levante. To the right, as you face the island, is the small Vulcanello peninsula. To reach the mud baths walk right along the *lungomare* (seafront road) and at the end, hidden behind a small hillock, are the pools. All facilities are concentrated between Porto di Levante and Porto di Ponente, where you will find the Spiaggia Sabbia Nera (Black Sand Beach), the only smooth, sandy beach on the islands.

Information

Emergency Doctor (☎ 090 985 22 20)
Tourist Office (☎ 090 985 20 28; Via Provinciale 41; ⊗ 8am-1.30pm & 2.45-3.45pm Jun-Aug)

Activities

The top attraction on Vulcano is the trek up the **Gran Cratere**. Follow the signs south along Via Provinciale out of town. It's about an hour's scramble and sections of the climb are demanding, but once you reach the top the sight of the steaming crater encrusted with red and yellow crystals is reward enough. A half-hour walk around the crater gives excellent views of the other islands. The walk is best done early in the day when the trail is mostly in the shade; you will need to wear sturdy boots, take plenty to drink and a hat is a must. If you want to hire a guide, contact the **Gruppo Nazionale Vulcanologia Marcello Carapessa** (☎ 090 985 25 28).

Praised for centuries for its therapeutic qualities, the mud of **Laghetto di Fanghi** (admission €1.50, groups of 10 €1) is said to treat arthritis, rheumatism and skin disorders. You can wallow in the hot, sulphurous mud pools – alongside many health-conscious Germans – but don't wear your best bathing costume (you'll never get the smell out) or any silver jewellery (it will tarnish). The pool is next to Vulcanello, so when you've had enough you can hop into the water at the adjacent beach where **acquacalda** (underwater hot springs) create a natural Jacuzzi effect.

At Porto di Ponente is **Spiaggia Sabbia Nera**, a black-sand beach curving around a pretty bay. **Pino & Giuseppe** (☎ 090 985 24 19; Via Comunale Levante), near Porto di Levante,

organises **boat trips** around the island for around €12 per person. Otherwise you can hire your own motorised dinghy from **Centro Nautico Baia di Levante** (☎ 090 982 2197), in a shed on the beach near the hydrofoil dock. A four-person zodiac costs €60/150 for a half/full day.

Sleeping & Eating

Vulcano is not a great place to stay for any extended period of time: the town has little character (it exists solely to serve the tourist industry), the landscape is barren and unforgiving and the mud baths really smell. If you do decide to stay the best hotels are situated around Spiaggia Sabbia Nera.

La Giara (☎ 090 985 22 29; fax 090 985 24 51; Via Provinciale 18; r per person €31) Towards the Gran Cratere are these pleasant furnished rooms. Outside August there are significant discounts. The hotel is closed late October to early April.

Hotel Torre (☎ /fax 090 985 23 42; Via Favaloro 1; d low/high season €38/75; ☒) This good-value hotel has large rooms that all come with kitchen and terrace. Its proximity to the beach at Laghetto di Fanghi may prove too potent for some.

Villagio Club Nautico Baiazzurra (☎ 090 985 2602; baia.azzurra@tiscalinett.it; Baia di Ponente; 2-/4-bed apartments per week €480/775; ☒) This attractive complex of self-catering cottages is situated at the south side of the bay and has its own private beach. It offers loads of activities from windsurfing and diving to fishing. The complex has pedalos and boats for hire, or you can enjoy one of the treatments in the Thalasso-Wellness spa.

Vulcano has a few overpriced restaurants where you eat some average food; the one exception is **Trattoria Maniaci Pina** (☎ 090 985 22 42; Gelso; meals €18). Although right on the south side of the island, this down-to-earth trattoria serves ubiquitous Sicilian dishes and is the best restaurant on Vulcano.

Cafe Piazetta (☎ 090 985 32 67; Piazzetta Faraglione) This large outdoor café is a convenient stop for a drink or gelato. In summer music booms out from the sound system and in July and August there is live music in the evenings.

Getting There & Around

Vulcano is an intermediate stop between Milazzo and Lipari and a good number of vessels go both ways throughout the day. See p726 for more details.

Scooters, bikes and small motorised cars can be rented from **Da Paolo** (☎ 090 985 21 12) or **Sprint** (☎ 090 985 22 08) at the intersection of Via Provinciale and Via Porto Levante. Scooters cost around €20 per day, although this varies with season and demand.

SALINA
pop 2500
In stark contrast to Vulcano's barren landscape, Salina's twin craters of Monte dei Porri and Monte Fossa delle Felci are lushly wooded. Wild flowers, thick yellow gorse bushes and serried ranks of vines carpet the island in vibrant colours and cool greens. Its high coastal cliffs plunge into dramatic beaches, and its quiet towns are a world away from the tourist bustle of Lipari and Vulcano. A few excellent small hotels and good restaurants make for total rest and relaxation.

Orientation & Information
Most boats dock at Santa Marina Salina. The main road, Via Risorgimento, runs parallel to the *lungomare* and is filled with small boutiques. Accommodation can be found in Salina's three main towns: Santa Marina Salina, Malfa and Rinella, a fishing hamlet on the southern coast.

In summer, tourist booths operate in the three main towns; the rest of the year, contact the Lipari bureau (p727). There is an ATM at **Banco Antoveneta** (Via Lungomare Notar Giuffre; ☺ 8.40am-1.20pm Mon-Sat) to the right along the *lungomare*. Emergency phone numbers include **medical assistance** (☎ 090 984 40 05), and the **police station** (☎ 090 984 30 19).

Sights & Activities
If you're feeling energetic, you could climb the **Fossa delle Felci** volcano and visit the **riserva naturale** (nature reserve). From Santa Marina Salina, head for Lingua, a small village 3km south, from where paths lead up the mountain. The excellent **Eolie Adventure** (☎ 090 984 41 34; 333 469 95 30; www.eolieadventure.com; table at Santa Marina harbour during summer) organises nature hikes on Salina as well as the other islands. A one-day hike costs €20 per person, or if you feel adventurous you can take the wonderful

three-day hike to Filicudi, which involves crossing a lava trail (€75 per person including tent and sleeping bag).

The **Santuario della Madonna del Terzito** at Valdichiesa, just south of Malfa, is a place of pilgrimage, particularly around the Feast of the Assumption on 15 August.

Rinella is a popular spot for spear-gun fishing. For information, contact the tourist booths. Boats are available for hire from June to August at **Nautica Levante** (☎ 090 984 30 83; Via Risorgimento, Santa Marina).

Don't miss a trip to the beach at **Pollara**, the setting for much of Massimo Troisi's last film, *Il Postino*. The climb down is a bit tricky but the beach itself, with its backdrop of volcanic cliffs, is absolutely unbeatable (visit in the afternoon as the beach is in shadow in the morning).

Sleeping & Eating
Hotel L'Ariana (☎ 090 980 90 75; www.hotelariana.it, Italian only; Via Rotabile 11; B&B/half board per person €45/65) A patrician villa overlooking the sea at Rinella is the setting for this lovely little hotel, which is hugely popular with a backpacking crowd. Its huge terrace is the place to be for sundowners as the sun sets on this side of the island. It also has a bar and restaurant, with good deals on half and full board in summer.

Pensione Mamma Santina (☎ 090 984 30 54; www.mammasantina.it; Via Sanità 40; half board low/high season per person €47/83) A family atmosphere, spotless rooms and great views are the features of this *pensione* in Santa Marina. Head for Via Risorgimento (the narrow main street) and walk north for a few hundred metres. Its highly regarded restaurant has been featured in *Cucina Italiana*.

Hotel Signum (☎ 090 984 42 22; www.hotelsignum .it; Via Scalo 15, Malfa; d low/high season €94/164; ☒) Surrounded by vineyards and overlooking the sea, the Signum is the best hotel on Salina. The building is a series of interlinking Aeolian houses and the interior is decorated with antiques. The rooms cluster around the stunning swimming pool with its invisible edge and views straight out to smoking Stromboli. The no-smoking restaurant, which serves up home-cooked Aeolian dishes, is also excellent.

Camping Tre Pini (☎ 090 980 91 55; Frazione Rinella-Leni; person/tent €8/8) Right on the beach at Rinella, the terraced sites here overlook the sea. Reserve in July and August as it is popular. There is also a market, bar and restaurant, and most people decamp to nearby Hotel L'Ariana (above) for sundowners.

Portobello (☎ 090 984 31 25; Via Bianchi 1, Santa Marina; meals €26; ☽ 12.30-3pm & 8-10.30pm Tue-Sat) Without doubt the best restaurant in town, where you can tuck into the daily catch for reasonable prices. The terrace looks out over the sea.

Getting There & Around
Hydrofoils and ferries service Santa Marina Salina and Rinella from Lipari. You'll find ticket offices in both places.

Regular buses run from Santa Marina Salina to Malfa and Lingua and from Malfa to Leni and Rinella. Timetables are posted at the ports. Motorcycles are available for hire from **Antonio Bongiorno** (☎ 090 984 34 09; Via Risorgimento 240, Santa Marina Salina). A scooter costs €26 per day.

PANAREA
pop 320

Tiny Panarea is 3km long and 2km wide and feels more like a Greek island with its adobe-style whitewashed houses. Exclusive and expensive, it is popular with the international jet set who come here for one reason only – Hotel Raya. In summer luxury yachts fill the tiny harbour while flocks of day-trippers dock at San Pietro, where you'll find most of the accommodation.

At the rocky outcrop of Punta Milazzese (about a half-hour walk) there are the remains of a **Bronze Age village**, made up of 23 huts, which was discovered in 1948. The **beaches** of Cala Junco and Spiaggia Fumarola are easily accessible, otherwise hire a boat at the port to explore the inaccessible coves. **Amphibia** (☎ 335 613 85 29), also at the port, organises scuba dives.

Da Francesco (☎ 090 98 30 23; San Pietro; r low/high season per person €21/52) One of the few budget options on the island and all rooms have views of the sea.

Hotel Raya (☎ 090 98 30 13; www.hotelraya.it; Via San Pietro; d low/high season €112/210; ☒) This is *the* hotel on Panarea. A complex of whitewashed villas climbing up the seashore, the Raya is pure, understated luxury. Each room has its own sunbathing terrace with views of Stromboli. In the evening diners eat by the intimate light of oil lamps and

tables are in such demand that you need to reserve ahead. The Raya's disco (open July to August) is known all over the islands.

Trattoria da Pina (☎ 090 98 30 32; Via San Pietro; mains €15; ☽ 12.30-3.30pm & 8.30-11pm Tue-Sat) Just up from the harbour, the tables of this family-run restaurant spill out onto a large covered terrace. It attracts a good crowd in season and is definitely worth a try.

Hydrofoils and the occasional ferry link the island with Stromboli to the north and Salina (and on to Lipari and Milazzo) to the south.

STROMBOLI
pop 400

Made famous in the 1950s film *Stromboli: Terra di Dio*, Stromboli's treacle-like lava oozing down the northwestern flank creates special effects more exciting than anything Hollywood could conjure up. Volcanic activity has scarred and blackened one side of the island, while the eastern side is green and dotted with white houses. At the time of writing, the most recent eruptions had just taken place on 5 April 2003 and showered the town of Ginostra with rocks. However, lava flow is confined to the Sciara del Fuoco (Trail of Fire), leaving the villages of San Bartolo, San Vincenzo and Scari (which merge into one town) to the east and Ginostra to the south quite safe. Some 5000 people lived on the island until the massive eruption of 1930, when most took fright and left. Permanent residents now number about 400.

Orientation
Boats arrive at Scari/San Vincenzo, downhill from the town. Accommodation is a short walk up the Scalo Scari to Via Roma, or, if you plan to head straight for the crater, follow the road along the waterfront.

Information
ATM (Ficogrande, Via Nunziante; ☽ Jun-Sep)
Police (emergency ☎ 090 98 60 21; Via Roma)
Medical Services (☎ 090 98 60 97; Via Vittorio Emanuele) Doctor.
Post Office (Via Roma)
Tourist Office (Ossidiana Hotel, Via Roma; ☽ summer)

Activities
The recent activity of the craters makes climbing the volcano without an official guide an act of pure recklessness. In recent

years the authorities have been tightening the controls and in the future unguided walkers may be fined. It must also be said that treks with a knowledgeable guide only enhance the experience of the volcano and increase one's awareness of the dramatic environment.

At the time of writing, access to the volcano was severely restricted, even for experienced guides, and where once you could trek nearly to the summit (920m), now you can only venture up to 400m. However, from here you can still get a good view of the **Sciara del Fuoco** (Trail of Fire). Most of the treks go up in the early evening so that the glow of the molten lava is visible. The climb is a totally different experience at night, when darkness throws the molten lava of the Sciara del Fuoco and the volcanic explosions into dramatic relief. However, at the time of writing night excursions had been suspended. For up-to-date information check the Magmatrek website (www.magmatrek.it).

Make your way to the beach of rocks and black volcanic sand at **Ficogrande** to swim and sunbathe. **La Sirenetta Diving Center** (☎ 090 98 60 25, ☎ 0347 353 47 14; La Sirenetta Park Hotel, Via Marina 33) offers diving courses and accompanied dives.

Tours

Magmatrek (☎ 090 98 65 768; www.magmatrek.it; Via Vittorio Emanuele; excursion to 400m €12, night excursions €34) Experienced vulcanological guides (speaking English, German and French) take groups of 10 or more to the crater; contact the office around noon to make a booking. For the night climb you'll need sturdy shoes, clothing for cold, wet weather, a torch (flashlight), food and a good supply of water. Equipment can be hired from **Totem Trekking** (☎ 090 986 57 52; Piazza San Vincenzo).

Società Navigazione Pippo (☎ 090 98 61 35; Via Roma 47; cruises per person around €12.90) The boat *Pippo* takes visitors for a 2½-hour gander at the Sciara del Fuoco from the sea. It leaves at 10pm from the port and at 10.10pm from Ficogrande. The same company also runs daytime trips leaving at 10am and 3pm.

Sleeping & Eating

Casa del Sole (☎ /fax 090 98 60 17; Via Soldato Cincotta; d low/high season €20.65/41.30) Off the road to the volcano, before you reach Ficogrande, Casa del Sole is one of the cheapest options on the island and is popular with young travellers. Prices include use of the kitchen.

Locanda del Barbablù (☎ 090 98 61 18; barbablu@hpe.it; Via Vittorio Emanuele 17; d low/high season €90/175) This charming little Aeolian guesthouse has comfortable rooms, some with four-poster beds. There's also a terrace looking out onto the volcano.

Park Hotel La Sirenetta (☎ 090 98 60 25; lasirenetta@netnet.it; Via Marina 33; d low/high season €115/190; ☻ closed Nov-Mar 22; ☒ ☒) This hotel is perfectly sited on the beach at Ficogrande in front of Strombolicchio, a towering rock rising out of the sea at San Vincenzo. It has a panoramic terrace with a highly regarded restaurant.

You'll also find a dozen *affittacamere* charging about €41 per person in the high season.

Ritrovo Ingrid (☎ 090 98 63 85; Piazza San Vincenzo; pizzas around €8; ☻ 8-1am, until 3am Jul & Aug) Situated at the high point of Piazza San Vincenzo with scenic views all around from its terrace, Ritrovo Ingrid is the heart of Stromboli. Trekkers come here for sundowners and pizza as well as the day's gossip.

Il Canneto (☎ 090 98 60 14; Via Roma 64; meals €20; ☻ noon-3pm & 8-11pm Tue-Sat) All the pastas in this charming restaurant are home-made. However, try the house special, *involtini di pesce spada* (rolled swordfish filled with bread and cheese stuffing and then baked).

Getting There & Away

Ticket offices for SNAV and Siremar are at the port. Bear in mind the cost and the distance if you're considering a day visit (which in any case will rob you of the opportunity to climb the volcano at night). Heavy seas can cause cancellation of ferry and hydrofoil services, so you could get stuck overnight.

FILICUDI & ALICUDI
pop 300

Filicudi is arguably the wildest and the prettiest of the Aeolian Islands, with crystal-clear waters and deep grottoes. The most attractive of these is **Grotta del Bue Marino** (Grotto of the Monk Seal). If you want to explore the grotto, boats are available for hire (€21) from the main port as well as from **I Delfini** (☎ 090 988 9077; Via Pecorini, Pecorini Mare). To the north-west **Scoglio della Canna** (Cane Reef) towers 71m out of the sea. On Capo Graziano, south of the port, are the remains of a **pre-historic village** dating from 1800 BC.

If you're trying to escape the summer crowds then Alicudi, home to a handful of farmers and fishermen, is the place to come. While on the island, walk up **Monte Filo dell'Arpa** (String of the Harp; 672m) to see the **crater** of the extinct Montagnola volcano and the **Timpone delle Femmine**, huge fissures where women are said to have taken refuge during pirate raids.

Sleeping & Eating

Filicudi has two hotels, both of which serve meals and offer half-board options (a good idea as the island's restaurant possibilities are very limited).

La Canna (☎ 090 988 99 56; vianast@tin.it; Via Rosa 43; s/d €40/80; 🕸 🗟) After an exhausting walk uphill (you can be picked up from the port), La Canna appears like a private paradise. Magnificent panoramic views, its own pool and some wonderful home cooking make this a highly recommended hotel. Reservations are advised.

Hotel Phenicusa (☎ 090 988 99 46; fax 090 988 99 55; Via Porto; s/d €60/75; 🕙 May-Sep) This imposing hotel dominates the port and provides nice accommodation. Some rooms have water views and the staff are friendly.

Isolated Alicudi is the furthest from Lipari and the least developed of the Aeolian group.

Ericusa (☎ 090 988 99 02; fax 090 988 96 71; Via Regina Elena, Alicudi; d €62, half board per person €60; 🕙 Jun-Sep) This pleasant hotel, with 12 rooms and a good restaurant, is the only place to stay on Alicudi so booking is strongly advised.

EASTERN COAST

MESSINA

pop 272,000

Known to the ancient Greeks as Zankle (Sickle) for its beautiful curved harbour, Messina is situated at the northernmost point of the Ionian coast, where Greek influence is still strongly felt both in the atmosphere of the cities and the character of the people.

Looking out at mainland Italy, Messina is all about the straits that separate them, now a veritable highway of seafaring traffic. Greeks mythologised the clashing currents in the straits as the twin monsters of Charbydis (the whirlpool) and Scylla (the six headed monster), and strong currents still lurk in the attractive waters, making swimming unadvisable.

In 1908, Messina suffered one of the worst natural disasters to hit Sicily – an earthquake sank the shore by half a metre and killed 84,000 people. The city had barely been rebuilt when it was flattened by bombing during WWII. Such calamity has engendered in the people a resilience and determination that now makes Messina a centre of industry and business.

Orientation

Wide boulevards, a practical grid system and elegant belle epoque buildings make Messina an easy and pleasant city to navigate. The main transport hub is Piazza della Repubblica, at the southern end of the long waterfront. You will find the train station here and the Trenitalia car and truck ferries also arrive here. The main intercity bus station is outside the train station, to the left on the piazza. To get to the city centre from Piazza della Repubblica, walk either straight across the piazza and directly ahead along Via I Settembre to the Piazza del Duomo, or turn left into Via La Farina and take the first right into Via Cannazzaro to reach Piazza Cairoli.

Those coming by hydrofoil from Reggio di Calabria arrive about 1km north of the city on Corso Vittorio Emanuele II, while drivers on the private car ferry from Villa San Giovanni land a few kilometres further along, just north of the trade-fair area (Fiera).

Information

EMERGENCIES

Police Station (☎ 090 36 611, foreigners ☎ 090 36 65 19; Via Placida 2)

INTERNET ACCESS

Internet Point (Via dei Mille 200; from €4/hr)

MEDICAL SERVICES

Ospedale Piemonte (☎ 090 699 53 01, casualty ☎ 090 222 42 38; Viale Europa)

Ospedale R Margherita (☎ 090 34 54 22; Viale Libertà)
Pharmacy (☎ 090 34 54 22; cnr Via Cesare Battisti & Via Canicattí)

MONEY
There are numerous banks in the city centre (most with ATMs) and a currency exchange booth at the timetable information office at the train station.

POST & TELEPHONE
Paritel Telecommunicazioni (Via Centonze 74) Telephones and Internet connection.
Post Office (Piazza Antonello, Corso Cavour; 🕑 8.30am-6.30pm Mon-Sat)

TOURIST INFORMATION
Tourist Office (☎ 090 67 42 36; Via Calabria 301, right from train station when exiting; 🕑 8am-2pm & 3.30-7pm Mon-Sat May-Oct) Friendly, English-speaking staff with good information about Messina and onward travel.

TRAVEL AGENCIES
Messina is full of travel agencies.
CTS (☎ 090 292 67 61; Via Ugo Bassi 93)
Lisciotti Viaggi (☎ 090 71 90 01; Piazza Cairoli 13) Can assist with theatre tickets for performances at venues such as Taormina's Greek theatre.

Sights
The Norman **cathedral** (Piazza del Duomo; admission free; 🕑 8am-6pm daily) is one of the most attractive churches in Sicily, situated as it is in a leafy and spacious piazza. Built in the 12th century, it was almost completely destroyed by the combined effects of the 1908 earthquake and WWII bombing. Since then it has been rebuilt faithfully in the style of the original basilica with three apses featuring mosaics. The additional decorative elements inside include an impressive carved altar and an inlaid organ. Other treasures, such as the magnificent **Golden Mantle** designed for the picture of the Madonna and Child, now on the altar, are kept in the cathedral **treasury** (admission €3; 🕑 9am-1pm Mon-Sat). Outside, the 90m clock tower houses what is thought to be the world's largest astronomical clock, which strikes at noon – watch out for the comical roaring lion and crowing cockerel. A booklet from the tourist office explains the symbolism of each of the different scenes. Below the tower, the pale marble **Fontana di Orione**,

complete with lounging Neptunes and ice-cream-licking tourists, commemorates Orion, the mythical founder of Messina. Another church of interest, and tiny by comparison, is the **Chiesa della Santissima Annunziata dei Catalani** (Piazza Catalani; admission free; 🕑 8am-noon & 4-6.30pm).

Picking up the **free city tram** at Piazza Carioli (or the train station), you can take a laid-back look up the sickle-shaped harbour. Halfway up is Messina's other great fountain, the 16th-century **Fontana del Nettuno**. Get off here and cross over to the small park of Piazzale Batteria Masotto, where you can enjoy the views over the harbour and admire the huge golden statue of the **Madonnino del Porto**. Alternatively, continue to the end of the tram line to the **Museo Regionale** (☎ 090 36 12 92; Viale della Libertà 465; admission €4.50; 🕑 9am-1.30pm Mon, Wed & Fri, 9am-1.30pm & 3-5.30pm Tue, Thu & Sat, 9am-12.30pm Sun). It houses works of art including the *Virgin and Child with Saints* by Antonello da Messina (born here in 1430) and two masterpieces by Caravaggio – *Adorazione dei Pastori* and *Resurrezione di Lazzaro*.

If you have your own transport, the drive north along the coast from Messina to Capo Peloro and then round to the east is pretty, and there are some reasonable **beaches** between the Cape and Acquarone. Where the coast road meets the A20 heading for Milazzo, take the tollway, as the S113 can be incredibly congested from this point. Alternatively, you can take bus No 79 or 80 to the lighthouse at **Torre del Faro** (8km north) and the popular summer resort of **Mortelle**.

Sleeping & Eating
Despite being a major transport hub, Messina is not a tourist city and hotels and restaurants cater for businesspeople and tend to lack charm.

Touring (☎ 090 293 88 51; Via N Scotto 17; s/d €35/45) Clean and well run, Touring is nothing fancy but is convenient for the station if you're just overnighting in town. The rooms without baths are fairly basic, but those with private facilities are decent.

Hotel Cairoli (☎ 090 67 37 55; www.hotel-cairoli .com; Viale San Martino 63; s/d 46/77; 🐾) This is by far the most convenient and comfortable budget accommodation in Messina and the reception staff are efficient and helpful. Breakfast is included in the price.

Grand Hotel Liberty (☎ 090 640 94 36; ricevimento .liberty@framon.hotels.it; Via I Settembre 15; s/d 145/214; Ⓟ ☒) A four-star hotel, the Grand is a renovated villa with luxurious rooms, mod cons and helpful English-speaking staff. Parking is in the car park of the sister hotel (the Royal Palace Hotel) 200m down the road.

There are few good restaurants accessible on foot in the town; in addition many of them close in August.

Mario's (☎ 090 424 77; Via Vittorio Emanuele 108; meals €20; ☽ noon-3.30pm & 8-11pm Tue-Sat) Opposite the hydrofoil dock, this specialist fish restaurant is highly regarded and popular with the locals. The antipasto – help yourself – is a delicious mixture of fish and vegetables. This is also a great place to while away the time before the hydrofoil leaves.

Lepanto (Via Lepanto 14; meals €10; ☽ 8pm-midnight Mon-Sat) Tucked behind the cathedral, this tiny cocktail bar in a cave-like basement is one of the only lively places of an evening. Drinks are served with crudités and there is a small selection of different platters to complement the wine list.

La Piazzetta (☎ 329 165 6083; Via Centonze, cnr of Via Dogali; meals €15; ☽ 12.30-3.30pm & 8-11pm Tue-Sat) This elegant trattoria, close to Piazza Cairoli, serves a tasty selection of pizza and pasta. Service is friendly and efficient.

Getting There & Around
BOAT
Messina is the main point of arrival for ferries and hydrofoils from the Italian mainland, only a 20-minute trip across the straits. Trenitalia runs 20 hydrofoils daily from Monday to Saturday and 10 on Sunday (the boats are still marked with the old FS insignia). The trip costs one way/return €2.58/ 4.65. **Navigazione Generale Italiana** (☎ 0335 842 77 84) has car ferries between Messina and Reggio di Calabria (foot passengers/ cars €0.52/7.75, 40 minutes, 12 daily). **SNAV** (☎ 090 36 40 44; www.snavali.com; Via Vittorio Emanuele at the hydrofoil dock) runs up to 20 hydrofoils on weekdays to Reggio di Calabria (€2.84 one way, 15 minutes). In summer SNAV hydrofoils also connect Messina with the Aeolian Islands (€19.15 one way, 1½ hours to Lipari, one daily).

BUS
Interbus (☎ 090 66 17 54; Piazza della Reppublica 6) runs a regular service to Taormina (€2.60

one way, 1½ hours, hourly Monday to Saturday) and has a direct connection to Rome (€29 one way, eight hours, two daily). Palermo, Catania and Catania's airport are served by **SAIS** (☎ 090 77 19 14; Piazza della Repubblica 6). The journeys cost €12.50, €6.20 and €6.70 respectively. **Giuntabus** (☎ 090 67 37 82; Via Terranova 8) runs a service to Milazzo (€3.10, 45 minutes, 14 daily) to catch the ferries and hydrofoils to the Aeolian Islands.

CAR & MOTORCYCLE
If you arrive in Messina by Trenitalia ferry with a vehicle, it is simple to make your way out of town. For Palermo (or Milazzo and the Aeolian Islands), turn right from the docks and follow Via Garibaldi along the waterfront. After about 1km, turn left into Viale Boccetta and follow the green autostrada (tollway) signs for Palermo. To reach Taormina and Syracuse, turn left from the docks into Via La Farina and follow the autostrada signs for Catania.

If you arrive by private ferry, turn right along Viale della Libertà for Palermo and Milazzo and left for Taormina and Catania – follow the green autostrada signs. You can also take the S113 (busy in summer). Streets in Messina are well signposted.

TRAIN
Regular trains connect Messina with places such as Catania (€5.68, 1¾ hours, 27 per day), Taormina (€2.48, 50 minutes, 26 per day), Syracuse (€6.70, three hours, 14 per day), Palermo (€11, 3½ hours, 15 per day) and Milazzo (€2.40, 45 minutes, 15 per day), but buses are generally faster. The train stations for Milazzo and Taormina are inconveniently located away from the city centre and the bus is generally faster and cheaper.

TRAM
A free tram serves the city from Piazza Cairoli to the Museo Regionale.

TAORMINA
pop 11,000
Spectacularly located on a terrace of Monte Tauro, dominating the sea with views westwards to Mt Etna, it is difficult to exaggerate the charming beauty of Taormina, Sicily's glitziest resort. Over the centuries Taormina has seduced an exhaustive line of writers and artists, aristocrats and royalty,

and these days it is host to a summer film festival (p739) that packs the town with international visitors.

Perched on its eyrie, sophisticated and chic, Taormina is far removed from the banal economic realities of other Sicilian cities, comfortably cushioned as it is by some serious wealth. But the charm and beauty are not manufactured. As capital of Byzantine Sicily in the 9th century, Taormina is an almost perfectly preserved medieval town, and if you can tear yourself away from the shopping and sunbathing it has a wealth of small but perfect tourist sites.

Orientation

The train station (Taormina-Giardini) is at the bottom of Monte Tauro. You'll need to hop on an Interbus outside the station, which will take you up to the main bus terminal on Via Pirandello. This is where you arrive if you catch the bus from Messina or Catania. Exit left out of the bus station car park and a short walk up the hill will bring you into the centre of Taormina and the start of Corso Umberto I, the main pedestrian thoroughfare.

Information

EMERGENCIES
Police Station (☎ 0942 2 232 32, ☎ 113)

INTERNET ACCESS
Internet Café (Corso Umberto 214; from €5/hr)

MEDICAL SERVICES
Emergency Medical Service (☎ 0942 62 54 19; Piazza San Francesco di Paola; ☼ 1 Jul–30 Sep) Only available in summer.
Ospedale San Vincenzo (☎ 0942 537 45; Piazza San Vincenzo) Call the same number for an ambulance.

MONEY
There are numerous banks in Taormina, mostly along Corso Umberto I; all have ATMs. You'll also find currency exchange places along the same street.
La Duca Viaggi (☎ 0942 62 52 55; Via Don Bosco 39 on Piazza Aprile IX; ☼ 9am-1pm & 4-7.30pm Mon-Fri Apr-Oct, closes 6pm Nov-Mar) Represents American Express but they don't change money.

POST & TELEPHONE
Avis (☎ 0942 2 30 41; Via San Pancrazio 7) To the right off Via Pirandello; has public telephones.

Post Office (Piazza Sant'Antonio; ☼ 8.30am-6.30pm Mon-Sat)

TOURIST INFORMATION
Tourist Office (☎ 0942 2 32 43; www.gate2 taormina.com; Palazzo Corvaja, Corso Umberto I; ☼ 8.30am-2pm & 4-7pm)

TRAVEL AGENCIES
CTS (☎ 0942 62 60 88; Corso Umberto I 101) Runs tours to Mt Etna (€27), Agrigento and Piazza Armerina (€50), Alcantara & Castiglione (€25) and Lipari & Vulcano (€52).
SAT (☎ 0942 2 46 53; www.sat-group.it; Corso Umberto I 73) This company also runs tours to Mt Etna (€35), Palermo & Monreale (€45) and other destinations.

Sights

One of the chief delights of Taormina is simply wandering along its narrow, medieval main drag, browsing among antique and craft shops, delis and designer boutiques. When these have exhausted their charms most folk retire to the obscenely pretty Piazza IX Aprile, from where you can enjoy stunning panoramic views and pop your head into the cutest rococo church, **Chiesa San Giuseppe**, which overflows with fashionable Taormitans on Sunday.

More serious tourists should head straight for **Teatro Greco** (☎ 0942 2 32 20; Via Teatro Greco; admission €4.50; ☼ 9am-7pm Mon-Sat, 9am-1pm Sun), Taormina's premier attraction. This perfect horseshoe theatre, suspended between sea and sky, was built in the 3rd century BC and is the second largest in Sicily (after Syracuse), although its lofty position makes it the most dramatically situated Greek theatre in the world. In summer the theatre is used as the venue of the international arts festival, Taormina Arte (p739). In peak season the site is best explored early in the morning to avoid the crowds.

The other great show in town is the **Piazza del Duomo**, where teenagers congregate around the ornate baroque fountain – sporting a two-legged centaur – in front of the **cathedral** (Piazza del Duomo; admission free; ☼ 8am-noon & 4-7pm). Constructed in the 13th century, the cathedral has survived much of the Renaissance remodelling undertaken by the Spanish aristocracy in the 15th century, which is better illustrated in the **Palazzo Duca di Santo Stefano** with its Norman-Gothic windows and decorative wood inlay. Although it is not possible to access

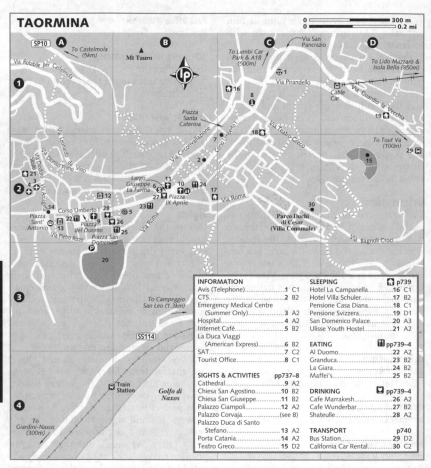

TAORMINA

INFORMATION	
Avis (Telephone)......................1 C1	
CTS..2 B2	
Emergency Medical Centre	
(Summer Only).....................3 A2	
Hospital...................................4 A2	
Internet Café............................5 B2	
La Duca Viaggi	
(American Express)...............6 B2	
SAT...7 C2	
Tourist Office...........................8 C1	
SIGHTS & ACTIVITIES pp737–8	
Cathedral.................................9 A2	
Chiesa San Agostino...............10 B2	
Chiesa San Giuseppe...............11 B2	
Palazzo Ciampoli....................12 A2	
Palazzo Corvaja....................(see 8)	
Palazzo Duca di Santo	
Stefano..............................13 A2	
Porta Catania.........................14 A2	
Teatro Greco..........................15 D2	

SLEEPING p739	
Hotel La Campanella...............16 C1	
Hotel Villa Schuler.................17 B2	
Pensione Casa Diana...............18 C1	
Pensione Svizzera...................19 D1	
San Domenico Palace..............20 A3	
Ulisse Youth Hostel.................21 A2	
EATING pp739–4	
Al Duomo...............................22 A2	
Granduca................................23 B2	
La Giara..................................24 B2	
Maffei's..................................25 B2	
DRINKING pp739–4	
Cafe Marrakesh.......................26 A2	
Cafe Wunderbar......................27 B2	
Shateulle.................................28 A2	
TRANSPORT p740	
Bus Station.............................29 D2	
California Car Rental...............30 C2	

this *palazzo*, you can take a look at other examples like **Palazzo Corvaja** (the tourist office) and **Palazzo Ciampoli** (now the Hotel Palazzo Vecchio).

To get away from the crowds, wander down to the beautiful Parco Duchi di Cesarò, more commonly referred to as the **Villa Comunale** (Via Bagnoli Croci; admission free; 9am-7pm summer, 9am-4.30pm winter). Created by Englishwoman Florence Trevelyan, these hanging gardens are a lush paradise of tropical plants and delicate flowers. Take a picnic and enjoy the best panorama in town. In summer the gardens stay open into the evening.

Panorama fanatics should head 5km up Via Leonardo da Vinci to **Castelmola**,

literally the high point of the area, with a ruined castle and sweeping views of, well, everything. Interbus runs an hourly service (€1.80 return) up the hill.

Activities

Many visitors to Taormina come for the beach life. To reach **Lido Mazzaró**, directly under Taormina, take the cable car (€2.70 return, operates 8am to 1am) from Via Pirandello. This beach is well serviced with bars and restaurants, and private operators charge a fee for rental of an umbrella and deckchair (€13 per day). To the right of the beach past the Sant'Andrea hotel is the miniscule **Isola Bella**, set in a stunning cove. You can walk here in a few minutes but it's more fun to rent a small boat from Mazzaró to paddle round Capo Sant'Andrea.

Naxos Diving Centre (☎ 360 28 95 55; info@dive sicily.com; Lido Mazzaró) can be found left along the beach and it offers a whole range of courses from introductory (€50) to advanced open water diver (€230).

Other activities involve short excursions around Taormina, one of the most popular being to the **Gole Alcantara**, a series of vertiginous lava gorges swirling with rapids and waterfalls. The Gole Alcantara office has a monopoly on **tours** (☎ 0942 98 50 10; admission €4.50) and hires out the necessary wellies and wetsuits. Take the bus from Taormina (€4.30 return, four daily). It is forbidden to enter the gorges from around November to May because of the risk of unexpected floods.

Festivals & Events
JULY/AUGUST
Taormina Arte (☎ 0942 2 11 42; www.taormina-arte .com; Corso Umberto I 19) Films, theatrical events and music concerts from an impressive list of international names. Contact Taormina Arte for details, programs and bookings.

SEPTEMBER/OCTOBER
Raduno del Costume e del Carretto Siciliano A parade featuring traditional Sicilian carts and folkloric groups. Usually held in autumn. Ask at the tourist office for details.

Sleeping
Taormina has plenty of accommodation, but in summer you should book in advance as rooms fill rapidly, particularly during August when the town reaches saturation point.

Ulisse Youth Hostel (☎ /fax 0942 2 31 93; Vico San Francesco di Paola 9; dm with breakfast €15) This is the cheapest place to stay in Taormina and it is extremely well run. Book well ahead in August.

Pensione Casa Diana (☎ 0942 2 38 98; Via D Giovanni 6; d €42) The lovely Signora Diana has only four rooms, and at these prices they are quickly snapped up. It's a stone's throw from the Greek theatre.

Hotel La Campanella (☎ 0942 233 81; fax 0942 62 5248; Via Circonvallazione 3; d €60) Furnished with an eclectic collection of antiques and modernist furniture, this charming hotel has a beautiful roof terrace and some of the rooms enjoy panoramic views.

Pensione Svizzera (☎ 0942 2 37 90; svizzera@tao.it; Via Pirandello 26; s/d €60/90; Feb-Nov) Barely 100m from the bus station, this *pensione* teeters on the edge of the cliff, giving some rooms great views. Rooms are comfortable and breakfast is served on a garden terrace.

Campeggio San Leo (☎ 0942 2 46 58; Via Nazionale, Località San Leo; person/tent €4.15/14.45) The facilities at this camp site near the beach are minimal. Take the bus from Taormina to the train station and ask the driver to drop you off at the entrance. Kids stay free.

Hotel Villa Schuler (☎ 0942 234 81; schuler@tao.it; Piazzetta Bastione, Via Roma 1; s/d €88/124; P) Surrounded by shady terraced gardens with views out over Mt Etna and the Ionian Sea, the rose-pink Villa Schuler represents fantastic value. The villa is family owned and offers a huge range of facilities from its gardens and sun terrace to access to the Tennis Club Taormina opposite. It also provides a shuttle service down to the beach.

Eating & Drinking
Eating out in Taormina goes hand in hand with posing. There are some excellent restaurants serving some very good food but there are also many overpriced establishments. Be aware that cafés in Taormina

---

SOMETHING SPECIAL

San Domenico Palace (☎ 0942 61 31 11; www.sandomenico.thi.it; Piazza San Domenico 5; d low/high season €274/423; P) Converted into a hotel in 1896, the San Domenico is Italy's oldest and perhaps most famous monastery hotel, with a guest list to prove it. Over the years it has hosted an illustrious list of names from Marshal Kesselring, who used it as his WWII headquarters, to a host of statesmen and celebrities including King Edward VII, Kaiser Wilhelm II, the Grand Duke of Russia, François Mitterand, Ava Gardner, Cary Grant and Audrey Hepburn. Situated on the cliff-edge, a thousand feet above sea level, the monastery complex commands spectacular views, while inside the lushly planted gardens, colonnaded courtyards and old vaulted ceilings create an atmosphere of such beauty and luxury that it is hard to think of its equal.

charge extraordinarily high prices even for coffee.

La Giara (☎ 0942 233 60; Vico la Floresta 1; mains €15-25; 🕑 8.15-11pm Tue-Sun Apr-Jul & Sep-Oct) This stylish Art Deco restaurant serves up perfectly grilled fish and delicious pasta with inventive sauces such as lemon and shrimps. A well-heeled clientele and seductive atmosphere make for a perfect meal. Reservations are required.

Granduca (☎ 0942 249 83; Corso Umberto 172; mains €10; 🕑 12.30-3pm & 7.30pm-midnight, closed Tue winter) Eating delicious pizza *al forno* on the spectacular terrace of Granduca is an experience not easily forgotten. A reservation is highly recommended if you want to be sure of getting a table.

Al Duomo (☎ 0942 62 56 56; Vico Ebrei 11; mains €10-15; 🕑 noon-2.30pm & 7-11pm Mon-Sat Nov-Mar, Thu-Mon Apr-Oct) Completely different from the above two restaurants but no less attractive is the discreet Al Duomo. The intimate terrace overlooks the cathedral and the restaurant has hosted a number of celebrities. The stewed lamb and fried calamari are simply delicious. Reservations are required.

Maffei's (☎ 0942 240 55; Via San Domenico de Guzman 1; mains €20-30; 🕑 noon-3pm & 7-11pm) With only 10 tables and some of the best fish dishes in Taormina, it is often hard to get into Maffei's and reservations are a must. Once in, you can sit down and enjoy a cornucopia of fish cooked to your liking, however it's always a good bet to go for the house special.

Cafe Marrakesh (☎ 0942 62 56 92; Piazza Garibaldi 2; cocktails €5.50; 🕑 6pm-3am) This Arabian-themed cocktail bar and club draws a cosmopolitan crowd each night with its novelty Sahara-style tents.

Shateulle (☎ 0942 61 61 75; Piazza Garibaldi; cocktails around €6, crepes €7; 🕑 6pm-3.30am) Next to Cafe Marrakesh is another popular cocktail bar serving light snacks. These two bars make Piazza Garibaldi one of the most swinging evening spots.

Tout Va (☎ 0942 238 24; Via Pirandello 70; 🕑 6pm-3.30am) Down by the water, this open-air club sees the hottest summer action. It also serves food late into the night on its panoramic terrace.

Cafe Wunderbar (Piazza IX Aprile; 🕑 9am-10pm) Situated in Piazza IX Aprile, this is a poseur's paradise. The cafe serves delicious granita and has the best view in Taormina.

Getting There & Around

BUS

The bus is the easiest way to reach Taormina. **Interbus** (☎ 0942 62 53 01; Via Pirandello) services leave for Messina (€2.50 one way, 1½ hours, 12 per day) and Catania (€3.80, 1½ hours, hourly). The same buses service the train station and Giardini-Naxos (€1.20). Fours buses run to the Gole Alcantara (€4.30 return).

CAR & MOTORCYCLE

Taormina is on the A18 tollway and the S114 between Messina and Catania. Parking can be a problem in Taormina, particularly during summer. The Lumbi car park is open 24 hours and there is a shuttle service to the centre from Porta Messina.

There are several car rental agencies in Taormina, including Avis, Hertz and Maggiore. **California** (☎ 0942 2 37 69; Via Bagnoli Croci 86) hires out cars and motorcycles at reasonable prices. A small car will cost around €270 per week, a Vespa around €37 per day.

TRAIN

There are also regular trains to/from Messina (€2.85, one hour, 26 per day) and Catania (€2.85, 45 minutes, every half-hour), but the awkward location of Taormina's station is a strong disincentive. If you arrive this way, catch an Interbus service up to the town. They run roughly every 30 to 90 minutes (much less frequently on Sunday).

CATANIA

pop 385,000

Bold, entrepreneurial Catania once earned the title 'Milan of South', and it is still the only city in Sicily that can really lay claim to that title today. At once a youthful university city full of bars and small businesses, it is also an elegant baroque affair where fur-clad Catanians *passeggiata* with a purpose. The resilience of the residents and their hard-nosed realism owes much to the brooding shadow of Etna that has forever dominated the city, razing it to its foundations in the disastrous 1669 eruption, when 12,000 people lost their lives. The rebuilding was largely undertaken by the baroque master Giovanni Vaccarini and resulted in a surprisingly coherent city of spacious boulevards and piazzas in a unique chiaroscuro baroque. Today Catanians still live with the unavoidable realities of

Etna and adhere very much to the motto of *carpe diem* (seize the day).

Orientation

The main train station is near the port at Piazza Giovanni XXIII, and the intercity bus terminal is one block up at Via d'Amico. From here, Corso Martiri della Libertà heads west towards the city centre, about a 15-minute walk (1km). Follow the road to Piazza della Repubblica and continue along Corso Sicilia to Via Etnea, the main thoroughfare running north off Piazza del Duomo. Most sights are concentrated around and west of Piazza del Duomo, while the commercial centre of Catania is further north around Via Pacini and Via Umberto I.

Information

EMERGENCIES

Police Station (☎ 095 736 71 11; Piazza San Nicolella)

INTERNET ACCESS

Prices are from €2 per hour.
Internet Caffetteria (Via Penninello 44) A nice café serving snacks and drinks; it has speedy computers.
Net.globe (Via Michele Rapisardi 10; ☺ 10.30am-1pm & 5pm-1am Tue-Fri, 5pm-1am Mon) Right next to Teatro Massimo Bellini.

MEDICAL SERVICES

Del Centro (☎ 095 31 36 85; Via Etnea 107; ☺ Sep-Jul) Late-night pharmacy.
Ospedale Garibaldi (☎ 095 759 43 66; Piazza Santo Maria di Gesú) Emergency room.
Ospedale Vittorio Emanuele (☎ 091 743 54 52; Via Plebiscito 628) Emergency room.

MONEY

Banks, several of which have currency exchanges, are concentrated along Corso Sicilia. There is also an exchange office at the train station. Plenty of ATMs can be found along Via Etnea.
Banco Nazionale del Lavoro Corso Sicilia (☺ 8.30am-1.30pm Mon-Fri); Train Station (☺ 8am-8pm)
La Duca Viaggi (☎ 095 31 61 55; Via Etnea 63-65) Represents American Express.

POST & TELEPHONE

Post Office (Via Etnea 215; ☺ 8am-6.30pm Mon-Fri, 8.30am-12.30pm Sat)
RAS Phone Centre (Via Corridoni 1b; ☺ 9am-7pm) Also has Internet access (€5/hr).

Telecom Office (Corso Sicilia 67; ☺ 9am-1pm & 4-7.30pm Mon-Sat)

TOURIST INFORMATION

Tourist Office (☎ 095 730 62 22, ☎ 095 730 62 11; www.apt.catania.it, Italian only; Via Cimarosa 10-12; ☺ 8am-7pm Mon-Sat); Train Station (☎ 095 730 62 55; ☺ 8am-7pm Mon-Sat); Airport (☎ 095 730 62 66; ☺ 8am-7pm Mon-Sat) Offer a huge selection of brochures and maps on the city and Etna. Some English spoken.

TRAVEL AGENCIES

You can book train, ferry and air tickets at the following agencies:
CIT (☎ 095 31 35 77; Via Antonino di San Giuliano 205)
Sestante Vacanze (☎ 095 31 35 17; Via Antonino di San Giuliano 208)

Sights

Catania's central square, **Piazza del Duomo**, has recently been declared a Unesco Heritage Site. Surrounded by magnificent sinuous buildings, the piazza is a sumptuous example of Catania's own peculiar style of baroque, with its contrasting lava and limestone. In the centre of the piazza is Catania's most memorable monument, the smiling **Fontana dell'Elefante**. This extraordinary statue is composed of a naive black-lava elephant, dating from the Roman period, surmounted by an improbable Egyptian obelisk. The elephant, with its comical upturned trunk, is known locally as Liotru and is believed to have belonged to the magician Eliodorus (8th century AD) who made his living turning men into animals. Liotru is also believed to possess magical powers that help to calm the restless activity of Mt Etna.

Facing the statue is Catania's other defence against the volcano, St Agata's **cathedral** (☎ 095 32 00 44; Piazza del Duomo; admission free; ☺ 8am-noon & 4-7pm) with its impressive marble facade. Inside the huge, cool vaulted interior lie the remains of the city's patron saint, the young virgin Agata, who resisted the advances of the nefarious Quintian (AD 250) and was horribly mutilated (her breasts were hacked off and her body was rolled in hot coals). She was imprisoned in the dungeons of **Sant'Agata al Carcere** (admission free; ☺ 8am-noon & 4-7pm Tue-Sat) during her torture and you can ask the custodian to take a peak at the gloomy prison cell below the church. The saint's jewel-drenched effigy is

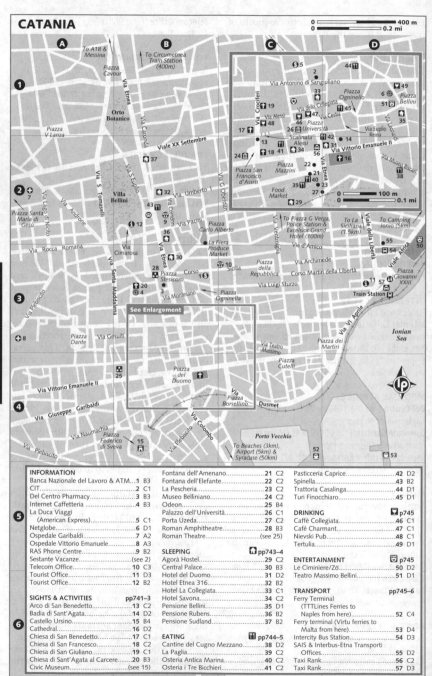

CATANIA

SICILY

ecstatically venerated in February (see following) in one of Sicily's largest festas.

A few blocks northeast you'll stumble onto Piazza Bellini. Its centrepiece is the **Teatro Massimo Bellini** (☎ 095 730 61 11; Via Perrotta 12; open for performances only), named after Vincenzo Bellini, Catania's most famous export and the father of a vibrant modern musical scene. There is a small museum, **Museo Belliniano** (☎ 095 715 05 35; Piazza San Francesco d'Assisi; admission free; ☼ 9am-1pm Mon-Fri & 3-6pm Tue & Thu), which houses a collection of memorabilia from the composer's life.

Today the best show in town is the bustling **La Pescheria**, the bustling **fish market** (☼ 5-11am) and adjoining **food market** (☼ all day). Here is the vision captured by Renato Guttuso's famous painting, *Vucciria*: carcasses of fish, meat, sheep's heads, rolls of sausages, huge cartwheels of cheese and piles of luscious vegetables are all rolled together in a few noisy, jam-packed alleyways. This street-show is not to be missed at any cost. The **Fontana dell'Amenano** at the entrance to the market is Tito Angelini's commemoration of the River Amenano, which once ran overground and on whose banks the Greeks first founded the city of Katáne.

Catania also has a number of very ruinous Roman remains dotted throughout the city. West along Via Vittorio Emanuele II is the **Roman theatre** and a small rehearsal theatre, the **Odeon** (Via V Emanuele II 266; admission free; ☼ 9am-1pm & 3-7pm). North of Piazza del Duomo, more leftovers from Roman days include a modest **amphitheatre** on Piazza Stesicoro. For relief from the madding crowd, continue north along Via Etnea and cut in to the left behind the post office for the lovely **Villa Bellini gardens** (☼ 8am-8pm) with its views of Mt Etna.

Museo Civico (☎ 095 34 58 30; Piazza Federico II di Svevia; admission free; ☼ 9am-1pm & 3-8pm Mon-Sat, 9am-12.30pm Sun) is housed in the grim-looking, moated **Castello Ursino**. It's in an equally grim neighbourhood southwest of Piazza del Duomo, just over the train line. The castle was once on a cliff top overlooking the sea; following the earthquake of 1693, the whole area to the south was reclaimed and the castle became landlocked. The museum inside contains finds from the Roman era up to the 18th century.

Catania's latest project is the renovation of its old sulphur refineries, **Le Ciminiere**

(☎ 095 734 99 11; Viale Africa). Fancifully called 'industrial archaeology', the refineries (covering 25,000 sq m) were transformed by Catanian architect Giacomo Leone into a vast cultural centre. Relatively new, it already has a permanent exhibition of WWII and you should watch this space in the future for more exhibitions and cultural events.

Festivals & Events
FEBRUARY
Festa di Sant'Agata (3-5 February) Hysterical celebrations where one million Catanians and tourists follow as the Fercolo (a silver reliquary bust of the saint covered in marvellous jewels) is carried along the main street of the city. There are also spectacular fireworks during the celebrations.

JULY
Catania Musica Estate Classical music festival.
Settimana Barocca A week of baroque concerts, pageants and other performances.
Etna Jazz Ask at the tourist office for information on this jazz festival.

Sleeping
Catania is served by a good range of reasonably priced places to stay, making it an excellent base for exploring the Ionian coast and Etna. Quality top-end hotels, however, are a bit thin on the ground.

BUDGET
Pensione Bellini (☎ 095 715 09 69; Via Landolini 41; s/d €32/46; ✖) This friendly little *pensione*, just off Piazza Bellini, is an excellent budget option and provides good, comfortable accommodation. The young couple who run it try their utmost to be helpful. Breakfast is included if requested.

Agorà Hostel (☎ 095 723 30 10; agorahostel@ hotmail.com; Piazza Currò 6; dm/d €15.50/41; ☐) A classic youth hostel with a ubiquitous reggae soundtrack. At night the live music, cheap food and bar get good reviews. Lock-out between 11am and 3pm.

Pensione Sudland (☎ 095 31 13 43; Via Etnea 270; s/d €26/40) Opposite the post office, the Pensione Sudland is real budget accommodation. It's popular and its proximity to the wonderful Villa Bellini gardens is a real bonus.

Camping Jonio (☎ 095 49 11 39; fax 095 49 22 77; Via Villini a Mare 2; adult/tent €5.40/11.90) This place is about 5km out of the city, close to a beautiful

SICILY

rocky beach. To get here, catch bus No 334 from Via Etnea.

MID-RANGE

Hotel Etnea 316 (☎ 095 250 30 76; www.hoteletnea 316.com; Via Etnea 316; s/d €70/100; ☒) The charming Hotel Etnea represents real value for money. The sunny lounge and breakfast room are inviting, the service is good and all the rooms are tastefully decorated and have comfortable beds.

Hotel del Duomo (☎ 095 250 31 77; www.hotel delduomo.it; Via Etnea 28; s/d €73/124; ☒) A classy three-star hotel occupying the whole wing of an ancient *palazzo*. Front rooms have great views over Piazza del Duomo.

Pensione Rubens (☎ 095 31 70 73; fax 095 715 17 13; Via Etnea 196; s/d €45/78; ☒) With only seven rooms and a well-deserved reputation for hospitality, you'll do well to book in advance here. Rooms are very comfortable. Another bonus is Signore Caviezel, who knows Catania inside out and could give a masterclass on hotel management.

Hotel Savona (☎ 095 32 69 82; fax 095 715 81 69; Via Vittorio Emanuele 210; d €93; ☒) Recently refurbished, the Savona is now an impressive mid-range option. Comfortable rooms overlook a quiet inner courtyard.

Hotel La Collegiata (☎ 095 31 52 56, ☎ 095 32 28 48; Via Paolo Vasta 10; s/d €50/78; ☒) This hotel is in a prime location near the Piazza del Duomo. Its rooms are perfectly adequate although nothing imaginative. For breakfast you will need to ask for a coupon from reception for one of the bars on Via Etnea.

TOP END

Excelsior Grand Hotel (☎ 095 747 61 11; excelsior -catania@thi.it; Piazza G Verga 39; s/d €145/197; ☒) Catania's top luxury hotel is the newly renovated Excelsior, in a Fascist building on Piazza Verga – much less attractive on the outside than it is on the inside. Although rated five-star, it lacks the real charm that is required to make you part with your money.

Central Palace (☎ 095 32 53 44; fax 095 715 89 39; Via Etnea 218; s/d €98/140; ☒) This is five-star luxury straight from the groovy 1970s. It's one for fans of the era rather than connoisseurs of top hotels.

Eating

Catania is renowned for its huge number of restaurants and bars that cater for every budget (pick up a copy of *Lapis* from the tourist office for full listings). Don't miss the savoury *arancini* (breaded rice balls filled with *ragù* and peas, then fried), *cartocciate* (focaccia stuffed with ham, mozzarella, olives and tomato) or baked onions, available for around €1.30 a piece from a *tavola calda*, found all over town.

La Siciliana (☎ 095 37 64 00; Viale Marco Polo 52; mains €20; ✆ 12.30-3.30pm & 8.30-11pm Tue-Sat, 12.30-3.30pm Sun) Considered Catania's best restaurant, La Siciliana serves traditional fare cooked to perfection. Try the breaded cutlets or roast lamb. Reservations required.

Osteria i Tre Bicchieri (☎ 095 715 35 40; Via S Giuseppe al Duomo 31; cheese/meat plates €10, fondue €20; ✆ 1-3pm & 8-11.30pm Mon evening-Sat) The dark wood-panelled interior creates the perfect atmosphere for this classy wine bar stocking over 1000 different labels. Huge glasses of wine are served with tasty crudités, and the fondue is great fun on evenings of live jazz.

Cantine del Cugno Mezzano (☎ 095 715 87 10; Via Museo Biscari 8; meals €25; ✆ noon-3pm & 8.30-10.30pm Tue-Sun Sep-Jul) Located in the former stables of Palazzo Biscari (the finest civic building in the city), this restaurant has a great atmosphere and an extensive wine list featuring some of the best Sicilian wines.

Turi Finocchiaro (☎ 095 715 35 73; Via Euplio Reina 13; meals €18; ✆ 8am-late) Simultaneously a restaurant, meeting place and pizzeria, Turi Finocchiaro has been around for years and is as popular as ever. The courtyard is a nice place to chill out on a hot evening.

Osteria Antica Marina (☎ 095 34 81 97; Via Pardo 29; meals €20; ✆ 12.30-3pm & 8-midnight Thu-Tue) A rustic-style trattoria behind the fish market, this is the restaurant to come to for fish. The decor features solid wooden tables and rough stones walls. Reservations are essential.

La Paglia (☎ 09534 68 38; Via Pardo 23; meals €15; ✆ 12.30-3.30pm) This is a great, cheap trattoria with an in-your-face view of the action around La Pescheria market.

Every morning except Sunday, Piazza Carlo Alberto is flooded by the chaos of a **produce market**, known locally as La Fiera, not dissimilar to a Middle-Eastern kasbah. The other major fresh-produce market is **La Pescheria**, off Piazza del Duomo.

CAFÉS

Try mouth-watering Sicilian sweets at the following cafés.

Pasticceria Caprice (Via Etnea 30) An old-style *pasticceria*, this café is highly recommended. Try a selection of mini-tarts filled with fresh fruit.

Spinella (☎ 095 32 72 47; Via Etnea 300) This is probably Catania's most famous *pasticceria*; one taste of its produce – especially the ricotta-filled *cannoli* – will tell you why. However, its fame has got the better of its service.

Café Charmant (Via Etnea 19-23) This elegant café with street-side tables is the perfect place for people-watching.

Drinking

Not surprisingly for a busy university town, Catania has a reputation for great nightlife. There are literally dozens of bars and other nightspots that offer a good mix of music and drinking. Via Etnea and Piazza Bellini are where a lot of the action takes place.

Tertulia (☎ 095 715 2603; Via M Rapisardi 1-3; ☺ 10am-11pm Tue-Sat) Adjoining a bookshop, this relaxing café is a pleasant mixture of tea house (serving great cakes) and bar depending on the time of day. There is also occasional live music.

Caffè Collegiata (☎ 095 32 12 30; Via della Collegiata 3; ☺ 7pm-4am Tue-Sat) In the basement of an elegant Art Nouveau building is this popular student hang-out.

Nievski Pub (Scalinata Alessi 15; ☺ 1-4pm & 7.30pm-1.30am Tue-Sat) On the heaving Scalinata Alessi, this is a good place to mingle with Catania's alternative crowd – that is, if you can get near the bar.

Entertainment

Zō (☎ 095 53 38 71; www.zoculture.it; Piazzale Asia 6; ☺ 1-3pm & 8.30pm-12.30am Tue-Sat) Zō is a new Catanian initiative set to take off. Part of a cultural complex hosting events and exhibitions, the bar/café/restaurant serves good food in an impressive venue – the converted sulphur works, Le Ciminiere (see p743). Weekends are the best time to come as there is live music and dancing.

Teatro Massimo Bellini (☎ 095 730 6111, Via Perrotta 12; www.teatromassimobellini.it) Opening in 1890 with Bellini's first opera, *Norma*, Teatro Massimo Bellini continues to honour Catania's finest operatic export with a full program of events. The opera season runs from October to June, followed by a symphony season in September. For information on performances ask at the tourist office or visit the theatre's website.

Getting There & Away

AIR

Catania's airport, Fontanarossa (CTA), is 7km southwest of the city centre and services domestic and European flights (many of the latter via Rome or Milan). Catania is well served with daily direct flights from Holland and Germany, Meridiana flies between London and Catania. In summer you may be able to dig up the odd direct charter flight to London (£240 to £300) or Paris (€275 to €300).

BOAT

The ferry terminal is south of the train station along Via VI Aprile. **Virtu Ferries** (☎ 095 31 67 11, ☎ 095 53 57 11) runs express ferries from Catania to Malta. Ferries depart Catania's Molo Centrale (one departure a week March to May and four weekly departures between late July and early September). The trip takes three hours and passenger tickets cost from €85.20 (from €103 for a car).

TTT Lines (☎ 095 746 21 87; www.tttlines.it, Italian only) has a daily ferry from Naples to Catania leaving at midnight. You can also buy tickets at local travel agencies (see p741).

BUS

Intercity buses terminate in the area around Piazza Giovanni XXIII, in front of the train station, and depart from Via d'Amico, one block north. Although initially intimidating in appearance, Catania's bus station is super-efficient and easy to navigate, far surpassing the rather plodding train service. **SAIS Autolinee** (☎ 095 53 62 01, ☎ 095 53 61 68; Via d'Amico 181-7) serves Syracuse (€4.10, one hour, 18 per day), Palermo (€11.62, 2¾ hours, 17 daily) and Agrigento (€9.18, three hours, five daily). It also has a service to Rome (€38.75 one way, 14 hours) leaving at 8pm. **AST** (☎ 095 746 10 96, ☎ 095 53 17 56; Via L Sturzo 232) also services these destinations and many smaller provincial towns around Catania, including Nicolosi. **Interbus-Etna Trasporti** (☎ 095 53 27 16, ☎ 095 746 13 33), at the same address as SAIS, runs buses to Piazza Armerina (€6.20), Taormina (€3.10) and Ragusa (€6.20).

SICILY

CAR & MOTORCYCLE
Catania can be easily reached from Messina on the A18 and from Palermo on the A19. From the A18, signs for the centre of Catania will bring you to Via Etnea.

TRAIN
Frequent trains connect Catania with Messina (€5.05, two hours, half-hourly) and Syracuse (€4.65, 1½ hours, 18 daily), and there are less-frequent services to Palermo (€11.25, 3½ hours, two daily), Enna (€4.50, 1¾ hours, four daily) and Agrigento (€9.20, an agonisingly slow four hours, two daily).

The private Circumetnea train line circles Mt Etna, stopping at the towns and villages on the volcano's slopes. See p747.

Getting Around
To reach the airport, take the special Alibus No 457 (€2.30) from outside the train station.

Many of the more useful **AMT city buses** (☎ 095 736 01 11) terminate in front of the

---

VOLCANIC RUMBLINGS

Italy's southern coast with its three active volcanoes, Etna, Stromboli and Vesuvius, forms Europe's biggest pressure cooker. Since September 1999 Etna has regularly given off signs of stirring activity, spitting ash into the skies and releasing rivers of molten rock. Etna's most recent eruption occurred at the end of 2002, when lava flows destroyed a pine forest on the northern slope and engulfed the refuge at Piano Provenzana. The southern side faired only marginally better with a huge lava trail just missing the Rifugio Sapienza and running over the road – the authorities have now carved a gap through the cooling lava. Shortly afterwards, Stromboli, Etna's terrible twin, changed its behavioural pattern – two of the three craters that regularly erupt fell silent until 5 April 2003, when the build-up of pressure resulted in a dramatic explosion, showering the sea with rocks that even reached Ginostra. Islanders were evacuated for a month and the sea around Panarea boiled for two weeks. Vulcanologists wait and wonder if the two events are connected and if we are in for some more devastating fireworks.

---

train station. These include: Alibus (station–airport every 20 minutes); Nos 1 to 4 (station–Via Etnea); Nos 4 to 7 (station–Piazza del Duomo). A ticket costs €0.80. In summer, a special service (D) runs from Piazza G Verga to the sandy beaches. Bus No 334 from Via Etnea takes you to the Riviera dei Ciclopi and the beautiful Norman castle at Acicastello (admission is free).

For drivers, some words of warning: there are complicated one-way systems around the city and the centre has now been pedestrianised. This means that the narrow streets get terribly clogged in rush hour and parking is a problem.

MT ETNA
Dominating the landscape in eastern Sicily between Taormina and Catania, Mt Etna (3350m) is Europe's largest live volcano and one of the world's most active. Eruptions occur frequently, both from the four live craters at the summit (one, the Bocca Nuova, was formed in 1968) and on the slopes of the volcano, which is littered with fissures and old craters. The volcano's most devastating eruptions occurred in 1669 and lasted 122 days. A huge river of lava poured down its southern slope, engulfing a good part of Catania and dramatically altering the landscape.

Activity at the end of 2002 has meant more disruption to services and visitors should be aware that excursions are at the mercy of volcanic activity. The volcano's unpredictability means people are no longer allowed to climb to the craters. It is possible to climb one of the peaks in front of the Rifugio Sapienza to get a small taste of the real thing.

There are several groups that organise tours up towards the craters, involving both trekking and 4WD vehicles with a vulcanologist or alpine guide. They include **Gruppo Guide Alpine Etna Sud** (☎ 095 791 47 55) and **Natura e Turismo** (☎ 095 33 35 43; natetur@tin.it; Via Quartararo 11, Catania).

The Craters
With a daily bus from Catania via Nicolosi, the southern side of the volcano presents the easier option for an ascent towards the craters. From Rifugio Sapienza (the closest the surfaced road comes to the summit) **SITAS** (☎ 095 91 11 58) has 4WD minibuses

going up Mt Etna for a hefty €38 per person. The vehicles take you through the eerie lavascape to 2900m and the **Torre del Filosofo** (Philosopher's Tower) where you can view the smoking landscape (on foot this trek takes 2½ hours). It is forbidden to go beyond this point. The cable cars that used to run up the volcano to 2600m are still suspended and the cabins have been removed from their cables to prevent them melting! Plans are afoot to reinstate them in the winter of 2003 but it all depends on Etna. The previous price for the cable car was €18. In winter you could ski back down (snow permitting) and a one-day ski pass cost €20.

The **Etna Sud tourist office** (☎ 095 91 63 56) is at Rifugio Sapienza and opens daily (closed at the time of writing due to the recent volcanic activity). For information you can also try the local **tourist office** (☎ 095 91 15 05; Via Garibaldi 63) in Nicolosi.

The recent lava flows on the northern side of Etna wiped out Piano Provenzana and its ski lift. Now the only tours run from Linguaglossa. Inquire at the **tourist office** (☎ 095 64 30 94; www.prolocolinguaglossa.it, Italian only; Piazza Annunziata 7) about hiring a guide or going on an organised tour.

Sleeping

Accommodation around Etna is scant; you're probably better off in Catania. For the following, be sure to book in advance in summer.

Etna Camping (☎ 095 91 43 09; fax 095 791 51 86; Via Goethe; per person €6.20) This camp site, based in Nicolosi, is about as close as campers will get to Etna. Well shaded and cool, it has a particularly nice quiet area for tents under pine trees.

Etna Youth Hostel (☎ 095 791 46 86; etnahostel@ hotmail.com; Via della Quercia 7, Nicolosi; dm/d €16/46) The most popular option with budget travellers, this establishment is HI-affiliated and offers dorm rooms and family rooms. It also has hotel rooms on offer and is open year-round.

Gemmellaro (☎ 095 91 13 73; fax 095 91 10 71; Via Etnea 160, Nicolosi; s/d €38/60; 🖭) This three-star hotel has comfortable rooms and is one of the better options in Nicolosi.

There are small hotels in some of the towns along the Circumetnea train line, including Linguaglossa and Randazzo.

Getting There & Away
BUS & CAR

Having your own transport will make life much easier around Mt Etna, but there are some public transport options. The easiest approach is from the south.

An **AST bus** (☎ 095 746 10 96, ☎ 095 53 17 56) departs from the car park in front of the main train station in Catania at 8.30am for Rifugio Sapienza via Nicolosi. It returns from the *rifugio* at 4.45pm. The return ticket costs €3.56. The **AST office** (☎ 095 91 15 05; Via Etnea 32, Nicolosi) is open 8am to 2pm Monday to Saturday. You can also drive the same route (take Via Etnea north out of town and follow the signs for Nicolosi and Etna).

SAIS and FCE buses connect Linguaglossa with Fiumefreddo on the coast (from where other SAIS buses run north to Taormina and Messina and south to Catania).

AROUND THE MOUNTAIN BY TRAIN

Another option is to circle Mt Etna on the private **Ferrovia Circumetnea** (☎ 095 54 12 50; www.circumetnea.it; Via Caronda 352a, Catania) train line. The line runs around the mountain from Catania to the coastal town of Riposto, passing through numerous towns and villages on its slopes, including Linguaglossa. You can reach Riposto (or the neighbouring Giarre) from Taormina by train or bus if you want to make the trip from that end.

Catania–Riposto is about a 3½-hour trip, but you needn't go that far. If you're leaving from Catania, consider finishing the trip at Randazzo (two hours), a small medieval town noted for the fact that it has consistently escaped destruction despite its proximity to the summit.

SOUTHEASTERN SICILY

SYRACUSE
pop 126,000

Sultry, civilised Syracuse, stranded at the southernmost tip of the island, was considered by Cicero to be the most beautiful city in the ancient world, rivalling Athens in power and prestige. Settled by colonists from Corinth in 734 BC, the city reached its zenith (4th century BC) under the demagogue Dionysius the Elder, who defeated the Athenians at sea and set about building a capital worthy of his illustrious name. Luminaries such as Cicero, Livy, Plato and Archimedes flocked to his capital, cultivating the sophisticated urban culture that was to see the birth of comic Greek theatre. As the sun set on ancient Greece, Syracuse became a Roman colony under Marcellus who looted its treasures and art. Since then the city has been in a free-fall of decline and its modern suburban squalor disguises its remaining treasure, the island of Ortigia. Lacking the drama of Palermo and the energy of Catania, Syracuse still manages to seduce visitors with its quiet decrepitude, excellent hotels and fascinating sites.

Orientation

The main sights of Syracuse are in two areas: on the island of Ortigia and 2km across town in the Parco Archeologico della Neapolis (archaeological zone). From the train station, walk east along Via F Crispi to Piazzale Marconi. Heading straight through the piazza to Corso Umberto will bring you to Ortigia, about 1km away. Alternatively, turn left from Piazzale Marconi into Via Catania, cross the train line and follow the busy shopping street, Corso Gelone, to Viale Paolo Orsi and the Parco Archeologico. If you arrive by bus, you'll be dropped in or near Piazza della Posta in Ortigia.

Information

EMERGENCIES
Police Station (☎ 0931 46 35 56; Via San Sebastiano)

MEDICAL SERVICES
Ospedale Generale Provinciale (☎ 0931 72 41 11; Via Testaferrata 1)

INTERNET ACCESS
Prices are from €4 per hour.
Cybercafe (Via del Crocifisso 44/46, Ortigia; ☽ 7.30pm-midnight Tue-Sat) Situated in a separate room off Ortigia's best wine bar, Fermento (p752).
Web and Work (Via Roma 16-18, Ortigia) Other multimedia services available.

MONEY
Numerous banks (all with ATMs) line Corso Umberto. There are others on Corso Gelone and on Ortigia around Piazza Archimede. The exchange rates at the train station booth are poor.
Banca Nazionale del Lavoro (Corso Umberto 29)

POST & TELEPHONE
There are plenty of public phones on the streets.
Post Office (Piazza della Posta 15; ☽ 8am-6.30pm Mon-Fri, 8.30am-1pm Sat) Also offers currency exchange.
Telecom Office (Viale Teracati 46; ☽ 8.30am-7.30pm Mon-Sat)

TOURIST INFORMATION
Main Tourist Office(☎ 0931 48 12 00; www.apt-siracusa.it; Via San Sebastiano 43; ☽ 8.30am-1.30pm & 3.30-6.30pm Mon-Sat) English-speaking staff and a useful city map – ask about the cumulative tickets for the sites. There is also an information booth at the Parco Archeologico.
Ortigia Tourist Office (☎ 0931 46 42 55; Via Maestranza 33; ☽ 8am-2pm & 2.30-5.30pm Mon-Fri, mornings only Sat)

TRAVEL AGENCIES
Syrako Porta Marina Tourist Point (☎ 0931 2 41 33; Largo Porta Marina; ☽ 9am-1pm & 3-8pm Mon-Sat) This information/tourist centre can help travellers without cars see more of the province.

Sights
ORTIGIA
The island of Ortigia is the spiritual and physical heart of the city. Despite its baroque veneer the Greek essence of Syracuse is everywhere in evidence, from the formal civility of the people to disguised architectural relics. The most obvious of these is the **cathedral** (Piazza del Duomo; admission free; ☽ 8am-noon & 4-7pm), which is in fact a Greek temple converted into a church when the island was evangelised by St Paul. The baroque carapace, designed by Andrea Palma, barely hides the solid Temple of Athena beneath. Huge 5th-century-BC Doric columns are visible both inside and out and still support the roof. Inside, the statue of the Virgin Mary (to whom the church is dedicated) stands in exactly the same spot where 2500 years ago a massive statue of the goddess Athena stood.

Just down the winding main street from the cathedral is the **Fontana Aretusa**, where fresh water bubbles up just as it did in ancient times when it was the city's main water supply. Legend has it that the goddess Artemis transformed her beautiful handmaiden Aretusa into the spring to protect her from the unwelcome attention of the river-god Alpheus. Now populated

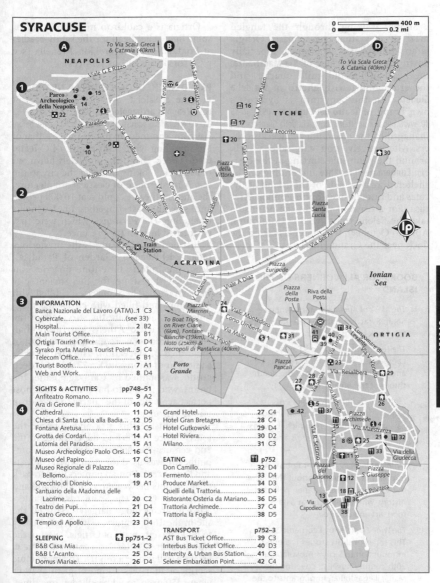

SYRACUSE

0 ———— 400 m
0 ———— 0.2 mi

INFORMATION
Banca Nazionale del Lavoro (ATM)..**1** C3
Cybercafe.................................(see 33)
Hospital..**2** B2
Main Tourist Office.........................**3** B1
Ortigia Tourist Office......................**4** D4
Syrako Porta Marina Tourist Point.**5** C4
Telecom Office...............................**6** B1
Tourist Booth.................................**7** A1
Web and Work................................**8** D4

SIGHTS & ACTIVITIES   pp748–51
Anfiteatro Romano..........................**9** A2
Ara di Gerone II.............................**10** A2
Cathedral......................................**11** D4
Chiesa di Santa Lucia alla Badia.....**12** D5
Fontana Aretusa............................**13** C5
Grotta dei Cordari..........................**14** A1
Latomia del Paradiso......................**15** A1
Museo Archeologico Paolo Orsi......**16** C1
Museo del Papiro............................**17** C1
Museo Regionale di Palazzo
  Bellomo.....................................**18** D5
Orecchio di Dionisio.......................**19** A1
Santuario della Madonna delle
  Lacrime......................................**20** A1
Teatro dei Pupi.............................**21** D4
Teatro Greco.................................**22** A1
Tempio di Apollo...........................**23** D4

SLEEPING   🏠 pp751–2
B&B Casa Mia................................**24** C3
B&B L'Acanto................................**25** D4
Domus Mariae...............................**26** D4

Grand Hotel..................................**27** C4
Hotel Gran Bretagna......................**28** C4
Hotel Gutkowski............................**29** D4
Hotel Riviera.................................**30** D2
Milano..**31** C3

EATING   🍴 p752
Don Camillo...................................**32** D4
Fermento......................................**33** D4
Produce Market.............................**34** D3
Quelli della Trattoria.....................**35** D4
Ristorante Osteria da Mariano........**36** D5
Trattoria Archimede.......................**37** D4
Trattoria la Foglia.........................**38** D5

TRANSPORT   p752–3
AST Bus Ticket Office.....................**39** C3
Interbus Bus Ticket Office..............**40** D3
Intercity & Urban Bus Station........**41** C3
Selene Embarkation Point..............**42** C4

by ducks, grey mullet and papyrus plants, the fountain is *the* place to hang out on summer evenings.

Just up Via Capodieci from the fountain is the **Museo Regionale di Palazzo Bellomo** (☎ 0931 6 96 17; Via Capodieci 14; admission €2.50; ⏰ 9am-1.30pm Tue-Sun, 9am-1.30pm & 3-7pm Wed), which houses a sizable collection of sculp-

ture and paintings dating from the Middle Ages to the 20th century. Highlights include Byzantine icons and Spanish paintings as well as the beautiful *Annunciazione* (Annunciation; 1474) by Antonello da Messina and *La Sepoltura di Santa Lucia* (The Burial of St Lucy; 1609) by Caravaggio. The *palazzo* itself is Ortigia's finest Catalan-Gothic mansion.

Simply walking through the tangled maze of alleys that characterises Ortigia is an atmospheric experience, especially down the narrow lanes of **Via Maestranza**, the heart of the old guild quarter, and the crumbling Jewish ghetto of **Via della Giudecca**. In this labyrinth is Syracuse's own brand of **Teatro dei Pupi** (☎ 0931 46 55 40; www.pupari.com, Italian only; Via della Giudecca 17), managed by the charming Mauceri brothers. Alternatively, you can take a walk around the peninsula starting at the eastern **Lungomare di Levante** and ending on the sheltered western side of the island at the cafés and restaurants around Fontana Aretusa. For a seaward view of the peninsula take the Selene **cruise** (€5.50, 45 minutes, April to October), which departs from the dock near the Grand Hotel.

Ortigia is a cauldron in summer so for some light relief head for the sandy **beaches** at Fontana Bianche or Lido Arenella (see p752 for details of bus services).

PARCO ARCHEOLOGICO DELLA NEAPOLIS
For the classicist, Syracuse's treasures at the **Neapolis archaeological park** (☎ 0931 6 62 06, Viale Paradisa; admission €4.50; 🕑 9am-2hrs before sunset) are summed up in one image – that of the sparkling white, 5th-century-BC **Teatro Greco** (Greek Theatre), completely hewn out of the rock, looking out over the city to the sea. A masterpiece of classical architecture, the ancient theatre could seat 16,000 people and saw the last tragedies of Aeschylus (including *The Persians*), which were first performed here in his presence.

Just beside the theatre is the mysterious **Latomia del Paradiso** (Garden of Paradise): deep, precipitous limestone quarries out of which the stone for the ancient city was extracted. These quarries, riddled with catacombs and filled with citrus and magnolia trees, are where the survivors of the 413 BC Syracuse–Athens war (more than 7000 Athenians) were imprisoned. Most of them died of starvation. The **Orecchio di Dionisio** (Ear of Dionysius), a 23m by 3m deep grotto, was named by Caravaggio after the tyrant, who is said to have used the almost perfect acoustics of the quarry to eavesdrop on his prisoners.

Back outside this area and opposite the tourist office you'll find the entrance to the 2nd-century-AD **Anfiteatro Romano**. The amphitheatre was used for gladiatorial combats and horse races. Roman punters used to park their chariots between the amphitheatre and Viale Paolo Orsi. The Spaniards, little interested in archaeology, largely destroyed the site in the 16th century, using it as a quarry to build the city walls of Ortigia. West of the amphitheatre is the 3rd-century-BC **Ara di Gerone II** (Altar of Hieron II). The monolithic sacrificial altar was a kind of giant abattoir where 450 oxen could be killed at one time.

To get here, catch a bus (No 1 and several others) from Riva della Posta on Ortigia.

MUSEO ARCHEOLOGICO PAOLO ORSI & MUSEO DEL PAPIRO
Located in the grounds of Villa Landolina, about 500m east of the Parco Archeologico, is the **Museo Archeologico Paolo Orsi** (☎ 0931 46

BOOKS FOR ALL CORNERS OF THE ISLAND

- *The Mask of Apollo* by Mary Renault – Set in Syracuse in the 5th century BC, this book brings the stones to life.

- *The Leopard* by Giuseppe Tomasi di Lampedusa – Sicily's most famous book and a delicious insight into the death throes of the great feudal nobility.

- *Mattanza* by Teresa Maggio – A sentimental paean to the vanishing Favignana tuna fishery, which includes personal portraits of the *rais* and his fishermen.

- *Midnight in Sicily* by Peter Robb – A gripping documentary about the Mafia, the 1990s maxi-trials, Italian politics and history, with loads of great asides on food, art and culture.

- *The Wine-Dark Sea* by Leornardo Sciascia – This series of short stories is a good introduction to Sicily's most famous 20th-century novelist, covering the Mafia, illegal Italian immigrants to the US, and Mussolini. The realist tradition at its best.

- *A House in Sicily* by Daphne Phelps – A feel-good recollection, studded with plenty of famous names, of one Englishwoman's 50 years in residence at Taormina.

40 22; Viale Teocrito; admission €4.50; ⊙ 9am-1pm Tue-Sun). It contains the best-organised and most interesting archaeological collection in Sicily (and is one of the most extensive archaeological collections in Europe) and certainly merits a visit. The opening hours are all over the place and often get extended in summer; check with one of the tourist offices.

Around the corner, the **Museo del Papiro** (☎ 0931 616 16; Viale Teocrito 66; admission free; ⊙ 9am-1.30pm) includes papyrus documents and products. The plant grows in abundance around the Ciane River, near Syracuse, and was used to make paper in the 18th century.

Festivals & Events
MAY/JUNE
Greek Classical Drama (☎ 0931 6 74 15; Teatro Greco) Today Syracuse boasts the only school of Classical Greek drama outside Athens and the performances attract some of Italy's finest performers. All performances are in Italian. Tickets (€12-31) are available from the tourist office or at the booth at the entrance to the theatre.

DECEMBER
Festa di Santa Lucia On the 13th December a festival commemorates the city's patron saint. Her enormous silver statue is paraded through the streets from Piazza del Duomo on Ortigia to Piazza Santa Lucia on the mainland. It is accompanied by fireworks.

Sleeping
BUDGET
B&B Casa Mia (☎ 0931 46 33 49; Corso Umberto 112; s/d €45/75) This home-away-from-home is a great choice, situated in an old mansion with nicely furnished rooms and a lovely breakfast area. Rooms are limited so it is advisable to book ahead.

B&B L'Acanto (☎ /fax 0931 46 11 29; lacanto@tiscali net.it; Via Roma 15; s/d €55/75; ✗) The family-run L'Acanto has delightful rooms (with TV) off a pretty courtyard. It is a small, cosy place.

Milano (☎ 0931 6 69 81; Corso Umberto 10; s/d €36/57; ✗) The Milano is a stone's throw from Ortigia and is also within easy access of the archaeological area. Rooms are fairly spartan but clean.

Fontane Bianche (☎ 0931 79 03 33; Via dei Lidi 476; Località Fontane Bianche; person/tent €6/4.50; ⊙ May-Sep) This camp site is about 18km southwest of Syracuse, at the beach of the same name. This is where all the action happens in summer when the beach is lined with dis-

THE AUTHOR'S CHOICE

Hotel Gutkowski (☎ 0931 46 58 61; www .guthotel.it; Lungomare Vittorini 26; s/d €65/90; ✗ 🖳) Facing the sea, this charming pastel-blue hotel on the eastern side of Ortigia has received rave reviews. Funded by EU grants and hard-earned private cash, the Gutkowski is one of numerous entrepreneurial ventures embarked upon by young Syracusans in an attempt to revive and restore the crumbling *palazzi*. Decorated with real verve, the hotel's pure white, minimalist rooms bring a touch of surprising modernity to this antique island. A family-run venture, it bears the hallmark of careful attention to detail. Multilingual staff are unbelievably helpful and breakfast is a quaint experience presided over by *nonna*, who skips from French to German to Italian and English with confusing ease. Ask for sea-view rooms or the room with the roof terrace.

cos and bars. Catch bus Nos 21 or 22 from Corso Umberto.

MID-RANGE & TOP END
Syracuse prides itself on discerning tourism and the hotels in this range certainly present great value for money. Many are on Ortigia, where young entrepreneurs are returning and breathing life into the decrepit streets.

Hotel Gran Bretagne (☎ 0931 687 65; Via Savoia 21; s/d €70/98; ✗) This small, swanky hotel has friendly management and is situated in a great location on Ortigia.

Hotel Riviera (☎ 0931 6 70 50; Via Eucleida 7; s/d €76/80; ✗) Situated right at the top of town near the Neapolis, the Riviera has been recommended by LP readers. It has stunning views of the sea from its 1st-floor terrace, and the rooms are large and elegant.

Domus Mariae (☎ 0931 2 48 54; htldomus@ sistemia.it; Via V Veneto 76; s/d €98/135; P ✗) This restored former school for nuns on Ortigia has been transformed into an elegant, comfortable hotel. Some rooms have sea views and there's free parking outside.

Grand Hotel (☎ 0931 46 46 00; fax 0931 46 46 11; Viale Mazzini 12; s/d €139/217; P ✗) This is Ortigia's top hotel and is the only one with access for the disabled. It has lovely rooms and all the facilities that you would expect.

Eating

There is no shortage of restaurants on Ortigia, where all the best eateries are located.

Trattoria Archimede (☎ 0931 697 01; Via Gemellaro 8; mains €8-15; ⏱ 12.30-3pm & 7.30-11pm Mon-Sat, closed 3 weeks Jul) The most authentic restaurant on Ortigia, with three large, formal dining rooms serving an array of seafood dishes and pasta. The menu changes constantly so you never get bored.

Fermento (☎ 0931 607 62; Via Crocifisso 44/46; meals €15; ⏱ 7.30pm-midnight Wed-Mon) This moody, vaulted wine bar is hidden in the crumbling Jewish quarter of Ortigia. It doesn't get going until about 10.30pm, when it suddenly fills up with fashionably-late Syracusans. The cheese and ham platters are great accompaniments to the wine. Try the *nero d'avola*, produced just down the road in Pachino, or the silky damaskino grape.

Trattoria la Foglia (☎ 0931 6 62 33; Via Capodieci 21; meals €25; ⏱ noon-3pm & 8.30-10.30pm Wed-Mon, daily summer) Here the eccentric owner/chef and her vegetarian husband bake their own bread and serve whatever seafood and vegetables are fresh that day. The *tagliolini pesce* (seafood pasta) is tasty and the ambience is delightful, with hand-embroidered tablecloths and fine porcelain plates.

Don Camillo (☎ 0931 6 71 33; Via Maestranza 96; meals around €30; ⏱ 12.30-3pm & 8-11pm Mon-Sat) Situated in the old guild quarter, this is a formal upmarket trattoria serving traditional Sicilian food with an excellent selection of wines. Very popular on Friday and Saturday nights so reservations are recommended.

Ristorante Osteria da Mariano (☎ 0931 6 74 44; Vicolo Zuccalà 9; meals €25; ⏱ 1-3.30pm & 7.30-11pm) Tucked away in an alleyway south of the cathedral on Ortigia, this restaurant serves very good traditional Sicilian fare. It is a small place and fills up quickly so be sure to book ahead, especially at the weekend.

Quelli della Trattoria (Via Cavour 28; meals €15; ⏱ 1-3.30pm & 8-11.30pm Mon-Sat) A tiny rustic restaurant that specialises in all manner of fresh pasta dishes (try the speciality of the house, seafood ravioli). It fills up quickly in the evenings so reservations are advised.

In the streets near the post office, there's a **produce market** until 1pm Monday to Saturday. There are several **grocery shops** and **supermarkets** along Corso Gelone.

Getting There & Away

BUS

Unless you're coming from Catania or Messina, you'll find buses faster and more convenient than trains. **Interbus** (☎ 0931 6 67 10; Via Trieste 28) services leave from Riva della Posta or near the company's office on Via Trieste. They connect with Catania (€4.10, one hour, 15 daily Monday to Saturday) and its airport, Palermo (€13.40, four hours, five daily), Enna and surrounding small towns including Noto (€2.60, one hour, nine per day). Interbus also has a daily service to Rome (€36, 12 hours) via Catania.

AST (☎ 0931 46 48 20; Riva della Posta 9/11) has buses for Catania (€4.10), Piazza Armerina (€7.50, three hours, one daily), Noto (€2.60) and Ragusa (€5.45, three hours, six daily).

CAR & MOTORCYCLE

If arriving from the north by car, you will enter Syracuse on Via Scala Greca. To reach the centre of the city, turn left at Viale Teracati and follow it around to the south; it eventually becomes Corso Gelone. There is ongoing confusion over the *superstrada* (superhighway) connection between Catania, Syracuse and towns such as Noto further along the coast. An autostrada is supposed to connect the towns but starts and ends virtually in the middle of nowhere, some kilometres out of Syracuse.

TRAIN

More than a dozen trains depart daily for Messina (€8.25, three hours) via Catania (€4.40, 1½ hours). Some go on to Rome, Turin, Milan and other long-distance destinations. There is only one direct connection to Palermo (€18, 6½ hours). If you miss this one, you'll have to go to Catania and wait for a connection. There are several slow trains to Modica (€4.90, 1¾ hours) and Ragusa (€5.70, two hours).

Getting Around

Only a few kilometres separate the Parco Archeologico and Ortigia, so it's possible to walk. Otherwise, bus Nos 1 and 2 make the trip from Piazza della Posta. Alternatively, take bus No 10 from Piazza Archimede. The tourist office has local timetables. AST bus Nos 21, 22 and 24 serve the beach at Fontane Bianche and No 23 takes you to Arenelle (€0.80).

AROUND SYRACUSE

Just south of the city, 5km along Via Elorina, is the **Fiume Ciane**, a mythical river dedicated to the nymph Ciane who tried to thwart the abduction of Proserpina by Hades – the spring, upriver, is said to have been formed by her tears. The river habitat, a tangle of lush papyrus, is unique and endangered – the only place outside north Africa where papyrus grows wild. Boat trips (May to September) are possible and start from about €40. For bookings and information call ☎ 0931 6 90 76. To get there take bus No 21, 22 or 23 from Piazza della Posta on Ortigia.

In the hills above is the region's foremost prehistoric site, **Necropoli di Pantalica**, 40km west of Syracuse. It's where more than 5000 tombs dating from the 13th to 8th century BC honeycomb the cliffs and where many of the treasures in the archaeological museum in Syracuse were excavated. The tombs lie in a gorge carved by the Anapo River and offer excellent tracks for walkers (paths marked A are unchallenging, those marked B challenging). The windswept plateaus, awash with wild flowers, and the sheer rock faces and deep ravines are a haven of peace and tranquillity. The site is difficult to get to without a car, but you can ask at any travel agent in Syracuse or at the tourist office about organised tours.

NOTO

pop 23,000

Flattened by the 1693 earthquake, Noto was rebuilt by its noble families in the grand baroque style and is now the finest and most coherent baroque town in Sicily. The local limestone gives the buildings a warm golden hue and the town is much vaunted by its tourist office as 'a garden of stone'. The florid architecture is the work of Rosario Gagliardi and his assistant Vincenzo Sinatra, local architects who also worked in Ragusa and Modica. Recently added to Unesco's list of World Heritage Sites, Noto is currently undergoing extensive restoration, as the soft tufa stone requires

constant maintenance. In 1996 the town was shocked when the dome and roof of its splendid baroque cathedral collapsed after a thunderstorm. Since then major works were implemented to stabilise the church and eventually fix the roof; these continue today.

Intercity buses drop you in the Porta Reale, which is at the beginning of Corso Vittorio Emanuele, the town's main street.

Information

EMERGENCIES

Ambulance (☎ 0931 89 02 35)
Police Station (☎ 0931 83 52 02)

MEDICAL SERVICES

Hospital (☎ 0931 890 111, first aid ☎ 0931 890 235; Via dei Mille) On the way out of town towards Noto Antica.

TOURIST INFORMATION

Tourist Office (☎ 0931 57 37 79; Piazza XVI Maggio; ☼ 8am-2pm & 3.30-6.15pm Mon-Sat) Can supply maps of the local area.

TRAVEL AGENCIES

Allakatakka (☎ 0931 83 50 05; Corso Vittorio Emanuele 47) This office wears various hats, including tour guide and renter of bikes (€10.30 per day) and scooters (€31 per day).

Sights

The **San Nicoló Cathedral** (still clad in scaffolding) stands centre stage in Noto's most graceful square, Piazza Municipio. It is surrounded on all sides by elegant town houses such as Palazzo Ducezio and Palazzo Landolina, once home to Noto's oldest noble family. The only *palazzo* that has been restored to its former glory is **Palazzo Villadorata** (also known as Palazzo Nicolaci; ☎ 0931 83 50 05; Via Corrado Nicolaci; adult/concession €3/1.50; ☼ 10am-1pm & 3-7pm Tue-Sun), whose wrought-iron balconies are supported by a swirling pantomime of grotesque figures – mythical monsters, griffons, cherubs and sirens. Inside, richly brocaded walls and frescoed ceilings give an idea of the sumptuous lifestyle of Sicilian nobles brought to life in Tomasi di Lampedusa's novel, *The Leopard* (see p750). Further along Corso Vittorio Emanuele are **Chiesa del Santissimo Salvatore** (Corso Vittorio Emanuele; admission free; ☼ 8am-12.30pm & 3.30-7pm) and an adjoining **monastery**. The interior of the church is the most impressive in Noto and the monastery was reserved for the daughters of local nobility. The **Giardino Pubblico** at the end of the road is a pleasant way to end the walk.

If you're interested in taking home a few pieces of Sicilian ceramics, **All'Angolo** (cnr Piazza dell'Immacolata & Corso Vittorio Emanuele) has an excellent selection of pieces from Caltagirone.

Festivals & Events
Infiorata (held on the third Sunday in May) sees Corso Vittorio Emanuele transformed into a sea of flowers as town residents welcome spring. Each of the palazzo's richly sculpted balconies is decorated differently and artists line Via Corrada Nicolaci with artwork made entirely of flower petals.

Sleeping & Eating
Be aware that accommodation is a problem as there is not a lot of choice in town.

Il Castello Noto (☎ /fax 0931 57 15 34; ostellodi noto@tin.it; Via F Bandiera 1; dm €14.50, HI members only) This hostel has good facilities and is the pride of Noto.

Al Canisello Rooms (☎ 0931 83 57 93; mazzone@ polosud.it; Via Pavese 1; d €65) This quiet farmhouse is at the end of Corso Vittorio Emanuele, past Piazza N Bixio. It has a lovely garden area and tastefully decorated rooms.

There are a handful of hotels down by the sea at Noto Marina, a 15-minute drive or bus trip (buses run only in summer).

President (☎ 0931 81 25 43; fax 0931 81 25 78; Località Falconara; s/d €56/84) This three-star hotel has top-quality rooms at reasonable prices.

Noto is particularly renowned for its cakes and pastries. Round the corner from each other, **Caffè Sicilia** (☎ 0931 83 50 13; Corso Vittorio Emanuele 125) and **Corrado Costanzo** (☎ 0931 83 52 43; Via Silvio Spaventa 9) are neck and neck when it comes to the best gelato and cakes in Noto. Both make superb *dolci di mandorle* (almond cakes and sweets), real cassata cake and *torrone* (nougat).

Trattoria del Carmine (☎ 0931 83 87 05; Via Ducezio 9; meals €15; ☺ noon-3.30pm & 7.30-10.30pm Tue-Sat) This place serves excellent home-style meals. Try the *coniglio alla stimpirata* (rabbit in local sauces).

Ristorante Neas (☎ 0931 57 35 38; Via Rocco Pirri 30; meals €25; ☺ noon-3pm & 8-11pm) You'll find a high standard of both food and service at this place, which opens up its lovely

terrace in summer. Try the *linguine allo scoglio* (with mixed seafood), or the legendary fish soup.

Getting There & Around
Noto is easily accessible by AST and Interbus from Catania (€5.70, 2¼ hours) and Syracuse (€2.50, one hour, nine per day). Buses run frequently between Noto and Noto Marina from May to September.

AROUND NOTO
Ragusa
The region around Noto is typified by lushly cultivated fields and refined baroque towns such as **Ragusa** and **Modica**. Ragusa is the more prosperous provincial capital and is virtually two towns in one: Ragusa Ibla, a curious cocktail of medieval and baroque, and the 18th-century 'new' town, simply known as Ragusa. Ragusa was appropriately described by novelist Gesualdo Bufalino as *'un isola nell'isola'* (an island within an island) and its hushed streets, filled with *circolo* (men's clubs), are reminiscent of a more formal and sedate age. The lower town, Ibla, has most of the sights but transport and accommodation are in the newer upper town.

Like Noto, Ragusa boasts a sumptuous cathedral, the **Basilica San Giorgio** (Piazza del Duomo; admission free; ☺ 10am-1pm & 4-6pm) designed by the same architect, Rosario Gagliardi. This huge wedding-cake concoction is only surpassed by the magnificent **Chiesa San Giorgio** (admission free; ☺ 9am-noon & 4-7pm) in Modica. Gagliardi's masterpiece is a vision of pure rococo splendour perched at the top of a flight of 250 steps. These gentrified towns offer an insight into a less-troubled Sicily, where a prosperous farming industry has sustained a fairly happy and healthy local population. In October, Ragusa also hosts a yearly **Busker's Festival** in Giardino Ibleo.

Ragusa is accessible by not-so-regular trains from Syracuse (€5.70, 2¼ hours) and Noto (€4.25, 1¾ hours). Buses are better. **AST** (☎ 0932 68 18 18) runs regular services to Noto and Syracuse (€5.40, 2½ hours, seven daily). An AST timetable is posted at the spot on Piazza Gramsci where AST and SAIS buses stop.

City bus Nos 1 and 3 run from Piazza del Popolo in the upper town to Piazza Pola and the gardens in the lower town of

Ragusa Ibla. It's only a 10-minute walk down to Ragusa Ibla, but it will take you at least 30 minutes to ascend.

CENTRAL & SOUTHWESTERN SICILY

ENNA
pop 29,500

Remote and ethereal, Enna dominates the centre of the island, a natural crossroads separating the three main provinces of western, eastern and southern Sicily. A rich agricultural centre, Enna has long been the seat of a sacred cult of Demeter (the goddess of fertility) and throughout the Greek, Roman and Arab periods it supplied far-flung places with grain and wheat, cotton and cane – a tradition it continues on a smaller scale today. Taken by the unearthly beauty of the place, Ovid declared that here 'Nature decks herself in all her varied hues', and the rolling hills around Enna are filled with a profusion of flowers in the springtime. Jealously guarded, the town's massive Norman fortifications are the most obvious physical manifestation of the inward-looking nature of Sicily's mountain villages, close-knit societies full of religious confraternities and impenetrable silences – which, although ostensibly accessible to tourism, remain just beyond one's grasp.

Orientation

The principal road into the town is Via Pergusa, which eventually links with Via Roma, the main street of historic Enna. The intercity bus station is on Viale Diaz. To get to the town centre, turn right from the station and follow Viale Diaz to Corso Sicilia, turn right again and follow it to Via Sant'Agata to the left, which heads down to Via Roma.

Information

EMERGENCIES

Police Station (☎ 0935 52 21 11; Via San Giuseppe 2)

MEDICAL SERVICES

Farmacia del Centro (☎ 0935 50 06 50; Via Roma 315) Pharmacy.

Ospedale Civile Umberto I (☎ 0935 4 52 45, ☎ first aid 0935 50 08 96; Via Trieste)

MONEY

There are several banks with ATMs around the city centre.

Banco di Sicilia (Via Roma 367)

POST & TELEPHONE

Public telephones are scattered around the town.

Post Office (Via Volta 1; ☽ 8am-6.30pm Mon-Fri, 8am-12.30pm Sat)

TOURIST INFORMATION

Tourist Office (☎ 0935 52 82 88; Via Roma 413; ☽ 9am-1pm & 3.30-6.30pm Mon-Sat) Provides a map and information about the province.

Sights

Cloaked by mist for much of the year, the streets of Enna feel like they might just float away if it wasn't for the huge solid mass of the rampart walls and the steadying bulwark of **Castello di Lombardia** (☎ 0935 50 09 62; Piazza Mazzini; admission free; ☽ 9am-1pm & 3-5pm). Built by the Swabians and altered by Frederick III of Aragon, it was one of the most important defensive structures in medieval Sicily. It retains six of its original 20 towers, and the views from Torre Pisano (the tallest tower) are spectacular – you can make out Mt Etna in the distant northeast. Closer and across the valley rises the town of Calascibetta, erected by the Arabs in the 9th century. The castle is now part-theatre. Secret passageways once led to the octagonal **Torre di Federico** (Tower of Frederick II; Via Torre di Federico), also part of the town's old defence system.

Back along Via Roma, the 14th-century **cathedral** (admission free; ☽ 9am-1pm & 4-7pm) is an illustration of the waves of invaders who sought to possess this mountain eyrie. Graeco-Roman remains are overlaid with medieval walls, Gothic doors and apses, Renaissance artwork and baroque carvings such as the elaborate pulpit. Ironically, the iron gate to the sacristy was taken from the *seraglio* (women's quarters) in the Castello di Lombardia. Behind the cathedral is the **Museo Alessi** (☎ 0935 50 31 65; Via Roma; adult/concession €2.60/1.50; ☽ 8am-8pm), which houses the contents of the cathedral's treasury.

For a pleasant evening stroll, head for Piazza Francesco Crispi and wander along **Viale Marconi** to enjoy the view.

SICILY

Festivals & Events

APRIL

Holy Week A living reminder of Enna's esoteric past. Thousands of people wearing hoods and capes representing the town's different religious confraternities participate in a solemn procession to the cathedral. Undertones of pagan rites and occultism.

JULY/AUGUST

Festa di Maria Santissimi della Visitazione (2 July) An effigy of Enna's patron saint was traditionally dragged through the town by farmers wearing only a white band over their hips! Today the band has been replaced by a long sheet. The feast is accompanied by fireworks.

Castello di Lombardia The *castello* hosts nightly plays and performances of a medieval nature. Ask the tourist office for details.

Grand Prix (☎ 0935 2 56 60) Formula 3 racing at the Autodromo di Pergusa, 9km south of Enna. Take bus No 5.

Sleeping

Enna has only one hotel, the **Grande Albergo Sicilia** (☎ 0935 50 08 50; fax 0935 50 04 88; Piazza N Colajanni 7; s/d €57/91), a nice place with well-appointed rooms and good views of the surrounding countryside.

For other options, catch city bus No 5 from Piazza Vittorio Emanuele to Lago di Pergusa (a small, touristy lake with beaches about 10km south).

Eating

San Gennaro da Gino (☎ 0935 240 67; Viale Belvedere Marconi 6; meals €15; 12.30-3pm & 8pm-12.30am) A room with a view, this restaurant specialises in meat and vegetables. The antipasto is a must.

Ristorante Pizzeria L'Ariston (☎ 0935 2 60 38; Via Roma 353; pizza €4; 1-2.30pm & 8-10.30pm Mon-Sat) This is one of Enna's better restaurants with elegant decor and good solid food at very reasonable prices.

Ristorante Centrale (☎ 0935 50 09 63; Piazza VI Dicembre 9; meals €20; 12.30-3.30pm & 8-11pm) This place has friendly service and dishes up traditional Sicilian food, with a menu that changes daily.

There is a morning **market,** Monday to Saturday, on Via Mercato Sant'Antonio, where you can find fresh produce.

Getting There & Away

Buses arrive and leave from the **bus station** (☎ 0935 50 09 05; Viale Diaz). **SAIS Autolinee** (☎ 0935 50 09 02) has buses connecting Enna with Catania (€7, two hours, six daily Monday to Saturday) and Palermo (€8, two hour, nine daily). It is possible to reach Agrigento via Caltanissetta (€3.50, one hour, four daily Monday to Saturday). Regular SAIS buses also run to Piazza Armerina (€2.60, 45 minutes, eight daily). Don't take a train – the station is 5km away at the foot of the mountain-top town.

AROUND ENNA

Villa Romana del Casale

Situated in the environs of Piazza Armerina is the **Villa Imperiale** (☎ 0935 68 00 36; 5km from Piazza Armerina; admission €4.50; 8am-6.30pm), a stunning 3rd-century Roman villa and one of the few remaining relics of Roman Sicily. Probably a hunting lodge, the sumptuous villa is thought to have belonged to Diocletian's co-emperor Marcus Aurelius Maximianus. Buried under mud in a 12th-century flood, it remained hidden for 700 years before its magnificent floor mosaics were discovered in the 1950s. It is worth arriving early or during the lunch hour to avoid the hordes of tourist groups that descend on the villa.

Covering about 3500 sq metres, the villa was designed in line with the lie of the hill on which it stands, creating three main areas. The mosaics cover almost its entire floor and are considered unique for their fluid narrative style of composition, range of subject and variety of colour – many of them clearly influenced by African themes. The villa's centrepiece is a huge courtyard, which leads off to the differently themed rooms. Along the eastern end of this is the wonderful **Corridor of the Great Hunt** depicting chariots, rhinos, cheetahs and lions in rich golden colours. The stylised animals seem ready to jump out of the scene, watched by the voluptuously beautiful Queen of Sheba. On the other side of the corridor is a series of apartments, whose floor illustrations reproduce scenes from Homer. But perhaps the most captivating of the mosaics include the erotic depictions in what was probably a private apartment on the northern side of the great peristyle (colonnaded garden), and the villa's most notorious piece, **The Ten Maidens**, clad in what must have been the world's earliest bikinis.

The **tourist office** (☎ 0935 68 02 01; Via Cavour 15; 8am-2pm & 2.30-6pm Mon-Sat) in Piazza

Armerina, 5km away, hands out brochures of the villa with a floor plan and an explanation of the mosaics. Three **ATAN** (☎ 0935 68 22 72) buses leave for the villa from Piazza Senatore Marescalchi in Piazza Armerina (10am to 4pm daily, last return 4.30pm). If you have a car, you will be charged €1 to park outside the villa's entrance.

AGRIGENTO
pop 55,500

Busy, brutish, beleaguered Agrigento is Sicily's oldest tourist site (it was first put on the map by Goethe in the 18th century). In ancient times Pindar declared the people of Akragas 'built for eternity but feasted as if there were no tomorrow' – nowadays the modern town, with its savvy inhabitants, has more in common with the character rather than the aesthetics of its ancient counterpart. Overshadowed by towering modern apartment blocks on the hill above, the splendid Valle dei Templi (Valley of the Temples) loses much of its immediate impact and it is only when you get down among the ruins that you can appreciate their monumentality. Still the modern town – encasing its medieval predecessor – is one of the most lively and aggressive in Sicily and if you are up for Naples you will be able to handle the *furbo* (cunning) Agrigentans.

Orientation

Intercity buses arrive on Piazza Rosselli and the train station is slightly south on Piazza Marconi. Lying between Piazzale Aldo Moro and Piazza Pirandello is the main street of the medieval town, Via Atenea. Frequent city buses run to the Valle dei Templi below the town (see p760).

Information
EMERGENCIES
Ambulance (☎ 0922 40 13 44)
Police Station (☎ 0922 59 63 22; Piazzale Aldo Moro 2)

MEDICAL SERVICES
Azienda Ospedaliera San Giovanni di Dio
(☎ 0922 40 13 44; Via Giovanni XXII)

MONEY
Out of hours, there's a currency exchange booth at the post office and another at the train station.

Monte dei Paschi di Siena (Piazza Vittorio Emanuele 1) Has an ATM.

POST & TELEPHONE
Post Office (Piazza Vittorio Emanuele; ◷ 8.30am-6.30pm Mon-Sat)
Telecom Office (Via A de Gasperi 25, ◷ 9am-7pm Mon-Fri)

TOURIST INFORMATION
Tourist Office (☎ 0922 2 04 54; Via Cesare Battisti 15, ◷ 8.30am-1.30pm Mon-Fri) Staff have maps and brochures and little else.
Information Booth (Piazzale Aldo Moro, ◷ 9am-1pm & 3-7pm) More maps and a little more information, if pushed.
Information Booth (Valle dei Templi, adjacent to car park; ◷ 8am-7.30pm summer)

Valley of the Temples (Valle dei Templi)

Despite its name the five Doric temples stand along a ridge, designed to be visible from all around and a beacon for homecoming sailors. In varying states of ruin, the temples give a tantalising glimpse of what must truly have been on of the most luxurious cities in Magna Graecia. The most scenic time to come is in February and March when the valley is awash with almond blossom.

The **archaeological park** (☎ 0922 261 91; admission €2; ◷ 8.30am-1hr before sunset) is divided

---

ETHICS & AESTHETICS

Illegal construction (known as *abusivismo*) has long been a Mafia favourite for laundering money, and the province of Agrigento has suffered some of the worst excesses. In 2000, over 4,790 illegal houses sprang up in Sicily, a staggering figure that contributes to making Italy the largest consumer of concrete in the world. Ironically, tourism provides a strong incentive for such abuses as hotels and restaurants rake in far more money than picturesque farm land. Nowadays the country as a whole, and especially Sicily, has an unusual problem – there are simply too many houses for a declining population. In 2001 the government and local campaigners took extreme measures and bulldozed many of these illegal buildings – but the abuse still continues.

SICILY

AGRIGENTO

into two sections. East of Via dei Templi are the most spectacular temples. The first temple you will come to is **Tempio di Ercole** (Temple of Hercules), built towards the end of the 6th century BC and believed to be the oldest of the temples. Eight of its 38 columns were raised in 1924 to reveal a structure that was roughly the same size as the Parthenon. The magnificent **Tempio della Concordia** (Temple of Concord) is the only one to survive relatively intact. Built around 440 BC, it was transformed into a Christian church in the 6th century AD. Its name is taken from a Roman inscription found nearby. The **Tempio di Giunone** (Temple of Juno) stands high on the edge of the ridge, a five-minute walk to the east. Part of its colonnade remains

and there is an impressive sacrificial altar. This section of the valley is open to 11pm.

Across Via dei Templi, to the west, is what remains of the massive **Tempio di Giove** (Temple of Jupiter), never actually completed and now totally in ruins. It covered an area 112m by 56m with columns 20m high. Between the columns stood *telamoni* (colossal statues), one of which was reconstructed and is now in the Museo Archeologico. A copy lies on the ground among the ruins, giving an idea of the immense size of the structure. Work began on the temple around 480 BC and it was probably destroyed during the Carthaginian invasion in 406 BC. The nearby **Tempio di Castore e Polluce** (Temple of Castor and Pollux) was partly reconstructed in the 19th century, although probably using pieces from other constructions. All the temples are atmospherically lit up at night.

The **Museo Archeologico** (☎ 0922 40 15 65, ☎ 0922 49 72 21; Via dei Templi, Contrada San Nicola; admission €4.50; ☷ 9am-1.30pm), just north of the temples, has a collection of artefacts from the area worth inspecting.

Medieval Agrigento

Roaming around the town's narrow, winding streets is relaxing after a day among the temples. The **Chiesa di Santa Maria dei Greci** (Salita Santa Maria dei Greci; admission free; ☷ 8am-noon & 3-6pm Mon-Sat), uphill from Piazza Lena (at the end of Via Atenea), is an 11th-century Norman church built on the site of a 5th-century-BC Greek temple. Note the remains of the wooden Norman ceiling and some Byzantine frescoes. If the church is closed, check with the custodian at Salita Santa Maria dei Greci 1, who'll open the doors for you (with a tip expected).

A not-so-relaxing walk further uphill leads to the fragile-looking **cathedral** (Via Duomo; admission free; ☷ 9am-noon & 4-7pm). Built in AD 1000, it has been restructured many times, and is dedicated to the Norman San Gerlando. The unfinished campanile was erected in the 15th century and the panelled ceiling inside dates from the 17th century.

Back towards Piazza Vittorio Emanuele, the **Monastero del Santo Spirito** was founded by Cistercian nuns at the end of the 13th century. Giacomo Serpotta is responsible for the stuccoes in the chapel. There is a small ethnographic **museum** (☎ 0922 59 03 71; Via Foderà; admission free; ☷ 9am-1pm & 4-7pm Mon-Sat) above the old church. You can buy cakes and pastries from the nuns here (see p760).

Festivals & Events

Agrigento's big annual shindig is the **Sagra del Mandorlo in Fiore**, a folk festival set on the first Sunday in February with open-air performances of drama and music staged in the Valle dei Templi.

The **Festa di San Calógero**, on the first Sunday in July, commemorates San Calógero, who saved Agrigento from the plague. Spectators throw spiced loaves of bread at a statue of the saint.

Sleeping

Rapacious tourism has made the modern town expensive and the services lousy. Most of Agrigento's better hotels are out of town around the Valle dei Templi or near the sea.

B&B Atenea 191 (☎ 0922 271 23; Via Atenea 191; r per person with breakfast €30) Due to open in summer 2003, a sneak preview revealed well-decorated rooms (some with ceiling frescoes, others with views over the valley), a huge communal kitchen and, unusually, access for the disabled. This place is right in the centre of town and will certainly be a welcome addition to the rather dreary hotel scene in medieval Agrigento.

Antica Foresteria Catalana (☎ 0922 204 35; Piazza Lena 5; s/d €45/75; ✸) A new venture by the owners of the Bella Napoli hotel (located virtually next door), the Catalana purports to be more upmarket and is thus more expensive. However, although it is newer than the Napoli and as a result offers slightly better accommodation, it hardly lives up to its fancy business card.

Hotel Akrabello (☎ 0922 60 62 77; fax 0922 60 61 86; Parco Angeli; s/d €78/114; P ✸ ✺) The modern and comfortable Akrabello is in the Parco Angeli area, east of the temples. The rooms all have mod cons and there are tennis courts to boot.

Hotel Kaos (☎ 0922 59 86 22; fax 0922 59 87 70; Contrada L Pirandello; s/d €104/165; P ✸ ✺) This large resort complex in a restored villa is by the sea, about 2km from the temples. It is a good choice if you have your own car.

Foresteria Baglio della Luna (☎ 0922 51 10 61; bagliodellaluna@tin.it; Contrada Maddalusa; d €233; P ✸) This handsome converted *baglio* lies in the middle of the Valle dei Templi and is Agrigento's best hotel. The interior is tastefully decorated with antiques and chintz and there is a good restaurant.

There are some good camp sites by the sea at San Leone, a few kilometres south of Agrigento. Take bus No 2 or 2/ from Agrigento or drive down Via dei Templi, continue along Viale Emporium towards the sea and turn left at Lungomare Akragas.

Camping Nettuno (☎ 0922 41 62 68; Viale Le Dune, San Leone; person/tent €5/5) Open year-round, this camp site is situated on a magnificent stretch of golden sand, within cycling distance (5km) of the Valle dei Templi. A map is available from the English-speaking staff at reception. It also has a market, bar and pizzeria.

Eating & Drinking

Da Giovanni (☎ 0922 2 11 10; Piazzetta Vadalá 2; meals €30; ☺ noon-3.30pm & 8-11pm Tue-Sat) With piazza seating, smooth service and mind-blowing cassata (cake filled with ricotta cheese, chocolate and candied fruits), this is a great restaurant if you want to treat yourself.

La Corte degli Sfizzi (☎ 0922 59 55 20; Via Atenea 4; meals €10; ☺ 11am-3.30pm & 7pm-midnight, closed Wed winter) A trendy pizzeria with several good-value set menus and a garden setting.

Manhattan Trattoria (☎ 0922 2 09 11; Salita Santa Maria degli Angeli 9; mains €8; ☺ noon-3pm & 7.30-10.30pm Mon-Sat) If it's a pizza or light lunch you're after, the Manhattan, in a steep street off Via Atenea, is a good choice.

Kalos (☎ 0922 2 63 89; Piazza San Calógero; meals €35; ☺ 12.30-3.30pm & 7.30-11pm Mon-Sat) This is a top-end restaurant close to the centre of town serving excellent *involtini di pesce spada* (rolled swordfish in breadcrumbs). It only picks up later in the evening.

Café Girasole (Via Atenea 68-70; ☺ 11am-midnight Mon-Sat) A popular wine bar in the heart of the medieval town. Light table snacks are served with cocktails and wine and it has a busy atmosphere and some outdoor seating.

Monastero del Santo Spirito (Via Foderà) For the best pastries, and just for the experience, go to the end of Via Foderà. The nuns in this convent have been baking heavenly *dolce di mandorle* (almond cakes and pastries) to a secret recipe for centuries. Press the door bell (to the right of the entrance to the convent/museum) and say 'Vorrei comprare qualche dolce' – and see how you go.

The daily **produce market** is held on Piazza San Francesco.

Getting There & Away

BUS

For most destinations, bus is the easiest way to get to and from Agrigento. The intercity bus station is on Piazza Rosselli, just off Piazza Vittorio Emanuele, and tickets and timetables for most services are available at the ticket booth on the piazza. The tourist office also has timetables.

Autoservizi Cuffaro (☎ 0922 41 82 31) runs buses to Palermo (€6.70, two hours, seven daily). **Lumia** (☎ 0922 2 04 14) has departures to Trapani (€9.30, three daily Monday to

Saturday). **SAIS** (☎ 0922 59 52 60; Via Ragazzi del '99 12) buses serve Catania (€9.80, 2½ hours, 11 daily), and Caltanissetta (€4.20, one hour, 13 daily Monday to Saturday).

CAR & MOTORCYCLE

Agrigento is easily accessible by road from all of Sicily's main towns. The S189 links the town with Palermo, while the S115 runs along the coast, northwest towards Sciacca and southeast for Gela and eventually Syracuse. For Enna, take the S640 via Caltanissetta. There is plenty of parking on Piazza Vittorio Emanuele in the centre.

TRAIN

Trains run to Palermo (€6.70, two hours, 11 daily), Catania (€8.90, 3½ hours, three daily) and Enna. For Palermo, the train is fine, if a little slow. For anywhere else the bus is recommended.

Getting Around

City buses run down to the Valle dei Templi and the beach at San Leone from in front of the train station. For the Valle dei Templi take bus No 1, 1/, 2, 2/ (every 30 minutes) or 3 and get off at either the museum or further downhill at Piazzale dei Templi. Bus No 2 and 2/ will take you on to San Leone.

The Linea Verde (green line) bus runs every hour from the train station to the cathedral, for those who prefer not to make the uphill walk. Tickets cost €0.77 and are valid for 1½ hours.

SELINUNTE

The ruins of Selinunte are some of the most impressive ruins in Sicily and are more atmospherically situated than those at Agrigento. The huge city was built (628 BC) on hills immediately above the sea, and for two-and-a-half centuries it was one of the richest and most powerful in the world. The spectacular remains of its many temples are proof of its influence. It was destroyed by the Carthaginians in 409 BC and finally fell to the Romans in about 350 BC when it went into rapid decline and disappeared from historical accounts. Its temples were then further damaged by earthquake.

Sights

The **ruins** (admission €4.50; ☺ 9am-1 hr before sunset) are extremely impressive: vast fragments of

Doric columns have been hurled about in all directions and colossal piles of carved marble lie where once the massive temples stood. The city's past is so remote that the names of the various temples have been forgotten and they are now identified by the letters A to G, M and O. Five are huddled together in the acropolis at the western end of the site, accessible by road from the ticket office, or on foot across the depression known as the Gorgo di Cottone – once Selinunte's harbour.

The most impressive, **Temple E**, has been partially rebuilt: its columns pieced together from their fragments with part of its tympanum. Many of the carvings, particularly from **Temple C**, are now on display in the archaeological museum in Palermo. Their quality is on a par with the Elgin marbles from Athen's Parthenon and clearly demonstrates the high artistic and cultural levels reached by many Greek colonies in Sicily.

No visit to Selinunte is complete without a walk along the **beach** below the city, from where there are marvellous panoramas of the temples. The path down is to the left of the parking area.

There is an **information office** (☎ 094 4 62 77; ⏰ 8am-8pm Mon-Sat, 9am-noon & 3-6pm Sun) just outside the entrance to the site.

Sleeping & Eating

Selinunte is close to the village of Marinella di Selinunte, where you can find accommodation.

Hotel Garzia (☎ 0924 4 66 60; fax 0924 4 61 96; Via Pigafetta 6; s/d €45/80; 🌐) With nice rooms on the seafront and good facilities, this is the best value in its class here.

Hotel Alceste (☎ 0924 4 61 84; fax 0924 4 61 43; Via Alceste 21; s/d €65/85; P 🌐) This place has some of the more upmarket rooms around as well as disabled access.

Il Maggiolino (☎ /fax 0924 4 60 44; magiol@potin.it; Località Marinella di Selinunte; person/tent €7/8) This is one of a couple of camp sites in the area. It has an eating area and disabled access. It is located on the S115, as you come into Selinunte.

There are some pleasant little restaurants along the beachfront.

Lido Azzurro (☎ 0924 4 62 11; Via Marco Polo 51; meals €25; ⏰ closed Sun & Mon) Also known as Baffo's, this eatery serves good pizza,

pasta and fresh seafood virtually beside the water's edge.

Getting There & Away

Regular AST buses link Selinunte and Marinella di Selinunte to Castelvetrano (€0.77, five daily), which can be reached by bus from Agrigento, Mazara del Vallo, Marsala and Trapani. Very slow trains also run from Palermo and Trapani to Castelvetrano. The tourist office has timetables.

NORTHWESTERN SICILY

MARSALA
pop 80,000

Best known for its sweet dessert wines, Marsala is a surprisingly pleasant town with an interesting historic centre. If you have a car, it's a good alternative to Trapani as a base for exploring Sicily's northwest. Founded as Lilybaeum on Cape Lilibeo by Carthaginians who had fled nearby Mothia (Mozia or Motya) after its destruction by Syracuse, the city was eventually conquered by the Arabs, who renamed it Marsa Allah (Port of God). It was at Marsala that Garibaldi landed with his One Thousand in 1860.

Information

Police Station (☎ 0923 92 43 71; Via Gramsci)

Hospital (☎ 0923 71 60 31, emergencies ☎ 0923 95 14 10; Piazza San Francesco)

Tourist Office (☎ 0923 71 40 97; Via XI Maggio 100; ⏰ 8am-2pm & 3-8pm Mon-Sat, 9am-noon Sun)

Information Booth (Lungomare Boeo; ⏰ 8am-2pm & 4-8pm Tue-Sun, mornings only Mon Jun-Sep) Next to the Museo Archeologico Regionale Baglio Anselmi.

Sights & Activities

Marsala's finest treasure, and worth the trip alone, is the partially reconstructed **Carthaginian warship** in the **Museo Archeologico Regionale Baglio Anselmi** (☎ 0923 95 25 35; Lungomare Boeo; admission €2; ⏰ 9am-1.30pm Mon, Tue & Thu, 9am-1.30pm & 4-6.30pm Wed, Fri, Sat & Sun). Sunk off the Egadi Islands during the First Punic War nearly 3000 years ago, this huge, strangely delicate ship is the only remaining physical evidence of the Phoenician seafaring superiority in the 3rd century BC. After visiting the excavations on Mothia (p763) the ship resonates with history, giving the slightest glimpse into a civilisation that was quite literally extinguished by the Romans after their victory over Carthage (Tunisia). North of the museum, along Viale Vittorio Veneto, is the partly excavated **Insula Romana** (closed at the time of research, due to reopen summer 2003), which was a 3rd-century AD Roman house.

Damaged during the war, Marsala's other sights are limited to the **Museo degli Arazzi Fiammingi** (☎ 0923 71 29 03; Via Garaffa 57; adult/student €1.50/0.50; ☺ 9am-1pm & 4-6pm Tue-Sun), which displays eight 16th-century Flemish tapestries, woven for the Spanish King Philip II and depicting scenes from the war of Titus against the Jews. The magnificent adjoining **cathedral** (under scaffolding at the time of writing) on Piazza della Repubblica was built in the 17th and 18th centuries.

Tipplers should head to **Cantine Florio** (☎ 0923 78 11 11; fax 0923 98 23 80; Lungomare Florio; ☺ 9am-1pm & 2.30-5pm Mon-Thu, 9am-1pm Fri) on

the road to Mazara del Vallo (bus No 16 from Piazza del Popolo). This is the place to buy the cream of Marsala's wines. Florio opens its doors to visitors to explain the process of making Marsala and to give you a taste of the goods (fax to make a reservation for one of the free tours). Pellegrino, Rallo, Mavis and Intorcia are four of the other producers in the same area, and all have an *enoteca* (wine bar) where you can select a bottle or two (usually open from about 9am to 12.30pm). Booking is recommended; ask the tourist office.

If you're travelling with small children, you might enjoy a break in the **Villa Cavalotti**, a large park just outside Porta Nuova with a playground and acres of space for a relaxing walk.

Festivals & Events
Preceding Trapani's Easter extravaganza, Marsala's **Processione del Giovedí** (Holy Thursday Procession) depicts the events leading up to Christ's crucifixion.

Held in the historic centre in July, the **Marsala Jazz Festival** is sponsored by Marsala wine companies and increasingly attracts major artists.

Sleeping & Eating
Marsala has few hotels within the city centre; most tend to be on the roads exiting the city.

Hotel Garden (☎ /fax 0923 98 23 20; Via Gambini 36; s/d without bathroom €30/51) A run-down exterior disguises the newly renovated Hotel Garden, one of the only centrally located hotels in Marsala.

Baglio Vajarassa (☎ /fax 0923 96 86 28; Contrada Spagnola 176; d B&B/half board €75/100) A great choice if you have a car is the seven-bedroom Vajarassa. It's in a traditional manor house 6km north of Marsala, near Mothia.

Delfino Beach Hotel (☎ 0923 75 10 76; delfino@ delfinobeach.com; Via Lungomare Mediterraneo 672; s/d €80/130; P) South of Marsala, the sumptuous Delfino is situated overlooking the sea near a wonderful sandy beach. The rooms are tastefully decorated and have marble bathrooms.

Trattoria Garibaldi (☎ 0923 95 30 06; Via Rubbino 35; mains €6; ☺ 12.30-2.30pm & 8-10.30pm Mon-Fri, 8-10.30pm Sat, 12.30-2.30pm Sun) This place is a reliable trattoria serving hearty Sicilian fare and is popular with the locals.

SICILY

THE BOY OF MOTHIA

In 1979 the statue of a young boy was discovered on the island of San Pantaleo, lying on its back in the dirt, headless, armless and legless. The head was found nearby, and its restoration completed one of the greatest surviving Greek sculptures in the world.

Carved in the early 5th century BC from imported Anatolian marble from Turkey, the statue of the young boy is unique, namely because he is clothed in a sensual long tunic, cinched around his chest with a wide band. Hundreds of delicate vertical grooves render the gossamer fabric realistic as it clings to his muscular body as he stands askance, hand on hip, his fingers visibly pressing into his flesh. Compared with the usual robust, vigorous nudity of other Greek sculpture of the period the boy is extraordinarily graceful and sensuous, capturing the ineffable physical ease of a young boy on the brink of manhood.

The enigma for scholars is that nothing comparable was to come out of ancient Greece for hundreds of years and, when it did, the delicate tension between grace and strength visible in the Boy of Mothia had vanished. What is even more remarkable is that this extremely fine work of art should be housed in a tiny museum on the small island of San Pantaleo.

Capo Lilybeo (☎ 0923 71 28 81; Via Lungomare Boeo 40; meals €25; ♈ 12.30-3pm & 8-10.30pm Tue-Sat, 12.30-3pm Sun) With very good food and delightful sea views, this is the place to come if you feel like treating yourself, especially on a sunny day.

Getting There & Away
Buses head for Marsala from Trapani (AST or Lumia, €2.60, 30 minutes, four daily), Agrigento (Lumia, €6.60, 3½ hours, three daily) and Palermo (Salemi, €7.25, 2½ hours, half-hourly). Palermo buses arrive at Piazza del Popolo, off Via Mazzini, in the centre of town. All other buses stop on Piazza Pizzo. The Agrigento buses generally stop at Castelvetrano, from where you can get another to Selinunte.

Trains serve Marsala from Trapani (€2.30, 30 minutes) and Palermo (€6.70), although from the latter you have to change at Alcamo (nine per day Monday to Saturday, two Sunday).

Between June and September, **Sandokan** (☎ 0923 71 20 60, ☎ 0923 95 34 34) runs a boat service from Molo Dogana to the Egadi Islands (€13.45 return to Favignana). Ustica Lines also runs daily hydrofoils (€6.70 to Favignana and Levanzo).

NEAR MARSALA & TRAPANI
The site of ancient **Mothia** (also known as Motya or Mozia), on the island of San Pantaleo in the Stagnone lagoon, is about 11km north along the scenic coast from Marsala. The island and lagoon form part of the **Riserva Naturale di Stagnone**, a wetlands area with a large population of water birds. Mothia was the site of one of the most important Phoenician settlements in the Mediterranean, coveted for its strategic position and eventually destroyed by Dionysius the Elder, tyrant of Syracuse, in 379 BC. The island is accessible by a ferry (€3 return), which operates 9am to around 6pm (mornings only in winter).

Today, it is the island's picturesque position in the saltpans, dotted with windmills, that attracts visitors. At the end of the pier is **Museo Saline Ettore e Inferza** (☎ 0923 96 69 36; admission €2.60; ♈ 9.30am-6pm), a museum demonstrating salt extraction. It also rents canoes (€5.50/hour; summer) so you can weave your way in and out of the saltpans. A local bus (No 4, direction Birgi) runs between Marsala's Piazza del Popolo and the ferry landing.

Little remains of the city of Mothia, but it is interesting to follow the path around the island to the various excavations, including the ancient port and dry dock. Note the submerged road at the port, which connects the island to the mainland. The island is home to the **Whitaker Museum** (☎ 0923 71 25 98; admission €6; ♈ 9am-1pm & 3-6pm Apr-Oct, 9am-3pm Nov-Mar), first established by Joseph Whitaker, a rich English entrepreneur who started the excavations on the island and established the small museum. Its main treasure is **Il Giovinetto di Mozia** (see the boxed text, p762), a sensuous 5th-century-BC sculpture of a young boy – one of the best examples of Greek sculpture in the world.

TRAPANI
pop 72,500
Arriving in Trapani through extensive and unattractive suburbs, one's first impression is of an uninspiring town that has suffered some of the worst abuses of unchecked Mafia construction. However, once ensconced in the tight-knit historic centre it is easy to be charmed by the laid-back Moorish atmosphere of what is, essentially, a large Arab fishing village. Situated on an attractive curving spit of land, Trapani sits opposite the Egadi Islands and is a good base from which to explore the northwest. From the ancient Greek city of Segesta and the medieval town of Erice to the beaches of the Golfo di Castellammare and the Riserva Naturale dello Zingaro, this small corner is a smorgasbord of Sicily's main delights.

Orientation
The main bus station is on Piazza Montalto, with the train station around the corner on Piazza Umberto I. The cheaper hotels are in the heart of the old centre, about 500m west. Make for Piazza Scarlatti down Corso Italia. The narrow streets of the old part of town can be a nightmare to negotiate if you're driving, so head for the port and park near there.

Information
EMERGENCIES
Police Station (☎ 0923 59 81 11; Piazza V Veneto)

MEDICAL SERVICES
Emergency Doctor (☎ 0923 2 96 29; Piazza Generale Scio 1)

SICILY

Ospedale Sant'Antonio Abate (☎ 0923 80 91 11, casualty ☎ 0923 80 94 50; Via Cosenza)

Telecom Office (Via Agostino Pepoli 82, ⊗ 9am-12.30pm & 4.30-8pm Mon-Sat)

INTERNET ACCESS
Prices from €5 per hour.
Internet Centre (Stazione Marettima) 1st floor in the ferry terminal; also a phone centre.
World Sport Line (Via Regina Elena 26-28)

TOURIST INFORMATION
Tourist Office (☎ 0923 2 90 00; www.apt.trapani.it, Italian only; Piazzetta Saturno1/2; ⊗ 8am-8pm Mon-Sat, 9am-noon Sun) This well-organised and friendly office gets the prize for the most hard-working tourist office in Sicily.

MONEY
There are several banks in the town with ATMs.
Banca di Roma (Corso Italia 38) Has an ATM.
Monte dei Paschi di Siena (Via XXX Gennaio 80)

TRAVEL AGENCIES
Egatours (☎ 0923 2 17 54; Via Ammiraglio Staiti 13) For bus and ferry tickets.
Salvo Viaggi (☎ 0923 54 54 55; Corso Italia 48)

POST & TELEPHONE
Post Office (Piazza V Veneto; ⊗ 8am-6.30pm Mon-Sat)

Sights
The narrow network of streets in Trapani's historic centre remain a Moorish labyrinth,

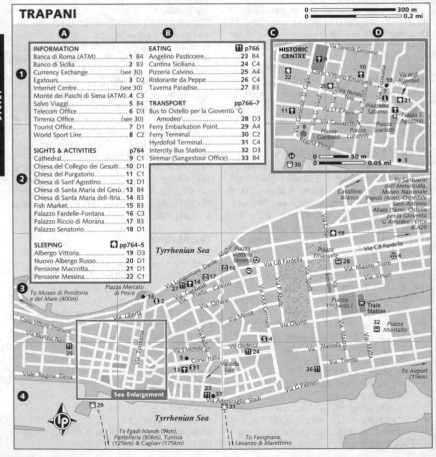

TRAPANI

0 — 300 m
0 — 0.2 mi

INFORMATION
Banca di Roma (ATM)................1 B4
Banco di Sicilia.........................2 B3
Currency Exchange..............(see 30)
Egatours...................................3 D2
Internet Centre.....................(see 30)
Monte dei Paschi di Siena (ATM)..4 C3
Salvo Viaggi.............................5 B4
Telecom Office.........................6 D3
Tirrenia Office.......................(see 30)
Tourist Office...........................7 D1
World Sport Line......................8 C2

SIGHTS & ACTIVITIES p764
Cathedral................................9 C1
Chiesa del Collegio dei Gesuiti...10 D1
Chiesa del Purgatorio..............11 C1
Chiesa di Sant'Agostino...........12 D1
Chiesa di Santa Maria del Gesù..13 B4
Chiesa di Santa Maria dell'Itria...14 B3
Fish Market.............................15 B3
Palazzo Fardelle-Fontana.........16 C3
Palazzo Riccio di Morana.........17 B3
Palazzo Senatorio....................18 D1

SLEEPING pp764-5
Albergo Vittoria......................19 D3
Nuovo Albergo Russo..............20 D1
Pensione Maccotta..................21 D1
Pensione Messina....................22 C1

EATING p766
Angelino Pasticcere.................23 B4
Cantina Siciliana.....................24 C4
Pizzeria Calvino......................25 A4
Ristorante da Peppe.................26 C4
Taverna Paradiso.....................27 B3

TRANSPORT pp766-7
Bus to Ostello per la Gioventù 'G
    Amodeo'...........................28 D3
Ferry Embarkation Point...........29 A4
Ferry Terminal.........................30 C2
Hyrdofoil Terminal...................31 C4
Intercity Bus Station................32 D3
Siremar (Sangestour Office)......33 B4

HISTORIC CENTRE
Via Tenente Genovese
Corso Vittorio Emanuele
Via degli Argentieri
Via Generale D. Giglio
Via Verdi
Via Nunzio Nasi
Via S F d'Assisi
Piazzetta Saturno
Piazza S Agostino
Via Cassaretto
Piazza Scarlatti
Piazza Garibaldi
Piazza Lucatelli
Via Regina Elena
0 — 50 m
0 — 0.05 mi

Tyrrhenian Sea

Cavallino Bianco

To Santuario dell'Annunziata, Museo Nazionale Pepoli (4km), Ospedale Sant-Antonio Abate (5km), Ostello per la Gioventù 'G Amodeo', Erice & A29

Via Crispi
Piazza Vittorio Veneto
Via GB Fardella
Piazza Emanuele
Via GB Fardella
Via Marino Torre
Via Spalti
Via Vespri

Tyrrhenian Sea

Via Lungomare Dante Alighieri
Piazza Mercato di Pesce
Via Garibaldi
Via Poeta Calvino
Via Orfane
Via XXX Gennaio
Via P Abate
Via Scontrino

To Museo di Preistoria e del Mare (400m)

Corso Vittorio Emanuele
Via Nunzio Nasi
Viale Regina Elena
Via Libertà
Via Torrearsa
Via S Michele
Corso Italia
Via della Luce
Via Giudecca
Via Merce
Via Osorio

Piazza Umberto I
Train Station
32 Piazza Montalto

Via Marinella
Via Marsala
Via Trento
Via Malta

To Airport (15km)

Via G Palmeri
Via Ammiraglio Staiti

Tyrrhenian Sea

To Egadi Islands (9km), Pantelleria (80km), Tunisia (125km) & Cagliari (175km)

To Favignana, Levanzo & Marettimo

See Enlargement

although they take much of their character from the fabulous 18th-century baroque of the Spanish period – a catalogue of examples can be found down the pedestrianised **Via Garibaldi**, most notably the Palazzo Riccio di Morana and Palazzo Fardelle Fontana. The best time to walk down here is in the early evening (7pm) when the *passeggiata* is in full swing.

Trapani's other main street is Corso Vittorio Emanuele, where you will find the imposing **cathedral** (admission free; ☺ 8am-4pm), with its baroque facade and iced-Christmas-cake-style stuccoed interior, and the elaborate facade of the **Palazzo Senatorio**, with its columns and clocks. Off the corso, south along Via Generale Dom Giglio, **Chiesa del Purgatorio** (☎ 0923 56 28 82; Via D'Assisi; admission free; ☺ 9am-noon & 4-7pm) houses the Misteri, 18th-century life-sized wooden figures depicting Christ's Passion. On Good Friday they are carried in procession (see the boxed text, this page).

Trapani's major sight is the 14th-century **Santuario dell'Annunziata** (☎ 0923 53 91 84; Via Conte Agostino Pepoli; admission free; ☺ 7am-noon & 4-7pm), some way from the centre on Via A Pepoli. Remodelled in baroque style in the 17th century, it retains its original Gothic rose window and doorway. The Cappella della Madonna, behind the high altar, contains the venerated Madonna di Trapani, carved, it's thought, by Nino Pisano.

Adjacent to the Santuario dell'Annunziata, in a former Carmelite monastery, is the **Museo Nazionale Pepoli** (☎ 0923 55 32 69; Via Conte Agostino Pepoli 2000; admission €4.50; ☺ 9am-1.30pm Mon-Sat plus 3-6.30pm Tue & Thu, 9am-12.30pm Sun). It has an archaeological collection, numerous statues by Antonella Gagini and some exquisite coral carvings unique to Trapani.

Trapani's other museum is the **Museo di Preistoria e del Mare** (☎ 0923 2 23 00; Via Torre di Ligny; admission €1.50; ☺ 9.30am-12.30pm) at the tip of the promontory in the Spanish fortress Torre di Ligny. It houses a collection of prehistoric artefacts and medieval objects recovered from shipwrecks off the coast. From the top of the tower there are great views over the town.

Festivals & Events

I Misteri (the Procession of the Misteri) begins the Tuesday before Easter Sunday and reaches its climax Good Friday afternoon (see boxed text).

I MISTERI

Sicily's most venerated Easter procession is a four-day festival of extraordinary religious fervour. Since the 17th century, the ordinary citizens of Trapani – represented by 20 traditional *maestranze* or guilds – have begun the celebration of the Passion of Christ on the Tuesday before Easter Sunday. The festival begins with the procession of a remarkable, life-sized wooden statue of the Virgin Mary.

Over the course of the next three evenings, processions make their way through the old quarter and port to a temporary chapel in Piazza Lucatelli specially erected for the celebrations, where the icons are stored overnight. Each statue is carried on the shoulders of the town's men and is accompanied by barefoot women and a local band, which plays dirges to the slow, steady beat of a drum.

The high point of the celebration is on Friday, when the 20 guilds emerge from the Chiesa del Purgatorio and descend the steps of the church carrying each of the statues, to begin the 1km-long all-night procession up to Via GB Fardella and back to the church the following morning. The massive crowds that gather to witness the slow march often reach a peak of delirious fervour.

Sleeping

Ostello per la Gioventù G Amodeo (☎ /fax 0923 55 29 64; Strada Provinciale Trapani-Erice, Contrada Raganzili; dm €13; ☺ year-round) This hostel gets a good report from its guests. Six kilometres north of the train station on the Erice road, it's a 15-minute ride on bus No 23 from Via GB Fardella to the Ospedale Villa dei Gerani. From there, turn right and then take the second right and walk about 500m uphill.

Pensione Messina (☎ 0923 2 11 98; Corso Vittorio Emanuele 71; s/d without shower €15/30, breakfast €3.50) The hilarious Pensione Messina, situated in a 17th-century building, is run by an ancient Trapanesi couple. It is cheap and basic but very central and a real insight into 1950s Italy. Beware of being let in by an irascible old guy in his dressing-gown – he's your host!

Pensione Maccotta (☎ 0923 2 84 18; albergo maccota@comeg.it; Via degli Argentieri 4; d €55; ⊠) Located near Piazza S Agostino, this small place is probably the most centrally located in Trapani. Its renovated rooms are clean and comfortable but you almost need shades for the blindingly white corridors.

Nuovo Albergo Russo (☎ 0923 2 21 66; fax 0923 2 66 23; Via Tintori 4; s/d €40/75; ✖) With gilded antiques in the lobby and a classic 1950s vibe in some of the rooms, this place is slightly more upmarket than Trapani's other options.

Albergo Vittoria (☎ 0923 87 30 44; fax 0923 2 98 70; Via Francesco Crispi 40; s/d €52/78) The rooms here are spotlessly clean and come with swish bathrooms. The management is extremely friendly and some rooms have a view of the sea. Breakfast is an additional €5.

Eating

Sicily's Arab heritage and Trapani's unique position on the sea route to Tunisia has made couscous (or cuscus/kuscus as they spell it around here) something of a speciality, particularly when served with a fish sauce that includes tomatoes, garlic and parsley.

Cantina Siciliana (☎ 0923 2 86 73; Via Giudecca 52; meals €15; ✖ 12.30-3pm & 8.30-11pm) This rustic trattoria has a limited but finely tuned menu. The service is extremely friendly and the desserts with Passito di Pantelleria (a sweet dessert wine) are heavenly.

Pizzeria Calvino (☎ 0923 2 14 64; Via N Nasi 77; pizza from €3.50; ✖ 7pm-midnight Wed-Mon) You

can't get a much better recommendation than being told this place (towards the port off Corso Vittorio Emanuele) is the town's favourite takeaway pizza spot.

Ristorante da Peppe (☎ 0923 2 82 46; Via Spalti 50; meals €20; ✖ 12.30-3pm & 7.30-11pm Tue-Sat) Lots of stained glass and fresh seafood, and in particular tuna specialities from May to early July. It has a justifiably good reputation.

Angelino Pasticcere (☎ 0923 2 80 64; Via A Staiti 87; ✖ 9am-6pm) This lovely little café serves a delicious array of cakes, chocolates, Sicilian sweets and light savoury meals. Opposite the hydrofoil dock, it's a great place to pick up a snack before heading off to the islands.

An open-air **fish market** is held Monday to Saturday morning on Piazza Mercato di Pesce, on the northern waterfront. The area around Piazza Lucatelli is a pleasant place for a sandwich and coffee.

Getting There & Around

AIR

Trapani has a small airport (TPS), 16km out of town at Birgi. AST buses leave from Piazza Montalto to coincide with flights. **Segesta** (☎ 091 34 20 55) has a daily bus for the island's main airport, Falcone-Borsellino, at Punta Raisi west of Palermo. Its timetable changes regularly, so check with the tourist office.

BOAT

Siremar (☎ 0923 54 54 55; www.siremar.it, Italian only; Via Ammiraglio Staiti 61) runs ferries and hydrofoils to Favignana (€3.10/5.20 ferry/hydrofoil) and Levanzo. The journey to Marettimo is much further and takes nearly three hours by ferry (€7) and one hour by hydrofoil (€11.70). Siremar also runs a daily ferry to Pantelleria (€25.70 one way for a *poltrona*, or airline-style seat, six hours) at midnight June to September (with a reduced service the rest of the year). The boat returns (usually) at noon, reaching Trapani at 4.45pm.

Ustica Lines (☎ 0923 2 22 00; www.usticalines.it, Italian only; Via Ammiraglio Staiti 23) runs regular hydrofoils to Favignana (€5.08, 20 minutes), Levanzo (€5.08, 20 minutes) and Marettimo (€10.45, one hour, three per day June to September) as well as a service from Naples to Trapani (€83 one way, once a day, three days a week June to September). It also has a ferry to Pantelleria (€34). Get tickets at **Egatours** (Via Ammiraglio Staiti 13),

---

THE AUTHOR'S CHOICE

Taverna Paradiso (☎ 0923 87 37 51; Lungomare Dante Alighieri 24; meals €30; ✖ noon-3pm & 8pm-1am Feb-Dec) Deceptively hidden behind workshop shutters is Taverna Paradiso, Trapani's best restaurant and arguably one of the best in Sicily. The taverna serves up excellent seafood dishes in what is almost a paean to Trapani's vanishing history as a fishing port. Dolce and Gabbana-clad women and besuited, bejewelled men gorge themselves on the seafood specialities, surrounded by paintings depicting the ancient mattanza slaughter (see p769). The atmosphere is heavily charged by influential patrons who all know the host and receive warm and personal attention, almost to the exclusion of other diners. During the mattanza season, late in the evening the tables are cleared for traditional music. Reservations are essential, as is appropriate dress.

or directly at the Ustica Lines embarkation point (on the seafront).

Tirrenia (☎ 0923 52 18 96; www.tirrenia.it; Stazione Marettima) runs weekly ferries to Tunisia from Trapani (€51.38 for a *poltrona*, €63.78 for a bed in a 2nd-class cabin), leaving at 10am on Monday. The return boat leaves Tunisia at 9pm Monday. There is also a weekly Tirrenia service to Cagliari (€38.21 for a *poltrona*, €51.64 for a bed in a 2nd-class cabin), leaving at 9pm on Tuesday. Tickets can be purchased at Salvo Viaggi (see p764 for details) or directly from the ferry terminal ☎ 0923 54 54 11.

BUS
Segesta (☎ 0923 2 17 54) runs express buses (around eight daily) connecting Trapani with Palermo (€7, two hours). **Lumia** (☎ 0923 2 17 54) serves Agrigento (€9.30, three hours, four daily). All intercity buses use Piazza Montalto, from where **AST** (☎ 0923 232 22) buses serve Erice (€1.80, hourly), San Vito lo Capo (€3.10, 1½ hours, eight daily), Castelvetrano (€5.70, seven daily) and Marsala (€2.60, four daily). Autoservizi Tarantola runs a bus service to Segesta and Calatafimi (six daily Monday to Friday, two Sunday).

The tourist office has updated timetables of all bus routes.

A free bus (No 11) does a circular trip through Trapani, leaving from the bus station and stopping at the train station on the return leg.

TRAIN
Trains connect Trapani to Palermo (€7.50, nine daily; note that some trains run via Marsala and are therefore slow), Castelvetrano (€4.15, one hour, 17 daily) and Marsala (€3, 30 minutes, 15 daily). For Segesta, you can either get off at Segesta Tempio (one train daily), from where you'll have to walk 3km to the temple, or Calatafimi (there are many each day) on the way to Palermo. The stations are roughly equidistant from the ancient Greek site.

AROUND TRAPANI
Segesta
The ancient Elymians must have been great aesthetes if their choice of sites for cities is any indication. Along with Erice and Entella, they founded Segesta on and around Monte Barbaro. Set on the edge of a deep canyon in the midst of wild, desolate mountains, this huge 5th-century-BC temple is a magical site. On windy days its 36 giant columns are said to act like an organ, producing mysterious notes.

The city was in constant conflict with Selinunte in the south and this rivalry led it to seek assistance from a succession of allies, including Carthage, Athens, Syracuse and the Romans, and eventually Selinunte was destroyed. Time has done to Segesta what violence inflicted on Selinunte, and little remains save the theatre and the never-completed **Doric temple** (☎ 0924 95 23 56; admission €4.50; ☼ 9am-4pm Nov-Mar, 9am-7pm Apr-Aug), the latter dating from around 430 BC and remarkably well preserved. Obsessed with Greek culture and style, the people of Segesta claimed to be descended from the defeated Trojans, but although they wrote in Greek their spoken language remains a mystery. The only other site to survive intact is the Hellenistic **theatre** inside the old city walls. A shuttle bus runs every 30 minutes from the entrance 1.5km uphill to the theatre and costs an additional €1.20. If you've got the energy, walk up instead – the views are magical.

During July and August, performances of Greek plays are staged in the theatre. For information, contact the tourist office in Trapani (p764).

Segesta is accessible by **AST bus** (☎ 0924 3 10 20) from Piazza Montalto in Trapani (€4.15, 25 minutes). Otherwise catch an train from Trapani (€4.70 return, 25 minutes, 10 daily) or Palermo to Segesta Tempio; the site is then a 20-minute walk away. There are signs to direct you.

Golfo di Castellammare
Saved from development and road projects by local protests, the tranquil **Riserva Naturale dello Zingaro** (☎ 0923 2 61 11; admission €4.50; ☼ 7am-9pm May-Aug, 7am-6pm Sep-Apr) is the star attraction on the gulf. Sicily's, and Italy's, first nature reserve, Zingaro was created with the support of local people and ecologists. Now it's wild coastline is a haven for the rare Bonelli eagle along with 40 other species of bird. Mediterranean flora dusts the hillsides with wild carob and bright yellow euphorbia, and hidden coves, like **Marinella bay**, provide excellent swimming spots. **Cetaria Diving Centre** (☎ 0924 54 10 73;

cetaria@tiscalnet.it; Via Marco Polo 3, Scopello) organises dives and underwater tours of the nature reserve from the Tonnara di Scopello (where there are toilets and showers) in summer. The main entrance of the park is 2km from Scopello. A **walk** up the coast between San Vito lo Capo and the little fishing village of Scopello (the park's two main entrances) will take about four hours along a clearly marked track. There are also several trails inland, which are detailed on maps available for a small fee at the information offices at the park's two entrances.

Once home to tuna fishers, **Scopello** now mainly hosts tourists, although its sleepy village atmosphere remains unspoiled. Its port is interesting to visit, with an abandoned *tonnara* (tuna processing plant) and *faraglione* (rock towers rising out of the sea).

There are numerous **camp sites** in the area, all of which have good facilities.

AST buses run to San Vito lo Capo and Castellammare del Golfo from Trapani's Piazza Montalto. From Castellammare, it is possible to catch a bus to Scopello (€1.80/2.85 one way/return). There is no road through the Zingaro park.

ERICE
pop 30,000
Erice sits on the legendary Mount Eryx (750m) and despite its rather puritanical appearance – all forts and churches – it has a notorious history as a centre for the cult of Venus. Settled by the mysterious Elymians of Segesta fame, Erice amid its fertile fields was an obvious abode for the goddess of love, and the town followed the peculiar ritual of sacred prostitution with the sacred prostitutes themselves accommodated in the temple. Needless to say, despite countless invasion the sacred site remained inviolate – no guesses why.

The **tourist office** (☎ 0923 86 93 88; Viale Conte Pepoli 56; ☼ 9am-1pm Mon-Fri) is conveniently near the bus terminus and is friendly and helpful.

Sights
The best views can be had from the quaint **Giardino del Balio**, which overlooks rugged turrets and wooded hillsides down to the salt-pans of Trapani and the sea. Adjacent to the gardens is the Norman **Castello di Venere** (Castle of Venus; Via Castello di Venere; admission free, donations

requested; ☼ 8am-7pm), built in the 12th and 13th centuries over the notorious temple of Venus where those ancients were busy in their devotions. Not much more than a ruin, the castle is upstaged by the panoramic vistas.

Of the several churches and other monuments in the small, quiet town, the 14th-century **Chiesa Matrice** (Via V Carvini; admission free; ☼ 10am-1pm & 3.30-6pm), just inside Porta Trapani, is probably the most interesting by virtue of its separate campanile (€1) with mullioned windows. The interior of the church was remodelled in neogothic style in the 19th century (with heavy use of decorative stucco that looks like royal icing).

Sleeping & Eating
Staying in Erice is both a privilege and an eye-opener. Once the busy crowds have left the walled medieval town the streets revert to an almost ancient silence. This period, and the early morning, are the best times to see the town, although accommodation is limited and prices tend to reflect this.

B&B Agora (☎ 0923 86 01 33; www.agoraerice.com; Via Vittorio Emanuele 111; d €62) A lovely little B&B within the medieval walls of the town. Comfortable bedrooms with balconies and stunning views.

Moderno (☎ 0923 86 93 00; fax 0923 86 91 39; Via Vittorio Emanuele 63; s/d €77/115) Another good option in Erice, the Moderno has all the comforts you'd want in a three-star hotel, and is ideally located in the centre of the medieval town.

Erice has a tradition of *dolci ericini* and there are numerous excellent pastry shops and cafés in the town.

Caffé Maria (☎ 0923 86 96 96; Via Vittorio Emanuele 4) Regardless of the length of your stay – hours or days – you cannot leave without a visit here. It's run by Maria Grammatico, who learnt the trade as a novice nun, and the *cannoli* here are to die for. If you go to the actual *pasticceria* a few doors down, you might get a glimpse of the pastry cooks at work.

Taverna di Ré Aceste (Via R de Martini; meals €20; ☼ 12.30-3pm & 7.30-10.30pm, closed Wed & Sun) Try this typical taverna with its lovely terrace and long-standing reputation. It is located in a small lane off Conte Pepoli.

Getting There & Away
Regular AST buses (hourly summer) run to Trapani (one way/return €1.80/2.85).

EGADI ISLANDS

For centuries the Egadi islanders have lived from the sea – and more famously from the tuna-slaughter in the spring. The Arabs used the Egadi Islands (Isole Egade) islands as a stepping-stone for their invasions, and the lucrative industry caused later conquerors to fortify them heavily until the 17th century, when the islands were sold to Genovese bankers and ultimately passed into the hands of business tycoon Ignazio Florio, who made his fortune from them. Nowadays, the waters around the islands have been overfished and the tuna fishery (once the only cannery in Europe) is long closed. Tourism looks set to be the main earner – even the *mattanza*, the ritual slaughtering of tuna, has become a spectator sport (see opposite), although the future of this is by no means certain.

Getting There & Away

Ferries and hydrofoils run between the islands and to Trapani. See p726 for details.

Levanzo, Favignana & Marettimo

Closest to Trapani lies Levanzo, the smallest island of the archipelago, inhabited by a handful of people and the site of ancient rock carvings at **Grotta del Genovese**. The cave can be visited by sea (if you negotiate with one of the fishermen at the port) or by taking the track between the peaks of Pizzo del Monaco and Pizzo del Corvo. Alternatively, contact the **custodian of the cave** (☎ 0923 92 40 32); he does guided tours (€13) for small groups. The huge cave – representing some of Italy's finest prehistoric paintings – is covered with Mesolithic etchings of bison and deer and a series of fascinating figures dating from the Neolithic period. The figures of women and men were 'painted' using animal fat and carbon and, fittingly, there is one image of the tuna that even then must have been revered.

The largest of the islands is butterfly-shaped Favignana, dominated by Monte Santa Caterina. It is pleasant to explore on bicycle as it's almost completely flat, and around the coast tufa quarries are carved out of the crystal-clear waters – most notably around **Cala Rossa** and **Cavallo**. Wander around the **tonnara** (tuna processing plant) at the port. It was closed at the end of the 1970s due to the general crisis in the local tuna fishing industry.

LA MATTANZA

A centuries-old tradition, the Egadi Islands' *mattanza* (the ritual slaughter of tuna) survives despite the ever-decreasing number of tuna fish. For centuries, schools of tuna have used the waters around western Sicily as a mating ground. Locals recall the golden days of the islands' fishing industry, when it wasn't uncommon to catch giant breeding tuna of between 200kg and 300kg. Fish that size are rare these days.

Now that the slaughter of tuna can no longer support the islands' economy, it is re-inventing itself as a tourist attraction. From around 20 May to 10 June, tourists flock to the Egadi Islands to witness the event. For a fee you can join the fishers in their boats and watch them catching the tuna at close hand – note that you'll need a strong stomach. This is no ordinary fishing expedition: the fishers organise their boats and nets in a complex formation designed to channel the tuna into a series of enclosures that culminate in the *camera della morte* (chamber of death). Once enough tuna are imprisoned here, the fishers close in and the *mattanza* begins (the word is derived from the Spanish word for killing). It is a bloody affair – up to eight or more fishers at a time will sink huge hooks into a tuna and drag it aboard. Anyone who has seen Rossellini's classic film *Stromboli* will no doubt recall the famous *mattanza* scene.

There is a **tourist office** (☎ 0923 92 16 47; Piazza Matrice 8; ☐ 9am-12.30pm & 4.30-7pm Mon-Sat year-round, 9.30am-12.30pm Sun Jun-Sep) in Favignana town. You'll find dive hire outlets and bicycles or scooters for rent around the town and at the small harbour.

The last of the islands and the most distant is Marettimo. A few hundred people live mostly in the tiny village on the eastern coast and there are no roads. You can go with fishing boats along the coast to explore some 400 grottoes or follow mule tracks across the island either to **Monte Falcone** or to **Case Romane** (a Roman ruin). But it is the island's beaches and its crystal-clear waters that are the main attractions.

SLEEPING & EATING

There's plenty of accommodation on Favignana and a limited amount on Levanzo.

SICILY

There are no hotels on Marettimo, but you should be able to dig up a room with the locals.

During the *mattanza* and in August you'll have trouble finding a bed without a booking. Many local people rent out rooms.

Albergo Egadi (☎ /fax 0923 92 12 32; Via Colombo 17; s/d €25/51) Run by the Guccione sisters, this small *albergo* on Favignana has only 12 rooms. It also has an acclaimed restaurant, where you'll eat one of your best meals in Sicily at a very reasonable price. Advance bookings are recommended.

Albergo Aegusa (☎ 0923 92 24 30; aegusa@cinet.it; Via Garibaldi 11; d low/high season €45/85; 🟥) Comfortable, well-furnished rooms right in the centre of Favignana. There is also a good restaurant in an attractive outdoor courtyard.

Camping Egad (☎ 0923 92 15 55; fax 0923 92 15 67; www.egadi.com/egad; Località Arena; person/4-bed bungalow €5.80/76) This well-equipped camp site is situated in the centre of Favignana, a particularly attractive location in the spring when wild flowers abound. The diving centre Atlantide is conveniently located opposite the camp site.

Levanzo has only two hotels, including the newly renovated **Albergo Paradiso** (☎ 0923 92 40 80; Via Lungomare; s/d half board €50/67). The Paradiso has comfortable rooms and is attractively situated on the seafront. It has a restaurant where you'll eat very well for around €21 per head.

PANTELLERIA

Known to the Arabs as 'daughter of the winds', this volcanic outcrop is Sicily's biggest island, although it lies closer to Tunisia than it does to Sicily. Buffeted by winds, even in August, the island is characterised by jagged lava stone, low-slung caper bushes, dwarf vines, steaming fumaroles and the **Lago Specchio di Venere** (The Mirror of Venus) mud baths near Bugeber. At Siba there is also a steaming natural sauna, **Stufa del Bagno di Arturo**, at the summit of Montagna Grande, the island's highest peak (signs guide you from Siba). The cave can get extremely hot so be prepared.

However, the island is more famous for its secluded coves, which are perfect for snorkelling and diving. The northeastern end of the island provides the best spots with a popular **acquacalda** at Gadir. Here you can while away your day wallowing like a walrus in the hot, shallow springs. Slightly further down the coast you will find ever-more scenic spots such as Cala di Tramontana and Cala di Levante. **Boat excursions**, available at the dock, are the perfect way to visit some of the more inaccessible grottoes around the island; contact **Minardi Adriano** (☎ 0923 91 15 02; Via Borgo Italia 5) for day trips costing €25 per person.

The only archaeological site on the island is at **Mursia**, where the remnants of *sesi* (ancient funerary monuments) are the only remaining evidence of a Bronze Age settlement. Many of the tombs have been destroyed and the rock used to build the domed *dammusi* (houses) that now offer accommodation to tourists. The exoticism and remoteness of Pantelleria has long made it a favourite with celebrities from Truman Capote and Henry Cartier-Bresson to the likes of Madonna and Sting.

There is a small **tourist office** (☎ 0923 91 18 38; www.pantelleria.it; Piazza Cavour; 🕙 Mon-Sat Jun-Sep) on Pantelleria that is way ahead of many offices on the mainland. Its excellent website has a good range of *dammusi* to rent. Summer accommodation bookings should be made at least a month in advance.

Albergo Papuscia (☎ 0923 91 54 63; www.papuscia.com; Corso da Sopra Portella 48, Località Tracino; d low/high season €59/89; 🟥) Situated on the eastern side of the island, this lovely little *albergo* in an 18th-century *dammusi* is surrounded by a flower-filled garden. Run by a mother and daughter, the hotel also has a good restaurant serving up mamma's own cooking.

In addition to the tourist office's website, most bars and restaurants have notices advertising *dammusi* rentals, although many require a minimum stay of around one week.

Siremar boats go to Trapani (see p766).

The island is 30 minutes by plane with **Gandalf Air** (toll free ☎ 848 84 88 80; www.gandalfair.it) from Trapani. Tickets cost €80. **Si Fly** (toll free ☎ 800 53 55 85) has a flight from Palermo. Plane tickets can be purchased at Salvo Viaggi in Trapani (p764). Local buses (€0.77) depart from Piazza Cavour in Pantelleria town at regular intervals daily (except Sunday) and service all the towns on the island. Alternatively, you can rent scooters from **Autonoleggio Policardo** (☎ 0923 91 28 44; Vicolo Messina 35) for €20 per day.

Sardinia (Sardegna)

SARDINIA (SARDEGNA)

Sardinia
(Sardegna)

This island mini-continent is just a few hours by ferry but a world away from mainland Italy. Nearly always dominated by outside forces, the proud Sardinians have never lost their sense of identity. Around its coast Sardinia boasts some of the most idyllic beaches in the Mediterranean and many of them are unspoiled. A growing troupe of European tourists come for fun in the sun but away from the sea this island remains a wild and seemingly impenetrable place.

Its history is as inscrutable as its interior is forbidding. Across the island are scattered 7000 *nuraghi*, strange conical stone fortresses, some extended into grand settlements that predate the arrival of the Romans by more than 1000 years. Curious temples, *domus de janus* (fairy house) tombs, *tombe dei giganti* (giants' tombs), mysterious menhirs, and remains of entire Bronze Age villages complete this ancient picture. Phoenicians, Carthaginians and finally Romans landed here, leaving their mark in Nora and Tharros. Later masters also left reminders. The northwest is strewn with Pisan Romanesque churches and Cagliari and Alghero retain much of their Catalan and Spanish feel. The island distinguishes itself in the kitchen, with hearty pastas and a love for suckling pig, kid and lamb. Sardinians produce notable wines and a rugged firewater, *filu e ferru*.

Avoid the broiling, crowded months of July and August. Dirt cheap accommodation, particularly in summer, is uncommon; it is advisable to book ahead in July and August.

HIGHLIGHTS

■ **Walking**
Wander around the coastal medieval Catalan town of Alghero (pp790–4)

■ **City Life**
Check out the medieval Il Castello in Cagliari (pp776–7)

■ **Roman World**
Delve into history at Tharros (p788) and Nora (pp782–3)

■ **Wild Coast**
Enjoy the pristine beaches of the Costa Verde (pp785–6)

■ **Feasting**
Enjoy a traditional meal of *porcetto* (roast suckling pig) washed down with a good Cannonau red

■ **Island-hopping**
Journey around the Arcipelago di la Maddalena (pp797–8) Speedboat Tour or whiz past the Golfo di Orosei's splendid beaches and coves (p802)

★ Isola La Maddalena
★ Alghero
Grotta di Ispingoli ★
Gola su Gorroppu ★
★ Golfo di Orosei
★ Santa Christina Temple
★ Tharros
★ Su Nuraxi
★ Costa Verde
★ Cagliari
★ Nora

■ POPULATION: 1.65 MILLION

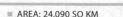
■ AREA: 24,090 SQ KM

HISTORY

Our primitive forebears may have been wandering around Sardinia as long as 400,000 years ago. Their Bronze Age descendents, known as the Nuraghic peoples after the bewildering stone towers and fortresses, or *nuraghi*, they built long dominated the interior of the island, even after the arrival of Phoenician traders around 850 BC. Their settlements (like Karalis, or modern Cagliari, Nora and Tharros) were later taken over by the Carthaginians and Romans. The latter managed to take control of much of the island and the indigenous people slowly melted into history.

The departure of the Romans and the ensuing chaos left Sardinia at the mercy of Vandal raiders, Byzantine occupiers and Arab corsairs. Four more or less independent kingdoms, or *giudicati*, emerged in the Middle Ages but by the 13th-century outsiders were again at the door. Pisans and Genoese vied for control but were finally replaced by the Catalano-Aragonese from northern Spain. They arrived in 1323 and only snuffed out the last resistance in 1478. Eleanora d'Arborea (1340–1404) offered the greatest challenge and she has gone down as Sardinia's Joan of Arc.

Sardinia became a Spanish territory after the unification of the Spanish kingdoms in 1479. In the ensuing centuries Sardinia decayed as the fleeting might of Spain crumbled. After the disastrous War of the Spanish Succession the north Italian Savoy kingdom took possession of this rough and difficult island in 1720. After Italian unity in 1861, Sardinia found itself under the disinterested boot of Rome.

In WWI the island's Sassari Brigade fought heroically in northern Italy against the Austro-Hungarians and in 1943, during WWII, Cagliari was heavily bombed by the Allies. One of the most important postwar successes was the elimination of malaria from the coast in the 1950s – this allowed the development of coastal tourism that today forms a pillar of Sardinia's economy.

TRANSPORT
Getting There & Away
AIR

The airports at Cagliari, Olbia, Alghero and Arbatax-Tortoli link Sardinia with major Italian and European cities. **Ryanair** (www.ryanair.com) in particular does a brisk business on its London Stansted–Alghero route. It flies up to twice a day.

BOAT

The island is accessible by ferry from the Italian ports of Genoa, Savona, La Spezia, Livorno, Piombino, Civitavecchia, Fiumicino, Naples, Palermo and Trapani.

MAINLAND ITALY–SARDINIA FERRY CROSSINGS

Route	adult/car (€)	car duration
Genoa to Arbatax	47.25/90.84	19 hours
Genoa to Porto Torres or Olbia	45.19/90.84	eight to 11 hours
Genoa to Porto Torres or Olbia (new ferries)	63.13/98.38	eight to 11 hours
Genoa to Olbia (fast ferry)	77.98/98.38	six hours
Civitavecchia to Arbatax	34.09/69.72	10½ hours
Civitavecchia to Olbia	24.53/85.47	eight hours
Civitavecchia to Olbia (fast ferry)	46.99/98.59	four hours
Livorno to Golfo Aranci	57/109	10 hours
Livorno to Olbia	56/109	seven to 11 hours
Naples to Cagliari	40.80/77.98	16¼ hours
Palermo to Cagliari	38.21/77.98	13½ hours
Piombino to Olbia	35/77	eight hours
Trapani to Cagliari	38.21/77.98	11 hours

These are sample fares on a selection of the main routes. The fares given are standard high-season one-way (in *poltrona*, or reclining seat). Children aged four to 12 generally pay around half and those under four go free. Also given is the high-season cost of transporting a small car. Port taxes of a few euros (it varies from port to port) have to be added on to these fares.

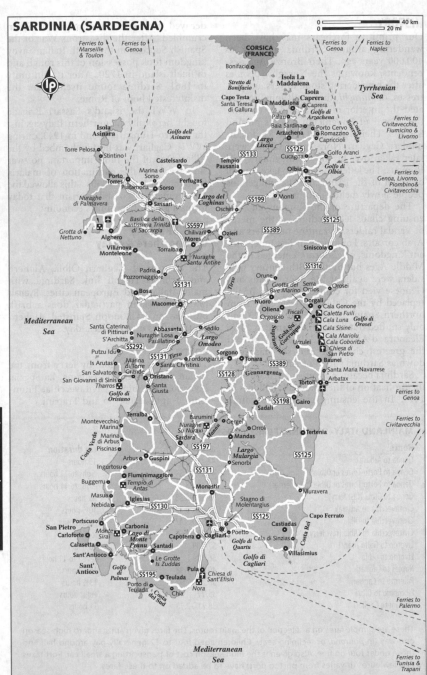

SARDINIA (SARDEGNA)

SARDINIA (SARDEGNA)

Ferries also run from Bonifacio and Porto Vecchio in Corsica. French ferries running from Marseille and Toulon sometimes call in at the Corsican ports of Ajaccio and Propriano en route for Sardinia. A ferry runs between Tunis and Cagliari via Trapani (Sicily).

The arrival points in Sardinia are Olbia, Golfo Aranci, Palau, Santa Teresa di Gallura and Porto Torres in the north, Arbatax on the east coast and Cagliari in the south.

Italy's main ferry company is **Tirrenia** (☎ 199 12 31 99; www.tirrenia.it). It runs year-round to various Sardinian ports from all the above Italian ports except Savona, La Spezia, Livorno and Piombino.

Moby Lines (☎ 010 254 15 13; www.mobylines.it) operates year-round between Olbia and Genoa, Livorno and Civitavecchia. **Grandi Navi Veloci** (Grimaldi; ☎ 010 2 54 65; www1.grimaldi.it) has year-round luxury ferry services from Genoa to Porto Torres and Olbia.

Sardinia Ferries (☎ 019 21 55 11; www.corsica ferries.com) operates from Civitavecchia and Livorno to Golfo Aranci and Cagliari. It also has boats on the Bonifacio run to Santa Teresa di Gallura. They run from May to September.

Enermar (☎ 899 20 00 01; www.enermar.it) runs between the northern ports of Genoa, Savona and La Spezia to Palau (some via Corsica). **Linea dei Golfi** (☎ 0565 22 23 00; www .lineadeigolfi.it) operates from Livorno and Piombino to Olbia from April to September. **Linee Lauro** (☎ 081 551 33 52; www.lineelauro.it) has two weekly boats from Naples to Palau, stopping in Corsica.

For an idea of the fares you might pay, see Mainland Italy–Sardinia Ferry Crossings (p773).

SNCM (France ☎ 08 91 70 18 01, Sardinia ☎ 079 51 44 77; www.sncm.fr) and **CMN La Méridionale** (☎ 08 10 20 13 20; www.cmn.fr) together operate ferries from Marseille to Porto Torres (via Corsica) from April to October. There are from nine to 16 sailings each month, but in July and August some leave from Toulon instead. Crossing time is 15 to 17 hours (12½ hours from Toulon) depending on the vessel. A seat costs €72 in high season (July to August) and a small car €104. A basic cabin for two costs €173.

For tickets and information in Porto Torres, go to **Agenzia Paglietti** (☎ 079 51 44 77; fax 079 51 40 63; Corso Vittorio Emanuele 19).

There are regular links between Sardinia (Santa Teresa di Gallura) and Bonifacio across the straits in Corsica. **Saremar** (☎ 0789 75 41 56) has from four to eight daily departures each way depending on the season. Adult one-way fares range up to €8.52 one-way, depending on the season. A small car costs up to €27.89. The trip takes 50 minutes. **Moby Lines** (☎ 0789 75 14 49) has 10 daily crossings in July and August and four during the rest of the year. Prices are virtually the same.

Once a week a Tirrenia vessel from Tunis arrives in Cagliari. The trip takes around 36 hours and costs €57.48 on the deck in high season. Sleeping berths start at €73.08. A small car costs €93.73.

Getting Around

BUS

The main bus company is the Azienda Regionale Sarda Trasporti or **ARST** (☎ 0800 86 50 42; www.arst.sardegna.it), which operates extensive services throughout the island. **PANI** (☎ 070 65 23 26, ☎ 079 23 69 83) links Cagliari, Oristano, Sassari, Nuoro and Porto Torres.

Other companies include Ferrovie della Sardegna (FdS) and Ferrovie Meridionale Sardegna (FMS). Buses are generally faster than trains.

CAR & MOTORCYCLE

The only way to really explore Sardinia is by road. For details about rental agencies, see Cagliari (p782) and some other towns around the island.

TRAIN

The main **Trenitalia** (www.trenitalia.it) train lines link Cagliari with Oristano, Sassari and Olbia, and are generally reliable but can be fairly slow. The FdS links some of the smaller towns with even slower narrow-gauge trains. In summer there are several *Trenino Verde* (Little Green Train) services that use the scenic lines long since out of standard commercial action. Some are particularly pretty, especially the Arbatax–Mandas line. The others are; Palau–Tempio Pausania; Tempio Pausania–Nulvi (from where you can connect with a regular service to Sassari); Bosa–Macomer (which links with the Macomer–Nuoro line); Isili–Sorgono.

CAGLIARI

pop 175,000

Even a brief exploration of the island's capital and largest city reveals it as a cosmopolitan enclave quite apart from the rest of the island. This is *the* city.

The hilly labyrinth of the sandy-coloured medieval Castello district, the bright pastel colours of restored facades, the taverns and restaurants jostling for your attention (especially around the Marina district); all draw you in like a magnet. Several fine monuments, including the archaeology museum with its priceless Nuraghic collections, will keep you occupied for a day or two. And the city's long Poetto beach is good for a city-side splash. The nearby salt marshes occasionally attract flocks of pink flamingos.

ORIENTATION

The main port, bus and train stations are near Piazza Matteotti, where the useful city tourist office is also. Running through the square is Via Roma, part of the principal route to Poetto and Villasimius in the east and Pula and the south coast to the west.

The warren of lanes just inland from Via Roma is known as Marina, with most of the cheaper and mid-range hotels and a plethora of eateries of all categories.

INFORMATION
Bookshops
Libreria Dattena (☎ 070 67 02 20; Via Garibaldi 175) Novels and other books in languages other than Italian.

Emergency
Police Station (☎ 070 49 21 69; Via Amat 9) The main police station behind the imposing law courts.

Internet Access
Internet Cafe (Via San Domenico 28; €2.60/hr; ☺ 8am-9am Mon-Sat) A handful of clunky computers.
Intermedia Point (Via Eleonora d'Arborea 4; €2.60/hr; ☺ 10am-1pm & 4-9pm Mon-Fri, 11am-1pm & 5-9pm Sat)

Laundry
Lavanderia Ghilbi (Via Sicilia 20; ☺ 8am-10pm; 6kg wash €3) On the island, this laundrette is a rare beast!

Medical Services
Guardia Medica (☎ 070 50 29 31) For a night-time emergency callout doctor.

Ospedale Brotzu (☎ 070 54 32 66; Via Peretti) This hospital is northwest of the city centre. Take Bus No 1 from Via Roma if you need to make a non-emergency visit.

Money
Banco di San Paolo Handily located next to the main train station. There are also ATMs inside the station.
Banco di Sardegna (Piazza del Carmine 28)
Mail Boxes Etc (☎ 070 67 37 04; Viale Trieste 65/b) You can send or receive money via Western Union here.

Post & Telephone
Main Post Office (Piazza del Carmine; ☺ 8.15am-6.40pm Mon-Fri, 8.15am-1.20pm Sat) It has a fax service and *fermo posta* (poste restante). You'll find telephones scattered across the city centre.

Tourist Information
Tourist Office (☎ 070 66 92 55; Piazza Matteotti; ☺ 8am-8pm Mon-Sat Apr-Sep, 8am-2pm Sun Jul-Aug, 9am-2pm & 3-6pm Mon-Fri, 9am-2pm Sat Oct-Mar)
Tourist Office (☎ 070 66 83 52; Stazione Marittima; ☺ 8.30am-1.30pm & 3-7pm)

SIGHTS
Il Castello
The precipitous white stone walls of medieval Cagliari, with two of the grand-looking Pisan towers still standing watch, enclose **Il Castello** (the Castle), a once virtually impregnable fortress town. The walls are best admired from beyond – one good spot is the Roman amphitheatre to the west.

One approach is from Piazza Costituzione. Climb the monumental stairway entrance to the Bastione San Remy, a grand belvedere offering views across the city.

A brisk march north brings you into Piazza Palazzo and face to face with the neo-Pisan Romanesque facade (1938) of the **Cattedrale di Santa Maria** (☎ 070 66 38 37; Piazza Palazzo 4; ☺ 8am-12.30pm & 4.30-8pm). Little remains of the original 13th-century church, buried in a heavy baroque remake in the 17th century. Then in 1933–38 they tried to turn the clocks back with the throwback facade. The square-based bell-tower *does* date to the 13th century. Inside are two magnificent stone pulpits on either side of the central entrance, sculpted by Guglielmo da Pisa and donated by Pisa to Cagliari in 1312.

The grand white **Torre di San Pancrazio** (Piazza Indipendenza; admission free; ☺ 9am-1pm & 3.30-7.30pm Tue-Sun Apr-Oct, 9am-5pm Tue-Sun Nov-Mar), to

SARDINIA (SARDEGNA)

the right of the northern city gate, is one of two medieval Pisan defensive towers still standing. Under the Catalano-Aragonese it became an office block with a view for public servants and in the 17th century was downgraded to a prison.

Beyond the city gate you are in Piazza dell'Arsenale. Cross the square into what was once the city's arsenal (the Regio Arsenale). Four museums constituting the **Citadella dei Musei**, including the island's most important archaeological and art collections are located here amid remains of the old arsenal and city walls.

The **Museo Archeologico Nazionale** (☎ 070 68 40 00; admission €4, with Pinacoteca Nazionale €5; ☼ 9am-8pm Tue-Sun) contains precious material dating from pre-Nuraghic to late Roman times, found at sites across Sardinia. Without doubt the single most impressive part of the collection is the *bronzetti*, astonishing bronze figurines that (in the absence of any written record) provide one of the few clues to Nuraghic people. There are two separate displays of the statuettes on the ground and 2nd floors. Of all the figures, the 'chieftain' stands out. He is depicted with a flowing mantle, staff and sword. Roman artefacts include mosaics, statuary, jewellery and coins.

The **Pinacoteca Nazionale** (☎ 070 68 40 00; admission €2, with Museo Archeologico Nazionale €5; ☼ 9am-8pm Tue-Sun) is the place to acquaint yourself with Sardinian art history, especially works from the 15th to 17th centuries. The four works by Pietro Cavaro, father of the so-called Stampace school and possibly Sardinia's most important artist, are outstanding. They include a moving *Deposizione* (Deposition) and portraits of Saints Peter, Paul and Augustine.

The other museums are curious *amuse-gueules* (appetisers). The **Raccolta di Cere Anatomiche** (admission €1.50; ☼ 9am-1pm & 4-7pm Tue-Sun) contains anatomical cross-section wax models while the **Museo d'Arte Siamese** (☎ 070 65 18 88; admission €2; ☼ 9am-1pm & 4-8pm Tue-Sun Jun-Sep; 9am-1pm & 3.30-7.30pm Tue-Sun Oct-May) houses a hodgepodge of Asian art and crafts.

Return to Piazza Indipendenza and head south along Castello's canyon-like streets to the **Torre dell'Elefante**, the other Pisan watchtower that takes its name from a small sculpted elephant at the tower's base as you enter from Via Università.

Marina, Stampace & Around

Just south of Piazza Costituzione an untidy jumble of lanes leads you to the Cagliari waterfront. Known as Marina, it bursts not only with all sorts of eateries and a handful of hotels but is also remarkably blessed with churches. The **Chiesa di Sant'Eulalia** is most interesting for its attached **Museo del Tesoro e Area Archeologica di Sant'Eulalia** (☎ 070 66 37 24; Vico del Collegio 2; admission €2.50; ☼ 10am-1pm & 5-11pm Jul-Sep, 10am-1pm & 5-8pm Tue-Sun Oct-Jun). In the underground area you can see evidence of Roman roads discovered when restoration work began on the church. Upstairs is the church's treasury, a particularly rich collection of religious art.

From Marina head up Largo Carlo Felice to the busy Piazza Yenne and veer west along Via Azuni into the centuries-old working class district of Stampace. Of the various churches here the most impressive is the **Chiesa di San Michele** (Via Ospedale 2; admission free; ☼ 7-11am & 6-8.30pm), the best example of rococo in Sardinia and scene of a rousing pre-war speech by the Hapsburg Emperor Carlos V before he set off on a fruitless campaign against Arab corsairs in Tunisia.

Of the few reminders of the Roman presence in Cagliari the most important is the **Anfiteatro Romano** (☼ 10am-1pm & 3-6pm Tue-Sun Apr-Oct, 10am-4pm Tue-Sun Nov-Mar). It's a bit of a climb to this marvellous 2nd-century outdoor theatre carved largely out of the hillside. Much of the original theatre was cannibalised for other constructions over the centuries but enough survived to pique the imagination. In summer it regains something of its original vocation, hosting summer concerts.

From here you can head further north and back downhill for a dose of contemporary culture at the **Galleria Comunale d'Arte** (☎ 070 49 07 27; Viale Regina Elena - Giardini Pubblici; adult/child €3.10/1.03; ☼ 9am-1pm & 5-9pm Wed-Mon) dedicated to the Collezione Ingrao, with more than 650 works of Italian art from mid-19th century to the late 20th century.

Villanova

The humdrum 'new town' of Villanova spreads away to the north and east of the old traditional quarters of Castello, Marina and Stampace. In among the apartments are such curios as the **Basilica di San Saturno**

CAGLIARI

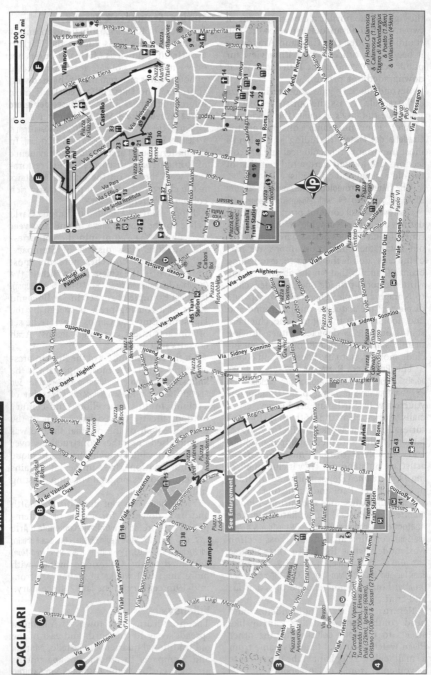

(Piazza San Cosimo; ☽ 9am-1pm Mon-Sat), the site of a 6th-century church, one of the island's oldest. Nearby, the former abattoir now serves as the **Exma** (☎ 070 66 63 99; Via San Lucifero 11; exhibitions around €3; ☽ 10am-2pm & 5pm-midnight Tue-Sun Jun-Sep, 9am-8pm Tue-Sun Oct-May) art exhibition space.

The **Santuario & Basilica di Nostra Signora di Bonaria** (Viale Bonaria; ☽ 6.30am-noon & 4.30-7.30pm Apr-Oct, 6.30am-noon & 4-6.30pm Nov-Mar) houses the miraculous statue of the Virgin Mary and Christ child that washed ashore in the 14th century. The sanctuary is dwarfed by the basilica to its right. It was bombed in 1943 and restoration was only completed in 1998.

Beaches
You can spend a day at either the little **Calamosca** or longer **Poetto** beaches, about 3km east of the centre, where several small bars have outside tables. Alternatively, amble over to the **Stagno di Molentargius**, just west of Poetto, to see the pink flamingos on the salt lake.

FESTIVALS & EVENTS
The **Festa di Sant'Efisio** has been held annually in May since the 17th century. For more details, see pp800–1.

SLEEPING
Hotel A&R Bundes Jack (☎/fax 070 66 79 70; Via Roma 75; s/d €40/60, with bathroom €47/72) This is the pick of the crop in Marina. The high-ceilinged rooms are spotless and comfortable.

Hotel Aurora (☎ 070 65 86 25; Salita Santa Chiara 19; s/d €25/40, with bathroom €37/51) A cheerful spot just off busy Piazza Yenne, which you can espy from most of the rooms' windows.

Hotel Regina Margherita (☎ 070 67 03 42; www.hotelreginamargherita.com; Viale Regina Margherita 44; s/d €125/160) Comfortable rooms hidden behind tinted glass in a rather ugly sprawling block; but from the inside you don't have to look at it, do you!

Hotel Calamosca (☎ 070 37 16 28; www.hotelcalamosca.it; Viale Calamosca 50; s/d €64/84) A great option right by the sea at this, the nearest beach to Cagliari's city centre. Rooms have heating in winter, TV and views over the cove.

EATING
Restaurants
The Marina area is peppered with good little restaurants to suit all tastes and budgets. At the cheaper ones you can get a full set meal for under €10.

Lillicu (☎ 070 65 29 70; Via Sardegna 78; meals €25; ☽ Mon-Sun Sep-Jul, Mon-Sat Aug) A down-to-earth trattoria frequently packed to the rafters. Fish and meat dishes are available and punters rarely leave dissatisfied.

SARDINIA (SARDEGNA)

Il Buongustaio (☎ 070 66 81 24; Via Concezione 7; meals €25-30; ✆ Wed-Sun & lunch Mon) Although specialising in home cooking, this place attracts foodies. Land and sea critters get an even run, and the homemade pasta is especially tasty.

Dal Corsaro (☎ 070 66 43 18; Viale Regina Margherita 28; meals €40-50; ✆ Mon-Sat) A classic of Cagliari's fine dining scene. Eat a la carte or choose from a range of set meal options starting at €45. Service is close to impeccable.

Crackers (☎ 070 65 39 12; Corso Vittorio Emanuele 193; meals €25; ✆ Thu-Tue) Crackers has a big creamy coloured vault beneath which you sit down to northern Italian specialities, including a variety of risottos.

Ristorante Royal (☎ 070 34 13 13; Via Bottego 24; meals €25-30) Tuck into a succulent Florentine steak or choose from a range of other meat and vegetable dishes in this window on Tuscany. Fish lovers should stay away.

Cafés & Gelato

Antico Caffè (☎ 070 65 82 06; Piazza Costituzione) The city's most elegant café. If the traffic puts you off the terrace, head for the charming interior with its marble topped tables. A breakfast splurge will set you back €8.20, while in the evening sip cocktails at around €4 to €5.

Sotto La Torre (Piazza San Giuseppe 2; ✆ 8am-3am Thu-Tue) Trip through the centuries as you sip anything from coffee and tea to grappa (grape-based liqueur). The decor is 17th century and you can peer into a couple of cisterns dating to Roman and Punic times.

Isola del Gelato (☎ 070 65 98 24; Piazza Yenne 35; ✆ 9am-2am Tue-Sun) An incredible 280 variations on the ice-cream theme, including several soy-based concoctions.

DRINKING

Al Merlo Parlante (☎ 070 65 39 81; Via Portoscalas 69; ✆ Tue-Sun) Home to a rollicking beer scene

---

THE AUTHOR'S CHOICE

Antica Hostaria (☎ 070 66 58 60; Via Cavour 60; meals €45; ✆ closed Aug) This is without doubt one of the strongholds of fine dining in Cagliari. Antique furnishings create a warm ambience and set the scene for simple but classic Italian cooking as well as rare treats such as those dishes served *al tartufo* (with truffles).

---

for a mostly young clientele. Anyone for Amsterdam Maximator (11.9% proof)?

Forum Caffè (Piazza Yenne; ✆ Tue-Sun) A popular bar on this busy square. It has a distinctly blue hue and hip sounds filter outside. This square is the nerve centre of Cagliari's pre-club doings, with young night owls firmly in control until the wee hours.

Brasserie Vecchia Bruxelles (☎ 070 68 20 37; Via Sulcis 4; ✆ Mon-Sat) An elegant spot with long sofas beneath stone vaulting; a comfy choice for a beer, snack or one of a dozen whiskies.

For nine months of the year, the bulk of the club action takes place in six locales in Assemini, 16km northwest of Cagliari. Most shut down in summer as the seaside takes over. Cagliaritani make for clubs, many of them open air, along the coast as far east as Villasimius and west to Pula and Santa Margherita. The latter include Pirata, along the SS195 in Pula and Corte Noa, 3km further along.

ENTERTAINMENT

Teatro Comunale (☎ 070 408 22 30; Via Sant' Alexinedda) is the main stage for classical music concerts and opera.

SHOPPING

For Sardinian crafts your best first stop is the regional crafts body, **Isola** (☎ 070 49 27 56; Via Bacaredda 176-178), where you can take a look at a range of quality products. It has other branches around the island.

Cagliari is the only place in Sardinia to do big city shopping. Italy's quality department store, **La Rinascente** (Via Roma 141) has one retail therapy branch here.

A good outlet for Sardinian music is **Grand Wazoo** (☎ 070 66 60 39; Via Garibaldi 143).

GETTING THERE & AWAY
Boat

Boats run to Cagliari from Civitavecchia, Livorno and Naples on the Italian mainland, as well as Palermo and Trapani in Sicily.

Bus

The main ARST intercity bus station is on Piazza Matteotti.

PANI buses to Oristano (€5.84, one hour 35 minutes), Nuoro (€5.84, 3½ hours), Sassari (€13.43 nonstop, 3¼ hours) leave from outside the Stazione Marittima. The ticket office is in the port building itself.

DIANA MAYFIELD

Picnicking on the vast Piano Grande beneath the hilltop village of **Castelluccio** (p545), Umbria

The beautiful Amalfi coast beckons from the rooftops of **Ravello** (p637)

STEPHEN SAKS

Study the unique conical-shaped houses of the **Trulli area** (p664)

OLIVER STREWE

MARTIN LLA

Spend a few days with the unreal scenery at **Taormina** (p736)

BETHUNE CARMICHAEL

Marvellous mosaics at **Monreale** (p721)

Join a tour (if you dare) up to the heights of **Mt Etna** (p746)

CHRISTOPHER W

The **Valley of the Temples** (p757) sparkles on Agrigento's coastline

IONAS KALTENBACH

A MEATY SUBJECT

Sardinia's cuisine was born of poverty and is traditionally based on what is local, practical and cost-effective.

Broths (*minestra* or *minestrone*) are common starters. On the coast this often comes in the form of fish soup or stews such as *brodetto* and *burrida*.

Another fishy speciality is *bottarga* – dried, pressed tuna roe – which is served finely grated over piping hot spaghetti. Traditional pasta dishes tend to be on the heavy side and include *culurgiones*, delicious parcels of pasta filled with potato and wild mint. Also common are *mallodoreddus*, a dense seashell-shaped pasta usually served with *salsa alla campidanese* (a sausage and tomato sauce). *Maccarones de busa,* or just plain *busa,* are shaped by wrapping the pasta around knitting needles. Thus 'pierced', the pasta can soak up as much sauce or broth as possible.

A long history of invasion and coastal malaria turned most Sardinians away from the sea. As a result, traditional Sardinian cuisine is based on meat dishes. Locals love *porcetto* (also called *porchetto* or *porceddu*), which is roast suckling pig, *capretto* (kid) and *agnello* (lamb, a pre-Christmas special). Demand for these, especially in high tourist season is such that quality is often poor. Horse and donkey meat are also sometimes on the menu, especially in little eateries in Sassari. Sardinians are also great lovers of tripe and other innards. And what about *granelle*, or sliced calf's testicles?

Seafood is now a common element along the coast but has more to do with tourism than Sardinian tradition.

The most common bread, especially in the north, is the crisp, paper-thin *pane carasau* (often sprinkled with oil and salt). Shepherds would carry it with them for weeks at a time. When soaked, *pane carasau* becomes malleable. Topped with tomato, soft-boiled egg and *pecorino* (the ever-present ewe's milk cheese), it becomes *pane frattau,* a cheap and protein-filled meal.

Sardinia produces about 80% of Italy's *pecorino. Pecorino romano* (originally from Lazio) is a dense pale cheese with a pale crust and is the cheese of choice for accompanying pasta. *Pecorino sardo* is a semi-cooked, nutty-flavoured cheese.

The most widespread dessert are *seadas* (or *sebadas*), a delightfully light pastry (vaguely like a turnover) filled with ricotta or sour cheese and drenched in honey.

For Iglesias (€2.89, one to 1½ hours), Carbonia, Portovesme (€4.44, two hours) and the Sulcis area, FMS buses leave from Via Colombo 24. Buy tickets at the bar. Some FdS buses leave from FdS train station.

Car & Motorcycle

The SS131 Carlo Felice highway links the capital with Porto Torres via Oristano and Sassari. It is the island's main dual-carriage artery. Another, the SS130, scoots east to Iglesias.

Train

The main Trenitalia station is found on Piazza Matteotti. Trains service both Iglesias (€2.56) and Carbonia (€3.35) in the southwest, while the main line proceeds northwards as far as Sassari (€12.10, 4¼ hours) and Porto Torres via the towns of Oristano (€4.55, one to two hours) and Macomer. A branch line from Chilivani heads out for Olbia (€12.95, four hours) and Golfo Aranci.

The FdS train station for trains travelling north to Dolianova, Mandas and Isili is located on Piazza Repubblica. In summer, a *Trenino Verde* scenic service runs between Mandas and Arbatax on the east coast – this is quite a slow ride through some wild country, mostly in the province of Nuoro. A similar line runs north from Isili to Sorgono.

GETTING AROUND
To/From the Airport

Cagliari's **Elmas airport** (☎ 070 2 10 51) is 6km northwest of the centre. Up to 24 daily buses connect with the city centre (ARST station in Piazza Matteotti). The trip normally takes 10 to 15 minutes and costs €0.77. A taxi will cost up to €10.

Bus

CTM (☎ 070 209 12 10) buses run on routes across the city and surrounding area. They come in handy for the Calamosca and Poetto beaches. A ticket costs €0.77.

Car & Motorcycle

Parking in the city centre generally means paying. Parking in blue zones costs €0.52 for the first hour and €1.03 for each hour thereafter. Either buy special tickets to leave on the dash from newspaper stands or pay one of the attendants.

The big international car rental agencies are represented at the airport and there are several at the port. You'll also find a few local outfits. **Ruvioli** (☎ 070 65 89 55; www.ruvioli.it; Via dei Mille 9) charges €166 for a Fiat Panda for three days.

Taxi

There are taxi ranks at Piazza Matteotti, Piazza della Repubblica and on Largo Carlo Felice. You can call for one on ☎ 070 40 01 01 from 5.30am to 2am. Outside those times you might have difficulty.

SOUTHEAST OF CAGLIARI

Once past the Poetto strand, the road east pretty much hugs the coast all the way around to Villasimius and then north along the Costa Rei.

The landscape is bare and hilly and the more clicks you put between yourself and Cagliari the more enticing the beaches become. There are numerous nondescript hotels along here that can put you up but you are better off pushing on to Villasimius and the Costa Rei.

Villasimius & Costa Rei

A few kilometres short of Villasimius, the heart of the tourist coast in these parts, a road veers off south along the peninsula that leads to **Capo Carbonara**, the most southeasterly point of Sardinia. On the way is a camp site and what remains of a square Spanish tower. South of the tower are a few stretches of beach, although the main strand on this side of the peninsula is **Spiaggia del Riso**. The east side is dominated by the **Stagno Notteri** lagoon. On its seaward side is a nice long beach, **Spiaggia del Simius**.

Villasimius is the most developed town in this area and makes a comfortable base for exploring the attractive coastline.

The only nearby camp site is **Campeggio Spiaggia del Riso** (☎ 070 79 10 52; fax 070 79 71 50; per person/site €7.50/27; ☼ May-Oct; P) on the beach of the same name about halfway down the

west side of the Capo Carbonara peninsula. It gets hellishly crowded in midsummer.

Albergo Stella d'Oro (☎ 070 79 12 55; fax 070 79 26 32; Via Vittorio Emanuele 25; s/d €36.50/67.50; P ☼) is a simple but pleasant enough deal about 50m east off Piazza Gramsci. Rooms are of a reasonable size and all have own bathroom.

Ristorante Carbonara (☎ 070 79 12 70; Via Umberto I 60; meals €30) is a cheerful pale blue place to submerge in for fish meals. The watery critters are on display for you to choose the subject of your main course.

ARST has up to nine buses daily in summer from Cagliari (€2.58, 1½ hours).

To take the wonderful high coast road west and then north towards Costa Rei, head *south* out of Villasimius and follow the signs. About 25km out of Villasimius you hit **Cala Sinzias**, a lovely sandy strand that has two camp sites. About 6km north you hit the resort of **Costa Rei**, with villas, shops and bars. **Spiaggia Costa Rei** is, like those to its south and north, a dazzling white strand lapped by impossibly clear blue-green water.

Camping Capo Ferrato (☎ /fax 070 99 10 12; per person/tent €8.50/12.90, 4-person bungalows €75.50; ☼ Mar-Oct) is a good-value ground at the southern entrance to the Costa Rei resort.

North of the resort scene, **Spiaggia Piscina Rei** has blinding white sand and turquoise water with a camp site fenced in just behind it. More beaches fill the remaining length of coast up to **Capo Ferrato** beyond which driveable dirt trails lead north.

The same ARST buses from Cagliari to Villasimius continue around to Costa Rei, taking about half an hour and costing €3.46.

SOUTHWEST OF CAGLIARI
Nora

Possibly founded as long ago as the 11th century by Phoenicians, the port town of Nora was later occupied by Carthaginians and Romans and only finally abandoned in the Middle Ages. What you see in the **ancient site** (adult/child including Pula museum €5.50/2.50; ☼ 9am-7pm) mostly dates to Roman times. Upon entry you pass by a single standing column of a former temple and then the small theatre now used for summer evening concerts. Towards the west are the substantial remains of the Terme al Mare (Baths by the Sea). Four columns (a

SARDINIA (SARDEGNA)

tetrastyle) stand at the heart of what was a patrician villa whose surrounding rooms retain their mosaic floor decoration.

In nearby Pula, the **Civico Museo Archeologico** (☎ 070 920 96 10; Corso Vittorio Emanuele 67; adult/child incl Nora site €5.50/2.50; ☸ 9am-8pm Sep-Jul, 9am-midnight Aug), near the central Piazza Municipio, has selected finds taken from Nora – mostly ceramics found in Punic and Roman tombs, a few bits of gold and bone jewellery, Roman glassware and the like.

The best sleeping option here is **Hotel Su Guventuddu** (☎ 070 920 90 92; fax 070 920 94 68; s/d €52/78; **P**), 2km from the Nora site on the road leading around to Su Guventeddu beach. It is a comfortable country house with pleasant rooms and a decent restaurant.

Zio Dino (☎ 070 920 91 59; Viale Segni 14; meals €30; ☸ Mon-Sat) is one of central Pula's best eateries, with a tempting mix of seafood and meat dishes. Meals are best begun with the *spaghetti alla Zio Dino*, a seafood special.

Regular ARST buses run from Cagliari to Pula (€2.01, 50 minutes). The last one back to Cagliari leaves at 9.30pm. Up to 16 local shuttle buses circulate between Pula and Nora (you can walk the 3km).

Costa del Sud & Around

The small town and beach of **Chia** marks the start of the beautiful Costa del Sud. It winds its way west to Porto Teulada and offers several enticing beaches, like Cala Teuradda, en route. Make sure to stop for the magnificent views at the lookout point high above Capo Malfatano.

Campeggio Torre Chia (☎ 070 923 00 54; www .campeggiotorrechia.it; per person/tent €8.50/13, 4-person villa up to €115) is a few hundred metres back from Spiaggia Su Portu and often full in August.

ARST buses to/from Chia run along the Costa del Sud a couple of times daily in summer. Up to eight buses run between Cagliari and Chia daily (€2.89, 1¼ hours).

Inland you could visit **Le Grotte Is Zuddas** (☎ 0781 95 57 41; adult/child €6.50/3.62; ☸ 9.30am-noon & 2.30-6pm Apr-Sep, noon-4pm Mon-Sat, 9.30am-noon & 2.30-7pm Sun & holidays Oct-Mar) are one of the island's many spectacular natural sculpture museums. The largely limestone rock lends the stalactites and stalagmites a particularly translucent quality.

SOUTHWESTERN SARDINIA

IGLESIAS

pop 29,700

As mining towns go, Iglesias is a surprisingly charming spot. The Spaniards are long gone but the place retains an Iberian feel, with chatter in the air, deep summer heat, Aragonese-style wrought iron balconies and that touch of decay you find in many a Spanish town.

The Romans called it Metalla, for around here they mined precious metals, especially lead and silver. The Romans were not the first to work mines around here. At the San Giorgio mines just outside Iglesias, mining equipment dating to the Carthaginian era was discovered when the mines were reopened in the 19th century. Mining operations in the Iglesias area ground to a halt in the 1970s.

The **Pro Loco** (☎ 0781 4 17 95; Via Gramsci 11-13; ☸ 9.30am-1pm & 4-7pm Mon-Fri, 9.30am-12.30pm Sat) has information on the town and the rest of the Iglesiente region around it.

Sights

The grand Piazza Sella, laid out in the 19th century, is something of a noisy meeting place for locals. Just off the piazza, amid pleasant hillside sculpted gardens, stand the remains of **Castello Salvaterra**, a Pisan fortress finished under Catalano-Aragonese rule. A stretch of the 14th-century northwestern perimeter walls survives along Via Campidano.

The **Duomo** (cathedral) dominates the eastern flank of Piazza del Municipio and retains its Pisan flavoured Romanesque-Gothic facade, as does the belltower with its chequerboard variety of stone. At the time of writing the cathedral was closed, making it impossible to view the internal makeover Catalan architects gave it in the 16th century. It is one of several churches in the old town (hence its Spanish name).

The **Museo dell'Arte Mineraria** (☎ 333 447 99 80; www.museoartemineraria.it; Via Roma 17; admission free; ☸ 7-10.30pm Wed-Sun Jun-Aug, 6-8.30pm Sat-Sun Sep-May) was a mining school and many of the materials and displays downstairs that recreate the reality of the mines were used by the school to train senior mine workers.

Sleeping & Eating

Hotel Artu (☎ 0781 2 24 92; www.hotelartuiglesias.it; Piazza Sella 15; s/d €55/82.50; ⓟ ⚇) The only central option. An ugly building, its rooms are fine and of a reasonable size, some looking out on to the busy square.

Volters & Murion (☎ 0781 3 37 88; Piazza Collegio 1; meals €25) A cheerful eatery tucked into a corner of Piazza del Collegio. It has a nice range of pasta and main courses. While, it's not fine cuisine, it's perfectly reasonable. The place is one of the best for an evening tipple in summer.

Getting There & Away

Intercity buses arrive at the Via Oristano side of the Giardini Pubblici. You can get information and tickets from Bar Giardini across the road. As many as 10 FMS buses run from Cagliari to Iglesias (€2.89, one to 1½ hours). As many as 16 trains run between Iglesias and Cagliari (€2.56). The train station on Via Garibaldi is a 15-minute walk along Via Matteotti from the town centre.

TEMPIO DI ANTAS

This Carthaginian-Roman **temple** (☎ 347 817 49 89; adult/child €2.60/1.30; ⓣ 9am-1pm & 3-8pm May-Sep, 9am-1pm & 3-6pm Sat, Sun & holidays Oct-Apr), about 15km north of Iglesias on the twisting road towards Fluminimaggiore, is set in a wide, picturesque valley. What you see, including the eight resurrected columns, dates to Roman times. You can take the FMS bus (€1.76, 45 minutes) from Iglesias for Fluminimaggiore and get off just after the village of Sant'Angelo. The temple is then a 3km walk along a dirt road.

Nearby and only reached by car is the **Grotta de Su Mannau** (☎ 0781 58 01 89; admission €4.50; ⓣ 9.30am-6.30pm), an 8km-long cave.

IGLESIENTE COAST

Just 8km west of Iglesias is the local golden beach of **Funtanamare** facing the Golfo di Gonnesa. Swing north from Funtanamare along the coast road, which quickly climbs the rocky walls of the Iglesiente coast to give you spectacular views northwards. Even before you reach the former mining settlement of Nebida, 5.5km away, three

faraglioni (craggy outcrops jutting out of the sea) and the bizarre **Scoglio Pan di Zucchero** (Sugarloaf Rock) islet come into view against a majestic backdrop of sheer rugged cliffs.

Nebida is a sprawling place with great views and a useful hotel. **Hotel Pan di Zucchero** (☎ /fax 0781 4 71 14; Via Centrale 366; s/d €36/46) has functional rooms and some have balconies with stunning coastal views. The restaurant serves up copious helpings from a limited menu of mostly seafood pasta dishes (try the fish-stuffed *ravioli al pomodoro*).

A few kilometres north **Masua** boasts wonderful close-up views of the Scoglio Pan di Zucchero and the chance to visit a singular mining 'port'. In 1924 a 600m twin tunnel was dug into the cliff here towards the open sea. An ingenious mobile 'arm' shoved the raw minerals from a conveyor belt to ships moored directly below. **Porto Flavia** (☎ 348 661 51 92; adult/child €8/4.50) can be visited daily for one-hour tours (the staff provide the hard hats!) in July and August (four or five visits a day depending on demand). In other months it is generally only possible for groups by calling ahead.

Up to 11 FMS buses run between Iglesias and Masua, just up from Nebida (€1.19, 30 minutes).

Beach-lovers should call in at the deep-set **Cala Domestica** on the way north to the former mining town of Buggerru and the broad **Spiaggia Portixeddu** beach at the northern end of the Iglesiente coast.

CARBONIA & AROUND
pop 32,700

The listless grid plan town of Carbonia was to have been the pride and joy of the island. In 1936 work began on the island's coal capital (*carbone* means coal). Shame that the local product was so poor. The idea of attaining coal self-sufficiency had no chance and today the town is barely worth stopping by. About 4km northwest of Carbonia is **Monte Sirai** (admission €2.60; ⓣ 9am-5pm Oct-Apr, 9am-1pm & 4-8pm May-Sep). The high plateau was a natural spot for a fort and the Phoenicians built one in 650BC. Dislodged by local Sardinian tribes, they were later replaced by the Carthaginians. You can make out the placement of the Carthaginian acropolis and defensive tower, a necropolis and *tophet* (where deceased children were interred).

SANT'ANTIOCO & SAN PIETRO

These islands, off the southwestern coast of Sardinia, have sandy beaches and quiet coves, as well as the pleasant towns of Calasetta (Sant'Antioco) and Carloforte (San Pietro), both with whitewashed or pastel-coloured houses lining narrow streets. The town of Sant'Antioco is more developed.

Information

Tourist Office Carloforte (☎ 0781 85 40 09; Piazza Carlo Emanuele III 19; ☽ 9.30am-12.30pm & 5-8pm Mon-Sat, 10am-noon Sun)

Tourist Office Sant'Antioco (☎ 0781 8 20 31; Piazza Repubblica 31a; ☽ 9am-noon & 5.30-9pm Mon-Fri)

Sights & Activities

In Sant'Antioco the **Chiesa di Sant'Antioco** is worth visiting for its **Catacombe** (admission €2.50; ☽ 9am-12.30pm & 3-8pm Mon-Sat), where the early Christians buried their dead and sometimes held Mass. A few doors down is a small archaeology museum and across town are scattered some Carthaginian sites.

Some beaches worth seeking out include **Maladroixa** and **Spiagga Coa Quaddus** along the east coast. The town of Calasetta on the northwest of the island is a sleepy town with a boat across to the Isola San Pietro, whose main settlement, **Carloforte** is a rather elegant spot with some fine restaurants.

The tourist offices can point you in the direction of **sailing** and **diving** outfits, especially on the Carloforte waterfront.

Sleeping

On both islands you will find a few camping grounds and a handful of hotels outside the main towns.

Hotel Eden (☎ 0781 84 07 68; Piazza Parrocchia 15; s/d €50/80; ⊠) A charming option in a modest mansion opposite the Chiesa di Sant'Antioco. Rooms are not particularly big but furnished with a touch of charm.

Hotel Hieracon (☎ 0781 85 40 28; www.hotelhieracon.cjb.net; Corso Cavour 63; s/d €57/98; ⊠) Carloforte's faded jewel, a grey art nouveau mansion at the northern end of the waterfront. It has all sorts of rooms with up to four beds.

Eating

Ristorante Sette Nani (☎ 0781 84 09 00; Via Garibaldi 139, Sant'Antioco; meals €25-30) Spread out over several floors and boasting a garden dining area to boot. Dishes lean to the sea and are good without being magnificent. You will be offered a selection of Sardinian sweets and a glass of *mirto* (local liqueur) to finish.

Tonno di Corsa (☎ 0781 85 51 06; Via Marconi 47, Carloforte; meals €35-40; ☽ Tue-Sun) Up a few blocks from the seaside along Via Caprera (then turn right) is paradise for tuna lovers. One of the best is the delicious *ventresca di tonno*, a sublime cut of the best tuna meat.

Dau Bobba (☎ 0781 85 40 37; Lungocanale delle Saline, Carloforte; meals €45-50; ☽ Wed-Mon) Dau Bobba, 500m south of the main waterfront, has a little courtyard garden inside that makes for an inviting shelter to taste anything from a great pesto to fresh catch of the day.

Getting There & Around

Sant'Antioco is connected to the mainland by a land bridge and is accessible by FMS bus from Cagliari and Iglesias. Regular ferries connect Calasetta and Carloforte. From Carloforte boats run to Portovesme on the mainland. The one-way trip on any of these costs around €2.50 a person. Local buses run around Sant'Antioco. Limited summer services operate on San Pietro.

COSTA VERDE

From Capo Pecora in the south to Capo Frasca in the north, the Costa Verde (Green Coast) boasts some of the least spoiled and most beautiful beaches in Sardinia.

From the south head inland along the SS126 and turn west at the turn-off for Bau and Gennamari. A high hill road winds out towards the coast. Keep an eye out for signs to **Spiaggia Scivu**, a spectacular golden strand. Almost 4km north of the Bau and Gennamari turn-off is another for the ghost town of **Ingurtosu**. Follow this and the track that winds out west to the coast to reach the magnificent dune-backed **Spiaggia Piscinas**.

In summer a few kiosk-cafés and fresh-water showers are set up on the beach. People park their campervans here or stay in the nearby stylish **Hotel Le Dune** (☎ 070 97 71 30; www.leduneingurtosu.it; r up to €165), carved out of mining buildings that were at the head of a mini-railway used to ferry ore to the coast for transport.

From there the road winds north through green *macchia* bush and pine stands past several beaches until you reach the scruffy

SARDINIA (SARDEGNA)

Torre dei Corsari resort. The broad beach that sweeps north below this high promontory, is another gem. At its northern end the beach is also known as **Pistis**.

Ostello della Torre (☎ /fax 070 97 71 55; Viale della Torre; s/d €25/47, half-board €45) is perched on a high point behind the southern headland that seals off the beach. Rooms are nicely arranged and amazingly good value. You can sit on terraces with sea views or in the garden.

It is difficult to get around by public transport. A couple of buses run to Ingurtosu from the inland town of Guspini (reached in turn from Cagliari or Oristano) but from there you must walk. Your own transport is the only seriously workable option.

ORISTANO & THE WEST

Oristano was only created as a province in 1974. The focal point for most visitors is the ancient site of Tharros on the Sinis peninsula and the beaches to the north. But the sleepy capital, Oristano, is also worth a stopover, as are several towns and Nuraghic sites in the interior.

ORISTANO
pop 32,900

Oristano was founded in the early Middle Ages as the inhabitants of Tharros wearied of repeated raids by North African corsairs. By the 11th century it had become the capital of the Giudicato d'Arborea (which reflects the area of the modern province), one of four such entities into which Sardinia was divided in the Middle Ages prior to its takeover by the Crown of Aragon. Eleonora di Arborea (c1340–1404) became head of the *giudicato* in 1383 and has gone down in history for her wise administration and resistance to the Catalano-Aragonese. Her death in 1404 led to capitulation but her Carta de Logu, an extraordinary law code, outlived her.

Information
BOOKSHOP
La Pergomena (☎ /fax 0783 7 50 58; Via Vittorio Emanuele 24) An excellent range of books on all aspects of Sardinia, plus a handful of novels in English, French and German.

INTERNET ACCESS
Internet Haus (Via Brancaleone Doria 28; €4/hr;
🕑 9.30am-1pm & 5.30-9.30pm Mon-Fri, 9.30am-1pm Sat)

MEDICAL SERVICES
Guardia Medica (☎ 0783 7 43 33; Via Carducci) For medical assistance.
Hospital (Viale Fondazione Rockefeller) The main hospital is south of the town centre.
Pharmacy (Corso Umberto 51)

POST
Post Office (Via Mariano IV; 🕑 8.15am-6.15pm Mon-Fri, 8.15am-noon Sat)

TOURIST INFORMATION
Information Booth (Piazza Roma; 🕑 9am-1pm & 4-9pm Mon-Sat, 9am-1pm & 4-10pm Sun & holidays Jul–mid-Sep)
Tourist Office (☎ 0783 3 68 31; enturismo.oristano@tiscali.it; Piazza Eleonora 19; 🕑 8am-2pm & 4-7pm Mon-Fri)
Tourist Office (☎ 0783 7 06 21; Via Vittorio Emanuele 8; 🕑 9am-noon & 5-8pm Mon-Fri, 9am-noon Sat May-Sep, 9am-noon & 4.30-7.30pm Mon-Fri, 9am-noon Sat Oct-Apr)

Sights
The 13th-century **Torre di Mariano II** (Piazza Roma) is one of the only vestiges of Oristano's medieval walls. The shopping street of Corso Umberto leads from Piazza Roma to **Piazza Eleonora d'Arborea**, presided over by a 19th-century statue of Oristano's heroine. The neoclassical **Chiesa di San Francesco** (Via Sant'Antonio; 🕑 8am-noon & 5-7pm Mon-Sat; 8am-noon Sun) is home to the *Crocifisso di Nicodemoa*, a 14th-century wooden sculpture by an unknown Catalan artist.

Follow Via Duomo to the cathedral or **Duomo** (Piazza del Duomo; 🕑 7am-noon & 4-7pm Mon-Sat, 8am-1pm Sun), built in the 13th century but remodelled in the 18th century. Its baroque bell tower is topped by a multi-coloured dome.

Museo Antiquarium Arborense (☎ 0783 79 12 62; Piazzetta Corrias; adult/child €3/1; 🕑 9am-1.30pm & 3-8pm), in the heart of the town, contains one of the most important collections found on the island. Artefacts dug up at Tharros and on the Sinis peninsula range from pre-Nuraghic aretfacts to early medieval pieces. A section hosts a small collection of *retablos* (painted altar pieces). One series of panels, the Retablo del Santo Cristo, done by the

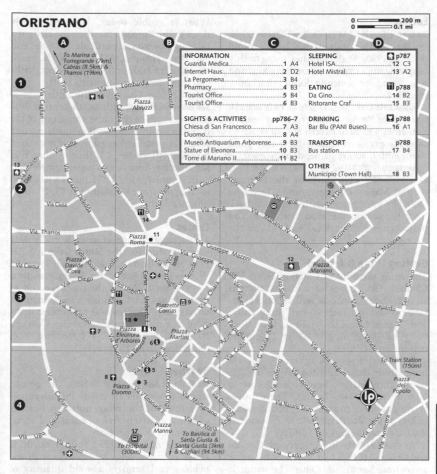

ORISTANO

INFORMATION
Guardia Medica....................................1 A4
Internet Haus.......................................2 D2
La Pergomena.....................................3 B4
Pharmacy...4 B3
Tourist Office..5 B4
Tourist Office..6 B3

SIGHTS & ACTIVITIES   pp786–7
Chiesa di San Francesco.................7 A3
Duomo..8 A4
Museo Antiquarium Arborense.....9 B3
Statue of Eleonora.........................10 B3
Torre di Mariano II........................11 B2

SLEEPING   p787
Hotel ISA..12 C3
Hotel Mistral.....................................13 A2

EATING   p788
Da Gino...14 B2
Ristorante Craf.................................15 B3

DRINKING   p788
Bar Blu (PANI Buses)....................16 A1

TRANSPORT   p788
Bus station..17 B4

OTHER
Municipio (Town Hall)..................18 B3

---

workshop of Cagliari's Pietro Cavaro in 1533, depicts a series of Franciscan saints.

About 3km south of Oristano at Santa Giusta, easily accessible by local ARST buses, is **Basilica di Santa Giusta**. Built from 1135 to 1145, it was one of the earliest Tuscan-style Romanesque churches built in Sardinia.

Festivals & Events
Oristano bursts into life with **Sa Sartiglia**, held on the last Sunday of carnival (late February or early March) and repeated on Shrove Tuesday. See the boxed text, pp800–1.

Sleeping
Camping Torregrande (☎/fax 0783 2 22 28; camping person/tent €5.20/7.80, bungalows €65.50; ⚘ May-Sep)

This camp site is a few hundred metres short of the waterfront at Marina di Torregrande as you come in from Oristano, 7km away.

Hotel Mistral (☎ 0783 21 25 05; fax 0783 21 00 58; Via Martiri di Belfiore; s/d €45/70; ⚙) Probably the ugliest option you'll encounter in town, at least it's ugly on the outside. Rooms are generally stock standard and comfortable enough, with en suite bathroom, TV and phone.

Hotel ISA (☎/fax 0783 36 01 01; Piazza Mariano 50; s/d €50/83) The most appealing hotel, even if it's getting a little crumbly around the edges. The better rooms have little semicircular balconies looking on to the square.

SARDINIA (SARDEGNA)

Eating

Da Gino (☎ 0783 7 14 28; Via Tirso 13; meals €25-30; ☻ Mon-Sat) This stalwart has been around since the 1930s. Seafood dishes, using freshly caught beasties from the nearby lagoons and coast, stand out. *Aragosta* (lobster) is a house speciality.

Ristorante Craf (☎ 0783 37 06 89; Via De Castro 34; meals €30; ☻ Mon-Sat) Another quality option. You enter a vaulted cavern and sit down to carefully prepared dishes, including good soups if, you're game, donkey meat.

Giovanni (☎ 0783 2 20 51; Via Colombo 8; meals €35; ☻ Tue-Sun) The pick of the culinary crop at Marina de Torregrande. Don't be fooled by its unprepossessing location back from the sea on the road to Cabras. The pasta courses using local seafood are the strong suit.

Getting There & Around

The main intercity bus station is on Via Cagliari. ARST buses leave for destinations all over the province as well as longer distance objectives like Sassari (four daily) and Cagliari (three daily). Buses leave once every half-hour for the 10- to 15-minute trip to Santa Giusta.

PANI buses serve Cagliari (€5.84, 1¼ hours, four daily) and Sassari (€7.18, 2½ hours, three daily). Several head east to Nuoro (€5.84, two hours). These buses arrive and leave from Via Lombardia. Buy tickets at **Bar Blu** (Via Lombardia 30; ☻ 6am-10pm Mon-Sat) or on the bus on Sunday.

As many as 20 trains run between Cagliari and Oristano (€4.55, two hours). Some trains arrive from Sassari and Olbia. The station is west of the centre on Piazza Ungheria.

Oristano city buses on the *azzurra* (blue) line run from Via Cagliari to Marina di Torregrande.

SINIS PENINSULA

West of Oristano stretches the Sinis Peninsula (Penisola di Sinis), with sandy beaches, the ruins of the ancient Tharros and the chance to see flamingos.

Tharros & Around

The ancient city of **Tharros** (☎ 0783 37 00 19; admission incl Museo Civico in Cabras €4; ☻ 9am-sunset), set impeccably by the sea at the southern extreme of the peninsula, reached the height of its importance under the Carthaginians.

What is visible today, however, largely dates to the Roman era, when the city got a thorough overhaul, particularly in the 2nd and 3rd centuries AD. The city's basalt streets were laid, and the aqueduct, baths and other major monuments built.

Just before Tharros is the settlement of **San Giovanni di Sinis**, with its 6th-century Byzantine church of the same name, one of the oldest in Sardinia. Some 4km north in a tiny village of pastel-coloured houses once used for spaghetti westerns, is the tiny church of **San Salvatore**, built over a pagan temple.

In summer, four ARST buses a day head to Tharros from Oristano (€1.45, 20 to 30 minutes).

Cabras

This straggling lagoon town is really only worth a stop for the **Museo Civico** (☎ 783 29 06 36; Via Tharros 121; admission incl Tharros €4; ☻ 9am-1pm & 4-8pm Tue-Sun Jun-Sep, 9am-1pm & 3-7pm Tue-Sun Oct-May) at the southern end of town. It has Carthaginian and Roman artefacts from Tharros and prehistoric items from a nearby archaeological site, Cuccuru is Arrius. Regular ARST buses run from Oristano (€0.67, 15 minutes).

Beaches

Spiaggia di San Giovanni di Sinis, the golden strand nearest Tharros has the advantage over most of the more northern beaches of being relatively free of rocks and algae; however, it does get busy.

Of the many beaches further north, **Is Arutas** is interesting. Mingled in with the pebbles and sand is a good quantity of quartz – walking along the beach is like getting a foot massage (making a souvenir of some of the quartz is illegal). The beach is signposted and is 5km west off the main road leading north from San Salvatore.

At **Putzu Idu** a long and sandy, if untidy, strand is backed by a motley set of holiday homes and beach bars. The lagoon inland from Putzu Idu often hosts some of Sardinia's flamingo population.

A trio of hotels (one each in Putzu Idu, Mandriola and Su Pallosu) offers the option of staying here and a handful of restaurant-pizzerias keep hunger at bay. Up to three ARST buses run from Oristano to Putzu Idu (30 minutes) in summer. The summer service to Tharros goes on as far as Is Arutas.

NORTH ORISTANO COAST

Further north of the Sinis Peninsula are some still better beaches around the low-key resort of **Santa Caterina di Pittinuri**. The town itself has a decent beach closed off by dramatic cliffs. The emerald waters in the cove of **S'Archittu** are tempting, or you could head a few kilometres south for the long expanse of the **Is Arenas** beach, which you reach along tracks threading past three camp sites. Buses between Oristano and Bosa stop at Santa Caterina, S'Archittu and Cuglieri. They will stop on request at the camp sites.

LAGO OMEDEO CIRCUIT

Following the SS131 highway north out of Oristano you come across the **Santa Cristina** (admission incl Paulilatino archaeological museum €3.10; 8.30am-11pm May-Sep, 8.30am-9pm Oct-Apr), site of a small pilgrims' church, Nuraghic village and, most importantly, an ancient Nuraghic well temple whose lines are so perfect it looks like it was made yesterday. Finds from the Santa Cristina site can be seen at a small archaeological museum in **Paulilatino**, a few kilometres north. Just north of Paulilatino is one of the island's most important *nuraghi*, the **Nuraghe Losa** (0785 5 48 23; admission €3.50; 9am-1pm & 3-7pm).

About 14km northeast of the Nuraghe Losa past Lago Omedeo is the unremarkable rural town of **Sedilo**, which crackles to life for the **Ardia** festival (see the boxed text, pp800–1).

About 30km south of Sedilo on the banks of the Tirso river is strange red town of **Fordongianus**, where everything seems to be made of the local trachyte stone except the **Terme Romane** (0783 6 01 57; admission €3; 9.30am-1pm & 3-7.30pm summer, 9.30am-1pm & 3-5.30pm winter). From below these Roman baths piping hot water still bubbles forth and into the river.

Your own transport is needed to get around most of these sights, although several ARST buses run from Oristano to Fordongianus (€1.76, 40 minutes). Buses from Oristano to Abbasanta (via Paulilatino; €2.32, 55 minutes) put you within potential walking distance of Nuraghe Losa, although it's a hassle.

BARUMINI & AROUND

One of the most important and most visited of the island's *nuraghi* is the **Nuraghe Su Nuraxi**

MYSTERY TOWERS, FAIRY HOUSES & SACRED WELLS

As early as 1800 BC Sardinians started raising rudimentary defensive towers. These Bronze Age structures, usually made of great slabs of dark basalt or trachyte, have defied explanation down through the centuries but their creators were fine engineers. In their more complex form, consisting of several levels, these conical towers are held together by the force of gravity.

Even before they started building *nuraghi*, the Sardinians were busy digging tombs into the rock across the island. These cavities later came to be known to the superstitious as *domus de janas* (fairy houses). More elaborate were the common graves fronted by what appears to be great ceremonial entrance ways known as *tombe di giganti* (giants' tombs).

From about 1100 BC the island's people began to construct elaborate *pozzi sacri* or sacred well temples. Those that have been discovered display many common traits. These include a keyhole shaped opening in the ground with a triangular stairwell leading down to the well. The wells always face the sun and are so oriented that at the solstices the sun shines directly down the stairs. The building techniques were more refined than those employed in the *nuraghi* and nowhere is this more evident than in the Santa Cristina site northeast of Oristano.

(admission over/under 25 €4.20/3.10; 9am-8pm), barely half a kilometre to the west of the village of Barumini on the road to Tuili. The hulk of the central tower of the complex stands as a prominent landmark but what makes it impressive is not so much the central tower but the extent of the village ruins around it, a veritable beehive of circular buildings, most not more than a metre high.

Albergo Sa Lolla (070 936 84 19; fax 070 936 11 07; Via Cavour 49; s/d €42/62; Jul-Aug) is a lovely renovated mansion with seven rooms in Barumini. It also has a restaurant. It's a few hundred metres east of the Chiesa di Santa Tecla.

To its north is the high **Giara di Gesturi** plateau, home to some 500 wild *cavallini* ('minihorses' or ponies), most likely seen by shallow *pauli* (seasonal lakes) at the break of daylight or dusk.

About 24km by road to the east (you have to double back through Serri) is the **Santuario Santa Vittoria di Serri** (adult/child €4/2; ☼ 9am-7pm), the most extensive Nuraghic settlement unearthed in Sardinia.

You need your own transport to get around this area as buses are rare and could leave you stranded.

BOSA
pop 7856

Bosa lies within the fat finger of Nuoro province that slips its way to the west coast between Sassari and Oristano provinces. The only important Sardinian town on a river, Bosa is a pretty stop that combines the curiosity of the medieval town and its monuments with the broad sandy beach nearby. It lies 3km inland from a fine beach on the banks of the Temo river.

Information

Medical Services (☎ 0785 37 46 15; Viale Italia) Just off the beach at Bosa Marina.

Tourist Office (☎ 0785 37 71 08; Bosa Marina train station; ☼ 10am-1pm & 7-10pm Jun-Sep)

Tourist Office (☎ 0785 37 61 07; www.infobosa.it; cnr Via Alberto Azuni & Via F Romagna; ☼ 9.30am-1pm & 6-8.30pm May-Sep)

Sights

Bosa's old centre, known as Sa Costa and bunched on a hill side, is all narrow lanes, little squares and a sprinkling of elegant baroque churches. The imposing medieval **castle** was built in 1112 by the Malaspina, a noble Tuscan family, to control the Temo valley. The Temo, with its 8km of navigable waters, made a local tanning industry possible. Also of interest is the Romanesque church of **San Pietro Extramuros** (☼ 10am-7pm), 2km from the old bridge on the south bank of the Temo. Bosa Marina's broad, sandy **beach** is the perfect place to end a tough morning's sightseeing. Windsurfers like this spot and it is possible to hire gear on the beach.

The coastline between Bosa and Alghero is stunning, with rugged cliffs dropping down to coves. It makes for a great drive and a couple of buses do the route too.

Sleeping & Eating

Hotel Sa Pischedda (☎ 0785 37 30 65; fax 0785 37 70 54; Via Roma 2; s/d €55/60) The most attractive choice in town. The wine-red facade of this restored house greets you just on the south side of the Ponte Vecchio. Some rooms have arched balconies out the back. It is the only place in Bosa that can be said to have character.

Hotel Miramare (☎ /fax 0785 37 34 00; Via Colombo; s/d up to €60/80) Virtually on the beach. Rooms are clean and simple, with TV and bathroom. Prices are often substantially lower.

Tatore (☎ 0785 37 31 04; Via Giuseppe Mannu 13; meals €25-30) This place offers whatever its owners find in the fish markets that day. Hardly surprisingly the seafood pasta is good, as is the *zuppa di pesce* (fish soup).

Borgo Sant'Ignazio (☎ 0785 37 46 62; Via Sant' Ignazio 33; meals €24; ☼ Tue-Sun) Hiding amid the web of lanes in the heart of the old town, the tastefully decorated dining area in this eatery provides an enticing setting for typical Sardinian dishes.

Getting There & Away

All buses terminate at Piazza Zanetti. Most services are run by FdS, which has a ticket office on the square. Up to four buses run to/from Alghero. The quicker ones take the scenic coastal route (€2.89, 55 minutes). Sassari is a long haul (€5.84, 2¼ hours).

NORTHERN SARDINIA

ALGHERO
pop 40,400

In the years after their arrival in Sardinia in 1323, the conquerors of the Crown of Aragon tried to 'ethnically cleanse' several Sardinian cities, replacing the local populace with Catalan colonists. The attempts largely failed, except in the northwestern port town of Alghero, where even today the Catalan tongue is still spoken. The medieval centre, with its sea walls still intact, is one of the most charming of Sardinian towns, although you may well feel like you have landed somewhere in Spain. It makes an agreeable base for exploring the northwest but can get crowded in summer, when the population more than doubles.

Orientation

Alghero's historic centre is on a small promontory jutting into the sea, with the new town stretching out behind it and along the coast to the north. Intercity buses arrive in Via Catalogna, just outside the historic centre. The train station is about 1km north, on Via Don Minzoni.

Information

INTERNET ACCESS
Poco Loco (Via Gramsci 8; €5/hr; 7.30pm-1am) It has just three terminals.

MEDICAL SERVICES
Farmacia Bulla (Via Garibaldi 13)
Farmacia Cabras (Piazza Sulis 11)
Ospedale Civile (☎ 079 99 62 00; Via Don Minzoni) The main hospital.

POST
Post Office (Via Carducci 35; 8.15am-6.15pm Mon-Fri, 8.15am-1pm Sat)

TOURIST INFORMATION
Tourist Office (☎ 079 97 90 54; www.infoalghero.it; Piazza Porta Terra 9; 8am-8pm Mon-Sat, 9am-1pm Sun Apr-Oct, 8am-2pm Mon-Sat Nov-Mar)

Sights
The cobbled lanes and honey-coloured walls of this former outpost of the Catalan merchant empire preserve more than a whiff of the centuries of Catalan presence here.

The **Cattedrale di Santa Maria** has been ruined by constant remodelling, but its **bell tower** (admission €1.50; 7-9.30pm Jun-Jul & Sep, 6-11pm Aug) remains a fine example of Catalan Gothic architecture. The **Museo Diocesano** next door to the cathedral houses religious treasures in a former chapel.

On old town's main street is the engaging **Chiesa di San Francesco** (Via Carlo Alberto; 7.30am-noon & 5-8.30pm), a combination of Romanesque and Gothic with an austere stone facade.

Several landward towers remain, including what was the main land entrance, or **Torre Porta a Terra**, now an information office and the **Torre di San Giovanni**, which houses a small multimedia display on the town's history. To the north the **Bastione della Maddalena**, with its like-named tower, form the only extant remnant of the city's former land battlements. The Mediterranean crashes up against the seaward walls of the **Bastioni di San Marco** and **Bastioni di Cristoforo Colombo**. Along these seaward bulwarks are some delightful eateries and

bars – wonderful for watching a summer sunset.

North of Alghero's port, jammed with yachts, Via Garibaldi sweeps up to the town's beaches, **Spiaggia di San Giovanni** and the adjacent **Spiaggia di Maria Pia**. Indeed, the line of strands continues pretty much uninterrupted around the coast to Fertilia.

Festivals & Events
The **Estate Musicale Internazionale di Alghero** (International Summer of Music) is staged in July and August, featuring classical music concerts in the contemplative setting of the Chiesa di San Francesco cloister.

Sleeping
It is virtually impossible to find a room in August unless you book in advance.

Camping La Mariposa (☎ 079 95 03 60; Via Lido 22; per person/tent €10.50/5, bungalows up to €72; Apr-Oct) About 2km north of the centre, this camp site is on the beach.

Pensione Normandie (☎/fax 079 97 53 02; Via Enrico Mattei 6; s/d €27/55, d with bathroom €62) The cheapest option. It's awkwardly placed south of the centre and the rooms are basic.

Hotel San Francesco (☎/fax 079 98 03 30; Via Ambrogio Machin 2; s/d €47/85; P) The only place in the old town, and alone in exuding real charm. Housed in the former convent of the Chiesa di San Francesco, the rooms are simple but comfortable.

Hotel El Balear (☎ 079 97 52 29; fax 079 97 48 47; Lungomare Dante 32; s/d €48/78; Mar-Oct;) A modest waterfront option south of the centre, with well-maintained, if not luxurious, rooms in a good position. In August half-board is compulsory at €73 per person.

Hotel Carlos V (☎ 079 97 95 01; www.hotelcarlosv.it; Lungomare Valencia 24; s €70-119, d €88-166; P) In a fine position, with its own pool and tennis court and the rooms, with all mod cons, are inviting.

Eating
Osteria Macchiavello (☎ 079 98 06 28; Bastioni Marco Polo 57; meals €30; Wed-Mon) A long tunnel of a place stretching to Via Cavour, but in summer you will want to dine right up on the fortress walls, watch the sunset and listen to the waves crashing below.

Da Ninetto (☎ 079 97 80 62; Via Gioberti 4; meals €25-30; Wed-Mon) A bright hole-in-the-wall arrangement and not a bad spot to indulge

SARDINIA (SARDEGNA)

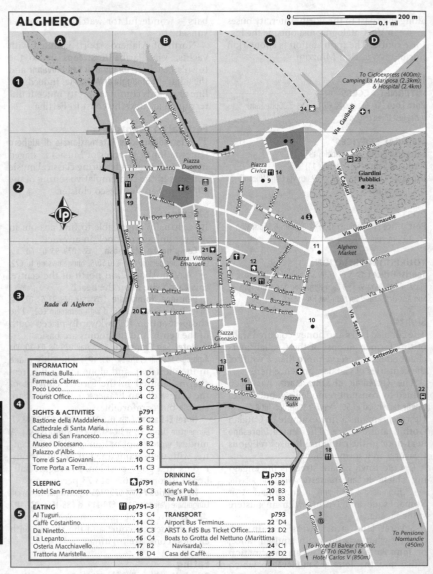

ALGHERO

To Cicloexpress (400m);
Camping La Mariposa (2.3km);
& Hospital (2.4km)

Piazza
Duomo

Piazza
Civica

Giardini
Pubblici

Rada di Alghero

Piazza Vittorio
Emanuele

Piazza
Ginnasio

Piazza
Sulis

To Hotel El Balear (190m);
El Trò (625m) &
Hotel Carlos V (850m)

To Pensione
Normandie
(450m)

INFORMATION	
Farmacia Bulla	1 D1
Farmacia Cabras	2 C4
Poco Loco	3 C5
Tourist Office	4 C2

SIGHTS & ACTIVITIES	p791
Bastione della Maddalena	5 C2
Cattedrale di Santa Maria	6 B2
Chiesa di San Francesco	7 C3
Museo Diocesano	8 B2
Palazzo d'Albis	9 C2
Torre di San Giovanni	10 C3
Torre Porta a Terra	11 C3

SLEEPING	p791
Hotel San Francesco	12 C3

EATING	pp791–3
Al Tuguri	13 C4
Caffè Costantino	14 C2
Da Ninetto	15 C3
La Lepanto	16 C4
Osteria Macchiavello	17 B2
Trattoria Maristella	18 D4

DRINKING	p793
Buena Vista	19 B2
King's Pub	20 B3
The Mill Inn	21 B3

TRANSPORT	p793
Airport Bus Terminus	22 D4
ARST & FdS Bus Ticket Office	23 D2
Boats to Grotta del Nettuno (Marittima Navisarda)	24 C1
Casa del Caffè	25 D2

in some lobster, which comes in at €9.50 per 100g.

Trattoria Maristella (☎ 079 97 81 72; Via Fratelli Kennedy 9; meals €22-25; ☽ Mon-Sat & lunch Sun) One of the best deals in town if you are looking for moderately-priced but reliable grub. The Mediterranean burnt-orange decor is cheerful and in summer

you can sit out in the street. Locals pour in so book ahead.

Al Tuguri (☎ 079 97 67 72; Via Maiorca 113; meals €35-40; ☽ Mon-Sat) This eatery and its near neighbours all involve greater fiscal effort but offer exquisite dining experiences. Try the *maltagliati con carciofi e fave* – a local pasta with artichokes and fava beans.

La Lepanto (☎ 079 97 91 16; Via Carlo Alberto 135; meals €35-40; ⊙ Tue-Sun) Check out the grand assortment of fish on display and the table overflowing with delicious dessert options.

The classiest coffee stop in town is the **Caffè Costantino** (Piazza Civica 31) located in the basement of the late Gothic Palazza d'Albis.

Drinking

The Mill Inn (Via Maiorca 37; ⊙ Thu-Tue) One of the busiest and cosiest bars in the old town, with punters crowding in below the stone vaults for a Guinness.

King's Pub (Via Cavour 123) This venue has two faces, one the terrace looking over the sea out the back on Bastioni di San Marco, the other a pink-lit horseshoe bar approached from Via Cavour.

Buena Vista (Bastioni San Marco 47) The prime drinking spot for taking in the sunset over an early evening aperitif...or two. If it gets too chilly, retire into the cavernous tavern below decks.

El Trò (Lungomare Valencia 3; ⊙ Tue-Sun) Less than 1km south of the centre is a kind of beach bar without the beach (but settled right on a rocky outcrop by the sea). People flock here and, late at night, start to loosen up for a dance. On Friday and Saturday they have you dancing until 7am the next day.

Getting There & Away

AIR
Fertilia airport (☎ 079 93 50 39) is about 12km north of Alghero. Domestic flights from Italy and Ryanair flights from London land here. Six FdS buses a day run between Piazza della Mercede in Alghero and the airport (€0.57, 20 minutes).

BUS
Intercity buses stop at Via Catalogna, by the Giardini Pubblici. Buy tickets for ARST and FdS buses at the booth in the gardens.

A few buses (ARST and FdS) run to/from Sassari and take 50 minutes to an hour depending on the route (€2.32 to €2.58). ARST runs up to eight buses to Porto Torres (€2.58, 55 minutes). Turmo Travel operates one direct bus to Olbia a day (€7.64, two hours).

TRAIN
The train station is 1.5km north of the old town on Via Don Minzoni. Up to 11 trains run to/from Sassari (€1.81, 35 minutes).

Getting Around
Line AO runs from Via Cagliari (by the Giardini Pubblici) to the beaches. Urban buses also operate to Fertilia and several places beyond. You can pick up these buses at stops around the Giardini Pubblici. Tickets (€0.57) are available at Casa del Caffè and most *tabacchi* outlets.

Cicloexpress (☎ 079 98 69 50; Via Garibaldi), on the port side of the road, has bicycles and mountain bikes from €8 to €13 a day and road bikes for up to €75 a day.

AROUND ALGHERO
About 10km west of Alghero on the road to Porto Conte is the **Nuraghe di Palmavera** (admission €2.10, with Necropoli di Anghelu Ruiu €3.60; ⊙ 9am-7pm Apr-Oct, 9.30am-4pm Nov-Mar). At the heart of this 3500-year-old Nuraghic village stands a central limestone tower and an elliptical building with a secondary sandstone tower that was added later. The AF local bus from Alghero to Porto Conte passes by here (€0.57, 15 to 20 minutes).

About 7km north of Alghero, just to the left (west) of the road to Porto Torres, lie scattered the ancient burial chambers of the **Necropoli di Anghelu Ruiu**. The tombs, 38 in all and carved into the rock, date to between 2700 BC and 3300 BC. This sort of tomb came to be known as *domus de janus*, or fairy houses. You need your own vehicle. Just 2km further up the road are the beautiful vineyards of the **Tenute Sella & Mosca** (⊙ 8.30am-8pm), the island's best known winemakers. Join a tour of the **cellars** (☎ 079 99 77 00; admission free; ⊙ tours 5.30pm Mon-Sat mid-Jun–Sep).

The road west from the *nuraghe* heads to **Porto Conte**, a lovely bay, and on around to **Capo Caccia**, a dramatic cape jutting out high above the Mediterranean. The end of the road is marked by the entrance to the **Grotta di Nettuno** (☎ 079 94 65 40; adult/child €8/4; ⊙ 9am-7pm Apr-Sep, 10am-5pm Oct, 9am-2pm Nov-Mar). You climb down several hundred steps along the seaward face of Capo Caccia – worthwhile in itself. The grotto is an underground fairyland that can also be accessed by sea. **Traghetti Navisarda** (☎ 079 95 06 03) runs several boats a day from April to October and allows you a fish-eye view of the coast from Alghero to Capo Caccia before depositing you at the grotto. The round-trip costs €10 (not including entry to the grotto) and takes about

2½ hours. Otherwise, one FdS bus from Via Catalogna in Alghero (€3.25 return, 50 minutes) leaves daily at 9.15am (returning at midday) and a couple of extra services are put on from June to September.

Those with transport should explore the coast north of Capo Caccia. Just a few kilometres north of the turn-off for Alghero, the road continues north. After 2km turn off west for the delightful little bay of **Torre di Porticciolo** (which has a decent camp site). About 7km further north is **Porto Ferro**, an unspoiled beach that even gets a few small waves on wilder days.

SASSARI
pop 121,500

Sardinia's second city, although no stunning beauty, warrants a day of your time. Little of the medieval city remains but some jewels are intact. Two grand churches, the cathedral and Santa Maria di Betlem, are impressive and the important archaeological museum is a must. Stick around for lunch and dinner too, as the old city hides some wonderful traditional locales.

Sassari rose to importance as its coastal counterpart, Porto Torres declined. Capital of the medieval Giudicato di Logudoro, it resisted both Genoese and Catalano-Aragonese rule. A university was set up here in the 16th century but this could not arrest the city's slow decline. More recently, Sassari has been a breeding ground for lawyers and politicians, among them former Italian presidents Antonio Segni and Francesco Cossiga. Communist leader, Enrico Berlinguer (1922–84), was another notable Sassarese.

Orientation

Sassari has a compact centre concentrated around its cathedral, but most services are in the busy newer part of town in the area around the vast 18th-century Piazza Italia. The main bus and train stations are just west of the centre.

Information
EMERGENCY
Police Station (☎ 079 283 55 00, Via Angioi 16)

INTERNET ACCESS
Phonecar (Via Roma 33; €5/hr; ⊙ 9am-1pm & 5-8pm Mon-Fri)

MEDICAL SERVICES
Farmacia Simon (Piazza Castello)
Nuovo Ospedale Civile (☎ 079 206 10 00; Viale Italia)

MONEY
Banca Comerciale Italiana (Piazza Italia 23)
Banca di Sassari (Piazza Castello 8) Western Union representative.

POST
Post Office (Via Brigata di Sassari; ⊙ 8.15am-6.15pm Mon-Fri, 8.15am-1pm Sat)

TOURIST INFORMATION
Tourist Office (☎ 079 23 13 31; www.regione.sardegna.it/azstss; Via Roma 62; ⊙ 9am-1.30pm & 4-6pm Mon-Thu, 9am-1.30pm Fri) Information is patchy.

Sights

In the heart of the medieval quarter the extraordinary baroque facade of Sassari's cathedral, the **Duomo di San Nicola**, seems to emanate its own radiant light. Busy with bulging sculptural caprice, it bears an uncanny resemblance to the ebullient baroque style of Apulia, in southeastern Italy.

Just beyond what were the city walls stands the proud **Chiesa di Santa Maria di Betlem**. The mostly Romanesque facade betrays Gothic and vaguely Oriental admixtures. Inside, the Catalan Gothic vaulting has been preserved but much baroque silliness has crept in.

In the new part of the city, the **Museo Nazionale Sanna** (☎ 079 27 22 03; Via Roma 64; adult over/under 25 €2/1; ⊙ 9am-8pm Tue-Sun) holds one of the island's most important archaeological collections, covering the Nuraghic period in depth.

Festivals & Events

The **Cavalcata Sarda** in May and **I Candelieri** on 14 August are the city's big festivals. For more details, see pp800–1.

Sleeping

Hotel Giusy (☎ 079 23 33 27; fax 079 23 84 90; Piazza Sant'Antonio 21; s/d €31/41.50) Giusy has the dual advantage of being cheap and handy for the train station. The modern brick building is anything but inspiring and rooms are a little clinical. Still they are perfectly acceptable and have balconies.

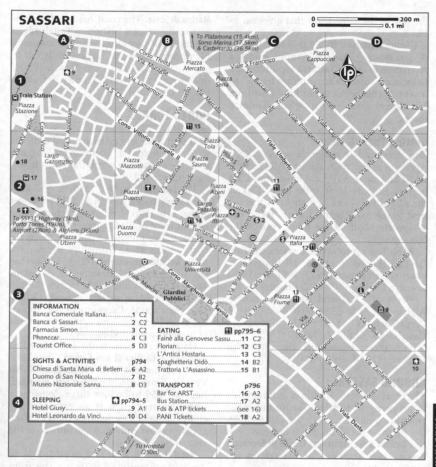

SASSARI

To Platamona (15.4km),
Sorso Marina (17.5km)
& Castelsardo (36.5km)

INFORMATION	
Banca Comerciale Italiana	.1 C2
Banca di Sassari	.2 C2
Farmacia Simon	.3 C2
Phonecar	.4 C3
Tourist Office	.5 D3

SIGHTS & ACTIVITIES	p794
Chiesa di Santa Maria di Betlem	..6 A2
Duomo di San Nicola	.7 B2
Museo Nazionale Sanna	.8 D3

SLEEPING	pp794–5
Hotel Giusy	.9 A1
Hotel Leonardo da Vinci	.10 D4

EATING	pp795–6
Fainè alla Genovese Sassu	.11 C2
Florian	.12 C3
L'Antica Hostaria	.13 C3
Spaghetteria Didò	.14 B2
Trattoria L'Assassino	.15 B1

TRANSPORT	p796
Bar for ARST	.16 A2
Bus Station	.17 A2
Fds & ATP tickets	(see 16)
PANI Tickets	.18 A2

To Hospital
(250m)

SARDINIA (SARDEGNA)

Hotel Leonardo da Vinci (☎ 079 28 07 44; www
.leonardodavincihotel.it; Via Roma 79; s/d €72/98; P ☒)
A spring clean here has left the rooms spick
and span. Skip the breakfast, which is rich
in fiscal terms.

Eating

Eating is a pleasure and all tastes and budgets are catered for. A local curiosity is *fainè*,
a sort of poor man's pizza made of chickpea
flour. It was introduced by the Genoese and
is similar to their *farinata*.

Fainè alla Genovese Sassu (Via Usai 17; ☜ Mon-Sat)
Sassari's original purveyor of fine *fainè*. Students and lunch-time snackers pile in for one
or two (€4 a throw), washed down with beer.
Via Usai is crowded with other eateries.

Trattoria L'Assassino (☎ 079 23 50 41; Via Ospizio
Cappuccini 1a; set dinner €18; ☜ Mon-Sat) This trattoria hidden away in a back alley off Piazza
Tola. The more adventurous will step beyond the set meal and try a selection of six
starters (€13). These can include classics
like *zimino rosso* (everything from braised
calf's heart to diaphragm) and *lumaconi*
(big snails). If you get really lucky you may
find calf's testicles on the menu too.

Spaghetteria Didò (Largo Pazzola 8; meals €18-22;
☜ Mon-Sat) A guaranteed hit. Apart from
the pasta, you can eat abundant, straightforward fish and meat courses.

Florian (☎ 079 20 80 56; Via Capitano Bellieni 27;
meals €35-40; ☜ Mon-Sat) A classic, with the
elegant dining area stretching back behind

the café of the same name that gives on to Via Roma.

L'Antica Hostaria (☎ 079 20 00 60; Via Mazzini 27; meals €40-45; ✆ Mon-Sat) L'Antica enjoys a reputation as one of Sassari's top addresses. In intimate surroundings you are treated to inventive cuisine rooted in local tradition. Meat lovers should try the *tagliata di manzo* (beef).

Getting There & Away
The intercity bus station is on Via XXV Aprile near the train station. ARST, FdS, PANI and some ATP local buses travelling beyond the city leave from here. Tickets for all but PANI can be bought at the bar next to the AGIP petrol station. PANI has a separate booth at the other end of the bus station.

PANI has up to seven services to/from Cagliari (€12.60 to €13.43, 3¾ hours). Six buses run to Nuoro (€6.77, 2½ hours) and seven to Oristano (€7.18, 2¼ hours).

Plenty of ARST and FdS buses run to Alghero (€2.32 to €2.58, 50 to 60 minutes), Porto Torres (€1.45, 20 to 30 minutes) and Castelsardo (€2.01, one hour).

Two direct trains link the city with Cagliari (€12.10, 4¼ hours).

AROUND SASSARI
The northwestern Sardinian countryside is peppered with delightful Romanesque churches built in a rough Tuscan style by the Pisans. One of the more impressive is the **Basilica della Santissima Trinità di Saccargia** about 18km southeast of Sassari on the SS597 road to Olbia.

About 2.5km back towards Sassari, where the SS597 branches off the SS131, head south along the latter about 23km to Torralba, just outside of which stands one of the island's major ancient sites, the **Nuraghe Santu Antine** (☎ 079 84 72 96; admission €3; ✆ 8.30am-sunset). Set in the so-called Valle dei Nuraghi (Nuraghes Valley), it is a unique blast from the past – at least 1600 years BC! If you only see one *nuraghe* in Sardinia, this one rivals Su Nuraxi at Barumini. Not far off to the northwest, just outside the village of Borutta, is another fine Romanesque church, **Chiesa di San Pietro Sorres**. ARST buses from Sassari call in at Torralba.

North of Sassari stretch the locals' favourite beaches, such as **Platamona** and

Marina di Sorso. The coast road leads northeast to the coastal bastion of **Castelsardo**, a confusion of tiny lanes wrapped around a high promontory that juts defiantly out to sea. ARST buses run from Sassari (€2.01, one hour) and Santa Teresa di Gallura (€4.44, 1½ hours).

PORTO TORRES
pop 21,440
This port town and petrochemical centre is unlikely to hold your attention for long, but a couple of sites are worth the effort if you have time to kill.

The **tourist office** (☎ 079 51 06 59; ✆ 7.30am-1pm & 4-8pm May-Sep, 9am-1pm & 3.30-7.30pm Mon-Sat Oct-Apr) is in an odd yellow structure in the port in front of the Capitaneria building.

Just a five-minute walk from the main port towards where Grimaldi's ferries dock is the **Antiquarium** (admission €3; ✆ 9am-8pm Tue-Sat), which houses artefacts discovered in Turris Libisonis, the present city's Roman predecessor. More interesting is what's outside, the excavated remains of the Roman city's public baths. You can see remnants of Roman streets and mosaics.

Of greater interest is the limestone Romanesque **Basilica di San Gavino** (✆ 8.30am-1pm & 3-7pm), about 1.5km inland on Corso Vittorio Emanuele, the town's main road. Built in 1050 to honour three Roman-era Christian martyrs, it is an extraordinary church, notable among other things for the apses on either end – you can only enter the church by side doors!

Hotel Elisa (☎ 079 51 32 60; fax 079 51 37 68; Via Mare 2; s/d with breakfast €46.50/73) is a spit from the port. Rooms are comfortable and come with TV and phone, and in some cases views across to the port.

Cristallo (☎ 079 51 49 09; Piazza XX Settembre 11; meals €35; ✆ Tue-Sun) is an unassuming looking place where you can enjoy good seafood and a selection of Sardinian favourites, such as lamb.

Most buses leave from Piazza Colombo, virtually at the port. Plenty go to Sassari (€1.45, 30 to 40 minutes). Up to six head for Alghero (€2.58, 50 minutes) and another six to Stintino (€2.01, 30 minutes). Trains also run south to Sassari (€1.20, 15 minutes) and beyond.

For information on ferries, see Mainland Italy–Sardinia Ferry Crossings (p773).

DALLAS STRIBLEY

Island hop your way around the **Arcipelago di la Maddalena** (p797)

ROCCO FASANO

Hike up the steep slopes of Cagliari's famed **Castello District** (p776)

EMILY RIDDELL

Savour the Catalan influence still pervading the small town of **Alghero** (p790)

Be a bronzed beach babe for a while on the magnificent cost of **Golfo di Orosei** (p805)

ROCCO FASANO

NICK TAPP

Spend some leisure time in Italy's World Heritage–listed **Cinque Terre** (p192)

ALAN BENSON

Quaff a quality red in the wine-making town of **Alba** (p219)

ALAN BEN

Taste that coveted Italian delicacy, the **truffle** (p221)

Join in the fray at Ivrea's **Battaglia delle Arance** (Battle of Oranges; p223)

DAMIEN SIM

STINTINO & ISOLA ASINARA

A small fishing village lies at the core of this peninsula resort area. People come above all for the magnificent azure waters of the **Spiaggia della Pelosa** towards the northern end of the peninsula. The main island stretching off to the north, **Isola Asinara** (Donkey Island) is so named after the remarkable white donkeys that are native there. Until recently the island was off limits as a penitentiary but now has been converted to a national park. You can join organised visits. Get tickets at **Agenzia La Nassa** (☎ 079 52 00 60; Via Sassari 6) in Stintino or the tourist office in Porto Torres. You can also book by phone number or online (☎ 800 56 11 66; www.parcoasinara.it). Bring lunch as there is nowhere on the island to buy anything.

There are three hotels in Stintino town and another dozen mostly medium- to upper-range places dotted along the coast.

Albergo Geranio Rosso (☎ 079 52 32 92; fax 079 52 32 93; Via XXI Aprile 4; s/d up to €70/105, half-board €80; ⊠) is an immaculately kept place two streets back from Porto Minori. The rooms are comfortable.

Ristorante L'Ancora (☎ 079 527 90 09; meals €35; ☉ Jun-Sep) has a charming veranda with magnificent sea views where you can indulge in good seafood. It's north of Stintino town on the way to Spiaggia della Pelosa – turn right into the Ancora residential complex and follow the signs.

Up to eight buses run from Sassari to Stintino and Spiaggia della Pelosa in summer (€3.15). As many as six run from Porto Torres (€2.01, 30 minutes).

SANTA TERESA DI GALLURA
pop 4060

Together with Palau, about 20km to the east, this seaside resort is an affordable alternative to the jet-set hangouts on the Costa Smeralda and a pleasant enough spot. Head for the weird granite rock forms of nearby Capo Testa. You can see Corsica across the Stretto di Bonifacio or even catch a ferry to Bonifacio for a day trip.

The town was founded in 1808 by the island's Savoy rulers to combat smugglers – the neat grid streets were designed by an army officer. Beyond it tourism-boom housing has spread since the 1960s. In summer as many as 50,000 tourists hang around!

The **tourist office** (☎ 0789 75 41 27; www .regione.sardega.it/aaststg; Piazza Vittorio Emanuele I 24) has information on the town and surrounding area.

After wandering the tidy streets you can head for the 16th-century Spanish watchtower, the **Torre Longonsardo** (admission €1.50; ☉ 10am-12.30pm & 4-7pm Jun-Sep) and plonk on the local beach, the Spiaggia Rena Bianca.

Four kilometres west of Santa Teresa, the granite headland of **Capo Testa** seems more like a divine sculpture garden. The place also has a couple of beaches. Five daily buses run from Santa Teresa from June to September. If you have transport, you could follow the coast road west towards Castelsardo and choose any of a number of wild and barely visited beaches.

There are plenty of hotels although most only open from about Easter to October. In August you may have to pay *mezza pensione* (half-board).

Camping La Liccia (☎ /fax 0789 75 51 90; camping per person/tent €11/15.70, 4-person bungalows €88; ☉ late Apr–Sep) is a pleasant spot about 8km west of town. It has a restaurant and swings for the kids.

Hotel Bellavista (☎ /fax 0789 75 41 62; Via Sonnino 8; s/d €33.60/57; half-board €59.40; ☉ May-Oct) is a surprise deal given its location looking down to the sea. You will have to take half-board in high season.

Ristorante Papé Satan (☎ 0789 75 50 48; Via Lamarmora 20; pizzas up to €8), with its wood-fired oven, is one of the best pizza options in town. The place has a nice internal courtyard and the service is prompt and friendly.

Ristorante La Torre (☎ 0789 75 46 00; Via del Mare 36; meals €30) is at its best with risotto and seafood dishes. Locals recommend it.

Buses terminate at Via Eleonora d'Arborea, near the post office. ARST buses operate up to seven times a day between Olbia and Santa Teresa (€3.72, one hour 50 minutes) and five times daily to/from Sassari (€5.85, 2½ hours). Get tickets from the nearby Baby Bar.

For the frequent ferries across to Bonifacio in Corsica, see p773.

PALAU & ARCIPELAGO DI LA MADDALENA

Close to the Costa Smeralda, **Palau** is little more than a conglomeration of expensive hotels and private apartment blocks. But it also has ferries to the **Isola della Maddalena**, the principal island of an archipelago of seven islands and 40 islets. The magic lies in exploring these islands by boat, although the two main islands warrant some closer attention.

The **tourist office** (☎ 0789 73 63 21; Cala Gavetta; ☼ 8.30am-1pm & 4.30-7.30pm Jun-Sep, reduced hrs Oct-May) in the main town of La Maddalena has information on the entire archipelago. The town is worth a wander and the island has some reasonable beaches.

Sights & Activities

Linked to La Maddalena by a narrow causeway is **Isola Caprera**, where legendary revolutionary Giuseppe Garibaldi made his home. You can visit this **Compendio Garibaldi** (admission €2; ☼ 9am-1.30pm & 4-7pm Tue-Sun Jun-Sep, 9am-1.30pm Tue-Sun Oct-May; guided visits in Italian), which is an object of pilgrimage for many Italians. Giuseppe Garibaldi, professional revolutionary and apotheosised in the folklore of Italian unification, bought half the island in 1855 (he got the rest 10 years later). Here he made his home and refuge, the place he would return to after yet another daring campaign in the pursuit of liberty and Italian unification. It is filled with personal memorabilia. A walking trail north of Garibaldi's pad leads down to the secluded **Cala Coticcio** beach.

The five remaining main islands can only be reached by boat. Numerous excursions leave from Isola della Maddalena and Palau. Or you can hire motorised dinghies and do it yourself. The three northernmost islands are **Isola Budelli**, **Isola Razzoli** and **Isola di Santa Maria**.

Windsurfers go to town on the windswept waters of Porto Pollo. You can hire the gear at several shops near Camping Isola dei Gabbiani (see under Sleeping).

Sleeping

Camping Abbatoggia (☎ 0789 73 91 73; www.camp ingabbatoggia.it; per person €10.50; ☼ Jun-Sep), The best of Isola della Maddalena's handful of camping grounds is in the north. It has access to a couple of good beaches, including Lo Strangolato.

Hotel Il Gabbiano (☎ 0789 72 25 07; Via Giulio Cesare 20; half-board €69-75) is a nice option just outside the western end of town. Rooms are comfortable and some have good sea views.

Back on the mainland there are plenty of options available in Palau. Seven kilometres west of Palau is **Camping Isola dei Gabbiani** (☎ 0789 70 40 19; www.isoladeigabbiani.it; per person €16, 2-person bungalow up to €79; ☼ Apr-Oct), on the peninsula of the same name. In high season you must book the bungalows for a minimum of two weeks. Prices halve in the low season.

Eating

La Maddalena offers a few worthwhile dining options.

Osteria Enoteca da Liò (☎ 0789 73 75 07; Corso Vittorio Emanuele 2-6; meals €25-30) A quiet eatery just off Piazza Santa Maria Maddalena, where you can indulge in Liò's culinary whims, which might run from *carpaccio di salmone* to various fish options in a white-wine sauce.

Ristorante Il Galleone (☎ 0789 73 51 52; Via Zonza 7; meals €25-30) There are signs pointing the way to this place from all over town. It needs them, as you'd be unlikely to stumble on it otherwise. What you find is an earthy back-street diner where you can eat good seafood.

In Palau try **La Taverna** (☎ 0789 70 92 89; Via Rossini 6; meals €25), which is a cosy side-street dining option. Pop in for some *risotto marinaro* (seafood risotto) at €10.

Getting There & Around

ARST buses connect Palau with destinations around the north and east coast, including Olbia, the Costa Smeralda, Santa Teresa di Gallura and Castelsardo. **Caramelli** (☎ 0789 70 94 95) buses run frequently to nearby destinations like Isola dei Gabbiani and Capo d'Orso. All buses leave from the port.

The **Trenino Verde** (☎ 079 24 57 40; www .treninoverde.com) is an 'olde worlde' train (sometimes of the steam variety) that runs from Palau twice a day inland to Tempio Pausania (€13 return, 1¾ hours) from mid-June to mid-September.

Several companies have regular car ferries to Isola della Maddalena. **Enermar** (☎ 899 200001; www.enermar.it) has runs from 7.10am to 10.20pm (€2, 20 minutes). A small car costs €5.50. **Saremar** (☎ 199 12 31 99) and **Tremar** (☎ 0789 73 00 32) also operate regular services. The latter has an hourly service late at night until dawn. Ticket prices are similar on all vessels.

COSTA SMERALDA & AROUND

Back in 1961 the Aga Khan and some pals bought a strip of beautiful Sardinian coast from struggling farmers and created the Costa Smeralda (Emerald). With its 'capital' in the yachtie haven of **Porto Cervo**, it is well beyond the scope of most of us mere mortals. Who wants to hang around posy Italian VIPs anyway? Among the nicest beaches are **Spiaggia Liscia Ruia**, **Capriccioli** (both near the exclusive Moorish-style Hotel Cala di Volpe 6km south of Porto Cervo) and **Spiagga del Principe**, a couple of kilometres further around the headland near Romazzino. The oft-crowded beach of **Baia Sardinia**, just outside the Costa Smeralda area 5km west of Porto Cervo, boasts waters of an incredible blue hue. So, if driving through, enjoy the beaches and head off to sleep elsewhere!

Inland is another world. **Arzachena**, a sprawling town 19km inland from Porto Cervo, is the launch pad for a driving tour to explore ancient Nuraghic sites. Among the most interesting of a series of *nuraghi* and burial grounds is **Coddu Ecchju** (☎ 0789 8 15 37; admission €2; ⏰ 9am-8pm Jun-Sep), a so-called *tomba dei giganti* (giants' tomb) that is in fact an ancient burial ground fronted by a what indeed seems like a giant's door. To get here take the Arzachena–Luogosanto road south out of Arzachena and follow the signs.

As if in defiance of all the wealth on the Costa Smeralda, a highly strategic camp site has been placed on the road running along the south side of Golfo di Cugnana, between Porto Rotondo and the north–south road leading to Porto Cervo. **Villaggio Camping La Cugnana** (☎ 0789 3 31 84; www.campingcugnana.it; Località Cugnana; per 2-people & car €33.60, 2-person bungalows per week €526; ⏰ May-Sep) has a supermarket, backs onto the sea and, perhaps best of all, puts on a free shuttle bus to Costa Smeralda beaches like Capriccioli, Liscia Ruia and Spiaggia del Principe.

OLBIA

pop 44,000

For many, this chaotic port and industrial centre is the first sight of Sardinia. While not altogether awful, unless you have to stick around the best thing you can do is hit the road and leave.

Orientation & Information

Ferries arrive at the Stazione Marittima (terminal) 1km east of town and a local bus (No 3) takes you into the centre. Trains run from the station to the port to coincide with ferry departures. Intercity buses terminate at the end of Corso Umberto next to the main train station. A handful of hotels and eateries are clustered in the narrow streets around Corso Umberto.

The **tourist office** (☎ 0789 2 14 53; fax 0789 2 22 21; Via Catello Piro 1; ⏰ 8am-1pm & 3.30-7pm Mon-Sat, 8.30am-12.30pm & 5-7pm Sun Jun-Sep, 8am-1pm Mon-Sat Oct-May) is handily located just off the port end of Corso Umberto I.

Sights

There's precious little to visit in Olbia apart from the **Chiesa di San Simplicio** (Via San Simplicio; ⏰ 9am-1pm & 4-7pm), a Romanesque jewel set aside from the town hubbub. Built entirely of granite, it is a curious mix of Tuscan and Lombard styles.

Sleeping & Eating

Hotel Terranova (☎ 0789 2 23 95; fax 0789 2 72 55; Via Garibaldi 6; s/d €55/83; ❌) Right in the middle of town. Rooms come with phone and TV and most have balconies over the narrow cobbled lane below.

Hotel Cavour (☎ 0789 20 40 33; www.cavourhotel.it; Via Cavour 22; s/d €57/83; Ⓟ) Nicely appointed rooms lie behind double-glazed windows (handy in this part of town) in this stylishly renovated building. Breakfast is included.

Ristorante Gallura (☎ 0789 2 46 48; Corso Umberto I 145; meals €30-35) This restaurant, in the hotel of the same name, has a reputation for fine seafood and homemade pasta. Booking ahead is essential and neat casual dress advised, as this restaurant has quite a name. It is also a rather romantic outing.

Barbagia (☎ 0789 5 1 64 02; Via Galvani; meals €30) Out of the centre you'll find one of the best spots in Olbia to get a taste of the traditional Sardinian cuisine of the interior. All sorts of odd names in Sardinian, which no amount of Italian will help you recognise, pop out of the menu at you.

Getting There & Away

AIR

Olbia's **Aeroporto di Costa Smeralda** (☎ 0789 6 90 00) is about 5km southeast of the centre and handles flights from most important

SARDINIA (SARDEGNA)

Italian mainland destinations. A handful of international flights from London, Paris and Frankfurt also land here.

BOAT
Regular ferries arrive in Olbia from Genoa, Civitavecchia and Livorno. For more details, see p773.

BUS
Bizarrely, for bus tickets you need to go to the train ticket window next door. ARST has buses travelling to destinations all over the island including Arzachena (€1.76, 11 daily); Golfo Aranci (€1.19, eight daily, summer only); and Porto Cervo (€2.58,

five daily). Further afield you can get to Dorgali (€6.30, three daily); Nuoro (€6.30, seven daily); and Santa Teresa di Gallura (€3.72, six daily).

CAR & MOTORCYCLE
Holiday Car (☎ 0789 2 84 96; Via Genova 71) will rent you a Fiat Panda from €35 a day in high season, or a Fiat Punto for €40. This includes 150km and insurance.

TRAIN
The Trenitalia station lies parallel to Via Gabriele D'Annunzio – walk through the bus station. One direct train a day runs to Cagliari (€12.95, four hours). Otherwise

---

FEAST OF FESTIVALS

Sardinia has hung on more tenaciously to its traditions than almost anywhere else in Italy and this is borne out in the rich calendar of festivals held around the island. A few of the more important ones are listed here.

January
Festa di Sant'Antonio Abate With the winter solstice passed, people of many towns and villages across Sardinia, especially in Nuoro province, seem intent on giving the chill weather a push towards spring with great bonfires lit up in central squares on the evening of 16 January. After the blessing of the fire and perhaps a procession, townsfolk turn to the serious business of drinking. Among the places where you can be sure of seeing a good bonfire are Orosei, Orgosolo, Sedilo and Paulilatino.
Mamuthones Warranting special mention are the celebrations that take place in the otherwise nondescript town of Mamoiada, south of Nuoro. Traditional costumes are used in processions here to represent the *mamuthones*, disturbing animal-like characters with fearsome masks and a heavy belt of cowbells with which they create an infernal din. They generally come out to play again in Carnevale.

February
Carnevale During the period running up to Ash Wednesday, many towns stage carnivals and enjoy their last opportunity to indulge before the 40 days of Lent. Traditionally processions and parties take place from Thursday to *martedí grasso* ('fat Tuesday', the last chance to eat and drink whatever you want before Ash Wednesday).
Sa Sartiglia This is the highlight of Carnevale celebrations at Oristano, held on the Sunday and Tuesday before Lent. It involves a medieval tournament of horsemen in masquerade.

March/April
Pasqua (Easter) Holy Week, which can take place any time from 22 March to 25 April depending on the lunar calendar, is marked by solemn processions and Passion plays all over the island. The people of Iglesias celebrate Easter with Iberian vigour. The most engaging Easter procession is probably Castelsardo's Lunissanti (Monday of Holy Week), an evocative torch-lit parade through the old town.

May
Festa di Sant'Efisio One of the island's most colourful festivals takes place to honour the memory of Sardinia's patron saint in Cagliari. On 1 May the saint's effigy is paraded around the city on a bullock-drawn carriage amid a colourful costume procession. It is then accompanied out of the city to

you have to change at Chilivani (and sometimes Macomer as well!). Up to three trains run to Sassari (€5.60, one hour 50 minutes) and up to seven to Golfo Aranci (€1.75, 25 minutes).

GOLFO ARANCI

Sardinia Ferries and Tirrenia run ferries from Livorno, Civitavecchia and Fiumicino to this ferry terminal located on the promontory northeast of Olbia. There's not a great deal else to say about this place, although there are some pleasant enough beaches on the coastal route to Olbia. Regular buses and trains connect the two places.

NUORO & THE EAST

If Sardinia is a world apart from the Italian mainland, Nuoro is an island within the island. Much of Sardinia's most rugged mountain territory is concentrated in this defiant and inward-looking province filling up the central eastern part of the island. More than anywhere else in Sardinia the people of this region are firmly attached to their traditions. You will never hear so much Sardinian spoken as here and it is in the remoter villages of Nuoro that you are most likely to come across the occasional local still sporting traditional dress.

---

the ancient site of Nora, where St Ephisius, a Roman commander who converted to Christianity, is said to have been decapitated on Diocletian's orders in AD 303. On 4 May the effigy is returned to Cagliari by the same road.

Cavalcata Sarda (Sardinian Parade) Hundreds of Sardinians wearing colourful traditional costume gather at Sassari on the second-last Sunday in May to mark a victory over the Saracens in the year 1000. They are followed by horsemen who make a spirited charge through the streets at the end of the parade.

July

Ardia More dangerous than Siena's famed Il Palio horse race, this impressive and mostly chaotic equestrian event at Sedilo on Sardinia on 6–7 July celebrates the victory of the Roman Emperor Constantine over Maxentius in AD 312 (the battle took place at the Ponte Milvio in Rome). An unruly pack of skilled horsemen races around a dusty track not far from the chapel erected in Constantine's name (Santu Antine) just outside the town. Onlookers drink, hoot and fire their guns into the air.

August

I Candelieri (The Candlesticks) Held on 14 August at Sassari, I Candelieri features town representatives in medieval costume bearing huge wooden columns (the 'candlesticks') through the town. The celebrations are held to honour a vow made in 1652 for deliverance from a plague but are also connected with the Feast of the Assumption (15 August).

Festa del Redentore Possibly what is the island's grandest procession of traditional Sardinian costume, this parade dominates this festival in Nuoro in the last week of the month. Groups from towns and villages all over the island proudly parade their festive dress on the last or second last Sunday of the month. Joining them in the parade are strapping horsemen and dance groups. The religious side of the festivities has its roots in the placement of a statue of Christ at the top of Monte Ortobene at the turn of the 20th century. A torchlight procession winds through the city on the evening of 28 August and an early morning pilgrimage to Monte Ortobene takes place the following day.

September

Festa di San Salvatore On the first Sunday of the month several hundred young fellows clothed in white set off on the Corsa degli Scalzi (Barefoot Race), an 8km run to the hamlet and sanctuary of San Salvatore. They bear with them an effigy of the Saviour and the whole event commemorates an episode in 1506, when townspeople raced to the San Salvatore sanctuary to collect the effigy and save it from Moorish sea raiders.

The dark majesty of the Supramonte and Gennargentu mountains and the inland Barbagia region (also known as the Barbagie, a plural collective noun indicating the several distinct areas that make it up) is matched by the extraordinary beauty of the Golfo di Orosei coast, a series of magical coves and beaches accessible only by sea or long inland treks. The breathtaking gorges of the Gola Su Gorroppu are a hiker's delight and indeed the entire mountainous province presents some of Sardinia's best walking country.

The people of this proud territory can be reserved but, once the ice is broken, incredibly hospitable. When visiting the villages and country do so with respect.

Fine country restaurants of all classes purvey heaped dishes of solid comfort food and you will want to wash it down with a robust Cannonau red.

Larger towns are accessible by bus, but you need your own transport to truly get to grips with this part of the island. If you have time, hire a guide for long walking excursions.

NUORO

pop 37,600

A handful of museums and churches and the town's pleasant hilly position in the shadow of Monte Ortobene make the provincial capital worth a stopover. Relax in the birthplace of Sardinia's most celebrated writer, Grazia Deledda.

By the end of the 18th century Nuoro barely counted 3000 inhabitants but was the only real 'urban' centre in a world of subsistence farming and banditry that had changed little in the preceding centuries. It took off after being made provincial capital in 1927.

Orientation

The old centre of the town is bunched in the northeastern corner of the city on a high spur of land that swings eastward to become Monte Ortobene. The heart of the town is contained in the warren of tidy streets and lanes around Piazza San Giovanni and Corso Garibaldi, the main street. The train and main bus stations are west of the city centre.

Information

Tourist Office (☎ 0784 3 87 77; www.viazzos.it; Corso Garibaldi 155; ☼ 9am-1pm & 3.30-7pm Mon-Sat)
Tourist Office (☎ 0784 3 00 83; Piazza Italia 19; ☼ 9am-1pm & 4-7pm Mon-Sat)

Sights

The **Museo della Vita e delle Tradizioni Sarde** (☎ 0784 25 70 35; Via Antonio Mereu 56; adult/child €2.58/0.52; ☼ 9am-8pm Tue-Sat, 9am-1pm Sun mid-Jun–Sep, 9am-1pm & 3-7pm Oct–mid-Jun) is the most interesting in town. It is a broad ethnographic collection with everything from traditional costumes to household implements of a bygone age.

Recently opened, the **Museo Archeologico Nazionale** (Via Mannu 1; admission free; ☼ 9am-1.30pm & 3-6pm Wed & Fri, 9am-1.30pm Tue, Thu & Sat) has a collection of artefacts ranging from ancient ceramics and fine *bronzetti* to a drilled skull from 1600 BC and early medieval finds.

About 7km out of Nuoro rises **Monte Ortobene**, a favourite picnic spot with locals. The No 8 local bus runs up to the mountain seven times a day from Piazza Vittorio Emanuele.

Festivals & Events

For the remarkably colourful **Festa del Redentore** at the end of August, see the boxed text, pp800–1.

Sleeping & Eating

Casa Solotti (☎ 0784 3 39 54; www.casasolotti.it; s/d €29/50) A charming house set in a grand garden on Monte Ortobene and exposed to wonderful views down into the valleys below. Three of the five rooms have balconies with views and you can use the kitchen.

Hotel Grillo (☎ 0784 3 86 78; fax 0784 3 20 05; Via Monsignor Melas 14; s/d up to €60/72) The most central spot. A biggish place with comfortable, spacious rooms (the colour green predominates), it is the best first port of call.

Hostaria Massimo (☎ 0784 3 38 60; Via Ugo Foscolo 3; pizzas up to €7; meals €25) The 30 or so pizza variations attract packs of punters into the bustling terrace.

Il Rifugio (☎ 0784 23 23 55; Via Antonio Mereu 28-36; meals €25-30; ☼ Thu-Tue) An age-old trattoria in a brand new locale (opened in 2002). It has been serving up delicious *malloreddus* (pasta that looks like shrivelled sea shells) in a tomato and basil sauce, and many other fine dishes, since the late 1980s.

Getting There & Away

PANI buses run from Cagliari (€11.31, 3½ hours) four times a day via Oristano (€5.84; two hours) and Sassari (€6.77, 2½ hours) up to six times a day. You can get tickets at Via Brigata di Sassari 19, where the buses terminate.

ARST buses run from a station on Viale Sardegna. There are two or three daily runs to places like Baunei (€4.91), Santa Maria Navarrese (€5.37) and Tortolì-Arbatax (€5.84). Regular buses make the trip to Oliena (€0.88, 20 minutes) and Orgosolo (€1.45, 30 minutes). Up to nine buses run to/from Dorgali (€2.01, 45 minutes).

AROUND NUORO
Fonte Sacra Su Tempiesu

This **well temple** (☎ 0784 27 67 16; adult/child €2/1; ☉ 9am-6pm) is unique among the Nuraghic temples for the A-shaped housing rising above the typical keyhole-shaped well. It is a masterpiece of ancient engineering and was only unearthed in 1953. You need transport to get here. Head for **Orune**, 18km northeast of Nuoro (buses come this far), from where it is a 7km drive southeast down a narrow country route (signposted).

Oliena

From Nuoro you can see this fetching town across a deep valley to the south. Behind it rises the magnificent spectacle of Monte Corrasi.

In Piazza Santa Maria, where buses stop and the town's 13th-century church of the same name is located, you will find **Servizi Turistici Corrasi** (☎ 0784 28 71 44; Piazza Santa Maria 30), which has information on the town and mountains. It organises treks to Tiscali, the Gola Su Gorroppu and elsewhere.

Hotel Cikappa (☎ /fax 0784 28 87 33; Corso Martin Luther King; s/d €36/49; ❄) is a cheerful hikers' hotel. Rooms are surprisingly comfortable and the hotel also hosts a hearty restaurant.

Hotel Monte Maccione (☎ 0784 28 83 63; fax 0784 28 84 73; s/d €33.50/55; **P**), run by the Cooperativa Eris, is buried deep in the woods of Monte Maccione (700m), 4km south of Oliena and good way uphill. The restaurant, where you can eat well for about €25 to €30, is a favourite getaway for locals. Oliena is a centre of good Cannonau reds, so always ask for local drops.

Orgosolo

Some 18km further south and backed by the dramatic grey wall of the Supramonte, Orgosolo means sheep-rustlers and bandits

THE AUTHOR'S CHOICE

Hotel Su Gologone (☎ 0784 28 75 12; fax 0784 28 76 68; s/d €119/176, half-board €101-139; ☉ Mar-Sep & mid-Dec–early-Jan; **P** ❄) Seven kilometres east of Oliena, this is one of the best hotel/restaurant complexes on the island. A discreet series of ivy-covered buildings contains the comfortable and charmingly decorated rooms. The restaurant, which concentrates on fine reinventions of local cuisine, is rated as one of Sardinia's best and is likely to relieve you of €50 including wine.

to most people. More recently this dusty, chaotic town has gained a little fame for its *murales*, lively wall paintings that express the social and political concerns of locals. They range from Sardinian issues to world politics and new ones still appear every now and then, 30 years after the first ones were done. The leftist murals were the brainchild of Francesco del Casino, an art teacher from Siena who has lived in Orgosolo for many years.

Petit Hotel (☎ /fax 0784 40 20 09; Via Mannu; s/d €28.50/38.80) is a basic place in the centre of the sprawling town. Don't expect much else but the bed and loo.

Mamoiada

Just 14km south of Nuoro, this undistinguished town is the scene of a remarkable winter celebration that dates to pagan times.

For the **Festa di Sant'Antonio** on 17 January the townspeople turn out to behold the frightful *mamuthones* as they parade about the town. For more information, see pp800–1.

You can get an idea of what it's all about at the **Museo delle Maschere** (☎ 0784 56 90 18; www.museodellemaschere.it; Piazza Europa 15; adult/child €4/2.60; ☉ 9am-1pm & 3-7pm Tue-Sun).

Buses service Mamoiada from Nuoro.

DORGALI & AROUND

Although of no real intrinsic interest, Dorgali is a handy base at the crossroads for traffic south to Arbatax and beyond, north to the coast and Olbia, east 10km to Cala Gonone and west towards Oliena and Nuoro.

The **tourist office** (☎ 0784 9 62 43; Via La Marmora 108b) can book rooms in hotels and

B&Bs in Dorgali and Cala Gonone on the coast – a handy service when things fill up in summer.

Dorgali is also a handy take-off point for hiking excursions. Several groups can take you on to 4WD excursions, hikes and caving expeditions. **Gennargentu Escursioni** (☎ 0784 9 43 85; Via La Marmora 197) organises one-day trips into the Gola Su Gorroppu (€25) and into the Supramonte (€41) for instance. Another is **Escursioni Ghivine** (☎ 349 442 55 52; www.ghivine.com; Via La Marmora 69E).

Hotel S'Adde (☎ 0784 9 44 12; fax 0784 9 41 35; Via Concordia; s/d up to €58/90; P 🐾) is an attractive hotel option at the northeastern end of town and next to a small park with kids' rides. Rooms are comfortable and the hotel restaurant opens out on to a first-floor terrace.

Ristorante Colibrì (☎ 0784 9 60 54; Via Gramsci 14; meals €27-30; 🕑 Mon-Sat) is tucked away off the main drag (follow the signs) and is a slightly overlit haven for carnivores. Mains range from *porcetto* through lamb to goat (done in thyme).

Grotta di Ispinigoli

Mexico is home to the world's tallest stalagmite (40m) but you shouldn't worry about settling for second best here – the natural spectacle of its slightly shorter counterpart here is every bit as awe-inspiring. The **Grotta di Ispinigoli** (adult/child €7/4.50; 🕑 9am-7pm Aug, reduced hrs Apr-Jul & Sep-Nov, closed Dec-Feb) is just 4km north of Dorgali.

Serra Orrios & Thomes

The Nuraghic village of **Serra Orrios** (adult/child €5/2; 🕑 9am-1pm & 4-6pm for hourly visits), while not as remarkable as the site at Santa Vittoria di Serri, is worth a stop. The remnants of more than 70 huts are clustered around what is left of two temples. The site lies 11km northwest of Dorgali (3km north off the Dorgali–Oliena road).

From Sierra Orrios you could continue north to see a fine example of a 'giants' tomb'. Continue 3km north of the crossroads with the Nuoro–Orosei route and the **Tomba dei Giganti S'Ena e Thomes** is signposted to the right. Just open the gate and walk on for about 200m. The stone monument is dominated by a central oval-shaped stone stele that closed off an ancient burial chamber. It is generally open from dawn to dusk.

OGLIASTRA

The southeastern sector of Nuoro province is known as the Ogliastra. From Dorgali the SS125 (Orientale Sarda) highway winds south through the high mountain terrain of the eastern end of the **Parco Nazionale del Golfo di Orosei e del Gennargentu**. The 18km stretch south to the Genna 'e Silana pass (1017m) is the most breathtaking. A useful local web site for this area is **Welcome in Ogliastra** (www.turinforma.it).

Tiscali

A first detour comes a few kilometres south of Dorgali with a road dropping off to the southwest past Monte Sant'Elene towards the Nuraghic village of **Tiscali** (admission €5; 🕑 9am-7pm May-Sep, 9am-5pm Oct-Apr). The village is thought to date only to the 3rd or 4th century BC, and was built in the white limestone *dolina* (sinkhole) inside the modest Monte Tiscali (515m) at an altitude of 360m.

From Dorgali, you drive about 14km to a bridge where a walking trail (1.5km) to the site is signposted. Another, tougher approach for walkers is from the north down the Valle di Lanaitto. If on a 4WD tour, you will be taken by 4WD down this valley and to within about an hour's walk of the site.

Gola Su Gorroppu

When you reach the **Genna 'e Silana** pass (hard to miss as a hotel and restaurant mark the spot on the east side of the road), you could stop for a morning's hike to the **Gola Su Gorroppu** (Gorroppu Gorge). The trail is signposted to the right (east) side of the road and is easy to follow. You reach the gorge with its claustrophobically tight high walls after about two hours' hiking. There's nothing to stop you wandering a little either way along the Rio Fluminedda river bed, but beyond that you need harnesses and proper equipment to get in any deeper.

To get to the gorge entrance by car, head south off Dorgali along the SS125 and turn right for the Hotel Sant'Elene. Follow this dirt road into the valley for about 8km (don't head uphill for the hotel) and you'll get to a small bridge. Here you'll have to park the car and continue on foot. Walk for about 1½ hours to two small lakes and the entrance to the gorge – one of the most spectacular and romantic landscapes in Sardinia. The huge boulders scattered around the entrance are a reminder that nature can be harsh as well as beautiful. Allow a full day for the expedition, which will give you time for the walk, a picnic and a swim in the lakes.

Cooperativa Gorropu (☎ 0782 64 92 82; Via Sa Preda Lada 2; Urzulei), whom you will find also in the Sa Domu 'e S'Orcu building on the SS125 just north of Urzulei turn-off, guide trekkers into the gorge and on other walks around the Golfo di Orosei and the Supramonte. It also organises meals with shepherds in the countryside and might be able to swing rooms in private houses for you.

For more tips on hiking in this area see also Lonely Planet's *Walking in Italy* guide.

Hotel Sant'Elene (☎ 0784 9 45 72; fax 0784 9 53 85; Località Sant'Elene; s/d €33.50/61; ☟ Mar-Oct; ℗)) is a wonderful choice of place to stay, a cosy spot whose rooms offer some fine views across the valley.

Baunei & the Altopiano del Golgo

About 28km south of the Genna 'e Silana pass you roll into the town of **Baunei**. There is nothing of any particular interest to hold you up long here but you could sit at the Cafe Belvedere for a drink and soak in the mountain valley views to the west.

What is seriously worth your while in Baunei is a 10km detour up on to the mountain plateau known as the **Altopiano del Golgo**, signposted from the middle of town. A steep 2km (10° incline) set of switchbacks gets you up to the plateau and sailing north through heavily wooded terrain. After 8km you see a sign to your right to Su Sterru (Il Golgo). Follow the sign (less than 1km), leave your vehicle and head for this remarkable feat of nature – a 270m abyss just 40m wide at its base. Its funnel-like opening is now fenced off but, knowing the size of the drop, just peering into the dark and damp opening of this eroded karst phenomenon is enough to bring on a case of vertigo. Cavers who like abseiling just love it.

At the end of the dirt trail is the **Locanda Il Rifugio** (☎ /fax 0782 61 05 99, ☎ 368 702 89 80; d €40), which the Cooperativa Goloritzè has carved out of a one-time shepherd's farmstead. You can opt for full board and take your meals in the excellent restaurant, where the staff prepare such specialities as *capretto* (kid meat) and *porcetto*. All the meat is raised

by the shepherds' cooperative – the place is surrounded by cattle, pigs and donkeys. And horses. The cooperative organises horse riding, excursions in 4WD and hiking. 4WD trails from the plateau lead to within 20 minutes' hiking distance of the marvellous Cala Goloritzè and Cala Sisine beaches. The place opens roughly for spring and summer. The staff can arrange to pick you up in Baunei if you don't have your own transport.

Just beyond their stables is the late 16th-century **Chiesa di San Pietro**, a humble affair flanked to one side by even humbler *cumbessias*, rough, largely open stone affairs – not at all comfortable for the passing pilgrims who traditionally sleep over here to celebrate the saint's day.

Santa Maria Navarrese

Located at the southern end of the Golfo di Orosei, this delightful spot is a tempting alternative to its busier northern counterpart, Cala Gonone. Basque sailors shipwrecked here built a small church in 1052, dedicated to Santa Maria di Navarra on the orders of the princess of Navarra who happened to be one of the survivors. The church was built in the shade of a grand olive tree that still thrives today.

The pleasant pine-backed beach (with more beaches stretching away further to the south) is lapped by transparent water and the setting is a gem. Offshore are several islets, including the **Isola dell'Ogliastra**, and the leafy northern end of the beach is topped by a watchtower built to look out for raiding Saracens.

About 500m further north is the small pleasure port, where **Nautica Centro Sub** (☎ 0782 61 55 22) organises dives and rents out *gommoni* (high-speed dinghies) for exploring the Golfo di Orosei coast to the north. They start at €100 a day for two people and allow to you inspect the same wonderful spots described below, but in reverse order. Similar excursions to those from Cala Gonone to some or all of these beauty spots also depart from here. Inquire at the kiosks in the port or at the **Tourpass office** (☎ 0782 61 53 30; Piazza Principessa di Navarra; ☟ 8.30am-1pm&5-8pm Sep-Jun, 8.30am-1pm&5-11.30pm Jul-Aug) in the centre of town.

Three hotels lie within 200m of one another. **Hotel Plammas** (☎ 0782 61 51 30; www .hotelplammas.com; Viale Plammas 59; d up to €76) is the cheapest deal and is a perfectly pleasant spot about 200m up the hill from the central square. The rooms are straightforward and a little sparsely furnished but fine. Single occupancy costs a little over half and in the off-season (ie June and September) prices halve! The restaurant has a name, especially for its pasta (try the fish-based *culurgiones*) and seafood mains.

You'll find several other little eateries and a handful of bars dotted about within quick strolling distance of the centre. **Bar L'Olivastro** has tables and chairs set up on shady terraces below the weird and wonderful branches of a huge olive tree at the northern end of the beach.

A handful of buses (sometimes only one a day) link Santa Maria Navarrese with Tortolì (€0.67, 15 minutes), Arbatax (€0.88, 30 minutes), Dorgali (€3.46, 1½ hours), Nuoro (€5.37, 2½ hours) and even Cagliari (€7.64, four hours).

Tortolì & Arbatax

The rather dispiriting sprawl of Tortolì and, 4km east, its industrial outgrowth and port Arbatax will be unlikely to enthral you, although you could find yourself passing through if you arrive at Arbatax by ferry. If you do find yourself in Arbatax killing time, head across the road from the port and behind the petrol station to the *rocce rosse* or 'red rocks'. These bizarre, weather-beaten rock formations dropping into the sea are well worth the brief wander. In the distance your gaze is attracted by the imperious cliffs of the southern Ogliastra and Golfo di Orosei.

Just by the port is the terminus for the FdS *Trenino Verde* summer tourist train to/from Mandas (4¾ hours, two daily), one of the most scenic of these rides. The train station also houses the tourist office, whose opening hours vary maddeningly with ferry arrival times.

Local buses No 1 & 2 run from Arbatax to Tortolì and, in the case of the latter service, to the beach and hotels at nearby **Porto Frailis**. If you need to stay around here, about the only cheapish option is the family-run **Hotel Il Gabbiano** (☎ 0782 66 76 22; d €58) in Porto Frailis. It has just four simple doubles without their own bathrooms but is a homey enough stopover. For single occupancy you pay a little less.

A few buses run from both these destinations to Santa Maria Navarrese, Dorgali, Nuoro and Cagliari, as well as many inland villages. Frequency is generally low, with sometimes only one departure a day.

CALA GONONE & AROUND

The fast-developing seaside resort of **Cala Gonone**, just 10km east of Dorgali, is an excellent base from which to explore the coves along the most startling stretch of the Golfo di Orosei's coastline.

The settlement, with its string of hotels and restaurants, is in itself nothing remarkable but pleasant enough. Most importantly, Cala Gonone's pleasure craft port is a starting point for boat excursions to the magical coves and cliffs to the south.

At the **tourist office** (☎ 0784 9 36 96; Viale Bue Marino 1a; ☯ 9am-6pm Apr-Oct, 9am-11pm Jul & Aug) there is plenty of info on the area.

Activities

Several decent beaches stretch to the immediate south of the port. Some better ones, including the sugar-white strand of the **Cala Cartoe** (where Madonna frolicked for her 2002 box office bomb, *Swept Away*), are accessible only by car – take Via Marco Polo away from the port and then follow the signs.

But if you do nothing else in Sardinia you should get on to a boat to explore the magical coves along a 20km stretch south of Cala Gonone. The first stop for many is **Grotta del Bue Marino**, touted as the last island refuge of the monk seal, although none have been seen around for a long time. The watery gallery is certainly impressive, with shimmering light playing on the strange shapes within the cave. Guided visits take place up to seven times a day.

There follows a string of coves and beaches, from the crescent-moon shaped **Cala Luna** and **Cala Sisine**, backed by a green valley, through to the incredible cobalt blue waters of **Cala Mariolu** and **Cala Goloritzè**. Indeed, the waters along this coast cover an exquisite spectrum from deep purple through emerald green to cerulean blue.

You can also walk to Cala Luna from Cala Gonone. The track starts at **Cala Fuili**, 3.5km from Cala Gonone. It's then 4km (about 1½ hours) between the two coves on rocky terrain but with breathtaking coastal views. Longer inland treks to some of these beaches can also be organised. Several local excursion and hiking outfits will put you on to this and other trails (on foot or in 4WD), including descents of the Gola Su Gorroppu gorge and visits to the Tiscali Nuraghic village. Try **Dolmen** (☎ 0784 9 32 60; www.sardegnadascoprire.it; Via Vasco da Gama 18).

Several operators offer diving courses and trips in the Golfo di Orosei. One is **Argonauta** (☎ /fax 0784 9 30 46; www.argonauta.it; Via dei Lecci 10), which also offers Professional Association of Diving Instructors (PADI) courses.

Sleeping & Eating

Free-camping is strictly forbidden in the area.

Camping Cala Gonone (☎ 0784 9 31 65; fax 0784 9 32 55; per person €16, bungalows up to €134; ☉ Apr-Oct) This camp site is a little way back from the waterfront along the main road from Dorgali. It gets crowded in August but is shady.

Piccolo Hotel (☎ 0784 9 32 32; fax 0784 9 32 35; Viale Colombo; s/d €31/51) The cheapest place in town and a cheerful enough option with simple but acceptable rooms a short stroll back from the port.

Pensione L'Oasi (☎ 0784 9 31 11; fax 0784 9 34 44; Via G Lorca; s/d up to €92/110; ☉ Jun-Oct) High up over the port this place is tucked away on the road to Cala Cartoe, about 1km from the centre. Rooms are big and fresh, most with balconies opening to privileged views of the gulf below.

Hotel Miramare (☎ 0784 9 31 40; fax 0784 9 34 69; Piazza Giardini; s/d up to €67/120; ☉ Apr-Oct) The first hotel to be built here in 1955 remains a good upper-range option. Rooms are arranged with style and have satellite TV, phone/fax and minibar. The garden restaurant is a shady retreat where good Sardinian dishes are served.

There are plenty of other hotels on or near the waterfront but you will definitely need to book ahead in July and August. Most close in winter.

Pizzeria 2P (☎ 0784 9 31 45; Via Vasco da Gama 7; pizzas from €4.50) A good spot for a pizza in a shady terrace just back from the more expensive (and frequently inferior) eateries on the waterfront. Pizzas are thin, crispy and delicious.

Ristorante Acquarius (☎ 0784 9 34 28; Lungomare Palmasera 34; meals €35) On the waterfront, this is one of the best dining options in

Cala Gonone, but portions are a trifle stingy for the prices asked. You can sit in a pleasant garden and choose between a mix of Sardinian and standard Italian dishes. Try the *anzelottos* (ricotta filled ravioli) followed by the *cozze alla marinara* (mussels).

Getting There & Away

In summer, as many as 10 ARST buses travel from Dorgali (€0.67, 20 minutes, 10km) and pull up at Via Marco Polo, near the port. Seven of these come in from Nuoro (€2.58, 70 minutes).

BOATING ALONG THE COAST

There are several ways to approach the coastal wonders from Cala Gonone. A fleet of boats, from large high-speed dinghies to small cruise boats and on to graceful sailing vessels are on hand, with a broad range of excursions on offer. The most basic option would see you joining a band of punters to be transported to one of the beaches along the coast.

The basic cost of such trips starts at €8.50 for the return trip only from Cala Luna (for those who elect to walk there). The round trip to Cala Luna or Grotta del Bue Marino is €14.50. The two together costs €23.50. The return trip to Cala Mariolu costs €22. Prices drop in the slower months.

Full-day cruises, with visits to various (but usually not all) the various beaches and other beauty spots can cost from €21.50 for a mini-cruise. Much nicer is the day-long trip on a sailing boat, costing €67 a head. If you want lunch on board (instead of taking your own), add €18. Contact **Cala Gonone Charter** (☎ 0784 9 37 37; Via S'Abba Irde 3).

The final option is the most tempting and the most expensive. For €60 to €80 a head, consider hiring a *gommone* (a big motorised dinghy). They start at €120 plus €10 to €15 for petrol. Nothing beats the freedom this offers you.

Boats operate from March until about November – dates depend a lot on demand. Prices vary according to season, of which there are four. 'Very high season' is around 11 to 25 August. You can get information at agencies around town or at a series of booths direct at the port.

Directory

CONTENTS

ACCOMMODATION

Accommodation in Italy ranges from the sublime to the ridiculous with prices to match. Hotels and *pensioni* make up the bulk of accommodation although there is a huge gulf between the luxury of top-end hotels and the numerous pokey and pricey budget options. A growing range of good, characterful B&Bs, villa rentals, hostels and *agriturismo* (farm stays) options are slowly addressing this problem.

In this book high-season prices are quoted and these are intended as a guide only. Prices fluctuate depending on the season, with Easter, the summer and Christmas being peak tourist times; it is advisable to book in advance during these periods. In budget hotels it can sometimes be worth bargaining in low season, although prices tend to be about 20% cheaper in general.

To make a reservation, hotels usually require confirmation by fax or letter as well as a deposit.

Agriturismo & B&Bs

A holiday on a working farm, or *agriturismo*, is quite well organised in Italy, especially in Trentino-Alto Adige, Tuscany and Umbria, and increasingly so in parts of Sicily and Sardinia. Local tourist offices can usually supply lists of operators. For detailed information on all *agriturismo* facilities available in Italy contact **Agriturist**

PRACTICALITIES

- Use the **metric** system for weights and measures.

- Buy or watch videos on the **PAL system**.

- Plugs have two or three round pins so bring an international adapter; the electric current is 220V, 50Hz but older buildings may still use 125V.

- If your Italian's up to it, try the following newspapers: *Corriere della Sera*, the country's leading daily; *Il Messaggero*, a popular Rome-based broadsheet; *L'Unità*, the former left-wing mouthpiece; or *La Repubblica*, a centre-left daily with a continuous flow of Mafia conspiracies and Vatican scoops.

- Tune into: Vatican Radio (1530 AM, 93.3 FM and 105 FM) for a run-down on what the pope is up to; state-owned Italian RAI-1 (1332 AM or 89.7 FM), RAI-2 (846 AM or 91.7 FM) and RAI-3 (93.7 FM) for classical and light music with news broadcasts; and commercial stations like Radio Centro Suono (101.3 FM), the Naples-based Radio Kiss Kiss (97.25 FM), and Radio Città Futura (97.7 FM) for contemporary music.

- Switch on the box to watch Italy's commercial stations Canale 5, Italia 1, Rete 4 and La 7, as well as state-run RAI 1, RAI 2 and RAI 3.

(☎ 06 685 23 337; www.agriturismo.it; Corso Vittorio Emanuele II 89, Rome).

Another increasingly popular option in Italy is bed and breakfast. Options include everything from restored farmhouses, city *palazzi* and seaside bungalows to rooms in family houses. Tariffs cover a wide price range typically in the €70 to €150 bracket. For more information contact **Bed & Breakfast Italia** (☎ 06 68 78 618; www.bbitalia.it; Palazzo Sforza Cesarini, Corso Vittorio Emanuele II 282, 00186 Rome).

Camping

Most camp sites in Italy are major complexes with swimming pools, restaurants and supermarkets. Like hotels, they are graded according to a star system. Charges range from €4 to €10 per adult, €3 to €8 for children aged under 12, and €5 to €12 for a site. In the major cities, camp sites are often a long way from the historic centres.

Independent camping is not permitted in protected areas but, out of the main tourist season, independent campers who choose spots not visible from the road and who don't light fires shouldn't have too much trouble. Always get permission from the landowner if you want to camp on private property.

Full lists of camp sites are available from local tourist offices or can be looked up on www.touringclub.it, the website of Touring Club Italiano (TCI). TCI publishes an annual book listing all camp sites in Italy, *Campeggi in Italia* (€13.50), and the Istituto Geografico de Agostini publishes the annual *Guida ai Campeggi in Europa*, sold together with *Guida ai Campeggi in Italia* (€13.50). These books are available in major bookshops.

Hostels

Ostelli per la gioventù (youth hostels) are run by the Associazione Italiana Alberghi per la Gioventù (AIG), which is affiliated to **Hostelling International** (HI; www.iyhf.org). A valid HI card is required in all associated youth hostels in Italy. You can get this in your home country or at the youth hostel in Rome.

Pick up a booklet on Italian hostels, with details of prices, locations and so on, from the national head office of **AIG** (☎ 06 487 11 52; www.ostellionline.org; Via Cavour 44, Rome). Nightly rates vary from €8 to €20, which often includes breakfast.

Accommodation is in segregated dormitories, although many hostels offer doubles or family rooms (at a higher price per person). Hostels usually have a lock-out period between 9am and 3.30pm. Check-in is 6pm to 10.30pm, although some hostels will allow you a morning check-in before they close for the day. Curfew is usually 10.30pm or 11pm in winter and 11.30pm or midnight in summer. It is usually necessary to pay before 9am on the day of your departure, otherwise you could be charged for another night.

Hotels & Pensioni

There is often no difference between a *pensione* and an *albergo* (hotel). However, a *pensione* will generally be of one- to three-star quality, while an *albergo* can be awarded up to five stars. *Locande* (inns) and *affittacamere* (rooms for rent) are cheaper and are not included in the star classification system, although in some areas (such as the Aeolian Islands and the Alps) the standard is very high.

While the quality of accommodation can vary a great deal, one-star hotels/*pensioni* tend to be very basic and usually do not have a private bathroom. Standards at two-star places are often only slightly better but rooms will generally have a private bathroom. Once you arrive at three stars you can assume that standards will be reasonable. Four- and five-star hotels offer facilities such as room service, laundry and dry-cleaning. Travellers should always check on prices before committing to stay in a place. Make a complaint to the local tourist office if you believe you're being overcharged.

Overall, prices are highest in major tourist destinations. They also tend to be higher in northern Italy. Prices can soar in the high season at beach resorts and during the ski season in the Alps. A *camera singola* (single room) costs from €30. A double room with *camera doppia* (twin beds) and a *camera matrimoniale* (double room with a double bed) will cost from around €50.

Tourist offices have booklets listing all local accommodation, including prices.

Mountain Refuges

The network of *rifugi* in the Alps, Apennines or other mountains in Italy are usually only open from July to September. Accommodation is generally in dormitories but some of the larger refuges do have double rooms for rent. The price per person for an overnight stay plus breakfast is around €20 (more if you are staying in a double room). A hearty post-walking dinner will set you back another €20.

The locations of *rifugi* are marked on good walking maps. Some are close to chair lifts and cable-car stations, which means they are usually expensive and crowded. Others are at high altitude and involve hours of hard walking. It is important to book a bed in advance. Additional information, including telephone numbers, can be obtained from local tourist offices.

The **Club Alpino Italiano** (CAI; www.cai.it, Italian only) owns and runs many of the mountain refuges. Members of organisations such as the Australian Alpine Club and British Mountaineering Council can enjoy discounted rates for accommodation and meals by obtaining (for a fee) a reciprocal rights card.

Rental Accommodation

Finding rental accommodation in the major cities can be difficult and time consuming – there are rental agencies that will assist, for a fee. Rental rates are higher for short-term leases. A small apartment anywhere near the centre of Rome will cost around €1000 per month and it is usually necessary to pay a deposit (generally one month in advance). Apartments and villas for rent are listed in local publications such as Rome's weekly *Porta Portese* and the fortnightly *Wanted in Rome*. Another option is to answer an advertisement in a local publication to share an apartment.

In major resort areas, such as the Aeolian Islands and other parts of Sicily, the coastal areas of Sardinia and in the Alps, the tourist offices have lists of local apartments and villas for rent. Most offices will be more than cooperative if you telephone beforehand for information on how to book an apartment.

VILLA RENTALS

People wanting to rent a villa in the countryside can seek information from specialist travel agencies such as the following:

Cuendet & Cie Spa (☎ 0577 57 63 30; www.cuendet .com; Strada di Strove 17, 53035 Monteriggioni, Siena)

One of the major companies in Italy with villas in Tuscany, Umbria, the Veneto, Rome, Marche, the Amalfi Coast, Puglia, Sicily and Sardinia. In the UK, you can order Cuendet's catalogues and make reservations by calling ☎ 0800 891573. In the USA, Cuendet bookings are handled by **Rentals in Italy** (☎ 805 987 5278; 1742 Calle Corva, Camarillo, CA 93010).

Cottages & Castles (☎ 61 3 9853 1142; www.cottages andcastles.com.au; 11 Laver St Kew, Victoria 3101) Australia's version of the above with a portfolio of properties throughout Italy.

The Parker Company (☎ 781-596 82 82; www.the parkercompany.com; Seaport Landing, 152 Lynnway, Lynn, MA 01902) This leading US provider of villa rentals has a huge portfolio ranging from apartments to farmhouses and castles. Their newest venture is **Actividayz** (www.actividayz.com) where travellers can book over 100 day trips online (from US$55 to $95).

Tuscany Now (☎ 020 7684 88 84; www.tuscany now.com; International House, 10-18 Vestry St, London N1 7RE) Established 11 years ago with only three Tuscan villas, this company has now grown to one of the world's largest with high-quality villas throughout Italy.

Think Sicily (☎ 020 7377 8518; www.thinksicily.com; The Old Truman Brewery, 91-95 Brick Lane, London E1 6QL) New to the scene with a fistful of Sicilian treasures, including a 14th-century *palazzo* in the heart of old Palermo and domed *dammusi* on Pantelleria. The company also runs guided walks through some of the most beautiful and unspoilt areas of the Sicilian countryside.

ACTIVITIES

Although Italy is famous for its cultural and historical treasures, there are a surprising number of outdoorsy activities as well. The stunning scenery, from the rolling hills of Tuscany and Umbria to dramatic mountain ranges and sinister volcanoes, offer a wealth of exciting activities off the beaten tourist track.

Cycling

Tourist offices will be able to offer information on mountain-bike trails and guided rides. For information on hiring or buying a bike and on travelling around Italy with one, see pp834–5.

The hills of Tuscany are very popular for cycling, particularly around Florence and Siena, from where you can explore the countryside around Fiesole, San Gimignano and Chianti. Try the one-day tour in Chianti offered by www.bicycletuscany.com. In Umbria, areas such as the Valnerina and the Piano Grande at Monte Vettore have beautiful trails and quiet country roads to explore and a bike would be particularly useful for getting around Sardinia. Serious cyclists will know where to go for the most challenging routes – the tortuous, winding road up to the Passo Stelvio is one of the most famous. At the end of May, the prestigious Giro d'Italia takes place and attracts a host of international participants.

Diving & Watersports

Windsurfing and sailing are extremely popular in Italy and at most beach resorts, as well as around the northern lakes, it is possible to hire boats and equipment. Canoeing and kayaking are also becoming increasingly popular – the **Amici del Fiume** (www.amicidelfiume.it, Italian only) has some interesting information.

Some of the best snorkelling and diving spots are in Campania, Calabria and Sicily, where the volcanic geology makes for rich marine life. The small island of Ustica is almost entirely devoted to diving and holds an annual marine festival from mid-June to August. It is also a popular pastime in the Aeolians and around Taormina.

Hiking & Walking

Italy is a walker's paradise with thousands of kilometres of *sentieri* (marked trails). The **Club Alpino Italiano** (CAI; www.cai.it) is a useful source of information. The Dolomites is the best known and most popular area with a multitude of stunning peaks. Parco Nazionale Gran Paradiso in Valle d'Aosta has a magnificent network of *sentieri* over high passes and through beautiful valleys. The Matterhorn (Monte Cervino) and Monte Rosa lie generally north of Valle d'Aosta, you can enjoy them from below along paths linking the fringing valleys. For wild and remote mountains, try the Maritime Alps in southwestern Piedmont and the Carniche and Giulie Alps in Friuli-Venezia Giulia. The long chain of the Apennines has some high-level walks, especially in Tuscany's Apuane Alps and Parco Nazionale d'Abruzzo. Sicily also has a number

of parks, which are rapidly improving their infrastructure and provide some wonderful seaside walks, particularly in the Riserva Naturale dello Zingaro. You can also brave the active volcanoes on foot – Vesuvius near Naples, Etna in Sicily and Stromboli and Vulcano on the Aeolian Islands.

Walking in the mountains and the valleys around the lakes of Garda, Como and Maggiore (mostly in Lombardy) is superb. Tuscany and, surprisingly, Sicily offer incomparable opportunities for combining scenic walks and finding food and wine. If you like to be near the sea, two great areas are the Cinque Terre in Liguria and the Amalfi-Sorrento peninsula in Campania where age-old paths follow precipitous hillsides.

Check out Lonely Planet's *Walking in Italy* for detailed descriptions of more than 50 walks. Guided walks are organised in many national parks, though you'd need to speak Italian (inquire at local tourist offices for details).

Skiing

There are numerous excellent ski resorts in the Italian Alps and, again, the Dolomites provide the most dramatic scenery. Options include *lo sci* (downhill skiing) and *sci di fondo* (cross-country skiing), as well as *sci alpinismo* (ski mountaineering).

Skiing is quite expensive because of the costs of ski lifts and accommodation but a Settimana Bianca (White Week) package can reduce the expense. It's not expensive, on the other hand, to hire ski equipment.

The season in Italy generally runs from December to late March. There is year-round skiing in areas such as the Marmolada glacier in Trentino-Alto Adige and on Mont Blanc (Monte Bianco) and the Matterhorn in the Valle d'Aosta.

The five major (read: most fashionable and expensive) ski resorts in Italy are Cortina d'Ampezzo in the Veneto; Madonna di Campiglio, San Martino di Castrozza and Canazei in Trentino; and Courmayeur in the Valle d'Aosta.

Spectator Sports

Italians are big on spectator sports – all the excitement and none of the pain. Top of the list has to be the national obsession, *calcio* (football), with the season starting at the end of August and finishing with the Italian Cup in June. The League is divided into different Series – A, B, C1 and C2 (with Series A representing the premiership). Matches normally take place on Sunday afternoon and tickets for Serie A matches range between €16 and €40. Check out the website www.football.it.

The other spectator sport with a die-hard following is motor-racing. The most famous track is the **Autodromo Nazionale Monza** (☎ 039 2 38 21; www.monzanet.it) near Milan. The other grand prix, San Marino, is held at **Imola** (☎ 0549 88 54 31; www.formula1.com). For classic-car enthusiasts the **Mille Miglia** (☎ 030 280 36; www.millemiglia.it, Italian only) takes place in mid-May, with nearly 1000 cars hurtling down from Brescia to Rome and back.

BUSINESS HOURS

Generally shops open 9am to 1pm and 3.30pm to 7.30pm (or 4pm to 8pm) Monday to Saturday. They may close on Saturday afternoon and on Thursday or Monday afternoon. In major towns most department stores and supermarkets now have continuous opening hours from 9am to 7.30pm Monday to Saturday. Some even open from 9am to 1pm on Sunday.

Banks tend to open 8.30am to 1.30pm and 3.30pm to 4.30pm Monday to Friday. They are closed at weekends but it is always possible to find a bureau de change open in the larger cities and in major tourist areas.

Major post offices open 8.30am to 5pm or 6pm Monday to Friday and also 8.30am to 1pm on Saturday. All post offices close two hours earlier than normal on the last business day of each month (not including Saturday).

Farmacie (pharmacies) are open 9am to 12.30pm and 3.30pm to 7.30pm. They are always closed on Sunday and usually on Saturday afternoon but are required to display a list of *farmacie* in the area that are open.

Bars (in the Italian sense, coffee and sandwich places) and cafés generally open 8am to 8pm, although some stay open after 8pm and turn into pub-style drinking-and-meeting places. Clubs and discos might open around 10pm but often there'll be no-one there until midnight. Restaurants open noon to 3pm and 7.30pm to 11pm (later in summer and in the south). Restaurants

and bars are required to close for one day each week with the day varying between establishments.

The opening hours of museums, galleries and archaeological sites vary, although there is a trend towards continuous opening from 9.30am to 7pm; many close on Monday. Increasingly, the major national museums and galleries remain open until 10pm during the summer.

CHILDREN
Practicalities

Italians love children but there are few special amenities for them. Always make a point of asking staff at tourist offices if they know of any special family activities and for suggestions on hotels that cater for kids. Discounts are available for children (usually aged under 12 but sometimes based on the child's height) on public transport and for admission to sites.

Book accommodation in advance to avoid any inconvenience and when travelling by train make sure to reserve seats to avoid finding yourselves standing up for the entire journey. You can hire car seats for infants and children from most car-rental firms, but you should always book them in advance.

You can buy baby formula in powder or liquid form, as well as sterilising solutions such as Milton, at *farmacie* (pharmacies). Disposable nappies (diapers) are widely available at supermarkets, *farmacie* and sometimes in larger *cartolerie* (stores selling paper goods). A pack of around 30 disposable nappies costs about €9.50. Fresh cow's milk is sold in cartons in bars that have a 'Latteria' sign and in supermarkets. If it is essential that you have milk, carry an emergency carton of UHT milk since bars usually close at 8pm. In many out-of-the-way areas in southern Italy, the locals use only UHT milk.

Sights & Activities

Successful travel with children can require a special effort. Don't try to overdo things and make sure activities include the kids – older children could help in the planning of these. Try to think of things that will capture their imagination like the sites at **Pompeii** (pp623–7), the **Colosseum** (pp93–4) and the **Forum** (pp89–91) in Rome, and Greek temples in the south and Sicily; another good bet are the volcanoes in the south and snorkelling or sailing is always popular. If you're travelling in northern Italy, you might want to make a stopover at **Gardaland** (p285), the amusement park near Lago di Garda in Lombardy, or at **Italia in Miniatura** (p429) at Viserba near Rimini in Emilia-Romagna. Always remember to allow some free-time for kids to play.

For more information, see Lonely Planet's *Travel with Children* or the websites www.travelwithyourkids.com and www.family travelnetwork.com.

CLIMATE CHARTS

Situated in the temperate zone and jutting deep into the Mediterranean, Italy is regarded by many tourists as a land of sunny, mild weather. However, due to the north–south orientation of the peninsula and the fact that it is largely mountainous, the country's climate is actually quite variable.

In the Alps, temperatures are lower and winters are long and severe. Generally the weather is warm from July to September, although rainfall can be high in September. While the first snowfall is usually in November, light snow sometimes falls in mid-September and the first heavy falls can occur in early October. Freak snowfalls in June are not unknown at high altitudes.

The Alps shield northern Lombardy and the Lakes area, including Milan, from the extremes of the northern European winter and Liguria enjoys a mild, Mediterranean climate similar to southern Italy because it is protected by both the Alps and the Apennine range.

Winters are severe and summers very hot in the Po Valley. Venice can be hot and humid in summer and, although not too cold in winter, it can be unpleasant as the sea level rises and acqua alta (literally 'high water') inundates the city.

Further south in Florence, which is encircled by hills, the weather can be extreme but, as you travel towards the tip of the boot, temperatures and weather conditions become milder. Rome, for instance, has an average July and August temperature in the mid-20°s (Celsius), although the impact of the sirocco (a hot, humid wind blowing from Africa) can produce stiflingly hot

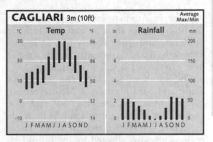

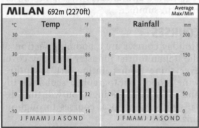

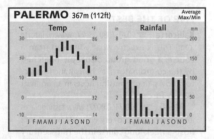

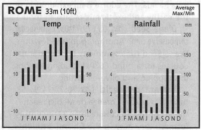

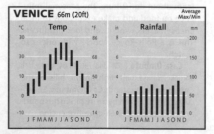

weather in August, with temperatures in the high 30°s for days on end. Winters are moderate and snow is very rare in Rome, although winter clothing (or at least a heavy overcoat) is still a requirement.

The south of Italy and the islands of Sicily and Sardinia have a Mediterranean climate. Summers are long, hot and dry, and winter temperatures tend to be quite moderate, averaging around 10°C. These regions are also affected by the humid sirocco in summer.

COURSES

Holiday courses are a booming section of the Italian tourist industry and they cover everything from painting, art, sculpture, wine, food, photography, scuba diving and even hang-gliding! You will find details on various local courses throughout this book.

FIVE OF THE BEST

Vallicorte (☎ 020 7680 13 77; www.vallicorte .com) This is exactly what you need from a course: a good group of people (matched by the co-ordinators), a charismatic instructor and a pair of amusing hosts in an ancient villa in Tuscany.

Menfi (☎ 020 7460 0077; www.tastingplaces .com) Published cookery writer Maxine Clark hosts a week-long course in the 18th-century Villa Ravidá. The course is an exploration of the earthy and exotic mix of Sicilian food.

Diane Seed (☎ 06 679 71 03; dianeseed@ compuserve.com) Another published writer, Diane Seed runs seven-day non-residential courses for around €680, including lessons in shopping and olive-oil tasting.

Lorenza de Medici (☎ 0577 74 94 98; cuisineint@aol.com) Lorenza de Medici teaches the art of Tuscan cuisine in an 11th-century former monastery in the Chianti. Students learn about agriculture, the seasonal influence on food and make excursions to local cheesemakers, wineries and food producers. This is a Rolls-Royce course with prices to match.

Casa Ombuto (☎ 348 736 38 64; www.itali ancookerycourse.com) High on the hills of the Casentino valley stands Casa Ombuto. Seven-day courses are run by an inspiring husband-and-wife team in their cave-like cucina.

Cooking

Many people come to Italy just for the food so it is hardly surprising that cookery courses are among the most popular. The useful website www.italycookingschools .com can help you evaluate hundreds of possibilities for free.

Language

Courses are run by private schools and universities throughout the country and are a great way to learn Italian while enjoying the opportunity to live in an Italian city or town. One of the cheapest options is the Università per Stranieri in Perugia. There are also extracurricular or full-time courses in painting, art history, sculpture and architecture available. Another school much praised by LP readers is **Saenaiulia** (☎ 0577 441 55; www.saenaiulia.it) in Siena.

The Istituto Italiano di Cultura (IIC), which has branches all over the world, is a government-sponsored organisation aimed at promoting Italian culture and language. This is a good place to start your search for places to study in Italy. Try the IIC's websites at www.iicmelau.org (Melbourne, Australia), www.iicsyd.org (Sydney, Australia), www.iicto-ca.org/istituto.htm (Canada), www.italynet.com/cultura/istcult (France) and www.italcultny.org (USA).

CUSTOMS

There is no limit on the amount of euros brought into the country. Goods brought in and exported within the EU incur no additional taxes, provided duty has been paid somewhere within the EU and the goods are for personal consumption.

Duty-free sales within the EU no longer exist. Visitors coming into Italy from non-EU countries can import, duty free, 1L of spirits, 2L wine, 60mL perfume, 250mL eau de toilette, 200 cigarettes and other goods up to a total of €175.50; anything over this limit must be declared on arrival and the appropriate duty paid. On leaving the EU, non-EU citizens can reclaim any Value Added Tax (VAT) on expensive purchases.

DANGERS & ANNOYANCES
Annoyances

It requires a lot of patience to deal with the Italian concept of service. What for Italians is simply a way of everyday life can be horrifying for the foreigner. Anyone in a uniform or behind a counter (including police officers, waiters and shop assistants) is likely to regard you with imperious contempt. Long queues are the norm in banks, post offices and any government offices. It pays to remain calm and patient. Aggressive, demanding and angry customers stand virtually no chance of getting what they want.

Pollution
Noise and air pollution are problems in the major cities, caused mainly by heavy traffic. A headache after a day of sightseeing in Rome is likely to be caused by breathing carbon monoxide and lead, rather than simple tiredness.

In summer there are periodic pollution alerts. The elderly, children and people who have respiratory problems are warned to stay indoors. If you fit into one of these categories, keep yourself informed through the tourist office or your hotel.

One of the most annoying things about cities such as Rome, Naples and Palermo is that the pavements are littered with dog pooh – so be careful where you plant your feet or roll your suitcase.

Italy's beaches are generally polluted by industrial waste, sewage and oil spills from the Mediterranean's considerable sea traffic. There are clean beaches on Sardinia, Sicily and in the less-populated areas of the south and around Elba.

Racism
As with nearly all European countries there has been a disturbing rise in racism in Italy (most notably in the port towns of the south). For decades Italy was one of the world's largest exporters of Italian immigrants around the world but now it has become the first port of call for a huge influx of refugees from the Balkans, Eastern Europe and North Africa. For such a homogenous society with one of the lowest birth rates in Europe the sudden influx has been traumatic and there are now an estimated half million *clandestini* (illegal immigrants) in the country. Travellers should be aware of this especially at key entry points on the Italian coast such as Brindisi; if subjected to any racial discrimination you should report it to your embassy immediately.

Sexual Harassment
Italy is not a dangerous country for women, but women travelling alone may find themselves plagued by unwanted attention, which is more annoying than anything else. Get used to being stared at as it's likely to happen.

Lone women will also find it difficult to remain alone. Usually the best response is to ignore unwanted approaches but if that doesn't work, politely tell them that you are waiting for your *marito* (husband) or *fidanzato* (boyfriend) and, if necessary, walk away. Avoid becoming aggressive as this may result in an unpleasant confrontation. If all else fails, approach the nearest member of the police.

Watch out for men with wandering hands on crowded buses. Either keep your back to the wall or make a loud fuss if someone starts fondling your backside. A loud 'Che schifo!' (How disgusting!) will usually do the trick. Similarly, in the case of flashers one should always make a fuss rather than accepting the situation in an embarrassed silence. If a more serious incident occurs, make a report to the police who are then required to press charges.

Women on their own should use their common sense. Avoid walking alone in dark streets, and look for hotels that are central (unsafe areas are noted throughout this book). Women should also avoid hitchhiking alone.

Women will find that the further south they travel, the more likely they are to be harassed. It is advisable to dress more conservatively – skimpy clothing is a sure attention-earner.

Theft
Pickpockets and bag-snatchers operate in most major cities and are particularly active in Naples and Rome. The best way to avoid being robbed is to wear a money belt under your clothing. Keep all important items, such as money, passport, other documents and tickets, in your money belt at all times and wear bags or cameras slung across the body.

You should also watch out for groups of dishevelled-looking women and children asking for money. Their favourite haunts are major train stations, tourist sights and in shopping areas. If you have been targeted by a group take evasive action (such as crossing the street) or shout '*Va via!*' (Go away!) in a loud voice. You should also be cautious of sudden friendships, particularly if your new-found *amico* or *amica* wants to sell you something.

Parked cars are also prime targets for thieves, particularly those with foreign number plates or rental-company stickers. Try not to leave anything in the car if you can help it and certainly not overnight. Car theft is a problem in Rome, Campania and Pulia. It is a good idea to leave your car in supervised car parks. Throughout Italy, particularly in the south, service stations along the motorways are a haunt of thieves. If possible park where you can keep an eye on your car.

Some Italians practise a more insidious form of theft: short-changing. If you are new to euros, take the time to acquaint yourself with the denominations. When paying keep an eye on the bills you hand over and then count your change.

In case of theft or loss, always report the incident at the police station within 24 hours and ask for a statement, otherwise your travel insurance company won't pay out.

Traffic

Italian traffic can at best be described as chaotic, at worst downright dangerous for the unprepared tourist. Drivers are not keen to stop for pedestrians, even at pedestrian crossings, and are more likely to swerve. Italians simply step off the footpath and walk through the (swerving) traffic with determination. It is a practice that seems to work, so if you feel uncertain about crossing a busy road, wait for the next Italian. (Better still, wait for a nun or priest to cross the road – most Italians seem to 'stop for God'.)

In many cities, roads that appear to be for one-way traffic have lanes for buses travelling in the opposite direction – always look both ways before stepping onto the road.

DISABLED TRAVELLERS

Italy is not an easy country for disabled travellers and getting around can be a problem for the wheelchair bound. Even a short journey in a city or town can become a major expedition if cobblestoned streets have to be negotiated. Although many buildings have lifts, they are not always wide enough to accommodate a wheelchair.

The Italian State Tourist Office (see p827) in your country may be able to provide advice on Italian associations for the disabled and information on what help is available. It may also carry a small brochure, *Services for Disabled Passengers*, published by the Italian railways company, Ferrovie dello Stato (FS), which details facilities at stations and on trains.

Organisations

Consorzio Cooperative Integrate (COIN; ☎ 06 712 90 11; www.coinsociale.it) Based in Rome, COIN is the best reference point for disabled travellers. It provides information on the capital (including transport and access) and is happy to share its contacts throughout Italy. It publishes a mulitilingual guide, *Roma Accessibile*, which lists available facilities at museums, shops and theatres. It is available by mail order and from some tourist offices.

The Associazione Italiana Assistenza Spastici (☎ 02 550 17 564; Via S Barnaba 29, Milan) Operates an information service for disabled travellers called the Sportello Vacanze Disabili.

Accessible Italy (☎ 011 309 63 63; www.accessible italy.com; Piazza Pitagora 9, 10137 Turin) A private company which specialises in holiday services for the disabled, ranging from tours to the hiring of adapted transport. There is also a branch in Rome called **La Viaggeria** (☎ 06 7158 29 45; Via Lemonia 161, 00174 Rome).

DISCOUNT CARDS

At museums, never hesitate to ask if there are discounts for students, young people, children, families or the elderly. When sightseeing and where possible buy a *biglietto cumulativo*, a ticket that allows admission to a number of associated sights for less than the combined cost of separate admission fees.

Senior Cards

Senior citizens are often entitled to public-transport discounts but usually only for monthly passes (not daily or weekly tickets); the minimum qualifying age is 65 years.

For rail travel on the FS, seniors (over 60) can get a 20% reduction on full fares by purchasing an annual seniors' pass called the Carta Argento (€20.66). You can purchase these at major train stations.

Admission to most museums in Rome is free for the over-60s but in other cities (such as Florence) often no concessions are made for nonresidents.

Student & Youth Cards

Free admission to galleries and sites is available to under 18s. Discounts (usually half the normal fee) are available to EU citizens aged between 18 and 25 (you will need to produce proof of your age). An ISIC (International Student Identity Card) is no longer sufficient at many tourist sites as prices are based on age so a passport, driving licence or **Euro<26** (www.euro26.org) card is preferable. An ISIC card will still, however, prove useful for cheap flights and theatre and cinema discounts; similar cards are available to teachers (ITIC). For nonstudent travellers who are under 25, there is the **International Youth Travel Card** (IYTC; www.istc.org) which offers the same benefits.

Student cards are issued by student unions, hostelling organisations and some youth travel agencies. In Rome, the office of the Centro Turistico Studentesco e Giovanile (CTS) will issue ISIC, ITIC and Euro<26 cards.

EMBASSIES & CONSULATES
Italian Embassies & Consulates

The following is a selection of Italian diplomatic missions abroad. Bear in mind that Italy maintains consulates in additional cities in many of the countries listed here.

Australia Canberra (☎ 02-6273 3333; www.ambitalia .org.au; 12 Grey St, Deakin ACT 2600); Sydney (☎ 02-9392 7900; itconsydn@itconsyd.org; Level 43, The Gateway, 1 Macquarie Place NSW 2000); Melbourne (☎ 03-9867 5744; itconmel@netlink.com.au; 509 St Kilda Rd VIC 3004)

Austria Vienna (☎ 01-712 51 21; ambitalviepress@ via.at; Metternichgasse 13, 1030)

Canada Ottawa (☎ 613-232 2401; www.italyincanada .com; 21st fl, 275 Slater St, Ontario, K1P 5H9); Vancouver (☎ 604-684 7288; consolato@italianconsulate.bc.ca; Standard Bldg 1100-510 West Hastings St, BC V6B 1L8)

France Paris (☎ 01 49 54 03 00; ambasciata@amb-italie .fr; 51 Rue de Varenne 75007)

Germany Berlin (☎ 030-254 40 0; www.botschaft -italien.de, Italian & German only; Dessauer Strasse 28-29, 10963)

Ireland Dublin (☎ 01-660 1744; www.italianembassy.ie; 63-65 Northumberland Rd, 4)

Japan Tokyo (☎ 03-3453 5291; www.embitaly.jp; 2-5-4 Mita, Minato-ku 108-8302)

Netherlands The Hague (☎ 070-302 10 30; www .italy.nl; Alexanderstraat 12, 2514 JL)

New Zealand Wellington (☎ 04-473 5339; www.italy -embassy.org.nz; 34-38 Grant Rd, Thorndon)

Switzerland Bern (☎ 031 350 07 77; www3.itu.int/ embassy/italy, Italian only; Elfenstrasse 14-3000, 16)

UK London (☎ 020-7312 2200; www.embitaly.org.uk; 14 Three Kings Yard, W1K 4EH); Edinburgh (☎ 0131-2263 631; consedimb@consedimb.demon.co.uk; 32 Melville St, EH3 7HW)

USA Washington (☎ 202-328 5500; www.italyemb.org; 1601 Fuller St, NW Washington, DC 20009); New York (☎ 212-737 9100; www.italconsulnyc.org; 690 Park Ave, 10021); Los Angeles (☎ 310-820 0727; www.conlang.com; Suite 300, 12400 Wilshire Blvd, 90025)

Embassies & Consulates in Italy

For other foreign embassies and consulates not listed here, look under 'Ambasciate' or 'Consolati' in the telephone directory. Alternatively, tourist offices generally have a list.

Australia Rome (☎ 06 85 27 21; Via Alessandria 215, 00198); Milan (☎ 02 77 70 41; australian -consulate-general@austrade.gov.au; 3rd fl, Via Borgogna 2, 20122)

Austria Rome (☎ 06 844 01 41; Via Pergolesi 3, 00198); Milan (☎ 02 481 20 66; Via Tranquillo Cremona 27, 20145)

Canada Rome (☎ 06 44 59 81; Via G B de Rossi 27, 00161); Milan (☎ 02 6 75 81; www.canada.it; Via Vittorio Pisani 19, 20124)

France Rome (☎ 06 68 60 11; Piazza Farnese 00186); Milan (☎ 02 655 91 41; Via C Mangile 1, 20121); Naples (☎ 081 761 22 75; Piazza della Repubblica 2, 80122); Venice (☎ 041 522 43 19; Ramo del Pestrin, Castello, 6140)

Germany Rome (☎ 06 49 21 31; Via San Martino della Battaglia 4, 00185); Florence (☎ 055 29 47 22; Lungarno Amerigo Vespucci 30, 50123); Milan (☎ 02 623 11 01; Via Solferino 40, 20121); Naples (☎ 081 61 33 93; Via Francesco Crispi 69, 80121); Venice (☎ 041 523 76 75; Campo Sant'Angelo 3816, San Marco)

Ireland Rome (☎ 06 697 91 21; Piazza Campitelli 3, 00186); Milan (☎ 02 551 87 569; Piazza F Pietro in Gessate 2, 20122)

Japan Rome (☎ 06 48 79 91; Via Quintino Sella 60, 00187); Milan (☎ 02 624 11 41; Via Privata Cesare Mangili 2/4, 20121)

Netherlands Rome (☎ 06 322 11 41; Via Michele Mercati 8, 00197); Milan (☎ 02 485 58 41; nlgovmil@iol.it; Via San Vittore 45, 20123); Naples (☎ 081 551 30 03; Via Agostino Depretis 114, 80133); Palermo (☎ 091 58 15 21; Via Roma 489, 90139)

New Zealand Rome (☎ 06 441 71 71; Via Zara 28, 00198); Milan (☎ 02 480 12 544; milano@tradenz.govt.nz; Via Guido d'Arezzo 6, 20145)

Switzerland Rome (☎ 06 80 95 71; Via Barnarba Oriani 61, 00197); Florence (☎ 055 22 24 34; Piazzale Galileo 5, 50125); Milan (☎ 02 777 91 61; Via Palestro 2, 20121); Naples (☎ 081 761 45 33; Via Pergolesi 1, 80122)

UK Rome (☎ 06 482 54 41; Via XX Settembre 80a, 00187); Florence (☎ 055 28 41 33; Lungarno Corsini 2, 50123); Milan (☎ 02 72 30 01; Via S Paolo 7, 20121); Naples (☎ 081 66 35 11; Via dei Mille 40, 80121); Venice (☎ 041 522 72 07; Palazzo Querini, Dorsoduro 1051, 30123)

USA Rome (☎ 06 467 41; www.usis.it; Via Vittorio Veneto 119a-121, 00187); Florence (☎ 055 266 951; Lungarno Vespucci 38, 50123); Milan (☎ 02 29 03 51; Largo Donegani 1); Naples (☎ 081 583 81 11; Piazza della Repubblica, 80122); Palermo (☎ 091 30 58 57; Via Vaccarini 1, 90141)

FESTIVALS & EVENTS

Italy's calendar bursts with cultural events ranging from colourful traditional celebrations, with a religious and/or historical flavour, through to festivals of the performing arts, including opera, music and theatre.

Among the important opera seasons are those at Verona's Arena and at La Scala in Milan. There are also significant opera seasons in Palermo and Catania. Major music festivals include Umbria Jazz in Perugia (July) and the Umbria Jazz Winter Festival in Orvieto (late December/early January) which hosts a fantastic party on New Year's Eve. There is also Siena Jazz, Vincenza Jazz and Maggio Musicale Fiorentino in Florence. International orchestras play annually at the **Festivale Musicale di Ravello** (www .ravelloarts.org).

FEBRUARY/MARCH/APRIL

Festa di Sant'Agata (p743; 3-5 Feb) Hysterical celebrations where one million Catanians and tourists follow as a silver reliquary bust of the saint covered in marvellous jewels is carried along the main street of Catania.

Sagra del Mandorlo in Fiore (p759; Festival of the Almond Blossoms; first Sun in Feb) A folk festival in Agrigento with open-air performances of drama and music.

Carnevale (Carnival) During the period before Ash Wednesday, many towns stage carnivals and enjoy their last opportunity to indulge before Lent. The carnival held in Venice (p346) during the 10 days before Ash Wednesday is the most famous.

Sa Sartiglia (p787; Sun & Tue before Lent) The highlight of carnival celebrations at Oristano. It involves a medieval tournament of horsemen in masquerade.

Settimana Santa (Holy Week) Holy Week in Italy is marked by solemn processions and Passion plays. Notable processions take place in Taranto (Puglia), Chieti (Abruzzo) and Trapani (Sicily). On Good Friday evening the Pope leads a candlelit procession to the Colosseum and on Easter Sunday he gives his traditional blessing.

Scoppio del Carro (p456; Explosion of the Cart; Easter Sat) A cartful of fireworks is exploded in the Piazza del Duomo in Florence – a tradition dating back to the crusades.

MAY

Festa di Sant'Efisio (p800; 1 May) An effigy of Sardinia's patron saint is paraded around Cagliari on a bullock-drawn carriage amid a colourful procession.

Festa di San Nicola (p662; 2-3 May) A procession in Bari follows a statue of the saint for a ceremony out at sea.

Processione dei Serpari (p579; Snake-Charmers' Procession; first Thu in May) Held at Cocullo, a statue of Saint Domenico is draped with live snakes and carried in procession.

Festa di San Gennaro (p600; first Sun in May, 19 Sep & 16 Dec) The faithful gather in Naples' cathedral to wait for the blood of San Gennaro to liquefy.

Festa dei Ceri (p539; Candles Festival; 15 May) Three teams, each carrying a *cero* (massive wooden pillars weighing about 400kg, bearing the statue of a rival saint) race through Gubbio's streets in commemoration of the city's patron Saint Sant'Ubaldo.

Cavalcata Sarda (p801; Sardinian Cavalcade; second last Sun in May) Hundreds of Sardi wearing colourful traditional costume gather at Sassari to mark a victory over the Saracens in the year 1000.

Palio della Balestra (p539; Crossbow Contest; last Sun in May) Held in Gubbio this contest is between the men of Gubbio and neighbouring Sansepolcro, who dress in medieval costume and use antique weapons.

Pavarotti & Friends (p407; end of May) A one-night mega-concert, in Modena, featuring international stars.

Greek Classical Drama (p751; mid May–mid June) During this unique yearly festival the works of Aristophanes and Euripedes, and other classical playwrights, once again bring to life the stones of Syracuse's ancient 5th-century amphitheatre. The festivals attract some of Italy's finest performers.

JUNE

Gioco del Ponte (p483; Game of the Bridge; last Sun in Jun) Two groups in medieval costume contend for the Ponte di Mezzo in Pisa.

Infiorata (Flower Festival; 21 Jun) To celebrate Corpus Domini some towns (including Bolsena and Genzano near Rome, Spello in Umbria and Noto in Sicily) decorate a street with colourful designs made with flower petals.

Festa di San Giovanni (p456; 24 Jun) Celebrated with the lively Calcio Storico, a series of medieval matches played on Florence's Piazza di Santa Croce.

Festival dei Due Mondi (p543; Festival of Two Worlds) An international arts event held in June and July in Spoleto, featuring music, theatre, dance and art.

Palio delle Quattro Antiche Repubbliche Marinare (Regatta of the Four Ancient Maritime Republics) A procession of boats and a race between the four historical maritime rivals: Pisa, Venice, Amalfi and Genoa. The event rotates between the four towns: Genoa in 2004, Amalfi in 2005, Pisa in 2006 and Venice in 2007. Although usually held in June, it has been known to be delayed as late as September.

JULY

Il Palio (p496; 2 Jul) A dangerous bareback horse race around the piazza in Siena, preceded by a parade of supporters in traditional costume.

Ardia (p801; 6-7 Jul) More dangerous than Il Palio, this impressive and chaotic horse race (accompanied by gunshots) at Sed ilo celebrates the victory of the Roman Emperor Constantine over Maxentius in AD 312.

Festa del Redentore (pp343-4; third weekend in Jul) There are fireworks and a procession over the bridge to the Chiesa del Redentore in Venice.

Festival Internazionale del Balleto (International Ballet Festival) This festival held in Nervi features international performers.

Taormina Arte (p739; www.taormina-arte.com) Films, theatrical events and music concerts from an impressive list of international names are on show in Sicily.

AUGUST

Quintana (p569; Medieval Joust; first Sun in Aug) A parade of hundreds of people in 15th-century costume, followed by a jousting tournament, is held at Ascoli Piceno.

I Candelieri (p801; The Candlesticks, 14 Aug) Town representatives in Sassari dress in medieval costume and carry huge wooden columns through the town.

Il Palio (p496; 16 Aug) A repeat of the famous horse race is held in Siena.

Festa del Redentore (p801; 28-29 Aug) Held in Nuoro, this folk festival is attended by thousands of people, dressed in traditional costume, from all over the island.

Mostra del Cinema di Venezia (pp346-7; Venice International Film Festival) Held at the Lido, the festival attracts the international film scene.

SEPTEMBER

Palio della Balestra (1st Sun Sep) Sansepolcro in Tuscany hosts a rematch with crossbow sharpshooters from Gubbio.

Regata Storica (p346; Historic Regatta; first Sun in Sep) A parade of boats followed by a gondola race along the Grand Canal in Venice.

NOVEMBER

Festa della Madonna (p347 ; 21 Nov) A procession – over a bridge of boats – to the Chiesa di Santa Maria della Salute in Venice gives thanks for the city's deliverance from plague in 1630.

Festa di Santa Cecilia (p496) A series of concerts and exhibitions in Siena honour the patron saint of musicians.

DECEMBER

Natale (Christmas) During the weeks preceding Christmas there are numerous processions and religious events. Many churches set up elaborate cribs or nativity scenes known as *presepi* – Naples is famous for these. From the first week in December there is a toy fair in Piazza Navona (Rome) where you can buy handmade Nativity scenes.

FOOD

Eating is one of life's great pleasures for Italians. Be adventurous and don't be intimidated by eccentric waiters or indecipherable menus and you will agree with the locals that nowhere in the world has food as good as Italy. For information on the staples of Italian food and regional varieties, see pp67–78.

For large cities and towns, restaurant listings in this book are given in the order: budget (€5 to €15), mid-range (€15 to €25) and top end (over €25). Within each section the restaurants are listed in order of preference, for small towns, listings are given in order of best first.

GAY & LESBIAN TRAVELLERS

Homosexuality is legal in Italy and well tolerated in major cities. However, overt displays of affection by homosexual couples could attract a negative response in the south and in smaller towns. The legal age of consent is 16. A few years ago the gay capitals of Italy were Milan and Bologna, but Rome is now giving both cities some strong competition.

There are gay clubs in Rome, Florence and Milan, which may be listed in newspapers but can be more reliably tracked down through local gay organisations or publications such as *Pride*, a national monthly magazine, and *AUT* published by Circolo Mario Mieli in Rome, both available at gay and lesbian organisations and bookshops. The international gay guide *Spartacus International Gay Guide* (US$32.95; available in bookshops worldwide) also has listings of gay venues all over Italy. The useful website www.gay.it /guida (Italian only) lists gay bars and hotels.

Organisations

ARCI-GAY & ARCI-Lesbica (☎ 051 644 7054; www.arcigay.it, Italian only; Piazza di Porta Saragozza 2, 20123 Bologna) National organisations for gay men and lesbians.

Circolo Mario Mieli di Cultura Omosessuale (☎ 06 541 39 85; info@mariomieli.it) Rome's main cultural and political organisation, organising cultural events such as Rome Pride which takes place every June. It also runs a free AIDS/HIV testing and care centre.

HOLIDAYS

Most Italians take their annual holiday in August. This means that many businesses and shops close for at least a part of that month. Larger cities, notably Milan and Rome, are left to the tourists, who may be frustrated that many restaurants and shops are closed until early September. The *Settimana Santa* (Easter Week) is another busy holiday period for Italians. Beware of school holiday periods (especially Easter) when large groups of children noisily prowl the cultural sights.

Individual towns have public holidays to celebrate the feasts of their patron saints (see pp818–19). National public holidays include the following:

New Year's Day 1 January
Epiphany 6 January
Easter Monday March/April
Liberation Day 25 April
Labour Day 1 May
Feast of the Assumption 15 August
All Saints' Day 1 November
Feast of the Immaculate Conception 8 December
Christmas Day 25 December
Feast of Santo Stefano 26 December

INSURANCE

A travel-insurance policy to cover theft, loss and medical problems is a good idea. It may also cover you for cancellation or delays to your travel arrangements. Paying for your ticket with a credit card can often provide limited travel accident insurance and you may be able to reclaim the payment if the operator doesn't deliver. Ask your credit card company what it will cover.

Emergency cover (including accidents) in Italy is available, by law, free of charge to all travellers. Medical care, such as consultations and prescriptions, are only freely available to EU nationals carrying an E111 form, although even with this form you will have to battle with the State Health Care system – not an easy task at the best of times. You can obtain this form from health centres and social security offices. For most short holidays private insurance is by far the best option. See p840 for more details.

Some policies specifically exclude 'dangerous activities', which can include scuba diving, motorcycling and even trekking. A locally acquired motorcycle licence is not valid under some policies.

You may prefer a policy which pays doctors or hospitals directly rather than you having to pay on the spot and claim later; if you have to claim later make sure you keep all documentation. Some policies ask you to call back (reverse charges) to a centre in your home country where an immediate assessment of your problem is made.

Check that the policy covers ambulances or an emergency flight home.

For details of car insurance, see p836.

INTERNET ACCESS

If you plan to carry your notebook or palmtop computer with you, remember that the power-supply voltage in the countries you visit may vary from that at home, risking damage to your equipment. The best investment is a universal AC adaptor for your appliance, which will enable you to plug it in anywhere. You'll also need a plug adaptor for each country you visit.

Also, your PC-card modem may not work once you leave your home country. The safest option is to buy a reputable 'global' modem before you leave home, or buy a local PC-card modem if you're spending an extended time in any one country. Keep in mind that the telephone socket in each country you visit will probably be different, so ensure that you have at least a US RJ-11 telephone adaptor that works with your modem. You can almost always find an adaptor that will convert from RJ-11 to the local variety. For more information on travelling with a portable computer, see www.teleadapt.com or www.warrior.com.

Major Internet service providers such as AOL (www.aol.com) and CompuServe (www.compuserve.com) have dial-in nodes in Rome and Milan; it's best to download a list of the dial-in numbers before you leave home. If you access your Internet email account at home through a smaller ISP or your office or school network, your best option is either to open account with a global ISP, like those mentioned above, or to rely on Internet cafés to collect your mail.

If you do intend to rely on Internet cafés, you'll need to carry three pieces of information: your incoming (POP or IMAP) mail server name, your account name and your password. Your ISP or network supervisor will be able to give you these.

You'll find Internet cafés throughout Italy; prices hover around €5 per hour. Check out www.netcafeguide.com for an up-to-date list. For more useful Internet addresses refer to p15.

LEGAL MATTERS

For many Italians, finding ways to get around the law (any law) is a way of life. Few people pay attention to speed limits; most motorcyclists and many drivers don't stop at red lights. No-one bats an eyelid about littering or dogs pooping in the middle of the pavement, even though many municipal governments have introduced laws against these things. But these are minor transgressions when measured up against the country's organised crime, the extraordinary levels of tax evasion and the corruption in government and business.

The average tourist will only have a brush with the law if they are robbed by a bag-snatcher or pickpocket.

Drink & Drugs

Although Italy's drug laws are relatively lenient, drugs are seriously frowned upon, in part due to the massive heroin problem (most notable in Naples and the poor south) created by the mafia's lucrative business. Although a 'few' grams of cannabis or marijuana are permissible for personal use, there is nothing to say how much a few grams is and it is better to avoid the risks altogether given the fact that the police can hold you for as long as it takes to analyse your case. If the police further decide that you are a pusher you could end up in prison.

The legal limit for blood-alcohol level is 0.05% and random breath tests do occur. See p837 for more information.

> **LEGAL AGE**
>
> - The right to vote: 18 years old
> - Age of consent: 16 years old (heterosexual and homosexual)
> - Driving age: 18 years old

Police

If you run into trouble in Italy, you're likely to end up dealing with either the *polizia statale* (state police) or the *carabinieri* (military police).

The *polizia* are a civil force, take their orders from the Ministry of the Interior, and deal generally with thefts, visa extensions and permissions. They wear powder-blue trousers with a fuchsia stripe and a navy-blue jacket. Their headquarters is called the *questura*, details of these are given throughout this book.

The *carabinieri*, on the other hand, are more concerned with civil obedience. They deal with general crime, public order and drug enforcement, and are therefore more visible on the street. They wear a black uniform with a red stripe and drive dark-blue cars with a red stripe. Their police station is called a *caserma* (barracks), a reflection of their military status.

Other police include the *vigili urbani*, who are basically traffic police. You will have to deal with them if you get a parking ticket or your car is towed away. The *guardia di finanza* are responsible for fighting tax evasion and drug smuggling. The *guardia forestale* or *corpo forestale* are responsible for enforcing laws concerning forests and the environment in general.

Addresses and local telephone numbers of police stations are given in the Emergency sections in this guide.

Your Rights

Italy still has some antiterrorism laws on its books that could make life very difficult if you happen to be detained by the police – for any alleged offence. You can be held for 48 hours without a magistrate being informed and you can be interrogated without the presence of a lawyer. It is difficult to obtain bail and you can be held legally for up to three years without being brought to trial.

MAPS

City Maps

The city maps in this book, combined with tourist office maps, are generally adequate. More detailed maps are available in Italy at good bookshops (such as Feltrinelli). Excellent city plans and maps are published by de Agostini, Touring Club Italiano (TCI) and Michelin. Other decent city-map publishers include FMB (with the yellow covers) and Milan's Vincitorio Editore. TCI publishes *200 Piante di Città*, a handy book of street plans covering pretty much any city. Lonely Planet publishes City Maps to Rome, Florence and Venice.

Road Atlases

If you are driving around Italy, the AA's *Road Atlas Italy*, available in the UK, is scaled at 1:250,000 and includes 39 town maps. Pretty much as good is Michelin's *Tourist and Motoring Atlas Italy*, which is scaled at 1:300,000, with 78 town maps.

In Italy, the Istituto Geografico de Agostini publishes a comprehensive *Atlante Turistico Stradale d'Italia* (1:250,000), which includes 145 city maps. TCI publishes an *Atlante Stradale d'Italia* (1:200,000) divided into three parts – Nord, Centro and Sud. It also publishes *Autoatlante d'Italia*, a road/street directory for the whole country which includes 206 city maps on a scale of 1:1,350,000.

Small-Scale Maps

Michelin has a series of good fold-out country maps. No 988 covers the whole country on a scale of 1:1,000,000. You could also consider the series of area maps at 1:400,000 – Nos 428 to 431 cover the mainland, 432 covers Sicily and 433 Sardinia. TCI publishes a decent map covering Italy, Switzerland and Slovenia at 1:800,000.

Walking Maps

Maps of walking trails in the Alps and Apennines are available in major bookshops in Italy, but the best by far are the TCI bookshops.

The best walking maps are the 1:25,000 scale series published by Tabacco (they mainly cover the north). Kompass publishes 1:25,000 scale maps of various parts of Italy, as well as a 1:50,000 series and several in other scales (including one at 1:7500

of Capri). Edizioni Multigraphic Florence produces a series of walking maps concentrating mainly on the Apennines.

The series of *Guide dei Monti d'Italia*, grey hardbacks published by the TCI and Club Alpino Italiano, are exhaustive walking guides with maps.

MONEY

On 1 January 2002, the euro became the currency of cash transactions in all of Italy and throughout the EU (except for the three foot-draggers: Denmark, Sweden and the UK). The euro is divided into 100 cents. Coin denominations are one, two, five, 10, 20 and 50 cents, €1 and €2. The notes are €5, €10, €20, €50, €100, €200 and €500.

Exchange rates are given on the inside front cover of this book and a guide to costs can be found on p13.

ATMs

Credit cards can also be used in a *bancomat* (ATM) displaying the appropriate sign or (if you have no PIN number) to obtain cash advances over the counter in many banks – Visa and MasterCard are among the most widely recognised. Check what charges you will incur with your bank.

It is possible to use your own ATM debit card in machines throughout Italy to obtain money from your own bank account. This is without doubt the simplest way to handle your money while travelling.

If an ATM rejects your card, don't despair. Try a few more ATMs displaying your credit card's logo before assuming the problem lies with your card. Italian ATMs are notoriously fickle.

Cash

There is little advantage in bringing foreign cash into Italy. True, exchange commissions are often lower than for travellers cheques but the danger of losing the lot far outweighs such gains.

Credit & Debit Cards

Credit and debit cards are the simplest way to organise your holiday funds. You can get money after hours and on weekends and the exchange rate is better than that offered for travellers cheques or cash exchanges.

Major credit cards, such as Visa, MasterCard, Eurocard, Cirrus and Eurocheques cards, are accepted throughout Italy. They can be used in many supermarkets, hotels and restaurants (although *pensioni*, smaller trattorie and *pizzerie* still tend to accept cash only).

If your credit card is lost, stolen or swallowed by an ATM, you can telephone toll free to have an immediate stop put on its use. For MasterCard the number in Italy is ☎ 800 870 866 or make a reverse-charges call to St Louis in the USA on ☎ 314-275 66 90. For Visa, phone ☎ 800 877 232 in Italy.

American Express is also widely accepted (although not as common as Visa or MasterCard). American Express's full-service offices (such as in Rome and Milan) will issue new cards, usually within 24 hours, if yours has been lost or stolen. Some American Express offices have ATMs that you can use to obtain cash advances if you have made the necessary arrangements prior to travel.

The toll-free emergency number to report a lost or stolen American Express card varies according to where the card was issued. Check with American Express in your country or contact American Express in Rome on ☎ 06 7 22 82, which has a 24-hour cardholders' service.

Moneychangers

You can change money in banks, at the post office or in a *cambio* (exchange office). Banks are generally the most reliable and tend to offer the best rates. Commission fluctuates and depends on whether you are changing cash or cheques.

While the post office charges a flat rate of €0.60 per cash transaction, banks charge at least €1.55 or more. Travellers cheques attract higher fees. Exchange booths often advertise 'no commission' but the rate of exchange is usually inferior.

The desire to save on such fees by making occasional large transactions should be balanced against a healthy fear of pickpockets.

Receipts

Laws aimed at tightening controls on the payment of taxes in Italy mean that the onus is on the buyer to ask for and retain receipts for all goods and services – this applies to everything. Although it rarely happens, you could be asked by an officer

of the *guardia di finanza* to produce the receipt immediately after you leave a shop. If you don't have it, you may be obliged to pay a fine of up to €155.

Taxes & Refunds

A value-added tax of around 19%, known as IVA (Imposta di Valore Aggiunto), is slapped onto just about everything in Italy. If you are a non-EU resident and you spend more than €335 on a purchase, you can claim a refund when you leave. The refund only applies to purchases from affiliated retail outlets which display a 'Tax free for tourists' sign. You have to complete a form at the point of sale, then get it stamped by Italian customs as you leave. At major airports you can then get an immediate cash refund; otherwise it will be refunded to your credit card. For information, pick up a pamphlet on the scheme from participating stores.

Tipping

You are not expected to tip on top of restaurant service charges but it is common to leave a small amount, perhaps €0.60 per person. If there is no service charge, the customer should consider leaving a 10-12% tip, but this is by no means obligatory. In bars, Italians often leave any small change as a tip, maybe only €0.10. Tipping taxi drivers is not common practice, but you are expected to tip the porter at top-end hotels.

Travellers Cheques

These are a safe way to carry money and are easily cashed at banks and exchange offices. Always keep the bank receipt listing the cheque numbers separate from the cheques themselves, and keep a list of the numbers of those you have already cashed – this will reduce problems in the event of loss or theft. Check the conditions applying to such circumstances before buying the cheques.

If you buy your travellers cheques in euros, you should not be charged commission when cashing them. Most hard currencies are widely accepted, although you may have occasional trouble with the New Zealand dollar.

Travellers using the better-known travellers cheques (such as Visa, American Express and Thomas Cook) will have little trouble in Italy. If you lose your American Express cheques, call toll free ☎ 800 872 000 (24 hours). For Thomas Cook or MasterCard cheques call ☎ 800 872 050 and for Visa cheques call ☎ 800 874 155.

Take along your passport as identification when you go to cash travellers cheques.

POST

Italy's postal system is notoriously unreliable. The most efficient service to use is *posta prioritaria* (priority mail).

Francobolli (stamps) are available at post offices and authorised tobacconists (look for the official *tabacchi* sign: a big 'T', usually white on black). Since letters often need to be weighed, what you get at the tobacconist's for international air mail will occasionally be an approximation of the proper rate. Tobacconists keep regular shop hours.

Information about postal services and rates can be obtained on ☎ 800 22 26 66 or online at www.poste.it (Italian only).

Postal Rates & Services

The cost of sending a letter *via aerea* (airmail) depends on its weight, destination and method of postage. The ordinary postal rates for letters up to 20g are divided into three zones: Zone 1 (Europe and the Mediterranean Basin) €0.41; Zone 2 (other countries in Africa, Asia and America) €0.52; and Zone 3 (the Pacific including Australia, Japan and New Zealand) €0.52. It can take up to two weeks for mail to arrive in the UK or USA, while a letter to Australia will take between two and three weeks. Postcards take even longer. Put them in an envelope and send them as letters.

For *posta prioritaria*, letters up to 20g cost €0.62 in Zone 1 and €0.77 in Zone 2 and 3. This service guarantees to deliver letters within Europe in three days and to the rest of the world within four to eight days.

For more important items, use *raccomandata* (registered mail) – €2.17 on top of the normal cost of the letter – or *assicurata* (insured mail), the cost of which depends on the value of the object being sent (€5.16 for objects up to the value of €51.65 in Zone 1).

Urgent mail can be sent by *postacelere* (also known as CAI Post), the Italian post office's courier service.

Receiving Mail

Poste restante (general delivery) is known as *fermo posta* in Italy. Letters marked thus will be held at the counter of the same name in the main post office in the relevant town. Poste restante mail to Verona, for example, should be addressed as follows:

John SMITH,
Fermo Posta,
37100 Verona,
Italy

You will need to pick up your letters in person and you must present your passport as ID.

American Express card or travellers cheque holders can use the free client mail-holding service at American Express offices. You can obtain a list of these from any American Express office. Take your passport when you go to pick up mail.

TELEPHONE
Mobile Phones

Italy has one of the highest levels of mobile phone penetration in Europe, and there are several companies through which you can get a temporary or prepaid account if you already own a GSM, dual- or tri-band cellular phone. You will usually need your passport to open an account.

Both TIM (Telecom Italia Mobile) and Omnitel offer *prepagato* (prepaid) accounts for GSM phones (frequency 900 mHz), whereby you can buy a SIM card (€51.65) for either network which gives you €25.80 worth of calls. You can then top up the account with multiples of €25.80 (plus a €5.15 service fee) as required. There are TIM and Omnitel retail outlets in virtually every Italian town. Calls on these plans cost around €0.10 per minute.

The dual-band operator Wind works on frequencies of 900mHz and 1800mHz and also offers prepaid accounts. You don't pay for Wind's SIM card but calls are more expensive than Telecom and Omnitel – around €0.25 per minute for the first three minutes, then €0.10 per minute. There are Wind retail outlets in most Italian towns.

Always check with your mobile service provider in your home country to ascertain whether your handset allows use of another SIM card.

TAKING YOUR MOBILE PHONE

Italy uses GSM 900/1800, which is compatible with the rest of Europe and Australia but not with North American GSM 1900 or the totally different system in Japan (although some GSM 1900/900 phones do work here). If you have a GSM phone, check with your service provider about using it in Italy and beware of calls being routed internationally (very expensive for a 'local' call).

Payphones & Phonecards

The state-run Telecom Italia is the largest telecommunications organisation in Italy and its orange public pay phones are liberally scattered about the country. The most common accept only *carte/schede telefoniche* (telephone cards), although you will still find plenty that accept cards and coins. Some card phones accept credit cards.

Telecom pay phones can be found in the streets, train stations and some stores as well as in Telecom offices. Where these offices are staffed, it is possible to make international calls and pay at the desk afterwards. Details of Telecom offices are included under Post & Telephone throughout this book. You can buy phonecards at post offices (usually a fixed euro rate of €5/10/20), tobacconists and newsstands. You must break the top left-hand corner of the card before you can use it. You need to be aware that phonecards have an expiry date, usually 31st December or 30th June depending on when you purchase the card.

Public phones operated by the private telecommunications companies Infostrada and Albacom can be found in airports and stations. These phones accept Infostrada or Albacom phonecards (available from post offices, tobacconists and newspaper stands). The rates are slightly cheaper than Telecom's for long-distance and international calls.

There are cut-price call centres all over Italy. These are run by various companies and the rates are lower than Telecom payphones for international calls. You simply place your call from a private booth inside the centre and pay for it when you've finished.

Domestic Calls

Rates, particularly for long-distance calls, are among the highest in Europe. The cheapest time for domestic calls is from 11pm to 8am and all of Sunday. A local call from a public phone will cost €0.10 for three to six minutes, depending on the time of day you call. Peak call times are 8am to 6.30pm Monday to Friday and 8am to 1pm on Saturday. Rates for long-distance calls within Italy depend on the time of day and the distance involved. At the worst, one minute will cost about €0.20 in peak periods.

Telephone area codes all begin with 0 and consist of up to four digits. The area code is followed by a number of anything from four to eight digits. Area codes, including the 0, are an integral part of all telephone numbers in Italy. Mobile phone numbers begin with a three-digit prefix such as 330. Toll-free (freephone) numbers are known as *numeri verdi* and usually start with 800. National call rate numbers start with 848 or 199.

For directory inquiries dial ☎ 12.

International Calls

If you need to call overseas, beware of the cost – calls to most European countries cost about €0.50 per minute, and closer to €1 from a public phone. Travellers from countries that offer direct-dialling services paid for at home-country rates (such as AT&T in the USA and Telstra in Australia) should think seriously about taking advantage of them.

Direct international calls can easily be made from public telephones by using a phonecard. Off-peak times are between 11pm and 8am and all of Sunday. Dial ☎ 00 to get out of Italy, then the relevant country and area codes, followed by the telephone number.

To make a reverse charges (collect) international call from a public telephone, dial ☎ 170. For European countries dial ☎ 15. All operators speak English.

Easier, and often cheaper, is using the Country Direct service for your country. You dial the number and request a reverse charges call through the operator in your country. Numbers for this service include:

Australia (Optus)	☎ 172 11 61
Australia (Telstra)	☎ 172 10 61
Canada	☎ 172 10 01

France	☎	172 00 33
New Zealand	☎	172 10 64
South Africa (Telkom)	☎	172 10 27
UK	☎	172 00 44
USA (AT&T)	☎	172 10 11
USA (MCI)	☎	172 10 22
USA (Sprint)	☎	172 18 77

For international directory inquiries call
☎ 176. To call Italy from abroad dial ☎ 39
and then the area code, including the 0.

TIME

Italy is one hour ahead of GMT. Daylight-
saving time, when clocks are moved forward one hour, starts on the last Sunday in
March. Clocks are put back an hour on the
last Sunday in October. Italy operates on a
24-hour clock.

TOURIST INFORMATION
Local Tourist Offices

The quality of tourist offices in Italy varies dramatically. One office might have
enthusiastic staff but no useful printed information, while indifferent staff in another
might have a gold mine of brochures.

Three tiers of tourist office exist: regional,
provincial and local. They have different
names (see below) but roughly offer the
same services, with the exception of the regional offices which are generally concerned
with promotion, planning and budgeting.
Throughout this book offices are referred to
as tourist offices rather than by their elaborate titles. Most offices will respond to written and telephone requests for information.

Azienda di Promozione Turistica (APT) The provincial – read: main – tourist office should have information
on the town you are in and the surrounding province.

**Azienda Autonoma di Soggiorno e Turismo
(AAST)** Otherwise known as Informazioni e Assistenza ai
Turisti, is the local tourist office. These local offices have
town-specific information and should also know about bus
routes and museum opening times.

Pro Loco This is the local office in small towns and villages and is similar to the AAST office.

Tourist offices are generally open 8.30am to
12.30pm or 1pm and 3pm to 7pm Monday
to Friday. Hours are usually extended in
summer, when some offices also open on
Saturday or Sunday.

Information booths at most major train
stations tend to keep similar hours but in
some cases operate only in summer. Staff
can usually provide a city map, list of hotels
and information on the major sights.

English, and sometimes French or German, is spoken at tourist offices in larger
towns and major tourist areas. German is,
of course, spoken in Alto Adige. Printed information is generally provided in a variety
of languages.

NATIONAL TOURIST OFFICE
Rome (☎ 06 4 97 11; www.enit.it; Via Marghera 2,
00185)

REGIONAL TOURIST AUTHORITIES
Abruzzo (☎ 0862 41 08 08; www.laquila.com, Italian
only; Piazza Santa Maria Paganica 5, L'Aquila)
Basilicata (☎ 0971 27 44 85; apt@powernet.it; Via
Cavour 15, Potenza)
Calabria (☎ 0965 2 11 71; apt.reggiocalabria@infinito
.it; Via Roma 3, Reggio di Calabria)
Campania (☎ 081 40 53 11; www.campaniafelix.it,
Italian only; Piazza dei Martiri 58, Naples)
Emilia-Romagna (☎ 051 24 65 41; www.emiliaromag
naturismo.it; Piazza Maggiore 1, Bologna)
Fruili (☎ 040 36 51 51; www.triestetourism.it; Via
Rossini 6, Trieste)
Lazio (☎ 06 488 99 253; www.romaturismo.it; Via
Parigi 5, Rome)
Liguria (☎ 919 24 87 11; www.turismo.liguriainrete.it;
Palazzina Santa Maria, Porto Antico, Genoa)
Lombardy (☎ 02 7252 43 50; www.milanoinfotourist.it;
Via Marconi 1, Milan)
Molise (☎ 0874 41 56 62; Piazza della Vittoria 14,
Campobasso)
Marche (☎ 071 35 89 81; www.le-marche.com/italia
/Marche/; Via Thaon de Revel 4, Ancona)
Piedmont (☎ 011 53 59 01; www.turismotorino.org;
Piazza Castello 161, Torino)
Puglia (☎ 080 524 23 61; www.pugliaturismo.com;
Piazza Aldo Moro 33a, Bari)
Sardinia (☎ 070 66 92 55; www.regione.sardegna.it
/eptca/, Italian only; Piazza Mateotti 9, Cagliari)
Sicily (☎ 091 605 81 11; www.regione.sicilia.it/turismo;
Piazza Castelnuovo 35, Palermo)
Trentino (☎ 0461 98 38 40; www.apt.trento.it; Via
Manci 2, Trento)
Tuscany (☎ 055 29 08 32; www.turismo.toscana.it; Via
Cavour 1r, Florence)
Umbria (☎ 075 572 33 27; www.umbria.org; Piazza IV
Novembre 3, Perugia)
Valle d'Aosta (☎ 01 65 23 66 27; www.regione.vda.it
/turismo, Italian only; Piazza Chanoux 8, Aosta)
Veneto (☎ 041 529 87 40; www.turismovenezia.it;
Piazza San Marco 71/f, Venice)

Tourist Offices Abroad

Information on Italy is available from the Italian State Tourist Office in the following countries.

Australia Sydney (☎ 02-9262 1666; enitour@ihug.com .au; Level 26, 44 Market St 2000)

Austria Vienna (☎ 01-505 16 30 12; delegation.wien@ enit.at; Kaerntnerring 4, A-1010)

Canada Toronto (☎ 416-925 4882; enit.canada@on .aibn.com; Suite 907, South Tower, 17 Bloor St E, Ontario M4W 3R8)

France Paris (☎ 01 42 66 66 68; enit.parigi@wanadoo.fr; 23 Rue de La Paix, 75002)

Germany Berlin (☎ 030-247 83 97; enit-berlin@ t-online.de; Karl Liebknecht Strasse 34, 10178) Munich (☎ 089-531 31 7; enit-muenchen@t-online.de; Goethes-trasse 20, 80336) Frankfurt (☎ 069-259 12 6; enit.ffm@ t-online.de; Kaiserstrasse 65, 60329)

Japan Tokyo (☎ 03-3478 2051; 2-7-14 Miami Ayoama, Minato-ku, 107)

Netherlands Amsterdam (☎ 020-616 82 44; enitams@ wirehub.nl; Stadhouderskade 2, 1054 ES)

Spain Madrid (☎ 91 559 9750; italiaturismo@retemail .es; Gran Via 84, Edificio Espagna 1-1, 28013)

Switzerland Zurich (☎ 01-211 79 17; enit@bluewin.ch; Uraniastrasse 32, 8001)

UK London (☎ 020-7408 1254; italy@italiantouristboard .co.uk; 1 Princes St, W1B 2AY)

USA Chicago (☎ 312-644 0996; www.italiantourism.com; 500 North Michigan Avenue, Suite 2240, IL 60611) Los Angeles (☎ 310-820 1898; 12400 Wilshire Blvd, Suite 550, CA 90025) New York (☎ 212-245 4822; 630 Fifth Ave, Suite 1565, NY 10111)

VISAS

Italy is among the 15 countries that have signed the Schengen Convention, an agreement whereby all EU member countries (except the UK and Ireland) plus Iceland and Norway agreed to abolish checks at common borders. Legal residents of one Schengen country do not require a visa for another. Citizens of the UK and Ireland are also exempt from visa requirements for Schengen countries. Nationals of Australia, Canada, Israel, Japan, New Zealand, Switzerland and the USA do not require visas for tourist visits of up to 90 days to any Schengen country.

The standard tourist visa is valid for up to 90 days. A Schengen visa issued by one Schengen country is generally valid for travel in other Schengen countries. However, individual Schengen countries may impose additional restrictions on certain nationalities. It is therefore worth checking visa regulations with the consulate of each country you plan to visit.

It's now mandatory that you apply for a Schengen visa in your country of residence. You can apply for no more than two Schengen visas in any 12-month period and they are not renewable inside Italy. If you are going to visit more than one Schengen country, you should apply for the visa at a consulate of your main destination country or the first country you intend to visit.

EU citizens do not require any permits to live or work in Italy. They are, however, required to register with a police station if they take up residence and obtain a *permesso di soggiorno* (see the following section).

Copies

All important documents (passport data page and visa page, credit cards, travel insurance policy, tickets, driving licence etc) should be photocopied before you leave home. Leave a copy with someone at home and keep one with you, separate from the originals.

Permesso di Soggiorno

If you plan to stay at the same address for more than one week you are obliged to report to the police station to receive a *permesso di soggiorno* (permit to remain in the country). Tourists who are staying in hotels are not required to do this.

A *permesso di soggiorno* only becomes a necessity if you plan to study, work (legally) or live in Italy. Obtaining one is never a pleasant experience; it involves queues and the frustration of arriving at the counter only to find you don't have the necessary documents.

The exact requirements, such as specific documents and *marche da bollo* (official stamps), can change from year to year. In general you will need: a valid passport containing a visa stamp indicating your date of entry into Italy, a special visa issued in your own country if you are planning to study, four passport-style photographs and proof of your ability to support yourself financially.

It is best to obtain precise information on what is required. Sometimes there is a list posted at the police station, otherwise you will need to go to the information counter. The main Rome **police station** (p83; Via Genova) is notorious for delays. You can, instead, apply at the *ufficio stranieri* (foreigners' bureau) of the police station closest to where you are staying.

Study Visas

Non-EU citizens who want to study at a university or language school in Italy must have a study visa. These visas can be obtained from your nearest Italian embassy or consulate. You will normally require confirmation of your enrolment, proof of payment of fees and adequate funds to support yourself before a visa is issued. The visa covers only the period of the enrolment. This type of visa is renewable within Italy but, again, only with confirmation of ongoing enrolment and proof that you are able to support yourself (bank statements are preferred).

WORK

It is illegal for non-EU citizens to work in Italy without a *permesso di lavoro* (work permit), but trying to obtain one can be time-consuming. EU citizens are allowed to work in Italy but they still need a *permesso di soggiorno* from the main police station in the town, ideally before they look for employment. See Permesso di Soggiorno, pp827–8, for more information.

Immigration laws require foreign workers to be 'legalised' through their employers, which can apply even to cleaners and babysitters. The employers then pay pension and health-insurance contributions. This doesn't mean that there aren't employers willing to take people without the right papers.

Work options depend on a number of factors (location, length of stay, nationality and qualifications, for example) but, in the major cities at least, job possibilities for English speakers can be surprisingly plentiful. Go armed with a CV (if possible in Italian) and be persistent.

Jobs are advertised in local newspapers and magazines, such as Rome's *Porta Portese* (weekly) and *Wanted in Rome* (fortnightly) or *Secondamano* in Milan, and you can also place an ad yourself.

A very useful guide is *Living, Studying and Working in Italy* by Travis Neighbor Ward and Monica Larner. You could also have a look at *Work Your Way Around the World* by Susan Griffith and *The Au Pair and Nanny's Guide to Working Abroad* by Susan Griffith and Sharon Legg.

The most easily secured jobs are short-term work in bars, hostels, on farms, babysitting and even volunteering (in return for accommodation and some expenses paid). The other obvious source for English-speaking foreigners is teaching English. However, most of the more reputable language schools will only hire people who hold a work permit. The more professional schools will require you to have a TEFL (Teaching English as a Foreign Language) certificate.

Organisations

Some useful organisations to start the job hunt:

Au Pair Italy (☎ 05 138 34 66; www.aupairitaly.com) Posts from three months to two years, living with an Italian family and working up to 30 hours per week. Italian not required.

British Institutes (☎ 02 439 00 41; www.britishinstitutes.org; Via Leopardi 8, Milan) Recruits English-speaking teachers. Italian essential.

The Cambridge School (☎ 0458 00 31 54; www.cambridgeschool.it; Via Rosmini 6, Verona) The other main employer of English teachers.

Center for Cultural Exchange (☎ 630-377 2272; www.cci-exchange.com; 17 North Second Ave, St. Charles, Illinois 60174) A non-profit making organisation dedicated to the promotion of cultural understanding. Offers internships in Italy.

Concordia International Volunteer Projects (☎ 01273 422218; www.concordia-iye.org.uk; 20-22 Boundary Rd, Hove, UK) Short-term community-based projects covering the environment, archaeology and the arts. UK applicants only.

Italian Association for Education, Exchanges & Intercultural Activities (AFSAI; ☎ 06 537 03 32; www.afsai.it; Viale dei Colli Portuensi 345, B2) Financed by the European Union this voluntary programme runs projects of 6-12 months for those aged between 16 and 25 years. Knowledge of Italian is required.

Mix Culture Au Pair Service (☎ 06 47 88 22 89; Via Nazionale 204, Rome) Posts from six months to a year. Enrolment in a language school is necessary to obtain the required visa.

Recruitaly (www.recruitaly.it) For graduates looking for long-term employment in Italy this useful website links up to professional employers.

World Wide Organisation of Organic Farming (www.wwoof.org) For a membership fee of euro25 this organisation provides a list of farms looking for volunteer workers. Recommended by LP readers.

Youth Info Centre (☎ 045 801 0796; Corso Porto Borsari 17, Verona) Finds local employment for travellers.

Transport

CONTENTS

GETTING THERE & AWAY

Competition between airlines means you should be able to pick up a reasonably priced fare to Italy, even if you are coming from as far away as Australia. If you live in Europe, you can also travel overland by car, bus or train.

Passport

Citizens of EU member states can travel to Italy with their national identity cards. People from countries that do not issue ID cards, such as the UK, must carry a valid passport. All non-EU nationals must have a full valid passport. If applying for a visa, check that the expiry date of your passport is at least some months off.

Entry stamps may not be stamped in your passport, but if you plan to remain in the country for an extended period or wish to work, you should insist on having one. Without a stamp you could encounter problems when trying to obtain a *permesso di soggiorno* – in effect, permission to remain in the country (see pp827-8).

If your passport is stolen or lost while you are in Italy, notify the police straight away and obtain a statement, and then contact your embassy or consulate as soon as possible.

AIR

High season in Italy is June to September and prices are at their highest during this period. Two months either side of this is the shoulder season, while low season is November to March. Holidays, such as Christmas and Easter, also see a (sometimes huge) jump in prices. Roughly speaking a return fare will cost you UK£70/375 in the low/high season from the UK; US$400/800 from North America; C$900/1800 from the Canadian east and C$1200/2000 from the Canadian west coast; and A$1600/2200 from Australia.

Airports & Airlines

Italy's main intercontinental gateway is the **Leonardo da Vinci Airport** (Fiumicino; ☎ 06 659 51; www.adr.it) in Rome, but regular intercontinental flights also serve Milan's **Linate Airport** (☎ 02 748 522 00; www.sea-aeroportimilano.it). Plenty of flights from other European cities also go direct to regional capitals around the country.

Many European and international airlines compete with the country's national carrier, Alitalia.

INTERNATIONAL AIRLINES IN ITALY

Alitalia (airline code AZ; ☎ 06 6 56 41, ☎ 848 86 56 41; www.alitalia.it)

WARNING

The information in this chapter is particularly vulnerable to change: prices for international travel are volatile, routes are introduced and cancelled, schedules change, special deals come and go, and rules and visa requirements are amended. You should check directly with the airline or a travel agent to make sure you understand how a fare (and ticket you may buy) works and be aware of the security requirements for international travel.

You should get quotes from as many airlines and travel agents as possible. The details given in this chapter should be regarded as pointers and are not a substitute for your own careful, up-to-date research.

Air Canada (AC; ☎ 06 55 1112, toll free ☎ 800 919091; www.aircanada.ca)

Air France (AF; ☎ 848 88 44 66; www.airfrance.com)

Air New Zealand (NZ; ☎ 06 48 79 11; www.airnz.co.nz)

American Airlines (AA; ☎ 02 6968 2464 Milan, ☎ 06 6605 3169 Rome; www.aa.com)

British Airways (BA; ☎ 199 712 266; www.british airways.com)

British Midland (BD; ☎ 44-1332 854 000; www .flybmi.com)

Delta Air Lines (DL; ☎ 800-477-999; www.delta.com)

EasyJet (U2; ☎ 848 887766 in Italy; www.easyjet.com)

KLM (KL; ☎ 06 6501 1147; www.klm.com)

Lufthansa (LH; ☎ 06 6568 4004; www.lufthansa.com)

Meridiana (IG; ☎ 199 11 13 33 call centre; www .meridiana.it)

Qantas (QF; ☎ 06 529 22 87; www.qantas.com)

Ryanair (FR; ☎ 899 89 98 44; www.ryanair.com)

Singapore Airlines (SQ; ☎ 06 478 55 360; www .singaporeair.com)

Thai Airways International (TG; ☎ 06 47 81 31; www.thaiair.com)

United Airlines (UA; ☎ 02 69 63 37 07; www.ual.com)

Virgin Express (TV; ☎ 02 482 960 00 Milan, ☎ 800 097 097 rest of Italy; www.virgin-express.com)

Tickets

World aviation has never been so competitive and the Internet is fast becoming the easiest way of locating and booking reasonably priced seats.

Full-time students and those under 26 years have access to discounted fares. You have to show a document proving your date of birth or a valid International Student Identity Card (ISIC) when buying your ticket. Other cheap deals are the discounted tickets released to travel agents and specialist discount agencies. One exception to this rule is the expanding number of 'no-frills' carriers, which sell direct to travellers. Many airlines also offer excellent fares to web surfers and there is an increasing number of online agents such as www.travelocity.co.uk, www.cheaptickets.com, www.travelcuts.com and www.expedia.com which operate only on the Internet.

From Africa

From South Africa there are a host of major airlines that service Italy; most notably: British Airways from Cape Town and Johannesburg through the UK; Air France with connections throughout Europe; and Lufthansa from Cape Town, Durban and

Johannesburg connecting through Germany. **Flight Centre** (☎ 0860 40 07 27; www.flightcentre.co.za) has offices in Johannesburg, Cape Town and Durban, and **STA Travel** (www.statravel.co.za) has offices in Johannesburg, Pretoria and Bloemfontein.

In Nairobi, **Flight Centres** (☎ 02-21 00 24) has been in business for many years.

From Asia

Bangkok, Singapore and Hong Kong are the best places to shop around for discount tickets. **STA Travel** (www.statravel.com) has offices in Hong Kong, Singapore, Taiwan and Thailand. In Hong Kong many travellers use the **Hong Kong Student Travel Bureau** (☎ 2730 3269; www.hkst.com.hk, Chinese only).

Singapore Air and Thai Airways serve most of Western Europe and also connect with Australia and New Zealand. Similarly, discounted fares can be picked up from Qantas which usually transits in Kuala Lumpur, Bangkok or Singapore.

From Australia

Cheap flights from Australia to Europe generally go via Southeast Asian capitals. Qantas, along with Alitalia, offer the only direct flights from Melbourne and Sydney to Rome but if you are looking for a bargain fare you will probably end up on Thai Air or Malaysia Airlines. Flights from Perth are generally a few hundred dollars cheaper.

Quite a few travel offices specialise in discount air tickets. Some travel agencies, particularly smaller ones, advertise cheap air fares in the travel sections of weekend newspapers, such as the *Age* in Melbourne and the *Sydney Morning Herald*.

STA Travel and Flight Centre are well known for cheap fares. **STA Travel** (☎ 1300 360 390; www.statravel.com.au) has offices in all major cities and on many university campuses. **Flight Centre** (☎ 1300 362 665; www.flightcentre.com.au) has dozens of offices throughout Australia.

From Canada

Alitalia has direct flights to Rome and Milan from Toronto and Montreal. Scan the budget travel agencies' advertisements in the *Toronto Globe & Mail*, the *Toronto Star* and the *Vancouver Province*.

Air Canada flies daily from Toronto to Rome, direct and via Montreal. British Airways, Air France, KLM and Lufthansa all fly to Italy via their respective home countries. Canada's main student travel organisation is **Travel Cuts** (☎ 800 667 2887; www.travelcuts.com), which has offices in all major cities.

From Continental Europe

All national European carriers offer services to Italy. The largest of these, Air France, Lufthansa and KLM, have representative offices in major European cities. Italy's national carrier, Alitalia, has a huge range of offers on all European destinations. Several airlines, including Alitalia, Qantas and Air France, offer cut-rate fares between cities on the European legs of long-haul flights.

In France the student travel agencies **OTU Voyages** (☎ 0820 817 817; www.otu.fr, French only) and **Travel Club Voyages** (☎ 0892 888 888; www.travelclub-voyages.com, French only) are a safe bet for cut-price travel. In Germany, Munich is a haven of budget travel outlets such as **STA Travel** (www.statravel.de, German only) which is one of the best and has offices throughout the country. **Kilroy Travel Group** (www.kilroygroups.com) offers discounted travel to people aged 16 to 33, and has representative offices in Denmark, Sweden, Norway, Finland and the Netherlands. In Athens **ISYTS** (☎ 010 322 12 67; www.isytstravel.gr) is the official International Student Youth Travel Service. **Virgin Express** (www.virgin-express.com) has a whole host of flights out of Brussels, including five daily flights to Rome. Details of its offices in Belgium, Denmark, France, Germany and Greece can be found on the website. If you are searching online, try www.budgettravel.com and www.airfair.nl (Dutch only). Getting cheap flights between Spain and Italy is difficult, frequently the best value flights are routed through another European city (such as Munich). In Madrid, one of the most reliable budget travel agencies is **Viajes Zeppelin** (☎ 902 38 42 53; www.viajeszeppelin.com, Spanish only) which also offers onward flights to South American destinations. The Italian airline Meridiana has direct flights from Barcelona to Milan (Linate).

From New Zealand

Air New Zealand flies direct from Auckland to Italy. The *New Zealand Herald* has a travel section in which travel agencies advertise fares. **Flight Centre** (☎ 0800 24 35 44; www.flightcentre.co.nz) has a large central office in Auckland and many other branches throughout the country. **STA Travel** (☎ 0800 24 35 44; www.statravel.co.nz) has offices in Auckland, as well as in Hamilton, Palmerston North, Wellington, Christchurch and Dunedin.

From the UK & Ireland

Discount air travel is big business in London. Advertisements for many travel agencies appear in the travel pages of the weekend newspapers, such as the *Independent* and the *Guardian* on Saturday and the *Sunday Times*, as well as in publications such as *Time Out* and *Exchange & Mart*.

STA Travel (☎ 0870 160 0599, www.statravel.co.uk) and **Trailfinders** (☎ 020 7292 18 88; www.trailfinders .com), both of which have offices throughout the UK, sell discounted and student tickets. Other good sources of discounted fares are www.discount-tickets.com, www .ebookers.com and www.flynow.com.

No-frills airlines are increasingly big business for travel between the UK and Ireland and Italy. EasyJet, having taken over British Airways' Go, is now the biggest operator. Their main competitor is the Irish Ryanair, although British Midland also offers some excellent deals. Prices vary wildly according to season and depend on how far in advance you can book them.

The two national airlines linking the UK and Italy are British Airways and Alitalia. They both operate regular flights to Rome, Milan, Venice, Florence, Turin, Naples, Palermo and Pisa.

Most British travel agents are registered with ABTA (Association of British Travel Agents). If you have paid for your flight with an ABTA-registered agent who then goes bust, ABTA will guarantee a refund or an alternative.

From the USA

Both TWA and Delta Airlines have daily flights from New York to Milan and Rome, while United Airlines has a service from Washington to Rome. The enormous American Airlines (who have recently taken over TWA as well) offers seasonal flights to Rome and connects all major American cities through Chicago.

Discount travel agencies in the USA are known as consolidators. San Francisco is the ticket consolidator capital of America although some good deals can be found in other big cities. The *New York Times*, the *Los Angeles Times*, the *Chicago Tribune* and the *San Francisco Examiner* all produce weekly travel sections.

Council Travel (☎ 800 226 8624, www.council travel.com), the largest student travel organisation in America, has around 75 offices in the USA. **STA Travel** (☎ 800 781 4040; www.statravel.com) has offices in Boston, Chicago, Los Angeles, New York, Philadelphia and San Francisco. Fares vary wildly depending on season, availability and a little luck.

Discount and rock-bottom options from the USA include charter, stand-by and courier flights. Stand-by fares are often sold at 60% of the normal price for one-way tickets. **Courier Travel** (☎ 303 570 7586; www.couriertravel.org) is a comprehensive search engine for courier and stand-by flights. You can also check out **Now Voyager** (☎ 212 459 1616; www.nowvoyager travel.com) or the **International Association of Air Travel Couriers** (IAATC; ☎ 308 632 3273; www.courier .org).

LAND

There are plenty of options for entering Italy by train, bus or private vehicle. Bus is the cheapest option but services are less frequent and less comfortable than the train. You will need to check whether you require visas to the countries you intend to pass through on your way.

Border Crossings

The main points of entry to Italy are the Mont Blanc Tunnel from France at Chamonix which connects with the A5 for Turin and Milan; the Grand St Bernard tunnel from Switzerland, which also connects with the A5; and the Brenner Pass from Austria, which connects with the A22 to Bologna. Mountain passes are often closed in winter and sometimes in autumn and spring, making the tunnels a more reliable option. Make sure you have snow chains if driving in winter.

Regular trains on two lines connect Italy with main cities in Austria and on into Germany, France or Eastern Europe. Those crossing the frontier at the Brenner Pass go to Innsbruck, Stuttgart and Munich. Those crossing at Tarvisio in the east proceed to Vienna, Salzburg and Prague. Trains from Milan head for Switzerland and on into

France and the Netherlands. The main international train line to Slovenia crosses near Trieste.

From Continental Europe

BUS

Eurolines (www.eurolines.com) is a consortium of European coach companies that operates across Europe with offices in all major European cities. You can contact them in your own country or in Italy and their multilingual website gives comprehensive details of prices, passes and travel agencies where you can book tickets.

Another option is **Busabout** (☎ 020 7950 1661; www.busabout.com), which covers at least 60 European cities and towns. This company offers passes of varying duration allowing you to use their hop-on hop-off bus network in Western and Central Europe. The frequency of departures and the number of stops available goes up between April and October. You can book onward travel and accommodation on the bus or on their website.

CAR & MOTORCYCLE

When driving in Europe always carry proof of ownership of a private vehicle. Third-party motor insurance is also a minimum requirement in Italy and throughout Europe. Ask your insurer for a European Accident Statement form which can simplify matters in the event of an accident. A European breakdown assistance policy is a good investment. In Italy, assistance can be obtained through the **Automobile Club Italiano** (ACI; ☎ 06 4 99 81, 24-hour info line ☎ 166 664 477).

Every vehicle travelling across an international border should display a nationality plate of its country of registration. A warning triangle (to be used in the event of a breakdown) is compulsory throughout Europe. Recommended accessories are a first-aid kit, spare-bulb kit and fire extinguisher.

Pre-booking a rental car before leaving home will enable you to find the cheapest deals (multinational agencies are listed on p836). No matter where you hire your car, make sure you understand what is included in the price and what your liabilities are. Since the most common way to pay for rental is by credit card, check whether or not you have car insurance with the credit-card provider and what the conditions are.

Italy is made for motorcycle touring and motorcyclists swarm into the country in summer to tour the scenic roads. With a bike you rarely have to book ahead for ferries and can enter restricted traffic areas in cities. Crash helmets are compulsory. **Beach's Motorcycle Adventures** (☎ 1-716 773 49 60; www.beachs-mca.com) can arrange two-weekly tours within Italy.

An interesting website which is loaded with advice for people planning to drive around Europe is www.ideamerge.com.

For help with route planning check out the website: www.euroshell.com.

TRAIN
The *Thomas Cook European Timetable* has a complete listing of train schedules. It is updated monthly and available from Thomas Cook offices worldwide. It is always advisable, and sometimes compulsory, to book seats on international trains to and from Italy. Some of the main international services include transport for private cars. On overnight hauls you can book a couchette for around €18 to €25.

RAIL PASSES

The InterRail Pass and Rail Europe Senior Card are available to people who have lived in Europe for six months or more. They can be bought at most major stations and student travel outlets.

Eurail passes and Eurail Selectpass are for those who have lived in Europe for less than six months and are supposed to be bought outside Europe. They are available from leading travel agencies. You can review passes and special deals on Eurail International's website at www.eurail.com.

InterRail Pass
The InterRail map of Europe is divided into zones, one of which comprises the countries Italy, Greece, Slovenia and Turkey. The pass is designed for people aged under 26, but there is a more expensive version for older folk: the InterRail 26+. Twenty-two days of unlimited 2nd-class travel in one zone costs UK£125/182 under 26/over 26. Better value is the one-month ticket for two zones for UK£195/275.

Cardholders get discounts on travel in the country where they purchase the ticket.

Senior Railcard
Seniors can get a Rail Europe Senior Card (available at all major stations), which is valid for a year for trips that cross at least one border and which entitles you to 30% off standard fares. In the UK the card costs UK£5 but you must already have a **Senior Railcard** (☎ 0845 748 4950; www.senior -railcard.co.uk; UK£18). The Europe-wide card is known in Italy as Carta Rail Plus and it costs €20.

Eurail Passes
Eurail passes are good for travel in 17 European countries (not including the UK) but forget it if you intend to travel mainly in Italy. People aged over 26 pay for a 1st-class pass (Eurailpass) and those aged under 26 for a 2nd-class pass (Eurailpass Youth). Passes are valid for 15 or 21 days or for one, two or three months. These cost US$588/762/946/1338/1654 respectively for the Eurailpass. Children aged between four and 11 pay half-price for 1st-class passes. The Eurailpass Youth comes in at US$414/534/664/938/1160. You'll need to cover more than 2400km within two weeks to get value for money.

Discounts are available for group travel (up to 5 people) in the form of a Eurailpass Saver and the Eurailpass Saver Flexi.

Eurail Selectpass
Previously the Europass, this provides between five and 15 days of unlimited travel within a two-month period in 17 European countries. As with Eurail passes, those aged over 26 pay for a 1st-class pass while those aged under 26 can get a cheaper Europass Youth for travel in 2nd class. The basic five-day pass costs US$438/307 for the adult/youth version. There is also a Europass Saver which works like the Eurailpass Saver and costs US$374 per person.

TRANSPORT

From the UK

CAR & MOTORCYCLE

Coming from the UK, you can take your car across to France by ferry or via the Channel Tunnel on **Eurotunnel** (☎ 08705 35 35 35; www.eurotunnel.com). The latter runs four crossings (35 minutes) an hour between Folkestone and Calais in the high season. You pay for the vehicle only and fares vary according to time of day and season but you can be looking at paying as much as UK£312 return (valid for a year).

UK drivers holding the old-style green driving licence will need to obtain an International Driving Permit (IDP) before they can drive on the continent. For breakdown assistance both the **AA** (☎ 0870 600 03 71; www.theaa.co.uk) and the **RAC** (☎ 0870 010 63 82; www.rac.co.uk) offer comprehensive cover in Europe.

TRAIN

The passenger-train service **Eurostar** (☎ 0870 518 6186; www.eurostar.com) travels between London and Paris and London and Brussels. Alternatively you can get a train ticket that includes crossing the Channel by ferry, SeaCat or hovercraft.

For the latest fare information on journeys to Italy, including the Eurostar, contact the **Rail Europe Travel Centre** (☎ 0870 848 848; www.raileurope.co.uk). Another source of rail information for all of Europe is **Rail Choice** (www.railchoice.com).

SEA

Ferries connect Italy with other Mediterranean countries. Tickets are the most expensive in summer and prices for vehicles vary according to their size. Eurail and Inter-Rail pass holders pay only a supplement on the Italy to Greece routes from Ancona and Bari.

Blue Star Ferries (www.greekferries.gr) and **Minoan Lines** (☎ 210 414 57 00; www.minoan.gr) service Venice, Brindisi and Ancona from Igoumenitsa, Corfu or Patras, while **Fragline Ferries** (☎ 210 821 41 71; www.fragline.gr) connects Corfu to Brindisi. Turkish **Marmara Lines** (www.marmaralines.com) connects Cesme to Brindisi and on to Venice.

Tirrenia Navigazione (☎ 199 12 31 99 call centre; www.tirrenia.it) services all major Italian ports and connects them with Tunisia, while **Grandi Navi Veloci** (www.grimaldi.it, Italian only; Livorno

☎ 058 640 98 94; Genoa ☎ 010 58 93 31; Palermo ☎ 091 58 74 04) services Barcelona and Valencia in Spain. The Maltese **Virtu Ferries** (☎ 356 31 88 54; www.virtuferries.com) has ferries from Malta to Catania between March and October. Prices for an airline-style seat range from €40 to €90. There are a burgeoning number of ferries between Croatia (Split and Dubrovnik) and Slovenia and the Italian ports of Ancona, Bari and Pescara. The incredibly helpful search engine **Traghettionline** (☎ 010 58 20 80; www.traghettionline.net) covers all the ferry companies in the Mediterranean; you can also book online.

GETTING AROUND

You can reach almost any destination in Italy by train or bus and services are efficient and cheap, for longer distances there are plenty of domestic air services. Your own wheels give you the most freedom. However, be aware that both petrol and autostrada (motorway) tolls are expensive and that the stress of driving and parking your car in a big Italian city could easily ruin your trip.

AIR

The domestic airlines in Italy are **Alitalia** (☎ 06 6 56 41, ☎ 848 86 56 41 in Rome; www.alitalia.it), **Meridiana** (☎ 0789 5 26 00 in Olbia, ☎ 199 11 13 33 call centre; www.meridiana.it) and also **Air One** (☎ toll free 800 900 966, ☎ 06 48 88 00 66; www.flyairone.it).

The main airports are in Rome, Pisa, Milan, Naples, Palermo, Catania and Cagliari; there are other, smaller airports throughout the country. Domestic flights can be booked through any travel agency (listed throughout this guide).

Alitalia offers a range of discounts for young people, families, seniors and weekend travellers, as well as advance purchase deals. A one-way fare is generally half the cost of the return fare.

All applicable airport taxes are factored into the price of your ticket.

BICYCLE

Cycling is a national pastime in Italy. There are no special road rules for cyclists but you would be wise to equip yourself with a helmet and lights. You cannot take bikes onto the autostrade. If you plan to bring your own bike, check with your airline for any additional costs. The bike will need to be disassembled and packed for the journey. Make sure you include a few tools, spare parts and a bike lock and chain.

Bikes can be taken very cheaply on trains for €5, although only certain trains will actually carry them. Fast trains (Intercity and Eurostar) will generally not accommodate bikes so they must be sent as registered luggage. Bikes can be transported for free on ferries.

In the UK **Cyclists' Touring Club** (☎ 0870 873 00 60; www.ctc.org.uk) can help you plan your own bike tour or organise guided tours for you. Membership costs UK£27.

Hire & Purchase

Bikes are available for hire in most Italian towns and many places have both city and mountain bikes. Rental costs for a city bike start at €5.50/25 per day/week.

If you shop around, bargain prices for bikes range from about €100 for a standard ladies' bike without gears to €210 for a mountain bike with 16 gears. A good place to shop for bargains is Tacconi Sport, which buys in bulk. It has large outlets near Perugia, Arezzo, Trento and in the Republic of San Marino.

BOAT

Navi (large ferries) service Sicily and Sardinia, and *traghetti* (smaller ferries) and *aliscafi* (hydrofoils) service the smaller islands. The main embarkation points for Sardinia are Genoa, Livorno (Leghorn), Civitavecchia and Naples; for Sicily the main points are Naples and Villa San Giovanni in Calabria. The main points of arrival in Sardinia are Cagliari, Arbatax, Olbia and Porto Torres; in Sicily they are Palermo and Messina.

Tirrenia Navigazione (☎ 199 12 31 99 call centre; www.tirrenia.it) services nearly all Italian ports. Other companies include Siremar, SNAV, Ustica Lines and Grandi Navi Veloci. The state railway service, Trenitalia (previously Ferrovie dello Stato), operates ferries to Sicily and Sardinia. Detailed information on ferry companies, prices and times is provided in the Getting There & Away sections of the Sicily and Sardinia chapters and other relevant destinations.

You can use **Traghettionline** (☎ 010 58 20 80; www.traghettionline.net) to search for and book tickets online.

Many ferry services are overnight and travellers can choose between cabin accommodation or a *poltrona*, an airline-type armchair. Deck class (which allows you to sit/sleep in the general lounge areas or on deck) is available only on some ferries. All ferries carry vehicles.

BUS

Bus services within Italy are provided by numerous companies and vary from local routes linking small villages to fast and reliable intercity connections. Buses can be a cheaper and faster way to get around if your destination is not on a main train line.

It is usually possible to get bus timetables from local tourist offices. In larger cities most of the intercity bus companies have ticket offices or operate through agencies. In some smaller towns and villages, tickets are sold in bars or on the bus. Note that buses almost always leave on time.

Major companies that run long-haul services include Marozzi (Rome to Brindisi); SAIS, Segesta and Interbus (Rome to Sicily); and Lazzi and SITA (from Lazio, Tuscany and other regions to the Alps).

Although it is usually not necessary to make reservations on buses, it is advisable in the high season for overnight or long-haul trips.

CAR & MOTORCYCLE

There is an excellent network of autostrade in Italy. The main north–south link is the Autostrada del Sole, which extends from Milan to Reggio di Calabria (called the A1 from Milan to Naples and the A3 from Naples to Reggio di Calabria).

There's a toll to use most of Italy's autostrade. You can pay by cash or credit card as you leave the autostrada; to avoid lengthy queues buy a pre-paid card (Telepass or Viacard) from banks, post offices and tobacconists. For information on road tolls and passes check online at www.autostrade.it or call the **Società Autostrade** (☎ 06 436 31).

Travellers with time to spare could consider using the system of *strade statali* (state roads), which are often multilane dual carriageways and are toll free. They are represented on maps as 'S' or 'SS'. The *strade*

Road Distances (km)

Note
Distances between Palermo and mainland towns do not take into account the ferry from Reggio di Calabria to Messina. Add an extra hour to your journey time to allow for this crossing.

	Bari	Bologna	Brindisi	Florence	Genoa	Livorno	Milan	Naples	Palermo	Perugia	Reggio di Calabria	Rome	Siena	Turin	Trento	Trieste	Venice	Verona
Bari	---																	
Bologna	670	---																
Brindisi	114	785	---															
Florence	662	101	776	---														
Genoa	889	291	1004	227	---													
Livorno	742	176	857	84	179	---												
Milan	877	207	992	296	146	296	---											
Naples	253	568	368	466	694	547	762	---										
Palermo	665	1234	669	1132	1360	1213	1429	683	---									
Perugia	565	235	679	150	378	231	447	369	1036	---								
Reggio di Calabria	445	1014	449	912	1140	993	1209	463	220	816	---							
Rome	413	369	527	267	495	305	563	217	884	170	664	---						
Siena	616	168	731	70	275	118	362	420	1087	103	867	221	---					
Turin	995	325	1109	394	168	345	139	860	1527	545	1307	661	460	---				
Trento	890	220	1005	309	354	384	223	775	1442	459	1222	576	375	355	---			
Trieste	891	290	1006	390	536	465	405	857	1523	465	1303	658	457	536	284	---		
Venice	754	154	868	255	400	329	269	721	1388	327	1168	522	321	401	159	153	---	
Verona	808	137	922	226	289	301	158	693	1359	377	1139	494	293	290	97	250	114	---

provinciali (provincial roads) are sometimes little more than country lanes but provide access to many small towns and villages. They are represented as 'P' or 'SP' on maps.

Driving Licence & Insurance

All EU member states' driving licences are fully recognised throughout Europe. Those with a non-EU licence are supposed to obtain an IDP to accompany their national licence which your national automobile association can issue. It is valid for 12 months and must be kept with your proper licence. People who have held residency in Italy for one year or more must apply for an Italian driving licence. If you want to hire a car or motorcycle you will need to produce your driving licence. To drive your own vehicle in Italy you need an International Insurance Certificate, also known as a Carta Verde (Green Card); your car insurance company will issue this.

Purchase

It is illegal for nonresidents to purchase a car in Italy. You can get round this by asking a friend who is resident in Italy to buy one for you. You'll pay up to around €3700 for a reasonable five-year-old Fiat Uno. Look in the classified section of local newspapers to find cars for sale.

The same laws apply to owning and registering a motorcycle as apply to purchasing a car. The cost of a second-hand Vespa ranges from €260 to €780.

Hire

CARS

The most competitive multinational car rental agencies are listed below.

Autos Abroad (☎ 44-8700 667 788; www.autos abroad.com)

Avis (☎ 02 754 197 61; www.avis.com)

Budget (☎ 1-800 472 33 25; www.budget.com)

Europe by Car (☎ 1-800 223 15 16; www.europe bycar.com)

Europcar (☎ 06 481 71 62; www.europcar.com)

Hertz (☎ 199 11 22 11 national; www.hertz.com)

Most tourist offices and hotels can provide information about car or motorcycle rental. To rent a car in Italy you have to be aged

21 or over (23 for some companies) and you have to have a credit card. Most firms will accept your standard licence or IDP.

MOTORCYCLE
You'll have no trouble hiring a small Vespa or moped. There are numerous rental agencies in cities where you'll also be able to hire larger motorcycles for touring. The average cost for a 50cc scooter (per person) is around €26/150 per day/week.

Most agencies will not rent motorcycles to people aged under 18. Note that many places require a sizeable deposit and that you could be responsible for reimbursing part of the cost of the bike if it is stolen.

Road Rules
In Italy, as in the rest of continental Europe, drive on the right side of the road and overtake on the left. Unless otherwise indicated, you must always give way to cars entering an intersection from a road on your right. It is compulsory to wear seat belts if fitted to the car. If you are caught not wearing a seat belt, you will be required to pay an on-the-spot fine.

Random breath tests now take place in Italy. If you're involved in an accident while under the influence of alcohol, the penalties can be severe. The blood-alcohol limit is 0.05%.

Speed limits on the autostrade are 130km/h, and on all non-urban highways 110km/h. In built-up areas the limit is 50km/h. Speeding fines follow EU standards and are proportionate with the number of kilometres that you are caught driving over the speed limit, reaching up to €260.

You don't need a licence to ride a moped under 50cc but you should be aged 14 or over. You can't carry passengers or ride on the autostrade. The speed limit for a moped is 40km/h. To ride a motorcycle or scooter up to 125cc, you must be aged 16 or over and have a licence (a car licence will do). Helmets are compulsory. For motorcycles over 125cc you will need a motorcycle licence.

You will be able to enter restricted traffic areas in Italian cities on a motorcycle without any problems, and traffic police generally turn a blind eye to motorcycles or scooters parked on footpaths. There is no lights-on requirement for motorcycles during the day.

Motoring organisations in various countries have publications that detail road rules for foreign countries. If you get an IDP, it should also include a road rules booklet.

HITCHING
Hitching is not particularly common in Italy as most Italians, living in their home towns, have a wide network of friends and family and there is always someone available to give the necessary lift. At weekends it is common to see Fiat Puntos filled to bursting with groups of friends out and about. On a cultural level, it is extremely unlikely for Italian girls to hitchhike, particularly in the south, and the added bonus of an extremely good network of public transport, especially the buses, makes it largely unnecessary. Travellers who make friends with locals will find it easy to get a lift but once on the road most Italians are loath to leave the racetrack to pick someone up.

LOCAL TRANSPORT
All the major cities have good transport systems, with bus and underground-train networks usually integrated. However, in Venice your only options are by boat or on foot.

Bus & Underground Trains
You must buy bus tickets before you board the bus and validate them once aboard. If you get caught with an unvalidated ticket you will be fined on the spot (up to €25.80 in most cities).

There are underground systems in Rome (Metropolitana), Milan (MM) and Naples (Metropolitana). You must buy tickets and validate them before getting on the train. You can get a map of the network from tourist offices in the relevant city.

Efficient provincial and regional buses also operate between towns and villages.

TICKETS
Tickets can be bought at most *tabacchi* (tobacconists), newsstands, from ticket booths or dispensing machines at bus stations and in underground stations. Tickets cost from €0.77 for two hours (it varies from city to city). Most cities offer 24-hour or daily tourist tickets which can mean big savings.

TRANSPORT

TRANSPORT

Taxi

You can usually find taxi ranks at train and bus stations or you can telephone for radio taxis. Taxis will rarely stop when hailed on the street (it's illegal for them to do so) and generally will not respond to telephone bookings if you are calling from a public phone.

With a minimum charge of approximately €3.10 (covering the first 3km) most short city journeys end up costing between €5 and €10. In Rome, there's a supplement of €7.80 on travel to and from the airports, because they are outside the city limits. No more than four or five people are allowed in one taxi.

TRANSPORT

TRENITALIA

Trenitalia was previously knows as the Ferrovie dello Stato (the State Railway Service). Now partially privatised, renamed and rebranded, the old FS name is theoretically redundant. However, this grand make-over has not completely come into effect on the ground and you may still come across the FS insignia, such as on the train ferries across the straits of Messina or the still-active website: www.fs-on-line.com. Despite being slightly confusing, the two names are synonymous and should make little difference to travellers.

TRAIN

The **Trenitalia** (☎ 848 88 80 88, Italian only; www .trenitalia.com) is the partially privatised state train system which runs most of the services in Italy. Other private Italian train lines are noted throughout this book.

There are several types of trains. Some stop at all stations, such as *regionale* or *interregionale* trains, while faster trains, such as the Intercity (IC) or the very fast Eurostar Italia (ES), stop only at major cities. It is cheaper to buy all local train tickets in-country.

All tickets must be validated *before* you board your train. You simply punch them in the yellow machines installed at the entrance to all train platforms. If you don't validate them you risk a fine. This rule does not apply to tickets purchased outside Italy.

There are left-luggage facilities at all train stations. They are usually open 24 hours or close only for a few hours after midnight. They charge from €3.10 per day for each piece of luggage.

Cost & Classes

There are 1st and 2nd classes on all Italian trains; a 1st-class ticket costs just under double the price of a 2nd-class ticket.

To travel on Intercity and Eurostar trains you are required to pay a supplement (€3 to €16) determined by the distance you are travelling. On the Eurostar the cost of the ticket includes the supplement and booking fee. Check up-to-date prices of routes on www.fs-on-line.com.

On overnight trips within Italy it can be worth paying extra for a *cuccetta* – a sleeping berth in a six- or four-bed compartment which costs €18 and €25 respectively.

Train Passes

Trenitalia offers its own discount passes for travel within the country. These include the Carta Verde (€20.66; valid for one year), which offers a 20% discount for people aged from 12 to 26 years. Similarly, the Carta d'Argento (€20.66; valid for one year) offers the same discount to people aged 60 years and over. Children aged between four and 12 years are entitled to a 50% discount; those aged under four travel free.

The new Trenitalia Pass allows for four to 10 days of travel within a two month period. Passes should be available from all major train stations. Prices are detailed below.

Category	4 days	6 days	8 days	10 days
1st Class	€217	€261	€305	€349
2nd Class	€174	€210	€246	€282
Youth	€145	€175	€205	€235
Groups (2–5 passengers)	€149	€164	€209	€239

Reservations

Reservations are not essential but without one you may not be able to find a seat. Bookings can be made when you buy your ticket, and usually cost an extra €2.50. Reservations are obligatory for many of the Eurostar trains.

You can make train bookings at most travel agencies or you can simply buy your ticket on arrival at the station (allow plenty of time for this). There are special booking offices for Eurostar trains at the relevant train stations.

Health

CONTENTS

BEFORE YOU GO

While Italy has excellent health care, prevention is the key to staying healthy while abroad. A little planning before departure, particularly for pre-existing illnesses, will save trouble later. Bring medications in their original, clearly labelled, containers. A signed and dated letter from your physician describing your medical conditions and medications, including generic names, is also a good idea. If carrying syringes or needles, be sure to have a physician's letter documenting their medical necessity. If you are embarking on a long trip, make sure your teeth are OK (dental treatment is particularly expensive in Italy) and take your optical prescription with you.

INSURANCE

If you're an EU citizen, an E111 form, available from health centres (and post offices in the UK), covers you for most medical care but not emergency repatriation home or non-emergencies. Citizens from other countries should find out if there is a reciprocal arrangement for free medical care between their country and Italy. If you do need health insurance, make sure you get a policy that covers you for the worst possible

scenario, such as an accident requiring an emergency flight home. Find out in advance if your insurance plan will make payments directly to providers or reimburse you later for overseas health expenditures.

RECOMMENDED VACCINATIONS

No jabs are required to travel to Italy. The WHO, however, recommends that all travellers should be covered for diphtheria, tetanus, measles, mumps, rubella and polio, as well as hepatitis B.

ONLINE RESOURCES

The WHO's publication *International Travel and Health* is revised annually and is available online at www.who.int/ith. Other useful websites include www.mdtravelhealth.com (travel health recommendations for every country; updated daily), www.fitfortravel.sc ot.nhs.uk (general travel advice for the layman), www.ageconcern.org.uk (advice on travel for the elderly) and www.mariestopes .org.uk (information on women's health and contraception).

IN TRANSIT

DEEP VEIN THROMBOSIS (DVT)

Blood clots may form in the legs during plane flights, chiefly because of prolonged immobility (the longer the flight, the greater the risk). The chief symptom of DVT is swelling or pain of the foot, ankle, or calf, usually but not always on just one side. When a blood clot travels to the lungs, it may cause chest pain and breathing difficulties. Travellers with any of these symptoms should immediately seek medical attention. To prevent the development of DVT on long flights you should walk about the cabin, contract the leg muscles while sitting, drink plenty of fluids and avoid alcohol and tobacco.

JET LAG

To avoid jet lag try drinking plenty of non-alcoholic fluids and eating light meals. Upon arrival, get exposure to natural sunlight and readjust your schedule (for meals, sleep etc) as soon as possible.

IN ITALY

AVAILABILITY & COST OF HEALTH CARE

If you need an ambulance anywhere in Italy call ☎ 118. For emergency treatment, go straight to the *pronto soccorso* (casualty) section of a public hospital, where you can also get emergency dental treatment.

Excellent health care is readily available throughout Italy but standards can vary. Pharmacists can give valuable advice and sell over-the-counter medication for minor illnesses. They can also advise when more specialised help is required and point you in the right direction. In major cities you are likely to find English-speaking doctors or a translator service available.

TRAVELLERS' DIARRHOEA

If you develop diarrhoea, be sure to drink plenty of fluids, preferably in the form of an oral rehydration solution such as Dioralyte. If diarrhoea is bloody, persists for more than 72 hours or is accompanied by fever, shaking, chills or severe abdominal pain you should seek medical attention.

ENVIRONMENTAL HAZARDS
Heatstroke

Heatstroke occurs following excessive fluid loss with inadequate replacement of fluids and salt. Symptoms include headache, dizziness and tiredness. Dehydration is already happening by the time you feel thirsty – aim to drink sufficient water to produce pale, diluted urine. To treat heatstroke drink water and/or fruit juice, and cool the body with cold water and fans.

Hypothermia

Hypothermia occurs when the body loses heat faster than it can produce it. As ever, proper preparation will reduce the risks of getting it. Even on a hot day in the mountains, the weather can change rapidly so carry waterproof garments, warm layers and a hat, and inform others of your route. Hypothermia starts with shivering, loss of judgment and clumsiness. Unless rewarming occurs, the sufferer deteriorates into apathy, confusion and coma. Prevent further heat loss by seeking shelter, warm dry clothing, hot sweet drinks and shared bodily warmth.

Bites, Stings & Insect-Borne Diseases

Italian beaches are occasionally inundated with jellyfish. Their stings are painful but not dangerous. Dousing in vinegar will deactivate any stingers that have not fired. Calamine lotion, antihistamines and analgesics may reduce the reaction and relieve pain.

Italy's only dangerous snake, the viper, is found throughout the country except on Sardinia. To minimise the possibilities of being bitten, always wear boots, socks and long trousers when walking through undergrowth where snakes may be present. Don't put your hands into holes and crevices, and be careful when collecting firewood. Viper bites do not cause instantaneous death and an antivenin is widely available in pharmacies. Keep the victim calm and still, wrap the bitten limb tightly, as you would for a sprained ankle, and attach a splint to immobilise it. Seek medical help, if possible with the dead snake for identification. Don't attempt to catch the snake if there is a possibility of being bitten again. Tourniquets and sucking out the poison are now comprehensively discredited.

Always check all over your body if you have been walking through a potentially tick-infested area as ticks can cause skin infections and other more serious diseases such as Lyme disease and tick-borne encephalitis. If a tick is found attached, press down around the tick's head with tweezers, grab the head and gently pull upwards. Avoid pulling the rear of the body as this may squeeze the tick's gut contents through the attached mouth parts into the skin, increasing the risk of infection and disease. Lyme disease begins with the spreading of a rash at the site of the bite, accompanied by fever, headache, extreme fatigue, aching joints and muscles and severe neck stiffness. If untreated, symptoms usually disappear but disorders of the nervous system, heart and joints can develop later. Treatment works best early in the illness – medical help should be sought. Symptoms of tick-borne encephalitis include blotches around the bite, which is sometimes pale in the middle, and headaches, stiffness and other flu-like symptoms (as well as extreme tiredness) appearing a week or two after the bite. Again, medical help must be sought.

Rabies is still found in Italy but only in isolated areas of the Alps. Any bite, scratch

HEALTH

or even lick from a mammal in an area where rabies does exist should be scrubbed with soap and running water immediately and then cleaned thoroughly with an alcohol solution. Medical help should be sought.

Leishmaniasis is a group of parasitic diseases transmitted by sandflies and found in coastal parts of Italy. Cutaneous leishmaniasis affects the skin tissue and causes ulceration and disfigurement; visceral leishmaniasis affects the internal organs. Avoiding sandfly bites by covering up and using repellent is the best precaution against this disease.

TRAVELLING WITH CHILDREN

Make sure children are up to date with routine vaccinations and discuss possible travel vaccines well before departure as some vaccines are not suitable for children under a year. Lonely Planet's *Travel with*

Children includes travel health advice for younger children.

WOMEN'S HEALTH

Emotional stress, exhaustion and travelling through different time zones can all contribute to an upset in the menstrual pattern.

If using oral contraceptives, remember some antibiotics, diarrhoea and vomiting can stop the pill from working. Time zones, gastrointestinal upsets and antibiotics do not affect injectable contraception.

Travelling during pregnancy is usually possible but always consult your doctor before planning your trip. The most risky times for travel are during the first 12 weeks of pregnancy and after 30 weeks.

SEXUAL HEALTH

Condoms are readily available but emergency contraception is not, so take the necessary precautions.

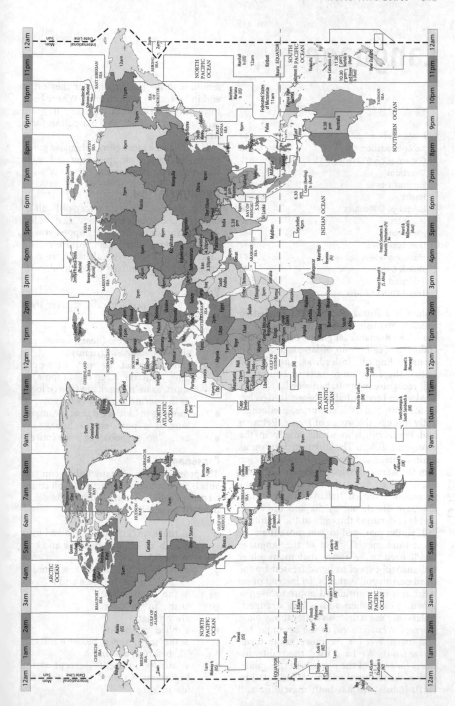

Language

CONTENTS

Italian is a Romance language related to French, Spanish, Portuguese and Romanian. The Romance languages belong to the Indo-European group of languages, which includes English. Indeed, as English and Italian share common roots in Latin, you will recognise many Italian words.

Modern literary Italian began to develop in the 13th and 14th centuries, predominantly through the works of Dante, Petrarch and Boccaccio, who wrote chiefly in the Florentine dialect. The language drew on its Latin heritage and many dialects to develop into the standard Italian of today. Although many dialects are spoken in everyday conversation, standard Italian is the national language of schools, media and literature, and is understood throughout the country.

If you've managed to gain more than the most fundamental grasp of the language you'll need to be aware that many older Italians still expect to be addressed by the third person polite, that is, *lei* instead of *tu*. Also, it is not considered polite to use the greeting *ciao* when addressing strangers, unless they use it first; it's better to say *buon giorno* (or *buona sera*, as the case may be) and *arrivederci* (or the more polite form, *arrivederla*). We have used the polite address for most of the phrases in this guide. Use of the informal address is indicated by (inf). Italian also has both masculine and feminine forms (in the singular they often end in 'o' and 'a' respectively). Where both forms are given in this guide, they are separated by a slash, the masculine form first.

If you'd like a more comprehensive guide to the language, pick up a copy of Lonely Planet's *Italian phrasebook*.

PRONUNCIATION

Italian pronunciation isn't very difficult to master once you learn a few easy rules. Although some of the more clipped vowels and stress on double letters require careful practice for English speakers, it is easy enough to make yourself understood.

Vowels

Vowels sounds are generally shorter than English equivalents:

a	as in 'art', eg *caro* (dear); sometimes short, eg *amico/a* (friend)
e	short, as in 'let', eg *mettere* (to put); long, as in 'there', eg *mela* (apple)
i	short, as in 'it', eg *inizio* (start); long, as in 'marine', eg *vino* (wine)
o	short, as in 'dot', eg *donna* (woman); long, as in 'port', eg *ora* (hour)
u	as the 'oo' in 'book', eg *puro* (pure)

Consonants

The pronunciation of many Italian consonants is similar to that of their English counterparts. Pronunciation of some consonants depends on certain rules:

c	as the 'k' in 'kit' before **a**, **o** and **u**; as the 'ch' in 'choose' before **e** and **i**
ch	as the 'k' in 'kit'
g	as the 'g' in 'get' before **a**, **o**, **u** and **h**; as the 'j' in 'jet' before **e** and **i**
gli	as the 'lli' in 'million'
gn	as the 'ny' in 'canyon'
h	always silent
r	a rolled 'rr' sound
sc	as the 'sh' in 'sheep' before **e** and **i**; as 'sk' before **a**, **o**, **u** and **h**
z	as the 'ts' in 'lights', except at the beginning of a word, when it's as the 'ds' in 'suds'

LANGUAGE

Note that when **ci**, **gi** and **sci** are followed by **a**, **o** or **u**, the 'i' is not pronounced unless the accent falls on the 'i'. Thus the name 'Giovanni' is pronounced joh-*vahn*-nee.

A double consonant is pronounced as a longer, more forceful sound than a single consonant. This can directly affect the meaning of a word, eg *sono* (I am), *sonno* (sleep), but the context of a sentence will usually get the message across.

Word Stress

Stress is indicated in our pronunciation guide by italics. Word stress generally falls on the second-last syllable, as in spa-*ghet*-ti, but when a word has an accent, the stress falls on that syllable, as in cit-*tà* (city).

ACCOMMODATION

I'm looking for a ...	Cerco ...	*cher*·ko ...
guesthouse	una pensione	oo·na pen·*syo*·ne
hotel	un albergo	oon al·*ber*·go
youth hostel	un ostello per la gioventù	oon os·*te*·lo per la jo·ven·*too*

Where is a cheap hotel?
Dov'è un albergo   do·ve oon al·*ber*·go
a buon prezzo?   a bwon *pre*·tso
What is the address?
Qual'è l'indirizzo?   kwa·*le* leen·dee·*ree*·tso
Could you write the address, please?
Può scrivere l'indirizzo,   pwo *skree*·ve·re leen·dee·*ree*·tso
per favore?   per fa·*vo*·re
Do you have any rooms available?
Avete camere libere?   a·*ve*·te *ka*·me·re *lee*·be·re

I'd like (a) ...	Vorrei ...	vo·*ray* ...
bed	un letto	oon *le*·to
single room	una camera singola	oo·na *ka*·me·ra *seen*·go·la
double room	una camera matrimoniale	oo·na *ka*·me·ra ma·tree·mo·*nya*·le
room with two beds	una camera doppia	oo·na *ka*·me·ra *do*·pya
room with a bathroom	una camera con bagno	oo·na *ka*·me·ra kon *ba*·nyo
to share a dorm	un letto in dormitorio	oon *le*·to een dor·mee·*to*·ryo

How much is it ...?	Quanto costa ...?	*kwan*·to *ko*·sta ...
per night	per la notte	per la *no*·te
per person	per persona	per per·*so*·na

MAKING A RESERVATION
(for inclusion in letters, faxes and emails)

To ...	A ...
From ...	Da ...
Date	Data
I'd like to book ...	Vorrei prenotare ... (see the list on this page for bed/room options)
in the name of ...	nel nome di ...
for the night/s of ...	per la notte/le notti di ...
credit card ...	carta di credito ...
number	numero
expiry date	data di scadenza
Please confirm availability and price.	Vi prego di confirmare disponibilità e prezzo.

May I see it?
Posso vederla?   *po*·so ve·*der*·la
Where is the bathroom?
Dov'è il bagno?   do·*ve* eel *ba*·nyo
I'm/We're leaving today.
Parto/Partiamo oggi.   *par*·to/par·*tya*·mo *o*·jee

CONVERSATION & ESSENTIALS

Hello.	Buon giorno.	bwon *jor*·no
	Ciao. (inf)	chow
Goodbye.	Arrivederci.	a·ree·ve·*der*·chee
	Ciao. (inf)	chow
Yes.	Sì.	see
No.	No.	no
Please.	Per favore/	per fa·*vo*·re/
	Per piacere.	per pya·*chay*·re
Thank you.	Grazie.	*gra*·tsye
That's fine/ You're welcome.	Prego.	*pre*·go
Excuse me.	Mi scusi.	mee skoo·zee
Sorry (forgive me).	Mi scusi/ Mi perdoni.	mee skoo·zee/ mee per·*do*·nee

What's your name?
Come si chiama?   *ko*·me see *kya*·ma
Come ti chiami? (inf)   *ko*·me tee *kya*·mee
My name is ...
Mi chiamo ...   mee *kya*·mo ...
Where are you from?
Da dove viene?   da *do*·ve *vye*·ne
Di dove sei? (inf)   dee *do*·ve se·ee
I'm from ...
Vengo da ...   *ven*·go da ...
I (don't) like ...
(Non) Mi piace ...   (non) mee *pya*·che ...

Just a minute.
Un momento. | oon mo-*men*-to

DIRECTIONS

Where is ...?
Dov'è ...? | do-*ve* ...
Go straight ahead.
Si va sempre diritto. | see va *sem*-pre dee-*ree*-to
Vai sempre diritto. (inf) | va-ee *sem*-pre dee-*ree*-to
Turn left.
Giri a sinistra. | jee-ree a see-*nee*-stra
Turn right.
Giri a destra. | jee-ree a *de*-stra
at the next corner
al prossimo angolo | al pro-see-mo *an*-go-lo
at the traffic lights
al semaforo | al se-*ma*-fo-ro

SIGNS

Ingresso/Entrata	Entrance
Uscita	Exit
Informazione	Information
Aperto	Open
Chiuso	Closed
Proibito/Vietato	Prohibited
Camere Libere	Rooms Available
Completo	Full/No Vacancies
Polizia/Carabinieri	Police
Questura	Police Station
Gabinetti/Bagni	Toilets
Uomini	Men
Donne	Women

---

behind	dietro	dye-tro
in front of	davanti	da-*van*-tee
far (from)	lontano (da)	lon-*ta*-no (da)
near (to)	vicino (di)	vee-*chee*-no (dee)
opposite	di fronte a	dee *fron*-te a
beach	la spiaggia	la *spya*-ja
bridge	il ponte	eel *pon*-te
castle	il castello	eel kas-*te*-lo
cathedral	il duomo	eel *dwo*-mo
island	l'isola	*lee*-so-la
(main) square	la piazza (principale)	la *pya*-tsa (preen-chee-*pa*-le)
market	il mercato	eel mer-*ka*-to
old city	il centro storico	eel *chen*-tro *sto*-ree-ko
palace	il palazzo	eel pa-*la*-tso
ruins	le rovine	le ro-*vee*-ne
sea	il mare	eel *ma*-re
tower	la torre	la *to*-re

EMERGENCIES

Help!
Aiuto! | a-*yoo*-to
There's been an accident!
C'è stato un incidente! | che *sta*-to oon een-chee-*den*-te
I'm lost.
Mi sono perso/a. | mee *so*-no *per*-so/a
Go away!
Lasciami in pace! | la-sha-mi een *pa*-che
Vai via! (inf) | va-ee *vee*-a

Call ...! | Chiami ...! | kee-*ya*-mee ...
 | Chiama ...! (inf) | kee-*ya*-ma ...
 a doctor | un dottore/ | oon do-*to*-re/
 | un medico | oon *me*-dee-ko
 the police | la polizia | la po-lee-*tsee*-ya

HEALTH

I'm ill. | Mi sento male. | mee *sen*-to *ma*-le
It hurts here. | Mi fa male qui. | mee fa *ma*-le *kwee*

I'm ... | Sono ... | *so*-no ...
 asthmatic | asmatico/a | az-*ma*-tee-ko/a
 diabetic | diabetico/a | dee-a-*be*-tee-ko/a
 epileptic | epilettico/a | e-pee-*le*-tee-ko/a

I'm allergic ... | Sono allergico/a ... | *so*-no a-*ler*-jee-ko/a ...
 to antibiotics | agli antibiotici | a-lyee an-tee-bee-o-tee-chee
 to aspirin | all'aspirina | a-la-spe-*ree*-na
 to penicillin | alla penicillina | a-la pe-nee-see-*lee*-na
 to nuts | ai noci | a-ee *no*-chee

antiseptic	antisettico	an-tee-*se*-tee-ko
aspirin	aspirina	as-pee-*ree*-na
condoms	preservativi	pre-zer-va-*tee*-vee
contraceptive	contraccetivo	kon-tra-che-*tee*-vo
diarrhoea	diarrea	dee-a-*re*-a
medicine	medicina	me-dee-*chee*-na
sunblock cream	crema solare	*kre*-ma so-*la*-re
tampons	tamponi	tam-*po*-nee

LANGUAGE DIFFICULTIES

Do you speak English?
Parla inglese? | *par*-la een-*gle*-ze
Does anyone here speak English?
C'è qualcuno che parla inglese? | che kwal-*koo*-no ke *par*-la een-*gle*-ze
How do you say ... in Italian?
Come si dice ... in italiano? | *ko*-me see *dee*-che ... een ee-ta-*lya*-no

What does ... mean?
Che vuol dire ...?   ke vwol *dee*-re ...
I understand.
Capisco.   ka-*pee*-sko
I don't understand.
Non capisco.   non ka-*pee*-sko
Please write it down.
Può scriverlo, per favore?   pwo skree-ver-lo per fa-*vo*-re
Can you show me (on the map)?
Può mostrarmelo   pwo mos-*trar*-me-lo
(sulla pianta)?   (soo-la *pyan*-ta)

NUMBERS

0	zero	dze-ro
1	uno	oo-no
2	due	doo-e
3	tre	tre
4	quattro	kwa-tro
5	cinque	cheen-kwe
6	sei	say
7	sette	se-te
8	otto	o-to
9	nove	no-ve
10	dieci	dye-chee
11	undici	oon-dee-chee
12	dodici	do-dee-chee
13	tredici	tre-dee-chee
14	quattordici	kwa-tor-dee-chee
15	quindici	kween-dee-chee
16	sedici	se-dee-chee
17	diciassette	dee-cha-se-te
18	diciotto	dee-cho-to
19	diciannove	dee-cha-no-ve
20	venti	ven-tee
21	ventuno	ven-too-no
22	ventidue	ven-tee-doo-e
30	trenta	tren-ta
40	quaranta	kwa-ran-ta
50	cinquanta	cheen-kwan-ta
60	sessanta	se-san-ta
70	settanta	se-tan-ta
80	ottanta	o-tan-ta
90	novanta	no-van-ta
100	cento	chen-to
1000	mille	mee-le
2000	due mila	doo-e mee-la

PAPERWORK

name	nome	no-me
nationality	nazionalità	na-tsyo-na-lee-ta
date/place of birth	data/luogo di nascita	da-ta/lwo-go dee na-shee-ta
sex (gender)	sesso	se-so
passport	passaporto	pa-sa-por-to
visa	visto	vee-sto

QUESTION WORDS

Who?	Chi?	kee
What?	Che?	ke
When?	Quando?	kwan-do
Where?	Dove?	do-ve
How?	Come?	ko-me

SHOPPING & SERVICES

I'd like to buy ...
Vorrei comprare ...   vo-ray kom-pra-re ...
How much is it?
Quanto costa?   kwan-to ko-sta
I don't like it.
Non mi piace.   non mee pya-che
May I look at it?
Posso dare   po-so da-re
un'occhiata?   oo-no-kya-ta
I'm just looking.
Sto solo guardando.   sto so-lo gwar-dan-do
It's cheap.
Non è caro/cara.   non e ka-ro/ka-ra
It's too expensive.
È troppo caro/a.   e tro-po ka-ro/ka-ra
I'll take it.
Lo/La compro.   lo/la kom-pro

Do you accept credit cards?	Accettate carte di credito?	a-che-ta-te kar-te dee kre-dee-to
I want to change ...	Voglio cambiare ...	vo-lyo kam-bya-re ...
money	del denaro	del de-na-ro
travellers cheques	assegni dee viaggio	a-se-nyee dee vee-a-jo
more	più	pyoo
less	meno	me-no
smaller	più piccolo/a	pyoo pee-ko-lo/la
bigger	più grande	pyoo gran-de
I'm looking for ...	Cerco ...	cher-ko ...
a bank	un banco	oon ban-ko
the church	la chiesa	la kye-za
the city centre	il centro	eel chen-tro
the ... embassy	l'ambasciata di ...	lam-ba-sha-ta dee ...
my hotel	il mio albergo	eel mee-o al-ber-go
the market	il mercato	eel mer-ka-to
the museum	il museo	eel moo-ze-o
the post office	la posta	la po-sta
a public toilet	un gabinetto	oon ga-bee-ne-to
the telephone centre	il centro telefonico	eel chen-tro te-le-fo-nee-ko
the tourist office	l'ufficio di turismo	loo-fee-cho dee too-reez-mo

LANGUAGE

TIME & DATES

What time is it?	Che ore sono?	ke o·re so·no
It's (8 o'clock).	Sono (le otto).	so·no (le o·to)

in the morning	di mattina	dee ma·tee·na
in the afternoon	di pomeriggio	dee po·me·ree·jo
in the evening	di sera	dee se·ra
When?	Quando?	kwan·do
today	oggi	o·jee
tomorrow	domani	do·ma·nee
yesterday	ieri	ye·ree

Monday	lunedì	loo·ne·dee
Tuesday	martedì	mar·te·dee
Wednesday	mercoledì	mer·ko·le·dee
Thursday	giovedì	jo·ve·dee
Friday	venerdì	ve·ner·dee
Saturday	sabato	sa·ba·to
Sunday	domenica	do·me·nee·ka

January	gennaio	je·na·yo
February	febbraio	fe·bra·yo
March	marzo	mar·tso
April	aprile	a·pree·le
May	maggio	ma·jo
June	giugno	joo·nyo
July	luglio	loo·lyo
August	agosto	a·gos·to
September	settembre	se·tem·bre
October	ottobre	o·to·bre
November	novembre	no·vem·bre
December	dicembre	dee·chem·bre

TRANSPORT
Public Transport

What time does the ... leave/ arrive?	A che ora parte/ arriva ...?	a ke o·ra par·te/ a·ree·va ...
boat	la nave	la na·ve
(city) bus	l'autobus	low·to·boos
(intercity) bus	il pullman	eel pool·man
plane	l'aereo	la·e·re·o
train	il treno	eel tre·no

I'd like a ... ticket.	Vorrei un biglietto ...	vo·ray oon bee·lye·to ...
one-way	di solo andata	dee so·lo an·da·ta
return	di andata e ritorno	dee an·da·ta e ree·toor·no
1st class	di prima classe	dee pree·ma kla·se
2nd class	di seconda classe	dee se·kon·da kla·se

I want to go to ...		
Voglio andare a ...		vo·lyo an·da·re a ...

The train has been cancelled/delayed.

Il treno è soppresso/ in ritardo.		eel tre·no e so·pre·so/ een ree·tar·do

the first	il primo	eel pree·mo
the last	l'ultimo	lool·tee·mo
platform (two)	binario (due)	bee·na·ryo (doo·e)
ticket office	biglietteria	bee·lye·te·ree·a
timetable	orario	o·ra·ryo
train station	stazione	sta·tsyo·ne

Private Transport

I'd like to hire a/an ...	Vorrei noleggiare ...	vo·ray no·le·ja·re ...
car	una macchina	oo·na ma·kee·na
4WD	un fuoristrada	oon fwo·ree·stra·da
motorbike	una moto	oo·na mo·to
bicycle	una bici(cletta)	oo·na bee·chee·(kle·ta)

Is this the road to ...?

Questa strada porta a ...?		kwe·sta stra·da por·ta a ...

Where's a service station?

Dov'è una stazione di servizio?		do·ve oo·na sta·tsyo·ne dee ser·vee·tsyo

Please fill it up.

Il pieno, per favore.		eel pye·no per fa·vo·re

I'd like (30) litres.

Vorrei (trenta) litri.		vo·ray (tren·ta) lee·tree

diesel	gasolio/diesel	ga·zo·lyo/dee·zel
leaded petrol	benzina con piombo	ben·dzee·na kon pyom·bo
unleaded petrol	benzina senza piombo	ben·dzee·na sen·dza pyom·bo

(How long) Can I park here?

(Per quanto tempo) Posso parcheggiare qui?		(per kwan·to tem·po) po·so par·ke·ja·re kwee

ROAD SIGNS

Dare la Precedenza	Give Way
Deviazione	Detour
Divieto di Accesso	No Entry
Divieto di Sorpasso	No Overtaking
Divieto di Sosta	No Parking
Entrata	Entrance
Passo Carrabile	Keep Clear
Pedaggio	Toll
Pericolo	Danger
Rallentare	Slow Down
Senso Unico	One Way
Uscita	Exit

LANGUAGE

Where do I pay?
Dove si paga?   *do*·ve see *pa*·ga

I need a mechanic.
Ho bisogno di un   o bee·*zo*·nyo dee oon
meccanico.   me·*ka*·nee·ko

The car/motorbike has broken down (at ...).
La macchina/moto   la *ma*·kee·na/*mo*·to
si è guastata (a ...).   see e gwas·*ta*·ta (a ...)

The car/motorbike won't start.
La macchina/moto   la *ma*·kee·na/*mo*·to
non parte.   non *par*·te

I have a flat tyre.
Ho una gomma bucata.   o oo·na *go*·ma boo·*ka*·ta

I've run out of petrol.
Ho esaurito la benzina.   o e·zo·*ree*·to la ben·*dzee*·na

I've had an accident.
Ho avuto un incidente.   o a·*voo*·to oon een·chee·*den*·te

TRAVEL WITH CHILDREN

Is there a/an ...?   *C'è ...?*   che ...
I need a/an ...   *Ho bisogno di ...*   o bee·*zo*·nyo dee ...
  baby change   *un bagno con*   oon *ba*·nyo kon
    room   *fasciatoio*   fa·sha·*to*·yo

car baby seat	*un seggiolino*	oon se·jo·*lee*·no
	per bambini	per bam·*bee*·nee
child-minding	*un servizio*	oon ser·*vee*·tsyo
service	*di babysitter*	dee be·bee·*see*·ter
children's menu	*un menù per*	oon me·*noo* per
	bambini	bam·*bee*·nee
(disposable)	*pannolini*	pa·no·*lee*·nee·
nappies/diapers	*(usa e getta)*	(*oo*·sa e *je*·ta)
formula (milk)	*latte in polvere*	*la*·te in *pol*·ve·re
(English-	*un/una*	oon/*oo*·na
speaking)	*babysitter (che*	be·bee·*see*·ter
babysitter	*parli inglese)*	(ke *par*·lee
		een·*gle*·ze)
highchair	*un seggiolone*	oon se·jo·*lo*·ne
potty	*un vasino*	oon va·*zee*·no
stroller	*un passeggino*	oon pa·se·*jee*·no

Do you mind if I breastfeed here?
Le dispiace se allatto   le dees·*pya*·che se a·*la*·to
il/la bimbo/a qui?   eel/la *beem*·bo/a kwee

Are children allowed?
I bambini sono   ee bam·*bee*·nee so·no
ammessi?   a·*me*·see

Also available from Lonely Planet:
Italian phrasebook

Lonely planet
phrasebooks
Italian
with 2000-word two-way dictionary

Glossary

A

AAST – Azienda Autonoma di Soggiorno e Turismo; local tourist office

abbazia – abbey

ACI – Automobile Club Italiano; Italian Automobile Association

affittacamere – rooms for rent

affresco – the painting method in which watercolour paint is applied to wet plaster

agriturismo – tourist accommodation on working farms

AIG – Associazione Italiana Alberghi per la Gioventù; Italian Youth Hostel Association

albergo (s), **alberghi** (pl) – hotel (up to five stars)

alimentari – grocery shop

aliscafo (s), **aliscafi** (pl) – hydrofoil

Alleanza Nazionale – National Alliance; neo-Fascist political party

al taglio – by the slice

alto – high

ambasciata – embassy

ambulanza – ambulance

anfiteatro – amphitheatre

APT – Azienda di Promozione Turistica; provincial tourist office

ASL – Azienda Sanitaria Locale; Provincial Health Agency

autonoleggio – car hire

autostrada (s), **autostrade** (pl) – motorway (highway)

B

bambino (s), **bambini** (pl) – child

battistero – baptistry

bene – well, good; the smart set

benzina – petrol

benzina senza piombo – unleaded petrol

bianco – white

biglietto – ticket

biglietto cumulativo – a ticket that allows entrance to a number of associated sights

bivacchi – unattended mountain hut

borgo (s), **borghi** (pl) – cluttered towns and villages, little changed over hundreds of years

Brigate Rosse (BR) – Red Brigades (terrorist group)

C

campanile – bell tower

campo – field

cappella – chapel

carabinieri – police with military and civil duties

carnevale – carnival period between Epiphany and Lent

carretti – carts

carta – menu

carta d'identità – identity card

carta geografica – map

casa – house

castello – castle

cattedrale – cathedral

cena – evening meal

centro – city centre

centro storico – historic centre

chiesa (s), **chiese** (pl) – church

chiostro – cloister; covered walkway, usually enclosed by columns, around a quadrangle

cima – summit

CIT – Compagnia Italiana di Turismo; Italy's national travel agency

città – town, city

colle – hill (**colle** in place names)

colonna – column

comune – equivalent to a municipality or county; town or city council; historically, a self-governing town or city

consolato – consulate

contrada – district

coperto – cover charge in restaurants

corso – main street

CTS – Centro Turistico Studentesco e Giovanile; Centre for Student and Youth Tourists

cuccetta – couchette

cupola – dome

D

Democrazia Cristiana (DC) – Christian Democrats; political party

Democratici di Sinistra (DS) – Left Democrats; political party

deposito bagagli – left luggage

diretto – direct; slow train

duomo – cathedral

E

ENIT – Ente Nazionale per il Turismo; Italian Tourist Board

enoteca – wine bar

EPT – Ente Provinciale per Il Turismo; local tourist bureau

ES – Eurostar; very fast train

espresso – express mail; express train; short black coffee

estiva – summer

F

fermoposta – poste restante

ferramenta – hardware store

ferrovia – train station

festa – feast day; holiday
Feste di Pasqua – Holy Week
fiume – river
fontana – fountain
fornaio – bakery
foro – forum
Forza Italia – Go Italy; political party
francobollo – postage stamp
frazione – small area
fresco – see affresco
FS – Ferrovie dello Stato; State Railways
funicolare – funicular railway
funivia – cable car

G
gabinetto – toilets, WC
garni – B&Bs
gasauto or **GPL** – liquid petroleum gas (LPG)
gasolio – diesel
gettoni – telephone tokens
giardino (s), **giardini** (pl) – gardens
golfo – gulf
grotta – cave
guardia forestale – forest ranger

G
HI – Hostelling International

I
IAT – Informazioni e Assistenza ai Turisti; local tourist office
IC – Intercity; fast train
IDP – International Driving Permit
interregionale – long-distance train that stops frequently
inverno – winter
isola – island
IVA – Imposta di Valore Aggiunto; value-added tax of around 19%

L
lago – lake
largo – (small) square
lavanderia – laundrette
Lega Nord – Northern League; federalist political party
lido – beach
lingua originale – original language
locanda – inn, small hotel
loggia – covered area on the side of a building; porch; lodge
lo sci – downhill skiing
lungomare – seafront road, promenade

M
mar or **mare** – sea
mercato – market

Metropolitana – the Rome and Naples underground transport systems
Mezzogiorno – literally midday; name for the south of Italy
MM – Metropolitana Milano; Milan's underground transport system
monte – mountain
motorini – scooters
motoscafo – motorboat
municipio – town hall
musico – musician

N
Natale – Christmas
nave (s), **navi** (pl) – large ferry, ship
necropoli – (ancient) cemetery, burial site
nuraghi – megalithic stone fortresses (on Sardinia)

O
oggetti smarriti – lost property
ostello per la gioventù – youth hostel
osteria – a snack bar; cheap restaurant

P
Pagine Gialle – Yellow Pages; phone directory
palazzo (s) **palazzi** (pl) – mansion, palace; large building of any type, including an apartment block
palio – contest
panetteria – bakery
paninoteche – cafés
parco – park
passeggiata – traditional evening stroll
pasticceria – cake/pastry shop
patrician – a member of the hereditary aristocracy of ancient Rome
Partito Comunista Italiano (PCI) – Italian Communist Party; political party
Partito Socialista Italiano (PSI) – Italian Socialist Party; political party
pellicola – film
permesso di lavoro – work permit
permesso di soggiorno – permit to stay in Italy for a nominated period
piazza – square
piazzale – (large) open square
pietà – literally pity or compassion; sculpture, drawing or painting of the dead Christ supported by the Madonna
pinacoteca – art gallery
Polo per le Libertà – Freedom Alliance; right-wing political coalition
poltrona – airline-type chair on a ferry
ponte – bridge
pontile – jetty
porta – gate, door

portico – portico; covered walkway, usually attached to the outside of buildings
porto – port
posta – post office
Partito Rifondazione Comunista (PRC) – Refounded Communist Party; political party
presepio – nativity scene
pronto soccorso – first aid; **riparto di pronto soccorso** is a casualty/emergency ward

Q
quartieri – districts
questura – police station

R
reale – royal
regionale – slow local train
rifugio (s), **rifugi** (pl) – mountain huts; accommodation in the Alps
riserva marina – marine reserve
riva – river bank
rocca – fortress
ronda – roundabout
rosticceria – shop selling roast meats

S
sala – room, hall
salumeria – delicatessen
santuario – sanctuary
sassi – stone houses built in two ravines in Matera (in Basilicata)
scala mobile – escalator, moving staircase
scalinata – staircase
sci alpinismo – ski mountaineering
sci di fondo – cross-country skiing
servizio – service charge in restaurants
sestiere – city section (in Venice)
Settimana Bianca – White Week; skiing package
soccorso alpino – mountain rescue
soccorso stradale – highway rescue
sovrintendenza – supervisor
spiaggia – beach
stazione – station

stazione di servizio – petrol or service station
stazione marittime – ferry terminal
strada – street, road
strada provinciale – main road; sometimes just a country lane
strada statale – main road; often multi-lane and toll free
superstrada – expressway; highway with divided lanes
supplemento – supplement; payable on a fast train

T
tabaccheria – tobacconist's shop
tavola calda – literally `hot table'; pre- prepared meat, pasta and vegetable selection, often self-service
teatro – theatre
tempio – temple
tempietto – small temple
terme – thermal baths
tesoro – treasury
torre – tower
torrente – stream
traghetto (s), **traghetti** (pl) – small ferry
trattoria – cheap restaurant

U
ufficio postale – post office
ufficio stranieri – foreigners bureau
uffizi – offices
Ulivo – Olive Tree Alliance; centre-left political coalition

V
vaporetto – small passenger boat/ferry (in Venice)
via – street, road
viale – avenue
vico – alley, alleyway
vigili del fuoco – fire brigade
vigili urbani – traffic police, local police
villa – town house or country house; also the park surrounding the house

Z
Zona Rimozione – Vehicle Removal Zone

Behind the Scenes

THIS BOOK

The 1st edition of Lonely Planet's *Italy* was written by Helen Gillman and John Gillman. Helen Gillman and Damien Simonis updated the 2nd edition. The 3rd edition was revised and expanded by Helen Gillman, Damien Simonis and Stefano Cavedoni. The 4th edition was updated by Helen Gillman, Damien Simonis, Sally Webb and Stefano Cavedoni. The 5th edition was worked on by Damien Simonis, Sally Webb, Fiona Adams, Miles Roddis and Nicola Williams. This mammoth 6th edition was updated by Duncan Garwood, Paula Hardy, Wendy Owen, Miles Roddis, Damien Simonis and Nicola Williams.

THANKS FROM THE AUTHORS

Duncan Garwood Lots of people helped me on this trip. A big thank you to Michala Green for giving me the job and then answering all my ridiculous questions; Miles Roddis for his helpful advice; Rebecca Lennox for so generously giving me the time off and Richard McKenna for his tips on Italian music. In Bari, Andrea and Maria Rosaria were the perfect hosts while Sheena and Pasquale entertained as only they can. Thanks also to Angela and Emmanuelle for their company in Lecce.

Tourist office staff were generally helpful, particularly so Katia Marcantonio (L'Aquila), Franca Leone (Sulmona), Laura Vigilante (Naples), Lorena De Pascale (Capri), Alfonso Mignone and Alessandro Memoli (Salerno), Leonilde Folliero (Lucera), Luisa Rinaldi (Trani) and Vincenzo Santilio (Matera). Sergio Mastrototaro and Romina Gioffré (Isole Tremiti) were also a help.

Finally, *grazie di cuore* to Lidia for so calmly giving birth to our beautiful baby boy Ben and to Ma and Pa Salvati for taking such good care of them both.

Readers whose letters were useful: Cie Sharp, Kathleen Epeldi, Carsten Kern, Renae Grasso, David Williams, S Eltaher, Jason Woods, Friederike, Juan Casabonne, Cheryl Passmore, Jessica Connell, Andreas Willeke and Fiona Duffy.

Paula Hardy Thanks go to all LP readers who write in with all the compliments and criticisms that keep us on our toes – thanks in particular to Diana Brown and her husband Salvatore, Shamus Sillar and Charles Manton. To the tourist offices in Palermo and Trapani – thank you for the time of day, the fantastic restaurant recommendations and the reliable (!) information. More specifically, thank you to Alfredo and Eleanora Durante at the embassy in Rome, the Benghazi-Sicily connections of the Dahmani's, and the warm hospitality of Angela, Ermeno and Laura, Mohammed and Julia, and Francesco. For a blissful day in paradise thank you to Emanuele of Eolie Adventures and for nerve-wracking info on volcanoes thank you to Lorenzo Russo at Magmatrek. As ever, heartfelt thanks to Ali – I await the next history of empires – and to my sister, Sandra, who held the fort in difficult times. Last, but by no means least, thank you Michala for soul-boosting editorial reassurance and support along the way.

Wendy Owen To my *carissimi amici* Christine Georgeff, Denis Redmont, Sari Gilbert, Fabrizio Coletti – thanks for still being there and for all

---

THE LONELY PLANET STORY

The story begins with a classic travel adventure: Tony and Maureen Wheeler's 1972 journey across Europe and Asia to Australia. There was no useful information about the overland trail then, so Tony and Maureen published the first Lonely Planet guidebook to meet a growing need.

From a kitchen table, Lonely Planet has grown to become the largest independent travel publisher in the world, with offices in Melbourne (Australia), Oakland (USA), London (UK) and Paris (France).

Today Lonely Planet guidebooks cover the globe. There is an ever-growing list of books and information in a variety of media. Some things haven't changed. The main aim is still to make it possible for adventurous travellers to get out there – to explore and better understand the world.

At Lonely Planet we believe travellers can make a positive contribution to the countries they visit – if they respect their host communities and spend their money wisely.

your invaluable help and knowledge both now and then. *Il Gruppo delle Merende*, new friends, reminded me that work can still be fun and that eating and drinking are indeed art forms and fundamental to an understanding of Italy. *Grazie infinite* to *la famiglia* Antonini/Consegni for their tremendous hospitality and *un abbraccio affettuoso* for Roberto, who knows how to make me laugh as well as smile. Many thanks also to Jocelyn Harewood for her sensitive approach to my verbal enthusiasm.

Miles Roddis Very special thanks to, as always, Ingrid, my staunchest backup and most critical reader. Also, to Paola Lazzarini for invaluable help in chasing up wayward facts and to Sam and Joan Baily for both hospitality and an eagle eyed read through of my Florence draft. Elizabeth Garvey of the British Council, Bologna, passed on some useful lowdown and tourist office staff were almost invariably helpfulness itself. My thanks to Maria Laura Billeri (Florence), Silvia Mangarelli (Fiesole), Rosemary McAra (Lucca), Roberta Favilla (Pisa), Claudia Verdolini (San Gimignano), Emanuela Lorenzetti (Siena), Michele Moscato (Montalcino), Roberto Ragazzini (Centro Visite del Parco Regionale della Maremma), Alocci Mazareno (Porto Santo Stefano), Luisa Foschetti (Pitigliano), Agnes del Gamba (Arezzo), Alessio Scioscia and Mariangela Regazzi (Parma), Loredana Troiani (Rimini), Daniela Baldini (Ravenna and Faenza), Marina Bruni (Bologna), Elena Bottoni (Ferrara), and Massimo Campobianchi (Reggio Emiliana).

Damien Simonis I would like to thank the following in Venice, the Veneto and Sardinia: Dr Alberto Stassi, Irina Freguia & family, Michela Scibilia, Roberta Guarnieri, Caterina de Cesero, Susanne Sagner, Bernhard Klein & Federica Centulani, Federica Rocco, Antonella Dondi dall'Orologio, William Gasparini & Cristina Vallin, Andrea Branca, Gian Paolo Epifani, Mattea Usai, Raimondo Cossa & Olga, Professore Mario Cubeddu & Carla, Francesco & Doloretta Cubeddu, Stefano Melone, Professore Salvatore Rubino, Stefano Cavedoni, Marco, Lucia, Laura and all the other Marcos at The Monastery, and Gigi and the bar gang in Desulo.

In London big thanks to my brother Desmond for looking after business on the home front during my absences and also a very big thank you to Michala Green of Lonely Planet's London office, who took on coordinating duties for this tome and maintained an exemplary sense of humour throughout an at times trying process.

Finally, this is for Janique, who came along for some of the rather bumpy rides, provided a home base and makes it all worthwhile.

Nicola Williams *Grazie mille* in Piedmont to Angelo Pittro and Claudio Peruccio from Lonely Planet's Turin-based Italian publisher EDT, Nicola Assetta for his local Turin insights, and Paola Galasso from the Regione Piemonte; in the Valle d'Aosta to Robberto Donatelli and his pals for some fine wine recommendations; in Genoa to Patricia Pesci from Pesci Viaggi e Turismo and Paolo Berardi; in Lombardy to outdoor enthusiast Matilde at Mennagio tourist office, Alberto Ferrario from Menaggio's Ostello La Primula, and Daniella from the Residence La Limonera in Bellagio; and in northern Italy's wildest climes, to Lorenzo Mosca from the Sant'Antonio di Mavignol visitors centre in the Parco Naturale Adamello-Brenta. Last but not least, many thanks to Omi and Opa for entertaining Niko.

CREDITS

The 6th edition of Lonely Planet's *Italy* was worked on by a cast of thousands. Editing was co-ordinated by Melanie Dankel with expert assistance by Carolyn Bain, Dan Caleo, Lara Morcombe, Kalya Ryan, Sally Steward and Katrina Webb. Cartography was co-ordinated by James Ellis with dedicated assistance from Yvonne Bischofberger, Csanad Csutoros, Hunor Csutoros, Tony Fankhauser, Daniel Fennessy, Anneka Imkamp, Birgit Jordan, Joelene Kowalski, Valentina Kremenchutskaya, Laurie Mikkelsen, Wayne Murphy, Jacqueline Nguyen, Adrian Persoglia, Anthony Phelan, Lachlan Ross, Jacqui Saunders, Julie Sheridan, Amanda Sierp, Sarah Sloane, Simon Tillema, Chris Tsismetzis and Celia Wood. The layout team consisted of Sonya Brooke, Katie Cason, Jacqui Saunders and Steven Cann. Thanks also to Ray Thomson, Bruce Evans, Stefanie di Trocchio, Barbara Delissen, Quentin Frayne for the Language chapter and LPI.

Series Publishing Manager Virginia Maxwell oversaw the redevelopment of the country guides series with help from Maria Donohoe. Regional Publishing Manager Katrina Browning steered the development of this title. The series was designed by James Hardy, with mapping development by Paul Piaia. The series development team included Shahara Ahmed, Susie Ashworth, Gerilyn Attebery, Jenny Blake, Anna Bolger, Erin Corrigan, Nadine Fogale, Dave McClymont, Leonie Mugavin, Lynne Preston, Rachel Peart, Howard Ralley and Verity Campbell.

Last but not least, *tante grazie* to the authors – thanks for all your hard work and patience.

THANKS FROM LONELY PLANET

Many thanks to the hundreds of travellers who used the last edition and wrote to us with helpful hints, useful advice and interesting anecdotes:

A Tal Alon, Gene Anderson, Murdoch Anderson, Johanna Arnorsdottir, John Arwe **B** Arnold Bake, Hugh Barber, Frank Barendregt, Istvan Barta & Erika Hartmann, Montse Baste-Kraan, Dennis Bateman, Michel Beauchemin Gérard Beaudry, Gillian Bell, Amy Best, Donna Bliss, Alessandro Borgogna, Simon Boscarino, Maarten Bosker, Jacqueline Bosma, Kevin Brandstetter, David Brett, Kieran Briggs, Laura Brillinger, Damon Burn **C** Margot Callahan, Ingrid Campos, Yo-Han Cha, Kim Chatfield, Mark Chillingworth, Cindy Cho, Nikitas Chondroyannos, Lily Chrywenstrom, Antonio Cioffi, Hilary Clarke, Ruth Colmer, F Colyer, Jessica Connell, Barbara Conners, Costas Constantinou, Mathew Costin, Geoff Craig, John Crocker, Sarah Cummins, Lionel Curin, Stella Cushing **D** Amy Dahl, Elizabeth Brooke Dankel, V Davies, Bill Davis, Luk De Rop, Snehal Desai, Anne Dicker, Simon Dicker, Francesco Diodato, Sandra Dittrich, PP Drew, Carolyn Duff, Fiona Duffy, Wesley Duke **E** Colin Easom, Margaret Eaton, Claire Edwardes, Alexander Ekvall, Kathleen Epeldi **F** Kenneth Fan, Simon Fenwick, Chris Fileman, Marcelle Fileman, Peter J Fish, Alan Fishman, Robert Fitzthum, Bruno Franchetti, Elinor Franchetti, David F. Freeman, Matias Friburg, Ronald J Friedman, Rosie Frost, Kathy Fulcher **G** Gretchen Gaede, Ron Gagliano, Marisol Gagliano, TJ Galda, Danielle Gerson, Andy and Nicky Gibb, Carey Gibbs, Jill & Ian Gibson, Greta Gillies, Renae Grasso, Jason Graham, Meahan Grande, Debbie Gray, Jaime Green, Judy Green **H** Ros Halliday, Marina Hansson, Bob Hatcher, Stuart Hedges, Megan Heim, Adrian Hervey, Wendy Hewitson, Larissa Hoerzer, Michael Hoexter, Steph Holbeck, David Hollingsworth, Rececca Hollister, Gerry T Hooning, Sue Humphreys **J** Tahirah Johnson, Emma Jorgenson, Peter Jowett **K** Benjamin Keay, Melanie Kelly, Abby Kennedy, Malcolm Kennedy, Pascal Keogh, Carsten Kern, Glenn Kerrigan, Sukey Kielman, Joshua King, Anna Klimi, Shelley Kloppenburg, Sonia Knox, Claire Koenig, Rainer Koester Barbara Konig, Bronwen Koolik, Ofer Kot, Olaf Kuhnemann **L** Beverly La Ferla, Elaine Lam, Anna Larsson, Ula Laspas, Jenny Lawrence, Keith Lawson, Emily Ledger, Paul Levatino, Sarah Lee, Geraldine Lum, Robyn Lyall, Peter Lysaught **M** Adam Mackstaller, Helen Madden, Andrea Maiolla, Bernard Mandile, Joanna Mandrides, Sonya Marinoni, Jane Martini, Klaus Matzka, Kennon McDonnell, Louise McSorley, Lori Mendel, Helene Mercier, Paul Mes, Ron Miller, Anna Moller, Jimena Moreno Letelier, Chris Morton, Fiona Morton, Ian Muncaster, Karla Murray **N** Jade Newbold, Anna Newton, Michael Nielsen **O** Anna Oberhofer, Kathi Olsen, Elaine O'Mullane, Henry O'Neal **P** Cheryl Passmore, Jean-François Patry, Jemma Pearce, Renate Pelzl, Susan Pempek, Jurgen Peppel, Jet Petersen, Allan Phillips, Anthony Pirraglia, Mike Pollard, Pat Pollard, Korbinian Poschl, Janice Potten, Jacqui Powell, Nicole Power, Charles Prêcheur, Joe Puccio **R** Chara Ragland, Gail Rahn, Margaret Rapoport, Benedict Rich, Michael Ridpath, Angela Rivalta, Carlos Rodriguez, Leslie Root, Karen Rose, Mark Rothwell, Suzanne Rutledge **S** Carmen Salazar, Nigel Sale, Erwin Salemink, Stritof Samo, Richard Sanderson, Rita Sanderson, Barb Satink, Michiel Schoen, Harvey Schwartz, J.M. Scott, Donna Scriven, Derek Seow, James Seymour, Shirley Sheaton, James Shields, Susan Shields, Amelia Shindelar, Jacqui Shoffner, Ross Shotton, Benoit Simard, Amanda Smith, Rachel Smyth, Jacalyn Soo, Tom Steger, John Spears, Mary Spears, Assen Stefanov, Sonya Stephens, Deborah Sterpin, Debbie Stokoe, Samo Stritof, Wendy Stronge, Leonore Swanson, Pete Symons **T** Jennifer Tamaddon, Don Tatum, Warwick Taylor, Betsy Thayer, Luke Torre, Penny Teutenberg, Sarah Turnbull, Jean-Pierre Turschwell, Ann Tuxford **U** Rolando Uliana de Oliveria **V** Marc van der Laan, Philip Vandenbroeck, Toby Vanhegan, Ivan Jose Varzinczak, Alex Vaulkhard **W** Richard Watson, Sasti Watson, Margo Weerdenburg, Demaris Wehr, Gail Weinkauf, Dorit Weissberg-Kasav, Andri Wikdahl, Andreas Willeke, David Williams, Elmar Winterberg, Keefe Wong, Gina Woolf, Margaret Wright, Susan Wuchter-Stein **Y** Einat Yaari, Jim Young

ACKNOWLEDGMENTS

Many thanks to the following for the use of their content:

Mountain High Maps® Copyright © 1993 Digital Wisdom, Inc.

Grateful acknowledgment is made for reproduction permission: ATAC S.P.A.© Rome Metro Map 2001

SEND US YOUR FEEDBACK

We love to hear from travellers – your comments keep us on our toes and help make our books better. Our well-travelled team reads every word on what you loved or loathed about this book. Although we cannot reply individually to postal submissions, we always guarantee that your feedback goes straight to the appropriate authors, in time for the next edition. Each person who sends us information is thanked in the next edition – and the most useful submissions are rewarded with a free book.

To send us your updates – and find out about LP events, newsletters and travel news – visit our award-winning website: **www.lonelyplanet.com**.

Note: We may edit, reproduce and incorporate your comments in Lonely Planet products such as guidebooks, websites and digital products, so let us know if you don't want your comments reproduced or your name acknowledged. For a copy of our privacy policy, email privacy@lonelyplanet.com.au.

Index

000 Map pages
000 Location of colour photographs

INDEX

INDEX

INDEX

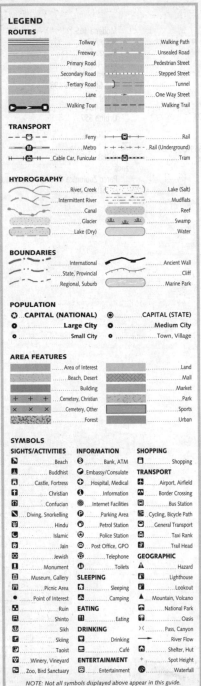

LEGEND

ROUTES

Tollway	Walking Path
Freeway	Unsealed Road
Primary Road	Pedestrian Street
Secondary Road	Stepped Street
Tertiary Road	Tunnel
Lane	One Way Street
Walking Tour	Walking Trail

TRANSPORT

Ferry	Rail
Metro	Rail (Underground)
Cable Car, Funicular	Tram

HYDROGRAPHY

River, Creek	Lake (Salt)
Intermittent River	Mudflats
Canal	Reef
Glacier	Swamp
Lake (Dry)	Water

BOUNDARIES

International	Ancient Wall
State, Provincial	Cliff
Regional, Suburb	Marine Park

POPULATION

CAPITAL (NATIONAL)	CAPITAL (STATE)
Large City	Medium City
Small City	Town, Village

AREA FEATURES

Area of Interest	Land
Beach, Desert	Mall
Building	Market
Cemetery, Christian	Park
Cemetery, Other	Sports
Forest	Urban

SYMBOLS

SIGHTS/ACTIVITIES
- Beach
- Buddhist
- Castle, Fortress
- Christian
- Confucian
- Diving, Snorkelling
- Hindu
- Islamic
- Jain
- Jewish
- Monument
- Museum, Gallery
- Picnic Area
- Point of Interest
- Ruin
- Shinto
- Sikh
- Skiing
- Taoist
- Winery, Vineyard
- Zoo, Bird Sanctuary

INFORMATION
- Bank, ATM
- Embassy/Consulate
- Hospital, Medical
- Information
- Internet Facilities
- Parking Area
- Petrol Station
- Police Station
- Post Office, GPO
- Telephone
- Toilets

SLEEPING
- Sleeping

EATING
- Eating

DRINKING
- Drinking
- Café

ENTERTAINMENT
- Entertainment

SHOPPING
- Shopping

TRANSPORT
- Airport, Airfield
- Border Crossing
- Bus Station
- Cycling, Bicycle Path
- General Transport
- Taxi Rank
- Trail Head

GEOGRAPHIC
- Hazard
- Lighthouse
- Lookout
- Mountain, Volcano
- National Park
- Oasis
- Pass, Canyon
- River Flow
- Shelter, Hut
- Spot Height
- Waterfall

NOTE: Not all symbols displayed above appear in this guide.

LONELY PLANET OFFICES

Australia
Head Office
Locked Bag 1, Footscray, Victoria 3011
☎ 03 8379 8000, fax 03 8379 8111
talk2us@lonelyplanet.com.au

USA
150 Linden St, Oakland, CA 94607
☎ 510 893 8555, toll free 800 275 8555
fax 510 893 8572, info@lonelyplanet.com

UK
72–82 Rosebery Ave,
Clerkenwell, London EC1R 4RW
☎ 020 7841 9000, fax 020 7841 9001
go@lonelyplanet.co.uk

France
1 rue du Dahomey, 75011 Paris
☎ 01 55 25 33 00, fax 01 55 25 33 01
bip@lonelyplanet.fr, www.lonelyplanet.fr

Published by Lonely Planet Publications Pty Ltd
ABN 36 005 607 983

© Lonely Planet 2004

© photographers as indicated 2004

Cover photographs by Lonely Planet Images: The Colosseum, illuminated at dusk, Martin Moos (front); Yellow Fiat 500 – Gubbio, Umbria, Damien Simonis (back). Many of the images in this guide are available for licensing from Lonely Planet Images: www.lonely planetimages.com.

All rights reserved. No part of this publication may be copied, stored in a retrieval system, or transmitted in any form by any means, electronic, mechanical, recording or otherwise, except brief extracts for the purpose of review, and no part of this publication may be sold or hired, without the written permission of the publisher.

Printed through Colorcraft Ltd, Hong Kong.
Printed in China

Lonely Planet and the Lonely Planet logo are trademarks of Lonely Planet and are registered in the US Patent and Trademark Office and in other countries.

Lonely Planet does not allow its name or logo to be appropriated by commercial establishments, such as retailers, restaurants or hotels. Please let us know of any misuses: www.lonelyplanet.com/ip

Although the authors and Lonely Planet have taken all reasonable care in preparing this book, we make no warranty about the accuracy or completeness of its content and, to the maximum extent permitted, disclaim all liability arising from its use.